# Civil Liberties
# Under the Constitution

# Civil Liberties Under the Constitution

**FIFTH EDITION**

By
## M. GLENN ABERNATHY
### UNIVERSITY OF SOUTH CAROLINA

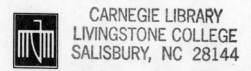

UNIVERSITY OF SOUTH CAROLINA PRESS

123569

Copyright © 1977, 1985, 1989 by M. Glenn Abernathy

Fifth Edition

Published in Columbia, South Carolina, by the
University of South Carolina Press

Manufactured in the United States of America

**Library of Congress Cataloging in Publication Data**

Abernathy, M. Glenn (Marba Glenn), 1921-
    Civil liberties under the Constitution / by M. Glenn Abernathy.—
5th ed.
        p.   cm.
    Bibliography: p.
    Includes index.
    ISBN 0-87249-617-1
    1. Civil rights—United States.      I. Title.
KF4748.A2 1989
342.73'085'02643—dc 19
[347.3028502643]                                            88-27011
                                                                  CIP

*In Memory of*
*my Mother and Father*

# CONTENTS

# PREFACE

The proper study of civil liberties in America involves virtually the whole range of social science techniques and subject matter. It should include constitutional law, political theory, political action, sociology, economics, psychology, history, and the behavioral approaches to decision making, both public and private. Obviously one who attempts to treat civil liberties in a single volume is forced to omit most of these approaches and, to that extent, excludes substantial areas of highly relevant and important material necessary to a solid understanding of civil liberties in America. Choice must be made, however, and for reasons both of personal preference and pedagogical utility, this study concentrates primarily on the constitutional law aspect of civil liberties. Given the importance of the "rule of law" concept in Anglo-American history, it is felt that a firm grasp of the *law* with respect to civil liberties will provide a useful anchor, and a base will be established from which the student can more competently and fruitfully explore other modes of investigating the subject. In short, no limited approach to civil liberties can be more than an introduction to the broad subject, and the student should be warned of this fact at the outset. If this introductory analysis provides a framework for and stimulates interest in further study of so vital a subject, the venture will have been a success.

This fifth edition incorporates some 75 additional cases and covers decisions through the end of the 1987–88 Term of Court. The approach used is to integrate case cuttings and descriptive text to achieve a coherent chronological development of the law in each area covered. An effort is made to provide textual background for each topic to prepare the student properly for the issues presented in the case cuttings. For the more complex cases, a follow-up analysis is provided to insure understanding. Collections of cases alone often present problems of discerning relationships and differences between the various decisions. And purely descriptive texts deprive the student of the flavor of the actual opinions delivered. The attempt here is to combine the advantages of each approach and avoid their disadvantages. Article and book citations are included in the text, and a chapter-by-chapter list of selected references is provided as an appendix.

# TABLE of CASES

# CHAPTER I

# *The Courts and Civil Rights*

Until relatively recently, the focal point for official pronouncements concerning the nature and extent of American civil rights has been the judiciary. This is not an unreasonable approach in view of the impact of the institution of judicial review and the habituation of Anglo-Americans to judicial policymaking through centuries of development of the common law. These factors, despite the fact that constitutional conventions or legislative bodies initiated the statements of rights found in the state and federal constitutions, inexorably operate to place the stress on the judiciary as the locus for definitive elaboration of rights. Constitutional challenges to laws or official behavior are expected to reach final resolution only in a court decision, and the higher the court the more nearly final the decision. Despite its oversimplification, there is some element of truth in the statement by presidential candidate Charles Evans Hughes, "We are under the Constitution, but the Constitution is what the judges say it is."

More recently, legislative bodies and administrative agencies have been recognized as important participants in the creation and delineation of rights. Congress, for example, can both create new rights and destroy old ones. In the adoption of the National Labor Relations Act in 1935 a new right of defined categories of workers to organize and bargain collectively was created. And the old right of employers to discharge workers for union activity was demolished. Similarly, in the Civil Rights Act of 1964 a new right of access to places of public accommodation, irrespective of race or religion, was created, while the old right of choice in the operators (absent state laws to the contrary) was removed. In administering the nondiscrimination-in-education provisions of the Civil Rights Act of 1964, the Office of Education has essentially extended the meager phraseology of the Act to embrace additional rights. In great part, however, such participation in the process of rights-definition does not appear to displace the judiciary from its position of primacy in the public mind.

Unfortunately, this attitude sometimes engenders as a corollary the belief that the courts are the omnipresent *guardians* of civil rights. In other words, it is not uncommonly assumed that the courts of the nation stand ever ready to right all wrongs suffered to one's person or liberty or property. In a strictly limited sense this is true. If one has suffered an injury recognized by the law, and if he has the time, money, energy, witnesses, and evidence to prosecute his cause successfully in court, then a remedy is available to him. But this statement camouflages a multitude of barriers to the realization of effective judicial remedies for wronged individuals. Thus, while the bulk of this volume places heavy stress on judicial pronouncements defining and analyzing civil rights, it is well to enter a *caveat* initially concerning a number of important factors which serve to limit the effectiveness of courts as *guardians* of civil rights. The purpose of this chapter is to examine these factors, some of which are external to the judicial process while others stem from the courts' own evaluation of the limits to their appropriate role, and then to define the area in which courts *can* act to protect civil rights. [For an excellent discussion of the limitations on the impact of the United States Supreme Court on practices affecting criminal suspects, see Anthony G. Amsterdam, "The Rights of Suspects," in Norman Dorsen, ed., *The Rights of Americans* (New York: Random House, 1972,) pp. 401–432.]

## LIMITATIONS ON JUDICIAL POWER TO PROTECT RIGHTS

**1. Failure to litigate.** At the outset it is clear that the initiative in a civil suit must be taken by the injured party if the courts are to offer any assistance in righting the wrong. Even in criminal actions, a substantial burden rests on the injured party to push forward his cause if he expects satisfaction. If one suffers a criminal wrong, his complaint and testimony (if he is alive to give them) are usually a prerequisite to successful prosecution. And if, instead, he is the victim of an improper prosecution, it is up to him to carry the appeals necessary to try to get a reversal of the conviction. Thus our adversary system demands action, not childlike faith in some future retribution for one's enemies, if the judicial machinery is to be set in motion to safeguard rights. But every day sees abridgments of rights in some form take place with only a very small portion of these leading to actual litigation. Why is this so? Among the more obvious answers are cost, fear of reprisals, delay in reaching final settlement, and perhaps the bad character of the victim. Other factors as well contribute to this reluctance.

Most of us have from time to time suffered an actionable wrong from either private persons or public officials. But we recognize that a certain amount of friction is inevitable in the multitudinous contacts of modern living and prefer to ignore the minor encroachments on our rights. More to the point, one does not lightly undertake a lawsuit if he takes the time to calculate the potential costs in lawyer's fees, witnesses' fees, court costs, and his own time. Particularly is this true when the defendant in such proceedings is "judgment proof"—in other words, out of reach of any judgment against him for lack of money.

Delay in getting a decision more often than not works in favor of the defendant in civil actions. And the courts in many sections of the nation are falling further behind each year in disposing of cases on the dockets. In some of the larger cities, for example, the civil docket for jury trials is three to four years behind. Equity actions, such as a suit for an injunction to prevent impending injury, do not face this problem because they are disposed of without jury determinations. The magistrates' courts and other limited jurisdiction courts are much speedier in their handling of cases, but the quality of their decisions is frequently suspect, and these courts can normally handle only cases at law (no equity jurisdiction) involving relatively small amounts of money. Under such circumstances it is hard to criticize the injured party who throws up his hands in despair and either puts aside any thought of bringing suit or, after filing the action, settles out of court for considerably less than the alleged damages. [See Hans Zeisel, Harry Kalven, Jr., and Bernard Buchholz, *Delay in the Court* (Boston: Little, Brown, 1959).]

In the case of various unpopular minority groups or those dependent on the good will of the defendant, there is still additional cause for caution—the fear of reprisals. Economic pressures or even violence may be the reward for attempts to redress grievances through court action. In such event, suffering in silence may well seem to be the wiser course.

In the evolution of the administration of workmen's compensation laws in the various states it was the recognition of just these factors of cost, delay, and fear of reprisals which led legislatures to conclude that the determination of awards to injured employees bringing suit against their employers should be transferred from the courts to administrative agencies. [See Walter F. Dodd, *Administration of Workmen's Compensation* (New York: Oxford University Press, 1936), chap. 4.]

The heavy hand of officialdom may be visited much more frequently on those who have already had a history of criminal behavior. It is easier for officials to slip beyond the bounds of their authority when dealing with the habitual offender. But this is the class which would be fighting the greatest odds in bringing an action against the offending officials. Thus the questionable character of the would-be plaintiff might lead him to doubt seriously whether he could successfully prosecute a suit to vindicate his rights. Convicts and ex-convicts seldom sue sheriffs and police officers.

To move into slightly more technical aspects than the failure to litigate, there are several factors implicit either in our judicial procedure or statutes which restrict the availability of judicial remedies. Among the more important of these are: the requirement of "standing" to bring suit, the nonreviewability by courts of many administrative acts, the presumption of validity of official acts, the presumption of constitutionality of acts of the legislature, the difficulty of extending decisions beyond the specific facts and parties involved, and, finally, the limited remedies for private interference with free choice.

**2. "Standing" to sue.**  The concept of "standing" to bring suit is a many-faceted problem. Basically, however, it is a requirement that the party bringing suit be able to show an injury recognized by the law, and one for which the law provides a remedy. Thus an individual cannot normally bring suit to redress a wrong suffered by another. (There are, of course, certain necessary exceptions, as in the case of parents, guardians, trustees, and others who may sue in behalf of those under their special care.) In addition, the injury must be real, not fancied, and must be one already suffered or immediately anticipated, not remote and speculative.

A standard illustration of the requirement that one must show injury to have "standing" to sue is the case of *Tileston* v. *Ullman,* 318 U.S. 44 (1943). Dr. Tileston, a Connecticut physician, challenged the constitutionality of a state law prohibiting "the use of drugs or instruments to prevent conception, and the giving of assistance or counsel in their use" on the ground that the law would prevent his giving professional advice to his patients whose lives would be endangered by childbearing. The United States Supreme Court dismissed the action, holding that no question was presented "which appellant has standing to assert." The allegations related to the potential dangers to his patients, not to him, and his patients were not parties to the proceeding. Thus, while the law might well present difficult questions of constitutionality, Dr. Tileston was not, in the context of this case, the appropriate person to raise them judicially.

The sequel to the case is *Griswold* v. *Connecticut,* 381 U.S. 479 (1965), in which the same law was again under attack in an appeal to the United States Supreme Court. This time, however, the appellants were appealing from a conviction in a Connecticut court for violation of the law. Since the injury was clear-cut and personal, they had the requisite "standing" to raise the constitutional issue, and the Court responded by rendering a decision on the merits. (A majority of five held the law to be an unconstitutional invasion of the right of privacy of married persons, while two other justices concurred on other grounds.)

The older rules relative to standing were somewhat restrictive, but beginning in 1968, several decisions of the Court have opened the way for broader access to the courts to attack governmental action. While the states have generally permitted suits by taxpayers attacking the validity of state appropriations, in *Frothingham* v. *Mellon,* 262 U.S. 447 (1923), the Court held that a *federal* taxpayer, merely as a taxpayer, did not have standing to challenge the constitutionality of a federal appropriation. But in *Flast* v. *Cohen,* 392 U.S. 83 (1968), the Court relaxed this rule to the extent of according standing when the plaintiff "alleges that congressional action under the taxing and spending clause is in derogation of those constitutional provisions which operate to restrict the exercise of the taxing and spending power." The case involved a challenge to the constitutionality of federal expenditures for textbooks and other instructional materials for religious schools, on the ground that such expenditures violated the establishment of religion clause of the First Amendment. In a more recent case, *Doe v. Bolton*, 410 U.S. 179 (1973), the Court held that both a married, pregnant woman and licensed physicians who had been consulted by pregnant women desiring abortions had standing to challenge Georgia's abortion laws.

In general, economic injury sustained as a result of competition has not been held sufficient to accord standing to sue. Thus, in *Tennessee Power Co. v. T.V.A.*, 306 U.S. 118 (1939), where private power companies sought to enjoin T.V.A. from operating, claiming that the statute under which it was created was unconstitutional, the Court denied the competitors standing. But the Administrative Procedure Act, 5 U.S.C.A. §702, grants standing to a person "aggrieved by agency action within the meaning of a relevant statute." And in *Association of Data Processing Service Organizations v. Camp*, 397 U.S. 150 (1970), the Court held that private data processing companies had standing to challenge a ruling by the Comptroller of the Currency that national banks, as an incident to their banking services, could make data processing services available to other banks and to bank customers. The decision, however, turned on the interpretation of a statutory provision stating that "No bank service corporation may engage in any activity other than the performance of bank services for banks." Thus, if the competitive injury can be challenged under a relevant statute, the Court is willing to accord standing. In *Linda R.S. v. Richard D.*, 410 U.S. 614 (1973), the Court pointed out that it is true that Congress may not confer jurisdiction on Article III federal courts to render advisory opinions, "but Congress may enact statutes creating legal rights, the invasion of which creates standing, even though no injury would exist without the statute."

In *Sierra Club v. Morton*, 405 U.S. 727 (1972), the Club sought a declaratory judgment and an injunction to restrain federal officials from approving the creation of an extensive ski-resort development in the scenic Mineral King Valley of the Sequoia National Forest. The Club claimed standing to maintain its "public interest" lawsuit because it had a special interest in the conservation and the sound maintenance of the national parks, game refuges, and forests of the country. The Court held those allegations insufficient since no specific injury to the members of the Club was alleged in the complaint. In a footnote to the opinion, however, it was suggested that the Club could easily rectify this error by amending the complaint to allege that the members actually used the area for hiking and camping and other recreational purposes, and that the development would cause direct, personal injury to the members.

What is the basis for the Court's requirement that a plaintiff have "standing" in order to receive a decision on his claim? The standard explanation is that the requirement is rooted in Article III, Section 2, of the Constitution which states that "The judicial power shall extend to . . . cases [and] . . . controversies. . . ." The Court has construed the terms "cases" and "controversies" as limiting its jurisdiction to situations where the plaintiff has shown direct and substantial injury to person or property, and the issue is presented in an adversary proceeding. In *Warth v. Seldin*, 422 U.S. 490, 498–500 (1975), Justice Powell addressed the topic:

> In essence the question of standing is whether the litigant is entitled to have the court decide the merits of the dispute or of particular issues. This inquiry involves both constitutional limitations on federal-court jurisdiction and prudential limitations on its exercise. . . . In both dimensions it is founded in concern about the proper—and properly limited—role of the courts in a democratic society. . . .
>
> In its constitutional dimension, standing imports justiciability: whether the plaintiff has made out a "case or controversy" between himself and the defendant within

the meaning of Art. III. This is the threshold question in every federal case, determining the power of the court to entertain the suit. As an aspect of justiciability, the standing question is whether the plaintiff has "alleged such a personal stake in the outcome of the controversy" as to warrant *his* invocation of federal-court jurisdiction and to justify exercise of the court's remedial powers on his behalf. . . . The Art. III judicial power exists only to redress or otherwise to protect against injury to the complaining party, even though the court's judgment may benefit others collaterally. A federal court's jurisdiction therefore can be invoked only when the plaintiff himself has suffered "some threatened or actual injury resulting from the putatively illegal action." . . .

Apart from this minimum constitutional mandate, this Court has recognized other limits on the class of persons who may invoke the court' decisional and remedial powers. First, the Court has held that when the asserted harm is a "generalized grievance" shared in substantially equal measure by all or a large class of citizens, that harm alone normally does not warrant exercise of jurisdiction. . . . Second, even when the plaintiff has alleged injury sufficient to meet the "case or controversy" requirement, this Court has held that the plaintiff generally must assert his own legal rights and interests, and cannot rest his claim to relief on the legal rights or interests of third parties. E.g., *Tileston* v. *Ullman*. . . . Without such limitations—closely related to Art. III concerns but essentially matters of judicial self-governance—the courts would be called upon to decide abstract questions of wide public significance even though other governmental institutions may be more competent to address the questions and even though judicial intervention may be unnecessary to protect individual rights. . . .

Closely akin to this limitation of "standing" is the rule followed by the federal courts and generally by state courts (unless constitutional provisions require otherwise) that they will not render advisory opinions. One must present a proper case or controversy to a court, in an adversary proceeding, in order to test the validity of a statute or administrative order. Still another facet of standing is the concept of "mootness." The Court will not decide a case if the decision will no longer affect the claimant in the case. In *Doremus* v. *Board of Education,* 342 U.S. 429 (1952), the issue presented was whether a New Jersey requirement of Bible-reading in the public high schools was unconstitutional as an establishment of religion. The New Jersey Supreme Court had held the practice constitutional in 1950, and the United States Supreme Court did not reach decision until 1952. By that time the student plaintiff in the case had graduated, so the Court held that the case was "moot" and dismissed. Justice Jackson, for the Court, (at 432-433) stated:

Obviously no decision we could render now would protect any rights she may once have had, and this Court does not sit to decide arguments after events have put them to rest.

Special situations may occur, however, that would demand a relaxation of this rule if the issue presented is to be decided at all through the lengthy appellate process. In the leading abortion case, for example, *Roe* v. *Wade*, 410 U.S. 113 (1973), Jane Roe had filed suit in 1970 challenging a Texas statute that prohibited abortion in her case. She was pregnant at the time of filing suit, but the United States Supreme Court did not reach decision until almost three years later, long past the end of her pregnancy. The State argued that the case was therefore moot, but the Court rejected the argument. Justice Blackmun, for the majority (at 125) stated:

The usual rule in federal cases is that an actual controversy must exist at stages of appellate or certiorari review, and not simply at the date the action is initiated. . . .

But when, as here, pregnancy is a significant fact in the litigation, the normal 266-day human gestation period is so short that the pregnancy will come to term before the usual appellate process is complete. If that termination makes a case moot, pregnancy litigation seldom will survive much beyond the trial stage, and appellate review will be effectively denied. Our law should not be that rigid. Pregnancy often comes more than once to the same woman, and in the general population, if man is to survive, it will always be with us. Pregnancy provides a classic justification for a conclusion of nonmootness. It truly could be "capable of repetition, yet evading review." . . .

[On standing generally, see Note, "Article III Justiciability and Class Action: Standing and Mootness," 59 *Tex. L. Rev.* (1981); James E. Radcliffe, *The Case-or-Controversy Provision* (State College: Pennsylvania State Univ. Press, 1978); Mark V. Tushnet, "The New Law of Standing: A Plea for Abandonment," 62 *Cornell L. Rev.* 663 (1977); Tinsley E. Yarbrough, "Litigant Access Doctrine and the Burger Court," 31 *Vanderbilt L. Rev.* 33 (1978). For the special standing problems of environmentalists, see Christopher D. Stone, "Should Trees Have Standing?—Toward Legal Rights for Natural Objects," 45 *So. Cal. L. Rev.* 450 (1972).]

**3. Presumption of validity of official acts.** Another feature of judicial operation which limits the chances for successful attack on official restraints lies in the courts' presumption that the acts of public officials are valid. The courts do not automatically presume that all restraints on free choice are improper. The burden is thrown on the person attacking such acts to *prove* that they are improper. This is most readily seen in cases involving the claim that an act of the legislature is unconstitutional. As Mr. Justice Bushrod Washington wrote, over a century ago, "It is but a decent respect to the wisdom, integrity, and patriotism of the legislative body, by which any law is passed, to presume in favor of its validity, until its violation of the Constitution is proved beyond a reasonable doubt." [*Ogden v. Saunders,* 12 Wheat. 213 (1827).]

In the same general direction is the view of judges that acts of administrative officials should be accorded some presumption of validity. Thus a health officer who destroys food alleged by him to be unfit for consumption is presumed to have good reason for his action. The person whose property is so destroyed must bear the burden of proving bad faith on the part of the official, if an action is brought as a consequence.

The point to be made here is that the claimant who protests the operation of a law or the act of a public official must not only show that his view of the matter is a reasonable one, but he must also show that the approach involved in the law or administrative act is clearly an unreasonable one. Thus, in *Powell v. Pennsylvania,* 127 U.S. 678 (1888), a manufacturer of oleomargarine in Pennsylvania was unable to challenge successfully a state law prohibiting the manufacture of such products in that state. He offered to show by clear and convincing tests that his product was not unhealthful and was clearly safe for human consumption. But since he could not go further and prove that the law was clearly an unreasonable approach to protecting the citizens from unsafe products of other manufacturers, he lost his case. Such a claimant, then, comes into court with the balances tilted against him. He must not merely equalize the weight in the opposite pan; he must add enough extra to tip the balance in his direction.

**4. Difficulty in extending decisions beyond specific facts and parties involved in litigation.** Technically, a decision rendered by a court binds only the parties to the suit then under consideration, and binds them only with respect to the controversy in which they are involved. If, however, the decision involves a constitutional question and is determined by the United States Supreme Court, then its effect may be considerably more far-reaching. Under our doctrine of precedent and the application of the national supremacy clause of Article VI of the United States Constitution, all state and federal judges are bound to apply the same constitutional rule if a case arises presenting a similar controversy. The point is, however, that a separate suit may be necessary to get a specific order directing that the Supreme Court's rule be followed. Two things then become apparent. First, a slight alteration of the facts presented may lead to a different decision by the Court in subsequent cases. Second, even if different parties present substantially the same fact situations, one Court decision does not by any means lead to a mass reaction on the part of legislators or administrators throughout the nation to bring their practices in line with the tenor of the Court's requirements.

The result is that inertia or opposition to a holding of a court, even the United States Supreme Court, could well mean that a prolonged period of litigation would be necessary to lead even to a partial acquiescence in the rule announced. This fact is nowhere better illustrated than in the long history of racial discrimination in according voting rights. The Fifteenth Amendment was proclaimed ratified in the year 1870. Yet until the implementation of the Voting Rights Act of 1965, almost a century later, many persons were still denied registration or voting rights solely on the grounds of race.

The words of the Fifteenth Amendment seem clear enough: "The right of citizens of the United States to vote shall not be denied or abridged by the United States or by any State on account of race, color, or previous condition of servitude." But a whole host of devices were employed to defeat the purposes of the Amendment. And in some parts of the South, as each device was held unconstitutional, a new one was substituted, which required a new course of litigation. A holding by the Court that denial of membership in the Democratic Party on account of race was unconstitutional did not preclude a state requirement that all applicants for registration give a "reasonable" interpretation of the United States Constitution. Thus a second case had to be brought and a second decision rendered on the new set of facts.

Even where the facts seem nearly identical, it still may be necessary to get a separate decree from a court in order to secure acquiescence. In *School District of Abington Township* v. *Schempp,* 374 U.S. 203 (1963), the Court held that the practices of schools in Pennsylvania and Maryland of beginning the public school day with Bible-reading and the recitation of the Lord's Prayer were an unconstitutional establishment of religion. It is clear, however, that similar programs are still in operation in various parts of the nation, but unless separate suits are brought to test the validity of such programs under the *Schempp* doctrine, they will continue indefinitely, in the absence of a legislative or administrative policy change. [See Kenneth M. Dolbeare and Phillip E. Hammond, *The School Prayer Decisions: From Court Policy to Local Practice* (Chicago: University of Chicago Press, 1971).] This lays open a key difference between the judicial process and the administrative process. The judicial process must await the sufficient irritation of the injured parties to energize its machinery. The administrative process has, by statutory grant, a built-in self-starting mechanism. Under the Occupational Safety and Health Act of 1970, for example, the Secretary of Labor may initiate inspections of workplaces to identify and seek correction of unsafe conditions. The agency need not wait for some workman to step forward and accuse his employer. In addition, the administrative agency has sufficient personnel to ensure, to a substantial degree at least, that its decisions are followed throughout all industries or areas where they may be applicable.

One way of broadening applications of decisions is to file a "class action" suit, the requirements for which are set out in Rule 23 of the Federal Rules of Civil Procedure. In general, the justification for bringing together a group of persons as a class to file as plaintiffs is that common questions of law may involve parties so numerous that joinder of all members is impractical and, further, that the risk of inconsistent disposition of separate cases or the refusal of the defendant to apply individual decisions to others similarly situated requires the issuance of a broader decree applicable to all members of the class. The courts have applied Rule 23 to permit a number of class action suits involving attacks on racial discrimination and have thus avoided the long delays occasioned by the requirement of separate suits by separate parties. In at least one area, however, the Court has applied the rule to restrict the opportunity for class actions. If the basis for federal jurisdiction is diversity of citizenship, the Congress has by statute provided that the amount in controversy must exceed $10,000 for the district courts to have jurisdiction. *Zahn* v. *International Paper Company,* 414 U.S. 291 (1973), involved a class action by petitioners, owners of property fronting on Lake Champlain in Vermont, on behalf of a class consisting of themselves and 200 lake-front property owners and lessees around the lake. They sought damages from International Paper Company, a New York corporation, for allegedly having permitted discharges from its pulp and paper-making plant to be carried into Lake Champlain, thereby polluting the waters of the lake and damaging the value and utility of the surrounding properties. The claim of each of the named plaintiffs was found to satisfy the $10,000 jurisdictional amount, but the District Court was convinced that not every individual owner in the class had suffered pollution damages in excess of $10,000. It then refused to permit the suit to proceed as a class action. The United States Supreme Court affirmed, with three justices dissenting. Thus each member of the class must claim the jurisdictional amount of damages, and if this cannot be shown, individual suits must be filed, with each plaintiff bearing the burden of expert testimony and with the additional drain on the resources of the judiciary.

**5. Limited remedies for private interference with free choice.** Another problem in the citizen's search for freedom from restriction lies in the fact that many types of interference stemming from private persons do not constitute actionable wrongs under the law. Private prejudice and private discrimination do not, in the absence of specific statutory provisions, offer grounds for judicial intervention in behalf of the sufferer. If one is denied admission to membership in a social club, for example, solely on the basis of his race or religion or political affiliation, he may understandably smart under the rejection, but the courts cannot help him (again assuming no statutory provision barring such distinctions). There are, then, many types of restraints on individual freedom of choice which are beyond the authority of courts to remove or ameliorate.

It should also be noted that the guarantees of rights in the United States Constitution only protect against *governmental* action and do not apply to purely private encroachments, except for the Thirteenth Amendment's prohibition of slavery. Remedies for private invasion must be found in statutes, the common law, or administrative agency regulations and adjudiciations.

**6. Political questions.** Another self-imposed limitation on the court's area of operation lies in the doctrine of political questions. In brief, this is the view that some problems are preeminently political in nature, and solutions should be sought in the political branches rather than in the courts. Even questions which turn on interpretations of the United States Constitution have occasionally been placed in this category, and the courts will refuse a remedy to those who claim injury. An illustration is found in the case of *Luther* v. *Borden* [7 Howard 1 (1849)] in which it was argued that the Article 4, Section

4, provision that "The United States shall guarantee to every State in this Union a Republican Form of Government" empowered the judiciary to decide which of two claimant groups was the lawful government of Rhode Island. The Court held this to be a political question outside the ambit of judicial power and one to be decided by the political branches.

In *Baker* v. *Carr* [369 U.S. 186 (1962)] the Court held that malapportionment in the lower house of a state legislature presented a proper question for judicial resolution under the Fourteenth Amendment's Equal Protection Clause. Earlier, in *Colegrove* v. *Green* [328 U.S. 549 (1946)], a minority of the Court had argued that this issue was a political question under the Guaranty Clause. In *Baker* Justice Brennan, for the majority, stated:

The nonjusticiability of a political question is primarily a function of the separation of powers. . . . Prominent on the surface of any case held to involve a political question is found a textually demonstrable constitutional commitment of the issue to a coordinate political department; or a lack of judicially discoverable and manageable standards for resolving it; or the impossibility of deciding without an initial policy determination of a kind clearly for nonjudicial discretion; or the impossibility of a court's undertaking independent resolution without expressing lack of the respect due coordinate branches of government; or an unusual need for unquestioning adherence to a political decision already made; or the potentiality of embarrassment from multifarious pronouncements by various departments on one question.

While there are factors which limit courts in protecting civil liberties, there is, nevertheless, much that they can do in this area. Even in their restricted scope of operation, the courts exercise a vast influence over the activities of both officials and private persons who themselves may never be a party to litigation. Americans have traditionally shown great respect for judicial opinion, despite occasional periods during which the courts have been under heavy fire, and it has sometimes been important in the formation of the public opinion.

One of the key powers of the courts is that of judicial review—that is, the authority to review acts of the coordinate branches (or the States, in the case of the federal courts), in appropriate cases, and to refuse to give effect to such acts on the ground of their unconstitutionality. This power of judicial review is more typically an American judicial power than one belonging to judges in all countries. Many nations today, however, permit the courts at least a limited exercise of this authority. [The standard work on judicial review in America is Charles G. Haines, *The American Doctrine of Judicial Supremacy* (Berkeley: University of California Press, 2d ed., 1959). See also Edward McWhinney, *Judicial Review in the English-Speaking World*, 4th ed. (Toronto: University of Toronto Press, 1969); Mauro Cappelletti, *Judicial Review in the Contemporary World* (Indianapolis: Bobbs-Merrill, 1971); John H. Ely, *Democracy and Distrust: A Theory of Judicial Review* (Cambridge: Harvard University Press, 1980); Stephen C. Halpern and Charles M. Lamb, eds., *Supreme Court Activism and Restraint* (Lexington, Mass.: Lexington Books, 1982); Michael J. Perry, *The Constitution, the Courts, and Human Rights* (New Haven: Yale University Press, 1982).]

Constitutional challenges may be directed to specific administrative practices rather than to a statute, and this, too, is an important aspect of the broad doctrine of judicial review. Most of the constitutional problems surrounding search and seizure cases involve challenges to police practices and not to statutes. And many of the appeals from administrative agency determinations are grounded in complaints that the agency did not follow statutory directives, not in challenges to the statutes themselves. While the bulk of challenged statutes or administrative actions are held valid, the threat of judicial review may serve as an important safeguard against improper or unconstitutional action.

## JUDICIAL REMEDIES FOR VIOLATIONS OF RIGHTS

Claims of denials of rights may be based on statutory or common-law grounds as well as on constitutional provisions. Whatever the basis for the alleged right, however, the more important specific *remedies* offered by the judicial process to wronged parties are encompassed in a relatively few procedures. And it is within the framework of these kinds of remedies that the courts serve to protect against injury or to assuage the wounds received.

**1. Mandamus.**   Mandamus is an old common-law writ which may be usefully employed against public officials in specified circumstances. Briefly put, it is a writ commanding a public officer to perform some duty which the laws require him to do but which he refuses or neglects to perform. If he has any discretion in the matter, mandamus cannot be used. But if the law is clear in requiring the performance of some ministerial function, then mandamus may properly be sought to nudge the reluctant or negligent official along in the performance of his duties.

As an illustration, one who is clearly qualified under the law to be registered as a qualified elector may use the remedy of mandamus to force the registrar who arbitrarily denies registration to place his name in the register. Since the writ cannot be employed where the official has discretion, however, it could not issue against the legislature on complaint by teen-age citizens that the voting age should be reduced to sixteen. As the United States Supreme Court stated, in *Wilbur v. United States*, 281 U.S. 206, 218 (1930):

> Where the duty in a particular situation is so plainly prescribed as to be free from doubt and equivalent to a positive command it is regarded as being so far ministerial that its performance may be compelled by mandamus, unless there be provision or implication to the contrary. But where the duty is not thus plainly prescribed but depends upon a statute the construction or application of which is not free from doubt, it is regarded as involving the character of a judgment or discretion which cannot be controlled by mandamus.

It is important to note as well that the writ does not issue to purely private persons, but can only be directed to public officials or persons performing some quasi-public function. Thus, while in its limited area it is useful, the restricted scope of application often makes it necessary for the citizen to seek other remedies.

**2. Injunction.**   The injunction is primarily a preventive remedy and issues from a court of equity. It is considerably broader in its applications than mandamus and is far more frequently employed in civil rights questions. It can apply to either ministerial or discretionary functions and to either public officials or private persons. Equity picks up where the law ends and enables a judge to frame an order or decree to fit the necessities of the case under consideration. The injunction is one of the most useful tools of the equity judge. The broad operation of the injunctive remedy is well illustrated by the school segregation cases. The complainants sought injunctions directed to various local school officials ordering them to refrain from enforcing laws requiring racial segregation in the public schools. The 1955 decision of the United States Supreme Court left the lower district court judges free to frame such decrees as appeared advisable to accomplish the ends indicated in the 1954 decision. In some areas of the South, judges issued injunctions to restrain all further attempts to enforce the school segregation laws of the areas involved. In others, special longer range programs of gradual integration were specified in the decrees. In a few instances blanket injunctions were issued to restrain any and all attempts by either officials or private persons to interfere with the integration process.

Thus the injunction is particularly useful where there is a claim that some constitutional right is abridged by the operation of a law or administrative practice and the victim desires the intervention of a court to stop the abridgment. Violation of the terms of either a mandamus or an injunction subjects the violator to the possibility of citation for contempt, with broad leeway given to the judge in determining what punishment to impose.

**3. Civil damage suit.**    Another important type of legal action to protect rights is the civil damage suit. If a citizen feels that he has been intentionally subjected to a deprivation of a right guaranteed by the law, he can initiate a suit for money damages against the offender. This is possible whether the defendant named is a private person or a public official. A person who without provocation assaults another leaves himself open to a damage suit in which the plaintiff may run up quite a list of items in the bill of damages: hospital or doctor's bills, mental and physical anguish, loss of time from work, and perhaps punitive damages as well. With the increasingly large jury verdicts in tort cases of various sorts, this type of action should pose a substantial deterrent against willful or malicious deprivation of rights. Exceptions are noted, of course, in those cases in which local sentiment runs against the plaintiff because of religion, race, past criminal activity, or some other factor which makes his cause unpopular.

While the civil suit for money damages might be useful in protecting private citizens against other private citizens, a more difficult problem is presented when the defendant is a public official, and the complaint arises from his official performance. If the official acts in good faith but makes an error of judgment, then the decision will normally run against the wronged citizen. The courts recognize that even competent, well-intentioned government personnel are sometimes known to err in the performance of their official duties. It would be a drastic rule indeed which would subject such persons to the expense of paying damages to all citizens who were inconvenienced by these mistakes. Officials might spend more time as defendants than in the pursuits of their vocations if this were allowed. Thus the plaintiff in such cases has an extra burden of proving willful or malicious deprivation of rights. This is much more difficult, and the difficulty is indicated in the relative rarity with which civil suits are successfully prosecuted against policemen, for example, for damages alleged to have been sustained by private persons in their contacts with these officials.

**4. Criminal prosecution.**    Where the deprivation of one's rights is declared by the law to be a criminal offense, the offender may not only be forced to pay damages, but he also can be put to trial for committing a crime. Suppose one is injured by the unprovoked physical assault of another. Clearly this is a situation which involves the commission of both a private and a public wrong. The victim of such treatment can sue in a civil action for damages, while the government can bring a criminal prosecution. Except in those situations where the victim is locally unpopular for one reason or another, the increasing probability of criminal prosecution has served as one factor, among others, in lessening the frequency of police brutality in the past two or three decades.

**5. Appellate court review.**    Deprivations of individual rights may take place or may be ignored in the course of judicial proceedings as well as elsewhere in life. Thus there must be some corrective which can operate on even the judicial process. The most important such device is to be found in the review of trial court proceedings by an appellate court. If errors of law are made in the trial court, or if a jury goes beyond its authority in rendering a verdict, then a case would be presented for the appropriate exercise of appellate court review and possible reversal. If a conviction is obtained under circumstances which render the possibility of a fair trial quite remote, such as mob domination or use of perjured testimony or "trial by newspaper," then an appellate court can reverse the conviction and demand a trial under more reasonable and proper conditions.

This power is a very important and highly valuable one. But it must be recognized that there are severe limitations on the effectiveness of this institution as a cure-all for mistakes in trial court proceedings. In the first place, less than five percent of the decisions of the trial courts in America are appealed. It is probably a fair assumption that in an appreciable number of the mass of unappealed cases reversible error occurred. But appellate review is not automatic, and if the losing party fails to perfect an appeal, the corrective powers of the higher courts cannot be brought to bear. In that event, the trial court decision, right or wrong, stands. In the second place, appellate courts as a general rule examine only the complaint that errors of *law* were made in the trial court, not errors in *fact-finding*. Since the disposition of large numbers of cases turns almost exclusively on the finding of facts, appeals would in most of these be completely futile.

Despite these limitations, the upper courts of both state and federal governments wield substantial powers to correct injustices in the trial courts. And it is argued by many that even where technically they might be powerless to act (e.g., under the rule of not disturbing a lower court finding of fact) there is always some point available on which a decision for reversal and an order for new trial can turn. At times the courts have even reversed on grounds which were not even raised by counsel seeking the review. These are very special cases, however, and the better view is to recognize that the power of review is useful but by no means a substitute for adequate staffing of the courts of first instance with competent personnel, and a high quality of advocacy on the part of counsel for both sides.

At this point the matter of how cases get to the United States Supreme Court deserves special treatment. Article III, Section 2, of the Constitution lists the kinds of cases and parties to which the federal judicial power extends. The Supreme Court has original jurisdiction in only two types of cases—those involving foreign ambassadors, ministers, or consuls and those in which a State is a party. In all the other cases listed in Section 2 the Court has appellate jurisdiction only, and even here the power to review is subject to "such exceptions" and "such regulations as the Congress shall make." Thus Congress has substantial authority to regulate the flow of appellate business to the Supreme Court. The previous provisions are included in Title 28, Chapter 81, of the United States Code. In general, Congress has divided the cases into two categories—those for which there is a "right" of review in the Supreme Court (called review by *appeal*) and those for which the Court has complete discretion as to whether it will grant or deny review (review by *writ of certiorari*). In applying these statutes, however, a third element comes into play. To understand fully the Court's appellate jurisdiction, then, one must look to three sources: (1) the Constitutional boundaries, which are set out in Article III, Section 2, (2) statutes of Congress which regulate appellate review, and (3) the Court's interpretations and applications of the constitutional and statutory provisions.

The Supreme Court's appellate business issues from a number of different courts: the various federal courts, including the District Courts, the ordinary Courts of Appeals, the United States Court of Appeals for the Federal Circuit, and also the state courts. While decisions of the District Courts normally reach the Supreme Court via the Courts of Appeals, Section 1253 of Title 28 provides for direct appeals from certain orders of District Courts in any civil action required by any act of Congress to be heard by a three-judge court. One illustration of such a case is a suit asking for an injunction to restrain, on grounds of unconstitutionality, the enforcement or operation of a state statute dealing with apportionment or reapportionment of legislative districts. In such a situation the case must be heard by a three-judge District Court, and the losing party has a right of appeal directly to the Supreme Court. Chief Justice Burger has argued that this provision for direct appeals places too great a burden on the Court and the Congress should at least make such direct review discretionary. While the Congress refused to go that far, it did restrict the type of cases requiring three judges in 1976 (PL 94-381), resulting in a decrease of almost fifty percent in their caseload over a two year period. In 1988 the Congress further restricted review by appeal (102 Stat. 662) by abolishing appeal from state courts and United States Courts of Appeals. Sections 1254 and 1257 of Title 28 had formerly provided for a right of appeal for certain cases in those courts. The 1988 law retains appeal only for United States District Court decisions in cases required by Congress to be heard by three judges.

All cases coming to the Court from the Courts of Appeals arrive by way of petitions for writs of certiorari, the granting of which is purely discretionary in the Court. (The matter of certified questions of law is omitted as relatively unimportant.) The writ of certiorari is an old common-law writ and historically was simply an order from a higher court to a lower court directing the latter to send up the record of a case for review. Thus, if a party has lost a decision in the United States Court of Appeals, he must petition the Supreme Court for a writ certiorari directed to the Court of Appeals if review is desired.

Aside from the various federal courts, the other source of appellate business for the Supreme Court is the state courts. But here the principle of federalism comes into play. As a broad generalization, the federal courts are established to deal with questions of federal law, and the state courts are established to handle questions of state law. There are obvious exceptions to this statement, since in diversity of jurisdiction cases the federal courts apply state law, and in many state cases questions of federal constitutional law are presented, but the generalization is still useful. The bulk of the cases decided in state courts do not involve questions of federal law, and therefore the decisions rendered in these courts will be final. Article VI of the Constitution states, however, that the United States Constitution, and the laws of the United States which shall be made in pursuance thereof, and all treaties made under the authority of the United States shall be the supreme law of the land, and the judges in every state shall be bound thereby. In the face of this doctrine of national supremacy, it would clearly be inappropriate to accord finality to State court decisions interpreting and applying federal laws, the United States Constitution, or treaties entered into by the United States. Thus provision is made for appellate review by the United States Supreme Court (not by any other federal court, however) of state court decisions which present "federal questions"—those involving federal laws, treaties, or the Constitution. Section 1257 of Title 28 provides that final judgments or decrees *rendered by the highest court of a state in which a decision could be had,* may be reviewed. All federal question decisions rendered by state courts must be reviewed by writ of certiorari. It is important to note three prerequisites for getting Supreme Court review of state court decisions. First, a federal question must be presented. If the only issue for decision is, for example, the proper distribution of property under a will as determined by the relevant state laws, then there is no federal question presented and no basis for review. Second, the losing party must have carried his case to the highest state court in which he could get a decision. While this normally means that he must have gone to the State Supreme Court, the state laws frequently provide that decisions of lower courts shall be final. Where this is true, Section 1257 of Title 28 simply requires that he go as far as he can before petitioning the United States Supreme Court for review. Third, the state court decision on the federal questions must be crucial to the decision, for if it rests on an independent state law basis, review by the Supreme Court would be fruitless. Thus if a state law is held by the state court to be violative of both the United States Constitution and the state constitution, then review of the decision regarding the application of the United States Constitution only would be pointless, since the decision would stand on an independent state law ground.

Whether the cases arrive from state or federal courts, and whether they come up on appeal or certiorari, the members of the Court examine the questions presented to determine whether they merit action. In a great many petitions the justices consider the questions to be so frivolous that they do not consider them sufficiently "reviewworthy" even to discuss at conference, and review is denied or the appeal dismissed. Justice Brennan, in an interesting article discussing the workload of the Court ["The National Court of Appeals: Another Dissent," 40 *Univ. of Chi. L. Rev.* 473 (1973)], cited several illustrations of such cases. Among the questions presented that he considered patently frivolous were: "Are Negroes in fact Indians and therefore entitled to Indians' exemptions from federal income taxes?" and "Are the federal income tax laws unconstitutional insofar as they do not provide a deduction for the depletion of the human body?"

The Court's own Rule 19, Section 1, gives the general policy regarding certiorari:

1.  A review on writ of certiorari is not a matter of right, but of sound judicial discretion, and will be granted only where there are special and important reasons therefor. The following, while neither controlling nor fully measuring the court's discretion, indicate the character of reasons which will be considered:

(a)  Where a state court has decided a federal question of substance not theretofore determined by this court, or has decided it in a way probably not in accord with applicable decisions of this court.

(b)  Where a court of appeals has rendered a decision in conflict with the decision of another court of appeals on the same matter; or has decided an important state or territorial question in a way in conflict with applicable state or territorial law; or has decided an important question of federal law which has not been, but should be, settled by this court; or has decided a federal question in a way in conflict with applicable decisions of this court; or has so far departed from the accepted and usual course of judicial proceedings, or so far sanctioned such a departure by a lower court, as to call for an exercise of this court's power of supervision.

At various times during the Term of Court, conferences are held at which all cases which seem to merit attention are discussed, and the Justices then vote on whether they should grant or deny the requests. If four or more of the Justices vote to grant certiorari, then the writ issues and the Court reviews the case. This "rule of four" is informal but has almost invariably been followed since the passage of the so-called Judges Act in 1925 which opened up the discretionary control by the Court of its appellate business. The necessity for such control is demonstrated by the fact that in the 1987 Term the Court had a total of 5,268 cases docketed. It would have been impossible to dispose of any large percentage of these cases on the merits, and the only manageable approach is to allow the Court to select the cases it deems important to decide, and to dismiss appeals and deny certiorari in all others. In that 1987 Term the Court disposed of 151 cases by signed opinion (although since some cases were combined, there were only 139 signed opinions), nine cases by per curiam opinion, and 87 cases by memorandum decision. [The statistics are reported in 57 *U.S. Law Week* 3074 (1988).] More than 90 percent of the petitions for certiorari are denied, and more than 50 percent of the appeals are dismissed. Thus one who loses a case in a trial court and exclaims vehemently, "I'll carry this all the way to the Supreme Court," has a very heavy statistical probability running against him. The opportunity for appellate review is important, and both state and national law normally provide avenues for at least one such review of trial court decisions. But the enormous volume of judicial determinations of all courts in the United States militates against United States Supreme Court review except for a minute fraction of the total number.

Mention should be made of the effect of a denial of certiorari and the dismissal of an appeal "for want of a substantial federal question." Since the granting of the writ of certiorari is purely discretionary, the accepted view is that a denial of the writ should not be construed in any way as a decision on the merits of the case. True, the result is that the decision of the court below stands, but denial of certiorari should not be interpreted as affirmance. The safe conclusion is that, for whatever reasons, there were not four members of the Court who wished to review the case, and nothing else should be read into the denial. On the other hand, it has been noted that in a substantial majority of the cases, the decision to *grant* certiorari results in a reversal of the lower court ruling. [See Stephen L. Wasby, *The Supreme Court in the Federal Judicial System*, pp. 151–152 (New York: Holt, Rinehart and Winston, 1978).]

Dismissal of appeals "for want of a substantial federal question," however, is a different matter. In *Hicks v. Miranda,* 422 U.S. 332 (1975), the Court stated that such action constitutes a binding precedent as to the federal questions presented. The majority opinion indicated that summary disposition of an appeal, either by affirmance or by dismissal for want of a substantial federal question, is a disposition on the merits. It should be noted that since late 1988 state cases are no longer reviewed by appeal, and such dismissals will no longer occur.

**6. Habeas Corpus.**   Another device available to vindicate one's legal rights is the writ of habeas corpus. Important though it is, it should be kept in mind that there are several limitations on its usefulness in the broad area of protecting personal liberties. Generally speaking, it is a device which can be used to test the legality of a physical restraint or detention. If a person is detained without any formal charge being placed against him, the writ may be used in effect to require that the man be released or a proper charge, supportable by some evidence or reliable information, be placed against him. If a prisoner has been tried and convicted, habeas corpus is still available as a potential remedy, since there is no time limit and no statute of limitations on its use. It cannot, however, be used as a substitute for ordinary appellate review, and the latter is a much broader device for raising issues concerning the interpretations of laws and the conduct of trials. Habeas corpus is referred to as a device for *collateral* attack on detention, since it opens up for investigation only such questions as are considered *jurisdictional* questions. Examples of such questions are whether the trial court which rendered judgment had authority over the person or the offense involved, or whether the prisoner was denied certain constitutional rights such as the right to counsel. On ordinary appellate review a great variety of additional points might be attacked which would be improper under habeas corpus, such as the judge's charge to the jury, the admissibility of evidence when the Fourth Amendment is not implicated, or the competency of certain witnesses to testify. [For an excellent discussion of the history and uses of the writ of habeas corpus, see David Fellman, *The Defendant's Rights Today* (Madison: Univ. of Wisconsin Press, 1976) chap. 5.] The writ is of special importance in dealing with detentions by the military, since there is no ordinary review of military court decisions by the civil courts. In 1983, however, amendments governing Supreme Court review authorized the parties to petition the Court to review decisions of the Court of Military Appeals through discretionary writs of certiorari.

While historically the writ had a relatively narrow application, the trend in the Court has been toward a definite liberalizing of the writ's uses. The "in custody" requirement for the availability of habeas corpus, for example, was held to have been met by one who was out of prison as a parolee, because of the stringent controls over the parolee exercised by the parole board. [*Jones* v. *Cunningham*, 371 U.S. 236 (1963).] And one formally charged with crime but released on bail would probably be held to meet the "in custody" test for habeas corpus purposes. In *Carafas* v. *LeVallee*, 391 U.S. 234 (1968), a prisoner filed an application for habeas corpus in federal court, alleging that illegally seized evidence had been used in securing his conviction in a state court. The application was dismissed by the District Court, and the Court of Appeals dismissed the appeal. Two weeks before filing a petition for certiorari in the United States Supreme Court, the petitioner was unconditionally released from the state prison. The Court held that the expiration of the sentence before the application for habeas corpus was finally adjudicated did not terminate federal jurisdiction, and because of the substantial disabilities which flowed from the conviction (ineligibility to engage in certain businesses, loss of voting rights, and others), the cause was not moot. Thus it was held that once federal jurisdiction attached in the District Court, it was not defeated by the release of the petitioner prior to completion of proceedings. (For a more detailed discussion of Habeas Corpus, see Chapter 3.)

## SOURCES OF INTERFERENCE WITH PERSONAL FREEDOM

Since it is clear that the courts alone cannot adequately safeguard the liberties of the people, the question naturally arises of what additional forces may be deployed to achieve the necessary protection. In approaching the problem it is convenient to look at the various *sources* of interference with our personal freedom. Some may call for a different attack than others.

One important source is the legislative body, and this includes all such bodies from the national Congress down to the municipal council. A rather flagrant example of arbitrary legislative abridgment of rights is that of a municipal ordinance which required labor union organizers to get a permit from the mayor and city council before recruiting new members and to pay a license fee of $2,000, plus $500 for each member obtained! [Held unconstitutional on its face in *Staub* v. *City of Baxley,* 355 U.S. 313 (1958).] The preventive remedies for this source of interference are easily stated but obviously rather difficult to maintain. First, we must elect a high-caliber legislature, and second, we must see that those members of the citizenry who are interested in the protection of civil rights, whether they be a majority or a minority, maintain continual pressure on the legislative body to thwart attempts to adopt such policies as that illustrated above. The ideal may be impossible to attain, but any progress in that direction represents stronger protection of civil liberties.

A second source of abridgments of rights is the administrative process. Modern government by bureaucracy involves a great deal of delegation of decision-making power to what might well be called the fourth branch of the government. Such officials, even when they act in good faith, have the power to impose a tremendous variety of improper limitations on the citizen's exercise of free choices. One example of this sort of restriction was the action of the Postmaster General some years past in withdrawing second-class mail privileges from *Esquire* magazine on the ground that it did not meet the statutory test of being "published for the dissemination of information of a public character, or devoted to literature, the sciences, arts, or some special industry." Actually, he simply disapproved of the contents. Such a withdrawal does not completely bar the designated periodical from the mails, but the first-class rates for mailing are well-nigh prohibitive for commercial publishers in a competitive market. [The Court unanimously held the action to be an unauthorized censorship: *Hannegan v. Esquire,* 327 U.S. 146 (1946).]

The nonjudicial remedies against administrative interference are similar to those applicable to the legislature. The prestige of governmental administrative service must be sufficiently enhanced to attract and keep the ablest personnel among the citizenry. Second, the people, both as individuals and as members of organizations, must maintain a continual watch over the actions of administrative officials in those areas where improper interference with private rights is apt to occur. Such abridgments as do occur should be brought promptly to the attention of both administrative supervisors and policy officials who control the agency involved. Similarly, special recognition should be accorded administrative personnel who show particular concern for the rights of the individual. Third, the legislature must be held responsible for exercising care both in its grants of statutory authority to administrators and in overseeing their functions.

Making the bureaucracy responsible to the people is one of the most difficult problems in government today. A novel approach to the problem was the development in Sweden of the office of the ombudsman. This official has discretion to investigate any administrative action or governmental agency omission impairing the rights of private persons, either on his own initiative or upon complaint filed with him. Denmark and Norway later adopted this institution, and considerable interest has been expressed in the United States. [See Donald C. Rowat, ed., *The Ombudsman: Citizen's Defender,* 2d ed. (London: Allen & Unwin, 1968); Walter Gellhorn, *When Americans Complain: Governmental Grievance Procedures* (Cambridge: Harvard University Press, 1966); and Roy V. Peel, ed., "The Ombudsman or Citizen's Defender: A Modern Institution," 377 *The Annals* (May, 1968), pp. iii–240.]

A third, and more widely publicized, source of violations of civil liberties lies in the personal malice or brutality of officials, particularly police officers. This is illustrated in peculiarly distasteful fashion by the case in which a city police chief and a sheriff's deputy forced a group of Jehovah's Witnesses to drink a half-pint of castor oil, in response to their request for police protection. [Held to come within the scope of acts punishable under the federal civil rights acts: *Catlette v. United States,* 132 F.2d 902 (4th C.A., 1943).] Many cases which are far more brutal come to light from time to time. In view of the vast number of daily contacts between police and citizen in the United States, the percentage of brutality cases must be extremely small. At least in this area, however, "small" must not be equated with "negligible." In discussing nonjudicial remedies, there is a strong tendency to propose that this type of evil will be adequately dispelled by the simple expedient of employing only well-educated young men who have passed rigid psychological tests for emotional stability. To some extent, more care in recruitment and training of policemen might well reduce the instances of police lawlessness. Assuredly this is an area in which progress can be made. But the habits and attitudes of the public toward police and law enforcement generally have a direct impact on the practices of the personnel involved. Low budgets and high pressures tend to push enforcement agencies into short-cut procedures. And community demands for unequal treatment of offenders, either on grounds of the character of the offender or of the offense, will usually find their response in the behavior of the enforcement agencies. Only if the community and the police maintain a genuine respect for following lawful procedures can such practices be minimized.

Unequal enforcement that is without brutality presents quite another problem. The average citizen is apt to hold that all criminal laws should be enforced against all offenders. A corollary would be the statement that selective enforcement constitutes a civil rights violation in that it denies equal protection of the laws. This same doctrinaire citizen would probably be enraged, however, if arrested for engaging in a penny-ante poker game on Saturday night with his close friends. As another illustration, laws against adultery are so rarely enforced in this country that one would surely hear indignant cries of "Discrimination!" if a prosecution were actually begun against one of the vast number of ordinary offenders. The suggestion is sometimes made that it would cleanse the consciences of both the police and the public if these rarely enforced criminal laws were repealed altogether. Then the laws remaining could be rewritten to make criminal *only* the specific acts which the community actively wants to see punished, and the police could push forward with full enforcement of *all* the laws.

There are several points at which these proposals are open to attack. First, the police, and (if closely questioned) in all probability the public, want to have available a full battery of weapons to use against persons in the community who are patently "undesirable." Then the prosecutor and the police who are forced by public pressures to act against a specific person can roam through the whole long list of criminal acts defined by the statutes or the common law to select the charges which can most easily be substantiated. A notorious but slippery racketeer might then be charged with adultery, when other offenders were overlooked. Admittedly, this is a sort of "The public will have its way" attitude on criminal law enforcement, but conversation with some students of the process would indicate that this conclusion is not too wide of the mark. A second difficulty with suggested remedies lies in the extreme complexity of the task of statute writing. If the reader will but sit down and try to draft a bill which would punish only the forms of gambling which the average community thinks ought to be subjected to the criminal process, he will see the problem. The attempt to exclude the church bingo game, the matching for coffee, the friendly poker game (do the stakes determine the degree of friendliness?) and the annual bet on the homecoming football game—all of which the average community would probably consider as outside the proper confines of the criminal process—will either leave the statute so ponderous as to be unwieldy (perhaps even unconstitutionally vague) or else will leave loopholes through which the professional gambler can escape. Many enforcement officers much prefer to take a flat prohibition in the law and use the law with discretion. This is another way of saying that what is desired is unequal enforcement, and a serious question may be raised as to whether there is any acceptable realistic alternative. Still a third objection to the remedies proposed lies in the budget process, mentioned above. The law enforcement process is unalterably tied to the appropriation bill. Whatever the criminal code may proscribe, the police can investigate, patrol, and prevent only to the extent that money is appropriated for these purposes. Doubling the appropriation thus could very well have the effect of markedly increasing the statistical crime rate, in the sense that the resulting step-up in police activity would normally lead to the apprehension of more criminals. More financial support should mean a nearer approach to full enforcement of the laws. But in all probability no community gives the enforcement agencies anything approaching the annual sum necessary really to approximate full enforcement of all criminal laws. The police chief simply has to stretch his appropriation to cover as nearly as possible the types of crimes which arouse the greatest public indignation and those which are cheapest to enforce. The twilight zone of unenforced laws is reserved for use against those persons who cannot effectively be reached by the other laws but who have aroused the antagonism of either the public or the officialdom.

The final source of interference with the free choice of individuals is the action of private persons. There are standard judicial remedies for a great many types of private encroachment on private rights, e.g., in the use of the laws of trespass, assault, tort, and others. Nonjudicial remedies which would increase the protection against private interference would basically go in two directions: better enforcement of existing laws and the creation of new rights. Just as government created a new right in the labor field by the laws guaranteeing protection against discrimination for union membership, so governments of the states could create rights in other aspects of man's relations with man. Attempts to go beyond the usual application of standard remedies, however, and reduce further the area of private discrimination touch on the most difficult and sensitive area of all. It is perfectly reasonable to insist that governments act without undue discrimination or favoritism. In the arena of private action, however, the individual should be allowed more room for choice, even though the basic decisions might be considered irrational by others. Governments have stepped in to remove some areas of "free" choice because of inherent inequalities in the bargaining positions of the parties involved and the severe hardships to which large numbers of people might be subjected by others. This has been true, for example, in the matter of minimum wages, maximum hours, and workmen's compensation. In matters generally considered less necessitous than the right to make a living, governments have less frequently interfered with private choices. In the equal accommodations title of the Civil Rights Act of 1964, however, the Congress took action to remove from the area of free choice one of the most exacerbating instances of private discrimination—choice of customers on the basis of race or religion in places of public accommodation.

Freedom to choose associates in either social or vocational activities often leads to exclusivity, and the excluded groups may complain that something must be done by the government to afford them a wider range of choice. The policy which would lead to wider choices for the excluded group must to that extent reduce the freedom of selection of the former. The task of the policy-maker is to weigh the importance of the activity and the number of people involved, and to balance out the conflicting gains and losses in order to make a decision as to whether governmental action will be more or less beneficial than inaction.

In conclusion, one can say that while there is a tremendous area for exploration in the nonjudicial protections which may be offered to civil liberties, the judicial arena is still of vast importance in the field. The Court is, normally, the final judge of what most of the Constitution means; the state and federal courts interpret and apply the laws in appropriate cases; and some of the finest statements in the literature on human rights are to be found in the official opinions of judges on the state and federal bench. Since this is the case, and since this work is predominantly designed to describe the present law in the field of civil rights, the material and comment to follow will center heavily on the questions which have been presented for judicial decision.

# CHAPTER 2

# *Civil Rights in the Federal System*

For the beginning student of American civil rights, one of the most perplexing features is the complication presented by the federal pattern of government. To such persons it may come as a shock to learn that even as recently as World War II the United States Constitution was construed as providing essentially a dual standard for national and state police or courts. Even today, the Constitution is interpreted as barring *federal* prosecution for serious crimes without grand jury indictment, but it permits a *state* to abolish the grand jury altogether. And until 1968 that same Constitution which guarantees the right of trial by jury to all persons charged with serious *federal* crimes allowed a *state*, if it chose to do so, to abolish the trial jury in all criminal cases, leaving the verdict to the judge. Further, until the decision in *Gideon* v. *Wainwright,* 372 U.S. 335 (1963), the state could send persons to trial accused of even serious noncapital felonies without benefit of counsel, unless they could afford their own, while the Sixth Amendment at that time was held to demand court-appointed counsel for indigent *federal* defendants in all cases more serious than "petty offenses." Thus it is necessary to understand both the basis for the dual standard originally applied and also the manner or vehicle by which the Court has moved its decisions in the direction of imposing a single standard for most of the Bill of Rights guarantees.

At the core of the matter is the fact that the Bill of Rights to the United States Constitution sets out various limitations on action by the *national* government, but it does not of its own terms in any way limit the *state* governments. Such protection as the Constitution provides against abridgment of civil rights by the state governments is to be found largely in the Civil War Amendments, and even these protections, with the exception of property rights, did not begin to take on substantial importance until the present century was well under way. Of course the most striking single development in the constitutional law of civil rights has been the "nationalization" of rights through the process of gradual "incorporation" of the various protections listed in the Bill of Rights into the due process clause of the Fourteenth Amendment. This process has been continuing, and today most of the safeguards against national action described in the Bill of Rights are similarly operative against state action through the Fourteenth Amendment. Despite this fact, there remain some differences between the two sets of guarantees, and a sophisticated understanding of civil rights in America requires an analysis of the emergence of that law in the framework of the federal system.

To begin with the Philadelphia Convention, the national Constitution was designed to describe the powers and organization of the national government, without attempting to set up simultaneously a general pattern of state government. Certain limitations on state powers are to be found in that document, to be sure, but they are largely due to the desire to protect the integrity of national powers from state interference or to ensure that the states would not thwart the flow of interstate activities by means of burdensome discriminations. It must be recalled that the states existing in 1787 already had their own constitutions and framework of government, and the framers of the national Constitution did not take it upon themselves to tamper with those going concerns except as certain transfers of power from state to nation appeared necessary. In view of the purpose for which the Philadelphia Convention assembled, it would be surprising to find the framers drawing up a detailed list of safeguards to protect the citizen against the *state* government.

From an examination of the general purposes of the framers, it is a relatively easy second step to a realization that the Bill of Rights, added in 1791, protects the citizen only against the actions of the national government. A federal system had been established. Each governmental entity, nation and state, had its own constitution defining governmental organization, powers, and limitations. The state constitutions customarily had bills of rights describing guarantees operating against state officials. The national Bill of Rights operated against the national government. It would have seemed as curious in 1791 to argue that these amendments limited the state governments as it would to have claimed that federal courts were strictly bound by the requirements of state constitutions. The clamor from north to south for the addition of a bill of rights to the proposed Constitution of 1787 stemmed from distrust of national officials, not state officials. And Hamilton's response to such critics is further support for the view that the demands were restricted to protection against national abridgment of rights. In *The Federalist*, No. 84, he stated:

> I go further, and affirm that bills of rights, in the sense and to the extent in which they are contended for, are not only unnecessary in the proposed Constitution, but would even be dangerous. They would contain various exceptions to powers not granted; and, on this very account, would afford a colorable pretext to claim more than were granted. For why declare that things shall not be done which there is no power to do? Why, for instance, should it be said that the liberty of the press shall not be restrained, when no power is given by which restrictions may be imposed?

Hamilton was stressing the point that the government was one of delegated powers only, and in the absence of a delegation of authority to restrain the press there was no power to do so. Clearly he was speaking only of the national government, since the states have broad *reserved* powers and are not held to a specific list of enumerated powers as is the national government.

Finally, the group of amendments proposed by the first House of Representatives numbered seventeen, of which only one specifically limited the states. It provided that "no state should infringe the right of trial by jury in criminal cases, nor the rights of conscience, nor the freedom of speech or of the press." It is at least a reasonable conclusion to draw from this fact that the other provisions which omitted any reference to states were not intended to apply to the states. [For possible counter-arguments to this logic, see Herman Pritchett, *The American Constitution* (New York: McGraw-Hill, 1959), p. 371.] Despite these arguments, a judicial decision was required to dispose of the question finally. The case was *Barron v. Baltimore*, decided in 1833.

### BARRON *v.* BALTIMORE
#### 7 *Peters 243 (1833)*

[The case arose out of alleged damage to a wharf owned by Barron in the course of a paving program carried out by the City of Baltimore. In the completion of the program, certain streams were diverted from their usual course, and deposits of sand

and gravel allegedly were built up at Barron's wharf to such an extent that access of vessels was prevented. A trial court verdict of $4,500 in Barron's favor was reversed by the Maryland Court of Appeals. Claiming that this action was a taking of his property for public use without just compensation, in violation of the Fifth Amendment to the United States Constitution, Barron took the question on writ of error to the United States Supreme Court. His contention was that the Fifth Amendment's broad language ought to be so construed as to restrain not only the power of the United States but also that of the State.]

Mr. Chief Justice Marshall delivered the opinion of the Court.

The judgment brought up by this writ of error having been rendered by the court of a State, this tribunal can exercise no jurisdiction over it, unless it be shown to come within the provisions of the twenty-fifth section of the Judicial Act.

The plaintiff in error contends that it comes within that clause in the Fifth Amendment to the Constitution, which inhibits the taking of private property for public use, without just compensation. He insists that this amendment, being in favor of the liberty of the citizen, ought to be so construed as to restrain the legislative power of a state, as well as that of the United States. If this proposition be untrue, the Court can take no jurisdiction of the cause.

The question thus presented is, we think, of great importance, but not of much difficulty.

The Constitution was ordained and established by the people of the United States for themselves, for their own government, and not for the government of the individual states. Each state established a constitution for itself, and, in that constitution, provided such limitations and restrictions on the powers of its particular government as its judgment dictated. The people of the United States framed such a government for the United States as they supposed best adapted to their situation, and best calculated to promote their interests. The powers they conferred on this government were to be exercised by itself; and the limitations on power, if expressed in general terms, are naturally, and, we think, necessarily applicable to the government created by the instrument. They are limitations of power granted in the instrument itself; not of distinct governments, framed by different persons and for different purposes.

If these propositions be correct, the Fifth Amendment must be understood as restraining the power of the general government, not as applicable to the states. In their several constitutions they have imposed such restrictions on their respective governments as their own wisdom suggested; such as they deemed most proper for themselves. It is a subject on which they judge exclusively, and with which others interfere no farther than they are supposed to have a common interest.

The counsel for the plaintiff in error insists that the Constitution was intended to secure the people of the several states against the undue exercise of power by their respective state governments; as well as against that which might be attempted by their general government. In support of this argument he relies on the inhibitions contained in the tenth section of the first article.

We think that section affords a strong if not a conclusive argument in support of the opinion already indicated by the Court.

[Here the Chief Justice compares some of the provisions of Article I, Section 9, with similar ones in Article I, Section 10. The former declares that "no bill of attainder or ex post facto law shall be passed." The latter declares that "no State shall pass any bill of attainder or ex post facto law." Marshall points out that despite the general wording of the prohibition in the former section it must be clear that it only applied to the Congress, because otherwise there would be no necessity for adding a separate phrase specifically forbidding the States to do these same things.]

If the original Constitution, in the ninth and tenth sections of the first article, draws this plain and marked line of discrimination between the limitations it imposes on the powers of the general government and on those of the states; if in every inhibition intended to act on state power, words are employed which directly express that intent, some strong reason must be assigned for departing from this safe and judicious course in framing the amendments, before that departure can be assumed.

We search in vain for that reason.

Had the people of the several states, or any of them, required changes in their constitutions; had they required additional safeguards to liberty from the apprehended encroachments of their particular governments, the remedy was in their own hands, and would have been applied by themselves. A convention would have been assembled by the discontented state, and the required improvements would have been made by itself. The unwieldly and cumbrous machinery of procuring a recommendation from two-thirds of Congress, and the assent of three-fourths of their sister states, could never have occurred to any human being as a mode of doing that which might be effected by the state itself. Had the framers of these amendments intended them to be limitations on the powers of the state governments, they would have imitated the framers of the original Constitution, and have expressed that intention. Had Congress engaged in the extraordinary occupation of improving the constitutions of the several states by affording the people additional protection from the exercise of power by their own governments in matters which concerned themselves alone, they would have declared this purpose in plain and intelligible language.

But it is universally understood, it is a part of the history of the day, that the great revolution which established the Constitution of the United States was not effected without immense opposition. Serious fears were extensively entertained that those powers which the patriot statesmen, who then watched over the interests of our country, deemed essential to union, and to the attainment of those invaluable objects for which union was sought, might be exercised in a manner dangerous to liberty. In almost every convention by which the Constitution was adopted, amendments to guard against the abuse of power were recommended. These amendments demanded security against the apprehended encroachments of the general government, not against those of the local governments.

In compliance with a sentiment thus generally expressed, to quiet fears thus extensively entertained, amendments were proposed by the required majority in Congress, and adopted by the states. These amendments contain no expression indicating an intention to apply them to the state governments. This Court cannot so apply them.

We are of opinion that the provision in the Fifth Amendment to the Constitution, declaring that privte property shall not be taken for public use without just compensation, is intended solely as a limitation on the exercise of power by the government of the United States, and is not applicable to the legislation of the states. We are therefore of opinion, that there is no repugnancy between the several acts of the general assembly of Maryland, given in evidence by the defendants at the trial of this cause, in the court of that state, and the Constitution of the United States. This Court, therefore, has no jurisdiction of the cause; and it is dismissed.

Despite Marshall's logic and his historical analysis, one might argue that since the First Amendment specifically restricts Congress and the next seven are general in their language, all of these latter amendments were intended to apply fully to all governments within the United States. The answer to this contention is that in reality all of the provisions embodied in the first eight amendments were one lengthy addition to the Constitution, with no necessary logic or subtle, unexpressed intent behind the separation into eight articles. Thus the specific application of the opening sentence to Congress should be carried right on through as a limitation on the appropriate arm of the *national* government in each of the provisions of the Bill of Rights.

The citizen of Barron's day might have been impelled by that decision to sit down and browse through the whole Constitution to see just what sort of safeguards that document offered against the improper interference with his rights by the agents of state governments. At that time, 1833, he would have noted the protections in Article I, Section 10, regarding ex post facto laws and bills of attainder, to which Marshall referred in the above case, but virtually nothing else. A keen observer, however, might have spotted a potential weapon in Article IV, which states in Section 2, "The citizens of each State shall be entitled to all privileges and immunities of citizens in the several States." This sentence is not noteworthy for its clarity. The lay reader might readily conjure up an interpretation which would serve as a massive barrier to state deprivations of rights. The judicial interpretations of this clause, however, gave no great encouragement to such a view.

The clause is really a shorthand version of Article 4 of the Articles of Confederation, which in long and somewhat quaint fashion declared:

**The better to secure and perpetuate mutual friendship and intercourse among the people of the different states in this Union, the free inhabitants of each of these states—paupers, vagabonds, and fugitives from justice, excepted—shall be entitled to all privileges and immunities of free citizens in the several states; and the people of each state shall have free ingress and regress to and from any other state, and shall enjoy therein all the privileges of trade and commerce, subject to the same duties, impositions, and restrictions, as the inhabitants thereof, respectively. . . .**

If one examines the Constitutional provision in the light of its predecessor in the Articles of Confederation, then it immediately becomes apparent that the purpose of the clause was to protect out-of-state residents from burdensome discriminations in favor of local residents. The framers quite reasonably anticipated an ever-increasing flow of interstate travel and interstate commerce and presumably inserted the Article IV provision to safeguard against the erection of improper barriers to that development. [See Roger Howell, "The Privileges and Immunities of State Citizenship," *Johns Hopkins University Studies in History and Political Science*, Vol. 36, No. 3 (1918).] Under such an interpretation, however, it is clear that this clause would afford no solace to the individual who claims that his rights are abridged by his own state. At the outset, then, there is a serious limitation on the usefulness of the clause to protect one's rights broadly against state deprivation.

There is another question to be answered even where the allegation is made that a state has abridged the rights of an out-of-state resident. The question is, just what kinds of rights are protected by the clause? Not until 1825 was there anything approaching an official interpretation of what rights were covered. The controversy leading to this decision arose in New Jersey and concerned rights to gather oysters.

A New Jersey statute prohibited any person not a resident of New Jersey from gathering oysters in the state. One Corfield sailed his boat into the waters of New Jersey and took oysters. His boat was seized, and he was sued in trespass. Was New Jersey's reservation of its oysters inconsistent with Article IV, Section 2, of the Constitution? Justice

Bushrod Washington, then on circuit, held the question under advisement from October term, 1824, until April term, 1825, and then gave his famous pronouncement on the meaning of the clause:

We feel no hesitation in confining these expressions to those privileges and immunities which are, in their nature fundamental; which belong, of right, to the citizens of all free governments; and which have, at all times, been enjoyed by the citizens of the several states which compose this Union, from the time of their becoming free, independent, and sovereign. What these fundamental principles are, it would perhaps be more tedious than difficult to enumerate. [The Justice then proceeds to risk tedium by recounting quite a list, including protection by the government; enjoyment of life and liberty; the right to acquire and possess property; the right of a citizen of one state to pass through, or reside in, other states for purposes of trade or profession; protection by the writ of habeas corpus; the right to institute and maintain court actions; exemption from higher taxes than are paid by other citizens of the state; and the elective franchise, as regulated by the laws of the particular state in which it is exercised.] These, and many others which might be mentioned, are, strictly speaking, privileges and immunities. [*Corfield* v. *Coryell*, 6 Fed. Cas. No. 3230, 546, 552 (1823).]

Considering the broad strokes with which Justice Washington outlined the "privileges and immunities" so protected, one might have expected him to have held oyster-taking in the protected category. He did not, however, and made a distinction between the private and personal rights covered and the common property of the people of a particular state, such as fish. He further held that the state was under no obligation to share property of this sort with citizens of other states. The precise holding of the case, with respect to fisheries, has been followed and even expanded to include game. One issue in *Baldwin* v. *Montana Fish and Game Commission*, 436 U.S. 371 (1978), was whether Montana's elk-hunting license fees, which were substantially higher for non-residents than for residents, violated the Privileges and Immunities Clause of Article IV. In upholding the law, Justice Blackmun stated for the majority:

We do not decide the full range of activities that are sufficiently basic to the 'livelihood of the Nation that the States may not interfere with a nonresident's participation therein without similarly interfering with a resident's participation. Whatever rights or activities may be "fundamental" under the Privileges and Immunities Clause, we are persuaded, and hold, that elk hunting by nonresidents in Montana is not one of them. (At 388.)

The State may also charge nonresidents a higher tuition for its schools. It may require a specified period of residence within the state before allowing divorce actions to be maintained in its courts, and this rule was upheld against claims of abridgment of the right to travel and violation of the due process clause in *Sosna* v. *Iowa*, 419 U.S. 393 (1975). The State may not generally, however, deny nonresidents access to its courts. [For an analysis of the clause and some of the major cases concerning it, see Lester S. Jayson, ed., *The Constitution of the United States of America*, revised and annotated (U.S. Government Printing Ofc., 1973), pp. 830–838.]

From both standpoints, then—the persons to whom the clause applies and the rights protected—the conclusion must be that this is a thin reed on which to rely for remedies against the State. To continue the search, what remained in the United States Constitution of the pre-Civil War period which would serve as a safeguard against abridgment of one's rights by his State? The answer is clear: nothing at all, except for the prohibitions against ex post facto laws and bills of attainder. The citizen of that period had to look to his own State laws and State constitution for redress of grievances against the officials of that government.

It should be apparent from this examination that not only did the pre-Civil War Constitution fail to restrain States in their general limitations on personal rights, but it also left the way open for the States to establish substantive and procedural standards in their respective bills of rights which were different from the protections afforded in the Bill of Rights to the United States Constitution. The fact that many of the guarantees in the state and national constitutions were in duplicate language should not lead one to the conclusion that his rights against the two governments were identical. The same phraseology was often construed differently by the separate court systems. And, as pointed out earlier, even today the State can abolish indictment by grand jury, while the Fifth Amendment makes it mandatory in federal felony cases. The net result was that the citizen had two separate packets of rights with two separate remedies for abuse, depending on which governmental entity committed the fault. This situation, then is the first complication introduced into the area of civil rights by our federal system of government.

A second complication, and the reason for the chronological references above, was introduced by the addition of the Fourteenth Amendment to the Constitution. The relevant portions of that amendment are found in Section 1:

**All persons born or naturalized in the United States, and subject to the jurisdiction thereof, are citizens of the United States and of the State wherein they reside. No State shall make or enforce any law which shall abridge the privileges or immunities of citizens of the United States; nor shall any State deprive any person of life, liberty, or property, without due process of law; nor deny to any person within its jurisdiction the equal protection of the laws.**

With the addition of this amendment in 1868 we have the first major *national* restraint upon the governments of the states in the field of civil rights. It is important to note, however, that even this protection does not reach the sort of deprivation caused by private persons. The Fourteenth Amendment is clearly a bar to certain interference occasioned by states, but does not reach the great area of injury inflicted by private action.

The immediate question presented by the addition of the Fourteenth Amendment was what kinds of rights and immunities were covered and to what extent they were covered. To be more specific, did this new amendment incorporate the long list of guarantees in the Bill of Rights and require exactly these same standards to be met by all the States? If so, then the troublesome problem of two separate packets of rights would no longer plague us. If not, then at least two alternative interpretations could be made, one of which would make the amendment merely a general statement of principle, and the other build up yet a *third* category of rights and still further complicate the problem. Let us take up the various stages of development to follow the actual line of interpretation.

Over a period of years, class after class of beginning students has been asked to select the phrase from the Fourteenth Amendment which would appear to offer the most substantial protection against encroachment by the state government upon their rights. Almost without fail, the clause selected is, "No State shall make or enforce any law which shall abridge the privileges or immunities of citizens of the United States." And it would seem to be a reasonable choice. The words have the ring of freedom about them. Unfortunately, judicial interpretation has shown this answer to be altogether wrong. The leading decision on what the privileges and immunities clause means was rendered in 1873 in the *Slaughter-House Cases.*

Despite the fact that the Fourteenth Amendment was primarily enacted to protect the newly freed Negro, it was a group of Southern whites who first invoked the amendment against the carpetbag laws of their own state.

## SLAUGHTER-HOUSE CASES
### 16 Wallace 36 (1873)

[In 1869 the Republican legislature of Louisiana passed an act "to protect the health of the city of New Orleans," which incorporated a slaughter-house company and gave it a twenty-five-year monopoly on the slaughtering business in that city. The law required that all other butchers in New Orleans come to that company and pay for the use of its abattoir. The case went up through the state courts with the Republican courts, of course, sustaining the statute. It was argued before the United States Supreme Court that the statute violated four parts of the United States Constitution: the Thirteenth Amendment and the "privileges and immunities" clause, the "due process" clause, and the "equal protection" clause of the Fourteenth Amendment. Since the main thrust of the opinion was in response to the "privileges and immunities" argument, the other portions of the opinion will be reserved for later discussion.]

On Writ of Error to the Supreme Court of the State of Louisiana.

Mr. Justice Miller delivered the opinion of the Court.

The plaintiffs in error. . .allege that the Statute is a violation of the Constitution of the United States in these several particulars:

That it creates an involuntary servitude forbidden by the Thirteenth Article of Amendment;

That it abridges the privileges and immunities of citizens of the United States;

That it denies to the plaintiffs the equal protection of the laws; and,

That it deprives them of their property without due process of law; contrary to the provisions of the first section of the Fourteenth Article of Amendment.

This Court is thus called upon for the first time to give construction to these Articles.

We do not conceal from ourselves the great responsibility which this duty devolves upon us. No questions so far-reaching and pervading in their consequences, so profoundly interesting to the people of this country, and so important in their bearing upon the relations of the United States and of the several states to each other, and to the citizens of the states and of the United States have been before this Court during the official life of any of its present members. . . .

[Here the Justice discusses the background of the citizenship clause of Section 1, and the holding in the Dred Scott case, to the effect that a man of African descent, whether a slave or not, was not and could not be a citizen of a state or of the United States.]

To remove this difficulty primarily, and to establish a clear and comprehensive definition of citizenship which should declare what should constitute citizenship of the United States, and also citizenship of a state, the first clause of the first section was framed.

"All persons born or naturalized in the United States, and subject to the jurisdiction thereof, are citizens of the United States and of the State wherein they reside."

The first observation we have to make on this clause is that it puts at rest both the questions which we stated to have been the subject of differences of opinion. It declares that persons may be citizens of the United States without regard to their citizenship of a particular state, and it overturns the Dred Scott decision by making all persons born within the United States and subject to its jurisdiction citizens of the United States. That its main purpose was to establish the citizenship of the Negro can admit of no doubt. The phrase "subject to its jurisdiction" was intended to exclude from its operation children of ministers, consuls, and citizens or subjects of foreign states born within the United States.

The next observation is more important in view of the arguments of counsel in the present case. It is, that the distinction beween citizenship of the United States and citizenship of a state is clearly recognized and established. Not only may a man be a citizen of the United States without being a citizen of a state, but an important element is necessary to convert the former into the latter. He must reside within the state to make him a citizen of it, but it is only necessary that he should be born or naturalized in the United States to be a citizen of the Union.

It is quite clear, then, that there is a citizenship of the United States, and a citizenship of a state, which are distinct from each other, and which depends upon different characteristics or circumstances in the individual.

We think this distinction and its explicit recognition in this Amendment of great weight in this argument, because the next paragraph of this same section, which is the one mainly relied on by the plaintiffs in error, speaks only of privileges and immunities of citizens of the United States, and does not speak of those of citizens of the several states. The argument, however, in favor of the plaintiffs rests wholly on the assumption that the citizenship is the same, and the privileges and immunities guaranteed by the clause are the same.

The language is: "No state shall make or enforce any law which shall abridge the privileges or immunities of citizens of the United States." It is a little remarkable, if this clause was intended as a protection to the citizen of a state against the legislative power of his own state, that the words "citizen of the state" should be left out when it is so carefully used, and used in contradistinction to "citizens of the United States" in the very sentence which precedes it. It is too clear for argument that the change in phraseology was adopted understandingly and with a purpose.

Of the privileges and immunities of the citizens of the United States, and of the privileges and immunities of the citizen of the state, and what they respectively are, we will presently consider; but we wish to state here that it is only the former which are placed by this clause under the protection of the Federal Constitution, and that the latter, whatever they may be, are not intended to have any additional protection by this paragraph of the Amendment.

If, then, there is a difference between the privileges and immunities belonging to a citizen of the United States as such, and those belonging to the citizen of the state as such, the latter must rest for their security and protection where they have heretofore rested; for they are not embraced by this paragraph of the Amendment.

The first occurrence of the words "privileges and immunities" in our constitutional history is to be found in the fourth of the Articles of the old Confederation.

[Here the Justice traces the development of the Article IV, Section 2, privileges and immunities clause in the Constitution, and cites Justice Washington's opinion in *Corfield* v. *Coryell,* discussed earlier in this chapter.]

In the case of *Paul* v. *Virginia,* the court, in expounding this clause of the Constitution, says that "the privileges and immunities secured to citizens of each state in the several states, by the provision in question, are those privileges and immunities which are common to the citizens in the latter states under their Constitution and laws by virtue of their being citizens."

The constitutional provision there alluded to did not create those rights, which it called privileges and immunities of citizens of the states. It threw around them in that clause no security for the citizen of the state in which they were claimed or exercised. Nor did it profess to control the power of the state governments over the rights of its own citizens.

Its sole purpose was to declare to the several states, that whatever those rights, as you grant or establish them to your own citizens, or as you limit or qualify, or impose restrictions on their exercise, the same, neither more nor less, shall be the measure of the rights of citizens of other states within your jurisdiction.

It would be the vainest show of learning to attempt to prove by citations of authority, that up to the adoption of the recent Amendments, no claim or pretense was set up that those rights depended on the Federal government for their existence or protection, beyond the very few express limitations which the Federal Constitution imposed upon the states—such, for instance, as the prohibition against ex post facto laws, bills of attainder, and laws impairing the obligation of contracts. But with the exception of these and a few other restrictions, the entire domain of the privileges and immunities of citizens of the states, as above defined, lay within the constitutional and legislative power of the states, and without that of the Federal government. Was it the purpose of the Fourteenth Amendment, by the simple declaration that no state should make or enforce any law which shall abridge the privileges and immunities of citizens of the United States, to transfer the security and protection of all the civil rights which we have mentioned, from the states to the Federal government? And where it is declared that Congress shall have the power to enforce that article, was it intended to bring within the power of Congress the entire domain of civil rights heretofore belonging exclusively to the states?

All this and more must follow, if the proposition of the plaintiffs in error be sound. For not only are these rights subject to the control of Congress whenever in its discretion any of them are supposed to be abridged by state legislation, but that body may also pass laws in advance, limiting and restricting the exercise of legislative power by the states, in their most ordinary and usual functions, as in its judgment it may think proper on all such subjects. And still further, such a construction followed by the reversal of the judgments of the supreme court of Louisiana in these cases would constitute this court a perpetual censor upon all legislation of the states, on the civil rights of their own citizens, with authority to nullify such as it did not approve as consistent with those rights, as they existed at the time of the adoption of this Amendment. The argument, we admit, is not always the most conclusive which is drawn from the consequences urged against the adoption of a particular construction of an instrument. But when, as in the case before us, these consequences are so serious, so far-reaching and pervading, so great a departure from the structure and spirit of our institutions; when the effect is to fetter and degrade the state governments by subjecting them to the control of Congress, in the exercise of powers heretofore universally conceded to them of the most ordinary and fundamental character; when in fact it radically changes the whole theory of the relations of the state and Federal governments to each other and of both these governments to the people; the argument has a force that is irresistible, in the absence of language which expresses such a purpose too clearly to admit of doubt.

We are convinced that no such results were intended by the Congress which proposed these amendments, nor by the legislatures of the states, which ratified them.

Having shown that the privileges and immunities relied on in the argument are those which belong to citizens of the states as such, and that they are left to the state governments for security and protection, and not by this article placed under the special care of the Federal government, we may hold ourselves excused from defining the privileges and immunities of citizens of the United States which no state can abridge, until some case involving those privileges may make it necessary to do so.

But lest it should be said that no such privileges and immunities are to be found if those we have been considering are excluded, we venture to suggest some which owe their existence to the Federal government, its national character, its Constitution, or its laws.

One of these is well described in the case of *Crandall* v. *Nevada.* It is said to be the right of the citizen of this great country, protected by implied guarantees of its Constitution, "to come to the seat of government to assert any claim he may have upon that government, to transact any business he may have with it, to seek its protection, to share its offices, to engage in administering its functions. He has the right of free access to its seaports, through which all operations of foreign commerce are conducted, to the sub-treasuries, land-offices, and courts of justice in the several states." And quoting from the language of Chief Justice Taney in another case, it is said "that, for all the great purposes for which the Federal government was established, we are one people with one common country; we are all citizens of the United States"; and it is as such citizens that their rights are supported in this court in *Crandall* v. *Nevada.*

Another privilege of a citizen of the United States is to demand the care and protection of the Federal government over his life, liberty, and property when on the high seas or within the jurisdiction of a foreign government. Of this there can be no doubt, nor that the right depends upon his character as a citizen of the United States. The right to peaceably assemble and petition for redress of grievances, the privilege of the writ of habeas corpus, are rights of the citizen guarantied by the Federal Constitution. The right to use the navigable waters of the United States, however they may penetrate the territory of the several states, and all rights secured to our citizens by treaties with foreign nations, are dependent upon citizenship of the United States, and not citizenship of a state. One of these privileges is conferred by the very article under consideration. It is that a citizen of the United States can, of his own volition, become a citizen of any state of the Union by a bona fide residence therein, with the same rights as other citizens of that state. To these may be added the rights secured by the thirteenth and fifteenth articles of amendment, and by the other clause of the fourteenth, next to be considered.

But it is useless to pursue this branch of the inquiry, since we are of opinion that the rights claimed by these plaintiffs in error, if they have any existence, are not privileges and immunities of citizens of the United States within the meaning of the clause of the fourteenth amendment under consideration. . . .

*Judgment affirmed.*

Justice Field, with Chief Justice Chase and Justices Swayne and Bradley concurring, rendered a dissenting opinion. He stated, in part:

The amendment does not attempt to confer any new privileges or immunities upon citizens, or to enumerate or define those already existing. It assumes that there are such privileges and immunities which belong of right to citizens as such, and ordains that they shall not be abridged by State legislation. If this inhibition has no reference to privileges and immunities of this character, but only refers, as held by the majority of the court in their opinion, to such privileges and immunities as were before its adoption specially designated in the Constitution or necessarily implied as belonging to citizens of the United States, it was a vain and idle enactment, which accomplished nothing, and most unnecessarily excited Congress and the people on its passage. With privileges and immunities thus designated or implied no State could ever have interfered by its laws, and no new constitutional provision was required to inhibit such interference. The supremacy of the Constitution and the laws of the United States always controlled any State legislation of that character.

Almost without exception, the interpretation given the privileges and immunities clause by the Court in the *Slaughter-House Cases* has remained the official view. The result has been that this clause affords no protection to the individual who claims that state officials have deprived him of rights which most of us consider the basic rights: freedom of speech, religious freedom, the right to engage in lawful occupations, freedom from improper police violence, and others of this nature. The initial reaction of many people to a reading of the opinion for the Court is frank surprise. One will frequently hear the remark that such a bad law *must* be unconstitutional, and the Court was derelict in its duty in refusing to hold it so. On the other hand, if Justice Miller's reasoning is carefully examined, it becomes clearer that the overall policy which he set out was beneficial in two important respects.

First, it recognized the existence of the two spheres of authority which the Constitution established in providing for the federal system of government. If we are to have a federal form, the agencies of the national government cannot be permitted to exercise a general supervisory power over every facet of state activity. This would make the states mere administrative subdivisions of the national government. A good case can be made for the unitary form of government, of course, but we have made no constitutional provision for such an arrangement. States are expected to operate more or less autonomously in many areas of policy-making, and it is improper for the arms of the national government to reach down to the purely local level to interfere with this discretionary power. State experiments in unemployment compensation or the use of the merit system of public employment which were dubbed "crackpot" in one period were in a later period adopted by all other states and the national government as well. And policies which are quite congenial to the residents of one state may find stubborn resistance in another. Thus Justice Miller's opinion shows a conscious refusal to stay the power of the state to experiment or to differ with its neighbors in the Union. It can quite properly be characterized as a strong "states-rights" decision.

A second beneficial aspect of the decision lies in the fact that the Court recognized the importance of judicial restraint in matters where the local citizenry should assume responsibility. The federal judges, with life tenure, are largely outside the control of the citizenry. The bench of even the states is not responsive to popular pressures to the degree to which the legislative and executive branches are. Thus errors committed by the judges may take longer to correct than would be the case with the other branches. The judge, then, must be constantly mindful of the ballot box as a remedy at least as important and perhaps more appropriate than judicial review for correcting the policy mistakes of governors and legislators.

An important consequence of the decision—whether beneficial or not depends upon the point of view—was its impact upon the possible enforcement legislation which Section 5 of the Fourteenth Amendment empowers Congress to enact. The fact of the matter seems to be that by the narrow coverage allowed to the privileges and immunities clause, the Court cut the heart out of one of the most potentially powerful weapons which Congress might have used to legislate in the civil rights area. The only remaining clauses of the amendment of importance for this purpose are the due process and equal protection clauses. Looking at these three clauses from the legislator's viewpoint, which would afford the simplest framework for enforcement legislation? It would appear that the privileges and immunities clause is tailor-made for such a purpose. All one need do would be to set out a comprehensive list of the vast number of rights which the average person considers to flow from possession of United States citizenship, and then make it a crime for any agent of the State to abridge such rights. The restrictive decision in Slaughter-House, however, effectively blocked such an approach. The remaining two clauses are far more elusive as reference points for enforcement legislation. How does one frame a statute to protect a person from state deprivation of his liberty "without due process of law"? Except, perhaps, in the area of racial discrimination, how can a bill-drafter come to grips with the requirement of "equal protection of the laws," which allows so much flexibility in classifying the objects of legislation? Even leaving aside the important political barriers to passing civil rights laws, the technical difficulties in phrasing bills to accomplish the purposes without being unconstitutionally vague are formidable.

The decision in the Slaughter-House Cases is thus in the same vein as Barron v. Baltimore. Federal rights and state rights are two different things, and one must take care to make the proper distinction so that the correct remedy can be selected when abridgment is alleged. To this day, the rule of the Slaughter-House Cases with respect to the privileges and immunities clause is still good law. The only aberration was in 1935, when the Court held in Colgate v. Harvey, 296 U.S. 404 (1935), that the right of a citizen of the United States to do business in, or place a loan in, a state other than that of his residence was a privilege of national citizenship. Only five years later, however, the Court expressly overruled that decision in Madden v. Kentucky, 309 U.S. 83 (1940), and returned to the old interpretation. Madden held that for a state to impose on its citizens a higher tax on out-of-state bank deposits than on those deposited within the state was not a violation of the privileges or immunities of national citizenship, since "the right to carry out an incident to a trade, business or calling such as the deposit of money in banks is not a privilege of national citizenship." And in Snowden v. Hughes, 321 U.S. 1 (1944), the Court held that the right to become a candidate for, and to be elected to, a state office was not among the privileges of United States citizenship but was an attribute of state citizenship. The complainant, then, had to look to his own state constitution and laws for redress of his injury, at least so far as this clause of the Constitution was concerned.

But what of the other two clauses in the Fourteenth Amendment—the due process and equal protection clauses? Are these no more useful as guarantees against state interference than the privileges and immunities clause proved to be? Again, the starting point is the Slaughter-House opinion of Justice Miller, but the subsequent developments have been vastly different. The appellants in the case argued most vigorously on the privileges and immunities ground, but the latter two clauses were tossed in for good measure. As to these claims, Justice Miller stated:

> The argument has not been much pressed in these cases that the defendant's charter deprives the plaintiffs of their property without due process of law, or that it denies to them the equal protection of the law. The first of these paragraphs has been in the Constitution since the adoption of the Fifth Amendment, as a restraint upon the federal power. It is also to be found in some form of expression in the constitutions of nearly all the states, as a restraint upon the power of the states. This law, then, has practically been the same as it now is during the existence of the government, except so far as the present Amendment may place the restraining power over the states in this matter in the hands of the federal government.
>
> We are not without judicial interpretation, therefore, both state and national, of the meaning of this clause. And it is sufficient to say that under no construction of that provision that we have ever seen, or any that we deem admissible, can the re-

straint imposed by the state of Louisiana upon the exercise of their trade by the butchers of New Orleans be held to be a deprivation of property within the meaning of that provision.

"Nor shall any State deny to any person within its jurisdiction the equal protection of the laws."

In the light of the history of these Amendments, and the pervading purpose of them, which we have already discussed, it is not difficult to give a meaning to this clause. The existence of laws in the states where the newly emancipated Negroes resided, which discriminated with gross injustice and hardship against them as a class, was the evil to be remedied by this clause, and by it such laws are forbidden.

If, however, the states did not conform their laws to its requirements, then by the fifth section of the Article of Amendment Congress was authorized to enforce it by suitable legislation. We doubt very much whether any action of a state not directed by way of discrimination against the Negroes as a class, or on account of their race, will ever be held to come within the purview of this provision. It is so clearly a provision for that race and that emergency, that a strong case would be necessary for its application to any other. But as it is a state that is to be dealt with, and not alone the validity of its laws, we may safely leave that matter until Congress shall have exercised its power, or some case of state oppression, by denial of equal justice in its courts, shall have claimed a decision at our hands. We find no such case in the one before us, and do not deem it necessary to go over the argument again, as it may have relation to this particular clause of the Amendment. . . .

In almost perfunctory fashion, then, Justice Miller denied the contention that the due process clause barred the state from enforcing the butcher monopoly law. Except for his statements concerning the recognition of the federal form of government, it is not really clear just why such a law would not constitute a taking of property without due process of law. To fill the gap here, however, one may look to another opinion for the Court filed by Justice Miller a few years later. The case was *Davidson v. New Orleans,* 96 U.S. 97 (1878), and it dealt with the question of whether a special assessment on certain real estate, for the purpose of draining swamp lands, which allegedly would not benefit the assessed landowner, constituted a taking of property without due process of law. The Louisiana Supreme Court had held against the owner, and the United States Supreme Court reviewed the decision under the question stated. Justice Miller, speaking for the Court, gave a very narrow construction to the clause. In essence, his argument is summarized in the following statements:

It is not possible to hold that a party has, without due process of law, been deprived of his property, when, as regards the issues affecting it, he has, by the laws of the State, a fair trial in a court of justice, according to the modes of proceeding applicable to such a case. . . .

This proposition covers the present case. Before the assessment could be collected, or become effectual, the statute required that the tableau of assessments should be filed in the proper District Court of the State; that personal service of notice, with reasonable time to object, should be served on all owners who were known and within reach of process, and due advertisement made as to those who were unknown, or could not be found. This was compiled with; and the party complaining here appeared, and had a full and fair hearing in the court of the first instance, and afterwards in the Supreme Court. If this be not due process of law, then the words can have no definite meaning as used in the Constitution.

It is clear from this excerpt of Justice Miller's opinion that to him all that the term "due" process required of the state was "legal" process. If all the forms required by state constitution or statute were met, and if the injured party had his "day in court," then he could not successfully contend that the substance of the law should concern the federal courts under a claim of Fourteenth Amendment violation.

Unlike the privileges and immunities clause, however, the due process clause underwent a radical change from the interpretation which Justice Miller gave it. The concurring opinion of Justice Bradley in *Davidson* v. *New Orleans* foretold the direction in which later interpretations of the clause would move:

> In the conclusion and general tenor of the opinion just read, I concur. But I think it narrows the scope of inquiry as to what is due process of law more than it should do.
>
> It seems to me that private property may be taken by a State without due process of law in other ways than by mere direct enactment, or the want of a judicial proceeding. . . . I think, therefore, we are entitled, under the fourteenth amendment, not only to see that there is some process of law, but "due process of law," provided by the State law when a citizen is deprived of his property; and that, in judging what is "due process of law," respect must be had to the cause and object of the taking, whether under the taxing power, the power of eminent domain, or the power of assessment for local improvements, or none of these; and if found to be suitable or admissible in this special case, it will be adjudged to be "due process of law"; but if found to be arbitrary, oppressive, and unjust, it may be declared to be not "due process of law." Such an examination may be made without interfering with that large discretion which every legislative power has of making wide modifications in the forms of procedure in each case, according as the laws, habits, customs, and preferences of the people of the particular State may require.

The two cases just discussed indicate the strong reluctance of the majority on the United States Supreme Court in the 1870s to allow the Fourteenth Amendment to become a vehicle for wholesale judicial review by the Court of the laws and policies adopted by the states. However, the opinion of Justice Bradley, just quoted, contained the seeds of development of the due process clause into quite a different and stronger weapon of supervision. Beginning in the economic area, with careful scrutiny of state laws interfering with the owner's use of property, the Court gradually toward the end of the nineteenth century assumed the power to determine whether such laws were so "arbitrary, oppressive, and unjust" as to amount to a deprivation of property without due process of law. Thus the Court moved away from a mere test of *procedural* regularity to an examination of the *substance* of the challenged law in the determination of constitutional validity. And so was born the concept of "*substantive* due process of law" to expand the scope of review beyond the narrower test of "*procedural* due process of law."

The classic case illustrative of the substantive due process approach is *Lochner* v. *New York*, 198 U.S. 45 (1905), in which the issue was whether a New York law limiting the hours of work for bakers to ten hours per day or sixty hours per week was a deprivation of liberty without due process of law under the Fourteenth Amendment. In holding the law invalid the Court made no mention whatever of procedures. The whole thrust of the opinion by Justice Peckham was that the law was an unreasonable interference with the liberty of persons or the right of free contract. He stated further:

> It is impossible for us to shut our eyes to the fact that many of the laws of this character, while passed under what is claimed to be the police power for the purpose of

protecting the public health or welfare, are, in reality, passed from other motives. . . .

. . . It seems to us that the real object and purpose were simply to regulate the hours of labor between the master and his employees (all being men, *sui juris*), in a private business, not dangerous in any degree to morals, or in any real and substantial degree to the health of the employees. Under such circumstances the freedom of master and employee to contract with each other in relation to their employment, and in defining the same, cannot be prohibited or interfered with, without violating the federal Constitution.

This highly subjective approach to judicial review of state economic regulations continued until the late 1930s. At that time the Court virtually adopted a "hands-off" attitude to state economic regulation unless there was a conflict with federal law. [See *West Coast Hotel Co.* v. *Parrish,* 300 U.S. 379 (1937), upholding a state law fixing minimum wages for women and minors, for example.]

More and more frequently during the latter years of the nineteenth century the Court was criticized for placing the property protection of the Fourteenth Amendment ahead of protection to life and liberty. Efforts were made in arguing some of the cases to prove that at least in the area of criminal procedure the Fourteenth Amendment really represented a shorthand adoption of the procedural guarantees listed in the Bill of Rights.

One of the most important cases involving this approach was *Twining* v. *New Jersey,* decided in 1908. Counsel for Twining in effect tried to convince the Court that either the privileges and immunities clause or the due process clause, or both of them, included the whole list of rights which the Bill of Rights protects from national abridgment. The Court's analysis of the issues readily breaks into two parts to answer the contentions made under these two clauses of the Fourteenth Amendment.

## TWINING *v.* NEW JERSEY
### *211 U.S. 78 (1908)*

[Twining and Cornell, directors of a bank in New Jersey, were indicted for having knowingly exhibited a false paper to a state bank examiner with intent to deceive him as to the condition of the bank. At the trial the defendants called no witnesses and did not testify in their own behalf. In his charge to the jury the judge said: "Because a man does not go upon the stand you are not necessarily justified in drawing an inference of guilt. But you have a right to consider the fact that he does not go upon the stand where a direct accusation is made against him."

The defendants were convicted and sentenced to imprisonment for six and four years respectively. This was affirmed by the Court of Errors and Appeals, and the case was then carried to the United States Supreme Court on the claim that the charge to the jury constituted a form of self-incrimination which abridged their privileges and immunities as United States citizens and led to a deprivation of liberty without due process of law. The attempt was to show that the Fifth Amendment's protection against self-incrimination had been included in the Fourteenth Amendment as a protection against the states.]

Justice Moody delivered the opinion of the Court.

[On the "privileges and immunities" issue:]

The defendants contend, in the first place, that the exemption from self-incrimination is one of the privileges and immunities of citizens of the United States which the Fourteenth Amendment forbids the States to abridge. It is not argued that the defendants are protected by that part of the Fifth Amendment which provides that "no person . . . shall be compelled in any criminal case to be a witness against himself," for it is recognized by counsel that by a long line of decisions the first ten Amendments are not operative on the States. *Barron* v. *Baltimore,* 7 Pet. 243; . . . But it is argued that this privilege is one of the fundamental rights of National citizenship, placed under National protection by the Fourteenth Amendment, and it is specifically argued that the "privileges and immunities of citizens of the United States," protected against State action by that Amendment, include those fundamental personal rights which are protected against National action by the first eight Amendments; that this was the intention of the framers of the Fourteenth Amendment, and that this part of it would otherwise have little or no meaning and effect. These arguments are not new to this court and the answer to them is found in its decisions. The meaning of the phrase "privileges and immunities of citizens of the United States," as used in the Fourteenth Amendment, came under early consideration in the *Slaughter-House Cases,* 16 Wall. 36. . . .

. . . If, then, it be assumed, without deciding the point, that an exemption from compulsory self-incrimination is what is described as a fundamental right belonging to all who live under a free government, and incapable of impairment by legislation or judicial decision, it is, so far as the states are concerned, a fundamental right inherent in state citizenship, and is a privilege or immunity of that citizenship only. Privileges and immunities of citizens of the United States, on the other hand, are only such as arise out of the nature and essential character of the national government, or are specifically granted or secured to all citizens or persons by the Constitution of the United States. *Slaughter-House Cases* . . .

Thus, among the rights and privileges of national citizenship recognized by this court are the right to pass freely from state to state (*Crandall* v. *Nevada,* 6 Wall. 35); the right to petition Congress for a redress of grievances (*U.S.* v. *Cruikshank*); the right to vote for national officers (Ex parte *Yarbrough,* 115 U.S. 651); the right to enter the public lands (*U.S.* v. *Waddell,* 112 U.S. 76); the right to be protected against violence while in the lawful custody of a United States marshal (*Logan* v. *U.S.,* 144 U.S. 263); and the right to inform the United States authorities of violation of its laws (*Re Quarles,* 158 U.S. 532). . . . But assuming it to be true that the exemption from self-incrimination is not, as a fundamental right of national citizenship, included in the privileges and immunities of citizens of the United States, counsel insist that, as a right specifically granted or secured by the Federal Constitution, it is included in them. This view is based upon the contention which must now be examined, that the safeguards of personal rights which are enumerated in the first eight articles of amendment to the Federal Constitution, sometimes called the Federal Bill of Rights, though they were by those Amendments originally secured only against national action, are among the privileges and immunities of citizens of the United States, which this clause of the Fourteenth Amendment protects against state action. This view has been, at different times, expressed by justices of this court . . . and was undoubtedly that entertained by some of those who framed the Amendment. It is, however, not profitable to examine the weighty arguments in its favor, for the question is no longer open in this court. The right of trial by jury in civil cases, guaranteed by the Seventh Amendment (*Walker* v. *Sauvinet,* 92 U.S. 90), and the right to bear arms, guaranteed by the Second Amendment (*Presser* v. *Illinois,* 116 U.S. 252), have been distinctly held not to be privileges and immunities of citizens of the United States, guaranteed by the Fourteenth Amendment against abridgment by the states, and in effect the same decision was made in respect of the guaranty against prosecution, except by indictment of a grand jury, contained in the Fifth Amendment (*Hurtado* v. *California,* 110 U.S. 516), and in respect of the right to be confronted with witnesses, contained in the Sixth Amendment (*West* v. *Louisiana,* 194 U.S. 258). In *Maxwell* v. *Dow* (176 U.S. 606), where the plaintiff in error had been convicted in a state court of a felony upon an information, and by a jury of eight persons, it was held that the indictment made indispensable by the Fifth Amendment, and the trial by jury, guaranteed by the Sixth Amendment, were not privileges and immunities of citizens of the United States, as those words were used in the Fourteenth Amendment. The discussion in that case ought not to be repeated. All the arguments for the other view were considered and answered, the authorities were examined and analyzed, and the decision rested upon the ground that this clause of the Fourteenth Amendment did not forbid the states to abridge the personal rights enumerated in the first eight Amendments, because those rights were not within the meaning of the clause "privileges and immunities of citizens of the United States.". . . We conclude, therefore, that the exemption from compulsory self-incrimination is not a privilege or immunity of national citizenship guaranteed by this clause of the Fourteenth Amendment against abridgment by the states.

[On the "due process" issue:]

The defendants, however, do not stop here. They appeal to another clause of the Fourteenth Amendment, and insist that the self-incrimination which they allege the instruction to the jury compelled was a denial of due process of law. This contention requires separate consideration, for it is possible that some of the personal rights safeguarded by the first eight Amendments against national action may also be safeguarded against state action, because a denial of them would be a denial of due process of law. . . . If this is so, it is not because those rights are enumerated in the first eight Amendments, but because they are of such a nature that they are included in the conception of due process of law. Few phrases of the law are so elusive of exact apprehension as this. Doubtless the difficulties of ascertaining its connotation have been increased in American jurisprudence, where it has been embodied in constitutions and put to new uses as a limit on legislative power. This court has always declined to give a comprehensive definition of it, and has preferred that its full meaning should be gradually ascertained by the process of inclusion and exclusion in the course of the decisions of cases as they arise. There are certain general principles, well settled, however, which narrow the field of discussion, and may serve as helps to correct conclusions. These principles grow out of the proposition universally accepted by American courts on the authority of Coke, that the words "due process of law" are equivalent in meaning to the words "law of the land," contained in that chapter of Magna Charta which provides that "no freeman shall be taken, or imprisoned, or disseised, or outlawed, or exiled, or any wise destroyed; nor shall we go upon him, nor send upon him, but by the lawful judgment of his peers or by the law of the land.". . . From the consideration of the meaning of the words in the light of their historical origin this court has drawn the following conclusions:

First. What is due process of law may be ascertained by an examination of those settled usages and modes of proceedings existing in the common and statute law of England before the emigration of our ancestors, and shown not to have been unsuited to their civil and political condition by having been acted on by them after the settlement of this country. . . . "A process of law," said Mr. Justice Matthews, . . . "which is not otherwise forbidden, must be taken to be due process of law, if it can show the sanction of settled usage both in England and in this country." *Hurtado* v. *California,* 110 U.S. 516, 528.

Second. It does not follow, however, that a procedure settled in English law at the time of the emigration, and brought to this country and practised by our ancestors, is an essential element of due process of law. If that were so, the procedure of the first half of the seventeenth century would be fastened upon the American jurisprudence like a straight-jacket, only to be unloosed by constitutional amendment. That, said Mr. Justice Matthews, in the same case, p. 529, "would be to deny every quality of the law but its age, and to render it incapable of progress or improvement.". . .

Third. But consistently with the requirements of due process, no change in ancient procedure can be made which disregards those fundamental principles, to be ascertained from time to time by judicial action, which have relation to process of law, and protect the citizen in his private right, and guard him against the arbitrary action of government. This idea has been many times expressed in differing words by this court, and it seems well to cite some expressions of it. . . . "This court has never attempted to define with precision the words 'due process of law.'. . . It is sufficient to say that there are certain immutable principles of justice which inhere in the very idea of free government which no member of the Union may disregard." *Holden* v. *Hardy,* 169 U.S. 366, 389. . . . "The limit of the full control which the state has in the proceedings of its courts, both in civil and criminal cases, is subject only to the qualification that such procedure must not work a denial of fundamental rights or conflict with specific and applicable provisions of the Federal Constitution." *West* v. *Louisiana,* 194 U.S. 258, 263.

The question under consideration may first be tested by the application of these settled doctrines of this court. If the statement of Mr. Justice Curtis, as elucidated in *Hurtado* v. *California,* is to be taken literally, that alone might almost be decisive. For nothing is more certain, in point of historical fact, than that the practice of compulsory self-incrimination in the courts and elsewhere existed for four hundred years after the granting of Magna Charta, continued throughout the reign of Charles I (though then beginning to be seriously questioned), gained at least some foothold among the early colonists of this country, and was not entirely omitted at trials in England until the eighteenth century. . . .

. . . We think it is manifest, from this review of the origin, growth, extent and limits of the exemption from compulsory self-incrimination in the English law, that it is not regarded as a part of the law of the land of Magna Charta or the due process of law, which has been deemed an equivalent expression, but, on the contrary, is regarded as separate from and independent of due process. It came into existence not as an essential part of due process, but as wise and beneficent rule of evidence developed in the course of judicial decision. This is a potent argument when it is remembered that the phrase was borrowed from English law and that to that law we must look at least for its primary meaning.

But . . . we prefer to rest our decision on broader grounds, and inquire whether the exemption from self-incrimination is of such a nature that it must be included in the conception of due process. Is it a fundamental principle of liberty and justice which inheres in the very idea of free government and is the inalienable right of a citizen of such a government? . . . One aid to the solution of the question is to inquire how the right was rated during the time when the meaning of due process was in a formative state, and before it was incorporated in American constitutional law. Did those who then were formulating and insisting upon the rights of the people entertain the view that the right was so fundamental that there could be no due process without it?

[The Court here reviews the historical background of state law on the subject and especially the attitude of the states at the time of the adoption of the Constitution and the Bill of Rights.] This survey does not tend to show that it was then in this country the universal or even general belief that the privilege ranked among the fundamental and inalienable rights of mankind; and what is more important here, it affirmatively shows that the privilege was not conceived to be inherent in due process of law, but, on the other hand, a right separate, independent, and outside of due process. Congress, in submitting the Amendments to the several states, treated the two rights as exclusive of each other. Such also has been the view of the states in framing their own Constitutions. . . . The inference is irresistible that it has been the opinion of constitution makers that the privilege, if fundamental in any sense, is not fundamental in due process of law, nor an essential part of it. . . .

. . . The essential elements of due process of law . . . are singularly few, though of wide application and deep significance. . . . Due process requires that the court which assumes to determine the rights of parties shall have jurisdiction . . . and that there shall be notice and opportunity for hearing given the parties. . . . Subject to these two fundamental conditions, which seem to be universally prescribed in all systems of law established by civilized countries, this court has, up to this time, sustained all state laws, statutory or judicially declared, regulating procedure, evidence, and methods of trial, and held them to be consistent with due process of law.

Even if the historical meaning of due process of law and the decisions of this court did not exclude the privilege from it, it would be going far to rate it as an immutable principle of justice which is the inalienable possession of every citizen of a free government. Salutary as the principle may seem to the great majority, it cannot be ranked with the right to hearing before condemnation, the immunity from arbitrary power not acting by general laws, and the inviolability of private property. The wisdom of the exemption has never been universally assented to since the days of Bentham; many doubt it today, and it is best defended not as an unchangeable principle of universal justice but as a law proved by experience to be expedient. . . .

*Judgment affirmed.*

Once again the Court refused to reconsider its narrow construction of the privileges and immunities clause laid down in *Slaughter-House Cases*. Further, the opinion clearly states that the Court did not construe the due process clause as a total incorporation of all the Bill of Rights guarantees to be applied against the states. But the door was opened to some extent in the area of criminal procedure, and subsequent developments have widened the opening still further.

Justice Moody cautioned that the phrase "due process of law" was "elusive of exact apprehension." But he tried to give a few general guidelines. He pointed out that if a practice is of ancient origin and usage, and if it is not prohibited by law, then it is to be accepted as due process of law. He was unwilling to adopt as a corollary, however, the conclusion that *only* ancient practices could meet the test. Such a view would operate like a straitjacket to stop progress or improvement. Then what is the proper test to apply to newer criminal procedures? Justice Moody quoted two earlier opinions, and then gave his own summary statement: quoting from *Holden* v. *Hardy,* "There are certain immutable principles of justice which inhere in the very idea of free government which no member of the Union may disregard;" and, quoting from *West* v. *Louisiana,* "Such procedure must not work a denial of fundamental rights or conflict with specific and applicable provisions of the Federal Constitution." His own statement was, "Due process requires that the court which assumes to determine the rights of parties shall have jurisdiction . . . and that there shall be notice and opportunity for hearing given the parties."

Justice Cardozo expressed a similar view of the limited scope of the due process clause in *Palko* v. *Connecticut,* 302 U.S. 319 (1937), holding that the clause did not bar appeal by the state based on alleged errors of law in criminal cases and subsequent retrial if the state won the appeal. He stated that the only rights covered by the due process clause were those which "have been found to be implicit in the concept of ordered liberty, and thus, through the Fourteenth Amendment, become valid as against the States."

To say that the state can run its own affairs as long as it does not violate "immutable principles of justice" or "fundamental rights" is an invitation to every disappointed litigant to claim that in his case the state violated just such principles or rights. The pressures in this direction gradually increased, and in the period since *Twining* hundreds of cases have been reviewed by the Court in which every conceivable facet of the Bill of Rights guarantees has been described by eloquent counsel as an "immutable principle of justice" or a "fundamental right" or as a necessary feature of the requirement of "notice and opportunity for hearing," and therefore forever embedded in the Fourteenth Amendment concept of "due process of law."

Some of these pleas have been sufficiently convincing to lead a majority of the Court to agree with the contentions, and to this extent the procedural guarantees of the Bill of Rights have been incorporated into the Fourteenth Amendment. Thus the cases incorporating guarantees such as the right to counsel and freedom from self-incrimination are the doctrinal offspring of *Twining* v. *New Jersey.* In *Powell* v. *Alabama,* 287 U.S. 45 (1932), for example, holding that due process requires that counsel be afforded by the state to ignorant, illiterate, indigent defendants accused of a capital crime, Justice Sutherland paraphrased the *Twining* opinion in stating:

It never has been doubted by this court, or any other so far as we know, that notice and hearing are preliminary steps essential to the passing of an enforceable judgment, and that they, together with a legally competent tribunal having jurisdiction of the case, constitute basic elements of the constitutional requirement of due process of law. . . .

What, then, does a hearing include? Historically and in practice, in our own country at least, it has always included the right to the aid of counsel when desired and provided by the party asserting the right. The right to be heard would be, in many cases, of little avail if it did not comprehend the right to be heard by counsel. . . .

. . . All that it is necessary now to decide, as we do decide, is that in a capital case, where the defendant is unable to employ counsel, and is incapable adequately of making his own defense because of ignorance, feebie-mindedness, illiteracy, or the like, it is the duty of the court, whether requested or not, to assign counsel for him as a necessary requisite of due process of law. . . .

The first actual incorporation of one of the Bill of Rights guarantees took place in *Chicago, Burlington & Quincy RR. Co.* v. *Chicago,* 166 U.S. 226 (1897), holding that the compensation clause of the Fifth Amendment applied to the states by way of the Fourteenth Amendment due process clause.

The *substantive* rights guaranteed by the Bill of Rights, such as speech, press, and assembly, have also been incorporated into the Fourteenth Amendment, but the vehicle for the expansion here has been the word "liberty" and not the phrase "due process of law." Thus in *Gitlow* v. *New York,* 268 U.S. 652 (1925), although the conviction for the crime of criminal anarchy was affirmed, the majority opinion stated that, "For present purposes we may and do assume that freedom of speech and of the press—which are protected by the First Amendment from abridgment by Congress—are among the fundamental personal rights and 'liberties' protected by the due process clause of the Fourteenth Amendment from impairment by the States." For our purposes here, however, it is immaterial which portion of the full due process clause has been the vessel to contain the new right. The important point is the extent to which the Fourteenth Amendment now includes Bill of Rights guarantees against state abridgment.

In *Near* v. *Minnesota,* 283 U.S. 697 (1931), the majority opinion stated, "It is no longer open to doubt that the liberty of the press and of speech is within the liberty safeguarded by the due process clause of the Fourteenth Amendment from invasion by state action." By 1937 the Court was willing to add freedom of assembly to the list. In *De Jonge* v. *Oregon,* 299 U.S. 353 (1937), Chief Justice Hughes, speaking for the Court, stated:

The right of peaceable assembly is a right cognate to those of free speech and free press and is equally fundamental. . . . [T]he right is one that cannot be denied without violating those fundamental principles of liberty and justice which lie at the base of all civil and political institutions,—principles which the Fourteenth Amendment embodies in the general terms of its due process clause.

Rounding out the incorporation of First Amendment rights into the Fourteenth, the Court in 1940 included religious freedom in the list. The case was *Cantwell* v. *Connecticut,* 310 U.S. 296 (1940), and Justice Roberts, speaking for a unanimous Court, stated:

We hold that the statute, as construed and applied to the appellants, deprives them of their liberty without due process of law in contravention of the Fourteenth Amendment. The fundamental concept of liberty embodied in that Amendment embraces the liberties guaranteed by the First Amendment. The First Amendment declares that Congress shall make no law respecting as establishment of religion or prohibiting the free exercise thereof. The Fourteenth Amendment has rendered the legislatures of the states as incompetent as Congress to enact such laws.

Although Justice Roberts included the prohibition against establishment of religion in his statement, *Cantwell* technically did not present that issue. The issue was squarely presented, however, in *Everson* v. *Board of Education,* 330 U.S. 1 (1947), and the Court held the establishment clause of the First Amendment to be applicable to the states through the Fourteenth Amendment.

We see in these decisions a judicial approach that has been designated "selective incorporation." The *Twining-Palko* formula was followed in a case-by-case determination of which of the Bill of Rights guarantees should be classified as so fundamental as to be included in the protection of the Fourteenth Amendment's due process clause. Justice Black, appointed to the Court in 1937, was in his first term on the Court when *Palko* was decided, and he did not dissent. But rather early in his tenure he began to develop opposition to the process of selective incorporation and argued that it was too subjective a "natural law" approach to the Bill of Rights. He felt that such wide-ranging discretion in the Court to pick and choose among the various guarantees was inappropriate to the judicial role and argued for full incorporation of the entire Bill of Rights. To support this position, however, he needed to determine whether this construction was congenial to the intent of the framers of the Fourteenth Amendment, and of the States which ratified it. He spent a great deal of time on a study of the various bills and resolutions proposed by the Congress on civil rights matters in the 1860s, including debates in Congress, speeches by leading proponents of the Fourteenth Amendment and correspondence of the major participants in the committees dealing with the proposals. His conclusion was that the Amendment *was* intended to incorporate the entire Bill of Rights, and he launched a campaign to persuade a majority of the Court to adopt this position. The official statement of his construction appeared in *Adamson* v. *California,* 332 U.S. 46 (1947), in which he made an impressive defense of his theory along with a lengthy appendix providing documentary support. He could not garner a majority, however, and the Court has continued to proceed in its pattern of selective incorporation. The *Adamson* case involved again, as in *Twining,* the issue of self-incrimination— whether judicial and prosecutorial comment on the failure of a defendant to take the witness stand in his defense as evidence of guilt was a violation of the Fourteenth Amendment's due process clause. By a five to four vote the Court held that the privilege was not incorporated, and the State had not violated due process. In dissent, Justice Black stated:

This decision reasserts a constitutional theory spelled out in *Twining* v. *New Jersey* . . . that this Court is endowed by the Constitution with boundless power under "natural law" periodically to expand and contract constitutional standards to conform to the Court's conception of what at a particular time constitutes "civilized decency" and "fundamental principles of liberty and justice." Invoking this *Twining* rule, the Court concludes that although comment upon testimony in a federal court would violate the Fifth Amendment, identical comment in a state court does not violate today's fashion in civilized decency and fundamentals and is therefore not prohibited by the Federal Constitution as amended.

. . . I would not reaffirm the *Twining* decision. I think that decision and the "natural law" theory of the Constitution upon which it relies, degrade the constitutional safeguards of the Bill of Rights and simultaneously appropriate for this Court a broad power which we are not authorized by the Constitution to exercise. . . .

My study of the historical events that culminated in the Fourteenth Amendment, and the expressions of those who sponsored and favored, as well as those who opposed its submission and passage, persuades me that one of the chief objects that the provisions of the Amendment's first section, separately, and as a whole, were intended to accomplish was to make the Bill of Rights applicable to the states. With full knowledge of the import of the *Barron* decision, the framers and backers of the Fourteenth Amendment proclaimed its purpose to be to overturn the constitutional rule that case had announced. This historical purpose has never received full consideration or exposition in any opinion of this Court interpreting the Amendment.

Professor Charles Fairman published a rebuttal to Black's conclusions, "Does the Fourteenth Amendment Incorporate the Bill of Rights? The Original Understanding," 2 *Stanford Law Review* 5 (1949), in which he concludes that on that broad issue "Mr. Justice Black's position is fatally weak." The opinion of most constitutional scholars seems to be that Fairman's analysis is the correct one.

Another conflict within the Court was over the issue of whether incorporation of a particular guarantee resulted in *full* incorporation (the imposition of exactly the same standard required in federal proceedings) or only *partial* incorporation (a requirement of some minimal standard, but one less rigorous than that required by the Bill of Rights in a federal proceeding). Justice Harlan (the second Harlan) was the leading exponent on the Court of the partial incorporation doctrine. He had a strong conviction that one of the basic elements of our federal system of government was appreciation of the value of experimentation and innovation in the policy laboratories of the States. Thus he was unwilling to fasten upon those States, as constitutional commands, the specific procedures that the Bill of Rights imposed upon the national government. When the Court held in *Duncan* v. *Louisiana,* 391 U.S. 145 (1968), that the Sixth Amendment's guarantee of jury trial in criminal cases was fully incorporated into the Fourteenth Amendment, Justice Harlan dissented, stating:

. . . I have raised my voice many times before against the Court's continuing undiscriminating insistence upon fastening on the States federal notions of criminal justice, and I must do so again in this instance. . . .

Apart from the approach taken by the absolute incorporationists, I can see only one method of analysis that has any internal logic. That is to start with the words "liberty" and "due process of law" and attempt to define them in a way that accords with American tranditions and our system of government. This approach, involving a much more discriminating process of adjudication than does "incorporation," is, albeit difficult, the one that was followed throughout the 19th and most of the present century. It entails a "gradual process of judicial inclusion and exclusion," seeking, with due recognition of constitutional tolerance for state experimentation and disparity, to ascertain those "immutable principles . . . of justice which inhere in the very idea of free government which no member of the Union may disregard." Due process was not restricted to rules fixed in the past, for that "would be to deny every quality of the law but its age, and to render it incapable of progress or improvement." Nor did it impose nationwide uniformity in details.

Justice Harlan's position has not prevailed, however, and today all of the guarantees of the Bill of Rights thus far incorporated have been fully incorporated.

The Fourth Amendment's protection against unreasonable searches and seizures was *partially* incorporated into the Fourteenth Amendment by the holding in *Wolf* v. *Colorado,* 338 U.S. 25 (1949), that the security of one's privacy against arbitrary intrusion by the police is "implicit in 'the concept of ordered liberty' and as such enforceable against the States through the Due Process Clause." Not until the decision in *Mapp* v. *Ohio,* 367 U.S. 643 (1961), however, did the Court presumably *fully* incorporate the Fourth Amendment by its holding that not only was an arbitrary search and seizure conducted by state officers unconstitutional, but it was also a violation of the Fourteenth Amendment for them to use evidence so obtained in a criminal prosecution.

In *Malloy* v. *Hogan,* 378 U.S. 1 (1964), the Court held that the Fifth Amendment's exemption from compulsory self-incrimination is also protected by the Fourteenth Amendment against abridgment by the States. And, lest any doubt remained that it was *full* incorporation which was intended, the Court in *Griffin* v. *California,* 380 U.S. 609(1965), held that adverse comment by the judge on the failure of the accused to take the stand in his defense would violate the Fifth Amendment if occurring in a federal proceeding and, therefore, violated the Fourteenth Amendment in the case under review. The holding of the *Twining* case, then, is no longer ruling law.

In *Benton* v. *Maryland,* 395 U.S. 784 (1969), the Court specifically overruled *Palko* v. *Connecticut* and held that the double jeopardy clause of the Fifth Amendment is applicable to the States through the Fourteenth Amendment.

The Sixth Amendment's guarantee of a jury trial in criminal cases has long been considered inapplicable to state trials, but this right has now been incorporated as a result of the decision in *Duncan* v. *Louisiana,* 391 U.S. 145 (1968). The right to a "public trial" was employed as a Fourteenth Amendment right in *In re Oliver,* 333 U.S. 257 (1948), to reverse a contempt citation imposed during a secret proceeding. The Sixth Amendment also guarantees the accused the right "to be confronted with the witnesses against him," including the right of cross-examination. In *Pointer* v. *Texas,* 380 U.S. 400 (1965), the majority opinion stated:

We hold that petitioner was entitled to be tried in accordance with the protection of the confrontation guarantee of the Sixth Amendment, and that that guarantee, like the right against compelled self-incrimination, is "to be enforced against the States under the Fourteenth Amendment according to the same standards that protect those personal rights against federal encroachment." *Malloy* v. *Hogan.* . . .

A further protection of the Sixth Amendment for the criminal defendant is the right "to have compulsory process for obtaining witnesses in his favor," In *Washington* v. *Texas,* 388 U.S. 14 (1967), the Court incorporated this right into the Fourteenth Amendment. It further held that this right was denied by Texas statutes which provided that persons charged or convicted as coparticipants in the same crime could not testify for one another, although there was no bar to their testifying for the state. The final clause of the Sixth Amendment guarantees to defendants in federal prosecutions the right to have "the assistance of counsel" for their defense. As stated earlier, *Powell* v. *Alabama* partially incorporated this right into the Fourteenth Amendment by applying it to certain kinds of capital cases. Shortly thereafter it was extended to all capital cases, and in *Gideon* v. *Wainwright,* 372 U.S. 335 (1963), to all felony trials. In *Argersinger* v. *Hamlin,* 407 U.S. 25 (1972), the Court held that both the Sixth and Fourteenth Amendments guaranteed the right to counsel in all criminal cases in which a jail term might be assessed.

The right to an "impartial jury" was incorporated in *Parker* v. *Gladden,* 385 U.S. 363 (1966), and in *Klopfer* v. *North Carolina,* 386 U.S. 213 (1967), the Court incorporated the "speedy trial" provision of the Sixth Amendment, stating: "We hold here that the right to a speedy trial is as fundamental as any of the rights secured by the Sixth Amendment." Thus the entire Amendment is now within the coverage of the Fourteenth.

Finally, in *Louisiana ex rel. Francis* v. *Resweber,* 329 U.S. 459 (1947), the majority "assumed" that the Eighth Amendment's prohibition against cruel and unusual punishments was binding on the State through the Fourteenth Amendment. This was accepted as a firm holding in *Robinson* v. *California,* 370 U.S. 660 (1962). While the Court has not yet ruled squarely that Fourteenth Amendment due process includes the Eighth Amendment prohibition of excessive bail, a number of lower federal courts have taken that prohibition for granted to such an extent that one can say that the bail provision probably does apply to the States.

The incorporation process has continued until at this juncture virtually all of the guarantees of the Bill of Rights have been drawn into the Fourteenth Amendment. There are a few of those guarantees, however, which still do not apply to the States through the absorption process. The Second Amendment right "to keep and bear arms" has not been incorporated, nor has the Third Amendment protection against the quartering of soldiers. And if the State wishes to abolish grand jury indictment and try criminals upon an information (a sworn written accusation by the prosecutor), the Fourteenth Amendment does not bar it, although the Fifth Amendment would prohibit such a substitution in a federal prosecution for a "capital or otherwise infamous crime." [*Hurtado* v. *California,* 110 U.S. 516 (1884).] While the right to jury trial in criminal cases has been incorporated, the Seventh Amendment guarantee of jury trial in civil suits at common law has not, so the State could abolish the civil jury altogether without, as yet, violating the Fourteenth Amendment. (See Table 1.)

It should also be noted that the phrase "due process of law" includes the concept of "fundamental fairness" in criminal proceedings and thus has been construed to include standards not listed in the Bill of Rights at all. For example, due process demands that the trial be conducted by an unbiased judge. *Tumey* v. *Ohio,* 273 U.S. 510 (1927), involved a conviction for violation of the liquor laws of the state. The mayor was authorized to try such offenses without a jury, and he received, in addition to his salary, the costs imposed on the defendant in case of conviction, but nothing if he were acquitted. The Court held that this pecuniary interest of the judge in conviction was a violation of due process. And in *Mooney* v. *Holohan,* 294 U.S. 103 (1935), the Court held that when a conviction is obtained by the presentation of testimony known to the prosecuting authorities to have been perjured, due process is violated. While the Court will not weigh the sufficiency of evidence in reviewing state cases, convictions that are not supported by any evidence at all are void under the due process clause. *Thompson* v. *City of Louisville,* 362 U.S. 199 (1960), involved the conviction of Sam Thompson in police

## TABLE 1
## THE INCORPORATION PROCESS

| Amendment | Guarantee | Case and Date |
|---|---|---|
| I | No establishment of religion<br>Free exercise of religion<br>Free speech<br>Free press<br>Freedom of assembly<br>Freedom of association | *Everson* v. *Board of Educ.,* 330 U.S. 1 (1947)<br>*Cantwell* v. *Connecticut,* 310 U.S. 296 (1940)<br>*Gitlow* v. *New York,* 268 U.S. 652 (1925)<br>*Near* v. *Minnesota,* 283 U.S. 697 (1931)<br>*DeJonge* v. *Oregon,* 299 U.S. 353 (1937)<br>*NAACP* v. *Alabama,* 357 U.S. 449 (1958) |
| II | Right to bear arms | Not incorporated |
| III | No quartering of soldiers | Not incorporated |
| IV | Freedom from unreasonable<br>searches and seizures<br>Exclusionary rule | *Wolf* v. *Colorado,* 338 U.S. 25 (1949)<br><br>*Mapp* v. *Ohio,* 367 U.S. 643 (1961) |
| V | Indictment by grand jury<br>No double jeopardy<br>Privilege against self-<br>incrimination<br>No taking of private property<br>for public use without just<br>compensation | Not incorporated<br>*Benton* v. *Maryland,* 395 U.S. 784 (1969)<br><br>*Malloy* v. *Hogan,* 378 U.S. 1 (1964)<br><br><br>*Chicago, B. & Q. Ry. Co.* v. *Chicago,* 166 U.S.<br>226 (1897) |
| VI | Speedy trial<br>Public trial<br>Impartial jury<br>Jury trial in serious crimes<br>Right to be informed of<br>nature of criminal charge<br>Confrontation of witnesses<br>Compulsory process for<br>obtaining witnesses<br>Right to counsel in capital<br>cases<br>Right to counsel in all felony<br>cases<br>Right to counsel in all<br>criminal cases involving a<br>jail term | *Klopfer* v. *North Carolina,* 386 U.S. 213 (1967)<br>*In re Oliver,* 333 U.S. 257 (1948)<br>*Parker* v. *Gladden,* 385 U.S. 363 (1966)<br>*Duncan* v. *Louisiana,* 391 U.S. 145 (1968)<br>Implicit in fair trial aspect of due process.<br>See *Cole* v. *Arkansas,* 333 U.S. 196 (1948)<br>*Pointer* v. *Texas,* 380 U.S. 400 (1965)<br><br>*Washington* v. *Texas,* 388 U.S. 14 (1967)<br><br>*Powell* v. *Alabama,* 287 U.S. 45 (1932)<br><br>*Gideon* v. *Wainwright,* 372 U.S. 335 (1963)<br><br><br>*Argersinger* v. *Hamlin,* 407 U.S. 25 (1972) |
| VII | Right to jury trial in civil cases<br>at common law | Not incorporated |
| VIII | No excessive bail or fines<br>No cruel or unusual<br>punishment | Not incorporated<br><br>*Robinson* v. *California,* 370 U.S. 660 (1962) |

court on the charge of "loitering." The evidence and testimony showed only that he had gone into a small cafe while waiting for his bus, had eaten a dish of macaroni, and was "shuffling" about a small dance floor in time to juke-box music. The Court held that "there simply is no semblance of evidence" from which one could infer a violation of the city ordinance on loitering, and thus the conviction violated the Fourteenth Amendment.

Despite the advance of incorporation, there still remain some differences between the standards set up by the Bill of Rights for federal proceedings and those which the Fourteenth Amendment has been construed as imposing upon states. The result of the line of decisions amplifying the due process clause of the Fourteenth Amendment is that the student of American civil rights must deal with *three separate* packets of constitutional rights: (1) the rights and safeguards which the Bill of Rights to the national Constitution guarantees against abridgment by the national government; (2) the rights which the state cannot abridge without violating the Fourteenth Amendment; and (3) the rights which the state constitution guarantees against abridgment by the state government. In addition to the constitutional guarantees, there are both federal and state statutes and state common law provisions which establish legal rights against governmental *and* private action beyond those covered by the constitutions. [While the Bill of Rights and the Fourteenth Amendment cover the bulk of the rights protected against governmental interference, there are, of course, a few rights specifically guaranteed in the main body of the Constitution and in other Amendments: in Article I, Sections 9 and 10 (safeguards against ex post facto laws, bills of attainder, and suspension of the writ of habeas corpus); in Article III, Section 2 (trial by jury in criminal cases); in the Thirteenth Amendment (barring slavery); and in the Fifteenth, Nineteenth, Twenty-fourth and Twenty-sixth Amendments (barring various restrictions on the right to vote).] Recognition of the threefold pattern of civil rights in the American system is a prerequisite to a full understanding of the legal problems in the field. Federalism does, indeed, introduce a number of complications into the picture.

# CHAPTER 3

# *The Rights of the Accused*

One of the hardest tasks for the nonlawyer is the full appreciation of the value of procedural regularity. A commonly heard criticism of appellate courts is that they reverse criminal convictions "because of some technicality." Procedural requirements are sometimes viewed impatiently as mere obstructions to the efficient administration of criminal justice. What is being overlooked in these attacks on procedural "technicalities" is the realization that over the long pull of centuries these requirements have served as the gradually accumulating building blocks to form our most effective barrier against arbitrary governmental deprivation of life and liberty. As Justice Frankfurter succinctly stated it, "The history of liberty has largely been the history of observance of procedural safeguards." [*McNabb v. United States,* 318 U.S. 332, 347 (1943).]

The primary constitutionally guaranteed procedures in federal prosecutions are fairly explicitly stated in the Bill of Rights. But the Fifth Amendment also contains the broad guarantee that no one can be deprived of life or liberty "without due process of law." The primary constitutionally guaranteed procedures in state prosecutions are contained in the due process and equal protection clauses of the Fourteenth Amendment. The Court has time and time again been faced with the task of giving content to the nebulous phrase "due process of law" in testing the validity of criminal procedures employed by the state or the federal government. In *Davidson* v. *New Orleans,* 96 U.S. 97, 104 (1877) Justice Miller said that if it were possible to define with precision the exact requirements of due process, "no more useful construction could be furnished to any part of the fundamental law." Since the courts of the nation have uniformly agreed that no such definition is possible, they have followed a course of defining the phrase, to quote Justice Miller again, "by the gradual process of judicial inclusion and exclusion, as the cases presented for decision shall require." In recognition of this practice, the approach here is to break up the criminal process into the more or less successive stages through which an accused may travel and examine the constitutional requirements at each stage. It will be seen that despite the absence of a precise definition of procedural due process, there is in the concept a general requirement that the procedures used at each stage must meet the test of "fundamental fairness."

In *Twining* v. *New Jersey,* 211 U.S. 78 (1908), the United States Supreme Court, through Justice Moody, made a tentative effort to point the way in approaching due process questions:

> The essential elements of due process of law . . . are singularly few, though of wide application and deep significance. . . . Due process requires that the court which assumes to determine the rights of parties shall have jurisdiction . . . and that there shall be notice and opportunity for hearing given the parties. . . . Subject to these two fundamental conditions, which seem to be universally prescribed in all systems of law established by civilized countries, this court has, up to this time, sustained all state laws, statutory or judicially declared, regulating procedure, evidence, and methods of trial, and held them to be consistent with due process of law.

We have in this statement what might be called the "hard core of due process"—jurisdiction, notice, and hearing. Taking these essential elements, along with the concept of fundamental fairness, the Court has over the years gradually elaborated the rules and principles which are followed today. At the same time, it must be noted that decisions expressing new requirements are often merely the bases for still further developments. Due process is by no means a static concept. Every term of Court sees refinements, modifications, and even reversals of former positions.

## NOTICE OF WHAT CONDUCT IS MADE CRIMINAL

### The "Void for Vagueness" Rule

To begin with the law which defines a crime, fairness demands that the law spell out with sufficient clarity just what it is that the legislature is trying to prohibit. Without this basic notice, the citizen surely should not be held accountable in a criminal prosecution which may result in a forfeiture of life, liberty, or property. Thus, in *United States* v. *Cohen Grocery Co.*, 255 U.S. 81 (1921), a World War I price-control statute which made it a crime to make "any unjust or unreasonable rate or charge" for "necessaries" was held unconstitutionally vague because it fixed no ascertainable standard of guilt. Similarly, in *Connally* v. *General Construction Company*, 269 U.S. 385 (1926), an Oklahoma statute was held invalid which made it a crime to pay "less than the current rate of per diem wages in the locality where the work is performed." The Court stated the controlling rule as follows:

That the terms of a penal statute creating a new offense must be sufficiently explicit to inform those who are subject to it what conduct on their part will render them liable to its penalties, is a well-recognized requirement, consonant alike with ordinary notions of fair play and the settled rules of law. And a statute which either forbids or requires the doing of an act in terms so vague that men of common intelligence must necessarily guess at its meaning and differ as to its application, violates the first essential of due process of law.

In holding the Oklahoma statute void, the Court found that such vague directions as "current rate" and "locality where the work is performed" were not sufficiently clear to apprise an employer of just what rates of pay would be so low as to violate the law. Prosecutions under such a law, then, would be in violation of the due process clause because insufficient notice was given. [See Note, "The Void-for-Vagueness Doctrine in the Supreme Court," 109 *U. Pa. L. Rev.* 67 (1960).]

Of course a great many vague statutes have been upheld by the Court. Statute-making is hardly an exact science, and even areas of regulation which might appear to be relatively simple may turn out to present complexities in drafting which render absolute clarity impossible. And normally the Court takes into account the problem faced by the legislature. Thus a provision which proscribed the sale of goods at "unreasonably low prices for the purpose of destroying competition or eliminating a competitor" was upheld as applied because the statute required (and the indictment alleged) a "predatory intent" to sell below cost without a justifying business reason and therefore adequately notified the defendant of the nature of the offense. [*United States* v. *National Dairy Prod. Corp.*, 372 U.S. 29 (1963).] And in *Nash* v. *United States*, 229 U.S. 373 (1913), upholding the Sherman Act's prohibition against unreasonable restraints of trade, Justice Holmes pointed out that "the law is full of instances where a man's fate depends on his estimating rightly, that is, as the jury subsequently estimates it, some matter of degree." (It should be noted, however, that the Court is much more demanding of particularity when the statute may impinge on First Amendment freedoms.) The Court has also examined the statutes for the requirement of *scienter* in the definition of the crime, and words such as "willfully" or "knowingly" coupled with the proscribed conduct have been held to overcome the vice of vagueness.

A more recent application of the vagueness rule has been with respect to ordinances punishing "vagrancy" or "loitering." At least as such laws are generally written, the decision in *Papachristou v. City of Jacksonville*, 405 U.S. 156 (1972), would seem to render them invalid. The Jacksonville ordinance punished as vagrants

rogues and vagabonds, or dissolute persons who go about begging, . . . common night walkers, . . . lewd, wanton and lascivious persons, . . . persons wandering or strolling around from place to place without any lawful purpose or object, habitual loafers, . . . persons neglecting all lawful business and habitually spending their time by frequenting houses of ill fame, gaming houses, or places where alcoholic beverages are sold or served, persons able to work but habitually living upon the earnings of their wives or minor children. . . .

The case involved eight defendants who were convicted in municipal court of vagrancy, most of whom were either employed or were students. Four of the defendants were charged with "vagrancy—prowling by auto" for driving down the main street of Jacksonville early Sunday morning. The Court unanimously held the ordinance void for vagueness, both in the sense that "it 'fails to give a person of ordinary intelligence fair notice that his contemplated conduct is forbidden by the statute,' . . . and because it encourages arbitrary and erratic arrests and convictions." The opinion also stressed the unfettered discretion which the ordinance placed in the hands of the police. Justice Douglas, for the Court, gave an interesting essay on the value of "wandering or strolling about," and also pointed out that the punishment of persons neglecting all lawful business and frequenting places where alcoholic beverages are served might be applied to members of golf clubs or city clubs.

## The Prohibition Against Ex Post Facto Laws

While ex post facto laws are normally considered separately from due process questions, the basic defect inherent in such laws is the failure to give adequate notice. To apply a criminal law retroactively, to the disadvantage of the accused, is to violate the most fundamental notions of fairness. Thus, even without the prohibitions against ex post facto laws in Article I, Sections 9 and 10 of the Constitution, the "due process" clauses of the Fifth and Fourteenth Amendments might be considered adequate to bar the application of such laws.

Whatever the framers of the Constitution might have intended, the Court has consistently held that only criminal laws can come within the meaning of ex post facto prohibitions. Retroactive civil laws, then, do not run afoul of this provision of the Constitution. The leading case on the subject is *Calder v. Bull*, 3 Dall. 386, decided in 1798 and still ruling law. In holding that a Connecticut statute, which set aside a probate court ruling and granted a new hearing on the disposition of a will, was not ex post facto, Justice Chase stated the rule:

I will state what laws I consider ex post facto laws, within the words and the intent of the prohibition. 1st. Every law that makes an action done before the passing of the law, and which was innocent when done, criminal; and punishes such action. 2d. Every law that aggravates a crime, or makes it greater than it was, when committed. 3d. Every law that changes the punishment, and inflicts a greater punishment, than the law annexed to the crime, when committed. 4th. Every law that alters the legal rules of evidence, and receives less, or different, testimony, than the law required at the time of the commission of the offense, in order to convict the offender. All these, and similar laws, are manifestly unjust and oppressive. In my opinion, the true distinction is between ex post facto laws, and retrospective laws. Every ex post facto law must necessarily be retrospective; but every retrospective law is not an ex post facto law; the former, only, are prohibited.

In determining whether a particular retroactive criminal law is ex post facto, within the rule of *Calder* v. *Bull,* the Court requires a showing that the new law will disadvantage defendants generally, as a class, rather than merely a particular defendant. Thus to reduce the size of the criminal jury from twelve to eight, and apply the reduction retroactively, was held to come within the bar against ex post facto laws in *Thompson* v. *Utah,* 170 U.S. 343 (1898). This was on the theory that defendants generally could be convicted more easily with eight jurors than twelve under a requirement of unanimity. And in *Weaver* v. *Graham,* 450 U.S. 24 (1981), the Court held a Florida statute, which reduced the time off for good behavior for prisoners and applied it to persons whose crime was committed before the new statute was enacted, unconstitutional as an ex post facto law. But in *Thompson* v. *Missouri,* 171 U.S. 380 (1898), the Court held that a change in the rules of evidence, to permit admission of letters written by the accused to his wife, was not ex post facto, despite the fact that a comparison of the handwriting showed that Thompson wrote a prescription for strychnine used to commit murder. The conviction was sustained on the ground that under the new rule both the state and the defendant were allowed to avail themselves of this additional evidence, and since it would not *uniformly* operate to the disadvantage of the accused, it was not ex post facto. [See Oliver P. Field, "Ex Post Facto in the Constitution," 20 *Mich. L. Rev.* 315 (1922).]

### Notice to the Accused of the Offense Charged Against Him

In addition to the general requirement that a statute be sufficiently clear to warn the citizenry of what the legislature is prohibiting, there is a more specific requirement of the Sixth Amendment (and of due process under the Fourteenth Amendment) that the accused in a criminal proceeding "be informed of the nature and cause of the accusation." Fairness demands that he know in advance just what the prosecution is for, in order that he may adequately attempt a defense. At an earlier stage in America this rule was carried to such extremes that indictments could be quashed unless the most minute details of the alleged crime were set forth—the manufacturer, the caliber, the color, and the model of the gun used to commit a murder, for example, and the physical location of the wound which was caused. The courts of today no longer require such lengthy descriptive essays in the indictments, but there still must appear a charge of sufficient clarity to apprise the accused of the nature of the offense charged. A good statement of the matter is found in *State* v. *Popolos,* 103 A.2d 511 (Maine, 1954), where the defendant questioned the adequacy of his indictment for perjury:

The essentials of an indictment for *perjury* in this State are set forth in a prescribed form by the legislature. But such a form is subject to constitutional restrictions and must be in compliance therewith. The statutes prescribing forms of indictment have removed many of the niceties of technical pleading and the indictment is made little more than a simple statement of the offense couched in ordinary language and with due regard for the rights of the accused. But they cannot change the requirements that the indictment must, as at common law, contain every averment that is necessary to inform the defendant of the particular circumstances of the charge against him. . . .

Under the Constitution of the United States and by provision of the Constitution of Maine the accused is entitled to be informed of the nature and cause of the accusation against him. These provisions are based on the presumption of innocence and require such certainty in indictments as will enable an innocent man to prepare for trial. But no greater particularity of allegation that may be of service to the accused in understanding the charge and preparing his defense is necessary. However, all the elements or facts necessary to the crime charged must be set out fully and clearly. . . .

The issue of adequate notice was brought to the United States Supreme Court in 1948 in a rather curious case. As the case appeared to that Court, the Supreme Court of Arkansas held that a conviction under one section of a law could not be sustained, but it was affirmed, nonetheless, since there appeared to be sufficient evidence to convict under another section, even though the defendant was never charged with the latter violation.

## COLE *v.* ARKANSAS
### 333 U.S. 196 (1948)

[Arkansas adopted a law in 1943 making it a felony to interfere in specified ways with one's right to work. The two key sections provided, in part:

Section 1. It shall be unlawful for any person by the use of force or violence . . . to prevent or attempt to prevent any person from engaging in any lawful vocation within this State. . . .

Section 2. It shall be unlawful for any person acting in concert with one or more other persons, to assemble at or near any place where a "labor dispute" exists and by force or violence prevent . . . any person from engaging in any lawful vocation, or for any person acting . . . in concert with one or more other persons, to promote, encourage or aid any such unlawful assemblage.]

Mr. Justice Black delivered the opinion of the Court.

The petitioners were convicted of a felony in an Arkansas state court and sentenced to serve one year in the state penitentiary. . . . We granted certiorari because the record indicated that at least one of the questions presented was substantial. That question, in the present state of the record, is the only one we find it appropriate to consider. The question is: "Were the petitioners denied due process of law . . . in violation of the Fourteenth Amendment by the circumstance that their convictions were affirmed under a criminal statute for violation of which they had not been charged?"

The present convictions are under an information. The petitioners urge that the information charged them with a violation of Section 2 of Act 193 of the 1943 Arkansas Legislature and that they were tried and convicted of violating only Section 2. The State Supreme Court affirmed their convictions on the ground that the information had charged and the evidence had shown that the petitioners had violated Section 1 of the Arkansas Act which describes an offense separate and distinct from the offense described in Section 2. . . .

We therefore have this situation. The petitioners read the information as charging them with an offense under Section 2 of the Act, the language of which the information had used. The trial judge construed the information as charging an offense under Section 2. He instructed the jury to that effect. He charged the jury that petitioners were on trial for the offense of promoting an unlawful assemblage, not for the offense "of using force and violence." Without completely ignoring the judge's charge, the jury could not have convicted petitioner for having committed the separate, distinct, and substantially different offense defined in Section 1. Yet the State Supreme Court refused to consider the validity of the convictions under Section 2, for violation of which petitioners were tried and convicted. It affirmed their convictions as though they had been tried for violating Section 1, an offense for which they were neither tried nor convicted.

No principle of procedural due process is more clearly established than that notice of the specific charge, and a chance to be heard in a trial of the issues raised by that charge, if desired, are among the constitutional rights of every accused in a criminal proceeding in all courts, state or federal. . . . If, as the State Supreme Court held, petitioners were charged with a violation of Section 1, it is doubtful both that the information fairly informed them of that charge and that they sought to defend themselves against such a charge; it is certain that they were not tried for or found guilty of it. It is as much a violation of due process to send an accused to prison following conviction of a charge on which he was never tried as it would be to convict him upon a charge that was never made. . . .

We are constrained to hold that the petitioners have been denied safeguards guaranteed by due process of law—safeguards essential to liberty in a government dedicated to justice under law.

In the present state of the record we cannot pass upon those contentions which challenge the validity of Section 2 of the Arkansas Act. The judgment is reversed and remanded to the State Supreme Court for proceedings not inconsistent with this opinion.

*Reversed and remanded.*

## SEARCHES AND SEIZURES

The Fourth Amendment to the United States Constitution begins with the phrase, "The right of the people to be secure in their persons, houses, papers, and effects, against unreasonable searches and seizures, shall not be violated . . ." The clear purport of the phrase is that not all seizures or searches are prohibited; it is only those which are *unreasonable* which are barred. The second part of the sentence states, "and no warrants shall issue, but upon probable cause, supported by oath or affirmation, and particularly describing the place to be searched, and the persons or things to be seized."

The phraseology of the Fourth Amendment raises two important questions of interpretation. First, what kinds of searches and seizures are "unreasonable"? Second, what sorts of information or observation are sufficient to constitute "probable cause" to believe that an offense was committed and that the things sought are in the place specified? The general bounds of the "probable cause" requirement become additionally important because of the fact that while not all searches require a warrant, even the exceptions usually demand that the officer meet this same test before proceeding, just as though he were attempting to obtain a warrant. [See Nelson B. Lasson, *The History and Development of the Fourth Amendment to the United States Constitution* (Baltimore: John Hopkins University Press, 1937) and Jacob W. Landynski, *Search and Seizure and the Supreme Court* (Baltimore: Johns Hopkins University Press, 1966).]

### Arrest

The Fourth Amendment prohibits unreasonable searches and seizures. While "arrest" is not specifically mentioned, an arrest is, of course, a seizure, and an illegal arrest is an unconstitutional seizure under the Fourth Amendment, as indicated in *Henry* v. *United States,* 361, U.S. 98 (1959). The terms "arrest" and "seizure" are not synonymous, however. "An arrest is the taking of a person into custody 'for the actual or purported purpose of bringing [him] before a court, or of otherwise securing the administration of justice.' " [David Fellman, *The Defendant's Rights Today* (Madison: University of Wisconsin Press, 1976), quoting from *Restatement, Torts,* §112 (1934).] But not every seizure of a person is for the purpose of "bringing [him] before a court." Thus an investigative stop by the police, without formal arrest, constitutes a "seizure" within the meaning of the Fourth Amendment. In *Terry* v. *Ohio,* 392 U.S. 1, at 16 (1968), the majority opinion stated: "Whenever a police officer accosts an individual and restrains his freedom to walk away, he has 'seized' that person."

In *Brown* v. *Texas,* 443 U.S. 47 (1979), the question presented was whether the appellant was validly convicted for refusing to comply with a policeman's demand that he identify himself pursuant to a provision of Texas law which made it a crime to refuse such identification on request. Officers had observed Brown and another man walking in opposite directions away from each other in an alley. Brown was asked for identification and an explanation of his presence in the alley, but he refused. The officers did not claim to suspect him of any specific misconduct, but they stated that this was in a "high drug problem area," the situation "looked suspicious and we had never seen that subject in that area before." In holding the stop violative of the Fourth Amendment, Chief Justice Burger, for a unanimous Court, stated: "When the officers detained appellant for the purpose of requiring him to identify himself, they performed a seizure of his person subject to the requirements of the Fourth Amendment." The reasonableness of the seizure, however, depends on a balancing of the public interest and the individual's right to freedom from arbitrary interference by law officers. In some circumstances an officer may detain a suspect briefly for questioning although he does not have probable cause to believe that the suspect is involved in criminal activity, as is required for a traditional arrest. "However, we have required the officers to have a reasonable suspicion, based on objective facts, that the individual is involved in criminal activity." In this case the application of the Texas law was held to have violated the Fourth Amendment because the officers lacked any reasonable suspicion to believe appellant was engaged or had engaged in criminal conduct. "Accordingly, appellant may not be punished for refusing to identify himself, and the conviction is reversed."

In *Tennessee* v. *Garner,* 471, U.S. 1 (1985), the Court held that a statute that allowed police officers to employ deadly force to prevent a felon from escaping was unconstitutional insofar as it authorized the use of such force to stop an apparently unarmed and nondangerous suspect. The majority opinion stated that "there can be no question that apprehension by the use of deadly force is a seizure subject to the reasonableness requirement of the Fourth Amendment."

While a quick reading of the Fourth Amendment might suggest, as a generalization, that arrests without warrants are unreasonable, there are certain important exceptions to such a generalization. Most arrests are made without warrants. At common law a warrant was required to arrest for any *misdemeanor* except a breach of the peace committed in the presence of the officer, and continuing at the time of the arrest. An arrest could be made for a *felony* without a warrant if the officer had reasonable ground to believe that a felony had been committed and the arrested person committed it. These rules have been modified by statute in most of the states. The general rule today is that an officer may arrest without warrant for *all* offenses committed in the presence of the officer, and may arrest a person for a *felony* without a warrant when he has reasonable cause to believe that a felony has been committed and reasonable cause to believe that such person has committed it. These are the exceptions, then, to a general requirement of a warrant prior to an *arrest.* [See Wayne R. LaFave, *Arrest* (Boston: Little, Brown, 1965).]

The argument that the Fourth Amendment permits warrantless arrests for felonies, based upon probable cause, only when exigent circumstances make obtaining a warrant impracticable was specifically rejected by the Court in *United States* v. *Watson*, 423 U.S. 411 (1976). A postal inspector, having reliable information that respondent Watson possessed stolen credit cards, arrested him, without a warrant, in a public restaurant. A subsequent consent search of his nearby car revealed two such cards which were introduced in evidence against him. The trial court denied the motion to suppress, and he was convicted. The Court of Appeals held the warrantless arrest violative of the Fourth Amendment and ruled the evidence inadmissible as having been seized illegally. The Supreme Court reversed. The majority opinion pointed out that a statute specifically authorized postal inspectors to make warrantless felony arrests based upon probable cause, and the Fourth Amendment did not change the common-law rule to require that a warrant be obtained where practicable, at least when the arrest occurs in a *public place.*

In *United States* v. *Santana*, 427 U.S. 38 (1976), the issue of the validity of a warrantless arrest turned on the question of whether the police action occurred in a public place and was thus governed by the *Watson* rule. On the basis of information that one "Mom" Santana had in her possession marked money used by an undercover agent to make a heroin "buy," police officers went to Santana's house. They saw her standing in the doorway of a building with a brown paper bag in her hand. As the officers approached, shouting "police," she retreated into the vestibule of her house, where they caught her. When she tried to escape, envelopes containing what was later determined to be heroin fell to the floor from the paper bag, and she was found to have been carrying some of the marked money on her person. After indictment, Santana moved to suppress the heroin and the marked money. The District Court granted the motion on the ground that although the officers had probable cause to make the arrest, Santana's retreat into the vestibule did not justify a warrantless entry into the house. The Supreme Court reversed, holding first that the threshold of the house came under the "public place" rule of *Watson*, and, second, that Santana could not defeat an otherwise proper arrest that had been set in motion in a public place "by the expedient of escaping to a private place" in the vestibule. The conclusion was that this was a true case of "hot pursuit." Justice Marshall, joined by Justice Brennan, dissented on the ground that warrantless arrests must be justified by exigent circumstances, and none was asserted in this case.

In *Payton* v. *New York*, 445 U.S. 573 (1980), however, the Court held that a warrantless, nonconsensual entry into a suspect's home to make a routine felony arrest violated the Fourth Amendment and that evidence obtained after the illegal entry fell under the exclusionary rule. Detectives, with probable cause to believe that Payton had committed murder, went to his apartment to arrest him, without having obtained a warrant. Although light and music emanated from the apartment, there was no response to their knock on the metal door. They summoned assistance and used crowbars to break open the door and enter the apartment. No one was there, but in plain view was a 30-caliber shell casing that was seized and later admitted into evidence at Payton's murder trial. The Court held the entry unconstitutional and reversed the conviction. Justice Stevens, for the majority, stated that a study of the common law on the question "reveals a surprising lack of judicial decisions and a deep divergence among scholars." Nonetheless, he concluded that "neither history nor this Nation's experience requires us to disregard the overriding respect for the sanctity of the home that has been embedded in our traditions since the origins of the Republic." The opinion stated, however, that for Fourth Amendment purposes, an arrest *warrant* founded on probable cause implicitly carries with it the limited authority to enter a dwelling in which the suspect lives when there is reason to believe the suspect is within. Justice White, speaking for the three dissenters, concluded that the common law *did* authorize such entries and disagreed with the majority holding. "This hard-and-fast rule, founded on erroneous assumptions concerning the intrusiveness of home arrest entries, finds little or no support in the common law or in the text and history of the Fourth Amendment."

It should be noted that even *with* an arrest warrant, in the absence of consent or emergency circumstances, a law enforcement officer may not constitutionally search for the individual named in the warrant in the home of a third party without first obtaining a search warrant. This was the holding in *Steagald* v. *United States,* 451 U.S. 204 (1981).

## Searches

As in the case of arrest, a reading of the Fourth Amendment might seem to indicate that the general rule with regard to the conduct of searches (and subsequent seizure) is that they are to be executed pursuant to a warrant. There are, however, several well-recognized exceptions to such a generalization that will be discussed below. The two main procedural points involved in obtaining a warrant are: first, the application for the warrant must specifically describe the place to be searched, and the person or things to be seized, and second, the warrant must issue from a nonpolice officer in order to guarantee a somewhat more detached and neutral view of the matter. The first requirement, that of particularity, was a response to the despised "writs of assistance" under which the British made general searches during the colonial period. The affidavit must cite sufficient facts to enable the issuing authority to determine that probable cause exists, and thus more is demanded than a mere belief on the part of the applicant. The second requirement has generally been thought to demand that a judicial officer issue the warrant. But in *Shadwick* v. *City of Tampa,* 407 U.S. 345 (1972), the Court made it clear that this was not necessarily the case and upheld the issuance of an arrest warrant (for the violation of a municipal ordinance) by a court clerk—a person who was not a judge or even a lawyer, but one who was attached to the court and was independent of the police.

A question arising with respect to searches under a warrant is: What things are subject to seizure? Since the warrant must describe the articles to be seized, it would seem reasonable to conclude that *only* such items described are subject to seizure. As a general rule, however, this interpretation is too restrictive, since the "plain view" doctrine permits seizure of other items as well, and this doctrine is applicable whether the search is with a warrant or a lawful warrantless search. In *Coolidge* v. *New Hampshire,* 403 U.S. 443 (1971), Justice Stewart, for the majority, discussed the doctrine:

What the "plain view" cases have in common is that the police officer in each of them had a prior justification for an intrusion in the course of which he came inadvertently across a piece of evidence incriminating the accused. The doctrine serves to supplement the prior justification—whether it be a warrant for another object, hot pursuit, search incident to lawful arrest, or some other legitimate reason for being present unconnected with a search directed against the accused—and permits the warrantless seizure. Of course, the extension of the original justification is legitimate only where it is immediately apparent to the police that they have evidence before them; the "plain view" doctrine may not be used to extend a general exploratory search from one object to another until something incriminating at last emerges.

It is important to note that the search must be *reasonable* in order to trigger the "plain view" doctrine. A search under a warrant to seize a stolen television set would not justify an officer in prowling about through desk drawers, while a warrant to seize stolen checks would permit a much more exhaustive search that might well disclose incriminating items in "plain view" that could also be seized. Finally, contraband is always subject to seizure since by definition it covers property illegal to possess. (The question of admissibility of evidence so seized is another matter, however, and is discussed in the section on the exclusionary rule, below.)

The plain view exception to the warrant requirement was construed very narrowly in *Arizona* v. *Hicks*, 55 LW 4258 (1987). Police officers entered the defendant's second-floor apartment without a warrant after a shot fired through the floor wounded a person in the apartment below. They found several weapons, drug paraphernalia, and a stocking-cap mask. The mask and some stereo components that seemed so expensive as to be out of place led the officers to believe that the equipment might be stolen. An officer moved some of the components in order to read and record several serial numbers. A phone check confirmed that one of the items was stolen, and it was seized immediately; others were seized later pursuant to a warrant, which police obtained through use of the serial numbers. The Arizona Court of Appeals held that the police actions violated the Fourth Amendment by moving equipment to obtain the serial numbers. It was conceded, however, that the initial entry and search, although warrantless, were justified by the exigent circumstances of the shooting.

Justice Scalia, for the 6–3 majority, agreed that the intrusion was justified, but held that moving the equipment constituted a "search" separate and apart from the search "for the shooter, victims, and weapons that was the lawful objective" of the officer's entry into the apartment. He stated that it was clear that the search was valid if the plain view doctrine would have sustained a seizure of the equipment. And it would have done so if the officer had probable cause to believe that the equipment was stolen. The State conceded, however, that he had only a "reasonable suspicion," by which it meant something less than probable cause. "We have not ruled on the question whether probable cause is required in order to invoke the 'plain view' doctrine. . . . We now hold that probable cause is required." He stated further, "No reason is apparent why an object should routinely be seizable on lesser grounds, during an unrelated search and seizure, than would have been needed to obtain a warrant for that same object if it had been known to be on the premises."

In dissent, Justice Powell stated:

With all respect, this distinction between "looking" at a suspicious object in plain view and "moving" it even a few inches trivializes the Fourth Amendment. . . . Apart from the importance of rationality in the interpretation of the Fourth Amendment, today's decision may handicap law enforcement without enhancing privacy interests.

Some of the basic aspects of Fourth Amendment application were treated in *Boyd* v. *United States*, 116 U.S. 616 (1886), and it is the leading case on one aspect of what may constitute an "unreasonable" search. While the case involved the validity of a production order issued by a court, rather than a search warrant as such, the primary issue was still the question of whether the Fourth Amendment was violated by an attempted seizure of private papers to be used in evidence against the owner. In the course of the majority opinion for the Court, it was pointed out that while it would be proper to authorize seizure of stolen goods or implements of crime or contraband, it would violate the Fourth and Fifth Amendments to seize "mere evidence" in the form of private papers in order to establish a criminal charge against the owner. This would be a seizure in order to compel self-incrimination.

Carried to its logical conclusion, the "mere evidence" rule as a protection against self-incrimination would appear to prohibit the taking of fingerprints or requiring one accused of drunken driving to take a breathalyzer test. The problem turns on a determination of just what kinds of inculpatory evidence taken from the person are contemplated in the term "self-incrimination." The Court reached this question in *Schmerber* v. *California*, 384 U.S. 757 (1966), and decided that the taking of a blood sample, under protest, of one accused of drunken driving, and the introduction of the results of the test in a prosecution, did not constitute a violation of the self-incrimination clause. The Court read the clause as a protection only against the use of matters of a "testimonial" or "communicative" nature, and thus did not extend to ordinary physical items of an evidentiary nature. This decision led to a reexamination of the "mere evidence" rule in *Warden* v. *Hayden* in 1967. While the case involved a search and seizure *without* a warrant, it has obvious relevance to the search with a warrant as well. In addition, it is a case of "hot pursuit" and illustrates one of the "exigent circumstances" that the Court indicates is an exception to the warrant requirement.

## WARDEN *v.* HAYDEN
### 387 U.S. 294 (1967)

[Following the armed robbery of a cab company in Baltimore, Maryland, two cab drivers, attracted by shouts of "Holdup," followed a man who fled the company premises, and watched him enter a residence. One driver notified the company dispatcher by radio that the man was a Negro about 5'8" tall, wearing a light cap and dark jacket, and that he had entered the house on Cocoa Lane. The dispatcher relayed the information to police. Within minutes, police arrived at the house in a number of patrol cars. They searched the first and second floors and the cellar for the suspect. Hayden was found in an upstairs bedroom, and he was arrested when the officers on the first floor reported that no other man was in the house. One officer discovered a shotgun and a pistol in a flush tank in a bathroom adjoining the bedroom. Another officer, who was searching the cellar for "a man or the money" found, in a washing machine, a jacket and trousers of the type the fleeing man was said to have worn. A clip of ammunition for the pistol and a cap were found under the mattress of Hayden's bed. All these items of evidence were introduced against him at his trial.]

Mr. Justice Brennan delivered the opinion of the Court.

We review in this case the validity of the proposition that there is under the Fourth Amendment a "distinction between merely evidentiary materials, on the one hand, which may not be seized either under the authority of a search warrant or during the course of a search incident to arrest, and on the other hand, those objects which may validly be seized including the instrumentalities and means by which a crime is committed, the fruits of crime such as stolen property, weapons by which escape of the person arrested might be effected, and property the possession of which is a crime.". . .

We agree with the Court of Appeals that neither the entry without warrant to search for the robber, nor the search for him without warrant was invalid. . . . The police . . . acted reasonably when they entered the house and began to search for a man of the description they had been given and for weapons which he had used in the robbery or might use against them. The Fourth Amendment does not require police officers to delay in the course of an investigation if to do so would gravely endanger their lives or the lives of others. Speed here was essential, and only a thorough search of the house for persons and weapons could have insured that Hayden was the only man present and that the police had control of all weapons which could be used against them or to effect an escape. . . .

It is argued that, while the weapons, ammunition, and cap may have been seized in the course of a search for weapons, the officer who seized the clothing was searching neither for the suspect nor for weapons when he looked into the washing machine in which he found the clothing. . . .

We come, then, to the question whether, even though the search was lawful, the Court of Appeals was correct in holding that the seizure and introduction of the items of clothing violated the Fourth Amendment because they are "mere evidence." . . . We today reject the distinction as based on premises no longer accepted as rules governing the application of the Fourth Amendment. . . .

Nothing in the language of the Fourth Amendment supports the distinction between "mere evidence" and instrumentalities, fruits of crime, or contraband. On its face, the provision assures the "right of the people to be secure in their persons, houses, papers, and effects . . . ," without regard to the use to which any of these things are applied. This "right of the people" is certainly unrelated to the "mere evidence" limitation. Privacy is disturbed no more by a search directed to a purely evidentiary object than it is by a search directed to an instrumentality, fruit, or contraband. . . . Indeed, the distinction is wholly irrational, since, depending on the circumstances, the same "papers and effects" may be "mere evidence" in one case and "instrumentality" in another. See Comment, 20 *U. Chi. L. Rev.* 319, 320–322 (1953).

In *Gouled* v. *United States* . . . the Court said that search warrants "may not be used as a means of gaining access to a man's house or office and papers solely for the purpose of making search to secure evidence to be used against him in a criminal or penal proceeding. . . ." The Court derived from *Boyd* v. *United States, supra,* the proposition that warrants "may be resorted to only when a primary right to such search and seizure may be found in the interest which the public or the complainant may have in the property to be seized, or in the right to the possession of it, or when a valid exercise of the police power renders possession of the property by the accused unlawful and provides that it may be taken." . . .

The items of clothing involved in this case are not "testimonial" or "communicative" in nature, and their introduction therefore did not compel respondent to become a witness against himself in violation of the Fifth Amendment. *Schmerber* v. *California,* 384 U.S. 757. This case thus does not require that we consider whether there are items of evidential value whose very nature precludes them from being the object of a reasonable search and seizure. . . .

The premise in *Gouled* that government may not seize evidence simply for the purpose of proving crime has . . . been discredited. The requirement that the Government assert in addition some property interest in material it seizes has long been a fiction, obscuring the reality that government has an interest in solving crime. *Schmerber* settled the proposition that it is reasonable, within the terms of the Fourth Amendment, to conduct otherwise permissible searches for the purpose of obtaining evidence which would aid in apprehending and convicting criminals. The requirements of the Fourth Amendment can secure the same protection of privacy whether the search is for "mere evidence" or for fruits, instrumentalities or contraband. There must, of course, be a nexus—automatically provided in the case of fruits, instrumentalities or contraband—between the item to be seized and criminal behavior. Thus in the case of "mere evidence," probable cause must be examined in terms of cause to believe that the evidence sought will aid in a particular apprehension or conviction. . . . The clothes found in the washing machine matched the description of those worn by the robber and the police therefore could reasonably believe that the items would aid in the identification of the culprit. . . .

The judgment of the Court of Appeals is

*Reversed.*

Mr. Justice Black concurs in the result.

Mr. Justice Fortas, with whom the Chief Justice joins, concurring. . . .

Mr. Justice Douglas, dissenting. . . .

As already noted, there are certain clear exceptions to the requirement of a search warrant prior to conducting a lawful search. One of these is the situation of "hot pursuit," illustrated by the *Warden* case. When police are chasing a suspect and he flees into a building, they are not required to halt the chase to get a warrant and thereby risk losing him.

A second exception, and more obvious, is presented by voluntary consent of the suspect. The matter of voluntariness is crucial to the legality of the search, however. Consent must be genuine, not coerced or obtained by deception. In *Bumper* v. *North Carolina,* 391 U.S. 543 (1968), police, without a valid warrant, went to an elderly Negro woman's house and announced that they had a search warrant to search the house. The woman responded, "Go ahead." When the use of the evidence obtained following the search was challenged, the State contended that the search was based on consent. In holding the evidence inadmissible, the Court stated, "When a law enforcement officer claims authority to search a home under a warrant, he announces in effect that the occupant has no right to resist the search. The situation is instinct with coercion—albeit colorably lawful coercion. Where there is coercion there cannot be consent."

In *Schneckloth* v. *Bustamonte,* 412 U.S. 218 (1973), the issue presented was whether consent given to search an automobile should be considered as "voluntary" if the accused was not aware that he had a right to refuse such consent. A police officer on routine patrol stopped a car for a minor traffic violation and found it to contain six men. When the driver could not produce a driver's license, the officer asked if any of the other five had any evidence of identification. One of the passengers produced a license and explained that the car was borrowed from his brother. The officer asked him if he could search the car, and the reply was, "Sure, go ahead." Prior to the search no one was threatened with arrest. The owner's brother opened the trunk and even assisted in the search. Under the rear seat were found three checks that had previously been stolen from a car wash. At subsequent trial upon a charge of possessing a check with intent to defraud, the defendant moved to suppress the evidence on the ground that the search and seizure were unconstitutional. The motion was denied, and accused was convicted. It was argued in the Supreme Court that consent could not be considered voluntary unless the accused was at the time aware of his right to refuse consent, and thus his permission would represent a "knowing and intelligent" waiver of such right—in effect, a Fourth Amendment *Miranda* warning. The majority of the Court rejected this argument, stating that "neither this Court's prior cases, nor the traditional definition of 'voluntariness' requires proof of knowledge of a right to refuse as the sine qua non of an effective consent to a search." It stated further: "Voluntariness is a question of fact to be determined from all the circumstances, and while the subject's knowledge of a right to refuse is a factor to be taken into account, the prosecution is not required to demonstrate such knowledge as a prerequisite to establishing a voluntary consent." Three justices dissented, with Justice Brennan stating: "It wholly escapes me how our citizens can meaningfully be said to have waived something as precious as a constitutional guarantee without ever being aware of its existence." The dissenters were not impressed with the majority's view that a consent search is fundamentally different in nature from the waiver of a trial right.

It may be noted that some state courts, as a matter of state constitutional law, have ruled the other way on this issue. See, for example, *State* v. *Johnson,* 68 N.J. 349, 346 A.2d 66 (1975); *State* v. *Kaluna,* 520 P.2d 51 (Hawaii, 1974); and *People* v. *Brisendine,* 13 Cal.3rd 528, 531 P.2d 1099 (1975).

There is also the question of who is authorized to give consent. In *Chapman* v. *United States,* 365 U.S. 610 (1961), the Court held that a landlord could not validly consent to a search of a house he had rented to another, and in *Stoner* v. *California,* 376 U.S. 483 (1964), it was held that a night hotel clerk could not validly consent to a search of a customer's room. But in *United States* v. *Matlock,* 415 U.S. 164 (1974), the Court ruled that consent for the search of a home could be given by a woman who was living in the home and occupying the same bedroom with the defendant, even though they were not married. The majority made clear that the consent of one who possesses common authority over premises or effects is valid against the absent, nonconsenting person with whom that authority is shared.

A third exception to the warrant requirement is a search incident to a lawful arrest. This exception is of ancient origin and is justified on two grounds. First, the officer should search the person of the accused and the immediate vicinity to be certain that there are no weapons by which the arrestee can effect an escape. In addition, the courts are agreed that an officer has the authority, following a lawful arrest, to make a search, similarly limited, in order to prevent the destruction or loss of evidence. It is important to keep in mind, however, that for such a search to be justified without warrant, the arrest must be lawful on grounds independent of what the search turns up. The protection against unreasonable searches would be undermined if the arrest could be justified on the basis of evidence turned up by the search.

Two other questions concerning search incident to arrest were dealt with in *United States* v. *Rabinowitz,* 339 U.S. 56 (1950). These were the issues of the legitimate extent of such a search and also the legality of a search without a warrant which goes beyond the person of the accused to include his room, where the police have time to obtain a search warrant but fail to do so. The majority held that a thorough search of desk, safe, and file cabinets in a one-room office following arrest on a valid arrest warrant was not an unreasonable search within the bar of the Fourth Amendment. It further held that the fact that the police had ample time to procure a search warrant but failed to do so did not make the search unreasonable. Contradictions and vacillations in the line of decisions on these points led the Court to make yet another attempt at resolution in 1969.

### CHIMEL v. CALIFORNIA
### 395 U.S. 752 (1969)

Mr. Justice Stewart delivered the opinion of the Court.

This case raises basic questions concerning the permissible scope under the Fourth Amendment of a search incident to a lawful arrest.

The relevant facts are essentially undisputed. Late in the afternoon of September 13, 1965, three police officers arrived at the Santa Ana, California, home of the petitioner with a warrant authorizing his arrest for the burglary of a coin shop. The officers knocked on the door, identified themselves to the petitioner's wife, and asked if they might come inside. She ushered them into the house, where they waited 10 or 15 minutes until the petitioner returned home from work. When the petitioner entered the house, one of the officers handed him the arrest warrant and asked for permission to "look around." The petitioner objected, but was advised that "on the basis of the lawful arrest," the officers would nonetheless conduct a search. No search warrant had been issued.

Accompanied by the petitioner's wife, the officers then looked through the entire three-bedroom house, including the attic, the garage, and a small workshop. In some rooms the search was relatively cursory. In the master bedroom and sewing room, however, the officers directed the petitioner's wife to open drawers and "to physically move contents of the drawers from side to side so that [they] might view any items that would have come from [the] burglary." After completing the search, they seized numerous items—primarily coins, but also several medals, tokens, and a few other objects. The entire search took between 45 minutes and an hour.

At the petitioner's subsequent state trial on two charges of burglary, the items taken from his house were admitted into evidence against him, over his objection that they had been unconstitutionally seized. He was convicted, and the judgments of conviction were affirmed by both the California District Court of Appeal . . . and the California Supreme Court.

Without deciding the question, we proceed on the hypothesis that the California courts were correct in holding that the arrest of the petitioner was valid under the Constitution. This brings us directly to the question whether the warrantless search of the petitioner's entire house can be constitutionally justified as incident to that arrest. The decisions of this Court bearing upon that question have been far from consistent, as even the most cursory review makes evident.

Approval of a warrantless search incident to a lawful arrest seems first to have been articulated by the Court in 1914 as dictum in *Weeks* v. *United States,* 232 U.S. 383. . . .

[Here the opinion traces the decisions, and their inconsistencies, from *Weeks* v. *United States* to *Harris* v. *United States*].

In [*Harris* v. *United States,* 331 U.S. 145 (1947)] officers had obtained a warrant for Harris' arrest on the basis of his alleged involvement with the cashing and interstate transportation of a forged check. He was arrested in the living room of his four-room apartment, and in an attempt to recover two canceled checks thought to have been used in effecting the forgery, the officers undertook a thorough search of the entire apartment. . . . The Court rejected Harris' Fourth Amendment claim, sustaining the search as "incident to arrest." . . .

Only a year after Harris, however, the pendulum swung again. In *Trupiano* v. *United States,* 334 U.S. 699 (1948), agents raided the site of an illicit distillery, saw one of several conspirators operating the still, and arrested him, contemporaneously "seizing the illicit distillery." . . . The Court held that the arrest and others made subsequently had been valid, but that the unexplained failure of the agents to procure a search warrant—in spite of the fact that they had had more than enough time before the raid to do so—rendered the search unlawful. . . .

In 1950, two years after Trupiano, came *United States* v. *Rabinowitz,* 339 U.S. 56, the decision upon which California primarily relies in the case now before us. In Rabinowitz, federal authorities had been informed that the defendant was dealing in stamps bearing forged overprints. On the basis of that information they secured a warrant for his arrest, which they executed at his one-room business office. At the time of the arrest, the officers "searched the desk, safe, and file cabinets in the office for about an hour and a half," . . . and seized 573 stamps with forged overprints. The stamps were admitted into evidence at the defendant's trial, and this Court affirmed his conviction, rejecting the contention that the warrantless search had been unlawful. The Court held that the search in its entirety fell within the principle giving law enforcement authorities "[t]he right 'to search the place where the arrest is made in order to find and seize things connected with the crime. . . .' " Harris was regarded as "ample authority" for that conclusion. . . .

Rabinowitz has come to stand for the proposition, inter alia, that a warrantless search "incident to a lawful arrest" may generally extend to the area that is considered to be in the "possession" or under the "control" of the person arrested. And it was on the basis of that proposition that the California courts upheld the search of the petitioner's entire house in this case. That doctrine, however, at least in the broad sense in which it was applied by the California courts in this case, can withstand neither historical nor rational analysis.

Even limited to its own facts, the Rabinowitz decision was, as we have seen, hardly founded on an unimpeachable line of authority. As Mr. Justice Frankfurter commented in dissent in that case, the "hint" contained in Weeks was, without persuasive justification, "loosely turned into dictum and finally elevated to a decision." . . .

Only last Term in *Terry* v. *Ohio*, 392 U.S. 1, we emphasized that "the police must, whenever practicable, obtain advance judicial approval of searches and seizures through the warrant procedure," . . . and that "[t]he scope of [a] search must be 'strictly tied to and justified by' the circumstances which rendered its initiation permissible." . . . The search undertaken by the officer in that "stop and frisk" case was sustained under that test, because it was no more than a "protective . . . search for weapons." . . . But in a companion case, *Sibron* v. *New York*, 392 U.S. 40, we applied the same standard to another set of facts and reached a contrary result, holding that a policeman's action in thrusting his hand into a suspect's pocket had been neither motivated by nor limited to the objective of protection. Rather, the search had been made in order to find narcotics, which were in fact found.

A similar analysis underlies the "search incident to arrest" principle, and marks its proper extent. When an arrest is made, it is reasonable for the arresting officer to search the person arrested in order to remove any weapons that the latter might seek to use in order to resist arrest or effect his escape. Otherwise, the officer's safety might well be endangered, and the arrest itself frustrated. In addition, it is entirely reasonable for the arresting officer to search for and seize any evidence on the arrestee's person in order to prevent its concealment or destruction. And the area into which an arrestee might reach in order to grab a weapon or evidentiary items must, of course, be governed by a like rule. A gun on a table or in a drawer in front of one who is arrested can be as dangerous to the arresting officer as one concealed in the clothing of the person arrested. There is ample justification, therefore, for a search of the arrestee's person and the area "within his immediate control"—construing that phrase to mean the area from within which he might gain possession of a weapon or destructible evidence.

There is no comparable justification, however, for routinely searching rooms other than that in which an arrest occurs—or, for that matter, for searching through all the desk drawers or other closed or concealed areas in that room itself. Such searches, in the absence of well-recognized exceptions, may be made only under the authority of a search warrant. The "adherence to judicial processes" mandated by the Fourth Amendment requires no less. . . .

The petitioner correctly points out that one result of decisions such as Rabinowitz and Harris is to give law enforcement officials the opportunity to engage in searches not justified by probable cause, by the simple expedient of arranging to arrest suspects at home rather than elsewhere. We do not suggest that the petitioner is necessarily correct in his assertion that such a strategy was utilized here, but the fact remains that had he been arrested earlier in the day, at his place of employment rather than at home, no search of his house could have been made without a search warrant. In any event, even apart from the possibility of such police tactics, the general points so forcefully made by Judge Leonard Hand in *United States* v. *Kirchenblatt*, 16 F.2d 202, remains:

"After arresting a man in his house, to rummage at will among his papers in search of whatever will convict him, appears to us to be indistinguishable from what might be done under a general warrant; indeed, the warrant would give more protection, for presumably it must be issued by a magistrate. True, by hypothesis the power would not exist, if the supposed offender were not found on the premises; but it is small consolation to know that one's papers are safe only so long as one is not at home." Id., at 203.

Rabinowitz and Harris have been the subject of critical commentary for many years, and have been relied upon less and less in our own decisions. It is time, for the reasons we have stated, to hold that on their own facts, and insofar as the principles they stand for are inconsistent with those that we have endorsed today, they are no longer to be followed.

Application of sound Fourth Amendment principles to the facts of this case produces a clear result. The search here went far beyond the petitioner's person and the area from within which he might have obtained either a weapon or something that could have been used as evidence against him. There was no constitutional justification, in the absence of a search warrant, for extending the search beyond that area. The scope of the search was, therefore, "unreasonable" under the Fourth and Fourteenth Amendments, and the petitioner's conviction cannot stand.

*Reversed.*

Mr. Justice Harlan, concurring. . . .
Mr. Justice White, with whom Mr. Justice Black joins, dissenting. . . .

The question of the extent of a search of the person, following arrest for a traffic violation, was considered in *United States* v. *Robinson* in 1973.

## UNITED STATES *v.* ROBINSON
### *414 U.S. 218 (1973)*

[A Washington, D.C. police officer, having reason to believe that Robinson was operating a motor vehicle after the revocation of his operator's permit, signaled him to stop the automobile. Robinson stopped, and the three occupants got out of the car. At that point the officer informed the defendant that he was under arrest for "operating after revocation and obtaining a permit by misrepresentation." It was assumed by lower courts, and conceded by the defendant, that the officer had probable cause to arrest and that he effected a full custody arrest. In accordance with police procedures, the officer then conducted a "patdown" of the defendant, during which the officer felt an object in the breast pocket of the heavy coat the defendant was wearing. He testified that he couldn't tell what the object was, nor actually the size of it. He reached into the pocket and pulled out a crumpled cigarette package. Upon looking in the package, he found fourteen gelatin capsules of white powder which he thought to be, and which later analysis proved to be, heroin. The heroin seized from the defendant was admitted into evidence at the trial which resulted in his conviction in the District Court. The Court of Appeals reversed, holding that the heroin had been obtained as a result of an unconstitutional search. The case came on certiorari to the Supreme Court.]

Mr. Justice Rehnquist delivered the opinion of the Court. . . .

It is well settled that a search incident to a lawful arrest is a traditional exception to the warrant requirement of the Fourth Amendment. This general exception has historically been formulated into two distinct propositions. The first is that a search may be made of the *person* of the arrestee by virtue of the lawful arrest. The second is that a search may be made of the area within the control of the arrestee.

Examination of this Court's decisions in the area show that these two propositions have been treated quite differently. The validity of the search of a person incident to a lawful arrest has been regarded as settled from its first enunciation, and has remained virtually unchallenged until the present case. The validity of the second proposition, while likewise conceded in principle, has been subject to differing interpretations as to the extent of the area which may be searched. . . .

[T]he broadly stated rule [regarding search of the person incident to lawful arrest], and the reasons for it, have been repeatedly affirmed in the decisions of this Court since *Weeks* v. *United States* nearly 60 years ago. Since the statements in the cases speak not simply in terms of an exception to the warrant requirement, but in terms of an affirmative authority to search, they clearly imply that such searches also meet the Fourth Amendment's requirement of reasonableness.

In its decision of this case, the majority of the Court of Appeals decided that even after a police officer lawfully places a suspect under arrest for the purpose of taking him into custody, he may not ordinarily proceed to fully search the prisoner. He must instead conduct a limited frisk of the outer clothing and remove such weapons that he may, as a result of that limited frisk, reasonably believe the suspect has in his possession. While recognizing that *Terry* v. *Ohio* . . . dealt with a permissible "frisk" incident to an investigative stop based on less than probable cause to arrest, the Court of Appeals felt that the principles of that case should be carried over to this probable cause arrest for driving while one's license is revoked. Since there would be no further evidence of such a crime to be obtained in a search of the arrestee, the Court held that only a search for weapons could be justified.

*Terry* v. *Ohio* did not involve an arrest for probable cause, and it made quite clear that the "protective frisk" for weapons which it approved might be conducted without probable cause. . . . The Court's opinion explicitly recognized that there is a "distinction in purpose, character, and extent between a search incident to an arrest and a limited search for weapons":

"The former, although justified in part by the acknowledged necessity to protect the arresting officer from assault with a concealed weapon, . . . is also justified on other grounds, and can therefore involve a relatively extensive exploration of the person. A search for weapons in the absence of probable cause to arrest, however, must, like any other search, be strictly circumscribed by the exigencies which justify its initiation. . . . Thus it must be limited to that which is necessary for the discovery of weapons which might be used to harm the officer or others nearby, and may realistically be characterized as something less than a "full" search even though it remains a serious intrusion. . . ."

*Terry,* therefore, affords no basis to carry over to a probable cause arrest the limitations this Court placed on a stop-and-frisk search permissible without probable cause. . . .

. . . [O]ur more fundamental disagreement with the Court of Appeals arises from its suggestion that there must be litigated in each case the issue of whether or not there was present one of the reasons supporting the authority for a search of the person incident to a lawful arrest. We do not think the long line of authorities of this Court dating back to *Weeks,* nor what we can glean from the history of practice in this country and in England, requires such a case by case adjudication. A police officer's determination as to how and where to search the person of a suspect whom he has arrested is necessarily a quick ad hoc judgment which the Fourth Amendment does not require to be broken down in each instance into an analysis of each step in the search. The authority to search the person incident to a lawful custodial arrest, while based upon the need to disarm and to discover evidence, does not depend on what a court may later decide was the probability in a particular arrest situation that weapons or evidence would in fact be found upon the person of the suspect. A custodial arrest of a suspect based on probable cause is a reasonable intrusion under the Fourth Amendment; that intrusion being lawful, a search incident to the arrest requires no additional justification. It is the fact of the lawful arrest which establishes the authority to search, and we hold that in the case of a lawful custodial arrest a full search of the person is not only an exception to the warrant requirement of the Fourth Amendment, but is also a "reasonable" search under that Amendment. . . .

*Reversed*

Mr. Justice Powell, concurring. . . .

. . . [There] are areas of an individual's life about which he entertains legitimate expectations of privacy. I believe that an individual lawfully subjected to a custodial arrest retains no significant Fourth Amendment interest in the privacy of his person. . . . The search incident to arrest is reasonable under the Fourth Amendment because the privacy interest protected by that constitutional guarantee is legitimately abated by the fact of arrest.

Mr. Justice Marshall, with whom Mr. Justice Douglas and Mr. Justice Brennan join, dissenting.

Certain fundamental principles have characterized this Court's Fourth Amendment jurisprudence over the years. Perhaps the most basic of these was expressed by Mr. Justice Butler, speaking for a unanimous Court in *Go-Bart Co.* v. *United States,* . . . : "There is no formula for the determination of reasonableness. Each case is to be decided on its own facts and circumstances." . . . The majority's approach represents a clear and marked departure from our long tradition of case-by-case adjudication of the reasonableness of searches and seizures under the Fourth Amendment. I continue to believe that "[t]he scheme of the Fourth Amendment becomes meaningful only when it is assured that at some point the conduct of those charged with enforcing the laws can be subjected to the more detached, neutral scrutiny of a judge who must evaluate the reasonableness of a particular search or seizure in light of the particular circumstances." *Terry* v. *Ohio.* . . . Because I find the majority's reasoning to be at odds with these fundamental principles, I must respectfully dissent. . . .

The majority also suggests that the Court of Appeals reached a novel and unprecedented result by imposing qualifications on the historically recognized authority to conduct a full search incident to a lawful arrest. Nothing could be further from the truth, as the Court of Appeals itself was so careful to point out. . . . The fact is that this question has been considered by several state and federal courts, the vast majority of which have held that absent special circumstances a police officer has no right to conduct a full search of the person incident to a lawful arrest for violation of a motor vehicle regulation. . . .

The underlying rationale of a search incident to arrest of a traffic offender initially suggests as reasonable a search whose scope is similar to the protective weapons frisk permitted in *Terry*. . . .

The Government does not now contend that the search of respondent's pocket can be justified by any need to find and seize evidence in order to prevent its concealment or destruction, for as the Court of Appeals found, there are no evidence or fruits of the offense with which the respondent was charged. The only rationale for a search in this case, then, is the removal of weapons which the arrestee might use to harm the officer and attempt to escape. This rationale, of course, is identical to the rationale of the search permitted in *Terry*. . . .

The majority opinion fails to recognize that the search conducted by Officer Jenks did not merely involve a search of respondent's person. It also included a separate search of effects found on his person. And even were we to assume, arguendo, that it was reasonable for Jenks to remove the object he felt in respondent's pocket, clearly there was no justification consistent with the Fourth Amendment which would authorize his opening the package and looking inside.

To begin with, after Jenks had the cigarette package in his hands, there is no indication that he had reason to believe or did in fact believe that the package contained a weapon. More importantly, even if the crumpled up cigarette package had in fact contained some sort of small weapon, it would have been impossible for respondent to have used it once the package was in the officer's hands. Opening the package therefore did not further the protective purpose of the search. . . .

The Government argues that it is difficult to see what constitutionally protected "expectation of privacy" a prisoner has in the interior of a cigarette pack. One wonders if the result in this case would have been the same were respondent a businessman who was lawfully taken into custody for driving without a license and whose wallet was taken from him by the police. Would it be reasonable for the police officer, because of the possibility that a razor blade was hidden somewhere in the wallet, to open it, remove all the contents, and examine each item carefully? Or suppose a lawyer lawfully arrested for a traffic offense is found to have a sealed envelope on his person. Would it be permissible for the arresting officer to tear open the envelope in order to make sure that it did not contain a clandestine weapon—perhaps a pin or a razor blade? . . . Would it not be more consonant with the purpose of the Fourth Amendment and the legitimate needs of the police to require the officer, if he has any question whatsoever about what the wallet or letter contains, to hold onto it until the arrestee is brought to the precinct station? . . .

The search conducted by Officer Jenks in this case went far beyond what was reasonably necessary to protect him from harm or to ensure that respondent would not effect an escape from custody. In my view, it therefore fell outside the scope of a properly drawn "search incident to arrest" exception to the Fourth Amendment's warrant requirement. I would affirm the judgment to the Court of Appeals holding that the fruits of the search should have been suppressed at respondent's trial.

It should be noted that some state courts have specifically refused to follow the rather harsh *Robinson* rule. [See, for example, *People* v. *Marsh*, 20 N.Y.2d 98, 228 N.E.2d 783 (1967).]

A fourth exception involves the police practice of "stop and frisk" which the Court examined in *Terry* v. *Ohio*, 392 U.S. 1 (1968), a case referred to extensively in the *Chi-*

*mel* and *Robinson* cases above. A police officer with thirty years experience patrolling an area of downtown Cleveland for shoplifters and pickpockets observed two men alternately walking back and forth along a line of stores, stopping each time to examine a particular store window. After this had gone on for ten to twelve minutes, the officer became thoroughly suspicious that the men were "casing a job, a stick-up." He approached the men, identified himself as a police officer and asked for their names. When the men "mumbled something," he grabbed Terry and patted down the outside of his clothing. In the left breast pocket of Terry's overcoat he felt a pistol. He retrieved the pistol, and Terry was charged with carrying a concealed weapon. The trial court rejected a motion to suppress the evidence, and the Supreme Court held that the "stop and frisk" under these circumstances did not violate the Fourth Amendment. Chief Justice Warren, for the majority, agreed that at the point that Terry was frisked there was no probable cause to arrest. But he stated:

Our evaluation of the proper balance that has to be struck in this type of case leads us to conclude that there must be a narrowly drawn authority to permit a reasonable search for weapons for the protection of the police officer, where he has reason to believe that he is dealing with an armed and dangerous individual, regardless of whether he has probable cause to arrest the individual for a crime. The officer need not be absolutely certain that the individual is armed; the issue is whether a reasonably prudent man in the circumstances would be warranted in the belief that his safety or that of others was in danger. . . . And in determining whether the officer acted reasonably in such circumstances, due weight must be given, not to his inchoate and unparticularized suspicion or "hunch," but to the specific reasonable inferences which he is entitled to draw from the facts in light of his experience.

On the same day, the Court decided *Sibron* v. *New York*, 392 U.S. 40 (1968), and stressed the point that the "stop and frisk" upheld in *Terry* was limited to a weapons check. Sibron was suspected of possession of narcotics, and when an officer approached Sibron, stating "You know what I am after," he reached into Sibron's pocket and discovered envelopes of heroin. The Court held that the nature and scope of the search were so clearly unrelated to a weapons search that the heroin could not be considered as admissible.

In *Adams* v. *Williams*, 407 U.S. 143 (1972), the Court upheld a stop and frisk where the officer's suspicions rested on an informer's tip. The officer was alone in a patrol car in a high crime area when a person known to the officer approached his cruiser and informed him that an individual seated in a nearby vehicle was carrying narcotics and had a gun at his waist. The informant had apparently provided the officer with information in the past. The officer approached the vehicle, tapped on the car window, and asked the occupant to open the door. When he rolled down the window instead, the officer reached into the car and removed a fully loaded revolver from the occupant's waistband. The gun had not been visible from outside the car, but it was in precisely the place indicated by the informant. The officer then arrested him, and a search incident to the arrest uncovered substantial quantities of heroin on the defendant's person and in the car, and a machete and a second revolver were found hidden in the automobile. The defendant contended that absent a more reliable informant, or some corroboration of the tip, the policeman's actions were unreasonable under *Terry* standards. The Court disagreed, stating that "while the Court's decisions indicate that this informant's unverified tip may have been insufficient for a narcotics arrest or search warrant, . . . the information carried enough indicia of reliability to justify the officer's forcible stop of Williams." Three justices dissented, arguing, first, that the informant was not shown to have been reliable and, second, that the mere presence of the pistol was not sufficient to justify the arrest, since Williams might have been licensed to carry the gun legally. [See Paul G. Chevigny, "Police Abuses in Connection with the Law of Search and Seizure," 5 *Crim. L. Bull.* 3 (1969).]

The fifth general exception to the requirement of a warrant prior to search is the situation of movable vehicles, such as automobiles, airplanes, or boats. The leading United States Supreme Court decision on the subject is *Carroll* v. *United States,* 267 U.S. 132 (1925), involving the admissibility of bottles of liquor seized from an automobile by federal prohibition agents without a warrant. Chief Justice Taft, after examining various federal statutes, stated for the Court:

> We have made a somewhat extended reference to these statutes to show that the guaranty of freedom from unreasonable searches and seizures by the Fourth Amendment has been construed, practically since the beginning of the government, as recognizing a necessary difference between a search of a store, dwelling house, or other structure in respect of which a proper official warrant readily may be obtained, and a search of a ship, motor boat, wagon, or automobile for contraband goods, where it is not practicable to secure a warrant because the vehicle can be quickly moved out of the locality or jurisdiction in which the warrant must be sought.

In that same opinion, however, it was stressed that such an exception should not be construed by the police as carte blanche to search movable vehicles out of curiosity or mere suspicion: "In cases where seizure is impossible except without warrant, the seizing officer acts unlawfully and at his peril unless he can show the court probable cause."

In *Brinegar* v. *United States,* 338 U.S. 160 (1949), the Court reaffirmed the principle announced in *Carroll* and also gave some attention to the matter of defining "probable cause." Justice Rutledge stated for the majority:

> In dealing with probable cause . . . , as the very name implies, we deal with probabilities. These are not technical; they are the factual and practical considerations of everyday life on which reasonable and prudent men, not legal technicians, act. The standard of proof is accordingly correlative to what must be proved.
>
> "The substance of all the definitions" of probable cause "is a reasonable ground for belief of guilt." . . . And this "means less than evidence which would justify condemnation" or conviction, as Marshall, Ch. J., said for the Court more than a century ago. . . . Since Marshall's time, at any rate, it has come to mean more than bare suspicion: Probable cause exists where "the facts and circumstances within their [the officers'] knowledge, and of which they had reasonably trustworthy information, [are] sufficient in themselves to warrant a man of reasonable caution in the belief that" an offense has been or is being committed. *Carroll* v. *United States.* . . . Requiring more would unduly hamper law enforcement. To allow less would be to leave law-abiding citizens at the mercy of the officers' whim or caprice.

Searches for illegal aliens conducted by the United States Border Patrol have presented some special problems in the area of warrantless searches of automobiles. In *Almeida-Sanchez* v. *United States,* 413 U.S. 266 (1973), the defendant, while driving on a state highway in California, about twenty-five miles from the Mexican border, was stopped by a roving border patrol of the United States Immigration and Naturalization Service, and his automobile was searched for aliens. The patrol had no search warrant and had no probable cause to believe that the defendant had committed any offense. In the course of the search, marijuana was found in the automobile. In a Federal District Court the defendant was convicted of concealing and transporting illegally imported marijuana. The conviction was affirmed by the Court of Appeals, which held that under a federal statute and a regulation adopted by the Service under the statute, the patrol was authorized to look for aliens by stopping and searching automobiles within 100 miles of an international border, without either a warrant or probable cause. The United States Supreme Court reversed, holding that in the absence of probable cause or consent, the warrantless search of the automobile violated his Fourth Amendment rights, and that the search could not be justified either as the "functional equivalent" of a border search or under the Court's decisions allowing certain warrantless searches of automobiles and warrantless administrative inspections.

Justice Stewart, for the majority, stated that it is "undoubtedly within the power of the Federal Government to exclude aliens from the country," and that this power "can be effectuated by routine inspections and searches of individuals or conveyances seeking to cross our borders." Further, such searches may, in certain instances, take place not only at the border itself, but at its "functional equivalents" as well, as, for example, a search of the passengers and cargo of an airplane arriving at a St. Louis airport after a nonstop flight from Mexico City. But the search of petitioner's automobile on a road that lies at all points at least twenty miles from the Mexican border was of a wholly different sort and violated the Fourth Amendment right of petitioner to be free of unreasonable searches and seizures.

In *United States* v. *Ortiz,* 422 U.S. 891 (1975), the Court extended the rule of *Almeida-Sanchez* to bar searches of automobiles by the Border Patrol at an official checkpoint at San Clemente, California, some sixty-six road miles north of the Mexican border, where the choice of cars to be searched was purely discretionary in the Border Patrol officers, and probable cause was not shown to determine which cars were selected for search at the checkpoint. In a footnote to his opinion for the majority, however, Justice Powell pointed out that the Court was not deciding the issue of whether Border Patrol officers may lawfully stop motorists for *questioning* at an established checkpoint without reason to believe that a particular vehicle is carrying aliens, nor did the opinion suggest that probable cause would be required for all inspections of private motor vehicles. "It is quite possible, for example, that different considerations would apply to routine safety inspections required as a condition of road use."

In both *Almeida-Sanchez* and *Ortiz* the Government had argued vigorously that the public interest demands effective measures to control the illegal entry of aliens at the Mexican border. The Immigration and Naturalization Service estimates that there may be as many as ten or twelve million aliens illegally in the country, and that some 85 percent of these are from Mexico. The Service argued that their special search measures were vital to achieve a reduction in such illegal entries. In *United States* v. *Brignoni-Ponce,* 422 U.S. 873 (1975), decided on the same day as *Ortiz,* the Court again reversed a conviction on Fourth Amendment grounds, but the majority stated that the full standard of "probable cause" would not be required of the Border Patrol when stopping cars without warrants in the border areas to check for illegal aliens. The defendant was convicted of knowingly transporting illegal immigrants into the country. The facts showed that the only ground for suspicion leading to the stopping of the car by the roving patrol was that the occupants appeared to be of Mexican ancestry. The Court held this to be insufficient. The majority opinion stated, "The likelihood that any given person of Mexican ancestry is an alien is high enough to make Mexican appearance a relevant factor, but standing alone it does not justify stopping all Mexican-Americans to ask if they are aliens." Justice Powell, for the Court, considered *Terry* v. *Ohio* and *Adams* v. *Williams* to be appropriate analogies, however, and stated:

These cases together establish that in appropriate circumstances the Fourth Amendment allows a properly limited "search" or "seizure" on facts that do not constitute probable cause to arrest or to search for contraband or evidence of crime. . . . [B]ecause of the importance of the governmental interest at stake, the minimal intrusion of a brief stop, and the absence of practical alternatives for policing the border, we hold that when an officer's observations lead him reasonably to suspect that a particular vehicle may contain aliens who are illegally in the country, he may stop the car briefly and investigate the circumstances that provoke suspicion. As in *Terry,* the stop and inquiry must be "reasonably related in scope to the justification for their initiation." . . . The officer may question the driver and passengers about their citizenship and immigration status, and he may ask them to explain suspicious circumstances, but any further detention or search must be based on consent or probable cause. . . .

. . . Except at the border and its functional equivalents, officers on roving patrol may stop vehicles only if they are aware of specific articulable facts, together with rational inferences from those facts, that reasonably warrant suspicion that the vehicles contain aliens who may be illegally in the country.

In *United States* v. *Martinez-Fuerte,* 428 U.S. 543 (1976), appellees had been stopped by the Border Patrol at a roadblock checkpoint and were charged and convicted of illegal transportation of aliens. The practice involved slowing all oncoming traffic "to a virtual, if not a complete, halt," at a highway roadblock, and referring vehicles chosen at the discretion of Border Patrol agents to an area for secondary inspection. The Court held that the stops, at a permanent checkpoint located on a major highway away from the Mexican border for brief questioning of the occupants was not violative of the Fourth Amendment even though there was no individualized suspicion that the vehicle contained illegal aliens. It held further that it was constitutional to refer motorists selectively to a secondary inspection area for limited inquiry on the basis of criteria that would not sustain a roving-patrol stop, since the intrusion was sufficiently minimal that no particularized reason need exist to justify it. *Brignoni-Ponce* was distinguished since it involved random stops and the greater possibility of abuse of discretion. "Routine checkpoint stops do not intrude similarly on the motoring public."

*Brignoni-Ponce* suggests, although it does not decide, that random stops by police for the purpose of license or registration checks may violate the Fourth Amendment. This issue was addressed by the Court in the following case.

DELAWARE *v.* PROUSE

*440 U.S. 648 (1979)*

[A Delaware patrolman stopped an automobile occupied by Prouse. The patrolman smelled marihuana smoke as he was walking toward the stopped vehicle, and he seized marihuana in plain view on the car floor. Prouse was subsequently indicted for illegal possession of a controlled substance. At a hearing on respondent's motion to suppress, the patrolman testified that prior to stopping the car he had observed neither traffic or equipment violations nor any suspicious activity, and that he made the stop only in order to check the driver's license and registration. The trial court granted the motion, and the Delaware Supreme Court affirmed on Fourth and Fourteenth Amendment grounds. The State sought review on certiorari.]

Mr. Justice White delivered the opinion of the Court.

The question is whether it is an unreasonable seizure under the Fourth and Fourteenth Amendments to stop an automobile, being driven on a public highway, for the purpose of checking the driving license of the operator and the registration of the car, where there is neither probable cause to believe nor reasonable suspicion that the car is being driven contrary to the laws governing the operation of motor vehicles or that either the car or any of its occupants is subject to seizure or detention in connection with the violation of any other applicable law. . . .

In this case . . . the State of Delaware urged that patrol officers be subject to no constraints in deciding which automobiles shall be stopped for a license and registration check because the State's interest in discretionary spot checks as a means of ensuring the safety of its roadways outweighs the resulting intrusion on the privacy and security of the persons detained.

[The opinion then discusses the decisions in *Brignoni-Ponce* and *Martinez-Fuerte*.]

Although not dispositive, these decisions undoubtedly provide guidance in balancing the public interest against the individual's Fourth Amendment interests implicated by the practice of spot checks such as occurred in this case. We cannot agree that stopping or detaining a vehicle on an ordinary city street is less intrusive than a roving-patrol stop on a major highway and that it bears greater resemblance to a permissible stop and secondary detention at a checkpoint near the border. In this regard, we note that *Brignoni-Ponce* was not limited to roving-patrol stops on limited access roads, but applied to any roving-patrol stop by Border Patrol agents on any type of roadway on less than reasonable suspicion. . . . We cannot assume that the physical and psychological intrusion visited upon the occupants of a vehicle by a random stop to check documents is of any less moment than that occasioned by a stop by border agents on roving patrol. Both of these stops generally entail law enforcement officers signaling a moving automobile to pull over to the side of the roadway, by means of a possibly unsettling show of authority. Both interfere with freedom of movement, are inconvenient, and consume time. Both may create substantial anxiety. For Fourth Amendment purposes, we also see insufficient resemblance between sporadic and random stops of individual vehicles making their way through city traffic and those stops occasioned by roadblocks where all vehicles are brought to a halt or to a near halt, and all are subjected to a show of the police power of the community. "At traffic checkpoints the motorist can see that other vehicles are being stopped, he can see visible signs of the officers' authority, and he is much less likely to be frightened or annoyed by the intrusion." . . .

. . . Absent some empirical data to the contrary, it must be assumed that finding an unlicensed driver among those who commit traffic violations is a much more likely event than finding an unlicensed driver by choosing randomly from the entire universe of drivers. . . . In terms of actually discovering unlicensed drivers or deterring them from driving, the spot check does not appear sufficiently productive to qualify as a reasonable law enforcement practice under the Fourth Amendment. . . .

Accordingly, we hold that except in those situations in which there is at least articulable and reasonable suspicion that a motorist is unlicensed or that an automobile is not registered, or that either the vehicle or an occupant is otherwise subject to seizure for violation of law, stopping an automobile and detaining the driver in order to check his driver's license and the registration of the automobile are unreasonable under the Fourth Amendment. This holding does not preclude the State of Delaware or other States from developing methods for spot checks that involve less intrusion or that do not involve the unconstrained exercise of discretion. Questioning of all oncoming traffic at roadblock-type stops is one possible alternative. We hold only that persons in automobiles on public roadways may not for that reason alone have their travel and privacy interfered with at the unbridled discretion of police officers. The judgment below is affirmed.

So ordered.

Mr. Justice Blackmun, with whom Mr. Justice Powell joins, concurring. . . .

Mr. Justice Rehnquist, dissenting.

The Court holds, in successive sentences, that absent an articulable, reasonable suspicion of unlawful conduct, a motorist may not be subjected to a random license check, but that the States are free to develop "methods for spot checks that . . . do not involve the unconstrained exercise of discretion," such as "[q]uestioning . . . all oncoming traffic at roadblock-type stops." . . . Because motorists, apparently like sheep, are much less likely to be "frightened" or "annoyed" when stopped en masse, a highway patrolman needs neither probable cause nor articulable suspicion to stop *all* motorists on a particular thoroughfare, but he cannot without articulable suspicion stop *less* than all motorists. The Court thus elevates the adage "misery loves company" to a novel role in Fourth Amendment jurisprudence. The rule becomes "curiouser and curiouser" as one attempts to follow the Court's explanation for it. . . .

Neither the Court's opinion, nor the opinion of the Supreme Court of Delaware, suggests that the random stop made in this case was carried out in a manner inconsistent with the Equal Protection Clause of the Fourteenth Amendment. Absent an equal protection violation, the fact that random stops may entail "a possibly unsettling show of authority," . . . and "may create substantial anxiety," . . . seems an insufficient basis to distinguish for Fourth Amendment purposes between a roadblock stopping all cars and the random stop at issue here. Accordingly, I would reverse the judgment of the Supreme Court of Delaware.

It should be noted that the case is illustrative of one of the basic requirements of the application of the "plain view" doctrine—that the officer be lawfully in a position to see the items seized. Since the random stop was a Fourth Amendment violation, the subsequent approach to the car which permitted the observation of the marihuana was not lawful.

An additional problem concerns the permissible extent of searches following a lawful stop of movable vehicles. *United States* v. *Robinson,* above, held that an officer could lawfully search the person of the driver of a car after making a *custodial arrest* for a motor vehicle violation. And in *New York* v. *Belton,* 453 U.S. 454 (1981), the Court held valid a warrantless search of the passenger compartment of a car as a contemporaneous incident of a lawful custodial arrest of the occupant. A New York policeman had stopped an automobile for speeding and, in the course of checking the driver's license and registration, smelled burnt marijuana and observed an envelope on the floor of the car which he associated with marijuana. He directed the four occupants to get out of the car and placed them under arrest for the unlawful possession of marijuana. He searched each of the four and then searched the passenger compartment of the car. On the back seat he found a leather jacket belonging to one of the occupants, unzipped one of the pockets and discovered cocaine. The majority of the Court held that an officer who has made a lawful custodial arrest of the occupant of an automobile may, as a contemporaneous incident of that arrest, search the passenger compartment of the automobile and may examine the contents of the containers found within the passenger compartment. Justice Stewart, for the majority, stated: " 'Container' here denotes any object capable of holding another object. It thus includes closed or open glove compartments, consoles, or other receptacles located anywhere within the passenger compartment, as well as luggage, boxes, bags, clothing, and the like. Our holding encompasses only the interior of the passenger compartment of an automobile and does not encompass the trunk."

Decisions by the Court in several cases during the period 1977–1981 left the law of vehicular searches in a somewhat confused state, and an attempt to clarify that law was made in *United States* v. *Ross* in 1982.

### UNITED STATES *v.* ROSS
### *456 U.S. 798 (1982)*

[Acting on information from a reliable informant that a described individual was selling narcotics kept in the trunk of a car parked at a specified location, District of Columbia police officers immediately drove to the location and found the car there. Failing to observe anyone matching the informant's description, they left the area. The officers returned five minutes later and observed the car being driven off. They noticed that the driver matched the informant's description and stopped the car, and the driver, Ross, was ordered to get out of the car. One officer discovered a bullet on the car's front seat and a search of the interior of the car revealed a pistol in the glove compartment. Ross was then arrested and handcuffed. The other officer opened the car's trunk, found a closed brown paper bag and after opening the bag discovered glassine bags containing white powder which was later determined to be heroin. The officer then drove the car to headquarters, where another warrantless search of the trunk revealed a zippered leather pouch containing $3,200 in cash. The motion to suppress the heroin and currency was denied, and Ross was convicted of possession of heroin with intent to distribute. The Court of Appeals reversed, holding that while the officers had probable cause to stop and search respondent's car—including its trunk—without a warrant, they should not have opened either the paper bag or the leather pouch found in the trunk without first obtaining a warrant.]

Justice Stevens delivered the opinion of the Court.

In *Carroll* v. *United States* . . . the Court held that a warrantless search of an automobile stopped by police officers who had probable cause to believe the vehicle contained contraband was not unreasonable within the meaning of the Fourth Amendment. The Court in *Carroll* did not explicitly address the scope of the search that is permissible. In this case, we consider the extent to which police officers—who have legitimately stopped an automobile and who have probable cause to believe that contraband is concealed somewhere within it—may conduct a probing search of compartments and containers within the vehicle whose contents are not in plain view. We hold that they may conduct a search of the vehicle that is as thorough as a magistrate could authorize in a warrant "particularly describing the place to be searched." . . .

### III

The rationale justifying a warrantless search of an automobile that is believed to be transporting contraband arguably applies with equal force to any movable container that is believed to be carrying an illicit substance. That argument, however, was squarely rejected in *United States* v. *Chadwick*, 433 U.S. 1 [1977].

*Chadwick* involved the warrantless search of a 200-pound footlocker secured with two padlocks. Federal railroad officials . . . became suspicious when they noticed that a brown footlocker loaded onto a train bound for Boston was unusually heavy and leaking talcum powder, a substance often used to mask the odor of marijuana. Narcotics agents met the train in Boston and a trained police dog signaled the presence of a controlled substance inside the footlocker. The agents did not seize the footlocker, however, at this time; they waited until respondent Chadwick arrived and the footlocker was placed in the trunk of Chadwick's automobile. Before the engine was started, the officers arrested Chadwick and his two companions. The agents then removed the footlocker to a secured place, opened it without a warrant, and discovered a large quantity of marijuana. . . .

The Court in *Chadwick* specifically rejected the argument that the warrantless search was "reasonable" because a footlocker has some of the mobile characteristics that support warrantless searches of automobiles. The Court recognized that "a person's expectations of privacy in personal luggage are substantially greater than in an automobile," . . . and noted that the practical problems associated with the temporary detention of a piece of luggage during the period of time necessary to obtain a warrant are significantly less than those associated with the detention of an automobile. . . . In ruling that the warrantless search of the footlocker was unjustified, the Court reaffirmed the general principle that closed packages and containers may not be searched without a warrant. . . . In sum, the Court in *Chadwick* declined to extend the rationale of the "automobile exception" to permit a warrantless search of any movable container found in a public place.

The facts in *Arkansas* v. *Sanders,* 442 U.S. 753 [1979], were similar to those in *Chadwick.* In *Sanders,* a Little Rock police officer received information from a reliable informant that Sanders would arrive at the local airport on a specified flight that afternoon carrying a green suitcase containing marijuana. The officer went to the airport. Sanders arrived on schedule and retrieved a green suitcase from the airline baggage service. Sanders gave the suitcase to a waiting companion who placed it in the trunk of a taxi. Sanders and his companion drove off in the cab; police officers followed and stopped the taxi several blocks from the airport. The officers opened the trunk, seized the suitcase, and searched it on the scene without a warrant. As predicted, the suitcase contained marijuana.

The Arkansas Supreme Court ruled that the warrantless search of the suitcase was impermissible under the Fourth Amendment, and this Court affirmed. As in *Chadwick,* the mere fact that the suitcase had been placed in the trunk of the vehicle did not render the automobile exception of *Carroll* applicable; the police had probable cause to seize the suitcase before it was placed in the trunk of the cab and did not have probable cause to search the taxi itself. . . . As the Chief Justice noted in his opinion concurring in the judgment: "Because the police officers had probable cause to believe that respondent's green suitcase contained marijuana before it was placed in the trunk of the taxicab, their duty to obtain a search warrant before opening it is clear under *United States* v. *Chadwick*. . . . Here, as in *Chadwick,* it was the *luggage* being transported by respondent at the time of the arrest, not the automobile in which it was being carried, that was the suspected locus of the contraband. The relationship between the automobile and the contraband was purely coincidental, as in *Chadwick.* The fact that the suitcase was resting in the trunk of the automobile at the time of respondent's arrest does not turn this into an "automobile" exception case. . . ."

*Robbins* v. *California,* 453 U.S. 420 [1981], however, was a case in which suspicion was not directed at a specific container. In that case the Court for the first time was forced to consider whether police officers who are entitled to conduct a warrantless search of an automobile stopped on a public roadway may open a container found within the vehicle. In the early morning . . . police officers stopped Robbins' station wagon because he was driving erratically. Robbins got out of the car, but later returned to obtain the vehicle's registration papers. When he opened the car door, the officers smelled marijuana smoke. One of the officers searched Robbins and discovered a vial of liquid; in a search of the interior of the car the officer found marijuana. The police officers then opened the tailgate of the station wagon and raised the cover of a recessed luggage compartment. In the compartment they found two packages wrapped in green opaque plastic. The police unwrapped the packages and discovered a large amount of marijuana in each. . . .

. . . Writing for a plurality, Justice Stewart rejected the argument that the outward appearance of the packages precluded Robbins from having a reasonable expectation of privacy in their contents. He also squarely rejected the argument that there is a constitutional distinction between searches of luggage and searches of "less worthy" containers. Justice Stewart reasoned that all containers are equally protected by the Fourth Amendment unless their contents are in plain view. The plurality concluded that the warrantless search was impermissible because *Chadwick* and *Sanders* had established that "a closed piece of luggage found in a lawfully searched car is constitutionally protected to the same extent as are closed pieces of luggage found anywhere else." . . .

. . . Unlike *Chadwick* and *Sanders,* in this case police officers had probable cause to search respondent's entire vehicle. Unlike *Robbins,* in this case the parties have squarely addressed the question whether, in the course of a legitimate warrantless search of an automobile, police are entitled to open containers found within the vehicle. We now address that question. Its answer is determined by the scope of the search that is authorized by the exception to the warrant requirement set forth in *Carroll.*

IV

In *Carroll* itself, the whiskey that the prohibition agents seized was not in plain view. It was discovered only after an officer opened the rumble seat and tore open the upholstery of the lazyback. The Court did not find the scope of the search unreasonable. Having stopped Carroll and Kiro on a public road and subjected them to the indignity of a vehicle search—which the Court found to be a reasonable intrusion on their privacy because it was based on probable cause that their vehicle was transporting contraband—prohibition agents were entitled to tear open a portion of the roadster itself. The scope of the search was no greater than a magistrate could have authorized by issuing a warrant based on the probable cause that justified the search. Since such a warrant could have authorized the agents to open the rear portion of the roadster and to rip the upholstery in their search for concealed whiskey, the search was constitutionally permissible. . . .

A lawful search of fixed premises generally extends to the entire area in which the object of the search may be found and is not limited by the possibility that separate acts of entry or opening may be required to complete the search. Thus, a warrant that authorizes an officer to search a home for illegal weapons also provides authority to open closets, chests, drawers, and containers in which the weapon might be found. . . .

As Justice Stewart stated in *Robbins,* the Fourth Amendment provides protection to the owner of every container that conceals its contents from plain view. . . . But the protection afforded by the Amendment varies in different settings. The luggage carried by a traveler entering the country may be searched at random by a customs officer; the luggage may be searched no matter how great the traveler's desire to conceal the contents may be. A container carried at the time of arrest often may be searched without a warrant and even without any specific suspicion concerning its contents. A container that may conceal the object of a search authorized by a warrant may be opened immediately; the individual's interest in privacy must give way to the magistrate's official determination of probable cause.

In the same manner, an individual's expectation of privacy in a vehicle and its contents may not survive if probable cause is given to believe that the vehicle is transporting contraband. Certainly the privacy interests in a car's trunk or glove compartment may be no less than those in a movable container. An individual undoubtedly has a significant interest that the upholstery of his automobile will not be ripped or a hidden compartment within it opened. These interests must yield to the authority of a search, however, which—in light of *Carroll*—does not itself require the prior approval of a magistrate. The scope of a warrantless search based on probable cause is no narrower—and no broader—than the scope of a search authorized by a warrant supported by probable cause. Only the prior approval of the magistrate is waived; the search otherwise is as the magistrate could authorize.

The scope of a warrantless search of an automobile thus is not defined by the nature of the container in which the contraband is secreted. Rather, it is defined by the object of the search and the places in which there is probable cause to believe that it may be found. Just as probable cause to believe that a stolen lawnmower may be found in a garage will not support a warrant to search an upstairs bedroom, probable cause to believe that undocumented aliens are being transported in a van will not justify a warrantless search of a suitcase. Probable cause to believe that a container placed in the trunk of a taxi contains contraband or evidence does not justify a search of the entire cab.

### V

Our decision today is inconsistent with the disposition in *Robbins* v. *California,* and with the portion of the opinion in *Arkansas* v. *Sanders* on which the plurality in *Robbins* relied. . . .

. . . We hold that the scope of the warrantless search authorized by [the exception recognized in *Carroll*] is no broader and no narrower than a magistrate could legitimately authorize by warrant. If probable cause justifies the search of a lawfully stopped vehicle, it justifies the search of every part of the vehicle and its contents that may conceal the object of the search.

The judgment of the Court of appeals is reversed. The case is remanded for further proceedings consistent with this opinion.

It is so ordered.

Justice Blackmun, concurring.

My dissents in prior cases have indicated my continuing dissatisfaction and discomfort with the Court's vacillation in what is rightly described as "this troubled area." . . .

I adhere to the views expressed in those dissents. It is important, however, not only for the Court as an institution, but also for law enforcement officials and defendants, that the applicable legal rules be clearly established. Justice Stevens' opinion for the Court now accomplishes much in this respect, and it should clarify a good bit of the confusion that has existed. In order to have an authoritative ruling, I join the Court's opinion and judgment.

Justice Powell, concurring. . . .

It became evident last Term . . . from the five opinions written in *Robbins*—in none of which the Chief Justice joined—that it is essential to have a Court opinion in *automobile* search cases that provides "specific guidance to police and courts in this reoccuring situation." . . . The Court's opinion today, written by Justice Stevens and now joined by four other Justices, will afford this needed guidance. It is fair also to say that, given *Carroll* v. *United States* . . . and *Chambers* v. *Maroney* . . . , the Court's decision does not depart substantially from Fourth Amendment doctrine in automobile cases. Moreover, in enunciating a readily understood and applied rule, today's decision is consistent with the similar step taken last Term in *Belton* v. *New York* . . . (1981).

I join the Court's opinion.

Justice White, dissenting.

I would not overrule *Robbins* v. *California*. . . . For the reasons stated by Justice Stewart in that case, I would affirm the judgment of the Court of Appeals. I also agree with much of Justice Marshall's dissent in this case.

Justice Marshall, with whom Justice Brennan joins, dissenting.

The majority today not only repeals all realistic limits on warrantless automobile searches, it repeals the Fourth Amendment warrant requirement itself. By equating a police officer's estimation of probable cause with a magistrate's, the Court utterly disregards the value of a neutral and detached magistrate. . . .

A police officer on the beat hardly satisfies these standards. In adopting today's new rule, the majority opinion shows contempt for these Fourth Amendment values, ignores this Court's precedents, is internally inconsistent, and produces anomalous and unjust consequences. I therefore dissent. . . .

A different automobile search problem is presented with respect to impounded cars. If a car is illegally parked in a restricted zone, or if police make a custodial arrest of a driver who is alone in a car, the practice is customarily to impound the car. In *South Dakota* v. *Opperman,* 428 U.S. 364 (1976), the Court held that since cars afford much less expectation of privacy than homes, police can routinely search and inventory contents of impounded cars so as adequately to secure and guard the contents, even if the car was locked, where some valuables on the dashboard and the rear seat were visible.

In *Colorado* v. *Bertine,* 55 LW 4105 (1987), the Court held 7–2 that warrantless inventories of impounded motor vehicles may encompass any container found inside, as well as the entire vehicle itself. Such inventories do not violate the Fourth Amendment as long as they are conducted pursuant to a standard police policy requiring such inventories and are not undertaken in bad faith or for the sole purpose of uncovering evidence of criminality. The defendant in this case was arrested for drunk driving and was taken into custody. An officer inventoried the contents of defendant's van before it was taken to an impoundment lot, pursuant to a departmental procedure requiring inspection and inventory of impounded vehicles. The officer found a backpack behind the seat of the car. He opened it, took out a nylon bag and removed metal cannisters. Chief Justice Rehnquist, for the majority explained that *Sanders* and *Chadwick* were inapposite, inasmuch as they "concerned searches conducted solely for the purpose of investigating criminal conduct." This case, he said, was more akin to *Opperman,* which upheld inventories of the glove compartment of an impounded car. And the governmental interests justifying the inventory in *Opperman*—protection of property from interference and thus guarding against claims of loss or theft, and averting danger to the police or others—are also relevant in this situation.

In *California* v. *Carney,* 471 U.S. 386 (1985), the Court expanded the automobile exception to include mobile motor homes. A Drug Enforcement Administration agent had information that respondent's motor home, parked on a public lot in downtown San Diego, was being used to exchange marijuana for sex. The agent watched the owner and a youth enter the vehicle and close the window shades. When the youth left the vehicle, more than an hour later, the officer stopped him. He told the officer that he had received marijuana in return for allowing sexual contacts. The officer, with others, entered the vehicle without a warrant and noted marijuana and accompanying paraphernalia on a table. Respondent was charged with possession of marijuana for sale. On certiorari the Court examined the issue of whether enforcement agents violated the Fourth Amendment when they conducted a warrantless search, based on probable cause, of a fully mobile motor home located in a public place. Rejecting respondent's argument that a warrant should have been required since the motor home was capable of functioning as a home, the Court held 6–3 that the automobile exception should apply. The holding was limited, however, to a motor home capable of being used on the road and located in a place not regularly used for residential purposes.

A sixth exception to the warrant requirement inheres in the "open fields" doctrine announced in *Hester* v. *United States,* 265 U.S. 57 (1924), which held that the Fourth Amendment requires neither a warrant nor probable cause in order for law enforcement officers to enter and conduct a search of unoccupied or undeveloped areas outside of the curtilage of a dwelling. This doctrine was reexamined in *Oliver* v. *United States* in 1984.

OLIVER *v.* UNITED STATES
*466 U.S. 170 (1984)*

[Acting on reports that marihuana was being raised on Oliver's farm, narcotics agents of the Kentucky State Police went to the farm to investigate. Arriving at the farm, they drove past the house to a locked gate with a "No Trespassing" sign. A footpath led around one side of the gate. The agents walked around the gate and along the road and found a field of marihuana over a mile from petitioner's house. Oliver was arrested and indicted for "manufacturing" a controlled substance in violation of a federal statute. The District Court suppressed the evidence on the ground that Oliver had a reasonable expectation that the fields would remain private. The Court of Appeals reversed on authority of *Hester* v. *United States,* and the Supreme Court granted certiorari.]

Justice Powell delivered the opinion of the Court.

The "open fields" doctrine, first enunciated by this Court in *Hester* v. *United States* . . . permits police officers to enter and search a field without a warrant. We granted certiorari in these cases to clarify confusion that has arisen as to the continued vitality of the doctrine. . . .

II

The rule announced in *Hester* v. *United States* was founded upon the explicit language of the Fourth Amendment. That Amendment indicates with some precision the places and things encompassed by its protections. As Justice Holmes explained for the Court in his characteristically laconic style: "[T]he special protection accorded by the Fourth Amendment to the people in their 'persons, houses, papers, and effects,' is not extended to the open fields. The distinction between the latter and the house is as old as the common law." . . .

III

This interpretation of the Fourth Amendment's language is consistent with the understanding of the right to privacy expressed in our Fourth Amendment jurisprudence. Since *Katz* v. *United States* . . . (1967), the touchstone of Amendment analysis has been the question whether a person has a "constitutionally protected reasonable expectation of privacy." . . . The Amendment does not protect the merely subjective expectation of privacy, but only "those expectations that society is prepared to recognize as 'reasonable.' " . . .

A

. . .

. . . [O]pen fields do not provide the setting for those intimate activities that the Amendment is intended to shelter from government interference or surveillance. There is no societal interest in protecting the privacy of those activities, such as the cultivation of crops, that occur in open fields. Moreover, as a practical matter these lands usually are accessible to the public and the police in ways that a home, an office or commercial structure would not be. It is not generally true that fences or no trespassing signs effectively bar the public from viewing open fields in rural areas. And [petitioner Oliver concedes] that the public and police lawfully may survey lands from the air. For these reasons, the asserted expectation of privacy in open fields is not an expectation that "society recognizes as reasonable."

The historical underpinnings of the "open fields" doctrine also demonstrate that the doctrine is consistent with respect for "reasonable expectations of privacy." As Justice Holmes, writing for the Court, observed in *Hester*, . . . the common law distinguished "open fields" from the "curtilage," the land immediately surrounding and associated with the home. . . . The distinction implies that only the curtilage, not the neighboring open fields, warrants the Fourth Amendment protections that attach to the home. At common law, the curtilage is the area to which extends the intimate activity associated with the "sanctity of a man's home and the privacies of life," . . . and therefore has been considered part of home itself for Fourth Amendment purposes. . . .

IV

. . .

. . . Initially, we reject the suggestion that steps taken to protect privacy establish that expectations of privacy in an open field are legitimate. It is true, of course, that petitioner Oliver . . . , in order to conceal [his] criminal activities, planted the marijuana upon secluded land and erected fences and no trespassing signs around the property. And it may be that because of such precautions, few members of the public stumbled upon the marijuana crops seized by the police. Neither of these suppositions demonstrates, however, that the expectation of privacy was *legitimate* in the sense required by the Fourth Amendment. The test of legitimacy is not whether the individual chooses to conceal assertedly "private" activity. Rather, the correct inquiry is whether the government's intrusion infringes upon the personal and societal values protected by the Fourth Amendment. As we have explained, we find no basis for concluding that a police inspection of open fields accomplishes such an infringement.

Nor is the government's intrusion upon an open field a "search" in the constitutional sense because that intrusion is a trespass at common law. The existence of a property right is but one element in determining whether expectations of privacy are legitimate. . . . "[E]ven a property interest in premises may not be sufficient to establish a legitimate expectation of privacy with respect to particular items located on the premises or activity conducted thereon." *Rakas* v. *Illinois* . . .

V

We conclude that the open fields doctrine, as enunciated in *Hester,* is consistent with the plain language of the Fourth Amendment and its historical purposes. Moreover, Justice Holmes' interpretation of the Amendment in *Hester* accords with the "reasonable expectation of privacy" analysis developed in subsequent decisions of this Court. We therefore affirm *Oliver* v. *United States*. . . .

*It is so ordered.*

Justice White, concurring in part and in the judgment. . . .

Justice Marshall, with whom Justice Brennan and Justice Stevens join, dissenting.

In each of these consolidated cases, police officers, ignoring clearly visible "no trespassing" signs, entered upon private land in search of evidence of a crime. At a spot that could not be seen from any vantage point accessible to the public, the police discovered contraband, which was subsequently used to incriminate the owner of the land. In neither case did the police have a warrant authorizing their activities.

The Court holds that police conduct of this sort does not constitute an "unreasonable search" within the meaning of the Fourth Amendment. The Court reaches that startling conclusion by two independent analytical routes. First, the Court argues that, because the Fourth Amendment by its terms renders people secure in their "persons, houses, papers, and effects," it is inapplicable to trespasses upon land not lying within the curtilage of a dwelling. . . . Second, the Court contends that "an individual may not legitimately demand privacy for activities conducted out of doors in fields, except in the area immediately surrounding the home.". . . Because I cannot agree with either of these propositions, I dissent. . . .

. . . If a person has not marked the boundaries of his fields or woods in a way that informs passersby that they are not welcome, he cannot object if members of the public enter onto the property. There is no reason why he should have any greater rights as against government officials. Accordingly, we have held that an official may, without a warrant, enter private land from which the public is not excluded and make observations from that vantage point. . . . Fairly read, the case on which the majority so heavily relies, *Hester* v. *United States* . . . , affirms little more than the foregoing unremarkable proposition. From aught that appears in the opinion in that case, the defendants, fleeing from revenue agents who had observed them committing a crime, abandoned incriminating evidence on private land from which the public had not been excluded. Under such circumstances, it is not surprising that the Court was unpersuaded by the defendants' argument that the entry onto their fields by the agents violated the Fourth Amendment.

A very different case is presented when the owner of undeveloped land has taken precautions to exclude the public. As indicated above, a deliberate entry by a private citizen onto private property marked with "no trespassing" signs will expose him to criminal liability. I see no reason why a government official should not be obliged to respect such unequivocal and universally understood manifestations of a landowner's desire for privacy. . . .

The Fourth Amendment, properly construed, embodies and gives effect to our collective sense of the degree to which men and women, in civilized society, are entitled "to be let alone" by their governments. . . . The Court's opinion bespeaks and will help to promote an impoverished vision of that fundamental right.

I dissent.

Since the manufacturers of controlled substances often operate in rural areas, to try to avoid detection, the distinction between the "open fields" doctrine and designation of residential "curtilage" has become more important for law enforcement purposes. In *California* v. *Ciraolo*, 476 U.S. 207 (1986), the Court held 5–4 that the Fourth Amendment was not violated by an aerial search for marijuana plants in defendant's backyard. The fact that the backyard and its crop were within the "curtilage" of the home did not bar officers from observing the area from public navigable airspace in a physically nonintrusive manner. Justice Powell, for the dissenters, argued that the search was an unconstitutional invasion of privacy, and the fact that it was "physically nonintrusive" did not validate the warrantless search.

In 1987, in *United States* v. *Dunn,* 55 LW 4251, the Court set out a four-point analysis to be employed in determining whether a particular area is within the home's curtilage and hence entitled to its Fourth Amendment protection. Federal drug agents discovered that a person had purchased large quantities of chemicals and equipment used to make controlled substances. The agents placed tracking "beepers" in some of these items, and the signals led agents to follow a truck to Dunn's ranch. Aerial photographs of the ranch showed the truck backed up to a barn behind the ranch house. The ranch was completely encircled by a perimeter fence, and contained several interior barbed wire fences, including one around the house approximately fifty yards from the barn, and a wooden fence enclosing the front of the barn. The barn itself had a locked waist-high gate with netting extending from the top of the gate to the ceiling. Drug agents, without a warrant, entered the property at night, crossing a number of fences, including the wooden fence surrounding the barn. They noticed a strong odor of what was believed to be phenylacetic acid. Shining a flashlight through the netting, they peered into the barn and observed what the agents thought to be a drug laboratory. At this point they left the property but returned twice more to confirm the presence of the laboratory. They then obtained a search warrant, arrested Dunn and seized chemicals and equipment, as well as bags of amphetamines they discoved in the house. The Court held that the area near the barn is not within the curtilage of the house for Fourth Amendment purposes. Justice White, for the majority, cited *Oliver* in stating: "We identified the central component of this inquiry as whether the area harbors the 'intimate activity associated with the sanctity of a man's home and the privacies of life." The four factors to be considered in determining whether an area comes under the umbrella of the home's protection are: (1) the proximity of the area to the home; (2) whether the area is within an enclosure surrounding the home; (3) the nature and uses to which the area is put; and (4) the steps taken by the resident to protect the area from observation by passersby. "Applying these factors to the respondent's barn and to the area immediately surrounding it, we have little difficulty in concluding that this area lay outside the curtilage of the ranch house." As to the fourth factor, Justice White concluded that the various fences were designed to corral livestock, not to prevent persons from observing what lay inside the enclosed areas.

### Administrative Searches

In addition to the well-recognized exceptions to the requirement of a search warrant, another situation was considered by the Court in 1959—the right of a health inspector to examine private premises without a warrant. The case was *Frank* v. *Maryland,* 359 U.S. 360 (1959), holding that conviction and fine for refusal to permit a health inspector to inspect the premises for rat infestation did not violate the Fourteenth Amendment. The majority opinion, through Justice Frankfurter, first stressed the point that the inspection was conducted solely to determine whether there were conditions existing which were forbidden by ordinance—not to gather evidence for a criminal prosecution. He further pointed to the long history of administrative inspections:

Inspection without a warrant, as an adjunct to a regulatory scheme for the general welfare of the community and not as a means of enforcing the criminal law, has antecedents deep in our history. For more than 200 years Maryland has empowered its officers to enter upon ships, carriages, shops, and homes in the service of the common welfare. . . .

Justice Douglas, joined by three others, filed a vigorous dissent. The close vote of five-to-four suggested a tenuous status for the Court's holding. Justice Frankfurter had indicated that as the complexities and problems of urban life increased, so would the need for freer governmental right to inspect. Others, however, argued that for the same reasons the government should be more severely limited in order to forestall mounting invasions of privacy without some probable cause requirement as included in the issuance of a search warrant. The controversy culminated in a reexamination of the question in 1967 and the overruling of *Frank* v. *Maryland.*

## CAMARA *v.* MUNICIPAL COURT OF SAN FRANCISCO
### 387 U.S. 523 (1967)

[An inspector of the Division of Housing Inspection of the San Francisco Department of Public Health entered an apartment building to make a routine annual inspection for possible violations of the city's Housing Code. The building's manager informed the inspector that appellant, lessee of the ground floor, was using the rear of his leasehold as a personal residence. Claiming that the building's occupancy permit did not allow residential use of the ground floor, the inspector confronted appellant and demanded that he permit an inspection of the premises. Appellant refused to allow the inspection because the inspector lacked a search warrant. The inspector returned two days later, again without a warrant, and appellant again refused to allow an inspection. A citation was then mailed ordering appellant to appear at the district attorney's office. When appellant failed to appear, two inspectors returned to his apartment and informed him that he was required to permit an inspection under §503 of the Housing Code, which set up a right of entry for authorized city employees "at reasonable times" for the purpose of performing any duty imposed upon them by the Municipal Code. Appellant still refused to permit the search without a warrant. Therefore he was arrested and charged with refusing to permit a lawful inspection. When his demurrer to the criminal complaint was denied, appellant filed this petition for a writ of prohibition.]

Mr. Justice White delivered the opinion of the Court. . . .

In *Frank* v. *Maryland,* this Court upheld the conviction of one who refused to permit a warrantless inspection of private premises for the purposes of locating and abating a suspected public nuisance. Although *Frank* can arguably be distinguished from these cases on its facts, the *Frank* opinion has generally been interpreted as carrying out an additional exception to the rule that warrantless searches are unreasonable under the Fourth Amendment. . . . The District Court of Appeal so interpreted *Frank* in this case, and that ruling is the core of appellant's challenge here. We proceed to a re-examination of the factors which persuaded the *Frank* majority to adopt this construction of the Fourth Amendment's prohibition against unreasonable searches. . . .

We may agree that a routine inspection of the physical condition of private property is a less hostile intrusion than the typical policeman's search for the fruits and instrumentalities of crime. . . . But we cannot agree that the Fourth Amendment interests at stake in these inspection cases are merely "peripheral.' . . . [E]ven the most law-abiding citizen has a very tangible interest in limiting the circumstances under which the sanctity of his home may be broken by official authority, for the possibility of criminal entry under the guise of official sanction is a serious threat to personal and family security. And even accepting *Frank's* rather remarkable premise, inspections of the kind we are here considering do in fact jeopardize "self-protection" interests of the property owner. Like most regulatory laws, fire, health, and housing codes are enforced by criminal processes. In some cities, discovery of a violation by the inspector leads to a criminal complaint. . . .

In summary, we hold that administrative searches of the kind at issue here are significant intrusions upon the interests protected by the Fourth Amendment, that such searches when authorized and conducted without a warrant procedure lack the traditional safeguards which the Fourth Amendment guarantees to the individual, and that the reasons put forth in *Frank* v. *Maryland* and in other cases for upholding these warrantless searches are insufficient to justify so substantial a weakening of the Fourth Amendment's protections. Because of the nature of the municipal programs under consideration, however, these conclusions must be the beginning, not the end of our inquiry. . . .

.[The opinion then discusses the "probable cause" requirement of the Fourth Amendment, and the conclusion is reached that this requirement would not necessarily be the same for municipal code inspection programs as for criminal investigations. The standard of reasonableness is weighed in terms of the needs and goals of code enforcement. Thus "area inspections" would not be justified in a search for stolen goods, but in the enforcement of fire, sanitation, and housing codes, "such programs have a long history of judicial and public acceptance."]

The judgment is vacated and the case is remanded for further proceedings not inconsistent with this opinion.

*It is so ordered.*

Mr. Justice Clark, with whom Mr. Justice Harlan and Mr. Justice Stewart join, dissenting. . . .

. . . As I read it, the Fourth Amendment guarantee of individual privacy is, by its language, specifically qualified. It prohibits only those searches that are "unreasonable." The majority seem to recognize this for they set up a new test for the long-recognized and enforced Fourth Amendment's "probable cause" requirement for the issuance of warrants. They would permit the issuance of paper warrants, in area inspection programs, with probable cause based on area inspection standards as set out in municipal codes, and with warrants issued by the rubber stamp of a willing magistrate. In my view, this degrades the Fourth Amendment.

Moreover, history supports the *Frank* disposition. Over 150 years of city *in rem* inspections for health and safety purposes have continuously been enforced. In only one case during all that period have the courts denied municipalities this right. . . .

. . . The majority seems to hold that warrants may be obtained after a refusal of initial entry; I can find no such constitutional distinction or command. This boxcar warrant will be identical as to every dwelling in the area, save the street number itself. I daresay they will be printed up in pads of a thousand or more—with space for the street number to be inserted—and issued by magistrates in broadcast fashion as a matter of course. . . .

In the companion case of *See* v. *Seattle*, 387 U.S. 541 (1967), the Court held that the *Camara* rule applied to commercial structures as well as private residences.

A peculiar aspect of the administrative search is the unannounced latenight "bed-check" by welfare agencies to ensure that deserted wives who are recipients of family support payments are not being visited by their husbands, thus forfeiting benefit rights. No warrant is used, but failure of the recipient to permit the search in itself is sufficient to withdraw support payments. In *Wyman* v. *James*, 400 U.S. 309 (1971), the Court held that such searches, with the coercive aspect of threatened termination of benefits, did not violate Fourth Amendment protections. [For criticism of the practice, see Albert M. Bendich, "Privacy, Poverty, and the Constitution," 54 *Calif. L. Rev.* 407 (1966), and Charles A. Reich, "Midnight Welfare Searches and the Social Security Act," 72 *Yale L. J.* 1347 (1963).]

WYMAN *v.* JAMES

*400 U.S. 309 (1971)*

Mr. Justice Blackmun delivered the opinion of the Court.

This appeal presents the issue whether a beneficiary of the program for Aid to Families with Dependent Children (AFDC) may refuse a home visit by the case worker without risking the termination of benefits.

The New York State and City social services commissioners appeal from a judgment and decree of a divided three-judge District Court holding invalid and unconstitutional in application §134 of the New York Social Services Law . . . and granting injunctive relief . . . The beneficiary's thesis, and that of the District Court majority, is that home visitation is a search and, when not consented to or when not supported by a warrant based on probable cause, violates the beneficiary's Fourth and Fourteenth Amendment rights. . . .

When a case involves a home and some type of official intrusion into that home, as this case appears to do, an immediate and natural reaction is one of concern about Fourth Amendment rights and the protection which that Amendment is intended to afford. . . .

This natural and quite proper protective attitude, however, is not a factor in this case, for the seemingly obvious and simple reason that we are not concerned here with any search by the New York social service agency in the Fourth Amendment meaning of that term. It is true that the governing statute and regulations appear to make mandatory the initial home visit and the subsequent periodic "contacts" (which may include home visits) for the inception and continuance of aid. It is also true that the caseworker's posture in the home visit is perhaps, in a sense, both rehabilitative and investigative. But this latter aspect, we think, is given too broad a character and far more emphasis than it deserves if it is equated with a search in the traditional criminal law context. We note, too, that the visitation in itself is not forced or compelled, and that the beneficiary's denial of permission is not a criminal act. If consent to the visitation is withheld, no visitation takes place. The aid then never begins or merely ceases, as the case may be. There is no entry of the home and there is no search. . . .

There are a number of factors which compel us to conclude that the home visit proposed for Mrs. James is not unreasonable:

1. The public's interest in this particular segment of the area of assistance to the unfortunate is protection and aid for the dependent child whose family requires such aid for that child. The focus is on the *child* and, further, it is on the child who is *dependent.* There is no more worthy object of the public's concern. The dependent child's needs are paramount, and only with hesitancy would we relegate those needs, in the scale of comparative values, to a position secondary to what the mother claims as her rights.

2. The agency, with tax funds provided from federal as well as from state sources, is fulfilling a public trust. The State, working through its qualified welfare agency, has appropriate and paramount interest and concern in seeing and assuring that the intended and proper objects of that tax-produced assistance are the ones who benefit from the aid it dispenses. Surely it is not unreasonble, in the Fourth Amendment

sense or in any other sense of that term, that the State have at its command a gentle means, of limited extent and of practical and considerate application, of achieving that assurance.

3. One who dispenses purely private charity naturally has an interest in and expects to know how his charitable funds are utilized and put to work. The public, when it is the provider, rightly expects the same. It might well expect more, because of the trust aspect of public funds, and the recipient, as well as the caseworker, has not only an interest but an obligation. . . .

7. Mrs. James, in fact, on this record presents no specific complaint of any unreasonable intrusion on her home and nothing which supports an inference that the desired home visit had as its purpose the obtaining of information as to criminal activity. She complains of no proposed visitation at an awkward or retirement hour. She suggests no forcible entry. She refers to no snooping. . . . What Mrs. James appears to want from the agency which provides her and her infant son with the necessities for life is the right to receive those necessities upon her own informational terms, to utilize the Fourth Amendment as a wedge for imposing those terms, and to avoid questions of any kind. . . .

Mr. Justice Douglas, dissenting. . . .

Mr. Justice Marshall, whom Mr. Justice Brennan joins, dissenting. . . .

Although the Court does not agree with my conclusion that the home visit is an unreasonable search, its opinion suggests that even if the visit were unreasonable, appellee has somehow waived her right to object. Surely the majority cannot believe that valid Fourth Amendment consent can be given under the threat of the loss of one's sole means of support. . . .

In deciding that the homes of AFDC recipients are not entitled to protection from warrantless searches by welfare caseworkers, the Court declines to follow prior case law and employs a rationale that, if applied to the claims of all citizens, would threaten the vitality of the Fourth Amendment. . . . I find no little irony in the fact that the burden of today's departure from principled adjudication is placed upon the lowly poor. Perhaps the majority has explained why a commercial warehouse deserves more protection than does this poor woman's home. I am not convinced; and therefore, I must respectfully dissent.

In *Marshall* v. *Barlow's, Inc.*, 436 U.S. 307 (1978), the Court applied the *Camara* and *See* rules in holding that the provisions of the Occupational Safety and Health Act of 1970 permitting warrantless inspections were violative of the Fourth Amendment. The Act empowers agents of the Secretary of Labor to search the work area of any employment facility within the Act's jurisdiction to inspect for safety hazards and violations of OSHA regulations. The president of Barlow's sued for an injunction to prevent an OSHA inspector from entering his electrical and plumbing business without a warrant. A three-judge District Court held the statutory provisions unconstitutional, and, on direct appeal, the Supreme Court affirmed. In so doing, however, the Court recognized certain exceptions to the rule of *See* v. *Seattle*. An exception from the search warrant requirement has been recognized for "pervasively regulated businesses" [*United States* v. *Biswell,* 406 U.S. 311 (1972)] and for "closely regulated" industries "long subject to close supervision and inspection" [*Colonnade Catering Corp.* v. *United States,* 397 U.S. 72 (1970)]. Justice White stated in *Marshall* v. *Barlow's, Inc.*:

These cases are indeed exceptions, but they represent responses to relatively unique circumstances. Certain industries have such a history of government oversight that no reasonable expectation of privacy . . . could exist for a proprietor over the stock of such an enterprise. Liquor *(Colonnade)* and firearms *(Biswell)* are industries of this type; when an entrepreneur embarks upon such a business, he has voluntarily chosen to subject himself to a full arsenal of governmental regulation.

In *Donovan* v. *Dewey,* 452 U.S. 594 (1981), the Court held that warrantless inspections of stone quarries by federal mine inspectors under the Federal Mine Safety and Health Act of 1977 are compatible with the Fourth Amendment in view of the pervasiveness of federal regulation of mining and the hazardous nature of the occupation. But in *Michigan* v. *Tyler,* 436 U.S. 499 (1978), the Court held that except for "certain carefully defined classes of cases," official entries on private property to investigate the cause of a fire must adhere to the warrant procedures of the Fourth and Fourteenth Amendments. Some two hours after a fire had broken out in a furniture store and while firemen were still engaged in dousing smoldering embers, the fire chief arrived on the scene. The discovery of plastic containers of flammable liquid was reported to him, and he summoned a police detective to investigate possible arson. The detective took several pictures but ceased further investigation because of the smoke and steam. Later in the morning, after the fire had been extinguished, the assistant chief and the detective examined the premises and removed pieces of evidence. About three weeks later a member of the arson section returned for a further inspection, and this was followed by other visits during which additional evidence and information were obtained. The store owners were subsequently charged with conspiracy to burn real property and other offenses. The evidence obtained in the various inspections was introduced over objections that no warrants or consent had been obtained. Justice Stewart, for the Court, stated:

A burning building clearly presents an exigency of sufficient proportions to render a warrantless entry "reasonable." Indeed, it would defy reason to suppose that firemen must secure a warrant or consent before entering a burning structure to put out the blaze. And once in a building for this purpose, firefighters may seize evidence of arson that is in plain view. . . . Thus, the Fourth and Fourteenth Amendments were not violated by the entry at Tyler's Auction, nor by Chief See's removal of the two plastic containers of flammable liquid found on the floor of one of the showrooms.

The opinion stated further that a warrant was unnecessary for the early morning visits after the fire had been extinguished, and evidence obtained at that time was also admissible. But evidence obtained in the inspections that occurred three weeks later was not admissible since the entries "were clearly detached from the initial exigency and warrantless entry," and thus those entries demanded that a warrant be obtained.

In *Michigan* v. *Clifford,* 464 U.S. 287 (1984), the Court reaffirmed *Tyler* but distinguished the cases on the facts. The Clifford's private residence was damaged by an early morning fire while they were out of town. Firefighters extinguished the blaze at 7:04 A.M., at which time all fire officials and police left the scene. Five hours later, a team of arson investigators arrived at the residence to investigate the cause of the blaze. They found a work crew boarding up the house and pumping water out of the basement. The crew had been sent by the owners' insurance company when the Cliffords had been notified of the fire. Nevertheless, the investigators entered the house and conducted an extensive search without obtaining either consent or a warrant. In the basement they found two Coleman fuel cans and a crock pot attached to an electrical timer and concluded that the fire had been set deliberately. They seized the evidence and extended their search to the upper portion of the house where they found additional evidence of arson. Respondents were charged with arson and moved to suppress all the evidence seized in the warantless search. Five members of the Court held that there were no exi-gent circumstances to justify the warrantless return visit five hours after the fire was ex-tinguished, and therefore the evidence should be suppressed. The four dissenters argued that since the initial re-entry in *Tyler* was a continuation of the earlier investiga-tion, the re-entry here should be viewed in the same light. Justice Rehnquist said: "I would hold that the 'exigent circumstances' doctrine enunciated in *Tyler* authorized the search of the basement of the Clifford home, although the remaining parts of the house could not have been searched without the issurance of a warrant issued upon probable cause." He stated further:

In my view, the utility of requiring a magistrate to evaluate the grounds for a search following a fire is so limited that the incidental protection of an individual's privacy interests simply does not justify imposing a warrant requirement. Here the inspection was conducted within a short time of extinguishing of the flames, while the owners were away from the premises, and before the premises had been fully se-cured from trespass. In these circumstances the search of the basement to determine the cause and origin of the fire was reasonable.

### Admissibility of Evidence Obtained Illegally—The "Exclusionary Rule"

The distinction between the question of unreasonable searches and the question of ad-missibility of illegally obtained evidence is important, because in *Weeks* v. *United States*, 232 U.S. 383 (1914), the Court held that the Fourth Amendment did not, accord-ing to the rule of *Weeks*, constitute a rule of evidence. The Court went on to state, how-ever, that unless such evidence were excluded, the Fourth Amendment would present no effective bar to improper searches and seizures. Thus *Weeks* held that as a federal rule of evidence, which in its supervisory function the Supreme Court can lay down for all federal courts, evidence illegally obtained by federal officers could not be used in a federal prosecution. [A majority of the Court, however, has now construed the *Weeks* rule as a Fourth Amendment requirement.]

At this point the complications of the federal system again enter the picture. Fourth Amendment limitations do not necessarily spell out the coverage of Fourteenth Amend-ment due process limitations on the States. And federal exclusionary rules are not appli-cable to the States' criminal procedures unless they rise to the level of constitutional requirements. The Fourteenth Amendment test, in the words of Justice Cardozo in *Palko* v. *Connecticut*, is whether a particular procedure or safeguard is "of the very es-sence of a scheme of ordered liberty." In 1949, the United States Supreme Court in *Wolf* v. *Colorado*, 338 U.S. 25, held that for the States to permit the use of evidence obtained illegally in a criminal prosecution was not a violation of the Fourteenth Amendment. Justice Frankfurter's opinion for the majority adverted to the *Weeks* doctrine, pointing out that as of 1949, thirty states rejected the *Weeks* doctrine, while seventeen states were in agreement with it. In view of this survey, he stated:

The jurisdictions which have rejected the *Weeks* doctrine have not left the right of privacy without other means of protection. Indeed, the exclusion of evidence is a remedy which directly serves only to protect those upon whose person or premises something incriminating has been found. We cannot, therefore, regard it as a depar-ture from basic standards to remand such persons, together with those who emerge scatheless from a search, to the remedies of private action and such protection as the internal discipline of the police, under the eyes of an alert public opinion, may af-ford. Granting that in practice the exclusion of evidence may be an effective way of deterring unreasonable searches, it is not for this Court to condemn as falling below the minimal standards assured by the Due Process Clause a State's reliance upon other methods which, if consistently enforced, would be equally effective. . . .

We hold, therefore, that in a prosecution in a State court for a State crime the Fourteenth Amendment does not forbid the admission of evidence obtained by an unreasonable search and seizure.

Despite the holding that illegally obtained evidence was not barred in a subsequent prosecution, Justice Frankfurter's opinion pointed out that "were a State affirmatively to sanction such police incursion into privacy it would run counter to the guaranty of the Fourteenth Amendment violation." Thus the majority held that arbitrary and illegal searches and seizures by the state constituted a Fourteenth Amendment violation, but this did not bar the introduction of the evidence so obtained in a prosecution. The apparent contradiction can be resolved in one way by making such conduct on the part of state officers actionable under the civil or criminal provisions of the Civil Rights Acts. This, of course, is exactly what the Court held in 1961 in the case of *Monroe* v. *Pape*, 365 U.S. 167.

Justice Murphy, in one of the three dissenting opinions in the *Wolf* case, said:

The conclusion is inescapable that but one remedy exists to deter violations of the search and seizure clause. That is the rule which excludes illegally obtained evidence. Only by exclusion can we impress upon the zealous prosecutor that violation of the Constitution will do him no good. And only when that point is driven home can the prosecutor be expected to emphasize the importance of observing constitutional demands in his instructions to the police.

The frustrations experienced by some members of the Court, occasioned by adherence to the *Wolf* rule, were brought sharply to focus in the case of *Irvine* v. *California*, 374 U.S. 128 (1954). In *Irvine* the police, after having made a key to fit the door, made repeated illegal entries into the home of a suspected bookmaker. They installed a secret microphone in the home and moved it from room to room, including the Irvines' bedroom. For over a month the police eavesdropped on conversations in this way, and on the basis of information thus obtained Irvine was tried and convicted. The United States Supreme Court affirmed, on authority of the *Wolf* rule, but Justice Jackson, who announced the judgment of the Court and wrote the principal opinion, thoroughly excoriated the behavior of the police. He stated that what was done "would be almost incredible if it were not admitted. Few police measures have come to our attention that more flagrantly, deliberately, and persistently violated the fundamental principle declared by the Fourth Amendment as a restriction on the Federal Government." Justice Jackson made a novel suggestion in the case, indicating his strong feeling that the officers should not escape unscathed, even though the evidence was admissible:

If the officials have willfully deprived a citizen of the United States of a right or privilege secured to him by the Fourteenth Amendment, that being the right to be secure in his home against unreasonable searches, as defined in *Wolf* v. *Colorado*, their conduct may constitute a federal crime. . . . We believe the Clerk of this Court should be directed to forward a copy of the record in this case, together with a copy of this opinion, for attention of the Attorney General of the United States.

The dissatisfaction with *Wolf's* bifurcation of the Fourth Amendment culminated in 1961 in a landmark case in the area of searches and seizures. The case was *Mapp* v. *Ohio,* and a majority of the Court officially adopted the conclusion expressed by Justice Murphy in his dissent in the *Wolf* case.

MAPP *v.* OHIO
*367 U.S. 643 (1961)*

[Three Cleveland police officers had come to appellant's residence in 1957, demanding entry on information that "a person was hiding out in the home who was wanted for questioning in connection with a recent bombing" and that policy paraphernalia was hidden in the home. Appellant, after phoning her attorney, refused to admit them without a search warrant. They returned later with several additional officers and forcibly broke into the house. Mrs. Mapp demanded to see a warrant. A paper, claimed to be a warrant, was held up by one of the officers. She grabbed the "warrant" and placed it in her bosom. A struggle ensued in which the officers recovered the piece of paper and handcuffed appellant because she had been "belligerent" in resisting their official rescue of the "warrant" from her person. The entire first and second floors of the house were thoroughly searched, and the search spread to the basement. In a trunk in the basement officers found the obscene material, for possession of which she was ultimately convicted. At the trial no search warrant was produced by the prosecution, nor was the failure to produce one explained or accounted for. The Ohio Supreme Court stated that there was "considerable doubt as to whether there ever was any warrant for the search of defendant's home." That court, however, followed *Wolf* v. *Colorado* in holding that despite the illegal seizure, the evidence was admissible.]

Mr. Justice Clark delivered the opinion of the Court.

Appellant stands convicted of knowingly having had in her possession and under her control certain lewd and lascivious books, pictures, and photographs in violation of . . Ohio's Revised Code. As officially stated in the syllabus to its opinion, the Supreme Court of Ohio found that her conviction was valid though "based primarily upon the introduction in evidence of lewd and lascivious books and pictures unlawfully seized during an unlawful search of defendant's home. . . ."

I

Seventy-five years ago, in *Boyd* v. *United States* . . . , considering the Fourth and Fifth Amendments as running "almost into each other" on the facts before it, this Court held that the doctrines of those Amendments "apply to all invasions on the part of the government and its employees of the sanctity of a man's home and the privacies of life." . . .

The Court noted that "constitutional provisions for the security of person and property should be liberally construed. . . . It is the duty of courts to be watchful for the constitutional rights of the citizen, and against any stealthy encroachments thereon." . . .

Less than 30 years after *Boyd*, this Court, in *Weeks* v. *United States*, . . . stated that "the Fourth Amendment . . . put the courts of the United States and Federal officials, in the exercise of their power and authority, under limitations and restraints [and] . . . forever secure[d] the people, their persons, houses, papers and effects against all unreasonable searches and seizures under the guise of law . . . and the duty of giving to it force and effect is obligatory upon all entrusted under our Federal system with the enforcement of the laws." . . .

Finally, the Court in that case clearly stated that use of the seized evidence involved "a denial of the constitutional rights of the accused." At p. 398. Thus, in the year 1914, in the *Weeks* case, this Court "for the first time" held that "in a federal prosecution the Fourth Amendment barred the use of evidence secured through an illegal search and seizure." *Wolf* v. *Colorado* . . . This Court has ever since required of federal law officers a strict adherence to that command which this Court has held to be a clear, specific, and constitutionally required—even if judicially implied—deterrent safeguard without insistence upon which the Fourth Amendment would have been reduced to "a form of words." *Holmes, J., Silverthorne Lumber Co.* v. *United States*. . . .

II

In 1949, 35 years after *Weeks* was announced, this court, in *Wolf* v. *Colorado* . . . , again for the first time, discussed the effect of the Fourth Amendment upon the States through the operation of the Due Process Clause of the Fourteenth Amendment. It said:

"We have no hesitation in saying that were a State affirmatively to sanction such police incursion into privacy it would run counter to the guaranty of the Fourteenth Amendment." At p. 28.

Nevertheless, after declaring that the "security of one's privacy against arbitrary intrusion by the police" is "implicit in the 'concept of ordered liberty' and as such enforceable agaisnt the States through the Due Process Clause," . . . and announcing that it "stoutly adhere[d]" to the *Weeks* decision, the Court decided that the *Weeks* exclusionary rule would not then be imposed upon the States as "an essential ingredient of the right." . . . The Court's reasons for not considering essential to the right to privacy, as a curb imposed upon the States by the Due Process Clause, that which decades before had been posited as part and parcel of the Fourth Amendment's limitation upon federal encroachment of individual privacy, were bottomed on factual considerations.

While they are not basically relevant to a decision that the exclusionary rule is an essential ingredient of the Fourteenth Amendment as the right it embodies is vouchsafed against the States by the Due Process Clause, we will consider the current validity of the factual grounds upon which *Wolf* was based. . . .

. . . While in 1949, prior to the *Wolf* case, almost two-thirds of the States were opposed to the exclusionary rule, now, despite the *Wolf* case, more than half of those since passing upon it, by their own legislative or judicial decision, have wholly or partly adopted or adhered to the *Weeks* rule. . . . Significantly, among those now following the rule is California which, according to its highest court, was "compelled to reach that conclusion because other remedies have completely failed to secure compliance with the constitutional provisions. . . ." In connection with this California case, we note that the second basis elaborated in *Wolf* in support of its failure to enforce the exclusionary doctrine against the States was that "other means of protection" have been afforded "the right to privacy." . . . The experience of California that such other remedies have been worthless and futile is buttressed by the experience of other States. The obvious futility of relegating the Fourth Amendment to the protection of other remedies has, moreover, been recognized by this Court since *Wolf*. See *Irvine* v. *California*. . . .

Likewise, time has set its face against what *Wolf* called the "weighty testimony" of *People* v. *Defore*. . . . There Justice (then Judge) Cardozo, rejecting adoption of the *Weeks* exclusionary rule in New York, had said that "[t]he Federal rule as it stands is either too strict or too lax." . . . However, the force of that reasoning has been largely vitiated by later decisions of this Court. These include the recent discarding of the "silver platter" doctrine which allowed federal judicial use of evidence seized in violation of the Constitution by state agents, *Elkins* v. *United States*, 364 U.S. 206, *supra*; the relaxation of the formerly strict requirements as to standing to challenge the use of evidence thus seized, so that now the procedure of exclusion, "ultimately referable to constitutional safeguards," is available to anyone even "legitimately on [the] premises" unlawfully searched, *Jones* v. *United States*, 362 U.S. 257 (1960); and, finally, the formulation of a method to prevent state use of evidence unconstitutionally seized by federal agents, *Rea* v. *United States*, 350 U.S. 214 (1956). . . .

It, therefore, plainly appears that the factual considerations supporting the failure of the *Wolf* Court to include the *Weeks* exclusionary rule when it recognized the enforceability of the right to privacy against the States in 1949, while not basically relevant to the constitutional consideration, could not, in any analysis, now be deemed controlling.

### III

. . . And only last Term, after again carefully re-examining the *Wolf* doctrine in *Elkins* v. *United States* . . . the Court pointed out that "the controlling principles" as to search and seizure and the problem of admissibility "seemed clear" until the announcement in *Wolf* "that the Due Process Clause of the Fourteenth Amendment does not itself require state courts to adopt the exclusionary rule" of the *Weeks* case. . . . At the same time the Court pointed out, "the underlying constitutional doctrine which *Wolf* established . . . that the Federal Constitution . . . prohibits unreasonable searches and seizures by state officers" had undermined the "foundation upon which the admissibility of state-seized evidence in a federal trial originally rested. . . ." The Court concluded that it was therefore obliged to hold, although it chose the narrower ground on which to do so, that all evidence obtained by an unconstitutional search and seizure was inadmissible in a federal court regardless of its source. Today we once again examine *Wolf's* constitutional documentation of the right to privacy free from unreasonable state intrusion, and, after its dozen years on our books, are led by it to close the only courtroom door remaining open to evidence secured by official lawlessness in flagrant abuse of that basic right, reserved to all persons as a specific guarantee against that very same unlawful conduct. We hold that all evidence obtained by searches and seizures in violation of the Constitution is, by that same authority, inadmissible in a state court. . . .

### V

. . . Moreover, our holding that the exclusionary rule is an essential part of both the Fourth and Fourteenth Amendments is not only the logical dictate of prior cases, but it also makes very good sense. There is no war between the Constitution and common sense. Presently, a federal prosecutor may make no use of evidence illegally seized, but a State's attorney across the street may, although he supposedly is operating under the enforceable prohibitions of the same Amendment. Thus, the State, by admitting evidence unlawfully seized, serves to encourage disobedience to the Federal Constitution which it is bound to uphold. Moreover, as was said in *Elkins* "[t]he very essence of a healthy federalism depends upon the avoidance of needless conflict between state and federal courts." . . . Such a conflict, hereafter needless, arose this very Term, in *Wilson* v. *Schnettler*, 355 U.S. 381 (1961), in which, and in spite of the promise made by *Rea*, we gave full recognition to our practice in this regard by refusing to restrain a federal officer from testifying in a state court as to evidence unconstitutionally seized by him in the performance of his duties. Yet the double standard recognized until today hardly put such a thesis into practice. In nonexclusionary States, federal officers, being human, were by it invited to and did, as our cases indicated, step across the street to the State's attorney with their unconstitutionally seized evidence. Prosecution on the basis of that evidence was then had in a state court in utter disregard of the enforceable Fourth Amendment. If the fruits of an unconstitutional search had been inadmissible in both state and federal courts, this inducement to evasion would have been sooner eliminated. There would be no need to reconcile such cases as *Rea* and *Schnettler*, each pointing up the hazardous uncertainties of our heretofore ambivalent approach. . . .

There are those who say, as did Justice (then Judge) Cardozo that under our constitutional exclusionary doctrine "[t]he criminal is to go free because the constable has blundered." . . . In some cases this will undoubtedly be the result. But, as was said in *Elkins*, "there is another consideration—the imperative of judicial integrity." . . . The criminal goes free, if he must, but it is the law that sets him free. Nothing can destroy a government more quickly than its failure to observe its own laws, or worse, its disregard of the charter of its own existence. . . .

The judgment of the Supreme Court of Ohio is reversed and the cause remanded for further proceedings not inconsistent with this opinion.

*Reversed and Remanded.*

Mr. Justice Black, concurring.

. . . I am still not persuaded that the Fourth Amendment, standing alone, would be enough to bar the introduction into evidence against an accused of papers and effects seized from him in violation of its commands. For the Fourth Amendment does not itself contain any provision expressly precluding the use of such evidence, and I am extremely doubtful that such a provision could properly be inferred from nothing more than the basic command against unreasonable searches and seizures. Reflection on the problem, however, in the light of cases coming before the Court since *Wolf*, has led me to conclude that when the Fourth Amendment's ban against unreasonable searches and seizures is considered together with the Fifth Amendment's ban against compelled self-incrimination, a constitutional basis emerges which not only justifies but actually requires the exclusionary rule. . . .

Mr. Justice Douglas, concurring. . . .

Mr. Justice Harlan, whom Mr. Justice Frankfurter and Mr. Justice Whittaker join, dissenting.

In overruling the *Wolf* case the Court, in my opinion, has forgotten the sense of judicial restraint which, with due regard for *stare decisis*, is one element that should enter into deciding whether a past decision of this Court should be overruled. Apart from that I also believe the *Wolf* rule represents sounder Constitutional doctrine than the new rule which now replaces it.

I

From the Court's statement of the case one would gather that the central, if not controlling, issue on this appeal is whether illegally state-seized evidence is Constitutionally admissible in a state prosecution, an issue which would of course face us with the need for re-examining *Wolf*. However, such is not the situation. For, although that question was indeed raised here and below among appellant's subordinate points, the new and pivotal issue brought to the Court by this appeal is whether Section 2905.34 of the Ohio Revised Code making criminal the *mere* knowing possession or control of obscene material, and under which appellant has been convicted, is consistent with the rights of free thought and expression assured against state action by the Fourteenth Amendment. That was the principal issue which was decided by the Ohio Supreme Court, which was tendered by appellant's Jurisdictional Statement, and which was briefed and argued in this Court.

In this posture of things, I think it fair to say that five members of this Court have simply "reached out" to overrule *Wolf*. With all respect for the views of the majority, and recognizing that *stare decisis* carries different weight in Constitutional adjudication than it does in nonconstitutional decision, I can perceive no justification for regarding this case as an appropriate occasion for re-examining *Wolf*. . . .

The occasion which the Court has taken here is in the context of a case where the question was briefed not at all and argued only extremely tangentially. . . . I would think that our obligation to the States, on whom we impose this new rule, as well as the obligation of orderly adherence to our own processes would demand that we seek that aid which adequate briefing and argument lends to the determination of an important issue. . . .

The preservation of a proper balance between state and federal responsibility in the administration of criminal justice demands patience on the part of those who might like to see things move faster among the States in this respect. Problems of criminal law enforcement vary widely from State to State. . . . For us the question remains, as it has always been, one of state power, not one of passing judgment on the wisdom of one state course or another. In my view this Court should continue to forbear from fettering the States with an adamant rule which may embarrass them in coping with their own peculiar problems in criminal law enforcement. . . .

[Memorandum of Mr. Justice Stewart concurring in the reversal on the ground that the conviction was not consistent with "the rights of free thought and expression" guaranteed by the Fourteenth Amendment.]

*Ker* v. *California*, 374 U.S. 23 (1963), held that "the standard of reasonableness is the same under the Fourth and Fourteenth Amendments," thus clearly "incorporating" the Fourth Amendment.

The opinion in *Mapp*, however, left unanswered the question of whether the bar to admission of illegally obtained evidence should be applied retroactively and thus open the way for those in prison to attack their convictions where such evidence was used by the prosecution. The Court did not reach this issue until four years later, in *Linkletter* v. *Walker*, 381 U.S. 618 (1965), and by a seven-to-two vote held that the *Mapp* rule did not operate retrospectively upon cases finally decided prior to the *Mapp* case. Justice Clark, for the Court, pointed out that while the various federal courts of appeals had split on the issue, the "state courts which have considered the question have almost unanimously decided against application to cases finalized prior to *Mapp*." The petitioner contended that prior cases demonstrated that an absolute rule of retroaction prevails in the area of constitutional adjudication. Justice Clark gave a brief but instructive "outline of the history and theory of the problem presented" and concluded that "the Constitution neither prohibits nor requires retrospective effect." The doctrine of "void *ab initio*" was well stated in *Norton* v. *Shelby Co.*, 118 U.S. 425 (1886), in which the Court held that unconstitutional action "confers no rights; it imposes no duties; it affords no protection; it creates no office; it is, in legal contemplation, as inoperative as though it had never been passed." This Blackstonian view was opposed by the Austinian view that Judges do more than merely discover law; they make law. And thus one cannot deny the existence of an overruled law as a juridical fact. Justice Clark stated, "We believe that the existence of the *Wolf* doctrine prior to *Mapp* is 'an operative fact and may have consequences which cannot justly be ignored. The past cannot always be erased by a new judicial declaration.' " He pointed out that the purpose in *Mapp* was to deter the lawless action of the police, and that purpose would not be served at this late date by the wholesale release of the guilty victims. He further suggested that retrospective application "would tax the administration of justice to the utmost." He concluded:

Finally, in each of the three areas in which we have applied our rule retrospectively the principle that we applied went to the fairness of the trial—the very integrity of the fact-finding process. Here, as we have pointed out, the fairness of the trial is not under attack. All that petitioner attacks is the admissibility of evidence, the reliability and relevancy of which is not questioned, and which may well have had no effect on the outcome.

[Justice Black, joined by Justice Douglas, dissented. He stated, "I am at a loss to understand why those who suffer from the use of evidence secured by a search and seizure in violation of the Fourth Amendment should be treated differently from those who have been denied other guarantees of the Bill of Rights."]

[See Oliver P. Field, *The Effect of an Unconstitutional Statute* (Minneapolis: University of Minnesota Press, 1935); Paul Freund, "New Vistas in Constitutional Law," 112 *U. Pa. L. Rev.* 631 (1964); Note, "Prospective Overruling and Retroactive Application in the Federal Courts," 71 *Yale L. J.* 907 (1962); Thomas S. Currier, "Time and Change in Judge-Made Law: Prospective Overruling," 51 *Va. L. Rev.* 201 (1965); and G. Gregory Fahlund, "Retroactivity and the Warren Court: The Strategy of a Revolution," 35 *Journal of Politics* 570 (1973).]

The exclusionary rule of *Weeks* and *Mapp* has been subjected to considerable criticism and it has been argued that irrespective of the manner in which evidence is obtained, if it has probative value, it should be admissible. Other remedies than suppressing the evidence should be employed to stop illegal seizures. The classic statement of this position was made by Judge Cardozo while on the New York Court of Appeals: "Is the criminal to go free because the constable has blundered?" The need for modification of the exclusionary rule was strongly urged by Chief Justice Burger in a dissenting opinion in *Bivens* v. *Six Unknown Fed. Narcotics Agents*, 403 U.S. 388 (1971). The Court held that a violation of the Fourth Amendment's prohibition against unreasonable searches and seizures, by a federal agent acting under color of federal authority, gave rise to a federal cause of action for damages. In dissent, the Chief Justice took the occasion to attack the exclusionary rule:

This evidentiary rule is unique to American jurisprudence. Although the English and Canadian legal systems are highly regarded, neither has adopted our rule. . . . Williams, *The Exclusionary Rule Under Foreign Law*—England, 52 *J. Crim. L. C. & P. S.* 272 (1961).

I do not question the need for some remedy to give meaning and teeth to the constitutional guarantees against unlawful conduct by government officials. Without some effective sanction, these protections would constitute little more than rhetoric. . . . But the hope that this objective could be accomplished by the exclusion of reliable evidence from criminal trial was hardly more than a wistful dream. Although I would hesitate to abandon it until some meaningful substitute is developed, the history of the suppression doctrine demonstrates that it is both conceptually sterile and practically ineffective in accomplishing its stated objective. . . .

Some clear demonstration of the benefits and effectiveness of the exclusionary rule is required to justify it in view of the high price it extracts from society—the release of countless guilty criminals. . . . But there is no empirical evidence to support the claim that the rule actually deters illegal conduct of law enforcement officials. . . .

As the Chief Justice stated, England has refused to adopt the exclusionary rule. In the course of debates in the House of Lords on the proposed Police and Criminal Evidence

Act (adopted in 1984), Lord Scarman offered an amendment that would allow exclusion of illegally obtained evidence unless the offense was grave or "the circumstances in which the evidence was obtained are such that the public interest in the fair administration of the criminal law requires the evidence to be given." In discussing the American rule, he stated:

Of course, a rule so inflexible is bound to result in some cases in guilty men going free. Grave charges on which there is abundant evidence will fail because of some technical irregularity by the police in the obtaining of the evidence. That is a rule which nobody in his senses would propose for the United Kingdom and this amendment does not propose any such rule. (House of Lords, *Hansard,* 31 July, 1984, Vol. 455, col. 654.)

On the other hand, there are those who strongly defend the rule. At least some of the available statistics indicate that the cost to society of the exclusionary rule is slight. According to one study, the charges most likely to be dismissed when particular evidence is suppressed are possessory offenses; in Chicago, for instance, 78 percent of all motions to suppress evidence were made in such cases. [See Dallin Oaks, "Studying the Exclusionary Rule in Search and Seizure," 37 *U. Chi. L. Rev.* 665, 682 (1970).] And even if these types of charges were not dismissed, many of those convicted, it is argued, would receive only a small fine or a suspended sentence from the judge.

Professor Anthony Amsterdam, rather than restricting the rule, would expand it not only to punish police who had behaved improperly, but also to make sure that there is no incentive for them to do so. Thus, if police observed a sawed-off shotgun on the floor of an automobile during a legitimate vehicle stop for a license check, the evidence would be suppressed. The reason would be to assure that decisions to institute license checks would not be tainted by any impermissible motive. [See his article, "Perspectives on the Fourth Amendment," 58 *Minn. L. Rev.* 349 (1974); also see John Kaplan, "Limits of the Exclusionary Rule," 26 *Stan. L. Rev.* 1027 (1974).]

Although its full impact remains to be seen, the long-expected decision modifying the exclusionary rule was announced on the last day of the Court's Term in 1984.

### UNITED STATES *v.* LEON et al.
### *468 U.S. 897 (1984)*

[Acting on the basis of information from a confidential informant of unproven reliability, Burbank, California, police officers initiated a drug-trafficking investigation involving surveillance of respondents' activities. Based on an affidavit summarizing the police officers' observations, one of the officers prepared an application for a warrant to search three residences and respondents' automobiles for an extensive list of items. A facially valid search warrant was issued by a state court judge, and ensuing searches produced large quantities of drugs and other evidence. Respondents were indicted for federal drug offenses and filed motions to suppress the evidence seized pursuant to the warrant, based on two grounds: first, the credibility of the informant was not established, and second, the information as to drug sales supplied by the informant was more than five months old and could not be used to establish probable cause to support a warrant. The District Court granted the motions in part, concluding that the affidavit was insufficient to establish probable cause. The Court of Appeals affirmed, refusing the Government's invitation to recognize a good-faith exception to the exclusionary rule. The Government's petition for certiorari presented only the question whether a good-faith exception to the exclusionary rule should be recognized.]

Justice White delivered the opinion of the Court.

This case presents the question whether the Fourth Amendment exclusionary rule should be modified so as not to bar the use in the prosecution's case-in-chief of evidence obtained by officers acting in reasonable reliance on a search warrant issued by a detached and neutral magistrate but ultimately found to be unsupported by probable cause. To resolve this question, we must consider once again the tension between the sometimes competing goals of, on the one hand, deterring official misconduct and removing inducements to unreasonable invasions of privacy and, on the other, establishing procedures under which criminal defendants are "acquitted or convicted on the basis of all the evidence which exposes the truth." . . .

I

. . .

We have concluded that, in the Fourth Amendment context, the exclusionary rule can be modified somewhat without jeopardizing its ability to perform its intended functions. Accordingly, we reverse the judgment of the Court of Appeals.

II

. . .

A

The Fourth Amendment contains no provision expressly precluding the use of evidence obtained in violation of its commands, and an examination of its origin and purposes makes clear that the use of fruits of a past unlawful search or seizure "work[s] no new Fourth Amendment wrong." . . . The rule thus operates as "a judicially created remedy designed to safeguard Fourth Amendment rights generally through its deterrent effect, rather than a personal constitutional right of the person aggrieved." . . .

Whether the exclusionary sanction is appropriately imposed in a particular case, our decisions make clear, is "an issue separate from the question whether the Fourth Amendment rights of the party seeking to invoke the rule were violated by police conduct." . . . Only the former question is currently before us, and it must be resolved by weighing the costs and benefits of preventing the use in the prosecution's case-in-chief of inherently trustworthy tangible evidence obtained in reliance on a search warrant issued by a detached and neutral magistrate that ultimately is found to be defective.

The substantial social costs exacted by the exclusionary rule for the vindication of Fourth Amendment rights have long been a source of concern. . . . An objectionable collateral consequence of this interference with the criminal justice system's truth-finding function is that some guilty defendants may go free or receive reduced sentences as a result of favorable plea bargains. Particularly when law enforcement officers have acted in objective good faith or their transgressions have been minor, the magnitude of the benefit conferred on such guilty defendants offends basic concepts of the criminal justice system. . . . Indiscriminate application of the exclusionary rule, therefore, may well "generat[e] disrespect for the law and the administration of justice." . . .

B

. . . The Court has, to be sure, not seriously questioned, "in the absence of a more efficacious sanction, the continued application of the rule to suppress evidence from the [prosecution's] case where a Fourth Amendment violation has been substantial and deliberate." . . . Nevertheless, the balancing approach that has evolved in various contexts—including criminal trials—"forcefully suggest[s] that the exclusionary rule be more generally modified to permit the introduction of evidence obtained in the reasonable good-faith belief that a search or seizure was in accord with the Fourth Amendment." . . . [Here the opinion lists several situations in which the Court has limited application of the rule as an absolute bar to the use of unlawfully obtained evidence. E.g., standing to invoke the rule has been limited to cases in which the defendant was himself subjected to the illegal search or seizure but is not applicable to cases in which the illegally obtained evidence was gotten from someone else. And unlawfully obtained evidence may be used to impeach defendant's testimony.]

### III

. . .

### C

We conclude that the marginal or nonexistent benefits produced by suppressing evidence obtained in objectively reasonable reliance on a subsequently invalidated search warrant cannot justify the substantial costs of exclusion. We do not suggest, however, that exclusion is always inappropriate in cases where an officer has obtained a warrant and abided by its terms. . . . [T]he officer's reliance on the magistrate's probable-cause determination and on the technical sufficiency of the warrant he issues must be objectively reasonable, . . . and it is clear that in some circumstances the officer will have no reasonable grounds for believing that the warrant was properly issued.

Suppression therefore remains an appropriate remedy if the magistrate or judge in issuing a warrant was misled by information in an affidavit that the affiant knew was false or would have known was false except for his reckless disregard of the truth. . . . The exception we recognize today will also not apply in cases where the issuing magistrate wholly abandoned his judicial role . . . ; in such circumstances, no reasonably well-trained officer should rely on the warrant. Nor would an officer manifest objective good faith in relying on a warrant based on an affidavit "so lacking in indicia of probable cause as to render official belief in its existence entirely unreasonable." . . . Finally, depending on the circumstances of the particular case, a warrant may be so facially deficient—*i.e.*, in failing to particularize the place to be searched or the things to be seized—that the executing officers cannot reasonably presume it to be valid. . . .

In so limiting the suppression remedy, we leave untouched the probable-cause standard and the various requirements for a valid warrant. Other objections to the modification of the Fourth Amendment exclusionary rule we consider to be insubstantial. The good-faith exception for searches conducted pursuant to warrants is not intended to signal our unwillingness strictly to enforce the requirements of the Fourth Amendment, and we do not believe that it will have this effect. As we have already suggested, the good-faith exception, turning as it does on objective reasonableness, should not be difficult to apply in practice. When officers have acted pursuant to a warrant, the prosecution should ordinarily be able to establish objective good faith without a substantial expenditure of judicial time. . . .

Accordingly, the judgment of the Court of Appeals is

*Reversed.*

Justice Blackmun, concurring. . . .

Justice Brennan, with whom Justice Marshall joins, dissenting.

Ten years ago in *United States* v. *Calandra* . . . I expressed the fear that the Court's decision "may signal that a majority of my colleagues have positioned themselves to reopen the door [to evidence secured by official lawlessness] still further and abandon altogether the exclusionary rule in search-and-seizure cases." . . . Since then, in case after case, I have witnessed the Court's gradual but determined strangulation of the rule. It now appears that the Court's victory over the Fourth Amendment is complete. That today's decision represents the *pièce de résistance* of the Court's past efforts cannot be doubted, for today the Court sanctions the use in the prosecution's case-in-chief of illegally obtained evidence against the individual whose rights have been violated—a result that had previously been thought to be foreclosed.

The Court seeks to justify this result on the ground that the "costs" of adhering to the exclusionary rule in cases like those before us exceed the "benefits." But the language of deterrence and of cost/benefit analysis, if used indiscriminately, can have a narcotic effect. It creates an illusion of technical precision and ineluctabilty. It suggests that not only constitutional principle but also empirical data supports the majority's result. When the Court's analysis is examined carefully, however, it is clear that we have not been treated to an honest assessment of the merits of the exclusionary rule, but have instead been drawn into a curious world where the "costs" of excluding illegally obtained evidence loom to exaggerated heights and where the "benefits" of such exclusion are made to disappear with a mere wave of the hand. . . .

. . . A chief consequence of today's decision will be to convey a clear and unambiguous message to magistrates that their decisions to issue warrants are now insulated from subsequent judicial review. Creation of this new exception for good faith reliance upon a warrant implicitly tells magistrates that they need not take much care in reviewing warrant applications, since their mistakes will from now on have virtually no consequence: If their decision to issue a warrant was correct, the evidence will be admitted; if their decision was incorrect, but the police relied in good faith on the warrant, the evidence will also be admitted. Inevitably, the care and attention devoted to such an inconsequential chore will dwindle. Although the Court is correct to note that magistrates do not share the same stake in the outcome of a criminal case as the police, they nevertheless need to appreciate that their role is of some moment in order to continue performing the important task of carefully reviewing warrant applications. Today's decision effectively removes that incentive. . . .

Justice Stevens, . . . dissenting. . . .

. . . [T]he Government now admits—at least for the tactical purpose of achieving what it regards as a greater benefit—that the substance, as well as the letter, of the Fourth Amendment was violated. The Court, therefore assumes that the warrant in that case was not supported by probable cause, but refuses to suppress the evidence obtained thereby because it considers the police conduct to satisfy a "newfangled" nonconstitutional standard of reasonableness. Yet if the Court's assumption is correct—if there was no probable cause—it must follow that it was "unreasonable" for the authorities to make unheralded entries into and searches of private dwellings and automobiles. The Court's conclusion that such searches undertaken without probable cause can nevertheless be "reasonable" is totally without support in our Fourth Amendment jurisprudence. . . .

The notion that a police officer's reliance on a magistrate's warrant is automatically appropriate is one the Framers of the Fourth Amendment would have vehemently rejected. The precise problem that the Amendment was intended to address was *the unreasonable issuance of warrants.* As we have often observed, the Amendment was actually motivated by the practice of issuing general warrants—warrants which did not satisfy the particularity and probable cause requirements. The resentments which led to the Amendment were directed at the issuance of *warrants* unjustified by particularized evidence of wrongdoing. Those who sought to amend the Constitution to include a Bill of Rights repeatedly voiced the view that the evil which had to be addressed was the issuance of warrants on insufficient evidence. . . .

In short, the Framers of the Fourth Amendment were deeply suspicious of warrants; in their minds the paradigm of an abusive search was the execution of a warrant not based on probable cause. The fact that colonial officers had magisterial authorization for their conduct when they engaged in general searches surely did not make their conduct "reasonable." The Court's view that it is consistent with our Constitution to adopt a rule that it is presumptively reasonable to rely on a defective warrant is the product of constitutional amnesia. . . .

The exclusionary rule is designed to prevent violations of the Fourth Amendment. "Its purpose is to deter—to compel respect for the constitutional guaranty in the only effectively available way, by removing the incentive to disregard it." . . . If the police cannot use evidence obtained through warrants issued on less than probable cause, they have less incentive to seek those warrants, and magistrates have less incentive to issue them.

Today's decisions do grave damage to that deterrent function. Under the majority's new rule, even when the police know their warrant application is probably insufficient, they retain an incentive to submit it to a magistrate, on the chance that he may take the bait. No longer must they hestitate and seek additional evidence in doubtful cases. . . .

We could, of course, facilitate the process of administering justice to those who violate the criminal laws by ignoring the commands of the Fourth Amendment—indeed, by ignoring the entire Bill of Rights—but it is the very purpose of a Bill of Rights to identify values that may not be sacrificed to expediency. In a just society those who govern, as well as those who are governed, must obey the law. . . .

Although the majority opinion states that the only issue was whether the exclusionary rule was to be modified in this case, and not whether the Fourth Amendment was violated, the decision in fact relaxes the strictures of the Amendment. Justice Stevens is correct on this point. Actual modification of the rule will take place when the Court holds that a search or seizure violates the Amendment, but the evidence will nonetheless be admitted. Thus the fewer searches or seizures the Court holds to be "unreasonable" (as under the open fields doctrine or in the case of aerial searches) the less often the exclusionary rule comes into play. This seems to be the contemporary direction rather than the overt modification of the exclusionary rule.

In *Illinois* v. *Krull,* 55 LW 4291 (1987), the Court extended the "good faith" exception of *Leon* to searches conducted under a statute later held to be unconstitutional. A statute required automobile parts dealers to permit state officials to enter their premises to inspect required records. On authority of this statute, officers entered the defendant's wrecking yard without a warrant and found evidence of stolen vehicles. The next day, however, a federal court held the statute unconstitutional under the Fourth Amendment. The Illinois Supreme Court agreed and held that the evidence should be suppressed in *Krull,* refusing to apply the good faith exception. The United States Supreme Court reversed. The majority opinion stressed that the primary rationale for the exclusionary rule was deterrence of police misconduct, and the rationale of *Leon* was equally applicable to cases of police reliance on a statute later found to be unconstitutional. Justice O'Connor, speaking for the four dissenters, argued that the decision provided "a grace period for unconstitutional search and seizure legislation during which the state is permitted to violate constitutional requirements with impunity."

In 1987, in *Maryland* v. *Garrison*, 55 LW 4190, the Court held that evidence seized by the police was admissible even though they searched the wrong apartment. A warrant was issued to search the apartment of one McWebb on the third floor of a specified address. The police thought that there was only one apartment on the third floor, but in fact there were two. They entered an open door, and before they were aware that they were in Garrison's apartment, they discovered contraband, and Garrison's arrest and conviction followed. The Court held that although the warrrant was broader than appropriate, the information available to the officers at the time the warrant issued was sufficient to validate the warrant. The officers' conduct was consistent with a reasonable effort to ascertain and identify the place intended to be searched within the meaning of the Fourth Amendment.

(Special cases involving warrantless searches—searches of probationers' homes, pocketbooks of public school students and desks and offices of government employees—are discussed in Chapter 8, The Right of Privacy.)

Brief mention should be made of the issue of who has standing to challenge the admission of evidence allegedly seized in violation of the Fourth Amendment. While the earlier position of the Court provided an "automatic standing" rule, in *United States* v. *Salvucci*, 448 U.S. 83 (1980), the Court held that defendants in a criminal prosecution who are charged with crimes of possession may only claim the benefits of the exclusionary rule to exclude evidence against them that was obtained as a result of an illegal search and seizure if their *own* Fourth Amendment rights were violated. Thus the defendant could not challenge the admission of evidence against him that was seized illegally from a third party.

## Wiretapping and Electronic Surveillance

The question of whether the Fourth Amendment was applicable to wire taps was first taken up by the Court in *Olmstead* v. *United States*, 277 U.S. 438 (1928), and by a five-to-four vote it was held that phone taps by federal officers did not violate the Fourth Amendment. Chief Justice Taft, speaking for the majority, stated:

> The well known historical purpose of the Fourth Amendment, directed against general warrants and writs of assistance, was to prevent the use of governmental force to search a man's house, his person, his papers, and his effects, and to prevent their seizure against his will. . . .
>
> The Amendment itself shows that the search is to be of material things—the person, the house, his papers or his effects. The description of the warrant necessary to make the proceeding lawful is that it must specify the place to be searched and the person or *things* to be seized. . . .
>
> The United States takes no such care of telegraph or telephone messages as of mailed sealed letters. The Amendment does not forbid what was done here. There was no searching. There was no seizure. The evidence was secured by the use of the sense of hearing and that only. There was no entry of the houses or offices of the defendants. . . .
>
> Congress may, of course, protect the secrecy of telephone messages by making them, when intercepted, inadmissible in evidence in Federal criminal trials, by direct legislation, and thus depart from the common law of evidence. But the courts may not adopt such a policy by attributing an enlarged and unusual meaning to the Fourth Amendment. The reasonable view is that one who installs in his house a telephone instrument with connecting wires intends to project his voice to those quite

outside, and that the wires beyond his house and messages while passing over them are not within the protection of the Fourth Amendment. Here those who intercepted the projected voices were not in the house of either party to the conversation. . . .

A standard which would forbid the reception of evidence if obtained by other than nice ethical conduct by government officials would make society suffer and give criminals greater immunity than has been known heretofore. In the absence of controlling legislation by Congress, those who realize the difficulties in bringing offenders to justice may well deem it wise that the exclusion of evidence should be confined to cases where rights under the Constitution would be violated by admitting it. . . .

[Justice Holmes gave a vigorous dissenting opinion, in the course of which he said:]

. . . It is desirable that criminals should be detected, and to that end that all available evidence should be used. It also is desirable that the government should not itself foster and pay for other crimes, when they are the means by which the evidence is to be obtained. If it pays its officers for having got evidence by crime I do not see why it may not as well pay them for getting it in the same way, and I can attach no importance to protestations of disapproval if it knowingly accepts and pays and announces that in the future it will pay for the fruits. We have to choose, and for my part I think it a less evil that some criminals should escape than that the government should play an ignoble part.

For those who agree with me, no distinction can be taken between the government as prosecutor and the government as judge. If the existing code does not permit district attorneys to have a hand in such dirty business, it does not permit the judge to allow such iniquities to succeed. . . . And if all that I have said so far be accepted, it makes no difference that in this case wire tapping is made a crime by the law of the state, not by the law of the United States. It is true that a state cannot make rules of evidence for courts of the United States, but the state has authority over the conduct in question, and I hardly think that the United States would appear to greater advantage when paying for an odious crime against state law than when inciting to the disregard of its own. . . .

[Justice Brandeis, also dissenting, made some prophetic statements about the "progress" of the various sciences in the art of prying into private lives:]

. . . The progress of science in furnishing the government with means of espionage is not likely to stop with wire-tapping. Ways may some day be developed by which the government, without removing papers from secret drawers, can reproduce them in court, and by which it will be enabled to expose to a jury the most intimate occurrences of the home. Advances in the psychic and related sciences may bring means of exploring unexpressed beliefs, thoughts and emotions. . . . Can it be that the Constitution affords no protection against such invasions of individual security? . . .

Decency, security, and liberty alike demand that government officials shall be subjected to the same rules of conduct that are commands to the citizen. In a government of laws, existence of the government will be imperiled if its fails to observe the law scrupulously. Our government is the potent, the omnipresent, teacher. For good or for ill, it teaches the whole people by its example. Crime is contagious. If the government becomes a law-breaker, it breeds contempt for law; it invites every man to become a law unto himself; it invites anarchy. To declare that in the administration of the criminal law the end justifies the means—to declare that the government may commit crimes in order to secure the conviction of a private criminal—would bring terrible retribution. Against that pernicious doctrine this Court should resolutely set its face.

[For an interesting treatment of the *Olmstead* case—"its genesis, its unfolding, and its impact"—see Walter F. Murphy, *Wiretapping on Trial: A Case Study in the Judicial Process* (New York: Random House, 1965).]

In his opinion for the majority, Chief Justice Taft suggested that if Congress so desired, it could bar the admission of intercepted telephone messages in federal criminal trials. Congress adopted the suggestions in passing the Federal Communications Act of 1934. The relevant portion of the Act is Section 605:

Unauthorized publication or use of communications. No person receiving or assisting in receiving, or transmitting, . . . any interstate or foreign communication by wire or radio shall divulge or publish the existence, contents, substance, purport, effect, or meaning thereof, . . . to any person other than the addressee . . . ; and no person not being authorized by the sender shall intercept any communication and divulge or publish the existence, contents, substance, purport, effect, or meaning of such intercepted communication to any persons; . . . and no person having received such intercepted communication or having become acquainted with the contents, . . . or meaning of the same or any part thereof, knowing that such information was so obtained, shall divulge or publish the existence, contents, . . . or meaning of the same or any part thereof, or use the same . . . for his own benefit or for the benefit of another not entitled thereto. . . .

Section 501 of the Act made the willful and knowing violation of this section punishable by a fine of not more than $10,000 or by imprisonment for a term of not more than two years or both.

By the late 1960s both legislation and post-*Olmstead* judicial decisions made it clear that wiretapping and electronic surveillance has been brought within Fourth and Fourteenth Amendment protection as "searches" necessitating the use of warrants.

In *Berger* v. *New York*, 388 U.S. 41 (1967), the Court considered the validity of New York's permissive eavesdrop statute which permitted certain courts to issue "an ex parte order for eavesdropping," upon oath or affirmation of a district attorney or ranking police officers that there was reasonable ground to believe that evidence of crime might be thus obtained, and particularly describing the person whose communications, conversations, or discussions were to be overheard or recorded and the purpose thereof. The order would be effective for a period of no more than two months unless extended by the judge who signed the original order. In view of the rather widespread support for a "middle position" of outlawing eavesdrop testimony instigated by the government, except for that obtained under a special court order, the decision in *Berger* v. *New York* was awaited with more than usual interest. When it was announced, the square holding of the majority was that the New York statute was violative of the Fourth and Fourteenth Amendments. The vote was five-to-four on this point, although Justice Stewart joined the majority on other grounds.

The majority opinion stated that while the statute satisfied the Fourth Amendment's requirement that a neutral and detached authority be interposed between the police and the public, "the broad sweep of the statute is immediately observable." The wiretapping, possibly extending to two months, was condemned as a series of intrusions with only one showing of probable cause and with no notice. Further, the statute was held to lack the particularization required by the Fourth Amendment. "It lays down no requirement for particularity in the warrant as to what specific crime has been or is being committed, nor 'the place to be searched,' or 'the persons or things to be seized'."

It was clear that the Court in *Berger* found the New York eavesdrop statute defective, but the more general impact of the decision was demonstrated later in the year in *Katz* v. *United States*, the "telephone booth" case.

## KATZ *v.* UNITED STATES
### *389 U.S. 347 (1967)*

Mr. Justice Stewart delivered the opinion of the Court.

The petitioner was convicted in the District Court of the Southern District of California under an eight-count indictment charging him with transmitting wagering information by telephone from Los Angeles to Miami and Boston, in violation of a federal statute. At trial the government was permitted, over the petitioner's objection, to introduce evidence of the petitioner's end of telephone conversations, overheard by FBI agents who had attached an electronic listening and recording device to the outside of the public telephone booth from which he had placed his calls. In affirming his conviction, the Court of Appeals rejected the contention that the recordings had been obtained in violation of the Fourth Amendment, because "[t]here was no physical entrance into the area occupied by [the petitioner]." We granted certiorari in order to consider the constitutional questions thus presented. . . .

. . . [T]he Fourth Amendment cannot be translated into a general constitutional "right to privacy." That Amendment protects individual privacy against certain kinds of government intrusion, but its protections go further, and often have nothing to do with privacy at all. Other provisions of the constitution protect personal privacy from other forms of governmental invasion. But the protection of a person's *general* right to privacy—his right to be let alone by other people—is, like the protection of his property and of his very life, left largely to the law of the individual States.

Because of the misleading way the issues have been formulated, the parties have attached great significance to the characterization of the telephone booth from which the petitioner placed his calls. The petitioner has strenuously argued that the booth was "a constitutionally protected area." The Government has maintained with equal vigor that it was not. But this effort to decide whether or not a given "area," viewed in the abstract, is "constitutionally protected" deflects attention from the problem presented by this case. For the Fourth Amendment protects people, not places. What a person knowingly exposes to the public, even in his own home or office, is not a subject of Fourth Amendment protection. . . . But what he seeks to preserve as private, even in an area accessible to the public, may be constitutionally protected. . . .

The Government stresses the fact that the telephone booth from which the petitioner made his calls was constructed partly of glass, so that he was as visible after he entered it as he would have been if he had remained outside. But what he sought to exclude when he entered the booth was not the intruding eye—it was the uninvited ear. He did not shed his right to do so simply because he made his calls from a place where he might be seen. No less than an individual in a business office, in a friend's apartment, or in a taxicab, a person in a telephone booth may rely upon the protection of the Fourth Amendment. One who occupies it, shuts the door behind him, and pays the toll that permits him to place a call is surely entitled to assume that the words he utters into the mouthpiece will not be broadcast to the world. To read the Constitution more narrowly is to ignore the vital role that the public telephone has come to play in private communication.

The Government contends, however, that the activities of its agents in this case should not be tested by Fourth Amendment requirements, for the surveillance technique they employed involved no physical penetration of the telephone booth from which the petitioner placed his calls. It is true that the absence of such penetration was at one time thought to foreclose further Fourth Amendment inquiry, *Olmstead* v. *United States*, . . . for that Amendment was thought to limit only searches and seizures of tangible property. But "[t]he premise that property interests control the right of the Government to search and seizure has been discredited." *Warden* v. *Hayden*. . . .

We conclude that the underpinnings of Olmstead and Goldman have been so eroded by our subsequent decisions that the "trespass" doctrine there enunciated can no longer be regarded as controlling. The Government's activities in electronically listening to and recording the petitioner's words violated the privacy upon which he justifiably relied while using the telephone booth and thus constituted a "search and seizure" within the meaning of the Fourth Amendment. . . .

The question remaining for decision, then, is whether the search and seizure conducted in this case complied with constitutional standards. . . . [T]he surveillance was limited, both in scope and in duration, to the specific purpose of establishing the contents of the petitioner's unlawful telephonic communications. The agents confined their surveillance to the brief periods during which he used the telephone booth, and they took great care to overhear only the conversations of the petitioner himself.

Accepting this account of the Government's actions as accurate, it is clear that this surveillance was so narrowly circumscribed that a duly authorized magistrate, properly notified of the need for such investigation, specifically informed of the basis on which it was to proceed, and clearly apprised of the precise intrusion it would entail, could constitutionally have authorized, with appropriate safeguards, the very limited search and seizure that the Government asserts in fact took place. . . .

The Government . . . argues that surveillance of a telephone booth should be exempted from the usual requirement of advance authorization by a magistrate upon a showing of probable cause. We cannot agree. . . . The government agents here ignored "the procedure of antecedent justification . . . that is central to the Fourth Amendment," a procedure that we hold to be a constitutional precondition of the kind of electronic surveillance involved in this case. Because the surveillance here failed to meet that condition, and because it led to the petitioner's conviction, the judgment must be reversed.

*It is so ordered.*

Mr. Justice Marshall took no part in the consideration or decision of this case.

Mr. Justice Douglas, with whom Mr. Justice Brennan joins, concurring. . . .

Mr. Justice Harlan, concurring. . . .

Mr. Justice Black, dissenting.

If I could agree with the Court that eavesdropping carried on by electronic means . . . constitutes a "search" or "seizure," I would be happy to join the Court's opinion. . . .

My basic objection is twofold: (1) I do not believe that the words of the Amendment will bear the meaning given them by today's decision, and (2) I do not believe that it is the proper role of this Court to rewrite the Amendment in order "to bring it into harmony with the times" and thus reach a result that many people believe to be desirable. . . .

In 1968 Congress responded to increasing public pressures calling for action to reduce the high incidence of crime, by enacting the Omnibus Crime Control and Safe Streets Act of 1968, 82 Stat. 197. While a major thrust of the Act was the establishment of the Law Enforcement Assistance Administration to provide assistance to state and local law enforcement agencies, Title III of the Act was an attempt to regulate governmental wiretapping and electronic surveillance (and to prohibit private interception) in accord with the guidelines laid down by the Court in *Berger* and *Katz*. In general terms, the Act prohibits electronic surveillance by any federal agency unless first authorized by "the Attorney General, or any Assistant Attorney General specially designated by the Attorney General" and then submitted to a federal judge who is empowered to issue the order approving the interception of communications. Detailed provisions cover the documents and information necessary to accompany the application, as well as the regulations surrounding the issuance of the order itself. There are several exceptions to the requirement of judicial authorization prior to interception, but the two more important ones are (1) prior consent of one of the parties to the communication for the interception, and (2) any situation in which the President deems it necessary, to protect national security, to obtain foreign intelligence information or to protect national security information against foreign intelligence.

In the cases which have thus far reached the Supreme Court, the Court has demanded absolute adherence to the letter of the Act. In *United States* v. *Giordano*, 416 U.S. 505 (1974), the Court held that evidence of narcotics violations obtained by a court-ordered wiretap would have to be suppressed as unlawfully intercepted because the application had been approved by the Attorney General's Executive Assistant instead of by the Attorney General or an "Assistant Attorney General specially designated" by him as required by the Act.

The question of whether the President could, without a warrant, direct a wiretap to gather information on alleged attempts of *domestic* organizations to subvert the government was answered in *United States* v. *United States District Court* in 1972.

## UNITED STATES *v.* UNITED STATES DISTRICT COURT
### *407 U.S. 297 (1972)*

[The case arose out of a criminal proceeding in which the United States charged three defendants with conspiracy to destroy government property. One of the defendants, Plamondon, was charged with the dynamite bombing of an office of the Central Intelligence Agency in Ann Arbor, Michigan. The defendants moved to compel the United States to disclose whether wiretap evidence had been obtained for use as evidence and to conduct a hearing to determine whether it had been obtained illegally. The government conceded that it had intercepted communications without a warrant, but argued that the surveillance was lawful under the President's power to protect the national security. The District Court held that the evidence was illegally obtained, and the government filed for a writ of mandamus to set aside the court's order.]

Mr. Justice Powell delivered the opinion of the Court. . . .

I

Title III of the Omnibus Crime Control and Safe Streets Act, 18 USC §§2510–2520, authorizes the use of electronic surveillance for classes of crimes carefully specified in 18 USC §2516. Such surveillance is subject to prior court order. Section 2518 sets forth the detailed and particularized application necessary to obtain such an order as well as carefully circumscribed conditions for its use. The Act represents a comprehensive attempt by Congress to promote more effective control of crime while protecting the privacy of individual thought and expression. Much of Title III was drawn to meet the constitutional requirements for electronic surveillance enunciated by this court in *Berger* v. *New York* . . . and *Katz* v. *United States*. . . .

Together with the elaborate surveillance requirements in Title III, there is the following proviso, 18 USC §2511 (3):

"Nothing contained in this chapter or in section 605 of the Communications Act of 1934 shall limit the constitutional power of the President to take such measures as he deems necessary to protect the Nation against actual or potential attack or other hostile acts of a foreign power, to obtain foreign intelligence information deemed essential to the security of the United States, or to protect national security information against foreign intelligence activities. *Nor shall anything contained in this chapter be deemed to limit the constitutional power of the President to take such measures as he deems necessary to protect the United States against the overthrow of the Government by force or other unlawful means, or against any other clear and present danger to the structure or existence of the Government.* The contents of any wire or oral communication intercepted by authority of the President in the exercise of the foregoing powers may be received in evidence in any trial, hearing or other proceeding where such interception was reasonable, and shall not be otherwise used or disclosed except as is necessary to implement that power." (Emphasis supplied.)

The Government relies on §2511 (3). It argues that "in excepting national security surveillances from the Act's warrant requirement Congress recognized the President's authority to conduct such surveillances without prior judicial approval." . . . The section thus is viewed as a recognition or affirmance of a constitutional authority in the President to conduct warrantless domestic security surveillance such as that involved in this case.

We think the language of §2511 (3), as well as the legislative history of the statute, refutes this interpretation. The relevant language is that: "Nothing contained in this chapter . . . shall limit the constitutional power of the President to take such measures as he deems necessary to protect . . ." against the dangers specified. At most, this is an implicit recognition that the President does have certain powers in the specified areas. Few would doubt this . . . But so far as the use of the President's electronic surveillance power is concerned, the language is essentially neutral.

Section 2511 (3) certainly confers no power, as the language is wholly inappropriate for such purpose. It merely provides that the Act shall not be interpreted to limit or disturb such power as the President may have under the Constitution. In short, Congress simply left presidential powers where it found them. . . . The legislative history of §2511 (3) supports this interpretation. . . . The debate . . . explicitly indicates that nothing in §2511 (3) was intended to *expand* or to *contract* or to *define* whatever presidential surveillance powers existed in matters affecting the national security. . . . [W]e hold that the statute is not the measure of the executive authority asserted in this case. Rather, we must look to the constitutional powers of the President.

II

It is important at the outset to emphasize the limited nature of the question before the Court. This case raises no constitutional challenge to electronic surveillance as specifically authorized by Title III of the Omnibus Crime Control and Safe Streets Act of 1968. Nor is there any question or doubt as to the necessity of obtaining a warrant in the surveillance of crimes unrelated to the national security interest. . . . Further, the instant case requires no judgment on the scope of the President's surveillance power with respect to the activities of foreign powers, within or without his country. The Attorney General's affidavit in this case states that the surveillances were "deemed necessary to protect the nation from attempts of *domestic organiza-*

*tions* to attack and subvert the existing structure of Government" (emphasis supplied). There is no evidence of any involvement, directly or indirectly, of a foreign power.

Our present inquiry, though important, is therefore a narrow one. It addresses a question left open by *Katz*: "Whether safeguards other than prior authorization by a magistrate would satisfy the Fourth Amendment in a situation involving the national security. . . . " The determination of this question requires the essential Fourth Amendment inquiry into the "reasonableness" of the search and seizure in question, and the way in which that "reasonableness" derives content and meaning through reference to the warrant clause. . . .

We begin the inquiry by noting that the President of the United States has the fundamental duty, under Art. II, §1, of the Constitution, "to preseve, protect, and defend the Constitution of the United States." Implicit in that duty is the power to protect our Government against those who would subvert or overthrow it by unlawful means. In the discharge of this duty, the President—through the Attorney General—may find it necessary to employ electronic surveillance to obtain intelligence information on the plans of those who plot unlawful acts against the Government. . . .

It has been said that "the most basic function of any government is to provide for the security of the individual and of his property." . . . And unless Government safeguards its own capacity to function and to preserve the security of its people, society itself could become so disordered that all rights and liberties would be endangered. . . .

But a recognition of these elementary truths does not make the employment by Government of electronic surveillance a welcome development—even when employed with restraint and under judicial supervision. There is, understandably, a deep-seated uneasiness and apprehension that this capability will be used to intrude upon cherished privacy of law-abiding citizens. We look to the Bill of Rights to safeguard this privacy. . . .

### III

As the Fourth Amendment is not absolute in its terms, our task is to examine and balance the basic values at stake in this case: the duty of Government to protect the domestic security, and the potential danger posed by unreasonable surveillance to individual privacy and free expression. If the legitimate need of Government to safeguard domestic security requires the use of electronic surveillance, the question is whether the needs of citizens for privacy and free expression may not be better protected by requiring a warrant before such surveillance is undertaken. We must also ask whether a warrant requirement would unduly frustrate the efforts of Government to protect itself from acts of subversion and overthrow directed against it. . . .

These Fourth Amendment freedoms cannot properly be guaranteed if domestic security surveillances may be conducted solely within the discretion of the executive branch. The Fourth Amendment does not contemplate the executive officers of Government as neutral and disinterested magistrates. Their duty and responsibility is to enforce the laws, to investigate and to prosecute. . . . But those charged with this investigative and prosecutorial duty should not be the sole judges of when to utilize constitutionally sensitive means in pursuing their tasks. The historical judgment, which the Fourth Amendment accepts, is that unreviewed executive discretion may yield too readily to pressures to obtain incriminating evidence and overlook potential invasions of privacy and protected speech.

It may well be that, in the instant case, the Government's surveillance of Plamondon's conversations was a reasonable one which readily would have gained prior judicial approval. But . . . the Fourth Amendment contemplates a prior judicial judgment, not the risk that executive discretion may be reasonably exercised. . . . The independent check upon executive discretion is not satisfied, as the Government argues, by "extremely limited" post-surveillance judicial review. Indeed, post-surveillance review would never reach the surveillances which failed to result in prosecutions. Prior review by a neutral and detached magistrate is the time tested means of effectuating Fourth Amendment rights. . . .

It is true that there have been some exceptions to the warrant requirement. . . . But those exceptions are few in number and carefully delineated; in general they serve the legitimate needs of law enforcement officers to protect their own well-being and preserve evidence from destruction. . . .

The Government argues that the special circumstances applicable to domestic security surveillances necessitate a further exception to the warrant requirement. It is urged that the requirement of prior judicial review would obstruct the President in the discharge of his constitutional duty to protect domestic security. We are told further that these surveillances are directed primarily to the collecting and maintaining of intelligence with respect to subversive forces, and are not an attempt to gather evidence for specific criminal prosecutions. It is said that this type of surveillance should not be subject to traditional warrant requirements which were established to govern investigation of criminal activity, not on-going intelligence gathering. . . .

The Government further insists that courts "as a practical matter would have neither the knowledge nor the techniques necessary to determine whether there was probable cause to believe that surveillance was necessary to protect national security." These security problems, the Government contends, involve "a large number of complex and subtle factors" beyond the competence of courts to evaluate. . . .

As a final reason for exemption from a warrant requirement, the Government believes that disclosure to a magistrate of all or even a significant portion of the information involved in domestic security surveillances "would create serious potential dangers to the national security and to the lives of informants and agents. . . . Secrecy is the essential ingredient in intelligence gathering; requiring prior judicial authorization would create a greater 'danger of leaks . . . , because in addition to the judge, you have the clerk, the stenographer and some other official like a law assistant or bailiff who may be apprised of the nature' of the surveillance." . . .

These contentions in behalf of a complete exemption from the warrant requirement, when urged on behalf of the President and the national security in its domestic implications, merit the most careful consideration. We certainly do not reject them lightly, especially at a time of worldwide ferment and when civil disorders in this country are more prevalent than in the less turbulent periods of our history. There is, no doubt, pragmatic force to the Government's position.

But we do not think a case has been made for the requested departure from Fourth Amendment standards. The circumstances described do not justify complete exemption of domestic security surveillance from prior judicial scrutiny. Official surveillance, whether its purpose be criminal investigation or on-going intelligence gathering, risks infringement of constitutionally protected privacy of speech. Security surveillances are especially sensitive because of the inherent vagueness of the domestic security concept, the necessarily broad and continuing nature of intelligence gathering, and the temptation to utilize such surveillances to oversee political dissent. We recognize, as we have before, the constitutional basis of the President's domestic security role, but we think it must be exercised in a manner compatible with the Fourth Amendment. In this case we hold that this requires an appropriate prior warrant procedure.

We cannot accept the Government's argument that internal security matters are too subtle and complex for judicial evaluation. Courts regularly deal with the most difficult issues of our society. There is no reason to believe that federal judges will be insensitive to or uncomprehending of the issues involved in domestic security cases. Certainly courts can recognize that domestic security surveillance involves different considerations from the surveillance of ordinary crime. If the threat is too subtle or complex for our senior law enforcement officers to convey its significance to a court, one may question whether there is probable cause for surveillance.

Nor do we believe prior judicial approval will fracture the secrecy essential to official intelligence gathering. The investigation of criminal activity has long involved imparting sensitive information to judicial officers who have respected the confidentialities involved. Judges may be counted upon to be especially conscious of security requirements in national security cases. . . . Moreover, a warrant application involves no public or adversary proceedings: it is an ex parte request before a magistrate or judge. Whatever security dangers clerical and secretarial personnel may pose can be minimized by proper administrative measures, possibly to the point of allowing the Government itself to provide the necessary clerical assistance.

Thus, we conclude that the Government's concerns do not justify departure in this case from the customary Fourth Amendment requirement of judicial approval prior to initiation of a search or surveillance. Although some added burden will be imposed upon the Attorney General, this inconvenience is justified in a free society to protect constitutional values. Nor do we think the Government's domestic surveillance powers will be impaired to any significant degree. A prior warrant establishes presumptive validity of the surveillance and will minimize the burden of justification in post-surveillance judicial review. By no means of least importance will be the reassurance of the public generally that indiscriminate wiretapping and bugging of law-abiding citizens cannot occur.

IV

We emphasize, before concluding this opinion, the scope of our decision. As stated at the outset, this case involves only the domestic aspects of national security. We have not addressed, and express no opinion as to, the issues which may be involved with respect to activities of foreign powers or their agents. Nor does our decision rest on the language of §2511 (3) or any other section of Title III of the Omnibus Crime Control and Safe Streets Act of 1968. That Act does not attempt to define or delineate the powers of the President to meet domestic threats to the national security. . . .

Moreover, we do not hold that the same type of standards and procedures prescribed by Title III are necessarily applicable to this case. We recognize that domestic security surveillance may involve different policy and practical considerations from the surveillance of "ordinary crime." . . . The exact targets of such surveillance may be more difficult to identify than in surveillance operations against many types of crime specified in Title III. . . . Thus, the focus of domestic surveillance may be less precise than that directed against more conventional types of crime. . . .

V

As the surveillance of Plamondon's conversations was unlawful, because conducted without prior judicial approval, the courts below correctly held that *Alder-*

*man* v. *United States* . . . (1969) is controlling and that it requires disclosure to the accused of his own impermissibly intercepted conversations. As stated in *Alderman,* "the trial court can and should, where appropriate, place a defendant and his counsel under enforceable orders against unwarranted disclosure of the materials which they may be entitled to inspect."

The judgment of the Court of Appeals is hereby

*Affirmed.*

The Chief Justice concurs in the result.

Mr. Justice Rehnquist took no part in the consideration or decision of this case.

Mr. Justice Douglas, concurring. . . .

Mr. Justice White, concurring in the judgment. . . .

In *Dalia* v. *United States,* 441 U.S. 238 (1979), the Court held that where federal agents have obtained court authorization to install electronic bugging equipment in a suspect's office, neither the Crime Control Act nor the Fourth Amendment makes covert entry to install the equipment unlawful. Nor is the issuing judge required explicitly to authorize such an entry.

In *Smith* v. *Maryland,* 422 U.S. 735 (1979), the Court held that the installation and use of a pen register (a device which, when hooked up to a phone line, records the phone numbers but not the content of outgoing calls) does not constitute a "search" within the meaning of the Fourth and Fourteenth Amendments.

## Bail

The ancient common law extended bail in all cases, but exceptions were gradually introduced by statute, and by the later 18th Century bail was not permitted in the case of serious crimes. [See David Fellman, *The Defendant's Rights Today* (Madison: University of Wisconsin Press, 1976), pp. 49–65.] One may argue that in a system of criminal law where the accused is presumed innocent until found guilty, he should not be incarcerated until guilt is determined. But the accused might flee the jurisdiction or he might continue to commit crimes while awaiting trial, and thus the counterargument is that in some cases bail should be denied. For almost two decades the American law governing release on bail in federal proceedings was provided in the Bail Reform Act of 1966 (18 U.S.C. Sections 3141-3151). The Act granted a statutory right to bail to all persons charged with an offense, other than an offense punishable by death, unless the judicial officer determines, "in the exercise of his discretion, that such a release will not reasonably assure the appearance of the person as required." The primary thrust of the Act was to redress injustices to indigent defendants by ordering release on the defendant's personal recognizance or upon the execution of an unsecured appearance bond. In a Report of the House of Representatives (H.R. Rep. No. 1541, 89th Cong., 2d Sess. 5-6) it was stated:

This legislation does not deal with the problem of the preventive detention of the accused because of the possibility that his liberty might endanger the public, either because of the possibility of the commission of further acts of violence by the accused during the pretrial period, or because of the fact that he is at large might result in the intimidation of witnesses or the destruction of evidence.

The 1966 Act was criticized on the grounds that release was granted too liberally and judges were not given appropriate discretion to deny release of defendants who posed serious risks of flight or danger to the community. In response to continued criticisms, Congress passed the Bail Reform Act of 1984 that repealed the 1966 Act's statutory pre-

THE RIGHTS OF THE ACCUSED **139**

sumption of a right to reasonable bail in all noncapital cases. [On the 1984 Act, see K. F. Berg, "The Bail Reform Act of 1984," 34 *Emory L. J.* 685 (1985); J. S. Goldkamp, "Danger and Detention: a Second Generation of Law Reform," 76 *J. Crim. L. & Criminology* 1 (1985); S. R. Schlesinger, "Bail Reform: Protecting the Community and the Accused," 9 *Harv. J. L. & Pub. Policy* 173 (1986).]

The rationale of the 1984 Act is that the need to protect the community from further criminal activity by the defendant during release outweighs the right of certain defendants to release prior to trial. If the judicial officer determines that release without conditions will not reasonably assure the appearance of the defendant or will endanger the safety of any other person or the community, he may order the release subject to any or all of some fourteen conditions set forth in Section 3142(c), including such conditions as remaining in the custody of a designated person who agrees to supervise him, avoiding all contact with an alleged victim of the crime and with a potential witness who may testify concerning the offense, complying with a specified curfew, refraining from possessing a firearm or other dangerous weapon, refraining from excessive use of alcohol, or satisfying "any other condition that is reasonably necessary to assure the appearance of the person as required and to assure the safety of any other person and the community."

The most important provisions of the 1984 Act are those that permit a judicial officer to order detention prior to trial. Such detention cannot be ordered, however, without a hearing. Under Section 3142(f) there are two situations that set up a hearing: (1) upon motion of the attorney for the Government in a case that involves (A) a crime of violence; (B) an offense for which the maximum sentence is life imprisonment or death; (C) a drug offense punishable by at least ten years in prison; or (D) any felony committed after the person had been convicted of two or more prior offenses described in (A)–(C); and (2) upon motion of the attorney for the Government or upon the judicial officer's own motion, in circumstances that involve (A) a serious risk that the person will flee; or (B) a serious risk that the person will obstruct or attempt to obstruct justice, or threaten, injure, or intimidate a prospective witness or juror. The hearing is for the purpose of determining whether any condition or combination of conditions as set forth in subsection (c) will reasonably assure the appearance of the person and the safety of any other person and the community. The hearing is to be held immediately upon the person's first appearance before the judicial officer unless the defendant seeks a continuance. And, with certain exceptions, in a case described in situation (1) above, a rebuttable presumption arises that no condition or combination of conditions will reasonably assure the safety of any other person and the community. At the hearing, the person has the right to be represented by counsel, to testify, to present witnesses on his own behalf, to cross-examine witnesses who appear, and to present information. The rules of evidence in criminal trials do not apply at the hearing. The facts the judicial officer uses to support a decision to order detention are to be supported by clear and convincing evidence, and the defendant may be detained pending completion of the hearing.

Section 3412(g) sets out the factors to be considered by the judicial officer in determining whether there are conditions of release that will reasonably assure the defendant's appearance and the safety of any other person and the community. These include such factors as the nature of the offense charged, including whether the offense is a crime of violence or involves a narcotic drug, the weight of the evidence against the defendant, family ties, employment, past conduct and criminal history, and whether the defendant was on probation or other release for an offense under federal, state or local law, but particularly a determination of the nature and seriousness of the danger to any person or the community that would be posed by the person's release.

Although the 1984 Act is silent on the matter of a time limit on pretrial detention, it seems clear that the 90-day limit set by the Speedy Trial Act [18 U.S.C. Section 3161

(1982)] applies. That Act, however, does contain provision for continuance beyond 90 days in special circumstances.

## UNITED STATES v. SALERNO
### 55 LW 4663 (1987)

Chief Justice Rehnquist delivered the opinion of the Court. . . .

Respondents Anthony Salerno and Vincent Cafaro were arrested on March 21, 1986, after being charged in a 29-count indictment alleging various Racketeer Influenced and Corrupt Organizations Act (RICO) violations, mail and wire fraud offenses, extortion, and various criminal gambling violations. The RICO counts alleged 35 acts of racketeering activity, including fraud, extortion, gambling, and conspiracy to commit murder. At respondents' arraignment, the Government moved to have Salerno and Cafaro detained pursuant to §3142(e), on the ground that no condition of release would assure the safety of the community or any person. The District Court held a hearing at which the Government made a detailed proffer of evidence. The Government's case showed that Salerno was the "boss" of the Genovese Crime Family of La Cosa Nostra and that Cafaro was a "captain" in the Genovese Family. According to the Government's proffer, based in large part on conversations intercepted by a court-ordered wiretap, the two respondents had participated in wide-ranging conspiracies to aid their illegitimate enterprises through violent means. The Government also offered the testimony of two of its trial witnesses, who would assert that Salerno personally participated in two murder conspiracies. Salerno opposed the motion for detention, challenging the credibility of the Government's witnesses. He offered the testimony of several character witnesses as well as a letter from his doctor stating that he was suffering from a serious medical condition. . . .

The District Court granted the Government's detention motion, concluding that the Government had established by clear and convincing evidence that no condition or combination of conditions of release would ensure the safety of the community or any person. . . .

Respondents appealed, contending that to the extent that the Bail Reform Act permits pretrial detention on the ground that the arrestee is likely to commit future crimes, it is unconstitutional on its face. Over a dissent, the United States Court of Appeals for the Second Circuit agreed. . . .

Respondents first argue that the Act violates substantive due process because the pretrial detention it authorizes constitutes impermissible punishment before trial. . . . The Government, however, has never argued that pretrial detention could be upheld if it were "punishment." The Court of Appeals assumed that pretrial detention under the Bail Reform Act is regulatory, not penal, and we agree that it is. . . .

We conclude that the detention imposed by the Act falls on the regulatory side of the dichotomy. The legislative history of the Bail Reform Act clearly indicates that Congress did not formulate the pretrial detention provisions as punishment for dangerous individuals. . . . Congress instead perceived pretrial detention as a potential solution to a pressing societal problem. There is no doubt that preventing danger to the community is a legitimate regulatory goal.

Nor are the incidents of pretrial detention excessive in relation to the regulatory goal Congress sought to achieve. The Bail Reform Act carefully limits the circumstances under which detention may be sought to the most serious of crimes. . . . We conclude, therefore, that the pretrial detention contemplated by the Bail Reform Act is regulatory in nature, and does not constitute punishment before trial in violation of the Due Process Clause. . . .

The government's interest in preventing crime by arrestees is both legitimate and compelling. . . . The Bail Reform Act, . . . narrowly focuses on a particularly acute problem in which the government interests are overwhelming. The Act operates only on individuals who have been arrested for a specific category of extremely serious offenses. . . . Congress specifically found that these individuals are far more likely to be responsible for dangerous acts in the community after arrest. . . . Nor is the Act by any means a scattershot attempt to incapacitate those who are merely suspected of these serious crimes. The government must first of all demonstrate probable cause to believe that the charged crime has been committed by the arrestee, but that is not enough. In a full-blown adversary hearing, the government must convince a neutral decisionmaker by clear and convincing evidence that no conditions of release can reasonably assure the safety of the community or any person. . . While the government's general interest in preventing crime is compelling, even this interest is heightened when the government musters convincing proof that the arrestee, already indicted or held to answer for a serious crime, presents a demonstrable danger to the community. Under these narrow circumstances, society's interest in crime prevention is at its greatest.

On the other side of the scale, of course, is the individual's strong interest in liberty. We do not minimize the importance and fundamental nature of this right. But, as our cases hold, this right may, in circumstances where the government's interest is sufficiently weighty, be subordinated to the greater needs of society. We think that Congress' careful delineation of the circumstances under which detention will be permitted satisfies this standard. When the government proves by clear and convincing evidence that an arrestee presents an identified and articulable threat to an individual or the community, we believe that, consistent with the Due Process Clause, a court may disable the arrestee from executing that threat. Under these circumstancs, we cannot categorically state that pretrial detention "offends some principle of justice so rooted in the traditions and conscience of our people as to be ranked as fundamental." . . .

Finally, we may dispose briefly of respondents' facial challenge to the procedures of the Bail Reform Act. To sustain them against such a challenge, we need only find them "adequate to authorize the pretrial detention of at least some [persons] charged with crimes." . . .

[Here the opinion gives a detailed outline of the procedural requirements of the Act prior to the determination of detention.]

We think these extensive safeguards suffice to repel a facial challenge. . . . Given the legitimate and compelling regulatory purpose of the Act and the procedural protections it offers, we conclude that the Act is not facially invalid under the Due Process Clause of the Fifth Amendment.

Respondents also contend that the Bail Reform Act violates the Excessive Bail Clause of the Eighth Amendment. The Court of Appeals did not address this issue because it found that the Act violates the Due Process Clause. We think that the Act survives a challenge founded upon the Eighth Amendment.

The Eighth Amendment addresses pretrial release by providing merely that "Excessive bail shall not be required." This Clause, of course, says nothing about whether bail shall be available at all. Respondents nevertheless contend that this Clause grants them a right to bail calculated solely upon considerations of flight. They rely on *Stack* v. *Boyle,* 342 U.S. 1, 5 (1951), in which the Court stated that "Bail set at a figure higher than an amount reasonably calculated [to ensure the defendant's presence at trial] is 'excessive' under the Eighth Amendment." In respondents' view, since the Bail Reform Act allows a court essentially to set bail at an infinite amount for reasons not related to the risk of flight, it violates the Excessive Bail Clause. Respondents concede that the right to bail they have discovered in the Eighth Amendment is not absolute. A court may, for example, refuse bail in capital cases. And, as the Court of Appeals noted and respondents admit, a court may refuse bail when the defendant presents a threat to the judicial process by intimidating witnesses. . . . Respondents characterize these exceptions as consistent with what they claim to be the sole purpose of bail—to ensure integrity of the judicial process. . . .

Nothing in the text of the Bail Clause limits permissible government considerations solely to questions of flight. The only arguable substantive limitation of the Bail Clause is that the government's proposed conditions of release or detention not be "excessive" in light of the perceived evil. Of course, to determine whether the government's response is excessive, we must compare that response against the interest the goverment seeks to protect by means of that response. Thus, when the government has admitted that its only interest is in preventing flight, bail must be set by a court at a sum designed to ensure that goal, and no more. . . . We believe that when Congress has mandated detention on the basis of a compelling interest other than prevention of flight, as it has here, the Eighth Amendment does not require release on bail.

In our society liberty is the norm, and detention prior to trial or without trial is the carefully limited exception. We hold that the provisions for pretrial detention in the Bail Reform Act of 1984 fall within that carefully limited exception. . . .

The judgment of the Court of Appeals is therefore

*Reversed.*

Justice Marshall, with whom Justice Brennan joins, dissenting. . . .

The essence of this case may be found, ironically enough, in a provision of the Act to which the majority does not refer. Title 18 U.S.C. §3142(j) (1982 ed., Supp. III) provides that "[n]othing in this section shall be construed as modifying or limiting the presumption of innocence." But the very pith and purpose of this statute is an abhorrent limitation of the presumption of innocence. The majority's untenable conclusion that the present Act is constitutional arises from a specious denial of the role of the Bail Clause and the Due Process Clause in protecting the invaluable guarantee afforded by the presumption of innocence. . . .

The statute now before us declares that persons who have been indicted may be detained if a judicial officer finds clear and convincing evidence that they pose a danger to individuals or to the community. The statute does not authorize the government to imprison anyone it has evidence is dangerous; indictment is necessary. But let us suppose that a defendant is indicted and the government shows by clear and convincing evidence that he is dangerous and should be detained pending a trial, at which trial the defendant is acquitted. May the government continue to hold the defendant in detention based upon its showing that he is dangerous? The answer cannot be yes, for that would allow the government to imprison someone for uncommitted crimes based upon "proof" not beyond a reasonable doubt. The result must therefore be that once the indictment has failed, detention cannot continue. But our fundamental principles of justice declare that the defendant is as innocent on the day before his trial as he is on the morning after his acquittal. Under this statute an untried indictment somehow acts to permit a detention, based on other charges, which after an acquittal would be unconstitutional. The conclusion is inescapable that the indictment has been turned into evidence, if not that the defendant is guilty of the crime charged, then that left to his own devices he will soon be guilty of something else. . . .

Honoring the presumption of innocence is often difficult; sometimes we must pay substantial social costs as a result of our commitment to the values we espouse. But at the end of the day the presumption of innocence protects the innocent; the short-cuts we take with those whom we believe to be guilty injure only those wrongfully accused and, ultimately, ourselves. . . .

I dissent.

Justice Stevens, dissenting. . . .

## SELF-INCRIMINATION

The privilege against self-incrimination is generally accepted as a landmark in the development of procedural guarantees. It became established in the common law as a revolt against procedures in which accused persons were questioned under oath by judges, both to get evidence and to obtain confessions. Immunity from such interrogation was written into the Fifth Amendment of the Constitution and provides that "no person . . . shall be compelled in any criminal case to be a witness against himself."

While it is sometimes suggested that the purpose of the privilege was simply to prevent torture, there is another reason as well. It lies in the general feeling that the concept of fair play demands that the individual not be required to accuse and convict himself out of his own mouth. The case against him must be built by the government without requiring of the accused that he make their case for them by his own testimony. This aspect of the privilege has important consequences. It is not confined, for example, merely to cases of criminal prosecution, but extends to all sorts of proceedings where testimony might be required and where the divulgences might lead to a later criminal prosecution of the witness. Thus the privilege can operate in civil cases and in legislative investigations, as well as in a criminal prosecution. The first case to rule squarely on the application of the privilege to testimony before congressional investigating committees was *Quinn* v. *United States*, 349 U.S. 155 (1955). In the opinion of the Court, upholding the application of the privilege, Chief Justice Warren said:

The privilege against self-incrimination is a right that was hard-earned by our forefathers. The reasons for its inclusion in the Constitution—and the necessities for its preservation—are to be found in the lessons of history. As early as 1650, remembrance of the horror of Star Chamber proceedings a decade before had firmly established the privilege in the common law of England. Transplanted to this country as part of our legal heritage, it soon made its way into various state constitutions and ultimately in 1791 into the federal Bill of Rights. The privilege, this Court has stated, "was generally regarded then, as now, as a privilege of great value, a protection to the innocent though a shelter to the guilty, and a safeguard against heedless, unfounded or tyrannical prosecutions." Coequally with our other constitutional guarantees, the Self-Incrimination Clause "must be accorded liberal construction in favor of the right it was intended to secure." Such liberal construction is particularly warranted in a prosecution of a witness for a refusal to answer, since the respect normally accorded the privilege is then buttressed by the presumption of innocence accorded a defendant in a criminal trial. To apply the privilege narrowly or begrudingly—to treat it as an historical relic, at most merely to be tolerated—is to ignore its development and purpose.

## The Invocation of the Privilege

In the case of a criminal defendant, invocation of the privilege is a very simple matter—he merely refuses to take the stand. By so doing, he precludes the prosecution from asking him any questions at all, incriminating or not. The defendant's counsel must weigh this advantage against the disadvantage that the jury may interpret such failure to defend himself as a sign of guilt, but the privilege is there if he chooses to use it. One problem which has arisen on this point is the constitutionality of permitting the trial judge to comment to the jury on the defendant's failure to take the stand. In *Twining* v. *New Jersey*, 211 U.S. 78 (1908), the Court held that it was not violative of the Fourteenth Amendment's privilege against self-incrimination for a state judge to charge the jury: "Because a man does not go upon the stand you are not necessarily justified in drawing an inference of guilt. But you have a right to consider the fact that he does not go upon the stand where a direct accusation is made against him." No case involving the Fifth Amendment's application directly to such a comment has been decided, since Congress by statute has required that federal judges specifically instruct juries that failure to take the stand should *not* be considered as evidence of guilt. But it was generally presumed that the Fifth Amendment would bar adverse comment in federal courts. In *Malloy* v. *Hogan*, 378 U.S. 1 (1964), the Court "incorporated" the Fifth Amendment privilege into the Fourteenth Amendment, thus imposing the federal standard upon the States. This inevitably led to the reexamination of the *Twining* rule, and in *Griffin* v. *California*, 380 U.S. 609 (1965), the Court held that "the Fifth Amendment, in its direct application to the federal government and its bearing on the States by reason of the Fourteenth Amendment, forbids either comment by the prosecution on the accused's silence or instructions by the court that such silence is evidence of guilt."

Suppose the person who is to be questioned is not a criminal defendant, but is instead a witness before a grand jury or a congressional committee. If he is under subpoena, he does not have the choice of refusing to "take the stand." How, then, does he invoke the privilege? The answer is that he must make a decision on each question as it is asked, as to whether he thinks his answer might incriminate him. If he concludes that it might do so, then he can refuse to answer, but he must in some way indicate that his refusal is based on the privilege.

As to whether the questioning body is absolutely bound by the witness' answer that his response might incriminate him, the answer is a qualified no. If the refusal is followed by a citation for contempt, and the question is before a court, the judge must make some sort of judgment as to whether there is any basis for fearing that an answer might incriminate the witness. The problem was discussed by Chief Justice Marshall while on circuit in the treason trial of Aaron Burr in 1807. During the course of the trial the attorney for the United States offered in evidence a paper in code. Burr's secretary was asked whether he understood the paper and declined to answer on the ground that he might incriminate himself. The court was asked to decide whether the excuse offered was sufficient to prevent his answering. In *United States* v. *Burr* [In re *Willie*], 25 Fed. Cas. 38, No. 14,692e (C.C.D. Va. 1807), the Chief Justice said:

When a question is propounded, it belongs to the court to consider and to decide whether any direct answer to it can implicate the witness. If this be decided in the negative, then he may answer it without violating the privilege which is secured to him by law. If a direct answer to it may criminate himself, then he must be the sole judge what his answer would be. The court cannot participate with him in this judgment, because they cannot decide on the effect of his answers without knowing what it would be; and a disclosure of that fact to the judges would strip him of the privilege which the law allows, and which he claims. It follows necessarily then, from this statement of things, that if the question be of such a description that an answer to it may or may not criminate the witness, according to the purport of that answer, it must rest with himself, who alone can tell what it would be, to answer the question or not. . . .

On examination of the question, the Chief Justice concluded that it could be answered without implicating the witness.

A similar approach was taken by Justice Clark, for the Court, in *Hoffman* v. *United States*, 341 U.S. 479 (1951), who stated: "The witness is not exonerated from answering merely because he declares that in so doing he would incriminate himself—his say-so does not of itself establish the hazard of incrimination. It is for the court to say whether his silence is justified . . . and to require him to answer if 'it clearly appears to the court that he is mistaken.' " He went on to say, however, just as did Chief Justice Marshall, that the witness cannot be required to make a complete revelation to prove his contention, or else the privilege is lost. By way of instruction, he stated: "[T]o sustain the privilege, it need only be evident from the implications of the question, in the setting in which it is asked, that a responsive answer to the question or an explanation of why it cannot be answered might be dangerous because injurious disclosure could result."

On occasion witnesses seem to plead the Fifth Amendment privilege when there would appear to be no basis whatever for a prosecution irrespective of the answer given. The general rule is that for the privilege to be invoked, there must be a real possibility of incrimination. However, this sometimes leaves the witness with the difficult problem of deciding when to stop answering questions after he has already answered several of them in a particular line of questioning. This was the problem presented in *Blau* v. *United States*, 340 U.S. 159 (1950). In response to questions by a grand jury about her employment by the Communist Party, the witness refused to answer and invoked the privilege. The government contended that it is not a crime merely to be an employee of the Party, and that she could not properly invoke the privilege. Petitioner was upheld in her refusal to answer:

At the time petitioner was called before the grand jury, the Smith Act was on the statute books making it a crime among other things to advocate knowingly the desirability of overthrow of the Government by force or violence. . . . These provisions made future prosecution of petitioner far more than "a mere imaginary possibility. . . ." Whether such admissions by themselves would support a conviction under a criminal statute is immaterial. Answers to the questions asked by the grand jury would have furnished a link in the chain of evidence needed in a prosecution.

While in *Blau* the witness was charged with having invoked the privilege before it was necessary, in a subsequent case the question presented was whether the witness had waited too long to permit its invocation, thereby in effect waiving it by already answering incriminating questions. The case was *Rogers* v. *United States*, 340 U.S. 367 (1951), arising out of a federal grand jury investigation in Colorado. Petitioner testified that she had held the position of Treasurer of the Communist Party of Denver and had been in possession of the membership lists and dues records of the Party. At the time of the investigation she no longer held such position and denied having possession of the records. But she refused to identify the person to whom she had given the Party's books, stating to the court as her only reason: "I don't feel that I should subject a person or persons to the same thing that I'm going through." She later repeated her refusal, asserting this time the privilege against self-incrimination.

She was sentenced for contempt, the court of appeals affirmed, and the United States Supreme Court affirmed, three justices dissenting. Chief Justice Vinson, for the majority, first pointed out that the petitioner had no privilege with respect to the books of the Party. "Books and records kept 'in a representative rather than in a personal capacity cannot be the subject of the personal privilege against self-incrimination, even though production of the papers might tend to incriminate [their keeper] personally.' " He stated further that the *Blau* rule did not apply since she had already freely described her membership, activities, and office in the Party. "Since the privilege against self-incrimination presupposes a real danger of legal detriment arising from the disclosure, petitioner cannot invoke the privilege where response to the specific question in issue here would not further incriminate her. Disclosure of a fact waives the privilege as to details." Thus after admitting to office-holding in the Party, disclosure of acquaintance with her successor "presents no more than 'a mere imaginary possibility' of increasing the danger of prosecution."

### The Scope of the Privilege

While the privilege "must be accorded liberal construction" and is "of great value," it does not extend to every divulgence which might have injurious consequences. In the first place, as the Court pointed out in *Rogers* v. *United States*, above, the privilege is purely personal and cannot be invoked to protect others. Similarly, the privilege can be claimed only by natural persons and not by corporations or other organizations. As was stated in *United States* v. *White*, 322 U.S. 694 (1944):

[T]he papers and effects which the privilege protects must be the private property of the person claiming the privilege, or at least in his possession in a purely personal capacity. . . . But individuals, when acting as representatives of a collective group, cannot be said to be exercising their personal rights and duties nor to be entitled to their purely personal privileges. . . . In their official capacity, therefore, they have no privilege against self-incrimination. And the official records and documents of the organization that are held by them in a representative rather than in a personal capacity cannot be the subject of the personal privilege against self-incrimination, even though production of the papers might tend to incriminate them personally.

Governments are, of course, empowered to grant immunity from prosecution to witnesses whom they wish to question. A Fifth Amendment problem may arise, however, if the extent of the immunity granted is too narrowly drawn and thus results in an abridgment of the privilege if the witness is compelled to testify. In 1954 Congress passed an immunity act which enabled Congress to compel testimony from witnesses in certain national security investigations. The immunity provision extended to a prohibition against prosecution for "any transaction, matter, or thing concerning which he is compelled to testify." In *Ullmann* v. *United States*, 350 U.S. 422 (1956), the Court upheld the act against claims of unconstitutionality on the grounds that: (1) the Fifth Amendment prohibits compulsion of what would otherwise be self-incriminating testimony irrespective of the grant of immunity, and (2) the grant of immunity was inadequate, since it did not extend to such injuries as loss of job or reputation. The majority held that the privilege is not a broad guarantee of a right to silence, and, further, the privilege only extends to a protection against criminal prosecution, not to other injurious consequences which might follow from divulgence of information.

In 1970 Congress passed another immunity act, but in so doing the "transactional immunity" provision found in the 1954 act was omitted. In *Kastigar* v. *United States* in 1972 the new act was tested.

## KASTIGAR *v.* UNITED STATES
### *406 U.S. 441 (1972)*

[A United States District Court ordered petitioners to appear before a grand jury and to answer its questions under a grant of immunity. The immunity was based upon a provision of the Organized Crime Control Act of 1970 stating that neither the compelled testimony nor any information directly or indirectly derived from such testimony could be used against the witness. Petitioners refused to answer the grand jury's questions and were found in contempt. The court rejected the contention that the Act abridged the privilege in that it still permitted prosecution for any crimes about which the petitioners might testify. The Court of Appeals affirmed, and the case came on certiorari to the Supreme Court.]

Mr. Justice Powell delivered the opinion of the Court. . . .

I

The power of government to compel persons to testify in court or before grand juries and other governmental agencies is firmly established in Anglo-American jurisprudence. . . . But the power to compel testimony is not absolute. There are a number of exemptions from the testimonial duty, the most important of which is the Fifth Amendment privilege against compulsory self-incrimination. . . .

Immunity statutes, which have historical roots deep in Anglo-American jurisprudence, are not incompatible with these values. Rather they seek a rational accommodation between the imperatives of the privilege and the legitimate demands of government to compel citizens to testify. The existence of these statutes reflects the importance of testimony, and the fact that many offenses are of such a character that the only persons capable of giving useful testimony are those implicated in the crime. . . . As Mr. Justice Frankfurter observed, speaking for the Court in *Ullmann* v. *United States*, . . . such statutes have "become part of our constitutional fabric." . . .

II

Petitioners contend first that the Fifth Amendment's privilege against compulsory self-incrimination . . . deprives Congress of power to enact laws which compel self-incrimination, even if complete immunity from prosecution is granted prior to the compulsion of the incriminatory testimony. In other words, petitioners assert that no immunity statute, however drawn, can afford a lawful basis for compelling incriminatory testimony. They ask us to reconsider and overrule *Brown* v. *Walker* . . . and *Ullmann* v. *United States* . . . , decisions which uphold the constitutionality of immunity statutes. We find no merit to this contention and reaffirm the decisions in *Brown* and *Ullmann*.

III

Petitioners' second contention is that the scope of immunity provided by the federal witness immunity statute . . . is not co-extensive with the scope of the Fifth Amendment privilege against compulsory self-incrimination, and therefore is not sufficient to supplant the privilege and compel testimony over a claim of the privilege. The statute provides that when a witness is compelled by district court order to testify over a claim of the privilege: "the witness may not refuse to comply with the order on the basis of his privilege against self-incrimination; but no testimony or other information compelled under the order (or any information directly or indirectly derived from such testimony or other information) may be used against the witness in any criminal case, except a prosecution for perjury, giving a false statement, or otherwise failing to comply with the order."

The constitutional inquiry, rooted in logic and history, as well as in the decisions of this court, is whether the immunity granted under this statute is co-extensive with the scope of the privilege. If so, petitioners' refusals to answer based on the privilege were unjustified, and the judgments of contempt were proper. . . . If, on the other hand, the immunity granted is not as comprehensive as the protection afforded by the privilege, petitioners were justified in refusing to answer, and the judgments of contempt must be vacated. . . .

Petitioners draw a distinction between statutes which provide transactional immunity and those which provide, as does the statute before us, immunity from use and derivative use. They contend that a statute must at a minimum grant full transactional immunity in order to be co-extensive with the scope of the privilege. . . .

The statute's explicit proscription of the use in any criminal case of "testimony or other information compelled under the order (or any information directly or indirectly derived from such testimony or other information)" is consonant with Fifth Amendment standards. We hold that such immunity from use and derivative use is co-extensive with the scope of the privilege against self-incrimination, and therefore is sufficient to compel testimony over a claim of the privilege. While a grant of immunity must afford protection commensurate with that afforded by the privilege, it need not be broader. Transactional immunity, which accords full immunity from prosecution for the offense to which the compelled testimony relates, affords the witness considerably broader protection than does the Fifth Amendment privilege. The privilege has never been construed to mean that one who invokes it cannot subsequently be prosecuted. Its sole concern is to afford protection against being "forced to give testimony leading to the infliction of 'penalties affixed to . . . criminal acts.' " Immunity from the use of compelled testimony and evidence derived directly and indirectly therefrom affords this protection. It prohibits the prosecutorial authorities from using the compelled testimony in *any* respect, and it therefore insures that the testimony cannot lead to the infliction of criminal penalties on the witness. . . .

IV

. . . Petitioners argue that use and derivative use immunity will not adequately protect a witness from various possible incriminating uses of the compelled testimony: for example, the prosecutor or other law enforcement officials may obtain leads, names of witnesses, or other information not otherwise available which might result in a prosecution. It will be difficult and perhaps impossible, the argument goes, to identify, by testimony or cross-examination, the subtle ways in which the compelled testimony may disadvantage a witness, especially in the jurisdiction granting the immunity.

This argument presupposes that the statute's prohibition will prove impossible to enforce. The statute provides a sweeping proscription of any use, direct or indirect, of the compelled testimony and any information derived therefrom. . . . This total prohibition on use provides a comprehensive safeguard, barring the use of compelled testimony as an "investigatory lead," and also barring the use of any evidence obtained by focusing investigation on a witness as a result of his compelled disclosures.

A person accorded this immunity . . . and subsequently prosecuted, is not dependent for the preservation of his rights upon the integrity and good faith of the prosecuting authorities. As stated in *Murphy*: "Once a defendant demonstrates that he has testified, under a state grant of immunity, to matters related to the federal prosecution, the federal authorities have the burden of showing that their evidence is not tainted by establishing that they had an independent, legitimate source for the disputed evidence." . . . This burden of proof, which we reaffirm as appropriate, is not limited to a negation of taint; rather it imposes on the prosecution the affirmative duty to prove that the evidence it proposes to use is derived from a legitimate source wholly independent of the compelled testimony.

This is very substantial protection, commensurate with that resulting from invoking the privilege itself. . . . The statute, like the Fifth Amendment, grants neither pardon nor amnesty. Both the statute and the Fifth Amendment allow the government to prosecute using evidence from legitimate independent sources.

The statutory proscription is analogous to the Fifth Amendment requirement in cases of coerced confessions. A coerced confession, as revealing of leads as testimony given in exchange for immunity, is inadmissible in a criminal trial, but it does not bar prosecution. . . .

We conclude that the immunity provided by [the Act] leaves the witness and the prosecutorial authorities in substantially the same position as if the witness had claimed the Fifth Amendment privilege. . . . The judgment of the Court of Appeals . . . accordingly is

*Affirmed.*

Mr. Justice Brennan and Mr. Justice Rehnquist took no part in the consideration or decision of this case.

Mr. Justice Douglas, dissenting. . . .

When we allow the prosecution to offer only "use" immunity we allow it to grant far less than it has taken away. For while the precise testimony that is compelled may not be used, leads from that testimony may be pursued and used to convict the witness. My view is that the Framers put it beyond the power of Congress to *compel* anyone to confess his crimes. The Self-Incrimination Clause creates, as I have said before, "the federally protected right of silence," making it unconstitutional to use a law "to pry open one's lips and make him a witness against himself." *Ullmann* v. *United States* . . . That is indeed one of the chief procedural guarantees in our accusatorial system. Government acts in an ignoble way when it stoops to the end which we authorize today.

I would . . . hold that this attempt to dilute the Self-Incrimination Clause is unconstitutional.

Mr. Justice Marshall, dissenting. . . .

The Fifth Amendment gives a witness an absolute right to resist interrogation, if the testimony sought would tend to incriminate him. A grant of immunity may strip the witness of the right to refuse to testify, but only if it is broad enough to eliminate all possibility that the testimony will in fact operate to incriminate him. It must put him in precisely the same position, vis-a-vis the government that has compelled his testimony, as he would have been in had he remained silent in reliance on the privilege. . . .

I do not see how it can suffice merely to put the burden of proof on the Government. First, contrary to the Court's assertion, the Court's rule does leave the witness "dependent for the preservation of his rights upon the integrity and good faith of the prosecuting authorities." . . . Second, even their good faith is not a sufficient safeguard. For the paths of information through the investigative bureaucracy may well be long and winding, and even a prosecutor acting in the best of faith cannot be certain that somewhere in the depths of his investigative apparatus, often including hundreds of employees, there was not some prohibited use of the compelled testimony. . . . The Court today sets out a loose net to trap tainted evidence and prevent its use against the witness, but it accepts an intolerably great risk that tainted evidence will in fact slip through that net. . . .

The distinction between "transactional" immunity and "use" immunity is important, since the latter affords substantially less protection. If one is given transactional immunity, then he cannot be prosecuted for any crime for which he has given incriminating testimony. But if he is afforded only use immunity, then he may still be subject to prosecution for such crimes so long as the prosecution can build its case on evidence or testimony obtained independently of any use of the witness's testimony. As pointed out in the Douglas dissent, it may be impossible to determine whether the prosecution has pursued leads from the testimony in order to convict.

### The Problem of Immunity and Federalism

Both the States and the federal government have statutes trading immunity for information, and these date back more than a century. Some of the provisions apply to specific kinds of crimes, while others are more broadly drawn to cover any criminal offense. It is not uncommon to find a multiplicity of statutes in a single State dealing with the matter of immunity. New York, for example, has more than twoscore provisions under which witnesses may obtain immunity in return for giving testimony.

Since a single act can constitute both a federal and a state crime, the familiar complications of federalism arise in connection with immunity granted by one but not both jurisdictions. Does a grant of immunity by one jurisdiction carry with it insulation against prosecutions by the other based on the testimony? If not, is that fact sufficient to support a refusal to testify grounded on fear of incrimination?

As stated earlier, it was not until the decision in Malloy v. Hogan, 378 U.S. 1 (1964), that the Court fully incorporated the Fifth Amendment privilege into the Fourteenth Amendment. Justice Brennan, for the majority, stated: "The Fourteenth Amendment secures against state invasion the same privilege that the Fifth Amendment guarantees against federal infringement—the right of a person to remain silent unless he chooses to speak in the unfettered exercise of his own will, and to suffer no penalty, as held in Twining, for such silence." In so holding, the Court reversed a contempt conviction for petitioner's refusal to answer questions relating to gambling activities, and held that the Twining rule can no longer be accepted as the appropriate standard for the exercise of the privilege. Under the double standard of Fifth and Fourteenth Amendment self-incrimination protection, a form of legalized coerced confession had been supported by the Court where the federal government could force testimony by extending immunity and subsequently the state government could prosecute for state crimes revealed. Conversely, the federal prosecutor could use testimony exacted by state officials in return for the limited immunity from state prosecution. These cases were reconsidered, and overruled, in light of Malloy v. Hogan, in a decision rendered on the same day as that case, in Murphy v. Waterfront Commission of New York Harbor.

MURPHY *v.* WATERFRONT COMMISSION OF NEW YORK HARBOR
*378 U.S. 52 (1964)*

[Petitioners were subpoenaed to testify at a hearing conducted by the Waterfront Commission of New York Harbor concerning a work stoppage at the Hoboken piers.

After refusing to respond to certain questions on the ground that the answers might tend to incriminate them, petitioners were granted immunity from prosecution under the laws of New Jersey and New York. Notwithstanding this grant of immunity, they still refused to respond to the questions on the ground that the answers might tend to incrimiante them under *federal* law, to which the grant of immunity did not purport to extend. Petitioners were thereupon held in civil and criminal contempt of court. The New Jersey Supreme Court affirmed the civil contempt judgments, holding that a state may constitutionally compel a witness to give testimony which might be used in a federal prosecution against him.]

Mr. Justice Goldberg delivered the opinion of the Court.

We have held today that the Fifth Amendment privilege against self-incrimination must be deemed fully applicable to the States through the Fourteenth Amendment. *Malloy* v. *Hogan*. . . . This case presents a related issue: whether one jurisdiction within our federal structure may compel a witness, whom it has immunized from prosecution under its laws, to give testimony which might then be used to convict him of a crime against another such jurisdiction. . . .

## I.  The Policies of the Privilege

The privilege against self-incrimination "registers an important advance in the development of our liberty—'one of the great landmarks in man's struggle to make himself civilized.' ". . . It reflects many of our fundamental values and most noble aspirations: our unwillingness to subject those suspected of crime to the cruel trilemma of self-accusation, perjury or contempt; our preference for an accusatorial rather than an inquisitorial system of criminal justice; our fear that self-incriminating statements will be elicited by inhumane treatment and abuses; our sense of fair play which dictates "a fair state-individual balance by requiring the government to leave the individual alone until good cause is shown for disturbing him and by requiring the government in its contest with the individual to shoulder the entire load,". . . ; our respect for the inviolability of the human personality and of the right of each individual "to a private enclave where he may lead a private life,". . . ; our distrust of self-deprecatory statements; and our realization that the privilege, while sometimes "a shelter to the guilty," is often "a protection to the innocent.". . .

Most, if not all, of these policies and purposes are defeated when a witness "can be whipsawed into incriminating himself under both state and federal law even though" the constitutional privilege against self-incrimination is applicable to each. . . . This has become especially true in our age of "cooperative federalism," where the Federal and State Governments are waging a united front against many types of criminal activity.

Respondent contends . . . that we should adhere to the "established rule" that the constitutional privilege against self-incrimination does not protect a witness in one jurisdiction against being compelled to give testimony which could be used to convict him in another jurisdiction. This "rule" has three decisional facets: *United States* v. *Murdock*, 284 U.S. 141 [1931], held that the Federal Government could compel a witness to give testimony which might incriminate him under state law; *Knapp* v. *Schweitzer*, 357 U.S. 371 [1958], held that a State could compel a witness to give testimony which might incriminate him under federal law; and *Feldman* v. *United States*, 322 U.S. 487 [1944], held that testimony thus compelled by a State could be introduced into evidence in the federal courts.

Our decision today in *Malloy* v. *Hogan, supra*, necessitates a reconsideration of this rule. Our review of the pertinent cases in this Court and of their English antecedents reveals that *Murdock* did not adequately consider the relevant authorities and has been significantly weakened by subsequent decisions of this Court, and, further, that the legal premises underlying *Feldman* and *Knapp* have since been rejected. . . .

[The opinion here gives a lengthy history of English and American cases on the self-incrimination issues through *Murdock, Knapp,* and *Feldman*, and then points out that in *Malloy* v. *Hogan* "the Court has today rejected" the rule which permits one government to use evidence obtained by another government under an immunity statute, "and with it, all the earlier cases resting on that rule."]

The foregoing makes it clear that there is no continuing legal vitality to, or historical justification for, the rule that one jurisdiction within our federal structure may compel a witness to give testimony which could be used to convict him of a crime in another jurisdiction.

## IV. Conclusions

In light of the history, policies and purposes of the privilege against self-incrimination, we now accept as correct the construction given the privilege by the English courts and by Chief Justice Marshall and Justice Holmes. . . . We reject—as unsupported by history or policy—the deviation from that construction only recently adopted by this Court in *United States* v. *Murdock*, and *Feldman* v. *United States*. We hold that the constitutional privilege against self-incrimination protects a state witness against incrimination under federal as well as state law and a federal witness against incrimination under state as well as federal law.

We must now decide what effect this holding has on existing state immunity legislation. In *Counselman* v. *Hitchcock*, 142 U.S. 547 [1892], this Court considered a federal statute which provided that no "evidence obtained from a party or witness by means of a judicial proceeding . . . shall be given in evidence, or in any manner used against him . . . in any court of the United States . . ." Notwithstanding this statute, appellant, claiming his privilege against self-incrimination, refused to answer certain questions before a grand jury. The Court said "that legislation cannot abridge a constitutional privilege, and that it cannot replace or supply one, at least unless it is so broad as to have the same extent in scope and effect.". . . Applying this principle to the facts of that case, the Court upheld appellant's refusal to answer on the ground that the statute: "could not, and would not, prevent the use of his testimony to search out other testimony to be used in evidence against him or his property, in a criminal proceeding in such court . . .", that it: "could not prevent the obtaining and the use of witnesses and evidence which should be attributable directly to the testimony he might give under compulsion, and on which he might be convicted, when otherwise, and if he had refused to answer, he could not possibly have been convicted . . .", and that it: "affords no protection against that use of compelled testimony which consists in gaining therefrom a knowledge of the details of a crime, and of sources of information which may supply other means of convicting the witness or party.". . .

Applying the holding of that case to our holdings today that the privilege against self-incrimination protects a state witness against federal prosecution . . . and that "the same standards must determine whether [a witness'] silence in either a federal or state proceeding is justified," *Malloy* v. *Hogan*, . . . we hold the constitutional rule to be that a state witness may not be compelled to give testimony which may be incriminating under federal law unless the compelled testimony and its fruits cannot be used in any manner by federal officials in connection with a criminal prosecution against him. We conclude, moreover, that in order to implement this constitutional rule and accommodate the interests of the State and Federal Governments in investigating crime, the Federal Government must be prohibited from making any such use of compelled testimony and its fruits. This exclusionary rule, while permitting the States to secure information necessary for effective law enforcement, leaves the witness and the Federal Government in substantially the same position as if the witness had claimed his privilege in the absence of a state grant of immunity.

It follows that petitioners here may now be compelled to answer the questions propounded to them. At the time they refused to answer, however, petitioners had a reasonable fear, based on this Court's decision in *Feldman* v. *United States*, that the federal authorities might use the answers against them in connection with a federal prosecution. We have now overruled *Feldman* and hold that the Federal Government may make no such use of the answers. Fairness dictates that petitioners should now be afforded an opportunity, in light of this development, to answer the questions. . . . Accordingly, the judgment of the New Jersey courts ordering petitioners to answer the questions may remain undisturbed. But the judgment of contempt is vacated and the cause remanded to the New Jersey Supreme Court for proceedings not inconsistent with this opinion.

*It is so ordered.*

Mr. Justice Black concurs in the judgment and opinion of the Court. . . .

Mr. Justice Harlan, whom Mr. Justice Clark joins, concurring in the judgment.

Unless I wholly misapprehend the Court's opinion, its holding that testimony compelled in a state proceeding over a witness' claim that such testimony will incriminate him may not be used against the witness in a federal criminal prosecution rests on *constitutional* grounds. On that basis, the contrary conclusion of *Feldman* v. *United States* . . . is overruled.

I believe that the constitutional holding of *Feldman* was correct, and would not overrule it. To the extent, however, that the decision in that case may have rested also on a refusal to exercise this Court's "supervisory power" over the administration of justice in federal courts, I think that it can no longer be considered good law. . . .

Part I of this opinion shows, I believe, that the Court's analysis of prior cases hardly furnishes an adequate basis for a new departure in constitutional law. Even if the Court's analysis were sound, however, it would not support reversal of the *Feldman* rule on *constitutional* grounds.

If the Court were correct in asserting that the "separate sovereignty" theory of self-incrimination should be discarded, that would, as the Court says, lead to the conclusion that "a state witness [is protected] against incrimination under federal as well as state law and a federal witness against incrimination under state as well as federal law.". . . However, dealing strictly with the situation presented by this case, that conclusion does *not* in turn lead to a constitutional rule that the testimony of a state witness (or evidence to which his testimony leads) who is compelled to testify in state proceedings may not be used against him in a federal prosecution. Protection which the Due Process Clause affords against the *States* is quite obviously not any basis for a constitutional rule regulating the conduct of *federal* authorities in *federal* proceedings.

The Court avoids this problem by mixing together the Fifth Amendment and the Fourteenth and talking about "the constitutional privilege against self-incrimination." Such an approach, which deals with "constitutional" rights at large, unrelated either to particular provisions of the Constitution or to relevant differences between the

States and the Federal Government warns of the dangers for our federalism to which the "incorporation" theory of the Fourteenth Amendment leads. . . .

The Court's reasons for overruling *Feldman* thus rest on an entirely new conception of the *Fifth Amendment*, namely that it applies to federal use of state-compelled incriminating testimony. The opinion, however, contains nothing at all to contradict the traditional, well-understood conception of the Fifth Amendment, to which, therefore, I continue to adhere. . . .

Accordingly, I cannot accept the majority's conclusion that a rule prohibiting federal authorities from using in aid of a federal prosecution incriminating testimony compelled in state proceedings is constitutionally required.

I would, however, adopt such a rule in the exercise of our supervisory power over the administration of federal criminal justice. . . . On this basis, I concur in the judgment of the Court.

Mr. Justice White, with whom Mr. Justice Stewart joins, concurring. . . .

### The Privilege, Registration Laws, and Compulsory Filing

Following the Kefauver Crime Committee investigation into crime and racketeering, Congress enacted the Gamblers' Occupational Tax Act in 1951. The Act levied a tax on persons engaged in the business of accepting wagers and required that they register with the Collector of Internal Revenue. In *United States* v. *Kahriger*, 345 U.S. 22 (1953), the Court, by a six-to-three vote, upheld the registration requirement against the claim that it violated the protection against self-incrimination. The majority reasoned that the privilege "has relation only to past acts, not to future acts that may or may not be committed." In dissenting, Justice Black said he was sure that the Act "creates a squeezing device contrived to put a man in federal prison if he refuses to confess himself into a state prison as a violator of state gambling law."

In *Marchetti* v. *United States*, 390 U.S. 39 (1968), and *Grosso* v. *United States*, 390 U.S. 62 (1968), the Court overruled *Kahriger*. Justice Harlan, writing for the majority in both cases, stated:

Substantial hazards of incrimination as to past or present acts plainly may stem from the requirements to register and to pay the occupational tax. . . . In the first place, satisfaction of those requirements increases the likelihood that any past or present gambling offenses will be discovered and successfully prosecuted. It both centers attention upon the registrant as a gambler, and compels "injurious disclosures" which may provide or assist in the collection of evidence admissible in a prosecution for past or present offenses. . . .

In *Leary* v. *United States*, 395 U.S. 6 (1969), the Court held, without dissent, that the elaborate registration provisions of the Marihuana Tax Act violated the defendant's privilege against self-incrimination. There was a "real and appreciable" risk where the law required an order form which issued only upon identification as a transferee of marijuana, and further provided for notification of such status to state law officers.

In the context of Communist activities controls the Court has considered other federal registration requirements. The Subversive Activities Control Act of 1950 required Communist-action organizations, as defined by the statute, to register with the Attorney General, such registration to include a list of individual members. The Act further provided that if the officers of a Communist-action organization failed to register, then the individual members become criminally liable if they fail to register themselves within sixty days after the registration order issued. After lengthy litigation, the self-incrimination issues were substantially settled by the Court. (The cases are treated at some length in Chapter 6 and will only briefly be reviewed here.)

In *Communist Party of the United States* v. *Subversive Activities Control Board*, 367 U.S. 1 (1961), the Court held that as to the officers of the Communist Party, the issue of whether the registration order violated the privilege against self-incrimination was premature. Justice Frankfurter, for the Court, stated:

> We cannot know now that the Party's officers will ever claim the privilege. . . . If a claim of privilege is made, it may or may not be honored by the Attorney General. We cannot, on the basis of supposition that the privilege will be claimed and not honored, proceed now to adjudicate the constitutionality under the Fifth Amendment of the registration provisions.

In *Albertson* v. *Subversive Activities Control Board*, 382 U.S. 70 (1965), however, the Court faced the issue squarely and ruled that as to the individual member of a Communist-action organization required to register, the requirement violated the privilege against self-incrimination. Justice Brennan, for the Court, noted that the Act had an immunity provision applicable to registrants, but he found that the immunity offered was incomplete. "It does not preclude the use of the admission as an investigatory lead, a use which is barred by the privilege."

## CONFESSIONS

While a confession is clearly a way in which one can incriminate himself, our present rules with respect to the use of confessions are not simply applications of the privilege to the subject of confessions. The privilege and the rule barring coerced confessions are different both in point of historical development and in the way they are applied. The privilege was firmly established by the late seventeenth century, but the rule barring forced confessions did not come until the late eighteenth century. In barring such confessions in federal proceedings, the Court did not rely on the Fifth Amendment privilege, but, instead, adopted a rule of evidence binding on the lower federal courts to accomplish the purpose. The phraseology of the privilege indicates strongly that it is to operate in official proceedings only—"in any criminal case." Such an interpretation would permit the use of a confession so long as it was obtained outside the formal proceedings of the court, grand jury, or legislative hearing. Thus a different basis than the privilege was considered necessary to afford the desired protection against coerced confessions. The federal bar to admission of coerced confessions originated, therefore, simply as a rule of evidence. Both this bar and the privilege against self-incrimination point in the same direction, of course, of guaranteeing to the accused fair play in the proceedings against him. As will be seen in the cases to follow, the prohibition against the use of coerced confessions has now been elevated to constitutional status as a requirement of due process of law.

Although the practice of barring coerced confessions in federal trials is an old one, it was not until 1936 that the court held that the introduction of coerced confessions in state prosecutions violated the Fourteenth Amendment's due process clause. The case was *Brown* v. *Mississippi*, and the Court was faced with the problem of qualifying an earlier statement made in *Twining* v. *New Jersey* relative to self-incrimination and due process. In *Twining* the Court had held that in a state criminal case, judicial comment to the jury concerning defendant's refusal to take the stand in his defense was not a violation of due process of law. In the last sentence of his opinion for the Court, Justice Moody had stated "We think that the exemption from compulsory self-incrimination in the courts of the States is not secured by any part of the Federal Constitution." In *Brown* v. *Mississippi* the state used this statement to support their argument that coerced confessions were within the holding of the *Twining* case and thus their admission as evidence did not violate the due process clause.

BROWN *v.* MISSISSIPPI
*297 U.S. 278 (1936)*

[Three Negroes were arrested on March 30, 1934, for the murder of one Raymond Stewart. Testimony indicated that police officers administered sustained and brutal whippings to all three men until they confessed to the crime. They were then told that if they changed their story at any time, additional beatings would be given. They were indicted on April 4, 1934, and were then arraigned and pleaded not guilty. Counsel were appointed by the court to defend them, and trial was begun the next morning. Aside from the confessions, there was no evidence sufficient to warrant the submission of the case to the jury. Testimony as to the confessions was received over the objection of defendants' counsel. Defendants then testified that the confessions were false and had been procured by physical torture. The case went to the jury with instructions, upon the request of defendants' counsel, that if the jury had reasonable doubt as to the confessions having resulted from coercion, *and that they were not true*, they were not to be considered as evidence. The jury found the three defendants guilty, and they were sentenced to death. The Mississippi Supreme Court affirmed the judgment.]

Mr. Chief Justice Hughes delivered the opinion of the Court.

The question in this case is whether convictions, which rest solely upon confessions shown to have been extorted by officers of the state by brutality and violence, are consistent with the due process of law required by the Fourteenth Amendment of the Constitution of the United States. . . .

The grounds of the decision were (1) that immunity from self-incrimination is not essential to due process of law; and (2) that the failure of a trial court to exclude the confessions after the introduction of evidence showing their incompetency, in the absence of a request for such exclusion, did not deprive the defendants of life or liberty without due process of law; and that even if the trial court had erroneously overruled a motion to exclude the confessions, the ruling would have been mere error reversible on appeal, but not a violation of constitutional right. . . .

1. The state stresses the statement in *Twining* v. *New Jersey*, 211 U.S. 78, 114, that "exemption from compulsory self-incrimination in the courts of the states is not secured by any part of the Federal Constitution," and the statements in *Snyder* v. *Massachusetts*, 291 U.S. 97, 105, that "the privilege against self-incrimination may be withdrawn and the accused put upon the stand as a witness for the state." But the question of the right of the state to withdraw the privilege against self-incrimination is not here involved. The compulsion to which the quoted statements refer is that of the process of justice by which the accused may be called as a witness and required to testify. Compulsion by torture to extort a confession is a different matter.

The state is free to regulate the procedure of its courts in accordance with its own conceptions of policy, unless in so doing it "offends some principle of justice so rooted in the traditions and conscience of our people as to be ranked as fundamental." *Snyder* v. *Massachusetts, supra*. . . . The state may abolish trial by jury. It may dispense with indictment by a grand jury and substitute complaint or information. *Walker* v. *Sauvinet*, 92 U.S. 90; *Hurtado* v. *California*, 110 U.S. 516; *Snyder* v. *Massachusetts, supra*. But the freedom of the state in establishing its policy is the freedom of constitutional government and is limited by the requirement of due process of law. Because a state may dispense with a jury trial, it does not follow that it may substitute trial by ordeal. The rack and torture chamber may not be substituted for the witness stand. The state may not permit an accused to be hurried to conviction under mob domination—where the whole proceeding is but a mask—without supplying corrective process. *Moore* v. *Dempsey*, 261 U.S. 86. The state may not deny to the accused the aid of counsel. *Powell* v. *Alabama*, 287 U.S. 45. Nor may a state, through the action of its officers, contrive a conviction through the pretense of a trial which in truth is "but used as a means of depriving a defendant of liberty through a deliberate deception of court and jury by the presentation of testimony known to be perjured." *Mooney* v. *Holohan*, 294 U.S. 103. And the trial equally is a mere pretense where the state authorities have contrived a conviction resting solely upon confessions obtained by violence. The due process clause requires "that state action, whether through one agency or another, shall be consistent with the fundamental principles of liberty and justice which lie at the base of all our civil and political institutions." *Hebert* v. *Louisiana*, 272 U.S. 312. It would be difficult to conceive of methods more revolting to the sense of justice than those taken to procure the confessions of these petitioners, and the use of the confessions thus obtained as the basis for conviction and sentence was a clear denial of due process.

2. It is in this view that the further contention of the State must be considered. That contention rests upon the failure of counsel for the accused, who had objected to the admissibility of the confessions, to move for their exclusion after they had been introduced and the fact of coercion had been proved. It is a contention which proceeds upon a misconception of the nature of petitioners' complaint. That complaint is not of the commission of mere error, but of a wrong so fundamental that it made the whole proceeding a mere pretense of a trial and rendered the conviction and sentence wholly void. . . .

In the instant case, the trial court was fully advised by the undisputed evidence of the way in which the confessions had been procured. The trial court knew that there was no other evidence upon which conviction and sentence could be based. Yet it proceeded to permit conviction and to pronounce sentence. . . . The court thus denied a federal right fully established and specially set up and claimed, and the judgment must be reversed.

*It is so ordered.*

The Court has further made it clear that even though a coerced confession be considered truthful and reliable, its admission into evidence will void a conviction. Justice Frankfurter, speaking for the Court in *Rogers* v. *Richmond*, 365 U.S. 534 (1961), said:

Our decisions under [the Fourteenth] Amendment have made clear that convictions following the admission into evidence of confessions which are involuntary . . . cannot stand. This is so not because such confessions are unlikely to be true but because the methods used to extract them offend an underlying principle in the enforcement of our criminal law: that ours is an accusatorial and not an inquisitorial system—a system in which the State must establish guilt by evidence independently and freely secured and may not by coercion prove its charge against an accused out of his own mouth. . . .

From a fair reading of [expressions of the courts below], we cannot but conclude that the question whether Rogers' confessions were admissible into evidence was answered by reference to a legal standard which took into account the circumstance of probable truth or falsity. And this is not a permissible standard under the Due Process Clause of the Fourteenth Amendment.

Before proceeding further, a brief look should be taken at federal practice regarding admissibility of confessions. The Court has held coerced confessions inadmissible as a rule of evidence in federal prosecutions. In *McNabb* v. *United States*, 318 U.S. 332 (1943), the Court took another step and held inadmissible a confession obtained by federal authorities who had not promptly taken the accused before a committing officer (as required by Rule 5 of the Federal Rules of Criminal Procedure). Thus the rule laid down was that a confession was inadmissible in a federal prosecution if secured during a period of unlawful detention. In *Upshaw* v. *United States*, 333 U.S. 410 (1948), the Court held that such confessions are inadmissible even though there is no proof of improper pressures brought to bear in obtaining the confessions. This was not construed as a requirement of the Constitution, but was in the exercise of the Court's supervisory power over the lower federal courts. The rule was followed in the highly controversial decision in *Mallory* v. *United States*, 354 U.S. 449 (1957), which reversed a conviction and death sentence for rape in a federal case. Washington, D.C., police had apprehended petitioner and others around two-thirty one afternoon. Petitioner was questioned for some forty-five minutes by four officers and strenuously denied his guilt. Around four o'clock the suspects were asked to submit to "lie detector" tests, and they agreed. Petitioner's questioning began at about eight o'clock, and after an hour and a half of interrogation he stated that he had committed the crime. At ten o'clock that evening the police attempted to reach a United States Commissioner for the purpose of arraignment. Failing in this, they had petitioner examined by a deputy coroner, who noted no indications of physical or psychological coercion, and around midnight he dictated his confession to a typist. Not until the following morning was he brought before a commissioner, although, as the Court stated, "arraignment could easily have been made in the same building in which the police headquarters were housed."

Justice Frankfurter, speaking for the Court, cited Rule 5 (a), requiring that officers take an arrested person "without unnecessary delay before the nearest available commissioner," and 5 (b) relative to the commissioner's function:

The commissioner shall inform the defendant of the complaint against him, of his right to retain counsel and of his right to have a preliminary examination. He shall also inform the defendant that he is not required to make a statement and that any statement made by him may be used against him. The commissioner shall allow the defendant reasonable time and opportunity to consult counsel and shall admit the defendant to bail as provided in these rules.

We see, this time in congressional legislation, the juxtaposition of the privilege and the right to counsel. In pointing out the purpose of Rule 5 (a) and (b), Justice Frankfurter said, "Not until he had confessed, when any judicial caution had lost its purpose, did the police arraign him." Thus the Court followed the *McNabb* rule in holding the confession inadmissible as a device to force the police to follow the congressional requirement of prompt arraignment and avoid the "tempting utilization of intensive interrogation, easily gliding into the evils of 'the third degree'."

A great deal of criticism from a variety of sources was leveled at the Court following both the *McNabb* and the *Mallory* decisions, and bills were introduced in Congress after each decision to protect the admissibility of voluntary confessions. Exhaustive hearings were conducted on the matter by a Senate subcommittee and, the published material contains a wealth of information on problems of confessions and police detention, proposed legislation, and journal articles. [See Hearings before the Subcommittee on Constitutional Rights of the Committee on the Judiciary, United States Senate, 85th Cong., 2nd Sess., *Confessions and Police Detention* (U.S. Government Printing Ofc., 1958).]

It has been pointed out by many writers that the *McNabb-Mallory* rule would not necessarily bar the use of damaging *admissions* (as opposed to confessions, or complete acknowledgment of guilt), such as the names of witnesses or a hidden weapon or the location of a buried body. [See, for example, M. C. Slough, "Confessions and Admissions," 28 *Fordham L. Rev.* 96 (1959).] Rather than abandon the rule because of such weakness, however, the Court has moved to strengthen it in an attempt to close the loophole. *Gideon* v. *Wainwright*, 372 U.S. 335 (1963), had held that the Sixth Amendment's right to counsel was "incorporated" into the Fourteenth Amendment. But the key counsel decision in the context of the privilege against self-incrimination during police interrogation came in *Escobedo* v. *Illinois*, 378 U.S. 478 (1964).

Petitioner was arrested at 2:30 A.M. with a warrant and interrogated. He was released that afternoon pursuant to a writ of habeas corpus obtained by his lawyer. Several days later, he was again arrested and interrogated further. He asked to see his lawyer, who had arrived shortly thereafter at police headquarters, but the police refused. The lawyer asked permission to see Escobedo, and this request was refused. Notwithstanding repeated requests by each, the petitioner and his retained lawyer were afforded no opportunity to consult with each other during the course of the entire interrogation. During the course of the interrogation the petitioner made several damaging admissions implicating himself in the crime, and these statements were introduced into evidence. At no time was he advised of his constitutional right to remain silent. In reversing the conviction, Justice Goldberg stated for the majority of the Court:

We hold . . . that where, as here, the investigation is no longer a general inquiry into an unsolved crime but has begun to focus on a particular suspect, the suspect has been taken into police custody, the police carry out a process of interrogations that lends itself to eliciting incriminating statements, the suspect has requested and been denied an opportunity to consult with his lawyer, and the police have not effectively warned him of his absolute constitutional right to remain silent, the accused has been denied "the Assistance of Counsel" in violation of the Sixth Amendment to the Constitution as "made obligatory upon the States by the Fourteenth Amendment," *Gideon* v. *Wainwright*, and that no statement elicited by the police during the interrogation may be used against him at a criminal trial.

The logical conclusion suggested by *Escobedo* came in *Miranda* v. *Arizona*, 384 U.S. 436 (1966). Four cases were brought together for decision, and without specific concentration on the facts of these cases, the Court sought to lay down the governing principles concerning interrogation and the Fifth Amendment privilege.

### MIRANDA *v.* ARIZONA
### *384 U.S. 436 (1966)*

Mr. Chief Justice Warren delivered the opinion of the Court.

The cases before us raise questions which go to the roots of our concepts of American criminal jurisprudence: the restraints society must observe consistent with the Federal Constitution in prosecuting individuals for crime. More specifically, we deal with the admissibility of statements obtained from an individual who is subjected to custodial police interrogation and the necessity for procedures which assure that the individual is accorded his privilege under the Fifth Amendment to the Constitution not to be compelled to incriminate himself.

We dealt with certain phases of this problem recently in *Escobedo* v. *Illinois*. . . . There, as in the four cases before us, law enforcement officials took the defendant into custody and interrogated him in a police station for the purpose of obtaining a confession. The police did not effectively advise him of his right to remain silent or of his right to consult with his attorney. . . . We held that the statements thus made were constitutionally inadmissible.

This case has been the subject of judicial interpretation and spirited legal debate since it was decided two years ago. Both state and federal courts, in assessing its implications, have arrived at varying conclusions. . . . We granted certiorari in these cases . . . in order further to explore some facets of the problems, thus exposed, of applying the privilege against self-incrimination to in-custody interrogation, and to give concrete constitutional guidelines for law enforcement agencies and courts to follow.

We start here, as we did in *Escobedo*, with the premise that our holding is not an innovation in our jurisprudence, but is an application of principles long recognized and applied in other settings. We have undertaken a thorough reexamination of the *Escobedo* decision and the principles it announced, and we reaffirm it. . . . It was necessary in *Escobedo*, as here, to insure that what was proclaimed in the Constitution had not become but a "form of words,". . . in the hands of government officials. And it is in this spirit, consistent with our role as judges, that we adhere to the principles of *Escobedo* today.

Our holding will be spelled out with some specificity in the pages which follow, but briefly stated it is this: the prosecution may not use statements, whether exculpatory or inculpatory, stemming from custodial interrogation of the defendant unless it demonstrates the use of procedural safeguards effective to secure the privilege against self-incrimination. By custodial interrogation, we mean questioning initiated by law enforcement officers after a person has been taken into custody or otherwise deprived of his freedom of action in any significant way. As for the procedural safeguards to be employed, unless other fully effective means are devised to inform accused persons of their right of silence and to assure a continuous opportunity to exercise it, the following measures are required. Prior to any questioning, the person must be warned that he has a right to remain silent, that any statement he does make may be used as evidence against him, and that he has a right to the presence of an attorney, either retained or appointed. The defendant may waive effectuation of these rights, provided the waiver is made voluntarily, knowingly and intelligently. If, however, he indicates in any manner and at any stage of the process that he wishes to consult with an attorney before speaking, there can be no questioning. Likewise, if the individual is alone and indicates in any manner that he does not wish to be interrogated, the police may not question him. The mere fact that he may have answered some questions or volunteered some statements on his own does not deprive him of the right to refrain from answering any further inquiries until he has consulted with an attorney and thereafter consents to be questioned. . . .

An understanding of the nature and setting of this in-custody interrogation is essential to our decisions today. The difficulty in depicting what transpires at such interrogations stems from the fact that in this country they have largely taken place incommunicado. From extensive factual studies undertaken in the early 1930s including the famous Wickersham Report to Congress by a Presidential Commission, it is clear that police violence and the "third degree" flourished at that time. In a series of cases decided by this Court long after these studies, the police resorted to physical brutality—beatings, hanging, whipping—and to sustained and protracted questioning incommunicado in order to extort confessions. The Commission on Civil Rights in 1961 found much evidence to indicate that "some policemen still resort to physical force to obtain confessions.". . . The use of physical brutality and violence is not, unfortunately, relegated to the past or to any part of the country.

Only recently in Kings County, New York, the police brutally beat, kicked and placed lighted cigarette butts on the back of a potential witness under interrogation for the purpose of securing a statement incriminating a third party. . . .

. . . [W]e stress that the modern practice of in-custody interrogation is psychologically rather than physically oriented. As we have stated before, "Since *Chambers* v. *Florida* . . . this Court has recognized that coercion can be mental as well as physical, and that the blood of the accused is not the only hallmark of an unconstitutional inquisition." . . . Interrogation still takes place in privacy. Privacy results in secrecy and this in turn results in a gap in our knowledge as to what in fact goes on in the interrogation rooms. A valuable source of information about present police practices, however, may be found in various police manuals and texts which document procedures employed with success in the past, and which recommend various other effective tactics. [The opinion here quotes at length from a number of manuals and texts on criminal investigation.]

Even without employing brutality, the "third degree" or the specific strategems described above, the very fact of custodial interrogation exacts a heavy toll on individual liberty and trades on the weakness of individuals. . . .

It is obvious that such an interrogation environment is created for no purpose other than to subjugate the individual to the will of his examiner. This atmosphere carries its own badge of intimidation. To be sure, this is not physical intimidation, but is equally destructive of human dignity. The current practice of incommunicado interrogation is at odds with one of our Nation's most cherished principles—that the individual may not be compelled to incriminate himself. Unless adequate protective devices are employed to dispel the compulsion inherent in custodial surroundings, no statement obtained from the defendant can truly be the product of his free choice.

From the foregoing, we can readily perceive an intimate connection between the privilege against self-incrimination and police custodial questioning. . . .

. . . Our decision in no way creates a constitutional straightjacket which will handicap sound efforts at reform, nor is it intended to have this effect. We encourage Congress and the States to continue their laudable search for increasingly effective ways of protecting the rights of the individual while promoting efficient enforcement of our criminal laws. However, unless we are shown other procedures which are at least as effective in apprising accused persons of their right of silence and in assuring a continuous opportunity to exercise it, the following safeguards must be observed.

At the outset, if a person in custody is to be subjected to interrogation, he must first be informed in clear and unequivocal terms that he has a right to remain silent. For those unaware of the privilege, the warning is needed simply to make them aware of it—the threshold requirement for an intelligent decision as to its exercise. More important, such a warning is an absolute prerequisite in overcoming the inherent pressures of the interrogation atmosphere. It is not just the subnormal or woefully ignorant who succumb to an interrogator's imprecations, whether implied or expressly stated, that the interrogation will continue until a confession is obtained or that silence in the face of accusation is itself damning and will bode ill when presented to a jury. Further, the warning will show the individual that his interrogators are prepared to recognize his privilege should he choose to exercise it. . . .

The warning of the right to remain silent must be accompanied by the explanation that anything said can and will be used against the individual in court. This warning is needed in order to make him aware not only of the privilege, but also of the consequences of foregoing it. . . .

The circumstances surrounding in-custody interrogation can operate very quickly to overbear the will of one merely made aware of his privilege by his interrogators. Therefore, the right to have counsel present at the interrogation is indispensable to the protection of the Fifth Amendment privilege under the system we delineate today. Our aim is to assure that the individual's right to choose between silence and speech remains unfettered throughout the interrogation process. . . .

An individual need not make a pre-interrogation request for a lawyer. While such request affirmatively secures his right to have one, his failure to ask for a lawyer does not constitute a waiver. No effective waiver of the right to counsel during interrogation can be recognized unless specifically made after the warnings we here delineate have been given. The accused who does not know his rights and therefore does not make a request may be the person who most needs counsel. . . .

Accordingly we hold that an individual held for interrogation must be clearly informed that he has the right to consult with a lawyer and to have the lawyer with him during interrogation. . . . As with the warnings of the right to remain silent and that anything stated can be used in evidence against him, this warning is an absolute prerequisite to interrogation. No amount of circumstantial evidence that the person may have been aware of this right will suffice to stand in its stead. Only through such a warning is there ascertainable assurance that the accused was aware of this right.

If an individual indicates that he wishes the assistance of counsel before any interrogation occurs, the authorities cannot rationally ignore or deny his request on the basis that the individual does not have or cannot afford a retained attorney. The financial ability of the individual has no relationship to the scope of the rights involved here. The privilege against self-incrimination secured by the Constitution applies to all individuals. The need for counsel in order to protect the privilege exists for the indigent as well as the affluent. . . .

In order fully to apprise a person interrogated of the extent of his rights under this system then, it is necessary to warn him not only that he has the right to consult with an attorney, but also that if he is indigent a lawyer will be appointed to represent him. Without this additional warning, the admonition of the right to consult with counsel would often be understood as meaning only that he can consult with a lawyer if he has one or has the funds to obtain one. . . .

This does not mean, as some have suggested, that each police station must have a "station house lawyer" present at all times to advise prisoners. It does mean, however, that if police propose to interrogate a person they must make known to him that he is entitled to a lawyer and that if he cannot afford one, a lawyer will be provided for him prior to any interrogation. If authorities conclude that they will not provide counsel during a reasonable period of time in which investigaton in the field is carried out, they may refrain from doing so without violating the person's Fifth Amendment privilege so long as they do not question him during that time.

If the interrogation continues without the presence of an attorney and a statement is taken, a heavy burden rests on the government to demonstrate that the defendant knowingly and intelligently waived his privilege against self-incrimination and his right to retained or appointed counsel. . . .

The warnings required and the waiver necessary in accordance with our opinion today are, in the absence of a fully effective equivalent, prerequisites to the admissibility of any statement made by a defendant. No distinction can be drawn between statements which are direct confessions and statements which amount to "admissions" of part or all of an offense. The privilege against self-incrimination protects the individual from being compelled to incriminate himself in any manner; it does not distinguish degrees of incrimination. . . .

Our decision is not intended to hamper the traditional function of police officers in investigating crime. . . . When an individual is in custody on probable cause, the police may, of course, seek out evidence in the field to be used at trial against him. Such investigation may include inquiry of persons not under restraint. General on-the-scene questioning as to facts surrounding a crime or other general questioning of citizens in the fact-finding process is not affected by our holding. It is an act of responsible citizenship for individuals to give whatever information they may have to aid in law enforcement. In such situations the compelling atmosphere inherent in the process of in-custody interrogation is not necessarily present.

In dealing with statements obtained through interrogation, we do not purport to find all confessions inadmissable. Confessions remain a proper element in law enforcement. Any statement given freely and voluntarily without any compelling influences is, of course, admissible in evidence. The fundamental import of the privilege while an individual is in custody is not whether he is allowed to talk to the police without the benefit of warnings and counsel, but whether he can be interrogated. There is no requirement that police stop a person who enters a police station and states that he wishes to confess to a crime, or a person who calls the police to offer a confession or any other statement he desires to make. Volunteered statements of any kind are not barred by the Fifth Amendment and their admissibility is not affected by our holding today.

To summarize, we hold that when an individual is taken into custody or otherwise deprived of his freedom by the authorities in any significant way and is subjected to questioning, the privilege against self-incrimination is jeopardized. Procedural safeguards must be employed to protect the privilege, and unless other fully effective means are adopted to notify the person of his right of silence and to assure that the exercise of the right will be scrupulously honored, the following measures are required. He must be warned prior to any questioning that he has the right to remain silent, that anything he says can be used against him in a court of law, that he has the right to the presence of an attorney, and that if he cannot afford an attorney one will be appointed for him prior to any questioning if he so desires. Opportunity to exercise the rights must be afforded to him throughout the interrogation. After such warnings have been given, and such opportunity afforded him, the individual may knowingly and intelligently waive these rights and agree to answer questions or make a statement. But unless and until such warnings and waiver are demonstrated by the prosecution at trial, no evidence obtained as a result of interrogation can be used against him. . . .

[The Court finds that in each of the four cases under review confessions were obtained without appropriate warnings of constitutional rights.]

Mr. Justice Clark, dissenting [in part]. . . .

Such a strict constitutional specific inserted at the nerve center of crime detection may well kill the patient. Since there is at this time a paucity of information and an almost total lack of empirical knowledge on the practical operation of requirements truly comparable to those announced by the majority, I would be more restrained lest we go too far too fast. . . .

Mr. Justice Harlan, whom Mr. Justice Stewart and Mr. Justice White join, dissenting.

I believe the decision of the Court represents poor constitutional law and entails harmful consequences for the country at large. How serious these consequences may prove to be only time can tell. . . .

What the Court largely ignores is that its rules impair, if they will not eventually serve wholly to frustrate, an instrument of law enforcement that has long and quite reasonably been thought worth the price paid for it. There can be little doubt that the Court's new code would markedly decrease the number of confessions. To warn the suspect that he may remain silent and remind him that his confession may be used in court are minor obstructions. To require also an express waiver by the suspect and an end to questioning whenever he demurs must heavily handicap questioning. And to suggest or provide counsel for the suspect simply invites the end of the interrogation. . . .

How much harm this decision will inflict on law enforcement cannot fairly be predicted with accuracy. Evidence on the role of confessions is notoriously incomplete. . . . , and little is added by the Court's reference to the FBI experience and the resources believed wasted in interrogation. . . . We do know that some crimes cannot be solved without confessions, that ample expert testimony attests to their importance in crime control, and that the Court is taking a real risk with society's welfare in imposing its new regime on the country. The social costs of crime are too great to call the new rules anything but a hazardous experimentation. . . .

Mr. Justice White, with whom Mr. Justice Harlan and Mr. Justice Stewart join, dissenting. . . .

It may be noted that after Miranda's conviction was reversed, the State of Arizona retried him. His confession was not introduced in evidence, but the prosecution found a new witness—Miranda's common-law wife—who gave testimony sufficiently damaging to result in a second conviction and a resulting sentence of from twenty to thirty years on each count of kidnapping and rape. [For an excellent description of the entire Miranda case, from commission of the crime to final disposition, see Richard C. Cortner and Clifford M. Lytle, *Modern Constitutional Law* (New York: Free Press, 1971), pp. 158–198.]

In *Johnson* v. *New Jersey,* 384 U.S. 719 (1966), the Court held that *Miranda* and *Escobedo* would not be applied retroactively, and thus the rules of those cases would apply prospectively from the dates the decisions were handed down.

In *Berkemer* v. *McCarty,* 468 U.S. 420 (1984), the Court held that the roadside questioning of a motorist detained pursuant to a routine traffic stop does not constitute "custodial interrogation" for the purposes of the *Miranda* rule. However, if a motorist who has been detained pursuant to a traffic stop thereafter is subjected to treatment that renders him "in custody" for practical purposes, he is entitled to the full panoply of protections prescribed by *Miranda*. McCarty had been stopped for driving erratically, and was asked to get out of the car. When he could not perform a field sobriety test without falling, the officer asked him if he had been using intoxicants. He replied that he had drunk two beers and had smoked marihuana a short time before. The officer then formally arrested him, drove him to a county jail, and resumed questioning without providing *Miranda* warnings. The Court held that the incriminating statements made after arrest were inadmissible, but that since he was not taken into custody for the pruposes of *Miranda* until he was formally arrested, his statements made prior to that point were admissible against him.

In *New York* v. *Quarles,* 467 U.S. 649 (1984), the Court made yet another exception to the *Miranda* rule. The record in the case showed that a woman approached police officers who were on road patrol, told them that she had just been raped, described her assailant, and told them that the man had just entered a nearby supermarket and was carrying a gun. One officer entered the store and spotted Quarles, who matched the description given by the woman. Quarles ran toward the rear of the store, and the officer pursued him with a drawn gun, but lost sight of him for several seconds. Upon catching up with him, the officer ordered him to stop and put his hands over his head. He then frisked Quarles and discovered that he was wearing an empty shoulder holster. After handcuffing him, he asked where the gun was. Quarles nodded toward some empty cartons and responded that "the gun is over there." The officer retrieved the gun, formally arrested Quarles and read him his *Miranda* rights. He indicated that he would answer questions without an attorney present and admitted that he owned the gun. The trial court excluded his initial statement and the gun because of failure to give the *Miranda* warning and also excluded his other statements as evidence tainted by the *Miranda* violation. The New York Court of Appeals affirmed, but the Supreme Court reversed. Justice Rehnquist, for the majority, stated: "We believe that this case presents a situation where concern for public safety must be paramount to adherence to the literal language of the prophylactic rules enunciated in *Miranda*." He thus announced a "public safety" exception to the rule, pointing out that so long as the gun was concealed somewhere in the supermarket, with its actual whereabouts unknown, "it obviously posed more than one danger to the public safety: an accomplice might make use of it, a customer or employee might later come upon it." And had *Miranda* warnings deterred Quarles from answering, danger to the public might have resulted. In response to the charge that the decision would lessen the desirable clarity of the *Miranda* rule, the opinion stated:

The exception will not be difficult for police officers to apply because in each case it will be circumscribed by the exigency which justifies it. We think police officers can and will distinguish almost instinctively between questions necessary to secure their own safety or the safety of the public and questions designed solely to elicit testimonial evidence from a suspect.

Justice Marshall, speaking for three dissenters, charged that the majority had abandoned the clear guidelines of *Miranda* and "condemns the American judiciary to a new era of *post hoc* inquiry into the propriety of custodial interrogations." He noted that New York had failed to prosecute on the rape charge, and the sole charge was criminal possession of a weapon. He also expressed doubt that police officers can "distinguish almost instinctively" questions tied to public safety and questions designed to elicit testimonial evidence. "In many cases—like this one—custodial questioning may serve both purposes. It is therefore wishful thinking for the majority to suggest that the intuitions of police officers will render its decision self-executing."

In *Colorado* v. *Spring*, 55 LW 4162 (1987), the Court held 7–2 that officers need not inform a defendant of the subject matter of an interrogation for a waiver to be "knowing and intelligent." Federal firearms agents received information linking the defendant to two different crimes: a federal crime of transporting guns in interstate commerce and a Colorado homicide. The agents arrested him, warned him of his rights, received a waiver and began questioning. They began with the weapons offense and then switched to questions about the Colorado murder. The defendant said, "I shot another guy once," but when asked whether he had shot a man named Walker, he said, "No." Two months later, Colorado police brought Spring in for questioning and gave him the *Miranda* warnings. He signed a waiver and then confessed to the Colorado murder. The Colorado Supreme Court excluded the confession as invalid because the federal agents failed to inform the defendant of the subject matter of the interrogation, and thus the Colorado confession was the "fruit of the poisonous tree." Justice Powell, for the majority on the United States Supreme Court, said that knowledge of what the questioning will be about is not necessary to make a waiver "voluntary," and to label the defendant's first statement "compelled" in violation of the Fifth Amendment would "strain the meaning of compulsion beyond the breaking point."

Another problem which is sometimes treated in the context of coerced confessions, although not involving testimonial utterances in any way, is the question of the legality of obtaining evidence from the actual person of the accused. Use of the person for identification purposes has long been sanctioned. The point was discussed by Justice Holmes in *Holt* v. *United States*, 218 U.S. 245, 252–253, in 1910:

Another objection is based upon an extravagant extension of the Fifth Amendment. A question arose as to whether a blouse belonged to the prisoner. A witness testified that the prisoner put it on and it fitted him. It is objected that he did this under the same duress that made his statements inadmissible, and that it should be excluded for the same reasons. But the prohibition of compelling a man in a criminal court to be witness against himself is a prohibition of the use of physical or moral compulsion *to extort communications from him,* not an exclusion of his body as evidence when it may be material. The objection in principle would forbid a jury to look at a prisoner and compare his features with a photograph in proof. (Italics added.)

As Justice Holmes stated, the person may even be used in supplying evidentiary proof over and above mere identification—as in trying on a blouse found at the scene of the crime. The problem is really one of coerced *evidence* rather than coerced confessions, although it is frequently put in the latter category. The question of how far the police can go in obtaining evidence from the person of the accused is thus better viewed as simply a due process question rather than in the context of self-incrimination. In this framework it is easier to distinguish the holdings in the two cases to follow: *Rochin* v. *California* and *Breithaupt* v. *Abram*.

### ROCHIN *v.* CALIFORNIA
### *342 U.S. 165 (1952)*

Mr. Justice Frankfurter delivered the opinion of the Court.

Having "some information that [the petitioner] was selling narcotics," three deputy sheriffs of the County of Los Angeles, on the morning of July 1, 1949, made for the two-story dwelling house in which Rochin lived with his mother, his common-law wife, brothers and sisters. Finding the outside door open, they entered and then forced open the door to Rochin's room on the second floor. Inside they found petitioner sitting partly dressed on the side of the bed, upon which his wife was lying. On a "night stand" beside the bed the deputies spied two capsules. When asked "Whose stuff is this?" Rochin seized the capsules and put them in his mouth. A struggle ensued, in the course of which the three officers "jumped upon him" and attempted to extract the capsules. The force they applied proved unavailing against Rochin's resistance. He was handcuffed and taken to a hospital. At the direction of one of the officers a doctor forced an emetic solution through a tube into Rochin's stomach against his will. This "stomach pumping" produced vomiting. In the vomited matter were found two capsules which proved to contain morphine.

Rochin was brought to trial before a California Superior Court, sitting without a jury, on the charge of possessing "a preparation of morphine". . . . Rochin was convicted and sentenced to sixty days' imprisonment. The chief evidence against him was the two capsules. They were admitted over petitioner's objection, although the means of obtaining them was frankly set forth in the testimony by one of the deputies, substantially as here narrated.

On appeal, the District Court of Appeal affirmed the conviction, despite the finding that the officers "were guilty of unlawfully breaking into and entering defendant's room and were guilty of unlawfully assaulting and battering, torturing and falsely imprisoning the defendant at the alleged hospital." . . . The Supreme Court of California denied without opinion Rochin's petition for a hearing. Two justices dissented from this denial. . . .

This Court granted certiorari. . . because a serious question is raised as to the limitations which the Due Process Clause of the Fourteenth Amendment imposes on the conduct of criminal proceedings by the States. . . .

. . . Regard for the requirements of the Due Process Clause "inescapably imposes upon this Court an exercise of judgment upon the whole course of the proceedings [resulting in a conviction] in order to ascertain whether they offend those canons of decency and fairness which express the notions of justice of English-speaking peoples even toward those charged with the most heinous offenses." *Malinski* v. *New York*. . . . These standards of justice are not authoritatively formulated anywhere as though they were specifics. Due process of law is a summarized constitutional guarantee of respect for those personal immunities which, as Mr. Justice Cardozo twice wrote for the Court, are "so rooted in the traditions and conscience of our people as to be ranked as fundamental," *Snyder* v. *Massachusetts,* 291 U.S. 97, 105, or are "implicit in the concept of ordered liberty." *Palko* v. *Connecticut,* 302 U.S. 319, 325. . . .

Applying these general considerations to the circumstances of the present case, we are compelled to conclude that the proceedings by which this conviction was obtained do more than offend some fastidious squeamishness or private sentimentalism about combatting crime too energetically. It is conduct that shocks the conscience. Illegally breaking into the privacy of the petitioner, the struggle to open his mouth and remove what was there, the forcible extraction of his stomach's contents—this course of proceeding by agents of government to obtain evidence is bound to offend even hardened sensibilities. They are methods too close to the rack and the screw to permit of constitutional differentiation.

It has long since ceased to be true that due process of law is heedless of the means by which otherwise relevant and credible evidence is obtained. Even before the series of recent cases enforced the constitutional principle the States could not base convictions upon confessions, however much verified, but obtained by coercion. These decisions are not arbitrary exceptions to the comprehensive right of States to fashion their own rules of evidence for criminal trials. They are not sports in our constitutional law but applications of a general principle. They are only instances of the general requirement that States in their prosecutions respect certain decencies of civilized conduct. Due process of law, as a historic and generative principle, precludes defining, and thereby confining, these standards of conduct more precisely than to say that convictions cannot be brought about by methods that offend "a sense of justice." See Mr. Chief Justice Hughes, speaking for a unanimous Court in *Brown* v. *Mississippi,* 297 U.S. 278, 285, 286. It would be a stultification of the responsibility which the course of constitutional history has cast upon this Court to hold that in order to convict a man the police cannot extract by force what is in his mind but can extract what is in his stomach.

To attempt in this case to distinguish what lawyers call "real evidence" from verbal evidence is to ignore the reasons for excluding coerced confessions. Use of involuntary verbal confessions in State criminal trials is constitutionally obnoxious not only because of their unreliability. They are inadmissible under the Due Process Clause even though statements contained in them may be independently established as true. Coerced confessions offend the community's sense of fair play and decency. So here, to sanction the brutal conduct which naturally enough was condemned by the court whose judgment is before us, would be to afford brutality the cloak of law. Nothing would be more calculated to discredit law and thereby to brutalize the temper of a society. . . .

We are not unmindful that hypothetical situations can be conjured by shading imperceptibly from the circumstances of this case and by graduations producing practical differences despite seemingly logical extensions. But the Constitution is "intended to preserve practical and substantial rights, not to maintain theories." *Davis* v. *Mills,* 194 U.S. 451, 457.

On the facts of this case the conviction of the petitioner has been obtained by methods that offend the Due Process Clause. The judgment below must be

*Reversed.*

Mr. Justice Minton took no part in the consideration or decision of this case.

Mr. Justice Black, concurring.

*Adamson* v. *California,* 332 U.S. 46, 68–123, sets out reasons for my belief that state as well as federal courts and law enforcement officers must obey the Fifth Amendment's command that "No person . . . shall be compelled in any criminal case to be a witness against himself." I think a person is compelled to be a witness against himself not only when he is compelled to testify, but also when, as here, incriminating evidence is forcibly taken from him by a contrivance of modern science. Cf. *Boyd* v. *United States,* 116 U.S. 616; . . . California convicted this petitioner by using against him evidence obtained in this manner, and I agree with Mr. Justice Douglas that the case should be reversed on this ground. . . .

Mr. Justice Douglas, concurring. . . .

As an orginal matter it might be debatable whether the provision in the Fifth Amendment that no person "shall be compelled in any criminal case to be a witness against himself" serves the ends of justice. Not all civilized legal procedures recognize it. But the choice was made by the Framers, a choice which sets a standard for legal trials in this country. The Framers made it a standard of due process for prosecutions by the Federal Government. If it is a requirement of due process for a trial in the federal court house, it is impossible for me to say it is not a requirement of due process for a trial in the state court house. . . . Of course an accused can be compelled to be present at the trial, to stand, to sit, to turn this way or that, and to try on a cap or a coat. See *Holt* v. *United States,* 218 U.S. 245, 252. 253. But I think that words taken from his lips, capsules taken from his stomach, blood taken from his veins are all inadmissible provided that are taken from him without his consent. They are inadmissible because of the command of the Fifth Amendment. . . .

In this concurring opinion, Justice Douglas put "blood taken from his veins" in the same area of constitutional protection as capsules taken from the stomach. He stated that in either case they are inadmissible if taken from the accused without his consent. Five years later the Court was faced with this exact question in *Breithaupt* v. *Abram,* 352 U.S. 432 (1957). Differences in approach among the justices which were indicated in *Rochin* resulted in a sharp split in the vote in *Breithaupt.*

While driving a pickup truck in New Mexico, Breithaupt was involved in a collision with a passenger car. Three occupants of the car were killed, and Breithaupt was seriously injured. He was taken to a hospital and while lying unconscious in the emergency room the smell of liquor was detected on his breath. A state patrolman requested that a sample of petitioner's blood be taken. An attending physician, while petitioner was unconscious, withdrew a blood sample, and subsequent laboratory analysis showed his blood to contain about .17 percent alcohol. Testimony regarding the blood test was admitted, over petitioner's objection, in a trial for involuntary manslaughter. He was convicted and sentenced and later, on a petition for habeas corpus, contended that the use of the blood test deprived him of his liberty without due process of law. By a six-to-three vote the Supreme Court held that there was no violation of the Fourteenth Amendment, and that there was no proper analogy to *Rochin.* Justice Clark, for the majority, stated:

Basically the distinction rests on the fact that there is nothing "brutal" or "offensive" in the taking of a sample of blood when done, as in this case, under the protective eye of a physician. To be sure, the driver here was unconscious when the blood was taken, but the absence of conscious consent, without more, does not necessarily render the taking a violation of a constitutional right; and certainly the test as administered here would not be considered offensive by even the most delicate. . . . The blood test procedure has become routine in our everyday life. It is a ritual for those going into the military service as well as those applying for marriage licenses. Many colleges require such tests before permitting entrance and literally millions of us have voluntarily gone through the same, though a longer routine, in becoming blood donors. . . . We therefore conclude that a blood test taken by a skilled technician is not such "conduct that shocks the conscience," *Rochin*, . . . nor such a method of obtaining evidence that it offends a "sense of justice," *Brown* v. *Mississippi*. . . .

Chief Justice Warren, joined by Justices Black and Douglas, dissented. He stated:

The judgment in this case should be reversed if *Rochin* v. *California*. . . is to retain its vitality and stand as more than an instance of personal revulsion against particular police methods. . . .

Only personal reaction to the stomach pump and the blood test distinguish them. To base the restriction which the Due Process Clause imposes on state criminal procedures upon such reactions is to build on shifting sands. We should, in my opinion, hold that due process means at least that law enforcement officers in their efforts to obtain evidence from persons suspected of crime must stop short of bruising the body, breaking skin, puncturing tissue or extracting body fluids, whether they contemplate doing it by force or by stealth.

In *Schmerber* v. *California*, 384 U.S. 757 (1966) the Court ruled on the admissibility of a blood test report on intoxication where the blood sample was taken from the injured petitioner despite his refusal, on the advice of counsel, to consent to the test. He contended that the admission of such evidence violated due process under the Fourteenth Amendment, his privilege against self-incrimination under the Fifth Amendment, his right to counsel under the Sixth Amendment, and the prohibitions against unreasonable searches and seizures under the Fourth Amendment, as these have been incorporated into the Fourteenth Amendment. The Court stated that in view of the important decisions rendered since *Breithaupt* v. *Abram* (viz., *Escobedo* v. *Illinois*, *Malloy* v. *Hogan*, and *Mapp* v. *Ohio*), certiorari was granted to reconsider the questions. Justice Brennan, speaking for a majority of five, stated: "We hold that the privilege protects an accused only from being compelled to testify against himself, or otherwise provide the State with evidence of a testimonial or communicative nature, and that the withdrawal of blood and use of the analysis in question in this case did not involve compulsion to these ends." The due process contention was rejected squarely on the basis of *Breithaupt*, and the majority concluded that no substantial right to counsel issue was presented. On the Fourth Amendment claim, the Court stated that there was probable cause to believe petitioner to be intoxicated, that the officer therefore made a lawful arrest, and that the ordering of the blood test without a warrant was "an appropriate incident to petitioner's arrest" in order to prevent the "destruction of evidence" by normal physiological elimination of blood alcohol. Justices Harlan and Stewart concurred, with the only additional comment that "While agreeing with the Court that the taking of this blood test involved no testimonial compulsion, I would go further and hold that apart from this consideration the case in no way implicates the Fifth Amendment." Chief Justice Warren and Justices Black and Douglas dissented, following their views expressed in *Breithaupt*.

Questions have also been raised as to whether the use of the breathalyzer on persons suspected of driving while intoxicated violated the privilege against self-incrimination. *South Dakota* v. *Neville*, 459 U.S. 553 (1983), in effect answered the question in the context of blood-alcohol tests. A South Dakota statute permits a person suspected of driving while intoxicated to refuse to submit to a blood-alcohol test, but authorizes revocation of the driver's license of a person so refusing the test and permits such refusal to be used against him at trial. When Neville was arrested, the officers asked him to submit to the test and warned him that he could lose his license if he refused, but did not warn him that the refusal could be used against him at trial. He refused to take the test, stating "I'm too drunk, I won't pass the test." The South Dakota Supreme Court held that the use of the refusal to take the test at the trial violated the privilege against self-incrimination, and on certiorari the United States Supreme Court reversed on a seven-to-two vote. Justice O'Connor, for the majority, argued that the rule of *Schmerber* v. *California* clearly supported the law.

*Schmerber* . . . clearly allows a State to force a person suspected of driving while intoxicated to submit to a blood alcohol test. South Dakota, however, has declined to authorize its police officers to administer a blood-alcohol test against the suspect's will. Rather, to avoid violent confrontations, the South Dakota statute permits a suspect to refuse the test, and indeed requires police officers to inform the suspect of his right to refuse. . . . This permission is not without a price, however. South Dakota law authorizes the department of public safety, after providing the person who has refused the test an opportunity for a hearing, to revoke for one year both the person's license to drive and any nonresident operating privileges he may possess. . . . Such a penalty for refusing to take a blood-alcohol test is unquestionably legitimate, assuming appropriate procedural protections. . . .

. . . [T]he officers specifically warned respondent that failure to take the test could lead to loss of driving privileges for one year. It is true the officers did not inform respondent of the further consequence that evidence of refusal could be used against him in court, but we think it unrealistic to say that the warnings given here implicitly assure a suspect that no consequences other than those mentioned will occur. . . . [W]e hold that such a failure to warn was not the sort of implicit promise to forego use of evidence that would unfairly "trick" respondent if the evidence were later offered against him at trial.

In *Winston* v. *Lee*, 470 U.S. 753 (1985), the Court followed *Schmerber* in employing a balancing test to determine whether the state's interest was sufficient to justify a surgical intrusion in the body of the suspect. A shopkeeper was wounded during an attempted robbery, but he managed to shoot his assailant in the side. The assailant then ran from the scene. Shortly after the vicitim was taken to a hospital, police officers found Lee, who was suffering from a gunshot wound to his left chest area, eight blocks away from the shooting. He was taken to the hospital, where the victim identified him as the assailant. After investigation, the police charged Lee with attempted robbery. The State then moved for a court order directing him to undergo surgery to remove a bullet lodged under his left collarbone, asserting that the bullet would provide evidence of his guilt or innocence. The state court granted the motion. X-rays taken later showed that the bullet was lodged deeply enough to require that general anesthetic would be necessary during the surgery. The Supreme Court reversed by a unanimous vote, holding that a compelled surgical intrusion into an individual's body for evidence implicated expectations of privacy and security of such magnitude that the intrusion may be "unreasonable" under the Fourth Amendment even if likely to produce evidence of a crime.

While taking fingerprints may not implicate the Fifth Amendment, the procedures employed may still run afoul of the protection of the Fourth Amendment. *Davis* v. *Mississippi,* 394 U.S. 721 (1969), involved the admissibility of fingerprints taken at a police station in a trial and conviction for rape. The victim could give no better description of her assailant than that he was a Negro youth. Fingerprints were found on a window sill, and over a period of ten days the police, without warrants, took at least twenty-four Negro youths to police headquarters where they were questioned briefly, fingerprinted, and released. The petitioner's prints matched those taken from the window sill, and he was tried and convicted. The Court reversed the conviction, holding that the unauthorized detention and fingerprinting of large numbers of persons, without probable cause to arrest, violated the Fourth Amendment.

In *United States* v. *Dionisio,* 410 U.S. 1 (1973), however, the Court held that a grand jury witness could be compelled to furnish a voice exemplar, and the fact that some twenty persons were subpoenaed for this purpose, without probable cause, did not require a holding of violation of either the Fourth or the Fifth Amendments. Dionisio had been held in contempt for refusing to comply with the instruction, but the Court of Appeals reversed on authority of *Davis,* reasoning that the dragnet effect had the same invidious effect on Fourth Amendment rights as had occurred in that case. The Supreme Court held, through Justice Stewart, that "Since neither the summons to appear before the grand jury, nor its directive to make a voice recording infringed upon any interest protected by the Fourth Amendment, there was no justification for requiring the grand jury to satisfy even the minimal requirement of 'reasonableness' imposed by the Court of Appeals." A person's voice, like his facial characteristics or handwriting, "is repeatedly produced for others to hear." And there is no intrusion which would present a Fourth Amendment violation. In *United States* v. *Mara,* 410 U.S. 19 (1973), the Court upheld the right of a grand jury to require the production of handwriting exemplars even though no preliminary showing of reasonableness was made.

The Court has also held admissible fingernail scrapings taken in a police station from one who was not under arrest but where probable cause to arrest existed. The case was *Cupp* v. *Murphy,* 412 U.S. 291 (1973). Murphy's wife was killed by strangulation in her home, and abrasions and lacerations were found on her throat. There was no sign of a break-in or robbery. Murphy, who was not living with his wife, was notified, and he voluntarily went to the station house for questioning. There the police noticed a dark spot on Murphy's finger and suspected that it might be dried blood. They asked if they might take a sample of scrapings and were refused. They took a sample anyhow, over his protest, and found it to contain traces of skin and blood cells and also fabric from the victim's nightgown. This evidence was admitted at the trial and Murphy was convicted of second-degree murder. In reversing the District Court's denial of habeas corpus, the Court of Appeals concluded that, absent arrest or other exigent circumstances, the search was unconstitutional. The Supreme Court reversed, holding that "on the facts of the case, considering the existence of probable cause, the very limited intrusion undertaken incident to the station-house detention, and the ready destructibility of the evidence," there was no violation of the Fourth Amendment.

## THE RIGHT TO COUNSEL

One of the most important rights of one accused of crime is the right to be represented by counsel. At common law a defendant had the right to employ counsel when charged with a misdemeanor, but not in cases of treason or felony. The theory apparently was that the Crown might err in petty offenses, but in the graver charges no case would be brought unless the evidence was so clear that guilt was evident. Therefore no lawyer was necessary, and the judge would see that procedures were fair. Full right of counsel was not extended by Parliament until 1836, much later than in the United States. Congress provided for the assistance of counsel in the original Judiciary Act of 1789, and in most of the original states the right was granted to accused persons whether in misdemeanor or felony cases.

It should be noted, however, that the original meaning of the right to counsel extended only to permission for the accused to employ and bring in to the trial a lawyer of his choosing. No general provision was made for the indigent defendant who might want and even badly need counsel, but who was too poor to employ a lawyer. Thus the Sixth Amendment provision for "assistance of counsel for his defense" in "all criminal prosecutions" was permissive only. It imposed no duty on the government to provide free counsel. The Federal Crimes Act of 1790, however, provided that counsel must be appointed in all capital cases at the request of the defendant. And Delaware, Pennsylvania, and South Carolina by 1789 had similar provisions. Connecticut apparently went further and the judges appointed counsel upon request if they felt that the accused needed it. With these exceptions, the "right to counsel" only gave the accused the right to hire a lawyer. In construing the federal requirement under the Sixth Amendment and under the Act of 1790, the Court held that neither the Constitution nor the statutes made court-appointed counsel mandatory in noncapital cases. Referring to the 1790 statute, which required counsel in all capital cases, the Court said, "There would appear to be a negative pregnant here." *United States* v. *Van Duzee*, 140 U.S. 169, 173 (1891). Thus it concluded that no appointment need be made in any other type of case. It did leave the trial court with discretion to appoint counsel in noncapital cases if the judge saw fit, but it held that there was neither constitutional nor statutory duty to do so. As recently as 1931 this interpretation received official recognition. The Wickersham Commission, appointed by President Hoover to investigate law enforcement, stated in its report in that year: "[T]he right guaranteed is one of employing counsel, not one of having counsel provided by the Government." [U.S. National Commission on Law Observance and Enforcement, *Report on Prosecution* 30 (U.S. Government Printing Ofc., 1931). See J. A. C. Grant, "Our Common Law Constitution," 40 *B. U. L. Rev.* 1, 5–10 (1960); David Fellman, *The Defendant's Rights Today* (Madison: Univ. of Wisconsin Press, 1976), chap. 7.]

While the exact scope of the Sixth Amendment's right to counsel was as yet undefined, the Court had occasion in 1932 to examine the question of the application of the Fourteenth Amendment's due process clause to the matter of counsel in state criminal proceedings. This was in the famous Scottsboro case of *Powell* v. *Alabama*.

### POWELL *v.* ALABAMA
#### 287 U.S. 45 (1932)

Mr. Justice Sutherland delivered the opinion of the Court.

These cases were argued together and submitted for decision as one case.

The petitioners, hereafter referred to as defendants, are negroes charged with the crime of rape, committed upon the persons of two white girls. The crime is said to have been committed on March 25, 1931. The indictment was returned in a state court of first instance on March 31, and the record recites that on the same day the defendants were arraigned and entered pleas of not guilty. There is a further recital to the effect that upon the arraignment they were represented by counsel. But no counsel had been employed, and aside from a statement made by the trial judge several days later during a colloquy immediately preceding the trial, the record does not disclose when, or under what circumstances, an appointment of counsel was made, or who was appointed. During the colloquy referred to, the trial judge, in response to a question, said that he had appointed all the members of the bar for the purpose of arraigning the defendants and then of course anticipated that the members of the bar would continue to help the defendants if no counsel appeared. Upon the argument here both sides accepted that as a correct statement of the facts concerning the matter.

There was a severance upon the request of the state, and the defendants were tried in three several groups, as indicated above. As each of the three cases was called for trial, each defendant was arraigned, and, having the indictment read to him, entered a plea of not guilty. Whether the original arraignment and pleas were regarded as ineffective is not shown. Each of the three trials was completed within a single day. Under the Alabama statute the punishment for rape is to be fixed by the jury, and in its discretion may be from ten years' imprisonment to death. The juries found defendants guilty and imposed the death penalty upon all. The trial court overruled motions for new trials and sentenced the defendants in accordance with the verdicts. The judgments were affirmed by the state supreme court. . . .

. . . It is perfectly apparent that the proceedings, from beginning to end, took place in an atmosphere of tense, hostile and excited public sentiment. During the entire time, the defendants were closely confined or were under military guard. The record does not disclose their ages, except that one of them was nineteen; but the record clearly indicates that most, if not all, of them were youthful, and they are constantly referred to as "the boys." They were ignorant and illiterate. All of them were residents of other states, where alone members of their families or friends resided.

However guilty defendants, upon due inquiry, might prove to have been, they were, until convicted, presumed to be innocent. It was the duty of the court having their cases in charge to see that they were denied no necessary incident of a fair trial. . . . The sole inquiry which we are permitted to make is whether the federal Constitution was contravened . . . whether the defendants were in substance denied the right of counsel, and if so, whether such denial infringes the due process clause of the Fourteenth Amendment. . . .

It is hardly necessary to say that, the right to counsel being conceded, a defendant should be afforded a fair opportunity to secure counsel of his own choice. Not only was that not done here, but such designation of counsel as was attempted was either so indefinite or so close upon the trial as to amount to a denial of effective and substantial aid in that regard. This will be amply demonstrated by a brief review of the record.

[The opinion then quotes from the record, indicating clearly that no specific designation of counsel was made until the time of trial, and even then on the basis of a volunteer who stated, "I will go ahead and help do anything I can do."]

And in this casual fashion the matter of counsel in a capital case was disposed of. . . .

. . . In any event, the circumstance lends emphasis to the conclusion that during perhaps the most critical period of the proceedings against these defendants, that is to say, from the time of their arraignment until the beginning of their trial, when consultation, thorough-going investigation and preparation were vitally important, the defendants did not have the aid of counsel in any real sense, although they were as much entitled to such aid during that period as at the trial itself. . . .

. . . The defendants, young, ignorant, illiterate, surrounded by hostile sentiment, haled back and forth under guard of soldiers, charged with an atrocious crime regarded with especial horror in the community where they were to be tried, were thus put in peril of their lives within a few moments after counsel for the first time charged with any degree of responsibility began to represent them. . . .

It never has been doubted by this court, or any other so far as we know, that notice and hearing are preliminary steps essential to the passing of an enforceable judgment, and that they, together with a legally competent tribunal having jurisdiction of the case, constitute basic elements of the constitutional requirement of due process of law. . . .

What, then, does a hearing include? Historically and in practice, in our own country at least, it has always included the right to the aid of counsel when desired and provided by the party asserting the right. The right to be heard would be, in many cases, of little avail if it did not comprehend the right to be heard by counsel. Even the intelligent and educated layman has small and sometimes no skill in the science of law. If charged with crime, he is incapable, generally, of determining for himself whether the indictment is good or bad. He is unfamiliar with the rules of evidence. Left without the aid of counsel he may be put on trial without a proper charge, and convicted upon incompetent evidence, or evidence irrelevant to the issue or otherwise inadmissible. He lacks both the skill and knowledge adequately to prepare his defense, even though he have a perfect one. He requires the guiding hand of counsel at every step in the proceedings against him. Without it, though he be not guilty, he faces the danger of conviction because he does not know how to establish his innocence. If that be true of men of intelligence, how much more true is it of the ignorant and illiterate, or those of feeble intellect. If in any case, civil or criminal, a state or federal court were arbitrarily to refuse to hear a party by counsel, employed by and appearing for him, it reasonably may not be doubted that such a refusal would be a denial of a hearing, and, therefore, of due process in the constitutional sense. . . .

In the light of the facts outlined in the forepart of this opinion—the ignorance and illiteracy of the defendants, their youth, the circumstances of public hostility, the imprisonment and the close surveillance of the defendants by the military forces, the fact that their friends and families were all in other states and communication with them necessarily difficult, and above all that they stood in deadly peril of their lives—we think the failure of the trial court to give them reasonable time and opportunity to secure counsel was a clear denial of due process.

But passing that, and assuming their inability, even if opportunity had been given to employ counsel, as the trial court evidently did assume, we are of opinion that, under the circumstances just stated, the necessity of counsel was so vital and imperative that the failure of the trial court to make an effective appointment of counsel was likewise a denial of due process within the meaning of the Fourteenth Amendment. Whether this would be so in other criminal prosecutions, or under other circumstances, we need not determine. All that it is necessary now to decide, as we do decide, is that in a capital case, where the defendant is unable to employ counsel, and is incapable adequately of making his own defense because of ignorance, feeble-mindedness, illiteracy, or the like, it is the duty of the court, whether requested or not, to assign counsel for him as a necessary requisite of due process of law; and that duty is not discharged by an assignment at such a time or under such circumstances as to preclude the giving of effective aid in the preparation and trial of the case. . . . In a case such as this, whatever may be the rule in other cases, the right to have counsel appointed, when necessary, is a logical corollary from the constitutional right to be heard by counsel. . . .

The judgments must be reversed and the causes remanded for further proceedings not inconsistent with this opinion.

*Judgments reversed.*

[Justice Butler, joined by Justice McReynolds, dissented.]

Justice Sutherland was careful in stating the decision to confine the ruling to the peculiar facts of the case. At the same time, there was dictum which could give encouragement to those who wished to see the Fourteenth Amendment right to counsel for the indigent defendant broadened. Further encouragement was offered by the decision in *Johnson* v. *Zerbst,* 304 U.S. 458 (1938), which clarified the Sixth Amendment right to counsel. Johnson was charged with passing counterfeit notes and tried in federal court. At trial, he stated that he had no lawyer, and—in response to an inquiry of the court—stated that he was ready for trial. The judge neither advised him of his right to counsel nor offered a court-appointed attorney. Johnson was convicted of the felony and sentenced to four and one-half years in prison. While in prison, he filed a petition for habeas corpus, alleging that his trial without counsel violated the Sixth Amendment. The Supreme Court held that the Sixth Amendment right to counsel extends to the *appointment* of counsel for indigent defendants in federal criminal proceedings unless the accused waives the right. The holding also involved two important subsidiary points. First, the defendant may waive counsel, but such waiver must be "intelligent and competent." The duty placed on the trial judge is clear; he must make certain that under the circumstances of the charge, the possible penalties, and the capabilities of the accused, that a request to proceed without counsel would not result in serious disability to the accused. Second, failure to meet the Sixth Amendment requirement with respect to counsel is a jurisdictional defect, and therefore the collateral remedy of habeas corpus may properly be employed.

In 1942, however, the majority made it clear that they did not intend to equate the Fourteenth Amendment requirement with that of the Sixth Amendment. The case was *Betts* v. *Brady,* 316 U.S. 455 (1942), which dealt with a trial for robbery in the state court of Maryland. Petitioner was too poor to employ counsel, so informed the judge at his arraignment, and requested that counsel be appointed for him. The judge refused, pointing out that counsel was appointed for indigent defendants only in prosecutions for murder and rape. The trial proceeded, without a jury, and the judge found him guilty. The sentence imposed was eight years. A majority of the United States Supreme Court held that under the circumstances of the case, no denial of a fair trial could be inferred. Thus counsel was not a constitutional necessity. Justice Black, joined by Justices Douglas and Murphy, dissented, and thus began a sustained campaign by a minority of the justices to equate the Fourteenth Amendment rule with that of the Sixth Amendment as announced in *Johnson* v. *Zerbst.* The campaign culminated in victory in 1963, when *Betts* v. *Brady* was squarely overruled in the case of *Gideon* v. *Wainwright.*

One additional case out of the host of cases between *Powell* and *Gideon* is worthy of note because of the peculiar twist it gave to the rule announced by Justice Sutherland in *Powell* v. *Alabama.* The case was *Bute* v. *Illinois,* 333 U.S. 640 (1948). Roy Bute, a fifty-seven-year-old man, pleaded guilty and was convicted of "taking indecent liberties with children." He was sentenced to one to twenty years in jail. After he had served eight years in jail, in 1946, he filed a writ of error in the Supreme Court of Illinois, claiming that he had been denied representation by counsel. His writ was denied, and the United States Supreme Court granted certiorari. In a five-to-four decision the denial was affirmed. The majority could find no fundamental unfairness in the trial and nothing unusual in the status of the defendant which would have demanded counsel. Justice Sutherland had stated in *Powell* that the accused must have appointed counsel if it is a capital case *and* if the accused is ignorant, feeble-minded, illiterate, "or the like." Justice Burton, for the majority in the *Bute* case, changed this "and" to "or." The result was two rules: counsel must be furnished in every capital case and also in every noncapital felony case where special facts seem to make it mandatory for a fair trial. His statement was:

> In a noncapital state felony case, this Court has recognized the constitutional right of the accused to the assistance of counsel for his defense when there are special circumstances showing that, otherwise, the defendant would not enjoy that fair notice and adequate hearing which constitute the foundation of due process of law in the trial of any criminal charge.

As more and more "special circumstances" requiring counsel impressed themselves upon the majority of the Court (such as youth, inability to speak English, complexity of the issues involved in the case, "loaded" suggestions by officers of the state to plead guilty), the pressures both of argument and case-load pushed almost inexorably in the direction of a more clear-cut rule. The decision was unanimous when it finally came in 1963 in *Gideon* v. *Wainwright.*

GIDEON *v.* WAINWRIGHT

*372 U.S. 335 (1963)*

Mr. Justice Black delivered the opinion of the Court.

Petitioner was charged in a Florida state court with having broken and entered a poolroom with intent to commit a misdemeanor. This offense is a felony under Florida law. Appearing in court without funds and without a lawyer, petitioner asked the court to appoint counsel for him, [a request denied by the court on the ground that the law of Florida required appointment only in capital cases].

Put to trial before a jury, Gideon conducted his defense about as well as could be expected from a layman. He made an opening statement to the jury, cross-examined the State's witnesses, presented witnesses in his own defense, declined to testify himself, and made a short argument "emphasizing his innocence to the charge contained in the Information filed in this case." The jury returned a verdict of guilty, and petitioner was sentenced to serve five years in the state prison. Later, petitioner filed in the Florida Supreme Court this habeas corpus petition attacking his conviction and sentence on the ground that the trial court's refusal to appoint counsel for him denied him rights "guaranteed by the Constitution and the Bill of Rights by the United States Government." Treating the petition for habeas corpus as properly before it, the State Supreme Court, "upon consideration thereof" but without an opinion, denied all relief. Since 1942, when *Betts* v. *Brady,* 316 U.S. 455, was decided by a divided Court, the problem of a defendant's federal constitutional right to counsel in a state court has been a continuing source of controversy and litigation in both state and federal courts. To give this problem another review here, we granted certiorari. . . . Since Gideon was proceeding *in forma pauperis,* we appointed counsel to represent him and requested both sides to discuss in their briefs and oral arguments the following: "Should this Court's holding in *Betts* vs. *Brady* . . . be reconsidered?"

I

The facts upon which Betts claimed that he had been unconstitutionally denied the right to have counsel appointed to assist him are strikingly like the facts upon which Gideon here bases his federal constitutional claim. . . . Since the facts and circumstances of the two cases are so nearly indistinguishable, we think the *Betts* v. *Brady* holding if left standing would require us to reject Gideon's claim that the

Constitution guarantees him the assistance of counsel. Upon full reconsideration we conclude that *Betts* v. *Brady* should be overruled.

## II

. . . We accept *Betts* v. *Brady's* assumption, based as it was on our prior cases, that a provision of the Bill of Rights which is "fundamental and essential to a fair trial" is made obligatory upon the States by the Fourteenth Amendment. We think the Court in *Betts* was wrong, however, in concluding that the Sixth Amendment's guarantee of counsel is not one of these fundamental rights. Ten years before *Betts* v. *Brady,* this Court, after full consideration of all the historical data examined in *Betts,* had unequivocally declared that "the right to the aid of counsel is of this fundamental character." *Powell* v. *Alabama,* 287 U.S. 45, 68, (1932). While the Court at the close of its *Powell* opinion did by its language, as this Court frequently does, limit its holding to the particular facts and circumstances of that case, its conclusions about the fundamental nature of the right to counsel are unmistakable. Several years later, in 1936, the Court reemphasized what it had said about the fundamental nature of the right to counsel in this language:

"We concluded that certain fundamental rights, safeguarded by the first eight amendments against federal action, were also safeguarded against state action by the due process clause of the Fourteenth Amendment, and among them the fundamental right of the accused to the aid of counsel in a criminal prosecution." *Grosjean* v. *American Press Co.,* 297 U.S. 233, 243, 244 (1936).

And again in 1938 this Court said:

"[The assistance of counsel] is one of the safeguards of the Sixth Amendment deemed necessary to insure fundamental human rights of life and liberty. . . . The Sixth Amendment stands as a constant admonition that if the constitutional safeguards it provides be lost, justice will not 'still be done.' " *Johnson* v. *Zerbst,* 304 U.S. 458, 462 (1938). . . .

In light of these and many other prior decisions of this Court, it is not surprising that the *Betts* Court, when faced with the contention that "one charged with crime, who is unable to obtain counsel, must be furnished counsel by the State," conceded that "expressions in the opinions of this court lend color to the argument. . . . " 316 U.S., at 462, 463. The fact is that in deciding as it did—that "appointment of counsel is not a fundamental right, essential to a fair trial"—the Court in *Betts* v. *Brady* made an abrupt break with its well-considered precedents. In returning to these old precedents, sounder we believe than the new, we but restore constitutional principles established to achieve a fair system of justice. Not only these precedents but also reason and reflection require us to recognize that in our adversary system of criminal justice, any person haled into court, who is too poor to hire a lawyer, cannot be assured a fair trial unless counsel is provided for him. This seems to us to be an obvious truth. Governments, both state and federal, quite properly spend vast sums of money to establish machinery to try defendants accused of crime. Lawyers to prosecute are everywhere deemed essential to protect the public's interest in an orderly society. Similarly, there are few defendants charged with crime, few indeed, who fail to hire the best lawyers they can get to prepare and present their defenses. That government hires lawyers to prosecute and defendants who have the money hire lawyers to defend are the strongest indications of the widespread belief that lawyers in criminal courts are necessities, not luxuries. The right of one charged with crime to counsel may not be deemed fundamental and essential to fair trials in some countries, but it is in ours. From the very beginning, our state and national constitutions and laws have laid great emphasis on procedural and substantive safeguards designed to assure fair trials before impartial tribunals in which every defendant stands equal before the law. This noble idea cannot be realized if the poor man charged with crime has to face his accusers without a lawyer to assist him. A defendant's need for a lawyer is nowhere better stated than in the moving words of Mr. Justice Sutherland in *Powell* v. *Alabama*. . . .

The Court in *Betts* v. *Brady* departed from the sound wisdom upon which the Court's holding in *Powell* v. *Alabama* rested. Florida, supported by two other States, has asked that *Betts* v. *Brady* be left intact. Twenty-two States, as friends of the Court, argue that *Betts* was "an anachronism when handed down" and that it should now be overruled. We agree.

The judgment is reversed and the cause is remanded to the Supreme Court of Florida for further action not inconsistent with this opinion.

*Reversed.*

[Justices Douglas, Clark, and Harlan each filed separate concurring opinions.]

[For an excellent treatment of the *Gideon* case, see Anthony Lewis, *Gideon's Trumpet* (New York: Random House, 1964).]

Another aspect of the right to counsel to be considered is the minimal offense to which it applies. Since the Sixth Amendment extends the right to "all criminal prosecutions," it is arguably a right enforceable even in cases involving petty offenses. The Court did not rule squarely on the question until 1972 in *Argersinger* v. *Hamlin*.

## ARGERSINGER *v.* HAMLIN
### *407 U.S. 25 (1972)*

Mr. Justice Douglas delivered the opinion of the Court.

Petitioner, an indigent, was charged in Florida with carrying a concealed weapon, an offense punishable by imprisonment up to six months and a $1,000 fine. The trial was to a judge and petitioner was unrepresented by counsel. He was sentenced to serve 90 days in jail and brought this habeas corpus action in the Florida Supreme Court, alleging that, being deprived of his right to counsel, he was unable as an indigent layman properly to raise and present to the trial court good and sufficient defenses to the charges for which he stands convicted. The Florida Supreme Court . . . , in ruling on the right to counsel, followed the line we marked out in *Duncan* v. *Louisiana* . . . as respects the right to trial by jury and held that the right to court-appointed counsel extends to trials "for nonpetty offenses punishable by more than six months imprisonment." . . .

The case is here on a petition for certiorari which we granted. We reverse.

The Sixth Amendment, which in enumerated situations has been made applicable to the States by reason of the Fourteenth Amendment, . . . provides specified standards for "all criminal prosecutions."

One is the requirement of a "public trial." *In re Oliver, supra,* held that the right to a "public trial" was applicable to a state proceeding even though only a 60-day sentence was involved. . . .

Another guarantee is the right to be informed of the nature and cause of the accusation. Still another, the right of confrontation. . . . And another, compulsory process for obtaining witnesses in one's favor. . . . We have never limited these rights to felonies nor to lesser but serious offenses. . . .

The right to trial by jury, also guaranteed by the Sixth Amendment by reason of the Fourteenth, was limited by *Duncan* v. *Louisiana, supra,* to trials where the potential punishment was imprisonment of six months or more. But as the various opinions in *Baldwin* v. *New York* . . . make plain, the right to trial by jury has a different genealogy and is brigaded with a system of trial to a judge alone. . . .

While there is historical support for limiting the "deep commitment" to trial by jury to "serious criminal cases," there is no such support for a similar limitation on the right to assistance of counsel:

"Originally, in England, a person charged with treason or felony was denied the aid of counsel, except in respect of legal questions which the accused himself might suggest. At the same time parties in civil cases and persons accused of misdemeanors were entitled to the full assistance of counsel. . . . [It] appears that in at least twelve of the thirteen colonies the rule of the English common law, in the respect now under consideration, had been definitively rejected and the right to counsel fully recognized in all criminal prosecutions, save that in one or two instances the right was limited to capital offenses or to the more serious crimes. . . ." *Powell* v. *Alabama*.

The Sixth Amendment thus extended the right to counsel beyond its common law dimensions. But there is nothing in the language of the Amendment, its history, or in the decisions of this Court, to indicate that it was intended to embody a retraction of the right in petty offenses wherein the common law previously did require that counsel be provided. . . .

We reject, therefore, the premise that since prosecutions for crimes punishable by imprisonment for less than six months may be tried without a jury, they may always be tried without a lawyer. The assistance of counsel is often a requisite to the very existence of a fair trial. . . . even in a petty offense prosecution. We are by no means convinced that legal and constitutional questions involved in a case that actually leads to imprisonment even for a brief period are any less complex than when a person can be sent off for six months or more. . . .

The trial of vagrancy cases is illustrative. While only brief sentences of imprisonment may be imposed, the cases often bristle with thorny constitutional questions. See *Papachristou* v. *Jacksonville*. . . .

Beyond the problem of trials and appeals is that of the guilty plea, a problem which looms large in misdemeanor as well as in felony cases. Counsel is needed so that the accused may know precisely what he is doing, so that he is fully aware of the prospect of going to jail or prison, and so that he is treated fairly by the prosecution.

In addition, the volume of misdemeanor cases, far greater in number than felony prosecutions, may create an obsession for speedy dispositions, regardless of the fairness of the result. The Report by the President's Commission on Law Enforcement and Administration of Justice, *The Challenge of Crime in a Free Society,* p. 128 (1967), states: "For example, until legislation last year increased the number of judges, the District of Columbia Court of General Sessions had four judges to process the preliminary stages of more than 1,500 felony cases, 7,500 serious misdemeanor cases, and 38,000 petty offenses and an equal number of traffic offenses per year. An inevitable consequence of volume that large is the almost total preoccupation in such a court with the movement of cases. The calendar is long, speed often is substituted for care, and casually arranged out-of-court compromise too often is substituted for adjudication. . . ."

That picture is seen in almost every report. "The misdemeanor trial is characterized by insufficient and frequently irresponsible preparation on the part of the defense, the prosecution, and the court. Everything is rush, rush." . . .

There is evidence of the prejudice which results to misdemeanor defendants from this "assembly-line justice." One study concluded that "Misdemeanants represented by attorneys are five times as likely to emerge from police court with all charges dismissed as are defendants who face similar charges without counsel." ACLU, Legal Counsel for Misdemeanants, Preliminary Report, 1 (1970). . . .

We hold, therefore, that absent a knowing and intelligent waiver, no person may be imprisoned for any offense, whether classified as petty, misdemeanor, or felony, unless he was represented by counsel at his trial. . . .

We do not sit as an ombudsman to direct state courts how to manage their affairs but only to make clear the federal constitutional requirement. How crimes should be classified is largely a state matter. The fact that traffic charges technically fall within the category of "criminal prosecutions" does not necessarily mean that many of them will be brought into the class where imprisonment actually occurs. . . .

Under the rule we announce today, every judge will know when the trial of a misdemeanor starts that no imprisonment may be imposed, even though local law permits it, unless the accused is represented by counsel. He will have a measure of the seriousness and gravity of the offense and therefore know when to name a lawyer to represent the accused before the trial starts.

The run of misdemeanors will not be affected by today's ruling. But in those that end up in the actual deprivation of a person's liberty, the accused will receive the benefit of "the guiding hand of counsel" so necessary when one's liberty is in jeopardy.

*Reversed.*

Mr. Justice Brennan, with whom Mr. Justice Douglas and Mr. Justice Stewart join, concurring.

I join the opinion of the Court and add only an observation upon its discussion of legal resources. . . . Law students as well as practicing attorneys may provide an important source of legal representation for the indigent. The Council on Legal Education for Professional Responsibility (CLEPR) informs us that more than 125 of the country's 147 accredited law schools have established clinical programs in which faculty-supervised students aid clients in a variety of civil and criminal matters. . . . These programs supplement practice rules enacted in 38 States authorizing students to practice law under prescribed conditions. . . . Given the huge increase in law school enrollments over the past few years, . . . I think it plain that law students can be looked to to make a significant contribution, quantitatively and qualitatively, to the representation of the poor in many areas, including cases reached by today's decision.

Mr. Chief Justice Burger, concurring in the result. . . .

Trial judges sitting in petty and misdemeanor cases—and prosecutors—should recognize exactly what will be required by today's decision. Because no individual can be imprisoned unless he is represented by counsel, the trial judge and the prosecutor will have to engage in a predictive evaluation of each case to determine whether there is a significant likelihood that, if the defendant is convicted, the trial judge will sentence him to a jail term. The judge can preserve the option of a jail sentence by offering counsel to any defendant unable to retain counsel on his own. This need to predict will place a new load on courts already overburdened and already compelled to deal with far more cases in one day than is reasonable and proper. Yet the prediction is not one beyond the capacity of an experienced judge, aided as he should be by the prosecuting officer. . . .

Mr. Justice Powell, with whom Mr. Justice Rehnquist joins, concurring in the result. . . .

The Court has stressed that a waiver of counsel must be "intelligent and competent." And in *Faretta* v. *California*, 422 U.S. 806 (1975), it held that a competent person accused of crime has a constitutional right to refuse a free, court-appointed lawyer and conduct his own defense.

A landmark decision was rendered in 1967 which extended the right to counsel to juvenile court proceedings where delinquency is charged. The case was In re *Gault*, 387 U.S. 1 (1967). The majority opinion is excerpted in the section "The Right to a Fair Hearing," below.

## Stage at Which the Right to Counsel Accrues

The Sixth Amendment refers to "criminal prosecutions" but makes no mention of detention, interrogation, preliminary hearings, or the other pretrial stages which an accused must face. Then when does the right to counsel accrue? In 1932, in *Powell* v. *Alabama*, Justice Sutherland stated that the defendant "requires the guiding hand of counsel at every step in the proceedings against him." It was not until the decision in *Miranda* v. *Arizona* in 1966, however, that the Court officially adopted the view that the right extends to the interrogation stage. And, as already pointed out, incriminating statements derived from interrogation in violation of the *Miranda* rule are not admissible. Problems of admissibility of statements have arisen, however, when, after defendant has refused to talk without a lawyer present, police have elicited incriminating statements not by direct interrogation, but by suggesting the unfortunate consequences of failure to locate a loaded weapon or the body of a victim. In *Brewer* v. *Williams*, 430 U.S. 387 (1977), the defendant was being transported from one city in Iowa to another, and his lawyer had advised him not to make any statements until he consulted a lawyer at his destination. He was to stand trial for murder, but the body of the victim had not been recovered. Enroute a detective expressed the view that given the poor weather conditions it might be impossible to find the body and that "the parents of this little girl should be entitled to a Christian burial for the little girl who was snatched away from them on Christmas Eve and murdered." The defendant then made incriminating statements, which also led to the recovery of the body. The Court held five-to-four that there was a violation of the right to counsel and that the statements were inadmissible. The majority held that the "Christian burial" speech was tantamount to interrogation and that there was no reasonable basis for finding that the prisoner had waived his right to counsel.

In *Rhode Island* v. *Innis*, 446 U.S. 291 (1980), defendant, who was identified as the armed robber of a cab driver, was given a *Miranda* warning three different times. He indicated that he wanted to speak to a lawyer and was driven to the police station by several police officers who had been instructed not to interrogate or intimidate him in any way. The sawed-off shotgun reportedly used in the robbery had not been recovered by the police. Enroute to the station, two of the officers made "off-hand remarks" that there were "a lot of handicapped children running around this area" and "God forbid one of them might find a weapon with shells and they might hurt themselves." The defendant then led the police to the location of the gun, after having been given the *Miranda* warning for the fourth time. The Court held that the gun was admissible at the trial as the fruit of a legitimate waiver of rights and that the defendant was not "interrogated" within the meaning of *Miranda* or subjected to the "functional equivalent" of questioning.

In *Brewer* v. *Williams*, above, the Court held that Wiliams' incriminating statements were inadmissible, but that evidence of the body's location and condition "might well be admissible on the theory that the body would have been discovered in any event, even had incriminating statements not been elicited from Williams." This prediction was based on the fact that some 200 volunteers who were searching for the body had been instructed to "check all the roads, the ditches, any culverts" in their search, and the body was located by Williams in a culvert along the road the volunteers were proceeding. At Williams' second trial, the prosecution did not offer Williams' statements into evidence, nor did it seek to show that Williams had directed the police to the child's body. However, evidence of the condition of her body as it was found, articles and photographs of her clothing, and the results of post mortem medical and chemical tests on the body were admitted. Over Williams' objection, this evidence was admitted, and Williams was again convicted of first-degree murder. In *Nix* v. *Williams,* 467 U.S. 431 (1984), the Court held the evidence admissible and adopted an "inevitable discovery" exception to the exclusionary rule. Chief Justice Burger, for the majority, stated:

It is clear that the cases implementing the Exclusionary Rule "begin with the premise that the challenged evidence is *in some sense* the product of illegal governmental activity." . . . Of course, this does not end the inquiry. If the prosecution can establish by a preponderance of the evidence that the information ultimately or inevitably would have been discovered by lawful means—here the volunteers' search—then the deterrence rationale has so little basis that the evidence should be received. Anything less would reject logic, experience, and common sense. . . .

Williams contends that because he did not waive his right to the assistance of counsel, the Court may not balance competing values in deciding whether the challenged evidence was properly admitted. He argues that, unlike the Exclusionary Rule in the Fourth Amendment context, the essential purpose of which is to deter police misconduct, the Sixth Amendment Exclusionary Rule is designed to protect the right to a fair trial and the integrity of the factfinding process. Williams contends that, when those interests are at stake, the societal costs of excluding evidence obtained from responses presumed involuntary are irrelevant in determining whether such evidence should be excluded. We disagree.

Exclusion of physical evidence that would inevitably have been discovered adds nothing to either the integrity or fairness of a criminal trial. The Sixth Amendment right to counsel protects against unfairness by preserving the adversary process in which the reliability of proffered evidence may be tested in cross-examination. . . . Here, however, Detective Leaming's conduct did nothing to impugn the reliability of the evidence in question. . . . No one would seriously contend that the presence of counsel in the police car when Leaming appealed to Williams' decent human instincts would have had any bearing on the reliability of the body as evidence. Suppression, in these circumstances, would do nothing whatever to promote the integrity of the trial process, but would inflict a wholly unacceptable burden on the administration of criminal justice.

The separate opinions in the case did not present objections to the "inevitable discovery" rule *per se,* but would have demanded that the prosecution bear a clear burden of proof that in fact the evidence *would* have been discovered without police misconduct.

It should not be assumed that interrogation is a factor in the bulk of criminal cases. In most such cases there is no interrogation whatever. After all, it is hardly necessary to subject a defendant to questioning if he is captured while climbing out of a window at two A.M. with a television set under his arm and a mask over his face. A *Miranda* warning must be given, of course, in the event that inculpatory statements might be made, but interrogation surely is superfluous. If no interrogation takes place, when does the right to counsel begin? Prior to the decision in *Gideon*, the primary thrust of litigation in the counsel cases was to broaden the categories of cases in which appointed counsel was guaranteed at the *trial* stage. Even so, the issue of when the right first obtained in the chronology of criminal procedure began to appear in some of the pre-*Gideon* cases. In *Hamilton* v. *Alabama*, 368 U.S. 52 (1961), for example, the Court held that appointment of counsel for indigent defendants must be made as early as the arraignment stage if this is "a critical stage in a criminal proceeding." Petitioner was convicted of the capital crime of breaking and entering a dwelling at night with intent to ravish, and was not afforded counsel until the trial stage. In reversing, the Court pointed out that under Alabama law the arraignment was the only stage at which the defense of insanity could be pleaded, that pleas in abatement could be made, or that motions to quash based on the ground that the grand jury was improperly drawn could be made. (An interesting dilemma is presented by the requirement that an uncounseled defendant who is in fact insane be at the same time sufficiently competent to enter a plea of insanity at arraignment.) In *United States* v. *Wade*, 388 U.S. 218 (1967), the Court held that a post-indictment police lineup was a "critical stage of the prosecution" at which the defendant was as much entitled to the aid of counsel as at the trial itself, and the police conduct of such a lineup without notice to and in the absence of his counsel denied the accused his Sixth Amendment right to counsel.

To what extent does the right to appointed counsel apply *after* trial and conviction? In 1956 the Court held in *Griffin* v. *Illinois,* 351 U.S. 12, that indigent defendants have a constitutional right to a free transcript on appeal: "destitute defendants must be afforded as adequate appellate review as defendants who have money enough to buy transcripts." This holding suggested that indigents might also have a right to counsel on appeal, and the Court so held in *Douglas* v. *California*, 372 U.S. 353 (1963). But in *Ross* v. *Moffitt*, 417 U.S. 600 (1974), the Court distinguished *Douglas* and held that neither the due process clause nor the equal protection clause of the Fourteenth Amendment required that a State, after appointing counsel for an indigent's first appeal of right from his conviction to an intermediate state court, must also appoint counsel for the indigent's subsequent discretionary appeal to the highest state court.

*Gagnon* v. *Scarpelli*, 411 U.S. 778 (1973), presented the questions whether a previously sentenced probationer is entitled to a hearing when his probation is revoked and, if so, whether he is entitled to be represented by appointed counsel at such a hearing. The Court held that the probationer was entitled to a hearing, but refused to lay out a firm requirement of counsel. The opinion stated that the decision as to the need for counsel "must be made on a case-by-case basis in the exercise of a sound discretion by the state authority charged with responsibility for administering the probation and parole system." It was stated further that "Although the presence and participation of counsel will probably be both undesirable and constitutionally unnecessary in most revocation hearings, there will remain certain cases in which fundamental fairness . . . will require that the State provide at its expense counsel for indigent probationers or parolees."

## Effective Representation by Counsel

In the majority opinion in *Powell* it was pointed out that "the failure of the trial court to make an effective appointment of counsel" was a denial of due process. Appointment must be made in time to be of some assistance to the accused. "That duty is not discharged by an assignment at such time or under such circumstances as to preclude the giving of effective aid in the preparation and trial of the case." *Miranda* held that assignment must be made at the interrogation stage if the right is not waived. And in the case where the police feel that evidence is sufficient that no interrogation is necessary, *Ham-*

*ilton* v. *Alabama* indicates that assignment must be made early enough to protect the interests of the defendant fully. A second interpretation of the requirement of "effective" representation raises the question of the competence of counsel handling the case. A losing defendant may protest that, through inefficiency or neglect, counsel was so incompetent that the conviction was obtained without due process of law. Obviously, appellate courts will be reluctant to overturn convictions under such a claim, both out of consideration for the orderly disposition of cases and also out of concern for the lawyer's standing as a professional man, heavily dependent upon his reputation. In retrospect, most trials could probably have been conducted more effectively had certain changes in strategy been made. But such a conclusion standing alone is insufficient to support a claim of denial of due process. The deficiencies must be so glaring and gross that the appellate court can see that on its face the trial was patently unfair. Thus, in *Sanchez* v. *Indiana,* 199 Ind. 235, 157 N.W. 1 (1927), reversal was obtained where counsel, hired by friends of an eighteen-year-old illiterate Mexican, was unaware of forcible process for obtaining witnesses, failed to object to obviously incompetent evidence, failed to submit instructions, and failed to produce character witnesses for the defendant, who had no previous criminal record.

It has been held that proper representation is not satisfied by the appointment of nonlawyers, even though they are law students, in *Jones* v. *Georgia,* 57 Ga. App. 344, 195 S.E. 316 (1938). And in *Glasser* v. *United States,* 315 U.S. 60 (1942), the Court held that if the trial judge appoints a single lawyer to represent two or more defendants being tried jointly, there must not be a conflict of interest as to the defendants which would result in a deprivation of fair representation. On the whole, however, the burden on the claimant of proving gross incompetence has only rarely been successfully met. [See Joel J. Finer, "Ineffective Assistance of Counsel," 58 *Cornell L. Rev.* 1077 (1973); Comment, "Effective Assistance of Counsel for the Indigent Defendant," 78 *Harv. L. Rev.* 1434 (1965).]

In *Strickland* v. *Washington,* 466 U.S. 668 (1984), the Court laid down a general test for judging ineffectiveness of counsel. Justice O'Connor, for the majority, stated:

A convicted defendant's claim that counsel's assistance was so defective as to require reversal of a conviction or death sentence has two components. First, the defendant must show the counsel's performance was deficient. This requires showing that counsel made errors so serious that counsel was not functioning as the "counsel" guaranteed the defendant by the Sixth Amendment. Second, the defendant must show that the deficient performance prejudiced the defense. This requires showing that counsel's errors were so serious as to deprive the defendant of a fair trial, a trial whose result is reliable. Unless a defendant makes both showings, it cannot be said that the conviction or death sentence resulted from a breakdown in the adversary process that renders the result unreliable.

Further elaborating on the second prong of the test, Justice O'Connor said, "The defendant must show that there is a reasonable probability that, but for counsel's unprofessional errors, the result of the proceeding would have been different."

The test was applied in *Kimmelman* v. *Morrison,* 477 U.S. 465 (1986), and the Court concluded that counsel's performance was both deficient and possibly prejudicial, although the case was remanded for a determination of the latter. The defendant was tried and convicted of rape. At the trial a police officer testified that a few hours after the rape she accompanied the victim to the defendant's apartment where the rape had occurred. He was not there but another tenant admitted them, and the officer seized a sheet from the defendant's bed. At this point defense counsel sought to suppress introduction of the sheet and any testimony about it on the ground that the seizure without a warrant was unconstitutional. The judge ruled the motion untimely under state law and rejected counsel's arguments that he had not heard of the seizure until the day of the trial and that it was the State's obligation to inform him of its case, even though he had made no pretrial request for discovery. Further, he had not expected to go to trial because he had been told that the victim did not wish to proceed. In a habeas review of the issue of the effectiveness of counsel in the case, Justice Brennan, for the majority, said that counsel's failure to conduct any discovery was "unreasonable, that is, contrary to prevailing professional norms." The justifications Morrison's attorney offered for his omission "betray a startling ignorance of the law—or a weak attempt to shift blame for inadequate preparation." While the first prong of the test was thus met, the Court felt that "We simply do not know" whether introduction of the sheet into evidence "tipped the balance" toward guilt and therefore met the prejudice test. Thus the case was remanded on that issue.

## THE RIGHT TO A FAIR HEARING

In addition to the guarantees already discussed, there are other requirements of the Sixth Amendment, and of due process generally, which are held to be requirements of a fair hearing. The Sixth Amendment guarantees the accused in a federal prosecution the right to a "public trial." The due process clause of the Fourteenth Amendment also assures this right in state proceedings. The Court so ruled in In re Oliver, 333 U.S. 257 (1948), holding invalid the criminal contempt conviction of a witness before a Michigan judge, sitting as a "one-man grand jury," and conducting the proceeding in secret. The Court stated:

The traditional Anglo-American distrust for secret trials has been variously ascribed to the notorious use of this practice by the Spanish Inquisition, to the excesses of the English Court of Star Chamber, and to the French monarchy's abuse of the *lettre de cachet*. All of these institutions obviously symbolized a menace to liberty.

Further, since publicity may be given to the proceedings, both witnesses and officials may tend to operate in more honest and trustworthy fashion. [See Max Radin, "The Right to a Public Trial," 6 *Temp. L. Q.* 381 (1932) and Charles W. Quick, "A Public Criminal Trial," 60 *Dick L. Rev.* 21 (1955).]

Due process also includes the right of the accused to be present at his trial in order to face his accusers and advise with his lawyer. Thus trials *in absentia* would seem normally to be unconstitutional in the United States. But in *Illinois v. Allen*, 397 U.S. 337 (1970), the Court held that the removal of a disruptive defendant from the courtroom during a criminal trial was not violative of his constitutional right to be present at trial.

ILLINOIS *v.* ALLEN

*397 U.S. 337 (1970)*

Mr. Justice Black delivered the opinion of the Court. . . .

One of the most basic of the rights guaranteed by the Confrontation Clause is the accused's right to be present in the courtroom at every stage of his trial. . . . The question presented in this case is whether an accused can claim the benefit of this constitutional right to remain in the courtroom while at the same time he engages in speech and conduct which is so noisy, disorderly, and disruptive that it is exceedingly difficult or wholly impossible to carry on the trial. . . . [The opinion here describes in detail the obstreperous conduct, the interruptions, and abusive language on the part of the defendant, resulting in the judge's order of removal from the courtroom for substantial portions of the trial.]

. . . Although mindful that courts must indulge every reasonable presumption against the loss of constitutional rights, . . . we explicitly hold today that a defendant can lose his right to be present at trial if, after he has been warned by the judge that he will be removed if he continues his disruptive behavior, he nevertheless insists on conducting himself in a manner so disorderly, disruptive, and disrespectful of the court that his trial cannot be carried on with him in the courtroom. Once lost, the right to be present can, of course, be reclaimed as soon as the defendant is willing to conduct himself consistently with the decorum and respect inherent in the concept of courts and judicial proceedings.

It is essential to the proper administration of criminal justice that dignity, order, and decorum be the hallmarks of all court proceedings in our country. The flagrant disregard in the courtroom of elementary standards of proper conduct should not and cannot be tolerated. We believe trial judges confronted with disruptive, contumacious, stubbornly defiant defendants must be given sufficient discretion to meet the circumstances of each case. No one formula for maintaining the appropriate courtroom atmosphere will be best in all situations. We think there are at least three constitutionally permissible ways for a trial judge to handle an obstreperous defendant like Allen: (1) bind and gag him, thereby keeping him present; (2) cite him for contempt; (3) take him out of the courtroom until he promises to conduct himself properly.

Trying a defendant for a crime while he sits bound and gagged before the judge and jury would to an extent comply with that part of the Sixth Amendment's purposes that accords the defendant an opportunity to confront the witnesses at the trial. But even to contemplate such a technique, much less see it, arouses a feeling that no person should be tried while shackled and gagged except as a last resort. . . .

It is not pleasant to hold that the respondent Allen was properly banished from the court for a part of his own trial. But our courts, palladiums of liberty as they are, cannot be treated disrespectfully with impunity. Nor can the accused be permitted by his disruptive conduct indefinitely to avoid being tried on the charges brought against him. It would degrade our country and our judicial system to permit our courts to be bullied, insulted, and humiliated and their orderly progress thwarted and obstructed by defendants brought before them charged with crimes. . . . Being manned by humans, the courts are not perfect and are bound to make some errors. But, if our courts are to remain what the Founders intended, the citadels of justice, their proceedings cannot and must not be infected with the sort of scurrilous, abusive language and conduct paraded before the Illinois trial judge in this case. The record shows that the Illinois judge at all times conducted himself with that dignity, decorum, and patience that befits a judge. Even in holding that the trial judge had erred, the Court of Appeals praised his "commendable patience under severe provocation."

We do not hold that removing this defendant from his own trial was the only way the Illinois judge could have constitutionally solved the problem he had. We do hold, however, that there is nothing whatever in this record to show that the judge did not act completely within his discretion. . . .

The judgment of the Court of Appeals is

*Reversed.*

Mr. Justice Brennan concurring. . . .

Mr. Justice Douglas, concurring. . . .

The mere fact that the superficial formalities of a trial are adhered to is not sufficient to meet the test of due process, if the result is dictated by external pressures. In *Moore* v. *Dempsey*, 261 U.S. 86 (1923), the Court reviewed the conviction of five Negroes in an Arkansas court for the murder of a white man. The trial court and the neighborhood were "thronged with an adverse crowd that threatened the most dangerous consequences to anyone interfering with the desired result." The trial lasted about forty-five minutes, and in less than five minutes the jury brought in a verdict of guilty of murder. According to the allegations and affidavits "no juryman could have voted for an acquittal and continued to live in Phillips County and if any prisoner by any chance had been acquitted by a jury he could not have escaped the mob." In reversing the denial of habeas corpus, Justice Holmes, for the Court, quoted from an earlier case, stating that "if the State, supplying no corrective process, carries into execution a judgment of death or imprisonment based upon a verdict thus produced by mob domination, the State deprives the accused of his life or liberty without due process of law."

Due process also demands that the trial be conducted by an unbiased judge. The best-known case on the point is *Tumey* v. *Ohio*, 273 U.S. 510 (1927), involving a conviction for violation of the liquor laws of the state. The mayor was authorized to try such offenses without a jury, and he received, in addition to his salary, the costs imposed on the defendant in case of conviction. Further, also in the event of conviction, the municipality received half the fine levied. In reversing, Chief Justice Taft stated for the Court:

All questions of judicial qualification may not involve constitutional validity. Thus matters of kinship, personal bias, state policy, remoteness of interest would seem generally to be matters merely of legislative discretion. . . . But it certainly violates the Fourteenth Amendment and deprives a defendant in a criminal case of due process of law to subject his liberty or property to the judgment of a court, the judge of which has a direct, personal, substantial pecuniary interest in reaching a conclusion against him in his case. . . .

. . . Every procedure which would offer a possible temptation to the average man as a judge to forget the burden of proof required to convict the defendant, or which might lead him not to hold the balance nice, clear, and true between the state and the accused denies the latter due process of law.

In *Dugan* v. *Ohio*, 277 U.S. 61 (1928), however, the Court, in refusing to reverse a conviction, emphasized that the judge's pecuniary interest had to be "direct, personal, and substantial" in order to disqualify him under the *Tumey* rule. It held that the interest was too remote in this case, which involved a mayor-judge on a fixed salary, who was a member of the city commission and was paid from the city's general fund, into which one-half of the fines of convicted persons was paid. [See John P. Frank, "Disqualification of Judges," 56 *Yale L. J.* 605 (1947).]

*Ward* v. *Monroeville*, 409 U.S. 57 (1972), presented a situation where the mayor was given broad executive powers and was also the chief conservator of the peace. In addition, a major part of the village income was derived from the fines, forfeitures, costs, and fees imposed by him in his mayor's court. The Court found that the "possible temptation" to forget the burden of proof required to convict defendants was too great in this case to be constitutionally acceptable.

The Sixth Amendment guarantees the accused a right "to be confronted with the witnesses against him," and, as a corollary thereto, the right to cross-examine them. In fact, the right of "confrontation" is intended primarily to afford to the accused an opportunity to cross-examine. The policy behind this requirement is well stated in Wigmore's *Textbook on the Law of Evidence* (Brooklyn: Foundation Press, 1935), Sec. 242:

[It is insisted upon because] the experience of the last three centuries of judicial trials has demonstrated convincingly that in disputed issues one cannot depend on the mere assertion of anybody, however plausible, without scrutiny into its bases. All the weaknesses that may affect a witness' trustworthiness—observation, memory, bias, interest, and the like—may otherwise lurk unrevealed; modifying circumstances omitted in his tale may give his facts an entirely different effect, if disclosed; and cross-examination is the best way to get at these.

In *Jencks* v. *United States,* 353 U.S. 657 (1957), the Court held that when the government calls its informers to the stand as witnesses in a criminal prosecution, it cannot refuse to produce the statements and reports of such informers in the possession of the government, if requested by the defendant as necessary aids to adequate cross-examination. The decision was criticized on the ground that it would open up the confidential and secret files of the government to general inspection by criminals, but the Court stated that the government must make the choice of either granting defendants full rights of cross-examination or proceeding without the desired testimony. [See Robert B. McKay, "The Right of Confrontation," 1959 *Wash. U. L. Q.* 122 (1959) and Barrie M. Karen, "The Right to Production for Inspection of Documents in Possession of the Government: Guaranteed by the Due Process Clause?" 31 *So. Calif. L. Rev.* 78 (1957).]

In *Pointer* v. *Texas,* 380 U.S. 400 (1965), the Court "incorporated" the Sixth Amendment right of confrontation into the Fourteenth Amendment due process clause. At the defendant's trial in a state court on a charge of robbery, the state, over defendant's objections, introduced the transcript of a witness' testimony given at the preliminary hearing, at which defendant was not represented by counsel and had no opportunity to cross-examine the witness. The state showed that the witness had moved out of Texas with no intention of returning. Defendant was convicted, and his conviction affirmed by the appellate court. On certiorari, the United States Supreme Court reversed. Justice Black, for the Court, stated:

It cannot seriously be doubted at this late date that the right of cross-examination is included in the right of an accused in a criminal case to confront the witnesses against him. And probably no one, certainly no one experienced in the trial of lawsuits, would deny the value of cross-examination in exposing falsehood and bringing out the truth in the trial of a criminal case. . . .

There are few subjects, perhaps, upon which this Court and other courts have been more nearly unanimous than in their expressions of belief that the right of confrontation and cross-examination is an essential and fundamental requirement for the kind of fair trial which is this country's constitutional goal. . . .

. . . We hold that petitioner was entitled to be tried in accordance with the protection of the confrontation guarantee of the Sixth Amendment, and that that guarantee, like the right against compelled self-incrimination, is "to be enforced against the States under the Fourteenth Amendment according to the same standards that protect those personal rights against federal encroachment." *Malloy v. Hogan.* . . .

The Court followed *Pointer* in *Douglas* v. *Alabama,* 380 U.S. 415 (1965). Defendant was charged with assault with intent to murder. An accomplice, who had been tried separately and found guilty, was called as a witness by the state but invoked his privilege against self-incrimination because he planned to appeal his conviction. The solicitor then produced a confession purportedly signed by the witness and, under the guise of cross-examination to refresh the witness' recollection, read from the document, pausing after every few sentences to ask him, before the jury, "Did you make that statement?" Each time, the witness invoked the privilege. Defendant's counsel objected to the reading, but defendant was convicted and the state supreme court affirmed. The

Court unanimously reversed, holding that in the circumstances, petitioner's inability to cross-examine the witness as to the alleged confession "plainly denied him the right of cross-examination secured by the Confrontation Clause."

In *Washington v. Texas,* 388 U.S. 14 (1967), the Court "incorporated" the Sixth Amendment right to have compulsory process for obtaining witnesses in his favor into the Fourteenth Amendment. It further held that this right was denied by Texas statutes which provided that persons charged or convicted as coparticipants in the same crime could not testify for one another, although there was no bar to their testifying for the state. The witness Washington wished to call had previously been convicted of the same crime, sentenced to fifty years in prison, and was confined in the Dallas County jail. On the basis of the statutes, the trial judge refused to allow the witness to testify. The United States Supreme Court unanimously reversed. Chief Justice Warren, for eight of the members, stated:

The right to offer the testimony of witnesses, and to compel their attendance, if necessary, is in plain terms the right to present a defense, the right to present the defendant's version of the facts as well as the prosecution's to the jury so it may decide where the truth lies. Just as an accused has the right to confront the prosecution's witnesses for the purpose of challenging their testimony, he has the right to present his own witnesses to establish a defense. The right is a fundamental element of due process of law.

It was argued that such witnesses should be disqualified on the ground that they are particularly likely to commit perjury. The Chief Justice pointed out that "the absurdity of the rule" is demonstrated by the fact that the accused accomplice could testify for the prosecution. It was further suggested that such witnesses would be more apt to lie for their coparticipants. The response by the Chief Justice was: "To think that criminals will lie to save their fellows but not to obtain favors from the prosecution for themselves is indeed to clothe the criminal class with more nobility than one might expect to find in the public at large."

One of the most important decisions of recent years involving criminal procedure came in 1967 in *In re Gault,* 387 U.S. 1 (1967). In that case the Court held that juvenile delinquency proceedings which may lead to commitment in state institutions must measure up to the essentials of due process and fair treatment. An Arizona juvenile court had committed a fifteen-year-old boy to the state industrial school for the period of his minority, unless officially discharged sooner. The boy was taken into custody by the county sheriff, without notice to his parents, on a complaint charging the defendant with making an obscene telephone call. The juvenile judge held a hearing at which the boy, his mother, his older brother, and two probation officers appeared. No transcript or recording was made, the complainant was not present, and no one was sworn. Later testimony by the juvenile judge was to the effect that the judge questioned the defendant at this hearing and that he admitted making lewd statements over the telephone. Neither the boy nor his parents was advised of his right to counsel or to remain silent. At a second hearing the following week, still without transcript or recording, the defendant and another boy, charged with participating in the same telephone call, were questioned further. Witnesses differed in their recollections of the defendant's testimony at this hearing. His parents recalled that he admitted only to having dialed the number, and that the other boy had made the remarks. The mother asked that the complainant be present to testify as to which boy had done the talking. The judge stated that she did not have to be present. At the conclusion of the hearing the defendant was committed to the state industrial school. Since no appeal was permitted by statute, the commitment was attacked by habeas corpus. The trial court dismissed, and the Arizona Supreme Court affirmed. The United States Supreme Court considered the case on appeal and reversed.

IN RE GAULT

*387 U.S. 1 (1967)*

Mr. Justice Fortas delivered the opinion of the Court. . . .

[Appellants] urge that we hold the Juvenile Code of Arizona invalid on its face or as applied in this case because, contrary to the Due Process Clause of the Fourteenth Amendment, the juvenile is taken from the custody of his parents and committed to a state institution pursuant to proceedings in which the Juvenile Court has virtually unlimited discretion, and in which the following basic rights are denied:

1. Notice of the charges;
2. Right to counsel;
3. Right to confrontation and cross-examination;
4. Privilege against self-incrimination;
5. Right to a transcript of the proceedings; and
6. Right to appellate review. . . .

We do not in this opinion consider the impact of these constitutional provisions upon the totality of the relationship of the juvenile and the state. . . . We consider only the problems presented to us by this case. These relate to the proceedings by which a determination is made as to whether a juvenvile is a "delinquent" as a result of alleged misconduct on his part, with the consequence that he may be committed to a state institution. . . .

From the inception of the juvenile court system, wide differences have been tolerated—indeed insisted upon—between the procedural rights accorded to adults and those of juveniles. . . .

The early reformers were appalled by adult procedures and penalties, and by the fact children could be given long prison sentences and mixed in jails with hardened criminals. . . . The apparent rigidities, technicalities, and harshness which they observed in both substantive and procedural criminal law were therefore to be discarded. The idea of crime and punishment was to be abandoned. The child was to be "treated" and "rehabilitated" and the procedures, from apprehension through institutionalization, were to be "clinical" rather than punitive.

These results were to be achieved, without coming to conceptual and constitutional grief, by insisting that the proceedings were not adversary, but that the State was proceeding as *parens patriae*. The Latin phrase proved to be a great help to those who sought to rationalize the exclusion of juveniles from the constitutional scheme; but its meaning is murky and its historic credentials are of dubious relevance. . . .

Accordingly, the highest motives and most enlightened impulses led to a peculiar system for juveniles, unknown to our law in any comparable context. The constitutional and theoretical basis for this peculiar system is—to say the least—debatable. And in practice. . . the results have not been entirely satisfactory. Juvenile court history has again demonstrated that unbridled discretion, however benevolently motivated, is frequently a poor substitute for principle and procedure. In 1937, Dean Pound wrote: "The powers of the Star Chamber were a trifle in comparison with those of our juvenile courts. . . . " The absence of substantive standards has not necessarily meant that children receive careful, compassionate, individualized treatment. The absence of procedural rules based upon constitutional principle has not always produced fair, efficient, and effective procedures. Departures from established principles of due process have frequently resulted not in enlightened procedure, but in arbitrariness. . . .

It is claimed that juveniles obtain benefits from the special procedures applicable to them which more than offset the disadvantages of denial of the substance of normal due process. As we shall discuss, the observance of due process standards, intelligently and not ruthlessly administered, will not compel the States to abandon or displace any of the substantive benefits of the juvenile process. . . .

. . . For example, the commendable principles relating to the processing and treatment of juveniles separately from adults are in no way involved or affected by the procedural issues under discussion. Further, we are told that one of the important benefits of the special juvenile court procedures is that they avoid classifying the juvenile as a "criminal." The juvenile offender is now classed as a "delinquent." There is, of course, no reason why this should not continue. It is disconcerting, however, that this term has come to involve only slightly less stigma than the term "criminal" applied to adults. . . .

Beyond this, it is frequently said that juveniles are protected by the process from disclosure of their deviational behavior. . . . This claim of secrecy, however, is more rhetoric than reality. Disclosure of court records is discretionary with the judge in most jurisdictions. . . .

In any event, there is no reason why, consistently with due process, a State cannot continue, if it deems it appropriate, to provide provision for the confidentiality of records of police contacts and court action relating to juveniles. . . .

Further, it is urged that the juvenile benefits from informal proceedings in the court. The early conception of the juvenile court proceeding was one in which a fatherly judge touched the heart and conscience of the erring youth by talking over his problems, by paternal advice and admonition, and in which, in extreme situations, benevolent and wise institutions of the State provided guidance and help "to save him from a downward career." . . . But recent studies have, with surprising unanimity, entered sharp dissent as to the validity of this gentle conception. They suggest that the appearance as well as the actuality of fairness, impartiality and orderliness— in short, the essentials of due process—may be a more impressive and more therapeutic attitude so far as the juvenile is concerned. . . .

Ultimately, however, we confront the reality of that portion of the juvenile court process with which we deal in this case. A boy is charged with misconduct. The boy is committed to an institution where he may be restrained of liberty for years. . . .

In view of this, it would be extraordinary if our Constitution did not require the procedural regularity and the exercise of care implied in the phrase "due process." Under our Constitution, the condition of being a boy does not justify a kangaroo court. . . .

If Gerald had been over 18, he would not have been subject to Juvenile Court proceedings. For the particular offense immediately involved, the maximum punishment would have been a fine of $5 to $50, or imprisonment in jail for not more than two months. Instead, he was committed to custody for a maximum of six years. If he had been over 18 and had committed an offense to which such a sentence might apply, he would have been entitled to substantial rights under the Constitution of the United States as well as under Arizona's laws and constitution. . . . So wide a gulf between the State's treatment of the adult and of the child requires a bridge sturdier than mere verbiage, and reasons more persuasive than cliche can provide. . . .

## Notice of Charges

. . . The applicable Arizona statute provides for a petition to be filed in Juvenile Court, alleging in general terms that the child is "neglected, dependent, or delinquent." The statute explicitly states that such a general allegation is sufficient, "without alleging the facts." . . .

We cannot agree with the court's conclusion that adequate notice was given in this case. . . . Due process of law requires notice of the sort we have described—that is, notice which would be deemed constitutionally adequate in a civil or criminal proceeding. . .

## Right to Counsel

Appellants charge that the Juvenile Court proceedings were fatally defective because the court did not advise Gerald or his parents of their right to counsel, and proceeded with the hearing, the adjudication of delinquency and the order of commitment in the absence of counsel for the child and his parents or an express waiver of the right thereto. . . . The court argued that "The parent and the probation officer may be relied upon to protect the infant's interests." Accordingly it rejected the proposition that "due process requires that an infant have a right to counsel." . . . We do not agree. . . . The child "requires the guiding hand of counsel at every step in the proceedings against him." . . .

### Confrontation, Self-Incrimination, Cross-Examination

Appellants urge that the writ of habeas corpus should have been granted because of the denial of the rights of confrontation and cross-examination in the Juvenile Court hearings, and because the privilege against self-incrimination was not observed. The Juvenile Court Judge testified at the habeas corpus hearing that he had proceeded on the basis of Gerald's admissions at the two hearings. . . .

It would indeed be surprising if the privilege against self-incrimination were available to hardened criminals but not to children. The language of the Fifth Amendment, applicable to the States by operation of the Fourteenth Amendment, is unequivocal and without exception. And the scope of the privilege is comprehensive. . . .

Against the application to juveniles of the right to silence, it is argued that juvenile proceedings are "civil" and not "criminal," and therefore the privilege should not apply. . . .

. . . For this purpose, at least, commitment is a deprivation of liberty. It is incarceration against one's will, whether it is called "criminal" or "civil." . . .

We conclude that the constitutional privilege against self-incrimination is applicable in the case of juveniles as it is with respect to adults. . . .

. . . Apart from the "admission," there was nothing upon which a judgment or finding might be based. There was no sworn testimony. Mrs. Cook, the complainant, was not present. . . .

. . . We now hold that, absent a valid confession, a determination of delinquency and an order of commitment to a state institution cannot be sustained in the absence of sworn testimony subjected to the opportunity for cross-examination in accordance with our law and constitutional requirements. . . .

[Justices Black and White concurred. Justice Harlan concurred in part and dissented in part. Justice Stewart dissented.]

In *In re Winship*, 397 U.S. 358 (1970), the Court examined the New York rule permitting conviction in juvenile delinquency proceedings based on a "preponderance of evidence." The Court reversed, holding that the due process clause protected an accused juvenile in a criminal prosecution against conviction except upon proof beyond a reasonable doubt. But in *McKeiver* v. *Pennsylvania,* 403 U.S. 528 (1971), the Court held that the Fourteenth Amendment does not require a jury trial in delinquency proceedings in juvenile courts.

Although the case did not involve criminal proceedings, in *Goss* v. *Lopez* in 1975 the Court examined the issue of whether the due process clause of the Fourteenth Amendment demanded a hearing prior to the suspension from school of public school students.

GOSS *v.* LOPEZ

*419 U.S. 565 (1975)*

Mr. Justice White delivered the opinion of the Court. . . .

Ohio law. . . empowers the principal of an Ohio public school to suspend a pupil for misconduct for up to 10 days or to expel him. In either case, he must notify the student's parents within 24 hours and state the reasons for his actions. A pupil who is expelled, or his parents, may appeal the decision to the Board of Education and in connection therewith shall be permitted to be heard at the board meeting. The board may reinstate the pupil following the hearing. No similar procedure is provided . . . for a suspended student. . . .

The nine named appellees, each of whom alleged that he or she had been suspended from public high school in Columbus for up to 10 days without a hearing . . . filed an action against the Columbus Board of Education and various administrators . . . under 42 USC §1983. The complaint sought a declaration that [the Ohio law] was unconstitutional in that it permitted public school administrators to deprive plaintiffs of their rights to an education without a hearing of any kind, in violation of the procedural due process component of the Fourteenth Amendment. It also sought to enjoin the public school officials from issuing future suspensions pursuant to [the law] and to require them to remove references to the past suspensions from the records of the students in question.

The proof below established that the suspensions in question arose out of a period of widespread student unrest. . . during February and March of 1971. Six of the named plaintiffs . . . were students at the Marion-Franklin High School and were each suspended for 10 days on account of disruptive or disobedient conduct committed in the presence of the school administrator who ordered the suspension. One of these, Tyrone Washington, was among a group of students demonstrating in the school auditorium while a class was being conducted there. He was ordered by the school principal to leave, refused to do so and was suspended. Rudolph Sutton, in the presence of the principal, physically attacked a police officer who was attempting to remove Tyrone Washington from the auditorium. He was immediately suspended. The other four Marion-Franklin students were suspended for similar conduct. None was given a hearing to determine the operative facts underlying the suspension, but each, together with his or her parents, was offered the opportunity to attend a conference, subsequent to the effective date of the suspension, to discuss the student's future. . . .

[A three-judge District Court granted the relief sought by plaintiffs.]

At the outset, appellants contend that because there is no constitutional right to an education at public expense, the Due Process Clause does not protect against expulsions from the public school system. This position misconceives the nature of the issue and is refuted by prior decisions. . . .

Here, on the basis of state law, appellees plainly had legitimate claims of entitlement to a public education. [The Ohio Code] directs local authorities to provide a free education to all residents between six and 21 years of age, and a compulsory attendance law requires attendance for a school year of not less than 32 weeks. . . .

Although Ohio may not be constitutionally obligated to establish and maintain a public school system, it has nevertheless done so and has required its children to attend. Those young people do not "shed their constitutional rights" at the schoolhouse door. *Tinker* v. *Des Moines School District.* . . . The authority possessed by the State to prescribe and enforce standards of conduct in its schools, although concededly very broad, must be exercised consistently with constitutional safeguards. Among other things, the State is constrained to recognize a student's legitimate entitlement to a public education as a property interest which is protected by the Due Process Clause and which may not be taken away for misconduct without adherence to the minimum procedures required by that clause. . . .

Appellants proceed to argue that even if there is a right to a public education protected by the Due Process Clause generally, the clause comes into play only when the State subjects a student to a "severe detriment or grievous loss." The loss of 10 days, it is said, is neither severe nor grievous and the Due Process Clause is therefore of no relevance. . . .

A short suspension is of course a far milder deprivation than expulsion. But, "education is perhaps the most important function of state and local governments." *Brown* v. *Board of Education.* . . . , and the total exclusion from the educational process for more than a trivial period, and certainly if the suspension is for 10 days, is a serious event in the life of the suspended child. Neither the property interest in educational benefits temporarily denied nor the liberty interest in reputation, which is also implicated, is so insubstantial that suspensions may constitutionally be imposed by any procedure the school chooses, no matter how arbitrary. . . .

We do not believe that school authorities must be totally free from notice and hearing requirements if their schools are to operate with acceptable efficiency. Students facing temporary suspension have interests qualifying for protection of the Due Process Clause, and due process requires, in connection with a suspension of 10 days or less, that the student be given oral or written notice of the charges against him and, if he denies them, an explanation of the evidence the authorities have and an opportunity to present his side of the story. The clause requires at least these rudimentary precautions against unfair or mistaken findings of misconduct and arbitrary exclusion from school.

There need be no delay between the time "notice" is given and the time of the hearing. In the great majority of cases the disciplinarian may informally discuss the alleged misconduct with the student minutes after it has occurred. We hold only that, in being given an opportunity to explain his version of the facts at this discussion, the student first be told what he is accused of doing and what the basis of the accusation is. Lower courts which have addressed the question of the *nature* of the procedures required in short suspension cases have reached the same conclusion. . . .

Since the hearing may occur almost immediately following the misconduct, it follows that as a general rule notice and hearing should precede removal of the student from school. We agree with the District Court, however, that there are recurring situations in which prior notice and hearing cannot be insisted upon. Students whose presence pose a continuing danger to persons or property or an ongoing threat of disrupting the academic process may be immediately removed from school. In such cases, the necessary notice and rudimentary hearing should follow as soon as practicable, as the District Court indicated. . . .

We stop short of construing the Due Process Clause to require, countrywide, that hearings in connection with short suspensions must afford the student the opportunity to secure counsel, to confront and cross-examine witnesses supporting the charge or to call his own witnesses to verify his version of the incident. Brief disciplinary suspensions are almost countless. To impose in each such case even truncated trial type procedures might well overwhelm administrative facilities in many places and, by diverting resources, cost more than it would save in educational effectiveness. Moreover, further formalizing the suspension process and escalating its formality and adversary nature may not only make it too costly as a regular disciplinary tool but also destroy its effectiveness as part of the teaching process.

On the other hand, requiring effective notice and informal hearing permitting the student to give his version of the events will provide a meaningful hedge against erroneous action. At least the disciplinarian will be alerted to the existence of disputes about facts and arguments about cause and effect. He may then determine himself to summon the accuser, permit cross-examination and allow the student to present his own witnesses. In more difficult cases, he may permit counsel. In any event, his discretion will be more informed and we think the risk of error substantially reduced. . . .

We should also make it clear that we have addressed ourselves solely to the short suspension, not exceeding 10 days. Longer suspensions or expulsions for the remainder of the school term, or permanently, may require more formal procedures. Nor do we put aside the possibility that in unusual situations, although involving only a short suspension, something more than the rudimentary procedures will be required. . . .

*Affirmed.*

Mr. Justice Powell, with whom the Chief Justice, Mr. Justice Blackmun, and Mr. Justice Rehnquist join, dissenting. . . .

No one can foresee the ultimate frontiers of the new "thicket" the Court now enters. Today's ruling appears to sweep within the protected interest in education a multitude of discretionary decisions in the educational process. Teachers and other school authorities are required to make many decisions that may have serious consequences for the pupil. . . . [I]n many of these situations, the pupil can advance the same types of speculative and subjective injury given critical weight in this case. The District Court, relying upon generalized opinion evidence, concluded that a suspended student may suffer psychological injury in one or more of the ways set forth in the margin below. The Court appears to adopt this rationale. . . .

It hardly need be said that if a student, as a result of a day's suspension, suffers "a blow" to his "self-esteem," "feels powerless," views "teachers with resentment," or feels "stigmatized by his teachers," identical psychological harms will flow from many other routine and necessary school decisions. The student who is given a failing grade, who is not promoted, who is excluded from certain extracurricular activities, who is assigned to a school reserved for children of less than average ability, or who is placed in the "vocational" rather than the "college preparatory" track, is unlikely to suffer any less psychological injury than if he were suspended for a day for a relatively minor infraction.

If, as seems apparent, the Court will now require due process procedures whenever such routine school decisions are challenged, the impact upon public education will be serious indeed. The discretion and judgment of federal courts across the land will be substituted for that of the 50 state legislatures, the 14,000 school boards and the 2,000,000 teachers who heretofore have been responsible for the administration of the American public school system. If the Court perceives a rational and analytically sound distinction between the discretionary decision by school authorities to suspend a pupil for a brief period, and the types of discretionary school decisions described above, it would be prudent to articulate it in today's opinion. Otherwise, the federal courts should prepare themselves for a vast new role in society. . . .

## DOUBLE JEOPARDY

Protection against double jeopardy was firmly grounded in the common law well before the addition of the Fifth Amendment provision that no person shall be "subject for the same offense to be twice put in jeopardy of life or limb." In fact the English rule today, embodying the common law principle, is tighter than our own, since the law does not permit English appellate courts to send criminal cases back for new trials except in very special situations. The choice is between correction of errors below, if possible (such as revision of sentences), or simply vacating the judgment of conviction, so rigidly is the rule against double jeopardy construed.

Since jeopardy means the danger of conviction, *indictment* for crime does not put a person in jeopardy, and therefore repeated indictments do not constitute double jeopardy. Jeopardy does not attach until the trial actually begins. If trial is without a jury, jeopardy commonly attaches when the first witness is sworn or when the court has begun to hear evidence. In *Serfass* v. *United States,* 420 U.S. 377 (1975), the Court ruled that in a case of jury trial, jeopardy attaches when the court begins to hear evidence. The general rule is that only under exceptional circumstances can the trial be halted after this stage and the accused subjected later to a second trial. Such would be the case where a juror is disqualified or the jury fails to reach a verdict. The latter situation was involved in *United States* v. *Perez,* 9 Wheat. 579 (1824), in which the Court stated:

> The prisoner has not been convicted or acquitted, and may again be put upon his defense. We think, that in all cases of this nature, the law has invested courts of justice with the authority to discharge a jury from giving any verdict, whenever, in their opinion, taking all the circumstances into consideration, there is a manifest necessity for the act, or the ends of public justice would otherwise be defeated.

An ususual aspect of the problem was considered by the Court in *Smalis* v. *Pennsylvania,* 476 U.S. 140 (1986). Petitioners, husband and wife, were charged with various crimes in connection with a fire in a building that resulted in the killing of two tenants. At the close of the prosecution's case in a Pennsylvania state court, petitioners challenged the sufficiency of the evidence by filing a demurrer. The trial court sustained the demurrer, and the Pennsylvania Superior Court quashed the Commonwealth's appeal on the ground that it was barred by the Double Jeopardy Clause. The Pennsylvania Supreme Court reversed, holding that the granting of a demurrer is not the functional equivalent of an acquittal and that, for purposes of considering a plea of double jeopardy, a defendant who demurs at the close of the prosecution's case in chief "elects to seek dismissal on grounds unrelated to his factual guilt or innocence." The United States Supreme Court held unanimously that "the trial judge's granting a petitioners' demurrer was an acquittal under the Double Jeopardy Clause, and that the Commonwealth's appeal was barred because reversal would have led to further trial proceedings."

### Double Jeopardy and Criminal Appeals

The federal law is clear that the government has no right to appeal after a verdict of acquittal, since the protection against double jeopardy encompasses such an action. Such was the holding in *Kepner* v. *United States,* 195 U.S. 100 (1904). This reaffirmed a similar holding based on common law considerations in *United States* v. *Sanges,* 144 U.S. 310, 323 (1892). Since jeopardy does not attach merely upon indictment, however, a judgment to quash an indictment is appealable by the Government. The old Fourteenth Amendment rule (no longer valid) was laid down in *Palko* v. *Connecticut,* 302 U.S. 319 (1937). The Court held there that where errors of law, to the prejudice of the State, were committed in the trial court, the State could appeal for a new trial. In *Benton* v. *Maryland,* 395 U.S. 784 (1969), however, the Court incorporated the Fifth Amendment's protection against double jeopardy into the Fourteenth Amendment and overruled *Palko.*

At the common law, and still in England, the appellate court was barred from ordering a retrial following conviction, even if material error was found in the trial proceedings. American courts have followed a practice of ordering a wholly new trial if the convicted defendant appealed and "reversible errors" were found to have occurred in the first trial. In *United States* v. *Keen,* 6 Fed. Cas. 686 (1839), Justice McLean, on circuit, vigorously rejected the view that the constitutional provision prohibited a new trial on the defendant's motion after a conviction, or that it "guarantees to him the right of being hung, to protect him from the danger of a second trial." The theory followed here seems to be that since the request is made by the defendant, the claim of double jeopardy is implicitly waived. There is no particular difficulty with this approach if the defendant obtains a new trial on the same charge for which conviction resulted in the first trial. A problem arises, however, if the conviction is for a lesser included offense of the original charge and on subsequent retrial the defendant again faces the more serious original charge. In *Palko,* for example, the defendant was tried for first degree murder. He was convicted of second degree murder. At the new trial he was again tried, and convicted, of *first* degree murder. The Court held in 1957, in *Green* v. *United States,* that such a procedure in the federal courts would violate the Fifth Amendment's protection against double jeopardy.

## GREEN *v.* UNITED STATES
### 355 *U.S. 184 (1957)*

Opinion of the Court by Mr. Justice Black, announced by Mr. Justice Douglas.

This case presents a serious question concerning the meaning and application of that provision of the Fifth Amendment to the Constitution which declares that no person shall

" . . . be subject for the same offence to be twice put in jeopardy of life or limb. . . ."

The petitioner, Everett Green, was indicted by a District of Columbia grand jury on two counts. The first charged that he had committed arson by maliciously setting fire to a house. The second accused him of causing the death of a woman by this alleged arson which if true amounted to murder in the first degree punishable by death. Green entered a plea of not guilty to both counts and the case was tried by a jury. After each side had presented its evidence the trial judge instructed the jury that it could find Green guilty of arson under the first count and of either (1) first degree murder or (2) second degree murder under the second count. The trial judge treated second degree murder, which is defined by the District Code as the killing of another with malice aforethought, and is punishable by imprisonment for a term of years or for life, as an offense included within the language charging first degree murder in the second count of the indictment.

The jury found Green guilty of arson and of second degree murder but did not find him guilty on the charge of murder in the first degree. Its verdict was silent on that charge. The trial judge accepted the verdict, entered the proper judgments and dismissed the jury. Green was sentenced to one to three years' imprisonment for arson and five to twenty years' imprisonment for murder in the second degree. He appealed the conviction of second degree murder. The Court of Appeals reversed that conviction because it was not supported by evidence and remanded the case for a new trial. . . .

On remand Green was tried again for first degree murder under the original indictment. At the outset of this second trial he raised the defense of former jeopardy but the court overruled his plea. This time a new jury found him guilty of first degree murder and he was given the mandatory death sentence. Again he appealed. Sitting *en banc,* the Court of Appeals rejected his defense of former jeopardy . . . and affirmed the conviction. . . .

Green was in direct peril of being convicted and punished for first degree murder at his first trial. He was forced to run the gantlet once on that charge and the jury refused to convict him. When given the choice between finding him guilty of either first or second degree murder it chose the latter. In this situation the great majority of cases in this country have regarded the jury's verdict as an implicit acquittal on the charge of first degree murder. . . . In brief, we believe this case can be treated no differently, for purposes of former jeopardy, than if the jury had returned a verdict which expressly read: "We find the defendant not guilty of murder in the first degree but guilty of murder in the second degree."

After the original trial, but prior to his appeal, it is indisputable that Green could not have been tried again for first degree murder for the death resulting from the fire. A plea of former jeopardy would have absolutely barred a new prosecution even though it might have been convincingly demonstrated that the jury erred in failing to convict him of that offense. And even after appealing the conviction of second degree murder he still could not have been tried a second time for first degree murder had his appeal been unsuccessful.

Nevertheless the Government contends that Green "waived" his constitutional defense of former jeopardy to a second prosecution on the first degree murder charge by making a *successful appeal* of his improper conviction of second degree murder. We cannot accept this paradoxical contention. . . .

Reduced to plain terms, the Government contends that in order to secure the reversal of an erroneous conviction of one offense, a defendant must surrender his valid defense of former jeopardy not only on that offense but also on a different offense for which he was not convicted and which was not involved in his appeal. . . . The law should not, and in our judgment does not, place the defendant in such an incredible dilemma. Conditioning an appeal of one offense on a coerced surrender of a valid plea of former jeopardy on another offense exacts a forfeiture in plain conflict with the constitutional bar against double jeopardy. . . .

*Reversed.*

Mr. Justice Frankfurter, whom Mr. Justice Burton, Mr. Justice Clark and Mr. Justice Harlan join, dissenting. . . .

In 1969, in *Benton* v. *Maryland,* the Court incorporated the Fifth Amendment's protection against double jeopardy into the Fourteenth Amendment. Following the federal rule announced in *Green* v. *United States,* the Court held that due process barred the State from subjecting a defendant to charges on retrial other than those for which he was convicted at the initial trial. To this extent *Palko* was explicitly overruled.

BENTON *v.* MARYLAND
*395 U.S. 784 (1969)*

[In a Maryland state court trial on charges of burglary and larceny, the jury found the defendant not guilty of larceny, but convicted him on the burglary count, for which he was sentenced to ten years in prison. Because both the grand and petit juries in the case had been unconstitutionally selected, the Maryland Court of Appeals remanded the case to the trial court, where the defendant was given the option of demanding reindictment and retrial, which he did. At the second trial, again for both larceny and burglary, the defendant's motion to dismiss the larceny charge as subjecting him to double jeopardy was denied, he was found guilty of both offenses, and he was given concurrent sentences of fifteen years on the burglary count and five years for larceny. The newly created Maryland Court of Special Appeals rejected the defendant's double jeopardy claim on the merits, and the Maryland Court of Appeals denied discretionary review.]

Mr. Justice Marshall delivered the opinion of the Court.

In 1937, this Court decided the landmark case of *Palko* v. *Connecticut*. . . . Palko, although indicted for first-degree murder, had been convicted of murder in the second degree after a jury trial in a Connecticut state court. The State appealed and won a new trial. Palko argued that the Fourteenth Amendment incorporated, as against the States, the Fifth Amendment requirement that no person "be twice put in jeopardy of life or limb." The Court disagreed. Federal double jeopardy standards were not applicable against the States. Only when a kind of jeopardy subjected a defendant to "a hardship so acute and shocking that our polity will not endure it,". . . did the Fourteenth Amendment apply. The order for a new trial was affirmed. In subsequent appeals from state courts, the Court continued to apply this lesser *Palko* standard. . . .

Recently, however, this Court has "increasingly looked to the specific guarantees of the [Bill of Rights] to determine whether a state criminal trial was conducted with due process of law." *Washington* v. *Texas*. . . (1967). In an increasing number of cases, the Court "has rejected the notion that the Fourteenth Amendment applies to the States only a 'watered-down, subjective version of the individual guarantees of the Bill of Rights. . . . ' " . . . Only last Term we found that the right to trial by jury in criminal cases was "fundamental to the American scheme of justice," *Duncan* v. *Louisiana* . . . (1968), and held that the Sixth Amendment right to a jury trial was applicable to the States through the Fourteenth Amendment. For the same reasons, we today find that the double jeopardy prohibition of the Fifth Amendment represents a fundamental ideal in our constitutional heritage, and that it should apply to the States through the Fourteenth Amendment. Insofar as it is inconsistent with this holding, *Palko* v. *Connecticut* is overruled.

*Palko* represented an approach to basic constitutional rights which this Court's recent decisions have rejected. It was cut of the same cloth as *Betts* v. *Brady*. . . , the case which held that a criminal defendant's right to counsel was to be determined by deciding in each case whether the denial of that right was "shocking to the universal sense of justice." . . . Our recent cases have thoroughly rejected the *Palko* notion that basic constitutional right can be denied by the States as long as the totality of the circumstances does not disclose a denial of "fundamental fairness." Once it is decided that a particular Bill of Rights guarantee is "fundamental to the American scheme of justice," . . . the same constitutional standards apply against both the State and Federal Governments. *Palko's* roots had thus been cut away years ago. We today only recognize the inevitable.

The fundamental nature of the guarantees against double jeopardy can hardly be doubted. Its origins can be traced to Greek and Roman Times, and it became established in the common law of England long before this Nation's independence. . . . Today, every State incorporates some form of the prohibition in its consitution or common law. . . . This underlying notion has from the very beginning been part of our constitutional tradition. Like the right to trial by jury, it is clearly "fundamental to the American scheme of justice." The validity of petitioner's larceny conviction must be judged, not by the watered-down standard enunciated in *Palko*, but under this Court's interpretations of the Fifth Amendment double jeopardy provision.

It is clear that petitioner's larceny conviction cannot stand once federal double jeopardy standards are applied. Petitioner was acquitted of larceny in his first trial. Because he decided to appeal his burglary conviction, he is forced to suffer retrial on the larceny count as well. As this Court held in *Green* v. *United States*, . . . "conditioning an appeal of one offense on a coerced surrender of a valid plea of former jeopardy on another offense exacts a forfeiture in plain conflict with the constitutional bar against double jeopardy."

Maryland argues that *Green* does not apply to this case because petitioner's original indictment was absolutely void. One cannot be placed in "jeopardy" by a void indictment, the State argues. This argument sounds a bit strange, however, since petitioner could quietly have served out his sentence under this "void" indictment had he not appealed his burglary conviction. . . . Petitioner was acquitted of larceny. He has, under *Green,* a valid double jeopardy plea which he cannot be forced to waive. Yet Maryland wants the earlier acquittal set aside, over petitioner's objections, because of a defect in the indictment. This it cannot do. Petitioner's larceny conviction cannot stand.

Petitioner argues that his burglary conviction should be set aside as well. He contends that some evidence, inadmissible under state law in the trial for burglary alone, was introduced in the joint trial for both burglary and larceny, and that the jury was prejudiced by this evidence. This question was not decided by the Maryland Court. . . . Accordingly, we think it "just under the circumstances,". . . to vacate the judgment below and remand for consideration of this question. The judgment is vacated and the case is remanded for further proceedings not inconsistent with this opinion.

*It is so ordered.*

Mr. Justice White, concurring. . . .

Mr. Justice Harlan, whom Mr. Justice Stewart joins, dissenting. . . .

I would hold, in accordance with *Palko* v. *Connecticut* . . . that the due Process Clause of the Fourteenth Amendment does not take over the Double Jeopardy Clause of the Fifth, as such. Today *Palko* becomes another casualty in the so far unchecked march toward "incorporating" much, if not all, of the Federal Bill of Rights into the Due Process Clause. This march began, with a Court majority, in 1961 when *Mapp* v. *Ohio* . . . was decided and, before the present decision, found its last stopping point in *Duncan* v. *Louisiana* . . . , decided at the end of last Term. I have at each step in the march expressed my opposition . . . ; more particularly in the *Duncan* case I undertook to show that the "selective incorporation" doctrine finds no support either in history or in reason. Under the pressures of the closing days of the Term, I am content to rest on what I have written in prior opinions, save to raise my voice again in protest against a doctrine which so subtly, yet profoundly, is eroding many of the basics of our federal system. . . .

In *North Carolina* v. *Pearce,* 395 U.S. 711 (1969), the Court examined another double jeopardy issue—the problem of the successful appellant who is given more severe sentence upon retrial than at the first trial. The Court held that while such sentences were not *ipso facto* unconstitutional, any punishment already exacted must be "fully credited," and where more severe punishment is given, the judge's reasons for doing so must affirmatively appear, and the factual data upon which the increased sentence is based must be made a part of the record for the purpose of reviewing the constitutionality of such sentence.

Chaffin v. Stynchcombe, 412 U.S. 17 (1973), involved the imposition of a more severe sentence upon retrial, but in this case the sentence was set by the jury. The defendant was convicted of a felony in a Georgia criminal court, and the jury, pursuant to Georgia procedure, sentenced him to fifteen years in prison. A United States District Court, granting habeas corpus relief, ordered a new trial. After retrial, before a different judge and jury, he was again convicted, and the second jury sentenced him to life imprisonment. He again pursued habeas corpus relief, but the District Court denied his claim of due process violation. The Court of Appeals affirmed and, on certiorari, the Supreme Court also affirmed. The majority held that the higher sentence did not violate the due process clause so long as the jury was not informed of the prior sentence and the second sentence was not otherwise shown to be a product of vindictiveness. Further, there was no need for extending to jury resentencing the restrictions, applicable to judge resentencing, that the record must show the reasons for the higher sentence, based on the defendant's conduct after the original sentencing.

In Michigan v. Payne, 412 U.S. 47 (1973), the Court held that the Pearce rule was not retroactive. Justice Powell, for the majority, stated that the test repeatedly utilized to ascertain whether "new" constitutional protections in the area of criminal procedure are to be applied retroactively calls for the consideration of three criteria: (a) the purpose to be served by the new standards, (b) the extent of the reliance by law enforcement authorities on the old standards, and (c) the effect on the administration of justice of a retroactive application of the new standards. Applying these criteria, he found that Pearce should not be applied retroactively.

Blackledge v. Perry, 417 U.S. 21 (1974), dealt with the matter of prosecutor vindictiveness after one convicted of a misdemeanor filed an appeal. While serving a prison term in North Carolina, Perry became involved in an altercation with another inmate. Perry was charged with the misdemeanor of assult with a deadly weapon and was convicted in the State District Court. While his appeal was pending in the Superior Court, where he had the right to a trial de novo, the prosecutor obtained an indictment covering the same conduct for the felony offense of assault with a deadly weapon with intent to kill inflicting serious bodily injury. Perry entered a plea of guilty and was sentenced to a term of five to seven years in the penitentiary, instead of the six-month sentence he had received in the District Court. Later, in a habeas corpus action in the United States District Court, Perry claimed that the felony indictment violated the double jeopardy clause and also violated the due process clause as expressed in the Pearce rule. When the case came on to the Supreme Court, only the latter claim was discussed. The opinion for the majority, through Justice Stewart, stated that the lesson that emerges from Pearce and Chaffin is that "the Due Process Clause is not offended by all possibilities of increased punishment upon retrial after appeal, but only by those that pose a realistic likelihood of 'vindictiveness.' " The majority concluded that the facts justified such a finding in this case. It was pointed out that if the prosecutor may "up the ante" through a felony indictment whenever misdemeanant pursues his statutory appellate remedy, the State can insure that only the most hardy defendants will brave the hazards of a de novo trial.

## Trial for Multiple Related Offenses

Double jeopardy issues of a special sort may be presented when an accused is tried on multiple counts—entirely in a single trial or in successive trials—arising out of the execution of a single criminal plot. Three facets of this situation occur, each presenting separate problems. (1) The criminal law has developed in a fashion which results in a great deal of overlapping, and consequently a single criminal act may in fact be chargeable as two or more offenses. In defining criminal offenses the law has operated like the pathologist's knife in splitting the total transaction into several discrete parts, each of which constitutes a separate crime. Thus a burglary might actually be broken down into the separate charges of conspiracy to commit burglary, possession of burglar's tools with intent to commit burglary, and burglary. (2) A criminal may commit several crimes on a single occasion, as, for example, by robbing five different customers in a tavern. In so doing, he has committed five separate crimes and may be so charged. The problem arises when he is tried seriatim on these charges, rather than in one trial. (3) A third double jeopardy issue stems from the fact that we live under a federal system, and a single act may constitute both a state crime and a federal crime.

The constitutionality of trying a defendant on closely related charges is usually determined by whether additional facts must be proved in the additional charges. In Albernaz v. United States, 450 U.S. 333 (1981), two defendants, who were involved in an agreement to import marihuana and then to distribute it domestically, were convicted on separate counts of conspiracy to import marihuana and of conspiracy to distribute marihuana. These two conspiracy convictions were based on separate offenses with separate penalty provisions which were contained in distinct sections of the Drug Abuse Prevention and Control Act of 1970. The defendants received consecutive sentences for these convictions, and the length of the combined sentences exceeded the maximum sentence which could have been imposed for either conspiracy conviction. The Court held that (1) Congress intended to permit the imposition of consecutive sentences for violations of the two sections even where such violations arise from a single conspiracy since it had multiple objectives, and (2) that such cumulative punishment is not barred by the double jeopardy clause since there were two offenses, each of which required proof of a fact which the other did not. Justice Rehnquist, in the majority opinion, quoted Blockburger v. United States, 284 U.S. 299, 304 (1932):

**The applicable rule is that where the same act or transaction constitutes a violation of two distinct statutory provisions, the test to be applied to determine whether there are two offenses or only one, is whether each provision requires proof of a fact which the other does not.**

In Brown v. Ohio, 432 U.S. 161 (1977), the Court applied the Blockburger test in reversing a conviction on double jeopardy grounds. The defendant was arrested nine days after he had stolen an automobile and pleaded guilty to a misdemeanor charge of joyriding—operating a car without the owner's consent—the joyriding charge having been based on his driving the car on the last day of his nine-day joyride. Subsequently he was charged with felony auto theft, based on his original taking of the car. The trial court rejected his double jeopardy claim, and he pleaded guilty. The Ohio Court of Appeals affirmed, holding that while joyriding was a lesser included offense of auto theft, nevertheless the two prosecutions were based on two separate acts, nine days apart, and thus the double jeopardy clause did not bar the second prosecution. In a six-to-three vote, the United States Supreme Court reversed. Justice Powell, for the majority, stated:

**Applying the Blockburger test, we agree with the Ohio Court of Appeals that joyriding and auto theft, as defined by that court, constitute "the same statutory offense" within the meaning of the Double Jeopardy Clause. . . . For it is clearly not the case that "each [statute] requires proof of a fact which the other does not." . . . As is invariably true of a greater and lesser included offense, the lesser offense—joyrid-**

ing—requires no proof beyond that which is required for conviction of the greater—auto theft. The greater offense is therefore by definition the "same" for purposes of double jeopardy as any lesser offense included in it.

When a criminal robs several persons on a single occasion, he has committed multiple crimes of an identical nature. The question then arises of whether he can be tried in a series of trials under these circumstances or whether the prohibition against double jeopardy limits the government to a single trial. Two cases involving this issue under the Fourteenth Amendment were decided in 1958. They were *Hoag* v. *New Jersey,* 356 U.S. 464 (1958), and *Ciucci* v. *Illinois,* 356 U.S. 571 (1958).

The *Hoag* case involved the robbery of five persons one evening in a New Jersey tavern. Hoag was indicted separately for robbery of three of the victims, and the indictments were joined for trial. At this trial acquittal resulted. All five victims were called as witnesses in the trial. Subsequently, Hoag was indicted, tried, and convicted for robbing a fourth person at the tavern. The same issues of identification of Hoag as a participant in the robbery and the credibility of Hoag's alibi were presented at the second trial. Hoag argued that in these circumstances his second trial was in violation of the due process protection against double jeopardy. The Supreme Court of New Jersey sustained the conviction, and on certiorari the United States Supreme Court affirmed by a five-to-three vote. The majority took into account the fact that several of the witnesses, to the surprise of the State, failed to identify Hoag as one of the robbers after having done so during the police investigation, and concluded that this was not an attempt on the part of the State to wear the accused out by a multitude of cases with accumulated trials. The dissenters argued that "Hoag is made to run the gantlet twice," since the only contested issue was whether he was one of the robbers. This they felt clearly violated the constitutional protection against double jeopardy.

In the same term of Court, a similar holding followed in *Ciucci* v. *Illinois,* 356 U.S. 571 (1958). In this case the vote was five-to-four, with Mr. Justice Brennan participating and voting with the dissenters. Ciucci's wife and three children were found dead with bullet wounds in their heads in a burning building. Ciucci was charged on four separate murder indictments and tried three successive times, first for the murder of his wife, and then for the murder of two of the three children. At each of the trials the prosecution introduced into evidence details of all four deaths. Under Illinois law, the jury fixed the penalty for first degree murder. Ciucci was convicted in each of the three trials. The sentences by the three different juries increased successively from 20 years for the wife, to 45 years for the first child, to death for the second child. The same majority as in *Hoag,* in a per curiam opinion, affirmed the judgment on authority of *Hoag* and *Palko.* In 1970, in the wake of *Benton* v. *Maryland,* the Court overruled this position in *Ashe* v. *Swenson.*

### ASHE *v.* SWENSON
### *397 U.S. 436 (1970)*

[Six men engaged in a poker game were robbed by three or four masked gunmen. Six weeks after being acquitted in a state trial for the robbery of one of the players, the defendant was tried for the robbery of another of the players and was convicted. The witnesses in the two trials were for the most part the same, and the State's evidence establishing the facts of the robbery was uncontradicted, but the testimony identifying the defendant as one of the robbers was substantially stronger at the second trial. The Supreme Court of Missouri affirmed the conviction, holding that the "plea of former jeopardy must be denied." A collateral attack upon the conviction in the state courts five years later was also unsuccessful. The defendant then brought a habeas corpus proceeding in the United States District Court, claiming that the second prosecution had violated his right not to be twice put in jeopardy. The District Court denied the writ, the Court of Appeals affirmed, and the Supreme Court granted certiorari.]

Mr. Justice Stewart delivered the opinion of the Court.

As the District Court and the Court of Appeals correctly noted, the operative facts here are virtually identical to those of *Hoag* v. *New Jersey*. . . . Viewing the question presented solely in terms of Fourteenth Amendment due process—whether the course that New Jersey had pursued had "led to fundamental unfairness," . . . —this Court declined to reverse the judgment of conviction, because "in the circumstances shown by this record, we cannot say that petitioner's later prosecution and conviction violated due process." . . . The Court found it unnecessary to decide whether "collateral estoppel"—the principle that bars relitigation between the same parties of issues actually determined at a previous trial—is a due process requirement in a state criminal trial. . . . And in the view the Court took of the issues presented, it did not, of course, even approach consideration of whether collateral estoppel is an ingredient of the Fifth Amendment guarantee against double jeopardy.

The doctrine of *Benton* v. *Maryland* . . . puts the issues in the present case in a perspective quite different from that in which the issues were perceived in *Hoag* v. *New Jersey.* The question is no longer whether collateral estoppel is a requirement of due process, but whether it is a part of the Fifth Amendment's guarantee against double jeopardy. . . .

"Collateral estoppel" is an awkward phrase, but it stands for an extremely important principle in our adversary system of justice. It means simply that when an issue of ultimate fact has once been determined by a valid and final judgment, that issue cannot again be litigated between the same parties in any future lawsuit. . . . The federal decisions have made clear that the rule of collateral estoppel in criminal cases is not to be applied with the hypertechnical and archaic approach of a 19th century pleading book, but with realism and rationality. Where a previous judgment of acquittal was based upon a general verdict, as is usually the case, this appoach requires a court to "examine the record of a prior proceeding, taking into account the pleadings, evidence, charge, and other relevant matter, and conclude whether a rational jury could have grounded its verdict upon an issue other than that which the defendant seeks to foreclose from consideration." . . .

Straightforward application of the federal rule to the present case can lead to but one conclusion. . . . The single rationally conceivable issue in dispute before the jury was whether the petitioner had been one of the robbers. And the jury by its verdict found that he had not. . . .

The ultimate question to be determined, then, in the light of *Benton* v. *Maryland, supra,* is whether this established rule of federal law is embodied in the Fifth Amendment guarantee against double jeopardy. We do not hesitate to hold that it is. For whatever else that constitutional guarantee may embrace, . . . it surely protects a man who has been acquitted from having to "run the gantlet" a second time. . . .

The question is not whether Missouri could validly charge the petitioner with six separate offenses for the robbery of the six poker players. It is not whether he could have received a total of six punishments if he had been convicted in a single trial of robbing the six victims. It is simply whether, after a jury determined by its verdict that the petitioner was not one of the robbers, the State could constitutionally hale him before a new jury to litigate that issue again. . . .

The judgment is reversed, and the case is remanded to the Court of Appeals for the Eighth Circuit for further proceedings consistent with this opinion.

[Separate concurring opinions were written by Justice Black, Justice Harlan, and Justice Brennan, who was joined by Justices Douglas and Marshall. Chief Justice Burger dissented.]

Another multiple offense problem arises when a single act constitutes a crime under state law and also under municipal ordinance. The question of whether dual prosecution in such situations constitutes double jeopardy was considered in *Waller* v. *Florida*, decided on the same day as *Ashe*.

WALLER v. FLORIDA
*397 U.S. 387 (1970)*

Mr. Chief Justice Burger delivered the opinion of the Court. . . .

Petitioner was one of a number of persons who removed a canvas mural which was affixed to a wall inside the City Hall of St. Petersburg, Florida. After the mural was removed, the petitioner and others carried it through the streets of St. Petersburg until they were confronted by police officers. After a scuffle, the officers recovered the mural, but in a damaged condition.

The petitioner was charged by the City of St. Petersburg with the violation of two ordinances: first, destruction of city property; and second, disorderly breach of the peace. He was found guilty in the municipal court on both counts, and a sentence of 180 days in the county jail was imposed.

Thereafter an information was filed against the petitioner by the State of Florida charging him with grand larceny. It is conceded that this information was based on the same acts of the petitioner as were involved in the violation of the two city ordinances. . . . Thereafter petitioner was tried in the Circuit Court of Florida by a jury and was found guilty of the felony of grand larceny. . . .

On appeal, the District Court of Appeal of Florida considered and rejected petitioner's claim that he had twice been put in jeopardy because prior to his conviction of grand larceny, he had been convicted by the municipal court of an included offense of the crime of grand larceny. . . . [The District Court of Appeal quoted the Florida Supreme Court saying:]

" 'This double jeopardy argument has long been settled contrary to the claims of the petitioner. We see no reason to recede from our established precedent on the subject. Long ago it was decided that an act committed within municipal limits may be punished by city ordinance even though the same act is also proscribed as a crime by a state statute. An offender may be tried for the municipal offense in the city court and for the crime in the proper state court. Conviction or acquittal in either does not bar prosecution in the other.' ". . .

. . . Whether in fact and law petitioner committed separate offenses which could support separate charges was not decided by the Florida courts, nor do we reach that question. What is before us is the asserted power of the two courts within one State to place petitioner on trial for the same alleged crime.

In *Benton* v. *Maryland* . . . this Court declared the double jeopardy provisions of the Fifth Amendment applicable to the States. . . . Here, as in *North Carolina* v. *Pearce* . . . *Benton* should be applied to test petitioner's conviction. . . .

Florida does not stand alone in treating municipalities and the State as separate sovereign entities, each capable of imposing punishment for the same alleged crime. Here, respondent State of Florida seeks to justify this separate sovereignty theory by asserting that the relationship between a municipality and the state is analogous to the relationship between a State and the Federal Government. Florida's chief reliance is placed upon this Court's holdings in *Bartkus* v. *Illinois* . . . and *Abbate* v.

*United States* . . . which permitted successive prosecutions by the Federal and State Governments as separate sovereigns. . . .

[The] provisions of the Florida Constitution demonstrate that the judicial power to try petitioner on the first charges in municipal court springs from the same organic law that created the state court of general jurisdiction in which petitioner was tried and convicted for a felony. Accordingly, the apt analogy to the relationship between municipal and state governments is to be found in the relationship between the government of a Territory and the Government of the United States. The legal consequence of that relationship was settled in *Grafton* v. *United States,* 206 U.S. 333 (1907), where this Court held that a prosecution in a court of the United States is a bar to a subsequent prosecution in a territorial court, since both are arms of the same sovereign. . . .

Thus *Grafton,* not *Fox* v. *Ohio, supra,* or its progeny, *Bartkus* v. *Illinois* . . . or *Abbate* v. *United States* . . . controls, and we hold that on the basis of the facts upon which the Florida District Court of Appeal relied petitioner could not lawfully be tried both by the municipal government and by the State of Florida. In this context a "dual sovereignty" theory is an anachronism, and the second trial constituted double jeopardy violative of the Fifth and Fourteenth Amendments to the United States Constitution. . . . [Judgment in the second trial vacated, and the cause remanded for further proceedings in accord with this opinion.]

[Justices Black and Brennan wrote concurring opinions.]

In *Robinson* v. *Neil,* 409 U.S. 505 (1973), the Court held that the rule of *Waller* was fully retroactive, since it went to the issue of a second trial taking place at all and not merely to questions of procedural fairness during the trial.

The final aspect of the multiple offense problems to be considered is that of trial by both federal and state authority where a single act constitutes a crime against both jurisdictions. Beginning in 1852 in *Moore* v. *Illinois,* 14 How. 13, the Court has indicated in a number of cases that trials by both jurisdictions in such instances would not violate the prohibitions against double jeopardy.

## BARTKUS *v.* ILLINOIS
### *359 U.S. 121 (1959)*

Mr. Justice Frankfurter delivered the opinion of the Court.

Petitioner was tried in the Federal District Court for the Northern District of Illinois on December 18, 1953, for robbery of a federally insured savings and loan association . . . in violation of 18 U.S.C. Sec. 2113. The case was tried to a jury and resulted in an acquittal. On January 8, 1954, an Illinois grand jury indicted Bartkus. The facts recited in the Illinois indictment were substantially identical to those contained in the prior federal indictment. The Illinois indictment charged that these facts constituted a violation of Illinois Revised Statutes, 1951 c. 38, Sec. 501, a robbery statute. Bartkus was tried and convicted in the Criminal Court of Cook County and was sentenced to life imprisonment under the Illinois Habitual Criminal Statute. . . .

The Illinois trial considered and rejected petitioner's plea of *autrefois acquit.* That ruling and other alleged errors were challenged before the Illinois Supreme Court which affirmed the conviction. . . .

The state and federal prosecutions were separately conducted. It is true that the agent of the Federal Bureau of Investigation who had conducted the investigation on behalf of the Federal Government turned over to the Illinois prosecuting officials all the evidence he had gathered against the petitioner. Concededly, some of that evidence had been gathered after acquittal in the federal court. The only other connection between the two trials is to be found in a suggestion that the federal sentencing of the accomplices who testified against petitioner in both trials was purposely continued by the federal court until after they testified in the state trial. The record establishes that the prosecution was undertaken by state prosecuting officials within their discretionary responsibility and on the basis of evidence that conduct contrary to the penal code of Illinois had occurred within their jurisdiction. It establishes also that federal officials acted in cooperation with state authorities, as is the conventional practice between the two sets of prosecutors throughout the country. It does not support the claim that the State of Illinois in bringing its prosecution was merely a tool of the federal authorities, who thereby avoided the prohibition of the Fifth Amendment against a retrial of a federal prosecution after an acquittal. It does not sustain a conclusion that the state prosecution was a sham and a cover for a federal prosecution, and thereby in essential fact another federal prosecution. . . .

Constitutional challenge to successive state and federal prosecutions based upon the same transaction or conduct is not a new question before the Court though it has now been presented with conspicuous ability. The Fifth Amendment's proscription of double jeopardy has been invoked and rejected in over twenty cases of real or hypothetical successive state and federal prosecution cases before this Court. While *United States* v. *Lanza,* 260 U.S. 377 [1922], was the first case in which we squarely held valid a federal prosecution arising out of the same facts which had been the basis of a state conviction, the validity of such a prosecution by the Federal Government has not been questioned by this Court since the opinion in *Fox* v. *State of Ohio,* 5 How. 410, more than one hundred years ago. . . .

In a dozen cases decided by this Court [before *United States* v. *Lanza*] this Court had occasion to reaffirm the principle first enunciated in *Fox* v. *State of Ohio*. Since *Lanza* the Court has five times repeated the rule that successive state prosecutions are not in violation of the Fifth Amendment. Indeed Mr. Justice Holmes once wrote of this rule that it "is too plain to need more than statement.". . . .

The experience of state courts in dealing with successive prosecutions by different governments is obviously also relevant in considering whether or not the Illinois prosecution of Bartkus violated due process of law. Of the twenty-eight States which have considered the validity of successive state and federal prosecutions as against a challenge of violation of either a state constitutional double-jeopardy provision or a common-law evidentiary rule of *autrefois acquit* and *autrefois convict,* twenty-seven have refused to rule that the second prosecution was or would be barred. These States were not bound to follow this Court and its interpretation of the Fifth Amendment. The rules, constitutional, statutory, or common law which bound them drew upon the same experience as did the Fifth Amendment, but were and are of separate and independent authority. . . .

With this body of precedent as irrefutable evidence that state and federal courts have for years refused to bar a second trial even though there had been a prior trial by another government for a similar offense, it would be disregard of a long, unbroken, unquestioned course of impressive adjudication for the Court now to rule that due process compels such a bar. A practical justification for rejecting such a reading of due process also commends itself in aid of this interpretation of the Fourteenth Amendment. In *Screws* v. *United States,* 325 U.S. 91, defendants were tried and convicted in a federal court under federal statutes with maximum sentences of a year and two years respectively. But the state crime there involved was a capital offense. Were the federal prosecution of a comparatively minor offense to prevent state prosecution of so grave an infraction of state law, the result would be a shocking and untoward deprivation of the historic right and obligation of the States to maintain peace and order within their confines. It would be in derogation of our federal system to displace the reserved power of States over state offenses by reason of prosecution of minor federal offenses by federal authorities beyond the control of the States. . . .

Precedent, experience, and reason all support the conclusion that Alphonse Bartkus has not been deprived of due process of law by the State of Illinois.

*Affirmed.*

Mr. Justice Black, with whom the Chief Justice and Mr. Justice Douglas concur, dissenting. . .

The Court's holding further limits our already weakened constitutional guarantees against double prosecutions. *United States* v. *Lanza* . . . allowed federal conviction and punishment of a man who had been previously convicted and punished for the identical acts by one of our States. Today, for the first time in its history, this Court upholds the state conviction of a defendant who had been *acquitted* of the same offense in the federal courts. I would hold that a federal trial following either state acquittal or conviction is barred by the Double Jeopardy Clause of the Fifth Amendment. *Abbate* v. *United States,* 359 U.S. 187 (dissenting opinion). And, quite apart from whether that clause is as fully binding on the States as it is on the Federal Government, . . . I would hold that Bartkus' conviction cannot stand. For I think double prosecutions for the same offense are so contrary to the spirit of our free country that they violate even the prevailing view of the Fourteenth Amendment, expressed in *Palko* v. *Connecticut.* . . .

The Court apparently takes the position that a second trial for the same act is somehow less offensive if one of the trials is conducted by the Federal Government and the other by a State. Looked at from the standpoint of the individual who is being prosecuted, this notion is too subtle for me to grasp. If double punishment is what is feared, it hurts no less for two "Sovereigns" to inflict it than for one. If danger to the innocent is emphasized, that danger is surely no less when the power of State and Federal Governments is brought to bear on one man in two trials, than when one of these "Sovereigns" proceeds alone. In each case, inescapably, a man is forced to face danger twice for the same conduct.

The Court, without denying the almost universal abhorrence of such double prosecutions, nevertheless justifies the practice here in the name of "federalism." This, it seems to me, is a misuse and desecration of the concept. Our Federal Union was conceived and created "to establish Justice" and to "secure the Blessings of Liberty," not to destroy any of the bulwarks on which both freedom and justice depend. We should, therefore, be suspicious of any supposed "requirements" of "federalism" which result in obliterating ancient safeguards. I have been shown nothing in the history of our Union, in the writings of its Founders, or elsewhere, to indicate that individual rights deemed essential by both State and Nation were to be lost through the combined operations of the two governments. Nor has the Court given any sound reason for thinking that the successful operation of our dual system of government depends in the slightest on the power to try people twice for the same act.

Implicit in the Court's reliance on "federalism" is the premise that failure to allow double prosecutions would seriously impair law enforcement in both State and Nation. For one jurisdiction might provide minor penalties for acts severely punished by the other and by accepting pleas of guilty shield wrongdoers from justice. I believe this argument fails on several grounds. In the first place it relies on the unwarranted assumption that State and Nation will seek to subvert each other's laws. It has elsewhere been persuasively argued that most civilized nations do not and have not needed the power to try people a second time to protect themselves even when dealing with foreign lands. . . .

Ultimately, the Court's reliance on federalism amounts to no more than the notion that, somehow, one act becomes two because two jurisdictions are involved. Hawkins, in his Pleas of the Crown, long ago disposed of a similar contention made to justify two trials for the same offense by different counties as "a mere Fiction or Construction of Law, which shall hardly take Place against a Maxim made in Favour of Life." It was discarded as a dangerous fiction then, it should be discarded as a dangerous fiction now. . . .

I would reverse.

[Mr. Justice Brennan, joined by Chief Justice Warren and Mr. Justice Douglas, dissented on the ground that the unusual extent of federal assistance and participation in the state trial made it "actually a second federal prosecution" barred by the double jeopardy provisions of the Fifth Amendment.]

Immediately following the decisions in *Bartkus* and *Abbate,* in 1959, the then Attorney General, William P. Rogers, announced for the Department of Justice a policy that no federal prosecution would be initiated following a state prosecution on a charge arising out of the same act "unless the reasons are compelling." Even here, it was stated, no federal case should be tried unless the United States Attorney first submitted a recommendation to the appropriate Assistant Attorney General, and that recommendation could not be approved until it was "first brought to [the] attention" of the Attorney General. (Department of Justice Press Release, April 6, 1959.)

The majority and dissenting opinions in *Bartkus,* taken together with the action of Attorney General Rogers, raise the interesting question of the degree to which official discretion ought to be permitted, in order to retain flexibility, in the face of our traditional repugnance to double punishment. They are also illustrative of the point that care must be exercised in erecting any rule to the level of a constitutional requirement, since this tends to remove any "play at the joints" in the application of the rule.

Writing for the majority in a 1980 decision, Justice Blackmun stated "That the Clause is important and vital in this day is demonstrated by the host of recent cases." He listed twenty-one decisions on double jeopardy between 1971 and 1980, and pointed out that its application "has not proved to be facile or routine." The case was *United States* v. *DiFrancesco,* 449 U.S. 117 (1980), in which the Court upheld a provision of the Organized Crime Control Act of 1970 granting the government the right to appeal sentences imposed on "dangerous special offenders." The respondent was convicted of federal racketeering offenses and sentenced as a dangerous special offender to two 10-year prison terms, to be served concurrently with each other and with a 9-year sentence previously imposed on convictions at an unrelated federal trial. The United States sought review of the sentences under the Crime Control Act, claiming that the District Court abused its discretion in imposing sentences that amounted to additional imprisonment for only one year in the face of findings the court made after the dangerous special offender hearing. The Court of Appeals dismissed the appeal on double jeopardy grounds, and the Supreme Court reversed. Justice Blackmun canvassed the earlier cases and stated:

The Double Jeopardy Clause is *not* a complete barrier to an appeal by the prosecution in a criminal case. "[W]here a Government appeal presents no threat of successive prosecutions, the Double Jeopardy Clause is not offended." . . . From this it follows that the Government's taking a review of respondent's sentence does not in itself offend double jeopardy principles just because its success might deprive respondent of the benefit of a more lenient sentence. . . . This Court's decisions in the

sentencing area clearly establish that a sentence does not have the qualities of constitutional finality that attend an acquittal. . . .

. . . Judge Frankel . . . has observed that the "basic problem" in the present system is "the unbridled power of the sentencers to be arbitrary and discriminatory.". . . Appellate review creates a check upon this unlimited power, and should
lead to a greater degree of consistency in sentencing.

Justice Brennan, speaking for the four dissenters, stated:

Because the Court has demonstrated no basis for differentiating between the finality of acquittals and the finality of sentences, I submit that a punishment enhanced
by an appellate court is an unconstitutional multiple punishment. To conclude otherwise, as the Court does, is to create an exception to basic double jeopardy protection which, if carried to its logical conclusion, might not prevent Congress, on
double jeopardy grounds, from authorizing the Government to appeal verdicts of
acquittal. Such a result is plainly impermissible under the Double Jeopardy Clause.

[See Peter Westen and Richard Drubel, "Toward a General Theory of Double Jeopardy,"
in Philip B. Kurland and Gerhard Casper, eds., *The Supreme Court Review: 1978* (Chicago:
Univ. of Chicago Press, 1979), pp. 81–169; Peter Westen, "The Three Faces of Double
Jeopardy: Reflections on Government Appeals of Criminal Sentences," 78 *Mich. L. Rev.*
1001 (1980).]

## TRIAL BY JURY

Trial by jury in criminal cases has been probably the most venerated and often praised
of any of the procedural guarantees of the Constitution. It has undergone a slow ero-
sion, however, and is only used in the more important cases in England. In the United
States a similar trend is evident, and increasingly the jury trial is being waived. In addition, several states have reduced the number of jurors required or changed the unanimity requirement or both. But in federal trials the right to a jury is specifically guaranteed.
The guarantee of jury trial in criminal cases is found both in Article III and in the Sixth
Amendment of the Constitution. Article III, Section 2, Clause 3, states:

The trial of all crimes, except in cases of impeachment, shall be by jury; and such
trial shall be held in the State where the said crimes shall have been committed; but
when not committed within any State, the trial shall be at such place or places as the
Congress may by law have directed.

The Sixth Amendment states:

In all criminal prosecutions the accused shall enjoy the right to a speedy and public trial, by an impartial jury of the State and district wherein the crime shall have
been committed. . . .

While the Sixth Amendment guarantees the right of jury trial "in all criminal prosecutions," and Article III states that the trial "of all Crimes" shall be by jury, the Court has
uniformly held that the Constitution does not require that petty offenses be tried to a
jury. This, too, is a common-law feature of jury trial. The rule was stated in *District of
Columbia* v. *Colts*, 282 U.S. 63 (1930). Colts was charged with having operated a motor
vehicle in the district at a greater rate of speed than twenty-two miles an hour (the legal
limit) recklessly, "in such manner and condition so as to endanger property and individuals." He demanded trial by jury but was refused. In reviewing his conviction the court
of appeals reversed the judgment, holding that the offense went beyond the character

of a petty offense, and therefore the accused was constitutionally entitled to trial by jury. The United States Supreme Court affirmed this decision. Justice Sutherland, for a unanimous Court, stated:

It will be seen that the respondent is not charged merely with the comparatively slight offense of exceeding the twenty-two mile limit of speed . . . or merely with driving recklessly . . . ; but with the grave offense of having driven at the forbidden rate of speed and recklessly, "so as to endanger property and individuals."

By section 165 of title 18 of the D.C. Code, . . . the Constitution is made the test—as, of course, it must be—to determine whether the accused be entitled to a jury trial. Article 3, Section 2, Cl. 3, of the Constitution provides that, "The Trial of all Crimes, except in Cases of Impeachment, shall be by Jury." This provision is to be interpreted in the light of common law, according to which petty offenses might be proceeded against summarily before a magistrate sitting without a jury. See *Callan* v. *Wilson,* 127 U.S. 540, 557. That there may be many offenses called "petty offenses" which do not rise to the degree of crimes within the meaning of Article 3, and in respect of which Congress may dispense with a jury trial, is settled. . . .

Whether a given offense is to be classed as a crime, so as to require a jury trial, or as a petty offense, triable summarily without a jury, depends primarily upon the nature of the offense. The offense here charged is not merely *malum prohibitum,* but in its very nature is *malum in se.* It was an indictable offense at common law . . . when horses, instead of gasoline, constituted the motive power. The New Jersey Court of Errors and Appeals, in *State* v. *Rodgers, supra,* has discussed the distinction between traffic offenses of a petty character, subject to summary proceedings without indictment and trial by jury, and those of a serious character, amounting to public nuisances indictable at common law; and its examination of the subject makes clear that the offense now under review is of the latter character.

In *Cheff* v. *Schnackenberg,* 384 U.S. 373 (1966), a majority of the Court held that crimes carrying possible penalties up to six months do not require a jury trial if they otherwise qualify as petty offenses.

An interesting aspect of the right to a jury trial involves the question of whether the defendant has a right to waive jury trial and allow the judge to render the verdict. Rule 23 (a) of the Federal Rules of Criminal Procedure provides:

Cases required to be tried by jury shall be so tried unless defendant waives a jury trial in writing with the approval of the court and the consent of the government.

The validity of the requirement of the consent of the government to the waiver was challenged, and upheld, in *Singer* v. *United States,* 380 U.S. 24 (1965). Singer was charged with violations of the mail fraud statute and offered to waive a trial by jury. The trial court approved, but the government refused to give its consent. Petitioner was subsequently convicted by a jury, and the Court granted certiorari to consider his claim that the Sixth Amendment affords an unconditional right in a federal criminal case for the defendant to have his case decided by a judge alone if he considers it to be to his advantage. The Court unanimously denied this interpretation and held Rule 23(a) to be valid. Chief Justice Warren stated for the Court:

In light of the Constitution's emphasis on jury trial, we find it difficult to understand how the petitioner can submit the bald proposition that to compel a defendant in a criminal case to undergo a jury trial against his will is contrary to his right to a fair trial or to due process. A defendant's only constitutional right concerning the method of trial is to an impartial trial by jury. We find no constitutional impediment to conditioning a waiver of this right on the consent of the prosecuting attorney and the trial judge when, if either refuses to consent, the result is simply that the defendant is subject to an impartial trial by jury—the very thing that the Constitution guarantees him.

## Incorporation

Until 1968 the Court followed the *Palko* rule of "fundamental fairness" with respect to the use of jury trials in state prosecutions and even indicated in several cases that the State could abolish the criminal jury altogether without violating the Fourteenth Amendment. In *Duncan v. Louisiana* in 1968, however the Court incorporated the Sixth Amendment jury trial guarantee into the Fourteenth Amendment.

DUNCAN *v.* LOUISIANA

*391 U.S. 145 (1968)*

Mr. Justice White delivered the opinion of the Court.

Appellant, Gary Duncan, was convicted of simple battery in the . . . District Court of Louisiana. Under Louisiana law simple battery is a misdemeanor, punishable by a maximum of two years' imprisonment and a $300 fine. Appellant sought trial by jury, but because the Louisiana Constitution grants jury trials only in cases in which capital punishment or imprisonment at hard labor may be imposed, the trial judge denied the request. Appellant was convicted and sentenced to serve 60 days in the parish prison and pay a fine of $150. Appellant sought review in the Supreme Court of Louisiana, asserting that the denial of jury trial violated rights guaranteed to him by the United States Constitution. The Supreme Court . . . denied appellant a writ of certiorari. . . .

The test for determining whether a right extended by the Fifth and Sixth Amendments with respect to federal criminal proceedings is also protected against state action by the Fourteenth Amendment has been phrased in a variety of ways in the opinions of this Court. The question has been asked whether a right is among those " 'fundamental principles of liberty and justice which lie at the base of all our civil and political institutions,' " . . . ; whether it is "basic in our system of jurisprudence," . . . ; and whether it is "a fundamental right, essential to a fair trial," . . . . . Because we believe that trial by jury in criminal cases is fundamental to the American scheme of justice, we hold that the Fourteenth Amendment guarantees a right of jury trial in all criminal cases which—were they to be tried in a federal court—would come within the Sixth Amendment's guarantee. Since we consider the appeal before us to be such a case, we hold that the Constitution was violated when appellant's demand for jury trial was refused. . . .

We are aware of prior cases in this Court in which the prevailing opinion contains statements contrary to our holding today that the right to jury trial in serious criminal cases is a fundamental right and hence must be recognized by the States as part of their obligation to extend due process of all to all persons within their jurisdiction. . . . None of these cases, however, dealt with a State which had purported to dispense entirely with a jury trial in serious criminal cases. . . .

The guarantees of jury trial in the Federal and State Constitutions reflect a profound judgment about the way in which law should be enforced and justice administered. A right to jury trial is granted to criminal defendants in order to prevent oppression by the Government. Those who wrote our constitutions knew from history and experience that it was necessary to protect against unfounded criminal charges brought to eliminate enemies and against judges too responsive to the voice of higher authority. . . . The deep commitment of the Nation to the right of jury trial in serious criminal cases as a defense against arbitrary law enforcement qualifies for protection under the Due Process Clause of the Fourteenth Amendment, and must therefore be respected by the States. . . .

. . . It is doubtless true that there is a category of petty crimes or offenses which is not subject to the Sixth Amendment jury trial provision and should not be subject to the Fourteenth Amendment jury trial requirement here applied to the States. Crimes carrying possible penalties up to six months do not require a jury trial if they otherwise qualify as petty offenses. *Cheff* v. *Schnackenberg*, 384 U.S. 373 (1966). But the penalty authorized for a particular crime is of major relevance in determining whether it is serious or not and may in itself, if severe enough, subject the trial to the mandates of the Sixth Amendment. . . .

We need not, however, settle in this case the exact location of the line between petty offenses and serious crimes. It is sufficient for our purposes to hold that a crime punishable by two years in prison is, based on past and contemporary standards in this country, a serious crime and not a petty offense. Consequently, appellant was entitled to a jury trial and it was error to deny it.

The judgment below is reversed and the case is remanded for proceedings not inconsistent with this opinion.

Mr. Justice Fortas, concurring. . . .

Mr. Justice Black, with whom Mr. Justice Douglas joins, concurring. . . .

Mr. Justice Harlan, whom Mr. Justice Stewart joins, dissenting. . . .

As noted earlier, however, in *McKeiver* v. *Pennsylvania,* 403 U.S. 528 (1971), the Court held that the Fourteenth Amendment does not require a jury trial in delinquency proceedings in juvenile courts.

## Number of Jurors

At common law the jury numbered twelve, and it has long been assumed that the Sixth Amendment jury contemplated twelve as a constitutional requirement. In fact the Court stated in *Thompson* v. *Utah,* 170 U.S. 343 (1898) that the Sixth Amendment jury was constituted "of twelve persons, neither more nor less," and this was reiterated in 1930 in *Patton* v. *United States,* 281 U.S. 276. If so, then the decision in *Duncan* v. *Louisiana* would demand that state criminal juries also number twelve. The Court examined this question in 1970, in *Williams* v. *Florida,* and held that the Constitution did *not* require juries of twelve.

WILLIAMS *v.* FLORIDA

*399 U.S. 78 (1970)*

[Prior to his trial for robbery in the State of Florida, petitioner filed a pretrial motion to impanel a twelve-man jury instead of the six-man jury provided by Florida law in all but capital cases. That motion was denied, and in the subsequent trial petitioner was convicted as charged and was sentenced to life imprisonment. The District Court of Appeals affirmed, rejecting petitioner's claim that his Sixth Amendment rights had been violated.]

Mr. Justice White delivered the opinion of the Court.

In *Duncan* v. *Louisiana* . . . we held that the Fourteenth Amendment guarantees a right to trial by jury in all criminal cases which—were they to be tried in a federal court—would come within the Sixth Amendment's guarantee. Petitioner's trial for robbery . . . clearly falls within the scope of that holding. . . . The question in this case then is whether the constitutional guarantee of a trial by "jury" necessarily requires trial by exactly 12 persons, rather than some lesser number—in this case six. We hold that the 12-man panel is not a necessary ingredient of "trial by jury," and that respondent's refusal to impanel more than the six members provided for by Florida law did not violate petitioner's Sixth Amendment rights as applied to the States through the Fourteenth.

We had occasion in *Duncan* v. *Louisiana*, . . . to review briefly the oft-told history of the development of trial by jury in criminal cases. That history revealed a long tradition attaching great importance to the concept of relying on a body of one's peers to determine guilt or innocence as a safeguard against arbitrary law enforcement. That same history, however, affords little insight into the considerations which gradually led the size of that body to be generally fixed at 12. Some have suggested that the number 12 was fixed upon simply because that was the number of the presentment jury from the hundred, from which the petty jury developed. Other, less circular but more fanciful reasons for the number 12 have been given, "but they were all brought forward after the number was fixed," and rest on little more than mystical or superstitious insights into the significance of "12." Lord Coke's explanation that the "number of twelve is much respected in holy writ, as 12 apostles, 12 stones, 12 tribes, etc." is typical. In short, while sometime in the 14th century the size of the jury at common law came to be fixed generally at 12, that particular feature of the jury system appears to have been an historical accident, unrelated to the great purposes which gave rise to the jury in the first place. The question before us is whether this accidental feature of the jury has been immutably codified into our Constitution.

This Court's earlier decisions have assumed an affirmative answer to this question. The leading case so construing the Sixth Amendment is *Thompson* v. *Utah,* 170 U.S. 343 (1898). . . . In reaching its conclusion, the Court announced that the Sixth Amendment was applicable to the defendant's trial when Utah was a territory, and that the jury referred to in the Amendment was a jury "constituted, as it was at common law, of twelve persons, neither more nor less.". . .

While "the intent of the Framers" is often an elusive quarry, the relevant constitutional history casts considerable doubt on the easy assumption in our past decisions that if a given feature existed in a jury at common law in 1789, then it was necessarily preserved in the Constitution. . . .

We do not pretend to be able to devine precisely what the word "jury" imported to the Framers, the First Congress, or the States in 1789. It may well be that the usual expectation was that the jury would consist of 12, and that hence, the most likely conclusion to be drawn is simply that little thought was actually given to the specific question we face today. But there is absolutely no indication in "the intent of the Framers" of an explicit decision to equate the constitutional and common law characteristics of the jury. . . . The relevant inquiry, as we see it, must be the function which the particular feature performs and its relation to the purposes of the jury trial. Measured by this standard, the 12-man requirement cannot be regarded as an indispensable component of the Sixth Amendment.

[The opinion here examines the functions of group deliberation, cross-section representation of the community, and protection against governmental oppression, and concludes that these functions are equally well served with juries of six.]

We conclude, in short, as we began: the fact that the jury at common law was composed of precisely 12 is an historical accident, unnecessary to effect the purposes of the jury system and wholly without significance "except to mystics.". . .

*Affirmed.*

Mr. Justice Blackmun took no part in the consideration or decision of this case.

Mr. Chief Justice Burger, concurring. . . .

Mr. Justice Harlan, concurring. [Following his oft-stated position, Harlan concurred in the result as permitting the States "more elbow room in ordering their own criminal systems." But he objected vigorously to the majority's construction that the Sixth Amendment permitted less than twelve jurors, and found no justification for violating the rule of stare decisis, particularly one so "rooted in history."]

Mr. Justice Stewart, concurring. . . .

Mr. Justice Black, with whom Mr. Justice Douglas joins, concurring. . . .

Mr. Justice Marshall, dissenting. . . .

The majority in *Williams* held that six jurors would suffice in a state criminal case, but it set no minimum. As Justice Harlan queried, if six are permissible, why not three? The answer was provided in *Ballew v. Georgia*, 435 U.S. 223 (1978), involving a misdemeanor conviction by a five-person jury, pursuant to a Georgia statute. The Court held unanimously that such a jury was unconstitutional, but there was no majority opinion. There was general agreement, however, that a jury of less than six would not adequately represent a cross-section of the community. Justice Blackmun's lengthy opinion referred to a number of empirical studies and stated:

[R]ecent empirical data suggest that progressively smaller juries are less likely to foster effective group deliberation. At some point, this decline leads to inaccurate factfinding and incorrect application of the common sense of the community to the facts.

Justice Powell concurred separately, disavowing reliance on "numerology derived from statistical studies." Joining in the result, however, he stated "the line between five- and six-member juries is difficult to justify, but a line has to be drawn somewhere if the substance of jury trial is to be preserved."

In *Colgrove v. Battin*, 413 U.S. 149 (1973), the Court followed the *Williams* rationale in holding that the Seventh Amendment's guarantee of jury trial in civil suits at common law was not violated by a local United States District Court rule providing for juries of six in such cases. The petitioner contended that the local rule (1) violated the Seventh Amendment; (2) violated the statutory provision, 28 U.S.C. §2072, that rules "shall preserve the right of trial by jury as at common law and as declared by the Seventh Amendment"; and (3) was rendered invalid by Federal Rules of Civil Procedure 83 because "inconsistent with" Federal Rules of Civil Procedure 48 that provides for juries of less than twelve when stipulated by the parties. The majority of five held that the Seventh Amendment did not bind the federal courts to the exact procedural incidents or details of jury trial according to the common law. As in *Williams,* the majority then concluded that the results of studies of juries of six and of twelve indicated that there was no discernible difference between the results reached by the two different-sized juries, and that a jury of six satisfies the Seventh Amendment's guarantee of trial by jury in civil cases. As to the contention that the local rule was inconsistent with Rule 48, the Court held that Rule 48 deals only with stipulation *by the parties* and does not purport to prevent court rules which provide for civil juries of reduced size. Only two of the four dissenters reached the constitutional issue, while the other two argued that Congress had not intended to permit federal courts to use a jury of six unless the parties so stipulated.

## Requirement of Unanimity

### APODACA v. OREGON
### 406 U.S. 404 (1972)

[Pursuant to Oregon constitutional provisions authorizing a verdict by ten of twelve jurors in criminal cases, except for first degree murder verdicts, three defendants were convicted of criminal offenses other than first degree murder in separate state prosecutions. Two were convicted by eleven-to-one verdicts and one by a ten-to-two verdict. The Court of Appeals of Oregon affirmed the convictions, rejecting the defendants' contention that conviction by less than a unanimous jury violated the right to trial by jury specified by the Sixth Amendment and made applicable to the states by the Fourteenth Amendment. The Oregon Supreme Court denied review.]

Mr. Justice White announced the judgment of the Court and an opinion in which the Chief Justice, Mr. Justice Blackmun, and Mr. Justice Rehnquist joined. . . .

In *Williams* v. *Florida* . . . (1970), we had occasion to consider a related issue: whether the Sixth Amendment's right to trial by jury requires that all juries consist of 12 men. After considering the history of the 12-man requirement and the functions it performs in contemporary society, we concluded that it was not of constitutional stature. We reach the same conclusion today with regard to the requirement of unanimity.

### I

Like the requirement that juries consist of 12 men, the requirement of unanimity arose during the Middle Ages and had become an accepted feature of the common-law jury by the 18th century. But, as we observed in *Williams,* "the relevant constitutional history casts considerable doubt on the easy assumption . . . that if a given feature existed in a jury at common law in 1789, then it was necessarily preserved in the Constitution.". . .

As we observed in *Williams,* one can draw conflicting inferences from [the] legislative history. One possible inference is that Congress eliminated references to unanimity and to the other "accustomed requisites" of the jury because those requisites were thought already to be implicit in the very concept of jury. A contrary explanation, which we found in *Williams* to be the more plausible, is that the deletion was intended to have some substantive effect. . . . Surely one fact that is absolutely clear from this history is that, after a proposal had been made to specify precisely which of the common-law requisites of the jury were to be preserved by the Constitution, the Framers explicitly rejected the proposal and instead left such specification to the future. . . .

### II

Our inquiry must focus upon the function served by the jury in contemporary society. . . . As we said in *Duncan,* the purpose of trial by jury is to prevent oppression by the Government by providing a "safeguard against the corrupt or overzealous prosecutor and against the compliant, biased, or eccentric judge.". . . "Given this purpose, the essential feature of a jury obviously lies in the interposition between the accused and his accuser of the commonsense judgment of a group of laymen.". . . A requirement of unanimity, however, does not materially contribute to the exercise of this commonsense judgment. As we said in *Williams,* a jury will come to such a judgment as long as it consists of a group of laymen representative of a cross section of the community who have the duty and the opportunity to deliberate, free from outside attempts at intimidation, on the question of a defendant's guilt. In terms of this function we perceive no difference between juries required to act unanimously and those permitted to convict or acquit by votes of 10 to two or 11 to one. Requiring unanimity would obviously produce hung juries in some situations where nonunanimous juries will convict or acquit. But in either case, the interest of the defendant in having the judgment of his peers interposed between himself and the officers of the State who prosecute and judge him is equally well served.

### III

Petitioners nevertheless argue that unanimity serves other purposes constitutionally essential to the continued operation of the jury system. Their principal contention is that a Sixth Amendment "jury trial". . . should be held to require a unanimous jury verdict in order to give substance to the reasonable doubt standard otherwise mandated by the Due Process Clause. . . .

We are quite sure, however, that the Sixth Amendment itself has never been held to require proof beyond a reasonable doubt in criminal cases. The reasonable doubt standard developed separately from both the jury trial and the unanimous verdict. . . . The reasonable doubt argument is rooted, in effect, in due process and has been rejected in *Johnson* v. *Louisiana, ante.*

### IV

Petitioners also cite quite accurately a long line of decisions of this Court upholding the principle that the Fourteenth Amendment requires jury panels to reflect a cross section of the community. . . . They then contend that unanimity is a necessary precondition for effective application of the cross section requirement, because a rule permitting less than unanimous verdicts will make it possible for convictions to occur without the acquiescence of minority elements within the community. . . .

We . . . cannot accept petitioners' . . . assumption—that minority groups, even when they are represented on a jury, will not adequately represent the viewpoint of those groups simply because they may be outvoted in the final result. They will be present during all deliberations, and their views will be heard. We cannot assume that the majority of the jury will refuse to weigh the evidence and reach a decision upon rational grounds, just as it must now do in order to obtain unanimous verdicts, or that a majority will deprive a man of his liberty on the basis of prejudice when a minority is presenting a reasonable argument in favor of acquittal. We simply find no proof for the notion that a majority will disregard its instructions and cast its votes for guilt or innocence based on prejudice rather than the evidence.

We accordingly affirm the judgment of the Court of Appeals of Oregon.

*It is so ordered.*

Mr. Justice Blackmun, concurring.

I join the Court's opinion and judgment in each of these cases. I add only the comment . . . that in so doing I do not imply that I regard a State's split verdict system as a wise one. My vote means only that I cannot conclude that the system is constitutionally offensive. Were I a legislator, I would disfavor it as a matter of policy. Our task here, however, is not to pursue and strike down what happens to impress us as undesirable legislative policy.

I do not hesitate to say, either, that a system employing a 7–5 standard, rather than a 9–3 or 75% minimum, would afford me great difficulty. . . .

Mr. Justice Powell, concurring. . . .

. . . I concur in the plurality opinion in this case insofar as it concludes that a defendant in a state court may constitutionally be convicted by less than a unanimous verdict, but I am not in accord with a major premise upon which that judgment is based. Its premise is that the concept of a jury trial, as applicable to the States under the Fourteenth Amendment, must be identical in every detail to the concept required in federal courts by the Sixth Amendment. I do not think that all of the elements of jury trial within the meaning of the Sixth Amendment are necessarily embodied in or incorporated into the Due Process Clause of the Fourteenth Amendment. . . .

In an unbroken line of cases reaching back into the late 1800's, the Justices of this Court have recognized, virtually without dissent, that unanimity is one of the indispensable features of *federal* jury trial. . . . It therefore seems to me, in accord both with history and precedent, that the Sixth Amendment requires a unanimous jury verdict to convict in a federal criminal trial. . . .

The question, therefore, which should be addressed in this case is whether unanimity is in fact so fundamental to the essentials of jury trial that this particular requirement of the Sixth Amendment is necessarily binding on the States under the Due Process Clause of the Fourteenth Amendment. . . . Since I do not view Oregon's less than unanimous jury verdict requirement as violative of the due process guarantee of the Fourteenth Amendment, I concur in the Court's affirmance of these convictions.

Mr. Justice Douglas, with whom Mr. Justice Brennan and Mr. Justice Marshall concur, dissenting. . . .

The plurality approves a procedure which diminishes the reliability of a jury. First, it eliminates the circumstances in which a minority of jurors (a) could have rationally persuaded the entire jury to acquit, or (b) while unable to persuade the majority to acquit, nonetheless could have convinced them to convict only on a lesser-included offense. Second, it permits prosecutors in Oregon . . . to enjoy a conviction-acquittal ratio substantially greater than that ordinarily returned by unanimous juries.

The diminution of verdict reliability flows from the fact that nonunanimous juries need not debate and deliberate as fully as must unanimous juries. As soon as the requisite majority is attained, further consideration is not required . . . even though the dissident jurors might, if given the chance, be able to convince the majority. Such persuasion does in fact occasionally occur in States where the unanimous requirement applies. . . .

The rationale of *Williams* can have no application here. *Williams* requires that the change be neither more nor less advantageous to either the State or the defendant. It is said that such a showing is satisfied here since a . . . 2:10 verdict will result in acquittal. Yet experience shows that the less than unanimous jury overwhelmingly favors the States. . . .

The requirements of a unanimous jury verdict in criminal cases and proof beyond a reasonable doubt are so embedded in our constitutional law and touch so directly all the citizens and are such important barricades of liberty that if they are to be changed they should be introduced by constitutional amendment. . . .

Mr. Justice Brennan, with whom Mr. Justice Marshall joins, dissenting. . . .

Mr. Justice Stewart, with whom Mr. Justice Brennan and Mr. Justice Marshall join, dissenting. . . .

In *Duncan* v. *Louisiana* . . . the Court squarely held that the Sixth Amendment right to trial by jury in a federal criminal case is made wholly applicable to state criminal trials by the Fourteenth Amendment. Unless *Duncan* is to be overruled, therefore, the only relevant question here is whether the Sixth Amendment's guarantee of trial by jury embraces a guarantee that the verdict of the jury must be unanimous. The answer to that question is clearly "yes," as my Brother Powell has cogently demonstrated in that part of his concurring opinion that reviews almost a century of Sixth Amendment adjudication.

Until today, it has been universally understood that a unanimous verdict is an essential element of a Sixth Amendment jury trial. . . .

I would follow these settled Sixth Amendment precedents and reverse the judgment before us.

Mr. Justice Marshall, with whom Mr. Justice Brennan joins, dissenting. . . .

It should be noted that while five of the justices in *Apodaca* held that the Fourteenth Amendment did not impose a unanimity requirement on state criminal juries, there were also five justices who stated that they construed the Sixth Amendment to demand unanimity in *federal* criminal trials.

The Court thus held that the Constitution permits juries of less than twelve members, but that it requires at least six. And it approved the use of certain nonunanimous verdicts in cases involving twelve-person juries. The next question, then, is whether a nonunanimous verdict is permissible when using a six-person jury. In *Burch* v. *Louisiana*, 441 U.S. 130 (1979), the Court answered "No." Justice Rehnquist, for the majority, stated:

[M]uch the same reasons that led us in *Ballew* to decide that use of a five-member jury threatened the fairness of the proceeding and the proper role of the jury, lead us to conclude now that conviction for a nonpetty offense by only five members of a six-person jury presents a similar threat to preservation of the substance of the jury trial guarantee and justifies our requiring verdicts rendered by six-person juries to be unanimous.

In a footnote to the quoted passage he admonishes "We, of course, intimate no view as to the constitutionality of nonunanimous verdicts rendered by juries comprised of more than six members."

## Selection of Jurors

The Court has long held that the systematic and intentional exclusion of any class of persons, otherwise eligible to serve, from the jury lists is constitutionally invalid. Thus it was held as early as 1880 in *Strauder* v. *West Virginia*, 100 U.S. 303, that trial of a Negro defendant by a jury from which all Negroes were excluded by law was a denial of equal protection guaranteed by the Fourteenth Amendment. A long series of subsequent cases have uniformly followed this rule. *Avery* v. *Georgia*, 345 U.S. 559 (1953), presented a novel process for exclusion of Negroes. Prospective jurors had their names printed on tickets, with white persons on white tickets and Negroes on yellow tickets. The tickets were placed in a box, and a judge drew out the required number. These were given to the sheriff, who in turn handed them to the clerk, who typed up the final list for the panel. In the *Avery* case not a single Negro was selected to serve on a panel of sixty. The Court concluded that such a procedure established a prima facie case of discrimination, which the State failed to overcome. In *Hernandez* v. *Texas*, 347 U.S. 475 (1954), the Court reversed the conviction of Hernandez upon a finding that no person with a Mexican or Latin-American name had served on a jury in that county for twenty-five years. As the Court has often pointed out, however, there is no constitutional requirement of proportional representation or even that a particular jury have members of the race or economic class of the defendant. Carried to such an extreme, a bank robber would be able to claim one or more of his trade on the jury trying him. For the state to exclude any category, however, it must show reasons relevant to the function which the jury is required to perform, and not exclude merely on grounds of race or sex or whether one is salaried or an hourly wage earner.

A more recent case involved the issue of racial discrimination in the use of peremptory challenges by the prosecution. In the process of selecting a particular jury, any prospective juror may be challenged for cause, but in addition, each side has a number of peremptory challenges for which no cause need be shown. During the criminal trial of a black defendant in a Kentucky state court, the judge conducted *voir dire* examination of the jury venire and excused certain jurors for cause. The prosecutor then used his peremptory challenges to strike all four black persons on the venire, and a jury composed only of white persons was selected. Defense counsel moved to discharge the jury on the ground that the prosecutor's removal of the black veniremen violated the defendant's rights under the Sixth and Fourth Amendments to a jury drawn from a cross section of the community, and under the Fourteenth Amendment to equal protection of the laws. The trial judge denied the motion, and the defendant was convicted. Affirming the conviction, the Kentucky Supreme Court stated that in another case it had relied on *Swain* v. *Alabama,* 380 U.S. 202 (1965), and had held that a defendant alleging lack of a fair cross section must demonstrate systematic exclusion of a group of jurors from the *venire.* On certiorari the United States Supreme Court reviewed the decision in *Batson* v. *Kentucky,* 476 U.S. 79 (1986), and reversed and remanded. In the majority opinion by Justice Powell *Strauder* v. *West Virginia* was reaffirmed, and that portion of the *Swain* holding, requiring the defendant to make out a prima facie case that the peremptory challenge system *as a whole* was being perverted, was rejected. A defendant has no right to a petit jury composed in whole or in part of persons of his own race, but the equal protection clause forbids the prosecutor to challenge potential jurors solely on account of their race or on the assumption that black jurors as a group will be unable impartially to consider the State's case against a black defendant. Once the defendant makes a prima facie case of purposeful discrimination in the use of peremptory challenges at his trial, the burden shifts to the State to "come forward with a neutral explanation for challenging black jurors." The case was then remanded for a determination of this issue.

Until 1987 the Court generally took the position that a new constitutional rule would be applied retroactively to all cases under direct review unless the new rule represented a "clear break" with past decisions or long-standing practice. In *Griffith* v. *Kentucky,* 55 LW 4089 (1987), involving the retroactive application of *Batson,* the majority opinion stated: "We therefore hold that a new rule for the conduct of criminal prosecutions is to be applied retroactively to all cases, state or federal, pending on direct review or not yet final, with no exception for cases in which the new rule constitutes a 'clear break' with the past."

It should be noted that in the jury cases discussed above the Court made repeated reference to a requirement that the jury represent a cross-section of the community. A unanimous Court stated in *Smith* v. *Texas,* 311 U.S. 128 (1940), that "it is part of the established tradition in the use of juries as instruments of public justice that the jury be a body truly representative of the community." This was the basic rationale employed by the Court in *Taylor* v. *Louisiana* in 1975 in considering the issue of exclusion or exemption of women from jury service.

TAYLOR *v.* LOUISIANA

*419 U.S. 522 (1975)*

[Prior to trial in a state court in Louisiana on a kidnapping charge, the defendant, a male, sought to quash the petit jury venire from which his jury would be selected,

THE RIGHTS OF THE ACCUSED 221

contending that women had been systematically excluded from the venire, thus depriving him of his federal constitutional right to a fair trial by a properly selected jury. The Louisiana Constitution excluded women from jury service selection unless they had previously filed a written declaration of their desire to be subject to jury service. Of the persons eligible for jury service in the judicial district in which Taylor was tried, 53 percent were women, but no more than 10 percent of the persons on the jury wheel were women, and none was selected for service on the defendant's venire. The motion to quash was denied, and at a trial before an all-male jury the defendant was convicted. The Supreme Court of Louisiana affirmed, holding the constitutional provision valid.]

Mr. Justice White delivered the opinion of the Court. . . .

The Louisiana jury selection system does not disqualify women from jury service, but in operation its conceded systematic impact is that only a very few women, grossly disproportionate to the number of eligible women in the community, are called for jury service. In this case, no women were on the venire from which the petit jury was drawn. The issue we have, therefore, is whether a jury selection system which operates to exclude from jury service an identifiable class of citizens constituting 53% of eligible jurors in the community comports with the Sixth and Fourteenth Amendments.

The State first insists that Taylor, a male, has no standing to object to the exclusion of women from his jury. But Taylor's claim is that he was constitutionally entitled to a jury drawn from a venire constituting a fair cross section of the community and that the jury that tried him was not such a jury by reason of the exclusion of women. Taylor was not a member of the excluded class; but there is no rule that claims such as Taylor presents may be made only by those defendants who are members of the group excluded from jury service. In *Peters* v. *Kiff* . . . (1972), the defendant, a white man, challenged his conviction on the ground that Negroes had been systematically excluded from jury service. Six members of the Court agreed that petitioner was entitled to present the issue and concluded that he had been deprived of his federal rights. Taylor, in the case before us, was similarly entitled to tender and have adjudicated the claim that the exclusion of women from jury service deprived him of the kind of fact finder to which he was constitutionally entitled.

The background against which this case must be decided includes our holding in *Duncan* v. *Louisiana* . . . (1968), that the Sixth Amendment's provision for jury trial is made binding on the States by virtue of the Fourteenth Amendment. Our inquiry is whether the presence of a fair cross section of the community on venires, panels or lists from which petit juries are drawn is essential to the fulfillment of the Sixth Amendment's guarantee of an impartial jury trial in criminal prosecutions.

The Court's prior cases are instructive. Both in the course of exercising its supervisory powers over trials in federal courts and in the constitutional context, the Court has unambiguously declared that the American concept of the jury trial contemplates a jury drawn from a fair cross section of the community. A unanimous Court stated in *Smith* v. *Texas* . . . (1940), that "it is part of the established tradition in the use of juries as instruments of public justice that the jury be a body truly representative of the community.". . .

The unmistakable import of this Court's opinions, at least since 1941, *Smith* v. *Texas, supra,* and not repudiated by intervening decisions, is that the selection of a petit jury from a representative cross section of the community is an essential component of the Sixth Amendment right to a jury trial. . . .

We accept the fair cross-section requirement as fundamental to the jury trial guaranteed by the Sixth Amendment and are convinced that the requirement has solid foundation. The purpose of a jury is to guard against the exercise of arbitrary power—to make available the commonsense judgment of the community as a hedge against the overzealous or mistaken prosecutor and in preference to the professional or perhaps overconditioned or biased response of a judge. . . . This prophylactic vehicle is not provided if the jury pool is made up of only special segments of the populace or if large, distinctive groups are excluded from the pool. Community participation in the administration of the criminal law, moreover, is not only consistent with our democratic heritage but is also critical to public confidence in the fairness of the criminal justice system. Restricting jury service to only special groups or excluding identifiable segments playing major roles in the community cannot be squared with the constitutional concept of jury trial. . . .

We are also persuaded that the fair cross section requirement is violated by the systematic exclusion of women, who in the judicial district involved here amounted to 53% of the citizens eligible for jury service. This conclusion necessarily entails the judgment that women are sufficiently numerous and distinct from men that if they are systematically eliminated from jury panels, the Sixth Amendment's fair cross section requirement cannot be satisfied. . . .

There remains the argument that women as a class serve a distinctive role in society and that jury service would so substantially interfere with that function that the State has ample justification for excluding women from service unless they volunteer, even though the result is that almost all jurors are men. . . .

The States are free to grant exemptions from jury service to individuals in case of special hardship or incapacity and to those engaged in particular occupations the uninterrupted performance of which is critical of the community's welfare. . . . It would not appear that such exemptions would pose substantial threats that the remaining pool of jurors would not be representative of the community. A system excluding all women, however, is a wholly different matter. It is untenable to suggest these days that it would be a special hardship for each and every woman to perform jury service or that society cannot spare *any* women from their present duties. This may be the case with many, and it may be burdensome to sort out those who should not be exempted from those who should serve. But that task is performed in the case of men, and the administrative convenience in dealing with women as a class is insufficient justification for diluting the quality of community judgment represented by the jury in criminal trials. . . .

It should also be emphasized that in holding that petit juries must be drawn from a source fairly representative of the community we impose no requirement that petit juries actually chosen must mirror the community and reflect the various distinctive groups in the population. Defendants are not entitled to a jury of any particular composition . . . , but the jury wheels, pools of names, panels or venires from which juries are drawn must not systematically exclude distinctive groups in the community and thereby fail to be reasonably representative thereof.

The judgment of the Louisiana Supreme Court is reversed and the case remanded to that court for further proceedings not inconsistent with this opinion.

*So ordered.*

Mr. Chief Justice Burger concurred in the result.

Mr. Justice Rehnquist, dissenting.

The Court's opinion reverses a conviction without a suggestion, much less a showing, that the appellant has been unfairly treated or prejudiced in any way by the manner in which his jury was selected. In so doing, the Court invalidates a jury selection system which it approved by a substantial majority only 13 years ago. I disagree with the Court and would affirm the judgment of the Supreme Court of Louisiana.

The majority opinion canvasses various of our jury trial cases, beginning with *Smith* v. *Texas*. . . . Relying on carefully chosen quotations, it concludes that the "unmistakable import" of our cases is that the fair cross section requirement "is an essential component of the Sixth Amendment right to a jury trial." I disagree. Fairly read, the only "unmistakable import" of those cases is that due process and equal protection prohibit jury selection systems which are likely to result in biased or partial juries. . . .

Absent any suggestion that appellant's trial was unfairly conducted, or that its result was unreliable, I would not require Louisiana to retry him (assuming the State can once again produce its evidence and witnesses) in order to impose on him the sanctions which its laws provide.

In *Daniel* v. *Louisiana,* 420 U.S. 31 (1975), decided one week after *Taylor,* the Court held that the rule of *Taylor* v. *Louisiana* would not be applied retroactively.

[On jury trial generally, see James Bradley Thayer, *A Preliminary Treatise on Evidence at the Common Law* (Boston: Little, Brown, 1898); Sir Patrick Devlin, *Trial by Jury* (London: Stevens, 1956); Harry Kalven, Jr., and Hans Zeisel, *The American Jury* (Boston: Little, Brown, 1966); Rita James Simon, *The Jury: Its Role in American Society* (Lexington, Mass.: Lexington Books, 1980).]

## GUILTY PLEAS

The previous sections treating various aspects of trial procedures should not, of course, lead to the conclusion that the usual course of a criminal prosecution involves a full court trial. The far more common practice is for the defendant to plead guilty and for the judge to pass sentence, thus by-passing the trial aspects completely. The Task Force Report *The Courts,* prepared by the President's Commission on Law Enforcement and Administration of Justice in 1967, suggests that guilty pleas account for 90 percent of all convictions, and perhaps as high as 95 percent of misdemeanor convictions. A substantial percentage of guilty pleas are a result of negotiations between the prosecutor and the defendant (or his attorney)—a process commonly termed "plea bargaining." The three customary bargaining points are: (1) the recommendation of a lesser sentence than might normally be given; (2) the reduction of the charge to a lesser offense; and (3) the dismissal of some charges where multiple offenses or charges are listed in the indictment.

It is well-settled that plea agreements are consistent with the requirements of voluntariness. Since each side may obtain advantages when a guilty plea is exchanged for sentencing concessions, the agreement is no less voluntary than any other bargained-for exchange. In *Brady* v. *United States,* 397 U.S. 742 (1970), Justice White stated:

For a defendant who sees slight possibility of acquittal, the advantages of pleading guilty and limiting the probable penalty are obvious—his exposure is reduced, the correctional processes can begin immediately, and the practical burdens of a trial are eliminated. For the State there are also advantages—the more promptly imposed punishment after an admission of guilt may more effectively attain the objectives of punishment; and with the avoidance of trial, scarce judicial and prosecutorial resources are conserved for those cases in which there is a substantial issue of the defendant's guilt or in which there is substantial doubt that the State can sustain its burden of proof. It is this mutuality of advantage that perhaps explains the fact that at present well over three-fourths of the criminal convictions in this country rest on pleas of guilty, a great many of them no doubt motivated at least in part by the hope or assurance of a lesser penalty than might be imposed if there were a guilty verdict after a trial to judge or jury.

There is considerable unease and suspicion surrounding the process of plea bargaining, and in 1973 the United States National Advisory Commission on Criminal Justice Standards and Goals went so far as to recommend its abolition by 1978. This does not appear to be the view of most court specialists, however, who prefer to retain the process but provide certain reforms. (See the *Report on Courts* of the Advisory Commission, p. 49.) Certainly our system of criminal justice has come to rely upon a steady flow of guilty pleas. There are not enough personnel—judges, prosecutors, or defense counsel—or even enough courtrooms to operate a system in which most defendants go to trial. Despite this fact, it is clear that the process of plea bargaining carries with it certain problems. Some of these are: (1) suspicion that the process may be employed for purely political gain by the prosecutor; (2) the question of the propriety of offering a defendant an inducement to surrender his right to trial; (3) the gamble on the defendant's part that the judge will, in fact, assign a lesser sentence; or (4) the potential for deliberate overcharging by the prosecutor to exert pressure for a guilty plea.

The most important Supreme Court decision to date on the guilty plea and subsequent sentencing is *Santobello* v. *New York* in 1971.

### SANTOBELLO *v.* NEW YORK
#### *404 U.S. 257 (1971)*

[After being indicted on two felony gambling counts under New York statutes, and after negotiating with the prosecuting attorney, the defendant withdrew his not guilty plea and entered a guilty plea to a lesser included offense, the prosecutor agreeing to make no recommendation as to the sentence to be imposed. The New York trial court accepted the guilty plea and set a date for a sentencing hearing, which was subsequently postponed. Some six months later, after several delays, the hearing was held, at which a new prosecuting attorney appeared. Apparently unaware of the previous prosecutor's commitment, he recommended that the maximum one-year sentence be imposed. Although the defendant objected and sought adjournment of the sentencing hearing, the judge stated that he was not influenced by the prosecutor's recommendation and imposed the maximum sentence on the basis of a presentence report. The Appellate Division of the New York Supreme Court affirmed, and the Court of Appeals denied leave to appeal.]

Mr. Chief Justice Burger delivered the opinion of the Court.

We granted certiorari in this case to determine whether the State's failure to keep a commitment concerning the sentence recommendation on a guilty plea required a new trial. . . .

This record represents another example of an unfortunate lapse in orderly prosecutorial procedures, in part, no doubt, because of the enormous increase in the workload of the often understaffed prosecutor's offices. The heavy workload may well explain these episodes, but it does not excuse them. The disposition of criminal charges by agreement between the prosecutor and the accused, sometimes loosely called "plea bargaining," is an essential component of the administration of justice. Properly administered, it is to be encouraged. If every criminal charge were subjected to a full-scale trial, the States and the Federal Government would need to multiply by many times the number of judges and court facilities.

Disposition of charges after plea discussions is not only an essential part of the process but a highly desirable part for many reasons. It leads to prompt and largely final disposition of most criminal cases; it avoids much of the corrosive impact of enforced idleness during pretrial confinement for those who are denied release pending trial; it protects the public from those accused persons who are prone to continue criminal conduct even while on pretrial release; and, by shortening the time between charge and disposition, it enhances whatever may be the rehabilitative prospects of the guilty when they are ultimately imprisoned. . . .

However, all of these considerations presuppose fairness in securing agreement between an accused and a prosecutor. It is now clear, for example, that the accused pleading guilty must be counseled, absent a waiver. *Moore* v. *Michigan,* 355 U.S. 155 (1957). Fed. Rule Crim. Proc. 11, governing pleas in federal courts, now makes clear that the sentencing judge must develop, *on the record,* the factual basis for the plea, as, for example, by having the accused describe the conduct that gave rise to the charge. The plea must, of course, be voluntary and knowing and if it was induced by promises, the essence of those promises must in some way be made known. There is, of course, no absolute right to have a guilty plea accepted. . . . A court may reject a plea in exercise of sound judicial discretion. . . .

On this record, petitioner "bargained" and negotiated for a particular plea in order to secure dismissal of more serious charges, but also on condition that no sentence recommendation would be made by the prosecutor. It is now conceded that the promise to abstain from a recommendation was made, and at this stage the prosecution is not in a good position to argue that its inadvertent breach of agreement is immaterial. The staff lawyers in a prosecutor's office have the burden of "letting the left hand know what the right hand is doing" or has done. That the breach of agreement was inadvertent does not lessen its impact.

We need not reach the question whether the sentencing judge would or would not have been influenced had he known all the details of the negotiations for the plea. He stated that the prosecutor's recommendation did not influence him and we have no reason to doubt that. Nevertheless, we conclude that the interests of justice and appropriate recognition of the duties of the prosecution in relation to promises made in the negotiation of pleas of guilty will be best served by remanding the case to the state courts for further consideration. The ultimate relief to which petitioner is entitled we leave to the discretion of the state court, which is in a better position to decide whether the circumstances of this case require only that there be specific performance of the agreement on the plea, in which case petitioner should be resentenced by a different judge, or whether, in the view of the state court, the circumstances require granting the relief sought by petitioner, i.e., the opportunity to withdraw his plea of guilty. We emphasize that this is in no sense to question the fairness of the sentencing judge; the fault here rests on the prosecutor, not on the sentencing judge.

The judgment is vacated and the case is remanded for reconsideration not inconsistent with this opinion.

Mr. Justice Douglas, concurring. . . .

I join the opinion of the Court and favor a constitutional rule for this as well as for other pending or on-coming cases. Where the "plea bargain" is not kept by the prosecutor, the sentence must be vacated and the state court will decide in light of the circumstances of each case whether due process requires (a) that there be specific performance of the plea bargain or (b) that the defendant be given the option to go on trial on the original charges. One alternative may do justice on one case, and the other in a different case. In choosing a remedy, however, a court ought to accord a defendant's preference considerable, if not controlling, weight inasmuch as the fundamental rights flouted by a prosecutor's breach of a plea bargain are those of the defendant, not of the State.

Mr. Justice Marshall, with whom Mr. Justice Brennan and Mr. Justice Stewart join, concurring in part and dissenting in part.

I agree with much of the majority's opinion, but conclude that petitioner must be permitted to withdraw his guilty plea. . . .

Here, petitioner never claimed any automatic right to withdraw a guilty plea before sentencing. Rather, he tendered a specific reason why, in his case, the plea should be vacated. His reason was that the prosecutor had broken a promise made in return for the agreement to plead guilty. When a prosecutor breaks the bargain, he undercuts the basis for the waiver of constitutional rights implicit in the plea. This, it seems to me, provides the defendant ample justification for rescinding the plea. . . .

In *Henderson* v. *Morgan*, 426 U.S. 637 (1976), the Court held invalid a plea of guilty to a charge of second-degree murder on the ground that the defendant was not given adequate notice of the elements of the offense. He admitted killing the victim but claimed it was not intentional. Only after his guilty plea was accepted and sentence entered did he learn that intent to kill was an element of the crime of second-degree murder. The Court held that a plea cannot support a judgment of guilt unless it is voluntary in a constitutional sense. "And clearly the plea could not be voluntary in the sense that it constituted an intelligent admission that he committed the offense unless the defendant received 'real notice of the true nature of the charge against him, the first and most universally recognized requirement of due process.' "

*Bordenkircher* v. *Hayes*, 434 U.S. 357 (1978), dealt with a claim of prosecutorial vindictiveness after a refusal to plead guilty. The defendant refused to plead guilty to a felony indictment for uttering a forged instrument, a crime punishable by a term of two to ten years in prison. The state prosecutor then carried out his threat made during plea bargaining conferences to have the defendant reindicted to add the additional charge of habitual offender, thus subjecting him to a mandatory life sentence in view of his prior felony convictions. A jury found him guilty under both charges, and he was sentenced to a life term. By a five-to-four vote the Court held that where the defendant could clearly have been chargeable initially under the recidivist statute, the prosecutor's actions did not violate due process. Three of the dissenters argued that this was a clear case of prosecutorial vindictiveness, and that the Court should follow the principle of *Blackledge* v. *Perry* (discussed earlier) and hold the prosecutor's conduct violative of due process of law. Justice Powell, also dissenting, expressed the view that the threat to procure the habitual criminal indictment penalized the defendant for exercising his constitutional rights.

[See Donald J. Newman, *Conviction: The Determination of Guilt or Innocence Without Trial* (Boston: Little, Brown, 1966); Jerome Skolnick, *Justice Without Trial* (New York: Wiley, 1966).]

## CRUEL AND UNUSUAL PUNISHMENTS

The Eighth Amendment provides that "cruel and unusual punishments" shall not be inflicted. The phraseology derives from the English Bill of Rights of 1689, and similar provisions were found in colonial records in this country. Presumably the guarantee bars such ancient practices as branding, drawing and quartering, burning alive, or crucifixion. But the death penalty as such has not been held to violate the provision as long as it is carried out without unnecessary cruelty. In upholding execution by a firing squad, in *Wilkerson* v. *Utah*, 99 U.S. 130 (1879), the Court stated, "Difficulty would attend the effort to define with exactness the extent of the constitutional provision which provides that cruel and unusual punishments shall not be inflicted, but it is safe to affirm that punishments of torture, . . . and all others in the same line of unnecessary cruelty, are forbidden by that Amendment to the Constitution."

Not only the *manner* of punishment but also the severity of the penalty in relation to the crime has been considered an appropriate issue within the scope of the guarantee. In *Weems* v. *United States*, 217 U.S. 349 (1910), the Court held invalid a Philippine statute prescribing fine and imprisonment in irons from twelve to twenty years for entry of a known false statement in a public record, on the ground that the gross disparity between this punishment and that imposed for other more serious crimes violated the prohibition against cruel and unusual punishments.

In *Louisiana ex rel. Francis* v. *Resweber*, 329 U.S. 459 (1947), four members of the Court assumed, "but without so deciding," that the Eighth Amendment's prohibition was binding on the states through the Fourteenth Amendment. The case involved a claim of cruel and unusual punishment where petitioner had been placed in the electric chair and the switch thrown, without consequent death, and the subsequent setting of a second date for execution. The state contended that the failure was due to a mechanical defect, that it was unintended, and that a subsequent execution would not be a denial of due process. The petitioner contended that to force him to undergo the strain of preparing for execution, actually to place him in the electric chair and throw the switch, and then to send him back to prison to be subjected to the whole process again, was a cruel and unusual punishment even if unintentional. By a five-to-four vote the Court upheld the state's position, stressing that it was an unforeseeable accident with "no purpose to inflict unnecessary pain." Four justices dissented, pointing out that the intent of the executioner was immaterial to the issue of cruel and unusual punishment, and protesting "death by installments."

In *Trop* v. *Dulles*, 356 U.S. 86 (1958), the Court held invalid the denationalization of a native-born citizen convicted by a court-martial of desertion from the military or naval forces in time of war and dismissed or dishonorably discharged. One of the grounds for invalidation was that divestiture of citizenship in such case was a cruel and unusual punishment. Chief Justice Warren, speaking for four members of the Court, said, "This Court has had little occasion to give precise content to the Eighth Amendment," but the scope of the Amendment "is not static. The Amendment must draw its meaning from the evolving standards of decency that mark the progress of a maturing society."

On the merits, the Chief Justice stated that denationalization in this case was a violation of the Eighth Amendment:

> There may be involved no physical mistreatment, no primitive torture. There is instead the total destruction of the individual's status in organized society. It is a form of punishment more primitive than torture, for it destroys for the individual the political existence that was centuries in the development. . . . His very existence is at the sufferance of the country in which he happens to find himself. . . . In short, the expatriate has lost the right to have rights.

Concurring separately, Justice Brennan agreed that such punishment was unduly severe in relationship to the power Congress was exercising, but he stopped short of holding it violative of the Eighth Amendment.

More recently, in *Robinson* v. *California*, 370 U.S. 660 (1962), the Court held invalid a California statute making it a misdemeanor for a person to "be addicted to the use of narcotics," subject to a mandatory jail term of not less than ninety days. Justice Stewart, speaking for five members of the Court, pointed out that the statute was not the usual one which punished for the use, purchase, sale, or possession of narcotics, but it was rather a statute "which makes the 'status' of narcotic addiction a criminal offense, for which the offender may be prosecuted 'at any time before he reforms.' " He concluded:

We hold that a state law which imprisons a person thus afflicted as a criminal, even though he has never touched any narcotic drug within the State or been guilty of any irregular behavior there, inflicts a cruel and unusual punishment in violation of the Fourteenth Amendment. To be sure, imprisonment for ninety days is not, in the abstract, a punishment which is either cruel or unusual. But the question cannot be considered in the abstract. Even one day in prison would be a cruel and unusual punishment for the "crime" of having a common cold.

The *Robinson* decision led to a similar challenge to conviction for public drunkenness. In *Powell* v. *Texas,* 392 U.S. 514 (1968), testimony indicated that the appellant worked at a tavern shining shoes and made about $12 a week which he used to buy wine. He testified that he drank wine every day and got drunk about once a week. The contention was that he was a chronic alcoholic, that this condition was a disease, and therefore his conviction constituted cruel and unusual punishment. While there was no majority opinion, a majority of the Court held that Powell was not being punished for his "status" or "condition" as being a chronic alcoholic, but for being drunk in public, and thus the *Robinson* rule was not applicable. Justice Fortas, in an opinion for the four dissenters, argued that the Eighth Amendment was violated, since the trial court found that the defendant was a chronic alcoholic who could not resist the constant, excessive consumption of alcohol and did not appear in public by his own volition, but under a compulsion which was part of his condition.

While *Weems* v. *United States* appeared to establish a rule that grossly disproportionate sentences would violate the Eighth Amendment, the Court in *Rummel* v. *Estelle*, 445 U.S. 263 (1980), upheld a life sentence imposed under a Texas recidivist law for having been convicted of three property related felonies. Rummel had been convicted for fraudulent use of a credit card to obtain $80 worth of goods, and later for passing a forged check in the amount of $28.36, and subsequently for "felony theft" for obtaining $120.75 by false pretenses. Justice Rehnquist, for the majority, said that *Weems'* finding of disproportionality "cannot be wrenched from the extreme facts of that case." He stressed the point that it was not merely the length of the sentence in *Weems* but the "accessory punishments" which were too harsh—the confinement in chains at the ankle and wrist, hard and painful labor, no marital authority or parental rights or rights of property, for example. In *Rummel*, on the contrary, there was simply a lengthy prison sentence, and in addition Texas parole policy permitted eligibility in as little as twelve years. He concluded that in such cases "the length of the sentence actually imposed is purely a matter of legislative prerogative."

Three years later, however, in *Solem* v. *Helm*, 463 U.S. 277 (1983), the Court held that it was cruel and unusual punishment to impose a life sentence without possibility of parole on one who was convicted of passing a bad check in the amount of $100 and who had been previously convicted of six nonviolent felonies. Justice Powell, for the majority, stated that the proportionality principle could be found as early as 1215 in Magna Carta, and "The principle that a punishment should be proportionate to the crime is deeply rooted and frequently repeated in common-law jurisprudence." He set out three "objective factors" to be examined in Eighth Amendment cases. First, "we look to the gravity of the offense and the harshness of the penalty." Second, "it may be helpful to compare the sentences imposed on other criminals in the same jurisdiction." And third, "courts may find it useful to compare the sentences imposed for commission of the same crime in other jurisdictions." After examination of these factors, the conclusion was that the sentence was significantly disproportionate to the crime and therefore violative of the Eighth Amendment.

For many years campaigns have been waged to try to abolish capital punishment. It is argued that neither on grounds of morality nor utility can such a severe penalty be justified. While some measure of success has been achieved in the fact that over the past two decades a number of states have abolished the death penalty, the proponents of abolition have long sought a decision from the Supreme Court that capital punishment was a violation of the Eighth Amendment's bar to cruel and unusual punishments. The Court managed to avoid the issue for many years, however, by denial of certiorari, as in *Rudolph* v. *Alabama*, 375 U.S. 889 (1963), with three Justices registering a strong dissent. The decision finally came, although limited in scope, in 1972 in *Furman* v. *Georgia*, 408 U.S. 238. By a vote of five-to-four the Court held that the death penalty, *as then imposed*, constituted cruel and unusual punishment in violation of the Eighth Amendment. The four Nixon appointees dissented. Nine separate opinions were filed, and the majority was split on the rationale for the decision. Justices Brennan and Marshall were the only members to state that the death penalty was *per se* a violation of the Eighth Amendment. Others of the majority stressed the discriminatory aspects of the sentence, citing studies which showed that the poor, the disadvantaged, and the minorities were the primary recipients of such sentences, and the broad discretion in juries to mete out either the death penalty or a term in prison. Justice Stewart emphasized the point that the Eighth Amendment "cannot tolerate the infliction of a sentence of death under legal systems that permit this unique penalty to be so wantonly and so freakishly imposed." Following the decision, States with capital punishment laws began revision of their statutes to try to meet the objections outlined in *Furman*. Some read *Furman* as ordering a complete removal of sentencing discretion and adopted new laws making the death penalty mandatory for specified crimes. Others provided for various degrees of discretion in the sentencing body but specified guidelines to be used in the decision to order the death penalty.

On July 2, 1976, the Court rendered decisions on the constitutionality of the new death penalty statutes of five states—Georgia, Florida, Texas, Louisiana, and North Carolina. Some 600 prisoners on death row in various states had been anxiously awaiting the verdict. The statutes of North Carolina and Louisiana were held invalid on the ground that the mandatory death sentence did not allow for appropriate differentiation between persons convicted of the same crime, and thus violated the Eighth Amendment's requirement of "civilized standards" for punishment. The statutes of the other three states were upheld as providing for properly controlled sentencing discretion. A majority of seven held clearly that capital punishment *per se* was not unconstitutional. The Georgia case contains fuller analyses and is selected for illustration. (The other cases are *Proffitt* v. *Florida*, 428 U.S. 242, *Jurek* v. *Texas*, 428 U.S. 262, *Woodson* v. *North Carolina*, 428 U.S. 280, and *Roberts* v. *Louisiana*, 428 U.S. 325.)

### GREGG *v.* GEORGIA
### *428 U.S. 153 (1976)*

[The petitioner, Troy Gregg, was charged with committing armed robbery and murder on the basis of evidence that he had killed and robbed two men.]

Mr. Justice Stewart, Mr. Justice Powell, and Mr. Justice Stevens announced the judgment of the Court and filed an opinion delivered by Mr. Justice Stewart.

The issue in this case is whether the imposition of the sentence of death for the crime of murder under the law of Georgia violates the Eighth and Fourteenth Amendments.

## I

The trial judge submitted the murder charges to the jury on both felony-murder and nonfelony-murder theories. He also instructed on the issue of self-defense but declined to instruct on manslaughter. He submitted the robbery case to the jury on both an armed-robbery theory and on the lesser included offense of robbery by intimidation. The jury found the petitioner guilty of two counts of armed robbery and two counts of murder.

At the penalty stage, which took place before the same jury, neither the prosecutor nor the petitioner's lawyer offered any additional evidence. Both counsel, however, made lengthy arguments dealing generally with the propriety of capital punishment under the circumstances and with the weight of the evidence of guilt. The trial judge instructed the jury that it could recommend either a death sentence or a life prison sentence on each count. The judge further charged the jury that in determining what sentence was appropriate the jury was free to consider the facts and circumstances presented by the parties, if any, in mitigation or aggravation.

Finally, the judge instructed the jury that it "would not be authorized to consider [imposing] the sentence of death" unless it first found beyond a reasonable doubt one of these aggravating circumstances:

"One—That the offense of murder was committed while the offender was engaged in the commission o[f] two other capit[a]l felonies, to wit the armed ro[b]bery of [Simons and Moore].

"Two—That the offender committed the offense of murder for the purpose of receiving money and the automobile described in the indictment.

"Three—The offense of murder was outrageously and wantonly vile, horrible and inhuman, in that they [sic] involved the depravity of the mind of the defendant."

Finding the first and second of these circumstances, the jury returned verdicts of death on each count.

The Supreme Court of Georgia affirmed the convictions and the imposition of the death sentences for murder. . . . After reviewing the trial transcript and the record, including the evidence, and comparing the evidence and sentence in similar cases in accordance with the requirements of Georgia law, the court concluded that, considering the nature of the crime and the defendant, the sentences of death had not resulted from prejudice or any other arbitrary factor and were not excessive or disproportionate to the penalty applied in similar cases. The death sentences imposed for armed robbery, however, were vacated on the grounds that the death penalty had rarely been imposed in Georgia for that offense and that the jury improperly considered the murders as aggravating circumstances for the robberies after having considered the armed robberies as aggravating circumstances for the murders. . . .

## II

Before considering the issues presented it is necessary to understand the Georgia statutory scheme for the imposition of the death penalty. The Georgia statute, as amended after our decision in *Furman* v. *Georgia*, . . . retains the death penalty for six categories of crime: murder, kidnapping for ransom or where the victim is harmed, armed robbery, rape, treason, and aircraft hijacking. . . . The capital defendant's guilt or innocence is determined in the traditional manner, either by a trial judge or a jury, in the first stage of a bifurcated trial.

If a trial is by jury, the trial judge is required to charge lesser included offenses when they are supported by any view of the evidence. . . . After a verdict, finding, or plea of guilty to a capital crime, a presentence hearing is conducted before whomever made the determination of guilt. The sentencing procedures are essentially the same in both bench and jury trials. . . .

. . . Before a convicted defendant may be sentenced to death, however, the jury, or the trial judge in cases tried without a jury, must find beyond a reasonable doubt one of the 10 aggravating circumstances specified in the statute. * The sentence of death may be imposed only if the jury (or judge) finds one of the statutory aggravating circumstances and then elects to impose that sentence. . . . If the verdict is death the jury or judge must specify the aggravating circumstance(s) found. . . . In jury cases, the trial judge is bound by the jury's recommended sentence. . . .

In addition to the conventional appellate process available in all criminal cases, provision is made for special expedited direct review by the Supreme Court of Georgia of the appropriateness of imposing the sentence of death in the particular case. The court is directed to consider "the punishment as well as any errors enumerated by way of appeal," and to determine:

"(1) Whether the sentence of death was imposed under the influence of passion, prejudice, or any other arbitrary factor, and

"(2) Whether, in cases other than treason or aircraft hijacking, the evidence supports the jury's or judge's finding of a statutory aggravating circumstance as enumerated [in the law], and

"(3) Whether the sentence of death is excessive or disproportionate to the penalty imposed in similar cases, considering both the crime and the defendant." . . . If the court affirms a death sentence, it is required to include in its decision reference to similar cases that it has taken into consideration. . . .

---

*The statute provides in part: . . .

"(1)   The offense of murder, rape, armed robbery, or kidnapping was committed by a person with a prior record of conviction for a capital felony, or the offense of murder was committed by a person who has a substantial history of serious assaultive criminal convictions.

"(2)   The offense of murder, rape, armed robbery, or kidnapping was committed while the offender was engaged in the commission of another capital felony, or aggravated battery, or the offense of murder was committed while the offender was engaged in the commission of burglary or arson in the first degree.

"(3)   The offender by his act of murder, armed robbery, or kidnapping knowingly created a great risk of death to more than one person in a public place by means of a weapon or device which would normally be hazardous to the lives of more than one person.

"(4)   The offender committed the offense of murder for himself or another, for the purpose of receiving money or any other thing of monetary value.

"(5)   The murder of a judicial officer, former judicial officer, district attorney or solicitor or former district attorney or solicitor during or because of the exercise of his official duty.

"(6)   The offender caused or directed another to commit murder or committed murder as an agent or employee of another person.

"(7)   The offense of murder, rape, armed robbery, or kidnapping was outrageously or wantonly vile, horrible or inhuman in that it involved torture, depravity of mind, or an aggravated battery to the victim.

"(8)   The offense of murder was committed against any peace officer, corrections employee or fireman while engaged in the performance of his official duties.

"(9)   The offense of murder was committed by a person in, or who has escaped from, the lawful custody of a peace officer or place of lawful confinement.

"(10)   The murder was committed for the purpose of avoiding, interfering with, or preventing a lawful arrest or custody in a place of lawful confinement, of himself or another.

. . . Under its special review authority, the court may either affirm the death sentence or remand the case for resentencing. In cases in which the death sentence is affirmed there remains the possibility of executive clemency.

## III

We address initially the basic contention that the punishment of death for the crime of murder is, under all circumstances, "cruel and unusual" in violation of the Eighth and Fourteenth Amendments of the Constitution. . . . [Here the opinion reviews the history of the "cruel and unusual" provision of the Eighth Amendment and concludes with the statement that history and precedent strongly support a negative answer to the question of whether capital punishment is violative of that provision. "The imposition of the death penalty for the crime of murder has a long history of acceptance both in the United States and in England."]

Four years ago, the petitioners in *Furman* and its companion cases predicated their argument primarily upon the asserted proposition that standards of decency had evolved to the point where capital punishment no longer could be tolerated. The petitioners in those cases said, in effect, that the evolutionary process had come to an end, and that standards of decency required that the Eighth Amendment be construed finally as prohibiting capital punishment for any crime regardless of its depravity and impact on society. This view was accepted by two Justices. Three other Justices were unwilling to go so far; focusing on the procedures by which convicted defendants were selected for the death penalty rather than on the actual punishment inflicted, they joined in the conclusion that the statutes before the Court were constitutionally invalid.

The petitioners in the capital cases before the Court today renew the "standards of decency" argument, but developments during the four years since *Furman* have undercut substantially the assumptions upon which their argument rested. Despite the continuing debate, dating back to the 19th century, over the morality and utility of capital punishment, it is now evident that a large proportion of American society continues to regard it as an appropriate and necessary criminal sanction.

The most marked indication of society's endorsement of the death penalty for murder is the legislative response to *Furman*. The legislatures of at least 35 States have enacted new statutes that provide for the death penalty for at least some crimes that result in the death of another person. And the Congress of the United States, in 1974, enacted a statute providing the death penalty for aircraft piracy that results in death. . . .

The jury also is a significant and reliable objective index of contemporary values because it is so directly involved. . . . Indeed, the actions of juries in many states since *Furman* is fully compatible with the legislative judgments, reflected in the new statutes, as to the continued utility and necessity of capital punishment in appropriate cases. At the close of 1974 at least 254 persons had been sentenced to death since *Furman,* and by the end of March 1976, more than 460 persons were subject to death sentences.

As we have seen, however, the Eighth Amendment demands more than that a challenged punishment be acceptable to contemporary society. The Court also must ask whether it comports with the basic concept of human dignity at the core of the Amendment. . . .

The death penalty is said to serve two principal social purposes: retribution and deterrence of capital crimes by prospective offenders.

In part, capital punishment is an expression of society's moral outrage at particularly offensive conduct. This function may be unappealing to many, but it is essential in an ordered society that asks its citizens to rely on legal processes rather than self-help to vindicate their wrongs. . . . "Retribution is no longer the dominant objective of the criminal law," . . . but neither is it a forbidden objective nor one inconsistent with our respect for the dignity of men. . . . Indeed, the decision that capital punishment may be the appropriate sanction in extreme cases is an expression of the community's belief that certain crimes are themselves so grievous an affront to humanity that the only adequate response may be the penalty of death.

Statistical attempts to evaluate the worth of the death penalty as a deterrent to crimes by potential offenders have occasioned a great deal of debate. The results simply have been inconclusive. . . .

Although some of the studies suggest that the death penalty may not function as a significantly greater deterrent than lesser penalties, there is no convincing empirical evidence either supporting or refuting this view. We may nevertheless assume safely that there are murderers, such as those who act in passion, for whom the threat of death has little or no deterrent effect. But for many others, the death penalty undoubtedly is a significant deterrent. There are carefully contemplated murders, such as murder for hire, where the possible penalty of death may well enter into the cold calculus that precedes the decision to act. And there are some categories of murder, such as murder by a life prisoner, where other sanctions may not be adequate.

The value of capital punishment as a deterrent of crime is a complex factual issue the resolution of which properly rests with the legislatures, which can evaluate the results of statistical studies in terms of their own local conditions and with a flexibility of approach that is not available to the courts. . . . Indeed, many of the post-*Furman* statutes reflect just such a responsible effort to define those crimes and those criminals for which capital punishment is most probably an effective deterrent.

In sum, we cannot say that the judgment of the Georgia legislature that capital punishment may be necessary in some cases is clearly wrong. Considerations of federalism, as well as respect for the ability of a legislature to evaluate, in terms of its particular state the moral consensus concerning the death penalty and its social utility as a sanction, require us to conclude, in the absence of more convincing evidence, that the infliction of death as a punishment for murder is not without justification and thus is not unconstitutionally severe. . . .

We hold that the death penalty is not a form of punishment that may never be imposed, regardless of the circumstances of the offense, regardless of the character of the offender, and regardless of the procedure followed in reaching the decision to impose it.

## IV

We now consider whether Georgia may impose the death penalty on the petitioner in this case.

### A

While *Furman* did not hold that the infliction of the death penalty *per se* violates the Constitution's ban on cruel and unusual punishments, it did recognize that the penalty of death is different in kind from any other punishment imposed under our system of criminal justice. Because of the uniqueness of the death penalty, *Furman* held that it could not be imposed under sentencing procedures that created a substantial risk that it would be inflicted in an arbitrary and capricious manner. . . .

*Furman* mandates that where discretion is afforded a sentencing body on a matter so grave as the determination of whether a human life should be taken or spared, that discretion must be suitably directed and limited so as to minimize the risk of wholly arbitrary and capricious action. . . .

In summary, the concerns expressed in *Furman* that the penalty of death not be imposed in an arbitrary or capricious manner can be met by a carefully drafted statute that ensures that the sentencing authority is given adequate information and guidance. As a general proposition these concerns are best met by a system that provides for a bifurcated proceeding at which the sentencing authority is apprised of the information relevant to the imposition of sentence and provided with standards to guide its use of the information.

We do not intend to suggest that only the above-described procedures would be permissible under *Furman* or that any sentencing system constructed along these general lines would inevitably satisfy the concerns of *Furman,* for each distinct system must be examined on an individual basis. Rather, we have embarked upon this general exposition to make clear that it is possible to construct capital-sentencing systems capable of meeting *Furman's* constitutional concerns.

## B

We now turn to consideration of the constitutionality of Georgia's capital-sentencing procedures. . . .

These procedures require the jury to consider the circumstances of the crime and the criminal before it recommends sentence. No longer can a Georgia jury do as Furman's jury did: reach a finding of the defendant's guilt and then, without guidance or direction, decide whether he should live or die. Instead, the jury's attention is directed to the specific circumstances of the crime: Was it committed in the course of another capital felony? Was it committed for money? Was it committed upon a peace officer or judicial officer? Was it committed in a particularly heinous way or in a manner that endangered the lives of many persons? In addition, the jury's attention is focused on the characteristics of the person who committed the crime: Does he have a record of prior convictions for capital offenses? Are there any special facts about this defendant that mitigate against imposing capital punishment (e.g., his youth, the extent of his cooperation with the police, his emotional state at the time of the crime). As a result, while some jury discretion still exists, "the discretion to be exercised is controlled by clear and objective standards so as to produce nondiscriminatory application." . . .

As an important additional safeguard against arbitrariness and caprice, the Georgia statutory scheme provides for automatic appeal of all death sentences to the State's supreme court. That court is required by statute to review each sentence of death and determine whether it was imposed under the influence of passion or prejudice, whether the evidence supports the jury's finding of a statutory aggravating circumstance, and whether the sentence is disproportionate compared to those sentences imposed in similar cases. . . .

The petitioner contends, however, that the changes in the Georgia sentencing procedures are only cosmetic, that the arbitrariness and capriciousness condemned by *Furman* continue to exist in Georgia—both in traditional practices that still remain and in the new sentencing procedures adopted in response to *Furman.*

1

First, the petitioner focuses on the opportunities for discretionary action that are inherent in the processing of any murder case under Georgia law. He notes that the state prosecutor has unfettered authority to select those persons whom he wishes to prosecute for a capital offense and to plea bargain with them. Further, at the trial the jury may choose to convict a defendant of a lesser included offense rather than find him guilty of a crime punishable by death, even if the evidence would support a capital verdict. And finally, a defendant who is convicted and sentenced to die may have his sentence commuted by the Governor of the State and the Georgia Board of Pardons and Paroles.

The existence of these discretionary stages is not determinative of the issues before us. At each of these stages an actor in the criminal justice system makes a decision which may remove a defendant from consideration as a candidate for the death penalty. *Furman,* in contrast, dealt with the decision to impose the death sentence on a specific individual who had been convicted of a capital offense. Nothing in any of our cases suggests that the decision to afford an individual defendant mercy violates the Constitution. *Furman* held only that, in order to minimize the risk that the death penalty would be imposed on a capriciously selected group of offenders, the decision to impose it had to be guided by standards so that the sentencing authority would focus on the particularized circumstances of the crime and the defendant. . . .

V

The basic concern of *Furman* centered on those defendants who were being condemned to death capriciously and arbitrarily. Under the procedures before the Court in that case, sentencing authorities were not directed to give attention to the nature or circumstances of the crime committed or to the character or record of the defendant. Left unguided, juries imposed the death sentence in a way that could only be called freakish. The new Georgia sentencing procedures, by contrast, focus the jury's attention on the particularized nature of the crime and the particularized characteristics of the individual defendant. While the jury is permitted to consider any aggravating or mitigating circumstances, it must find and identify at least one statutory aggravating factor before it may impose a penalty of death. In this way the jury's discretion is channeled. No longer can a jury wontonly and freakishly impose the death sentence; it is always circumscribed by the legislative guidelines. In addition, the review function of the Supreme Court of Georgia affords additional assurance that the concerns that prompted our decision in *Furman* are not present to any significant degree in the Georgia procedure applied here.

For the reasons expressed in this opinion, we hold that the statutory system under which Gregg was sentenced to death does not violate the Constitution. Accordingly, the judgment of the Georgia Supreme Court is affirmed.

*It is so ordered.*

Mr. Justice White, with whom the Chief Justice and Mr. Justice Rehnquist join, concurring in the judgment. . . .

III

The threshold question in this case is whether the death penalty may be carried out for murder under the Georgia legislative scheme consistent with the decision in

*Furman* v. *Georgia*. . . . Petitioner argues that, as in *Furman,* the jury is still the sentencer; that the statutory criteria to be considered by the jury on the issue of sentence under Georgia's new statutory scheme are vague and do not purport to be all inclusive; and that, in any event, there are *no* circumstances under which the jury is required to impose the death penalty. Consequently, the petitioner argues that the death penalty will inexorably be imposed in as discriminatory, standardless, and rare a manner as it was imposed under the scheme declared invalid in *Furman.*

The argument is considerably overstated. The Georgia Legislature has made an effort to identify those aggravating factors which it considers necessary and relevant to the question whether a defendant convicted of capital murder should be sentenced to death. The jury which imposes sentence is instructed on all statutory aggravating factors which are supported by the evidence, and is told that it may not impose the death penalty unless it unanimously finds at least one of those factors to have been established beyond a reasonable doubt. The Georgia Legislature has plainly made an effort to guide the jury in the exercise of its discretion, while at the same time permitting the jury to dispense mercy on the basis of factors too intangible to write into a statute and I cannot accept the naked assertion that the effort is bound to fail. . . .

Petitioner also argues that decisions made by the prosecutor—either in negotiating a plea to some offense lesser than capital murder or in simply declining to charge capital murder—are standardless and will inexorably result in the wanton and freakish imposition of the penalty condemned by the judgment in *Furman.* I address this point separately because the cases in which no capital offense is charged escape the view of the Georgia Supreme Court and are not considered by it in determining whether a particular sentence is excessive or disproportionate.

Petitioner's argument that prosecutors behave in a standardless fashion in deciding which cases to try as capital felonies is unsupported by any facts. Petitioner simply asserts that since prosecutors have the power not to charge capital felonies they will exercise that power in a standardless fashion. This is untenable. Absent facts to the contrary, it cannot be assumed that prosecutors will be motivated in their charging decision by factors other than the strength of their case and the likelihood that a jury would impose the death penalty if it convicts. Unless prosecutors are incompetent in their judgments, the standards by which they decide whether to charge a capital felony will be the same as those by which the jury will decide the questions of guilt and sentence. Thus defendants will escape the death penalty through prosecutorial charging decisions only because the offense is not sufficiently serious; or because the proof is insufficiently strong. This does not cause the system to be standardless any more than the jury's decision to impose life imprisonment on a defendant whose crime is deemed insufficiently serious or its decision to acquit someone who is probably guilty but whose guilt is not established beyond a reasonable doubt. Thus the prosecutor's charging decisions are unlikely to have removed from the sample of cases considered by the Georgia Supreme Court any which are truly "similar." If the cases really were "similar" in relevant respects, it is unlikely that prosecutors would fail to prosecute them as capital cases; and I am unwilling to assume the contrary. . . .

I therefore concur in the judgment of affirmance.

Statement of The Chief Justice and Mr. Justice Rehnquist:

We join the opinion of Mr. Justice White, agreeing with its analysis that Georgia's system of capital punishment comports with the Court's holding in *Furman* v. *Georgia*. . . .

Mr. Justice Blackmun, concurring in the judgment. . . .

Mr. Justice Brennan, dissenting.

The Cruel and Unusual Punishments Clause "must draw its meaning from the evolving standards of decency that mark the progress of a maturing society." The opinions of Mr. Justice Stewart, Mr. Justice Powell, and Mr. Justice Stevens today hold that "evolving standards of decency" require focus not on the essence of the death penalty itself but primarily upon the procedures employed by the State to single out persons to suffer the penalty of death. . . .

In *Furman* v. *Georgia* . . . I read "evolving standards of decency" as requiring focus upon the essence of the death penalty itself and not primarily or solely upon the procedures under which the determination to inflict the penalty upon a particular person was made. . . .

This Court inescapably has the duty, as the ultimate arbiter of the meaning of our Constitution, to say whether, when individuals condemned to death stand before our Bar, "moral concepts" require us to hold that the law has progressed to the point where we should declare that the punishment of death, like punishments on the rack, the screw and the wheel, is no longer morally tolerable in our civilized society. My opinion in *Furman* v. *Georgia* concluded that our civilization and the law had progressed to this point and that therefore the punishment of death, for whatever crime and under all circumstances, is "cruel and unusual" in violation of the Eighth and Fourteenth Amendment of the Constitution. I shall not again canvass the reason that led to that conclusion. I emphasize only that foremost among the "moral concepts" recognized in our cases and inherent in the Clause is the primary moral principle that the State, even as it punishes, must treat its citizens in a manner consistent with their intrinsic worth as human beings—a punishment must not be so severe as to be degrading to human dignity. A judicial determination whether the punishment of death comports with human dignity is therefore not only permitted but compelled by the Clause. . . .

I do not understand that the Court disagrees that "[i]n comparison to all other punishments today . . . the deliberate extinguishment of human life by the State is uniquely degrading to human dignity." . . . For three of my Brethren hold today that mandatory infliction of the death penalty constitutes the penalty cruel and unusual punishment. I perceive no principled basis for this limitation. Death for whatever crime and under all circumstances "is truly an awesome punishment. The calculated killing of a human being by the State involves, by its very nature, a denial of the executed person's humanity. . . . An executed person has indeed 'lost the right to have rights.' " . . . Death is not only an unusually severe punishment, unusual in its pain, in its finality, and in its enormity, but it serves no penal purpose more effectively than a less severe punishment; therefore the principle inherent in the Clause that prohibits pointless infliction of excessive punishment when less severe punishment can adequately achieve the same purposes invalidates the punishment. . . .

The fatal constitutional infirmity in the punishment of death is that it treats "members of the human race as nonhumans, as objects to be toyed with and discarded. [It is] thus inconsistent with the fundamental premise of the Clause that even the vilest criminal remains a human being possessed of common human dignity." . . . As such it is a penalty that "subjects the individual to a fate forbidden by the principle of civilized treatment guaranteed by the [Clause]." I therefore would hold, on that ground alone, that death is today a cruel and unusual punishment prohibited by the Clause. "Justice of this kind is obviously no less shocking than the crime itself, and the new 'official' murder, far from offering redress for the offense committed against society, adds instead a second defilement to the first." . . .

Mr. Justice Marshall, dissenting.

In *Furman* v. *Georgia* . . . I set forth at some length my views on the basic issue presented to the Court in these cases. The death penalty, I concluded, is a cruel and unusual punishment prohibited by the Eighth and Fourteenth Amendments. That continues to be my view. . . .

In *Furman* I concluded that the death penalty is constitutionally invalid for two reasons. First, the death penalty is excessive. . . . And second, the American people, fully informed as to the purposes of the death penalty and its liabilities, would in my view reject it as morally unacceptable. . . .

Since the decision in *Furman,* the legislatures of 35 States have enacted new statutes authorizing the imposition of the death sentence for certain crimes, and Congress has enacted a law providing the death penalty for air piracy resulting in death. . . . I would be less than candid if I did not acknowledge that these developments have a significant bearing on a realistic assessment of the moral acceptability of the death penalty to the American people. But if the constitutionality of the death penalty turns, as I have urged, on the opinion of an *informed* citizenry, then even the enactment of new death statutes cannot be viewed as conclusive. In *Furman,* I observed that the American people are largely unaware of the information critical to a judgment on the morality of the death penalty, and concluded that if they were better informed they would consider it shocking, unjust, and unacceptable. . . . A recent study, conducted after the enactment of the post-*Furman* statutes, has confirmed that the American people know little about the death penalty, and that the opinions of an informed public would differ significantly from those of a public unaware of the consequences and effects of the death penalty.

Even assuming, however, that the post-*Furman* enactment of statutes authorizing the death penalty renders the prediction of the views of an informed citizenry an uncertain basis for a constitutional decision, the enactment of those statutes has no bearing whatsoever on the conclusion that the death penalty is unconstitutional because it is excessive. An excessive penalty is invalid under the Cruel and Unusual Punishments Clause "even though popular sentiment may favor" it. . . . The inquiry here, then, is simply whether the death penalty is necessary to accomplish the legitimate legislative purposes in punishment, or whether a less severe penalty—life imprisonment—would do as well. . . .

The two purposes that sustain the death penalty as nonexcessive in the Court's view are general deterrence and retribution. In *Furman,* I canvassed the relevant data on the deterrent effect of capital punishment. . . . The state of knowledge at that point, after literally centuries of debate, was summarized as follows by a United Nations Committee:

"It is generally agreed between the retentionists and abolitionists, whatever their opinions about the validity of comparative studies of deterrence, that the data which now exist show no correlation between the existence of capital punishment and lower rates of capital crime." . . .

The available evidence, I concluded in *Furman,* was convincing that "capital punishment is not necessary as a deterrent to crime in our society." . . .

The other principal purpose said to be served by the death penalty is retribution. The notion that retribution can serve as a moral justification for the sanction of death finds credence in the opinion of my Brothers Stewart, Powell, and Stevens, and that of my Brother White in *Roberts* v. *Louisiana, post.* . . . It is this notion that I find to be the most disturbing aspect of today's unfortunate decision. . . .

My Brothers Stewart, Powell, and Stevens offer the following explanation of the retributive justification for capital punishment:

"The instinct for retribution is part of the nature of man, and channeling that instinct in the administration of criminal justice serves an important purpose in promoting the stability of a society governed by law. When people begin to believe that organized society is unwilling or unable to impose upon criminal offenders the punishment they 'deserve,' then there are sown the seeds of anarchy—of self-help, vigilante justice, and lynch law." . . .

This statement is wholly inadequate to justify the death penalty. . . . It simply defies belief to suggest that the death penalty is necessary to prevent the American people from taking the law into their own hands.

In a related vein, it may be suggested that the expression of moral outrage through the imposition of the death penalty serves to reinforce basic moral values—that it marks some crimes as particularly offensive and therefore to be avoided. . . . This contention, like the previous one, provides no support for the death penalty. It is inconceivable that any individual concerned about conforming his conduct to what society says is "right" would fail to realize that murder is "wrong" if the penalty were simply life imprisonment. . . .

There remains for consideration, however, what might be termed the purely retributive justification for the death penalty—that the death penalty is appropriate, not because of its beneficial effect on society, but because the taking of the murderer's life is itself morally good. Some of the language of the plurality's opinion appears positively to embrace this notion of retribution for its own sake as a justification for capital punishment. . . . The mere fact that the community demands the murderer's life in return for the evil he has done cannot sustain the death penalty, for as the plurality reminds us, "the Eighth Amendment demands more than that a challenged punishment be acceptable to contemporary society." . . . . To be sustained under the Eighth Amendment, the death penalty must "[comport] with the basic concept of human dignity at the core of the Amendment," . . . ; the objective in imposing it must be "[consistent] with our respect for the dignity of other men." . . . Under these standards, the taking of life "because the wrong-doer deserves it" surely must fall, for such a punishment has as its very basis the total denial of the wrong-doer's dignity and worth.

The death penalty, unnecessary to promote the goal of deterrence or to further any legitimate notion of retribution, is an excessive penalty forbidden by the Eighth and Fourteenth Amendments. I respectfully dissent from the Court's judgment upholding the sentences of death imposed upon the petitioners in these cases.

In separate decisions the Court upheld the death penalty statutes of Texas and Florida. Although different from the Georgia statute, the majority of the Court found that in each case the sentencing body was guided by standards and was required to consider both aggravating and mitigating factors in reaching its decision on whether to impose the death penalty or life imprisonment. The North Carolina and Louisiana statutes were held unconstitutional because conviction for specified crimes mandated the death penalty with no latitude for discretion in the sentencing body to consider either aggravating or mitigating circumstances.

In *Coker* v. *Georgia*, 433 U.S. 584 (1977), the Court reversed a Georgia death sentence imposed on one convicted of rape of an adult woman during the commission of the felony of armed robbery. Justice White, in a plurality opinion, said that the penalty was grossly disproportionate to the crime of raping an adult woman, as long as the rapist did not take the life of his victim. He pointed out that Georgia was the only state authorizing the death penalty in such cases, and also that since 1973 Georgia juries had not imposed the death sentence in the vast majority (90%) of rape convictions. Justices

Brennan and Marshall continued their argument that the death penalty was always unconstitutional. Justice Powell concurred in the result but disagreed with the plurality that a death sentence for rape was *always* disproportionate in the case of an adult woman who was not killed. "Some victims are so grievously injured physically or psychologically that life *is* beyond repair. Thus, it may be that the death penalty is not disproportionate punishment for the crime of aggravated rape."

In *Enmund* v. *Florida,* 458 U.S. 782 (1982), the Court reviewed a Florida case in which an individual and a codefendant were found guilty of murder and robbery of two elderly persons at their farmhouse, and both were sentenced to death. The Supreme Court of Florida affirmed the defendant's death sentence, holding that even though the record supported no more than the inference that he was in a car by the side of the road at the time of the killings, waiting to help the robbers escape, this was enough under Florida law to make the defendant a constructive aider and abettor and hence a principal in first-degree murder upon whom the death penalty could be imposed. The United States Supreme Court reversed and remanded. A majority of five members held that the Eighth and Fourteenth Amendments were violated by the imposition of the death penalty on the defendant, who aided and abetted a felony in the course of which a murder was committed by others but who did not himself kill, attempt to kill, intend to kill, or contemplate that life would be taken. Justice White's opinion for the majority examined the laws of the thirty-six state and federal jurisdictions presently authorizing the death penalty and concluded: "Thus only a small minority of jurisdictions—eight—allow the death penalty to be imposed solely because the defendant somehow participated in a robbery in the course of which a murder was committed."

In *Ford* v. *Wainwright,* 477 U.S. 399 (1986), the Court held for the first time that a condemned prisoner who becomes insane while awaiting execution cannot be put to death unless and until he becomes competent again. There was no suggestion that the defendant was incompetent at the time of the offense, at trial, or at sentencing. But subsequently he began to manifest changes in behavior indicating a mental disorder. At counsel's request, the Governor, following statutory procedure, appointed three psychiatrists, who together interviewed the prisoner for thirty minutes in the presence of eight other people, including the prisoner's counsel. The Governor's order directed that the attorneys should not participate in the examination in any adversarial manner. All three psychiatrists reported that while the prisoner suffered from certain mental disorders, he was considered to be competent. A Federal District Court denied a petition for habeas corpus in which an evidentiary hearing was sought, and the Court of Appeals affirmed. The Supreme Court reversed and remanded, holding that since the defendant had been denied a factfinding procedure "adequate to afford a full and fair hearing" on the critical issue of his sanity, petitioner was entitled to an evidentiary hearing in the District Court, *de novo,* on the question of his competence to be executed. Four of the justices stated that the Eighth Amendment did not prohibit the execution of the insane, although Justices O'Connor and White concurred in the result because they found that the Florida statute did not provide adequate procedural protections to enforce its policy of prohibiting execution of the incompetent.

*Sumner* v. *Shuman,* 55 LW 4931 (1987), involved the validity of the mandatory death sentence for prison murder. In 1973 Nevada adopted a capital murder statute that mandated the death penalty for one who committed murder while under sentence for life imprisonment without possiblity of parole. Shuman was convicted in a Nevada state court of first degree murder for the shooting death of a truck driver during a roadside robbery. He was sentenced to life imprisonment without possibility of parole. While serving the sentence, he was convicted of the murder of a fellow prisoner and sentenced to death. The State Supreme Court affirmed. In a habeas corpus proceeding a

Federal District Court vacated the sentence, holding that the mandatory capital-punishment statute violated the Eighth and Fourteenth Amendments, and the Court of Appeals affirmed. By a 6–3 vote the Supreme Court affirmed, holding that under the individualized capital-sentencing doctrine, the Constitution demands that the sentencing authority consider relevant mitigating circumstances pertaining to the offense and a range of factors concerning the character of the defendant. The death penalty might still be imposed, but the jury could be persuaded that it was not appropriate. Justice White, for the three dissenters, argued that "a State does not violate the Eighth Amendment by maintaining the full deterrent effect of the death penalty in this kind of case and by insisting that those who murder while serving a life sentence without parole not be able to escape punishment for that crime."

## THOMPSON v. OKLAHOMA
### 56 LW 4892 (1988)

[Petitioner, when he was fifteen years old, actively participated in a brutal murder. Because petitioner was a "child" as a matter of Oklahoma law, the District Attorney filed a statutory petition seeking to have him tried as an adult, which the trial court granted. He was then convicted and sentenced to death, and the Court of Criminal Appeals of Oklahoma affirmed.]

Justice Stevens announced the judgment of the Court, and delivered an opinion in which Justice Brennan, Justice Marshall, and Justice Blackmun join.

Petitioner was convicted of first-degree murder and sentenced to death. The principal question presented is whether the execution of that sentence would violate the constitutional prohibition against the infliction of "cruel and unusual punishments" because petitioner was only 15 years old at the time of his offense. . . .

[I]n confronting the question whether the youth of the defendant—more specifically, the fact that he was less than 16 years old at the time of his offense—is a sufficient reason for denying the state the power to sentence him to death, we first review relevant legislative enactments, then refer to jury determinations, and finally explain why these indicators of contemporary standards of decency confirm our judgment that such a young person is not capable of acting with the degree of culpability that can justify the ultimate penalty. . . .

Most state legislatures have not expressly confronted the question of establishing a minimum age for imposition of the death penalty. In 14 States, capital punishment is not authorized at all, and in 19 others capital punishment is authorized but no minimum age is expressly stated in the death penalty statute. One might argue on the basis of this body of legislation that there is no chronological age at which the imposition of the death penalty is unconstitutional and that our current standards of decency would still tolerate the execution of 10-year-old children. We think it self-evident that such an argument is unacceptable; indeed, no such argument has been advanced in this case. If, therefore, we accept the premise that some offenders are simply too young to be put to death, it is reasonable to put this group of statutes to one side because they do not focus on the question of where the chronological age line should be drawn. When we confine our attention to the 18 States that have expressly established a minimum age in their death-penalty statutes, we find that all of them require that the defendant have attained at least the age of 16 at the time of the capital offense.

The conclusion that it would offend civilized standards of decency to execute a person who was less than 16 years old at the time of his or her offense is consistent with the views that have been expressed by respected professional organizations, by other nations that share our Anglo-American heritage, and by the leading members of the Western European community. . . .

The second societal factor the Court has examined in determining the acceptability of capital punishment to the American sensibility is the behavior of juries. . . .

While it is not known precisely how many persons have been executed during the 20th century for crimes committed under the age of 16, a scholar has recently compiled a table revealing this number to be between 18 and 20. All of these occurred during the first half of the century, with the last such execution taking place apparently in 1948. . . .

Department of Justice statistics indicate that during the years 1982 through 1986 an average of over 16,000 persons were arrested for willful criminal homicide (murder and nonnegligent manslaughter) each year. Of that group of 82,094 persons, 1,393 were sentenced to death. Only five of them, including the petitioner in this case, were less than 16 years old at the time of the offense. Statistics of this kind can, of course, be interpreted in different ways, but they do suggest that these five young offenders have received sentences that are "cruel and unusual in the same way that being struck by lightning is cruel and unusual." *Furman* v. *Georgia*. . . .

"Although the judgments of legislatures, juries, and prosecutors weigh heavily in the balance, it is for us ultimately to judge whether the Eighth Amendment permits imposition of the death penalty" on one such as petitioner who committed a heinous murder when he was only 15 years old. . . . In making that judgment, we first ask whether the juvenile's culpability should be measured by the same standard as that of an adult, and then consider whether the application of the death penalty to this class of offenders "measurably contributes" to the social purposes that are served by the death penalty.

It is generally agreed "that punishment should be directly related to the personal culpability of the criminal defendant." . . . There is also broad agreement on the proposition that adolescents as a class are less mature and responsible than adults. We stressed this difference in explaining the importance of treating the defendant's youth as a mitigating factor in capital cases: . . .

Thus, the Court has already endorsed the proposition that less culpability should attach to a crime committed by a juvenile than to a comparable crime committed by an adult. The basis for this conclusion is too obvious to require extended explanation. . . . The reasons why juveniles are not trusted with the privileges and responsibilities of an adult also explain why their irresponsible conduct is not as morally reprehensible as that of an adult.

"The death penalty is said to serve two principal social purposes: retribution and deterrence of capital crimes by prospective offenders." *Gregg* v. *Georgia*. . . . In *Gregg* we concluded that as "an expression of society's moral outrage at particularly offensive conduct," retribution was not "inconsistent with our respect for the dignity of men." Given the lesser culpability of the juvenile offender, the teenager's capacity for growth, and society's fiduciary obligations to its children, this conclusion is simply inapplicable to the execution of a 15-year-old offender.

For such a young offender, the deterrence rationale is equally unacceptable. The Department of Justice statistics indicate that about 98 percent of the arrests for willful homicide involved persons who were over 16 at the time of the offense. Thus, excluding younger persons from the class that is eligible for the death penalty will not diminish the deterrent value of capital punishment for the vast majority of potential offenders. And even with respect to those under 16 years of age, it is obvious that the potential deterrent value of the death sentence is insignificant for two reasons. The likelihood that the teenage offender has made the kind of cost-benefit analysis that attaches any weight to the possibility of execution is so remote as to be virtually nonexistent. And, even if one posits such a cold-blooded calculation by a 15-year-old, it is fanciful to believe that he would be deterred by the knowledge that a small number of persons his age have been executed during the 20th century. In short, we are not persuaded that the imposition of the death penalty for offenses committed by persons under 16 years of age has made, or can be expected to make, any measurable contribution to the goals that capital punishment is intended to achieve. It is, therefore, "nothing more than the purposeless and needless imposition of pain and suffering," . . . and thus an unconstitutional punishment. . . .

The judgment of the Court of Criminal Appeals is vacated and the case is remanded with instructions to enter an appropriate order vacating petitioner's death sentence.

*It is so ordered.*

Justice Kennedy took no part in the consideration or decision of this case.

Justice O'Connor, concurring in the judgment. . . .

The most salient statistic that bears on this case is that every single American legislature that has expressly set a minimum age for capital punishment has set that age at 16 or above. . . . When one adds these 18 States to the 14 that have rejected capital punishment completely, . . . it appears that almost two-thirds of the state legislatures have definitely concluded that no 15-year-old should be exposed to the threat of execution. . . . Where such a large majority of the state legislatures have unambiguously outlawed capital punishment for 15-year-olds, and where no legislature in this country has affirmatively and unequivocally endorsed such a practice, strong counterevidence would be required to persuade me that a national consensus aginst this practice does not exist.

The dissent argues that it has found such counterevidence in the laws of the 19 States that authorize capital punishment without setting any statutory minimum age. If we could be sure that each of these 19 state legislatures had deliberately chosen to authorize capital punishment for crimes committed at the age of 15, one could hardly suppose that there is a settled national consensus opposing such a practice. In fact, however, the statistics relied on by the dissent may be quite misleading. When a legislature provides for some 15-year-olds to be processed through the adult criminal justice system, and capital punishment is available for adults in that jurisdiction, the death penalty becomes at least theoretically applicable to such defendants. This is how petitioner was rendered death-eligible, and the same possiblity appears to exist in 18 other States. . . . As the plurality points out, however, it does not necessarily follow that the legislatures in those jurisdictions have deliberately concluded that it would be appropriate to impose capital punishment on 15-year-olds (or on even younger defendants who may be tried as adults in some jurisdictions). . . .

The day may come when we must decide whether a legislature may deliberately and unequivocally resolve upon a policy authorizing capital punishment for crimes committed at the age of 15. In the event, we shall have to decide the Eighth Amendment issue that divides the plurality and the dissent in this case, and we shall have to evaluate the evidence of societal standards of decency that is available to us at that time. In my view, however, we need not and should not decide the question today. . . .

Justice Scalia, with whom Chief Justice Rehnquist and Justice White join, dissenting. . . .

The text of the Eighth Amendment, made applicable to the states by the Fourteenth, prohibits the imposition of "cruel and unusual punishments." The plurality does not attempt to maintain that this was originally understood to prohibit capital punishment for crimes committed by persons under the age of 16; the evidence is unusually clear and unequivocal that it was not. . . .

Necessarily, therefore, the plurality seeks to rest its holding on the conclusion that Thompson's punishment as an adult is contrary to the "evolving standards of decency that mark the progress of a maturing society." . . . Of course the risk of assessing evolving standards is that it is all too easy to believe that evolution has culminated in one's own views. To avoid this danger we have, when making such an assessment in prior cases, looked for objective signs of how today's society views a particular punishment. . . . The most reliable objective signs consist of the legislation that the society has enacted. It will rarely if ever be the case that the members of this Court will have a better sense of the evolution in views of the American people than do their elected representatives.

It is thus significant that, only four years ago, in the Comprehensive Crime Control Act of 1984, . . . Congress expressly addressed the effect of youth upon the imposition of criminal punishment, and changed the law in precisely the opposite direction from that which the plurality's perceived evolution in social attitudes would suggest: It lowered from 16 to 15 the age at which a juvenile's case can, "in the interest of justice," be transferred from juvenile court to federal District Court, enabling him to be tried and punished as an adult. . . .

Turning to legislation at the state level, one observes the same trend of *lowering* rather than raising the age of juvenile criminal liability. As for the state *status quo* with respect to the death penalty in particular: The plurality chooses to "confine [its] attention" to the fact that all 18 of the States that establish a minimum age for capital punishment have chosen at least 16. But it is beyond me why an accurate analysis would not include within the computation the larger number of States (19) that have determined that no minimum age for capital punishment is appropriate, leaving that to be governed by their general rules for the age at which juveniles can be criminally responsible. A survey of state laws shows, in other words, that a majority of the States for which the issue exists (the rest do not have capital punishment) are of the view that death is not different insofar as the age of juvenile criminal responsibility is concerned. . . .

Even assuming that the execution rather than the sentencing statistics are the pertinent data, . . . the statistics are frail support for the existence of the *relevant* trend. There are many reasons that adequately account for the drop in executions other than the premise of general agreement that no 15-year-old murderer should ever be executed. Foremost among them, of course, was a reduction in public support for capital punishment in general. . . .

In sum, the statistics of executions demonstrate nothing except the fact that our society has always agreed that executions of 15-year-old criminals should be rare, and in more modern times has agreed that they (like all other executions) should be even rarer still. There is no rational basis for discerning in that a societal judgment that no one so much as a day under 16 can *ever* be mature and morally responsible enough to deserve that penalty; and there is no justification except our own predeliction for converting a statistical rarity of occurrence into an absolute constitutional ban. . . . One could readily run the same statistical argument with respect to other classes of defendants. Between 1930 and 1955, for example, 30 women were executed in the United States. Only 3 were executed between then and 1986—and none in the 22-year period between 1962 and 1984. Proportionately, the drop is as impressive as that which the plurality points to in 15-year-old executions. . . . Surely the conclusion is not that it is unconstitutional to impose capital punishment upon a woman. . . .

While issues of jury selection have been discussed earlier, special aspects of the problem have arisen in cases involving the possibility of a sentence of death. Some prospective jurors are adamantly opposed to the death penalty, while others express grave reservations about joining in a vote to impose such a sentence. Can either or both of these categories be challenged for cause in a capital case and still meet the constitutional requirement of a "cross-section of the community" for jury selection procedures? In *Witherspoon* v. *Illinois,* 391 U.S. 510 (1968), the Court reversed the imposition of the death penalty where the prosecution eliminated nearly half the venire of prospective jurors by challenging any venireman who expressed qualms about capital punishment. Justice Stewart, in the majority opinion, indicated that the issue did not involve the State's assertion of "a right to exclude from the jury in a capital case those who say that they could never vote to impose the death penalty," but it was the narrow issue of whether the State could exclude even those who expressed hesitancy in their willingness to impose such a penalty. This, he said, would result in a jury that fell "woefully short of that impartiality to which the petitioner was entitled under the Sixth and Fourteenth Amendments." In *Adams* v. *Texas,* 448 U.S. 38 (1980), Justice White, in his opinion for the Court, discussed *Witherspoon* and its progeny and concluded: "This line of cases establishes the general proposition that a juror may not be challenged for cause based on his views about capital punishment unless those views would prevent or substantially impair the performance of his duties as a juror in accordance with his instructions and his oath. The State may insist, however, that jurors will consider and decide the facts impartially and conscientiously apply the law as charged by the court."

In *Lockhart* v. *McCree,* 476 U.S. 162 (1986), the Court reached the issue left open in *Witherspoon.* At McCree's trial in Arkansas for capital felony murder, the judge at *voir dire* removed for cause, over McCree's objections, those prospective jurors who stated that they could not under any circumstances vote for the imposition of the death penalty. The jury convicted, but at the sentencing phase of the trial it rejected the State's request for the death penalty and set punishment at life imprisonment without parole. The conviction was affirmed on appeal. In a habeas corpus action in Federal District Court he argued that the "death qualification" of the jury by the removal for cause of the "*Witherspoon*-excludables" denied him his constitutional right to an impartial jury selected from a representative cross-section of the community. The District Court agreed, and the Court of Appeals affirmed. The Supreme Court reversed in a 6–3 vote. Justice Rehnquist, for the majority, stated:

In this case we address the question left open by our decision nearly 18 years ago in *Witherspoon* v. *Illinois* . . . : Does the Constitution prohibit the removal for cause, prior to the guilt phase of a bifurcated capital trial, of prospective jurors whose opposition to the death penalty is so strong that it would prevent or substantially impair the performance of their duties as jurors at the sentencing phase of the trial? . . . We hold that it does not.

McCree had argued successfully in the lower federal courts that the numerous social science studies submitted as evidence proved that "death qualification" produced juries that were more prone to convict capital defendants and that their use thus violated both the fair cross section and impartiality requirements of the Sixth and Fourteenth Amendments. Justice Rehnquist discussed the social science studies at some length and, in effect, dismissed them as either not relevant or "too tentative and fragmentary" to make out a claim of constitutional error. He went further to state that "The essence of a 'fair cross-section' claim is the systematic exclusion of 'a "distinctive" group in the community.' . . . In our view, groups defined solely in terms of shared attitudes that would prevent or substantially impair members of the group from performing one of their duties as jurors, such as the 'Witherspoon-excludables' at issue here, are not 'distinctive groups' for fair cross-section purposes."

*Spaziano* v. *Florida*, 468 U.S. 447 (1984), presented a challenge to Florida's capital sentencing statute. It provided that the jury's recommendation in a capital case was only advisory. The trial court was permitted to conduct its own weighing of the aggravating and mitigating circumstances and, notwithstanding the recommendaiton of a majority of the jury, to enter a sentence of life imprisonment or death. In the latter case, specified written findings were required. The jury found the defendant guilty of first-degree murder, and following a sentencing hearing returned a majority verdict recommending life imprisonment. The judge imposed the death sentence and entered his findings in support thereof. Justice Blackmun, for the majority, stated that nothing in the previous decisions of the Court "*requires* that the sentence [of death] be imposed by a jury." He stated further:

The fact that a majority of jurisdictions has adopted a different practice, however, does not establish that contemporary standards of decency are offended by the jury override. . . . We see nothing that suggests that the application of the jury-override procedure has resulted in arbitrary or discriminatory application of the death penalty, either in general or in this particular case.

Justice Stevens, joined by Justices Brennan and Marshall, dissented on this issue. "I am convinced that the danger of an excessive response can only be avoided if the decision to impose the death penalty is made by a jury rather than by a single governmental official." And, quoting *Witherspoon* v. *Illinois*, he argued that the question of whether a sentence of death is excessive in the circumstances of any particular case is one that must be answered by the decisionmaker that is best able to "express the conscience of the community on the ultimate question of life or death."

Many supporters of capital punishment have protested what they consider to be the inordinate delay between sentence and execution. For defendants who avail themselves of the various appellate remedies, the process reportedly averages eight years. [See C. Herman Pritchett, *Constitutional Civil Liberties* (Englewood Cliffs: Prentice-Hall, 1984), p. 247.] Justice Rehnquist, in *Coleman* v. *Balkcom*, 451 U.S. 949 (1981), has registered a strong protest at the delay. He stated:

Although this Court has determined that capital punishment statutes do not violate the Constitution, . . . and although 30-odd States have enacted such statutes, apparently in the belief that they constitute sound social policy, the existence of the death penalty in this country is virtually an illusion. Since 1976, hundreds of juries have sentenced hundreds of persons to death, . . . yet virtually nothing happens except endlessly drawn out legal proceedings. . . . Of the hundreds of prisoners condemned to die who languish on the various "death rows," few of them appear to face any imminent prospect of their sentence being executed. Indeed, in the five years since *Gregg* v. *Georgia*, there has been only one execution of a defendant who has persisted in his attack upon his sentence.

Justice Rehnquist refers to his in-chambers opinion in *Spenkelink* v. *Wainwright*, 442 U.S. 1301 (1979), in which he describes some of the many avenues of relief which can be pursued by one sentenced to death. Perhaps in response to such complaints, the Court in *Barefoot* v. *Estelle*, 463 U.S. 880 (1983), indicated its approval of several procedures for expediting the handling of appeals by those sentenced to the death penalty. If indeed time is running out on those hundreds of prisoners who are "languishing on the various death rows," the end of the decade may confront the nation with a massive number of executions.

*Ingraham* v. *Wright*, 430 U.S. 651 (1977), dealt with the issue of the application of the Eighth Amendment to corporal punishment in the public schools. As stated by Justice Powell in his opinion for the majority:

This case presents questions concerning the use of corporal punishment in public schools: First, whether the paddling of students as a means of maintaining school discipline constitutes cruel and unusual punishment in violation of the Eighth Amendment; and, second, to the extent that paddling is constitutionally permissible, whether the Due Process Clause of the Fourteenth Amendment requires prior notice and an opportunity to be heard.

The majority held that the Eighth Amendment did not apply nor did the Fourteenth Amendment require notice and hearing prior to punishment. The conclusion was that the history of the Eighth Amendment and the Court's decisions made it clear that the bar to cruel and unusual punishment was designed to protect those convicted of crime, and there was no need for "wrenching the Eighth Amendment from its historical context and extending it to traditional disciplinary practices in the public schools." It was pointed out that the openness of the public school and its supervision by the community afford significant safeguards against the kinds of abuses from which the Eighth Amendment protects the prisoner. Further, the common law permits school officials to administer only such punishment as is reasonably necessary for the proper education and discipline of the child. Any punishment beyond that may result in both civil and criminal liability.

The requirement of prior notice and hearing was considered to be too significant a burden and would entail "a significant intrusion into an area of primary educational responsibility." Four members of the Court vigorously dissented. It was pointed out that Ingraham, because he was slow to respond to his teacher's instructions, was subjected to more than twenty licks with a wooden paddle while being held over a table in the principal's office. He required medical attention and was out of school for several days. Justice White, for the dissenters, did not suggest that spanking in the public schools was in every case prohibited by the Eighth Amendment. But he took issue "with the extreme view of the majority that corporal punishment in public schools, no matter how barbaric, inhumane, or severe, is never limited by the Eighth Amendment." He also argued that prior notice and hearing should be required to minimize the risk of mistakes, particularly in view of his conclusion that the remedy of a tort action was "utterly inadequate to protect against erroneous infliction of punishment."

[On cruel and unusual punishments generally, see David Fellman, *The Defendant's Rights Today* (Madison: University of Wisconsin Press, 1976), Chap. 11; Michael Metsner, *Cruel and Unusual: The Supreme Court and Capital Punishment* (New York: Morrow, 1974); and Larry C. Berkson, *The Concept of Cruel and Unusual Punishment* (Lexington, Mass.: Heath, 1975).]

## HABEAS CORPUS

There are several varieties of writs of habeas corpus. The one which is commonly referred to, however, as "the" writ, when the shorthand title is employed, is *habeas corpus ad subjiciendum et recipiendum*. It stems from the common law, with certain important extensions made by the famous Habeas Corpus Act adopted by Parliament in 1679. The writ is purely procedural in character. Its primary function is to provide a procedure whereby a speedy inquiry may be made by a judge into the legality of a detention on a criminal charge. More broadly, however, it can be used to test the legality of any restraint of person.

Since the writ is available to test the legality of detentions, it may be brought into play either before trial or after conviction and sentence. In the latter situation, however, it should be noted that habeas corpus is not a substitute for appeal. Allegations of error may be properly considered on appeal which are outside the scope of attack by habeas corpus. As a generalization, habeas corpus represents only a collateral attack on the detention, and concerns contentions which mainly reach questions of the jurisdiction of the committing court or agency. The Court has, however, tended to broaden the category of issues which it will accept as "jurisdictional questions." Under older approaches, a showing in a return to a writ that the prisoner was held under final process based upon a judgment of a court of competent jurisdiction closed the inquiry. This same rule was carried over into the Judiciary Act of 1789. But in 1867 Congress made a major change in the law. It extended the availability of the writ to state as well as federal prisoners, and made it applicable to restraints of liberty "in violation of the constitution, or of any treaty or law of the United States."

It should be clear that a court could have jurisdiction over a specific party and cause of action, but the procedure might be employed in the course of the trial "in violation of the constitution." Thus the act of 1867 opened the way for a much broader scope of "review" than was formerly the case. It still, however, does not permit the use of habeas corpus to reach ordinary assignments of error, such as an erroneous charge to the jury or the admission of improper evidence, where such claims do not rise to the status of constitutional rights. Thus appellate review should not be neglected under the mistaken belief that habeas corpus can serve the same purposes. While there is no time limit on the availability of the writ, unlike the situation with respect to appeals, the writ is narrower in its application. At the same time, there are procedural aspects of the use of the writ which afford more flexibility than is the case with appeal. Appeals are normally carried to a specified court, while any coordinate trial court may entertain a petition for habeas corpus.

That the scope of the writ is not confined to common-law rules or even, for that matter, to earlier American judicial interpretation, was made clear in *Johnson* v. *Zerbst*, 304 U.S. 458 (1938), discussed earlier in this chapter. In holding that habeas corpus was an appropriate remedy for attacking a federal conviction denying the Sixth Amendment right to counsel, the majority, through Justice Black, stated:

> The scope of inquiry in habeas corpus proceedings has been broadened—not narrowed—since the adoption of the Sixth Amendment. . . . A court's jurisdiction at the beginning of trial may be lost "in the course of the proceedings" due to failure to complete the court—as the Sixth Amendment requires—by providing Counsel for an accused who is unable to obtain Counsel, who has not intelligently waived this constitutional guaranty, and whose life or liberty is at stake. If this requirement of the Sixth Amendment is not complied with, the court no longer has jurisdiction to proceed. The judgment of conviction pronounced by a court without jurisdiction is void, and one imprisoned thereunder may obtain release by habeas corpus.

More recently, a majority of the Court asserted the right to expand the writ by judicial interpretation and to permit its use for a purpose unknown to the common law, to bring a prisoner into court to argue his own appeal. Justice Murphy, for the majority, in *Price* v. *Johnston*, 334 U.S. 266, 282 (1948), stated:

[W]e do not conceive that a circuit court of appeals, in issuing a writ of habeas corpus under Section 262 of the Judicial Code, is necessarily confined to the precise forms of that writ in vogue at the common law or in the English judicial system. Section 262 says that the writ must be agreeable to the usages and principles of "law," a term which is unlimited by the common law or the English law. And since "law" is not a static concept, but expands and develops as new problems arise, we do not believe that the forms of the *habeas corpus* writ authorized by Section 262 are only those recognized in this country in 1789, when the original Judiciary Act containing the substance of this section came into existence.

A dramatic use for habeas corpus is illustrated by cases in which the evidence or testimony indicates that the whole trial proceedings are infected with basic unfairness. Such a case was *Moore v. Dempsey*, 261 U.S. 86 (1923), discussed earlier, where evidence showed the entire trial to have been under mob domination. Justice Holmes, for the majority, stated:

We assume . . . that the corrective process supplied by the state may be so adequate that interference by habeas corpus ought not to be allowed. It certainly is true that mere mistakes of law in the course of a trial are not to be corrected in that way. But if the case is that the whole proceeding is a mask,—that counsel, jury, and judge were swept to the fatal end by an irresistible wave of public passion, and that the state courts failed to correct the wrong,—neither perfection in the machinery for correction nor the possibility that the trial court and counsel saw no other way of avoiding an immediate outbreak of the mob can prevent this court from securing to the petitioners their constitutional rights.

The general rule is that the writ of habeas corpus is unavailable unless the petitioner is under detention or in custody in some fashion. Over the years, however, the Court has substantially liberalized the application of the "in custody" requirement for purposes of utilizing habeas corpus.

In *Jones v. Cunningham*, 371 U.S. 236 (1963), the Court faced the question of whether the "in custody" requirement of 28 U.S.C. 2241 was sufficiently met in the supervisory control exercised over a parolee by the state parole board. Petitioner had been sentenced as a recidivist in state court and filed a petition for habeas corpus in federal district court alleging the invalidity of his conviction on the ground of denial of right to counsel. The superintendent of the prison was named as respondent. The petition was dismissed and appeal was taken. Before the appeal was argued, the prisoner was paroled, and he moved to add the parole board as respondents. The court of appeals refused on the ground that the board did not have physical custody of the prisoner and dismissed the petition on the ground that the case was moot because the petitioner was out of prison. On certiorari, the United States Supreme Court unanimously reversed. The Court agreed that the case was moot as to the prison superintendent, but it held that the stringent controls over the parolee exercised by the parole board met the "in custody" requirement of the statute necessary to the issuance of habeas corpus. The lower courts were thus ordered to proceed to a decision on the merits of petitioner's case.

In *Carafas v. LaVallee*, 391 U.S. 234 (1968), a prisoner filed an application for habeas corpus in federal court, alleging that illegally seized evidence had been used in securing his conviction in a state court. The application was dismissed by the District Court, and the Court of Appeals dismissed the appeal. Two weeks before filing a petition for certiorari in the United States Supreme Court, the petitioner was unconditionally released from the state prison. The Court held that the expiration of the sentence before the application for habeas corpus was finally adjudicated did not terminate federal jurisdiction, and because of the substantial disabilities which flowed from the conviction (ineligibility to engage in certain businesses, loss of voting rights, and others), the cause was not moot. Thus it was held that once federal jurisdiction attached in the District Court, it was not defeated by the release of the petitioner prior to completion of proceedings.

For federal courts to intervene in state criminal process through the device of habeas corpus is, of course, to raise delicate questions of federal-state relations. For this reason, the federal code requires that state prisoners exhaust their state remedies, including habeas corpus, prior to petitioning federal courts for the writ. The normal appellate route for state prisoners is to proceed through the state courts as far as allowable, and then, if a federal question is presented, to petition the United States Supreme Court for certiorari.

Suppose a defendant convicted in a state court fails to appeal within the allotted time and then petitions in a federal court for habeas corpus. Is he barred by the code provision (28 U.S.C. §2254) which states that the writ shall not be granted "unless it appears that the applicant has exhausted the remedies available in the courts of the State"? The Court in *Fay v. Noia*, 372 U.S. 391 (1963), held that the writ could properly issue in such cases unless it appeared that the petitioner had "deliberately by-passed the orderly procedure of the state courts and in so doing has forfeited his state court remedies."

Justice Brennan, for the majority, stated:

We affirm the judgment of the Court of Appeals but reach that court's result by a different course of reasoning. We hold: (1) Federal courts have *power* under the federal habeas statute to grant relief despite the applicant's failure to have pursued a state remedy not available to him at the time he applies; the doctrine under which state procedural defaults are held to constitute an adequate and independent state law ground barring direct Supreme Court review is not to be extended to limit the power granted the federal courts under the federal habeas statute. (2) Noia's failure to appeal was not a failure to exhaust "the remedies available in the courts of the State" as required by §2254; that requirement refers only to a failure to exhaust state remedies still open to the applicant at the time he files his application for habeas corpus in the federal court. (3) Noia's failure to appeal cannot under the circumstances be deemed an intelligent and understanding waiver of his right to appeal such as to justify the withholding of federal habeas corpus relief.

*Fay v. Noia* appeared to remove the final barriers to broad collateral reexamination of state criminal convictions in federal habeas corpus proceedings. But in 1976 the Court made a major policy shift away from *Fay* and, at the same time, gave strong indications that the exclusionary rule of *Mapp* v. *Ohio* might be applied selectively "in the light of competing policies." In *Stone* v. *Powell*, 428 U.S. 465 (1976), a majority of six members held that "where the State has provided an opportunity for full and fair litigation of a Fourth Amendment claim, the Constitution does not require that a state prisoner be granted federal habeas corpus relief on the ground that evidence obtained in an unconstitutional search or seizure was introduced at his trial." Justice Powell, for the majority, stated that the rule was not absolute which barred illegally seized evidence, since it is admissible in grand jury proceedings and may be admitted to impeach the credibility of a defendant in the trial itself. He further pointed out some of the defects and costs in the application of the rule which "deflects the truthfinding process and often frees the guilty." Nonetheless, he concluded that the exclusionary rule should be implemented at trial and on direct appeal of state court convictions. "But the additional contribution, if any, of the consideration of search-and-seizure claims of state prisoners on collateral review is small in relation to the costs." Chief Justice Burger, in a concurring opinion, would have gone even further in the shift away from *Mapp*, stating that "it seems clear to me that the exclusionary rule has been operative long enough to demonstrate its flaws. The time has come to modify its reach, even if it is retained for a small and limited category of cases."

[See Zechariah Chafee, "The Most Important Human Right in the Constitution," 32 *B.U.L.Rev.* 144 (1952); David Fellman, *The Defendant's Rights Today* (Madison: University of Wisconsin Press, 1976), Chap. 5; William J. Brennan, Jr., "State Constitutions and the Protection of Individual Rights," 90 *Harv. L. Rev.* 489 (1977); Paul M. Bator, "Finality in Criminal Law and Federal Habeas Corpus for State Prisoners," 76 *Harv. L. Rev.* 441 (1963).]

A final aspect of the writ of habeas corpus concerns the form and the procedure accompanying its use. The prisoner or his lawyer or a friend petitions an appropriate judge to issue the writ. While there is no rigid requirement of a particular form, there are certain essential allegations and statements of fact which must be presented in order for consideration to be given the petition. [For sample forms, see 28 U.S.C. §2254 (Supp. 1983, p. 241).]

Upon receipt of such a petition alleging facts which would support a charge of illegal detention, the judge issues the writ, directed to the warden or other person detaining the petitioner, ordering him to bring the prisoner before the judge for hearing. While the judge may doubt the authenticity of the claims of petitioner, if a proper statement is made, the writ issues. However, as Justice Jackson pointed out in *Brown* v. *Allen*, 344 U.S. 443, 547 (1953), "Unless it states facts which, if proved, would warrant relief, the applicant is not entitled as of right to a hearing." This factor normally presents no problem to the prisoner, however, since most penitentiaries have among the inmates at least one expert on drawing petitions for habeas corpus. Judges have often complained, however, that since the issuance of the writ is very nearly automatic and since there is no limit on the number of petitions a prisoner may file, that the writ is all too often used merely as a device to get a few days vacation from the prison. Justice Jackson, again in *Brown* v. *Allen*, stated:

[T]his Court has sanctioned progressive trivialization of the writ until floods of stale, frivolous and repetitious petitions inundate the docket of the lower courts and swell our own. Judged by our own disposition of habeas corpus matters, they have, as a class, become peculiarly undeserving. It must prejudice the occasional meritorious application to be buried in a flood of worthless ones. He who must search a haystack for a needle is likely to end up with the attitude that the needle is not worth the search. Nor is it any answer to say that few of these petitions in any court really result in the discharge of the petitioner. That is condemnation of the procedure which has encouraged frivolous cases.

The "needle" referred to by Justice Jackson turns out to represent between 1 percent and 2 percent of the total petitions handled in federal courts. Many people, especially the prisoners concerned, feel that even this small return on the time invested is worth the effort.

## RIGHTS OF PRISONERS

Increasingly since the early 1960s persons confined in prisons have been filing suits requesting injunctive relief against a variety of restrictions imposed upon them during incarceration. The suits include complaints against censorship of mail, the failure to furnish library facilities and legal assistance to aid in the preparation of habeas corpus applications or civil rights actions, or the imposition of punishment while in prison without the alleged due process safeguards of notice, hearing, access to witnesses, or counsel. In *Johnson* v. *Avery*, 393 U.S. 483 (1969), a state prisoner in Tennessee who had repeatedly assisted other prisoners to prepare petitions for postconviction relief, was placed in disciplinary confinement and deprived of certain privileges for violating a prison regulation prohibiting inmates from helping other inmates to prepare writs or other legal papers. The Court held that Tennessee could not constitutionally adopt and enforce a rule "forbidding illiterate or poorly educated prisoners to file habeas corpus petitions," but the prison rule barring assistance from other prisoners "effectively does just that." Therefore, "unless and until the State provides some reasonable alternative to assist inmates in the preparation of petitions for post-conviction relief, it may not validly enforce a regulation such as that here in issue, barring inmates from furnishing such assistance to other prisoners." In *Bounds* v. *Smith*, 430 U.S. 817 (1977), the Court went further and held that the fundamental constitutional right of access to the courts required state prison authorities to assist inmates in the preparation and filing of meaningful legal papers by providing prisoners with adequate law libraries or adequate assistance from persons trained in the law.

*Procunier* v. *Martinez*, 416 U.S. 396 (1974), dealt with the issue of censorship of prisoners' incoming and outgoing personal mail in state prisons in California. The censorship regulations authorized censorship of statements that "unduly complain" or "magnify grievances," expression of "inflammatory political, racial, or religious, or other views," and matter deemed "defamatory" or "otherwise inappropriate." A three-judge District Court enjoined enforcement of the regulations as violative of the First Amendment, and the Supreme Court affirmed. In his opinion for the Court, Justice Powell first canvassed lower federal court decisions on prison regulations restricting freedom of speech, concluding that this "array of disparate approaches" dictated that the Court formulate a "standard of review for prisoner mail censorship." He stated:

[W]e hold that censorship of prisoner mail is justified if the following criteria are met. First, the regulation or practice in question must further an important or substantial governmental interest unrelated to the supression of expression. Prison officials may not censor inmate correspondence simply to eliminate unflattering or unwelcome opinions or factually inaccurate statements. Rather, they must show that a regulation authorizing mail censorship furthers one or more of the substantial governmental interests of security, order, and rehabilitation. Second, the limitation of First Amendment freedoms must be no greater than is necessary or essential to the protection of the particular governmental interest involved. . . . [T]he Department's regulations authorized censorship of prisoner mail far broader than any legitimate interest of penal administration demands and were properly found invalid by the District Court.

In *Turner* v. *Safley*, 55 LW 4719 (1987), inmates in a Missouri prison brought a class action challenging two regulations issued by the Missouri Division of Corrections. The first permitted correspondence between immediate family members who were inmates "concerning legal matters," but allowed other inmate correspondence only if each inmate's classification and treatment team deemed it in the best interests of the parties. The second regulation permitted an inmate to marry only with the prison superintendent's permission, which could be given only when there were "compelling reasons" to do so. Testimony indicated that generally only a pregnancy or the birth of an illegitimate child would be considered "compelling." The Court held 5–4 that the correspondence regulation was constitutional but held unanimously that the restrictions on marriage of inmates were invalid. Justice O'Connor, for the Court, stated that the proper standard for review of prisoners' constitutional complaints was not strict scrutiny but whether a prison regulation that impinges on inmates' constitutional rights was "reasonably related" to legitimate penological interests. She stated that there were several relevant factors for determining reasonableness: (a) whether there is a "valid, rational connection" between the regulation and the legitimate governmental interest put forward to justify it; (b) whether there are alternative means of exercising the right that remain open to prison inmates; (c) the impact that accommodation of the asserted constitutional right will have on guards and other inmates, and on the allocation of prison resources generally; and (d) the absence of alternatives that fully accommodate the prisoner's rights at *de minimis* cost to valid penological interests. Testimony indicated that the prison system had a growing problem with prison gangs, and that restricting communications among gang members, both by transferring gang members to different institutions and by restricting their correspondence, was an important element in combatting this problem. The majority concluded that the regulation was reasonably related to legitimate security interests. The marriage restriction, however, was held to constitute "an exaggerated response to petitioners' rehabilitation and security concerns." While the right to marry "is subject to substantial restrictions as a result of incarceration," it is still a fundamental right, and restrictions must be reasonably related to appropriate penological interests.

*Wolff* v. *McDonnell*, decided in 1974, addressed several issues of prisoners' rights arising from regulations imposed by the Nebraska Penal and Correctional Complex. Two of the allegations were that disciplinary proceedings did not comply with the due process clause of the Fourteenth Amendment and that the regulations governing the inspection of mail to and from attorneys for inmates were unconstitutionally restrictive. The respondent filed a complaint under 42 U.S.C. §1983 requesting damages and injunctive relief.

## WOLFF *v.* McDONNELL
### *418 U.S. 539 (1974)*

Mr. Justice White delivered the opinion of the Court. . . .

We begin with the due process claim. An understanding of the issues involved requires a detailing of the prison disciplinary regime set down by Nebraska statutes and prison regulations.

Section 16 of the Nebraska Treatment and Corrections Act . . . provides that the chief executive officer of each penal facility is responsible for the discipline of inmates in a particular institution. The statute provides for a range of possible disciplinary action. "Except in flagrant or serious cases, punishment for misconduct shall consist of deprivation of privileges. In cases of flagrant or serious misconduct, the chief executive officer may order that a person's reduction of term . . . [good-time credit] be forfeited or withheld and also that the person be confined in a disciplinary cell." Each breach of discipline is to be entered in the person's file together with the disposition or punishment therefor. . . .

[Major misconduct must be reported to an Adjustment Committee, composed of the Associate Warden Custody, the Correctional Industries Superintendent, and the Reception Center Director. This Committee is directed to review and evaluate all misconduct reports, conduct investigations, make findings, and impose disciplinary actions. Based on the testimony, the District Court found that the following procedures were in effect when an inmate is written up or charged with a prison violation: (a) the chief correction supervisor reviews the "write-ups" on the inmates by the officers of the Complex daily; (b) the convict is called to a conference with the chief correction supervisor and the charging party; (c) following the conference, a conduct report is sent to the Adjustment Committee: (d) there follows a hearing before the Adjustment Committee and the report is read to the inmate and discussed; (e) if the inmate denies the charge he may ask questions of the party writing him up; (f) the Adjustment Committee can conduct additional investigations if it desires; and (g) punishment is imposed.]

Petitioners assert that the procedure for disciplining prison inmates for serious misconduct is a matter of policy raising no constitutional issue. If the position implies that prisoners in state institutions are wholly without the protections of the Constitution and the Due Process Clause, it is plainly untenable. Lawful imprisonment necessarily makes unavailable many rights and privileges of the ordinary citizen, a "retraction justified by the considerations underlying our penal system." . . . But though his rights may be diminished by the needs and exigencies of the institutional environment, a prisoner is not wholly stripped of constitutional protections when he is imprisoned for crime. . . .

Of course, as we have indicated, the fact that prisoners retain rights under the Due Process Clause in no way implies that these rights are not subject to restrictions imposed by the nature of the regime to which they have been lawfully committed. . . . Prison disciplinary proceedings are not part of a criminal prosecution, and the full panoply of rights due a defendant in such proceedings does not apply. . . . In sum, there must be mutual accommodation between institutional needs and objectives and the provisions of the Constitution that are of general application. . . .

. . . But the State having created the right to good time and itself recognizing that its deprivation is a sanction authorized for major misconduct, the prisoner's interest has real substance and is sufficiently embraced within Fourteenth Amendment "liberty" to entitle him to those minimum proceedures appropriate under the circumstances and required by the Due Process Clause to insure that the state-created right is not arbitrarily abrogated. . . .

We hold that written notice of the charges must be given to the disciplinary-action defendant in order to inform him of the charges and to enable him to marshall the facts and prepare a defense. At least a brief period of time after the notice, no less than 24 hours, should be allowed to the inmate to prepare for the appearance before the Adjustment Committee.

We also hold that there must be a "written statement by the fact-finders as to the evidence relied on and reasons" for the disciplinary action. . . .

We are also of the opinion that the inmate facing disciplinary proceedings should be allowed to call witnesses and present documentary evidence in his defense when permitting him to do so will not be unduly hazardous to institutional safety or correctional goals. Ordinarily, the right to present evidence is basic to a fair hearing; but the unrestricted right to call witnesses from the prison population carries obvious potential for disruption and for interference with the swift punishment that in individual cases may be essential to carrying out the correctional program of the institution. . . .

Confrontation and cross-examination present greater hazards to institutional interests. If confrontation and cross-examination of those furnishing evidence against the inmate were to be allowed as a matter of course, as in criminal trials, there would be considerable potential for havoc inside the prison walls. Proceedings would inevitably be longer and tend to unmanageability. . . . Although some States do seem to allow cross-examination in disciplinary hearings, we are not apprised of the conditions under which the procedure may be curtailed; and it does not appear that confrontation and cross-examination are generally required in this context. We think that the Constitution should not be read to impose the procedure at the present time and that adequate bases for decision in prison disciplinary cases can be arrived at without cross-examination. . . .

The insertion of counsel into the disciplinary process would inevitably give the proceedings a more adversary cast and tend to reduce their utility as a means to further correctional goals. There would also be delay and very practical problems in providing counsel in sufficient numbers at the time and place where hearings are to be held. At this stage of the development of these procedures we are not prepared to hold that inmates have a right to either retained or appointed counsel in disciplinary proceedings.

Where an illiterate inmate is involved, however, or where the complexity of the issue makes it unlikely that the inmate will be able to collect and present the evidence necessary for an adequate comprehension of the case, he should be free to seek the aid of a fellow inmate, or if that is forbidden, to have adequate substitute aid in the form of help from the staff or from a sufficiently competent inmate designated by the staff. . . .

The issue of the extent to which prison authorities can open and inspect incoming mail from attorneys to inmates, has been considerably narrowed in the course of this litigation. . . . Petitioners now concede that they cannot open and *read* mail from attorneys to inmates, but contend that they may open all letters from attorneys as long as it is done in the presence of the prisoners. . . .

. . . We think it entirely appropriate that the State require any such communications to be specially marked as originating from an attorney, with his name and address being given, if they are to receive special treatment. It would also certainly be permissible that prison authorities require that a lawyer desiring to correspond with a prisoner, first identify himself and his client to the prison officials, to assure that the letters marked privileged are actually from members of the bar. As to the ability to open the mail in the presence of inmates, this could in no way constitute censorship, since the mail would not be read. Neither could it chill such communications, since the inmate's presence insures that prison officials will not read the mail. The possibility that contraband will be enclosed in letters, even those from apparent attorneys, surely warrants prison officials' opening the letters.

Inmates at a medium security prison in Massachusetts who had been transferred to a maximum security prison brought a civil rights action in a federal District Court alleging that the due process clause demanded an adequate factfinding hearing before such a transfer could constitutionally be made. The transfers were ordered following reports from informants that the prisoners were involved in planning and executing various fires at the prison. The District Court held that *Wolff* v. *McDonnell* required notice and hearing and that the inmates should be returned to their original prison until a proper hearing was held. The Supreme Court distinguished *Wolff* and reversed in *Meachum* v. *Fano*, 427 U.S. 215 (1976).

Justice White, for the majority, stated:

Confinement in any of the State's institutions is within the normal limits or range of custody which the conviction has authorized the State to impose. That life in one prison is much more disagreeable than in another does not in itself signify that a Fourteenth Amendment liberty interest is implicated when a prisoner is transferred to the institution with the more severe rules. . . . [T]o hold as we are urged to do that any substantial deprivation imposed by prison authorities triggers the procedural protections of the Due Process Clause would subject to judicial review a wide spectrum of discretionary actions that traditionally have been the business of prison administrators rather than of the federal courts. . . . Whatever expectation the prisoner may have in remaining at a particular prison so long as he behaves himself, it is too ephemeral and insubstantial to trigger procedural due process protections as long as prison officials have discretion to transfer him for whatever reason or for no reason at all.

The Eighth Amendment has also been the vehicle for a number of challenges by prisoners. In *Estelle* v. *Gamble*, 429 U.S. 97 (1976), the Court held that deliberate indifference to serious medical needs of prisoners constitutes the unnecessary and wanton infliction of pain proscribed by the Eighth Amendment. "This is true whether the indifference is manifested by prison doctors in their response to the prisoner's needs or by prison guards in intentionally denying or delaying access to medical care or intentionally interfering with the treatment once prescribed." In 1976 United States District Judge Frank Johnson held that Alabama's state prisons were "unfit for human habitation" and threatened to close them unless certain minimum standards were met. [The case is *Pugh* v. *Locke*, 406 F. Supp. 318 (DC, MD Ala., 1976). And see Tinsley E. Yarbrough, *Judge Frank Johnson and Human Rights in Alabama* (Tuscaloosa: University of Alabama Press, 1981).] Excerpts from Johnson's opinion describing the deplorable conditions in Alabama's prisons and references to "dozens of other cases" are found in Justice Brennan's concurring opinion in *Rhodes* v. *Chapman*, 452 U.S. 337 (1981). He also noted that "There are over 8,000 pending cases filed by inmates challenging prison conditions." The *Rhodes* case was brought by inmates of a maximum-security state prison in Ohio contending that housing two inmates in a cell designed for one person constituted cruel and unusual punishment. The District Court found an Eighth Amendment violation, although its findings of fact indicated that the double-celling did not lead to deprivations of essential food, medical care, or sanitation, nor did it lead to increased violence among inmates. The Supreme Court reversed, with the statement that "there is no evidence that double celling under these circumstances either inflicts unnecessary or wanton pain or is grossly disproportionate to the severity of crimes warranting imprisonment." Absent such a finding, the matter of housing prisoners was properly a subject to be weighed by the legislature and prison administration rather than a court. Justice Marshall, the only dissenter, stated:

In a doubled cell, each inmate has only some 30–35 square feet of floor space. Most of the windows in the Supreme Court building are larger than that. The conclusion of every expert who testified at trial and of every serious study of which I am aware is that a long-term inmate must have to himself, at the very least, 50 square feet of floor space—an area smaller than that occupied by a good-sized automobile— in order to avoid serious mental, emotional, and physical deterioration. . . . These conditions in my view go well beyond contemporary standards of decency and therefore violate the Eighth and Fourteenth Amendments.

Prison search procedures have also been challenged. In *Bell* v. *Wolfish*, 441 U.S. 520 (1979), pretrial detainees in a federally operated short-term custodial facility in New York alleged the unconstitutionality of (1) searches of the inmates' rooms during which they were not allowed to be present, and (2) strip searches of inmates conducted after every contact visit with a person from outside, including visual inspection of body cavities. The District Court enjoined the practices and the Court of Appeals affirmed. The Supreme Court reversed. On the issue of room searches, Justice Rehnquist for the majority stated:

It is difficult to see how the detainee's interest in privacy is infringed by the room-search rule. No one can rationally doubt that room searches represent an appropriate security measure and neither the District Court nor the Court of Appeals prohibited such searches. And even the most zealous advocate of prisoners' rights would not suggest that a warrant is required to conduct such a search. . . . Permitting detainees to observe the searches does not lessen the invasion of their privacy; its only conceivable beneficial effect would be to prevent theft or misuse by those conducting the search.

On the issue of body searches the Justice stated:

Admittedly, this practice instinctively gives us the most pause. However, . . . we nonetheless conclude that these searches do not violate [the Fourth] Amendment. . . . A detention facility is a unique place fraught with serious security dangers. Smuggling of money, drugs, weapons, and other contraband is all too common an occurrence. And inmate attempts to secrete these items into the facility by concealing them in body cavities are documented in this record. . . . That there has been only one instance where an MCC inmate was discovered attempting to smuggle contraband into the institution on his person may be more a testament to the effectiveness of this search technique as a deterrent than to any lack of interest on the part of the inmates to secrete and import such items when the opportunity arises.

We do not underestimate the degree to which these searches may invade the personal privacy of inmates. Nor do we doubt, as the District Court noted, that on occasion a security guard may conduct the search in an abusive fashion. . . . Such abuse cannot be condoned. . . . But we deal here with the question whether visual body-cavity inspections as contemplated by the MCC rules can *ever* be conducted on less than probable cause. Balancing the significant and legitimate security interests of the institution against the privacy interests of the inmates, we conclude that they can.

Justice Marshall, in dissent, was outraged by the body-searches.

In my view, the body-cavity searches of MCC inmates represent one of the most grievous offenses against personal dignity and common decency. After every contact visit with someone from outside the facility, including defense attorneys, an inmate must remove all of his or her clothing, bend over, spread the buttocks, and display the anal cavity for inspection by a correctional officer. Women inmates must assume a suitable posture for vaginal inspection. . . . And, as the Court neglects to note, because of time pressures, this humiliating spectacle is frequently conducted in the presence of other inmates. . . . A psychiatrist testified that the practice placed inmates in the most degrading position possible. . . . There was evidence, moreover, that these searches engendered among detainees fears of sexual assault. . . . , were the occasion for actual threats of physical abuse by guards, and caused some inmates to forego personal visits.

Justice Marshall was also unpersuaded of the necessity for the searches. He noted that inmates were required to wear one-piece jumpsuits with zippers in the front.

To insert an object into the vaginal or anal cavity, an inmate would have to remove the jumpsuit, at least from the upper torso. Since contact visits occur in a glass enclosed room and are continuously monitored by corrections officers . . . such a feat would seem extraordinarily difficult. . . . Additionally, before entering the visiting room, visitors and their packages are searched thoroughly by a metal detector and fluoroscope, and by hand [or may be required to leave packages with guards until the visit is over]. Only by blinding itself to the facts presented on this record can the Court accept the Government's security rationale.

In *Block* v. *Rutherford*, 468 U.S. 576 (1984), the Court upheld the practice of the Los Angeles County Central Jail officials in conducting irregular "shakedown" searches of cells while pretrial detainees were away at meals, recreation, or other activities, on authority of *Bell* v. *Wolfish*. The Court also held that the jail policy of denying the detainees contact visits with their spouses, relatives, children and friends did not constitute a deprivation of liberty without due process of law. Chief Justice Burger, for the majority stated:

[W]e do not in any sense denigrate the importance of visits from family or friends to the detainee. Nor do we intend to suggest that contact visits might not be a factor contributing to the ultimate reintegration of a detainee into society. We hold only that the Constitution does not require that detainees be allowed contact visits when responsible, experienced administrators have determined, in their sound discretion, that such visits will jeopardize the security of the facility.

Justice Marshall, speaking for the three dissenters, protested:

This case marks the third time in recent years that the Court has turned a deaf ear to inmates' claims that the conditions of their confinement violate the Federal Constitution. See *Rhodes* v. *Chapman*, . . . ; *Bell* v. *Wolfish*. . . . Guided by an unwarranted confidence in the good faith and "expertise" of prison administrators and by a pinched conception of the meaning of the Due Process Clauses and the Eighth Amendment, a majority of the Court increasingly appears willing to sanction any prison condition for which they can imagine a colorable rationale, no matter how oppressive or ill justified that condition is in fact.

Finally, the Court has held that the First Amendment is not violated by a prison rule barring the formation of a prisoners' union. In *Jones* v. *North Carolina Prisoners' Labor Union, Inc.*, 433 U.S. 119 (1977), the Court held that on balance the First Amendment guarantees of speech and assembly did not override the State's interest in the maintenance of prison decorum and security. Justice Rehnquist stated:

Prison life, and the relations between the inmates themselves and between the inmates and prison officials or staff, contain the ever-present potential for violent confrontation and conflagration. . . . Responsible prison officials must be permitted to take reasonable steps to forestall such a threat, and they must be permitted to act before the time when they can compile a dossier on the eve of a riot. The case of a prisoners' union, where the focus is on the presentation of grievances to, and encouragement of adversary relations with, institution officials surely would rank high on anyone's list of potential trouble spots.

The Court also held that there was no equal protection violation in the fact that officials permitted meeting rights to the Jaycees, Alcoholics Anonymous, and the Boy Scouts, since those could reasonably be considered to differ from the union "in fundamental respects."

# Chapter 4

# *Religious Freedom*

The part played by religious enthusiasts in the settlement and development of America is an oft-told story. What is sometimes overlooked, however, is the fact that religious liberty did not reach fruition with the landing of the Pilgrims. On the contrary, the attainment of the present broad measure of religious freedom in America is a story of long, and sometimes bitter, struggle extending over more than three centuries. Even today, there are controverted areas of policy and practice in which various minority sects are claiming abridgment of their constitutional guarantees of religious liberty.

The Puritans brought with them to New England the conviction that men have a right and a duty to associate voluntarily for religious purposes. For this group, however, religious freedom meant only freedom to practice the true faith—Puritanism. They not only did not accept the principle of religious toleration; they went further and used the arm of government both to prosecute dissenters and to enforce observance of certain of the church laws. Thus we have depicted in the history of the Massachusetts Bay Colony two of the primary enemies of religious freedom—active support of religion by the government and governmental suppression of certain religious exercises.

In Massachusetts Bay, Puritanism was the official faith. In the Virginia charter of 1609 the doctrine and rites of the Church of England were established by law. While most other faiths were apparently to be tolerated, the charter particularly excluded "persons who affected the 'superstitions of the Church of Rome.' " In New Netherlands the Dutch Reformed Church had the exclusive right of public worship. And in the Spanish colonies the Inquisition was imported to guarantee the repression of non-Catholic heresies.

At the mid-seventeenth century only two of the English colonies, Rhode Island and Maryland, offered substantial religious freedom. Not until almost the outbreak of the Revolutionary War did the attitude on religious liberty begin to soften and governmental policy toward minority sects show signs of easing. Changes in the law followed, with Virginia leading the way by its adoption of religious toleration in the Declaration of Rights accompanying its 1776 constitution. Pennsylvania in the same year and Massachusetts in 1780 guaranteed to all faiths the freedom to worship publicly. These were measures directed to *one* of the problems of religious freedom—that of *free exercise* of religion. And while they were important gains, they represented actually only a strong start along a long road. Some of the most important developments, in fact, have come in the period since 1940.

Another major hurdle to overcome in the advance toward religious freedom was disestablishment and the abolition of taxation for religious purposes. These problems arise from the presence of *active government support* of religion, especially where the support is for a specific religion. Modifications were made in the latter years of the Revolution, and in 1785 Jefferson's famous Act for Establishing Religious Freedom passed the Virginia legislature. Other states followed, although New England was much slower to succumb to the trend. The Connecticut constitution of 1818 provided for separation of church and state, but this chapter of the struggle was not closed until the last state, Massachusetts, adopted a constitutional amendment in 1833 to remove the state from active promotion of a particular religion.

Since 1833, and particularly since the end of World War II, the problem of governmental support of religion has broadened, and the controversies have presented issues more difficult of logical resolution. There is probably fairly general agreement in the United States that government should not actively show a preference for one religious sect. But suppose government promotes all religious sects equally. Does this present a threat to religious freedom? Does the fact that the overwhelming majority of people in the United States profess a preference for Christianity justify Sunday Closing Laws? Is religious liberty endangered by either promoting or permitting religious exercises in the public schools? Does government act improperly if it includes religious schools among the beneficiaries of aid-to-education appropriation bills? These questions are less easily disposed of than those involving the clear-cut issue of preferential treatment.

The theory behind the argument for virtually complete separation of church and state is fairly easy to state. It rests on a view that religious liberty is best protected when government remains absolutely neutral on matters of religion. The problem, however, is that one man's neutrality is another man's hostility. To some, government is neutral toward religion if it does not support or even permit religious exercises in public schools during the school day. It is neither promoting sectarian religion nor is it prohibiting the child from engaging in religious observance, so long as it takes place outside the ambit of public school activities. To others, the denial of permission to use a portion of the school day for religious exercises is to *interfere* with religious freedom and therefore is outright governmental hostility. The newer cases raising the separation issue have presented questions which are more and more difficult of logical resolution. The result has frequently been more readily defensible as simply a convenient place to draw the line, rather than the logical necessities of applying the broad principle of "separation of church and state."

The two aspects of religious liberty—freedom from governmental establishment of religion and the free exercise of religion—will be taken up separately in this chapter. In the First Amendment both aspects are covered in the phrase "Congress shall make no law respecting an establishment of religion, or prohibiting the free exercise thereof."

## SEPARATION OF CHURCH AND STATE

The establishment clause of the First Amendment has long since been rephrased in the general literature and in the popular mind to become simply a guarantee of "separation of church and state." The controversy over separation in America has its roots in the debate between John Cotton and Roger Williams in Massachusetts Bay Colony in the first half of the seventeenth century. It has continued at intervals ever since. But the first case to reach the United States Supreme Court in which the Court really came to grips with the question of applying the First Amendment's establishment clause (albeit through the Fourteenth Amendment) did not arrive until 1947. State courts for some years have been faced with establishment issues, although most of these are of twentieth century vintage. Thus we have the somewhat strange situation of a burgeoning body of relatively new case law on a controversy which in America is as old as the colonial settlements themselves.

**Aid to Religious Schools**

## EVERSON *v.* BOARD OF EDUCATION
### *330 U.S. 1 (1947)*

Mr. Justice Black delivered the opinion of the Court.

A New Jersey statute authorizes its local school districts to make rules and contracts for the transportation of children to and from schools.* The appellee, a township board of education, acting pursuant to this statute, authorized reimbursement to parents of money expended by them for the bus transportation of their children on regular buses operated by the public transportation system. Part of this money was for the payment of transportation of some children in the community to Catholic parochial schools. These church schools give their students, in addition to secular education, regular religious instruction conforming to the religious tenets and modes of worship of the Catholic Faith. The superintendent of these schools is a Catholic priest.

The appellant, in his capacity as a district taxpayer, filed suit in a State court challenging the right of the Board to reimburse parents of parochial school students. He contended that the statute and the resolution passed pursuant to it violated both the State and the Federal Constitutions. That court held that the legislature was without power to authorize such payment under the State constitution. 132 N.J.L. 98. The New Jersey Court of Errors and Appeals reversed, holding that neither the statute nor the resolution passed pursuant to it was in conflict with the State constitution or the provisions of the Federal Constitution in issue. 133 N.J.L. 350. The case is here on appeal under 28 U.S.C. Section 344(a). . . .

The only contention here is that the State statute and the resolution, insofar as they authorized reimbursement to parents of children attending parochial schools, violate the Federal Constitution in these two respects, which to some extent overlap. First. They authorize the State to take by taxation the private property of some and bestow it upon others, to be used for their own private purposes. This, it is alleged, violates the due process clause of the Fourteenth Amendment. Second. The statute and the resolution forced inhabitants to pay taxes to help support and maintain schools which are dedicated to, and which regularly teach, the Catholic Faith. This is alleged to be a use of State power to support church schools contrary to the prohibition of the First Amendment which the Fourteenth Amendment made applicable to the states. . . .

It is much too late to argue that legislation intended to facilitate the opportunity of children to get a secular education serves no public purposes. . . . The same thing is no less true of legislation to reimburse needy parents, or all parents, for payment of the fares of their children so that they can ride in public busses to and from schools rather than run the risk of traffic and other hazards incident to walking or "hitch-hiking.' . . . Nor does it follow that a law has a private rather than a public purpose because it provided that tax-raised funds will be paid to reimburse individuals on account of money spent by them in a way which furthers a public program. . . . Subsidies and loans to individuals such as farmers and home owners, and to privately owned transportation systems, as well as many other kinds of businesses, have been common-place practice in our state and national history. . . .

* "Whenever in any district there are children living remote from any schoolhouse, the board of education of the district may make rules and contracts for the transportation of such children to and from school, including the transportation of school children to and from school other than a public school, except such school as is operated for profit in whole or in part. . . . "

*Second.* The New Jersey statute is challenged as a "law respecting the establishment of religion." The First Amendment, as made applicable to the states by the Fourteenth, *Murdock* v. *Pennsylvania,* 319 U.S. 105, commands that a state "shall make no law respecting an establishment of religion, or prohibiting the free exercise thereof." . . . These words of the First Amendment reflected in the minds of early Americans a vivid mental picture of conditions and practices which they fervently wished to stamp out in order to preserve liberty for themselves and for their posterity. Doubtless their goal has not been entirely reached; but so far has the Nation moved toward it that the expression "law respecting the establishment of religion," probably does not so vividly remind present-day Americans of the evils, fears, and political problems that caused that expression to be written into our Bill of Rights. Whether this New Jersey law is one respecting the "establishment of religion" requires an understanding of the meaning of that language, particularly with respect to the imposition of taxes. Once again, therefore, it is not inappropriate briefly to review the background and environment of the period in which that constitutional language was fashioned and adopted. . . . [Here the opinion reviews the historical events and concludes with the interpretation that the First Amendment was intended to bar the government from adopting measures to "tax, to support, or otherwise to assist any or all religions. . . ."]

The "establishment of religion" clause of the First Amendment means at least this: Neither a state nor the Federal Government can set up a church. Neither can pass laws which aid one religion, aid all religions, or prefer one religion over another. Neither can force nor influence a person to go to or to remain away from church against his will or force him to profess a belief or disbelief in any religion. No person can be punished for entertaining or professing religious beliefs or disbeliefs, for church attendance or non-attendance. No tax in any amount, large or small, can be levied to support any religious activities or institutions, whatever they may be called, or whatever form they may adopt to teach or practice religion. Neither a state nor the Federal Government can, openly or secretly, participate in the affairs of any religious organizations or groups and vice versa. In the words of Jefferson, the clause against establishment of religion by law was intended to erect "a wall of separation between Church and State." *Reynolds* v. *United States,* 98 U.S. 145, 164.

We must consider the New Jersey statute in accordance with the foregoing limitations imposed by the First Amendment. But we must not strike that state statute down if it is within the State's constitutional power even though it approaches the verge of that power. . . . New Jersey cannot consistently with the "establishment of religion" clause of the First Amendment contribute tax-raised funds to the support of an institution which teaches the tenets and faith of any church. On the other hand, other language of the amendment commands that New Jersey cannot hamper its citizens in the free exercise of their own religion. Consequently, it cannot exclude individual Catholics, Lutherans, Mohammedans, Baptists, Jews, Methodists, Nonbelievers, Presbyterians, or the members of any other faith, *because of their faith, or lack of it,* from receiving the benefits of public welfare legislation. While we do not mean to intimate that a state could not provide transportation only to children attending public schools, we must be careful, in protecting the citizens of New Jersey against state-established churches, to be sure that we do not inadvertently prohibit New Jersey from extending its general state law benefits to all its citizens without regard to their religious belief.

Measured by these standards, we cannot say that the First Amendment prohibits New Jersey from spending tax-raised funds to pay the bus fares of parochial school pupils as a part of a general program under which it pays the fares of pupils attending public and other schools. It is undoubtedly true that children are helped to get to church schools. There is even a possibility that some of the children might not be sent to the church schools if the parents were compelled to pay their children's bus fares out of their own pockets when transportation to a public school would have been paid for by the state. The same possibility exists where the state requires a local transit company to provide reduced fares to school children including those attending parochial schools, or where a municipally owned transportation system undertakes to carry all school children free of charge. Moreover, state-paid policemen, detailed to protect children going to and from church schools from the very real hazards of traffic, would serve much the same purpose and accomplish much the same result as state provisions intended to guarantee free transportation of a kind which the state deems to be best for the school children's welfare. And parents might refuse to risk their children to the serious danger of traffic accidents going to and from parochial schools, the approaches to which were not protected by policemen. Similarly, parents might be reluctant to permit their children to attend schools which the state had cut off from such general government services as ordinary police and fire protection, connections for sewage disposal, public highways and sidewalks. Of course, cutting off church schools from these services, so separate and so indisputably marked off from the religious function, would make it far more difficult for the schools to operate. But such is obviously not the purpose of the First Amendment. That Amendment requires the state to be neutral in its relations with groups of religious believers and non-believers; it does not require the state to be their adversary. State power is no more to be used so as to handicap religions than it is to favor them.

This Court has said that parents may, in the discharge of their duty under state compulsory education laws, send their children to a religious rather than a public school if the school meets the secular educational requirements which the state has power to impose. See *Pierce* v. *Society of Sisters,* 268 U.S. 510. It appears that these parochial schools meet New Jersey's requirements. The state contributes no money to the schools. It does not support them. Its legislation, as applied, does no more than provide a general program to help parents get their children, regardless of their religion, safely and expeditiously to and from accredited schools.

The First Amendment has erected a wall between church and state. That wall must be kept high and impregnable. We could not approve the slightest breach. New Jersey has not breached it here.

*Affirmed.*

Mr. Justice Jackson, dissenting. . . .

Whether the taxpayer constitutionally can be made to contribute aid to parents of students because of their attendance at parochial schools depends upon the nature of those schools and their relation to the Church. . . .

It is no exaggeration to say that the whole historic conflict in temporal policy between the Catholic Church and non-Catholics comes to a focus in their respective school policies. The Roman Catholic Church, counseled by experience in many ages and many lands and with all sorts and conditions of men, takes what, from the viewpoint of its own progress and the success of its mission, is a wise estimate of the importance of education to religion. It does not leave the individual to pick up religion by chance. It relies on early and indelible indoctrination in the faith and order of the Church by the word and example of persons consecrated to the task. . . .

I should be surprised if any Catholic would deny that the parochial school is a vital, if not the most vital, part of the Roman Catholic Church. If put to the choice, that venerable institution, I should expect, would forego its whole service for mature persons before it would give up education of the young, and it would be a wise choice. Its growth and cohesion, discipline and loyalty, spring from its schools. Catholic education is the rock on which the whole structure rests, and to render tax aid to its Church school is indistinguishable to me from rendering the same aid to the Church itself.

It is of no importance in this situation whether the beneficiary of this expenditure of tax-raised funds is primarily the parochial school and incidentally the pupil, or whether the aid is directly bestowed on the pupil with indirect benefits to the school. The state cannot maintain a Church and it can no more tax its citizens to furnish free carriage to those who attend a Church. The prohibition against establishment of religion cannot be circumvented by a subsidy, bonus or reimbursement of expense to individuals for receiving religious instruction and indoctrination. . . .

Mr. Justice Frankfurter joins in this opinion.

Mr. Justice Rutledge, with whom Mr. Justice Frankfurter, Mr. Justice Jackson and Mr. Justice Burton agree, dissenting. . . .

This case forces us to determine squarely for the first time what was "an establishment of religion" in the First Amendment's conception; and by that measure to decide whether New Jersey's action violates its command.

[Here the opinion contains a survey of the "generating history" of the religious clause of the First Amendment.]

In view of this history no further proof is needed that the Amendment forbids any appropriation, large or small, from public funds to aid or support any and all religious exercises. But if more were called for, the debates in the First Congress and this Court's consistent expressions, whenever it has touched on the matter directly, supply it. . . .

Compulsory attendance upon religious exercises went out early in the process of separating church and state, together with forced observance of religious forms and ceremonies. Test oaths and religious qualification for office followed later. These things none devoted to our great tradition of religious liberty would think of bringing back. Hence today, apart from efforts to inject religious training or exercises and sectarian issues into the public schools, the only serious surviving threat to maintaining that complete and permanent separation of religion and civil power which the First Amendment commands is through use of the taxing power to support religion, religious establishments, or establishments having a religious foundation whatever their form or special religious function.

Does New Jersey's action furnish support for religion by use of the taxing power? Certainly it does, if the test remains undiluted as Jefferson and Madison made it, that money taken by taxation from one is not to be used or given to support another's religious training or belief, or indeed one's own. Today as then the furnishing of "contributions of money for the propagation of opinions which he disbelieves" is the forbidden exaction; and the prohibition is absolute for whatever measure brings that consequence and whatever amount may be sought or given to that end.

The funds used here were raised by taxation. The Court does not dispute, nor could it, that their use does in fact give aid and encouragement to religious instruction. It only concludes that this aid is not "support" in law. But Madison and Jefferson were concerned with aid and support in fact, not as a legal conclusion "entangled in precedents." . . . Here parents pay money to send their children to parochial school and funds raised by taxation are used to reimburse them. This not only helps the children to get to school and the parents to send them. It aids them in a substantial way to get the very thing which they are sent to the particular school to secure, namely, religious training and teaching. . . .

Despite the close vote in the case and the controversy aroused by the decision, *Everson* remains as ruling law on the bus transportation issue. However, the earlier cautions concerning the impact of federalism on civil rights must be called to mind here. All the Court held in *Everson* was that the New Jersey bus transportation scheme did not violate the United States Constitution. Obviously the case did not hold that the State was *required* to furnish such transportation. Less obviously, perhaps, it in no way foreclosed a decision by the state courts that such a scheme would violate *state* constitutional provisions relative to separation of church and state. In our federal system the state supreme court is the final judge of the construction of the state constitution. And a practice may be held violative of state constitutional provisions even though it does not offend against the United States Constitution, and even though the constitutional phraseology is identical. In fact, the bus transportation issue was litigated under state constitutional provisions in several states both before and after the *Everson* decision, and the weight of authority among the state courts is against such transportation. [The cases are canvassed in David Fellman, *Religion in American Public Law* (Boston: Boston University Press, 1965), pp. 81–83.]

The issue of aid to religion at the federal level arose in 1961 with President Kennedy's proposals to provide federal grants to assist *public* elementary and secondary schools. Pressure developed to extend the assistance to private schools as well, including sectarian schools. The positions of those who opposed and those who supported federal aid to church-related schools were compromised in the passage of the Elementary and Secondary School Improvement Act of 1965. About one-fourth of the more than $1,000,000,000 to be provided was to be earmarked for the purchase of textbooks and for the establishment of supplementary education centers, both of which would be under the control of the public schools, but the benefits to be shared by pupils in the parochial schools.

### BOARD OF EDUCATION *v.* ALLEN
### *392 U.S. 236 (1968)*

Mr. Justice White delivered the opinion of the Court.

A law of the State of New York requires local public school authorities to lend textbooks free of charge to all students in grades seven through 12; students attending private schools are included. This case presents the question whether this statute is a "law respecting an establishment of religion, or prohibiting the free exercise thereof," and so in conflict with the First and Fourteenth Amendments to the Constitution, because it authorizes the loan of textbooks to students attending parochial schools. We hold that the law is not in violation of the Constitution. . . .

*Everson* v. *Board of Education* . . . is the case decided by this Court that is most nearly in point for today's problem. . . .

*Everson* and later cases have shown that the line between state neutrality to religion and state support of religion is not easy to locate. . . . Based on *Everson, Zorach, McGowan,* and other cases, *Abington School District* v. *Schempp* . . . fashioned a test subscribed to by eight Justices for distinguishing between forbidden involvements of the State with religion and those contacts which the Establishment clause permits:

"The test may be stated as follows: what are the purpose and the primary effect of the enactment? If either is the advancement or inhibition of religion then the enactment exceeds the scope of legislative power as circumscribed by the Constitution. That is to say that to withstand the strictures of the Establishment Clause there must be a secular legislative purpose and a primary effect that neither advances nor inhibits religion. . . ."

The test is not easy to apply, but the citation of *Everson* by the *Schempp* Court to support its general standard made clear how the *Schempp* rule would be applied to the facts of *Everson*. The statute upheld in *Everson* would be considered a law having "a secular legislative purpose and a primary effect that neither advances nor inhibits religion." We reach the same result with respect to the New York law. . . .

Of course books are different from buses. Most bus rides have no inherent religious significance, while religious books are common. However, the language of Sec. 701 does not authorize the loan of religious books, and the State claims no right to distribute religious literature. Although the books loaned are those required by the parochial school for use in specific courses, each book loaned must be approved by the public school authorities; only secular books may receive approval. . . . In judging the validity of the statute on this record we must proceed on the assumption that books loaned to students are books that are not unsuitable for use in the public schools because of religious content. . . .

The judgment is affirmed.

Mr. Justice Harlan, concurring. . . .

Mr. Justice Black, dissenting. . . .

I still subscribe to the belief that tax-raised funds cannot constitutionally be used to support religious schools, buy their school books, erect their buildings, pay their teachers, or pay any other of their maintenance expenses, even to the extent of one penny. . . . And I still believe that the only way to protect minority religious groups from majority groups in this country is to keep the wall of separation between church and state high and impregnable as the First and Fourteenth Amendments provide. The Court's affirmance here bodes nothing but evil to religious peace in this country.

Mr. Justice Douglas, dissenting. . . .

Whatever may be said of *Everson,* there is nothing ideological about a bus. There is nothing ideological about a school lunch, or a public nurse, or a scholarship. . . . The textbook goes to the very heart of education in a parochial school. It is the chief, although not solitary, instrumentality for propagating a particular religious creed or faith. How can we possibly approve such state aid to a religion? . . .

The initiative to select and requisition "the books desired" is with the parochial school. Powerful religious-political pressures will therefore be on the state agencies to provide the books that are desired.

These then are the battlegrounds where control of textbook distribution will be won or lost. Now that "secular" textbooks will pour into religious schools, we can rest assured that a contest will be on to provide those books for religious schools which the dominant religious group concludes best reflect the theocentric or other philosophy of the particular church. . . .

It has long been the policy of governmental units to accord special treatment to religious and other charitable organizations in the form of exemptions from property taxes. While such exemptions do not constitute an appropriation of tax money for religious purposes, they obviously represent a valuable monetary benefit, and money not spent for taxes may be used to expand religious operations. The Court considered the First Amendment implications of such exemptions in *Walz* v. *Tax Commission of the City of New York* in 1970.

## WALZ *v.* TAX COMMISSION OF THE CITY OF NEW YORK
### *397 U.S. 664 (1970)*

[The plaintiff, an owner of real property, brought suit in the New York courts to enjoin the New York City Tax Commission from granting property tax exemptions to religious organizations for religious properties used solely for religious worship.

Such exemptions were authorized by state constitutional and statutory provisions, but the plaintiff contended that the exemptions indirectly required the plaintiff to make a contribution to religious bodies, thereby violating the religion clauses of the First Amendment. The court dismissed the complaint, and the New York Court of Appeals affirmed.]

Mr. Chief Justice Burger delivered the opinion of the Court.

The course of constitutional neutrality in this area cannot be an absolutely straight line; rigidity could well defeat the basic purpose of these provisions, which is to insure that no religion be sponsored or favored, none commanded, and none inhibited. . . .

The legislative purpose of a property tax exemption is neither the advancement nor the inhibition of religion; it is neither sponsorship nor hostility. New York, in common with the other States, has determined that certain entities that exist in a harmonious relationship to the community at large, and that foster its "moral or mental improvement," should not be inhibited in their activities by property taxation or the hazard of loss of those properties for nonpayment of taxes. It has not singled out one particular church or religious group or even churches as such; rather, it has granted exemption to all houses of religious worship within a broad class of property owned by nonprofit, quasi-public corporations which include hospitals, libraries, playgrounds, scientific, professional, historical and patriotic groups. The State has an affirmative policy that considers these groups as benficial and stabilizing influences in community life and finds this classification useful, desirable, and in the public interest. . . .

Determining that the legislative purpose of tax exemption is not aimed at establishing, sponsoring, or supporting religion does not end the inquiry, however. We must also be sure that the end result—the effect—is not an excessive government entanglement with religion. The test is inescapably one of degree. Either course, taxation of churches or exemption, occasions some degree of involvement with religion. Elimination of exemption would tend to expand the involvement of government by giving rise to tax valuation of church property, tax liens, tax foreclosures, and the direct confrontations and conflicts that follow in the train of those legal processes. . . . The exemption creates only a minimal and remote involvement between church and state and far less than taxation of churches. It restricts the fiscal relationship between church and state, and tends to complement and reinforce the desired separation insulating each from the other. . . .

All of the 50 States provide for tax exemption of places of worship, most of them doing so by constitutional guarantees. For so long as federal income taxes have had any potential impact on churches—over 75 years—religious organizations have been expressly exempt from the tax. . . .

Nothing in this national attitude toward religious tolerance and two centuries of uninterrupted freedom from taxation has given the remotest sign of leading to an established church or religion and on the contrary it has operated affirmatively to help guarantee the free exercise of all forms of religious beliefs. . . . If taxation can be seen as this first step toward "establishment" of religion, as Mr. Justice Douglas fears, the second step has been long in coming. Any move which realistically "establishes" a church or tends to do so can be dealt with "while this Court sits." . . .

*Affirmed.*

Mr. Justice Brennan, concurring. . . .

The existence from the beginning of the Nation's life of a practice, such as tax exemptions for religious organizations, is not conclusive of its constitutionality. But such practice is a fact of considerable import in the interpretation of abstract constitutional language. On its face, the Establishment Clause is reasonably susceptible of different interpretations regarding the exemptions. This Court's interpretation of the clause, accordingly, is appropriately influenced by the reading it has received in the practices of the Nation. As Mr. Justice Holmes observed in an analogous context, in resolving such questions of interpretation, "a page of history is worth a volume of logic." . . . The more longstanding and widely accepted a practice, the greater its impact upon constitutional interpretation. History is particularly compelling in the present case because of the undeviating acceptance given religious tax exemptions from our earliest days as a Nation. Rarely if ever has this Court considered the constitutionality of a practice for which the historical support is so overwhelming. . . .

The exemptions have continued uninterrupted to the present day. They are in force in all 50 States. No judicial decision, state or federal, has ever held that they violate the Establishment Clause. . . .

Tax exemptions and general subsidies . . . are qualitatively different. Though both provide economic assistance, they do so in fundamentally different ways. A subsidy involves the direct transfer of public monies to the subsidized enterprise and uses resources exacted from taxpayers as a whole. An exemption, on the other hand, involves no such transfer. It assists the exempted enterprise only passively, by relieving a privately funded venture of the burden of paying taxes. In other words, "in the case of direct subsidy, the state forcibly diverts the income of both believers and nonbelievers to churches," while "in the case of an exemption, the state merely refrains from diverting to its own uses income independently generated by the churches through voluntary contributions." . . .

. . . Moreover, the termination of exemptions would give rise, as the Court says, to the necessity for "tax valuation of church property, tax liens, tax foreclosures, and the direct confrontation and conflicts that follow in the train of those legal processes." . . . Whether Government grants or withholds the exemptions, it is going to be involved with religion. . . .

Mr. Justice Harlan, concurring. . . .

Mr. Justice Douglas, dissenting. . . .

It should be noted that while the Court in *Walz* reaffirmed the two-pronged test for Establishment Clause cases that it utilized in *Board of Education* v. *Allen* (a secular legislative purpose and a primary effect that neither advances nor inhibits religion), it added a third prong: "We must also be sure that the end result—the effect—is not an excessive government entanglement with religion."

There are many states in which private school (largely sectarian) enrollment at the elementary and secondary level represents a substantial percentage of the total school population. As costs have increased over the past several years, private schools have faced severe budgetary difficulties, and their supporters have mounted strong pressures for at least minimal financial aid from public funds. Three arguments have been forcefully presented: (1) as a matter of public policy, the government should promote a strong private school sector in order to encourage diversity of training and educational choice; (2) from the standpoint of equity, those who support both private and public schools, but who do not use or burden the public school system, should receive governmental assistance to at least some extent; and (3) in order to protect against the potentially substantial costs of increased public school enrollment occasioned by large-scale failures of financially beset private schools, some governmental assistance should be provided.

A number of proposals for aid to private schools have been adopted in response to these pleas, and almost immediately they have been challenged by persons or organizations who contend that such aid represents an unconstitutional establishment of religion insofar as it assists sectarian schools. The following cases represent the more important decisions with respect to these various school-aid devices.

## LEMON v. KURTZMAN
### 403 U.S. 602 (1971)

Mr. Chief Justice Burger delivered the opinion of the Court.

These two appeals raise questions as to Pennsylvania and Rhode Island statutes providing state aid to church-related elementary and secondary schools. Both statutes are challenged as violative of the Establishment and Free Exercise Clauses of the First Amendment and the Due Process Clause of the Fourteenth Amendment.

Pennsylvania has adopted a statutory program that provides financial support to nonpublic elementary and secondary schools by way of reimbursement for the cost of teachers' salaries, textbooks, and instructional materials in specified secular subjects. Rhode Island has adopted a statute under which the State pays directly to teachers in nonpublic elementary schools a supplement of 15% of their annual salary. Under each statute state aid has been given to church-related educational institutions as well as other private schools. We hold that both statutes are unconstitutional. . . .

### (a) Rhode Island Program

The District Court made extensive findings on the grave potential for excessive entanglement that inheres in the religious character and purpose of the Roman Catholic elementary schools of Rhode Island, to date the sole beneficiaries of the Rhode Island Salary Supplement Act. . . .

In *Allen* the Court refused to make assumptions, on a meager record, about the religious content of the textbooks that the State would be asked to provide. We cannot, however, refuse here to recognize that teachers have a substantially different ideological character than books. In terms of potential for involving some aspect of faith or morals in secular subjects, a textbook's content is ascertainable, but a teacher's handling of a subject is not. We cannot ignore the dangers that a teacher under religious control and discipline poses to the separation of the religious from the purely secular aspects of pre-college education.

In our view the record shows these dangers are present to a substantial degree. . . . The teacher is employed by a religious organization, subject to the direction and discipline of religious authorities, and works in a system dedicated to rearing children in a particular faith. These are not lessened by the fact that most of the lay teachers are of the Catholic faith. Inevitably some of a teacher's responsibilities hover on the border between secular and religious orientation.

We need not and do not assume that teachers in parochial schools will be guilty of bad faith or any conscious design to evade the limitations imposed by the statute and the First Amendment. We simply recognize that a dedicated religious person, teaching in a school affiliated with his or her faith and operated to inculcate its tenets, will inevitably experience great difficulty in remaining religiously neutral. . . .

### (b) Pennsylvania Program

The Pennsylvania statute also provides state aid to church-related schools for teachers' salaries. . . .

As we noted earlier, the very restrictions and surveillance necessary to ensure that teachers play a strictly nonideological role give rise to entanglements between church and state. The Pennsylvania statute, like that of Rhode Island, fosters this kind of relationship. Reimbursement is not only limited to courses offered in the public schools and materials approved by state officials, but the statute excludes "any subject matter expressing religious teaching, or the morals or forms of worship of any sect." In addition schools seeking reimbursement must maintain accounting procedures that require the State to establish the cost of the secular as distinguished from the religious instruction.

The Pennsylvania statute, moreover, has the further defect of providing state financial aid directly to the church-related school. This factor distinguishes both *Everson* and *Allen,* for in both those cases the Court was careful to point out that state aid was provided to the student and his parents—not to the church-related school. . . . The history of government grants of a continuing cash subsidy indicates that such programs have almost always been accompanied by varying measures of control and surveillance. . . .

A broader base of entanglement of yet a different character is presented by the divisive political potential of these state programs. In a community where such a large number of pupils are served by church-related schools, it can be assumed that state assistance will entail considerable political activity. . . . Candidates will be forced to declare and voters to choose. It would be unrealistic to ignore the fact that many people confronted with issues of this kind will find their votes aligned with their faith.

Ordinarily political debate and division, however vigorous or even partisan, are normal and healthy manifestations of our democratic system of government, but political division along religious lines was one of the principal evils against which the First Amendment was intended to protect. . . .

Mr. Justice Harlan, concurring. . . .

Mr. Justice Douglas, whom Mr. Justice Black joins, concurring. . . .

A measure of at least one state's concern and interest in helping the private schools is indicated by the rapidity with which the legislature of Pennsylvania reacted to the decision in *Lemon* v. *Kurtzman.* That decision came on June 28, 1971, and on August 27, 1971, the legislature promulgated a new aid law, entitled the "Parent Reimbursement Act for Nonpublic Education," providing funds to reimburse parents for a portion of tuition expenses incurred in sending their children to nonpublic schools. In *Sloan* v. *Lemon,* 413 U.S. 825 (1973), the Court held this act also unconstitutional because "at bottom its intended consequence is to preserve and support religion-oriented institutions." On the same day, in *Committee for Public Education* v. *Nyquist,* a more elaborate aid statute of New York was held invalid.

## COMMITTEE FOR PUBLIC EDUCATION *v.* NYQUIST
### *413 U.S. 756 (1973)*

[Amendments to New York's education and tax laws established three financial aid programs for nonpublic elementary and secondary schools. The first section provides for direct money grants to "qualifying" schools to be used for maintenance and repair of facilities and equipment. A "qualifying" school is a nonpublic, nonprofit elementary or secondary school serving a high concentration of pupils from low-income families. The annual grant is $30 per pupil, or $40 if the facilities are more than twenty-five years old, but not to exceed 50 percent of the average per-pupil cost for such services in the public schools. Section 2 establishes a tuition reimbursement plan for parents of children attending nonpublic elementary or secondary schools. Reimbursement is provided in amounts up to $50 per grade school child and $100 per high school student to parents with an annual taxable income of less than $5,000. Sections 3, 4, and 5 provide tax relief to parents failing to qualify for tuition reimbursement. Each taxpayer-parent is entitled to deduct a specified sum from his gross income for each child attending a nonpublic school. The amount of the deduction is unrelated to the amount of tuition actually paid and decreases as the amount of taxable income increases. Parents with adjusted gross incomes of more than $25,000 receive no deduction.

The Committee for Public Education filed for an injunction in the United States District Court for the Southern District of New York, alleging that each of the three aid provisions constituted an invalid aid to religion. A three-judge court found that the maintenance and tuition reimbursement provisions were unconstitutional, but that the income tax relief provided in the law was valid. Appeal to the Supreme Court.]

Mr. Justice Powell delivered the opinion of the Court. . . .

Most of the cases coming to this Court raising Establishment Clause questions have involved the relationship between religion and education. Among these religion-education precedents, two general categories of cases may be identified: those dealing with religious activities within the public schools, and those involving public aid in varying forms to sectarian institutions. . . . Taken together, these decisions dictate that to pass muster under the Establishment Clause the law in question, first must reflect a clearly secular legislative purpose . . . , second, must have a primary effect that neither advances nor inhibits religion, . . . and, third, must avoid excessive government entanglement with religion. . . .

In applying these criteria to the three distinct forms of aid involved in this case, we need touch only briefly on the requirement of a "secular legislative purpose." As the recitation of legislative purposes appended to New York's law indicates, each measure is adequately supported by legitimate, nonsectarian state interests. We do not question the propriety, and fully secular content, of New York's interest in preserving a healthy and safe educational environment for all of its school children. And we do not doubt—indeed, we fully recognize—the validity of the State's interests in promoting pluralism and diversity among its public and nonpublic schools. Nor do we hesitate to acknowledge the reality of its concern for an already overburdened public school system that might suffer in the event that a significant percentage of children presently attending nonpublic schools should abandon those schools in favor of the public schools.

But the propriety of a legislature's purposes may not immunize from further scrutiny a law which either has a primary effect that advances religion, or which fosters excessive entanglements between Church and State. Accordingly, we must weigh each of the three aid provisions challenged here against these criteria of effect and tanglement.

The "maintenance and repair" provisions of §1 authorize direct payments to nonpublic schools, virtually all of which are Roman Catholic schools in low-income areas. . . . So long as expenditures do not exceed 50% of comparable expenses in the public school system, it is possible for a sectarian elementary or secondary school to finance its entire "maintenance and repair" budget from state tax-raised funds. No attempt is made to restrict payments to those expenditures related to the upkeep of facilities used exclusively for secular purposes, nor do we think it possible within the context of these religion-oriented institutions to impose such restrictions. Nothing in the statute, for instance, bars a qualifying school from paying out of state funds the salaries of employees who maintain the school chapel, or the cost of renovating classrooms in which religion is taught, or the cost of heating and lighting those same facilities. Absent appropriate restrictions on expenditures for these and similar purposes, it simply cannot be denied that this section has a primary effect that advances religion in that it subsidizes directly the religious activities of sectarian elementary and secondary schools.

The state officials nevertheless argue that these expenditures for "maintenance and repair" are similar to other financial expenditures approved by this Court. Primarily they rely on *Everson* v. *Board of Education; Board of Education* v. *Allen* . . . ; and *Tilton* v. *Richardson*. In each of those cases it is true that the Court approved a form of financial assistance which conferred undeniable benefits upon private, sectarian schools. But a close examination of those cases illuminates their distinguishing characteristics. . . .

These cases simply recognize that sectarian schools perform secular, educational functions as well as religious functions, and that some forms of aid may be channeled to the secular without providing direct aid to the sectarian. But the channel is a narrow one, as the above cases illustrate. Of course, it is true in each case that the provision of such neutral, nonideological aid, assisting only the secular functions of sectarian schools, served indirectly and incidentally to promote the religious function by rendering it more likely that children would attend sectarian schools and by freeing the budgets of those schools for use in other nonsecular areas. But an indirect and incidental effect beneficial to religious institutions has never been thought a sufficient defect to warrant the invalidation of a state law. . . .

What we have said demonstrates that New York's maintenance and repair provisions violate the Establishment Clause because their effect, inevitably, is to subsidize and advance the religious mission of sectarian schools. . . .

New York's tuition reimbursement program also fails the "effect" test, for much the same reasons that govern its maintenance and repair grants. . . . There can be no question that these grants could not, consistently with the Establishment Clause, be given directly to sectarian schools, since they would suffer from the same deficiency that renders invalid the grants for maintenance and repair. In the absence of an effective means of guaranteeing that the state aid derived from public funds will be used exclusively for secular, neutral, and nonideological purposes, it is clear from our cases that direct aid in whatever form is invalid. . . . The controlling question here, then, is whether the fact that the grants are delivered to parents rather than schools is of such significance as to compel a contrary result. The State and intervenor-appellees rely on *Everson* and *Allen* for their claim that grants to parents, unlike grants to institutions, respect the "wall of separation" required by the Constitution. . . .

In *Everson*, the Court found the bus fare program analogous to the provision of services such as police and fire protection, sewage disposal, highways, and sidewalks for parochial schools. . . . Such services, provided in common to all citizens, are "so separate and so indisputably marked off from the religious function," . . . that they may fairly be viewed as reflections of a neutral posture toward religious institutions. *Allen* is founded upon a similar principle. The Court there repeatedly emphasized that upon the record in that case there was no indication that textbooks would be provided for anything other than purely secular courses. . . .

The tuition grants here are subject to no such restrictions. There has been no endeavor "to guarantee the separation between secular and religious educational functions and to ensure that State financial aid supports only the former." *Lemon* v. *Kurtzman*. . . . Indeed, it is precisely the function of New York's law to provide assistance to private schools, the great majority of which are sectarian. By reimbursing parents for a portion of their tuition bill, the State seeks to relieve their financial burdens sufficiently to assure that they continue to have the option to send their children to religion-oriented schools. And while the other purposes for that aid—to perpetuate a pluralistic educational environment and to protect the fiscal integrity of overburdened public schools—are certainly unexceptionable, the effect of the aid is unmistakably to provide desired financial support for nonpublic, sectarian institutions. . . .

Sections 3, 4, and 5 establish a system for providing income tax benefits to parents of children attending New York's nonpublic schools. . . .

In practical terms there would appear to be little difference, for purposes of determining whether such aid has the effect of advancing religion, between the tax benefit allowed here and the tuition grant allowed under §2. The qualifying parent under either program receives the same form of encouragement and reward for sending his children to nonpublic schools. The only difference is that one parent receives an actual cash payment while the other is allowed to reduce by an arbitrary amount the sum he would otherwise be obliged to pay over to the State. We see no answer to Judge Hays' dissenting statement below that "in both instances the money involved represents a charge made upon the state for the purpose of religious education." . . .

. . .[A]ppellees place their strongest reliance on *Walz* v. *Tax Comm'n* in which New York's property tax exemption for religious organizations was upheld. We think that *Walz* provides no support for appellees' position. Indeed, its rationale plainly compels the conclusion that New York's tax package violates the Establishment Clause.

Tax exemptions for church property enjoyed an apparently universal approval in this country both before and after the adoption of the First Amendment. . . . We know of no historical precedent for New York's recently promulgated tax relief program. Indeed, it seems clear that tax benefits for parents whose children attend parochial schools are a recent innovation, occasioned by the growing financial plight of such nonpublic institutions and designed, albeit unsuccessfully, to tailor state aid in a manner not incompatible with the recent decisions of this Court. . . . A proper respect for both the Free Exercise and the Establishment Clauses compels the State to pursue a course of "neutrality" toward religion. . . . Special tax benefits, however, cannot be squared with the principle of neutrality established by the decisions of this Court. To the contrary, insofar as such benefits render assistance to parents who send their children to sectarian schools, their purpose and inevitable effect are to aid and advance those religious institutions. . . .

One further difference between tax exemptions for church property and tax benefits for parents should be noted. The exemption challenged in *Walz* was not restricted to a class composed exclusively or even predominantly of religious institutions. Instead, the exemption covered all property devoted to religious, educational, or charitable purposes. As the parties here must concede, tax reductions authorized by this law flow primarily to the parents of children attending sectarian, nonpublic schools. . . .

In conclusion, we find the *Walz* analogy unpersuasive, and in light of the practical similarity between New York's tax and tuition reimbursement programs, we hold that neither form of aid is sufficiently restricted to assure that it will not have the impermissible effect of advancing the sectarian activities of religious schools. . . .

Mr. Chief Justice Burger, joined in part by Mr. Justice White, and joined by Mr. Justice Rehnquist, concurring in part and dissenting in part.

I join in that part of the Court's opinion . . . which holds the New York "maintenance and repair" provision unconstitutional under the Establishment Clause because it is a direct aid to religion. I disagree, however, with the Court's decisions in *Nyquist* and in *Sloan* v. *Lemon* . . . to strike down the New York and Pennsylvania tuition grant programs and the New York tax relief provisions. I believe the Court's decisions on those statutory provisions ignore the teachings of *Everson* v. *Board of Education* . . . and *Board of Education* v. *Allen,* . . . and fail to observe what I thought the Court had held in *Walz* v. *Tax Comm'n.* . . . I therefore dissent as to those aspects of the two holdings. . . .

The tuition grant and tax relief programs now before us are, in my view, indistinguishable in principle, purpose, and effect from the statutes in *Everson* and *Allen.* In the instant cases, as in *Everson* and *Allen,* the States have merely attempted to equalize the costs incurred by parents in obtaining an education for their children. The only discernible difference between the programs in *Everson* and *Allen* and these cases is in the method of the distribution of benefits: here the particular benefits of the Pennsylvania and New York statutes are given only to parents of private schoolchildren, while in *Everson* and *Allen* the statutory benefits were made available to parents of both public and private schoolchildren. But to regard that difference as constitutionally meaningful is to exalt form over substance. It is beyond dispute that the parents of public schoolchildren in New York and Pennsylvania presently receive the "benefit" of having their children educated totally at state expense; the statutes enacted in those States and at issue here merely attempt to equalize that "benefit" by giving to parents of private schoolchildren, in the form of dollars or tax deductions, what the parents of public schoolchildren receive in kind. It is no more than simple equity to grant partial relief to parents who support the public schools they do not use. . . .

Mr. Justice White, joined in part by the Chief Justice and Mr. Justice Rehnquist, dissenting. . . .

I am quite unreconciled to the Court's decision in *Lemon* v. *Kurtzman* . . . (1971). I thought then, and I think now, that the Court's conclusion there was not required by the First Amendment and is contrary to the long-range interests of the country. I therefore have little difficulty in accepting the New York maintenance grant, which does not and could not, by its terms, approach the actual repair and maintenance cost incurred in connection with the secular education services performed for the State in parochial schools. But, accepting *Lemon* and the invalidation of the New York maintenance grant, I would, with The Chief Justice and Mr. Justice Rehnquist, sustain the New York and Pennsylvania tuition grant statutes and the New York tax credit provisions. . . .

The reimbursement and tax benefit plans today struck down, no less than the plans in *Everson* and *Allen,* are consistent with the principle of neutrality. New York has recognized that parents who are sending their children to nonpublic schools are rendering the State a service by decreasing the costs of public education and by physically relieving an already overburdened public school system. Such parents are nonetheless compelled to support public school services unused by them and to pay for their own children's education. Rather than offering "an incentive to parents to send their children to sectarian schools," . . . as the majority suggests, New York is effectuating the secular purpose of the equalization of the costs of educating New York children that are borne by parents who send their children to nonpublic schools. . . .

The increasing difficulties faced by private schools in our country are no reason at all for this Court to readjust the admittedly rough-hewn limits on governmental involvement with religion which are found in the First and Fourteenth Amendments. But, quite understandably, these difficulties can be expected to lead to efforts on the part of those who wish to keep alive pluralism in education to obtain through legislative channels forms of permissible public assistance which were not thought necessary a generation ago. Within the limits permitted by the Constitution, these decisions are quite rightly hammered out on the legislative anvil. If the Constitution does indeed allow for play in the legislative joints, *Walz, supra,* . . . the Court must distinguish between a new exercise of power within constitutional limits and an exercise of legislative power which transgresses those limits. I believe the Court has failed to make that distinction here, and I therefore dissent.

In *Meek* v. *Pittenger,* 421 U.S. 349 (1975), the Court upheld that portion of a Pennsylvania law which provided for loan of textbooks "acceptable for use in" the public schools to children enrolled in nonpublic elementary and secondary schools. But the remainder of the act which provided various "auxiliary services" was held to be violative of the establishment clause. The services included counseling, testing, psychological services, speech and hearing therapy, and related services for exceptional, remedial, or educationally disadvantaged students, "and such other secular, neutral, nonideological services as are of benefit to nonpublic school-children" and are provided to those in the public schools. Further provision was made for instructional equipment (projectors, recorders, and laboratory paraphernalia) and instructional materials (periodicals, photographs, maps, charts, recordings, and films). The majority found that although such aid was ostensibly limited to secular materials, the massive aid provided was neither indirect nor incidental and amounted to a direct and substantial advancement of religious activity. It also found the auxiliary services unconstitutional since excessive entanglement would be required for Pennsylvania to be assured that the public school professional staff members providing the services did not advance the religious mission of the church-related schools in which they were to serve.

Two years later, in *Wolman* v. *Walter,* 433 U.S. 229 (1977), the Court examined an extensive school-aid program of the State of Ohio for nonpublic schools, to be funded by an $88,000,000 biennial appropriation. The diverse forms of assistance were: (1) the purchase and loan of secular textbooks (approved by state officials for the public schools) to students in nonpublic schools, (2) the provision of the standardized tests and scoring services employed in the public schools to nonpublic school pupils, (3) the provision of speech and hearing and psychological diagnostic services (which were available to public school pupils) to nonpublic school students, but such services to be performed by public employees and treatment off the nonpublic school premises, (4) therapeutic, guidance and remedial services for nonpublic school students (as available to public school pupils) to be performed by public employees in public schools, public centers, or mobile units off the nonpublic school premises, (5) purchase and loan to nonpublic school pupils or their parents secular instructional equipment such as projectors, tape recorders, maps and science kits (of the kind used in the public schools), and (6) the provision of such field trip transportation and services to nonpublic school students as are provided to public school students, with substantial discretion as to choice of destination given to the nonpublic school teacher. A three-judge District Court held the statute constitutional in all respects.

On direct appeal, the Supreme Court affirmed in part and reversed in part. The majority held the first four provisions valid, but found the sections dealing with instructional equipment and the field trips unconstitutional. The Court was badly fragmented, as is often the case on school-aid issues. The Chief Justice and Justices White and Rehnquist would have held all sections of the law constitutional. And Justice Brennan would have held all sections unconstitutional. Majorities of from six to eight did, however, agree to uphold the validity of the first four sections of the law.

After a New York statute that appropriated public funds to reimburse private schools, including sectarian schools, for administering and reporting various state-mandated test results had been held violative of the Establishment Clause in *Levitt* v. *Committee for Public Education,* 413 U.S. 472 (1973), the New York legislature adopted a new law on the subject. The new law provided direct cash reimbursement for meeting the testing and reporting requirements, but, unlike the old law, it covered only costs of administering state-prepared tests and not teacher-prepared tests. Further, it ensured that only actual costs would be reimbursed by establishing means for substantiating and auditing payments of state funds. In *Committee for Public Education* v. *Regan,* 444 U.S. 646 (1980), the Court held that the new law was constitutional and that the decision was controlled by *Wolman* v. *Walter.* "As in *Wolman* . . . '[t]he nonpublic school does not control the content of the test or its result'; and here, as in *Wolman,* this factor 'serves to prevent the use of the test as part of religious teaching,' thus avoiding the kind of direct aid forbidden by the Court's prior cases. The District Court was correct in concluding that there was no substantial risk that the examinations could be used for religious educational purposes."

In the *Nyquist* case, discussed earlier, the Court held that the New York tax-credit provision for parents of children attending *nonpublic* schools was unconstitutional. In 1983 the Court examined a Minnesota law that allowed taxpayers deductions in computing state income tax for expenditures for "tuition, textbooks and transportation" for their children attending *either* public or private elementary or secondary schools. A taxpayer suit was brought challenging the constitutionality of the statute.

MUELLER *v.* ALLEN

*463 U.S. 388 (1983)*

Justice Rehnquist delivered the opinion of the Court. . . .

Little time need be spent on the question of whether the Minnesota tax deduction has a secular purpose. Under our prior decisions, governmental assistance programs have consistently survived this inquiry even when they have run afoul of other aspects of the *Lemon* framework. . . .

We turn therefore to the more difficult but related question whether the Minnesota statute has "the primary effect of advancing the sectarian aims of the nonpublic schools." . . . In concluding that it does not, we find several features of the Minnesota tax deduction particularly significant. First, an essential feature of Minnesota's arrangement is the fact that [it] is only one among many deductions—such as those for medical expenses . . . and charitable contributions. . . . Under our prior decisions, the Minnesota legislature's judgment that a deduction for educational expenses fairly equalizes the tax burden of its citizens and encourages desirable expenditures for educational purposes is entitled to substantial deference.

Other characteristics of [the law] argue equally strongly for the provision's constitutionality. Most importantly, the deduction is available for educational expenses incurred by *all* parents, including those whose children attend public schools and those whose children attend non-sectarian private schools or sectarian private schools. Just as in *Widmar* v. *Vincent,* . . . where we concluded that the state's provision of a forum neutrally "open to a broad class of nonreligious as well as religious speakers" does not "confer any imprimatur of State approval," so here: "the provision of benefits to so broad a spectrum of groups is an important index of secular effect."

In this respect, as well as others, this case is vitally different from the scheme struck down in *Nyquist.* There, public assistance amounting to tuition grants, was provided only to parents of children in *nonpublic* schools. This fact had considerable bearing on our decision striking down the New York statute at issue; we explicitly distinguished both *Allen* and *Everson* on the grounds that "In both cases the class of beneficiaries included *all* schoolchildren, those in public as well as those in private schools." . . . Moreover, we intimated that "public assistance (e.g., scholarships) made available generally without regard to the sectarian-nonsectarian or public-nonpublic nature of the institution benefited," might not offend the Establishment Clause. We think the tax deduction adopted by Minnesota is more similar to this latter type of program than it is to the arrangement struck down in *Nyquist.* As *Widmar* and our other decisions indicate, a program . . . that neutrally provides state assistance to a broad spectrum of citizens is not readily subject to challenge under the Establishment Clause. . . .

Petitioners argue that, notwithstanding the facial neutrality of [the law], in application the statute primarily benefits religious institutions. Petitioners rely, as they did below, on a statistical analysis of the type of persons claiming the tax deduction. They contend that most parents of public school children incur no tuition expenses . . . and that other expenses deductible under [the law] are negligible in value; moreover, they claim that 96% of the children in private schools in 1978–1979 attended religiously-affiliated institutions. Because of all this, they reason, the bulk of deductions taken under [the law] will be claimed by parents of children in sectarian schools. . . .

We need not consider these contentions in detail. We would be loath to adopt a rule grounding the constitutionality of a facially neutral law on annual reports reciting the extent to which various classes of private citizens claimed benefits under the law. Such an approach would scarcely provide the certainty that this field stands in need of, nor can we perceive principled standards by which such statistical evidence might be evaluated. . . .

Turning to the third part of the *Lemon* inquiry, we have no difficulty in concluding that the Minnesota statute does not "excessively entangle" the state in religion. The only plausible source of the "comprehensive, discriminating, and continuing state surveillance," . . . necessary to run afoul of this standard would lie in the fact that state officials must determine whether particular textbooks qualify for a deduction. In making this decision, state officials must disallow deductions taken from "instructional books and materials used in the teaching of religious tenets, doctrines or worship, the purpose of which is to inculcate such tenets, doctrines or worship." . . . Making decisions such as this does not differ substantially from making the types of decisions approved in earlier opinions of this Court. In *Board of Education* v. *Allen* . . . , for example, the Court upheld the loan of secular textbooks to parents or children attending nonpublic schools; though state officials were required to determine whether particular books were or were not secular, the system was held not to violate the Establishment Clause. . . .

Justice Marshall, joined by Justices Brennan, Blackmun and Stevens, dissented. He argued that "The Minnesota tax statute violates the Establishment Clause for precisely the same reason as the statute struck down in Nyquist: it has a direct and immediate effect of advancing religion." He stated further:

That the Minnesota statute makes some small benefit available to all parents cannot alter the fact that the most substantial benefit provided by the statute is available only to those parents who send their children to schools that charge tuition. It is simply undeniable that the single largest expense that may be deducted under the Minnesota statute is tuition. The statute is little more than a subsidy of tuition masquerading as a subsidy of general educational expenses. The other deductible expenses are *de minimis* in comparison to tuition expenses. . . .

That this deduction has a primary effect of promoting religion can easily be determined without any resort to the type of "statistical evidence" that the majority fears would lead to constitutional uncertainty. . . . In this case, it is undisputed that well over 90% of the children attending tuition-charging schools in Minnesota are enrolled in sectarian schools. History and experience likewise instruct us that any generally available financial assistance for elementary and secondary school tuition expenses mainly will further religious education because the majority of the schools which charge tuition are sectarian. . . . More importantly, the assistance that flows to parochial schools as a result of the tax benefit is not restricted, and cannot be restricted, to the secular functions of those schools.

A Michigan school district adopted two programs—Shared Time and Community Education—that provided classes to nonpublic school students at public expense in classrooms located and leased from the nonpublic schools, forty of which out of the forty-one participating were identifiably religious schools. The Shared Time program offered classes during the regular school day that were intended to supplement the "core curriculum" courses required by the State. The Shared Time teachers were full-time employees of the public schools, but a "significant portion" of them had previously taught in nonpublic schools. The Community Education Program offered classes at the conclusion of the regular school day in voluntary courses, some of which were not offered at the public schools but others of which were. Community Education teachers were part-time public school employees who for the most part were otherwise employed full-time by the same nonpublic school in which their Community Education classes were held. In *Grand Rapids School District v. Ball,* 473 U.S. 373 (1985), the Court held that both programs had the "primary or principal" effect of advancing religion in violation of the Establishment Clause. Justice Brennan, for the majority, stated:

We do not question that the dedicated and professional religious school teachers employed by the Community Education program will attempt in good faith to perform their secular mission conscientiously. . . . Nonetheless, there is a substantial risk that, overtly or subtly, the religious message they are expected to convey during the regular school day will infuse the supposedly secular classes they teach after school. The danger arises "not because the public employee [is] likely deliberately to subvert his task to the service of religion, but rather because the pressures of the environment might alter his behavior from its normal course." *Wolman* v. *Walter.* . . . "The conflict of functions inheres in the situation." *Lemon* v. *Kurtzman.* . . .

The Shared Time program, though structured somewhat differently, nonetheless also poses a substantial risk of state-sponsored indoctrination. The most important difference between the programs is that most of the instructors in the Shared Time program are full-time teachers hired by the public schools. . . . Nonetheless, as with the Community Education program, no attempt is made to monitor the Shared Time courses for religious content. . . .

Thus, despite these differences between the two programs, our holding in *Meek* controls the inquiry with respect to Shared Time, as well as Community Education.

Chief Justice Burger and Justice O'Connor agreed that the Community Education program was unconstitutional but would have upheld the Shared Time program. Justices White and Rehnquist argued that neither program violated the Establishment Clause.

On the same day the Court held unconstitutional a New York City program in *Aguilar* v. *Felton,* 473 U.S. 402 (1985). The City, using funds made available by Title I of the Elementary and Secondary Education Act for teaching educationally deprived children from low income families, paid the salaries of public school teachers who taught remedial classes in parochial schools. The City provided materials and equipment and monitored Title I classes for religious content. It also worked with parochial school personnel to resolve class scheduling problems. The City made teacher assignments, and the instructors were supervised by field personnel, who attempted to pay at least one unannounced visit per month. By a 5–4 vote the Court held that the arrangement of "pervasive monitoring by public authorities in the sectarian schools infringes precisely those Establishment Clause values at the root of the prohibition of excessive entanglement."

At this writing, Justice Kennedy, the most recent appointee to the Court, has not participated in any school-aid cases. Since the vote in many of them in recent years has been 5–4, with Justice Powell in the majority, his replacement could well represent a swing in the other direction and change the whole pattern of school-aid decisions.

It is important to note that the cases discussed thus far have dealt with aid to private schools at the elementary and secondary grade levels—levels at which most of the students are subjected to state compulsory attendance laws. The Court has taken a different approach and is less stringent in its surveillance of financial assistance to institutions of higher education. The distinction is made clear in the leading case, *Tilton* v. *Richardson*, 403 U.S. 672 (1971), challenging the constitutionality of federal aid for church-related colleges and universities under the Higher Education Facilities Act of 1963, which provided construction grants for buildings and facilities used exclusively for secular educational purposes. Chief Justice Burger, for the plurality, stated:

The simplistic argument that every form of financial aid to church-sponsored activity violates the Religion Clauses was rejected long ago. . . . The crucial question is not whether some benefit accrues to a religious institution as a consequence of the legislative program, but whether its principal or primary effect advances religion. . . .

Appellants . . . rely on the argument that government may not subsidize any activities of an institution of higher learning that in some of its programs teaches religious doctrines. This argument rests on *Everson* where the majority stated that the Establishment Clause barred any "tax . . . levied to support any religious . . . institutions . . . whatever form they may adopt to teach or practice religion." . . .

Under this concept appellants' position depends on the validity of the proposition that religion so permeates the secular education provided by church-related colleges and universities that their religious and secular educational functions are in fact inseparable. . . .

There are generally significant differences between the religious aspects of church-related institutions of higher learning and parochial elementary and secondary schools. The "affirmative if not dominant policy" of the instruction in pre-college church schools is "to assure future adherents to a particular faith by having control of their total education at an early age." . . . There is substance to the contention that college students are less impressionable and less suceptible to religious indoctrination. Common observation would seem to support that view, and Congress may well have entertained it. The skepticism of the college student is not an inconsiderable barrier to any attempt or tendency to subvert the congressional objectives and limitations. Furthermore, by their very nature, college and postgraduate courses tend to limit the opportunities for sectarian influence by virtue of their own internal disciplines. Many church-related colleges and universities are characterized by a high degree of academic freedom and seek to evoke free and critical responses from their students.

The record here would not support a conclusion that any of these four institutions departed from this general pattern. All four schools are governed by Catholic religious organizations, and the faculties and student bodies at each are predominantly Catholic. Nevertheless, the evidence shows that non-Catholics were admitted as students and given faculty appointments. Not one of these four institutions requires its students to attend religious services. . . . In short, the evidence shows institutions with admittedly religious functions but whose predominant higher education mission is to provide their students with a secular education. . . .

A majority of the Court held valid the policy of aid for construction of secular buildings, but the provision in the Act that barred the use of such buildings for sectarian purposes for *only twenty years* was held unconstitutional. Chief Justice Burger pointed out that it "cannot be assumed that a substantial structure has no value after that period and hence the unrestricted use of a valuable property is in effect a contribution of some value to a religious body. If, at the end of 20 years, the building is, for example, converted into a chapel or otherwise used to promote religious interests, the original federal grant will in part have the effect of advancing religion."

In *Hunt* v. *McNair,* 413 U.S. 734 (1973), a South Carolina taxpayer sued state officials for declaratory and injunctive relief against the operation of the South Carolina Educational Facilities Act insofar as it authorized the state-created Educational Facilities Authority to issue revenue bonds for the benefit of the Baptist College at Charleston. Under the arrangement, the Authority was permitted to issue bonds (at the lower interest rates for tax-exempt state bonds than the private Baptist College could obtain), the proceeds of which would be used to finance the construction of buildings and facilities for the college. The plan provided that the college would convey title to such projects to the Authority, and the Authority would lease back to the college, with reconveyance to the college upon full repayment of the bonds.

The Court held that the scheme did not violate the establishment clause because (1) the statute had a secular purpose in seeking to aid institutions of higher education, whether or not they had religious affiliations; (2) the Baptist College's operations were not oriented significantly toward sectarian rather than secular education, since there were no religious qualifications for faculty membership or student admission, and its percentage of Baptist students was roughly equal to the percentage of Baptists in that area of the state; (3) the bond issuance would not have the primary effect of advancing or inhibiting religion, because the project would not include any buildings or facilities used for religious purposes; and (4) the transaction would not foster an excessive entanglement with religion merely because the college had a formalistic relationship with the state or because the Authority might foreclose if the college should fail to make the prescribed rental payments or otherwise default in its obligations.

At the same time, the Court added a refinement to the "primary effect" test, the second of the three tests applied in *Lemon* v. *Kurtzman:*

Aid normally may be thought to have a primary effect of advancing religion when it flows to an institution in which religion is so pervasive that a substantial portion of its functions are subsumed in the religious mission or when it funds a specifically religious activity in an otherwise substantially secular setting.

In 1971 a Maryland statute was enacted that authorized the payment of state funds to any private institution of higher education within the state that met certain minimum criteria and did not award "only seminarian or theological degrees." The aid was in the form of an annual fiscal year subsidy to qualifying colleges and universities. The amounts were based upon the number of students, excluding those in seminarian or theological academic programs. The grants were noncategorical, but could not be utilized by the institutions for sectarian purposes. The assistance program was primarily administered by the Maryland Council for Higher Education, which, in order to insure compliance with statutory restrictions, (1) determined the eligibility of applicant institutions, and (2) examined applications to insure that only nonsectarian uses for the money were planned. At the end of the fiscal year the recipient institution was required to file a financial statement showing the specific purposes for which the money was used.

Suit was brought by four Maryland citizens and taxpayers challenging the statutory scheme as violative of the establishment clause. In addition to the responsible state officials, plaintiffs joined as defendants four Roman Catholic colleges, claiming that they were constitutionally ineligible for this form of aid. The Federal District Court, applying the three-part requirement of *Lemon* v. *Kurtzman,* upheld the statute and denied relief. On direct appeal, the Supreme Court affirmed in *Roemer* v. *Board of Public Works of Maryland,* 426 U.S. 736 (1976). The vote was five to four, and there was no majority opinion. Appellants did not challenge the District Court's finding respecting the first part of *Lemon's* three-part test—that the purpose of Maryland's aid program was the secular one of supporting private higher education generally, as an economic alternative to a wholly public system. The focus of the argument was on the second and third parts, those concerning the primary effect of advancing religion and excessive church-state entanglement.

In the plurality opinion by Justice Blackmum, joined by the Chief Justice and Justice Powell, it was concluded that the picture painted of the four Maryland colleges was "similar in almost all respects to that of the church-affiliated colleges considered in *Tilton* and *Hunt,"* and that the institutions were not "so permeated by religion that the secular side cannot be separated from the sectarian." Further, it was concluded that the aid was extended only to the secular side and could not be used to support a "specially religious activity." Thus, the aid did not violate the "primary effect of advancing religion" test.

As to the "excessive entanglement" test, the plurality found no greater problem here than in *Tilton* and the statute was upheld against this claim.

As the District Court pointed out, ongoing, annual supervision of college facilities was explicitly foreseen in *Tilton* . . . and even more so in *Hunt.* . . . *Tilton* and *Hunt* would be totally indistinguishable, at least in terms of annual supervision, if funds were used under the present statute to build or maintain physical facilities devoted to secular use. The present statute contemplates annual decisions by the Council as to what is a "sectarian purpose," but, as we have noted, the secular and sectarian activities of the college are easily separated. Occasional audits are possible here, but we must accept the District Court's finding that they would be "quick and non-judgmental." . . . They and the other contacts between the Council and the colleges are not likely to be any more entangling than the inspections and audits incident to the normal process of the colleges' accreditations by the State.

Justice White, joined by Justice Rehnquist, concurred in the result but objected to the use of the "excessive entanglement" test. He stated that, "I have never understood the constitutional foundation for this added element; it is at once both insolubly paradoxical . . . and . . . a 'blurred, indistinct and variable barrier.' " He argued that if the purpose of the legislation is secular and if the primary effect of the aid program is not advancement of religion, that is enough to sustain the program against constitutional challenge, "and I would say no more."

Justice Brennan, joined by Justice Marshall, dissented on the ground that the statute provided a general subsidy to religious schools from public funds, and that such a provision exposes state money for use in advancing religion, no matter the vigilance to avoid it. In a separate dissent, Justice Stewart stressed the point that theology courses were a compulsory part of the curriculum at each of the appellee institutions, and that they were not taught merely as part of the academic discipline. Thus, the aid provided did in fact advance religion. Justice Stevens added an interesting reversal to the usual no-aid-to-religion argument in stating:

I would add emphasis to the pernicious tendency of a state subsidy to tempt religious schools to compromise their religious mission without wholly abandoning it. The disease of entanglement may infect a law discouraging wholesome religious activity as well as a law encouraging the propagation of a given faith.

### "Released Time" Programs

In many public school districts of the United States it was a long-established practice to include various kinds of religious exercises as a part of the school program. In some of these districts specific times were set aside during the school week when pupils were "released" from regular classes in order to attend some sort of religious program in the school building. An establishment of religion issue is clearly presented by such practices, but the first case on that issue to reach the United States Supreme Court did not arrive until 1948. It was *Illinois* ex rel. *McCollum* v. *Board of Education,* 333 U.S. 203, and dealt with the "released time" program adopted in Champaign, Illinois. Interested members of the Jewish, Roman Catholic, and a few of the Protestant faiths obtained permission from the Board of Education to offer classes in religious instruction to public school pupils in grades four to nine. Classes were taught weekly in three separate religious groups by Protestant teachers, Catholic priests, and, for a time, a Jewish rabbi, to pupils whose parents signed cards requesting that their children be permitted to attend. The classes were conducted in the regular classrooms of the school building, and students who did not choose to take part were required to leave their classrooms and go to some other place in the school building for pursuit of their secular studies. Attendance reports were required for pupils attending religious instruction.

With only one dissent, by Justice Reed, the Court held the program violative of the Establishment Clause. Justice Black, in the opinion of the Court, stated:

The foregoing facts, without reference to others that appear in the record, show the use of tax-supported property for religious instruction and the close cooperation between the school authorities and the religious council in promoting religious education. The operation of the state's compulsory education system thus assists and is integrated with the program of religious instruction carried on by separate religious sects. Pupils compelled by law to go to school for secular education are released in part from their legal duty upon the condition that they attend the religious classes. This is beyond all question a utilization of the tax-established and tax-supported public school system to aid religious groups to spread their faith. And it falls squarely under the ban of the First Amendment (made applicable to the States by the Fourteenth) as we interpreted it in *Everson* v. *Board of Education,* 330 U.S. 1. . . . The majority in the *Everson* case, and the minority . . . , agreed that the First Amendment's language, properly interpreted, had erected a wall of separation between Church and State. They disagreed as to the facts shown by the record and as to the proper application of the First Amendment's language to those facts. . . .

To hold that a State cannot consistently with the First and Fourteenth Amendments utilize its public school system to aid any or all religious faiths or sects in the dissemination of their doctrines and ideals does not, as counsel urge, manifest a governmental hostility to religion or religious teachings. A manifestation of such hostility would be at war with our national tradition as embodied in the First Amendment's guaranty of the free exercise of religion. For the First Amendment rests upon the premise that both religion and government can best work to achieve their lofty aims if each is left free from the other within its respective sphere. Or, as we said in the *Everson* case, the First Amendment has erected a wall between Church and State which must be kept high and impregnable.

Here not only are the state's tax-supported public school buildings used for the dissemination of religious doctrines. The State also affords sectarian groups an invaluable aid in that it helps to provide pupils for their religious classes through use of the state's compulsory public school machinery. This is not separation of Church and State.

Justice Frankfurter wrote a concurring opinion in which he stressed the inherent coerciveness in the program:

Religious education so conducted on school time and property is patently woven into the working scheme of the school. The Champaign arrangement thus presents powerful elements of inherent pressure by the school system in the interest of religious sects. The fact that this power has not been used to discriminate is beside the point. Separation is a requirement to abstain from fusing functions of Government and of religious sects, not merely to treat them all equally. That a child is offered an alternative may reduce the constraint; it does not eliminate the operation of influence by the school in matters sacred to conscience and outside the school's domain. The law of imitation operates, and non-conformity is not an outstanding characteristic of children. The result is an obvious pressure upon children to attend. Again, while the Champaign school population represents only a fraction of the more than two hundred and fifty sects of the nation, not even all the practicing sects in Champaign are willing or able to provide religious instruction. The children belonging to these non-participating sects will thus have inculcated in them a feeling of separatism when the school should be in the training ground for habits of community, or they will have religious instruction in a faith which is not that of their parents. As a result, the public school system of Champaign actively furthers inculcation in the religious tenets of some faiths, and in the process sharpens the consciousness of religious differences at least among some of the children committed to its care. These are consequences not amenable to statistics. But they are precisely the consequences against which the Constitution was directed when it prohibited the Government common to all from becoming embroiled, however innocently, in the destructive conflicts of which the history of even this country records some dark pages. . . .

We renew our conviction that "we have staked the very existence of our country on the faith that complete separation between the state and religion is best for the state and best for religion." *Everson* v. *Board of Education*. If nowhere else, in the relation between Church and State, "good fences make good neighbors."

The decision in the *McCollum* case was greeted with a storm of protest. One of America's most eminent scholars in constitutional law, Professor E. S. Corwin, argued that the establishment clause only barred the government from setting up an official church or showing preference for one religion over another. [See E. S. Corwin, "The Supreme Court as National School Board," 14 *Law & Contemp. Prob.* 3 (1949).] But groups supporting the viewpoint of the majority took encouragement from the decision and plans were soon under way to initiate suits testing the "released time" programs in other parts of the nation. The New York City program was brought before the Court for examination only four years after *McCollum*. In *Zorach* v. *Clauson* the Court beat a strategic retreat and upheld this "dismissed time" program in which the pupils were permitted to leave the school grounds during the school day for their religious instruction.

## ZORACH v. CLAUSON
### 343 U.S. 306 (1952)

Mr. Justice Douglas delivered the opinion of the Court.

New York City has a program which permits its public schools to release students during the school day so that they may leave the school buildings and school grounds and go to religious centers for religious instruction or devotional exercises. A student is released on written request of his parents. Those not released stay in the classrooms. The churches make weekly reports to the schools, sending a list of children who have been released from public school but who have not reported for religious instruction.

This "released time" program involves neither religious instruction in public school classrooms nor the expenditure of public funds. All costs, including the application blanks, are paid by the religious organizations. The case is therefore unlike *McCollum* v. *Board of Education,* 333 U.S. 203, which involved a "released time" program from Illinois. In that case the classrooms were turned over to religious instructors. We accordingly held that the program violated the First Amendment which (by reason of the Fourteenth Amendment) prohibits the states from establishing religion or prohibiting its free exercise.

Appellants, who are taxpayers and residents of New York City and whose children attend its public schools, challenge the present law, contending it is in essence not different from the one involved in the *McCollum* case. Their argument, stated elaborately in various ways, reduces itself to this: the weight and influence of the school is put behind a program for religious instruction; public school teachers police it, keeping tab on students who are released; the classroom activities come to a halt while the students who are released for religious instruction are on leave; the school is a crutch on which the churches are leaning for support in their religious training; without the cooperation of the schools this "released time" program, like the one in the *McCollum* case, would be futile and ineffective. The New York Court of Appeals sustained the law against this claim of unconstitutionality. . . .

There is a suggestion that the system involves the use of coercion to get public school students into religious classrooms. There is no evidence in the record before us that supports that conclusion. The present record indeed tells us that the school authorities are neutral in this regard and do no more than release students whose parents so request. If in fact coercion were used, if it were established that any one or more teachers were using their office to persuade or force students to take the religious instruction, a wholly different case would be presented. Hence we put aside the claim of coercion both as respects the "free exercise" of religion and "an establishment of religion" within the meaning of the First Amendment. . . .

. . . There cannot be the slightest doubt that the First Amendment reflects the philosophy that Church and State should be separated. And so far as interference with the "free exercise" of religion and an "establishment" of religion are concerned, the separation must be complete and unequivocal. The First Amendment within the scope of its coverage permits no exception; the prohibition is absolute. The First Amendment, however, does not say that in every and all respects there shall be a separation of Church and State. Rather, it studiously defines the manner, the specific ways, in which there shall be no concert or union or dependency one on the other. That is the common sense of the matter. Otherwise the state and religion would be aliens to each other—hostile, suspicious, and even unfriendly. Churches could not be required to pay even property taxes. Municipalities would not be permitted to render police or fire protection to religious groups. Policemen who helped parishioners into their places of worship would violate the Constitution. Prayers in our legislative halls; the appeals to the Almighty in the messages of the Chief Executive; the proclamations making Thanksgiving Day a holiday; "so help me God" in our courtroom oaths—these and all other references to the Almighty that run through our laws, our public rituals, our ceremonies would be flouting the First Amendment. A fastidious atheist or agnostic could even object to the supplication with which the Court opens each session: "God save the United States and this Honorable Court."

We would have to press the concept of separation of Church and State to these extremes to condemn the present law on constitutional grounds. The nullification of this law would have wide and profound effects. A Catholic student applies to his teacher for permission to leave the school during hours on a Holy Day of Obligation to attend a mass. A Jewish student asks his teacher for permission to be excused for Yom Kippur. A Protestant wants the afternoon off for a family baptismal ceremony. In each case the teacher requires parental consent in writing. In each case the teacher, in order to make sure the student is not a truant, goes further and requires a report from the priest, the rabbi, or the minister. The teacher in other words cooperates in a religious program to the extent of making it possible for her students to participate in it. Whether she does it occasionally for a few students, regularly for one, or pursuant to a systematized program designed to further the religious needs of all the students does not alter the character of the act.

We are a religious people whose institutions presuppose a Supreme Being. We guarantee the freedom to worship as one chooses. We make room for as wide a variety of beliefs and creeds as the spiritual needs of man deem necessary. We sponsor an attitude on the part of government that shows no partiality to any one group and that lets each flourish according to the zeal of its adherents and the appeal of its dogma. When the state encourages religious instruction or cooperates with religious authorities by adjusting the schedule of public events to sectarian needs, it follows the best of our traditions. For it then respects the religious nature of our people and accommodates the public service to their spiritual needs. To hold that it may not would be to find in the Constitution a requirement that the government show a callous influence to religious groups. That would be preferring those who believe in no religion over those who do believe. Government may not finance religious groups nor undertake religious instruction nor blend secular and sectarian education nor use secular institutions to force one or some religion on any person. But we find no constitutional requirement which makes it necessary for government to be hostile to religion and to throw its weight against efforts to widen the effective scope of religious influence. The government must be neutral when it comes to competition between sects. It may not thrust any sect on any person. It may not make a religious observance compulsory. It may not coerce anyone to attend church, to observe a religious holiday, or to take religious instruction. But it can close its doors or suspend its operations as to those who want to repair to their religious sanctuary for worship or instruction. No more than that is undertaken here.

This program may be unwise and improvident from an educational or a community viewpoint. That appeal is made to us on a theory, previously advanced, that each case must be decided on the basis of "our own prepossessions." . . . Our individual preferences, however, are not the constitutional standard. The constitutional standard is the separation of Church and State. The problem, like many problems in constitutional law, is one of degree. . . .

In the *McCollum* case the classrooms were used for religious instruction and the force of the public school was used to promote that instruction. Here, as we have said, the public schools do no more than accommodate their schedules to a program of outside religious instruction. We follow the *McCollum* case. But we cannot expand it to cover the present released time program unless separation of Church and State means that public institutions can make no adjustments of their schedules to accommodate the religious needs of the people. We cannot read into the Bill of Rights such a philosophy of hostility to religion.

*Affirmed.*

Mr. Justice Black, dissenting. . . .

I see no significant difference between the invalid Illinois system and that of New York here sustained. Except for the use of the school buildings in Illinois, there is no difference between the systems which I consider even worthy of mention. In the New York program, as that of Illinois, the school authorities release some of the children on the condition that they attend the religious classes, get reports on whether they attend, and hold the other children in the school building until the religious hour is over. . . . *McCollum* . . . held that Illinois could not constitutionally manipulate the compelled classroom hours of its compulsory school machinery so as to channel children into sectarian classes. Yet that is exactly what the Court holds New York can do. . . . .

Difficulty of decision in the hypothetical situations mentioned by the Court, but not now before us, should not confuse the issues in this case. Here the sole question is whether New York can use its compulsory education laws to help religious sects get attendants presumably too unenthusiastic to go unless moved to do so by the pressure of this state machinery. That this is the plan, purpose, design and consequence of the New York program cannot be denied. The state thus makes religious sects beneficiaries of its power to compel children to attend secular schools. Any use of such coercive power by the state to help or hinder some religious sects or to prefer all religious sects over nonbelievers or vice versa is just what I think the First Amendment forbids. In considering whether a state has entered this forbidden field the question is not whether it has entered too far but whether it has entered at all. New York is manipulating its compulsory education laws to help religious sects get pupils. This is not separation but combination of Church and State. . . .

Mr. Justice Frankfurter, dissenting. . . .

Mr. Justice Jackson, dissenting.

This released time program is founded upon a use of the State's power of coercion, which, for me, determines its unconstitutionality. Stripped to its essentials, the plan has two stages: first, that the State compel each student to yield a large part of his time for public secular education; and, second, that some of it be "released" to him on condition that he devote it to sectarian religious purposes.

No one suggests that the Constitution would permit the State directly to require this "released" time to be spent "under the control of a duly constituted religious body." This program accomplishes that forbidden result by indirection. If public education were taking so much of the pupils' time as to injure the public or the students' welfare by encroaching upon their religious opportunity, simply shortening everyone's school day would facilitate voluntary and optional attendance at Church classes. But that suggestion is rejected upon the ground that if they are made free many students will not go to the Church. Hence, they must be deprived of freedom for this period, with Church attendance put to them as one of the two permissible ways of using it.

The greater effectiveness of this system over voluntary attendance after school hours is due to the truant officer who, if the youngster fails to go to the Church school, dogs him back to the public schoolroom. Here schooling is more or less suspended during the "released time" so the nonreligious attendants will not forge ahead of the churchgoing absentees. But it serves as a temporary jail for a pupil who will not go to Church. It takes more subtlety of mind than I possess to deny that this is governmental constraint in support of religion. It is as unconstitutional, in my view, when exerted by indirection as when exercised forthrightly. . . .

A number of Justices just short of a majority of the majority that promulgates today's passionate dialectics joined in answering them in *Illinois* ex rel. *McCollum* v. *Board of Education,* 333 U.S. 203. The distinction attempted between that case and this is trivial, almost to the point of cynicism, magnifying its nonessential details and disparaging compulsion which was the underlying reason for invalidity. A reading of the Court's opinion in that case along with its opinion in this case will show such difference of overtones and undertones as to make clear that the *McCollum* case has passed like a storm in a teacup. The wall which the Court was professing to erect between Church and State has become even more warped and twisted than I expected. Today's judgment will be more interesting to students of psychology and of the judicial processes than to students of constitutional law.

As pointed out in the majority opinion, the New York courts refused to consider plaintiff's offers of proof of coercion. [A description of some of the practices under the released time program in New York City, with quotations from affidavits filed in the Supreme Court, Kings County, is given in Note, "Released Time Reconsidered: The New York Plan Is Tested," 61 *Yale L. J.* 405 (1952).] In one of the affidavits, for example, it was alleged that in one sixth grade classroom the students who did not attend the religious programs were given very difficult long division arithmetic problems during every released time hour, while those who went to their religious exercises were excused from this work. [On the released time issue generally, see George E. Reed, "Church-State and the Zorach Case," 27 *Notre Dame Law.* 529 (1952); Paul G. Kauper, "Church, State and Freedom: A Review," 52 *Mich. L. Rev.* 829 (1954); and Leo Pfeffer, "Released Time and Religious Liberty: A Reply," 53 *Mich. L. Rev.* 91 (1954).]

Some indication of the importance of the retention in school of nonparticipants is shown in the finding of one investigator that several such programs of religious instruction collapsed from nonattendance when they were shifted to the time immediately after school hours and the nonparticipating student was free to go home or play as the alternative to a religious program. [See Gordon Patric, "The Impact of a Court Decision: Aftermath of the McCollum Case," 6 *Journal of Public Law* 455 (1957).]

*Widmar* v. *Vincent,* 454 U.S. 263 (1981), presented the question whether a state university, which made its facilities generally available for the activities of registered student groups, could close its facilities to a registered student group desiring to use the facilities for religious worship and religious discussion. A Federal District Court found that the regulation banning such use was not only justified, but it was also required by the Establishment Clause. The Supreme Court held that in order to justify discriminatory exclusion from its facilities based on the religious content of intended speech, the State must show a compelling interest. This it failed to do. Further, an "equal access" policy would satisfy the three prongs of the *Lemon* test. Justice Powell, for the majority, stated:

The basis for our decision is narrow. Having created a forum generally open to student groups, the University seeks to enforce a content-based exclusion of religious speech. Its exclusionary policy violates the fundamental principle that a state regulation of speech should be content-neutral, and the University is unable to justify this violation under applicable constitutional standards.

In 1984 the Equal Access Act was passed by Congress. The Act made it unlawful for any public secondary school which receives Federal financial assistance and which has a limited open forum to deny equal access to students who wish to conduct a meeting therein if the denial is based on the content of the speech at such meetings. Certain regulations of the meetings are permissible, including provision that the meetings be voluntary and student-initiated, no sponsorship by the school or its employees, no control by nonschool persons, and "the meeting does not materially and substantially interfere with the orderly conduct of educational activities within the school."

## The Bible and Prayer in Public Schools

The decisions by the United States Supreme Court on the use of Bible-reading and prayer in the public schools have stirred protest and controversy to an extent rarely equaled in the history of the Court. It should not be forgotten, however, that litigation on these issues is by no means new. While these decisions were the first in which the Court ruled on the validity of such practices under the United States Constitution, the issues have been litigated in various forms under *state* constitutional provisions for over a hundred years, and in the appellate courts of nearly half the states. The earliest reported case is a Maine case, *Donahoe* v. *Richards,* 38 Me. 376 (1854), in which the court held that a regulation adopting the King James version of the Bible as a textbook, binding upon all pupils, was not a violation of the rights of conscience or religion guaranteed by the state constitution. By the time the first such issue reached the Supreme Court, the appellate courts of twenty-three states had considered the issue of Bible-reading in the public schools. Seventeen held that the practices challenged did not violate state or federal constitutional provisions, but the courts of six states held the practices invalid under state constitutional provisions. A Wisconsin decision, *State* ex rel. *Weiss* v. *District Board of Edgerton,* 76 Wis. 177, 44 N.W. 967 (1890), was the earliest of these decisions ruling against Bible-reading. [The cases are canvassed in David Fellman, *Religion in American Public Law* (Boston: Boston University Press, 1965), pp. 98–99. See also, Robert E. Cushman, "The Holy Bible and the Public Schools," 40 *Cornell L. Q.* 475 (1955).] Thus the issue was already a very old one even in the judicial arena by the time it reached the United States Supreme Court, and, further, twenty-five percent of the twenty-three states ruling on the question had ruled *against* the validity of Bible-reading in the public schools. The first decision to come from the Supreme Court did not come until 1962, however, and it involved the so-called Regents' prayer in the State of New York rather than Bible-reading.

The State Board of Regents of New York has broad supervisory powers over the public school system. The Board adopted the following prayer and recommended that the various school districts use it in daily exercises: "Almighty God we acknowledge our dependence upon Thee and we beg Thy blessings upon us, our parents, our teachers and our country." In *Engel* v. *Vitale,* 370 U.S. 421 (1962), the Court held that such a state-sponsored prayer program was an establishment of official religion in violation of the Constitution. In response to the claim that such a construction indicated hostility toward religion or toward prayer, Justice Black, for the Court, stated:

> Nothing, of course, could be more wrong. . . . It is neither sacrilegious nor antireligious to say that each separate government in this country should stay out of the business of writing or sanctioning official prayers and leave that purely religious function to the people themselves and to those the people choose to look to for religious guidance. . . .

The criticism which the Court received after the *McCollum* decision was mild by comparison with the tempest which blew up following *Engel* v. *Vitale.* Fresh charges were leveled that the members of the majority were atheistic or even Communist-inspired. And another round of proposals was aired calling for mass impeachments.

Much of the initial anger was dispelled, however, as more people actually read the opinions, and officials of a number of different religious organizations issued public statements pointing out that the decision gave constitutional status to what they had long argued—that the church and the home, rather than the public schools, should be the primary centers of religious instruction. On legal grounds, however, Professor Sutherland of the Harvard Law School criticized the decision on the ground that the *de minimis* rule should have been employed by the Court to avoid ruling on such a small religious exercise. [Arthur E. Sutherland, Jr., "Establishment According to Engel," 76 *Harv. L. Rev.* 25 (1962).] And Dean Erwin Griswold of the Harvard Law School criticized Justice Black for what he considered to be an extreme absolutist position in barring all religion from public activity. [Erwin Griswold, "Absolute Is in the Dark," 8 *Utah L. Rev.* 167 (1963).]

Despite the fact that the opinion was carefully written to apply only to governmentally written prayers, it was not difficult to make the necessary extension to predict the treatment to be accorded Bible-reading and the recitation of the Lord's Prayer as officially sponsored exercises in the public schools. One year later, almost to the day, the Court decided companion cases from Pennsylvania and Maryland and held such exercises unconstitutional.

SCHOOL DISTRICT OF ABINGTON TOWNSHIP *v.* SCHEMPP (NO. 142)
MURRAY *v.* CURLETT (NO. 119)
*374 U.S. 203 (1963)*

Mr. Justice Clark delivered the opinion of the Court.

Once again we are called upon to consider the scope of the provision of the First Amendment to the United States Constitution which declares that "Congress shall make no law respecting an establishment of religion or prohibiting the free exercise thereof. . . ." These companion cases present the issues in the context of state actions requiring that schools begin each day with readings from the Bible. While raising the basic questions under slightly different factual situations, the cases permit of joint treatment. In light of the history of the First Amendment and of our cases interpreting and applying its requirements, we hold that the practices at issue and the laws requiring them are unconstitutional under the Establishment Clause, as applied to the states through the Fourteenth Amendment. . . .

I

*The Facts in Each Case:* No. 142. The Commonwealth of Pennsylvania by law . . . requires that "At least ten verses from the Holy Bible shall be read, without comment, at the opening of each public school on each school day. Any child shall be excused from such Bible reading, or attending such Bible reading, upon the written request of his parent or guardian." . . .

On each school day at the Abington High School between 8:15 and 8:30 A.M., while the pupils are attending their home rooms or advisory sections, opening exercises are conducted pursuant to the statute. The exercises are broadcast into each room in the school building through an intercommunications system and are conducted under the supervision of a teacher by students attending the school's radio and television workshop. Selected students from this course gather each morning in the school's workshop studio for the exercises, which include readings by one of the students of 10 verses of the Holy Bible, broadcast to each room in the building. This is followed by the recitation of the Lord's Prayer, likewise over the intercommunications system, but also by the students in the various classrooms, who are asked to stand and join in repeating the prayer in unison. The exercises are closed with the flag salute and such pertinent announcements as are of interest to the students. Participation in the opening exercises, as directed by the statute, is voluntary. The student reading the verses from the Bible may select the passages and read from any version he chooses, although the only copies furnished by the school are the King James version, copies of which were circulated to each teacher by the school district. During the period in which the exercises have been conducted the King James, the Douay and the Revised Standard versions of the Bible have been used, as well as the Jewish Holy Scriptures. There are no prefatory statements, no questions asked or solicited, no comments or explanations made and no interpretations given at or during the exercises. The students and parents are advised that the student may absent himself from the classroom, or should he elect to remain, not participate in the exercises.

It appears from the record that in schools not having an intercommunications system the Bible reading and the recitation of the Lord's Prayer were conducted by the homeroom teacher, who chose the text of the verses and read them herself or had students read them in rotation or by volunteers. This was followed by a standing recitation of the Lord's Prayer, together with the Pledge of Allegiance to the flag by the class in unison and a closing announcement of routine school items of interest.

At the first trial Edward Schempp and the children testified as to specific religious doctrines purveyed by a literal reading of the Bible "which were contrary to the religious beliefs which they held and to their familial teaching." . . . The children testified that all of the doctrines to which they referred were read to them at various times as part of the exercises. Edward Schempp testified at the second trial that he had considered having Roger and Donna excused from attendance at the exercises but decided against it for several reasons, including his belief that the children's relationships with their teachers and classmates would be adversely affected.

Expert testimony was introduced by both appellants and appellees at the first trial, which testimony was summarized by the trial court as follows:

"Dr. Solomon Grayzel testified that there were marked differences between the Jewish Holy Scriptures and the Christian Holy Bible, the most obvious of which was the absence of the New Testament in the Jewish Holy Scriptures. Dr. Grayzel testified that portions of the New Testament were offensive to Jewish tradition and that, from the standpoint of Jewish faith, the concept of Jesus Christ as the Son of God was 'practically blasphemous.' He cited instances in the New Testament which, assertedly, were not only sectarian in nature but tended to bring the Jews into ridicule or scorn. . . .

"Dr. Luther A. Weigle, an expert witness for the defense, testified in some detail as to the reasons for and the methods employed in developing the King James and the Revised Standard Versions of the Bible. On direct examination, Dr. Weigle stated that the Bible was nonsectarian within the Christian faiths." . . .

No. 119. In 1905 the Board of School Commissioners of Baltimore City adopted a rule. . . . The rule provided for the holding of opening exercises in the schools of the city consisting primarily of the "reading, without comment, of a chapter of the Holy Bible and/or the use of the Lord's Prayer." The petitioners, Mrs. Madalyn Murray and her son, William J. Murray, III, are both professed atheists. Following unsuccessful attempts to have the respondent school board rescind the rule this suit was filed for mandamus to compel its rescission or cancellation. It was alleged that William was a student in a public school of the city and Mrs. Murray, his mother, was a taxpayer therein; that it was the practice under the rule to have a reading on each school morning from the King James version of the Bible; that at petitioners' insistence the rule was amended to permit children to be excused from the exercise on request of the parent and that William had been excused pursuant thereto; that nevertheless the rule as amended was in violation of the petitioners' rights "to freedom of religion under the First and Fourteenth Amendments" and in violation of "the principle of separation between church and state, contained therein. . . ." The petition particularized the petitioners' atheistic beliefs and stated that the rule, as practiced, violated their rights "in that it threatens their religious liberty by placing a premium on belief as against non-belief and subjects their freedom of conscience to the rule of the majority; it pronounces belief in God as the source of all moral and spiritual values, equating these values with religious values, and thereby renders sinister, alien and suspect the beliefs and ideas of your Petitioners, promoting doubt and question of their morality, good citizenship and good faith."

The respondents demurred and the trial court, recognizing that the demurrer admitted all facts well pleaded, sustained it without leave to amend. The Maryland Court of Appeals affirmed, the majority of four justices holding the exercise not in violation of the First and Fourteenth Amendments, with three justices dissenting. . . .

"The government is neutral, and, while protecting all, it prefers none, and it disparages none."

Before examining this "neutral" position in which the Establishment and Free Exercise Clauses of the First Amendment place our government it is well that we discuss the reach of the Amendment under the cases of this Court.

[The opinion here contains numerous quotations from the various previous cases on religious freedom.]

The wholesome "neutrality" of which this Court's cases speak thus stems from a recognition of the teachings of history that powerful sects or groups might bring about a fusion of governmental and religious functions or a concert or dependency of one upon the other to the end that official support of the State or Federal Government would be placed behind the tenets of one or of all orthodoxies. This the Establishment Clause prohibits. And a further reason for neutrality is found in the Free Exercise Clause, which recognizes the value of religious training, teaching and observance and, more particularly, the right of every person to freely choose his own course with reference thereto, free of any compulsion from the state. This the Free Exercise Clause guarantees. Thus, as we have seen, the two clauses may overlap. As we have indicated, the Establishment Clause has been directly considered by this Court eight times in the past score of years and, with only one Justice dissenting on the point, it has consistently held that the clause withdrew all legislative power respecting religious belief or the expression thereof. The test may be stated as follows: what are the purpose and the primary effect of the enactment? If either is the advancement or inhibition of religion then the enactment exceeds the scope of legislative power as circumscribed by the Constitution. That is to say that to withstand the strictures of the Establishment Clause there must be a secular legislative purpose and a primary effect that neither advances nor inhibits religion. . . . The Free Exercise Clause, likewise considered many times here, withdraws from legislative power, state and federal, the exertion of any restraint on the free exercise of religion. Its purpose is to secure religious liberty in the individual by prohibiting any invasions thereof by civil authority. Hence it is necessary in a free exercise case for one to show the coercive effect of the enactment as it operates against him in the practice of his religion. The distinction between the two clauses is apparent—a violation of the Free Exercise Clause is predicated on coercion while the Establishment Clause violation need not be so attended.

Applying the Establishment Clause principles to the cases at bar, we find that the States are requiring the selection and reading at the opening of the school day of verses from the Holy Bible and the recitation of the Lord's Prayer by the students in unison. These exercises are prescribed as part of the curricular activities of students who are required by law to attend school. They are held in the school buildings under the supervision and with the participation of teachers employed in those schools. None of these factors, other than compulsory school attendance, was present in the program upheld in *Zorach* v. *Clauson.* The trial court in No. 142 has found that such an opening exercise is a religious ceremony and was intended by the State to be so. We agree with the trial court's finding as to the religious character of the exercises. Given that finding the exercises and the law requiring them are in violation of the Establishment Clause.

There is no such specific finding as to the religious character of the exercises in No. 119, and the State contends (as does the State in No. 142) that the program is an effort to extend its benefits to all public school children without regard to their religious belief. Included within its secular purposes, it says, are the promotion of moral values, the contradictions to the materialistic trends of our times, the perpetuation of our institutions and the teaching of literature. The case came up on demurrer, of course, to a petition which alleged that the uniform practice under the rule had been to read from the King James version of the Bible and that the exercise was sectarian. The short answer, therefore, is that the religious character of the exercise was admitted by the State. But even if its purpose is not strictly religious, it is sought to be accomplished through readings, without comment, from the Bible. Surely the place of the Bible as an instrument of religion cannot be gainsaid, and the State's recognition of the pervading religious character of the ceremony is evident from the rule's specific permission of the alternative use of the Catholic Douay version as well as the recent amendment permitting nonattendance at the exercises. None of these factors is consistent with the contention that the Bible is here used either as an instrument for nonreligious moral inspiration or as a reference for the teaching of secular subjects.

The conclusion follows that in both cases the laws require religious exercises and such exercises are being conducted in direct violation of the rights of the appellees and petitioners. Nor are these required exercises mitigated by the fact that individual students may absent themselves upon parental request, for that fact furnishes no defense to a claim of unconstitutionality under the Establishment Clause. See *Engel* v. *Vitale, supra* (370 U.S. at 430). Further, it is no defense to urge that the religious practices here may be relatively minor encroachments on the First Amendment. The breach of neutrality that is today a trickling stream may all too soon become a raging torrent and, in the words of Madison, "it is proper to take alarm at the first experiment on our liberties." Memorial and Remonstrance Against Religious Assessments, quoted in *Everson, supra,* 330 U.S. at 65.

It is insisted that unless these religious exercises are permitted a "religion of secularism" is established in the schools. . . . We do not agree, however, that this decision in any sense has that effect. In addition, it might well be said that one's education is not complete without a study of comparative religion or the history of religion and its relationship to the advancement of civilization. It certainly may be said that the Bible is worthy of study for its literary and historic qualities. Nothing we have said here indicates that such study of the Bible or of religion, when presented objectively as part of a secular program of education, may not be effected consistent with the First Amendment. But the exercises here do not fall into those categories. They are religious exercises, required by the States in violation of the command of the First Amendment that the Government maintain strict neutrality, neither aiding nor opposing religion.

Finally, we cannot accept that the concept of neutrality, which does not permit a State to require a religious exercise even with the consent of the majority of those affected, collides with the majority's right to free exercise of religion. While the Free Exercise Clause clearly prohibits the use of state action to deny the rights of free exercise to *anyone,* it has never meant that a majority could use the machinery of the State to practice its beliefs. Such a contention was effectively answered by Mr. Justice Jackson for the Court in *West Virginia State Board of Education* v. *Barnette,* 319 U.S. 624, 638 (1943):

"The very purpose of a Bill of Rights was to withdraw certain subjects from the vicissitudes of political controversy, to place them beyond the reach of majorities and officials and to establish them as legal principles to be applied by the courts. One's right to . . . freedom of worship . . . and other fundamental rights may not be submitted to vote; they depend on the outcome of no elections." . . .

[Judgment in No. 142 affirmed. Judgment in No. 119 reversed and the cause remanded.]

Mr. Justice Douglas, concurring. . . .

Mr. Justice Brennan, concurring. . . .

Mr. Justice Goldberg, with whom Mr. Justice Harlan joins, concurring. . . .

Mr. Justice Stewart, dissenting. . . .

It might . . . be argued that parents who want their children exposed to religious influences can adequately fulfill that wish off school property and outside school time. With all its surface persuasiveness, however, this argument seriously misconceives the basic constitutional justification for permitting the exercises at issue in these cases. For a compulsory state educational system so structures a child's life that if religious exercises are held to be an impermissible activity in schools, religion is placed at an artificial and state-created disadvantage. Viewed in this light, permission of such exercises for those who want them is necessary if the schools are truly to be neutral in the matter of religion. And a refusal to permit religious exercises thus is seen, not as the realization of state neutrality, but rather as the establishment of a religion of secularism, or at the least, as government support of the beliefs of those who think that religious exercises should be conducted only in private. . . .

Our decisions made clear that there is no constitutional bar to the use of government property for religious purposes. On the contrary, this Court has consistently held that the discriminatory barring of religious groups from public property is itself a violation of First and Fourteenth Amendment guarantees. *Fowler* v. *Rhode Island,* 345 U.S. 67; *Niemotko* v. *Maryland,* 340 U.S. 268. . . .

It is clear that the dangers of coercion involved in the holding of religious exercises in a schoolroom differ qualitatively from those presented by the use of similar exercises or affirmations in ceremonies attended by adults. Even as to children, however, the duty laid upon government in connection with religious exercises in the public schools is that of refraining from so structuring the school environment as to put any kind of pressure on a child to participate in those exercises; it is not that of providing an atmosphere in which children are kept scrupulously insulated from any awareness that some of their fellows may want to open the school day with prayer, or of the fact that there exist in our pluralistic society differences of religious belief. . . .

. . . [R]eligious exercises are not constitutionally invalid if they simply reflect differences which exist in the society from which the school draws its pupils. They become constitutionally invalid only if their administration places the sanction of secular authority behind one or more particular religious or irreligious beliefs. . . .

Viewed in this light, it seems to me clear that the records in both of the cases before us are wholly inadequate to support an informed or responsible decision. Both cases involve provisions which explicitly permit any student who wishes, to be excused from participation in the exercises. There is no evidence in either case as to whether there would exist any coercion of any kind upon a student who did not want to participate. . . .

What our Constitution indispensably protects is the freedom of each of us, be he Jew or Agnostic, Christian or Atheist, Buddhist or Free-thinker, to believe or disbelieve, to worship or not worship, to pray or keep silent, according to his own conscience, uncoerced and unrestrained by government. It is conceivable that these school boards, or even all school boards, might eventually find it impossible to administer a system of religious exercises during school hours in such a way as to meet this constitutional standard—in such a way as completely to free from any kind of official coercion those who do not affirmatively want to participate. But I think we must not assume that school boards so lack the qualities of inventiveness and good will as to make impossible the achievement of that goal.

I would remand both cases for further hearings.

Opposition to the prayer decisions led to an enormous mail campaign demanding that members of Congress introduce constitutional amendments to permit prayer and Bible-reading in the public schools. During the 88th Congress, through the third week of March 1964, 146 proposals for such constitutional amendments were introduced in the House and sent to the House Judiciary. A group of House members supporting amendment met to join forces behind a single proposal. The result was the "Becker Amendment," named for representative Frank Becker of New York who had sponsored the first prayer amendment bill in the 88th Congress. The text was as follows (H. J. Res. 693):

Sec. 1. Nothing in this Constitution shall be deemed to prohibit the offering, reading from, or listening to prayers or Biblical Scriptures, if participation therein in on a voluntary basis, in any governmental or public school, institution or place.

Sec. 2. Nothing in this Constitution shall be deemed to prohibit making reference to belief in, reliance upon, or invoking the aid of God or a Supreme Being in any governmental or public document, proceeding, activity, ceremony, school, institution, or place, or upon any coinage, currency, or obligation of the United States.

Sec. 3. Nothing in this Article shall constitute an establishment of religion

Although the House Judiciary Committee held hearings on the proposals, action was delayed sufficiently long until supporters of the Court's decisions mounted strong counter pressures, and no amendment proposal has passed the Congress to date. [For an account of the legislative history of the proposals, the stands taken by various church groups, and testimony before the Judiciary Committee, see Congressional Quarterly Weekly Report, No. 18 (May 1, 1964), pp. 881–885.]

The House of Representatives last voted on a constitutional amendment to allow prayer in public schools in 1971, when support for the measure failed by twenty-nine votes to achieve the necessary two-thirds vote. A similar amendment was rejected by the Senate in March, 1984. But on July 26, 1984, the House approved a bill to require schools to allow silent prayer in the classroom. It was adopted as an amendment to an omnibus education bill and was considered to be a fall-back position for members who opposed the stronger amendment by conservatives that would have cut off federal funds to schools that prohibited silent or spoken prayer. [See Congressional Quarterly, Weekly Report, March 24, 1984, p. 643; July 28, 1984, p. 1809.] But when the bill went to conference committee, it was agreed to drop the silent prayer provision, and agreement was reached on October 1 on the education bill.

During his terms of office President Ronald Reagan repeatedly urged Congress to adopt a constitutional amendment permitting prayer in the public schools. And in his 1983 State of the Union address he said, "God never should have been expelled from America's classrooms."

The mere fact that the Court has ruled unconstitutional religious exercises in the public schools should not, of course, lead one to conclude that such practices were immediately halted. Opposition to those decisions continues, and in many areas they are either ignored or various attempts have been made to introduce schemes to circumvent the decisions. Professor Herman Pritchett states that by 1983 "at least eighteen state legislatures had required a daily minute of silence in schools as a way of circumventing the Supreme Court rulings." [*Constitutional Civil Liberties* (Englewood Cliffs, N.J.: Prentice-Hall, 1984), p. 153.] In *Treen* v. *Karen B.*, 653 F2d 897 (CA5, 1981), a federal Court of Appeals held unconstitutional a Louisiana school board policy, authorized by state statute, allowing students to participate in a one-minute prayer period at the start of the school day, upon request accompanied by parental consent. In 1982, in *Treen* v. *Karen B.*, 455 U.S. 913, the Supreme Court affirmed without opinion.

## WALLACE *v.* JAFFREE
### *472 U.S. 38 (1985)*

[An Alabama law authorized a period of silence "for meditation or voluntary prayer" in all public schools. A Federal District Court held the statute constitutional because, in its opinion, Alabama has the power to establish a state religion if it chooses to do so. The Court of Appeals reversed.]

Justice Stevens delivered the opinion of the Court. . . .

[T]he narrow question for decision is whether §16-1-20.1, which authorizes a period of silence for "meditation or voluntary prayer," is a law respecting the establishment of religion within the meaning of the First Amendment. . . .

When the Court has been called upon to construe the breadth of the Establishment Clause, it has examined the criteria developed over a period of many years. Thus, in *Lemon* v. *Kurtzman* . . . we wrote:

"Every analysis in this area must begin with consideration of the cumulative criteria developed by the Court over many years. Three such tests may be gleaned from our cases. First, the statute must have a secular legislative purpose; second, its principal or primary effect must be one that neither advances nor inhibits religion . . . ; finally, the statute must not foster 'an excessive government entanglement with religion.' "

It is the first of these three criteria that is most plainly implicated by this case. As the District Court correctly recognized, no consideration of the second or third criteria is necessary if a statute does not have a clearly secular purpose. For even though a statute that is motivated in part by a religious purpose may satisfy the first criterion, . . . the First Amendment requires that a statute must be invalidated if it is entirely motivated by a purpose to advance religion.

In applying the purpose test, it is appropriate to ask "whether government's actual purpose is to endorse or disapprove of religion." In this case, the answer to that question is dispositive. For the record not only provides us with an unambiguous affirmative answer, but it also reveals that the enactment of §16-1-20.1 was not motivated by any clearly secular purpose—indeed, the statute had *no* secular purpose.

The sponsor of the bill that became §16-1-20.1, Senator Donald Holmes, inserted into the legislative record—apparently without dissent—a statement indicating that the legislation was an "effort to return voluntary prayer" to the public schools. Later Senator Holmes confirmed this purpose before the District Court. In response to the question whether he had any purpose for the legislation other than returning voluntary prayer to public schools, he stated: "No, I did not have no other purpose in mind." The State did not present evidence of *any* secular purpose. . . .

The legislative intent to return prayer to the public schools is, of course, quite different from merely protecting every student's right to engage in voluntary prayer during an appropriate moment of silence during the schoolday. The 1978 statute [§16-1-20 authorizing a 1-minute period of silence "for meditation"] already protected that right, containing nothing that prevented any student from engaging in voluntary prayer during a silent minute of meditation. Appellants have not identified any secular purpose that was not fully served by §16-1-20 before the enactment of §16-1-20.1. Thus, only two conclusions are consistent with the text of §16-1-20.1: (1) the statute was enacted to convey a message of State endorsement and promotion of prayer; or (2) the statute was enacted for no purpose. No one suggests that the statute was nothing but a meaningless or irrational act. . . .

. . . The legislature enacted §16-1-20.1, despite the existence of §16-1-20 for the sole purpose of expressing the State's endorsement of prayer activities for one minute at the beginning of each schoolday. The addition of "or voluntary prayer" indicates that the State intended to characterize prayer as a favored practice. Such an endorsement is not consistent with the established principle that the government must pursue a course of complete neutrality toward religion. . . .

The judgment of the Court of Appeals is affirmed.

*It is so ordered.*

Justice Powell, concurring. . . .

I agree fully with Justice O'Connor's assertion that some moment-of-silence statutes may be constitutional, a suggestion set forth in the Court's opinion as well. . . .

I join the opinion and judgment of the Court.

Justice O'Connor, concurring in the judgment.

Nothing in the United States Constutition as interpreted by this Court or in the laws of the State of Alabama prohibits public school students from voluntarily praying at any time before, during, or after the schoolday. . . .

A state-sponsored moment of silence in the public schools is different from state-sponsored vocal prayer or Bible reading. First, a moment of silence is not inherently religious. Silence, unlike prayer or Bible reading, need not be associated with a religious exercise. Second, a pupil who participates in a moment of silence need not compromise his or her beliefs. During a moment of silence, a student who objects to prayer is left to his or her own thoughts, and is not compelled to listen to the prayers or thoughts of others. For these simple reasons, a moment of silence statute does not stand or fall under the Establishment Clause according to how the Court regards vocal prayer or Bible reading. Scholars and at least one member of this Court have recognized the distinction and suggested that a moment of silence in public schools would be constitutional. . . . As a general matter, I agree. It is difficult to discern a serious threat to religious liberty from a room of silent, thoughtful school-children. . . .

It is obvious that either of the two Religion Clauses, "if expanded to a logical extreme, would tend to clash with the other." *Walz*. . . . The Court has long exacerbated the conflict by calling for government "neutrality" toward religion. . . . It is difficult to square any notion of "complete neutrality" with the mandate of the Free Exercise Clause that government must sometimes exempt a religious observer from an otherwise generally applicable obligation. A government that confers a benefit on an explicitly religious basis is not neutral toward religion. See *Welsh* v. *United States*. . . .

The solution to the conflict between the Religion Clauses lies not in "neutrality," but rather in identifying workable limits to the government's license to promote the free exercise of religion. The text of the Free Exercise Clause speaks of laws that prohibit the free exercise of religion. On its face, the Clause is directed at government interference with free exercise. Given that concern, one can plausibly assert that government pursues Free Exercise Clause values when it lifts a government-imposed burden on the free exercise of religion. If a statute falls within this category, then the standard Establishment Clause text should be modified accordingly. It is disingenuous to look for a purely secular purpose when the manifest objective of a statute is to facilitate the free exercise of religion by lifting a government-imposed burden. Instead, the Court should simply acknowledge that the religious purpose of such a statute is legitimated by the Free Exercise Clause. . . . Thus individual perceptions, or resentment that a religious observer is exempted from a particular government requirement, would be entitled to little weight, if the Free Exercise Clause strongly supported the exemption.

While this "accommodation" analysis would help reconcile our Free Exercise and Establishment Clause standards, it would not save Alabama's moment of silence law. If we assume that the religious activity that Alabama seeks to protect is silent prayer, then it is difficult to discern any state-imposed burden on that activity that is lifted by Alabama Code §16-1-20.1.

Chief Justice Burger, dissenting. . . .

Justice White, dissenting. . . .

Justice Rehnquist, dissenting. . . .

[The opinion opens with a lengthy explication of the history of the Religion Clauses of the First Amendment.]

It would seem from this evidence that the Establishment Clause of the First Amendment had acquired a well-accepted meaning: it forbade establishment of a national religion, and forbade preference among religious sects or denominations. Indeed, the first American dictionary defined the word "establishment" as "the act of establishing, founding, ratifying or ordaining," such as in "[t]he episcopal form of religion, so called, in England." . . . The Establishment Clause did not require government neutrality between religion and irreligion nor did it prohibit the Federal Government from providing nondiscriminatory aid to religion. There is simply no historical foundation for the proposition that the Framers intended to build the "wall of separation" that was constitutionalized in *Everson*. . . .

The Court has more recently attempted to add some mortar to *Everson's* wall through the three-part test of *Lemon* v. *Kurtzman* . . . which served at first to offer a more useful test for purposes of the Establishment Clause than did the "wall" metaphor. Generally stated, the *Lemon* test proscribes state action that has a sectarian purpose or effect, or causes an impermissible governmental entanglement with religion. . . .

[Here the opinion cites the problems occasioned in applying each of the three prongs of the *Lemon* test.]

These difficulties arise because the *Lemon* test has no more grounding in the history of the First Amendment that does the wall theory upon which it rests. The three-part test represents a determined effort to craft a workable rule from a historically faulty doctrine; but the rule can only be as sound as the doctrine it attempts to service. The three-part test has simply not provided adequate standards for deciding Establishment Clause cases, as this Court has slowly come to realize. Even worse, the *Lemon* test has caused this Court to fracture into unworkable plurality opinions . . . depending upon how each of the three factors applies to a certain state action. The results from our school services cases show the difficulty we have encountered in making the *Lemon* test yield principled results.

For example, a State may lend to parochial schoolchildren geography textbooks that contain maps of the United States, but the State may not lend maps of the United States for use in geography class. A State may lend textbooks on American colonial history, but it may not lend a film on George Washington, or a projector to show it in history class. . . . A State may pay for bus transportation to religious schools but may not pay for bus transportation from the parochial school to the public zoo or natural history museum for a field trip. A State may pay for diagnostic services conducted in the parochial school but therapeutic services must be given in a different building; speech and hearing "services" conducted by the State inside the sectarian school are forbidden, . . . but the State may conduct speech and hearing diagnostic testing inside the sectarian school. . . .

If a constitutional theory has no basis in the history of the amendment it seeks to interpret, is difficult to apply and yields unprincipled results, I see little use in it. The "crucible of litigation" . . . has produced only consistent unpredictability, and today's effort is just a continuation of "the sisyphean task of trying to patch together the 'blurred, indistinct and variable barrier' described in *Lemon* v. *Kurtzman*." . . .

The State surely has a secular interest in regulating the manner in which public schools are conducted. Nothing in the Establishment Clause of the First Amendment, properly understood, prohibits any such generalized "endorsement" of prayer. I would therefore reverse the judgment of the Court of Appeals.

*Epperson* v. *Arkansas*, 393 U.S. 97 (1968), held that a state law banning the teaching of evolution in public schools violated the First Amendment, since "teaching and learning" must not "be tailored to the principles or prohibitions of any religious sect or dogma." In *Edwards* v. *Aguillard*, 55 LW 4860 (1987), the Court held Louisiana's "Creationism Act" violative of the Establishment Clause. The Act forbade the teaching of the theory of evolution in public schools unless accompanied by instruction in "creation science." No school was required to teach evolution or creation science, but if either was taught, then the other also had to be taught. The theories of evolution and creation science were statutorily defined as "the scientific evidences for [creation or evolution] and inferences from those scientific evidences." The Court held that the Act was designed *either* to promote the theory of creation science which embodied a particular religious tenet by requiring that creation science be taught whenever evolution was taught *or* to prohibit the teaching of a scientific theory disfavored by certain religious sects by forbidding the teaching of evolution when creation science was not also taught. "Because the primary purpose of the Creationism Act is to advance a particular religious belief, the Act endorses religion in violation of the First Amendment."

In *Stone* v. *Graham*, 449 U.S. 39 (1980), the Court held unconstitutional a Kentucky statute requiring the posting of a copy of the Ten Commandments on the wall of each public school classroom in the Commonwealth. The copies were purchased with private contributions, and the law required the following notation in small print at the bottom of each copy: "The secular application of the Ten Commandments is clearly seen in its adoption as the fundamental legal code of Western Civilization and the Common Law of the United States." In a Per Curiam opinion for the five-member majority it was stated:

We conclude that Kentucky's statute requiring the posting of the Ten Commandments in public school rooms has no secular legislative purpose, and is therefore unconstitutional. . . . If the posted copies of the Ten Commandments are to have any effect at all, it will be to induce the schoolchildren to read, meditate upon, perhaps to venerate and obey, the Commandments. However desirable this might be as a matter of private devotion, it is not a permissible state objective under the Establishment Clause.

Justice Rehnquist, in dissent, stated: "The Court's summary rejection of a secular purpose articulated by the legislature and confirmed by the state court is without precedent in Establishment Clause jurisprudence." He was particularly critical of the "cavalier summary reversal, without benefit of oral argument or briefs on the merits, of the highest court of Kentucky."

## Legislative Chaplains and the Establishment Clause

It is the practice in most state legislatures and in the Congress to begin their sessions with prayer, although most do not have a formal rule requiring this procedure. Several states choose a chaplain who serves for the entire legislative session, but in other states, the prayer is offered by a different clergyman each day. Under either system, some states pay their chaplains and others do not. The Congress elects chaplains for the two houses and provides compensation. In *Marsh* v. *Chambers*, 463 U.S. 783 (1983), a member of the Nebraska legislature challenged that State's practice of opening each legislative day with a prayer by a chaplain paid by the State. The federal District Court held that the First Amendment was not breached by the prayers, but was violated by paying the chaplain from public funds. The Court of Appeals held both aspects of the practice unconstitutional, and the Supreme Court reversed, holding that the practice was constitutional. Looking to the practice of Congress, Chief Justice Burger, for the majority of six, stated: "It can hardly be thought that in the same week Members of the First Congress voted to appoint and to pay a Chaplain for each House and also voted to approve the draft of the First Amendment for submission to the States, they intended the Establishment Clause of the Amendment to forbid what they had just declared acceptable." He stated further, "In light of the unambiguous and unbroken history of more than 200 years, there can be no doubt that the practice of opening legislative sessions with prayer has become part of the fabric of our society." Three points were stressed by the complainant: first, that a clergyman of only one denomination—Presbyterian—had been selected for sixteen years; second, that the chaplain was paid at public expense; and third, that the prayers were in the Judeo-Christian tradition. The majority opinion found that "Weighed against the historical background, these factors do not serve to invalidate Nebraska's practice." Justice Brennan wrote a lengthy dissent in which he concluded that the chaplaincy scheme in Nebraska violated all three of the *Lemon* tests. The "purpose" of legislative prayer was preeminently religious, the "primary effect" was clearly religious, and the "excessive entanglement" was clear in that the controversy between Senator Chambers and his colleagues "had reached the stage of difficulty and rancor long before this lawsuit was brought."

## Nativity Scenes Displayed Under Government Sponsorship

LYNCH *v.* DONNELLY
*465 U.S. 668 (1984)*

The Chief Justice delivered the opinion of the Court.

We granted certiorari to decide whether the Establishment Clause of the First Amendment prohibits a municipality from including a creche, or Nativity scene, in its annual Christmas display.

I

Each year, in cooperation with the downtown retail merchants' association, the City of Pawtucket, Rhode Island, erects a Christmas display as part of its observance of the Christmas holiday season. The display is situated in a park owned by a non-profit organization and located in the heart of the shopping district. The display is essentially like those to be found in hundreds of towns or cities across the Nation—often on public grounds—during the Christmas season. The Pawtucket display comprises many of the figures and decorations traditionally associated with Christmas, including, among other things, a Santa Claus house, reindeer pulling Santa's sleigh, candy-striped poles, a Christmas tree, . . . hundreds of colored lights, a large banner that reads "SEASONS GREETINGS," and the creche at issue here. All components of this display are owned by the City.

. . . In 1973, when the present creche was acquired, it cost the City $1365; it now is valued at $200. The erection and dismantling of the creche costs the City about $20 per year; nominal expenses are incurred in lighting the creche. No money has been expended on its maintenance for the past 10 years.

Respondents . . . brought this action in the United States District Court for Rhode Island, challenging the City's inclusion of the creche in the annual display. The District Court held that the City's inclusion of the creche in the display violates the Establishment Clause . . . [and the] City was permanently enjoined from including the creche in the display.

A divided panel of the Court of Appeals for the First Circuit affirmed. . . . We granted certiorari, . . . and we reverse. . . .

[Here the opinion describes "an unbroken history of official acknowledgment by all three branches of government of the role of religion in American life from at least 1789."]

Art galleries supported by public revenues display religious paintings of the 15th and 16th centuries, predominantly inspired by one religious faith. The National Gallery in Washington, maintained with Government support, for example, has long exhibited masterpieces with religious messages, notably the Last Supper, and paintings depicting the Birth of Christ, the Crucifixion, and the Resurrection, among many others with explicit Christian themes and messages. The very chamber in which oral arguments on this case were heard is decorated with a notably and permanent—not seasonal—symbol of religion: Moses with Ten Commandments. Congress has long provided chapels in the Capitol for religious worship and meditation. . . .

III

. . .

In this case, the focus of our inquiry must be on the creche in the context of the Christmas season. . . . Focus exclusively on the religious component of any activity would inevitably lead to its invalidation under the Establishment Clause. . . .

The District Court inferred from the religious nature of the creche that the City has no secular purpose for the display. In so doing, it rejected the City's claim that its reasons for including the creche are essentially the same as its reasons for sponsoring the display as a whole. The District Court plainly erred by focusing almost exclusively on the creche. When viewed in the proper context of the Christmas Holiday season, it is apparent that, on this record, there is insufficient evidence to establish that the inclusion of the creche is a purposeful or surreptitious effort to express some kind of subtle governmental advocacy of a particular religious message. In a pluralistic society a variety of motives and purposes are implicated. The City, like the Congresses and Presidents, however, has principally taken note of a significant historical religious event long celebrated in the Western World. The creche in the display depicts the historical origins of this traditional event long recognized as a National Holiday. . . .

The narrow question is whether there is a secular purpose for Pawtucket's display of the creche. The display is sponsored by the City to celebrate the Holiday and to depict the origins of that Holiday. These are legitimate secular purposes. The District Court's inference, drawn from the religious nature of the creche, that the City has no secular purpose was, on this record, clearly erroneous.

The District Court found that the primary effect of including the creche is to confer a substantial and impermissible benefit on religion in general and on the Christian faith in particular. . . . We can assume, arguendo, that the display advances religion in a sense; but our precedents plainly contemplate that on occasion some advancement of religion will result from governmental action. The Court has made it abundantly clear, however, that "not every law that confers an 'indirect,' 'remote,' or 'incidental' benefit upon [religion] is, for that reason alone, constitutionally invalid." *Nyquist*. . . . Here, whatever benefit to one faith or religion or to all religions, is indirect, remote and incidental; display of the creche is no more an advancement or endorsement of religion than the Congressional and Executive recognition of the origins of the Holiday itself as "Christ's Mass," or the exhibition of literally hundreds of religious paintings in governmentally supported museums. . . .

Entanglement is a question of kind and degree. In this case, however, there is no reason to disturb the District Court's finding on the absence of administrative entanglement. There is no evidence of contact with church authorities concerning the content or design of the exhibit prior to or since Pawtucket's purchase of the creche. . . . In many respects the display requires far less ongoing, day-to-day interaction between church and state than religious paintings in public galleries. . . .

We are satisfied that the City has a secular purpose for including the creche, that the City has not impermissibly advanced religion, and that including the creche does not create excessive entanglement between religion and government.

## IV

Justice Brennan describes the creche as a "re-creation of an event that lies at the heart of Christian faith," . . . The creche, like a painting, is passive; admittedly it is a reminder of the origins of Christmas. Even the traditional, purely secular displays extant at Christmas, with or without a creche, would inevitably recall the religious nature of the Holiday. The display engenders a friendly community spirit of good will in keeping with the season. . . .

Of course the creche is identified with one religious faith but no more so than the examples we have set out from prior cases in which we found no conflict with the Establishment Clause. See, e.g., *McGowan,* supra; *Marsh,* supra. It would be ironic, however, if the inclusion of a single symbol of a particular historic religious event, as part of a celebration acknowledged in the Western World for 20 centuries, and in this country by the people, by the Executive Branch, by the Congress, and the courts for two centuries, would so "taint" the City's exhibit as to render it violative of the Establishment Clause. To forbid the use of this one passive symbol—the creche—at the very time people are taking note of the season with Christmas hymns and carols in public schools and other public places, and while the Congress and Legislatures open session with prayers by paid chaplains would be a stilted overreaction contrary to our history and to our holdings. If the presence of the creche in this display violates the Establishment Clause, a host of other forms of taking official note of Christmas, and of our religious heritage, are equally offensive to the Constitution. . . .

Justice O'Connor, concurring. . . .

Justice Brennan, with whom Justice Marshall, Justice Blackmun and Justice Stevens join, dissenting. . . .

. . . Unlike such secular figures as Santa Claus, reindeer and carolers, a nativity scene represents far more than a mere "traditional" symbol of Christmas. The essence of the creche's symbolic purpose and effect is to prompt the observer to experience a sense of simple awe and wonder appropriate to the contemplation of one of the central elements of Christian dogma—that God sent His son into the world to be a Messiah. Contrary to the Court's suggestion, the creche is far from a mere representation of a "particular historic religious event." . . . It is, instead, best understood as a mystical re-creation of an event that lies at the heart of Christian faith. To suggest, as the Court does, that such a symbol is merely "traditional" and therefore no different from Santa's house or reindeer is not only offensive to those for whom the creche has profound significance, but insulting to those who insist for religious or personal reasons that the story of Christ is in no sense a part of "history" nor an unavoidable element of our national "heritage."

For these reasons, the creche in this context simply cannot be viewed as playing the same role that an ordinary museum display does. . . .

The American historical experience concerning the public celebration of Christmas, if carefully examined, provides no support for the Court's decision. The opening sections of the Court's opinion, while seeking to rely on historical evidence, do no more than recognize the obvious: because of the strong religious currents that run through our history, an inflexible or absolutistic enforcement of the Establishment Clause would be both imprudent and impossible. . . . This observation is at once uncontroversial and unilluminating. Simply enumerating the various ways in which the Federal Goverment has recognized the vital role religion plays in our society does nothing to help decide the question presented in *this* case. . . .

Justice Blackmun, with whom Justice Stevens joins, dissenting.

As Justice Brennan points out, the logic of the Court's decision in *Lemon* v. *Kurtzman* . . . *compels* an affirmance here. If that case and its guidelines mean anything, the presence of Pawtucket's creche in a municipally sponsored display must be held to be a violation of the First Amendment.

Not only does the Court's resolution of this controversy make light of our precedents, but also, ironically, the majority does an injustice to the creche and the message it manifests. While certain persons, including the Mayor of Pawtucket, undertook a crusade to "keep Christ in Christmas," . . . the Court today has declared that presence virtually irrelevant. The majority urges that the display, "with or without a creche," "recall[s] the religious nature of the Holiday," and "engenders a friendly community spirit of good will in keeping with the season." . . . Before the District Court, an expert witness for the city made a similar, though perhaps more candid, point, stating that Pawtucket's display invites people "to participate in the Christmas spirit, brotherhood, peace, and let loose with their money." . . . The creche has been relegated to the role of a neutral harbinger of the holiday season, useful for commercial purposes, but devoid of any inherent meaning and incapable of enhancing the religious tenor of a display of which it is an integral part. The city has its victory—but it is a Pyrrhic one indeed.

The import of the Court's decision is to encourage use of the creche in a municipally sponsored display, a setting where Christians feel constrained in acknowledging its symbolic meaning and non-Christians feel alienated by its presence. Surely, this is a misuse of a sacred symbol. Because I cannot join the Court in denying either the force of our precedents or the sacred message that is at the core of the creche, I dissent and join Justice Brennan's opinion.

Since *Lynch* was decided, three different Federal Courts of Appeals have held unconstitutional the placement of creches and other religious symbols on public property by local governments. The decisions seemingly turned largely on the location of the exhibits and the fact that they were not a part of a larger exhibit including nonreligious items: *ACLU* v. *City of Birmingham*, 791 F2d 1561 (CA 6, 1986), a city-owned creche placed on the front lawn of the city hall; *American Jewish Congress* v. *City of Chicago*, 827 F2d 120 (CA 7, 1987), a privately owned creche displayed in the lobby of the Chicago city-county building; and *ACLU* v. *County of Allegheny*, 56 LW 2549 (CA 3, 1988), a creche inside the main entrance of the county courthouse and a menorah to be placed on the steps of the main entrance of the city-county building owned jointly by the County and the City of Pittsburgh.

## Sunday Closing Laws and the Establishment Clause

One of the clearest legacies bequeathed to us by the American Puritans is the Sunday Blue Law. Whatever the errors perpetuated concerning the Puritan's capacity for sin and pleasure—and the adjective "puritanical" is illustrative of such error—the accounts of his rigid and sober Sabbath observance are grounded in solid fact. Now, more than three hundred years later, we still retain laws which bar many kinds of mercantile and manufacturing operations on Sunday. For those persons whose Sabbath observance is on Sunday this is a congenial arrangement. For others, it may introduce a certain conflict in accommodating their religious and business interests to the Sunday Closing Law. At the very least, they may feel that the state is adopting punitive legislation which favors certain religious sects and penalizes others. Despite the clear indication that Sunday Laws were originally adopted as a means of promoting Christian observance, the earlier court decisions have uniformly upheld such laws, as in the case of *Petit* v. *Minnesota*, 177 U.S. 164 (1900), where a state law forbidding Sunday labor except works of necessity or charity was upheld. The first detailed examination of Sunday Laws by the United States Supreme Court under the claims of establishment of religion and abridgment of free exercise of religion did not occur, however, until 1961. In that year four cases involving the Sunday Laws of Massachusetts, Pennsylvania, and Maryland were decided, and in each case the laws were upheld against the claims of violation of religious liberty. The Maryland case, *McGowan* v. *Maryland*, covers the establishment arguments most thoroughly and will be presented as illustrative of the Court's view on that issue. (Since the Sunday laws contain a myriad of exceptions and exemptions from the closing requirement, the question of improper classification under the equal protection clause naturally arises, but this issue has been omitted from the cutting below since it does not relate directly to the matter of religious liberty.)

McGOWAN *v.* MARYLAND

*366 U.S. 420 (1961)*

Mr. Chief Justice Warren delivered the opinion of the Court.

The issues in this case concern the constitutional validity of Maryland criminal statutes, commonly known as Sunday Closing Laws or Sunday Blue Laws. . . .

Appellants are seven employees of a large discount department store located on a highway in Anne Arundel County, Maryland. They were indicted for the Sunday sale of a three-ring loose-leaf binder, a can of floor wax, a stapler and staples, and a toy submarine in violation of Md. Ann. Code, Art. 27 §521. Generally, this section prohibited, throughout the State, the Sunday sale of all merchandise except the retail sale of tobacco products, confectioneries, milk, drugs and medicines, and newspapers and periodicals. Recently amended, this section also now excepts from the general prohibition the retail sale in Anne Arundel County of all foodstuffs, automobile and boating accessories, flowers, toilet goods, hospital supplies and souvenirs. It now further provides that any retail establishment in Anne Arundel County which does not employ more than one person other than the owner may operate on Sunday. . . .

. . . Appellants were convicted and each was fined five dollars and costs. . . .

### III

The final questions for decision are whether the Maryland Sunday Closing laws conflict with the Federal Constitution's provisions for religious liberty. . . . But appellants allege only economic injury to themselves; they do not allege any infringement of their own religious freedoms due to Sunday closing. In fact, the record is silent as to what appellants' religious beliefs are. Since the general rule is that "a litigant may only assert his own constitutional rights or immunities," *United States* v. *Raines,* 362 U.S. 17, 22, we hold that appellants have no standing to raise this contention. . . .

Secondly, appellants contend that the statutes violate the guarantee of separation of church and state in that the statutes are laws respecting an establishment of religion contrary to the First Amendment, made applicable to the states by the Fourteenth Amendment. . . . Appellants here concededly have suffered direct economic injury, allegedly due to the imposition on them of the tenets of the Christian religion. We find that, in these circumstances, these appellants have standing to complain that the statutes are laws respecting an establishment of religion.

The essence of appellant's "establishment" argument is that Sunday is the Sabbath day of the predominant Christian sects; that the purpose of the enforced stoppage of labor on that day is to facilitate and encourage church attendance; that the purpose of setting Sunday as a day of universal rest is to induce people with no religion or people with marginal religious beliefs to join the predominant Christian sects; that the purpose of the atmosphere of tranquility created by Sunday closing is to aid the conduct of church services and religious observance of the sacred day. In substantiating their "establishment" argument, appellants rely on the wording of the present Maryland statutes, on earlier versions of the current Sunday laws and on prior judicial characterizations of these laws by the Maryland Court of Appeals. Although only the constitutionality of §521, of the section under which appellants have been convicted, is immediately before us in this litigation, inquiry into the history of Sunday Closing Laws in our country, in addition to an examination of the Maryland Sunday closing statutes in their entirety and of their history, is relevant to the decision of whether the Maryland Sunday Law in question is one respecting an establishment of religion. There is no dispute that the original laws which dealt with Sunday labor were motivated by religious forces. But what we must decide is whether present Sunday legislation having undergone extensive changes from the earliest forms, still retains its religious character.

Sunday Closing Laws go far back into American history, having been brought to the colonies with a background of English legislation dating to the thirteenth century. . . . The law of the colonies to the time of the Revolution and the basis of the Sunday laws in the States was 29 Charles II, c. 7 (1677). It provided, in part:

"For the better observation and keeping holy the Lord's day, commonly called Sunday: be it enacted . . . that all the laws enacted and in force concerning the observation of the Lord's day, *and repairing to the church thereon,* be carefully put in execution; and that all and every person and persons whatsoever shall upon every Lord's day apply themelves to the observation of the same, by exercising themselves thereon in the duties of piety and true religion, publicly and privately; and that no tradesman, artificer, workman, laborer, or other person whatsoever, *shall do or exercise any worldly labor or business or work* of their ordinary callings upon the Lord's day, . . ." (Emphasis added.)

Observation of the above language, and of that of the prior mandates, reveals clearly that the English Sunday legislation was in aid of the established church.

The American colonial Sunday restrictions arose soon after settlement. Starting in 1650, the Plymouth Colony proscribed servile work, unnecessary travelling, sports, and the sale of alcoholic beverages on the Lord's day and enacted laws concerning church attendance. . . .

But, despite the strongly religious origin of these laws, beginning before the eighteenth century, nonreligious arguments for Sunday closing began to be heard more distinctly and the statutes began to lose some of their totally religious flavor. In the middle 1700's, Blackstone wrote, "[T]he keeping one day in the seven holy, as a time of relaxation and refreshment as well as for public worship, is of admirable service to a state considered merely as civil institution. It humanizes, by the help of conversation and society, the manners of the lower classes; which would otherwise degenerate into a sordid ferocity and savage selfishness of spirit; it enables the industrious workman to pursue his occupation in the ensuing week with health and cheerfulness." 4 Bl. Comm. 63. . . . With the advent of the First Amendment, the colonial provisions requiring church attendance were soon repealed. . . .

More recently, further secular justifications have been advanced for making Sunday a day of rest, a day when people may recover from the labors of the week just passed and may physically and mentally prepare for the week's work to come. In England, during the First World War, a committee investigating the health conditions of munitions workers reported that "if the maximum output is to be secured and maintained for any length of time, a weekly period of rest must be allowed. . . . On economic and social grounds alike this weekly period of rest is best provided on Sunday."

The proponents of Sunday closing legislation are no longer exclusively representatives of religious interests. Recent New Jersey Sunday legislation was supported by labor groups and trade associations. . . .

In light of the evolution of our Sunday Closing Laws through the centuries, and of their more or less recent emphasis upon secular considerations, it is not difficult to discern that as presently written and administered, most of them, at least, are of a secular rather than of a religious character, and that presently they bear no relationship to establishment of religion as those words are used in the Constitution of the United States.

Throughout this century and longer, both the federal and state governments have oriented their activities very largely toward improvements of the health, safety, recreation and general well-being of our citizens. Numerous laws affecting public health, safety factors in industry, laws affecting hours and conditions of labor of women and children, week-end diversion at parks and beaches, and cultural activities of various kinds, now point the way toward the good life for all. Sunday Closing Laws, like those before us, have become part and parcel of this great governmental concern wholly apart from their original purposes or connotations. The present purpose and effect of most of them is to provide a uniform day of rest for all citizens; the fact that this day is Sunday, a day of particular significance for the dominant Christian sects, does not bar the State from achieving its secular goals. To say that the States cannot prescribe Sunday as a day of rest for these purposes solely because centuries ago such laws had their genesis in religion would give a constitutional interpretation of hostility to the public welfare rather than one of mere separation of church and state.

We now reach the Maryland statutes under review. . . .

Considering the language and operative effect of the current statutes, we no longer find the blanket prohibition against Sunday work or bodily labor. To the contrary, we find . . . the Sunday sale of tobaccos and sweets and a long list of sundry articles which we have enumerated above; . . . the Sunday operation of bathing beaches, amusement parks and similar facilities; . . . the Sunday sale of alcoholic beverages, . . . Sunday bingo and the Sunday playing of pin-ball machines and slot machines, activities generally condemned by prior Maryland Sunday legislation. Certainly, these are not works of charity or necessity. . . . These provisions, along with those which permit various sports and entertainments on Sunday, seem clearly to be fashioned for the purpose of providing a Sunday atmosphere of recreation, cheerfulness, repose and enjoyment. Coupled with the general proscription against other types of work, we believe that the air of the day is one of relaxation rather than one of religion. . . .

But this does not answer all of appellants' contentions. We are told that the State has other means at its disposal to accomplish its secular purpose, other courses that would not even remotely or incidentally give state aid to religion. . . . It is true that if the State's interest were simply to provide for its citizens a periodic respite from work, a regulation demanding that everyone rest one day in seven, leaving the choice of the day to the individual, would suffice.

However, the State's purpose is not merely to provide a one-day-in-seven work stoppage. In addition to this, the State seeks to set one day apart from all others as a day of rest, repose, recreation and tranquility—a day which all members of the family and community have the opportunity to spend and enjoy together, a day in which there exists relative quiet and disassociation from the everyday intensity of commercial activities, a day in which people may visit friends and relatives who are not available during working days.

Obviously, a State is empowered to determine that a rest-one-day-in-seven statute would not accomplish this purpose; that it would not provide for a general cessation of activity, a special atmosphere of tranquility, a day which all members of the family or friends and relatives might spend together. Furthermore, it seems plain that the problems involved in enforcing such a provision would be exceedingly more difficult than those in enforcing a common-day-of-rest provision.

Moreover, it is common knowledge that the first day of the week has come to have special significance as a rest day in this country. . . . Sunday is a day apart from all others. The cause is irrelevant; the fact exists. It would seem unrealistic for enforcement purposes and perhaps detrimental to the general welfare to require a State to choose a common-day-of-rest other than that which most persons would select of their own accord. For these reasons, we hold that the Maryland statutes are not laws respecting an establishment of religion. . . .

Accordingly, the decision is

*Affirmed.*

Separate opinion of Mr. Justice Frankfurter, whom Mr. Justice Harlan joins, [concurring]. . . .

Mr. Justice Douglas, dissenting.

The question is not whether one day out of seven can be imposed by a State as a day of rest. The question is not whether Sunday can by force of custom and habit be retained as a day of rest. The question is whether a State can impose criminal sanctions on those who, unlike the Christian majority that make up our society, worship on a different day or do not share the religious scruples of the majority. . . .

With that as my starting point I do not see how a State can make protesting citizens refrain from doing innocent acts on Sunday because the doing of those acts offends sentiments of their Christian neighbors. . . .

. . . The "establishment" clause protects citizens also against any law which selects any religious custom, practice, or ritual, puts the force of government behind it, and fines, imprisons, or otherwise penalizes a person for not observing it. The Government plainly could not join forces with one religious group and decree a universal and symbolic circumcision. Nor could it require all children to be baptized or give tax exemptions only to those whose children were baptized.

Could it require a fast from sunrise to sunset throughout the Moslem month of Ramadan? I should think not. Yet why then can it make criminal the doing of other acts, as innocent as eating, during the day that Christians revere? . . .

The issue of these cases would therefore be in better focus if we imagined that a state legislature controlled by Orthodox Jews and Seventh Day Adventists, passed a law by making it a crime to keep a shop open on Saturdays. Would a Baptist, Catholic, Methodist, or Presbyterian be compelled to obey that law or go to jail or to pay a fine? Or suppose Moslems grew in political strength here and got a law through a state legislature making it a crime to keep a shop open on Fridays? Would the rest of us have to submit under the fear of criminal sanctions? . . .

It seems to me plain that by these laws the States compel one, under sanction of law, to refrain from work or recreation on Sunday because of the majority's religious views about that day. The State by law makes Sunday a symbol of respect or adherence. Refraining from work or recreation in deference to the majority's religious feelings about Sunday is within every person's choice. By what authority can government compel it?

Cases are put where acts that are immoral by our standards but not by the standards of other religious groups are made criminal. That category of cases, until today, has been a very restricted one confined to polygamy . . . and other extreme situations. . . . None of the actions made constitutionally criminal today involves the doing of any act that any society has deemed to be immoral. . . .

The State can of course require one day of rest a week: one day when every shop or factory is closed. Quite a few States make that requirement. Then the "day of rest" becomes purely and simply a health measure. But the Sunday laws operate differently. They force minorities to obey the majority's religious feelings of what is due and proper for a Christian community; they provide a coercive spur to the "weaker brethen," to those who are indifferent to the claims of a Sabbath through apathy or scruple. Can there be any doubt that Christians, now aligned vigorously in favor of these laws, would be as strongly opposed, if they were prosecuted under a Moslem law that forbade them from engaging in secular activities on days that violated Moslem scruples?

There is an "establishment" of religion in the constitutional sense if any practice of any religious group has the sanction of law behind it. There is an interference with the "free exercise" of religion if what in conscience one can do or omit doing is required because of the religious scruples of the community. Hence I would declare each of those laws unconstitutional as applied to the complaining parties, whether or not they are members of a sect which observes as their Sabbath a day other than Sunday.

When these laws are applied to Orthodox Jews . . . or to Sabbatarians their vice is accentuated. If the Sunday laws are constitutional. Kosher markets are on a five-day week. Thus those laws put an economic penalty on those who observe Saturday rather than Sunday as the Sabbath. For the economic pressures on these minorities, created by the fact that our communities are predominantly Sunday-minded, there is no recourse. When, however, the State uses its coercive powers—here the criminal law—to compel minorities to observe a second Sabbath, not their own, the State undertakes to aid and "prefer one religion over another" contrary to the commands of the Constitution. . . .

## THE "FREE EXERCISE" OF RELIGION

As previously pointed out, the First Amendment contains two clauses designed to safeguard religious liberty—the establishment clause and the free exercise clause. These are, of course, but complementary facets of the overall protection for religious freedom. While the one shades off into the other, it is still useful to separate the two facets for analysis. As Justice Frankfurter stated in his concurring opinion in *McGowan* v. *Maryland:*

Within the discriminating phraseology of the First Amendment, distinction has been drawn between cases raising "establishment" and "free exercise" questions. Any attempt to formulate a bright-line distinction is bound to founder. In view of the competition among religious creeds, whatever "establishes" one sect disadvantages another, and vice versa. But it is possible historically, and therefore helpful analytically—no less for problems arising under the Fourteenth Amendment, illuminated as that Amendment is by our national experience, than for problems arising under the First—to isolate in general terms the two largely overlapping areas of concern reflected in the two constitutional phrases, "establishment" and "free exercise." . . .

Religious minorities were too busy struggling for their existence during the earlier period of American development to feel that they could turn to the courts for protection against majority rules which merely pinched but did not destroy. As the major battles were won in the political arena—freedom to engage in public worship, freedom from taxes to support religion, and freedom from the onus of an established religion—the climate was prepared for settling the secondary sources of friction by the calmer method of litigation. Thus it was not until the latter quarter of the nineteenth century that the first major case on religious liberty reached the United States Supreme Court. The case was *Reynolds* v. *United States,* decided in 1879, and it dealt with the constitutionality of a law prohibiting polygamous marriages as applied to a Mormon whose religion encouraged such a practice.

### Permissible Areas of Restraint—Protection of Morals, Health, and Safety

Reynolds was convicted in a district court of the Territory of Utah of the crime of bigamy, in violation of federal statutes which prohibited bigamy in any place under exclusive jurisdiction of the United States. He admitted to having entered into a second marriage, but as a Mormon, he alleged that "it was the duty of male members of said Church, circumstances permitting, to practice polygamy," and for the United States to punish him for enjoying this prescription of his Church was to abridge his First Amendment right to free exercise of religion. In *Reynolds* v. *United States*, 98 U.S. 145 (1879), the Court unanimously denied his claim. Chief Justice Waite, for the Court, examined the statutory history relating to the practice and concluded: "Polygamy has always been odious among the Northern and Western Nations of Europe and, until the establishment of the Mormon Church, was almost exclusively a feature of the life of Asiatic and African people." He stated that since before, during, and after the adoption of the First Amendment the law had punished bigamous marriages, "it is impossible to believe that the constitutional guaranty of religious freedom was intended to prohibit legislation in respect to this most important feature of social life."

As the *Reynolds* opinion makes clear, the First Amendment was not intended, and has not been so construed, to set up an absolute right to engage in a course of action just because one's religion happens to dictate it. Reasonable restrictions adopted by governments in furtherance of the health, safety, and convenience of the community may be enforced even against claims of violation of religious freedom.

The State has a well-recognized interest in the proper care and maintenance of children, and every State has laws charging parents with due attention to the helath needs of their minor children. Issues have arisen, however, as a result of parental decisions to rely on prayer or special religious ceremony rather than normal medical assistance for the cure of sick children. Although some state courts have held differently in "special cases," the general rule is that a competent adult may freely choose whether to submit to medical treatment or not. [See William C. Cunningham, S.J., "Indicated Blood Transfusions and the Adult Jehovah's Witness: Trial Judge's Dilemma," 2 *Valparaiso U.L. Rev.* 55 (1967) and John J. Paris, S.J., "Compulsory Medical Treatment and Religious Freedom: Whose Law Shall Prevail?" 10 *Un. of San Franciso L. Rev.* 1 (1975).] The question arises, however, whether the parent is constitutionally free to make the same choices on religious grounds for his or her minor children.

As a matter of religious belief, Jehovah's Witnesses refuse to submit to blood transfusions, even in life-threatening situations. They rest this decision on the Bible's injunction against "eating blood," a prohibition found in several books of the Bible, but particularly in Leviticus 17: 10–14. But a special problem arises when Jehovah's Witness parents refuse to allow transfusions for their minor children even though accepted medical opinion dictates the procedure. In a number of state court decisions, courts have appointed non-Witness guardians for such children, and the guardians have given permission for the doctors to administer the transfusions. In *Jehovah's Witnesses in the State of Washington v. King County Hospital*, a three-judge federal District Court refused to enjoin a provision of Washington's Juvenile Court Act under which judges were authorized to declare children dependent wards of the state to permit administration of blood transfusions in cases where parents objected to the procedure on religious grounds. The Supreme Court affirmed in a *per curiam* opinion, 390 U.S. 598 (1968).

The major case thus far to reach the United States Supreme Court involving a conflict between child care laws and the claim of free exercise of religion is *Prince* v. *Massachusetts*, 321 U.S. 158 (1944). It concerned the validity of the application of the state's child labor law to the guardian of a nine-year-old girl, who was permitted by the guardian to engage in "preaching work" and the sale and distribution of religious literature on the public streets after school hours. The defendant objected on the ground of interference with her religious freedom. By a five-to-four vote the Court held the application of such a criminal law valid as a reasonable police regulation designed to protect the welfare of children, even against the competing claim of religious exercise. The Court noted that the authority of the State as *parens patriae* "is not nullified merely because the parent grounds his claim to control the child's course of conduct on religion or conscience." The Court stated further:

> The state's authority over children's activities is broader than over like actions of adults. This is peculiarly true of public activities and in matters of employment. A democratic society rests, for its continuance, upon the healthy, well-rounded growth of young people into full maturity as citizens, with all that implies. It may secure this against impeding restraints and dangers within a broad range of selection. Among evils most appropriate for such action are the crippling effects of child employment, more especially in public places, and the possible harms arising from other activities subject to all the diverse influences of the street. It is too late now to doubt that legislation appropriately designed to reach such evils is within the state's police power, whether against the parent's claim to control of the child or one that religious scruples dictate contrary action.

Justice Murphy dissented on the ground that the particular prohibition of religious activities by children in this case was unreasonable, suggesting that "the reasonableness that justifies the prohibition of the ordinary distribution of literature in the public streets by children is not necessarily the reasonableness that justified such a drastic restriction when the distribution is part of their religious faith."

Where religious practices endanger the health or safety of others in the community, the courts have had no difficulty applying the normal police power regulations to such practices. As one illustration, a number of state supreme courts have dealt with claims of violation of religious freedom in the convictions of persons who engage in handling poisonous snakes as a part of their religious ritual. Such convictions have uniformly been upheld against claims of violation of the free exercise clauses of state constitutions. Illustrative of the cases is *Harden v. State of Tennessee*, 188 Tenn. 17, 216 S.W.2d 708 (1949).

The Biblical reference in support of this practice is Mark 16: 18, which states: "they will take snakes in their hands, and if they drink poison it will not hurt them" if they are believers. Harden and others were convicted of violating a statute making in unlawful for any person to handle or display any poisonous or dangerous snake in such manner as to endanger the life or health of any person. They were members of a religious denomination believing that the handling of poisonous snakes was a method of confirming their faith and, further, that nonbelievers would be converted to their faith upon witnessing this miracle of safely handling such snakes. The Tennessee Supreme Court, in upholding the conviction, pointed out:

> Aside from the fact that such handling of a rattlesnake is commonly known to be fraught with danger, there is in this record affirmative evidence that at this particular church at least one worshipper was bitten by a poisonous snake and died from the effects thereof within a few hours.
>
> Reasonable minds must agree that the aforementioned practice of so handling poisonous snakes as a part of the religious services of this Church is dangerous to the life and health of people.

[See also *Tennessee ex rel. Swann v. Pack*, 527 S.W.2d 99 (1975), in which the Tennessee Supreme Court affirmed a lower court decision enjoining as a public nuisance the handling of rattlesnakes and drinking strychnine in public meetings.]

The courts of the States have also upheld state laws which require affirmative action to prevent disease, as well as the requirements of caring for ill minor children. The compulsory vaccination laws have been upheld in general in *Jacobson* v. *Massachusetts,* 197 U.S. 11 (1905), and convictions for failure to vaccinate children as a condition for admission to public school have been upheld against religious challenge, as in *Anderson* v. *State,* 84 Ga. App. 259, 65 S.E. 2d 848 (1951). Flouridation has been upheld against the challenge from members of religious sects opposed to medication that such a program violates their religious liberty, as in *Baer* v. *City of Bend,* 206 Ore. 221, 292 P. 2d 134 (1956). It is interesting to note that such groups do not normally oppose *chlorination* of water although they do oppose *fluoridation.* The distinction apparently is drawn on the basis that chlorination merely kills certain bacteria, while fluoridation specifically is designed to serve as a caries preventive and is therefore a form of medication.

Another area in which the police power has been deemed to take precedence over claims of religious liberty is protection against fraud. Spiritual healing and faith healing have probably been with us since the earliest case of illness. Since normal physiological processes will rectify three-fourths of an illness, and psychosomatic disorders may respond to readjustment of mental state, the reportable "cures" of healers may reach impressive percentage figures. Claimants of special supernatural powers to heal the sick have often been sincerely convinced that they possessed such talents. Others have formed religious sects which included as an article of faith the belief that participation in certain kinds of religious ritual would result in curing illness. Where there is a clear nexus between religious belief or practice and the attempts to heal the sick, government denies religious freedom if it attempts actively to intervene. On the other hand, there are those who, without any prompting of religious conviction, set up healing enterprises with all the panoply and trappings of religion and play upon the credulity of the ignorant and the desperation of the incurably ill solely for financial gain. The general view is that the latter category of healers can properly be made the object of prosecutions for fraud, although there are strong dissents from this view.

The United States Supreme Court in 1944 considered the issue of the constitutionality under the First Amendment of prosecution of faith healers for mail fraud. The "I Am" cult was established in California by one Guy Ballard. The founders and leaders of the movement were subjected to a mail fraud prosecution. Guy Ballard claimed that he and his wife Edna and their child had been selected by St. Germain (dead since A.D. 488) as earthly representatives of the true religion. As a consequence of such divine designation Guy Ballard could heal incurable diseases and take spots off clothing, or at least so their doctrine taught. Funds were received from believers to carry on the work of the cult, and the mails were used for this purpose, as well as for the sale of various types of printed matter describing the doctrines of the cult. Very substantial profits were made on the printed material.

The federal government charged that the mails had been used to defraud. The major question throughout was just what the jury was supposed to decide: whether the Ballards could cure the incurable, or whether the Ballards *believed* that they could cure the incurable. The trial judge decided that the jury could only examine the latter, that is, the question of whether the Ballards honestly believed what they taught.

Before the case was concluded Guy Ballard died, following an operation, but his wife and child were convicted, fined, and given suspended prison sentences. The Court of Appeals reversed on the ground that the trial judge improperly charged the jury as to the defendants' sincerity. This decision was appealed, and the United States Supreme Court, agreeing with the view of the trial judge, reversed the decision of the Court of Appeals. Justice Douglas, speaking for the Court in *United States* v. *Ballard,* 322 U.S. 78 (1944), stated that this approach was in line with the First Amendment protection of religious freedom. Clearly, he said, the Constitution did not countenance an examination into the truth or falsity of beliefs, for then any religious group could be brought into court to prove the validity of its teachings, and religious freedom would be at an end. The majority, however, voted to remand the case for the disposition of other issues, with three justices dissenting. Justice Jackson was the lone dissenter on the question of the government's right to try the Ballards. He was by no means impressed with what he called "humbug, untainted by any trace of truth," but he felt that a jury simply would not be able to distinguish the beliefs of the Ballards from the credibility of such beliefs in reaching their verdict. In view of this difficulty he felt that the only safe course from the standpoint of religious freedom was to rule out such trials altogether. Even the more orthodox ministers or clergymen might be hard pressed on occasion if they were subjected to a sincerity test for everything said in the pulpit before the collection plate was passed. [For an interesting treatment of *Ballard,* see David Fellman, *The Limits of Freedom* (New Brunswick: Rutgers Universitgy Press, 1959), pp. 6–19.]

A different form of restraint on religious institutions is exemplified by the application of the Internal Revenue Code. A section of that Code provides that corporations "organized and operated exclusively for religious, charitable . . . or educational purposes" are entitled to tax exemption. Until 1970, the IRS granted tax-exempt status under this section to private schools, independent of racial admissions policies, and granted charitable deductions for contributions to such schools. But in 1970 the IRS issued a ruling providing that a private school not having a racially nondiscriminatory policy as to students was not "charitable" within the common-law concepts reflected in the Code. Bob Jones University is a nonprofit corporation located in Greenville, South Carolina. It was founded in Florida in 1927 and moved to Greenville in 1940. It is not affiliated with any religious denomination, but is dedicated to the teaching and propagation of its fundamentalist Christian religious beliefs. It is both a religious and educational institution. Entering students are screened as to their religious beliefs, and their public and private conduct is strictly regulated by standards promulgated by University authorities.

The sponsors of the University genuinely believe that the Bible forbids interracial dating and marriage. Negroes were completely excluded until 1971. From 1971 to 1975, the University acccepted no applications from unmarried Negroes, but did accept applications from Negroes married within their race. Since 1975 (and the decision in *McCrary* v. *Runyon* in that year prohibiting racial exclusion from private schools), the University has permitted unmarried Negroes to enroll; but a disciplinary rule prohibits interracial dating and marriage or the advocacy of interracial dating or marriage. After revocation of its tax-exempt status, the University paid a portion of the federal unemployment taxes and sued for a refund, alleging that the decision of IRS was both improper and unconstitutional under the Religion Clauses of the First Amendment. The United States District Court so held, but the Court of Appeals reversed. In *Bob Jones University* v. *United States* (with the companion case *Goldsboro Christian Schools, Inc.* v. *United States*), 461 U.S. 574 (1983), the Supreme Court affirmed. Chief Justice Burger, for the majority, stated that it was not enough to look at the plain words of the statute, but that the Code section needed to be analyzed within the framework of the Internal Revenue Code and against the background of the Congress' purposes. "Such an examination reveals unmistakable evidence that, underlying all relevant parts of the Code, is the intent that entitlement to tax exemption depends on meeting certain common-law standards of charity—namely, that an institution seeking tax-exempt status must serve a public purpose and not be contrary to established public policy." He stated that there can no longer be any doubt that racial discrimination in education violates "deeply and widely accepted views of elementary justice." Further, over the past quarter of a century, "every pronouncement of this Court and myriad Acts of Congress and Executive Orders attest a firm national policy to prohibit racial segregation and discrimination in public education." It was held that, contrary to Bob Jones University's contention that it is not racially discriminatory, discrimination on the basis of racial affiliation and association is a form of racial discrimination. As to the First Amendment claim, the Court stated that the state may justify a limitation on religious liberty by showing that it is essential to accomplish an overriding governmental interest. "The governmental interest at stake here is compelling . . . the Government has a fundamental, overriding interest in eradicating racial discrimination in education." It held that this governmental interest "substantially outweighs whatever burden denial of tax benefits places on petitioners' exercise of their religious beliefs." Justice Rehnquist dissented on the ground that the Internal Revenue Code could not properly be interpreted to bar tax-exempt status to organizations that practice racial discrimination, although he agreed that Congress had the power to do so.

## Compulsory Patriotic Exercises and Religious Freedom

In the public schools of many states there are compulsory exercises which include the salute to the flag and the recitation of the pledge of allegiance. The Jehovah's Witnesses sect believes that such a gesture of respect for the flag as saluting is forbidden by the commands of Scripture. Reliance is especially placed on the third, fourth, and fifth verses of Chapter 20 of Exodus prohibiting false gods, graven images, and bowing down to such images. In 1940 the United States Supreme Court faced the issue of whether children in the public schools could be expelled for refusal on religious grounds to participate in the flag salute exercises. In *Minersville School District* v. *Gobitis,* 310 U.S. 586 (1940), the Court held that such provisions did not unconstitutionally abridge religious liberty. Justice Frankfurter, for the majority, stated:

We are dealing with an interest inferior to none in the hierarchy of legal values. National unity is the basis of national security. . . . To stigmatize legislative judgment in providing for this universal gesture of respect for the symbol of our national life in the setting of the common school as a lawless inroad on that freedom of conscience which the Constitution protects, would amount to no less than the pronouncement of pedagogical and psychological dogma in a field where courts possess no marked and certainly no controlling competence. The influences which help toward a common feeling for the common country are manifold. Some may seem harsh and others no doubt are foolish. Surely, however, the end is legitimate. And the effective means for its attainment are still so uncertain and so unauthenticated by science as to preclude us from putting the widely prevalent belief in flag-saluting beyond the pale of legislative power. It mocks reason and denies our whole history to find in the allowance of a requirement to salute our flag on fitting occasions the seeds of sanction for obeisance to a leader. . . . Where all the effective means of inducing political changes are left free from interference, education in the abandonment of foolish legislation is itself a training in liberty. To fight out the wise use of legislative authority in the forum of public opinion and before legislative assemblies rather than to transfer such a contest to the judicial arena, serves to vindicate the self-confidence of a free people.

Justice Stone was the only dissenter in the case. In a vigorous dissent he stated:

. . . [B]y this law the state seeks to coerce these children to express a sentiment which, as they interpret it, they do not entertain, and which violates their deepest religious convictions. . . . History teaches us that there have been but few infringements of personal liberty by the state which have not been justified, as they are here, in the name of righteousness and the public good, and few which have not been directed, as they are now, at politically helpless minorities. . . . I cannot conceive that in prescribing, as limitations upon the powers of government, the freedom of the mind and spirit secured by the explicit guarantees of freedom of speech and religion, [the framers] intended or rightly could have left any latitude for a legislative judgment that the compulsory expression of belief which violates religious convictions would better serve the public interest than their protection.

The *Minersville* decision was subjected to wide criticism. In an unusual step, three justices took the occasion of a dissenting opinion in a case arising in 1942 to announce that they felt the *Minersville* case was "wrongly decided." With Justice Stone, this made four members opposing that decision. Justice Byrnes, a member of the *Minersville* majority, resigned and was replaced by Justice Rutledge in 1943. In that same year the issue was relitigated in the case of *West Virginia State Board of Education v. Barnette.*

### WEST VIRGINIA STATE BOARD OF EDUCATION *v.* BARNETTE
### *319 U.S. 624 (1943)*

Mr. Justice Jackson delivered the opinion of the Court. . . .

The Board of Education on January 9, 1942, adopted a resolution containing recitals taken largely from the Court's *Gobitis* opinion and ordering that the salute to the flag become "a regular part of the program of activities in the public schools," that all teachers and pupils "shall be required to participate in the salute honoring the Nation represented by the Flag; provided, however that refusal to salute the Flag be regarded as an Act of insubordination, and shall be dealt with accordingly." . . .

Failure to conform is "insubordination" dealt with by expulsion. Readmission is denied by statute until compliance. Meanwhile the expelled child is "unlawfully absent" and may be proceeded against as a delinquent. His parents or guardians are liable to prosecution, and if convicted are subject to fine not exceeding $50 and jail term not exceeding thirty days.

Appellees, citizens of the United States and of West Virginia, brought suit in the United States District Court for themselves and others similarly situated asking its injunction to restrain enforcement of these laws and regulations against Jehovah's Witnesses. The Witnesses are an unincorporated body teaching that the obligation imposed by law of God is superior to that of laws enacted by temporal government. Their religious beliefs include a literal version of Exodus, Chapter 20, verses 4 and 5, which says: "Thou shalt not make unto thee any graven image, or any likeness of anything that is in heaven above, or that is in the earth beneath, or that is in the water under the earth; thou shalt not bow down thyself to them, nor serve them." They consider that the flag is an "image within this command." For this reason they refuse to salute it.

Children of this faith have been expelled from school and are threatened with exclusion for no other cause. Officials threaten to send them to reformatories maintained for criminally inclined juveniles. Parents of such children have been prosecuted and are threatened with prosecutions for causing delinquency.

. . . The cause was submitted on the pleadings to a District Court of three judges. It restrained enforcement as to the plaintiffs and those of that class. The Board of Education brought the case here by direct appeal.

This case calls upon us to reconsider a precedent decision, as the Court throughout its history often has been required to do. Before turning to the *Gobitis* case, however, it is desirable to notice certain characteristics by which this controversy is distinguished.

The freedom asserted by these appellees does not bring them into collision with rights asserted by any other individual. It is such conflicts which most frequently require intervention of the State to determine where the rights of one end and those of another begin. . . . The sole conflict is between authority and rights of the individual. The State asserts power to condition access to public education on making a prescribed sign and profession and at the same time to coerce attendance by punishing both parent and child. The latter stand on a right of self-determination in matters that touch individual opinion and personal attitude. . . .

There is no doubt that, in connection with the pledges, the flag salute is a form of utterance. . . .

. . . To sustain the compulsory flag salute we are required to say that a Bill of Rights which guards the individual's right to speak his own mind, left it open to public authorities to compel him to utter what is not in his mind. . . .

Nor does the issue as we see it turn on one's possession of particular religious views or the sincerity with which they are held. While religion supplies appellees' motive for enduring the discomforts of making the issue in this case, many citizens who do not share their religious views hold such a compulsory rite to infringe constitutional liberty of the individual. It is not necessary to inquire whether nonconformist beliefs will exempt from the duty to salute unless we first find power to make the salute a legal duty.

The *Gobitis* decision, however, *assumed,* as did the argument in that case and in this, that power exists in the State to impose the flag salute discipline upon school children in general. The Court only examined and rejected a claim based on religious beliefs of immunity from an unquestioned general rule. The question which underlies the flag salute controversy is whether such a ceremony so touching matters of opinion and political attitude may be imposed upon the individual by official authority under powers committed to any political organization under our Constitution. We examine rather than assume existence of this power and, against this broader definition of issues in this case, re-examine specific grounds assigned for the *Gobitis* decision. . . .

3. The *Gobitis* opinion reasoned that this is a field "where courts possess no marked and certainly no controlling competence," that it is committed to the legislatures as well as the courts to guard cherished liberties and that it is constitutionally appropriate to "fight out the wise use of legislative authority in the forum of public opinion and before legislative assemblies rather than to transfer such a contest to the judicial arena," since all the "effective means of inducing political changes are left free."

The very purpose a Bill of Rights was to withdraw certain subjects from the vicissitudes of political controversy, to place them beyond the reach of majorities and officials and to establish them as legal principles to be applied by the courts. One's rights to life, liberty, and property, to free speech, a free press, freedom of worship and assembly, and other fundamental rights may not be submitted to vote; they depend on the outcome of no elections. . . .

4. Lastly, and this is the very heart of the *Gobitis* opinion, it reasons that "national unity is the basis of national security," that the authorities have "the right to select appropriate means for its attainment," and hence reaches the conclusion that such compulsory measures toward "national unity" are constitutional. Upon the verity of this assumption depends our answer in this case.

National unity as an end which officials may foster by persuasion and example is not in question. The problem is whether under our Constitution compulsion as here employed is a permissible means for its achievement.

Struggles to coerce uniformity of sentiment in support of some end thought essential to their time and country have been waged by many good as well as by evil men. Nationalism is a relatively recent phenomenon but at other times and places the ends have been racial or territorial security, support of a dynasty or regime, and particular plans for saving souls. As first and moderate methods to attain unity have failed, those bent on its accomplishment must resort to an ever increasing severity. As governmental pressure toward unity becomes greater, so strife becomes more bitter as to whose unity it shall be. Probably no deeper division of our people could proceed from any provocation than from finding it necessary to choose what doctrine and whose program public educational officials shall compel youth to unite in embracing. Ultimate futility of such attempts to compel coherence is the lesson of every such effort from the Roman drive to stamp out Christianity as a disturber of its pagan unity, the Inquisition, as a means to religious and dynastic unity, the Siberian exiles as a means to Russian unity, down to the fast failing efforts of our present totalitarian enemies. Those who begin coercive elimination of dissent soon find themselves exterminating dissenters. Compulsory unification of opinion achieves only the unanimity of the graveyard.

It seems trite but necessary to say that the First Amendment to our Constitution was designed to avoid those ends by avoiding these beginnings. There is no mysticism in the American concept of the State or of the nature or origin of its authority. We set up government by consent of the governed, and the Bill of Rights denies those in power any legal opportunity to coerce that consent. Authority here is to be controlled by public opinion, not public opinion by authority.

The case is made difficult not because the principles of its decision are obscure but because the flag involved is our own. Nevertheless, we apply the limitations of the Constitution with no fear that freedom to be intellectually and spiritually diverse or even contrary will disintegrate the social organization. To believe that patriotism will not flourish if patriotic ceremonies are voluntary and spontaneous instead of a compulsory routine is to make an unflattering estimate of the appeal of our institutions to free minds. We can have intellectual individualism and the rich cultural diversities that we owe to exceptional minds only at the price of occasional eccentricity and abnormal attitudes. When they are so harmless to others or to the State as those we deal with here, the price is not too great. But freedom to differ is not limited to things that do not matter much. That would be a mere shadow of freedom. The test of its substance is the right to differ as to things that touch the heart of the existing order.

If there is any fixed star in our constitutional constellation, it is that no official, high or petty, can prescribe what shall be orthodox in politics, nationalism, religion, or other matters of opinion or force citizens to confess by word or act their faith therein. If there are any circumstances which permit an exception, they do not now occur to us.

We think the action of the local authorities in compelling the flag salute and pledge transcends constitutional limitations on their power and invades the sphere of intellect and spirit which it is the purpose of the First Amendment to our Constitution to reserve from all official control.

The decision of this Court in *Minersville School District* v. *Gobitis* and the holdings of those few *per curiam* decisions which preceded and foreshadowed it are overruled, and the judgment enjoining enforcement of the West Virginia Regulation is

*Affirmed.*

Mr. Justice Roberts and Mr. Justice Reed adhere to the views expressed by the Court in *Minersville School District* v. *Gobitis* . . . and are of the opinion that the judgment below should be reversed.

Mr. Justice Black and Mr. Justice Douglas concurring. . . .

Mr. Justice Murphy concurring. . . .

Mr. Justice Frankfurter, dissenting.

One who belongs to the most vilified and persecuted minority in history is not likely to be insensible to the freedoms guaranteed by our Constitution. Were my purely personal attitude relevant I should wholeheartedly associate myself with the general libertarian views in the Court's opinion, representing as they do the thought and action of a lifetime. But as judges we are neither Jew nor Gentile, neither Catholic nor agnostic. We owe equal attachment to the Constitution and are equally bound by our judicial obligations whether we derive our citizenship from the earliest or the latest immigrants to these shores. As a member of this Court I am not justified in writing my private notions of policy into the Constitution, no matter how deeply I may cherish them or how mischievous I may deem their disregard. The duty of a judge who must decide which of two claims before the Court shall prevail, that of a State to enact and enforce laws within its general competence or that of an individual to refuse obedience because of the demands of his conscience, is not that of the ordinary person. It can never be emphasized too much that one's own opinion about the wisdom or evil of a law should be excluded altogether when one is doing one's duty on the bench. The only opinion of our own even looking in that direction that is material is our opinion of whether legislators could in reason have enacted such a law. In the light of all the circumstances, including the history of this question in this Court, it would require more daring than I possess to deny that reasonable legislators could have taken the action which is before us for review. Most unwillingly, therefore, I must differ from my brethren with regard to legislation like this. I cannot bring my mind to believe that the "liberty" secured by the Due Process Clause gives this Court authority to deny to the State of West Virginia, the attainment of that which we all recognize as a legitimate legislative end, namely, the promotion of good citizenship, by employment of the means here chosen. . . .

[For a thorough treatment of the flag salute cases, see David Manwaring, *Render Unto Caesar: The Flag Salute Controversy* (Chicago: University of Chicago Press, 1962).]

### Free Exercise of Religion and the Problems of Sabbatarians

In *McGowan* v. *Maryland,* discussed earlier, Maryland's Sunday Laws were challenged on the ground that they represented an establishment of religion. In companion cases decided on the same day as *McGowan* (*Gallagher* v. *Crown Kosher Super Market of Massachusetts* and *Braunfeld* v. *Brown*) Sunday Closing Laws were challenged by members of the Orthodox Jewish faith on the ground that they were an interference with the free exercise of their religion. The essence of the claim was that their religion required them to remain closed on Saturday, and that if they were compelled to remain closed on Sunday as well, the effect of the law would be to compel them to make a choice between going out of business or violating their religious beliefs and remaining open on Saturday. In *Gallagher*, for example, it was testified that the market had been conducting about one-third of its weekly business on Sunday, and that to close on that day would be ruinous.

BRAUNFELD *v.* BROWN

*366 U.S. 599 (1961)*

Mr. Chief Justice Warren announced the judgment of the Court and an opinion in which Mr. Justice Black, Mr. Justice Clark, and Mr. Justice Whittaker concur.

This case concerns the constitutional validity of the application to appellants of the Pennsylvania criminal statute, enacted in 1959, which proscribes the Sunday retail sale of certain enumerated commodities. Among the questions presented are whether the statute is a law respecting an establishment of religion and whether the statute violates equal protection. Since both of these questions, in reference to this very statute, have already been answered in the negative, . . . and since appellants present nothing new regarding them, they need not be considered here. Thus, the only question for consideration is whether the statute interferes with the free exercise of appellants' religion.

Appellants are merchants in Philadephia who engage in the retail sale of clothing and home furnishings within the proscription of the statute in issue. Each of the appellants is a member of the Orthodox Jewish faith, which requires the closing of their places of business and a total abstention from all manner of work from nightfall each Friday until nightfall each Saturday. They instituted a suit in the court below seeking a permanent injunction against the enforcement of the 1959 statute. . . .

A three-judge court was properly convened and it dismissed the complaint. . . . On appeal brought under 28 USC Section 1253, we noted probable jurisdiction. . . .

Appellants contend that the enforcement against them of the Pennsylvania statute will prohibit the free exercise of their religion because, due to the statute's compulsion to close on Sunday, appellants will suffer substantial economic loss, to the benefit of their non-Sabbatarian competitors, if appellants also continue their Sabbath observance by closing their businesses on Saturday; that this result will either compel appellants to give up their Sabbath observance, a basic tenet of the Orthodox Jewish faith, or will put appellants at a serious economic disadvantage if they continue to adhere to the Sabbath. Appellants also assert that the statute will operate so as to hinder the Orthodox Jewish faith in gaining new adherents. And the corollary to these arguments is that if the free exercise of appellants' religion is impeded, that religion is being subjected to discriminatory treatment by the State. . . .

Concededly, appellants and all other persons who wish to work on Sunday will be burdened economically by the State's day of rest mandate; and appellants point out that their religion requires them to refrain from work on Saturday as well. Our inquiry then is whether, in these circumstances, the First and Fourteenth Amendments forbid application of the Sunday Closing Law to appellants.

Certain aspects of religious exercise cannot, in any way, be restricted or burdened by either federal or state legislation. Compulsion by law of the acceptance of any creed or the practice of any form of worship is strictly forbidden. The freedom to hold religious beliefs and opinions is absolute. . . .

However, the freedom to act, even when the action is in accord with one's religious convictions, is not totally free from legislative restrictions. . . . As pointed out in *Reynolds* v. *United States* . . . legislative power over mere opinion is forbidden but it may reach people's actions when they found to be in violation of important social duties or subversive of good order, even when the actions are demanded by one's religion. . . .

But . . . the statute at bar does not make unlawful any religious practices of appellants; the Sunday law simply regulates a secular activity and, as applied to appellants, operates so as to make the practice of their religious beliefs more expensive. Furthermore, the law's effect does not inconvenience all members of the Orthodox Jewish faith but only those who believe it necessary to work on Sunday. And even these are not faced with as serious a choice as forsaking their religious practices or subjecting themselves to criminal prosecution. Fully recognizing that the alternatives open to appellants and others similarly situated—retaining their present occupations and incurring economic disadvantage or engaging in some other commercial activity which does not call for either Saturday or Sunday labor—may well result in some financial sacrifice in order to observe their religious beliefs, still the option is wholly different than when the legislation attempts to make a religious practice itself unlawful.

To strike down, without the most critical scrutiny, legislation which imposes only an indirect burden on the exercise of religion, i.e., legislation which does not make unlawful the religious practice itself, would radically restrict the operating latitude of the legislature. Statutes which tax income and limit the amount which may be deducted for religious contributions impose an indirect economic burden on the observance of the religion of the citizen whose religion requires him to donate a greater amount to his church; statutes which require the courts to be closed on Saturday and Sunday impose a similar indirect burden on the observance of the religion of the trial lawyer whose religion requires him to rest on a weekday. The list of legislation of this nature is nearly limitless. . . .

Of course, to hold unassailable all legislation regulating conduct which imposes solely an indirect burden on the observance of religion would be a gross oversimplification. If the purpose or effect of a law is to impede the observance of one or all religions or is to discriminate invidiously between religions, that law is constitutionally invalid even though the burden may be characterized as being only indirect. But if the State regulates conduct by enacting a general law within its power, the purpose and effect of which is to advance the State's secular goals, the statute is valid despite its indirect burden on religious observance unless the State may accomplish its purpose by means which do not impose such a burden. . . .

As we pointed out in *McGowan* v. *Maryland* . . . we cannot find a State without power to provide a weekly respite from all labor and, at the same time, to set one day of the week apart from the others as a day of rest, repose, recreation and tranquility. . . .

However, appellants . . . contend that the State should cut an exception from the Sunday labor proscription for those people who, because of religious conviction, observe a day of rest other than Sunday. By such regulation, appellants contend, the economic disadvantages imposed by the present system would be removed and the State's interest in having all people rest one day would be satisfied.

A number of States provide such an exemption, and this may well be the wiser solution to the problem. But our concern is not with the wisdom of legislation but with its constitutional limitation. Thus, reason and experience teach that to permit the exemption might well undermine the State's goal of providing a day that, as best possible, eliminates the atmosphere of commercial noise and activity. Although not dispositive of the issue, enforcement problems would be more difficult since there would be two or more days to police rather than one and it would be more difficult to observe whether violations were occurring.

Additional problems might also be presented by a regulation of this sort. To allow only people who rest on a day other than Sunday to keep their businesses open on that day might well provide the people with an economic advantage over their competitors who must remain closed on that day; this might cause the Sunday-observers to complain that their religions are being discriminated against. With this competitive advantage existing, there could well be the temptation for some, in order to keep their businesses open on Sunday, to assert that they have religious convictions which compel them to close their businesses on what had formerly been their least profitable day. This might make necessary a state-conducted inquiry into the sincerity of the individual's religious beliefs, a practice which a State might believe would itself run afoul of the spirit of constitutionally protected religious guarantees. Finally, in order to keep the disruption of the day at a minimum, exempted employers would probably have to hire employees who themselves qualified for the exemption because of their own religious beliefs, a practice which a State might feel to be opposed to its general policy prohibiting religious discrimination in hiring. For all of these reasons, we cannot say that the Pennsylvania statute before us is invalid, either on its face or as applied.

Mr. Justice Harlan concurs in the judgment. Mr. Justice Brennan and Mr. Justice Stewart concur in our disposition of appellants' claims under the Establishment Clause and the Equal Protection Clause. Mr. Justice Frankfurter and Mr. Justice Harlan have rejected appellants' claim under the Free Exercise Clause in a separate opinion.

Accordingly, the decision is

*Affirmed.*

Separate opinion of Mr. Justice Frankfurter, whom Mr. Justice Harlan joins [relating to all four of the Sunday law cases]. . . .

Mr. Justice Brennan, concurring and dissenting.

I agree with the Chief Justice that there is no merit in appellants' establishment and equal-protection claims. I dissent, however, as to the claim that Pennsylvania has prohibited the free exercise of appellants' religion. . . .

[The complaint alleges that] "Plaintiff, Abraham Braunfeld, will be unable to continue in his business if he may not stay open on Sunday and he will thereby lose his capital investment." In other words, the issue in this case—and we do not understand either appellees or the Court to contend otherwise—is whether a State may put an individual to a choice between his business and his religion. The Court today holds that it may. But I dissent, believing that such a law prohibits the free exercise of religion. . . .

What, then, is the compelling state interest which impels the Commonwealth of Pennsylvania to impede appellants' freedom of worship? . . . It is the mere convenience of having everyone rest on the same day. It is to defend this interest that the Court holds that a State need not follow the alternative route of granting an exemption for those who in good faith observe a day of rest other than Sunday.

It is true, I suppose, that the granting of such an exemption would make Sundays a little noisier, and the task of police and prosecutor a little more difficult. It is also true that a majority—21—of the 34 States which have general Sunday regulations have exemptions of this kind. We are not told that those States are significantly noisier, or that their police are significantly more burdened, than Pennsylvania's. Even England, not under the compulsion of a written constitution, but simply influenced by considerations of fairness, has such an exemption for some activities. The Court conjures up several difficulties with such a system which seem to me more fanciful than real. . . .

In fine, the Court, in my view, has exalted administrative convenience to a constitutional level high enough to justify making one religion economically disadvantageous. . . .

I would reverse this judgment and remand for a trial of appellants' allegations, limited to the free-exercise-of-religion issue.

Mr. Justice Stewart, dissenting.

I agree with substantially all that Mr. Justice Brennan has written. Pennsylvania has passed a law which compels an Orthodox Jew to choose between his religious faith and his economic survival. That is a cruel choice. It is a choice which I think no State can constitutionally demand. For me this is not something that can be swept under the rug and forgotten in the interest of enforced Sunday togetherness. I think the impact of this law upon these appellants grossly violates their constitutional right to the exercise of their religion.

Mr. Justice Douglas, dissenting. [This dissent to the holding in *McGowan* v. *Maryland applies* to all four Sunday Law cases.]

The question is not whether one day out of seven can be imposed by a State as a day of rest. The question is not whether Sunday can by force of custom and habit be retained as a day of rest. The question is whether a State can impose criminal sanctions on those who, unlike the Christian majority that makes up our society, worship on a different day or do not share the religious scruples of the majority. . . .

[The Justice here takes up the "establishment" issue, included in the excerpts quoted earlier in *McGowan* v. *Maryland.*]

When these laws are applied to Orthodox Jews, as they are in [*Gallagher* and *Braunfeld*], or to Sabbatarians their vice is accentuated. If the Sunday laws are constitutional, Kosher markets are on a five-day week. Thus those laws put an economic penalty on those who observe Saturday rather than Sunday as the Sabbath. For the economic pressures on these minorities, created by the fact that our communities are predominantly Sunday-minded, there is no recourse. When, however, the State uses its coercive powers—here the criminal law—to compel minorities to observe a second Sabbath, not their own, the State undertakes to aid and "prefer one religion over another"—contrary to the command of the Constitution. . . .

The reverse side of an "establishment" is a burden on the "free exercise" of religion. Receipt of funds from the state benefits the established church directly; laying an extra tax on nonmembers benefits the established church indirectly. Certainly the present Sunday laws place Orthodox Jews and Sabbatarians under extra burdens because of their religious opinions or beliefs. Requiring them to abstain from their trade or business on Sunday reduces their work-week to five days, unless they violate their religious scruples. This places them at a competitive disadvantage and penalizes them for adhering to their religious beliefs.

. . . The special protection which Sunday laws give the dominant religious groups and the penalty they place on minorities whose holy day is Saturday constitute in my view state interference with the "free exercise" of religion.

An unusual aspect of the problem faced by a Sabbatarian in a Sunday-observing society is the question of eligibility for unemployment compensation in the face of a refusal to accept any job requiring Saturday work. Does denial by the state agency of such compensation constitute abridgment of religious freedom for the Saturday worshiper? The Court decided the issue in a case arriving from South Carolina in 1963, *Sherbert* v. *Verner,* 374 U.S. 398 (1963).

The appellant in the case became a member of the Seventh-Day Adventist Church in 1957 at a time when her employer permitted her to work a five-day week. In 1959 the work week was changed to six days, including Saturday, for all shifts in the mill. Appellant was discharged by her employer because she refused to work on Saturday, the Sabbath Day of her faith. She was unable to obtain other employment for which she was qualified because of her refusal to take Saturday work and filed for unemployment compensation benefits under the state law. The appellee Employment Security Commission found her disqualified for benefits by their interpretation of the provision disqualifying persons who fail to accept "suitable work when offered" by the employment office. The South Carolina Supreme Court sustained this finding.

With two dissenting votes, the United States Supreme Court reversed, holding the decision of the Commission to be an abridgment of the free exercise of religion. Justice Brennan, for the majority, stated:

Here not only is it apparent that appellant's declared ineligibility for benefits derives solely from the practice of her religion, but the pressure upon her to forego that practice is unmistakable. The ruling forces her to choose between following the precepts of her religion and forfeiting benefits, on the one hand, and abandoning one of the precepts of her religion in order to accept work, on the other hand. Governmental imposition of such a choice puts the same kind of burden upon the free exercise of religion as would a fine imposed against appellant for her Saturday worship.

The Court noted further that South Carolina law expressly saves the Sunday worshipper from penalties or from discrimination because of refusal, based on his religion, to work on Sunday. "The unconstitutionality of the disqualification of the Sabbatarian is thus compounded by the religious discrimination which South Carolina's general statutory scheme necessarily effects." The Court could find no strong state interest in enforcing the eligibility provisions against the claim of free exercise of religion. To this extent it found the state interest asserted "is wholly dissimilar to the interests which were found to justify the less direct burden upon religious practices in *Braunfeld* v. *Brown,*" namely, the provision of one uniform day of rest for all workers.

Justice Stewart concurred, but he stated that he did not see how the decision could be reconciled with that in *Braunfeld* v. *Brown,* since in both cases the state forced the citizen to make a choice between his religion and his economic welfare. Justice Harlan dissented, joined by Justice White, on the ground that Mrs. Sherbert's denial of benefits was no different from that of "any other claimant . . . denied benefits who was not 'available for work' for personal reasons." Justice Harlan also stated that the decision was inconsistent with that in *Braunfeld* v. *Brown.*

The Connecticut legislature decided to take a direct approach to the problem of Sabbath observance and employment and in 1976 passed a statute that provided: "No person who states that a particular day of the week is observed as his Sabbath may be required by his employer to work on such day. An employee's refusal to work on his Sabbath shall not constitute grounds for his dismissal." An employee of Calder, Inc., refused to work on Sunday and rejected an offer to transfer him to another store that was closed on Sunday. When he was transferred to another position at a lower salary, he resigned and filed a grievance with the State Board of Mediation and Arbitration alleging a violation of the statute. In *Thornton* v. *Caldor,* 472 U.S. 703 (1985), the Court held that the statute, by providing Sabbath observers with an absolute and unqualified right not to work on their chosen Sabbath, violated the Establishment Clause by impermissibly advancing a particular religious practice. Thus it would seem that the employee does not have a right not to be discharged for refusing to work on his Sabbath, but the State cannot deny him unemployment compensation if he is so discharged.

Although the case did not involve a Sabbatarian, in *Thomas* v. *Review Board,* 450 U.S. 707 (1981), the Court applied the rule of *Sherbert* to overturn a denial of unemployment benefits for a Jehovah's Witness who terminated his job because his religious beliefs forbade participation in the production of armaments. He was employed in a foundry which produced sheet steel. Subsequently the foundry closed and he was transferred to another department which produced turrets for military tanks. His request to be laid off was denied, and he quit his job. The Indiana Supreme Court held that his resignation did not suffice as "good cause" under the unemployment compensation statute, but the United States Supreme Court reversed, holding that "the coercive impact on Thomas is indistinguishable from *Sherbert.*"

The Civil Rights Act of 1964 prohibited employers from discriminating against employees on the basis of religion. Administrative regulations, as well as a 1972 amendment to the Act, require that employers, however, make "reasonable accommodations" to religious needs of employees so long as the accommodations do not impose undue hardship on the operation of the business.

### Religious Oaths—Conscientious Objectors

Whatever may be the constitutional status of formal governmental religious declarations or practices (as in the mottoes on coins or the religious exercises in governmental ceremonies), it is clear that when government requires an affirmation of religious belief, it oversteps the bounds of the Constitution. Article VI states that "no religious test shall ever be required as a qualification to any office or public trust under the United States." And in 1961 the Court held that the First and Fourteenth Amendments imposed a similar prohibition on States. The case was *Torcaso* v. *Watkins,* 367 U.S. 488 (1961), involving a Maryland constitutional provision requiring a belief in God as a qualification for holding public office. Citing *Everson* v. *Board of Education,* the Court held: "We repeat and again reaffirm that neither a State nor the Federal Government can constitutionally force a person 'to profess a belief or disbelief in any religion.' " It was also pointed out that "Among religions in this country which do not teach what would generally be considered a belief in the existence of God are Buddhism, Taoism, Ethical Culture, Secular Humanism and others."

Several of the justices in *United States* v. *Ballard* and the *Sunday Law Cases* and *Sherbert* v. *Verner* referred to the delicate ground of governmental inquiry into religious beliefs. *Torcaso* v. *Watkins* held that government may not condition office holding on the affirmation of a belief in the existence of God. A related problem is presented in the draft law exemption granted by statute to conscientious objectors. The constitutional issue of forcing one to perform military service against his religious convictions has not squarely arisen because of the exemption provided in all national conscription laws since the first one in 1917. But draft boards have been faced with the problems of applying the exemptions to claimant conscientious objectors. In so doing, they inquired into the beliefs of the claimant for exemption and the evidence indicating the tenacity with which he held to the principle of nonviolence—for example, whether he acquired his convictions before or after the outbreak of hostilities. Obviously the claimant cannot be given exemption merely for the asking, and the Court has held, in *Dickinson* v. *United States,* 346 U.S. 389 (1953), that the claim of ministerial exemption is subject to judicial review. A number of cases have reached the Supreme Court since World War II dealing with both the exemption from combatant service for conscientious objectors and the exemption for ordained ministers. In general the cases have dealt with either statutory construction or with the fairness of administrative procedures or findings. [For a collection of the cases dealing with conscientious objectors through 1964, see Annotation, "Who is Entitled to Exemption as a Conscientious Objector Within the Universal Military Training and Service Act," 13 L Ed 2d 1186.]

An interesting aspect of the problem was presented in *United States* v. *Seeger,* 380 U.S. 163 (1965), a consolidated group of cases which treats comprehensively the background of legislation as to conscientious objectors. The cases raised the question of the constitutionality, under the First Amendment, of the section of the Universal Military Training and Service Act which defines the term "religious training and belief" (for purposes of the exemption) as "an individual's belief in a relation to a Supreme Being involving duties superior to those arising from any human relation, but [not including] essentially political, sociological, or a merely personal moral code." Seeger stated that he was conscientiously opposed to war in any form by reason of his "religious" belief, but preferred to leave open the question as to his belief in a Supreme Being. He stated further that his was a "belief in and devotion to goodness and virtue for their own sakes, and a religious faith in a purely ethical creed," without belief in God, "except in the remotest sense." His belief was found to be sincere and made in good faith. He was classified 1-A and ordered to report for induction into the armed forces. Upon refusal he was tried and convicted for refusal to submit to induction. The court of appeals reversed, and the government sought review on writ of certiorari. In another of the cases Forest Peter was convicted in a federal district court in California on a charge of refusing to submit to induction. He had stated that he was not a member of a religious sect or organization, but that he conscientiously objected to war, and felt it a violation of his moral code to take human life. As to whether his conviction was religious, he quoted with approval the Reverend John Holmes' definition of a religion as "the consciousness of some power manifest in nature which helps man in the ordering of his life in harmony with its demands . . . ; it is man thinking his highest, feeling his deepest, and living his best." As to his belief in a Supreme Being, Peter stated that he supposed "you could call that a belief in the Supreme Being or God. These just do not happen to be the words I use." He was classified 1-A, convicted for failure to report for induction, and the court of appeals affirmed.

The United States Supreme Court unanimously affirmed the reversal of Seeger's conviction and reversed the conviction of Peter, without, however, reaching the constitutional issues raised. The Court concluded that the statutory purpose, in using the expression "Supreme Being" rather than the designation "God," was merely clarifying the meaning of religious training and belief so as to embrace all religions and to exclude essentially political, sociological, or philosophical views." Justice Clark, for the Court, then formulated the appropriate test: "We believe that under this construction, the test of belief 'in a relation to a Supreme Being' is whether a given belief that is sincere and meaningful occupies a place in the life of its possessor parallel to that filled by the orthodox belief in God of one who clearly qualifies for the exemption." He said further, "This construction avoids imputing to Congress an intent to classify different religious beliefs, exempting some and excluding others, and is in accord with the well-established congressional policy of equal treatment for those whose opposition to service is grounded in their religious tenets." In support of the construction given the Act, various theological authorities and even the Schema of the recent Ecumenical Council were cited to indicate the "ever-broadening understanding of the modern religious community." [See Francis Heisler, "The Law versus the Conscientious Objector," 20 U. Chi. L. Rev. 441 (1953); Selective Service System, Conscientious Objection (Special Monograph No. 11, 1950); and J. D. Tietz, "Jehovah's Witnesses: Conscientious Objectors," 28 So. Calif. L. Rev. 123 (1955).]

Several conscientious objector cases of note were decided in 1970 and 1971. Welsh v. United States, 398 U.S. 333 (1970) involved a draft registrant's application for exemption based on his conscientious scruples against participating in any war and on his belief that killing was morally wrong, but he stated that his views were not "religious" in the traditional sense. The application was denied, and he was convicted of refusing to submit to induction. The Supreme Court reversed the conviction, with five members agreeing that the proper test was whether the opposition to war stemmed from moral, ethical, or religious beliefs about what was right and wrong, and whether such beliefs were held with the strength of traditional convictions.

In *Gillette* v. *United States,* 401 U.S. 437 (1971), however, the Court held that the statutory conscientious objector status did not have to be accorded one who objects to the Vietnam War, but not to participation in a war of national defense or a war sponsored by the United Nations as a peacekeeping measure.

In *Clay (Ali)* v. *United States,* 403 U.S. 698 (1971), the Court reversed the conviction of Muhammad Ali for willful refusal to submit to induction. The *per curiam* opinion stated: "In order to qualify for classification as a conscientious objector, a registrant must satisfy three basic tests. He must show that he is conscientiously opposed to war in any form. *Gillette* v. *United States.* . . . He must show that this opposition is based upon religious training and belief, as the term has been construed in our decisions. *United States* v. *Seeger,* . . . *Welsh* v. *United States.* . . . And he must show that this objection is sincere." The Court found that Ali's case satisfied all three tests and that the conviction must be reversed.

In *Mulloy* v. *United States,* 398 U.S. 410 (1970), the Court held unanimously that when a local draft board is presented with a nonfrivolous, prima facie claim for a change in classification based on new factual allegations which were not conclusively refuted by other information in the registrant's file, the board's refusal to reopen the classification, thereby depriving the registrant of his right to an administrative appeal, constituted an abuse of discretion, rendering invalid a subsequent order to report for induction, and requiring reversal of a conviction for refusal to submit to induction.

In *Johnson* v. *Robinson,* 415 U.S. 361 (1974), the Court held that one who is exempted from military service as a conscientious objector, but who meets the statutory obligation by engaging in "alternative civilian service" can be denied educational benefits under the Veterans Act of 1966 without violation of the free exercise of religion clause.

It should be noted that the various exemption provisions deal with induction into the military, and do not excuse covered categories from the requirement of registering for the draft. Failure to register as required by law can lead to criminal prosecution. During the Vietnam conflict numbers of persons fled the country to avoid either registration or induction and thus were subject to prosecution if apprehended. In 1977 President Carter fulfilled a clear promise made during the election campaign and granted amnesty to draft-evaders of the Vietnam War. But in *Selective Service System* v. *Minnesota Public Interest Research Group,* 468 U.S. 841 (1984), the Court upheld a provision of the Department of Defense Authorization Act of 1983 which denied federal financial assistance under the Higher Education Act of 1965 to male students between the ages of eighteen and twenty-six who failed to register for the draft. The majority held that the provision was neither a bill of attainder nor a violation of the privilege against self-incrimination.

### Compulsory Public Education Laws and Religious Freedom

Aside from the Bible and prayer cases, which presented establishment issues primarily, and the flag salute controversy, two additional areas of conflict between educational policy and religious freedom should be noted. The first issue involved the attempt by a State to require all children to attend *public* schools through the eighth grade despite parental preference to send children to private sectarian elementary schools. The second issue was a challenge to a compulsory school law, brought by members of the Amish religion, contending that the requirement of school attendance beyond the eighth grade violated their religious principles.

An Oregon school law, adopted in 1922, required that persons having custody of children between the ages of eight and sixteen send the children to a *public* school, and failure to do so was declared a misdemeanor. In *Pierce* v. *Society of Sisters,* 268 U.S. 510 (1925), the Court held the law to be unconstitutional under the due process clause of the Fourteenth Amendment. Justice McReynolds stated:

No question is raised concerning the power of the state reasonably to regulate all schools, to inspect, supervise, and examine them, their teachers and pupils; to require that all children of proper age attend some school, that teachers shall be of good moral character and patriotic disposition, that certain studies plainly essential to good citizenship must be taught, and that nothing be taught which is manifestly inimical to the public welfare. . . .

[W]e think it entirely plain that the Act of 1922 unreasonably interferes with the liberty of parents and guardians to direct the upbringing and education of children under their control. As often heretofore pointed out, rights guaranteed by the Constitution may not be abridged by legislation which has no reasonable relation to some purpose within the competency of the state. The fundamental theory of liberty upon which all governments in this Union repose excludes any general power of the State to standardize its children by forcing them to accept instruction from public teachers only. . . .

As Justice McReynolds pointed out, *Pierce* held only that the State could not constitutionally prohibit parents from sending their children to a nonpublic school. It can require all children (with special exceptions) to attend *some* school through a specified grade or until reaching a specified age. And although *Pierce* offers substantial protections to the continued operation of the private school, the State clearly has the power to demand minimum standards in such schools, such as curriculum approval and teacher accreditation, if the private schools are to be allowed as alternatives to the public schools.

## WISCONSIN *v.* YODER
### 406 U.S. 205 (1972)

[Members of the Old Order Amish religion and the Conservative Amish Mennonite Church declined to send their children to school after they completed the eighth grade, although Wisconsin's school attendance law required attendance until the age of sixteen was reached. The parents were convicted of violation of the law and were fined five dollars. The law was challenged as a violation of the parents' and children's free exercise of religion. The Wisconsin Supreme Court reversed.]

Mr. Chief Justice Burger delivered the opinion of the Court. . . .

Amish objection to formal education beyond the eighth grade is firmly grounded in . . . religious concepts. They object to the high school, and higher education generally, because the values they teach are in marked variance with the Amish values and the Amish way of life; they view secondary school education as an impermissible exposure of their children to a "worldly" influence in conflict with their beliefs. The high school tends to emphasize intellectual and scientific accomplishments, self-distinction, competitiveness, worldly success, and social life with other students. Amish society emphasizes informal learning-through-doing; a life of "goodness," rather than a life of intellect; wisdom, rather than technical knowledge; community welfare, rather than competition; and separation from, rather than integration with, contemporary worldly society.

Formal high school education beyond the eighth grade is contrary to Amish beliefs, not only because it places Amish children in an environment hostile to Amish beliefs with increasing emphasis on competition in class work and sports and with pressure to conform to the styles, manners, and ways of the peer group, but also because it takes them away from their community, physically and emotionally, during the crucial and formative adolescent period of life. During this period, the children must acquire Amish attitudes favoring manual work and self-reliance and the specific skills needed to perform the adult role of an Amish farmer or housewife. . . . And, at this time in life, the Amish child must also grow in his faith and his relationship to the Amish community if he is to be prepared to accept the heavy obligations imposed by adult baptism. In short, high school attendance with teachers who are not of the Amish faith—and may even be hostile to it—interposes a serious barrier to the integration of the Amish child into the Amish religious community. . . .

The Amish do not object to elementary education through the first eight grades as a general proposition because they agree that their children must have basic skills in the "three R's" in order to read the Bible, to be good farmers and citizens, and to be able to deal with non-Amish people when necessary in the course of daily affairs. . . .

There is no doubt as to the power of a State, having a high responsibility for education of its citizens, to impose reasonable regulations for the control and duration of basic education. . . . Yet even this paramount responsibility was, in *Pierce,* made to yield to the right of parents to provide an equivalent education in a privately operated system. . . . Thus, a State's interest in universal education, however highly we rank it, is not totally free from a balancing process when it impinges on fundamental rights and interests, such as those specifically protected by the Free Exercise Clause of the First Amendment, and the traditional interest of parents with respect to the religious upbringing of their children so long as they, in the words of *Pierce,* "prepare [them] for additional obligations."

It follows that in order for Wisconsin to compel school attendance beyond the eighth grade against a claim that such attendance interferes with the practice of a legitimate religious belief, it must appear either that the State does not deny the free exercise of religious belief by its requirement, or that there is a state interest of sufficient magnitude to override the interest claiming protection under the Free Exercise Clause. . . .

The conclusion is inescapable that secondary schooling, by exposing Amish children to worldly influences in terms of attitudes, goals, and values contrary to beliefs, and by substantially interfering with the religious development of the Amish child and his integration into the way of life of the Amish faith community at the crucial adolescent stage of development, contravenes the basic religious tenets and practice of the Amish faith, both as to the parent and the child.

The impact of the compulsory-attendance law on respondents' practice of the Amish religion is not only severe, but inescapable, for the Wisconsin law affirmatively compels them, under threat of criminal sanction, to perform acts undeniably at odds with fundamental tenets of their religious beliefs. . . .

We turn, then, to the State's broader contention that its interest in its system of compulsory education is so compelling that even the established religious practices of the Amish must give way. . . .

The State advances two primary arguments in support of its system of compulsory education. It notes . . . that some degree of education is necessary to prepare citizens to participate effectively and intelligently in our open political system if we are to preserve freedom and independence. Further, education prepares individuals to be self-reliant and self-sufficient participants in society. We accept these propositions.

However, the evidence adduced by the Amish in this case is persuasively to the effect that an additional one or two years of formal high school for Amish children in place of their long-established program of informal vocational education would do little to serve those interests. . . . It is one thing to say that compulsory education for a year or two beyond the eighth grade may be necessary when its goal is the preparation of the child for life in modern society as the majority live, but it is quite another if the goal of education be viewed as the preparation of the child for life in the separated agrarian community that is the keystone of the Amish faith. . . .

The State attacks respondents' position as one fostering "ignorance" from which the child must be protected by the State. No one can question the State's duty to protect children from ignorance but this argument does not square with the facts disclosed in the record. Whatever their idiosyncrasies as seen by the majority, this record strongly shows that the Amish community has been a highly successful social unit within our society, even if apart from the conventional "mainstream." Its members are productive and very law-abiding members of society; they reject public welfare in any of its usual modern forms. The Congress itself recognized their self-sufficiency by authorizing exemption of such groups as the Amish from the obligation to pay social security taxes.

It is neither fair nor correct to suggest that the Amish are opposed to education beyond the eighth grade level. . . . To the contrary, not only do the Amish accept the necessity for formal schooling through the eighth grade level, but continue to provide what has been characterized by the undisputed testimony of expert educators as a "ideal" vocational education for their children in the adolescent years. There is nothing in this record to suggest that the Amish qualities of reliability, self-reliance, and dedication to work would fail to find ready markets in today's society. Absent some contrary evidence supporting the State's position, we are unwilling to assume that persons possessing such valuable vocational skills and habits are doomed to become burdens on society should they determine to leave the Amish faith. . . .

Insofar as the State's claim rests on the view that a brief additional period of formal education is imperative to enable the Amish to participate effectively and intelligently in our democratic process, it must fall. . . . When Thomas Jefferson emphasized the need for education as a bulwark of a free people against tyranny, there is nothing to indicate he had in mind compulsory education through any fixed age beyond a basic education. Indeed, the Amish communities singularly parallel and reflect many of the virtues of Jefferson's ideal of the "sturdy yeoman" who would form the basis of what he considered as the ideal of a democratic society. Even their idiosyncratic separateness exemplifies the diversity we profess to admire and encourage. . . .

For the reasons stated we hold, with the Supreme Court of Wisconsin, that the First and Fourteenth Amendments prevent the State from compelling respondents to cause their children to attend formal high school to age 16. . . .

Nothing we hold is intended to undermine the general applicability of the State's compulsory school-attendance statutes or to limit the power of the State to promulgate reasonable standards that, while not impairing the free exercise of religion, provide for continuing agricultural vocational education under parental and church guidance by the Old Order Amish or others similarly situated. . . .

*Affirmed.*

Mr. Justice Powell and Mr. Justice Rehnquist took no part in the consideration or decision of this case.

Mr. Justice Stewart, with whom Mr. Justice Brennan joins, concurring. . . .

Mr. Justice White, with whom Mr. Justice Brennan and Mr. Justice Stewart join, concurring. . . .

Mr. Justice Douglas, dissenting in part. . . .

On this important and vital matter of education, I think the children should be entitled to be heard. While the parents, absent dissent, normally speak for the entire family, the education of the child is a matter on which the child will often have decided views. He may want to be a pianist or an astronaut or an oceanographer. To do so he will have to break from the Amish tradition.

It is the future of the student, not the future of the parents, that is imperiled by today's decision. If a parent keeps his child out of school beyond the grade school, then the child will be forever barred from entry into the new and amazing world of diversity that we have today. The child may decide that that is the preferred course, or he may rebel. It is the student's judgment, not his parents', that is essential if we are to give full meaning to what we have said about the Bill of Rights and of the right of students to be masters of their own destiny. If he is harnessed to the Amish way of life by those in authority over him and if his education is truncated, his entire life may be stunted and deformed. The child, therefore, should be given an opportunity to be heard before the State gives the exemption which we honor today. . . .

[For a detailed treatment of the *Yoder* case, see Richard Cortner, *The Supreme Court and Civil Liberties Policy* (Palo Alto: Mayfield, 1975), pp. 153–182.]

## Prior Restraints on the Free Exercise of Religion

In many of the previous free exercise cases the judicial approach has been to make a determination of the interest the state may have in maintaining a specific policy and the kind and degree of restraint on the individual's exercise of religion. To say, therefore, that the individual may practice his religion freely so long as he does not violate the criminal laws of the state is too facile a generalization. If the statement were true as given, then no interference which took the form of a penal statute would violate the guarantee of religious freedom. The crux of the problem is the determination of whether the application of a criminal provision in a particular exercise of religion situation is an improper infringement of that exercise. And the weighing of interests involved in each separate fact situation can result in a decision either in favor of the claimed immunity or against it, depending on how a majority of the Court may view the weight of the state's and the individual's interests. Thus in *Reynolds* and *Prince* the Court upheld the application of criminal statutes barring polygamy and certain forms of child labor, respectively, against the claims of religious freedom. But in *West Virginia Board of Education* v. *Barnette* the Court held that to punish the parent and to expel the child who refused on religious grounds to salute the flag in public school exercises was violative of the constitutional protection to free exercise of religion. Whether a particular criminal law can constitutionally be applied to restrict religious exercise will turn on the kind and degree of interference and the value to the state of imposing the restraint.

There is one category of First Amendment restrictions, however, concerning which the Court has taken a virtually absolutist position—those laws or official practices which impose "prior restraints" on First Amendment freedoms. The theory here is that if a course of action is not *malum in se* or *malum prohibita* (is not, for example, in the category of human sacrifice or polygamy or forced child labor of certain kinds) then it is a violation of First Amendment guarantees to require permits or licenses as conditions of engaging in the religious activity. This is in essence the doctrine of "no previous restraints." It does not, of course, halt the application of the ordinary criminal provisions to the conduct of the participants. Delivering a religious sermon is not *per se* unlawful, but the time, the place, and the kind of language used may still be such as to justify criminal penalties. The point of the "no previous restraint" doctrine, however, is that one cannot be barred at the outset the right to participate in an ordinarily lawful religious exercise or have that right conditioned on obtaining a permit from some governmental official, unless issuance is nondiscretionary in nature. The first case to come to the United States Supreme Court involving the prior restraint doctrine as applied to religious freedom was *Cantwell* v. *Connecticut,* decided in 1940. It was also the case in which the Free Exercise Clause of the First Amendment was incorporated into the Fourteenth Amendment.

CANTWELL *v.* CONNECTICUT

*310 U.S. 296 (1940)*

Mr. Justice Roberts delivered the opinion of the Court.

Newton Cantwell and his two sons, Jessee and Russell, members of a group known as Jehovah's Witnesses, and claiming to be ordained ministers, were arrested in New Haven, Connecticut, and each was charged by information in five counts, with statutory and common-law offenses. After trial in the Court of Common Pleas of New Haven County each of them was convicted on the third count, which charged a violation of Section 6294 of the General Statutes of Connecticut, and on the fifth count, which charged commission of the common-law offenses of inciting a breach of the peace. . . .

The facts adduced to sustain the convictions on the third count follow. On the day of their arrest the appellants were engaged in going singly from house to house on Cassius Street in New Haven. They were individually equipped with a bag containing books and pamphlets on religious subjects, a portable phonograph and a set of records, each of which, when played, introduced, and was a description of, one of the books. Each appellant asked the person who responded to his call for permission to play one of the records. If permission was granted he asked the person to buy the book described and, upon refusal, he solicited such contribution towards the publication of the pamphlets as the listener was willing to make. If a contribution was received, a pamphlet was delivered upon condition that it would be read.

Cassius Street is in a thickly populated neighborhood, where about ninety per cent of the residents are Roman Catholics. A phonograph record, describing a book entitled "Enemies," included an attack on the Catholic religion. None of the persons interviewed were members of Jehovah's Witnesses.

The statute under which the appellants were charged provides:

"No person shall solicit money, services, subscriptions or any valuable thing for any alleged religious, charitable or philanthropic cause, from other than a member of the organization for whose benefit such person is soliciting or within the county in which such person or organization is located unless such cause shall have been approved by the secretary of the public welfare council. Upon application of any person in behalf of such cause, the secretary shall determine whether such cause is a religious one or is a bona fide object of charity or philanthropy and conforms to reasonable standards of efficiency and integrity, and, if he shall so find, shall approve the same and issue to the authority in charge a certificate to that effect. Such certificate may be revoked at any time. Any person violating any provision of this section shall be fined not more than one hundred dollars or imprisoned not more than thirty days or both."

The appellants claimed that their activities were not within the statute but consisted only of distribution of books, pamphlets, and periodicals. The State Supreme Court construed the finding of the trial court to be that "in addition to the sale of the books and the distribution of the pamphlets the defendants were also soliciting contributions or donations of money for an alleged religious cause, and thereby came within the purview of the statute." It overruled the contention that the Act, as applied to the appellants, offends the due process clause of the Fourteenth Amendment, because it abridges or denies religious freedom and liberty of speech and press. The court stated that it was the solicitation that brought the appellants within the sweep of the Act and not their other activities in the dissemination of literature. It declared the legislation constitutional as an effort by the State to protect the public against fraud and imposition in the solicitation of funds for what purported to be religious, charitable, or philanthropic causes. . . .

*First.* We hold that the statute, as construed and applied to the appellants, deprives them of their liberty without due process of law in contravention of the Fourteenth Amendment. The fundamental concept of liberty embodied in that Amendment embraces the liberties guaranteed by the First Amendment. . . . No one would contest the proposition that a State may not, by statute, wholly deny the right to preach or to disseminate religious views. Plainly such a previous and absolute restraint would violate the terms of the guarantee. It is equally clear that a State may by general and non-discriminatory legislation regulate the times, the places, and the manner of soliciting upon its streets, and of holding meeting thereon; and may in other respects safeguard the peace, good order and comfort of the community, without unconstitutionally invading the liberties protected by the Fourteenth Amendment. The appellants are right in their insistence that the Act in question is not such a regulation. If a certificate is procured, solicitation is permitted without restraint but, in the absence of a certificate, solicitation is altogether prohibited.

The appellants urge that to require them to obtain a certificate as a condition of soliciting support for their views amounts to a prior restraint on the exercise of their religion within the meaning of the Constitution. The State insists that the Act, as construed by the Supreme Court of Connecticut, imposes no previous restraint upon the dissemination of religious views or teaching but merely safeguards against the perpetration of frauds under the cloak of religion. Conceding that this is so, the question remains whether the method adopted by Connecticut to that end transgresses the liberty safeguarded by the Constitution.

The general regulation, in the public interest, of solicitation, which does not involve any religious test and does not unreasonably obstruct or delay the collection of funds, is not open to any constitutional objection, even though the collection be for a religious purpose. Such regulation would not constitute a prohibited previous restraint on the free exercise of religion or interpose an inadmissible obstacle to its exercise.

It will be noted, however, that the Act requires an application to the secretary of the public welfare council of the State; that he is empowered to determine whether the cause is a religious one, and that the issue of a certificate depends upon his affirmative action. If he finds that the cause is not that of religion, to solicit for it becomes a crime. He is not to issue a certificate as a matter of course. His decision to issue or refuse it involves appraisal of facts, the exercise of judgment, and the formation of an opinion. He is authorized to withhold his approval if he determines that the cause is not a religious one. Such a censorship of religion as the means of determining its right to survive is a denial of liberty protected by the First Amendment and included in the liberty which is within the protection of the Fourteenth.

Nothing we have said is intended even remotely to imply that, under the cloak of religion, persons may, with impunity, commit frauds upon the public. Certainly penal laws are available to punish such conduct. Even the exercise of religion may be at some slight inconvenience in order that the state may protect its citizens from injury. Without doubt a State may protect its citizens from fraudulent solicitation by requiring a stranger in the community, before permitting him publicly to solicit funds for any purpose, to establish his identity and his authority to act for the cause which he purports to represent. The State is likewise free to regulate the time and manner of solicitation generally, in the interest of public safety, peace, comfort or convenience. But to condition the solicitation of aid for the perpetuation of religious views or systems upon a license, the grant of which rests in the exercise of a determination by state authority as to what is a religious cause, is to lay a forbidden burden upon the exercise of liberty protected by the Constitution. . . .

*Reversed.*

It should be noted that the holding of *Cantwell* v. *Connecticut* reaches only those discretionary practices on the part of officials which would allow them to make distinctions between what is and what is not a religious cause. The Court did not hold that every requirement of obtaining a permit prior to embarking on religious solicitation would be unconstitutional. It did, however, point out that such requirements would have to be rather severely limited to such purposes as identification and notification in order to protect against fraud to escape the strictures of the First Amendment's protections to speech and religion.

In *Cox* v. *State of New Hampshire*, 312 U.S. 569 (1941), the Court reviewed a conviction of five Jehovah's Witnesses for violation of a statute prohibiting parades upon a public street without a special license. As construed by the state courts, the statute required prior application for a license and payment of a fee which was scaled according to a reasonable estimate of the expense of policing the particular parade. The statute was further construed as allowing no discretion in the licensing board except as necessity might dictate changes in time or route for such parades. The Court held the statute valid and found that it was administered in a fair and nondiscriminatory manner consistent with the requirements of the Constitution.

The issue of the validity of the fee requirement prior to parading was discussed separately in the *Cox* case and the requirement was upheld. The decision cannot be read, however, as supporting all license taxes on the exercise of First Amendment rights. The Court's discussion was confined to the problems of administering the municipal function of policing traffic in the public ways. Other types of religious exercise requiring no such special attention could be treated quite differently by the Court in dealing with license tax requirements. However, in the next year after *Cox*, the Court was faced with a challenge to a municipal ordinance which imposed a license tax on all persons who sold or canvassed for the sale of printed matter. There was no discrimination against sellers of religious literature; the license fee applied to all alike. Jehovah's Witnesses in Opelika, Alabama, raised the issue of abridgment of religious freedom in the application of such a fee requirement to their missionary efforts. In a five-to-four decision in *Jones* v. *Opelika,* 316 U.S. 584 (1942), the Court upheld the ordinance as applied to the Jehovah's Witnesses. The opinion for the majority stated that "The First Amendment does not require a subsidy in the form of fiscal exemption." This judgment was vacated in the following year, however, when in *Murdock* v. *Pennsylvania,* 319 U.S. 105 (1943), the Court reversed its position and held such fees unconstitutional as applied to the sale of religious literature. In this case Jehovah's Witnesses attacked the license requirement of the city of Jeannette, Pennsylvania. Justice Douglas, speaking for a majority of five, stated:

The hand distribution of religious tracts is an age-old form of missionary evangelism—as old as the history of printing presses. It has been a potent force in various religious movements down through the years. This form of evangelism is utilized today on a large scale by various religious sects whose colporteurs carry the Gospel to thousands upon thousands of homes and seek through personal visitations to win adherents to their faith. It is more than preaching; it is more than distribution of reli-

gious literature. It is a combination of both. Its purpose is as evangelical as the reviv-
al meeting. This form of religious activity occupies the same high estate under the
First Amendment as do worship in the churches and preaching from the pulpits. It
has the same claim to protection as the more orthodox and conventional exercises
of religion. It also has the same claim as the others to the guarantees of freedom of
speech and freedom of the press.

It was alleged in justification for the license fee that the religious literature was distributed with a solicitation of funds, and thus utilized ordinary commercial methods. Justice Douglas responded that the mere fact that the religious literature is "sold" by
itinerant preachers rather than "donated" does not transform evangelism into a commercial enterprise. "If it did, then the passing of the collection plate in church would
make the church service a commercial project. The constitutional rights of those
spreading their religious beliefs through the spoken and printed word are not to be
gauged by standards governing retailers or wholesalers of books." He stated further that
an itinerant evangelist does not become "a mere book agent by selling the Bible or religious tracts to help defray his expenses or to sustain him."

The Justice was careful to say, however, that he did not mean that religious groups
and the press are free from all financial burdens of government. Normal income taxes
or property taxes levied on one who engages in religious activities are a different matter.
But in this case, it was "a flat tax imposed on the exercise of a privilege granted by the
Bill of Rights," and therefore a prior restraint on the free exercise of religion.

The *Murdock* decision was followed in *Follett* v. *Town of McCormick,* 321 U.S. 573
(1944), invalidating a similar municipal tax imposed on a Jehovah's Witness who maintained his home in the municipality and who earned his living by means of the sale of
religious literature. [For discussions of some of the earlier Jehovah's Witnesses cases,
see Hollis W. Barber, "Religious Liberty v. Police Power—Jehovah's Witnesses," 41 *Am.
Pol. Sci. Rev.* 226 (1947); and Edward F. Waite, "The Debt of Constitutional Law to Jehovah's Witnesses," 28 *Minn. L. Rev.* 209 (1944).]

## Miscellaneous Free Exercise Issues

A qualified applicant sought a Nebraska driver's license but refused to have her photograph taken and affixed to the license as required by state law. Her application was denied, and she sued for relief, contending that the denial violated her First Amendment
right to the free exercise of religion.

Her refusal to be photographed was based on her religious conviction that it would
violate her literal interpretation of the Second Commandment: "Thou shalt not make
unto thee any graven image or likeness of anything that is in heaven above, or that is in
the earth beneath, or that is in the water under the earth." She was not a member of any
organized church but considered herself a Christian and attended church with her family. Her beliefs stemmed from her own study of the Bible. In *Quaring* v. *Peterson,* 728
F2d 1121 (CA 8, 1984), the Court of Appeals held the denial of the license violative of
the Free Exercise Clause. The majority opinion stated:

In this case, quick and accurate identification of motorists surely constitutes an
important state interest, but the court does not think that the interest is so compelling as to prohibit selective exemptions to the requirement. . . .

The state plainly has an interest in avoiding the administratively cumbersome task
of considering applications for religious exemptions, but its interest is not compelling. . . . This record contains no evidence that allowing religious exemptions will

jeopardize the state's administrative efficiency. Such persons are likely to be few in number.

In *Jenson* v. *Quaring,* 472 U.S. 478 (1985), the Supreme Court affirmed by an equally divided Court. (Justice Powell took no part in the decision.)

In *Goldman* v. *Weinberger,* 475 U.S. 503 (1986), the petitioner challenged on free exercise grounds, an Air Force regulation that barred him from wearing a yarmulke indoors while on duty. Goldman, an Orthodox Jew and ordained rabbi, was serving as a commissioned officer with the Air Force. An Air Force regulation provided that authorized headgear could be worn out of doors, but that indoors "[h]eadgear [may] not be worn . . . except by armed security police in the performance of their duties." He was ordered not to wear the yarmulke while on duty and in uniform, and he brought an action in Federal District Court claiming a violation of his First Amendment freedom to exercise his religious beliefs. The District Court permanently enjoined the Air Force from enforcing the regulation against Goldman, but the Court of Appeals reversed. In a 5–4 decision the Supreme Court affirmed. Justice Rehnquist, for the majority, stated:

> Our review of military regulations challenged on First Amendment grounds is far more deferential than constitutional review of similar laws or regulations designed for civilian society. The military need not encourage debate or tolerate protest to the extent that such tolerence is required of the civilian state by the First Amendment; to accomplish its mission the military must foster instinctive obedience, unity, commitment, and esprit de corps. . . .
>
> These aspects of military life do not, of course, render entirely nugatory in the military context the guarantees of the First Amendment. . . . But "within the military community there is simply not the same [individual] autonomy as there is in the larger civilian community." . . . The desirability of dress regulations in the military is decided by the appropriate military officials, and they are under no constitutional mandate to abandon their considered professional judgment. Quite obviously, to the extent the regulations do not permit the wearing of religious apparel such as a yarmulke, a practice described by petitioner as silent devotion akin to prayer, military life may be more objectionable for petitioner and probably others. But the First Amendment does not require the military to accommodate such practices in the face of its view that they would detract from the uniformity sought by the dress regulations. The Air Force has drawn the line essentially between religious apparel which is visible and that which is not, and we hold that those portions of the regulations challenged here reasonably and evenhandedly regulate dress in the interest of the military's perceived need for uniformity. The First Amendment therefore does not prohibit them from being applied to petitioner even though their effect is to restrict the wearing of the headgear required by his religious beliefs.

The dissenters argued that no such absolute deference to the military was necessary, and that the exemption for Goldman would present no substantial danger to discipline that would override his sincere attempt at religious exercise.

*Bowen* v. *Roy,* 476 U.S. 693 (1986), involved a federal statutory requirement that recipients of benefits under the Aid to Families with Dependent Children (AFDC) program and the Food Stamp program furnish their Social Security numbers and those of each member of their household as a condition of receiving benefits. The appellees had their benefits terminated when they refused to provide a Social Security number for their two-year old daughter. Roy was a Native American, and he contended that he had a religious objection to obtaining a Social Security number for the daughter, Little Bird of the Snow. In testimony before a Federal District Court he argued that in order to prepare his daughter for greater spiritual power, he felt that he must keep her person and spirit unique, and that the uniqueness of the Social Security number, coupled with the other uses of the number, would serve to "rob the spirit" of his daughter and prevent her from attaining greater spiritual power.

The Court held that the requirement does not violate the Free Exercise Clause. The requirement "is wholly neutral in religious terms and uniformly applicable," and clearly promotes a legitimate and important public interest—preventing fraud in these benefit programs.

In *Wisconsin* v. *Yoder*, discussed earlier, the Court held that Wisconsin's compulsory education law, as applied to members of the Amish sect, was violative of the Free Exercise Clause. But in *United States* v. *Lee*, 455 U.S. 252 (1982), the Court upheld the Social Security Act against a similar challenge. Lee, a carpenter and farmer, was a member of the Old Order Amish, which believe that there is a religiously based obligation to provide for their fellow members the kind of assistance comtemplated by the social security system. He employed other Amish on his farm and in his carpenter shop during several years and failed to withhold social security taxes from the employees or to pay the employer's taxes because he believed that payment of the taxes and receipt of benefits would violate the Amish faith. The Social Security Act provides an exemption for self-employed individuals who are members of a religious sect conscientiously opposed to acceptance of the benefits of private or public insurance programs, but it does not exempt employers and employees from its provisions. A Federal District Court held that the Act violated Lee's free exercise of religion. The Supreme Court unanimously reversed. Chief Justice Burger, for the Court, recognized that there was a conflict between the Amish faith and the obligations imposed by the social security system, but "The state may justify a limitation on religious liberty by showing that it is essential to accomplish an overriding governmental interest." Widespread individual voluntary coverage under social security would undermine the soundness of the social security system, and would make the system almost a contradiction in terms and difficult, if not impossible to administer. "Unlike the situation presented in *Wisconsin* v. *Yoder*, it would be difficult to accommodate the comprehensive social security system with myriad exceptions flowing from a wide variety of religious beliefs." Further, Congress has accommodated, to the extent compatible with a comprehensive national program, the practices of those who on religious grounds object to the system by exempting such persons from the tax on self-employed persons.

# CHAPTER 5

# *Freedom of Speech, Press, and Assembly*

The freedoms of speech, press, and assembly occupy a peculiar position relative to the democratic process, and one shared only by the various aspects of the right to participate in elections. Trial by jury, freedom from self-incrimination, and the right to counsel are assuredly important procedural guarantees against arbitrary deprivation of life and liberty. But the democratic process could be maintained even if these guarantees were changed. The First Amendment guarantees freedom from establishment of religion, and there is apparently widespread approval of this policy in the United States. But a change to some specific established church in this nation would have no necessary impact on the characterization of the United States as a democratic nation. England has an established church and yet is clearly democratic by the usual procedural standards. To restrict substantially the rights of speech, press, assembly, and voting, however, is to cut the arteries that feed the heart of the democratic model. However one may choose to define democracy, the list of characteristics must include at least certain minimal procedural features: widespread adult suffrage, reasonably frequent elections, reasonable access to the ballot on the part of candidates, popular selection of major policy-making officials, and decision by majority rule. Those rights which are necessary to ensure free interchange of ideas and to guarantee that a continuing and shifting majority may be arrived at freely would certainly seem to be in a special category in terms of constitutional immunity. The most important institutions for the preservation of the democratic process are those which safeguard the opportunity for the reversal of the public policy if a sufficient majority demands it. The important rights in this category would be access to the ballot, both as a voter and as a candidate, and the freedoms of speech, press, and assembly. Serious inroads on the exercise of any of these rights may result in a corresponding curtailment of the ease with which public policy can be changed, even though a majority may desire the change. Thus while encroachments on other types of personal rights might be inconvenient or even obnoxious, the dangers to democratic form must be considerably less as long as the channels for formulating public opinion and focusing majority demands remain open. It is this general proposition which accounts for the apparently paradoxical position in which many champions of personal liberties find themselves with respect to treatment of Communists in the United States. Free speech and association are vital in a democracy, but some restraints even on these must be permitted if there is a real danger that the group using them to gain political power will close off the channels and institutions by which reversal of policy can be accomplished by majority demand.

The conclusion that certain rights guaranteed in the Constitution are in a special position in a democracy is not drawn from any specific phraseology of the Constitution. It is derived logically from the assumption that the democratic system is the appropriate organizational scheme for a reasonably educated society but one in which knowledge will always be incomplete. The channels of communication, of receiving new information, and of persuasion, and the institutions for legally influencing the determination of public policy deserve special care if the democratic model is to function according to blueprint. Such a view is somewhat akin to the "preferred position" doctrine which for a time enjoyed considerable publicity in the opinions of the Court. That doctrine, however, was squarely tied to the First Amendment in its entirety and was never extended to cover voting rights as well, as does the statement here.

## THE SCOPE OF THE RIGHTS

The words "speech, press, and assembly" have certain obvious connotations which have required no special analysis to fit them under the First Amendment coverage of these words. A candidate's speech requesting votes, the publication of books and newspapers, and a meeting to discuss public questions are clearly within the scope of application of the First Amendment. Certain other aspects of these words have, however, been less clearly subsumed under the proper interpretation of the bare phraseology of the First Amendment, and their addition has been slower and somewhat more controversial. Probably the best illustration of this slow expansion of the scope of the rights is in the position of motion pictures under the First Amendment. The question of whether commercial movies were entitled to constitutional protection as speech and press first reached the Supreme Court in 1915, in *Mutual Film Corporation* v. *Industrial Commission*, 236 U.S. 230. The Court in that case held that the exhibition of motion pictures was a "business pure and simple, originated and conducted for profit like other spectacles, not to be regarded, nor intended to be regarded by the Ohio Constitution . . . as part of the press of the country or as organs of public opinion." This view held until 1952, when the Court overruled that portion of the *Mutual Film Corporation* decision in *Burstyn* v. *Wilson*, 343 U.S. 495. The court stated squarely in the latter case that the "liberty of expression by means of motion pictures is guaranteed by the First and Fourteenth Amendments."

In 1940 the Court held that picketing of a plant in the course of a labor dispute came within the meaning of "speech" in the First Amendment. The case was *Thornhill* v. *Alabama*, 310 U.S. 88, and the opinion for a nearly unanimous Court stated:

> In the circumstances of our times the dissemination of information concerning the facts of a labor dispute must be regarded as within that area of free discussion that is guaranteed by the Constitution. . . . The range of activities proscribed by Section 3448, whether characterized as picketing or loitering or otherwise, embraces nearly every practicable, effective means whereby those interested—including the employees directly affected—may enlighten the public on the nature and causes of a labor dispute. The safeguarding of these means is essential to the securing of an informed and educated public opinion with respect to a matter which is of public concern.

In *Cox* v. *State of New Hampshire*, 312 U.S. 569 (1941), the Court made the logical extension from *Thornhill* and accepted the view that parades could be properly brought under the rubric of speech and assembly protected by the Constitution.

The "press" protected by the First Amendment extends to handbills and circulars, as well as the standard forms of books and magazines and newspapers. As the Court stated in *Lovell* v. *Griffin*, 303 U.S. 444 (1938):

> The liberty of the press is not confined to newspapers and periodicals. It necessarily embraces pamphlets and leaflets. These indeed have been historic weapons in the

defense of liberty, as the pamphlets of Thomas Paine and others in our own history abundantly attest. The press in its historic connotation comprehends every sort of publication which affords a vehicle of information and opinion.

The Court has also accorded "symbolic" speech First Amendment protection. This approach was followed with respect to "sit-in" demonstrations protesting racial segregation in *Garner* v. *Louisiana,* 368 U.S. 157 (1961), the wearing of black armbands by public school students protesting the Vietnam War in *Tinker* v. *Des Moines School District,* 393 U.S. 503 (1969), and displaying the American flag upside down with a peace symbol attached in *Spence* v. *Washington,* 418 U.S. 405 (1974).

Nor has the Court ignored the impact of technological developments on the traditional forms of speech and press. As indicated earlier, in 1952 it held that movies were a form of expression guaranteed by the First and Fourteenth Amendments. And in 1948, in *Saia* v. *New York,* 334 U.S. 558, the Court held that the use of amplifying systems in delivering speeches did not take them out of the area of protection of the First Amendment. Justice Douglas stated for the Court, "Loud-speakers are today indispensable instruments of effective public speech. The sound truck has become an accepted method of political campaigning. It is the way people are reached."

Finally, the right of assembly has been expanded beyond the simple concept of a physical assemblage to include the even more significant right of association. In *NAACP* v. *Alabama,* 357 U.S. 449 (1958), Justice Harlan, speaking for a unanimous Court, stated:

Effective advocacy of both public and private points of view, particularly controversial ones, is undeniably enhanced by group association, as this Court has more than once recognized by remarking upon the close nexus between the freedoms of speech and assembly. . . . It is beyond debate that freedom to engage in association for the advancement of beliefs and ideas is an inseparable aspect of the "liberty" assured by the Due Process Clause of the Fourteenth Amendment, which embraces freedom of speech.

Even these few cases illustrate the breadth which the Court is willing to accord to the words of the First Amendment. The words "speech," "press," and "assembly" are not applied in coldly formalistic fashion. Instead, it is the substance of the rights which is examined and their importance in a free democratic system. Thus, as Justice Harlan put it in the NAACP case, what the First Amendment protects is "effective advocacy of both public and private points of view." To introduce novel vehicles of expression, then, is merely to change the angle from which resulting problems of reconciliation might be viewed; it is not to step outside the First Amendment's scope of application.

As has already been discussed, the rights guaranteed by the First Amendment are explicitly guaranteed against abridgment by Congress. It has also been noted that over the past several decades the Court has, through a succession of decisions, gradually "incorporated" these same rights into the liberties which the due process clause of the Fourteenth Amendment protects against invasion by the state. In the area of First Amendment rights, then, it is usually safe to use First Amendment cases and Fourteenth Amendment cases interchangeably in discussing the validity of restrictions placed by government—whether state or federal—on the exercise of those rights. The process of "incorporation" began with *Gitlow* v. *New York,* 268 U.S. 652 (1925). Benjamin Gitlow was indicted in the supreme court of New York for the crime of criminal anarchy, as defined by statute. His conviction was affirmed by the New York appellate courts. The case was taken on writ of error to the United States Supreme Court under the contention that the statute was repugnant to the due process clause of the Fourteenth Amendment. The Court affirmed the judgment of the New York Court of Appeals, but on the issue of whether a state law unduly restrictive of freedom of speech and press could be held to violate the Fourteenth Amendment the Court gave, almost casually, one of its most momentous decisions. Justice Sanford, for the Court, said, "For present purposes we may and do assume that freedom of speech and of the press—which are protected by the First Amendment from abridgment by Congress—are among the fundamental personal rights and liberties protected by the due process clause of the Fourteenth Amendment from impairment by the States." With such a modest statement did the Court begin the vastly important process of "incorporation" of the First Amendment rights into the Fourteenth Amendment's "liberty" safeguarded by the concept of due process of law.

Freedom of the press was officially incorporated in *Near v. Minnesota*, 283 U.S. 697 (1931), in which the Court held that an injunction against future publications of a periodical because past issues had contained "malicious, scandalous and defamatory" matter was an unconstitutional prior restraint. Chief Justice Hughes, for the majority, stated: "It is no longer open to doubt that the liberty of the press and of speech is within the liberty safeguarded by the due process clause of the Fourteenth Amendment from invasion by state action."

Freedom of assembly, the third of the rights covered in this chapter, was brought under the protection of the Fourteenth Amendment's due process clause in 1937 in *De Jonge v. Oregon*, 229 U.S. 353. The appellant in that case was indicted for violation of the Criminal Syndicalism Law of Oregon, was found guilty as charged, and was sentenced to imprisonment for seven years. The law defined "criminal syndicalism" as "the doctrine which advocates crime, physical violence, sabotage or any unlawful acts or methods as a means of accomplishing or effecting industrial or political change or revolution." The charge was that De Jonge assisted in the conduct of a meeting called under the auspices of the Communist Party. The defense contended that the meeting was lawful, orderly, and public, and that no unlawful conduct was taught or advocated at the meeting. In holding the Fourteenth Amendment applicable to assemblies, as well as to speech and press, the Court, through Chief Justice Hughes, first cited *Gitlow v. New York*. The opinion then stated:

> Freedom of speech and of the press are fundamental rights which are safeguarded by the due process clause of the Fourteenth Amendment of the Federal Constitution. . . . The right of peaceable assembly is a right cognate to those of free speech and free press and is equally fundamental. . . . The First Amendment of the Federal Constitution expressly guarantees that right against abridgment by Congress. But explicit mention there does not argue exclusion elsewhere. For the right is one that cannot be denied without violating those fundamental principles of liberty and justice which lie at the base of all civil and political institutions,—principles which the Fourteenth Amendment embodies in the general terms of its due process clause.

Two important points should be noted, then, concerning the Constitution's protection of speech, press, and assembly. First, the rights have been broadly construed to include picketing, parading, carrying placards, distributing handbills or circulars, using amplifying equipment, movies, and organizational associations as well as mere congregations of people. Second, the rights guaranteed in the First Amendment against abridgment by the national government have been incorporated totally into the "liberty" guaranteed in the Fourteenth Amendment against state encroachment.

## PREVIOUS RESTRAINTS

It should be obvious that the First Amendment was not intended and has not been construed to protect every utterance, publication, or assembly. The traditional approach is to consider that certain well-recognized exceptions to the exercise of First Amendment rights were tacitly included in defining the scope of the Amendment's protections. As

Justice Thomas M. Cooley stated, with respect to the Bill of Rights, "They are conservatory instruments rather than reformatory." [*Weimer* v. *Bunbury*, 30 Mich. 201, 214 (1874).] Despite the broad language, then, existing limitations on the exercise of those rights were not necessarily abolished.

Since the First Amendment rights are not absolute, the essential problem to be faced is the delineation of the kinds of restraints on speech, press, and assembly which are constitutionally permissible from those which are not. There are widely differing views on the appropriate answer to this problem, and the present chapter depicts the application of some of these views to the central areas of controversy surrounding First Amendment rights. There is one area, however, on which there seems to be fairly general agreement. This is in the theory that the First Amendment forbids the imposition of most *prior* restraints on the exercise of First Amendment rights. The standard citation is Blackstone's *Commentaries* (IV, 151), in which he states that "the liberty of the press . . . consists in laying no *previous* restraints upon publications and not in freedom from censure for criminal matter when published." Broadening the statement to include other rights, it would indicate that government cannot hinder speech or press or assembly *before* the speaking or printing or assembling takes place, but can punish or obstruct as it may choose *afterward*. As Thomas Jefferson often urged, Blackstone was no model for those interested in human liberty to follow. Probably the most trenchant statements on this aspect of Blackstone are those of Professor Zechariah Chafee, Jr., in his book *Free Speech in the United States*:[1]

This Blackstonian theory dies hard, but it ought 'o be knocked on the head once for all. In the first place, Blackstone was not interpreting a constitution, but trying to state the English law of his time, which had no censorship and did have extensive libel prosecutions. Whether or not he stated that law correctly, an entirely different view of the liberty of the press was soon afterwards enacted in Fox's Libel Act, . . . so that Blackstone's view does not even correspond to the English law of the last hundred and twenty-five years. Furthermore, Blackstone is notoriously unfitted to be an authority on the liberties of American colonists, since he upheld the right of Parliament to tax them, and was pronounced by one of his own colleagues to have been "we all know, an anti-republican lawyer."

Not only is the Blackstonian interpretation of our free speech clauses inconsistent with eighteenth-century history, . . . but it is contrary to modern decisions, thoroughly artificial, and wholly out of accord with a common-sense view of the relations of state and citizen. In some respects this theory goes altogether too far in restricting state action. The total prohibition of previous restraint would not allow the government to prevent a newspaper from publishing the sailing dates of transports or the number of troops in a sector. It would forbid the removal of an indecent poster from a billboard. . . .

On the other hand, it is hardly necessary to argue that the Blackstonian definition gives very inadequate protection to the freedom of expression. A death penalty for writing about socialism would be as effective suppression as a censorship. The government which holds twenty years in prison before a speaker and calls him free to talk resembles the peasant described by Galsworthy:

"The other day in Russia an Englishman came on a street-meeting shortly after the first revolution had begun. An extremist was addressing the gathering and telling them that they were fools to go on fighting, that they ought to refuse and go home, and so forth. The crowd grew angry, and some soldiers were for making a rush at

[1] Zechariah Chafee, Jr., *Free Speech in the United States* (Cambridge: Harvard University Press, 1948), pp. 9–11. Reprinted by permission of the publishers.

him; but the chairman, a big burly peasant, stopped them with these words: 'Brothers, you know that our country is now a country of free speech. We must listen to this man, we must let him say anything he will. But, brothers, when he's finished, we'll bash his head in!' "

Professor Chafee has thus pointed out that the Blackstonian statement is at the same time too extreme a restriction on governmental powers of censorship and too liberal in its grant of governmental power to punish after the fact. The Court has not treated the former issue definitively, but it has clearly refused to apply the First Amendment so as to permit the kinds of punishment which would have the same stifling effect as prior restraints. It is the impact of the restriction on the exercise of First Amendment rights which is the important consideration, rather than the mere formal determination of whether the restraining hand of government is laid on before or after the exercise of the right. Nevertheless, the Court has taken a near absolutist position on the invalidity of prior restraints. It is apt to use a balancing test on the issue of liability for punishment after the speech, publication, or assembly, but the rule generally is a firm one relative to prior restraints. A case illustrative of the Court's approach is *Near v. Minnesota*, dealing with limitations on the press.

## NEAR *v.* MINNESOTA
### 283 U.S. 697 (1931)

Mr. Chief Justice Hughes delivered the opinion of the Court.

Chapter 285 of the Session Laws of Minnesota for the year 1925 . . . provides for the abatement, as a public nuisance, of a "malicious, scandalous defamatory newspaper, magazine or other periodical." Section 1 of the act is as follows:

"Section 1: Any person who, as an individual, or as a member or employee of a firm, or association or organization, or as an officer, director, member or employee of a corporation, shall be engaged in the business of regularly or customarily producing, publishing or circulating, having in possession, selling or giving away,

(a) an obscene, lewd and lascivious newspaper, magazine, or other periodical, or

(b) a malicious, scandalous and defamatory newspaper, magazine or other periodical,

is guilty of a nuisance, and all persons guilty of such nuisance may be enjoined, as hereinafter provided. . . .

"In actions brought under (b) above, there shall be available the defense that the truth was published with good motives and for justifiable ends and in such actions the plaintiff shall not have the right to report [sic] to issues or editions of periodicals taking place more than three months before the commencement of the action." . . .

Under this statute, [section one, clause (b)], the county attorney of Hennepin county brought this action to enjoin the publication of what was described as a "malicious, scandalous and defamatory newspaper, magazine and periodical," known as "The Saturday Press," published by the defendants in the city of Minneapolis. . . .

Without attempting to summarize the contents of the voluminous exhibits attached to the complaint, we deem it sufficient to say that the articles charged in substance that a Jewish gangster was in control of gambling, bootlegging and racketeering in Minneapolis, and that law enforcing officers and agencies were not energetically performing their duties. Most of the charges were directed against the chief of police; he was charged with gross neglect of duty, illicit relations with gangsters, and with participation in graft. The county attorney was charged with knowing the existing conditions and with failure to take adequate measures to remedy them. The mayor was accused of inefficiency and dereliction. One member of the grand jury was stated to be in sympathy with the gangsters. A special grand jury and a special prosecutor were demanded to deal with the situation in general, and, in particular, to investigate an attempt to assassinate one Guilford, one of the original defendants, who, it appears from the articles, was shot by gangsters after the first issue of the periodical had been published. There is no question but that the articles made serious accusations against the public officers named and others in connection with the prevalence of crimes and the failure to expose and punish them. . . .

The district court made findings of fact, which followed the allegations of the complaint and found in general terms that the editions in question were "chiefly devoted to malicious, scandalous and defamatory articles," concerning the individuals named. The court further found that the defendants through these publications "did engage in the business of regularly and customarily producing, publishing and circulating a malicious, scandalous and defamatory newspaper," and that "the said publication under said name of The Saturday Press, or any other name, constitutes a public nuisance under the laws of the state." Judgment was thereupon entered adjudging that "the newspaper, magazine and periodical known as The Saturday Press," as a public nuisance, "be and is hereby abated." The judgment perpetually enjoined the defendants "from producing, editing, publishing, circulating, having in their possession, selling or giving away any publication whatsoever which is a malicious, scandalous or defamatory newspaper, as defined by law," and also "from further conducting said nuisance under the name and title of said The Saturday Press or any other name or title." . . .

This statute, for the suppression as a public nuisance of a newspaper or periodical, is unusual, if not unique, and raises questions of grave importance transcending the local interests involved in the particular action. It is no longer open to doubt that the liberty of the press and of speech is within the liberty safeguarded by the due process clause of the Fourteenth Amendment from invasion by state action. It was found impossible to conclude that this essential personal liberty of the citizen was left unprotected by the general guaranty of fundamental rights of person and property. . . .

First. The statute is not aimed at the redress of individual or private wrongs. Remedies for libel remain available and unaffected. The statute, said the state court, "is not directed at threatened libel but at an existing business which, generally speaking, involves more than libel." It is aimed at the distribution of scandalous matter as "detrimental to public morals and to the general welfare," tending "to disturb the peace of the community" and "to provoke assaults and the commission of crime." In order to obtain an injunction to suppress the future publication of the newspaper or periodical, it is not necessary to prove the falsity of the charges that have been made in the publication condemned. In the present action there was no allegation that the matter published was not true. It is alleged, and the statute requires the allegation, that the publication was "malicious." But, as in prosecutions for libel, there is no requirement of proof by the state of malice in fact as distinguished from malice inferred from the mere publication of the defamatory matter. The judgment in this case proceeded upon the mere proof of publication. The statute permits the defense, not of the truth alone, but only that the truth was published with good motives and for justifiable ends. It is apparent that under the statute the publication is to be regarded as defamatory if it injures reputation, and that it is scandalous if it circulates charges of reprehensible conduct, whether criminal or otherwise, and the publication is thus deemed to invite public reprobation and to constitute a public scandal. . . .

Second. The statute is directed not simply at the circulation of scandalous and defamatory statements with regard to private citizens, but at the continued publication by newspapers and periodicals of charges against public officers of corruption, malfeasance in office, or serious neglect of duty. Such charges by their very nature create a public scandal. They are scandalous and defamatory within the meaning of the statute, which has its normal operation in relation of publications dealing prominently and chiefly with the alleged derelictions of public officers.

Third. The object of the statute is not punishment, in the ordinary sense, but suppression of the offending newspaper or periodical. The reason for the enactment, as the state court has said, is that prosecutions to enforce penal statutes for libel do not result in "efficient repression or suppression of the evils of scandal." . . . Under this statute, a publisher of a newspaper or periodical, undertaking to conduct a campaign to expose and to censure official derelictions, and devoting his publication principally to that purpose, must face not simply the possibility of a verdict against him in a suit or prosecution for libel, but a determination that his newspaper or periodical is a public nuisance to be abated, and that this abatement and suppression will follow unless he is prepared with legal evidence to prove the truth of the charges and also to satisfy the court that, in addition to being true, the matter was published with good motives and for justifiable ends.

This suppression is accomplished by enjoining publication and that restraint is the object and effect of the statute.

Fourth. The statute not only operates to suppress the offending newspaper or periodical but to put the publisher under an effective censorship. . . .

If we cut through mere details of procedure, the operation and effect of the statute in substance is that public authorities may bring the owner or publisher of a newspaper or periodical before a judge upon a charge of conducting a business of publishing scandalous and defamatory matter—in particular that the matter consists of charges against public officers of official dereliction—and unless the owner or publisher is able and disposed to bring competent evidence to satisfy the judge that the charges are true and are published with good motives and for justifiable ends, his newspaper or periodical is suppressed and further publication is made punishable as a contempt. This is the essence of censorship.

The question is whether a statute authorizing such proceedings in restraint of publication is consistent with the conception of the liberty of the press as historically conceived and guaranteed. In determining the extent of the constitutional protection, it has been generally, if not universally, considered that it is the chief purpose of the guaranty to prevent previous restraints upon publication. The struggle in England, directed against the legislative power of the licenser, resulted in renunciation of the censorship of the press. . . . Here, as Madison said, "The great and essential rights of the people are secured against legislative as well as against executive ambition. They are secured, not by laws paramount to prerogative, but by constitutions paramount to laws. This security of the freedom of the press requires that it should be exempt not only from previous restraint by the executive, as in Great Britain, but from legislative restraint also." Report on the Virginia Resolutions, Madison's Works, vol. 4, p. 543. This court said, in *Patterson* v. *Colorado*, 205 U.S. 454, 462: "In the first place, the main purpose of such constitutional provisions is 'to prevent all such *previous restraints* upon publications as had been practised by other governments,' and they do not prevent the subsequent punishment of such as may be deemed contrary to the public welfare." . . .

. . . In the present case, we have no occasion to inquire as to the permissible scope of subsequent punishment. For whatever wrong the appellant has committed or may commit, by his publications, the state appropriately affords both public and private redress by its libel laws. As has been noted, the statute in question does not deal with punishments; it provides for no punishment, except in case of contempt for violation of the court's order, but for suppression and injunction, that is, for restraint upon publication.

The objection has also been made that the principle as to immunity from previous restraint is not absolutely unlimited. But the limitation has been recognized only in exceptional cases. "When a nation is at war many things that might be said in time of peace are such a hindrance to its effort that their utterance will not be endured so long as men fight and that no court could regard them as protected by any constitutional right." *Schenck* v. *United States*, 249 U.S. 47, 52. No one would question but that a government might prevent actual obstruction to its recruiting service or the publication of the sailing dates of transports or the number and location of troops. On similar grounds, the primary requirements of decency may be enforced against obscene publications. The security of the community life may be protected against incitements to acts of violence and the overthrow by force of orderly government. The constitutional guaranty of free speech does not "protect a man from an injunction against uttering words that may have all the effect of force. *Gompers* v. *Bucks Stove & Range Co.*, 221 U.S. 418, 439." *Schenck* v. *United States, supra*. These limitations are not applicable here. Nor are we now concerned with questions as to the extent of authority to prevent publications in order to protect private rights according to the principles governing the exercise of the jurisdiction of courts of equity. (See 29 *Harvard Law Rev.* 640.)

The exceptional nature of its limitations places in a strong light the general conception that liberty of the press, historically considered and taken up by the Federal Constitution, has meant, principally, although not exclusively, immunity from previous restraints or censorship. . . .

The importance of this immunity has not lessened. While reckless assaults upon public men, and efforts to bring obloquy upon those who are endeavoring faithfully to discharge official duties, exert a baleful influence and deserve the severest condemnation in public opinion, it cannot be said that this abuse is greater, and it is believed to be less, than that which characterized the period in which our institutions took shape. Meanwhile, the administration of government has become more complex, the opportunities for malfeasance and corruption have multiplied, crime has grown to most serious proportions, and the danger of its protection by unfaithful officials and of the impairment of the fundamental security of life and property by criminal alliances and official neglect, emphasizes the primary need of a vigilant and courageous press, especially in great cities. The fact that the liberty of the press may be abused by miscreant purveyors of scandal does not make any the less necessary the immunity of the press from previous restraint in dealing with official misconduct. Subsequent punishment for such abuses as may exist is the appropriate remedy, consistent with constitutional privilege. . . .

Equally unavailing is the insistence that the statute is designed to prevent the circulation of scandal which tends to disturb the public peace and to provoke assaults and the commission of crime. Charges of reprehensible conduct, and in particular of official malfeasance, unquestionably create a public scandal, but the theory of the constitutional guaranty is that even a more serious public evil would be caused by authority to prevent publication. . . .

*Judgment reversed.*

[Mr. Justice Butler wrote a dissenting opinion, concurred in by Justices Van Devanter, McReynolds, and Sutherland.]

In 1971 the Court faced the issue of freedom of the press versus the national security in *New York Times Co.* v. *United States*, the "Pentagon Papers Case."

## NEW YORK TIMES CO. *v.* UNITED STATES
### *403 U.S. 713 (1971)*

[In June 1971 Professor Daniel Ellsberg released to the press a large portion of a 47-volume Pentagon study entitled *History of the United States Decision-Making Process on Vietnam Policy*—some 7,000 pages of material still classified "Top Secret-Sensitive" by the Defense Department. On June 13 the *New York Times* published the first installment of a scheduled five-part series on how the United States got involved in Vietnam. On June 18 the *Washington Post* published the first in its series of articles based on the "Pentagon Papers." The Department of Justice in two separate District Courts requested temporary restraining orders to halt further publication of the papers by the *Times* and the *Post*. Both District Courts denied the requests. On June 19 the Court of Appeals, District of Columbia, temporarily restrained the *Post* from continuing its series, and the District Judge scheduled a hearing for June 21 on the Justice Department's request for an injunction. The Court of Appeals for the Second Circuit issued a restraining order against the *Times* to allow the Government to appeal the District Court decision in New York. After secret hearings in both District Courts, the Court of Appeals for the Second Circuit continued its restraining order and the *Times* filed an appeal to the Supreme Court, while the Court of Appeals in Washington upheld the District Court decision there that the government had failed to prove that the *Post* articles would endanger the national security, but extended the restraining order to give the government time for an appeal to the Supreme Court. Both cases were handled on writs of certiorari and decided on June 30, 1971.]

PER CURIAM.

We granted certiorari in these cases in which the United States seeks to enjoin the *New York Times* and the *Washington Post* from publishing the contents of a classified study entitled "History of U.S. Decision-Making Process on Viet Nam Policy."

"Any system of prior restraints of expression comes to this Court bearing a heavy presumption against its constitutional validity." *Bantam Books, Inc.* v. *Sullivan* . . . ; see also *Near* v. *Minnesota*. . . . The Government "thus carries a heavy burden of showing justification for the enforcement of such a restraint." *Organization for a Better Austin* v. *Keefe*. . . . The District Court for the Southern District of New York in the *New York Times* case and the District Court for the District of Columbia and the Court of Appeals for the District of Columbia Circuit in the *Washington Post* case held that the Government had not met that burden. We agree.

The judgment of the Court of Appeals for the District of Columbia Circuit is therefore affirmed. The order of the Court of Appeals for the Second Circuit is reversed and the case is remanded with directions to enter a judgment affirming the judgment of the District Court for the Southern District of New York. The stays entered June 25, 1971, by the Court are vacated. The mandates shall issue forthwith.

*So ordered.*

Mr. Justice Black, with whom Mr. Justice Douglas joins, concurring.

I adhere to the view that the Government's case against the *Washington Post* should have been dismissed and that the injunction against the *New York Times* should have been vacated without oral argument when the cases were first presented to this Court. I believe that every moment's continuance of the injunctions against these newspapers amounts to a flagrant, indefensible, and continuing violation of the First Amendment. . . . In my view it is unfortunate that some of my Brethren are apparently willing to hold that the publication of news may sometimes be enjoined. Such a holding would make a shambles of the First Amendment. . . .

In the First Amendment the Founding Fathers gave the free press the protection it must have to fulfill its essential role in our democracy. The press was to serve the governed, not the governors. . . . Only a free and unrestrained press can effectively expose deception in government. And paramount among the responsibilities of a free press is the duty to prevent any part of the government from deceiving the people and sending them off to distant lands to die of foreign fevers and foreign shot and shell. In my view, far from deserving condemnation for their courageous reporting, the *New York Times*, the *Washington Post*, and other newspapers should be commended for serving the purpose that the Founding Fathers saw so clearly. . . .

Mr. Justice Douglas, with whom Mr. Justice Black joins, concurring. . . .

The dominant purpose of the First Amendment was to prohibit the widespread practice of governmental suppression of embarrassing information. It is common knowledge that the First Amendment was adopted against the widespread use of the common law of seditious libel to punish the dissemination of material that is embarrassing to the powers-that-be. . . . The present cases will, I think, go down in history as the most dramatic illustration of that principle. A debate of large proportions goes on in the Nation over our posture in Vietnam. That debate antedated the disclosure of the contents of the present documents. The latter are highly relevant to the debate in progress.

Secrecy in government is fundamentally anti-democratic, perpetuating bureaucratic errors. Open debate and discussion of public issues are vital to our national health. On public questions there should be "open and robust debate." . . .

Mr. Justice Brennan, concurring.

I write separately in these cases only to emphasize what should be apparent: that our judgment in the present cases may not be taken to indicate the propriety, in the future, of issuing temporary stays and restraining orders to block the publication of material sought to be suppressed by the Government. . . .

The error which has pervaded these cases from the outset was the granting of any injunctive relief whatsoever, interim or otherwise. The entire thrust of the Government's claim throughout these cases has been that publication of the material sought to be enjoined "could," or "might," or "may" prejudice the national interest in various ways. But the First Amendment tolerates absolutely no prior judicial restraints of the press predicated upon surmise or conjecture that untoward consequences may result. . . . Thus, only governmental allegation and proof that publication must inevitably, directly and immediately cause the occurrence of an event kindred to imperiling the safety of a transport already at sea can support even the issuance of an interim restraining order. In no event may mere conclusions be sufficient: for if the Executive Branch seeks judicial aid in preventing publication, it must inevitably submit the basis upon which that aid is sought to scrutiny by the judiciary. And therefore, every restraint issued in this case, whatever its form, has violated the First Amendment—and none the less so because that restraint was justified as necessary to afford the court an opportunity to examine the claim more thoroughly. Unless and until the Government has clearly made out its case, the First Amendment commands that no injunction may issue.

Mr. Justice Stewart, with whom Mr. Justice White joins, concurring. . . .

In the absence of the governmental checks and balances present in other areas of our national life, the only effective restraint upon executive policy and power in the areas of national defense and international affairs may lie in an enlightened citizenry—in an informed and critical public opinion which alone can here protect the values of democratic government. . . .

Yet it is elementary that the successful conduct of international diplomacy and the maintenance of an effective national defense require both confidentiality and secrecy. . . .

I think there can be but one answer to this dilemma, if dilemma it be. The responsibility must be where the power is. If the Constitution gives the Executive a large degree of unshared power in the conduct of foreign affairs and the maintenance of our national defense, then under the Constitution the Executive must have the largely unshared duty to determine and preserve the degree of internal security necessary to exercise that power successfully. . . . [I]t is clear to me that it is the constitutional duty of the Executive—as a matter of sovereign prerogative and not as a matter of law as the courts know law—. . . to protect the confidentiality necessary to carry out its responsibilities in the fields of international relations and national defense. . . .

. . . [I]n the cases before us we are asked neither to construe specific regulations nor to apply specific laws. We are asked, instead, to perform a function that the Constitution gave to the Executive, not the Judiciary. . . . I join the judgments of the Court.

Mr. Justice White, with whom Mr. Justice Stewart joins, concurring.

I concur in today's judgments, but only because of the concededly extraordinary protection against prior restraints enjoyed by the press under our constitutional system. I do not say that in no circumstances would the First Amendment permit an injunction against publishing information about government plans or operations. Nor, after examining the materials the Government characterizes as the most sensitive and destructive, can I deny that revelation of these documents will do substantial damage to public interests. Indeed, I am confident that their disclosure will have that result. But I nevertheless agree that the United States has not satisfied the very heavy burden which it must meet to warrant an injunction against publication in these cases, at least in the absence of express and appropriately limited congressional authorization for prior restraints in circumstances such as these. . . .

Mr. Justice Marshall, concurring. . . .

The problem here is whether in this particular case the Executive Branch has authority to invoke the equity jurisdiction of the courts to protect what it believes to be the national interest. . . .

It would . . . be utterly inconsistent with the concept of separation of power for this Court to use its power of contempt to prevent behavior that Congress has specifically declined to prohibit. . . .

Either the Government has the power under statutory grant to use traditional criminal law to protect the country or, if there is no basis for arguing that Congress has made the activity a crime, it is plain that Congress has specifically refused to grant the authority the Government seeks from this Court. In either case this Court does not have authority to grant the requested relief. It is not for this Court to fling itself into every breach perceived by some Government official nor is it for this Court to take on itself the burden of enacting law, especially law that Congress has refused to pass. . . .

Mr. Chief Justice Burger, dissenting. . . .

Only those who view the First Amendment as an absolute in all circumstances—a view I respect, but reject—can find such a case as this to be simple or easy.

This case is not simple for another and more immediate reason. We do not know the facts of the case. No District Judge knew all the facts. No Court of Appeals judge knew all the facts. No member of this Court knows all the facts. . . .

I suggest we are in this posture because these cases have been conducted in unseemly haste. Mr. Justice Harlan covers the chronology of events demonstrating the hectic pressures under which these cases have been processed and I need not restate them. . . .

The consequence of all this melancholy series of events is that we literally do not know what we are acting on. As I see it we have been forced to deal with litigation concerning rights of great magnitude without an adequate record, and surely without time for adequate treatment either in the prior proceedings or in this Court. . . . I agree with Mr. Justice Harlan and Mr. Justice Blackmun but I am not prepared to reach the merits.

I would affirm the Court of Appeals for the Second Circuit and allow the District Court to complete the trial aborted by our grant of certiorari meanwhile preserving the *status quo* in the *Post* case. I would direct that the District Court on remand give priority to the *Times* case to the exclusion of all other business on that court but I would not set arbitrary deadlines. . . .

Mr. Justice Harlan, with whom the Chief Justice and Mr. Justice Blackmun join, dissenting. . . .

With all respect, I consider that the Court has been almost irresponsibly feverish in dealing with these cases. . . .

Forced as I am to reach the merits of these cases, I dissent from the opinion and judgments of the Court. . . .

It is plain to me that the scope of the judicial function in passing upon the activities of the Executive Branch of the Government in the field of foreign affairs is very narrowly restricted. This view is, I think, dictated by the concept of separation of powers upon which our constitutional system rests. . . .

I agree that, in performance of its duty to protect the values of the First Amendment against political pressures, the judiciary must review the initial Executive determination to the point of satisfying itself that the subject matter of the dispute does lie within the proper compass of the President's foreign relations power. . . . Moreover, the judiciary may properly insist that the determination that disclosure of the subject matter would irreparably impair the national security be made by the head of the Executive Department concerned—here the Secretary of State or the Secretary of Defense—after actual personal consideration by that officer. . . .

But in my judgment the judiciary may not properly go beyond these two inquiries and redetermine for itself the probable impact of disclosure on the national security. . . .

I can see no indication in the opinions of either the District Court or the Court of Appeals in the *Post* litigation that the conclusions of the Executive were given even the deference owing to an administrative agency, much less that owing to a co-equal branch of the Government operating within the field of its constitutional prerogative. . . .

Mr. Justice Blackmun, dissenting. . . .

With such respect as may be due to the contrary view, this, in my opinion, is not the way to try a law suit of this magnitude and asserted importance. It is not the way for federal courts to adjudicate, and to be required to adjudicate, issues that allegedly concern the Nation's vital welfare. . . .

The First Amendment, after all, is only part of an entire Constitution. Article II of the great document vests in the Executive Branch primary power over the conduct of foreign affairs and places in that branch the responsibility for the Nation's safety. Each provision of the Constitution is important, and I cannot subscribe to a doctrine of unlimited absolutism for the First Amendment at the cost of downgrading other provisions. First Amendment absolutism has never commanded a majority of this Court. . . . What is needed here is a weighing, upon properly developed standards, of the broad right of the press to print and of the very narrow right of the Government to prevent. Such standards are not yet developed. The parties here are in disagreement as to what those standards should be. But even the newspapers concede that there are situations where restraint is in order and is constitutional. . . .

I therefore would remand these cases. . . .

Both *Near* v. *Minnesota* and the *New York Times* case involved injunctions against future publications—"the essence of censorship." But suppose a statute presents no bar to publication, but permits the issuance of an injunction against sale or distribution of the published matter. Is there a constitutional difference or is this still an invalid prior restraint? Would carefully structured procedural safeguards in the equity action offset the threat to freedom of expression? In a case involving allegedly obscene books a majority of the Court agreed that it would.

KINGSLEY BOOKS, INC. *v.* BROWN
*354 U.S. 436 (1957)*

Mr. Justice Frankfurter delivered the opinion of the Court.

This is a proceeding under Sec. 22-a of the New York Code of Criminal Procedure. . . . This section supplements the existing conventional criminal provision dealing with pornography by authorizing the chief executive, or legal officer, of a municipality to invoke a "limited injunctive remedy," under closely defined procedural safeguards, against the sale and distribution of written and printed matter found after due trial to be obscene, and to obtain an order for the seizure, in default of surrender, of the condemned publications.

A complaint dated September 10, 1954, charged appellants with displaying for sale paper-covered obscene booklets, fourteen of which were annexed, under the general title of "Nights of Horror." The complaint prayed that appellants be enjoined from further distribution of the booklets, that they be required to surrender to the sheriff for destruction all copies in their possession, and, upon failure to do so, that the sheriff be commanded to seize and destroy those copies. The same day the appellants were ordered to show cause within four days why they should not be enjoined *pendente lite* from distributing the booklets. Appellants consented to the granting of an injunction *pendente lite* and did not bring the matter to issue promptly, as was their right under subdivision 2 of the challenged section, which provides that the persons sought to be enjoined "shall be entitled to a trial of the issues within two days of the conclusion of the trial." After the case came to trial, the judge, sitting in equity, found that the booklets annexed to the complaint and introduced in evidence were clearly obscene—were "dirt for dirt's sake"; he enjoined their further distribution and ordered their destruction. He refused to enjoin "the sale and distribution of later issues" on the ground that "to rule against a volume not offered in evidence would . . . impose an unreasonable prior restraint upon freedom of the press." . . .

Neither in the New York Court of Appeals, nor here, did appellants assail the legislation insofar as it outlaws obscenity. The claim they make lies within a very narrow compass. Their attack is upon the power of New York to employ the remedial scheme of Section 22-a. . . . Resort to this injunctive remedy, it is claimed, is beyond the constitutional power of New York in that it amounts to a prior censorship of literary product and as such is violative of that "freedom of thought, and speech" which has been "withdrawn by the Fourteenth Amendment from encroachment by the states." . . . Reliance is particularly placed upon *Near* v. *Minnesota*. . . .

We need not linger over the suggestion that something can be drawn out of the Due Process Clause of the Fourteenth Amendment that restricts New York to the criminal process in seeking to protect its people against the dissemination of pornography. It is not for this Court thus to limit the State in resorting to various weapons in the armory of the law. Whether proscribed conduct is to be visited by a criminal prosecution or by a *qui tam* action or by an injunction or by some or all of these remedies in combination, is a matter within the legislature's range of choice. . . . If New York chooses to subject persons who disseminate obscene "literature" to criminal prosecution and also to deal with such books as deodands of old, or both, with due regard, of course, to appropriate opportunities for the trial of the underlying issue, it is not for us to gainsay its selection of remedies. . . .

. . . The phrase "prior restraint" is not a self-wielding sword. Nor can it serve as a talismanic test. The duty of closer analysis and critical judgment in applying the thought behind the phrase has thus been authoritatively put by one who brings weighty learning to his support of constitutionally protected liberties: "What is needed," writes Professor Paul A. Freund, "is a pragmatic assessment of its operation in the particular circumstances. The generalization that prior restraint is particularly obnoxious in civil liberties cases must yield to more particularistic analysis." The Supreme Court and Civil Liberties, *4 Vand. L. Rev. 533, 539.*

Wherein does Section 22-a differ in its effective operation from the type of statute upheld in *Alberts?* Section 311 of California's Penal Code provides that "Every person who willfully and lewdly . . . keeps for sale . . . any obscene . . . book . . . is guilty of a misdemeanor. . . ." Section 1141 of New York's Penal Law is similar. One would be bold to assert that the *in terrorem* effect of such statutes less restrains booksellers in the period before the law strikes than does Section 22-a. Instead of requiring the bookseller to dread that the offer for sale of a book may, without prior warning, subject him to a criminal prosecution with the hazard of imprisonment, the civil procedure assures him that such consequences cannot follow unless he ignores a court order specifically directed to him for a prompt and carefully circumscribed determination of the issue of obscenity. Until then, he may keep the book for sale and sell it on his own judgment rather than steer "nervously among the treacherous shoals." . . .

Criminal enforcement and the proceeding under section Section 22-a interfere with a book's solicitation of the public precisely at the same stage. In each situation the law moves after publication; the book need not in either case have yet passed into the hands of the public. . . .

Nor are the consequences of a judicial condemnation for obscenity under Section 22-a more restrictive of freedom of expression than the result of conviction for a misdemeanor. In *Alberts*, the defendant was fined $500, sentenced to sixty days in prison, and put on probation for two years on condition that he not violate the obscenity statute. Not only was he completely separated from society for two months but he was also seriously restrained from trafficking in all obscene publications for a considerable time. Appellants, on the other hand, were enjoined from displaying for sale or distributing only the particular booklets theretofore published and adjudged to be obscene. Thus, the restraint upon appellants as merchants in obscenity was narrower than that imposed on Alberts.

Section 22-a's provision for the seizure and destruction of the instruments of ascertained wrongdoing expresses resort to a legal remedy sanctioned by the long history of Anglo-American law. See Holmes, The Common Law, 24–26. . . .

It only remains to say that the difference between *Near* v. *Minnesota, supra,* and this case is glaring in fact. The two cases are no less glaringly different when judged by the appropriate criteria of constitutional law. Minnesota empowered its courts to enjoin the dissemination of future issues of a publication because its past issues had been found offensive. In the language of Mr. Chief Justice Hughes, "This is of the essence of censorship." . . . As such, it was found unconstitutional. This was enough to condemn the statute wholly apart from the fact that the proceeding in *Near* involved not obscenity but matters deemed to be derogatory to a public officer. Unlike *Near*, Section 22-a is concerned solely with obscenity and, as authoritatively construed, it studiously withholds restraint upon matters not already published and not yet found to be offensive.

The judgment is

*Affirmed.*

Mr. Chief Justice Warren, dissenting. . . .

Mr. Justice Douglas, joined by Mr. Justice Black, dissenting.

There are two reasons why I think this restraining order should be dissolved.

First, the provision for an injunction *pendente lite* gives the State the paralyzing power of a censor. A decree can issue *ex parte*—without a hearing and without any ruling or finding on the issue of obscenity. This provision is defended on the ground that it is only a little encroachment, that a hearing must be promptly given and a finding of obscenity promptly made. But every publisher knows what awful effect a decree issued in secret can have. We tread here on First Amendment grounds. And nothing is more devastating to the rights that it guarantees than the power to restrain publication before even a hearing is held. This is prior restraint and censorship at its worst.

Second, the procedure for restraining by equity decree the distribution of all the condemned literature does violence to the First Amendment. . . . I think every publication is a separate offense which entitles the accused to a separate trial. Juries or judges may differ in their opinions, community by community, case by case. . . .

The regime approved by the Court goes far toward making the censor supreme. It also substitutes punishment by contempt for punishment by jury trial. In both respects it transgresses constitutional guarantees. . . .

[Justice Brennan, dissenting, argued that a jury determination of the issue of obscenity was constitutionally necessary.]

### Licensing and Taxation as Previous Restraint

It is not uncommon for governmental units to require a license or permit prior to engaging in parades or meetings in public parks or speeches on the public ways. Even the solicitation of funds may in some instances require a permit. *Cantwell v. Connecticut*, discussed in the previous chapter, held that the Connecticut statute requiring a permit prior to embarking upon solicitation of funds for religious purposes was an invalid prior restraint because it vested in the licensing authority the power to determine whether the cause was a religious one. A permit requirement in such cases that serves only the purpose of identification and notification, however, without the discretionary control over issuance, would presumably meet the test of constitutionality.

In *Cox v. New Hampshire*, also discussed earlier, the Court upheld a statute prohibiting parades upon a public street without a special license and the payment of a fee which was scaled according to a reasonable estimate of the expense of policing the particular parade. A determining factor in the decision was the construction of the statute as allowing no discretion in the licensing board except as necessity might dictate changes in time or route for such parades. The fee requirement was considered to be a reasonable imposition solely to offset the added cost of policing the event and was not construed as a tax on the exercise of a First Amendment right.

In *Niemotko v. Maryland*, 340 U.S. 268 (1951), involving the operation of an "amorphous practice" [in the language of the Chief Justice] of requiring a permit from the city council before holding a meeting in a public park, there is an indication that a permit requirement which is completely nondiscretionary and is used merely for the purpose of notification and for scheduling use in an orderly fashion would not be considered as an unconstitutional restraint. Chief Justice Vinson, speaking for the majority, stated:

This court has many times examined the licensing systems by which local bodies regulate the use of their parks and public places. . . . In those cases this Court condemned statutes and ordinances which required that permits be obtained from local officials as a prerequisite to the use of public places, on the grounds that a license requirement constituted a prior restraint on freedom of speech, press and religion, and, *in the absence of narrowly drawn, reasonable and definite standards for the officials to follow*, must be invalid. [Emphasis added.]

SHUTTLESWORTH *v.* BIRMINGHAM
*394 U.S. 147 (1969)*

[In April, 1963, three ministers, Martin Luther King, Jr., Fred L. Shuttlesworth and another, announced plans for a "march" on Good Friday in Birmingham, Alabama. A city ordinance required that a permit be obtained from the City Commission prior to holding any parade or procession on the streets or public ways. It stated further: "The Commission shall grant a written permit for such parade, procession or other public demonstration . . . unless in its judgment the public welfare, peace, safety, health, decency, and good order, morals or convenience require that it be refused." Shuttlesworth sent a representative to the City Hall to request a permit, and she was directed to Commissioner "Bull" Connor, who denied her request vehemently. He said, "No, you will not get a permit in Birmingham, Alabama, to picket. I will picket you over to the City Jail." Two days later, Shuttlesworth sent a telegram to Commissioner Connor requesting a permit to picket "against the injustices of segregation and discrimination." In reply, Connor sent a wire stating that permits were the responsibility of the entire Commission, and closed with the statement "I insist that you and your people do not start any picketing on the streets in Birmingham, Alabama."

On Good Friday afternoon fifty-two people, including the three ministers, began a march on the sidewalks of the city without interference with other pedestrians or with traffic when crossing streets. They were convicted of violation of the permit ordinance. Shuttlesworth was sentenced to 90 days' imprisonment at hard labor and an additional 48 days at hard labor in default of payment of a $75 fine and $24 costs. The Alabama Supreme Court affirmed the conviction.]

Mr. Justice Stewart delivered the opinion of the Court. . . .

There can be no doubt that the Birmingham ordinance, as it was written, conferred upon the City Commission virtually unbridled and absolute power to prohibit any "parade," "procession," or "demonstration" on the city's streets or public ways. For in deciding whether or not to withhold a permit, the members of the Commission were to be guided only by their own ideas of "public welfare, peace, safety, health, decency, good order, morals or convenience." This ordinance as it was written, therefore, fell squarely within the ambit of the many decisions of this Court over the last 30 years, holding that a law subjecting the exercise of First Amendment freedoms to the prior restraint of a license, without narrow, objective, and definite standards to guide the licensing authority, is unconstitutional. "It is settled by a long line of recent decisions of this Court that an ordinance which, like this one, makes the peaceful enjoyment of freedoms which the Constitution guarantees contingent upon the uncontrolled will of an official—as by requiring a permit or license which may be granted or withheld in the discretion of such official—is an unconstitutional censorship or prior restraint upon the enjoyment of those freedoms." . . . And our decisions have made clear that a person faced with such an unconstitutional licensing law may ignore it and engage with impunity in the exercise of the right of free expression for which the law purports to require a license. . . .

It is argued, however, that what was involved here was not "pure speech," but the use of public streets and sidewalks, over which a municipality must rightfully exercise a great deal of control in the interest of traffic regulation and public safety. That, of course, is true. We have emphasized before this that "the First and Fourteenth Amendments [do not] afford the same kind of freedom to those who would communicate ideas by conduct such as patrolling, marching, and picketing on streets and highways, as these amendments afford to those who communicate ideas by pure speech." *Cox* v. *Louisiana.* . . . "Governmental authorities have the duty and responsibility to keep their streets open and available for movement." . . .

But our decisions have also made clear that picketing and parading may nonetheless constitute methods of expression, entitled to First Amendment protection. . . . "Wherever the title of streets and parks may rest, they have immemorially been held in trust for the use of the public and, time out of mind, have been used for purposes of assembly, communicating thoughts between citizens, and discussing public questions. . . ." *Hague* v. *C.I.O.* . . . . (opinion of Mr. Justice Roberts, joined by Mr. Justice Black).

Accordingly, "[a]lthough this Court has recognized that a statute may be enacted which prevents serious interference with normal usage of streets and parks, . . . we have consistently condemned licensing systems which vest in an administrative official discretion to grant or withhold a permit upon broad criteria unrelated to proper regulation of public places." . . . Even when the use of its public streets and sidewalks is involved, therefore, a municipality may not empower its licensing officials to roam essentially at will, dispensing or withholding permission to speak, assemble, picket, or parade, according to their own opinions regarding the potential effect of the activity in question on the "welfare," "decency," or "morals" of the community. . . . The judgment is

*Reversed.*

Mr. Justice Black concurs in the result.

Mr. Justice Marshall took no part in the consideration or decision of this case.

Mr. Justice Harlan, concurring. . . .

As a separate facet of this same episode, Birmingham city officials applied for an injunction against parading without a permit, and the injunction was served on the day before Good Friday. The group of Negroes decided to ignore the injunction and marched on Good Friday and on Easter Sunday. They were convicted of violating the injunction in a separate proceeding from that involved in *Shuttlesworth*, and the case came to the Supreme Court two years earlier in *Walker* v. *Birmingham*, 388 U.S. 307 (1967). The Court in *Walker* affirmed the conviction, with the majority arguing that the petitioners should have attempted to have the injunction dissolved or modified rather then simply "ignore all the procedures of the law and carry their battle to the streets." If one accepts the outcomes in the two cases as ruling law, then the conclusion must be that one is free to violate an ordinance or statute that is unconstitutional on its face, but is not permitted to ignore an injunction based on that same ordinance or statute. The Court, however, refused to consider the constitutionality of the ordinance in the *Walker* case.

It is clear that a requirement of a license prior to the publication of a book would be an invalid prior restraint. Although movies were held to be within the protection of the First Amendment in *Burstyn* v. *Wilson* in 1952, the Court held in *Times Film Corporation* v. *City of Chicago*, 365 U.S. 43 (1961), that a municipal ordinance requiring the submission of all motion pictures for examination prior to their public exhibition, and the obtaining of a permit from a licensing board, was not unconstitutional. The corporation contended that the requirement could not validly be enforced. Justice Clark, for the majority, stated:

Petitioner would have us hold that the public exhibition of motion pictures must be allowed under any circumstances. The State's sole remedy, it says, is the invocation of criminal process under the Illinois pornography statute, . . . and then only after a transgression. But this position, as we have seen, is founded upon the claim of absolute privilege against prior restraint under the First Amendment—a claim without sanction in our cases. . . . Chicago emphasizes here its duty to protect its people against the dangers of obscenity in the public exhibition of motion pictures. To this argument petitioner's only answer is that regardless of the capacity for, or extent of such an evil, previous restraint cannot be justified. With this we cannot agree. We recognized in *Burstyn,* that "capacity for evil . . . may be relevant in determining the permissible scope of control," . . . and that motion pictures were not "necessarily subject to the precise rules governing any other particular method of expression. Each method," we said, "tends to present its own peculiar problems." . . . It is not for this Court to limit the State in its selection of the remedy it deems most effective to cope with such a problem, absent, of course, a showing of unreasonable strictures on individual liberty resulting from its application in particular circumstances. *Kingsley Books, Inc.,* v. *Brown*. . . . We, of course, are not holding that city officials may be granted the power to prevent the showing of any motion picture they deem unworthy of a license. . . .

In the 1960s four States and less than a score of cities had provisions requiring that an exhibitor obtain a permit prior to the showing of any motion picture publicly. The laws generally allowed the licensing agency to refuse a permit if the film was considered obscene or would "tend to corrupt morals" or incite to crime. In *Freedman* v. *Maryland*, 380 U.S. 51 (1965), the Court held the Maryland law invalid because of the heavy burden placed on the exhibitor in challenging the denial of a permit. The opinion stressed the fact that there was no statutory provision for judicial participation in the procedure which barred a film, nor even assurance of prompt judicial review. "Risk of delay is built into the Maryland procedure, as is borne out by experience." In the only reported case illustrating this delay, the initial judicial determination took four months and final vindication of the film on appellate review, six months. In view of the absence of safeguards against undue inhibition of expression, the requirement of prior submission was held to be an invalid previous restraint. The Court also suggested that Maryland might look to the procedures in *Kingsley Books, Inc.* v. *Brown* for a model. The aftermath of *Freedman* appears to be that permit requirements for motion pictures have now been rescinded.

[See John R. Verani, "Motion Picture Censorship and the Doctrine of Prior Restraint," 3 *Houston L. Rev.* 11 (1965), and Ernest Giglio, "Prior Restraint of Motion Pictures," 69 *Dick. L. Rev.* 379 (1965).]

As a general rule, it may be said that no tax can constitutionally be levied on the exercise of a First Amendment right. This does not, of course, bar the imposition of ordinary taxes such as an income tax on the profits realized from such exercise. Thus a law requiring the payment of a tax prior to making speeches would be invalid, but the fees received from such speeches are income and may properly be subject to taxation. In

*Murdock* v. *Pennsylvania*, 319 U.S. 105 (1943), the Court held unconstitutional an ordinance of the city of Jeannette, Pennsylvania, which required the payment of a license fee prior to engaging in the sale of religious literature. Justice Douglas, for the Court, stated that the fee was "a flat tax imposed on the exercise of a privilege granted by the Bill of Rights," and was thus a prior restraint on the free exercise of religion. The *Murdock* decision was followed in *Follett* v. *Town of McCormick*, 321 U.S. 573 (1944), invalidating a similar municipal tax imposed on a Jehovah's Witness who maintained his home in the municipality and who earned his living by means of the sale of religious literature.

Probably the best-known illustration of a tax levied to inhibit publication was dealt with in *Grosjean* v. *American Press Co.*, 297 U.S. 233 (1936). Huey Long, of Louisiana, was given very favorable treatment in the small rural newspapers but not so in the large city press. Apparently at his behest, the legislature enacted a 2 percent tax on gross receipts from advertising on all newspapers or periodicals having a circulation of more than 20,000 copies per week. The Court held the tax unconstitutional by a unanimous vote, characterizing the law as "a deliberate and calculated device in the guise of a tax to limit the circulation of information to which the public is entitled in virtue of the constitutional guaranties."

In 1971 Minnesota amended its sales and use tax law to provide for a "use tax" on the cost of paper and ink products consumed in the production of periodic publications. In *Minneapolis Star and Tribune Company* v. *Minnesota*, 460 U.S. 575 (1983), the Court held the tax unconstitutional as a violation of the First Amendment in singling out the press for special tax treatment. There was no finding of impermissible or censorial motive on the part of the Legislature, but the impact was considered to be too serious a burden on the press even though the *Grosjean* type of motivation was not present.

## Overbreadth

Two additional challenges to statutes on the ground that they are unconstitutional on their face involve the concepts of "void for vagueness" and "overbreadth." While sometimes confused, these concepts reach distinct and separable problems in statutory drafting. The vagueness doctrine applies when the law is written in such ambiguous terms that the citizen cannot divine just what conduct is prohibited, and thus there is no "ascertainable standard of guilt." The doctrine of "overbreadth" applies when a statute, even though clearly written, punishes *both* conduct which can legitimately be proscribed and conduct which is constitutionally protected. Of course, a statute may be held defective under both doctrines, as was the case in *Coates* v. *Cincinnati*, 402 U.S. 611 (1971). Coates and others were convicted of violating a Cincinnati ordinance making it a criminal offense for "three or more persons to assemble . . . on any of the sidewalks . . . and there conduct themselves in a manner annoying to persons passing by." The record showed only that Coates was a student involved in a demonstration and the other persons were pickets involved in a labor dispute. In holding the ordinance unconstitutional on its face, Justice Stewart, for the majority, stated:

[T]he only construction put upon the ordinance by the state court was its unexplained conclusion that "the standard of conduct which it specifies is not dependent upon each complainant's sensitivity." . . . But the court did not indicate upon whose sensitivity a violation does depend—the sensitivity of the judge or jury, the sensitivity of the arresting officer, or the sensitivity of a hypothetical reasonable man.

We are thus relegated, at best, to the words of the ordinance itself. If three or more people meet together on a sidewalk or street corner, they must conduct themselves so as not to annoy any police officer or other person who should happen to pass by. In our opinion this ordinance is unconstitutionally vague because it subjects the exercise of the right of assembly to an unascertainable standard, and unconstitutionally broad because it authorizes the punishment of constitutionally protected conduct.

Conduct that annoys some people does not annoy others. Thus, the ordinance is vague, not in the sense that it requires a person to conform his conduct to an imprecise but comprehensible normative standard, but rather in the sense that no standard of conduct is specified at all. As a result, "men of common intelligence must necessarily guess at its meaning." . . .

It is said that the ordinance is broad enough to encompass many types of conduct clearly within the city's constitutional power to prohibit. And so, indeed, it is. The city is free to prevent people from blocking sidewalks, obstructing traffic, littering streets, committing assaults, or engaging in countless other forms of antisocial conduct. It can do so through the enactment and enforcement of ordinances directed with reasonable specificity toward the conduct to be prohibited. . . . It cannot constitutionally do so through the enactment and enforcement of an ordinance whose violation may entirely depend upon whether or not a policeman is annoyed. . . .

. . . The First and Fourteenth Amendments do not permit a State to make criminal the exercise of the right of assembly simply because its exercise may be "annoying" to some people. If this were not the rule, the right of the people to gather in public places for social or political purposes would be continually subject to summary suspension through the good-faith enforcement of a prohibition against annoying conduct. . . .

The ordinance before us makes a crime out of what under the Constitution cannot be a crime. It is aimed directly at activity protected by the Constitution. We need not lament that we do not have before us the details of the conduct found to be annoying. It is the ordinance on its face that sets the standard of conduct and warns against transgression.

In *Airport Commissioners* v. *Jews for Jesus, Inc.*, 482 U.S.—(1987), the issue presented was whether a resolution adopted by the Board of Airport Commissioners banning all "First Amendment activities" at the Los Angeles International Airport (LAX) violated the First Amendment. An airport peace officer had stopped a minister from distributing free religious literature in the central terminal area, explained the resolution to him and requested him to leave the terminal. He was warned that the City would take legal action against him if he refused to leave. A Federal District Court held the resolution unconstitutional, and the Court of Appeals affirmed. The Supreme Court unanimously held that the resolution was facially unconstitutional under the overbreadth doctrine. Justice O'Connor, for the Court, stated:

Under the First Amendment overbreadth doctrine, an individual whose own speech or conduct may be prohibited is permitted to challenge a statute on its face "because it also threatens others not before the court—those who desire to engage in legally protected expression but who may refrain from doing so rather than risk prosecution or undertake to have the law declared partially invalid." . . . A statute may be invalidated on its face, however, only if the overbreadth is "substantial." . . . The requirement that the overbreadth be substantial arose from our recognition that application of the overbreadth doctrine is, "manifestly, strong medicine," . . . and that "there must be a realistic danger that the statute itself will significantly compromise recognized First Amendment protections of parties not before the Court for it to be facially challenged on overbreadth grounds." . . .

On its face, the resolution at issue in this case reaches the universe of expressive activity, and, by prohibiting *all* protected expression, purports to create a virtual "First Amendment Free Zone" at LAX. The resolution does not merely regulate expressive activity in the Central Terminal Area that might create problems such as congestion or the disruption of the activities of those who use LAX. . . . The resolution therefore does not merely reach the activity of respondents at LAX; it prohibits even talking and reading, or the wearing of campaign buttons or symbolic clothing. Under such a sweeping ban, virtually every individual who enters LAX may be found to violate the resolution by engaging in some "First Amendment activit[y]"

It may be seen from the various opinions expressed in the cases presented thus far that discussion of the specific doctrine of previous restraint tends to slide over into the more generalized concept of censorship. The latter word is quite commonly employed in the literature to denote any form of restraint, before or after publication, aside from criminal prosecutions, which effectively impairs consumption of the various forms of speech or press. What is the Court's attitude on restraints imposed after the speech is made or after the book has been made available to the public? As Chafee pointed out so clearly, the Blackstone approach would leave the speaker or the writer at the mercy of the law once he had exercised his right to put his ideas before the public. Such an attitude would make a mockery of the constitutional guarantees. Recognizing this, the Court and thoughtful writers have explored several approaches in their attempts to set out workable doctrines as decisional rules for determining the permissible area of restraint on First Amendment rights. The development of these approaches is taken up in the following section.

## DOCTRINES ADVANCED AS TESTS OF CONSTITUTIONALITY OF FIRST AMENDMENT RESTRAINTS

Probably the best known judicial test in the First Amendment area is the "clear and present danger" test formulated by Justice Holmes in *Schenck* v. *United States* in 1919. The case presented the delicate issue of the area of criticism and dissent allowable during time of war. The decision holds that the rights of speech and press are not and were not intended to be absolute rights, but must be subject to certain reasonable restraints. At the same time, Justice Holmes, for a unanimous Court, set out his controversial proposition regarding the requirements necessary to support such restraints.

SCHENCK *v.* UNITED STATES

*249 U.S. 47 (1919)*

Mr. Justice Holmes delivered the opinions of the Court.

This is an indictment in three counts. The first charges a conspiracy to violate the Espionage Act of June 15, 1917, . . . by causing and attempting to cause insubordination, etc., in the military and naval forces of the United States, and to obstruct the recruiting and enlistment service of the United States when the United States was at war with the German Empire, to-wit, that the defendants willfully conspired to have printed and circulated to men who had been called and accepted for military service under the Act of May 18, 1917, a document set forth and alleged to be calculated to cause such insubordination and obstruction. . . . The second count alleges a conspiracy to commit an offense against the United States, to-wit, to use the mails for the transmission of matter declared to be nonmailable by . . . the Act of June 15, 1917, to-wit, the above mentioned document, . . . The third count charges an unlawful use of the mails for the transmission of the same matter and otherwise as above. The defendants were found guilty on all the counts. They set up the First Amendment to the Constitution forbidding Congress to make any law abridging the freedom of speech, or of the press, and bringing the case here on that ground have argued some other points also of which we must dispose. . . .

The document in question upon its first printed side recited the first section of the Thirteenth Amendment, said that the idea embodied in it was violated by the Conscription Act and that a conscript is little better than a convict. In impassioned language it intimated that conscription was despotism in its worst form and a monstrous wrong against humanity in the interest of Wall Street's chosen few. It said, "Do not submit to intimidation," but in form at least confined iself to peaceful measures such as a petition for the repeal of the act. The other and later printed side of the sheet was headed "Assert Your Rights." It stated reasons for alleging that any one violated the Constitution when he refused to recognize "your right to assert your opposition to the draft," and went on, "If you do not assert and support your rights, you are helping to deny or disparage rights which it is the solemn duty of all citizens and residents of the United States to retain." It described the arguments on the other side as coming from cunning politicans and a mercenary capitalist press, and even silent consent to the conscription law as helping to support an infamous conspiracy. It denied the power to send our citizens away to foreign shores to shoot up the people of other lands, and added that words could not express the condemnation such cold-blooded ruthlessness deserves, &c., &c., winding up, "You must do your share to maintain, support and uphold the rights of the people of this country." Of course the document would not have been sent unless it had been intended to have some effect, and we do not see what effect it could be expected to have upon persons subject to the draft except to influence them to obstruct the carrying of it out. The defendants do not deny that the jury might find against them on this point.

But it is said, suppose that that was the tendency of the circular, it is protected by the First Amendment to the Constitution. Two of the strongest expressions are said to be quoted respectively from well-known public men. It well may be that the prohibition of laws abridging the freedom of speech is not confined to previous restraints, although to prevent them may have been the main purpose, as intimated in *Patterson* v. *Colorado*, 205 U.S. 454, 462. We admit that in many places and in ordinary times the defendants saying all that was said in the circular would have been within their constitutional rights. But the character of every act depends upon the circumstances in which it is done. *Aikens* v. *Wisconsin*, 195 U.S. 194, 205, 206. The most stringent protection of free speech would not protect a man in falsely shouting fire in a theatre and causing a panic. It does not even protect a man from an injunction against uttering words that may have all the effect of force. *Gompers* v. *Bucks Stove & Range Co.*, 221 U.S. 418, 439. The question in every case is whether the words used are used in such circumstances and are of such a nature as to create a clear and present danger that they will bring about the substantive evils that Congress has a right to prevent. It is a question of proximity and degree. When a nation is at war many things that might be said in time of peace are such a hindrance to its effort that their utterance will not be endured so long as men fight and that no Court could regard them as protected by any constitutional right. It seems to be admitted that if an actual obstruction of the recruiting service were proved, liability for words that produced that effect might be enforced. The Statute of 1917, in Section 4, punishes conspiracies to obstruct as well as actual obstruction. If the act (speaking, or circulating a paper), its tendency and the intent with which it is done, are the same, we perceive no ground for saying that success alone warrants making the act a crime. . . .

*Judgments affirmed.*

Nine months after the *Schenck* case the Court decided *Abrams* v. *United States*, 250 U.S. 616 (1919). (For an excellent treatment of this case see Chafee, *Free Speech in the United States*, pp. 108–140). In August 1918, while the United States was still at war with Germany, American troops were ordered to Vladivostok as a move to hinder the success of the Russian Revolution. Abrams and others began meeting in their "third-floor back" in New York's East Side and decided to protest against the attack on the Russian Revolution, with which they strongly sympathized. They printed several thousand leaflets and distributed them. There were general exhortations to munitions workers to strike in order to prevent American interference in the Revolution. There was no evidence that any of the leaflets reached any munitions workers or that anyone was led to stop war work. The five defendants were convicted and sentenced to twenty years imprisonment. The United States Supreme Court affirmed the convictions. The majority found that the defendants had intended to "urge, incite, and advocate" curtailment of production necessary to the war with Germany and were thus guilty of violation of the Sedition Act of 1918. Justice Holmes, with Justice Brandeis concurring, dissented. His opinion stated in part:

I never have seen any reason to doubt that the questions of law that alone were before this Court in the cases of *Schenck, Frohwerk* and *Debs*, . . . were rightly decided. I do not doubt for a moment that by the same reasoning that would justify punishing persuasion to murder, the United States constitutionally may punish speech that produces or is intended to produce a clear and imminent danger that it will bring about forthwith certain substantive evils that the United States constitutionally may seek to prevent. The power undoubtedly is greater in time of war than in time of peace because war opens dangers that do not exist at other times.

But as against dangers peculiar to war, as against others, the principle of the right to free speech is always the same. It is only the present danger of immediate evil or an intent to bring it about that warrants Congress in setting a limit to the expression of opinion where private rights are not concerned. Congress certainly cannot forbid all effort to change the mind of the country. Now nobody can suppose that the surreptitious publishing of a silly leaflet by an unknown man, without more, would present any immediate danger that its opinions would hinder the success of the government arms or have any appreciable tendency to do so. Publishing those opinions for the very purpose of obstructing, however, might indicate a greater danger and at any rate would have the quality of an attempt. So I assume that the second leaflet if published for the purposes alleged in the fourth count might be punishable. But it seems pretty clear to me that nothing less than that would bring these papers within the scope of this law. . . .

I do not see how anyone can find the intent required by the statute in any of the defendants' words. The second leaflet is the only one that affords even a foundation for the charge, and there, without invoking the hatred of German militarism expressed in the former one, it is evident from the beginning to the end that the only object of the paper is to help Russia and stop American intervention there against the popular government—not to impede the United States in the war that it was carrying on. To say that two phrases taken literally might import a suggestion of conduct that would have interference with the war as an indirect and probably undesired effect seems to be by no means enough to show an attempt to produce that effect. . . .

Persecution for the expression of opinions seems to me perfectly logical. If you have no doubt of your premises or your power and want a certain result with all your heart you naturally express your wishes in law and sweep away all opposition. To allow opposition by speech seems to indicate that you think the speech impotent, as when a man says that he has squared the circle, or that you do not care wholeheartedly for the result, or that you doubt either your power or your premises. But when men have realized that time has upset many fighting faiths, they may come to believe even more than they believe the very foundation of their own conduct that the ultimate good desired is better reached by free trade in ideas—that the best test of truth is the power of the thought to get itself accepted in the competition of the market, and that truth is the only ground upon which their wishes safely can be carried out. That at any rate is the theory of our Constitution. It is an experiment, as all life is an experiment. Every year if not every day we have to wager our salvation upon some prophecy based upon imperfect knowledge. While that experiment is part of our system I think that we should be eternally vigilant against attempts to check the expression of opinions that we loathe and believe to be fraught with death, unless they so imminently threaten immediate interference with the lawful and pressing purposes of the law that an immediate check is required to save the country. I wholly disagree with the argument of the Government that the First Amendment left the common law as to seditious libel in force. I had conceived that the United States through many years had shown its repentance for the Sedition Act of 1798, by repaying fines that it imposed. Only the emergency that makes it immediately dangerous to leave the correction of evil counsels to time warrants making any exception to the sweeping command, "Congress shall make no law . . . abridging the freedom of speech." Of course I am speaking only of expressions of opinion and exhortations, which were all that were uttered here, but I regret that I cannot put into more impressive words my belief that in their conviction upon this indictment the defendants were deprived of their rights under the Constitution of the United States.

It seems to be a reasonable inference from Justice Holmes' pronouncements in the two preceding cases that the Court itself would have the final word on whether a given speech or publication presented the requisite "clear and present danger"—at least where the issue was appropriately raised. In *Gitlow* v. *New York*, 268 U.S. 652 (1925), however, the majority gave the doctrine a different cast.

GITLOW *v.* NEW YORK
*268 U.S. 652 (1925)*

[Benjamin Gitlow was convicted in the Supreme Court of New York of the statutory crime of criminal anarchy, in that he and others published and distributed various papers advocating the revolutionary overthrow of the government. He was a member of the Left Wing section of the Socialist Party and participated in the publication and circulation of a Left Wing Manifesto in the official organ entitled "The Revolutionary Age." Several thousand copies of the paper were distributed by mail and by direct sale. The manifesto called for a "Communist revolution" and mobilizing the "power of the proletariat in action," through mass industrial revolts developing into mass political strikes and "revolutionary mass action" for the purpose of conquering and destroying the parliamentary state and establishing in its place the "system of Communist Socialism."]

Justice Sanford delivered the opinion of the Court. . . .

By enacting the present statute the state has determined, through its legislative body, that utterances advocating the overthrow of organized government by force, violence, and unlawful means, are so inimical to the general welfare, and involve such danger of substantive evil, that they may be penalized in the exercise of its police power. That determination must be given great weight. . . . That utterances inciting to the overthrow of organized government by unlawful means present a sufficient danger of substantive evil to bring their punishment within the range of legislative discretion is clear. Such utterances, by their very nature, involve danger to the public peace and to the security of the state. They threaten breaches of the peace and ultimate revolution. And the immediate danger is none the less real and substantial because the effect of a given utterance cannot be accurately foreseen. . . .

We cannot hold that the present statute is an arbitrary or unreasonable exercise of the police power of the state, unwarrantably infringing the freedom of speech or press; and we must and do sustain its constitutionality.

This being so it may be applied to every utterance—not too trivial to be beneath the notice of the law—which is of such a character and used with such intent and purpose as to bring it within the prohibition of the statute. . . . In other words, when the legislative body has determined generally, in the constitutional exercise of its discretion, that utterances of a certain kind involve such danger of substantive evil that they may be punished, the question whether any specific utterance coming within the prohibited class is likely, in and of itself, to bring about the substantive evil, is not open to consideration. It is sufficient that the statute itself be constitutional, and that the use of the language comes within its prohibition.

It is clear that the question in such cases is entirely different from that involved in those cases where the statute merely prohibits certain acts involving the danger of substantive evil, without any reference to language itself, and it is sought to apply its provisions to language used by the defendant for the purpose of bringing about the prohibited results. . . . And the general statement in the *Schenck* case that the "question in every case is whether the words are used in such circumstances and are of such a nature as to create a clear and present danger that they will bring about the substantive evils,"—upon which great reliance is placed in the defendant's argument,—was manifestly intended, as shown by the context, to apply only in cases of this class, and has no application to those like the present, where the legislative body itself has previously determined the danger of substantive evil arising from utterances of a specified character. . . .

Justice Holmes, joined by Justice Brandeis, dissenting. . . .

If I am right, then I think that the criterion sanctioned by the full court in *Schenck* v. *United States* . . . applies: "The question in every case is whether the words used are used in such circumstances and are of such a nature as to create a clear and present danger that they will bring about the substantive evils that [the state] has a right to prevent." It is true that in my opinion this criterion was departed from in *Abrams* v. *United States*, . . . but the convictions that I expressed in that case are too deep for it to be possible for me as yet to believe that it and *Schaefer* v. *United States* . . . have settled the law. If what I think the correct test is applied, it is manifest that there was no present danger of an attempt to overthrow the government by force on the part of the admittedly small minority who shared the defendant's views. It is said that this Manifesto was more than a theory, that it was an incitement. Every idea is an incitement. It offers itself for belief, and, if believed, it is acted on unless some other belief outweighs it, or some failure of energy stifles the movement at its birth. The only difference between the expression of an opinion and an incitement in the narrower sense is the speaker's enthusiasm for the result. Eloquence may set fire to reason. But whatever may be thought of the redundant discourse before us, it had no chance of starting a present conflagration. If, in the long run, the beliefs expressed in proletarian dictatorship are destined to be accepted by the dominant forces of the community, the only meaning of free speech is that they should be given their chance and have their way.

If the publication of this document had been laid as an attempt to induce an uprising against government at once, and not at some indefinite time in the future, it would have presented a different question. The object would have been one with which the law might deal, subject to the doubt whether there was any danger that the publication could produce any result; or, in other words, whether it was not futile and too remote from possible consequences. But the indictment alleges the publication and nothing more.

Since Justice Holmes had formulated the "clear and present danger" statement and had written the opinion for a unanimous Court when it first appeared in the official reports, and since Justice Sanford was not even on the Court when the *Schenck* case was decided, Justice Sanford's attempt to explain the appropriate application of the doctrine might seem to indicate considerable temerity. The majority in *Abrams* had disagreed with Justice Holmes, but no mention was made by them of the clear and present danger test.

It appears that the majority in *Gitlow* employed the normal test of reasonableness coupled with the presumption of validity accorded legislative determinations. Speech was to be accorded no different treatment than any other area subject to legislative restraint, and the statutory finding of clear and present danger was to be conclusive upon the courts. It seems equally clear that the Holmes test was either purposely designed or, at the very least, used as a judicial tool for according special protection to the rights of expression against overzealous application of restraints. It did not purport to set up an absolute freedom to speak and publish, but as Justice Holmes applied the phrase it was a useful mechanism for broadening the permissible area of speech and press and for allowing the courts to examine more critically than before the restraints on those rights. Justice Black's gloss on the doctrine affords the maximum scope. In his opinion for the Court in *Bridges* v. *California*, 314 U.S. 252 (1941), he stated, "What finally emerges from the 'clear and present danger' cases is a working principle that the substantive evil must be extremely serious and the degree of imminence extremely high before utterances can be punished." On the other hand, Justice Frankfurter minimized the utility of the phrase. In his concurring opinion in *Pennekamp* v *Florida*, 328 U.S. 331 (1946), he stated:

"Clear and present danger" was never used by Mr. Justice Holmes to express a technical legal doctrine or to convey a formula for adjudicating cases. It was a literary phrase not to be distorted by being taken from its context. In its setting it served to indicate the importance of freedom of speech to a free society but also to emphasize that its exercise must be compatible with the preservation of other freedoms essential to a democracy and guaranteed by our Constitution. When those other attributes of a democracy are threatened by speech, the Constitution does not deny power to the states to curb it.

The years since *Schenck* and *Gitlow* have seen a variety of different, even tortured, applications of the clear and present danger doctrine. [See, for example, the opinions in *Dennis* v. *United States*, 341 U.S. 494 (1951).] It has been subjected to criticism as well as praise, and to avoid this collateral controversy the Court today seems to feel that it can handle First Amendment cases more easily by simply omitting reference to the doctrine altogether. The one exception in recent years is *Wood* v. *Georgia*, 370 U.S. 375 (1962), in which the test was applied to invalidate a conviction for contempt of court based upon a sheriff's criticism of certain judges which allegedly interfered with a grand jury proceeding. Two justices dissented, but all justices accepted the application of the test in the case.

While the customary view has been that the clear and present danger doctrine had as its primary function the *broadening* of the permissible area of First Amendment freedoms, there have been some who have argued that to use such a test is to *restrict* First Amendment rights and therefore to violate the Constitution. The foremost exponent of this view has been Alexander Meiklejohn.

In his book *Free Speech and Its Relation to Self-Government*, Professor Meiklejohn argued that the protection accorded freedom of speech by the First Amendment was absolute, unqualified, and admits of no exceptions. But he made an interesting distinction between "public" speech (on matters concerning government, public policy, and the welfare of the nation) and "private" speech (on all other nonpublic matters). Public speech comes under the absolute protection of the First Amendment, while private speech is protected by the Fifth Amendment's protection accorded the "liberty" of the people, and thus such speech can be restricted if the restrictions meet the test of due process of law. He argued that the "clear and present danger" test, while better than the *Gitlow* approach, would still be an improper restraint on freedom of speech if employed in a case involving *public* discussion rather than speech concerning *private* matters. In 1962, in a public interview with Professor Edmond Cahn, Justice Black indicated an even stronger position in favor of freedom of speech than did Professor Meiklejohn. Some questions and Justice Black's answers follow:[2]

Suppose we start with one of the key sentences in your James Madison Lecture where you said, "It is my belief that there *are* 'absolutes' in our Bill of Rights, and that they were put there on purpose by men who knew what words meant and meant their prohibitions to be 'absolutes.' " Will you please explain your reasons for this.

JUSTICE BLACK: My first reason is that I believe the words do mean what they say. I have no reason to challenge the intelligence, integrity or honesty of the men who wrote the First Amendment. . . .

I learned a long time ago that there are affirmative and negative words. The beginning of the First Amendment is that "Congress shall make no law." I understand that it is rather old-fashioned and shows a slight naivete to say that "no law" means no law. It is one of the most amazing things about the ingeniousness of the times that strong arguments are made, which *almost* convince me, that it is very foolish of me to think "no law" means no law. But what it *says* is "Congress shall make no law respecting an establishment of religion," and so on.

I have to be honest about it. I confess not only that I think the Amendment means what it says but also that I may be slightly influenced by the fact that I do not think Congress *should* make any law with respect to these subjects. . . .

CAHN: Some of your colleagues would say that it is better to interpret the Bill of Rights so as to permit Congress to take what it considers reasonable steps to preserve the security of the nation even at some sacrifice of freedom of speech and association. Otherwise what will happen to the nation and the Bill of Rights as well? What is your view of this?

[2]"Justice Black and First Amendment 'Absolutes': A Public Interview," 37 *N.Y.U. L. Rev.* 549 (1962). Reprinted by permission of the *New York University Law Review* and Justice Black.

JUSTICE BLACK: . . . Of course, I want this country to do what will preserve it. I want it to be preserved as the kind of Government it was intended to be. I would not desire to live at any place where my thoughts were under the suspicion of government and where my words could be censored by government, and where worship, whatever it was or wasn't, had to be determined by an officer of the government. That is not the kind of government I want preserved.

I agree with those who wrote our Constitution, that too much power in the hands of officials is a dangerous thing. What was government created for except to serve the people? Why was a Constitution written for the first time in this country except to limit the power of government and those who were selected to exercise it at the moment?

My answer to the statement that this Government should preserve itself is yes. The method I would adopt is different, however, from that of some other people. I think it can be preserved only by leaving people with the utmost freedom to think and to hope and to talk and to dream if they want to dream. I do not think this Government must look to force, stifling the minds and aspirations of the people. Yes, I believe in self-preservation, but I would preserve it as the founders said, by leaving people free. I think here, as in another time, it cannot live half slave and half free. . . .

CAHN: Do you make an exception in freedom of speech and press for the law of defamation? That is, are you willing to allow people to sue for damages when they are subjected to libel or slander?

JUSTICE BLACK: My view of the First Amendment, as originally ratified, is that it said Congress should pass none of these kinds of laws. As written at that time, the Amendment applied only to Congress. I have no doubt myself that the provision, as written and adopted, intended that there should be no libel or defamation law in the United States under the United States Government, just absolutely none so far as I am concerned. . . .

My belief is that the First Amendment was made applicable to the states by the Fourteenth. I do not hesitate, so far as my own view is concerned, as to what should be and what I hope will sometime be the constitutional doctrine that just as it was not intended to authorize damage suits for mere words as distinguished from conduct as far as the Federal Government is concerned, the same rule should apply to the states. . . .

I believe with Jefferson that it is time enough for government to step in to regulate people when they *do* something, not when they *say* something, and I do not believe myself that there is *any* halfway ground if they enforce the protections of the First Amendment. . . .

CAHN: Is there any kind of obscene material, whether defined as hardcore pornography or otherwise, the distribution and sale of which can be constitutionally restricted in any manner whatever, in your opinion?

JUSTICE BLACK: I will say it can in this country, because the courts have held that it can.

CAHN: Yes, but you won't get off so easily. I want to know what you think.

JUSTICE BLACK: My view is, without deviation, without exception, without any ifs, buts, or whereases, that freedom of speech means that you shall not do something to people either for the views they have or the views they express or the words they speak or write.

There is strong argument for the position taken by a man whom I admire very greatly, Dr. Meiklejohn, that the First Amendment really was intended to protect *political* speech, and I do think that was the basic purpose; that plus the fact that they wanted to protect *religious* speech. Those were the two main things they had in mind.

It is the law that there can be an arrest made for obscenity. It was the law in Rome that they could arrest people for obscenity after Augustus became Caesar. Tacitus says that then it became obscene to criticize the Emperor. It is not any trouble to establish a classification so that whatever it is that you do not want said is within that classification. So far as I am concerned, I do not believe there is any halfway ground for protecting freedom of speech and press. If you say it is half free, you can rest assured that it will not remain as much as half free. Madison explained that in his great Remonstrance when he said in effect, "If you make laws to force people to speak the words of Christianity, it won't be long until the same power will narrow the sole religion to the most powerful sect in it." I realize that there are dangers in freedom of speech, but I do not believe there are any halfway marks.

CAHN: Do you subscribe to the idea involved in the clear and present danger rule?

JUSTICE BLACK: I do not.

The "absolutist" position on First Amendment rights has never gained the acceptance of a majority on the Court, but it is a recurring theme in many of the dissenting opinions of Justice Black, who was frequently joined by Chief Justice Warren and Justice Douglas.

Another approach to the judicial handling of restrictions on freedom of expression is the "preferred position" doctrine, which posits that First Amendment rights should be given priority by comparison with other guarantees in the Bill of Rights. Variations on this theme were presented at least as early as 1788 in letters of Thomas Paine and Thomas Jefferson. [Edmond Cahn gives an interesting historical analysis in "The Firstness of the First Amendment," 65 *Yale L. J.* 464 (1956).] The main thrust of the doctrine, although not the phrase itself, made its first appearance in judicial opinions in Justice Stone's now famous "footnote 4" in his opinion for the Court in *United States* v. *Carolene Products Company*, 304 U.S. 144, 152, n. 4 (1938). In it he stated:

There may be narrower scope for operation of the presumption of constitutionality when legislation appears on its face to be within a specific prohibition of the Constitution, such as those of the first ten Amendments, which are deemed equally specific when held to be embraced within the Fourteenth. . . .

It is unnecessary to consider now whether legislation which restricts those political processes which can ordinarily be expected to bring about repeal of undesirable legislation, is to be subjected to more exacting judicial scrutiny under the general prohibitions of the Fourteenth Amendment than are most other types of legislation.

In *Murdock* v. *Pennsylvania* in 1943 Justice Douglas, speaking for a majority of the Court, said: "Freedom of the press, freedom of speech, freedom of religion are in a preferred position." A more elaborate statement of the doctrine appeared two years later in *Thomas* v. *Collins*, 323 U.S. 516 (1945). The case dealt with the validity of a labor organizer's conviction for contempt of court for violating an order that he refrain from addressing a meeting until he first registered and obtained an organizer's card as required by Texas law. In holding the requirement invalid, and thus the conviction as well, Justice Rutledge, speaking for the majority, stated:

The case confronts us again with the duty our system places on this Court to say where the individual's freedom ends and the State's power begins. Choice on that border, now as always delicate, is perhaps more so where the usual presumption supporting legislation is balanced by the preferred place given in our scheme to the great, the indispensable democratic freedoms secured by the First Amendment. That priority gives these liberties a sanctity and a sanction not permitting dubious intrusions. And it is the character of the right, not of the limitation, which determines what standard governs the choice.

In effect, the theory of this doctrine is that the presumption of validity of legislation under attack is reversed when the questioned legislation affects adversely First Amendment freedom of expression. Thus, while formerly the Court took the view that state or federal laws were constitutional until proved otherwise, the "preferred position" concept would shift the burden of proof to the government to show that the attempted restriction was not unconstitutional. By the late 1940s, however, the Court was wavering on the use of this concept, and in 1949 Justice Frankfurter frankly expressed his distrust of its use. The occasion was the Court's consideration of a Trenton, New Jersey, sound truck ordinance in *Kovacs v. Cooper*, 336 U.S. 77 (1949). In the course of his opinion concurring with the majority in holding the ordinance constitutional, Justice Frankfurter took issue with Justice Reed's acceptance of the "preferred position" concept. He stated:

My brother Reed speaks of "The preferred position of freedom of speech," though, to be sure, he finds that the Trenton ordinance does not disregard it. This is a phrase that has uncritically crept into some recent opinions of this Court. I deem it a mischievous phrase, if it carries the thought, which it may subtly imply, that any law touching communication is infected with presumptive invalidity. It is not the first time in the history of constitutional adjudication that such a doctrinaire attitude has disregarded the admonition most to be observed in exercising the Court's reviewing power over legislation, "that it is a *constitution* we are expounding," *McCulloch* v. *Maryland.* . . . I say the phrase is mischievous because it radiates a constitutional doctrine without avowing it. . . .

Behind the notion sought to be expressed by the formula as to "the preferred position of freedom of speech" lies a relevant consideration in determining whether an enactment relating to the liberties protected by the Due Process Clause of the Fourteenth Amendment is violative of it. In law also, doctrine is illuminated by history. The ideas now governing the constitutional protection of freedom of speech derive essentially from the opinions of Mr. Justice Holmes.

The philosophy of his opinions on that subject arose from a deep awareness of the extent to which sociological conclusions are conditioned by time and circumstance. Because of this awareness Mr. Justice Holmes seldom felt justified in opposing his own opinion to economic views which the legislature embodied in law. But since he also realized that the progress of civilization is to a considerable extent the displacement of error which once held sway as official truth by beliefs which in turn have yielded to other beliefs, for him the right to search for truth was of a different order than some transient economic dogma. And without freedom of expression, thought becomes checked and atrophied. Therefore, in considering what interests are so fundamental as to be enshrined in the Due Process Clause, those liberties of the individual which history has attested as the indispensable conditions of an open as against a closed society come to this Court with a momentum for respect lacking when appeal is made to liberties which derive merely from shifting economic arrangements. Accordingly, Mr. Justice Holmes was far more ready to find legislative invasion where free inquiry was involved than in the debatable area of economics. See my Mr. Justice Holmes and the Supreme Court, 58 et seq.

The objection of summarizing this line of thought by the phrase "the preferred position of freedom of speech" is that it expresses a complicated process of constitutional adjudication by a deceptive formula. And it was Mr. Justice Holmes who admonished us that "To rest upon a formula is a slumber that, prolonged, means death." Collected Legal Papers, 306. Such a formula makes for mechanical jurisprudence. . . .

A careful reading of Justice Frankfurter's opinion might lead to the conclusion that he accepted the idea of a gradation of rights, with freedom of expression on public matters as foremost, but he disapproved of a shorthand "doctrine" to express the differentiation. [For further reading on the "preferred position" concept, as well as a detailed analysis of Justice Frankfurter's position, see Robert B. McKay, "The Preference for Freedom," 34 N.Y.U. L. Rev. 1182 (1959).]

More recently the Court has tended to stress a "balancing" test, although some members strongly object to its use, preferring instead something closer to the absolute position. It seems that the first use of the "balancing" test by the Court is to be found in Chief Justice Vinson's opinion for the majority in *American Communications Ass'n., CIO v. Douds*, 339 U.S. 382 (1950), in which the Court upheld the non-Communist affidavit provision of the Labor Management Relations Act of 1947. In the course of his opinion he stated:

So far as the *Schenck* case itself is concerned, imminent danger of any substantive evil that Congress may prevent justifies the restriction of speech. . . . But in suggesting that the substantive evil must be serious and substantial, it was never the intention of this Court to lay down an absolutist test measured in terms of danger to the Nation. When the effect of a statute or ordinance upon the exercise of First Amendment freedoms is relatively small and the public interest to be protected is substantial, it is obvious that a rigid test requiring a showing of imminent danger to the security of the Nation is an absurdity. . . .

When particular conduct is regulated in the interest of public order, and the regulation results in an indirect, conditional, partial abridgment of speech, the duty of the courts is to determine which of these two conflicting interests demands the greater protection under the particular circumstances presented. The high place in which the right to speak, think, and assemble as you will was held by the Framers of the Bill of Rights and is held today by those who value liberty both as a means and an end indicates the solicitude with which we must view any assertion of personal freedoms. . . .

On the other hand, legitimate attempts to protect the public, not from the remote possible effects of noxious ideologies, but from present excesses of direct, active conduct are not presumptively bad because they interfere with and, in some of its manifestations, restrain the exercise of First Amendment rights. . . . In essence, the problem is one of weighing the probable effects of the statute upon the free exercise of the right of speech and assembly against the congressional determination that political strikes are evils of conduct which cause substantial harm to interstate commerce and that Communists and others identified by Section 9(h) pose continuing threats to the public interest when in positions of union leadership. We must, therefore, undertake the "delicate and difficult task . . . to weigh the circumstances and to appraise the substantiality of the reason advanced in support of the regulation of the free enjoyment of the rights." *Schneider v. Irvington*, 308 U.S. 147, 161.

Justices Frankfurter, Harlan, and Clark were leading supporters of the "balancing" test in the period beginning in 1950. In *Dennis v. United States*, 341 U.S. 494 (1951), upholding sections of the Smith Act of 1940, Justice Frankfurter made the following statements in his concurring opinion:

The demands of free speech in a democratic society as well as the interest in national security are better served by candid and informed weighing of the competing interests, within the confines of the judicial process, than by announcing dogmas too inflexible for the non-Euclidian problems to be solved.

But how are competing interests to be assessed? Since they are not subject to quantitative ascertainment, the issue necessarily resolves itself into asking, who is to make the adjustment?—who is to balance the relevant factors and ascertain which interest is in the circumstances to prevail? Full responsibility for the choice cannot be given to the courts. Courts are not representative bodies. They are not designed to be a good reflex of a democratic society. Their judgment is best informed, and therefore most dependable, within narrow limits. Their essential quality is detachment, founded on independence. History teaches that the independence of the judiciary is jeopardized when courts become embroiled in the passions of the day and assume primary responsibility in choosing between competing political, economic and social pressures.

Primary responsibility for adjusting the interests which compete in the situation before us of necessity belongs to the Congress. The nature of the power to be exercised by this Court has been delineated in decisions not charged with the emotional appeal of situations such as that now before us. We are to set aside the judgment of those whose duty it is to legislate only if there is no reasonable basis for it. . . .

. . . Free-speech cases are not an exception to the principle that we are not legislators, that direct policy-making is not our province. How best to reconcile competing interests is the business of legislatures, and the balance they strike is a judgment not to be displaced by ours, but to be respected unless outside the pale of fair judgment. . . .

. . . A survey of the relevant decisions indicates that the results which we have reached are on the whole those that would ensue from careful weighing of conflicting interests. The complex issues presented by regulation of speech in public places by picketing, and by legislation prohibiting advocacy of crime have been resolved by scrutiny of many factors besides the imminence and gravity of the evil threatened. The matter has been well summarized by a reflective student of the Court's work. "The truth is that the clear-and-present-danger test is an oversimplified judgment unless it takes account also of a number of other factors: the relative seriousness of the danger in comparison with the value of the occasion for speech or political activity; the availability of more moderate controls than those which the state has imposed; and perhaps the specific intent with which the speech or activity is launched. No matter how rapidly we utter the phrase 'clear and present danger,' or how closely we hyphenate the words, they are not a substitute for the weighing of values. They tend to convey a delusion of certitude when what is most certain is the complexity of the strands in the web of freedoms which the judge must disentangle." Freund, *On Understanding the Supreme Court*, 27–28.

Justice Harlan made use of the "balancing" test in his opinion for a unanimous Court in *NAACP v. Alabama*, 357 U.S. 449 (1958), in which the Court held invalid the order of an Alabama court requiring the disclosure of membership rolls of the Alabama affiliates of the National Association for the Advancement of Colored People. Justice Harlan's opinion pointed out that "the production order, in the respects here drawn in question, must be regarded as entailing the likelihood of a substantial restraint upon the exercise by petitioner's members of their right to freedom of association." He then stated: "We turn to the final question whether Alabama has demonstrated an interest in obtaining the disclosures it seeks from petitioner which is sufficient to justify the deterrent effect which we have concluded these disclosures may well have on the free exercise by petitioner's members of their constitutionally protected right of association." The phraseology is thus clearly indicative of the employment of a "balancing" test of constitutionality. And Justice Clark, in his dissenting opinion in *Talley* v. *California*, 362 U.S. 60 (1960), dealing with the constitutionality of a Los Angeles ordinance requiring the name and address of sponsors on any handbills distributed, said: "[B]efore passing upon the validity of the ordinance, I would weigh the interests of the public in its enforcement against the claimed right of Talley."

Justices Black and Douglas were vigorous opponents of the use of the "balancing" test in the First Amendment area. In *Barenblatt* v. *United States*, 360 U.S. 109 (1959), in which the Court upheld the conviction for contempt of Congress for refusal to answer committee questions concerning Communist Party membership, and in which Barenblatt grounded his refusal on First Amendment protection to belief and associated activity, Justice Black dissented, saying:

The First Amendment says in no equivocal language that Congress shall pass no law abridging freedom of speech, press, assembly or petition. The activities of this Committee, authorized by Congress, do precisely that, through exposure, obloquy and public scorn. . . .

(A) I do not agree that laws directly abridging First Amendment freedoms can be justified by a congressional or judicial balancing process. There are, of course, cases suggesting that a law which primarily regulates conduct but which might also indirectly affect speech can be upheld if the effect on speech is minor in relation to the need for control of the conduct. With these cases I agree. Typical of them are *Cantwell* v. *State of Connecticut* 310 U.S. 296, and *Schneider* v. *Irvington*, 308 U.S. 147. Both of these involved the right of a city to control its streets. . . . In so holding, we, of course, found it necessary to "weigh the circumstances." But we did not in *Schneider*, any more than in *Cantwell*, even remotely suggest that a law directly aimed at curtailing speech and political persuasion could be saved through a balancing process. . . .

To apply the Court's balancing test under such circumstances is to read the First Amendment to say "Congress shall pass no law abridging freedom of speech, press, assembly and petition, unless Congress and the Supreme Court reach the joint conclusion that on balance the interests of the Government in stifling these freedoms is greater than the interest of the people in having them exercised." This is closely akin to the notion that neither the First Amendment nor any other provision of the Bill of Rights should be enforced unless the Court believes it is *reasonable* to do so. Not only does this violate the genius of our *written* Constitution, but it runs expressly counter to the injunction to Court and Congress made by Madison when he introduced the Bill of Rights.

Yet another facet of the Court's approach to restrictions on First Amendment rights is the "less drastic means" test. In *Shelton* v. *Tucker*, 364 U.S. 479 (1960), the Court held invalid, as an abridgment of the freedom of association, an Arkansas statute that compelled every teacher in a state-supported school to file annually an affidavit listing without limitation every organization to which he belonged or regularly contributed within the preceding five years. While it was agreed that the State could investigate the fitness and competence of its school teachers, the majority held that this law went too far:

In a series of decisions this Court has held that, even though the governmental purpose be legitimate and substantial, that purpose cannot be pursued by means that broadly stifle fundamental personal liberties when the end can be more narrowly achieved. The breadth of legislative abridgment must be viewed in the light of less drastic means for achieving the same basic purpose.

In *United States* v. *Robel*, 389 U.S. 258 (1967), Chief Justice Warren cited *Shelton* and said: "Our decision today simply recognizes that, when legitimate legislative concerns are expressed in a statute which imposes a substantial burden on protected First Amendment activities, Congress must achieve its goal by means which have a "less drastic" impact on the continued vitality of First Amendment freedoms." In *Robel* the Court held unconstitutional a section of the Subversive Activities Control Act of 1950 that made it a crime for a member of a Communist-action organization under a final order to register with the Attorney General "to engage in any employment in any defense facility." It was agreed that Congress could protect sensitive defense industries from those who would disrupt production, but the Court held this section of the law too broad. The Chief Justice gave an interesting justification for refusing to employ the "balancing" test:

It has been suggested that this case should be decided by "balancing" the governmental interests expressed in [the law] against the First Amendment rights asserted by the appellee. This we decline to do. We recognize that both interests are substantial, but we deem it inappropriate for this Court to label one as being more important or more substantial than the other. Our inquiry is more circumscribed. Faced with a clear conflict between a federal statute enacted in the interests of national security and an individual's exercise of his First Amendment rights, we have confined our analysis to whether Congress has adopted a constitutional means in achieving its concededly legitimate legislative goal. In making this determination we have found it necessary to measure the validity of the means adopted by Congress against both the goal it has sought to achieve and the specific prohibitions of the First Amendment. But we have in no way "balanced" those respective interests. We have ruled only that the Constitution requires that the rights be accommodated by legislation drawn more narrowly to avoid the conflict. . . . (at 268, fn. 20.).

It can be seen that there are a variety of "'doctrines," "principles," or "tests" which have been employed or suggested for determining the validity of restraints on First Amendment freedom of expression. But there is substantial disagreement among the members of the Court and among leading scholars as to the appropriate test to employ. The problem is further complicated by the fact that some of the members of the Court have stated that First Amendment cases must be categorized and different tests employed for the different categories. Justice Black indicated as much in the portion of his dissent in *Barenblatt* quoted above. Thus a street regulation which indirectly affects speech may be handled under a "balancing" test, but a straight restriction on First Amendment freedom of expression may not be. Justice Jackson, in his concurring opinion in the *Dennis* case, suggested a different division. Discussing the "clear and present danger" test, he stated:

I would save it, unmodified, for application as a "rule of reason" in the kind of case for which it was devised. When the issue is criminality of a hot-headed speech on a street corner, or circulation of a few incendiary pamphlets, or parading by some zealots behind a red flag, or refusal of a handful of school children to salute our flag, it is not beyond the capacity of the judicial process to gather, comprehend, and weigh the necessary materials for decision whether it is a clear and present danger of substantive evil or a harmless letting off of steam. It is not a prophecy, for the danger in such cases has matured by the time of trial or it was never present. The test applies and has meaning where a conviction is sought to be based on a speech or writing which does not directly or explicitly advocate a crime but to which such tendency is sought to be attributed by construction or by implication from external circumstances. The formula in such cases favors freedoms that are vital to our society, and, even if sometimes applied too generously, the consequences cannot be grave. But its recent expansion has extended, in particular to Communists, unprecedented immunities. Unless we are to hold our Government captive in a judge-made trap, we must approach the problem of a well-organized, nationwide conspiracy, such as I have described, as realistically as our predecessors faced the trivialities that were being prosecuted until they were checked with a rule of reason. . . .

The authors of the clear and present danger test never applied it to a case like this, nor would I. If applied as it is proposed here, it means that the Communist plotting is protected during its period of incubation; its preliminary stages of organization and preparation are immune from the law; the Government can move only after imminent action is manifest, when it would, of course, be too late.

A majority of the Court has more recently developed an exacting-scrutiny approach to restrictions on speech (in all its forms) where the restrictions are based on the *content* of the speech and the activity takes place on public forums, such as streets and parks. In *Perry Education Ass'n* v. *Perry Local Educators' Ass'n,* 460 U.S. 37 (1983), Justice White, for the majority, stated:

In these quintessential public forums, the government may not prohibit all communicative activity. For the State to enforce a content-based exclusion it must show that its regulation is necessary to serve a compelling state interest and that it is narrowly drawn to achieve that end. . . . The State may also enforce regulations of the time, place, and manner of expression which are content-neutral, are narrowly tailored to serve a significant government interest, and leave open ample alternative channels of communication.

[For further treatment of the various doctrines applied to freedom of expression, see Zechariah Chafee, Jr., *Free Speech in the United States, passim;* Thomas I. Emerson, "Toward a General Theory of the First Amendment," 72 *Yale L. J.* 877 (1963); and Charles B. Nutting, "Is the First Amendment Obsolete?" 30 *Geo. Wash. L. Rev.* 167 (1961). On the "clear and present danger" test, see Chester J. Antieau, "The Rule of Clear and Present Danger—Its Origin and Application," 13 *U. Det. L. J.* 198 (1950); Chester J. Antieau, "The Rule of Clear and Present Danger: Scope of Its Applicability," 48 *Mich. L. Rev.* 811 (1950); and Robert B. McKay, "The Preference for Freedom," 34 *N.Y.U. L. Rev.* 1182 (1959). On the "absolutist" approach, see Alexander Meiklejohn, "The Balancing of Self-Preservation Against Political Freedom," 49 *Calif. L. Rev.* 4 (1961), and "The First Amendment Is an Absolute," 1961 *Sup. Ct. Rev.* 245. On the "balancing" test, see Wallace Mendelson, "On the Meaning of the First Amendment: Absolutes in the Balance," 50 *Calif. L. Rev.* 821 (1962); and Laurent B. Frantz, "The First Amendment in the Balance," 71 *Yale L. J.* 1424 (1962).]

The contrapuntal application of these doctrines in the major areas of First Amendment controversy can be most easily seen in the categorized examination of the cases. The remaining portion of this chapter will be devoted to delineating the scope of protection offered in the more important areas of governmental restraint on freedom of expression.

## INTERNAL SECURITY

One of the most notorious instances of governmental repression of freedom of expression in American history was the enactment of the Sedition Act of 1798. There were a number of interesting aspects of the operation of the law. Although the verdict of history has been that it was unconstitutional, the act was never challenged in the United States Supreme Court. The act expired by its own terms in 1801, after two years of operation.

And despite the furor the act aroused, only ten persons were convicted under it, although many more were indicted but never tried. One Jared Peck was indicted under the act for circulating a petition to Congress asking that the act be repealed. [For the best account of the Alien and Sedition Acts, see James Morton Smith, *Freedom's Fetters* (Ithaca: Cornell University Press, 1956).] The important portions of the act prohibited the writing, printing, or uttering "any false, scandalous and malicious writings against the government of the United States, or either house of the Congress of the United States, or the President" with intent to defame them, or to bring them into contempt or disrepute, or "to excite any unlawful combinations therein, for opposing or resisting any law of the United States. . . ." The punishment was a fine not exceeding $2,000 and imprisonment not exceeding two years.

The next important pieces of federal legislation restricting speech and press did not come until World War I, with the enactment of the Espionage Act of 1917 and the Sedition Act of 1918. As indicated earlier, these acts were upheld in *Schenck* v. *United States* and *Abrams* v. *United States*, along with four other cases decided in the period 1919–1920. The Espionage Act penalized the circulation of false statements made with intent to interfere with military success, or attempts to cause insubordination in the military and naval forces of the United States, or to obstruct the recruiting and enlistment service of the United States. The Sedition Act further prohibited speeches or acts obstructing the sale of government bonds, or speaking or writing anything intended to cause contempt for the American form of government, the Constitution, the flag, or the military uniforms, or urging any curtailment of production of things necessary to the prosecution of the war with intent to hinder its prosecution, or supporting the cause of any country at war with us, or opposing the cause of the United States therein. The penalty was $10,000 fine or twenty years imprisonment or both. Nearly a thousand persons were convicted under these two acts, out of about two thousand cases prosecuted. In his *Free Speech in the United States* Professor Chafee devoted a chapter to these prosecutions. He stated:

. . . Almost all the convictions were for expressions of opinion about the merits and conduct of the war.

It became criminal to advocate heavier taxation instead of bond issues, to state that conscription was unconstitutional though the Supreme Court had not yet held it valid, to say that the sinking of merchant vessels was legal, to urge that a referendum should have preceded our declarations of war, to say that war was contrary to the teachings of Christ. Men have been punished for criticising the Red Cross and the Y.M.C.A., while under the Minnesota Espionage Act it has been held a crime to discourage women from knitting by the remark, "No soldier ever sees these socks." [p. 51.]

More recently the Congress enacted the Alien Registration Act of 1940, better known simply as the Smith Act. The Act contains provisions similar to those of New York's Criminal Anarchy Act of 1902, which was upheld in *Gitlow* v. *New York*. It was not until 1951, however, that the United States Supreme Court decided the issue of the constitutionality of the Smith Act. Prior to that case, *Dennis* v. *United States*, the Act had been invoked only twice. In 1941, eighteen Trotskyites were convicted under the Act, and their convictions were affirmed by the Court of Appeals. [*Dunne* v. *United States*, 138 F.2d 137 (C.A. 8th, 1943).] The Supreme Court denied certiorari. A second trial, involving alleged pro-Nazis, was dropped before completion in 1944. [*United States* v. *McWilliams*, 163 F.2d 695 (C.A. D.C., 1947).]

In 1948, eleven top members of the American Community Party were indicted for conspiracies prohibited by Section 3 of the Smith Act. The trial in the District Court in New York was a marathon proceeding, running for nine months and resulting in conviction. The convictions were affirmed by the court of appeals with an opinion by Judge Learned Hand. [*United States* v. *Dennis*, 183 F.2d 201 (C.A. 2d, 1950).] The Supreme Court granted certiorari, limiting review to the constitutional issues raised without examining such issues as the sufficiency of the evidence.

## DENNIS *v.* UNITED STATES
### *341 U.S. 494* (1951)

Mr. Chief Justice Vinson announced the judgment of the Court and an opinion in which Mr. Justice Reed, Mr. Justice Burton and Mr. Justice Minton join.

Petitioners were indicted in July, 1948, for violation of the conspiracy provisions of the Smith Act, 54 Stat. 671, 18 U.S.C. (1946 ed.) Section 11. . . . A verdict of guilty as to all the petitioners was returned by the jury. . . . The Court of Appeals affirmed the convictions. 183 F.2d 201. We granted certiorari . . . limited to the following two questions: (1) Whether either Section 2 or Section 3 of the Smith Act, inherently or as construed and applied in the instant case, violates the First Amendment and other provisions of the Bill of Rights; (2) whether either Section 2 or Section 3 of the Act, inherently or as construed and applied in the instant case, violates the First and Fifth Amendments because of indefiniteness.

Sections 2 and 3 of the Smith Act . . . provide as follows:

"Sec. 2.

"(a) It shall be unlawful for any person—

"(1) to knowingly or wilfully advocate, abet, advise, or teach the duty, necessity, desirability, or propriety of overthrowing or destroying any government in the United States by force or violence, or by the assassination of any officer of such government;

"(2) with intent to cause the overthrow or destruction of any government in the United States, to print, publish, edit, issue, circulate, sell, distribute, or publicly display any written or printed matter advocating, advising, or teaching the duty, necessity, desirability, or propriety of overthrowing or destroying any government in the United States by force or violence;

"(3) to organize or help to organize any society, group, or assembly of persons who teach, advocate, or encourage the overthrow or destruction of any government in the United States by force or violence; or to be or become a member of, or affiliate with, any such society, group, or assembly of persons, knowing the purpose thereof. . . .

"Sec. 3. It shall be unlawful for any person to attempt to commit, or to conspire to commit, any of the acts prohibited by the provisions of . . . this title."

The indictment charged the petitioners with wilfully and knowingly conspiring (1) to organize as the Communist Party of the United States of America a society, group and assembly of persons who teach and advocate the overthrow and destruction of the Government of the United States by force and violence, and (2) knowingly and wilfully to advocate and teach the duty and necessity of overthrowing and destroying the Government of the United States by force and violence. The indictment further alleged that Section 2 of the Smith Act proscribes these acts and that any conspiracy to take such action is a violation of Section 3 of the Act. . . .

### I

It will be helpful in clarifying the issues to treat next the contention that the trial judge improperly interpreted the statute by charging that the statute required an unlawful intent before the jury could convict. More specifically, he charged that the jury could not find the petitioners guilty under the indictment unless they found that petitioners had the intent "to overthrow . . . the Government of the United States by force and violence as speedily as circumstances would permit." . . .

. . . We hold that the statute requires as an essential element of the crime proof of the intention of those who are charged with its violation to overthrow the Government by force and violence. . . .

## II

The obvious purpose of the statute is to protect existing Government, not from change by peaceable, lawful and constitutional means, but from change by violence, revolution and terrorism. That it is within the *power* of the Congress to protect the Government of the United States from armed rebellion is a proposition which requires little discussion. Whatever theoretical merit there may be to the argument that there is a "right" to rebellion against dictatorial governments is without force where the existing structure of the government provides for peaceful and orderly change. We reject any principle of government helplessness in the face of preparation for revolution, which principle, carried to its logical conclusion, must lead to' anarchy. No one could conceive that it is not within the power of Congress to prohibit acts intended to overthrow the Government by force and violence. The question with which we are concerned here is not whether Congress has such *power*, but whether the *means* which it has employed conflict with the First and Fifth Amendments to the Constitution.

One of the bases for the contention that the means which Congress has employed are invalid takes the form of an attack on the face of the statute on the grounds that by its terms it prohibits academic discussion of the merits of Marxism-Leninism, that it stifles ideas and is contrary to all concepts of a free speech and a free press. Although we do not agree that the language itself has that significance, we must bear in mind that it is the duty of the federal courts to interpret federal legislation in a manner not inconsistent with the demands of the Constitution. . . .

The very language of the Smith Act negates the interpretation which petitioners would have us impose on that act. It is directed at advocacy, not discussion. Thus, the trial judge properly charged the jury that they could not convict if they found that petitioners did "no more than pursue peaceful studies and discussions or teachings and advocacy in the realm of ideas." He further charged that it was not unlawful "to conduct in an American college and university a course explaining the philosophical theories set forth in the books which have been placed in evidence." Such a charge is in strict accord with the statutory language, and illustrates the meaning to be placed on those words. Congress did not intend to eradicate the free discussion of political theories, to destroy the traditional rights of Americans to discuss and evaluate ideas without fear of governmental sanctions. Rather Congress was concerned with the very kind of activity in which the evidence showed these petitioners engaged.

## III

. . . No important case involving free speech was decided by this Court prior to *Schenck* v. *United States*, 249 U.S. 47 (1919). . . . Writing for a unanimous Court, Justice Holmes stated that the "question in every case is whether the words used are used in such circumstances and are of such a nature as to create a clear and present danger that they will bring about the substantive evils that Congress has a right to prevent." . . .

. . . But . . . neither Justice Holmes nor Justice Brandeis ever envisioned that a shorthand phrase should be crystallized into a rigid rule to be applied inflexibly without regard to the circumstances of each case. Speech is not absolute, above and beyond control by the legislature when its judgment, subject to review here, is that certain kinds of speech are so undesirable as to warrant criminal sanction. Nothing is more certain in modern society than the principle that there are no absolutes, that a name, a phrase, a standard has meaning only when associated with the considerations which give birth to the nomenclature. . . . To those who would paralyze our Government in the face of impending threat by encasing it in a semantic straitjacket we must reply that all concepts are relative.

In this case we are squarely presented with the application of the "clear and present danger" test, and must decide what that phrase imports. We first note that many of the cases in which this Court has reversed convictions by use of this or similar tests have been based on the fact that the interest which the State was attempting to protect was itself too insubstantial to warrant restriction of speech. . . . Overthrow of the Government by force and violence is certainly a substantial enough interest for the Government to limit speech. Indeed, this is the ultimate value of any society, for if a society cannot protect its very structure from armed internal attack, it must follow that no subordinate value can be protected. If, then, this interest may be protected, the literal problem which is presented is what has been meant by the use of the phrase "clear and present danger" of the utterances bringing about the evil within the power of Congress to punish.

Obviously, the words cannot mean that before the Government may act, it must wait until the *putsch* is about to be executed, the plans have been laid and the signal is awaited. If Government is aware that a group aiming at its overthrow is attempting to indoctrinate its members and to commit them to a course whereby they will strike when the leaders feel the circumstances permit, action by the Government is required. The argument that there is no need for Government to concern itself, for Government is strong, it possesses ample powers to put down a rebellion, it may defeat the revolution with ease needs no answer. For that is not the question. Certainly an attempt to overthrow the Government by force, even though doomed from the outset because of inadequate numbers or power of the revolutionists, is a sufficient evil for Congress to prevent. The damage which such attempts create both physically and politically to a nation makes it impossible to measure the validity in terms of the probability of success, or the immediacy of a successful attempt. In the instant case the trial judge charged the jury that they could not convict unless they found that petitioners intended to overthrow the Government "as speedily as circumstances would permit." This does not mean, and could not properly mean, that they would not strike until there was certainty of success. What was meant was that the revolutionists would strike when they thought the time was ripe. We must therefore reject the contention that success or probability of success is the criterion.

The situation with which Justices Holmes and Brandeis were concerned in *Gitlow* was a comparatively isolated event bearing little relation in their minds to any substantial threat to the safety of the community. . . . They were not confronted with any situation comparable to the instant one—the development of an apparatus designed and dedicated to the overthrow of the Government, in the context of world crisis after crisis.

Chief Judge Learned Hand, writing for the majority below, interpreted the phrase as follows: "In each case [courts] must ask whether the gravity of the 'evil,' discounted by its improbability, justifies such invasion of free speech as is necessary to avoid the danger." We adopt this statement of the rule. As articulated by Chief Judge Hand, it is as succinct and inclusive as any other we might devise at this time. It takes into consideration those factors which we deem relevant, and relates their significances. More we cannot expect from words.

Likewise, we are in accord with the court below, which affirmed the trial court's finding that the requisite danger existed. The mere fact that from the period 1945 to 1948 petitioner's activities did not result in an attempt to overthrow the Government by force and violence is of course no answer to the fact that there was a group that was ready to make the attempt. The formation by petitioners of such a highly organized conspiracy, with rigidly disciplined members subject to call when the leaders, these petitioners, felt that the time had come for action, coupled with the inflammable nature of world conditions, similar uprisings in other countries, and the touch-and-go nature of our relations with countries with whom petitioners were in the very least ideologically attuned, convince us that their convictions were justified on this score. And this analysis disposes of the contention that a conspiracy to advocate, as distinguished from the advocacy itself, cannot be constitutionally restrained, because it comprises only the preparation. It is the existence of the conspiracy which creates the danger. . . .

### IV

[The Chief Justice then considers the contention that the trial judge should have submitted for jury determination the question of whether sufficient danger existed to apply the law rather than making this decision himself as a matter of law.]

When facts are found that establish the violation of a statute the protection against conviction afforded by the First Amendment is a matter of law. The doctrine that there must be a clear and present danger of a substantive evil that Congress has a right to prevent is a judicial rule to be applied as a matter of law by the courts. The guilt is established by proof of facts. Whether the First Amendment protects the activity which constitutes the violation of the statute must depend upon a judicial determination of the scope of the First Amendment applied to the circumstances of the case. . . .

### V

There remains to be discussed the question of vagueness—whether the statute as we have interpreted it is too vague, not sufficiently advising those who would speak of the limitations upon their activity. . . .

We hold that Sections 2(a)(1), 2(a)(3) and 3 of the Smith Act, do not inherently, or as construed or applied in the instant case, violate the First Amendment and other provisions of the Bill of Rights, or the First and Fifth Amendments because of indefiniteness. Petitioners intended to overthrow the Government of the United States as speedily as the circumstances would permit. Their conspiracy to organize the Communist Party and to teach and advocate the overthrow of the Government of the United States by force and violence created a "clear and present danger" of an attempt to overthrow the Government by force and violence. They were properly and constitutionally convicted for violation of the Smith Act. The judgments of conviction are

*Affirmed.*

Mr. Justice Clark took no part in the consideration or decision of this case.

Mr. Justice Frankfurter, concurring in affirmance of the judgment. . . .

The language of the First Amendment is to be read not as barren words found in a dictionary but as symbols of historic experience illumined by the presuppositions of those who employed them. Not what words did Madison and Hamilton use, but what was it in their minds which they conveyed? Free speech is subject to prohibition of those abuses of expression which a civilized society may forbid. . . . Absolute rules would inevitably lead to absolute exceptions, and such exceptions would eventually corrode the rules. The demands of free speech in a democratic society as well as the interest in national security are better served by candid and informed weighing of the competing interests, within the confines of the judicial process, than by announcing dogmas too inflexible for the non-Euclidian problems to be solved. . . .

## II

We have recognized and resolved conflicts between speech and competing interests in six different types of cases. . . .

I must leave to others the ungrateful task of trying to reconcile all these decisions. In some instances we have too readily permitted juries to infer deception from error, or intention from argumentative or critical statements. . . . In other instances we weighed the interest in free speech so heavily that we permitted essential conflicting values to be destroyed. . . . Viewed as a whole, however, the decisions express an attitude toward the judicial function and a standard of values which for me are decisive of the case before us.

*First*.—Free-speech cases are not an exception to the principle that we are not legislators, that direct policy-making is not our province. How best to reconcile competing interests is the business of legislatures, and the balance they strike is a judgment not to be displaced by ours, but to be respected unless outside the pale of fair judgment. . . .

*Second*.—A survey of the relevant decisions indicates that the results which we have reached are on the whole those that would ensue from careful weighing of conflicting interests. The complex issues presented by regulation of speech. . . . have been resolved by scrutiny of many factors besides the imminence and gravity of the evil threatened. . . .

*Third*.—Not every type of speech occupies the same position on the scale of values. There is no substantial public interest in permitting certain kinds of utterances: "the lewd and obscene, the profane, the libelous, and the insulting or 'fighting' words—those which by their very utterance inflict injury or tend to incite an immediate breach of the peace." *Chaplinsky* v. *New Hampshire*, 315 U.S. 568, 572. We have frequently indicated that the interest in protecting speech depends on the circumstances of the occasion. . . .

The defendants have been convicted of conspiring to organize a party of persons who advocate the overthrow of the Government by force and violence. . . .

On any scale of values which we have hitherto recognized, speech of this sort ranks low. . . .

## III

These general considerations underlie decision of the case before us.

On the one hand is the interest in security. The Communist Party was not designed by these defendants as an ordinary political party. . . . The jury found that the Party rejects the basic premise of our political system—that change is to be brought about by nonviolent constitutional process. The jury found that the Party advocates the theory that there is a duty and necessity to overthrow the Government by force and violence. . . .

. . . . We may take judicial notice that the Communist doctrines which these defendants have conspired to advocate are in the ascendancy in powerful nations who cannot be acquitted of unfriendliness to the institutions of this country. We may take account of evidence brought forward at this trial and elsewhere, much of which has long been common knowledge. In sum, it would amply justify a legislature in concluding that recruitment of additional members for the Party would create a substantial danger to national security. . . .

On the other hand is the interest in free speech. The right to exert all governmental powers in aid of maintaining our institutions and resisting their physical overthrow does not include intolerance of opinions and speech that cannot do harm although opposed and perhaps alien to dominant, traditional opinion. . . .

. . . A public interest is not wanting in granting freedom to speak their minds even to those who advocate the overthrow of the Government by force. For, as the evidence in this case abundantly illustrates, coupled with such advocacy is criticism of defects in our society. Criticism is the spur to reform. . . . Suppressing advocates of overthrow inevitably will also silence critics who do not advocate overthrow but fear that their criticism may be so construed. No matter how clear we may be that the defendants now before us are preparing to overthrow our Government at the propitious moment, it is self-delusion to think that we can punish them for their advocacy without adding to the risks run by loyal citizens who honestly believe in some of the reforms these defendants advance. It is a sobering fact that in sustaining the conviction before us we can hardly escape restriction on the interchange of ideas. . . .

It is not for us to decide how we would adjust the clash of interests which this case presents were the primary responsibility for reconciling it ours. Congress has determined that the danger created by advocacy of overthrow justifies the ensuing restriction on freedom of speech. . . .

. . . [I]t is relevant to remind that in sustaining the power of Congress in a case like this nothing irrevocable is done. The democratic process at all events is not impaired or restricted. Power and responsibility remain with the people and immediately with their representation. All the Court says is that Congress was not forbidden by the Constitution to pass this enactment and a prosecution under it may be brought against a conspiracy such as the one before us. . . .

Mr. Justice Jackson, concurring.

This prosecution is the latest of never-ending, because never successful, quests for some legal formula that will secure an existing order against revolutionary radicalism. It requires us to reappraise, in the light of our own times and conditions, constitutional doctrines devised under other circumstances to strike a balance between authority and liberty. . . .

If we must decide that this Act and its application are constitutional only if we are convinced that petitioner's conduct creates a "clear and present danger" of violent overthrow, we must appraise imponderables, including international and national phenomena which baffle the best informed foreign offices and our most experienced politicians. We would have to foresee and predict the effectiveness of Communist propaganda, opportunities for infiltration, whether, and when, a time will come that they consider propitious for action, and whether and how fast our existing government will deteriorate. And we would have to speculate as to whether an approaching Communist *coup* would not be anticipated by a nationalistic fascist movement. No doctrine can be sound whose application requires us to make a prophecy of that sort in the guise of a legal decision. The judicial process simply is not adequate to a trial of such far-flung issues. The answers given would reflect our own political predilections and nothing more.

The authors of the clear and present danger test never applied it to a case like this, nor would I. If applied as it is proposed here, it means that Communist plotting is protected during its period of incubation; its preliminary stages of organization and preparation are immune from the law; the Government can move only after imminent action is manifest, when it would, of course, be too late. . . .

There is lamentation in the dissents about the injustice of conviction in the absence of some overt act. Of course, there has been no general uprising against the Government, but the record is replete with acts to carry out the conspiracy alleged, acts such as always are held sufficient to consummate the crime where the statute requires an overt act. . . .

Mr. Justice Black, dissenting. . . .

At the outset I want to emphasize what the crime involved in this case is, and what it is not. These petitioners were not charged with an attempt to overthrow the Government. They were not charged with overt acts of any kind designed to overthrow the Government. They were not even charged with saying anything or writing anything designed to overthrow the Government. The charge was that they agreed to assemble and to talk and publish certain ideas at a later date: The indictment is that they conspired to organize the Communist Party and to use speech or newspapers and other publications in the future to teach and advocate the forcible overthrow of the Government. No matter how it is worded, this is a virulent form of prior censorship of speech and press, which I believe the First Amendment forbids. I would hold Section 3 of the Smith Act authorizing this prior restraint unconstitutional on its face and as applied.

. . . The opinions for affirmance indicate that the chief reason for jettisoning the [clear and present danger] rule is the expressed fear that advocacy of Communist doctrine endangers the safety of the Republic. Undoubtedly, a governmental policy of unfettered communication of ideas does entail dangers. To the Founders of this Nation, however, the benefits derived from free expression were worth the risk. . . . I have always believed that the First Amendment is the keystone of our Government, that the freedoms it guarantees provide the best insurance against destruction of all freedom. At least as to speech in the realm of public matters, I believe that the "clear and present danger" test does not "mark the furthermost constitutional boundaries of protected expression" but does "no more than recognize a minimum compulsion of the Bill of Rights." *Bridges* v. *California*, 314 U.S. 252, 263.

So long as this Court exercises the power of judicial review of legislation, I cannot agree that the First Amendment permits us to sustain laws suppressing freedom of speech and press on the basis of Congress' or our own notions of mere "reasonableness." Such a doctrine waters down the First Amendment so that it amounts to little more than an admonition to Congress. The Amendment as so construed is not likely to protect any but those "safe" or orthodox views which rarely need its protection. . . .

Public opinion being what it now is, few will protest the conviction of these Communist petitioners. There is hope, however, that in calmer times, when present pressures, passions and fears subside, this or some later Court will restore the First Amendment liberties to the high preferred place where they belong in a free society.

Mr. Justice Douglas, dissenting. . . .

The next important case to come before the Court involving the Smith Act was *Yates* v. *United States,* 354 U.S. 298 (1957). Other prosecutions of lesser Communists had taken place in the interval since *Dennis,* but the Court had not reviewed any of the convictions. In *Yates* the Court imposed no limitations upon its grant of certiorari to review the convictions of fourteen Communists under the same Smith Act sections involved in the *Dennis* case. Thus it was free to examine the whole record and consider the sufficiency of the evidence supporting the convictions. Three primary issues were presented in the case. First, the petitioners contended that the conviction for "organizing" the Community Party was barred by the three-year statute of limitations, since the Party was "organized," within the meaning of the statute, by 1945 at the latest, and the indictment was returned in 1951. Justice Harlan, for the majority, agreed with this contention. He pointed out that the statute did not define what was meant by "organize," and that, "In these circumstances we should follow the familiar rule that criminal statutes are to be strictly construed and give to 'organize' its narrow meaning, that is, that the word refers only to acts entering into the creation of a new organization, and not to acts thereafter performed in carrying on its activities, even though such acts may loosely be termed 'organizational.'"

A second issue presented by petitioners was that the instructions to the jury were fatally defective in that the trial court refused to charge that, in order to convict, the jury must find that the advocacy which the defendants conspired to promote was directed at promoting unlawful action and not mere persuasion to accept forcible overthrow as abstract doctrine. The majority agreed with this second contention also. Justice Harlan stated:

In failing to distinguish between advocacy of forcible overthrow as an abstract doctrine and advocacy of action to that end, the District Court appears to have been led astray by the holding in *Dennis* that advocacy of violent action to be taken at some future time was enough. . . . [W]e are unable to regard the District Court's charge upon this aspect of the case as adequate. The jury was never told that the Smith Act does not denounce advocacy in the sense of preaching abstractly the forcible overthrow of the Government. We think that the trial court's statement that the proscribed advocacy must include the "urging," "necessity," and "duty" of forcible overthrow, and not merely its "desirability" and "propriety," may not be regarded as a sufficient substitute for charging that the Smith Act reaches only advocacy of action for the overthrow of government by force and violence. The essential distinction is that those to whom the advocacy is addressed must be urged to *do* something, now or in the future, rather than merely to *believe* in something.

Although the holding on the first two issues already required reversal of the convictions, the Court went one step further to consider the sufficiency of the evidence against the fourteen petitioners, "to see whether there are individuals as to whom acquittal is unequivocally demanded." After putting aside all evidence relating to the "organizing" charge alone as well as that not directly connected to a charge of advocacy in the sense of a call to forcible action, Justice Harlan found the record "strikingly deficient." As to five of the defendants he found no overt acts to support the conviction other than mere membership in the Party or as officers or functionaries, and their acquittal was ordered. As to the other nine defendants, the majority found evidence indicating "action" in their holding of classes teaching illegal action as well as other participation in "underground apparatus"—which might support a finding of guilty under a proper charge to the jury. The cases of these nine, then, were remanded for new trials.

The *Yates* decision represents somewhat of a withdrawal from the broad language of Chief Justice Vinson in the *Dennis* case and, in fact, draws in question the very validity of the convictions in the earlier case. Since the decision came off on statutory construction rather than constitutional issues, the Congress might have revised the Smith Act to reach any advocacy of overthrow of the government by violence, thus presenting the constitutional issue squarely, but such revision has not been made. Congress did disagree with the Court's construction of the "organizing" section, however, and in 1962 amended the Act to include within the meaning of that section the continued recruitment or expansion of organizational activity.

Neither *Dennis* nor *Yates*, however, reached the question of the validity of the "membership" section of the Smith Act. The section appeared to raise even more serious questions of constitutionality than the two preceding sections, and the Government was somewhat slow to proceed under the "membership" charge alone. In *Scales* v. *United States,* 367 U.S. 203 (1961), the Court ruled on the issue for the first time.

## SCALES *v.* UNITED STATES
### *367 U.S. 203 (1961)*

Mr. Justice Harlan delivered the opinion of the Court.

Our writ issued in this case . . . to review . . . petitioner's conviction under the so-called membership clause of the Smith Act. 18 USC Section 2385. The Act, among other things, makes a felony the acquisition or holding of knowing membership in any organization which advocates the overthrow of the Government of the United States by force or violence.

The validity of this conviction is challenged on statutory, constitutional, and evidentiary grounds, and further on the basis of certain alleged trial and procedural errors. . . . For reasons given in this opinion we affirm the Court of Appeals.

### I
### Statutory Challenge

Petitioner contends that the indictment fails to state an offense against the United States. The claim is that Section 4(f) of the Internal Security Act of 1950, 64 Stat 987, . . . constitutes a *pro tanto* repeal of the membership clause of the Smith Act by excluding from the reach of that clause membership in any Communist organization. . . .

We turn first to the provision itself, and find that, as to petitioner's construction of it, the language is at best ambiguous if not suggestive of a contrary conclusion. Section 4(f) provides that membership or office-holding in a Communist organization shall not constitute *"per se* a violation of subsection (a) or subsection (c) of this section or of any other criminal statute."* Petitioner would most plainly be correct if the statute under which he was indicted purported to proscribe membership in Communist organizations, as such, and to punish membership *per se* in an organization engaging in proscribed advocacy. . . .

. . . The natural tendency of the first sentence of subsection (f) as to the criminal provisions specifically mentioned is to provide clarification of the meaning of those provisions, that is, that an offense is not made out on proof of *mere* membership in a Communist organization. . . .

. . . Although we think that the membership clause on its face goes beyond making mere Party membership a violation, in that it requires a showing both of illegal Party purposes and of a member's knowledge of such purposes, we regard the first sentence of Section 4(f) as a clear warrant for construing the clause as requiring not only knowing membership, but active and purposive membership, purposive that is as to the organization's criminal ends. . . . By its terms, then, subsection (f) does not effect a *pro tanto* repeal of the membership clause; at most it modifies it. . . .

[The opinion then takes up an examination of the legislative history of the Internal Security Act of 1950, and Justice Harlan concludes that it does not bar this prosecution.]

### II

### Constitutional Challenge to the Membership Clause on its Face

Petitioner's constitutional attack goes both to the statute on its face and as applied. . . .

It will bring the constitutional issues into clearer focus to notice first the premises on which the case was submitted to the jury. The jury was instructed that in order to convict it must find that within the three-year limitations period (1) the Communist Party advocated the violent overthrow of the Government, in the sense of present "advocacy of action" to accomplish that end as soon as circumstances were propitious; and (2) petitioner was an "active" member of the Party, and not merely "a nominal, passive, inactive or purely technical" member, with knowledge of the Party's illegal advocacy and a specific intent to bring about violent overthrow "as speedily as circumstances would permit."

The constitutional attack upon the membership clause, as thus construed, is that the statute offends (1) the Fifth Amendment, in that it impermissibly imputes guilt to an individual merely on the basis of his associations and sympathies, rather than because of some concrete personal involvement in criminal conduct; and (2) the First Amendment, in that it infringes free political expression and association. . . .

### Fifth Amendment

Any thought that due process puts beyond the reach of the criminal law all individual associational relationships, unless accompanied by the commission of specific acts of criminality, is dispelled by familiar concepts of the law of conspiracy and complicity. . . .

What must be met, then, is the argument that membership, even when accompanied by the elements of knowledge and specific intent, affords an insufficient quantum of participation in the organization's alleged criminal activity, that is, an insufficiently significant form of aid and encouragement to permit the imposition of criminal sanctions on that basis. . . .

In an area of the criminal law which this Court has indicated more than once demands its watchful scrutiny. . . , these factors have weight and must be found to be overborne in a total constitutional assessment of the statute. We think, however, they are duly met when the statute is found to reach only "active" members having also a guilty knowledge and intent, and which therefore prevents a conviction on what otherwise might be regarded as merely an expression of sympathy with the alleged criminal enterprise, unaccompanied by any significant action in its support or any commitment to undertake such action. . . .

### First Amendment

Little remains to be said concerning the claim that the statute infringes First Amendment freedoms. It was settled in *Dennis* that the advocacy with which we are here concerned is not constitutionally protected speech, and it was further established that a combination to promote such advocacy, albeit under the aegis of what purports to be a political party, is not such association as is protected by the First Amendment. We can discern no reason why membership, when it constitutes a purposeful form of complicity in a group engaging in this same forbidden advocacy, should receive any greater degree of protection from the guarantees of that Amendment.

If it is said that the mere existence of such an enactment tends to inhibit the exercise of constitutionally protected rights, in that it engenders an unhealthy fear that one may find himself unwittingly embroiled in criminal liability, the answer surely is that the statute provides that a defendant must be proven to have knowledge of the proscribed advocacy before he may be convicted. . . . The clause does not make criminal all association with an organization, which has been shown to engage in illegal advocacy. There must be clear proof that a defendant "specifically intend[s] to accomplish [the aims of the organization] by resort to violence." *Noto* v. *United States*. . . . Thus the member for whom the organization is a vehicle for the advancement of legitimate aims and policies does not fall within the ban of the statute: he lacks the requisite specific intent "to bring about the overthrow of the government as speedily as circumstances would permit." Such a person may be foolish, deluded, or perhaps merely optimistic, but he is not by this statute made a criminal.

We conclude that petitioner's constitutional challenge must be overruled.

### III
### Evidentiary Challenge

Only in rare instances will this Court review the general sufficiency of the evidence to support a criminal conviction, for ordinarily that is a function which properly belongs to and ends with the Court of Appeals. We do so in this case and in . . . *Noto* v. *United States* . . . , our first review of convictions under the membership clause of the Smith Act—not only to make sure that substantive constitutional standards have not been thwarted, but also to provide guidance for the future to the lower courts in an area which borders so closely upon constitutionally protected rights. . . .

[Justice Harlan here examines the testimony introduced to prove the illegal purposes and general "character of the organization of which he is charged with being a member." As to the specific acts of the defendant, Justice Harlan cited testimony and evidence showing that Scales had recruited members, sent out Communist literature, instructed and guided new members, arranged for scholarships to study at official Communist Party schools, and advised one member to "infiltrate the Civilian Defense setup" in New York.]

We conclude that this evidence sufficed to make a case for the jury on the issue of illegal Party advocacy. *Dennis* and *Yates* have definitely laid at rest any doubt but that present advocacy of *future* action for violent overthrow satisfies statutory and constitutional requirements equally with advocacy of *immediate* action to that end. . . . Hence this record cannot be considered deficient because it contains no evidence of advocacy for immediate overthrow. . . .

The sufficiency of the evidence as to other elements of the crime requires no exposition. Scales' "active" membership in the Party is indisputable, and that issue was properly submitted to the jury under instructions that were entirely adequate. The elements of petitioner's "knowledge" and "specific intent" . . . require no further discussion of the evidence beyond that already given as to Scales' utterances and activities. Compare *Noto* v. *United States*. . . . They bear little resemblance to the fragmentary and equivocal utterances and conduct which were found insufficient in *Nowak* v. *United States*, 356 U.S. 660. . . .

We hold that this prosecution does not fail for insufficiency of the proof. . . .

The judgment of the Court of Appeals must be

*Affirmed.*

Mr. Justice Black, dissenting.

. . . My reasons for dissenting from this decision are primarily those set out by Mr. Justice Brennan—that Section 4(f) of the Subversive Activities Control Act bars prosecutions under the membership clause of the Smith Act—and Mr. Justice Douglas—that the First Amendment absolutely forbids Congress to outlaw membership in a political party or similar association merely because one of the philosophical tenets of that group is that the existing government should be overthrown by force at some distant time in the future when circumstances may permit. . . .

. . . I think it is important to point out the manner in which this case re-emphasizes the freedom-destroying nature of the "balancing test" presently in use by the Court to justify its refusal to apply specific constitutional protections of the Bill of Rights. In some of the recent cases in which it has "balanced" away the protections of the First Amendment, the Court has suggested that it was justified in the application of this "test" because no direct abridgment of First Amendment freedoms was involved, the abridgment in each of these cases being, in the Court's opinion, nothing more than "an incident of the informed exercise of a valid governmental function." A possible implication of that suggestion was that if the Court were confronted with what it would call a direct abridgment of speech, it would not apply the "balancing test" but would enforce the protections of the First Amendment according to its own terms. This case causes me to doubt that such an implication is justified. Petitioner is being sent to jail for the express reason that he has associated with people who have entertained unlawful ideas and said unlawful things, and that of course is a *direct* abridgment of his freedoms of speech and assembly—under any definition that has ever been used for that term. Nevertheless, even as to this admittedly direct abridgment, the Court relies upon its prior decisions to the effect that the Government has power to abridge speech and assembly if its interest in doing so is sufficient to outweigh the interest in protecting these First Amendment freedoms.

This, I think, demonstrates the unlimited breadth and danger of the "balancing test" as it is currently being applied by a majority of this Court. Under that "test," the question in every case in which a First Amendment right is asserted is not whether there has been an abridgment of that right, not whether the abridgment of that right was intentional on the part of the Government, and not whether there is any other way in which the Government could accomplish a lawful aim without an invasion of the constitutionally guaranteed rights of the people. It is, rather, simply whether the Government has an interest in abridging the right involved and, if so, whether that interest is of sufficient importance, in the opinion of a majority of this Court, to justify the Government's action in doing so. This doctrine, to say the very least, is capable of being used to justify almost any action Government may wish to take to suppress First Amendment freedoms.

Mr. Justice Douglas, dissenting.

When we allow petitioner to be sentenced to prison for six years for being a "member" of the Communist Party, we make a sharp break with traditional concepts of First Amendment rights and make serious Mark Twain's lighthearted comment that, "It is by the goodness of God that in our country we have those three unspeakably precious things: freedom of speech, freedom of conscience, and the prudence never to practice either of them." . . .

We legalize today guilt by association, sending a man to prison when he committed no unlawful act. Today's break with tradition is a serious one. It borrows from the totalitarian philosophy. . . .

The case is not saved by showing that petitioner was an active member. None of the activity constitutes a crime. . . .

Belief in the principle of revolution is deep in our traditions. The Declaration of Independence proclaims it. . . .

This right of revolution has been and is a part of the fabric of our institutions. . . .

Mr. Justice Brennan, with whom the Chief Justice and Mr. Justice Douglas join, dissenting. . . .

States, of course, have long had various kinds of sedition statutes of their own. No particular problems were presented by such laws, other than those taken up in the cases above, until the enactment of the Smith Act. The issue then presented was one of national supremacy: did the federal law supersede the state laws on sedition and thereby render them unenforceable? In *Pennsylvania* v. *Nelson*, 350 U.S. 497 (1956), the Court held that in passing the Smith Act Congress intended to occupy the field, and affirmed the Pennsylvania Supreme Court's reversal of a conviction under the state statute. The Court pointed out as additional support for its decision the strong possibility of interference by the state enforcement authorities with the overall program of the federal government.

Although the cases thus far discussed point up some rather sharp differences of opinion among the justices regarding the validity of some of the major antisubversion sections of the Smith Act, the Court is unanimous in its view that *overt acts* in aid of revolution may appropriately be punished. Justices Black and Douglas stressed, however, that restrictions imposed prior to engagement in overt action unconstitutionally inhibit freedom of thought and association. At the core of the differences of opinion on these questions appears to be the divergence of attitude on whether making speeches, organizing groups, and associating for common purposes can appropriately be considered as "overt action." A minority of the Court did not think such stages could be so held, and this conclusion led them to dissent in a number of cases involving a variety of restrictions primarily directed at subversive organizations. The important right of association was the central issue in many of these cases, particularly those involving the various kinds of non-Communist oaths. [On the validity of state criminal syndicalism laws, see *Brandenburg* v. *Ohio*, 395 U.S. 444 (1969), later in this chapter.]

In the Taft-Hartley Act of 1947 Congress provided that the services of the NLRB and the protections of the Act would be denied to labor organizations whose officers failed to file affidavits with the Board that they were not Communist Party members and did not believe in overthrow of the government by force. This requirement was upheld in *American Communications Ass'n., CIO* v. *Douds*, 339 U.S. 382 (1950). Chief Justice Vinson in his opinion for the Court stated:

Government's interest here is not in preventing the dissemination of Communist doctrine or the holding of particular beliefs because it is feared that unlawful action will result therefrom if free speech is practiced. Its interest is in protecting the free flow of commerce from what Congress considers to be substantial evils of conduct that are not the products of speech at all. Section 9(h), in other words, . . . regulates harmful conduct which Congress has determined is carried on by persons who may be identified by their political affiliations and beliefs.

Justices Jackson and Frankfurter concurred in the result as to the non-membership portion but dissented as to the "belief" portion of the affidavit. Justice Black dissented on the ground that both provisions were unconstitutional. He stated that "Never before has this Court held that the Government could for any reason attaint persons for their political beliefs or affiliations. It does so today."

Many States and cities have adopted policies demanding non-Communist oaths from governmental employees. In 1948 Los Angeles adopted an ordinance requiring all employees to file an oath stating that they had neither advocated overthrow of the government by violence nor been a member of an organization which advocated such action and also to file an affidavit stating whether they were or ever had been a member of the Communist Party. The validity of the ordinance was tested in *Garner* v. *Board of Public Works*, 341 U.S. 716 (1951). Five members of the Court held that both the oath and the affidavit were valid, although Justice Clark, for the majority, said, "We assume that *scienter* is implicit in each clause of the oath." Thus innocent membership was not to be punished. Two members of the Court felt that the affidavit was valid but not the oath, since the ordinance did not by its terms clearly specify "knowing" membership as the

basis for denial of employment. Justices Douglas and Black considered both requirements to be bills of attainder and ex post facto.

The following year, in *Wieman* v. *Updegraff*, 344 U.S. 183 (1952), the Court unanimously invalidated an oath requirement of Oklahoma which barred from governmental employment persons who were or had been members of proscribed organizations,
irrespective of their knowledge of the purposes of such organizations. Justice Clark, for
the Court, stated:

> Under the Oklahoma Act, the fact of association alone determines disloyalty and
> disqualification; it matters not whether association existed innocently or knowing-
> ly. To thus inhibit individual freedom of movement is to stifle the flow of democratic
> expression and controversy at one of its chief sources. We hold that the distinction
> observed between the case at bar and *Garner* . . . is decisive. Indiscriminate classifi-
> cation of innocent with knowing activity must fall as an assertion of arbitrary power.
> The oath offends due process.

Employees have also been removed from public positions when found to belong to
subversive organizations. New York's Feinberg Law, passed in 1949, provided that after
an inquiry and notice and hearing the Board of Regents should prepare a list of subversive organizations. Thereafter membership in any of these organizations should constitute prima facie evidence of disqualification for employment in the public schools. The
law was upheld by the Supreme Court in *Adler* v. *Board of Education of the City of New
York*, 342 U.S. 485 (1952). Justice Minton, speaking for the majority, stated that persons
have no right to work for the state in the school system on their own terms. If they do
not choose to work for the school system upon the reasonable terms laid down by the
proper authorities of New York, "they are at liberty to retain their beliefs and associations and go elsewhere."

Public employees have also been dismissed for refusal to answer questions about
membershp in subversive organizations, even when the alleged association took place
many years earlier. A Brooklyn College professor was discharged on the ground that
claiming the Fifth Amendment privilege before a Senate committee, which had questioned him concerning his political affiliations prior to 1941, was "equivalent to a resignation" under the Charter of the City of New York. In *Slochower* v. *Board of Higher
Education*, 350 U.S. 551 (1956), the Court reversed the judgment, but at the same time
it suggested that the city could use whatever facts it chose to make an inquiry to see
whether Slochower's continued employment was "inconsistent with a real interest of
the State."

New York City accepted the suggestion, and two employees who refused to answer
questions concerning Communist membership were discharged. Lerner, a subway con-
ductor, was removed as a person of "doubtful trust and reliability" for his "lack of candor," and Beilan, a public school teacher, was dismissed for "incompetency." The
judgments were affirmed by the Court in *Lerner* v. *Casey*, 357 U.S. 468 (1958), and *Beilan* v. *Board of Public Education*, 357 U.S. 399 (1958), respectively. A similar result obtained in a Los Angeles County employee's dismissal for refusal to testify concerning his
subversive activity before a subcommittee of the House Un-American Activities Committee in the face of a state statute requiring all public employees to give such testimony
"on pain of discharge." *Nelson* v. *County of Los Angeles*, 362 U.S. 1 (1960).

The cases above indicate a Court that was troubled over the proper approach to issues of official inquiry into the associational patterns of public employees. One explanation for the difficulty is that not until 1958 in the decision in *NAACP* v. *Alabama*
(discussed below) did the Court squarely recognize a constitutional right of association.
Once having accorded this right First Amendment status, however, subsequent deci-

sions demonstrate greater reluctance to uphold governmental restrictions which directly impinged on the right of association. Further, *Scales* v. *United States*, established a clear rule that only "active" membership in the Communist Party should be punishable. This decision, especially, triggered a shift in approach to the public employment cases.

In *Elfbrandt* v. *Russell*, 384 U.S. 11 (1966), the Court held unconstitutional an Arizona loyalty oath for state employees which subjected to discharge and prosecution for perjury any person who took the oath and "knowingly and willfully becomes or remains a member of the communist party" or any other organization having as one of its purposes the overthrow of the government of Arizona. A majority of five held the statute invalid since it did not require a showing that an employee was an active member with the specific intent of assisting in achieving the unlawful ends of a proscribed organization. Justice Douglas, for the majority, said, "This Act threatens the cherished freedom of association protected by the First Amendment." He said further:

Those who join an organization but do not share its unlawful purposes and who do not participate in its unlawful activities surely pose no threat, either as citizens or as public employees. Laws such as this which are not restricted in scope to those who join with the "specific intent" to further illegal action impose, in effect, a conclusive presumption that the member shares the unlawful aims of the organization.

The decision in *Elfbrandt* invited a new attack on New York's Feinberg Law. Several faculty members of the State University of New York brought suit in a federal district court for declaratory and injunctive relief against the New York plan, formulated partly in statutes and partly in administrative regulations. A three-judge court upheld the plan, but on direct appeal, in *Keyishian* v. *Board of Regents of New York*, 385 U.S. 589 (1967), the Supreme Court reversed, overruling *Adler* and holding the Feinberg Law to be unconstitutional.

Three sections of the New York law were challenged as being unconstitutionally vague: (1) a section requiring removal for "treasonable or seditious" utterances or acts; (2) a section barring employment of any person who "by word of mouth or writing willfully and deliberately advocates, advises or teaches the doctrine" of forceful overthrow of government; and (3) a section requiring the disqualification of an employee involved with the distribution of written material "containing or advocating, advising or teaching the doctrine" of forceful overthrow, and who himself "advocates, advises, teaches, or embraces the duty, necessity or propriety of adopting the doctrine contained therein."

A majority of five held these sections to be unconstitutionally vague, on the ground that they were "plainly susceptible to sweeping and improper application" and might "reasonably be construed to cover mere expression of belief." As to the provisions of the Feinberg Law making Communist Party membership, as such, prima facie evidence of disqualification, the majority followed *Elfbrandt* in holding that "legislation which sanctions membership unaccompanied by specific intent to further the unlawful goals of the organization or which is not active membership violates constitutional limitations."

In the course of his opinion for the majority, Justice Brennan gave an impressive statement in support of academic freedom:

Our Nation is deeply committed to safeguarding academic freedom, which is of transcendent value to all of us and not merely to the teachers concerned. That freedom is therefore a special concern of the First Amendment, which does not tolerate laws that cast a pall of orthodoxy over the classroom. "The vigilant protection of constitutional freedoms is nowhere more vital than in the community of American schools." . . . The classroom is peculiarly the "marketplace of ideas." The Nation's future depends upon leaders trained through wide exposure to that robust exchange of ideas which discovers the truth "out of a multitude of tongues, [rather] than through any kind of authoritative selection."

In *United States* v. *Robel*, 389 U.S. 258 (1967), the Court held unconstitutional a section of the Subversive Activities Control Act of 1950 which makes it a crime, when a Communist-action organization is under a final order to register, "for any member of that organization to engage in any employment in any defense facility." Robel was a member of the Communist Party and a machinist in a West Coast shipyard at the time the Communist Party was ordered to register and the yard was declared a "defense facility." In affirming the dismissal of Robel's indictment, Chief Justice Warren, for the majority, stated that the statute cast too broad a net "indiscriminately trapping membership which can be constitutionally punished and membership which cannot be so proscribed. It is made irrelevant to the statute's operation that an individual may be a passive or inactive member of a designated organization, that he may be unaware of the organization's unlawful aims, or that he may disagree with those unlawful aims." Thus the section contained the "fatal defect of overbreadth."

A special problem involving the right of association concerns governmental power, by statute or order, to compel individuals to disclose their membership in various organizations or to compel organizations to disclose their membership lists. The major recent cases on these questions have held that the Constitution protects against such compulsory disclosure.

*NAACP* v. *Alabama*, 357 U.S. 449 (1958) involved the validity of an Alabama court order directing the disclosure of membership lists in the Alabama affiliate of the NAACP. The organization offered to produce all requested papers and information except those showing names and addresses of officers and members. The Alabama court held the NAACP in contempt and a fine of $100,000 was adjudged. The United States Supreme Court unanimously held the registration requirement invalid. Speaking for the Court, Justice Harlan stated:

Effective advocacy of both public and private points of view, particularly controversial ones, is undeniably enhanced by group association, as this Court has more than once recognized by remarking upon the close nexus between the freedoms of speech and assembly. . . . It is beyond debate that freedom to engage in association for the advancement of beliefs and ideas is an inseparable aspect of the "liberty" assured by the Due Process Clause of the Fourteenth Amendment, which embraces freedom of speech. . . . Of course, it is immaterial whether the beliefs sought to be advanced by association pertain to political, economic, religious or cultural matters, and state action which may have the effect of curtailing the freedom to associate is subject to the closest scrutiny.

The main problem presented in the case was to distinguish the Alabama requirement from the Klan registration law of New York which the Court had held constitutional in *New York ex rel. Bryant* v. *Zimmerman*, 278 U.S. 63 (1928). On this point Justice Harlan stated:

That case involved markedly different considerations in terms of the interest of the State in obtaining disclosure. . . . In its opinion, the Court took care to emphasize the nature of the organization which New York sought to regulate. The decision was based on the particular character of the Klan's activities, involving acts of unlawful intimidation and violence, which the Court assumed was before the state legislature when it enacted the statute, and of which the Court itself took judicial notice. . . . And we conclude that Alabama has fallen short of showing a controlling justification for the deterrent effect on the free enjoyment of the right to associate which disclosure of membership lists is likely to have.

[See Joseph B. Robison, "Protection of Associations from Compulsory Disclosure of Membership," 58 *Col. L. Rev.* 614 (1958).]

Despite the distinction which the opinion indicated between the Klan registration law and the NAACP registration, the holding in the NAACP case raises doubts as to the continued vitality of the *Zimmerman* decision.

In *Shelton* v. *Tucker*, 364 U.S. 479 (1960), the Court dealt with an Arkansas statute which compelled every teacher in a state-supported school to file annually an affidavit listing every organization to which he had belonged or regularly contributed within the preceding five years. Plaintiffs challenged the validity of the statute under the Fourteenth Amendment due process clause. By the narrow margin of five-to-four the Court held the requirement unconstitutional. All members of the Court agreed that the State has a right to investigate the competence and fitness of those whom it hires to teach in its schools. They further appeared to agree that some check into the associational ties would be relevant to the matter of competence. But the majority felt that to inquire into *every* such organizational relationship—church affiliation, political party, social club and others—was to permit unlimited scope to such an inquiry and therefore to violate the freedom of association. As Justice Stewart stated for the majority, "Many such relationships could have no possible bearing upon the teacher's occupational competence or fitness."

Justice Frankfurter, dissenting, felt that the State was entitled to know whether a teacher might "have so many divers associations, so many divers commitments, that they consume his time and energy and interest at the expense of his work or even of his professional dedication." He also stated that, on the record, he could not attribute to the State a purpose to inhibit constitutional rights. But he added, "Of course, if the information gathered by the required affidavits is used to further a scheme of terminating the employment of teachers solely because of their membership in unpopular organizations, that use will run afoul of the Fourteenth Amendment."

The more recent issue of compulsory disclosure of membership involved the application of the Subversive Activities Control Act of 1950 (Title I of the Internal Security Act of 1950), which required the registration with the Attorney General of all Communist-action organizations, as well as all Communist-front organizations, as so designated by the Subversive Activities Control Board. Registration was to be accompanied by a statement containing, among other information, the names and addresses of each person who had been an officer or member during the past twelve months. Failure to meet the registration requirements was subject to criminal penalties: a fine of not more than $10,000 for each offense by an organization; a fine of not more than $10,000 or imprisonment for not more than five years or both for each offense by an officer or individual; and each day of failure to register constituted a separate offense.

In *Communist Party of the United States* v. *Subversive Activities Control Board*, 367 U.S. 1 (1961), the Party challenged the Act on the grounds that it was a bill of attainder and that it violated freedom of expression and association and also the privilege against self-incrimination. By a five-to-four vote the Court upheld the Act.

The majority, through Justice Frankfurter, held that many of the alleged consequences of the Act were prematurely presented and the prejudicial effects only speculative, without support in the record. They refused, therefore, to reach several of the claims of appellants. The majority specifically held, however, that the Act was not a bill of attainder, since the Act applies to a class of activity, not to the Communist Party as such. On the claim of violation of freedom of expression and association, Justice Frankfurter stated, "The present case differs from *Thomas* v. *Collins* and from *National Association for Advancement of Colored People, Bates,* and *Shelton* in the magnitude of the public interests which the registration and disclosure provisions are designed to protect and in the pertinence which registration and disclosure bear to the protection of those interests." He reviewed the legislative findings of the threat to national security from the Communist-action organizations and the purpose of the Act as preventing "the world-wide Communist conspiracy from accomplishing its purpose in this country." He stated further:

Congress, when it enacted the Subversive Activities Control Act, did attempt to cope with precisely such a danger. In light of its legislative findings, based on voluminous evidence collected during years of investigation, we cannot say that that danger is chimerical, or that the registration requirement of Section 7 is an ill-adjusted means of dealing with it. In saying this, we are not insensitive to the fact that the public opprobrium and obloquy which may attach to an individual listed with the Attorney General as a member of a Communist-action organization is no less considerable than that with which members of the National Association for the Advancement of Colored People were threatened in *National Association for Advancement of Colored People* and *Bates.* But while an angry public opinion, and the evils which it may spawn, are relevant considerations in adjudging . . . the validity of legislation that, in effecting disclosure, may thereby entail some restraints on speech and association, the existence of an ugly public temper does not, as such and without more, incapacitate government to require publicity demanded by rational interests high in the scale of national concern. Where the mask of anonymity which an organization's members wear serves the double purpose of protecting them from popular prejudice and of enabling them to cover over a foreign-directed conspiracy, infiltrate into other groups, and enlist the support of persons who would not, if the truth were revealed, lend their support, . . . it would be a distortion of the First Amendment to hold that it prohibits Congress from removing the mask.

An additional claim of the Party was that the registration requirements of the Act could not be imposed and exacted consistently with the Fifth Amendment's self-incrimination clause. It was argued that the officers of the Party are compelled, in the very act of filing a signed registration statement, to admit that they *are* Party officers—an admission which the Court has held incriminating. Justice Frankfurter's response was that the claim was premature:

Manifestly, insofar as this contention is directed against the provisions. . . requiring that designated officers file registration statements in default of registration by an organization, it is prematurely raised in the present proceeding. The duties imposed by those provisions will not arise until and unless the Party fails to register. At this time their application is wholly contingent and conjectural. . . .

The sequel to the case came in 1965 in the case of *Albertson* v. *Subversive Activities Control Board,* 382 U.S. 70 (1965). After the Communist Party had failed to comply with an order requiring it to furnish the Attorney General a list of the Party's members, the Attorney General, acting pursuant to provisions of the Subversive Activities Control Act, requested that the Subversive Activities Control Board grant orders requiring petitioners to register as individual members of the Party. The Board granted the orders, and the Court of Appeals for the District of Columbia affirmed, expressing the view that the constitutional issues raised by the petitioners were not ripe for adjudication and would be ripe only in a prosecution for failure to register if the petitioners did not register. The United States Supreme Court voted unanimously to reverse, holding that the orders violated the Fifth Amendment privilege against self-incrimination. Justice Brennan, for the Court, stated that admission of membership may be used to prosecute the registrant under the membership clause of the Smith Act. He stated further:

Section 4(f) of the Act, the purported immunity provision, does not save the registration orders from petitioners' Fifth Amendment challenge. . . . [T]he immunity granted by §4(f) is not complete. . . . With regard to the act of registering . . . §4(f) provides only that the admission of Party membership thus required shall not per se constitute a violation of §§4(a) and (c) or any other criminal statute, or "be received in evidence" against a registrant in any criminal prosecution; it does not preclude the use of the admission as an investigatory lead, a use which is barred by the privilege.

It is not an easy matter to sum up the Court's delineation of the constitutional rights to free expression when applied to matters touching on internal security, especially as related to restrictions on Communists. But a few signposts have been erected, indicating at least general directions. At the outset, it is apparent that in the hard cases involving the issue of freedom of expression versus internal security the Court takes a long, close look at the procedures used in applying the given restrictions. While procedural matters have generally been dealt with in a previous chapter, the point here is that where freedom of expression is being abridged, the statutory and constitutional procedural requirements are apt to be applied somewhat more rigorously than in some other areas. Once these requirements are met, however, the Court has permitted both the national and the state governments to impose a variety of restrictions on Communists. [For a compilation of such restrictions and court decisions relative to them, see the Fund for the Republic publication, *Digest of the Public Record of Communism in the United States* (New York: Fund for the Republic, 1955).] Both governments may bar *active* Communists from employment. In addition, a refusal to answer official inquiries concerning such participation can be taken into account in determining "competence" or "good moral character" in connection with retention of governmental employment or admission to the bar. But where associational tests range too widely and reach ordinarily lawful organizational ties, then the Court tends to hold that First Amendment rights of belief and association have been abridged. Thus it may be true that there is no "right" to government employment, but this is not to say that governments can set requirements which are unrelated to the proper performance of the employment position or which classify applicants in an unreasonable fashion.

The Court has upheld a congressional requirement that before becoming eligible for the services of the National Labor Relations Board, and thus the statutory benefits of the Wagner Act, a labor organization must file with the Board an affidavit executed by each officer of such organization that he is not a member of the Communist Party or affiliated with it. In 1959, however, this requirement of the Taft-Hartley Act was replaced by a provision making it a crime for a member of the Communist Party to serve as an officer or employee of a labor union (except in clerical or custodial positions). In *United States v. Brown*, 381 U.S. 437 (1965), the Court by a five-to-four vote held this section unconstitutional as a bill of attainder. The Chief Justice, for the majority, stated that the statute did not "set forth a generally applicable rule decreeing that any person who commits certain acts or possesses certain characteristics. . . . shall not hold union office, and leave to courts and juries the job of deciding what persons have committed the specified acts or possessed the specified characteristics." Instead it simply designated the persons—members of the Communist Party—and such designation "is not the substitution of a semantically equivalent phrase" and is therefore a bill of attainder.

In *Schneiderman* v. *United States*, 320 U.S. 118 (1943), the Court indicated that Congress might exclude all Communist aliens from entering the United States. And in *Hari-*

*siades* v. *Shaughnessy*, 342 U.S. 580 (1952), it was held that Congress could constitutionally deport all aliens who had been members of the Communist Party, including even those whose membership had ceased prior to the passage of the statute requiring such deportation. Thus aliens and immigrants are in a particularly vulnerable position. [See Milton R. Konvitz, *Civil Rights in Immigration* (Ithaca: Cornell University Press, 1953); Lena L. Orlow, "The Immigration and Nationality Act in Operation," 29 *Temple L.Q.* 153 (1956); Blanch L. Freedman, "The Loyalty-Security Program—Its Effect in Immigration and Deportation," 15 *Law. Guild Rev.* 135 (1955); and Comment, "The Alien and the Constitution," 20 *U. of Chi. L. Rev.* 547 (1953).]

The advocacy of revolution can constitutionally be punished unless it is limited to the advocacy of *belief in the doctrine* of overthrow of the government by violence. And organizing a group or becoming an active member of a group dedicated to teaching the overthrow of the government by violence may constitutionally be punished. Restrictions of Communists unsupported by a showing of potential danger to the nation or to maintenance of order appear to be subjected to close scrutiny, however. Thus in *Aptheker* v. *Secretary of State*, 378 U.S. 500 (1964), the Court held that Section 6 of the Subversive Activities Control Act, which bars the application for or use of a passport by a member of an organization ordered to register by the Board as a Communist-action organization, was an undue restriction on the right to travel abroad and therefore an unconstitutional abridgment of the liberty guaranteed by the Fifth Amendment. [See Leonard B. Boudin, "The Constitutional Right to Travel," 56 *Column, L. Rev.* 47 (1956).] More recently, in *Lamont* v. *Postmaster General*, 381 U.S. 301 (1965), the Court held unconstitutional a federal statute requiring a request in writing as a prerequisite to the delivery of nonsealed mail from abroad which was classified as containing Communist propaganda material. This case is particularly noteworthy in that for the first time in our history the United States Supreme Court held a *federal* statute unconstitutional as an abridgment of First Amendment rights. [See Jay A. Sigler, "Freedom of the Mails: a Developing Right," 54 *Geo. L. J.* 30 (1965).]

At least in the treatment of citizens, it appears that the Court is more willing to take up cases dealing with anti-Communist restrictions than it was in the decade following World War II and is requiring a relatively close relationship between the restriction and the protection of the nation's security before upholding the peripheral attacks on Communists.

[The literature on loyalty-security problems is enormous. See Thomas I. Emerson, David Haber, and Norman Dorsen, *Political and Civil Rights in the United States*, 3rd ed., 2 vols. (Boston: Little, Brown, 1967), chap. 3, especially the bibliographic references. See also John L. O'Brian, *National Security and Individual Freedom* (Cambridge: Harvard University Press, 1955); Harold W. Chase, *Security and Liberty: The Problem of Native Communists, 1947–1955* (Garden City: Doubleday, 1955); and Walter Gellhorn, ed., *The States and Subversion* (Ithaca: Cornell University Press, 1952).]

## REGULATION OF TRAFFIC AND MAINTENANCE OF PUBLIC PEACE AND ORDER

The State may place the exercise of speech and assembly under reasonable police regulations for a variety of purposes, and some of the most oft-cited illustrations of this power are in the areas of traffic control and the preservation of public order. Of course the previously treated decisions dealing with prior restraints are applicable in this area, just as in other types of expression, but if the State avoids this error, it is permitted a reasonable range of control.

A good illustration of the Court's view of an improper and a proper statutory handling of a permissible area of regulation is to be seen in two cases dealing with the regulation of sound amplification equipment in urban streets and parks. In *Saia v. New York,* 334 U.S. 558 (1948), the Court found a prior restraint in a city ordinance forbidding the use of sound amplification devices except for "public dissemination. . . of items of news and matters of public concern. . . provided that the same be done under permission obtained from the Chief of Police." Refused a second permit on the ground that complaints had been reported concerning his prior speeches and sermons using a loud-speaker, appellant, a minister of the Jehovah's Witnesses, delivered a speech, without a permit and again using a loud-speaker, in a park normally used for recreation purposes. By a five-to-four majority the Court held the ordinance unconstitutional on its face as a prior restraint on the right of free speech. It should be noted, however, that the opinion for the Court pointed out that reasonable regulation of the use of loud-speaker was within the range of state power. Justice Douglas, for the majority, stated:

Noise can be regulated by regulating decibels. The hours and place of public discussion can be controlled. But to allow the police to bar the use of loud-speakers because their use can be abused is like barring radio receivers because they too make a noise. The police need not be given the power to deny a man the use of his radio in order to protect a neighbor against sleepless nights. The same is true here.

Any abuses which loud-speakers create can be controlled by narrowly drawn statutes. When a city allows an official to ban them in his uncontrolled discretion, it sanctions a device for suppression of free communication of ideas. In this case a permit is denied because some persons were said to have found the sound annoying. In the next one a permit may be denied because some people find the ideas annoying. Annoyance at ideas can be cloaked in annoyance at sound. The power of censorship inherent in this type of ordinance reveals its vice.

Justice Frankfurter, joined in dissent by Justices Reed and Burton, pointed out that there is an important difference in ordinary human speech and the use of modern amplifying devices which "afford easy, too easy, opportunities for aural aggression." Considering this and the fact that people had complained, it did not seem to him unreasonable or unconstitutional to refuse a license to the appellant for the time and place requested. Justice Jackson dissented separately, stating that this was not even a free speech issue.

[C]an it be that society has no control of apparatus which, when put to unregulated proselyting, propaganda and commercial uses, can render life unbearable? It is intimated that the city can control the decibels; if so, why may it not prescribe zero decibels as appropriate to some places? It seems to me that society has the right to control, as to place, time and volume, the use of loud-speaking devices for any purpose, provided its regulations are not unduly arbitrary, capricious or discriminatory.

The second loud-speaker case also came on a five-to-four vote, but this time upholding a regulation. The case was *Kovacs v. Cooper,* 336 U.S. 77 (1949), involving the validity of a Trenton, New Jersey, ordinance which provided:

That it shall be unlawful for any person, firm or corporation. . . to play, use or operate for advertising purposes, or for any other purpose whatsoever, on or upon the public streets, alleys or thoroughfares in the City of Trenton, any device known as a sound truck, loud speaker or sound-amplifier, or radio or phonograph with a loud speaker or sound amplifier, or any other instrument known as a calliope or any instrument of any kind or character which emits therefrom loud and raucous noises and is attached to and upon any vehicle operated or standing upon said streets or public places aforementioned.

Although five justices held the regulation valid, there was no opinion for the Court. Justice Reed, speaking for three members, seemingly accepted the construction placed on the ordinance by the New Jersey Supreme Court, namely that the ordinance applied only to vehicles with sound amplifiers "emitting loud and raucous noises" and did not prohibit sound trucks altogether. On this basis he stated, "We think that the need for reasonable protection in the homes or business houses from the distracting noises of vehicles equipped with such sound amplifying devices justifies the ordinance."

Justice Frankfurter concurred, repeating the views expressed in his *Saia* dissent. Justice Jackson also concurred separately, saying:

> I join the judgment sustaining the Trenton ordinance because I believe that operation of mechanical sound-amplifying devices conflicts with quiet enjoyment of home and park and with safe and legitimate use of street and market place, and that it is constitutionally subject to regulation or prohibition by the state or municipal authority. . . .
>
> But I agree with Mr. Justice Black that this decision is a repudiation of that in *Saia* v. *New York*. . . . Like him, I am unable to find anything in this record to warrant a distinction because of "loud and raucous" tones of this machine. . . Trenton, as the ordinance reads to me, unconditionally bans all sound trucks from the city streets. Lockport relaxed its prohibition with a proviso to allow their use, even in areas set aside for public recreation, when and where the Chief of Police saw no objection. Comparison of this our 1949 decision with our 1948 decision, I think, will pretty hopelessly confuse municipal authorities as to what they may or may not do.

Justice Black, joined by Justices Douglas and Rutledge, dissented on the ground that the "ordinance is on its face, and as construed and applied in this case by that state's courts, an absolute and unqualified prohibition of amplifying devices on any of Trenton's streets at any time, at any place, for any purpose, and without regard to how noisy they may be." He indicated clearly, however, that reasonable regulation would meet the test of constitutionality. The opinion stated:

> I would agree without reservation to the sentiment that "unrestrained use throughout a municipality of all sound amplifying devices would be intolerable." And of course cities may restrict or absolutely ban the use of amplifiers on busy streets in the business area. A city ordinance that reasonably restricts the volume of sound, or the hours during which an amplifier may be used, does not in my mind infringe the constitutionally protected area of free speech. It is because this ordinance does none of these things, but is instead an absolute prohibition of all uses of an amplifier on any of the streets of Trenton at any time that I must dissent.

Justice Murphy dissented separately.

While reconciliation of the two cases may not be easy, a head-count of the voting in the cases shows that Chief Justice Vinson was the only member to change his vote from *Saia* to *Kovacs* relative to the power to enforce the respective ordinances. Since he did not write an opinion in either case, it is not possible to state precisely the basis for his shift. Once again, however, it is clear from a reading of the opinions that an ordinance limiting the volume, time, and place of the use of sound trucks or public sound amplification equipment in some reasonable manner would pass constitutional muster.

The problem of regulating street processions while at the same time avoiding the pitfall of prior restraint and affording broad protection to First Amendment rights was well illustrated in the case of *Cox v. New Hampshire,* 312 U.S. 569 (1941), discussed earlier. The Court upheld a reasonable and nondiscriminatory permit requirement for the holding of parades as a proper municipal regulation of the use of the streets.

*Feiner v. New York*, 340 U.S. 315 (1951) illustrates the application of a municipal ordinance prohibiting disorderly conduct to the attempted exercise of free speech. Feiner addressed a group of listeners on a street corner in Syracuse, New York. A racially mixed crowd of some seventy-five or eighty people gathered on the sidewalks and spilled into the street. He urged the audience to attend a speech later that night on the subject of racial discrimination, and during the appeal referred to President Truman as a "bum," to the American Legion as "a Nazi Gestapo," and to the Mayor of Syracuse as a "champagne-sipping bum." He also said that "colored people don't have equal rights and they should rise up in arms and fight for them."

Two officers were sent to the meeting and stated that the crowd was restless and there was some pushing, shoving, and milling around. One man said to the police officers, "If you don't get that S.O.B. off, I will go over and get him off there myself." The police officers told Feiner to stop speaking, and when he refused, arrested him for disorderly conduct. In finding Feiner guilty the trial judge concluded that the police officers were justified in taking action to prevent a breach of the peace, and the New York Court of Appeals affirmed.

A majority of six in the United States Supreme Court considered that the facts clearly indicated sufficient evidence of a possible breach of the peace to warrant Feiner's arrest for disorderly conduct. The Chief Justice, speaking for the majority, stated that "Petitioner was neither arrested nor convicted for the making or the content of his speech. Rather it was the reaction which it actually engendered." He stated further:

We are well aware that the ordinary murmurings and objections of a hostile audience cannot be allowed to silence a speaker, and are also mindful of the possible danger of giving overzealous police officials complete discretion to break up otherwise lawful public meetings. . . . But we are not faced here with such a situation. It is one thing to say that the police cannot be used as an instrument for the oppression of unpopular views, and another to say that, when as here the speaker passes the bounds of argument or persuasion and undertakes incitement to riot, they are powerless to prevent a breach of the peace.

Justices Black and Douglas gave vigorous dissenting opinions, Justice Minton concurring with the latter. Justice Black stated:

As to the existence of a dangerous situation on the street corner, it seems farfetched to suggest that the "facts" show any imminent threat of riot or uncontrollable disorder. It is neither unusual nor unexpected that some people at public street meetings mutter, mill about, push, shove, or disagree, even violently, with the speaker. Indeed, it is rare where controversial topics are discussed that an outdoor crowd does not do some or all of these things. Nor does one isolated threat to assault the speaker forbode disorder. . . .

Moreover, assuming that the "facts" did indicate a critical situation, I reject the implication of the Court's opinion that the police had no obligation to protect petitioner's constitutional right to talk. But if, in the name of preserving order, they ever can interfere with a lawful public speaker, they first must make all reasonable efforts to protect him. Here the policemen did not even pretend to try to protect petitioner. . . . Their duty was to protect petitioner's right to talk, even to the extent of arresting the man who threatened to interfere. Instead, they shirked that duty and acted only to suppress the right to speak.

The decision in the *Feiner* case indicates the importance of the fact-finding aspect of the cases. The members of the Court sometimes disagree on the law and sometimes on the way that the facts should be read. While the appellate courts do not as a rule upset lower court findings of fact, the United States Supreme Court has often pointed out that in First Amendment cases it will feel free to make its own determination of the facts. The majority in *Feiner* found the facts to support a conviction for disorderly conduct, while the minority read them differently and concluded that the problem was one of a hostile audience interfering with a lawful speech. [See Note, "Hostile Audience Confrontations: Police Conduct and First Amendment Rights," 75 *Michigan Law Rev.* 180 (1976), and Zechariah Chafee, "The Problem of the Hostile Audience," 49 *Colum. L. Rev.* 1118 (1949).]

We saw in *Cantwell v. Connecticut* that a permit requirement for solicitation for religious causes was unconstitutional where the law accorded the licensing official discretion to determine what was a religious cause. But in a case involving the Hare Krishna sect the Court upheld a Minnesota state fair rule regulating the locale for such solicitation.

HEFFRON *v.* INTERNATIONAL SOCIETY FOR
KRISHNA CONSCIOUSNESS, INC.
*452 U.S. 640 (1981)*

[Rule 6.05 of the Minnesota Agricultural Society, a public corporation that operates the annual state fair, provides that sale or distribution of any merchandise, including printed or written material, except from a duly licensed location on the fairgrounds shall be a misdemeanor. The respondents, an organization espousing the views of the Krishna religion, filed suit in a state court seeking injunctive relief on the ground that the rule, on its face and as applied, violated their First Amendment rights. The trial court upheld the constitutionality of the rule, but the Minnesota Supreme Court reversed.]

Justice White delivered the opinion of the Court. . . .

. . . As Rule 6.05 is construed and applied by the Society, "all persons, groups or firms which desire to sell, exhibit or distribute materials during the annual State Fair must do so only from fixed locations on the fairgrounds." Although the Rule does not prevent organizational representatives from walking about the fairgrounds and communicating the organization's views with fair patrons in face-to-face discussions, it does require that any exhibitor conduct its sales, distribution, and fund solicitation operations from a booth rented from the Society. Space in the fairgrounds is rented to all comers in a nondiscriminatory fashion on a first-come, first-served basis with the rental charge based on the size and location of the booth. The Rule applies alike to nonprofit, charitable, and commercial enterprises. . . .

. . . ISKCON asserted that the Rule would suppress the practice of Sankirtan, one of its religious rituals, which enjoins its members to go into public places to distribute or sell religious literature and to solicit donations for the support of the Krishna religion. . . . We granted the . . . petition for writ of certiorari in light of the important constitutional issues presented and the conflicting results reached in similar cases in various lower courts. [A footnote here lists the lower court cases involving regulations applying to booths, airports, the World Trade Center, highway rest stops and a performing arts center.]

The State does not dispute that the oral and written dissemination of the Krishnas' religious views and doctrines is protected by the First Amendment. . . .

It is also common ground, however, that the First Amendment does not guarantee the right to communicate one's views at all times and places or in any manner that may be desired. . . . As the Minnesota Supreme Court recognized, the activities of ISKCON, like those of others protected by the First Amendment, are subject to reasonable time, place, and manner restrictions. . . . *Kovacs* v. *Cooper* . . . *Cox* v. *New*

*Hampshire.* . . . ."We have often approved restrictions of that kind provided that they are justified without reference to the content of the regulated speech, that they serve a significant governmental interest, and that in doing so they leave open ample alternative channels for communication of the information.". . .

. . . Here, the principal justification asserted by the State in support of rule 6.05 is the need to maintain the orderly movement of the crowd given the large number of exhibitors and persons attending the Fair. . . . Because the Fair attracts large crowds—an average of 115,000 patrons on weekdays and 160,000 on Saturdays and Sundays—it is apparent that the State's interest in the orderly movement and control of such an assembly of persons is a substantial consideration. . . .

As we see it, the Minnesota Supreme Court took too narrow a view of the State's interest in avoiding congestion and maintaining the orderly movement of fair patrons on the fairgrounds. The justification for the Rule should not be measured by the disorder that would result from granting an exemption solely to ISKCON. That organization and its ritual of Sankirtan have no special claim to First Amendment protection as compared to that of other religions who also distribute literature and solicit funds. None of our cases suggest that the inclusion of peripatetic solicitation as part of a church ritual entitles church members to solicitation rights in a public forum superior to those of members of other religious groups that raise money but do not purport to ritualize the process. Nor for present purposes do religious organizations enjoy rights to communicate, distribute, and solicit on the fairgrounds superior to those of other organizations having social, political, or other ideological messages to proselytize. These nonreligious organizations seeking support for their activities are entitled to rights equal to those of religious groups to enter a public forum and spread their views, whether by soliciting funds or by distributing literature.

If Rule 6.05 is an invalid restriction on the activities of ISKCON, it is no more valid with respect to the other social, political, or charitable organizations that have rented booths at the Fair and confined their distribution, sale, and fund solicitation to those locations. . . . Obviously, there would be a much larger threat to the State's interest in crowd control if all other religious, nonreligious, and noncommercial organizations could likewise move freely about the fairgrounds distributing and selling literature and soliciting funds at will.

Given these considerations, we hold that the State's interest in confining distribution, selling, and fund solicitation activities to fixed locations is sufficient to satisfy the requirement that a place or manner restriction must serve a substantial state interest. . . .

Justice Brennan, with whom Justice Marshall and Justice Stevens join, concurring in part and dissenting in part. . . .

The State advances three justifications for its booth Rule. The justification relied upon by the Court today is the State's interest in maintaining the orderly movement of the crowds at the fair. . . . The second justification, relied upon by the dissenting justices below, . . . is the State's interest in protecting its fair goers from fraudulent, deceptive, and misleading solicitation practices. The third justification, based on the "captive audience" doctrine, is the State's interest in protecting its fairgoers from annoyance and harassment. . . . I join the judgment of the court insofar as it upholds Rule 6.05's restriction on sales and solicitations. However, because I believe that the booth Rule is an overly intrusive means of achieving the State's interest in crowd control, and because I cannot accept the validity of the State's third asserted justification, I dissent from the Court's approval of Rule 6.05's restriction on the distribution of literature. . . .

Justice Blackmun, concurring in part and dissenting in part. . . .

"Green River" ordinances (so called because of earlier adoption by the City of Green River, Wyoming) are those which prohibit various kinds of door-to-door solicitation without the prior permission of the householder. In *Martin* v. *Struthers*, 319 U.S. 141 (1943), a divided Court held that a municipality could not constitutionally prohibit a person from going from door to door knocking on doors and ringing doorbells for the purpose of distributing to the householder a handbill announcing a religious meeting. The community's interest in preventing crime and in assuring privacy in an industrial community where many residents worked night shifts and had to sleep during the day was held insufficient to justify the ordinance in the case of persons involved in religious communication by handbill. Justice Frankfurter filed a strong dissent stressing the need to recognize the householder's privacy.

In *Breard* v. *City of Alexandria*, 341 U.S. 622 (1951), however, the Court sustained a similar ordinance as applied to solicitation for magazine subscriptions. The majority opinion distinguished the case from *Martin*, since solicitation for the sale of subscriptions "brings into the transaction a commercial feature" that tilted the balance in favor of the householder's desire for privacy. *Hynes* v. *Mayor of Oradell*, 425 U.S. 610 (1976), dealt with a city ordinance requiring an identification permit for canvassing or soliciting from house to house for charitable or political purposes. The Court held that soliciting and canvassing from door to door were subject to reasonable regulation so as to protect the citizen against crime and undue annoyance, but that the First Amendment required such controls to be drawn with "narrow specificity." The ordinance was invalidated as unacceptably vague.

In *Village of Schaumburg* v. *Citizens for A Better Environment*, 444 U.S. 620 (1980), the Court held that an ordinance barring door-to-door solicitation of contributions by charitable organizations that did not use at least 75% of their receipts for "charitable purposes" (such purposes defined to exclude solicitation expenses, salaries, overhead, and other administrative expenses) was unconstitutionally overbroad. The Court pointed out that the ordinance would prohibit solicitation by certain organizations entitled to First Amendment protection but "whose purpose is not to provide money or services for the poor, the needy or other worthy objects of charity, but to gather and disseminate information about and advocate positions on matters of public concern." Organizations of this kind would necessarily spend more than 25 percent of their budgets on salaries and administrative expenses and would be barred from solicitation in the Village. Prevention of fraud was the Village's principal justification for the ordinance, but the opinion stated that the interest in preventing fraud "can be better served by measures less intrusive than a direct prohibition on solicitation."

In an attempt to avoid the defects of the ordinance in *Schaumburg,* North Carolina passed a Charitable Solicitations Act that defined the "reasonable fee" that professional fundraisers could charge according to a three-tiered schedule. A fee up to 20% of receipts collected was deemed reasonable. A fee between 20% and 35% was deemed unreasonable unless the solicitation involved the "dissemination of information, discussion, or advocacy relating to public issues as directed by the [charitable organization] which is to benefit from the solicitation." A fee exceeding 35% was presumed unreasonable, but the fundraiser could rebut the presumption by showing that the fee was necessary either because the solicitation involved the dissemination of information or advocacy on public issues directed by the charity, or because otherwise the charity's ability to raise money or communicate would be significantly diminished. In addition, professional fundraisers could not solicit without an approved license. In contrast, volunteer fundraisers could solicit immediately upon submitting a license application. And the Act set no time limit on the licensor's determination of whether to issue the license to professional fundraisers. Citing *Schaumburg,* the Court in *Riley* v. *National Federation of the Blind,* 56 LW 4869 (1988), held the Act unconstitutional as an infringement upon freedom of speech. "Our prior cases teach that the solicitation of charitable contributions is protected speech, and that using percentages to decide the legality of the fundraiser's fee is not narrowly tailored to the State's interest in preventing fraud." The opinion pointed out that North Carolina had an anti-fraud law, "and we presume that law enforcement officers are ready and able to enforce it." Further, the Act permits delay without limit with respect to the issuance of the license. "The statute on its face does not purport to require when a determination must be made, nor is there an administrative regulation or interpretation doing so."

### Profane and Abusive Language: The "Fighting Words" Doctrine

*Chaplinsky* v. *New Hampshire,* 315 U.S. 568 (1942), involved a state law providing that:

No person shall address any offensive, derisive or annoying word to any other person who is lawfully in any street or other public place, nor call him by any offensive or derisive name, nor make any noise or exclamation in his presence and hearing with intent to deride, offend or annoy him or to prevent him from pursuing his lawful business or occupation.

The state court construed the statute as prohibiting "words likely to cause an average addressee to fight," or "face-to-face words plainly likely to cause a breach of the peace by the addressee." Appellant was a Jehovah's Witness who, after getting into an argument on a public sidewalk, called a city marshal a "damned Fascist" and a "God-dammed racketeer." His conviction under the statute was unanimously upheld by the United States Supreme Court against a claim of invasion of First Amendment freedom of expression. Justice Murphy, for the Court, stated:

There are certain well-defined and narrowly limited classes of speech, the prevention and punishment of which have never been thought to raise any Constitutional problem. These include the lewd and obscene, the profane, the libelous, and the insulting or "fighting" words—those which by their very utterance inflict injury or tend to incite an immediate breach of the peace. It has been well observed that such utterances are no essential part of any exposition of ideas and are of such slight social value as a step to truth that any benefit that may be derived from them is clearly outweighed by the social interest in order and morality.

A case frequently cited in the context of "fighting words" is *Terminiello* v. *Chicago,* 337 U.S. 1 (1949), although the decision in the United States Supreme Court did not come off on that issue. Terminiello spoke in an auditorium in Chicago to a crowd of about 800 persons. He criticized Democrats, Jews, and Communists in a speech full of racial and political hatred. A crowd of over a thousand gathered outside in protest, yelling "Fascists, Hitlers!" A cordon of police assigned to the meeting was unable to stop the smashing of doors, the breaking of windows, and other acts of violence. Terminiello was arrested and convicted of violating a breach of the peace ordinance. In charging the jury, however, the judge defined breach of the peace to include speech which "stirs the public to anger, invites dispute, brings about a condition of unrest or creates a disturbance." By a five-to-four vote the Court reversed the conviction on the ground that the charge to the jury interpreting the statute permitted the punishment of speech that was protected by the Constitution. Justice Douglas, for the majority, stated:

A function of free speech under our system of government is to invite dispute. It may indeed best serve its high purpose when it induces a condition of unrest, creates dissatisfaction with conditions as they are, or even stirs people to anger. Speech is often provocative and challenging. It may strike at prejudices and preconceptions and have profound unsettling effects as it presses for acceptance of an idea. . . . The ordinance as construed by the trial court seriously invaded this province. It permitted conviction of petitioner if his speech stirred people to anger, invited public dispute, or brought about a condition of unrest. A conviction resting on any of these grounds may not stand.

There were dissents on the ground that no one had raised any issue regarding the charge to the jury at any stage of the proceedings, and thus the question was not open to them. Justices Jackson and Burton further dissented on the ground that the jury was justified in finding a breach of the peace in the facts of the case, and the conviction should have been affirmed.

In view of the basis for the majority decision, the *Terminiello* case must be confined to the issue of whether speech which invites dispute and stirs the public to anger can for those reasons only be restricted. Thus it stands as no authority for what a municipality can or cannot do to punish a man who says the things which Terminiello did under the circumstances of his speech. The Court simply did not reach that question in deciding the case.

### COHEN *v.* CALIFORNIA
### *403 U.S. 15 (1971)*

[On April 26, 1968, Cohen was observed in the Los Angeles County Courthouse in the corridor outside the Municipal Court wearing a jacket bearing the words "Fuck the Draft" which were plainly visible. There were women and children present in the corridor. Cohen was arrested and convicted of violating a state law which prohibits "maliciously and willfully disturbing the peace or quiet of any neighborhood or person, . . . by . . . offensive conduct . . ." and sentenced to thirty days imprisonment. The California Court of Appeals affirmed.]

Mr. Justice Harlan delivered the opinion of the Court.

This case may seem at first blush too inconsequential to find its way into our books, but the issue it presents is of no small constitutional significance. . . .

The conviction quite clearly rests upon the asserted offensiveness of the *words* Cohen used to convey his message to the public. The only "conduct" which the State sought to punish is the fact of communication. Thus, we deal here with a conviction resting solely upon "speech," . . . not upon any separated identifiable conduct. . . . Further, the State certainly lacks power to punish Cohen for the underlying content of the message the inscription conveyed. At least so long as there is no showing of an intent to incite disobedience to or disruption of the draft, Cohen could not, consistently with the First and Fourteenth Amendments, be punished for asserting the evident position on the inutility or immorality of the draft his jacket reflected. . . .

Appellant's conviction, then, rests squarely upon his exercise of the "freedom of speech" protected from arbitrary governmental interference by the Constitution and can be justified, if at all, only as a valid regulation of the manner in which he exercised that freedom, not as a permissible prohibition on the substantive message it conveys. . . .

In the first place, Cohen was tried under a statute applicable throughout the entire State. Any attempt to support this conviction on the ground that the statute seeks to preserve an appropriately decorous atmosphere in the courthouse where Cohen was arrested must fail in the absence of any language in the statute that would have put appellant on notice that certain kinds of otherwise permissible speech or conduct would nevertheless, under California law, not be tolerated in certain places. . . .

In the second place, as it comes to us, this case. . . is not an obscenity case. Whatever else may be necessary to give rise to the States' broader power to prohibit obscene expression, such expression must be, in some significant way, erotic. . . . It cannot plausibly be maintained that this vulgar allusion to the Selective Service System would conjure up such psychic stimulation in anyone likely to be confronted with Cohen's crudely defaced jacket.

This Court has also held that the States are free to ban the simple use, without a demonstration of additional justifying circumstances, of so-called "fighting words," those personally abusive epithets which, when addressed to the ordinary citizen, are, as a matter of common knowledge, inherently likely to provoke violent reaction. *Chaplinsky* v. *New Hampshire.* . . . While the four-letter word displayed by Cohen in relation to the draft is not uncommonly employed in a personally provocative fashion, in this instance it was clearly not "directed to the person of the hearer." . . . There is, as noted above, no showing that anyone who saw Cohen was in fact violently aroused or that appellant intended such a result.

Finally, in arguments before this Court much has been made of the claim that Cohen's distasteful mode of expression was thrust upon unwilling or unsuspecting viewers, and that the State might therefore legitimately act as it did in order to protect the sensitive from otherwise unavoidable exposure to appellant's crude form of protest. Of course, the mere presumed presence of unwitting listeners or viewers does not serve automatically to justify curtailing all speech capable of giving offense. . . . The ability of government, consonant with the constitution, to shut off discourse solely to protect others from hearing it is. . . dependent upon a showing that substantial privacy interests are being invaded in an essentially intolerable manner. Any broader view of this authority would effectively empower a majority to silence dissidents simply as a matter of personal predilections. . . .

. . . [T]he principle contended for by the State seems inherently boundless. How is one to distinguish this from any other offensive word? Surely the State has no right to cleanse public debate to the point where it is grammatically palatable to the most squeamish among us. Yet no readily ascertainable general principle exists for stopping short of that result were we to affirm the judgment below. For, while the particular four-letter word being litigated here is perhaps more distasteful than most others of its genre, it is nevertheless often true that one man's vulgarity is another's lyric. Indeed, we think it is largely because government officials cannot make principled distinctions in this area that the Constitution leaves matters of taste and style so largely to the individual.

Additionally, we cannot overlook the fact, because it is well illustrated by the episode involved here, that much linguistic expression serves a dual communicative function: it conveys not only ideas capable of relatively precise, detached explication, but otherwise inexpressible emotions as well. In fact, words are often chosen as much for their emotive as their cognitive force. We cannot sanction the view that the Constitution, while solicitous of the cognitive content of individual speech, has little or no regard for that emotive function which, practically speaking, may often be the more important element of the overall message sought to be communicated. . . .

Mr. Justice Blackmun, with whom The Chief Justice and Mr. Justice Black join, dissenting. [Mr. Justice White concurred in part.]

## GOODING v. WILSON
### 405 U.S. 518 (1972)

[Appellee Wilson was one of a group of persons who picketed a building housing the 12th Army Corps Headquarters, carrying signs opposing the war in Vietnam. When the police tried to remove the pickets from the door, a scuffle ensued. Testimony showed that Wilson addressed the police as follows: "White son of a bitch, I'll kill you." "You son of a bitch, I'll choke you to death." "You son of a bitch, if you ever put your hands on me again, I'll cut you all to pieces." Wilson was charged and convicted of using opprobrious words and abusive language in violation of a Georgia law which provides: "Any person who shall, without provocation, use to or of another, and in his presence. . . opprobrious words or abusive language, tending to cause a breach of the peace. . . shall be guilty of a misdemeanor." The Georgia Supreme Court affirmed the conviction. Wilson then sought habeas corpus relief in a federal District Court, which held that the Georgia statute was unconstitutionally vague and broad and set aside the conviction.]

Mr. Justice Brennan delivered the opinion of the Court. . . .

[The statute] punishes only spoken words. It can therefore withstand appellee's attack upon its facial constitutionality only if, as authoritatively construed by the Georgia courts, it is not susceptible of application to speech, although vulgar or offensive, that is protected by the First and Fourteenth Amendments, *Cohen* v. *California*. . . .

"Although a statute may be neither vague, overbroad, nor otherwise invalid as applied to the conduct charged against a particular defendant, he is permitted to raise its vagueness or unconstitutional overbreadth as applied to others. And if the law is found deficient in one of these respects, it may not be applied to him either, until and unless a satisfactory limiting construction is placed on the statute. The statute, in effect, is stricken down on its face. This result is deemed justified since the otherwise continued existence of the statute in unnarrowed form would tend to suppress constitutionally protected rights." *Coates* v. *City of Cincinnati*, . . . In other words, the statute must be carefully drawn or be authoritatively construed to punish only unprotected speech and not be susceptible of application to protected expression. . . .

Appellant does not challenge these principles but contends that the Georgia statute is narrowly drawn to apply only to a constitutionally unprotected class of words—"fighting" words—"those which by their very utterance inflict injury or tend to incite an immediate breach of the peace." . . . Our decisions since *Chaplinsky* have continued to recognize state power constitutionally to punish "fighting" words under carefully drawn statutes not also susceptible of application to protected expression. . . . We have, however, made our own examination of the Georgia cases, both those cited and others discovered in research. That examination brings us to the conclusion, in agreement with the courts below, that the Georgia appellate decisions have not construed [the statute] to be limited in application, as in *Chaplinsky*, to words that "have a direct tendency to cause acts of violence by the person to whom, individually, the remark is addressed.". . .

Mr. Justice Powell and Mr. Justice Rehnquist took no part in the consideration or decision of this case.

Mr. Chief Justice Burger, dissenting.

I fully join in Mr. Justice Blackmun's dissent against the bizarre result reached by the Court. It is not merely odd, it is nothing less than remarkable that the Court can find a state statute void on its face, not because of its language—which is the traditional test—but because of the way courts of that State have applied the statute in a few isolated cases, decided as long ago as 1905 and generally long before this Court's decision in *Chaplinsky* v. *New Hampshire*. . . . Even if all of those cases had been decided yesterday, they do nothing to demonstrate that the narrow language of the Georgia statute has any significant potential for sweeping application to suppress or deter important protected speech. . . .

. . . And if the early Georgia cases cited by the majority establish any proposition, it is that the statute, as its language so clearly indicates, is aimed at preventing precisely that type of personal, face-to-face, abusive and insulting language likely to provoke a violent retaliation—self-help, as we euphemistically call it—that the *Chaplinsky* case recognized could be validly prohibited. The facts of the case now before the Court demonstrate that the Georgia statute is serving that valid and entirely proper purpose. There is no persuasive reason to wipe the statute from the books, unless we want to encourage victims of such verbal assaults to seek their own private redress. . . .

Mr. Justice Blackmun, with whom The Chief Justice joins, dissenting.

It seems strange indeed, that in this day a man may say to a police officer, who is attempting to restore access to a public building, "White son of a bitch, I'll kill you" and "You son of a bitch, I'll choke you to death,". . . and yet constitutionally cannot be prosecuted and convicted under a state statute that makes it a misdemeanor to "use to or of another, and in his presence . . . opprobrious words or abusive languge, tending to cause a breach of the peace. . . . " This, however, is precisely what the Court pronounces as the law today.

The Supreme Court of Georgia, when the conviction was appealed, unanimously held the other way. . . . Surely any adult who can read—and I do not exclude this appellee-defendant from that category—should reasonably expect no other conclusion. The words . . . are clear. They are also concise. They are not in my view, overbroad or incapable of being understood. Except perhaps for the "big" word "opprobrious"—and no point is made of its bigness—any Georgia schoolboy would expect that this defendant's fighting and provocative words to the officers were covered. . . . Common sense permits no other conclusion. This is demonstrated by the fact that the appellee, and this Court, attack the statute, not as it applies to the appellee, but as it conceivably might apply to others who might utter other words. . . .

In *Eaton* v. *City of Tulsa*, 415 U.S. 697 (1974), the Court reversed a contempt citation which had been imposed on petitioner because of his use of an expletive during the course of a trial for an alleged violation of a Tulsa ordinance. During cross-examination, in response to a question asked him by the assistant city prosecutor, the following exchange occurred:

Q. What did you do?

A. I sensed something from behind me and I turned maybe enough to look over my shoulder. At the time I turned and looked over my shoulder I could see this guy's face and shoulders coming at me; almost simultaneously he hit me and he knocked me over on my back a bench down. Luckily, somebody grabbed him and pulled him back, and I got up off of my back after being knocked down on my back, wrenched my elbow, got up to a vertical posture where I would have some kind of defensibility and moved up to where I had some square footing.

Q. What's defensibility?

A. I think that would be a place where you were able to get your feet to stand square so you would be half ready for some chicken shit that had jumped you from behind.

THE COURT: Mr. Eaton, you will have until tomorrow morning to show me why you should not be held in direct contempt of this Court. I'm not going to put up with that kind of language in this Court.

THE WITNESS: That's fine, I don't feel as though I need to put up with why I received this.

THE COURT: Mr. Eaton, did you hear what I just said?

THE WITNESS: Yes, sir.

Petitioner was found guilty of contempt and fined $50 plus costs. The Oklahoma Court of Criminal Appeals affirmed. The Supreme Court reversed, and the Per Curiam opinion stated:

> This single isolated usage of street vernacular, not directed at the judge or any officer of the court, cannot constitutionally support the conviction of criminal contempt. . . . In using the expletive in answering the question on cross-examination "it is not charged that [petitioner] here disobeyed any valid court order, talked loudly, acted boisterously, or attempted to prevent the judge or any other officer of the court from carrying on his court duties.". . . In the circumstances, the use of the expletive thus cannot be held to "constitute an imminent. . . threat to the administration of justice."

Justice Powell, concurring, stated that "the controlling fact, in my view, and one that should be emphasized, is that petitioner received no prior warning or caution from the trial judge with respect to court etiquette."

In *Lewis v. New Orleans*, 415 U.S. 130 (1974), the Court held a New Orleans ordinance overbroad in violation of the First Amendment and therefore facially invalid. The ordinance provided:

> It shall be unlawful and a breach of the peace for any person wantonly to curse or revile or to use obscene or opprobrious language toward or with reference to any member of the city police while in the actual performance of his duty.

After words were exchanged between the appellant and a police officer, the appellant allegedly said, "You god damn m.f. police—I am going to [the Superintendent of Police] about this." She was charged and convicted of violation of the above ordinance. The Court reversed, citing *Gooding v. Wilson*. Justice Powell, in a concurring opinion, said:

> Quite apart from the ambiguity inherent in the term "opprobrious," words may or may not be "fighting words," depending upon the circumstances of their utterance. It is unlikely, for example, that the words said to have been used here would have precipitated a physical confrontation between the middle-aged woman who spoke them and the police officer in whose presence they were uttered.

The justice also cited the Model Penal Code suggestion that even "fighting words" as defined by *Chaplinsky* should not be punished when addressed to a police officer trained to exercise a higher degree of restraint than the average citizen. One might almost conclude from the cases that in the absence of a violent response to the vilifying language used the Court would probably conclude that the language therefore should not fall within the definition of "fighting words." Clearly, the mere use of profanity would not come within the definition. Justice Blackmun, writing for the three dissenters in *Lewis*, protested:

> The "overbreadth" and "vagueness" doctrines, as they are now being applied by the Court, quietly and steadily have worked their way into First Amendment parlance much as substantive due process did for the "old Court" of the 20's and 30's. These doctrines are being invoked indiscriminately without regard to the nature of the speech in question, the possible effect the statute or ordinance has upon such

speech, the importance of the speech in relation to the exposition of ideas, or the purported or asserted community interest in preventing that speech.

[See Annotation, "Supreme Court's View . . . of the Utterance of 'Fighting Words,' " 39 L.Ed.2d 925 (1974); Note, "Fighting Words or Free Speech," 50 N.C. L. Rev. 382 (1972);

## Demonstrations and Protest Speech

The decades of the 1960s and 1970s were marked by a substantial increase in the use of protest marches and demonstrations. These tactics were employed by a number of groups, but particularly by civil rights and peace advocates and, more recently, by groups opposed to nuclear plants in America. Marches, parades, picketing, and demonstrations are not newcomers to the American scene, of course. Labor groups, the Salvation Army, suffragists, and others have used one or another of these approaches at various periods in our history. Even the March on Washington was utilized as early as 1894 by Jacob S. Coxey, who led his "army" of some 500 unemployed to Washington to petition Congress for a public works appropriation. (The movement failed when Coxey and his lieutenants were arrested for "walking on the grass.") In 1932 President Hoover ordered federal troops and tanks, commanded by General Douglas MacArthur, to drive the World War I veterans' "bonus marchers" out of Washington.

Recent decades, however, have shown an increase in the use of the group or mass demonstration, and a new term in the vocabulary of protest—the "sit-in"—has been introduced. The law with respect to the older tactics has changed but little, although a number of previously unresolved issues have reached the Supreme Court for decision. A problem that proved particularly vexing for the Court was the matter of sit-in demonstrations protesting racial discrimination in privately owned establishments. The issue was substantially mooted by the enactment of the Civil Rights Act of 1964 with its broad guarantee of equal accommodations for all races.

*Shuttlesworth* v. *Birmingham* in 1969 involved a protest march on the streets and sidewalks of Birmingham, Alabama, and was discussed earlier as an illustration of an invalid ordinance regulating parades and processions. The *Edwards* case, below, dealt with a demonstration on the South Carolina State House grounds.

### EDWARDS *v.* SOUTH CAROLINA
### *372 U.S. 229 (1963)*

Mr. Justice Stewart delivered the opinion of the Court.

The petitioners, 187 in number, were convicted in a magistrate's court in Columbia, South Carolina, of the common-law crime of breach of the peace. Their convictions were ultimately affirmed by the South Carolina Supreme Court. . . . We granted certiorari. . . to consider the claim that these convictions cannot be squared with the Fourteenth Amendment of the United States Constitution.

There was no substantial conflict in the trial evidence. Late in the morning of March 2, 1961, the petitioners, high school and college students of the Negro race, met at the Zion Baptist Church in Columbia. From there, at about noon, they walked in separate groups of about 15 to the South Carolina State House grounds, an area of two city blocks open to the general public. Their purpose was "to submit a protest to the citizens of South Carolina, along with the Legislative Bodies of South Carolina, our feelings and our dissatisfaction with the present condition of discriminatory actions against Negroes, in general, and to let them know that we were dissatisfied and that we would like for the laws which prohibited Negro privileges in this State to be removed."

Already on the State House grounds when the petitioners arrived were 30 or more law enforcement officers, who had advance knowledge that the petitioners were coming. Each group of petitioners entered the grounds through a driveway and parking area known in the record as the "horseshoe." As they entered, they were told by the law enforcement officials that "they had a right, as a citizen, to go through the State House grounds, as any other citizen has, as long as they were peaceful." During the next half hour or 45 minutes, the petitioners, in the same small groups, walked single file or two abreast in an orderly way through the grounds, each group carrying placards bearing such messages as "I am proud to be a Negro," and "Down with segregation."

During this time a crowd of some 200 to 300 onlookers had collected in the horseshoe area and on the adjacent sidewalks. There was no evidence to suggest that these onlookers were anything but curious, and no evidence at all of any threatening remarks, hostile gestures, or offensive language on the part of any member of the crowd. The City Manager testified that he recognized some of the onlookers, whom he did not identify, as "possible trouble makers," but his subsequent testimony made clear that nobody among the crowd actually caused or threatened any trouble. There was no obstruction of pedestrian or vehicular traffic within the State House grounds. . . . Although vehicular traffic at a nearby street intersection was slowed down somewhat, an officer was dispatched to keep traffic moving. There were a number of bystanders on the public sidewalk adjacent to the State House grounds, but they all moved on when asked to do so, and there was no impediment of pedestrian traffic. Police protection at the scene was at all times sufficient to meet any foreseeable possibility of disorder.

In the situation and under the circumstances thus described, the police authorities [actually the order issued from the City Manager, as the footnote excerpts from the trial record show] advised the petitioners that they would be arrested if they did not disperse within 15 minutes. Instead of dispersing, the petitioners engaged in what the City Manager described as "boisterous," "loud," and "flamboyant" conduct, which, as his later testimony made clear, consisted of listening to a "religious harangue" by one of their leaders, and loudly singing "The Star Spangled Banner" and other patriotic and religious songs, while stamping their feet and clapping their hands. After 15 minutes had passed, the police arrested the petitioners and marched them off to jail.

Upon this evidence the state trial court convicted the petitioners of breach of the peace, and imposed sentences ranging from a $10 fine or five days in jail, to a $100 fine or 30 days in jail. In affirming the judgments, the Supreme Court of South Carolina said that under the law of that State the offense of breach of the peace "is not susceptible of exact definition," but that the "general definition of the offense" is as follows:

"In general terms, a breach of the peace is a violation of public order, a disturbance of the public tranquility, by any act or conduct inciting to violence . . . , it includes any violation of any law enacted to preserve peace and good order. It may consist of an act of violence or an act likely to produce violence. It is not necessary that the peace be actually broken to lay the foundation for a prosecution for this offense. If what is done is unjustifiable and unlawful, tending with sufficient directness to break the peace, no more is required. Nor is actual personal violence an essential element in the offense. . . ."

The petitioners contend that there was a complete absence of any evidence of the commission of this offense, and that they were thus denied one of the most basic elements of due process of law. . . . Whatever the merits of this contention, we need not pass upon it in the present case. The state courts have held that the petitioners' conduct constituted breach of the peace under state law, and we may accept their decision as binding upon us to that extent. *But it nevertheless remains our duty in a case such as this to make an independent examination of the whole record.* [Emphasis supplied.] . . . And it is clear to us that in arresting, convicting, and punishing the petitioners under the circumstances disclosed by this record, South Carolina infringed the petitioners' constitutionally protected rights of speech, free assembly, and freedom to petition for redress of their grievances.

. . . The circumstances in this case reflect an exercise of these basic constitutional rights in their most pristine and classic form. The petitioners felt aggrieved by laws of South Carolina which allegedly "prohibited Negro privileges in this State." They peaceably assembled at the site of the State Government and there peaceably expressed their grievances "to the citizens of South Carolina, along with the Legislative Bodies of South Carolina." Not until they were told by police officials that they must disperse on pain of arrest did they do more. Even then, they but sang patriotic and religious songs after one of their leaders had delivered a "religious harangue." There was no evidence or threat of violence on their part, or on the part of any member of the crowd watching them. Police protection was "ample."

This, therefore, was a far cry from the situation in *Feiner* v. *New York,* . . . where two policemen were faced with a crowd which was "pushing, shoving, and milling around," . . . where at least one member of the crowd "threatened violence if the police did not act," . . . where "the crowd was pressing closer around petitioner and the officer," . . . and where "the speaker passes the bounds of argument or persuasion and undertakes incitement to riot." . . . And the record is barren of any evidence of "fighting words." See *Chaplinsky* v. *New Hampshire.* . . .

We do not review in this case criminal convictions resulting from the evenhanded application of a precise and narrowly drawn regulatory statute evincing a legislative judgment that certain specific conduct be limited or proscribed. If, for example, the petitioners had been convicted upon evidence that they had violated a law regulating traffic, or had disobeyed a law reasonably limiting the periods during which the State House grounds were open to the public, this would be a different case. . . . These petitioners . . . were convicted upon evidence which showed no more than that the opinions which they were peaceably expressing were sufficiently opposed to the views of the majority of the community to attract a crowd and necessitate police protection. . . .

For these reasons we conclude that these criminal convictions cannot stand.

*Reversed.*

Mr. Justice Clark, dissenting. . . .

. . . Petitioners, of course, had a right to peaceable assembly, to espouse their cause and to petition, but in my view the manner in which they exercised those rights was by no means the passive demonstration which this Court relates; rather, as the City Manager of Columbia testified, "a dangerous situation was building up" which South Carolina's courts expressly found had created "an actual interference with traffic and an imminently threatened disturbance of the peace of the community." Since the Court does not attack the state courts' findings and accepts the convictions as "binding" to the extent that the petitioners' conduct constituted a breach of the peace, it is difficult for me to understand its understatement of the facts and reversal of the convictions. . . .

. . . Here the petitioners were permitted without hindrance to exercise their rights of free speech and assembly. Their arrests occurred only after a situation arose in which the law-enforcement officials on the scene considered that a dangerous disturbance was imminent. The County Court found that "the evidence is clear that the officers were motivated solely by a proper concern for the preservation of order and the protection of the general welfare in the face of an actual interference with traffic and an imminently threatened disturbance of the peace of the community." In affirming, the South Carolina Supreme Court said the action of the police was "reasonable and motivated solely by a proper concern for the preservation of order and prevention of further interference with traffic upon the public streets and sidewalks." . . .

. . . [I]n *Feiner* v. *New York*. . . we upheld a conviction for breach of the peace in a situation no more dangerous than that found here. There the demonstration was conducted by only one person and the crowd was limited to approximately 80. . . . Here 200 youthful Negro demonstrators were being aroused to a "fever pitch" before a crowd of some 300 people who undoubtedly were hostile. . . . It is my belief that anyone conversant with the almost spontaneous combustion in some Southern communities in such a situation will agree that the City Manager's action may well have averted a major catastrophe.

The gravity of the danger here surely needs no further explication. The imminence of that danger has been emphasized at every stage of this proceeding, from the complaints charging that the demonstrations "tended directly to immediate violence" to the State Supreme Court's affirmance on the authority of Feiner (US) *supra*. This record, then, shows no steps backward from a standard of "clear and present danger." But to say that the police may not intervene until the riot has occurred is like keeping out the doctor until the patient dies. I cannot subscribe to such a doctrine. . . .

I would affirm the convictions.

The "demonstration" has developed into a widely used weapon in the arsenal of peaceful protest. In many of its forms it is simply a variation of the old tool of the picket line. Since it has normally been used to protest a practice or custom much more widespread than the boundaries of a single company, however, and involves an attempt to change entire communities' practices, it carries with it more of the traditional aspects and justifications for considering it as an exercise of freedom of speech than do some of the more narrowly drawn picketing issues. Certainly the majority opinion in Edwards illustrates this interpretation. Justice Stewart said, "The circumstances in this case reflect an exercise of these basic constitutional rights in their most pristine and classic form." This is not to say that there is an absolute right to "demonstrate" in large crowds in any and every circumstance, but it is a clear warning that so long as the participants are not engaged in clearly unlawful conduct, the State must show a strong justification for any interference and the justification must be supported by the facts, subject to independent examination by the United States Supreme Court. The position was reiterated in Henry v. Rock Hill, 376 U.S. 776 (1964), reversing convictions for breach of the peace where there had been a peaceful assemblage at a city hall, with the participants carrying signs and singing songs to protest segregation and where no violence had occurred.

A touchier question was presented in the review of a conviction for picketing in front of a courthouse in Baton Rouge, Louisiana. The appellant Cox was convicted on three charges: (1) breach of the peace, (2) obstructing public passages, and (3) picketing before a courthouse. The charges were based on his conduct during a demonstration of some 2,000 Negro college students protesting racial discrimination. The convictions were separated into two appeals, the first, No. 24, dealing with the first two charges and the second, No. 49, dealing with the charge of picketing before the courthouse. The Court voted unanimously to reverse the convictions on the first charge of breach of the peace. While there was disagreement on the bases for reversal, most of the justices used reasoning similar to that in the *Edwards* case. Justice Black concurred on the ground that the breach of the peace statute on its face and as construed by the state courts was so broad as to be unconstitutionally vague. On the second charge the Court voted seven-to-two for reversal. *Cox v. Louisiana*, 379 U.S. 536 (1965). Justice Goldberg, for five members of the Court, held that the conviction for unlawfully obstructing public passages was an unwarranted abridgment of the leader's freedom of speech and assembly because the city authorities permitted or prohibited parades or street meetings in their completely uncontrolled discretion. He stated that, "Although the statute here involved on its face precludes all street assemblies and parades, it has not been so applied and enforced by the Baton Rouge authorities. City officials who testified for the state clearly indicated that certain meetings and parades are permitted in Baton Rouge, even though they have the effect of obstructing traffic, provided prior approval is obtained." Justices Black and Clark concurred on the separate ground that since the statute expressly permitted picketing for the publication of labor union views, to deny picketing for other free speech uses was forbidden by the equal protection clause of the Fourteenth Amendment. Justice White and Harlan dissented from the reversal of the conviction of obstructing public passages, stating that the statute had not been applied as an "open-ended licensing statute."

The appeal on the third charge of picketing before a courthouse is reported separately as *Cox v. Louisiana*, 379 U.S. 559 (1965), and the Court reversed by a vote of five-to-four. The conviction was for violations of a Louisiana statute which prohibited picketing or parading in or near a state court "with the intent of interfering with, obstructing or impeding the administration of justice, or with the intent of influencing any judge, juror, witness, or court officer, in the discharge of his duty." Justice Goldberg, speaking for the majority, denied appellant's contention that the statute was invalid on its face. He pointed out that the statute was modeled after an identical statute pertaining to the federal judiciary, passed by Congress in 1949 (64 Stat. 1018) and "unlike the two previously considered, is a precise, narrowly drawn regulatory statute which proscribes certain specific behavior."

The majority went on to find, further, that in applying the statute the state could properly arrest and convict for the kind of demonstration held in this instance—a protest gathering objecting to the arrest of a number of the students and held in the vicinity of the courthouse where the students' trials would take place and where the judges were located who would be trying the students' cases. Justice Goldberg made a distinction between regulations of "speech in its pristine form," such as newspaper comment or a telegram by a citizen to a public official, and "expression mixed with particular conduct." Noting that the case involved the latter form of expression, he concluded that appellant's argument that no clear and present danger was presented should be rejected on the ground that the legislature could properly have made a determination "based on experience that such conduct inherently threatens the judicial process."

Despite these statements in support of a general power to forbid what was done by the demonstrators in this case, however, the majority voted to reverse the convictions on the ground that prior permission was granted by the police and that the meeting did not acquire any illegal aspects afterward which would make refusal to obey a dispersal order a legitimate basis for arrest and conviction on the charge of picketing before a courthouse. The opinion pointed out that the demonstration took place on the far side of the street from the courthouse steps, and that the record showed that the officials present gave permission for Cox to conduct the demonstration at this point. This testimony "was corroborated by the State's witnesses themselves." Justice Goldberg said that "under all the circumstances of this case, after the public officials acted as they did, to sustain appellant's later conviction for demonstrating where they told him he could 'would be to sanction an indefensible sort of entrapment by the State—convicting a citizen for exercising a privilege which the State had clearly told him was available to him.' "

## ADDERLEY v. FLORIDA
### 385 U.S. 39 (1966)

Mr. Justice Black delivered the opinion of the Court.

Petitioners, Harriett Louise Adderley and 31 other persons, were convicted by a jury . . . on a charge of "trespass with a malicious and mischievous intent" upon the premises of the county jail contrary to . . . Florida statutes. . . . Petitioners, apparently all students of the Florida A. & M. University in Tallahassee, had gone from the school to the jail about a mile away, along with many other students, to "demonstrate" at the jail their protests of arrests of other protesting students the day before, and perhaps to protest more generally against state and local policies and practices of racial segregation, including segregation of the jail. The county sheriff, legal custodian of the jail and jail grounds, tried to persuade the students to leave the jail grounds. When this did not work, he notified them that they must leave, that if they did not leave he would arrest them for trespassing, and that if they resisted he would charge them with that as well. Some of the students left but others, including petitioners, remained and they were arrested. On appeal the convictions were affirmed. . . . [P]etitioners applied to us for certiorari contending that, in view of petitioners' purpose to protest against jail and other segregation policies, their conviction denied them "rights of free speech, assembly, petition, due process of law and equal protection of the laws as guaranteed by the Fourteenth Amendment. . . ."

Petitioners have insisted from the beginning of this case that it is controlled by and must be reversed because of our prior cases of *Edwards* v. *South Carolina* . . . and *Cox* v. *Louisiana* . . . We cannot agree. . . .

. . . The South Carolina breach-of-the-peace statute was. . . struck down as being so broad and all-embracing as to jeopardize speech, press, assembly and petition, under the constitutional doctrine enunciated in *Cantwell* v. *Connecticut* . . . and followed in many subsequent cases. And it was on this same ground of vagueness that in *Cox* v. *Louisiana* . . . the Louisiana breach-of-the-peace law used to prosecute Cox was invalidated.

The Florida trespass statute under which these petitioners were charged cannot be challenged on this ground. It is aimed at conduct of one limited kind, that is, for one person or persons to trespass upon the property of another with a malicious and mischievous intent. There is no lack of notice in this law, nothing to entrap or fool the unwary. . . .

Petitioners next argue that "petty criminal statutes may not be used to violate minorities' constitutional rights." This of course is true, but this abstract proposition gets us nowhere in deciding this case.

Petitioners here contend that "Petitioners' convictions are based on a total lack of relevant evidence." If true, this would be a denial of due process. . . . Both in the petition for certiorari and in the brief on the merits petitioners state that their summary of the evidence "does not conflict with the facts contained in the Circuit Court's opinion" which was in effect affirmed by the District Court of Appeal . . . That statement is correct and petitioner's summary of facts, as well as that of the Circuit Court, shows an abundance of facts to support the jury's verdict of guilty in this case. . . .

Under the foregoing testimony the jury was authorized to find that the State had proven every essential element of the crime, as it was defined by the state court. That interpretation is, of course, binding on us, leaving only the question of whether conviction of the state offense, thus defined, unconstitutionally deprives petitioners of their rights to freedom of speech, press, assembly or petition. We hold it does not. The sheriff, as jail custodian, had power, as the state courts have here held, to direct that this large crowd of people get off the grounds. There is not a shred of evidence in this record that this power was exercised, or that its exercise was sanctioned by the lower courts, because the sheriff objected to what was being sung or said by the demonstrators or because he disagreed with the objectives of their protest. The record reveals that he objected only to their presence on that part of the jail grounds reserved for jail uses. There is no evidence at all that on any other occasion had similarly large groups of the public been permitted to gather on this portion of the jail grounds for any purpose. Nothing in the Constitution of the United States prevents Florida from even-handed enforcement of its general trespass statute against those refusing to obey the sheriff's order to remove themselves from what amounted to the curtilage of the jailhouse. The State, no less than a private owner of property, has power to preserve the property under its control for the use to which it is lawfully dedicated. For this reason there is no merit to the petitioner's argument that they had a constitutional right to stay on the property, over the jail custodian's objections, because this "area chosen for the peaceful civil rights demonstration was not only 'reasonable' but also particularly appropriate. . . ." Such an argument has as its major unarticulated premise the assumption that people who want to propagandize protests or views have a constitutional right to do so whenever and however and wherever they please. That concept of constitutional law was vigorously and forthrightly rejected in two of the cases petitioners rely on. . . . We reject it again. The United States Constitution does not forbid a State to control the use of its own property for its own lawful nondiscriminatory purpose.

*Affirmed.*

Mr. Justice Douglas, with whom The Chief Justice, Mr. Justice Brennan, and Mr. Justice Fortas concur, dissenting. . . .

. . . When we allow Florida to construe her "malicious trespass" statute to bar a person from going on property knowing it is not his own and to apply that prohibition to public property, we discard *Cox* and *Edwards.* Would the case be any different if, as is common, the demonstration took place outside a building which housed both the jail and the legislative body? I think not.

There may be some public places which are so clearly committed to other purposes that their use for the airing of grievances is anomalous. There may be some instances in which assemblies and petitions for redress of grievances are not consistent with other necessary purposes of public property. A noisy meeting may be out of keeping with the serenity of the statehouse or the quiet of the courthouse. No one, for example, would suggest that the Senate gallery is the proper place for a vociferous protest rally. And in other cases it may be necessary to adjust the right to petition for redress of grievances to the other interests inhering in the uses to which the public property is normally put. . . . But this is quite different from saying that all public places are off limits to people with grievances. . . . And it is farther yet from saying that the "custodian" of the public property in his discretion can decide when public places shall be used for the communication of ideas, especially the constitutional right to assemble and petition for redress of grievances. . . . For to place such discretion in any public official, be he the "custodian" of the public property or the local police commissioner . . . is to place those who assert their First Amendment rights at his mercy. It gives him the awesome power to decide whose ideas may be expressed and who shall be denied a place to air their claims and petition their government. Such power is out of step with all our decisions prior to today. . . .

In 1972, Dr. Benjamin Spock and Julius Hobson were the candidates of the People's party for the offices of president and vice-president of the United States. They wrote to the commanding officer of Fort Dix requesting permission to enter the military reservation in order to distribute campaign literature and hold meetings to discuss election issues. The request was denied based on Fort Dix regulations prohibiting partisan political speeches and demonstrations. In *Greer* v. *Spock*, 424 U.S. 828 (1976), the Court upheld the regulations. Justice Stewart, for the majority, argued that it is the "primary business of armies and navies to fight or be ready to fight wars should the occasion arise," and thus "the business of a military installation like Fort Dix is to train soldiers, not to provide a public forum." He continued: "The notion that federal military reservations, like municipal streets and parks, have traditionally served as a place for free public assembly and communication of thoughts by private citizens is thus historically and constitutionally false."

A federal statute prohibits "the display [of] any flag, banner, or device designed or adapted to bring into public notice any party, organization, or movement" in the Supreme Court building or on its grounds, which are defined to include the sidewalk surrounding the block on which the Court is located. One person was threatened with arrest for distributing leaflets on the sidewalk, and another was similarly threatened for displaying on the sidewalk a picket sign containing the text of the First Amendment. In *United States* v. *Grace*, 457 U.S. 393 (1983), the Court upheld the ban on protests within the Court building and on Court grounds, but held that the prohibition of communicative activity on the public sidewalks did not substantially serve the purposes of providing for the maintenance of law and order on the Court grounds and could not be sustained.

### GREGORY v. CHICAGO
### 394 U.S. 111 (1969)

Mr. Chief Justice Warren delivered the opinion of the Court.

This is a simple case. Petitioners, accompanied by Chicago police and an assistant city attorney, marched in a peaceful and orderly procession from city hall to the mayor's residence to press their claims for desegregation of the public schools. Having promised to cease singing at 8:30 P.M., the marchers did so. Although petitioners and the other demonstrators continued to march in a completely lawful fashion, the onlookers became unruly as the number of bystanders increased. Chicago police, to prevent what they regarded as an impending civil disorder, demanded that the demonstrators, upon pain of arrest, disperse. When this command was not obeyed, petitioners were arrested for disorderly conduct.

Petitioners' march, if peaceful and orderly, falls well within the sphere of conduct protected by the First Amendment. . . . There is no evidence in this record that petitioners' conduct was disorderly. Therefore, under the principle first established in *Thompson* v. *City of Louisville*, . . . convictions so totally devoid of evidentiary support violate due process.

The opinion of the Supreme Court of Illinois suggests that petitioners were convicted not for the manner in which they conducted their march but rather for their refusal to disperse when requested to do so by Chicago police. . . . However reasonable the police request may have been and however laudable the police motives, petitioners were charged and convicted for holding a demonstration not for a refusal to obey a police officer. . . .

The judgments are

*Reversed.*

Mr. Justice Douglas, while joining the separate opinion of Mr. Justice Black, also joins this opinion.

Mr. Justice Stewart and Mr. Justice White concurring. . . .

Mr. Justice Black, with whom Mr. Justice Douglas joins, concurring.

This we think is a highly important case which requires more detailed consideration than the Court's opinion gives it. . . .

. . . [B]oth police and demonstrators made their best efforts faithfully to discharge their responsibilities as officers and citizens, but they were nevertheless unable to restrain these hostile hecklers within decent and orderly bounds. These facts disclosed by the record point unerringly to one conclusion, namely, that when groups with diametrically opposed, deep-seated views are permitted to air their emotional grievances, side by side, on city streets, tranquility and order cannot be maintained even by the joint efforts of the finest and best officers and of those who desire to be the most law-abiding protestors of their grievances.

It is because of this truth, and a desire both to promote order and to safeguard First Amendment freedoms, that this Court has repeatedly warned States and governmental units that they cannot regulate conduct connected with these freedoms through use of sweeping, dragnet statutes that may, because of vagueness, jeopardize these freedoms. In those cases, however, we have been careful to point out the Constitution does not bar enactment of laws regulating conduct, even though connected with speech, press, assembly, and petition, if such laws specifically bar only the conduct deemed obnoxious and are carefully and narrowly aimed at that forbidden conduct. The dilemma revealed by this record is a crying example of a need for some such narrowly drawn law. . . .

The disorderly conduct ordinance under which these petitioners were charged and convicted is not, however, a narrowly drawn law. . . . To the contrary, it might better be described as a meat ax ordinance, gathering in one comprehensive definition of an offense a number of words which have a multiplicity of meanings, some of which would cover activity specifically protected by the First Amendment. . . .

The so-called "diversion tending to a breach of the peace" here was limited entirely and exclusively to the fact that when the policeman in charge of the special police detail concluded that the hecklers observing the march were dangerously close to rioting and that the demonstrators and others were likely to be engulfed in that riot, he ordered Gregory and his demonstrators to leave, and Gregory—standing on what he deemed to be his constitutional rights—refused to do so. . . . To let a policeman's command become equivalent to a criminal statute comes dangerously near making our government one of men rather than of law. . . . There are ample ways to protect the domestic tranquility without subjecting First Amendment freedoms to such a clumsy and unwieldy weapon.

The city of Chicago, recognizing the serious First Amendment problems raised by the disorderly conduct ordinance as it is written, argues that these convictions should nevertheless be affirmed in light of the narrowing construction placed on the ordinance by the Illinois Supreme Court in this case. . . . Whatever the validity of the Illinois Supreme Court's construction, this was simply not the theory on which these petitioners were convicted. In explaining the elements of the offense to the jury, the trial judge merely read the language of the ordinance. The jury was not asked to find whether, as the Illinois Supreme Court's construction apparently requires, there was "an imminent threat of violence," or whether the police had "made all reasonable efforts to protect the demonstrators." Rather, it was sufficient for the jury to decide that petitioners had made "an improper noise" or a "diversion tending to a breach of the peace," or had "collect[ed] in bodies or crowds for unlawful purposes, or for any purpose, to the annoyance or disturbance of other persons.". . .

In agreeing to the reversal of these convictions, however, we wish once more to say that we think our Federal Constitution does not render the States powerless to regulate the conduct of demonstrators and picketers, conduct which is more than "speech," more than "press," more than "assembly," and more than "petition" as those terms are used in the First Amendment. Narrowly drawn statutes regulating the conduct of demonstrators and picketers are not impossible to draft. . . . Speech and press are, of course, to be free, so that public matters can be discussed with impunity. But picketing and demonstrating can be regulated like other conduct of men. We believe that the homes of men, sometimes the last citadel of the tired, the weary and the sick, can be protected by government from noisy, marching, tramping, threatening picketers and demonstrators bent on filling the minds of men, women, and children with fears of the unknown.

For these reasons we concur in the reversal. . . .

Mr. Justice Harlan, concurring in the result. . . .

Another Chicago parade problem arose when a group requested permission from the city to march to a white neighborhood park and there to proclaim their protest against events which, in their opinion, deprived black citizens of their constitutional rights. City authorities pointed out that on a previous march by the group bystanders had resorted to violence that damaged property and injured policemen and the march resulted in fifty-two arrests. For this reason, they offered the group an alternate parade route to a predominantly black neighborhood park. In *Dr. Martin Luther King, Jr., Movement, Inc. v. Chicago*, 419 F.Supp. 667 (N.D. Ill., 1976), the federal district court held that the directive to take the alternate route was "an ill-covered subterfuge" that discriminated on the basis of race and resulted in a protest before an audience which needed no persuasion to the views held by the members of the demonstrating group. As to the previous violence, the court held that it was well-settled law that the presence of hostile spectators or bystanders did not justify the restraint of otherwise legal First Amendment activities.

A more difficult problem was presented, also in the Chicago area, by the efforts of the National Socialist Party of America to engage in parades through areas heavily populated by Jews, and to do so in Nazi uniforms with swastikas on armbands and on banners. One such demonstration was planned for Skokie, Illinois, and was to consist of some thirty to fifty demonstrators marching back and forth in front of the village hall and carrying a party banner and signs containing such messages as "white free speech." The village is predominantly Jewish, and 5,000 to 7,000 of its residents at the time were survivors of German concentration camps. A number of Jewish organizations planned counter-demonstrations for the same day, and fears were expressed that a Nazi party demonstration would result in violence. A court order was entered enjoining party members from displaying the swastika during the demonstration, and this order was appealed to the Illinois Supreme Court. That court denied a stay order and refused the appeal. The United States Supreme Court reversed and remanded in *National Socialist Party of America* v. *Village of Skokie*, 432 U.S. 43 (1977). In *Village of Skokie* v. *National Socialist Party of America*, 373 N.E.2d 21 (Ill. Sup. Ct., 1978), the Illinois Supreme Court then reversed the lower court order on First Amendment grounds. The village argued that the exhibition of the swastika was tantamount to the use of "fighting words" and its bar was therefore a justifiable restraint on symbolic speech. The majority held that the swastika could not be considered so offensive and peace-threatening to the public that its display could be enjoined. It also pointed out that advance notice had been given, and those to whom sight of the swastika would be offensive were forewarned and need not view it. Thus the court concluded that the display of the swastika could not be enjoined under the fighting words doctrine, nor could anticipation of a hostile audience justify the prior restraint.

A similar result was reached by a federal Court of Appeals in a case challenging the validity of three village ordinances designed to curtail demonstrations by the American Nazi party in Skokie. The first ordinance required, as a condition precedent for a demonstration permit, $300,000 in public liability insurance. The second prohibited the dissemination of any material that promoted and incited hatred against persons by reason of their race, national origin, or religion. This prohibition extended to the use of signs, handbills, or clothing of symbolic significance. The third ordinance prohibited public demonstrations by members of political parties while wearing "military-style" uniforms. The District Court held the three ordinances violative of the First and Fourteenth Amendments, and the Court of Appeals affirmed in *Collin* v. *Smith*, 578 F.2d 1197 (C.A. 7, 1978). On the appeal Skokie had conceded the invalidity of the first and third ordinances, but contended that the second ordinance was valid under the rule of *Beauharnais* v. *Illinois*, 343 U.S. 250 (1952), which upheld a conviction under a statute prohibiting the dissemination of materials promoting racial or religious hatred. The Court of Appeals stated that the "tendency to induce violence" approach sanctioned in *Beauharnais* probably would not pass constitutional muster today, and even assuming that it would, it did not support this ordinance because the village did not assert the Nazis' possible violence, the audience's possible responsive violence, or possible violence against third parties by those incited by the Nazis as justification for the ordinance. Thus the rationale of *Beauharnais* did not apply. The village also argued that the march would create a substantive evil which the village had a right to prevent: the infliction of psychic trauma on resident holocaust survivors and other Jewish residents. Illinois recognizes the tort of intentional infliction of severe emotional distress. The Court of Appeals, however, held that even if persons could proceed in tort under this theory to recover damages, and that a First Amendment defense would not bar the action, it was nonetheless quite a different matter to criminalize protected First Amendment conduct in anticipation of such results. The United States Supreme Court denied a request for a stay, but three days before the demonstration was to take place, the Nazi leader canceled the program. Backed by the court decisions, however, the Nazis obtained a federal court order setting aside the Chicago Park District's requirement that the group obtain $60,000 in liability insurance before engaging in demonstrations in city parks.

Final action on the matter occurred when the Supreme Court refused to review the Seventh Circuit decision invalidating the Skokie ordinances, *Smith* v. *Collin*, 439 U.S. 916 (1978). Justice Blackmun, joined by Justice White, dissented, urging that certiorari be granted "in order to resolve any possible conflict that may exist between the ruling of the Seventh Circuit here and Beauharnais." He stated further "that the present case affords the Court an opportunity to consider whether . . . there is no limit whatsoever to the exercise of free speech. There indeed may be no such limit, but when citizens assert, not casually but with deep conviction, that the proposed demonstration is scheduled at a place and in a manner that is taunting and overwhelmingly offensive to the citizens of that place, that assertion, uncomfortable though it may be for judges, deserves to be examined."

A provision of the District of Columbia Code makes it unlawful, within 500 feet of a foreign embassy, either to display any sign that tends to bring the foreign government into "public odium" or "public disrepute," or to congregate and refuse to obey a police dispersal order. Three individuals who wished to carry signs critical of the governments of the Soviet Union and Nicaragua on the sidewalks within 500 feet of those embassies filed suit in the Federal District Court challenging the Code provision. The District Court upheld the ordinance. The Court of Appeals affirmed, although it gave a narrowing construction to the "congregation" section, stating that it should be construed to permit dispersal only of congregations that were directed againt the nearby embassy, and only when the police reasonably believed that a threat to the security or peace of the embassy was present. In *Boos* v. *Barry,* 56 LW 4255 (1988), the Supreme Court held the "display" section unconstitutional, but upheld the "congregation" section as construed by the Court of Appeals. Justice O'Conner, for the majority, held that the "display" provision was clearly a content-based restriction on freedom of speech. Such restrictions "must be subjected to the most exacting scrutiny," and the government must show that the regulation is necessary to serve a "compelling state interest." This it failed to do, particularly when an act of Congress was available that prohibits intimidating, coercing, or harassing foreign officials or obstructing them in the performance of their duties.

In *Gregory* v. *Chicago,* above, the Court reversed a conviction for disorderly conduct of demonstrators who had marched from the city hall to the residence of the mayor. Justice Black concurred, but he pointed out that picketing and demonstrating can be regulated. He stated: "We believe that the homes of men, sometimes the last citadel of the tired, the weary and the sick, can be protected by government from noisy, marching, tramping, threatening picketers and demonstrators. . . ." In Brookfield, Wisconsin, a group strongly opposed to abortion picketed the residence of a doctor who had performed abortions at two clinics in neighboring towns. On at least six occasions the group, varying in size from 11 to more than 40 people, engaged in picketing, for periods ranging from one to one and a half hours. The town Board adopted an ordinance providing: "It is unlawful for any person to engage in picketing before or about the residence or dwelling of any individual in the Town of Brookfield." Justice O'Connor, speaking for the majority, construed the ban "to be a limited one; only focused picketing taking place solely in front of a particular residence is prohibited." Thus, "marching through residential neighborhoods, or even walking a route in front of an entire block of houses, is not prohibited by this ordinance." As interpreted, the ordinance was constitutional as a protection for residential privacy against offensive and disturbing intrusions. *Frisby* v. *Schultz,* 56 LW 4785 (1988).

## BRANDENBURG *v.* OHIO
### 395 U.S. 444 (1969)

[The defendant, a leader of a Ku Klux Klan group, spoke at a Klan rally at which a large wooden cross was burned and some of the other persons present were carrying firearms. His remarks included such statements as: "Bury the niggers," "the niggers should be returned to Africa," and "send the Jews back to Israel." He was convicted under the Ohio Criminal Syndicalism statute of "advocat[ing] . . . the duty, necessity, or propriety of crime, sabotage, violence, or unlawful methods of terrorism as a means of accomplishing industrial or political reform" and of "voluntarily assembl[ing] with any society, group or assemblage of persons formed to teach or advocate the doctrines of criminal syndicalism." On appeal, he challenged the constitutionality of the statute under the First and Fourteenth Amendments, but the intermediate appellate court of Ohio affirmed, without opinion, and the Supreme Court of Ohio dismissed his appeal.]

PER CURIAM. . . .

In 1927, this Court sustained the constitutionality of California's Criminal Syndicalism Act, . . . the text of which is quite similar to that of the laws of Ohio. *Whitney* v. *California.* . . . The Court upheld the statute on the ground that, without more, "advocating" violent means to effect political and economic change involves such danger to the security of the State that the State may outlaw it. . . . But *Whitney* has been thoroughly discredited by later decisions. See *Dennis* v. *United States*. . . . These later decisions have fashioned the principle that the constitutional guarantees of free speech and free press do not permit a State to forbid or proscribe advocacy of the use of force or of law violation except where such advocacy is directed to inciting or producing imminent lawless action and is likely to incite or produce such action. As we said in *Noto.* v. *United States*, . . . "the mere abstract teaching . . . of the moral propriety or even moral necessity for a resort to force and violence, is not the same as preparing a group for violent action and steeling it to such action." . . . A statute which fails to draw this distinction impermissibly intrudes upon the freedoms guaranteed by the First and Fourteenth Amendments. . . .

. . . [W]e are here confronted with a statute which, by its own words and as applied, purports to punish mere advocacy and to forbid, on pain of criminal punishment, assembly with others merely to advocate the described type of action. Such a statute falls within the condemnation of the First and Fourteenth Amendments. The contrary teaching of *Whitney* v. *California, supra,* cannot be supported, and that decision is therefore overruled.

*Reversed.*

Mr. Justice Black, concurring. . . .
Mr. Justice Douglas, concurring. . . .

In *United States* v. *O'Brien*, 391 U.S. 367 (1968), the defendant was convicted for violating federal law by burning his draft card. The Court of Appeals reversed on the ground that the statute was unconstitutional as a law abridging freedom of speech. The Supreme Court reinstated the judgment and sentence of the District Court. Chief Justice Warren, for the majority, said, "We cannot accept the view that an apparently limitless variety of conduct can be labelled 'speech' whenever the person engaging in the conduct intends thereby to express an idea." He stated further that the power to classify and conscript manpower for military service is "beyond question," and that the issuance of draft cards was a legitimate and substantial administrative aid in the functioning of the system.

*Street* v. *New York*, 394 U.S. 576 (1969), involved a conviction for burning an American flag on a street corner. After learning that civil rights leader James Meredith had been shot by a sniper in Mississippi, the accused set fire to his flag. After a policeman approached and learned that Street had burned the flag, the accused stated: "If they did that to Meredith, we don't need an American flag." Following a nonjury trial in the New York City Criminal Court, the accused was convicted and given a suspended sentence for malicious mischief consisting of a violation of a New York statute making it a misdemeanor publicly to mutilate, defile, or cast contempt upon an American flag either by words or act. The conviction was affirmed by the New York Court of Appeals. On appeal, the United States Supreme Court reversed and remanded. A majority of five held that the accused had a constitutional right to express his opinion about the flag, even if his opinion was defiant or contemptuous, and that since he might have been convicted for the words used rather than merely the deed, the case would have to be remanded. Four judges dissented, arguing that the conviction was based on the deed rather than the words and was therefore constitutional.

In *Spence* v. *Washington*, 418 U.S. 405 (1974), the Court reversed a conviction under a Washington statute which prohibited the placing of any "word, figure, mark, picture, design, . . . of any nature upon any flag" of the United States. Spence had affixed to both surfaces of a flag a large peace symbol of removable tape and had then displayed the flag from his apartment window. The Per Curiam opinion for five members of the

Court stated that the defendant was not charged under a flag desecration statute, nor did he permanently disfigure the flag or destroy it. "His message was direct, likely to be understood, and within the contours of the First Amendment. Given the protected character of his expression and in light of the fact that no interest the State may have in preserving the physical integrity of a privately-owned flag was significantly impaired on these facts, the conviction must be invalidated."

## TINKER *v.* DES MOINES SCHOOL DISTRICT
### *393 U.S. 503 (1969)*

Mr. Justice Fortas delivered the opinion of the Court.

Petitioner John F. Tinker, 15 years old, and petitioner Christopher Eckhardt, 16 years old, attended high schools in Des Moines. Petitioner Mary Beth Tinker, John's sister, was a 13-year-old student in junior high school. [As part of a plan formulated by a group of adults and students in the city, the petitioners wore black armbands to their schools to publicize their objections to the hostilities in Vietnam and their support for a truce, despite the fact that they were aware that the school authorities a few days previously had adopted a policy that any student wearing an armband to school would be asked to remove it, on penalty of suspension until he returned without the armband. After refusal to remove the armbands, the students were suspended. Petitioners filed a suit for injunction in federal court. The District Court dismissed the complaint, holding the order a reasonable measure to prevent disturbance of school discipline. The Court of Appeals affirmed.]

The problem presented by the present case does not relate to regulation of the length of skirts or the type of clothing, to hair style or deportment. . . . It does not concern aggressive, disruptive action or even group demonstrations. Our problem involves direct, primary First Amendment rights akin to "pure speech."

The school officials banned and sought to punish petitioners for a silent, passive, expression of opinion, unaccompanied by any disorder or disturbance on the part of petitioners. There is here no evidence whatever of petitioners' interference, actual or nascent, with the school's work or of collision with the rights of other students to be secure and to be let alone. Accordingly, this case does not concern speech or action that intrudes upon the work of the school or the rights of other students. . . .

In order for the State in the person of school officials to justify prohibition of a particular expression of opinion, it must be able to show that its action was caused by something more than a mere desire to avoid the discomfort and unpleasantness that always accompany an unpopular viewpoint. Certainly where there is no finding and no showing that the exercise of the forbidden right would "materially and substantially interfere with the requirements of appropriate discipline in the operation of the school," the prohibition cannot be sustained. . . .

It is also relevant that the school authorities did not purport to prohibit the wearing of all symbols of political or controversial significance. The record shows that students in some of the schools wore buttons relating to national political campaigns, and some even wore the Iron Cross, traditionally a symbol of nazism. The order prohibiting the wearing of armbands did not extend to these. Instead, a particular symbol—black armbands worn to exhibit opposition to this Nation's involvement in Vietnam—was singled out for prohibition. Clearly, the prohibition of expression of one particular opinion, at least without evidence that it is necessary to avoid material and substantial interference with school work or discipline, is not constitutionally permissible.

In our system, state-operated schools may not be enclaves of totalitarianism. School officials do not possess absolute authority over their students. Students in school as well as out of school are "persons" under our Constitution. They are possessed of fundamental rights which the State must respect, just as they themselves must respect their obligations to the State. In our system, students may not be regarded as closed-circuit recipients of only that which the State chooses to communicate. They may not be confined to the expression of those sentiments that are officially approved. In the absence of a specific showing of constitutionally valid reasons to regulate their speech, students are entitled to freedom of expression of their views. . . .

*Reversed and remanded.*

Mr. Justice Stewart, concurring. . . .

Mr. Justice White, concurring. . . .

Mr. Justice Black, dissenting.

The Court's holding in this case ushers in what I deem to be an entirely new era in which the power to control pupils by the elected "officials of state supported public schools . . ." in the United States is in ultimate effect transferred to the Supreme Court. . . .

Assuming that the Court is correct in holding that the conduct of wearing armbands for the purpose of conveying political ideas is protected by the First Amendment . . . the crucial remaining questions are whether students and teachers may use the school at their whim as a platform for the exercise of free speech— "symbolic" or "pure"—and whether the Courts will allocate to themselves the function of deciding how the pupils' school day will be spent. While I have always believed that under the First and Fourteenth Amendments neither the State nor Federal Government has any authority to regulate or censor the content of speech, I have never believed that any person has a right to give speeches or engage in demonstrations where he pleases and when he pleases. This Court has already rejected such a notion. . . .

While the record does not show that any of these armband students shouted, used profane language or were violent in any manner, a detailed report by some of them shows their armbands caused comments, warnings by other students, the poking of fun at them, and a warning by an older football player that other, nonprotesting students had better let them alone. There is also evidence that the professor of mathematics had his lesson period practically "wrecked" chiefly by disputes with Beth Tinker, who wore her armband for her "demonstration." Even a casual reading of the record shows that this armband did divert students' minds from their regular lessons, and that talk, comments, etc., made John Tinker "self-conscious" in attending school with his armband. While the absence of obscene or boisterous and loud disorder perhaps justifies the Court's statement that the few armband students did not actually "disrupt" the classwork, I think the record overwhelmingly shows that the armbands did exactly what the elected school officials and principals foresaw it would, that is, took the students' minds off their classwork and diverted them to thoughts about the highly emotional subject of the Vietnam war. And I repeat that if the time has come when pupils of state-supported schools, kindergarten, grammar school or high school, can defy and flaunt orders of school officials to keep their minds on their own school work, it is the beginning of a new revolutionary era of permissiveness in this country fostered by the judiciary. The next logical step, it appears to me, would be to hold unconstitutional laws that bar pupils under 21 or 18 from voting, or from being elected members of the Boards of Education. . . .

. . . The truth is that a teacher of kindergarten, grammar school, or high school pupils no more carries into a school with him a complete right to freedom of speech and expression than an anti-Catholic or anti-Semitic carries with him a complete freedom of speech and religion into a Catholic church or Jewish synagogue. Nor does a person carry with him into the United States Senate or House, or to the Supreme Court, or any other court, a complete constitutional right to go into those places contrary to their rules and speak his mind on any subject he pleases. . . .

In my view, teachers in state-controlled public schools are hired to teach there. Although Mr. Justice McReynolds may have intimated to the contrary in *Myers* v. *Nebraska, supra,* certainly a teacher is not paid to go into school and teach subjects the State does not hire him to teach as a part of its selected curriculum. Nor are public school students sent to the schools at public expense to broadcast political or any other views to educate and inform the public. The original idea of schools, which I do not believe is yet abandoned as worthless or out of date, was that children had not yet reached the point of experience and wisdom which enabled them to teach all of their elders. It may be that the Nation has outworn the old-fashioned slogan that "children are to be seen not heard," but one may, I hope, be permitted to harbor the thought that taxpayers send children to school on the premise that at their age they need to learn, not teach. . . .

Change has been said to be truly the law of life but sometimes the old and the tried and true are worth holding. The schools of this Nation have undoubtedly contributed to giving us tranquility and to making us a more law-abiding people. Uncontrolled and uncontrollable liberty is an enemy to domestic peace. We cannot close our eyes to the fact that some of the country's greatest problems are crimes committed by the youth, too many of school age. . . . One does not need to be a prophet to know that after the Court's holding today that some students in Iowa schools and indeed in all schools will be ready, able, and willing to defy their teachers on practically all orders. This is the more unfortunate for the schools since groups of students all over the land are already running loose, conducting break-ins, sit-ins, lie-ins, and smash-ins. . . . Students engaged in such activities are apparently confident that they know far more about how to operate public school systems than do their parents, teachers, and elected school officials. It is no answer to say that the particular students here have not yet reached such high points in their demands to attend classes in order to exercise their political pressures. Turned loose with lawsuits for damages and injunctions against their teachers like they are here, it is nothing but wishful thinking to imagine that young, immature students will not soon believe it is their right to control the schools rather than the right of the States that collect the taxes to hire the teachers for the benefit of the pupils. This case, therefore, wholly without constitutional reasons in my judgment, subjects all the public schools in the country to the whims and caprices of their loudest-mouthed, but maybe not their brightest, students. I, for one, am not fully persuaded that school pupils are wise enough, even with this Court's expert help from Washington, to run the 23,390 public school systems in our 50 States. I wish, therefore, wholly to disclaim any purpose on my part, to hold that the Federal Constitution compels the teachers, parents, and elected school officials to surrender control of the American public school system to public school students. I dissent.

Mr. Justice Harlan, dissenting. . . .

## SPECIAL ASPECTS OF FREEDOM OF THE PRESS

While the broader aspects of the topics previously discussed apply to all forms of expression—speech, press, and assembly—and thus have not been dealt with in their applications to isolated First Amendment rights, there are certain special problems which have arisen in connection with the press and other news media which require separate treatment. Among the foremost is that of reconciling the demands of a free press with the need for fair administration of justice. Another is the definition and proper treatment of obscene publications within the demand of the First Amendment. In addition there are problems of delineating the appropriate area of regulation of the press in its character as a normal commercial enterprise, and the application of state laws in such areas as libel and the regulation of distribution of handbills. Insofar as regulations may run afoul of the general interdiction against prior restraints, the earlier discussion of that rule in this chapter applies, as in the important free press case *Near* v. *Minnesota*. In general, this section will deal with the constitutional issues presented by some of the postpublication regulations or burdens on the various facets of the press.

### Free Press v. Fair Administration of Justice

While a democratic society must accord a high place to the freedom of news media to inform the public, the right to a fair trial, both in civil and criminal cases, is entitled to no less regard. A conflict between these two values arises when newspaper or radio or television communications prior to a trial or during a trial are of such a nature as to threaten the impartiality of verdicts or sentences. The issue with respect to criminal cases has been dealt with to some extent in the earlier chapter on the rights of the accused.

Under his common-law powers the judge in Anglo-American courts has long had the power to punish for contempt persons who interfere with or obstruct the administration of justice. The application of this power to a newspaper, of course, raises First Amendment questions. In the companion cases of *Bridges* v. *California* and *Times-Mirror Company* v. *Superior Court of California,* 314 U.S. 252 (1941), the Court for the first time had occasion to review a state's exercise of the contempt power in punishing a publisher for statements appearing during the course of a trial. Justice Black, in his opinion for the Court, recited the facts:

The Los Angeles Times Editorials. The Times-Mirror Company, publisher of the Los Angeles Times, and L. D. Hotchkiss, its managing editor, were cited for contempt for the publication of three editorials. Both found by the trial court to be responsible for one of the editorials, the company and Hotchkiss were each fined $100. The company alone was held responsible for the other two, and was fined $100 more on account of one, and $300 more on account of the other.

The $300 fine presumably marks the most serious offense. The editorial thus distinguished was entitled "Probation for Gorillas?" After vigorously denouncing two members of a labor union who had previously been found guilty of assaulting nonunion truck drivers, it closes with the observation: "Judge A. A. Scott will make a serious mistake if he grants probation to Matthew Shannon and Kennan Holmes. This community needs the example of their assignment to the jute mill." Judge Scott had previously set a day (about a month after the publication) for passing upon the application of Shannon and Holmes for probation and for pronouncing sentence. . . .

The Bridges Telegram. While a motion for a new trial was pending in a case involving a dispute between an A.F. of L. union and a C.I.O. union of which Bridges was an officer, he either caused to be published or acquiesced in the publication of a telegram which he had sent to the Secretary of Labor. The telegram referred to the judge's decision as "outrageous"; said that attempted enforcement of it would tie up the port of Los Angeles and involve the entire Pacific Coast; and concluded with the announcement that the C.I.O. union, representing some twelve thousand members, did "not intend to allow state courts to override the majority vote of members in choosing its officers and representatives and to override the National Labor Relations Board."

Apparently Bridges' conviction is not rested at all upon his use of the word "outrageous." The remainder of the telegram fairly construed appears to be a statement that if the court's decree should be enforced there would be a strike. It is not claimed that such a strike would have been in violation of the terms of the decree, nor that in any other way it would have run afoul of the law of California. On no construction, therefore, can the telegram be taken as a threat either by Bridges or the union to follow an illegal course of action.

By a five-to-four vote the Court reversed the contempt citations in both cases. Justice Black, for the majority, examined and refuted the argument that "the power of judges to punish by contempt out-of-court publications tending to obstruct the orderly and fair administration of justice in a pending case was deeply rooted in English common law at the time the Constitution was adopted," and therefore the usual constitutional immunity guaranteed to other types of utterances could not be applied in this case. The opinion stated further:

. . . [W]e are convinced that the judgments below result in a curtailment of expression that cannot be dismissed as insignificant. If they can be justified at all, it must be in terms of some serious substantive evil which they are designed to avert. The substantive evil here sought to be averted has been variously described below. It appears to be double: disrespect for the judiciary; and disorderly and unfair administration of justice. The assumption that respect for the judiciary can be won by shielding judges from published criticism wrongly appraises the character of American public opinion. For it is a prized American privilege to speak one's mind, although not always with perfect good taste, on all public institutions. And an enforced silence, however limited, solely in the name of preserving the dignity of the bench, would probably engender resentment, suspicion, and contempt much more than it would enhance respect. . . .

The majority felt that there was no more danger of intimidation or interference with justice in the Bridges telegram than in the editorials and reversed the judgment in this case also. Justice Frankfurter filed a long dissenting opinion, concurred in by Chief Justice Stone and Justices Roberts and Byrnes. He said, "A trial is not a 'free trade in ideas,' nor is the best test of truth in a courtroom 'the power of the thought to get itself accepted in the competition of the market.' " He continued:

A court is a forum with strictly defined limits for discussion. It is circumscribed in the range of its inquiry and in its methods by the Constitution, by laws, and by age-old traditions. Its judges are restrained in their freedom of expression by historic compulsions resting on no other officials of government. They are so circumscribed precisely because judges have in their keeping the enforcement of rights and the protection of liberties which, according to the wisdom of the ages, can only be enforced and protected by observing such methods and traditions. . . .

It is suggested that threats, by discussion, to untrammeled decisions by courts are the most natural expressions when public feeling runs highest. But it does not follow that states are left powerless to prevent their courts from being subverted by outside pressure when the need for impartiality and fair proceeding is greatest. To say that the framers of the Constitution sanctified veiled violence through coercive speech directed against those charged with adjudications is not merely to make violence an ingredient of justice; it mocks the very ideal of justice by respecting its forms while stultifying its uncontaminated exercise.

The case illustrates the milder strictures employed in the United States against newspaper comment while a case is *sub judice*. In England the rule is much tighter, and the fines are apt to be far more severe. In 1949 the Lord Chief Justice fined the London *Daily Mirror* £10,000 and sentenced the editor to three months in jail for comments published concerning a murder trial then under way. [See Donald M. Gillmor, "Free Press and Fair Trial in English Law," 22 *Wash. & Lee L. Rev.* 17 (1965).] In the United States Supreme Court the cases indicate that the evidence supporting a contempt finding must point to a strong threat of subversion of justice before such a judgment will be upheld. In *Pennekamp* v. *Florida,* 328 U.S. 331 (1946), the publisher of the *Miami Herald* was fined for contempt for having published various editorials and a cartoon criticizing a local judge for interfering with the prosecutor's attempts to combat crime in the Miami area. The Supreme Court reversed. Even though some of the cases were still pending, the Court unanimously held that the criticism did not create a danger to fair judicial administration of the "clearness and immediacy necessary to close the doors of permissible public comment." And in *Craig* v. *Harney*, 331 U.S. 367 (1947), a divided Court held that publication, while a motion for a new trial was pending, of an unfair report of the facts of a civil case, accompanied by criticism of the judge for taking the case from the jury, was protected by the Constitution. The press called the action of the trial judge "arbitrary action" and a "travesty on justice." It deplored the fact that the elected judge was a "layman" and not a "competent attorney." The case dealt with an attempt by a property owner to evict a serviceman from business property for nonpayment of rent, and public opinion seemingly was strongly in favor of the serviceman. The jury had twice returned a verdict in his favor despite an instructed verdict for the plaintiff. The motion for new trial followed the jury's third verdict in compliance with the judge's instruction. Subsequently the newspaper personnel involved in the editorials and reports were adjudged guilty of contempt. Justice Douglas, speaking for the majority voting to reverse, stated:

A judge who is part of such a dramatic episode can hardly help but know that his decision is apt to be unpopular. But the law of contempt is not made for the protection of judges who may be sensitive to the winds of public opinion. Judges are supposed to be men of fortitude, able to thrive in a hardy climate. Conceivably a campaign could be so managed and so aimed at the sensibilities of a particular judge and the matter pending before him as to cross the forbidden line. But the episodes we have here do not fall in that category. Nor can we assume that the trial judge was not a man of fortitude.

[Justice Frankfurter, joined by Chief Justice Vinson, dissented, pointing out that the newspapers involved were under common control and were the only papers of general circulation in the area.]

[Justice Jackson dissented separately, saying:]

From our sheltered position, fortified by life tenure and other defenses to judicial independence, it is easy to say that this local judge ought to have shown more fortitude in the face of criticism. But he had no such protection. He was an elective judge who held for a short term. I do not take it that an ambition of a judge to remain a judge is either unusual or dishonorable. Moreover, he was not a lawyer, and I regard this as a matter of some consequence. A lawyer may gain courage to render a decision that temporarily is unpopular because he has confidence that his profession over the years will approve it, despite its unpopular reception, as has been the case with many great decisions. But this judge had no anchor in professional opinion. Of course, the blasts of these little papers in this small community do not jolt us, but I am not so confident that we would be indifferent if a news monopoly in our entire jurisdiction should perpetrate this kind of an attack on us.

The previous decisions have presented the problem of unusual pressures on judges by newspapers to have them dispose of cases in particular ways. A problem is also presented when pretrial publicity in criminal cases is of such a nature as to threaten impartial decisions by jurors. The usual procedure for developing this issue is to appeal a conviction on the ground that a fair trial was denied because of the prejudicial effect of the publicity. In *Shepherd* v. *Florida,* 341 U.S. 50 (1951), this was one of the grounds suggested in requesting a reversal of the conviction of four Negroes. The majority reversed, although the decision came on the ground that discrimination had been practiced in the selection of the grand jury. Justices Frankfurter and Jackson, however, argued further that inflammatory newspaper comment made a fair trial in the community impossible.

Contempt proceedings have also been initiated against persons publishing prejudicial comment upon pending criminal cases. A Maryland trial court, in 1949, punished for contempt a broadcasting company which prior to a murder trial had announced that the person arrested had confessed to the crime, that he had a long criminal record, and that he went to the scene of the crime with officers, re-enacted the crime, and dug up the knife which he had used to commit the murder. The Maryland court of appeals reversed the contempt conviction on the basis of *Bridges, Pennekamp,* and *Craig.* The United States Supreme Court denied certiorari, *Maryland* v. *Baltimore Radio Show,* 338 U.S. 912 (1950), but Justice Frankfurter filed an opinion stressing the point that such denial should not be construed as approving the decision below. He set out in an appendix the course of English decisions dealing with situations in which publications were claimed to have injuriously affected the prosecutions for crime awaiting jury determination, and as to freedom of press in England cited the Report of the Royal Commission on the Press, Cmd. No. 7700, and the debate thereon in the House of Commons, July 28, 1949 (467 H.C. Deb., 5th Ser., 2683–2794).

A flagrant example of pretrial publicity is presented in *Rideau* v. *Louisiana,* 373 U.S. 73 (1963). Following a confession televised from a jail cell, Rideau moved for a change of venue. The motion was denied, and the defendant was tried, convicted, and sentenced to death for murder. On certiorari, the United States Supreme Court reversed, with the majority holding that due process required a trial before a jury drawn from a community of people who had not seen and heard the televised interview. The facts are recited in Justice Stewart's opinion for the Court:

[A] man robbed a bank in Lake Charles, Louisiana, kidnapped three of the bank's employees, and killed one of them. A few hours later the petitioner . . . was apprehended by the police and lodged in . . . jail in Lake Charles. The next morning a moving picture film with a sound track was made of an "interview" in the jail between Rideau and the Sheriff of Calcasieu Parish. This "interview" lasted approximately 20 minutes. It consisted of interrogation by the sheriff and admissions by Rideau that he had perpetrated the bank robbery, kidnapping, and murder. Later the same day the filmed "interview" was broadcast over a television station in Lake Charles, and some 24,000 people in the community saw and heard it on television. The sound film was again shown on television the next day to an estimated audience of 53,000 people. The following day the film was again broadcast by the same television station, and this time approximately 29,000 people saw and heard the "interview" on their television sets. Calcasieu Parish has a population of approximately 150,000 people. . . .

Three members of the jury which convicted him had stated on *voir dire* that they had seen and heard Rideau's televised "interview" with the sheriff on at least one occasion. . . . Rideau's counsel had requested that three jurors be excused for cause, having exhausted all of their peremptory challenges, but these challenges for cause had been denied by the trial judge.

[In holding the denial of the motion for change of venue and the subsequent trial unconstitutional, Justice Stewart stated:]

For anyone who has ever watched television the conclusion cannot be avoided that this spectacle, to the tens of thousands of people who saw and heard it, in a very real sense *was* Rideau's trial—at which he pleaded guilty to murder. Any subsequent court proceedings in a community so pervasively exposed to such a spectacle could be but a hollow formality.

Justices Clark and Harlan dissented on the ground that the record did not show that the adverse publicity "fatally infected the trial."

The most vivid recent situation involving the clash between the freedom of the news media and the right of an accused to an impartial determination of his guilt took place following the assassination of President Kennedy in November, 1963. A crime of such magnitude was bound to lead to enormous pressures on the police and prosecutor for even the most trivial piece of information concerning the assassin which could be transmitted by radio, television, and newspaper to people all over the world. And much that would be considered of an evidentiary nature was released to these media prior to and after the arrest of Lee Harvey Oswald. Had he not been murdered prior to the trial, a serious question would have been presented of whether the three days of saturation coverage precluded an impartial jury determination. The President's Commission on the Assassination took cognizance of this aspect of the events and in the official report, issued in 1964, stated as the last of twelve recommendations:

The commission recommends that the representatives of the bar, law enforcement associations, and the news media work together to establish ethical standards concerning the collection and presentation of information to the public so that there will be no interference with pending criminal investigations, court proceedings, or the right to a fair trial.

In 1965 the Court faced the issue of whether televising and broadcasting a criminal trial of considerable notoriety denied the accused due process of law. The case involved a state prosecution for swindling against Billie Sol Estes in Texas. At a pretrial hearing the defense moved to prevent telecasting, broadcasting by radio and news photography and also moved for a continuance. In a two-day hearing arguments were heard on these motions. These hearings were carried live by both radio and television, and news photography was permitted throughout. At least twelve cameramen were present, "cables and wires were snaked across the courtroom floor, three microphones were on the judge's bench and others were beamed at the jury box and the counsel table," as Justice Clark described the scene. A venire of jurymen had been summoned and was present in the courtroom during the entire hearing. The motion for continuance was granted. At the trial itself, a booth was constructed at the back of the courtroom with an aperture to permit cameramen an unrestricted view of the courtroom. All television cameras and newsreel photographers were restricted to the area of the booth when shooting film or telecasting. Live telecasting was permitted only for the opening and closing arguments of the state, the return of the jury's verdict, and its receipt by the trial judge. Videotapes of the entire proceeding without sound were permitted, however, although the cameras operated only intermittently. Estes was convicted, and the Texas Court of Criminal Appeals affirmed, over the claim of denial of due process under the Fourteenth Amendment because of the televising and broadcasting of proceedings.

By a five-to-four vote the Court reversed in *Estes* v. *Texas*, 381 U.S. 532 (1965), although the majority was divided on the applicable rule governing the televising and broadcasting of criminal trials. Chief Justice Warren, joined by Justices Douglas and Goldberg, concurred in the result, stating that he believed "that it violates the Sixth

Amendment for federal courts and the Fourteenth Amendment for state courts to allow criminal trials to be televised to the public at large." By 1981, however, with all three of those members no longer on the Court, a Florida experimental program of televising a criminal trial was unanimously upheld in *Chandler* v. *Florida,* 449 U.S. 560. The Florida Supreme Court, following a pilot program, promulgated a revised Canon of the Florida Code of Judicial Conduct permitting electronic media and still photography coverage of judicial proceedings, subject to the control of the presiding judge within guidelines to protect the right of the accused to a fair trial. Appellants were convicted after a jury trial over objections that televising and broadcasting parts of the trial denied them a fair and impartial trial. The Court held that in the absence of a showing of prejudice of constitutional dimensions or any attempt to show that the presence of cameras impaired the ability of the jurors to decide the case solely on the basis of the evidence before them the defendants were not denied a fair trial. Chief Justice Burger, for the Court, pointed out that the jurors were asked if the presence of the camera would in any way compromise their ability to consider the case, and each juror answered in the negative. The trial court also instructed the jurors not to watch television accounts of the trial. The Chief Justice stated:

It is not necessary either to ignore or to discount the potential danger to the fairness of a trial in a particular case in order to conclude that Florida may permit the electronic media to cover trials in its state courts. Dangers lurk in this, as in most experiments, but unless we were to conclude that television coverage under all conditions is prohibited by the Constitution, the states must be free to experiment. We are not empowered by the Constitution to oversee or harness state procedural experimentation; only when the state action infringes fundamental guarantees are we authorized to intervene. We must assume state courts will be alert to any factors that impair the fundamental rights of the accused.

In an important decision in 1966, *Sheppard* v. *Maxwell,* the Court undertook to suggest some appropriate steps which trial judges should employ to safeguard against prejudicial reporting in criminal trials. The occasion was the review of proceedings at a notorious murder trial.

SHEPPARD *v.* MAXWELL
*384 U.S. 333 (1966)*

[Petitioner, accused of murdering his wife, was tried before a jury in the Court of Common Pleas of Cuyahoga County, Ohio. Both before and during the trial, which began two weeks before an election in which the trial judge and the chief prosecutor were candidates for judgeships, the petitioner was the subject of extensive newspaper, radio, and television publicity. The publicity included many matters unfavorable to the defendant which were never presented in court. The trial judge denied various requests by defense counsel for a continuance, change of venue, mistrial, and interrogation of the jurors as to their exposure to the publicity. During the trial, which lasted nine weeks, reporters were seated at a press table inside the bar, a few feet from the jury box, and most of the seats in the courtroom were filled with representatives of the news media. Radio broadcasting was done from a room next to the room where the jury recessed and deliberated. Courtroom proceedings which were supposed to be private were overheard and reported by the press, and the noise of newsmen moving in and out of the courtroom made it difficult for counsel and witnesses to be heard. The trial judge made no effort to control the release of leads, information, and gossip to the press by the prosecuting attorneys, the coroner, police officers, or witnesses. Petitioner was convicted of second degree murder. The Ohio

Supreme Court affirmed, and the United States Supreme Court denied certiorari. Several years later, petitioner instituted habeas corpus proceedings in a federal district court, which held that he had been denied a fair trial and was entitled to be released. The Court of Appeals reversed. The Supreme Court granted certiorari.]

Mr. Justice Clark delivered the opinion of the Court. . . .

The principle that justice cannot survive behind walls of silence has long been reflected in the "Anglo-American distrust for secret trials." . . . A responsible press has always been regarded as the handmaiden of effective judicial administration, especially in the criminal field. Its function in this regard is documented by an impressive record of service over several centuries. The press does not simply publish information about trials but guards against the miscarriage of justice by subjecting the police, prosecutors, and judicial processes to extensive public scrutiny and criticism. This Court has, therefore, been unwilling to place any direct limitations on the freedom traditionally exercised by the news media for "[w]hat transpires in the courtroom is public property." . . .

But the Court has also pointed out that "[l]egal trials are not like elections, to be won through the use of the meeting-hall, the radio, and the newspaper." . . .

While we cannot say that Sheppard was denied due process by the judge's refusal to take precautions against the influence of pretrial publicity alone, the court's later rulings must be considered against the setting in which the trial was held. In light of this background, we believe that the arrangements made by the judge with the news media caused Sheppard to be deprived of that "judicial serenity and calm to which [he] was entitled." . . . The fact is that bedlam reigned at the courthouse during the trial and newsmen took over practically the entire courtroom, hounding most of the participants in the trial, especially Sheppard. . . .

The carnival atmosphere at trial could easily have been avoided since the courtroom and courthouse premises are subject to the control of the court. As we stressed in *Estes,* the presence of the press at judicial proceedings must be limited when it is apparent that the accused might otherwise be prejudiced or disadvantaged. Bearing in mind the massive pretrial publicity, the judge should have adopted stricter rules governing the use of the courtroom by newsmen, as Sheppard's counsel requested. The number of reporters in the courtroom itself could have been limited at the first sign that their presence would disrupt the trial. They certainly should not have been placed inside the bar. Furthermore, the judge should have more closely regulated the conduct of newsmen in the courtroom. For instance, the judge belatedly asked them not to handle and photograph trial exhibits lying on the counsel table during recesses.

Secondly, the court should have insulated the witnesses. All of the newspapers and radio stations apparently interviewed prospective witnesses at will, and in many instances disclosed their testimony. . . .

Thirdly, the court should have made some effort to control the release of leads, information, and gossip to the press by police officers, witnesses, and the counsel for both sides. Much of the information thus disclosed was inaccurate, leading to groundless rumors and confusion. . . . Under such circumstances, the judge should have at least warned the newspapers to check the accuracy of their accounts. And it is obvious that the judge should have further sought to alleviate this problem by imposing control over the statements made to the news media by counsel, witnesses, and especially the Coroner and police officers. The prosecution repeatedly made evidence available to the news media which was never offered in the trial. Much of the "evidence" disseminated in this fashion was clearly inadmissible. The exclusion of such evidence in court is rendered meaningless when a news media makes it available to the public. . . .

More specifically, the trial court might well have proscribed extrajudicial statements by any lawyer, party, witness, or court official which divulged prejudicial matters, such as the refusal of Sheppard to submit to interrogation or take any lie detector tests; any statement by Sheppard to officials; the identity of prospective witnesses or their probable testimony; any belief in guilt or innocence; or like statements concerning the merits of the case. . . . In addition, reporters who wrote or broadcasted prejudicial stories, could have been warned as to the impropriety of publishing material not introduced in the proceedings. . . .

From the cases coming here we note that unfair and prejudicial news comment on pending trials has become increasingly prevalent. Due process requires that the accused receive a trial by an impartial jury free from outside influences. Given the pervasiveness of modern communications and the difficulty of effacing prejudicial publicity from the minds of the jurors, the trial courts must take strong measures to ensure that the balance is never weighed against the accused. . . . Neither prosecutors, counsel for defense, the accused, witnesses, court staff nor enforcement officers coming under the jurisdiction of the court should be permitted to frustrate its function. Collaboration between counsel and the press as to information affecting the fairness of a criminal trial is not only subject to regulation, but is highly censurable and worthy of disciplinary measures.

. . . The case is remanded to the District Court with instructions to issue the writ and order that Sheppard be released from custody unless the State puts him to its charges again within a reasonable time.

*It is so ordered.*

Mr. Justice Black dissents.

While the *Sheppard* case presented the situation of undue laxity on the part of a trial judge in dealing with the media, the Court in 1976 faced a problem at the other extreme—an absolute "gag rule" imposed by a Nebraska judge on the media and applicable until the trial jury was actually impanelled. The order was occasioned by a sensational murder case. Police had found the six members of a family murdered in their home in Sutherland, Nebraska, a town of about 850 people. On the following day a suspect was arrested. Three days later, upon request by the prosecuting and defense attorneys, the County Court entered an order prohibiting anyone in attendance at pretrial proceedings from releasing or authorizing for public dissemination any testimony given or evidence given. A preliminary hearing was held on the same day, open to the public but subject to the order. The defendant was bound over for trial in the District Court on charges that he had committed the murders in the course of a sexual assault. Several members of the media then petitioned the District Court for leave to intervene, asking that the restrictive order be vacated. District Judge Stuart entered his own restrictive order which, as modified by the Nebraska Supreme Court, prohibited reporting of three matters: (1) the existence and nature of any confessions or admissions made by the defendant to law enforcement officers, (2) any confessions or admissions made to any third parties, except members of the press, and (3) other facts "strongly implicative" of the accused. The Nebraska Supreme Court held that the order was necessary, in view of the publicity surrounding the crime, in order to assure trial by an impartial jury.

The United States Supreme Court reviewed the case on certiorari and in *Nebraska Press Association* v. *Stuart,* 427 U.S. 539 (1976), unanimously reversed. While the defendant had already been tried, convicted, and sentenced to death, the case was on appeal to the Nebraska Supreme Court, and the United States Supreme Court held that the "gag rule" issue was not moot, stating that "jurisdiction is not necessarily defeated simply because the order attacked has expired, if the underlying dispute between the parties is one 'capable of repetition, yet evading review.' " On the merits, the Court held that there was no finding that alternative measures short of prior restraint on the press would not have protected the accused's right to a fair trial. Such alternatives were "discussed with obvious approval in *Sheppard* v. *Maxwell.*" To the extent that the order prohibited the reporting of evidence at the open preliminary hearing, it violated the settled principle stated in *Sheppard* that "there is nothing that proscribes the press from reporting events that transpire in the courtroom." In some circumstances the hearing might have been closed to the public, but once it was open, "what transpired there could not be subject to prior restraint." Finally, the portion of the order restraining publication of other facts "strongly implicative" of the accused was held to be too vague and too broad to survive the scrutiny given to restraints on First Amendment rights.

In *Gannett Co, Inc.* v. *DePasquale,* 443 U.S. 368 (1979), the Court upheld a trial judge's decision to close a pre-trial hearing to the press and the public. The hearing was on a motion to suppress an allegedly involuntary confession and certain evidence in a murder case. The defendants requested that the hearing be closed to prevent the possibility of adverse publicity, and the prosecuting attorney did not oppose the request. A reporter protested, but the judge ruled that the defendants' right to a fair trial should prevail over the interest of the press and the public. In the United States Supreme Court the decision turned on the question of where the Sixth Amendment's guarantee of a "public trial" inhered—in the defendant (who might then waive the right) or in the public and the press. Justice Stewart, for the majority of five, stated that the Sixth Amendment's guarantee of a public trial was for the benefit of the defendant alone. "The Constitution nowhere mentions any right of access to a criminal trial on the part of the public; its guarantee, like the others enumerated, is personal to the accused." Further, he stated that even though historically trials were open to the public, pretrial proceedings were never characterized by the same degree of openness as were actual trials.

Speaking for the four dissenters, Justice Blackmun argued that the Sixth Amendment does guarantee to the accused a public trial, but this does not guarantee him a right to a private trial as well. The Sixth and Fourteenth Amendments prohibit the States from excluding the public from a proceeding without affording full and fair consideration to the public's interests in maintaining an open proceeding. On the record Justice Blackmun did not find a sufficient showing to establish the strict and inescapable necessity that supports an exclusion order.

The decision caused considerable controversy, and only one year later in *Richmond Newspapers, Inc.* v. *Virginia,* 448 U.S. 555 (1980), the Court, without overruling *Gannett,* held that the public and the press had a First and Fourteenth Amendment right to attend criminal *trials* in the absence of "overriding interest articulated in the findings." In a footnote to his opinion for the plurality, Chief Justice Burger stated:

> We have no occasion here to define the circumstances in which all or parts of a criminal trial may be closed to the public, . . . but our holding today does not mean that the First Amendment rights of the public and representatives of the press are absolute. . . . [A] trial judge [may], in the interest of the fair administration of justice, impose reasonable limitations on access to a trial.

There still remained the question of whether pretrial hearings carried a substantially lower right of access in the public and the press. In *Waller* v. *Georgia,* 467 U.S. 39 (1984), the Court held unanimously that the right to a public trial under the Sixth and Fourteenth Amendments applies to a hearing on a motion to suppress evidence. The trial court's findings to support its closure order for an entire seven-day hearing "were broad and general, and did not purport to justify closure of the entire hearing." Further, the court did not consider alternatives to immediate closure of the entire hearing: "direct-

ing the government to provide more detail about its need for closure, *in camera* if necessary, and closing only those parts of the hearing that jeopardized the interests
advanced."

In *Globe Newspaper Co.* v. *Superior Court,* 457 U.S. 596 (1982), the Court held unconstitutional a Massachusetts statute providing for exclusion of the public from trials of
various sexual offenses involving a victim under the age of 18. It held that the statute
could not be justified on the basis of either the State's interest in protecting minor victims of sex crimes from further trauma and embarrassment or its interest in encouraging
such victims to come forward and testify in a truthful and credible manner. As to the first
basis, "compelling as that interest is, it does not justify a *mandatory* closure rule." A trial
court "can determine on a case-by-case basis whether closure is necessary to protect
the welfare of a minor victim," weighing such factors as the age, psychological maturity
and understanding and the desires of the victim and the interests of parents and relatives. As to the second interest, its validity was considered open to serious question in
view of the fact that the press would have access to the transcript and could publish the
substance of the testimony, as well as the victim's identity.

[On the subject of fair trial and free press, see Carolyn Jaffee, "The Press and the Op-
pressed—A Study of Prejudicial News Reporting in Criminal Cases," 56 *J. Crim. L.* 1
(1965); A.B.A. Advisory Comm. on Fair Trial and Free Press, *Standards Relating to Fair
Trial and Free Press, Tentative Draft* (New York: Institute of Judicial Administration,
1966); Hearings on S.290 before the Subcommittee on Constitutional Rights and the
Subcommittee on Improvements in Judicial Machinery of the Senate Committee on the
Judiciary, *Free Press and Fair Trial,* 89th Cong., 1st Sess. (1965); Association of the Bar of
the City of New York, Special Committee on Radio, Television, and the Administration
of Justice, *Freedom of the Press and Fair Trial: Final Report with Recommendations* (New
York: Columbia Univ. Press, 1967); Andrew M. Schatz, "Gagging the Press in Criminal
Trials," 10 *Harv. Civil Rights-Civil Liberties* L. Rev. 608 (1975); and Alfred Friendly and
Ronald L. Goldfarb, *Crime and Publicity: The Impact of News on the Administration of
Justice* (New York: Twentieth Century Fund, 1967).]

### Newsman's Privilege

### BRANZBURG *v.* HAYES
### *408 U.S. 665 (1972)*

[The Supreme Court granted certiorari in three cases to consider newsmen's constitutional privilege from giving grand jury testimony. Branzburg, a reporter for the
*Louisville Courier-Journal,* published a story in 1969 describing in detail his observations of two young persons synthesizing hashish from marihauana, an activity
which, they asserted, earned them about $5,000 in three weeks. The article stated
that Branzburg had promised not to reveal the identity of the two hashish makers.
He was subpoenaed by the county grand jury but refused to identify the individuals
he had seen possessing marihuana or the persons he had seen making hashish. A state
trial court judge ordered petitioner to answer these questions and rejected his contention that the Kentucky reporters' privilege statute, the First Amendment, or the
Kentucky Constitution authorized his refusal to answer. Petitioner then sought prohibition and mandamus in the Kentucky Court of Appeals, but the Court denied the
petition.

A second case involving Branzburg arose from a later story which described in detail the use of drugs in Frankfort, Kentucky. A number of conversations with several
unnamed drug users were recounted. Subpoenaed to appear before another county

grand jury, petitioner moved to quash the summons. The Court of Appeals once again denied the requested writs.

The two other cases involved newsmen from Massachusetts and California, respectively, who carried out in-depth interviews with local Black Panther Party members and other black militant groups. In each case they were ordered to appear before grand juries and answer questions concerning possible violations of a number of criminal statutes. In the Massachusetts case, the courts refused the motion to quash. In the California case, involving a federal grand jury, the Court of Appeals held that absent compelling reasons for requiring his testimony, he was privileged to withold it. The United States petitioned for certiorari.]

Opinion of the Court by Mr. Justice White, announced by The Chief Justice.

The issue in these cases is whether requiring newsmen to appear and testify before State or federal grand juries abridges the freedom of speech and press guaranteed by the First Amendment. We hold that it does not. . . .

Petitioners Branzburg and Pappas and respondent Caldwell press First Amendment claims that may be simply put: that to gather news it is often necessary to agree either not to identify the source of information published or to publish only part of the facts revealed or both; that if the reporter is nevertheless forced to reveal these confidences to a grand jury, the source so identified and other confidential sources of other reporters will be measurably deterred from furnishing publishable information, all to the detriment of the free flow of information protected by the First Amendment. Although petitioners do not claim an absolute privilege against official interrogation in all circumstances, they assert that the reporter should not be forced either to appear or to testify before a grand jury or at a trial until and unless sufficient grounds are shown for believing that the reporter possesses information relevant to a crime the grand jury is investigating, that the information the reporter has is unavailable from other sources, and that the need for the information is sufficiently compelling to override the claimed invasion of First Amendment interests occasioned by the disclosure. . . . The heart of the claim is that the burden on news gathering resulting from compelling reporters to disclose confidential information outweighs any public interest in obtaining the information.

We do not question the significance of free speech, press or assembly to the country's welfare. Nor is it suggested that news gathering does not qualify for First Amendment protection; without some protection for seeking out the news, freedom of the press could be eviscerated. But this case involves no intrusions upon speech or assembly, no prior restraint or restriction on what the press may publish, and no express or implied command that the press publish what it prefers to withhold. . . .

The sole issue before us is the obligation of reporters to respond to grand jury subpoenas as other citizens do and to answer questions relevant to an investigation into the commission of crime. Citizens generally are not constitutionally immune from grand jury subpoenas; and neither the First Amendment nor other constitutional provision protects the average citizen from disclosing to a grand jury information that he has received in confidence. The claim is, however, that reporters are exempt from these obligations because if forced to respond to subpoenas and identify their sources or disclose other confidences, their informants will refuse or be reluctant to furnish newsworthy information in the future. This asserted burden on news gathering is said to make compelled testimony from newsmen constitutionally suspect and to require a privileged position for them.

It is clear that the First Amendment does not invalidate every incidental burdening of the press that may result from the enforcement of civil or criminal statutes of general applicability. Under prior cases, otherwise valid laws serving substantial public interests may be enforced against the press as against others, despite the possible burden that may be imposed. . . .

The prevailing view is that the press is not free with impunity to publish everything and anything it desires to publish. Although it may deter or regulate what is said or published, the press may not circulate knowing or reckless falsehoods damaging to private reputation without subjecting itself to liability for damages, including punitive damages, or even criminal prosecution. . . . A newspaper or a journalist may also be punished for contempt of court, in appropriate circumstances. . . .

It has generally been held that the First Amendment does not guarantee the press a constitutional right of special access to information not available to the public generally. . . . Despite the fact that news gathering may be hampered, the press is regularly excluded from grand jury proceedings, our own conferences, the meetings of other official bodies gathered in executive session, and the meetings of private organizations. . . .

It is thus not surprising that the great weight of authority is that newsmen are not exempt from the normal duty of appearing before a grand jury and answering questions relevant to a criminal investigation. At common law, courts consistently refused to recognize the existence of any privilege authorizing a newsman to refuse to reveal confidential information to a grand jury. . . . In 1958, a news gatherer asserted for the first time that the First Amendment exempted confidential information from public disclosure pursuant to a subpoena issued in a civil suit, . . . but the claim was denied, and this argument has been almost uniformly rejected since then, although there are occasional dicta that, in circumstances not presented, a newsman might be excused. . . .

A number of States have provided newsmen a statutory privilege of varying breadth, but the majority have not done so, and none has been provided by federal statute. Until now the only testimonial privilege for unofficial witnesses that is rooted in the Federal Constitution is the Fifth Amendment privilege against compelled self-incrimination. We are asked to create another by interpreting the First Amendment to grant newsmen a testimonial privilege that other citizens do not enjoy. This we decline to do. Fair and effective law enforcement aimed at providing security for the person and property of the individual is a fundamental function of government, and the grand jury plays an important, constitutionally mandated role in this process. On the records now before us, we perceive no basis for holding that the public interest in law enforcement and in ensuring effective grand jury proceedings is insufficient to override the consequential, but uncertain, burden on news gathering which is said to result from insisting that reporters, like other citizens, respond to relevant questions put to them in the course of a valid grand jury investigation or criminal trial. . . .

Accepting the fact, however, that an undetermined number of informants not themselves implicated in crime will nevertheless, for whatever reason, refuse to talk to newsmen if they fear identification by a reporter in an official investigation we cannot accept the argument that the public interest in possible future news about crime from undisclosed, unverified sources must take precedence over the public interest in pursuing and prosecuting those crimes reported to the press by informants and in thus deterring the commission of such crimes in the future.

[I]t is obvious that agreements to conceal information relevant to commission of crime have very little to recommend them from the standpoint of public policy. Historically, the common law recognized a duty to raise the "hue and cry" and report felonies to the authorities. Misprision of a felony—that is, the concealment of a felony . . . —was often said to be a common law crime. The first Congress passed a statute . . . which is still in effect, defining a federal crime of misprision. . . . It is apparent from this statute, as well as from our history and that of England, that concealment of crime and agreements to do so are not looked upon with favor. Such conduct deserves no encomium, and we decline now to afford it First Amendment protection by denigrating the duty of a citizen, whether reporter or informer, to respond to grand jury subpoena and answer relevant questions put to him. . . .

At the federal level, Congress has freedom to determine whether a statutory newsman's privilege is necessary and desirable and to fashion standards and rules as narrow or broad as deemed necessary to address the evil discerned and, equally important, to re-fashion those rules as experience from time to time may dictate. There is also merit in leaving state legislatures free, within First Amendment limits, to fashion their own standards in light of the conditions and problems with respect to the relations between law enforcement officials and press in their own areas. . . .

Finally, as we have earlier indicated, news gathering is not without its First Amendment protections, and grand jury investigations if instituted or conducted other than in good faith, would pose wholly different issues for resolution under the First Amendment. Official harassment of the press undertaken not for purposes of law enforcement but to disrupt a reporter's relationship with his news sources would have no justification. Grand juries are subject to judicial control and subpoenas to motions to quash. We do not expect courts will forget that grand juries must operate within the limits of the First Amendment as well as the Fifth. . . .

Mr. Justice Powell, concurring in the opinion of the Court. . . .

Mr. Justice Douglas, dissenting. . . .

It is my view that there is no "compelling need" that can be shown which qualifies the reporter's immunity from appearing or testifying before a grand jury, unless the reporter himself is implicated in a crime. His immunity in my view is therefore quite complete, for absent his involvement in a crime, the First Amendment protects him against an appearance before a grand jury, and if he is involved in a crime, the Fifth Amendment stands as a barrier. Since in my view there is no area of inquiry not protected by a privilege, the reporter need not appear for the futile purpose of invoking one to each question. And, since in my view a newsman has an absolute right not to appear before a grand jury it follows for me that a journalist who voluntarily appears before that body may invoke his First Amendment privilege to specific questions. . . .

The press has a preferred position in our constitutional scheme not to enable it to make money, not to set newsmen apart as a favored class, but to bring fulfillment to the public's right to know. The right to know is crucial to the governing powers of the people, to paraphrase Alexander Meiklejohn. Knowledge is essential to informed decisions. . . .

The record in this case is replete with weighty affidavits from responsible newsmen, telling how important are the sanctity of their sources of information. When we deny newsmen that protection, we deprive the people of the information needed to run the affairs of the Nation in an intelligent way. . . .

Mr. Justice Stewart, with whom Mr. Justice Brennan and Mr. Justice Marshall join, dissenting.

The Court's crabbed view of the First Amendment reflects a disturbing insensitivity to the critical role of an independent press in our society. . . . The Court thus invites state and federal authorities to undermine the historic independence of the press by attempting to annex the journalistic profession as an investigative arm of government. Not only will this decision impair performance of the press' constitutionally protected functions, but it will, I am convinced, in the long run, harm rather than help the administration of justice. . . .

The right to gather news implies . . . a right to a confidential relationship between a reporter and his source. This proposition follows as a matter of simple logic once three factual predicates are recognized: (1) newsmen require informants to gather news; (2) confidentiality—the promise or understanding that names or certain aspects of communications will be kept off-the-record—is essential to the creation and maintenance of a news-gathering relationship with informants; and (3) the existence of an unbridled subpoena power—the absence of a constitutional right protecting, in *any* way, a confidential relationship from compulsory process—will either deter sources from divulging information or deter reporters from gathering and publishing information. . . .

The reporter must speculate about whether contact with a controversial source or publication of controversial material will lead to a subpoena. In the event of a subpoena, under today's decision, the newsman will know that he must choose between being punished for contempt if he refuses to testify, or violating his profession's ethics and impairing his resourcefulness as a reporter if he discloses confidential information. . . .

Accordingly, when a reporter is asked to appear before a grand jury and reveal confidences, I would hold that the government must (1) show that there is probable cause to believe that the newsman has information which is clearly relevant to a specific probable violation of law; (2) demonstrate that the information sought cannot be obtained by alternative means less destructive of First Amendment rights; and (3) demonstrate a compelling and overriding interest in the information.

This is not to say that a grand jury could not issue a subpoena until such a showing were made, and it is not to say that a newsman would be in any way privileged to ignore any subpoena that was issued. Obviously, before the government's burden to make such a showing were triggered, the reporter would have to move to quash the subpoena, asserting the basis on which he considered the particular relationship a confidential one. . . .

[See Note, "Reporters and Their Sources: The Constitutional Right to a Confidential Relationship," 80 *Yale L. J.* 317 (1970).]

## Libel

In the past it has been commonplace to cite libelous and obscene publications as exceptions to the general rule of constitutional protection afforded the press. In more recent years, however, questions have been raised as to whether even these kinds of publications should necessarily be placed outside the pale of First Amendment protection. Justice Black, in a public interview quoted earlier [37 *N.Y.U. L. Rev.* 549 (1962)], stated that he had no doubt that the First Amendment intended that there should be no libel or defamation law·in the United States, and that the Constitution was not intended "to authorize damage suits for mere words as distinguished from conduct."

The Court has not yet adopted the absolute protection argued for by Justice Black, but when the allegedly libelous statements are directed toward official conduct, the Court indicated in *New York Times Co.* v. *Sullivan,* 376 U.S. 254 (1964), that actual malice must be shown to support a judgment against the press.

NEW YORK TIMES CO. *v.* SULLIVAN

*376 U.S. 254 (1964)*

[A civil libel action was filed in Montgomery, Alabama, by Montgomery's Commissioner of Public Affairs, whose duties included the supervision of the police department. The action was brought against the *New York Times* for publication of a paid advertisement describing the mistreatment of Negro students protesting segregation in Montgomery, and also against four individuals whose names, among others, appeared in the advertisement. The advertisement stated in part:

"In Montgomery, Alabama, after students sang 'My country, 'Tis of Thee' on the State Capitol steps, their leaders were expelled from school, and truckloads of police armed with shotguns and tear-gas ringed the Alabama State College Campus. When the entire student body protested to state authorities by refusing to re-register, their dining hall was padlocked in an attempt to starve them into submission." . . .

"Again and again the Southern violators have answered Dr. King's peaceful protests with intimidation and violence. They have bombed his home almost killing his wife and child. They have assaulted his person. They have arrested him seven times—for 'speeding,' 'loitering' and similar 'offenses.' And now they have charged him with 'perjury'—a *felony* under which they could imprison him for *ten years*. . . ."

Sullivan contended that both paragraphs accused the Montgomery police, and hence him, as the commissioner who supervised the police, of answering Dr. King's protests with intimidation and violence. It was uncontroverted that some of the statements contained in the two paragraphs were not accurate descriptions of events which occurred. For example, the campus dining hall was not padlocked, the police did not "ring" the campus, although there were large numbers deployed near it, and Dr. King had been arrested only four times rather than seven.

The jury awarded plaintiff damages of $500,000 against all defendants, and the judgment on the verdict was affirmed by the Supreme Court of Alabama on the grounds that the statements in the advertisement were libelous *per se,* false, and not privileged, and that the evidence showed malice on the part of the newspaper.]

Mr. Justice Brennan delivered the opinion of the Court.

We are required for the first time in this case to determine the extent to which the constitutional protections for speech and press limit a State's power to award damages in a libel action brought by a public official against critics of his official conduct. . . .

. . . We reverse the judgment. We hold that the rule of law applied by the Alabama courts is constitutionally deficient for failure to provide the safeguards for freedom of speech and of the press that are required by the First and Fourteenth Amendments in a libel action brought by a public official against critics of his official conduct. We further hold that under the proper safeguards the evidence presented in this case is constitutionally insufficient to support the judgment for the respondent. . . .

Respondent relies heavily, as did the Alabama courts, on statements of this Court to the effect that the Constitution does not protect libelous publications. Those statements do not foreclose our inquiry here. None of the cases sustained the use of libel laws to impose sanctions upon expression critical of the official conduct of public officials. . . .

Thus we consider this case against the background of a profound national commitment to the principle that debate on public issues should be uninhibited, robust, and wide-open, and that it may well include vehement, caustic, and sometimes unpleasantly sharp attacks on government and public officials. . . . The present advertisement, as an expression of grievance and protest on one of the major issues of our time, would seem clearly to qualify for the constitutional protection. The question is whether it forfeits that protection by the falsity of some of its factual statements and by its alleged defamation of respondent.

Authoritative interpretations of the First Amendment guarantees have consistently refused to recognize an exception for any test of truth—whether administered by judges, juries, or administrative officials—and especially one that puts the burden of proving truth on the speaker. . . . The constitutional protection does not turn upon "the truth, popularity, or social utility of the ideas and beliefs which are offered." . . .

Injury to official reputation affords no more warrant for repressing speech that would otherwise be free than does factual error. Where judicial officers are involved, this Court has held that concern for the dignity and reputation of the courts does not justify the punishment as criminal contempt of criticism of the judge or his decision. . . . This is true even though the utterance contains "half-truths" and "misinformation." . . . If judges are to be treated as "men of fortitude, able to thrive in a hardy climate," . . . surely the same must be true of other government officials, such as elected city commissioners. Criticism of their official conduct does not lose its constitutional protection merely because it is effective criticism and hence diminishes their official reputations.

If neither factual error nor defamatory content suffices to remove the constitutional shield from criticism of official conduct, the combination of the two elements is no less inadequate. . . .

A rule compelling the critic of official conduct to guarantee the truth of all his factual assertions—and to do so on pain of libel judgments virtually unlimited in amount—leads to a . . . "self-censorship." Allowance of the defense of truth, with the burden of proving it on the defendant, does not mean that only false speech will be deterred. Even courts accepting this defense as an adequate safeguard have recognized the difficulties of adducing legal proofs that tne alleged libel was true in all its factual particulars. . . . Under such a rule, would-be critics of official conduct may be deterred from voicing their criticism, even though it is believed to be true and even though it is in fact true, because of doubt whether it can be proved in court or fear of the expense of having to do so. They tend to make only statements which "steer far wider of the unlawful zone." . . . The rule thus dampens the vigor and limits the variety of public debate. It is inconsistent with the First and Fourteenth Amendments.

The constitutional guarantees require, we think, a federal rule that prohibits a public official from recovering damages for a defamatory falsehood relating to his official conduct unless he proves that the statement was made with "actual malice"— that is, with knowledge that it was false or with reckless disregard of whether it was false or not. . . .

We conclude that such a privilege is required by the First and Fourteenth Amendments. . . . [T]he judgment must be reversed and remanded. . . .

Since respondents may seek a new trial, we deem that considerations of effective judicial administration require us to review the evidence in the present record to determine whether it could constitutionally support a judgment for respondent. . . .

Applying these standards, we consider that the proof presented to show actual malice lacks the convincing clarity which the constitutional standard demands, and hence that it would not constitutionally sustain the judgment for respondent under the proper rule of law. . . . The statement by the Times' Secretary that, apart from the padlocking allegation, he thought the advertisement was "substantially correct," affords no constitutional warrant for the Alabama Supreme Court's conclusion that it was a "cavalier ignoring of the falsity of the advertisement [from which] the jury could not have but been impressed with the bad faith of the Times, and its maliciousness inferable therefrom." . . . We think the evidence against the Times supports at most a finding of negligence in failing to discover the misstatements, and is constitutionally insufficient to show the recklessness that is required for a finding of actual malice. . . .

*Reversed and remanded.*

Mr. Justice Black with whom Mr. Justice Douglas joins, concurring. . . .

. . . I base my vote to reverse on the belief that the First and Fourteenth Amendments not merely "delimit" a State's power to award damages to "a public official against critics of his official conduct" but completely prohibit a State from exercising such a power. The Court goes on to hold that a State can subject such critics to damages if "actual malice" can be proved against them. "Malice," even as defined by the Court, is an elusive, abstract concept, hard to prove and hard to disprove. The requirement that malice be proved provides at best an evanescent protection for the right critically to discuss public affairs and certainly does not measure up to the sturdy safeguard embodied in the First Amendment. Unlike the Court, therefore I vote to reverse exclusively on the ground that the Times and the individual defendants had an absolute, unconditional constitutional right to publish in the Times advertisement their criticisms of the Montgomery agencies and officials. . . . An unconditional right to say what one pleases about public affairs is what I consider to be the minimum guarantee of the First Amendment. . . .

Mr. Justice Goldberg, with whom Mr. Justice Douglas joins, concurring in the result. . . .

In my view, the First and Fourteenth Amendments to the Constitution afford to the citizen and to the press an absolute, unconditional privilege to criticize official conduct despite the harm which may flow from excesses and abuses. . . . In a democratic society, one who assumes to act for the citizens in an executive, legislative, or judicial capacity must expect that his official acts will be commented upon and criticized. Such criticism cannot, in my opinion, be muzzled or deterred by the courts at the instance of public officials under the label of libel. . . .

This is not to say that the Constitution protects defamatory statements directed against the private conduct of a public official or private citizen. Freedom of press and of speech insures that government will respond to the will of the people and that changes may be obtained by peaceful means. Purely private defamation has little to do with the political ends of a self-governing society. The imposition of liability for private defamation does not abridge the freedom of public speech or any other freedom protected by the First Amendment. . . .

The rule of the *New York Times* case was followed in *Garrison* v. *Louisiana,* 379 U.S. 64 (1964), in reversing a conviction for criminal defamation. During a dispute with the judges of a criminal court of New Orleans, the district attorney for the parish held a press conference at which he attributed a large backlog of pending criminal cases to the inefficiency, laziness, and excessive vacations of the judges, and accused them of hampering his enforcement of the vice laws by refusing to authorize the expenses for the necessary investigations. The Court held that the *New York Times* rule limiting the awarding of civil damages in cases of alleged false criticism of public officials to instances of actual malice was also applicable to criminal sanctions for such criticism.

The Court has also applied the *New York Times* standard to the reporting of incidents of "public interest," even though they did not involve "public officials." *Time, Inc.* v. *Hill,* 385 U.S. 374 (1967), arose from the publication in *Life* magazine of an article reporting that a new play portrayed a hostage experience suffered by James Hill and his family. The article was entitled "True Crime Inspires Tense Play," with the subtitle, "The ordeal of a family trapped by convicts gives Broadway a new thriller, 'The Desperate

Hours.' " Hill alleged that the article falsely reported that the play was based on his family's experience and sued for damages under a New York statute protecting the right of privacy. The Court reversed the award of damages below on the ground that an improper standard was employed by the trial court. Although this was an invasion of privacy action rather than libel, the majority opinion utilized similar language in stating: "We hold that the constitutional protections for speech and press preclude the application of the New York statute to redress false reports of matters of public interest in the absence of proof that the defendant published the report with knowledge of its falsity or in reckless disregard of the truth."

In *Curtis Publishing Co.* v. *Butts,* 388 U.S. 130 (1967), the Court extended the *Times* rule to cover "public figures." The *Saturday Evening Post* had published an article entitled "The Story of a College Football Fix," in which it was stated that "Wally" Butts, University of Georgia football coach, had revealed to "Bear" Bryant, University of Alabama football coach, Georgia's plays, defensive patterns, and all the significant secrets Georgia's football team possessed. This reportedly occurred shortly before the two teams were to play a conference game. Butts sued for libel in a diversity action in federal court and won a jury verdict of more than $3,000,000. The trial court reduced the award to $460,000, and the Court of Appeals affirmed. The Supreme Court affirmed, but there was no majority opinion. A majority of the justices did, however, hold that the rule of *New York Times* was constitutionally demanded in the case of "public figures" as well as public officials. It was further held that the evidence supported the jury verdict in view of the failure of the *Post* to check the accuracy of the very serious allegations made against a well-known football coach, although the majority on the merits was a different group of justices and included some who would require a lesser standard for "public figures" than for public officials.

*Greenbelt Cooperative Publishing Ass'n.* v. *Bresler,* 398 U.S. 6 (1970), involved a libel action against a newspaper brought by a private real-estate developer. News articles had reported that at city council meetings certain citizens had characterized as "blackmail" the plaintiff's negotiating position with the city council in seeking to obtain zoning variances for certain property owned by the plaintiff at the same time that the city was attempting to buy other property from the plaintiff for school building purposes. The plaintiff contended that the defendants should be held liable for the knowing use of falsehood, since the word "blackmail" was intended to charge the plaintiff with the crime of blackmail, and since the defendants knew that the plaintiff had committed no such crime. The trial court's charge to the jury stated that the plaintiff could recover if the publications had been made with malice *or* with a reckless disregard of whether they were true or false. Judgment was entered for the plaintiff, the Maryland Court of Appeals affirmed, and on certiorari the United States Supreme Court reversed and remanded. The majority held that the plaintiff's status in the course of the negotiations with school officials and the city council brought him clearly within the "public figure" category as defined in *Curtis Publishing Co.* v. *Butts.* Thus the constitutional standard permitted recovery only if it was established that the defamatory publication was false *and* that it was made with knowledge of its falsity or in reckless disregard of whether it was false or true. Further, the majority thought it "simply impossible to believe" that a reader who reached the word "blackmail" would have considered it to be more than "rhetorical hyperbole."

In *Monitor Patriot Co.* v. *Roy,* 401 U.S. 265 (1971), the Court held that the *Sullivan* test applied to a newspaper's characterization of a candidate for the United States Senate as a "former small-time bootlegger." The trial court had charged the jury that if the libel was in the "public sector" and concerned the plaintiff's fitness for office, then the *Sullivan* rule applied, but that if the libel was in the "private sector," the plaintiff need only show that the article was false and had not been published in good faith for a justifiable purpose with a belief founded on reasonable grounds of the truth of the matter published. The jury found against the newspaper, and the New Hampshire Supreme Court affirmed. The United States Supreme Court reversed and remanded, holding that the *Sullivan* test was the proper rule since, as a matter of constitutional law, a charge of criminal conduct, no matter how remote in time or place, could never be irrelevant to a candidate's fitness for office.

In 1971 the Court reworked the rule of *New York Times* v. *Sullivan* to extend even further the media's protection against libel action. *Rosenbloom* v. *Metromedia,* 403 U.S. 29 (1971), involved a libel action against a radio station as a result of news stories of petitioner's arrest for possession of obscene literature, and stories concerning petitioner's lawsuit against certain officials alleging that the magazines he distributed were not obscene and seeking injunctive relief from police interference with his business. The latter stories did not mention petitioner's name, but used the terms "smut literature racket" and "girlie-book peddlers." Following his acquittal of criminal obscenity charges, petitioner sued in a diversity suit in federal court seeking damages under Pennsylvania's libel law. The jury found for petitioner and awarded $25,000 in general damages and $725,000 in punitive damages, which was reduced by the court on remittitur to $25,000. The Court of Appeals reversed, and the Supreme Court affirmed by a five-to-three vote, with Justice Douglas not participating. There was no majority opinion. Justice Brennan wrote an opinion which was joined by the Chief Justice and Justice Blackmun, however, in which the "public official" or "public figure" test was revised to focus on whether the matter publicized was "an event of public or general concern." It was argued that this would protect the media under the *Sullivan* test if the subject matter was of public concern, whether the person involved was a "public official," "public figure," or "private individual," and in this case "police arrest of a person for distributing allegedly obscene magazines clearly constitutes an issue of public or general interest." Justice Black concurred, reiterating his position that the First Amendment bars all libel actions against the news media "even when statements are broadcast with knowledge they are false." Justice White concurred in the result.

The decision seemingly left no remedy even for private persons who are the victims of false and irresponsible attacks by the media, as long as the publication "concerns a matter of public or general interest." The Court retreated from this position three years later in *Gertz* v. *Welch.*

GERTZ *v.* WELCH

*418 U.S. 323 (1974)*

[A Chicago policeman named Nuccio was convicted of murder. The victim's family retained Gertz, a reputable attorney, to represent them in a civil suit against the officer. An article appearing in Welch's magazine alleged that the murder trial was part of a Communist conspiracy to discredit the local police, and it falsely stated that Gertz had arranged Nuccio's "frame-up," implied that Gertz had a criminal record and labeled him a "Communist-fronter." Petitioner brought this diversity libel action against respondent. After all the evidence had been presented but before submission of the case to the jury, the court ruled that Gertz was neither a public official nor a public figure. After the jury returned a verdict for petitioner for $50,000, the District Court decided that the standard announced in *New York Times* should have been applied to the suit. Concluding that this standard protects media discussion of a public issue without regard to whether the person defamed is a public official or a public figure, the court made its own finding that petitioner had failed to prove malice or reckless disregard for the truth and therefore entered judgment n.o.v. for respondent. The Court of Appeals affirmed.]

Mr. Justice Powell delivered the opinion of the Court. . . .

[The opinion begins with a lengthy analysis of the Court's libel decisions from *New York Times* v. *Sullivan* through *Rosenbloom* v. *Metromedia.*]

The *New York Times* standard defines the level of constitutional protection appropriate to the context of defamation of a public person. Those who, by reason of the notoriety of their achievements or the vigor and success with which they seek the public's attention, are properly classed as public figures and those who hold governmental office may recover for injury to reputation only on clear and convincing proof that the defamatory falsehood was made with knowledge of its falsity or with reckless disregard for the truth. This standard administers an extremely powerful antidote to the inducement to media self-censorship of the common-law rule of strict liability for libel and slander. And it exacts a correspondingly high price from the victims of defamatory falsehood. Plainly many deserving plaintiffs, including some intentionally subjected to injury, will be unable to surmount the barrier of the *New York Times* test. Despite this substantial abridgment of the state law right to compensation for wrongful hurt to one's reputation, the Court has concluded that the protection of the *New York Times* privilege should be available to publishers and broadcasters of defamatory falsehood concerning public officials and public figures. . . . We think that these decisions are correct, but we do not find their holdings justified solely by reference to the interest of the press and broadcast media in immunity from liability. Rather, we believe that the *New York Times* rule states an accommodation between this concern and the limited state interest present in the context of libel actions brought by public persons. For the reasons stated below, we conclude that the state interest in compensating injury to the reputation of private individuals requires that a different rule should obtain with respect to them. . . .

. . . [W]e have no difficulty in distinguishing among defamation plaintiffs. The first remedy of any victim of defamation is self-help—using available opportunities to contradict the lie or correct the error and thereby to minimize its adverse impact on reputation. Public officials and public figures usually enjoy significantly greater access to the channels of effective communication and hence have a more realistic opportunity to counteract false statements than private individuals normally enjoy. Private individuals are therefore more vulnerable to injury, and the state interest in protecting them is correspondingly greater.

More important than the likelihood that private individuals will lack effective opportunities for rebuttal, there is a compelling normative consideration underlying the distinction between public and private defamation plaintiffs. An individual who decides to seek governmental office must accept certain necessary consequences of that involvement in public affairs. He runs the risk of closer public scrutiny than might otherwise be the case. And society's interest in the officers of government is not strictly limited to the formal discharge of official duties. . . .

Those classed as public figures stand in a similar position. Hypothetically, it may be possible for someone to become a public figure through no purposeful action of his own, but the instances of truly involuntary public figures must be exceedingly rare. . . .

We hold that, so long as they do not impose liability without fault, the States may define for themselves the appropriate standard of liability for a publisher or broadcaster of defamatory falsehood injurious to a private individual. . . .

Our accommodation of the competing values at stake in defamation suits by private individuals allows the States to impose liability on the publisher or broadcaster of defamatory falsehood on a less demanding showing than that required by *New York Times*. . . . But this countervailing state interest extends no further than compensation for actual injury. . . [W]e hold that the States may not permit recovery of presumed or punitive damages, at least when liability is not based on a showing of knowledge of falsity or reckless disregard for the truth. . . .

We therefore conclude that the *New York Times* standard is inapplicable to this case and that the trial court erred in entering judgment for respondent. Because the jury was allowed to impose liability without fault and was permitted to presume damages without proof of injury, a new trial is necessary. We reverse and remand for further proceedings in accord with this opinion.

*It is so ordered.*

Mr. Justice Blackmun, concurring. . . .
Mr. Chief Justice Burger, dissenting. . . .
Mr. Justice Douglas, dissenting. . . .
Mr. Justice Brennan, dissenting. . . .
Mr. Justice White, dissenting. . . .

While Justice Powell stated that "the New York Times standard is inapplicable to this case," he said that in order to recover presumed or punitive damages there must be a showing of "knowledge of falsity or reckless disregard for the truth." And this, of course, *is* the New York Times standard. Further, in the determination of "actual injury," Powell stated that it was not limited to "out-of-pocket loss." "Indeed, the more customary types of actual harm inflicted by defamatory falsehood include impairment of reputation and standing in the community, personal humiliation, and mental anguish and suffering." This would appear to allow substantial latitude for jury discretion in awarding damages for "actual injury." In addition, the opinion disavowed application of the *Rosenbloom* plurality's "public or general interest" test. Thus private persons, under *Gertz*, presumably would only need to prove negligence on the part of the publisher—the failure to exercise normal care—to receive compensation for actual injury.

The *Gertz* rule was applied in *Time, Inc.* v. *Firestone*, 424 U.S. 448 (1976), although the case was remanded for reconsideration. Mary Alice Firestone sued her husband, "the scion of one of America's wealthier families," for separate maintenance. Her husband filed a counterclaim for divorce on grounds of extreme cruelty and adultery. A Florida Circuit Court granted the divorce. Although there was discussion of the allegations of adultery in the court's final judgment, there was some ambiguity concerning the actual finding on this point. *Time* magazine published a report stating that the divorce was granted "on grounds of extreme cruelty and adultery." The former wife demanded a retraction, but *Time* declined. She sued for libel and won a judgment for $100,000, and the Florida Supreme Court affirmed. The United States Supreme Court reversed and remanded. The majority held that Mary Alice Firestone was not a "public figure" because she did not meet the *Gertz* tests of occupying a role "of especial prominence in the affairs of society," nor had she "thrust [herself] to the forefront of particular public controversies in order to influence the resolution of the issues involved." Thus, the *New York Times* standard did not apply. The *Gertz* decision does state, however, that liability cannot be imposed without fault, and the Court did not discover in the opinions of the various Florida courts a specific finding of fault on the part of *Time* magazine. The judgment was reversed and the case remanded for reconsideration and a finding on the issue of negligence.

An interesting aspect of the defamation problem resulted from Senator William Proxmire's practice of designating his "Golden Fleece of the Month Award" for what he considered to be egregiously wasteful spending under various federal grant programs. One such award was made to the National Science Foundation, the National Aeronautics and Space Administration, and the Office of Naval Research for spending almost half a million dollars to fund a behavioral scientist's research to investigate the behavior patterns of animals (particularly monkeys) such as the clenching of their jaws when exposed to aggravating stressful stimuli. The award was announced by the Senator and later incorporated in a widely distributed press release, was referred to in newsletters sent out by the Senator, and was mentioned in a television interview program on which he appeared. The scientist, Ronald Hutchinson, sued for defamation, contending that he had suffered loss of respect in his profession and a loss of income and the ability to earn income in the future. The lower federal courts held that Hutchinson was a "public figure" and also that the Speech and Debate Clause protected Proxmire's comments in the press release and newsletters. Further, there was no showing of "malice" in the statements made on television, and thus Hutchinson as a public figure could not recover damages. In *Hutchinson* v. *Proxmire*, 443 U.S. 111 (1979), the Court reversed and remanded, holding that despite Hutchinson's professional reputation as a scientist, he could not properly be considered a public figure, and the Senator's immunity under the Speech or Debate Clause of the Constitution did not extend to remarks published in the newsletter or the press release or delivered over television.

In *Dun & Bradstreet* v. *Greenmoss Builders,* 472 U.S. 749 (1984), the Court reworked *Gertz* and seemingly resurrected a portion of *Rosenbloom.* Dun & Bradstreet, a credit reporting agency, sent a report to five subscribers indicating that Greenmoss had filed a voluntary petition for bankruptcy. The report was false and grossly misrepresented Greenmoss's assets and liabilities. Thereafter, the agency issued a corrective notice, but Greenmoss was dissatisfied and brought a defamation action in a Vermont state court seeking damages. The jury awarded both compensatory or presumed damages and punitive damages. But the trial court granted a new trial on the ground that the instructions to the jury permitted it to award damages on a lesser showing than "actual malice," as it believed was required by *Gertz.* The Vermont Supreme Court reversed, holding that *Gertz* was inapplicable to nonmedia defamation actions. The United States Supreme Court affirmed, although on a different rationale. Justice Powell, who had written the opinion for the Court in *Gertz,* also wrote the majority opinion here. He opened with the statement:

> In *Gertz* v. *Robert Welch, Inc.* . . . we held that the First Amendment restricted the damages that a private individual could obtain from a publisher for a libel *that involved a matter of public concern.* [Emphasis supplied.] More specifically, we held that in these circumstances the First Amendment prohibited awards of presumed and punitive damages for false and defamatory statements unless the plaintiff shows "actual malice," that is, knowledge of falsity or reckless disregard for the truth. The question presented in this case is whether this rule of *Gertz* applies when the false and defamatory statements do not involve matters of public concern.

In fact, Powell's opinion in *Gertz* in no way ties the actual malice requirement to "matters of public concern." Thus *Dun & Bradstreet* gives a new twist to the *Gertz* rule. The opinion proceeds, however, to state that *Gertz* is inapplicable because the agency's credit report "concerns no public issue," and the plaintiff is in the category of a private person. The emphasis in the opinion, however, was on the type of speech involved: "There is simply no credible argument that this type of credit reporting requires special protection to ensure that 'debate on public issues [will] be uninhibited, robust, and wide-open.' *New York Times Co.* v. *Sullivan.*"

## HUSTLER MAGAZINE *v.* JERRY FALWELL
### 56 LW 4180 (1988)

[The inside front cover of the November, 1983, issue of Hustler Magazine featured a "parody" of an advertisement for Campari Liqueur that contained the name and picture of Jerry Falwell, a nationally known minister who has been active as a commentator on politics and public affairs. The ad was entitled "Jerry Falwell talks about his first time." This parody was modeled after actual Campari ads that included interviews with various celebrities about their "first times." Although it was apparent by the end of each interview that this meant the first time they sampled Campari, the ads clearly played on the sexual double entendre of the general subject of "first times." Copying the form and layout of these Campari ads, Hustler's editors chose Falwell as the featured celebrity and drafted an alleged "interview" with him in which he states that his "first time" was during a drunken incestuous rendezvous with his mother in an outhouse. The Hustler parody portrays him and his mother as drunk and immoral, and suggests that he is a hypocrite who preaches only when he is drunk. In small print at the bottom of the page, the ad contains the disclaimer, "ad parody—not to be taken seriously."

Falwell sued the magazine and its publisher, Larry Flynt, to recover damages for, *inter alia,* libel and intentional infliction of emotional distress. The jury found for the defendants on the libel claim but found for Falwell on the emotional distress claim and awarded $100,000 in compensatory damages, as well as $50,000 in punitive damages from each defendant. The Court of Appeals affirmed.]

Chief Justice Rehnquist delivered the opinion of the Court. . . .

This case presents us with a novel question involving First Amendment limitations upon a State's authority to protect its citizens from the intentional infliction of emotional distress. We must decide whether a public figure may recover damages for emotional harm caused by the publication of an ad parody offensive to him, and doubtless gross and repugnant in the eyes of most. Respondent would have us find that a State's interest in protecting public figures from emotional distress is sufficient to deny First Amendment protection to speech that is patently offensive and is intended to inflict emotional injury, even when that speech could not reasonably have been interpreted as stating actual facts about the public figure involved. This we decline to do. . . .

The sort of robust political debate encouraged by the First Amendment is bound to produce speech that is critical of those who hold public office or those public figures who are "intimately involved in the resolution of important public questions or, by reason of their fame, shape events in areas of concern to society at large." . . . Justice Frankfurter put it succinctly . . . when he said that "[o]ne of the prerogatives of American citizenship is the right to criticize public men and measures." Such criticism, inevitably, will not always be reasoned or moderate; public figures as well as public officials will be subject to "vehement, caustic, and sometimes unpleasantly sharp attacks." . . . "[T]he candidate who vaunts his spotless record and sterling integrity cannot convincingly cry 'Foul!' when an opponent or an industrious reporter attempts to demonstrate the contrary." *Monitor Patriot Co.* v. *Roy.* . . . .

Of course, this does not mean that *any* speech about a public figure is immune from sanction in the form of damages. Since *New York Times Co.* v. *Sullivan,* we have consistently ruled that a public figure may hold a speaker liable for the damage to reputation caused by publication of a defamatory falsehood, but only if the statement was made "with knowledge that it was false or with reckless disregard of whether it was false or not." . . . False statements of fact are particularly valueless;

they interfere with the truth-seeking function of the marketplace of ideas, and they cause damage to an individual's reputation that cannot easily be repaired by counter-speech, however persuasive or effective. . . . But even though falsehoods have little value in and of themselves, they are "nevertheless inevitable in free debate," and a rule that would impose strict liability on a publisher for false factual assertions would have an undoubted "chilling" effect on speech relating to public figures that does have constitutional value. "Freedoms of expression require 'breathing space.' " . . . This breathing space is provided by a constitutional rule that allows public figures to recover the libel or defamation only when they can prove *both* that the statement was false and that the statement was made with the requisite level of culpability.

Respondent argues, however, that a different standard should apply in this case because here the State seeks to prevent not reputational damage, but the severe emotional distress suffered by the person who is the subject of an offensive publication. . . . In respondent's view, and in the view of the Court of Appeals, so long as the utterance was intended to inflict emotional distress, was outrageous, and did in fact inflict serious emotional distress, it is of no constitutional import whether the statement was a fact or an opinion, or whether it was true or false. It is the intent to cause injury that is the gravamen of the tort, and the State's interest in preventing emotional harm simply outweighs whatever interest a speaker may have in speech of this type.

Generally speaking the law does not regard the intent to inflict emotional distress as one which should receive much solicitude, and it is quite understandable that most if not all jurisdictions have chosen to make it civilly culpable where the conduct in question is sufficiently "outrageous." But in the world of debate about public affairs, many things done with motives that are less than admirable are protected by the First Amendment. . . . Thus while such a bad motive may be deemed controlling for purposes of tort liability in other areas of the law, we think the First Amendment prohibits such a result in the area of public debate about public figures.

Were we to hold otherwise, there can be little doubt that political cartoonists and satirists would be subjected to damages awards without any showing that their work falsely defamed its subject. . . . The appeal of the political cartoon or caricature is often based on exploration of unfortunate physical traits or politically embarrassing events—an exploration often calculated to injure the feelings of the subject of the portrayal. The art of the cartoonist is often not reasoned or evenhanded, but slashing and one-sided. . . .

Respondent contends, however, that the caricature in question here was so "outrageous" as to distinguish it from more tradtional political cartoons. There is no doubt that the caricature of respondent and his mother published in Hustler is at best a distant cousin of the political cartoons described above, and a rather poor relation at that. If it were possible by laying down a principled standard to separate the one from the other, public discourse would probably suffer little or no harm. But we doubt that there is any such standard, and we are quite sure that the pejorative description "outrageous" does not supply one. "Outrageousness" in the area of political and social discourse has an inherent subjectiveness about it which would allow a jury to impose liability on the basis of the jurors' tastes or views, or perhaps on the basis of their dislike of a particular expression. An "outrageousness" standard thus runs afoul of our longstanding refusal to allow damages to be awarded because the speech in question may have an adverse emotional impact on the audience. . . .

Here it is clear that respondent Falwell is a "public figure" for purposes of First Amendment law. The jury found against respondent on his libel claim when it decided that the Hustler ad parody could not "reasonably be understood as describing actual facts about [respondent] or actual events in which [he] participated." . . . The Court of Appeals interpreted the jury's finding to be that the ad parody "was not reasonably believable," . . . and in accordance with our custom we accept this finding. Respondent is thus relegated to his claim for damages awarded by the jury for the intentional infliction of emotional distress by "outrageous" conduct. But for reasons heretofore stated this claim cannot, consistently with the First Amendment, form a basis for the award of damages when the conduct in question is the publication of a caricature such as the ad parody involved here. The judgment of the Court of Appeals is accordingly

*Reversed.*

Justice Kennedy took no part in the consideration or decision of this case.

Justice White, concurring in the judgment. . . .

Cox Broadcasting Corporation v. Cohn, 420 U.S. 469 (1975), involved the question of the liability of a television newsman who had broadcast the identity of a rape victim. A Georgia statute made it a misdemeanor to publish or broadcast the name of any rape victim. The reporter attended the trial of the persons charged with the rape and murder of a seventeen-year-old girl and learned the name of the girl from the indictments, which were public records. Later that day, he broadcast a news report of the proceedings, during which he named the victim of the crime. The father of the victim sued for money damages. The Georgia Supreme Court held that the name of a rape victim was not a matter of public concern and that the statute was a legitimate limitation on the First Amendment's right of expression. On appeal, the United States Supreme Court reversed. Justice White, for the majority, stated that public records are of interest to those concerned with the administration of government, "and a public benefit is performed by the reporting of the true contents of the records by the media." He stated further that the "States may not impose sanctions for the publication of truthful information contained in official court records open to public inspection."

## Handbills, Posters, and Commercial Advertising

The earlier cases involving restraints on the distribution of handbills were largely decided on the basis that such limitations constituted prior restraints on free speech and press. Justice Frankfurter gives a brief résumé of the cases in his concurring opinion in Kunz v. New York, 340 U.S. 290 (1951):

The easiest cases have been those in which the only interest opposing free communication was that of keeping the streets of the community clean. This could scarcely justify prohibiting the dissemination of information by handbills or censoring their contents. In *Lovell* v. *City of Griffin*, 303 U.S. 444 (1937), an ordinance requiring a permit to distribute pamphlets was held invalid where the licensing standard was "not limited to ways which might be regarded as inconsistent with the maintenance of public order or as involving disorderly conduct, the molestation of the inhabitants, or the misuse or littering of the streets." . . . In *Hague* v. *C.I.O.*, 307 U.S. 496 (1939), a portion of the ordinance declared invalid prohibited the distribution of pamphlets. In *Schneider* v. *New Jersey, Town of Irvington*, 308 U.S. 147 (1939), three of the four ordinances declared invalid by the Court prohibited the distribution of pamphlets. In *Jamison* v. *Texas*, 318 U.S. 413 (1943), the Court again declared invalid a municipal ordinance prohibiting the distribution of all handbills.

In *Talley* v. *California*, 362 U.S. 60 (1960), the Court reviewed the conviction of appellant who was convicted in a Los Angeles Municipal Court for violating a municipal ordinance making it a criminal offense to distribute "any handbill in any place under any circumstances," unless it had printed on it the names and addresses of the persons who prepared, distributed, or sponsored it. The Court divided six-to-three in reversing the conviction. Justice Black, speaking for the Court, found the ordinance void on its face, citing *Lovell* v. *Griffin,* Counsel for the state urged that the ordinance was aimed at providing a way to identify those responsible for fraud, false advertising, and libel. Justice Black stated, however, that "the ordinance is in no manner so limited, nor have we been referred to any legislative history indicating such a purpose." He stated further:

There can be no doubt that such an identification requirement would tend to restrict freedom to distribute information and thereby freedom of expression. . . .

Anonymous pamphlets, leaflets, brochures and even books have played an important role in the progress of mankind. Persecuted groups and sects from time to time throughout history have been able to criticize oppressive practices and laws either anonymously or not at all. . . .

We have recently had occasion to hold in two cases that there are times and circumstances when States may not compel members of groups engaged in the dissemination of ideas to be publicly identified. *Bates* v. *Little Rock* . . . ; *National Association for Advancement of Colored People* v. *Alabama,* . . . The reason for those holdings was that identification and fear of reprisal might deter perfectly peaceful discussions of public matters of importance. This broad Los Angeles ordinance is subject to the same infirmity. We hold that it, like the Griffin, Georgia, ordinance, is void on its face.

Justice Clark, joined by Justices Frankfurter and Whittaker, dissented. He pointed out that Talley had made no showing that a restraint upon his freedom of speech would result from the enforcement of the ordinance and concluded that "the substantiality of Los Angeles' interest in the enforcement of the ordinance sustains its validity." He also stated that the case was controlled by prior decisions in which "this Court has approved laws requiring no less than Los Angeles' ordinance:" one upholding an Act of Congress requiring newspapers using the second-class mails to publish the names of their editors, publishers, and owners; a second upholding the Federal Regulation of Lobbying Act requiring registration; and, third, the stated policy of a majority of states prohibiting the anonymous distribution of materials relating to candidates and elections.

In *Los Angeles City Council* v. *Taxpayers for Vincent,* 466 U.S. 789 (1984), the Court upheld a Los Angeles ordinance prohibiting the posting of signs on public property against a claim that posting campaign signs on public utility poles was protected by the First Amendment. Justice Stevens, for the majority, stated:

It is true that the esthetic interest in preventing the kind of litter that may result from the distribution of leaflets on the public streets and sidewalks cannot support a prophylactic prohibition against the citizen's exercise of that method of expressing his views. In *Schneider* v. *State* . . . (1939), the Court held that ordinances that absolutely prohibited handbilling on the streets were invalid. . . . Taxpayers contend that their interest in supporting Vincent's political campaign, which affords them a constitutional right to distribute brochures and leaflets on the public streets of Los Angeles, provides equal support for their asserted right to post temporary signs on objects adjacent to the streets and sidewalks. They argue that the mere fact that their temporary signs "add somewhat" to the city's visual clutter is entitled to no more weight than the temporary unsightliness of discarded handbills and the additional street cleaning burden that were insufficient to justify the ordinances reviewed in *Schneider.* . . .

With respect to signs posted by appellees, however, it is the tangible medium of expressing the message that has the adverse impact on the appearance of the landscape. . . . Here, the substantive evil—visual blight—is not merely a possible by-product of the activity, but is created by the medium of expression itself. In contrast to *Schneider*, therefore, the application of ordinance in this case responds precisely to the substantive problem which legitimately concerns the City. The ordinance curtails no more speech than is necessary to accomplish its purpose.

In an earlier period the Court tended to afford less protection to commercial speech than to noncommercial speech. Despite the broad safeguards provided for distribution of handbills, for example, *Valentine* v. *Chrestensen*, 316 U.S. 52 (1942), upheld an ordinance which prohibited distribution of commercial and advertising matter in the streets. The ordinance, however, made an exception for literature devoted to "information" or to public matters. (The effort to circumvent the ordinance by printing on the reverse side of the handbills a protest against the city dock department for refusing wharfage facilities for conducting tours of a former navy submarine was denied.) The Court unanimously upheld the ordinance, clearly differentiating between the State's power to proscribe the dissemination of information and opinion and its power to regulate commercial advertising.

More recently the Court has moved strongly in the direction of affording more nearly equal protection for commercial speech. Publishers of books and newspapers are, after all, normally seeking to make a profit. They are engaged in a commercial enterprise, and the "free press" is not really free—one must pay for it. Nonetheless, the First Amendment is clearly applicable to protect those operations. And the Court has gradually extended the protection to other kinds of commercial speech or advertising as well. In *Virginia State Board of Pharmacy* v. *Virginia Citizens Consumer Council, Inc.*, 425 U.S. 748 (1976), the Court held unconstitutional a Virginia statute which prohibited pharmacists from advertising prices of prescription drugs. The suit was brought by consumers rather than by pharmacists, but the Court held that there was a First Amendment right of pharmacists to engage in truthful, nondeceptive advertising, and "If there is a right to advertise, there is a reciprocal right to receive the advertising, and it may be asserted by these appellees." Thus, commercial speech, while subject to reasonable regulation, is not wholly outside the protection of the First and Fourteenth Amendments. In a footnote to the majority opinion, however, it was stated that no opinion was being expressed as to regulations of commercial advertising by other professions, such as physicians and lawyers, which "render professional *services* of almost infinite variety and nature, with the consequent enhanced possibility for confusion and deception if they were to undertake certain kinds of advertising."

In the following year, despite those cautionary remarks, the Court upheld the right of lawyers to advertise. Two lawyers advertised in newspapers that they were offering "legal services at very reasonable fees," and listed their fees for a variety of services. They were suspended for one week, and the Supreme Court of Arizona rejected their claims that the action violated their First Amendment rights. In *Bates* v. *State Bar of Arizona*, 433 U.S. 350 (1977), the Court by a five-to-four vote reversed on authority of *Virginia Pharmacy.* Three of the dissenters expressed fear that permitting such advertisements would be injurious to the public and would result in inherently misleading advertisements. Justice Rehnquist argued that commercial advertising was not the sort of expression that the First Amendment was adopted to protect. "The *Valentine* distinction was constitutionally sound and practically workable, and I am still unwilling to take even one step down the 'slippery slope' away from it."

In *Linmark Associates, Inc.* v. *Willingboro*, 431 U.S. 85 (1977), the Court unanimously held invalid a municipal ordinance prohibiting the posting of "For Sale" or "Sold" signs in the township. The ordinance was designed to stop what was perceived as the flight of white homeowners from the racially integrated community of Willingboro. Justice Marshall, for the Court could find "no meaningful distinction" between the ordinance and the statute overturned in *Virginia Pharmacy.*

Special problems have arisen with respect to speech and handbill activities in privately owned "company towns" and in privately owned shopping centers, both of which are generally open to the public. In *Marsh* v. *Alabama,* 326 U.S. 501 (1946), the Court reversed a trespass conviction of a Jehovah's Witness who undertook to distribute religious literature on a sidewalk near a post office on property owned by the Gulf Shipbuilding Corporation. The majority opinion pointed out that there was nothing to distinguish the town and its shopping district from any other town and shopping center except the fact that the title to the property belonged to a private corporation. To apply trespass law to one distributing religious literature in such an area was held to violate his First and Fourteenth Amendment rights.

In *Amalgamated Food Employees Union* v. *Logan Valley Plaza,* 391 U.S. 308 (1968), the Court extended the rationale of *Marsh* to peaceful picketing of a store, located in a large shopping center, by nonemployees who were protesting the fact that the store was employing a wholly nonunion staff. The opinion, however, noted that the scope of the holding was limited and added, "We are, therefore, not called upon to consider whether respondents' property rights could, consistently with the First Amendment, justify a bar on picketing which was not thus directly related in its purpose to the use to which the shopping center property was being put."

The question of the right to deliver handbills in a privately owned shopping center came to the court in *Lloyd Corporation* v. *Tanner,* 407 U.S. 551 (1972). The respondents attempted to distribute handbills, which invited the public to a meeting to protest the draft and the Vietnam War, in the interior mall area of a large privately owned shopping center. The owner had a strict no-handbilling rule, and his security guards requested the respondents, under threat of arrest, to stop the distribution. They then secured an injunction from a United States District Court in Oregon against interference with their continued distribution of noncommercial handbills in a peaceful and orderly manner in areas open to general public access. The Court of Appeals affirmed, but the Supreme Court reversed and remanded with directions to vacate the injunction. In an opinion by Justice Powell for five members of the Court, it was held that while generally open to the public, the shopping center was not so dedicated to public use as to require the shopping center owner to permit handbilling in the center which was unrelated to the shopping center's operations. *Marsh* was distinguished on the ground that it involved a company town which had all the attributes of a municipality. *Logan Valley* was distinguished on the ground that the picketing there was designed to convey a message to patrons of a particular store, so located as to preclude other reasonable access to patrons of the store. The dissenters argued that the mall was the functional equivalent of a public business district, and that the First Amendment protected the right to distribute handbills. Justice Marshall, for the dissenters, stated, "As I read the opinion of the Court, it is an attack not only on the rationale of *Logan Valley,* but also on this Court's longstanding decision in *Marsh* v. *Alabama.*"

Any doubt as to the continued vitality of *Logan Valley* was removed in 1976 when the Court overruled that decision in *Hudgens* v. *N. L. R. B.,* 424 U.S. 507. Striking warehouse employees, who were members of a union, started to picket their employer's retail store located in a privately owned shopping center. They departed, however, when an agent of the owner of the shopping center threatened that they would be arrested for trespassing. The union then filed an unfair labor charge with the N.L.R.B., alleging interference with the employees' rights under the N.L.R.B. Relying on *Logan Valley* in addition to the Act, the Board held that union members could not be enjoined from exercising their First Amendment right to picket in a shopping center which was the equivalent of a municipality's business district. The Court of Appeals enforced the Board's cease-and-desist order, holding that the Board had met the requirement of *Lloyd Corp.* v. *Tanner* of proving that less intrusive locations for picketing were either unavailable or ineffective.

On certiorari, the Supreme Court reversed and remanded. The majority opinion indicated that a large self-contained shopping center was not the functional equivalent of a municipality, and therefore the First and Fourteenth Amendments had no application to this case. It stated further that the *Lloyd* case amounted to a total rejection of *Logan Valley*, and the striking employees in the case at bar "did not have a First Amendment right to enter this shopping center for the purpose of advertising their strike." It followed that the rights and liabilities of the parties were dependent exclusively upon the Labor Relations Act, and the case was remanded to the Board for a determination of those issues.

An interesting reversal of the problem of shopping center access was presented in *PruneYard Shopping Center* v. *Robins,* 447 U.S. 74 (1980), in which the Court held that a California Supreme Court decision requiring access to a shopping center for the exercise of the rights of expression and petition did not violate the owner's First, Fifth, or Fourteenth Amendment rights. High school students seeking to solicit support for their opposition to a United Nations resolution set up a table in a corner of the central courtyard of a shopping center in California and passed out pamphlets and asked passersby to sign a petition addressed to the president and members of Congress. A security guard informed them that their project was in violation of the shopping center's policy and directed them to cease. The California Supreme Court held that the state constitution's provisions regarding the right of free expression and the right to petition the government for redress of grievances entitled the high school students to conduct their activity on shopping center property, and that such construction of the constitution did not violate the owner's property rights under the Federal Constitution. The United States Supreme Court affirmed, holding that the decision did not amount to a "taking" of the owner's property nor did it violate the shopping center owner's free speech rights under the First and Fourteenth Amendments as forcing him to use his property as a forum for the speech of others, since the views expressed by members of the public in passing out pamphlets and seeking signatures would not likely be identified with those of the owner. Justice Marshall, concurring, said that in light of recent decisions of the Court wrongly prohibiting access to private shopping centers for the exercise of free expression rights, "I applaud the court's decision, which is a part of a very healthy trend of affording state constitutional provisions a more expansive interpretation than this Court has given to the Federal Constitution." Justice White also concurred, but pointed out that the U.S. Constitution does not *require* a shopping center owner to permit distributions or solicitations on his property, and that insofar as the Constitution is concerned, a State may decline to construe its own constitution so as to limit the property rights of a shopping center owner.

### A "Right of Reply" and Problems of the Broadcast Media

In 1973 the State of Florida adopted a "right of reply" statute which provided that if a candidate for nomination or election was assailed regarding his personal character or official record by any newspaper, the candidate had the right to demand that the newspaper print, free of cost to the candidate, any reply the candidate might make to the newspaper's charges. The reply had to appear in as conspicuous a place and in the same kind of type as the charges which prompted the reply, provided it did not take up more space than the charges. Failure to comply with the statute constituted a first-degree misdemeanor. In *Miami Herald Publishing Company* v. *Tornillo,* 418 U.S. 241 (1974), the Court held unanimously that the statute violated the First Amendment guarantee of a free press. [See Jerome A. Barron, *Freedom of the Press for Whom?* (Bloomington, Ind.: Indiana Univ. Press, 1973), and Francisco J. Lewels, "Restoring the Free Marketplace: Minority Access to the Media," 4 *Policy Studies Journal* 103 (1975).]

Controls over radio and television broadcasting are treated differently from the press since frequencies and channels are limited in number. The Federal Communications Act established the Federal Communications Commission and gave it authority to license stations and to adopt regulations concerning their operation. One policy of the FCC, the "fairness doctrine," requires that licensees devote some reasonable portion of air time to coverage of public issues and also provide an opportunity for presentation of contrasting points of view. The FCC additionally ruled that when personal attacks or political editorials were broadcast, the station must notify the persons involved and allow time over the station to respond. This rule was very similar to that challenged in the *Tornillo* case. In *Red Lion Broadcasting Co.* v. *Federal Communications Commission,* 395 U.S. 367 (1969), the Court upheld the fairness regulations, including the right-of-reply rule. In *Accuracy in Media* v. *NBC,* 516 F.2d 1101 (CA DC, 1974), however, a Court of Appeals for the District of Columbia reversed an FCC ruling requiring NBC to provide opportunity for the plaintiffs to present views in opposition to those expressed in an NBC documentary on the evils of private pension systems. The Supreme Court denied review. Despite *Red Lion,* then, the present status of radio and television broadcasting may be closer to the view expressed in *Tornillo.*

An aspect of the issue involving access to radio and television time was presented in a group of four cases, with the decision coming under *Columbia Broadcasting System* v. *Democratic National Committee,* 412 U.S. 94 (1973). The Federal Communications Commission had rejected contentions that the general policy of certain radio and television broadcast licensees of not selling any editorial advertising time to individuals or groups wishing to speak out on public issues violated the Federal Communications Act of 1934 and the First Amendment. The contentions were asserted in actions instituted by a national organization of businessmen opposed to United States involvement in Vietnam and by the Democratic National Committee. The complainants had argued that responsible individuals and groups had a right to purchase advertising time to comment on public issues without regard to whether the broadcaster had complied with the Commission's "fairness doctrine" requiring that a broadcaster provide adequate coverage of public issues, fairly reflecting differing viewpoints. The Court of Appeals reversed the Commission and remanded to the Commission to develop regulations governing the airing of editorial advertisements. The opinion stated that "a flat ban on paid public issue announcements is in violation of the First Amendment, at least when other sorts of paid announcements are accepted." The Supreme Court reversed, holding that neither the Communications Act nor the First Amendment requires broadcasters to accept paid editorial advertisements. Chief Justice Burger, speaking for six members of the Court, stated that great weight must be afforded to the decisions of Congress and the experience of the FCC. He noted that Congress has consistently rejected efforts to impose on broadcasters a "common carrier" right of access for all persons wishing to speak out on public issues. Instead, it reposed in the FCC regulatory authority by which the fairness doctrine was evolved to require that the broadcaster's coverage of important public issues must be adequate and must fairly reflect differing viewpoints. No private individual or group, therefore, has a right to command the use of broadcast facilities. Further, the FCC was justified in concluding that the public interest in having access to the marketplace of "ideas and experience" would not be served by ordering a right of access to advertising time. There is a substantial risk that such a system would be monopolized by those who were wealthy, and the public accountability which now rests with the broadcaster would be diluted.

Justice Brennan, joined by Justice Marshall, dissented. He stated that the First Amendment must be construed to safeguard "not only the right of the public to *hear* debate, but also the right of individuals to *participate* in that debate and to attempt to persuade others to their points of view. He pointed out that as the system now operates, any person wishing to market beer, soap, toothpaste, or deodorant has direct, personal, and instantaneous access to the electronic media. But a similar individual "seeking to discuss war, peace, pollution, or the suffering of the poor is denied this right to speak." He felt that the differential treatment accorded "commercial" and "controversial" speech clearly violated the First Amendment. [See Louis L. Jaffe, "The Editorial Responsibility of the Broadcaster: Reflections on Fairness and Access," 85 *Harv. L. Rev.* 768 (1972).]

One section of the Federal Communications Act, as amended in 1971 by the Federal Election Campaign Act, allows the FCC to revoke a broadcaster's license for willful failure to allow "reasonable access to or to permit purchase of reasonable amounts of time for the use of a broadcasting station" by a candidate for federal elective office. In October, 1979, the Carter-Mondale Committee requested each of the three major television networks to provide time for a 30-minute program. The networks declined, primarily on the ground that it was too early to begin a presidential campaign. The FCC ruled that the networks had violated the statute. In *CBS, Inc.* v. *FCC*, 453 U.S. 367 (1981), the Court upheld the FCC rule and rejected the network's First Amendment challenge to the statute as applied. [See Annotation, "First Amendment Guaranty of Free Speech and Press as Applied to Licensing and Regulation of Broadcast Media," 69 L Ed2d 1110 (1981).]

An act of Congress (18 USC §1464) prohibits the use of "any obscene, indecent, or profane language by means of radio communications." A radio station of Pacifica Foundation made an afternoon broadcast of a satiric monologue, entitled "Filthy Words," by George Carlin. The monologue listed and repeated a variety of colloquial uses of "words you couldn't say on the public airwaves." A complaint was filed by a listener to the Federal Communications Commission. The FCC did not impose formal sanctions, but issued a declaratory order granting the complaint and stated that the order would be filed with the station's license file to be considered in the event that future complaints were received. In *FCC* v. *Pacifica Foundation*, 438 U.S. 726 (1978), the Court upheld the FCC's finding that the monolgue was "indecent," and the order was not violative of the First Amendment. Of all forms of communication, "it is broadcasting that has received the most limited First Amendment protection." The broadcast media have established "a uniquely pervasive presence in the lives of all Americans" and confront the citizen not only in public, but also in the privacy of the home. Further, broadcasting is uniquely accessible to children, even those too young to read. (Students who have a scholarly interest in the content of the monologue may find it in an Appendix to the Opinion of the Court at 438 U.S. 751.)

The Public Broadcasting Act of 1967 established the Corporation for Public Broadcasting (CPB), a nonprofit corporation, to allocate federal funds to noncommercial television and radio stations for educational programming. Section 399 of the Act forbids any such station to "engage in editorializing." Various plaintiffs brought an action in federal court challenging the constitutionality of the prohibition. The District Court granted summary judgment, holding that the section violated the First Amendment. In *FCC* v. *League of Women Voters of California*, 468 U.S. 364 (1984), the Court affirmed on direct appeal. The Government argued that the ban was necessary, first, to protect noncommercial educational broadcasting stations from being coerced, as a result of federal financing, into becoming vehicles for government propagandizing; and, second, to keep these stations from becoming convenient targets for capture by private interest groups wishing to express their own partisan viewpoints. Justice Brennan, for the five-member majority, pointed out that the CPB stations air a wide variety of programs addressing controversial issues. The ban is not directed to such programs; instead it is directed solely at the expression of editorial opinion by local station management. He stated:

[T]he manifest imprecision of the ban imposed by §399 reveals that its proscription is not sufficiently tailored to the harms it seeks to prevent to justify its substantial interference with broadcasters' speech. Section 399 includes within its grip a potentially infinite variety of speech, most of which would not be related in any way to governmental affairs, political candidacies or elections. Indeed, the breadth of editorial commentary is as wide as human imagination permits. But the Government never explains how, say, an editorial by local station management urging improvements in a town's parks or museums will so infuriate Congress or other Federal officials that the future of public broadcasting will be imperiled unless such editorials are suppressed. Nor is it explained how the suppression of editorials alone serves to reduce the risk of governmental retaliation and interference when it is clear that station management is fully able to broadcast controversial views so long as such views are not labelled as its own.

In conclusion, he stated that the specific interests sought to be advanced by the ban "are either not sufficiently substantial or are not served in a sufficiently limited manner to justify the substantial abridgement of important journalistic freedoms which the First Amendment jealously protects."
[See generally, Richard E. Labunski, *The First Amendment Under Siege: The Politics of Broadcast Regulation* (Westport, Conn.: Greenwood Press, 1981).]

### Censorship of Public School Newspapers

HAZELWOOD SCHOOL DISTRICT *v.* KUHLMEIER
*56 LW 4079 (1988)*

[Respondents, former high school students who were staff members of the school's newspaper *Spectrum,* filed suit in Federal District Court against the school district and school officials, alleging that respondents' First Amendment rights were violated by the deletion from a certain issue of the paper of two pages that included an article describing school students' experiences with pregnancy and another article discussing the impact of divorce on students at the school. The newspaper was written and edited by a journalism class as part of the school's curriculum. Pursuant to the school's practice, the teacher in charge of the paper submitted page proofs to the school's principal who objected to the pregnancy story because the pregnant students, although not named, might be identified from the text, and because he believed that the article's references to sexual activity and birth control were inappropriate for some of the younger students. The principal objected to the divorce article because the page proofs he was furnished identified by name (deleted by the teacher from the final version) a student who complained of her father's conduct, and the principal believed that the student's parents should have been given an opportunity to respond to the remarks or to consent to their publication. Believing that there was no time to make necessary changes in the articles if the paper was to be issued before the end of the school year, the principal directed that the pages on which they appeared be withheld from publication even though other, unobjectionable articles were included on such pages. The District Court held that no First Amendment violation had occurred. The Court of Appeals reversed.]

Justice White delivered the opinion of the Court.

This case concerns the extent to which educators may exercise editorial control over the contents of a high school newspaper produced as part of the school's journalism curriculum. . . .

The [Court of Appeals] held at outset that Spectrum was not only a "part of the school adopted curriculum," . . . but also a public forum, because the newspaper was "intended to be and operated as a conduit for student viewpoint." . . . The court then concluded that Spectrum's status as a public forum precluded school officials from censoring its contents except when " 'necessary to avoid material and substantial interference with school work or discipline . . . or the rights of others.' " . . . (quoting *Tinker* v. *Des Moines Independent School Dist.*)

Students in the public schools do not "shed their constitutional rights to freedom of speech or expression at the schoolhouse gate." *Tinker*, . . . They cannot be punished merely for expressing their personal views on the school premises—whether "in the cafeteria, or on the playing field, or on the campus during the authorized hours."—unless school authorities have reason to believe that such expression will "substantially interfere with the work of the school or impinge upon the rights of other students." . . .

We have nonetheless recognized that the First Amendment rights of students in the public schools "are not automatically coextensive with the rights of adults in other settings," *Bethel School District No 403* v. *Fraser* . . . (1986), and must be "applied in light of the special characteristics of the school environment." . . . A school need not tolerate student speech that is inconsistent with its "basic educational mission," *Fraser* . . . , even though the government could not censor similar speech outside the school. Accordingly, we held in *Fraser* that a student could be disciplined for having delivered a speech that was "sexually explicit" but not legally obscene at an official school assembly, because the school was entitled to "dissociate itself" from the speech in a manner that would demonstrate to others that such vulgarity is "wholly inconsistent with the 'fundamental values' of public school education." . . . We thus recognized that "[t]he determination of what manner of speech in the classroom or in school assembly is inappropriate properly rests with the school board" . . . rather than with the federal courts. It is in this context that respondents' First Amendment claims must be considered.

We deal first with the question whether Spectrum may appropriately be characterized as a forum for public expression. The public schools do not possess all of the attributes of streets, parks, and other traditional public forums that "time out of mind, have been used for purposes of assembly, communicating thoughts between citizens, and discussing public question." . . . Hence, school facilities may be deemed to be public forums only if school authorities have "by policy or by practice" opened those facilities "for indiscriminate use by the general public" . . . or by some segment of the public, such as student organization. If the facilities have instead been reserved for other intended purposes, "communicative or otherwise," then no public forum has been created, and school officials may impose reasonable restrictions on the speech of students, teachers, and other members of the school community. . . .

The question whether the First Amendment requires a school to tolerate particular student speech—the question that we addressed in *Tinker*—is different from the question whether the First Amendment requires a school affirmatively to promote particular student speech. The former question addresses educators' ability to silence a student's personal expression that happens to occur on the school premises. The latter question concerns educators' authority over school-sponsored publications, theatrical productions, and other expressive activities that students, parents, and members of the public might reasonably perceive to bear the imprimatur of the school. These activities may fairly be characterized as part of the school curriculum, whether or not they occur in a traditional classroom setting, so long as they are supervised by faculty members and designed to impart particular knowledge or skills to student participants and audiences.

Educators are entitled to exercise greater control over this second form of student expression to assure that participants learn whatever lessons the activity is designed to teach, that readers or listeners are not exposed to material that may be inappropriate for their level of maturity, and that the views of the individual speaker are not erroneously attributed to the school. . . .

Accordingly, we conclude that the standard articulated in *Tinker* for determining when a school may punish student expression need not also be the standard for determining when a school may refuse to lend its name and resources to the dissemination of student expression. Instead, we hold that educators do not offend the First Amendment by exercising editorial control over the style and content of student speech in school-sponsored expressive activities so long as their actions are reasonably related to legitimate pedagogical concerns. . . .

The judgment of the Court of Appeals for the Eighth Circuit is therefore

*Reversed*

Justice Brennan, with whom Justice Marshall and Justice Blackmun join, dissenting. . . .

This Court applied the *Tinker* test just a Term ago in *Fraser, supra,* upholding an official decision to discipline a student for delivering a lewd speech in support of a student-government candidate. The Court today casts no doubt on *Tinker's* vitality. Instead it erects a taxonomy of school censorship, concluding that *Tinker* applies to one category and not another. On the one hand is censorship "to silence a student's personal expression that happens to occur on the school premises." . . . On the other hand is censorship of expression that arises in the context of "school-sponsored . . . expressive activities that students, parents and members of the public might reasonably perceive to bear the imprimatur of the school."

The Court does not, for it cannot, purport to discern from our precedents the distinction it creates. . . .

Even if we were writing on a clean slate, I would reject the Court's rationale for abandoning *Tinker* in this case. The Court offers no more than an obscure tangle of three excuses to afford educators "greater control" over school-sponsored speech than the *Tinker* test would permit: the public educator's prerogative to control curriculum; the pedagogical interest in shielding the high school audience from objectionable viewpoints and sensitive topics; and the school's need to dissociate itself from student expression. . . . None of the excuses, once disentangled, supports the distinction that the Court draws. *Tinker* fully addresses the first concern; the second is illegitimate; and the third is readily achievable through less oppressive means. . . .

## OBSCENITY AND PORNOGRAPHY

Earlier forms of censorship were primarily concerned with stamping out heresy or sedition. More recently, while considerations of security are important, the principal impetus for control of publications and movies is a concern for morality and the prohibition of obscenity. The common-law crime of "obscene libel" developed in England in the early part of the eighteenth century. The established rule of the old common law received its formulation in the opinion of Chief Justice Cockburn in the case of *Regina* v. *Hicklin* (1868), L.R. 3 Q.B. 360. The case dealt with a pamphlet purporting to describe the morals—or lack of morals—of Catholic priests in connection with the confessional. The long title was *The Confessional Unmasked: showing the depravity of the Roman Priesthood, the iniquity of the Confessional and the questions put to females in confession.* It was printed and circulated at cost by an anti-Catholic group which had as its main purpose the election of Protestants to Parliament. The case involved a request for a destruction order, rather than a prosecution, and in allowing the order the Chief Justice laid down the test for obscenity:

I think the test of obscenity is this, whether the tendency of the matter charged as obscenity is to deprave and corrupt those whose minds are open to such immoral influences, and into whose hands a publication of this sort may fall.

This rule has apparently been followed by the English courts down to the enactment of the Obscene Publications Act of 1959, which changed "tendency" to "effect" and omitted the application to "those whose minds are open to such immoral influences." [On the English law generally, see Norman St. John-Stevas, *Obscenity and the Law* (New York: Macmillan, 1956), and John Chandos, ed., *To Deprave and Corrupt* (New York: Association Press, 1962).]

The objection to the *Hicklin* test, of course, is that it fixes a standard for the community's reading matter geared to the feeblest mentality or most suggestible individual in the community. While the test may have been followed to some extent by American judges, it was explicitly rejected in 1933 by federal judge John Woolsey in *United States* v. *One Book Called Ulysses*, 5 F. Supp. 182 (1933), a case involving a customs official's denial of entry of James Joyce's *Ulysses*. [Aff'd. 72 F.2d 705 (1934) by Judges Augustus N. and Learned Hand.] Since then American judges have preferred to use as a standard of judgment the effect of the book upon normal, average, healthy persons.

The United States Supreme Court made a historic decision in 1957 when it ruled squarely for the first time on the subject of the censorship of books. The case was *Butler* v. *Michigan*, 352 U.S. 380 (1957). The state statute made it a misdemeanor to sell to the *general reading public* any obscene book, "tending to incite minors to violent or depraved or immoral acts," or "tending to the corruption of the morals of youth." The appellant was convicted of violating the statute by selling a copy of a paper-bound reprint of John Griffin's *The Devil Rides Outside*.

The Court unanimously voted to set aside the conviction. Justice Frankfurter, for the Court, stated:

The State insists that, by thus quarantining the general reading public against books not too rugged for grown men and women in order to shield juvenile innocence, it is exercising its power to promote the general welfare. Surely, this is to burn the house to roast the pig. . . . We have before us legislation not reasonably restricted to the evil with which it is said to deal. The incidence of this enactment is to reduce the adult population of Michigan to reading only what is fit for children.

At the same term of Court, and also for the first time, the problem of legislative control of publications alleged to be obscene was considered. The opinion was written jointly for the companion cases of *Roth* v. *United States* and *Alberts* v. *California*, 354 U.S. 476 (1957). Roth was convicted in a federal court of violating the federal statute which forbids the mailing of obscene literature, by sending a publication called *American Aphrodite*. Alberts was convicted for advertising such books as *Sword of Desire, She*

*Made It Pay,* and *The Business Side of the Oldest Business,* in violation of a California law which forbids the writing, publishing, or selling of obscene books.

ROTH *v.* UNITED STATES
ALBERTS *v.* CALIFORNIA
*354 U.S. 476 (1957)*

Mr. Justice Brennan delivered the opinion of the Court. . . .

The dispositive question is whether obscenity is utterance within the area of protected speech and press.* Although this is the first time the question has been squarely presented to this Court, either under the First Amendment or under the Fourteenth Amendment, expressions found in numerous opinions indicate that this Court has always assumed that obscenity is not protected by the freedoms of speech and press. . . .

The guaranties of freedom of expression in effect in 10 of the 14 States which by 1792 had ratified the Constitution, gave no absolute protection for every utterance. Thirteen of the 14 States provided for the prosecution of libel, and all of those States made either blasphemy or profanity, or both, statutory crimes. As early as 1712, Massachusetts made it criminal to publish "any filthy, obscene, or profane song, pamphlet, libel or mock sermon" in imitation or mimicking of religious services. . . . Thus, profanity and obscenity were related offenses.

In light of this history, it is apparent that the unconditional phrasing of the First Amendment was not intended to protect every utterance. . . . At the time of the adoption of the First Amendment, obscenity law was not as fully developed as libel law, but there is sufficiently contemporaneous evidence to show that obscenity, too, was outside the protection intended for speech and press. . . .

All ideas having even the slightest redeeming social importance—unorthodox ideas, controversial ideas, even ideas hateful to the prevailing climate of opinion—have the full protection of the guaranties, unless excludable because they encroach upon the limited area of more important interests. But implicit in the history of the First Amendment is the rejection of obscenity as utterly without redeeming social importance. This rejection for that reason is mirrored in the universal judgment that obscenity should be restrained, reflected in the international agreement of over 50 nations,** in the obscenity laws of all of the 48 States, and in the 20 obscenity laws enacted by the Congress from 1842 to 1956. . . . We hold that obscenity is not within the area of constitutionally protected speech or press.

It is strenuously urged that these obscenity statutes offend the constitutional guaranties because they punish incitation to impure sexual *thoughts,* not shown to be related to any overt antisocial conduct which is or may be incited in the persons stimulated to such *thoughts.* . . .

However, sex and obscenity are not synonymous. Obscene material is material which deals with sex in a manner appealing to prurient interest.*** The portrayal of

---

*No issue is presented in either case concerning the obscenity of the material involved.

**Agreement for the Suppression of the Circulation of Obscene Publications, 37 stat. 1511; Treaties in Force 209 (U.S. Department of State, October 31, 1956).

***I.e., material having a tendency to excite lustful thoughts. . . .

We perceive no significant difference between the meaning of obscenity developed in the case law and the definition of the A.L.I., Model Penal Code, Section 207.10 (2) (Tent. Draft No. 6, 1957), *viz.:*

". . . A thing is obscene if, considered as a whole, its predominant appeal is to prurient interest, i.e., a shameful or morbid interest in nudity, sex, or excretion, and if it goes substantially beyond customary limits of candor in description or representation of such matters. . . ." . . .

sex, *e.g.,* in art, literature and scientific works, is not itself sufficient reason to deny material the constitutional protection of freedom of speech and press. Sex, a great and mysterious motive force in human life, has indisputably been a subject of absorbing interest to mankind through the ages; it is one of the vital problems of human interest and public concern. . . .

The early leading standard of obscenity allowed material to be judged merely by the effect of an isolated excerpt upon particularly susceptible persons. *Regina* v. *Hicklin* [1868] L.R. 3 Q.B. 360. Some American courts adopted this standard but later decisions have rejected it and substituted this test: whether to the average person, applying contemporary community standards, the dominant theme of the material taken as a whole appeals to prurient interest. The *Hicklin* test, judging obscenity by the effect of isolated passages upon the most susceptible persons, might well encompass material legitimately treating with sex, and so it must be rejected as unconstitutionally restrictive of the freedoms of speech and press. On the other hand, the substituted standard provides safeguards adequate to withstand the charge of constitutional infirmity. . . .

It is argued that the statutes do not provide reasonably ascertainable standards of guilt and therefore violate the constitutional requirements of due process. . . .

Many decisions have recognized that these terms of obscenity statutes are not precise. This Court, however, has consistently held that lack of precision is not itself offensive to the requirements of due process. . . . These words [obscene, lewd, lascivious, or filthy or indecent], applied according to the proper standard for judging obscenity, already discussed, give adequate warning of the conduct proscribed and mark " . . . boundaries sufficiently distinct for judges and juries fairly to administer the law." . . .

[Chief Justice Warren concurred in the result.]

[Justice Harlan concurred in *Alberts* and dissented in *Roth*. He stated that "Congress has no substantive power over sexual morality," and such powers as the federal government has in this field are insufficient to support a statute so broadly phrased as to reach the transmission of books which, under the judge's charge "tend to stir sexual impulses and lead to sexually impure thoughts." He stated further that he did not think the federal statute could be constitutionally construed to reach other than "what the Government has termed as 'hard-core' pornography."]

Mr. Justice Douglas, with whom Mr. Justice Black concurs, dissenting.

When we sustain these convictions, we make the legality of a publication turn on the purity of thought which a book or tract instills in the mind of the reader. I do not think we can approve that standard and be faithful to the command of the First Amendment, which by its terms is a restraint on Congress and which by the Fourteenth is a restraint on the States. . . .

By these standards punishment is inflicted for thoughts provoked, not for overt acts nor antisocial conduct. This test cannot be squared with our decisions under the First Amendment. . . . This issue cannot be avoided by saying that obscenity is not protected by the First Amendment. The question remains what is the constitutional test of obscenity?

The tests by which these convictions were obtained require only the arousing of sexual thoughts. Yet the arousing of sexual thoughts and desires happens every day in normal life in dozens of ways. Nearly 30 years ago a questionnaire sent to college and normal school women graduates asked what things were most stimulating sexually. Of 409 replies, 9 said "music"; 18 said "pictures"; 29 said "dancing"; 40 said "drama"; 95 said "books"; and 218 said "man." Alpert, Judicial Censorship of Obscene Literature, 52 Harv. L. Rev. 40, 73. . . .

If we were certain that impurity of sexual thoughts impelled to action, we would be on less dangerous ground in punishing the distributors of this sex literature. But it is by no means clear that obscene literature, as so defined, is a significant factor in influencing substantial deviations from the community standards. . . .

The absence of dependable information on the effect of obscene literature on human conduct should make us wary. It should put us on the side of protecting society's interest in literature, except and unless it can be said that the particular publication has an impact on action that the government can control.

As noted, the trial judge in the *Roth* case charged the jury in the alternative that the federal obscenity statute outlaws literature dealing with sex which offends "the common conscience of the community." That standard is, in my view, more inimical still to freedom of expression.

. . . . Certainly that standard would not be an acceptable one if religion, economics, politics or philosophy were involved. How does it become a constitutional standard when literature treating with sex is concerned?

Any test that turns on what is offensive to the community's standards is too loose, too capricious, too destructive of freedom of expression to be squared with the First Amendment. Under that test, juries can censor, suppress what they don't like, provided the matter relates to "sexual impurity" or has a tendency "to excite lustful thoughts." This is community censorship in one of its worst forms. It creates a regime where in the battle between the literati and the Philistines, the Philistines are certain to win. If experience in this field teaches anything, it is that "censorship of obscenity has almost always been both irrational and indiscriminate." . . .

I would give the broad sweep of the First Amendment full support. I have the same confidence in the ability of our people to reject noxious literature as I have in their capacity to sort out the true from the false in theology, economics, politics, or any other field.

[Although published in 1956, still one of the most perceptive and entertaining treatments of the matter of censorship of obscenity is Walter Gellhorn, "Restraints on Book Reading," chap. 2 in *Individual Freedom and Governmental Restraints* (Baton Rouge: Louisiana State Univ. Press, 1956).]

A new gloss was added to the law of obscenity in three decisions in 1966. In *Ginzburg v. United States*, 383 U.S. 463 (1966), defendants challenged their convictions for having violated the federal obscenity statute by using the mail for distributing allegedly obscene literature—namely, the magazine *Eros*, containing articles and photo essays on love and sex; a biweekly newsletter, dedicated to "keeping sex an art and preventing it from becoming a science"; and "The Housewife's Handbook on Promiscuity." On certiorari, the Supreme Court by a five-to-four vote affirmed the convictions. In so holding, the majority stated that even through the publications, standing alone, might not be obscene, the question of obscenity "may include consideration of the setting in which the publications were presented as an aid to determining the question of obscenity, and assume without deciding that the prosecution could not have succeeded otherwise." "We view the publications against a background of commercial exploitation of erotica solely for the sake of their prurient appeal." The Court found ample evidence to support a finding that the publisher pointedly directed his advertising and distribution campaign to prurient appeal. Justice Brennen stated:

Besides testimony as to the merit of the material, there was abundant evidence to show that each of the accused publications was originated or sold as stock in trade of the sordid business of pandering—"the business of purveying textual or graphic matter openly advertised to appeal to the erotic interest of their customers."

With respect to the "Handbook," the government drew a distinction between the author's solicitation and that of petitioners. The author had printed the work privately and canvassed persons whose names appeared on membership lists of medical and psychiatric associations, asserting its value as an adjunct in therapy. According to the United States Attorney, the author "never had widespread indiscriminate distribution of the Handbook and, consequently, the Post Office Department did not interfere." The majority of the Court accepted this distinction in applying the definition of obscenity, stating:

> Petitioners, however, did not sell the book to such a limited audience, or focus their claims for it on its supposed therapeutic or educational value; rather, they deliberately emphasized the sexually provocative aspects of the work, in order to catch the salaciously disposed.

Thus the majority added to the *Roth* test of obscenity another consideration, whether in the context of the production, sale, and publicity for the publication there is substantial evidence of "exploitation by those who would make a business of pandering to 'the widespread weakness for titillation by pornography.' " And the finding of the latter fact "in close cases . . . may be probative with respect to the nature of the material in question and thus satisfy the *Roth* test."

There were four separate dissenting opinions. Justice Stewart expressed the views that (1) the defendants were denied due process because they were never charged with "commercial exploitation," or "pandering," or "titillation"; (2) no federal statute made conduct of this kind a criminal offense; (3) any such criminal statute would be unconstitutionally vague; and (4) the Court had no power to deny a defendant the First Amendment protections because it disapproves of his sordid business.

A second obscenity case, decided on the same day, was *Mishkin* v. *New York,* 383 U.S. 502 (1966). Mishkin was convicted of violating New York law by preparing obscene books, publishing obscene books, and possessing obscene books with intent to sell them. Fifty books were involved in the case. As stated by Justice Brennan, "They portray sexuality in many guises. Some depict relatively normal heterosexual relations, but more depict such deviations as sado-masochism, fetishism, and homosexuality." By a six-to-three vote the Court affirmed the conviction. Appellant attacked his conviction on three grounds: (1) the statutory proscriptions against "sadistic" or "masochistic" or "obscene" materials are impermissibly vague and thus the statute is invalid on its face; (2) the books were not in fact obscene; and (3) the proof of *scienter* was inadequate.

The Court stated that the New York courts have interpreted "obscenity" to cover only so-called hard-core pornography, and since this is a more rigorous test than the *Roth* definition, the constitutional criteria are satisfied. The second challenge rested in part on the *Roth* requirement that the material be judged on the basis of its appeal to the "average" or "normal" person. It was argued that material concerning deviant sexual practices, such as flagellation, fetishisms, and lesbianism, do not satisfy the prurient-appeal requirement because the "average" person would be disgusted rather than erotically stimulated. In response Justice Brennan, for the majority, stated:

> We adjust the prurient-appeal requirement to social realities by permitting the appeal of this type of material to be assessed in terms of the sexual interests of its intended and probable recipient group; and since our holding requires that the recipient group be defined with more specificity than in terms of sexually immature persons, it also avoids the inadequacy of the most susceptible-person facet of the *Hicklin* test.

On the issue of *scienter,* the Court quoted the New York Court of Appeals statement that "It is not innocent but *calculated purveyance* of filth which is exorcised," and stated that there was adequate proof that appellant was aware of the character of the material which he purposely had prepared and sold.

In a third case decided on the same day, *A Book Named "John Cleland's Memoirs of a Woman of Pleasure"* v. *Attorney General of Massachusetts*, 383 U.S. 413 (1966), the Court reviewed the judgment of a Massachusetts court of equity that the book *Memoirs of a Woman of Pleasure* (commonly known as *Fanny Hill*), written by John Cleland in about 1750, was obscene. By a six-to-three vote the Court reversed, but the majority was so badly split that there was no "opinion for the Court." Three justices, through Justice Brennan, held that the *Roth* test required a finding that the book be *"utterly* without redeeming social value" to be classified as obscene; that each of the three facets of the *Roth* test is to be applied independently; and that "the social value of the book can neither be weighed against nor canceled by its prurient appeal or patent offensiveness." Thus the Massachusetts court erred in holding that book need not be "unqualified worthless before it can be deemed obscene." The opinion brought this holding in line with *Ginzburg* by stating that there was no evidence presented that the book was "commercially exploited for the sake of prurient appeal, to the exclusion of all other values," but that such a finding might justify the conclusion that the book was utterly without redeeming social importance.

Another aspect of the enforcement of obscenity laws was the basis for reversal in *Smith* v. *California*, 361 U.S. 147 (1959). Smith was the proprietor of a bookstore and was convicted of violating a Los Angeles ordinance which made it unlawful to possess any obscene or indecent book in any place where books were sold or kept for sale. The ordinance was construed as imposing a strict criminal liability, without requiring any element of *scienter*, i.e., knowledge by the defendant of the contents of the book upon which the criminal charge was based. The Court unanimously reversed the conviction, although there were five separate opinions. Justice Brennan, speaking for five members, held that the requirement of strict liability on the bookseller unconstitutionally hindered freedom of speech and press. He stated:

[I]f the bookseller is criminally liable without knowledge of the contents, and the ordinance fulfills its purposes, he will tend to restrict the books he sells to those he has inspected; and thus the State will have imposed a restriction upon the distribution of constitutionally protected as well as obscene literature. . . . If the contents of bookshops and periodical stands were restricted to material of which their proprietors had made an inspection, they might be depleted indeed. . . . The bookseller's self-censorship, compelled by the State, would be a censorship affecting the whole public, hardly less virulent for being privately administered.

In *Bantam Books, Inc.* v. *Sullivan*, 372 U.S. 58 (1963), the Court dealt with the constitutionality of certain forms of informal suppression of distribution of books by a state commission. The Rhode Island legislature created the "Rhode Island Commission to Encourage Morality in Youth" which, among other duties, was charged with educating the public concerning any obscene publications and with investigating and recommending the prosecution of all violations of relevant statutes. The Commission evolved the practice of sending notices to distributors that certain designated books or magazines had been found to be objectionable for sale, distribution, or display to persons under 18 years of age, asking for their cooperation, and reminding them of the Commission's duty to recommend prosecution of sellers of obscenity. Copies of the lists of objectionable publications were also circulated to local police departments, and the distributors were so advised. The normal result of such notification was for the distributor to halt further circulation of the listed publications, to withdraw from retailers all unsold copies, and to return all unsold copies to the publishers.

Appellants, four New York publishers of paperback books, brought the action in the Superior Court of Rhode Island (1) to declare the law creating the Commission unconstitutional and (2) to declare unconstitutional and enjoin the acts and practices of the Commission under the law. With only one dissent, the Court held that the law creating the Commission was valid, but the practice of informal suppression constituted a system of prior administrative restraints. The opinion for the majority noted that "although the Commission's supposed concern is limited to youthful readers, the 'cooperation' it seeks from distributors invariably entails the complete suppression of the listed publications; adult readers are equally deprived of the opportunity to purchase the publications in the State." The fact that such a result could be accomplished without any judicial determination of the issue of obscenity was a fatal defect in its failure to furnish the procedural safeguards required for restricting the freedom of the press.

In *Ginsberg* v. *New York,* 390 U.S. 629 (1968), the Court examined the question of the constitutionality on its face of a New York criminal obscenity statute which prohibited the sale to minors under 17 years of age of material defined to be obscene on the basis of its appeal to them, whether or not it would be obscene to adults. Appellant was convicted under the statute for selling two "girlie" magazines to a sixteen-year-old boy. The Court upheld the statute against the claim that the *Roth-Memoirs* test was the appropriate standard, and held that the State could properly bar the sale of materials to minors which it could not constitutionally exclude from distribution to adults.

## STANLEY *v.* GEORGIA
### *394 U.S. 557 (1969)*

Mr. Justice Marshall delivered the opinion of the Court.

An investigation of appellant's alleged bookmaking activities led to the issuance of a search warrant for appellant's home. Under authority of this warrant, federal and state agents secured entrance . . . [W]hile looking through a desk drawer in an upstairs bedroom, one of the federal agents, accompanied by a state officer, found three reels of eight-millimeter film. Using a projector and screen found in an upstairs living room they viewed the films. The state officer concluded that they were obscene and seized them. Since a further examination of the bedroom indicated that appellant occupied it, he was charged with possession of obscene matter and placed under arrest. He was later indicted for "knowingly hav[ing] possession of obscene matter" in violation of Georgia law. Appellant was tried before a jury and convicted. The Supreme Court of Georgia affirmed. . . .

It is now well established that the Constitution protects the right to receive information and ideas. . . . The right to receive information and ideas, regardless of their social worth . . . is fundamental to our free society. Moreover, in the context of this case—a prosecution for mere possession of printed or filmed matter in the privacy of a person's own home—that right takes on an added dimension. For also fundamental is the right to be free, except in very limited circumstances, from unwanted governmental intrusions into one's privacy. . . .

These are the rights that appellant is asserting in the case before us. He is asserting the right to read or observe what he pleases—the right to satisfy his intellectual and emotional needs in the privacy of his own home. He is asserting the right to be free from state inquiry into the contents of his library. Georgia contends that appellant does not have these rights, that there are certain types of materials that the individual may not read or even possess. Georgia justifies this assertion by arguing that the films in the present case are obscene. But we think that mere categorization of these films as "obscene" is insufficient justification for such a drastic invasion of personal liberties guaranteed by the First and Fourteenth Amendments. Whatever may be the justifications for other statutes regulating obscenity, we do not think they reach into the privacy of one's own home. If the First Amendment means anything, it means that a State has no business telling a man, sitting alone in his own house, what books he may read or what films he may watch. Our whole constitutional heritage rebels at the thoughts of giving government the power to control men's minds.

And yet, in the face of these traditional notions of individual liberty, Georgia asserts the right to protect the individual's mind from the effects of obscenity. We are not certain that this argument amounts to anything more than the assertion that the State has the right to control the moral content of a person's thoughts. To some, this may be a noble purpose, but it is wholly inconsistent with the philosophy of the First Amendment. . . . Whatever the power of the State to control public dissemination of ideas inimical to the public morality, it cannot constitutionally premise legislation on the desirability of controlling a person's private thoughts. . . .

*Reversed and remanded.*

Mr. Justice Black, concurring. . . .

Mr. Justice Stewart, with whom Mr. Justice Brennan and Mr. Justice White join, concurring in the result. . . .

Even in the much criticized case of *United States* v. *Rabinowitz* . . . the Court emphasized that "exploratory searches . . . cannot be undertaken by officers, with or without a warrant." . . . This record presents a bald violation of that basic constitutional rule. To condone what happened here is to invite a government official to use a seemingly precise and legal warrant only as a ticket to get into a man's home, and, once inside, to launch forth upon unconfined searches and indiscriminate seizures as if armed with all the unbridled and illegal power of a general warrant. . . .

UNITED STATES *v.* REIDEL
*402 U.S. 351 (1971)*

Mr. Justice White delivered the opinion of the Court.

Section 1461 of Title 18, USC, prohibits the knowing use of the mails for the delivery of obscene matter. The issue presented by the jurisdictional statement in this case is whether Sec. 1461 is constitutional as applied to the distribution of obscene material to willing recipients who state that they are adults. The District Court held that it was not. We disagree and reverse the judgment. . . .

In *Roth* v. *United States.* . . . Roth was convicted under Sec. 1461 for mailing obscene circulars and advertising. The Court affirmed the conviction. . . . *Roth* has not been overruled. It remains the law on this Court and governs this case. . . .

*Stanley* v. *Georgia* . . . compels no different result. . . . [I]t neither overruled nor disturbed the holding in *Roth*. . . . The Court made its point expressly: *"Roth* and the cases following that decision are not impaired by today's holding. . . . "

The District Court ignored both *Roth* and the express limitations on the reach of the *Stanley* decision. Relying on the statement in *Stanley* that "the Constitution protects the right to receive information and ideas . . . regardless of their social worth," . . . the trial judge reasoned that "if a person has the right to receive and possess this material, then someone must have the right to deliver it to him." He concluded that Sec. 1461 could not be validly applied "where obscene material is not directed at children, or it is not directed at an unwilling public, where the material such as in this case is solicited by adults. . . . "

The District Court gave *Stanley* too wide a sweep. To extrapolate from Stanley's right to have and peruse obscene material in the privacy of his own home a First

Amendment right in Reidel to sell it to him would effectively scuttle *Roth*, the precise result that the *Stanley* opinion abjured. . . .

Reidel is in a wholly different position. He has no complaints about governmental violations of his private thoughts or fantasies, but stands squarely on a claimed First Amendment right to do business in obscenity and use the mails in the process. But *Roth* has squarely placed obscenity and its distribution outside the reach of the First Amendment and they remain there today. *Stanley* did not overrule *Roth* and we decline to do so now. . . .

The judgment of the District Court is

*Reversed.*

Mr. Justice Harlan, concurring. . . .

Mr. Justice Marshall, concurring. . . .

Mr. Justice Black, with whom Mr. Justice Douglas joins, dissenting. . . .

*Roth* v. *United States* was decided in 1957, and it represented the Court's first effort to provide a definition of that unprotected area of publication denoted as "obscenity." While that effort was subscribed to by a majority of the Court, it was not until 1973, in *Miller* v. *California,* that the Court could again marshal a clear majority behind a revised definition of obscenity. The *Memoirs* gloss, for example, which altered the *Roth* test to require that the prosecution must prove that a work was *"utterly* without redeeming social value," had only plurality support. The problem, of course, arose from the fact that the membership of the Court split into at least three different ideological camps for purposes of dealing with obscenity cases. One group argued from an absolutist position and contended that all such restraints were in violation of the First Amendment. At the other end of the constitutional spectrum, a second group took a more traditional due process approach and contended that unless state regulations of obscenity were irrational or unreasonable, they should be upheld. The middle group attempted to establish a definitional standard for obscenity and apply this to the specific publication or movie on a case-by-case approach. The result of this fragmentation was that cases could be *disposed* of by a majority vote, but it was nearly impossible to muster a majority behind a single rationale for the disposition. A shift in the personnel of the Court between 1957 and 1973, however, opened the way for a different alignment on the obscenity issue, and the redefinition which came in *Miller* v. *California* had the support of five of the Justices.

## MILLER *v.* CALIFORNIA
### *413 U.S. 15 (1973)*

Mr. Chief Justice Burger delivered the opinion of the Court.

This is one of a group of "obscenity-pornography" cases being reviewed by the Court in a re-examination of standards enunciated in earlier cases involving what Mr. Justice Harlan called "the intractable obscenity problem." . . .

Appellant conducted a mass mailing compaign to advertise the sale of illustrated books, euphemistically called "adult" material. After a jury trial, he was convicted of . . . a misdemeanor, by knowingly distributing obscene matter. . . . Appellant's conviction was specifically based on his conduct in causing five unsolicited advertising brochures to be sent through the mail in an envelope addressed to a restaurant in Newport Beach, California. The envelope was opened by the manager of the restaurant and his mother. They had not requested the brochures; they complained to the police.

The brochures advertise four books entitled "Intercourse," "Man-Woman," "Sex Orgies Illustrated," and "An Illustrated History of Pornography," and a film entitled

"Marital Intercourse." While the brochures contain some descriptive printed material, primarily they consist of pictures and drawings very explicitly depicting men and women in groups of two or more engaging in a variety of sexual activities, with genitals often prominently displayed.

This case involves the application of a State's criminal obscenity statute to a situation in which sexually explicit materials have been thrust by aggressive sales action upon unwilling recipients who had in no way indicated any desire to receive such materials. This Court has recognized that the States have a legitimate interest in prohibiting dissemination or exhibition of obscene material when the mode of dissemination carries with it a significant danger of offending the sensibilities of unwilling recipients or of exposure to juveniles. *Stanley* v. *Georgia* . . . *Ginsberg* v. *New York*. . . . It is in this context that we are called on to define the standards which must be used to identify obscene material that a State may regulate without infringing the First Amendment as applicable to the States through the Fourteenth Amendment.

[The opinion here discusses the standards announced in *Roth* v. *United States* and *Memoirs* v. *Massachusetts*.]

While *Roth* presumed "obscenity" to be "utterly without redeeming social value," *Memoirs* required that to prove obscenity it must be affirmatively established that the material is "utterly without redeeming social value." Thus, even as they repeated the words of *Roth*, the *Memoirs* plurality produced a drastically altered test that called on the prosecution to prove a negative, i.e., that the material was "*utterly* without redeeming social value"—a burden virtually impossible to discharge under our criminal standards of proof. . . .

Apart from the initial formulation in the *Roth case*, no majority of the Court has at any given time been able to agree on a standard to determine what constitutes obscene, pornographic material subject to regulation under the States' police power. . . . This is not remarkable, for in the area of freedom of speech and press the courts must always remain sensitive to any infringement on genuinely serious literary, artistic, political, or scientific expression. This is an area in which there are few eternal verities.

The case we now review was tried on the theory that the California Penal Code . . . approximately incorporates the three-stage *Memoirs* test, . . . But now the *Memoirs* test has been abandoned as unworkable by its author and no member of the Court today supports the *Memoirs* formulation.

This much has been categorically settled by the Court, that obscene material is unprotected by the First Amendment. . . . We acknowledge, however, the inherent dangers of undertaking to regulate any form of expression. State statutes designed to regulate obscene materials must be carefully limited. . . . As a result, we now confine the permissible scope of such regulation to works which depict or describe sexual conduct. That conduct must be specifically defined by the applicable state law, as written or authoritatively construed. A state offense must also be limited to works which, taken as a whole, appeal to the prurient interest in sex, which portray sexual conduct in a patently offensive way, and which, taken as a whole, do not have serious literary, artistic, political, or scientific value.

The basic guidelines for the trier of fact must be: (a) whether "the average person, applying contemporary community standards" would find that the work, taken as a whole, appeals to the prurient interest . . . , (b) whether the work depicts or describes, in a patently offensive way, sexual conduct specifically defined by the applicable state law and (c) whether the work, taken as a whole, lacks serious literary, artistic, political, or scientific value. We do not adopt as a constitutional standard the "*utterly* without redeeming social value" test of *Memoirs* v. *Massachusetts* . . . ; that concept has never commanded adherence of more than three Justices at one time. . . . If a state law that regulates obscene material is thus limited, as written or construed, the First Amendment values applicable to the States through the Fourteenth Amendment are adequately protected by the ultimate power of appellate courts to conduct an independent review of constitutional claims when necessary. . . .

We emphasize that it is not our function to propose regulatory schemes for the States. That must await their concrete legislative efforts. It is possible, however, to give a few plain examples of what a state statute could define for regulation under the second part (b) of the standard announced in this opinion, *supra:*

(a) Patently offensive representations or descriptions of ultimate sexual acts, normal or perverted, actual or simulated.

(b) Patently offensive representations or descriptions of masturbation, excretory functions, and lewd exhibition of the genitals.

Sex and nudity may not be exploited without limit by films or pictures exhibited or sold in places of public accommodation any more than live sex and nudity can be exhibited or sold without limit in such public places. At a minimum, prurient, patently offensive depiction or description of sexual conduct must have serious literary, artistic, political, or scientific value to merit First Amendment protection. . . .

It is certainly true that the absence, since *Roth,* of a single majority view of this Court as to proper standards for testing obscenity has placed a strain on both state and federal courts. But today, for the first time since *Roth* was decided in 1957, a majority of this Court has agreed on concrete guidelines to isolate "hard core" pornography from expression protected by the First Amendment. Now we may abandon the casual practice of *Redrup* v. *New York* . . . and attempt to provide positive guidance to the federal and state courts alike.

This may not be an easy road, free from difficulty. But no amount of "fatigue" should lead us to adopt a convenient "institutional" rationale—an absolutist, "anything goes" view of the First Amendment—because it will lighten our burdens. . . . Nor should we remedy "tension between state and federal courts" by arbitrarily depriving the States of a power reserved to them under the Constitution, a power which they have enjoyed and exercised continuously from before the adoption of the First Amendment to this day. . . .

Under a national Constitution, fundamental First Amendment limitations on the powers of the States do not vary from community to community, but this does not mean that there are, or should or can be, fixed, uniform national standards of precisely what appeals to the "prurient interest" or is "patently offensive." These are essentially questions of fact, and our nation is simply too big and too diverse for this Court to reasonably expect that such standards could be articulated for all 50 States in a single formulation, even assuming the prerequisite consensus exists. . . . The adversary system, with lay jurors as the usual ultimate factfinders in criminal prosecutions, has historically permitted triers-of-fact to draw on the standards of their community, guided always by limiting instructions on the law. To require a State to structure obscenity proceedings around evidence of a *national* "community standard" would be an exercise in futility. . . .

We conclude that neither the State's alleged failure to offer evidence of "national standards," nor the trial court's charge that the jury consider state community standards, were constitutional errors. Nothing in the First Amendment requires that a jury must consider hypothetical and unascertainable 'national standards" when attempting to determine whether certain materials are obscene as a matter of fact. . . .

It is neither realistic nor constitutionally sound to read the First Amendment as requiring that the people of Maine or Mississippi accept public depiction of conduct found tolerable in Las Vegas, or New York City. . . . People in different States vary in their tastes and attitudes, and this diversity is not to be strangled by the absolutism of imposed uniformity. . . . We hold the requirement that the jury evaluate the materials with reference to "contemporary standards of the State of California" serves this protective purpose and is constitutionally adequate.

The dissenting Justices sound the alarm of repression. But, in our view, to equate the free and robust exchange of ideas and political debate with commercial exploitation of obscene material demeans the grand conception of the First Amendment and its high purposes in the historic struggle for freedom. . . . The First Amendment protects works which, taken as a whole, have serious literary, artistic, political or scientific value, regardless of whether the government or a majority of the people approve of the ideas these works represent. . . . But the public portrayal of hard core sexual conduct for its own sake, and for the ensuing commerical gain, is a different matter. . . .

In sum we (a) reaffirm the *Roth* holding that obscene material is not protected by the First Amendment, (b) hold that such material can be regulated by the States, subject to the specific safeguards enunciated above, without a showing that the material is "*utterly* without redeeming social value," and (c) hold that obscenity is to be determined by applying "contemporary community standards," . . . not "national standards." . . .

*Vacated and remanded for further proceedings.*

Mr. Justice Douglas, dissenting.

Today we leave open the way for California to send a man to prison for distributing brochures that advertise books and a movie under freshly written standards defining obscenity which until today's decision were never the part of any law. . . .

Today the Court retreats from the earlier formulations of the constitutional test and undertakes to make new definitions. This effort, like the earlier ones, is earnest and well-intentioned. The difficulty is that we do not deal with constitutional terms, since "obscenity" is not mentioned in the Constitution or Bill of Rights. And the First Amendment makes no such exception from "the press" which it undertakes to protect nor, as I have said on other occasions, is an exception necessarily implied, for there was no recognized exception to the free press at the time the Bill of Rights was adopted which treated "obscene" publications differently from other types of papers, magazines, and books. So there are no constitutional guidelines for deciding what is and what is not "obscene." The Court is at large because we deal with tastes and standards of literature. What shocks me may be sustenance for my neighbor. What causes one person to boil up in rage over one pamphlet or movie may reflect only his neurosis, not shared by others. We deal here with problems of censorship which, if adopted, should be done by constitutional amendment after full debate by the people.

Obscenity cases usually generate tremendous emotional outbursts. They have no business being in the courts. If a constitutional amendment authorized censorship, the censor would probably be an administrative agency. Then criminal prosecutions could follow as, if and when publishers defied the censor and sold their literature. Under that regime a publisher would know when he was on dangerous ground. Under the present regime—whether the old standards or the new ones are used—the criminal law becomes a trap. A brand new test would put a publisher behind bars under a new law improvised by the courts after the publication. That was done in *Ginzburg* and has all the evils of an ex post facto law.

My contention is that until a civil proceeding has placed a tract beyond the pale, no criminal prosecution should be sustained. For no more vivid illustration of vague and uncertain laws could be designed than those we have fashioned. . . .

No such protective procedure has been designed by California in this case. Obscenity—which even we cannot define with precision—is a hodge-podge. To send men to jail for violating standards they cannot understand, construe, and apply is a monstrous thing to do in a Nation dedicated to fair trials and due process. . . .

The idea that the First Amendment permits government to ban publications that are "offensive" to some people puts an ominous gloss on freedom of the press. That test would make it possible to ban any paper or any journal or magazine in some benighted place. The First Amendment was designed "to invite dispute," to induce "a condition of unrest," to create dissatisfaction with conditions as they are," and even to stir "people to anger." . . . The idea that the First Amendment permits punishment for ideas that are "offensive" to the particular judge or jury sitting in judgment is astounding. . . .

Mr. Justice Brennan, with whom Mr. Justice Stewart and Mr. Justice Marshall join, dissenting. . . .

On the same date that the *Miller* decision was made, the Court decided *Paris Adult Theatre I* v. *Slaton,* 413 U.S. 49 (1973). The case involved a civil action for an injunction to restrain the Theatre from continued exhibition of an obscene film. The Theatre had displayed a sign on the door stating: "Adult Theatre—You must be 21 and able to prove it. If viewing the nude body offends you, Please Do Not Enter." Its contention was that the showing of obscene films was constitutionally protected since they were exhibited only to consenting adults. The Court refused to accept this application of the First Amendment and held the exhibitor bound by the state law as long as the law met the standards announced in *Miller* v. *California.* Chief Justice Burger for the majority stated:

We categorically disapprove the theory . . . that obscene, pornographic films acquire constitutional immunity from state regulation simply because they are exhibited for consenting adults only. This holding was properly rejected by the Georgia Supreme Court. Although we have often pointedly recognized the high importance of the state interest in regulating the exposure of obscene materials to juveniles and unconsenting adults, . . . this Court has never declared these to be the only legitimate state interests permitting regulation of obscene material. The States have a long-recognized legitimate interest in regulating the use of obscene material in local commerce and in all places of public accommodation, as long as these regulations do not run afoul of specific constitutional prohibitions. . . .

In particular, we hold that there are legitimate state interests at stake in stemming the tide of commercialized obscenity, even assuming it is feasible to enforce effective safeguards against exposure to juveniles and to the passerby. Rights and interests "other than those of the advocates are involved." . . . These include the interest of the public in the quality of life and the total community environment, the tone of commerce in the great city centers, and, possibly, the public safety itself. . . .

[See Walter Berns, "Pornography v. Democracy: The Case for Censorship," 22 *The Public Interest* 3 (1971).]

While the Court in *Miller* held that in defining the "community standard" the trial court was not required to employ a "national standard," it held in *Hamling* v. *United States,* 418 U.S. 87 (1974), that it was not reversible error for the trial judge to charge the jury to employ national community standards in determining obscenity, since there was nothing to indicate that the use of statewide community standards would have materially affected the deliberations of the jury in California.

*Jenkins* v. *Georgia,* 418 U.S. 153 (1974), involved the conviction of a Georgia theater manager for showing the motion picture *Carnal Knowledge* in violation of a state obscenity statute. The trial occurred before the *Miller* decision was rendered by the Court, and the trial court gave instructions directing the jury, which viewed the film, to apply "community standards" in determining obscenity without specifying what "community." Since the case was on appeal at the time the *Miller* decision was made, the Court held that the defendant was entitled to receive any benefit available to him under that ruling. The majority further held that in state obscenity prosecutions, juries could properly be instructed to apply "community standards" without specifying what "community" since "the Constitution does not require that juries be instructed in state obscenity cases to apply the standards of a hypothetical statewide community." *Miller* approved the use of such instructions; it did not mandate their use. What *Miller* makes clear is that state juries need not be instructed to apply "national standards." But after the Court viewed the film (as is its custom), the majority concluded that, the jury verdict to the contrary notwithstanding, the film "could not be found under the *Miller* standards to depict sexual conduct in a patently offensive way," and thus reversed the conviction. The dissenting opinion of Justice Brennan pointed to the obvious problem resulting from the new *Miller-Jenkins* approach to obscenity: any time a film is found to be obscene and comes to the Court on review, the Court will have to look at the film and decide whether to substitute judgment for the trial court. "One cannot say with certainty that material is obscene until at least five members of this Court, applying inevitably obscure standards, have pronounced it so."

[For a lively account of the Burger Court's views on obscenity cases, and particularly "movie day" on which members and their clerks viewed the films in cases under review, see Bob Woodward and Scott Armstrong, *The Brethren* (New York: Simon and Schuster, 1979), pp. 192–204.]

While some local officials interpreted the "community standard" test as permitting the juries complete discretion to ban books or films that they thought "bad" or "immoral," the *Jenkins* decision should make it clear that jury discretion runs in only one direction—permissiveness. Thus a jury can hold that material is not subject to a ban even though it would meet the *Miller* test of obscenity, but it cannot punish for distribution of books or films that fail to meet that test without violating the First Amendment.

Figure 1 is an attempt to illustrate the constitutional rule graphically, by categorizing books or films in terms of content.

*New York v. Ferber,* 458 U.S. 747 (1982), dealt with a statute prohibiting persons from knowingly promoting a sexual performance by a child under the age of sixteen by the production, sale or distribution of such material. The sexual conduct prohibited was defined as actual or simulated sexual intercourse, masturbation, lewd exhibition of the genitals, and others. Ferber was convicted for selling films that came under the statutory definition, but the New York Court of Appeals reversed on First Amendment grounds. The United States Supreme Court reversed, holding that States are entitled to greater leeway in the regulation of pornographic depictions of children, that *Miller v. California* does not provide a satisfactory test in dealing with the child pornography problem, and recognizing and classifying child pornography as a category of material outside the First Amendment's protection is not incompatible with the Court's decisions defining unprotected speech. The important consideration of the welfare of children permits the States to accord greater weight to the need for regulation than would be the case for adults.

Following the Court's decisions in a number of cases requiring a more careful definition and less restrictive application of obscenity laws, a substantial increase in the number of "adult book stores" and "'adult movies" occurred. In order to avoid development of blight resulting from high concentrations of such businesses in specific neighborhoods, some municipalities adopted zoning ordinances requiring that these businesses be scattered about the community rather than localized in certain areas. In

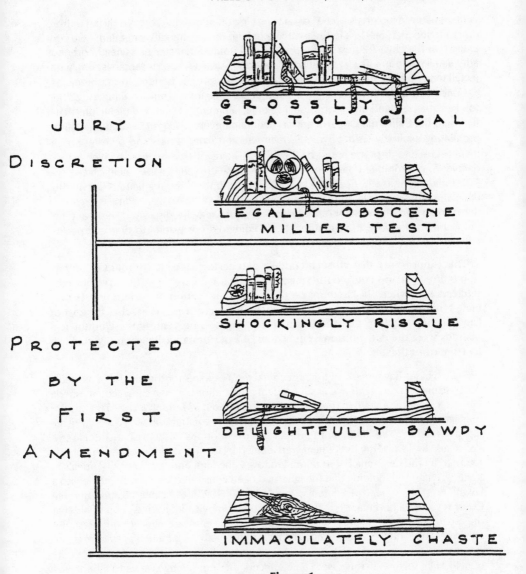

**Figure 1.**

(Courtesy of Duncan Abernathy)

1972 Detroit adopted amendments to its "Anti-Skid Row Ordinance" providing that adult movie theaters could not be located within 1000 feet of any two other "regulated uses (ten different kinds of establishments in addition to adult theaters, including adult book stores, bars, and taxi dance halls), and defining an "adult theater" as one which presents material "characterized by an emphasis on sexual activities." It also barred such theaters within 500 feet of a residential area. By a five-to-four vote the Court upheld the provisions in *Young v. American Mini Theatres,* 427 U.S. 50 (1976). Justice Stevens, for the majority, said: "Even though the First Amendment protects communication in this area from total suppression, we hold that the State may legitimately use the content of these materials as the basis for placing them in a different classification from other motion pictures." As to the rationale behind the ordinances, he stated: "we conclude that the city's interest in the present and future character of its neighborhoods adequately supports its classification of motion pictures." The dissenters strongly objected to permitting States to regulate motion pictures on the basis of their content.

Concerned with the progression in a few years' time from "topless" dancers to "bottomless" dancers and other forms of "live entertainment" in bars and nightclubs that it licensed, the California Department of Alcoholic Beverage Control issued regulations prohibiting explicitly sexual live entertainment and films in bars and other establishment licensed to dispense liquor by the drink. (The regulations were so explicit in their definitions of prohibited behavior as almost to raise obscenity issues themselves.) The Court in *California* v. *La Rue,* 409 U.S. 109 (1972), upheld the regulations as constitutional under the broad latitude granted States by the Twenty-first Amendment to control the manner and circumstances under which liquor may be dispensed. Justice Rehnquist, for the majority, indicated that the holding did not extend to dramatic performances in a theater where liquor was not served:

This is not to say that all such conduct and performance is without the protection of the First and Fourteenth Amendments. But we would poorly serve both the interests for which the State may validly seek vindication and the interests protected by the First and Fourteenth Amendments were we to insist that the sort of bacchanalian revelries that the Department sought to prevent by these liquor regulations were the constitutional equivalent of a performance by a scantily clad ballet troupe in a theater.

Several cases have involved the procedural requirements for the seizure of allegedly obscene materials as evidence in subsequent prosecutions. In one case a county sheriff viewed a movie at a drive-in theater, and, acting without a warrant, arrested the theater manager on a charge of exhibiting an obscene film to the public and seized a copy of the film as evidence. The defendant's pretrial and trial motions to suppress the film as evidence and to dismiss the indictment were denied by the trial court. A guilty verdict was returned by the jury, which was permitted to see the film, and the Court of Appeals of Kentucky affirmed, holding that the films had been constitutionally seized incident to a lawful arrest. In *Roaden* v. *Kentucky,* 413 U.S. 496 (1973), the United States Supreme Court reversed and remanded. The majority opinion by Chief Justice Burger held that the seizure of the film without a constitutionally sufficient warrant was a prior restraint on expression, and thus the film could not constitutionaly be admitted as evidence.

In *Heller* v. *New York,* 413 U.S. 483 (1973), decided on the same day, the Court upheld a film seizure. In this case, a New York criminal court judge viewed a motion picture as a patron of a theater, found it to be obscene, and issued warrants under which the theater manager was arrested and the film was seized as being obscene under New York criminal statutes. The trial court rejected the defendant's contention that the seizure of the film without a prior adversary hearing violated his constitutional rights, and he was found guilty. The United States Supreme Court vacated and remanded. Chief Justice Burger, for five members of the Court, held that the seizure, without a prior adversary hearing, of a film for the bona fide purpose of preserving it as evidence was constitutionally permissible under the First Amendment if such seizure was pursuant to a warrant issued after a determination of probable cause by a neutral magistrate, and if a prompt judicial determination of the obscenity issue was available at the request of any interested party. "In addition, on a showing to the trial court that other copies of the film are not available to the court should permit the seized film to be copied so that showing can be continued pending a judicial determination of the obscenity issue in an adversary proceeding. Otherwise, the film must be returned." The seizure in this case and its admission as evidence were held constitutional, but the case was remanded to allow the state courts to reconsider its obscenity standards in light of the intervening decision in *Miller v. California.*

In *New York v. P.J. Video, Inc.,* 475 U.S. 868 (1986), the Court faced a challenge to the validity of warrant where the defendants claimed that the affidavits accompanying the application were insufficient to meet the probable cause requirement. An investigator from a New York District Attorney's office viewed videocassette movies that had been rented from respondents' store by a member of the County Sheriff's Department. The investigator then executed affidavits summarizing the theme of, and conduct depicted in, each movie. These were attached to an application for a warrant to search the store, and a New York Supreme Court Justice issued the warrant authorizing the search and seizure of the movies. The respondents were charged with violating the state obscenity statute and moved to suppress the movies on the ground that the warrant was issued without probable cause to believe that the movies were obscene. The Justice Court granted the motion and dismissed the charges, and both the County Court and the New York Court of Appeals affirmed. The Court of Appeals held that there was a "higher standard for evaluation of a warrant application seeking to seize such things as books and films, as distinguished from one seeking to seize weapons or drugs, for example." In a 6–3 vote the Supreme Court reversed, holding that no higher probable cause standard was required by the First Amendment for the issuance of the warrant to seize films. Further, the majority's examination of the affidavits "convinces us that the issuing justice also was given more than enough information to conclude that there was a 'fair probability' that the movies satisfied" major elements of the statutory definition of obscenity. (The affidavits are included in an Appendix to the Opinion of the Court by Justice Rehnquist.)

[On obscenity questions generally, see: Martin Shapiro, "Obscenity Law: a Public Policy Analysis," 20 *J. Pub. L.* 503 (1971); Walter Gellhorn, "Dirty Books, Disgusting Pictures, and Dreadful Laws," 8 *Ga. L. Rev.* 291 (1974); Note, "Morality and the Broadcast Media: a Constitutional Analysis of FCC Regulatory Standards," 85 *Harv. L. Rev.* 664 (1971); Note, "Obscenity and the Right to Be Let Alone: the Balancing of Constitutional Rights," 6 *Ind. L. Rev.* 490 (1973); and *The Report of the Commission on Obscenity and Pornography* (Washington, D.C.: U.S. Gov't Printing Office, 1970).]

# CHAPTER 6

# *Equal Protection of the Law*

Much of the developing law in the area of civil rights can in essence be characterized as a drive for equality under the law. The concept of equality has played an important part in American legal and political development since its overt statement by Thomas Jefferson in the Declaration's famous words, "We hold these truths to be self-evident, that all men are created equal. . . ." The movement has been sporadic and has taken differing directions and emphases, sometimes stressing the economic, at other times the legal or the social. In the Revolutionary and post-Revolutionary periods substantial gains were made in the area of religious support, disestablishment, and the removal of restrictions on public worship for some of the minority sects. During the Jacksonian period religious tests for office-holding began to disappear and political equality was further extended by the removal of property qualifications for both voters and candidates for public office. In economic thought it was one of the firm tenets of Jacksonian democracy that progress could be assured for all if the legislative policy of granting exclusive grants of privilege could be stopped and everyone afforded equal opportunity to engage in business enterprise. The Civil War era saw the adoption of a minimal program of racial equality in the abolition of slavery. Even in the period of Manchester Liberalism in the latter third of the nineteenth century, when the doctrines of Herbert Spencer held sway, it was a somewhat twisted concept of equality which was interwoven into the fabric of social Darwinism. All men had an equal opportunity to compete for economic survival and leadership. By fencing off government from entering the struggle to lay down ground rules for the economic "game," equality was supposedly secured and the victors were entitled to the spoils because they were the fittest. The theory, of course, took no account of the fact that the competition could never be equal between persons who entered the struggle with substantially unequal financial assets. A great deal of legislation since the adoption of the Sherman Antitrust Act in 1980 has been prompted by the desire to equalize the competitive battle in the economic arena, including labor's bargaining position as against management.

Except in the area of voting rights and in certain aspects of economic rights, there was little governmental activity, either legislative or judicial, to extend the guarantees of equality prior to World War II. The Fourteenth Amendment, with it's equal protection clause, was ratified in 1868, but cases were rarely won by litigants who based their attacks on the invalidity of legislative classifications. Distinctions based on race were upheld unless they were found to abridge political or property rights. And virtually all distinctions based on sex, except for those impairing voting rights, could be validly imposed. With few exceptions, it was not until the post-World War II period that Congress and the federal courts began a concerted drive to eliminate some of the major inequalities based on race, sex, religion, and economic level.

It was not until the 1950s, during the Warren Court period, that the potential of the equal protection clause began to be realized. Beginning with *Brown v. Board of Education* in 1954, the Court has rendered key decisions under this clause resulting in prohibitions against governmental race discrimination, the requirement of fair apportionment of population in establishing election districts, substantial equality of rights for indigents in the criminal process, and the gradual elimination of a number of disabilities imposed by law on women.

While under the traditional view of the equal protection clause the State was allowed broad leeway to classify for purposes of legislation, a new and more rigid standard was developed during the period of the Warren Court to test the validity of state laws which affected special classes or special rights. Thus the discussion to follow will first take up cases illustrating the traditional approach and then will move to the "new" equal protection tests developed by the Warren Court, and, finally, to the more recent "three-tiered" approach.

## THE TRADITIONAL VIEW

In the traditional approach to the judicial treatment of equal protection cases, the issues raised could usually be resolved into two questions: (1) Did the legislature, in adopting a law providing for differential treatment of segments of the public, set up a reasonable classification of the objects or persons treated, in view of the overall purposes of the law? Stated differently, this question might be: Did the legislature make "invidious distinctions" in the law? and (2) Was the specific law involved administered impartially?

The first aspect of the problem of equal protection concerns actual classification by the legislature in the application of a statute. It is almost impossible to conceive of a law which does not in some way employ classification. And it would place an intolerable burden on the legislature to have to deal with all evils in the community at once, or even to deal with all aspects of a single evil, in order to meet the test of equal protection. Thus the legislature can, if it chooses, attack community ills more or less piecemeal. It can try to solve problems one at a time, and it can even deal with some aspects of a given problem while ignoring others. In short, the equal protection clause does not fasten upon the legislature an iron rule of uniform treatment.

The legislature is thus free to "classify" the objects of its attention, treating some in one fashion and others differently. It is, then, free to discriminate. But if it *does* discriminate, the equal protection requirement demands that the legislative classification not be arbitrary and unreasonable and that the distinctions employed bear some rational relationship to the lawful purposes to be accomplished. Even here, however, there is a strong presumption in the courts that discriminations in legislation are based on adequate grounds. As indicated in *Crescent Oil Company v. Mississippi*, 257 U.S. 129, 137 (1921), every set of facts sufficient to sustain a classification which can reasonably be conceived of as having existed when the law was adopted will be assumed. Further, since the legislature is free to try to correct one evil without reaching others, it is no defense to show that a challenged law could easily have been broadened to correct other very similar evils. As Justice Holmes stated in *Keokee Consolidated Coke Company v. Taylor* 234 U.S. 224 (1914), "it is established by repeated decisions that a statute aimed at what is deemed an evil, and hitting it presumably where experience shows it to be most felt, is not to be upset by thinking up and enumerating other instances to which it might have been applied equally well, so far as the Court can see."

A famous case which involved in part the equal protection issue was *Buck v. Bell*, 274 U.S. 200 (1927), in which a state law providing for the sterilization of mental defectives was challenged. A Virginia law of 1924 provided that after complying with very careful procedural requirements to protect patients from possible abuse, *institutionalized* mental defectives could be ordered sterilized. No provision was made for sterilization of such persons who were not living in various institutions specified in the law. The main thrust of argument in the case was that it deprived the affected persons of their liberty without due process of law, and in upholding the provisions the opinion was primarily directed to that issue. The law was also challenged, however, on the ground that the differential treatment accorded institutional inmates and those outside institutions violated the equal protection clause. In upholding the statute against this claim, Justice Holmes, for the Court, stated:

But, it is said, however it might be if this reasoning were applied generally, it fails when it is confined to the small number who are in the institutions named and is not applied to the multitudes outside. It is the usual last resort of constitutional arguments to point out shortcomings of this sort. But the answer is that the law does all that is needed when it does all that it can, indicates a policy, applies it to all within the lines, and seeks to bring within the lines all similarly situated so far and so fast as its means allow. Of course so far as the operations enable those who otherwise must be kept confined to be returned to the world, and thus open the asylum to others, the equality aimed at will be more nearly reached.

In 1942 the Court held that an Oklahoma law providing for the sterilization of certain kinds of criminals and not others went beyond the bounds of reasonable classification. The case was *Skinner* v. *Oklahoma*, 316 U.S. 535 (1942). The law provided for the sterilization of habitual criminals and defined such persons as those convicted three or more times for crimes "amounting to felonies involving moral turpitude." The act provided for exceptions, however, for "offenses arising out of the violation of the prohibitory laws, revenue acts, embezzlement, or political offenses." One of Skinner's felonies was that of stealing chickens. Upon conviction for his third felony, the State began sterilization proceedings under the act, and Skinner appealed. In holding the law invalid, the Court pointed out that while one who was convicted three times for stealing chickens could be sterilized, the law exempted the embezzler from such treatment even though he might have stolen large amounts of money. Justice Douglas, for the Court, said: "When the law lays an unequal hand on those who have committed intrinsically the same quality of offense and sterilizes one and not the other, it has made as invidious a discrimination as if it had selected a particular race or nationality for oppressive treatment." He stated further, "The equal protection clause would indeed be a formula of empty words if such conspicuously artificial lines could be drawn."

In matters of economic regulation, an area in which the Court has almost gone out of the business of invalidating legislation on due process grounds, the State has exceedingly large powers of classification. In *Williamson* v. *Lee Optical Company*, 348 U.S. 483 (1955), for example, the Court examined an Oklahoma law which made it unlawful for any person not a licensed optometrist or ophthalmologist to fit lenses to the face or to duplicate or replace lenses except upon written prescriptive authority of a licensed ophthalmologist or optometrist. Sellers of ready-to-wear glasses were exempt, however, from the regulations, and the claim was made that the exemption rendered the law invalid under the equal protection clause. The Court unanimously disallowed the claim. Justice Douglas, for the Court, stated:

The problem of legislative classification is a perennial one, admitting of no doctrinaire definition. Evils in the same field may be of different dimensions and proportions, requiring different remedies. Or so the legislature may think. . . . Or the reform may take one step at a time, addressing itself to the phase of the problem which seems most acute to the legislative mind. . . . The legislature may select one phase of one field and apply a remedy there, neglecting the others. . . . The prohibition of the Equal Protection Clause goes no further than the invidious discrimination. We cannot say that that point has been reached here. For all this record shows, the ready-to-wear branch of this business may not loom large in Oklahoma or may present problems of regulation distinct from the other branch.

The "hands-off" attitude implicit in Justice Douglas' statement is fairly typical of the judicial restraint exhibited by the Court when faced with classifications affecting the economic or related areas. Thus states may classify cities by population and provide different powers or obligations for each class. The Social Security Act may be applied to large firms and exempt small firms. And license-tax or property-tax laws may differentiate by size or function. The constitutional requirement in each case is that the classification not be arbitrary, capricious, or irrational. Thus the traditional view of the equal protection clause was fairly aptly described by Justice Holmes as "the usual last resort of constitutional arguments." And so long as the Court finds no "invidious discrimination," this pattern of judicial restraint still applies in many areas of governmental regulatory policy.

An early case on the second issue was *Yick Wo v. Hopkins*, 118 U.S. 356 (1886). The board of supervisors of San Francisco enacted an ordinance providing that no one should carry on a laundry within the county "without having first obtained the consent of the board of supervisors, except the same be located in a building constructed either of brick or stone." Yick Wo, a Chinese subject resident in San Francisco, petitioned for a license to carry on a laundry in the same building in which he had been doing so for twenty-two years. His application was refused, and he was arrested and fined $10 for continuing in business without the license. After failure to pay the fine he was committed to jail, where he petitioned for a writ of habeas corpus. He had received certificates from the fire wardens and the health officer showing that his premises were safe and in sanitary condition. At the time the ordinance was passed, there were about 320 laundries in San Francisco of which about 240 were owned and operated by Chinese. It was admitted that all applications for a license made by Chinese persons were refused, while the petitions of all others, with one exception, were granted. About 150 Chinese were arrested for noncompliance, while, as stated in Yick Wo's petition, "those who are not subjects of China and who are conducting eighty-odd laundries under similar conditions, are left unmolested." The Supreme Court of California discharged the writ, but the United States Supreme Court reversed, holding the application of the law violative of the equal protection clause.

Justice Matthews, for the Court, stated:

In the present cases we are not obliged to reason from the probable to the actual, and pass upon the validity of the ordinances complained of, as tried merely by the opportunities which their terms afford, of unequal and unjust discrimination in their administration. For the cases present the ordinances in actual operation, and the facts shown establish an administration directed so exclusively against a particular class of persons as to warrant and require the conclusion that . . . they are applied by the public authorities charged with their administration . . . with a mind so unequal and oppressive as to amount to a practical denial by the State of that equal protection of the laws which is secured . . . by the broad and benign provisions of the Fourteenth Amendment. . . . Though the law itself be fair on its face and impartial in appearance, yet, if it is applied and administered by public authority with an evil eye and an unequal hand, so as practically to make unjust and illegal discriminations between persons in similar circumstances, material to their rights, the denial of equal justice is still within the prohibition of the Constitution. . . .

A similar issue, although in quite another context, was presented in *Niemotko v. Maryland*, 340 U.S. 268 (1951). Niemotko and others, who were Jehovah's Witnesses, scheduled Bible talks in the public park of Havre de Grace, Maryland. Although there was no ordinance prohibiting or regulating the use of this park, it had been the custom for organizations and individuals desiring to use it for meetings and celebrations of various kinds to obtain a permit from the park commissioner. In conformity with this practice, the group requested permission to use the park on four consecutive Sundays. The park commissioner refused.

The group appealed this refusal to the city council, and a hearing was held by the council. The evidence indicated that the only questions asked of the Witnesses at the hearing pertained to their alleged refusal to salute the flag, their views on the Bible, and other issues irrelevant to unencumbered use of the public parks. After the hearing, the council denied the request, although permits had been customarily granted for similar purposes, including meetings of religious and fraternal organizations. Niemotko was later arrested for attempting to hold the meeting without a permit and convicted of disorderly conduct. The Maryland appellate court denied certiorari, and on appeal the United States Supreme Court unanimously held the convictions violative of equal protection of the laws. Chief Justice Vinson, for the Court stated:

**The conclusion is inescapable that the use of the park was denied because of the City Council's dislike for or disagreement with the Witnesses on their views. The right to equal protection of the laws, in the exercise of those freedoms of speech and religion protected by the First and Fourteenth Amendments, has a firmer foundation than the whims or personal opinions of a local governing body.**

Because of limited resources, enforcement agencies often follow policies of selective enforcement of various laws. Presumably if such selectivity is based on race or religion, it would run afoul of the equal protection clause, as in the two cases discussed above. But suppose the only basis for the policy is the judicious allocation of scarce policing resources. This situation presents a more difficult question, and one which the Court has not fully explored. In one case, however, the Court expressly recognized the dilemma of the enforcing agency and approved a selective enforcement order of the FTC. The Commission obtained a cease and desist order against one firm engaged in illegal price arrangements. The firm complained that several other business competitors were following the same practices, and that it was unfair to subject one to serious financial loss without at the same time punishing the others. In *Moog Industries* v. *FTC*, 335 U.S. 411 (1958), the Court rejected the argument, and, after stressing the "specialized experienced judgment" of the Commission, concluded that "the Commission alone is empowered to develop that enforcement policy best calculated to achieve the ends contemplated by Congress and to allocate its available funds and personnel in such a way as to execute its policy efficiently and economically." [See Wayne R. LaFave, "The Police and Nonenforcement of the Law" (Two Pts.), 1962 Wis. L. Rev. 104, 179.]

## THE NEW EQUAL PROTECTION

*Brown v. Board of Education* and its progeny held that governmental discrimination based on race was invalid under the equal protection clause. While the language of the opinion did not specifically suggest a new formula for considering equal protection claims generally, it at least opened the way for such a development. By the late 1960s, the Court began to apply its new, stricter standard. The rule is fairly easily stated although the application is more difficult. When government legislates or acts either on the basis of a "suspect" category or with respect to a "fundamental right," the traditional standard is ignored, and the Court subjects the action to a "strict scrutiny." If it is a state law which is being examined, the Court will demand that there be shown a "compelling state interest" justifying the law's classification. If the regulation does not set up a suspect category or restrict a fundamental right, then the lesser invidious-discrimination test is still the standard. Race is, of course, the most suspect of categories, but the Court has now included "alienage" in this group as well. In *Graham v. Richardson*, 403 U.S. 365 (1971), the Court struck down statutes of Arizona and Pennsylvania which substantially limited welfare benefits to United States citizens. In holding the laws violative of the equal protection clause, Justice Blackmun, for the Court, stated:

Under traditional equal protection principles, a State retains broad discretion to classify as long as its classification has a reasonable basis. . . . But the Court's decisions have established that classifications based on alienage, like those based on nationality or race, are inherently suspect and subject to close judicial scrutiny. Aliens as a class are a prime example of a "discrete and insular" minority. . . for whom such heightened judicial solicitude is appropriate.

In 1973 the Court applied the *Graham* rule to invalidate a Connecticut provision which denied aliens admission to the bar.

### IN RE GRIFFITHS
### *413 U.S. 717 (1973)*

[Appellant Fre Le Poole Griffiths, a citizen of the Netherlands, came to the United States in 1965 as a visitor. In 1967 she married a citizen of the United States and became a resident of Connecticut. After graduation from law school, she applied in 1970 for permission to take the Connecticut bar examination. The County Bar Association found her qualified in all respects except that she was not a citizen of the United States as required by the Connecticut Practice Book, and on that account refused to allow her to take the examination. The Superior Court denied her petition for a decree that she be permitted to take the examination and be declared eligible for admission, and the Supreme Court of Connecticut affirmed.]

Mr. Justice Powell delivered the opinion of the Court. . . .

The Court has consistently emphasized that a State which adopts a suspect classification "bears a heavy burden of justification," . . . a burden which, though variously formulated, requires the State to meet certain standards of proof. In order to justify the use of a suspect classification, a State must show that its purpose or interest is both constitutionally permissible and substantial, and that its use of the classification is "necessary . . . to the accomplishment" of its purpose or the safeguarding of its interest.

Resident aliens, like citizens, pay taxes, support the economy, serve in the armed forces, and contribute in myriad other ways to our society. It is appropriate that a State bear a heavy burden when it deprives them of employment opportunities.

We hold that the Committee, acting on behalf of the State, has not carried its burden. The State's ultimate interest here implicated is to assure the requisite qualifications of persons licensed to practice law. It is undisputed that a State has a constitutionally permissible and substantial interest in determining whether an applicant possesses " 'the character and general fitness requisite for an attorney and counselor-at-law.' " . . . But no question is raised in this case as to appellant's character or general fitness. Rather, the sole basis for disqualification is her status as a resident alien.

The Committee defends [the rule] that applicants for admission to the bar be citizens of the United States on the ground that the special role of the lawyer justifies excluding aliens from the practice of law. . . . In order to establish a link between citizenship and the powers and responsibilities of the lawyer in Connecticut, the Committee contrasts a citizen's undivided allegiance to this country with a resident alien's possible conflict of loyalties. From this, the Committee concludes that a resident alien lawyer might in the exercise of his functions ignore his responsibilities to the courts or even his clients in favor of the interest of a foreign power.

We find these arguments unconvincing. It in no way denigrates a lawyer's high responsibilities to observe that the powers "to sign writs and subpoenas, take recognizances, [and] administer oaths" hardly involve matters of state policy or acts of such unique responsibility as to entrust them only to citizens. Nor do we think that the practice of law offers meaningful opportunities adversely to affect the interest of the United States. Certainly the Committee has failed to show the relevance of citizenship to any likelihood that a lawyer will fail to protect faithfully the interest of his clients.

Nor would the possibility that some resident aliens are unsuited to the practice of law be a justification for a wholesale ban . . . .

. . . Although, as we have acknowledged, a State does have a substantial interest in the qualifications of those admitted to the practice of law, the arguments advanced by the Committee fall short of showing that the classification established . . . is necessary to the promoting or safeguarding of this interest. . . .

Mr. Chief Justice Burger, with whom Mr. Justice Rehnquist joins, dissenting. . . .

In recent years the Court, in a rather casual way, has articulated the code phrase "suspect classification" as though it embraced a reasoned constitutional concept. Admittedly, it simplifies judicial work as do "per se" rules, but it tends to stop analysis while appearing to suggest an analytical process. . . .

Mr. Justice Rehnquist, dissenting. . . .

In *Hampton* v. *Mow Sun Wong*, 426 U.S. 88 (1976), the Court held that a federal regulation, adopted not by the president or Congress but by the Civil Service Commission, generally barring noncitizens from employment in the federal civil service, deprives lawfully admitted resident aliens of liberty without due process in violation of the Fifth Amendment. In the opinion for the Court by Justice Stevens (his first on the Court), however, it was pointed out that the concept of equal justice under law, included in the Fifth Amendment's guarantee of due process, and the equal protection clause of the Fourteenth Amendment were not always coextensive. "There may be overriding national interests which justify selective federal legislation that would be unacceptable for an individual State." Justice Stevens stated further:

We do not agree, however, with the petitioners' primary submission that the federal power over aliens is so plenary that any agent of the National Government may arbitrarily subject all resident aliens to different substantive rules than those applied to citizens. . . . We may assume with the petitioners that if the Congress or the President had expressly imposed the citizenship requirement, it would be justified by the national interest in providing an incentive for aliens to become naturalized, or possibly even as providing the President with an expendable token for treaty negotiating purposes; but we are not willing to presume that the Chairman of the Civil Service Commission, or any of the other original defendants, was deliberately fostering an interest so far removed from his normal responsibilities.

In *Mathews* v. *Diaz*, 426 U.S. 67 (1976), the Court held that a federal statute which conditions permanent resident aliens' eligibility for Medicare supplemental insurance on five years continuous residence in the United States does not constitute invidious discrimination within a class of aliens or deprive ineligible aliens of liberty or property in violation of the Fifth Amendment's due process clause.

In *Cabell* v. *Chavez-Salido,* 454 U.S 432 (1982), the Court upheld a California law that required "peace officers," including probation officers, to be United States citizens, although there were four dissents. The majority held that while restriction on lawfully resident aliens that primarily affects economic interests is subject to strict judicial scrutiny, such scrutiny is out of place when the restriction primarily serves a political function. The conclusion was that probation officers "sufficiently partake of the sovereign's power to exercise coercive force over the individual that they may be limited to citizens." The Court cited *Foley* v. *Connelie,* 435 U.S. 291 (1978), upholding a New York law requiring citizenship for members of the state police, and *Ambach* v. *Norwick,* 441 U.S. 68 (1979), holding that a State may require citizenship for its public teachers, since they are performing a "governmental function" of special importance in its relation to the functions of the state.

At this writing only race (or national origin) and alienage have been declared to be "inherently suspect" categories, although one would certainly assume that religion would be included. While some members of the Court would include classifications based on sex as suspect, a majority of the Justices have not so held as yet. (See the treatment of the cases under "Sex Discrimination," below.)

In a number of cases the Court has declared that there is a constitutional right to travel across state lines. An application of the equal protection clause to a state law allegedly impairing this "fundamental right" is found in *Shapiro* v. *Thompson,* which dealt with residence requirements for the receipt of welfare assistance.

SHAPIRO *v.* THOMPSON
*394 U.S. 618 (1969)*

Mr. Justice Brennan delivered the opinion of the Court.

These three appeals were restored to the calendar for reargument . . . Each is an appeal from a decison of a three-judge District Court holding unconstitutional a State or District of Columbia statutory provision which denies welfare assistance to residents of the State or District who have not resided within their jurisdictions for at least one year immediately preceding their applications for such assistance. We affirm the judgments of the District Courts in the three cases. . . .

There is no dispute that the effect of the waiting-period requirement in each case is to create two classes of needy resident families indistinguishable from each other except that one is composed of residents who have resided a year or more, and the second of residents who have resided less than a year, in the jurisdiction. On the basis of this sole difference the first class is granted and the second class is denied welfare aid upon which may depend the ability of the families to obtain the very means to subsist—food, shelter, and other necessities of life. In each case, the District Court found that appellees met the test for residence in their jurisdictions, as well as all other eligibility requirements except the requirement of residence for a full year prior to their applications. On reargument, appellees' central contention is that the statutory prohibition of benefits to residents of less than a year creates a classification which constitutes an invidious discrimination denying them equal protection of the laws. We agree. The interests which appellants assert are promoted by the classification either may not constitutionally be promoted by government or are not compelling governmental interests.

Primarily, appellants justify the waiting-period requirement as a protective device to preserve the fiscal integrity of state public assistance programs. It is asserted that people who require welfare assistance during their first year of residence in a State are likely to become continuing burdens on state welfare programs. Therefore, the argument runs, if such people can be deterred from entering the jurisdiction by denying them welfare benefits during the first year, state programs to assist long-time residents will not be impaired by a substantial influx of indigent newcomers.

There is weighty evidence that exclusion from the jurisdiction of the poor who need or may need relief was the specific objective of these provisions. In the Congress, sponsors of federal legislation to eliminate all residence requirements have been consistently opposed by representatives of state and local welfare agencies who have stressed the fears of the States that elimination of the requirements would result in a heavy influx of individuals into States providing the most generous benefits. . . .

We do not doubt that the one-year waiting-period device is well suited to discourage the influx of poor families in need of assistance. . . . But the purpose of inhibiting migration by needy persons into the State is constitutionally impermissible.

This Court long ago recognized that the nature of our Federal Union and our constitutional concepts of personal liberty unite to require that all citizens be free to travel throughout the length and breadth of our land uninhibited by statutes, rules, or regulations which unreasonably burden or restrict this movement. . . .

We have no occasion to ascribe the source of this right to travel interstate to a particular constitutional provision. It suffices that, as Mr. Justice Stewart said for the Court in *United States* v. *Guest,* . . . : "The constitutional right to travel from one State to another . . . occupies a position fundamental to the concept of our Federal Union. It is a right that has been firmly established and repeatedly recognized. . . ."

Thus, the purpose of deterring the in-migration of indigents cannot serve as justification for the classification created by the one-year waiting period, since that purpose is constitutionally impermissible. . . .

Alternatively, appellants argue that even if it is impermissible for a State to attempt to deter the entry of all indigents, the challenged classification may be justified as a permissible state attempt to discourage those indigents who would enter the State solely to obtain larger benefits. We observe first that none of the statutes before us is tailored to serve that objective. . . .

More fundamentally, a State may no more try to fence out those indigents who seek higher welfare benefits than it may try to fence out indigents generally. Implicit in any such distinction is the notion that indigents who enter a State with the hope of securing higher welfare benefits are somehow less deserving than indigents who do not take this consideration into account. But we do not perceive why a mother who is seeking to make a new life for herself and her children should be regarded as less deserving because she considers, among other factors, the level of a State's public assistance. Surely such a mother is no less deserving than a mother who moves into a particular State in order to take advantage of its better educational facilities. . . .

Appellants next advance as justification certain administrative and related governmental objectives allegedly served by the waiting-period requirement. They argue that the requirement (1) facilitates the planning of the welfare budget; (2) provides an objective test of residency; (3) minimizes the opportunity for recipients fraudulently to receive payments from more than one jurisdiction; and (4) encourages early entry of new residents into the labor force.

At the outset, we reject appellants' argument that a mere showing of a rational relationship between the waiting period and these four admittedly permissible state objectives will suffice to justify the classification. . . . The waiting-period provision denies welfare benefits to otherwise eligible applicants solely because they have recently moved into the jurisdiction. But in moving from State to State or to the District of Columbia appellees were exercising a constitutional right, and any classification which serves to penalize the exercise of that right, unless shown to be necessary to promote a *compelling* government interest, is unconstitutional. . . . [Here the opinion takes up each of the four justifications claimed, and the conclusion is that they either are not achieved by the residence period or can be better achieved by other reasonable methods.]

We conclude therefore that appellants in these cases do not use and have no need to use the one-year requirement for the governmental purposes suggested. Thus, even under traditional equal protection tests a classification of welfare applicants according to whether they have lived in the State for one year would seem irrational and unconstitutional. But, of course, the traditional criteria do not apply in these cases. Since the classification here touches on the fundamental right of interstate movement, its constitutionality must be judged by the stricter standard of whether it promotes a *compelling* state interest. Under this standard, the waiting-period requirement clearly violates the Equal Protection Clause. . . .

*Affirmed.*

Mr. Justice Stewart, concurring. . . .

Mr. Chief Justice Warren, with whom Mr. Justice Black joins, dissenting. . . .

Mr. Justice Harlan, dissenting. . . .

In upholding the equal protection argument, the Court has applied an equal protection doctrine of relatively recent vintage: the rule that statutory classifications which either are based upon certain "suspect" criteria or affect "fundamental rights" will be held to deny equal protection unless justified by a "compelling" governmental interest. . . .

The "compelling interest" doctrine, which today is articulated more explicitly than ever before, constitutes an increasingly significant exception to the long-established rule that a statute does not deny equal protection if it is rationally related to a legitimate governmental objective. The "compelling interest" doctrine has two branches. The branch which requires that classifications based upon "suspect" criteria be supported by a compelling interest apparently had its genesis in cases involving racial classifications, which have, at least since *Korematsu* v. *United States* . . . , have been regarded as inherently "suspect." . . .

I think that this branch of the "compelling interest" doctrine is sound when applied to racial classifications, for historically the Equal Protection Clause was largely a product of the desire to eradicate legal distinctions founded upon race. However, I believe that the more recent extensions have been unwise. . . .

The second branch of the "compelling interest" principle is even more troublesome. For it has been held that a statutory classification is subject to the "compelling interest" test if the result of the classification may be to affect a "fundamental right," regardless of the basis of the classification. . . .

I think this branch of the "compelling interest" doctrine particularly unfortunate and unnecessary. It is unfortunate because it creates an exception which threatens to swallow the standard equal protection rule. Virtually every state statute affects important rights. This Court has repeatedly held, for example, that the traditional equal protection standard is applicable to statutory classifications affecting such fundamental matters as the right to pursue a particular occupation, the right to receive greater or smaller wages or to work more or less hours, and the right to inherit property. Rights such as these are in principle indistinguishable from those involved here, and to extend the "compelling interest" rule to all cases in which such rights are affected would go far toward making this Court a "superlegislature." This branch of the doctrine is also unnecessary. When the right affected is one assured by the Federal Constitution, any infringement can be dealt with under the Due Process Clause. But when a statute affects only matters not mentioned in the Federal Constitution and is not arbitrary or irrational, I must reiterate that I know of nothing which entitles this Court to pick out particular human activities, characterize them as "fundamental," and give them added protection under an unusually stringent equal protection test. . . .

While the Court has held that the right to travel interstate is a "fundamental right," it has not so categorized the right of international travel. In *Califano* v. *Aznavorian*, 439 U.S. 170 (1978), the Court upheld an act of Congress cutting off certain benefits to the needy aged, blind, and disabled for any month which the recipient spends entirely outside the United States. The majority opinion stated:

The constitutional right of interstate travel is virtually unqualified. . . . By contrast the "right" of international travel has been considered to be no more than an aspect of the "liberty" protected by the Due Process Clause of the Fifth Amendment. . . . As such, this "right," the Court has held, can be regulated within the bounds of due process.

In addition to the right to travel interstate, *Kramer* v. *Union Free School District No. 15* (1969) held that voting rights are clearly among the "fundamental rights" of citizens.

### KRAMER *v.* UNION FREE SCHOOL DISTRICT NO. 15
### *395 U.S. 621 (1969)*

Mr. Chief Justice Warren delivered the opinion of the Court.

In this case we are called on to determine whether §2012 of the New York Education Law . . . is constitutional. The legislation provides that in certain New York school districts residents who are otherwise eligible to vote in state and federal elections may vote in the school district election only if they (1) own (or lease) taxable real property within the district, or (2) are parents (or have custody) of children enrolled in the local public schools. Appellant, a bachelor who neither owns nor leases taxable real property, filed suit in federal court claiming that §2012 denied him equal protection of the laws in violation of the Fourteenth Amendment. With one judge dissenting, a three-judge District Court dismissed appellant's complaint. Finding that §2012 does violate the Equal Protection Clause of the Fourteenth Amendment, we reverse. . . .

. . . [I]n this case, we must give the statute a close and exacting examination. "[S]ince the right to exercise the franchise in a free and unimpaired manner is preservative of other basic civil and political rights, any alleged infringement of the right of citizens to vote must be carefully and meticulously scrutinized." *Reynolds* v. *Sims.* . . . This careful examination is necessary because statutes distributing the franchise constitute the foundation of our representative society. Any unjustified discrimination in determining who may participate in political affairs or in the selection of public officials undermines the legitimacy of representative government.

Thus, state apportionment statutes, which may *dilute* the effectiveness of some citizens' votes, receive close scrutiny from this Court. . . . No less rigid an examination is applicable to statutes *denying* the franchise to citizens who are otherwise qualified by residence and age. . . . Therefore, if a challenged state statute grants the right to vote to some bona fide residents of requisite age and citizenship and denies the franchise to others, the Court must determine whether the exclusions are necessary to promote a compelling state interest. . . .

And, for these reasons, the deference usually given to the judgment of legislators does not extend to decisions concerning which resident citizens may participate in the election of legislators and other public officials. Those decisions must be carefully scrutinized by the Court to determine whether each resident citizen has, as far as is possible, an equal voice in the selections. Accordingly, when we are reviewing statutes which deny some residents the right to vote, the general presumption of constitutionality afforded state statutes and the traditional approval given state classifications if the Court can conceive of a "rational basis" for the distinctions made are not applicable. . . .

Appellant . . . contends that he and others of his class are substantially interested in and significantly affected by the school meeting decisions. All members of the community have an interest in the quality and structure of public education, appellant says, and he urges that "the decisions taken by local boards . . . may have grave consequences to the entire population." . . .

. . . [A]ppellees argue that the State has a legitimate interest in limiting the franchise in school district elections to "members of the community of interest"—those "primarily interested in such elections." Second, appellees urge that the State may reasonably and permissibly conclude that "property taxpayers" (including lessees of taxable property who share the tax burden through rent payments) and parents of the children enrolled in the district's schools are those "primarily interested" in school affairs.

We do not understand appellees to argue that the State is attempting to limit the franchise to those "subjectively concerned" about school matters. Rather, they appear to argue that the State's legitimate interest is in restricting a voice in school matters to those "directly affected" by such decisions. The State apparently reasons that since the schools are financed in part by local property taxes, persons whose out-of-pocket expenses are "directly" affected by property tax changes should be allowed to vote. Similarly, parents of children in school are thought to have a "direct" stake in school affairs and are given a vote. . . .

. . . .[A]ssuming, arguendo, that New York legitimately might limit the franchise in these school district elections to those "primarily interested in school affairs," close scrutiny of the §2012 classifications demonstrates that they do not accomplish this purpose with sufficient precision to justify denying appellant the franchise. . . .

The classifications in §2012 permit inclusion of many persons who have, at best, a remote and indirect interest in school affairs and, on the other hand, exclude others who have a distinct and direct interest in the school meeting decisions.

. . . [T]he issue is not whether the legislative judgments are rational. A more exacting standard obtains. The issue is whether the §2012 requirements do in fact sufficiently further a compelling state interest to justify denying the franchise to appellant and members of his class. The requirements of §2012 are not sufficiently tailored to limiting the franchise to those "primarily interested" in school affairs to justify the denial of the franchise to appellant and members of his class.

The judgment . . . is therefore reversed. The case is remanded for further proceedings consistent with this opinion.

It is so ordered.

Mr. Justice Stewart, with whom Mr. Justice Black and Mr. Justice Harlan join, dissenting. . . .

In a variety of cases claimants have attempted to achieve the advantage of the "strict scrutiny" rule by contentions that challenged laws either set up "suspect" categories or impaired "fundamental rights." Laws discriminating on the basis of legitimacy of birth or on the basis of wealth have been so challenged, for example, but thus far the Court has not held these to be suspect classifications. It should not be assumed, however, that such a denial automatically results in a holding that the law meets the equal protection test. Laws which classify must still overcome the "invidious discrimination" claim even if they do not involve the strict scrutiny standard. In *Weber* v. *Aetna Casualty & Surety Co.*, 406 U.S. 164 (1972), for example, a Louisiana workman's compensation law was challenged which allowed illegitimate children to recover benefits only if there were not enough legitimate children to exhaust the maximum benefits under the statute. In holding the classification invalid, Justice Powell, for the Court, stated:

Obviously, no child is responsible for his birth and penalizing the illegitimate child is an ineffectual—as well as an unjust—way of deterring the parent. Courts are powerless to prevent the social opprobrium suffered by these hapless children, but the Equal Protection Clause does enable us to strike down discriminatory laws relating to status of birth where—as in this case—the classification is justified by no legitimate state interest, compelling or otherwise.

The problem of the indigent who is disadvantaged in his contacts with governmental action or policy may raise serious equal protection questions. The long history of the development of the right of the indigent to appointed counsel when charged with a jailable criminal offense took place largely within the context of the due process clause. But there were clearly equal protection overtones in much of the language employed by the Court in the various decisions. The issue was more clearly raised in a case involving a convicted indigent who was fined, but who was sentenced to a term in jail because of his inability to pay the fine. In *Tate* v. *Short,* 401 U.S. 395 (1971), the Court reversed the conviction, holding that the sentence of imprisonment "worked an invidious discrimination solely because the defendant was too poor to pay the fine, and therefore violated the Equal Protection Clause." The Court suggested alternatives for imprisonment, including the payment of fines in installments.

A case which combined the contentions that poverty (or wealth) is a suspect classification and that education is a fundamental right was *San Antonio* v. *Rodriguez,* 411 U.S. 1 (1973). At issue was the question of whether interdistrict disparities in school expenditures—with larger budgets in the richer districts and smaller budgets in the poorer districts—constituted a violation of the equal protection clause.

SAN ANTONIO *v.* RODRIGUEZ

*411 U.S. 1 (1973)*

[The financing of public schools in Texas is a combination of state aid and local contribution based on property taxes. Appellees brought this class action contending that the state's reliance on local property taxation favors the more affluent districts and violates the equal protection clause because of substantial interdistrict disparities in per-pupil expenditures in the school system. Appellees are residents of the Edgewood Independent School District, a predominantly Mexican-American area. The average assessed property value per pupil is $5,900—the lowest in the metropolitan area. At a tax rate of $1.05 per $100—the highest in the metropolitan area—the district contributed $26 per child for the 1967–1968 school year above the legal minimum required. The combined state-local total was $248 per pupil, and federal funds brought the total to $356 per pupil.

In Alamo Heights district the assessed property value per pupil was over $49,000. The local tax rate of $.85 per $100 yielded an excess of $333 per pupil over its required minimum. The combined state-local total was $558 per pupil, and federal funds brought the total to $594 per student.]

Mr. Justice Powell delivered the opinion of the Court. . . .

Despite . . . recent increases, substantial interdistrict disparities in school expenditures found by the District Court to prevail in San Antonio and in varying degrees throughout the State still exist. And it was these disparities, largely attributable to differences in the amounts of money collected through local property taxation, that led the District Court to conclude that Texas' dual system of public school finance violated the Equal Protection Clause. The District Court held that the Texas system discriminates on the basis of wealth in the manner in which education is provided for its people. Finding that wealth is a "suspect" classification and that education is a "fundamental" interest, the District Court held that the Texas system could be sustained only if the State could show that it was premised upon some compelling state interest. On this issue the court concluded that "not only are defendants unable to demonstrate compelling state interests . . . they fail even to establish a reasonable basis for these classifications." . . .

We are unable to agree that this case, which in significant aspects is *sui generis,* may be so neatly fitted into the conventional mosaic of constitutional analysis under the Equal Protection Clause. Indeed, for the several reasons that follow, we find neither the suspect classification nor the fundamental interest analysis persuasive.

The precedents of this Court provide the proper starting point. The individuals or groups of individuals who constituted the class discriminated against in our prior cases shared two distinguishing characteristics: because of their impecunity they were completely unable to pay for some desired benefit, and as a consequence, they sustained an absolute deprivation of a meaningful opportunity to enjoy that benefit. . . .

Only appellees' first possible basis for describing the class disadvantaged by the Texas school finance system—discrimination against a class of definably "poor" persons—might arguably meet the criteria established in these prior cases. Even a cursory examination, however, demonstrates that neither of the two distinguishing characteristics of wealth classifications can be found there. First, in support of their charge that the system discriminates against the "poor," appellees have made no effort to demonstrate that it operates to the peculiar disadvantages of any class fairly definable as indigent, or as composed of persons whose incomes are beneath any designated poverty level. Indeed, there is reason to believe that the poorest families are not necessarily clustered in the poorest property districts. . . .

Second, neither appellees nor the District Court addressed the fact that, unlike each of the foregoing cases, lack of personal resources has not occasioned an absolute deprivation of the desired benefit. The argument here is not that the children in districts having relatively low assessable property values are receiving no public education; rather, it is that they are receiving a poorer quality education than that available to children in districts having more assessable wealth. Apart from the unsettled and disputed question whether the quality of education may be determined by the amount of money expended for it, a sufficient answer to appellees' argument is that at least where wealth is involved the Equal Protection Clause does not require absolute equality or precisely equal advantages. Nor, indeed, in view of the infinite variables affecting the educational process, can any system assure equal quality of education except in the most relative sense. . . .

[The opinion here rejects the argument that the system discriminates on the basis of family income.]

This brings us, then, to the third way in which the classification scheme might be defined—*district* wealth discrimination. Since the only correlation indicated by the evidence is between district property wealth and expenditures, it may be argued that discrimination might be found without regard to the individual income characteristics of district residents. . . .

However described, it is clear that appellees' suit asks this Court to extend its most exacting scrutiny to review a system that allegedly discriminates against a large, diverse, and amorphous class, unified only by the common factor of residence in districts that happen to have less taxable wealth than other districts. The system of alleged discrimination and the class it defines have none of the traditional indicia of suspectness: the class is not saddled with such disabilities, or subjected to such a history of purposeful unequal treatment, or relegated to such a position of political powerlessness as to command extraordinary protection from the majoritarian political process.

We thus conclude that the Texas system does not operate to the peculiar disadvantage of any suspect class. But in recognition of the fact that this Court has never heretofore held that wealth discrimination alone provides an adequate basis for invoking strict scrutiny, appellees have not relied solely on this contention. They also assert that the State's system impermissibly interferes with the exercise of a "fundamental" right and that accordingly the prior decisions of this Court require the application of the strict standard of judicial review. . . .

In *Brown* v. *Board of Education*, . . . a unanimous Court recognized that "education is perhaps the most important function of state and local governments.". . . What was said there in the context of racial discrimination has lost none of its vitality with the passage of time. . . .

Nothing this Court holds today in any way detracts from our historic dedication to public education. We are in complete agreement with the conclusion of the three-judge panel below that "the grave significance of education both to the individual and to our society" cannot be doubted. But the importance of a service performed by the State does not determine whether it must be regarded as fundamental for purposes of examination under the Equal Protection Clause. . . .

. . . It is not the province of this Court to create substantive constitutional rights in the name of guaranteeing equal protection of the laws. Thus the key to discovering whether education is "fundamental" is not to be found in comparisons of the relative societal significance of education as opposed to subsistence or housing. Nor is it to be found by weighing whether education is as important as the right to travel. Rather, the answer lies in assessing whether there is a right to education explicitly or implicitly guaranteed by the Constitution. . . .

Education, of course, is not among the rights afforded explicit protection under our Federal Constitution. Nor do we find any basis for saying it is implicitly so protected. As we have said, the undisputed importance of education will not alone cause this Court to depart from the usual standard for reviewing a State's social and economic legislation. . . .

We need not rest our decision, however, solely on the inappropriateness of the strict scrutiny test. A century of Supreme Court adjudication under the Equal Protection Clause affirmatively supports the application of the traditional standard of review, which requires only that the State's system be shown to bear some rational relationship to legitimate state purposes. This case represents far more than a challenge to the manner in which Texas provides for the education of its children. We have here nothing less than a direct attack on the way in which Texas has chosen to raise and disburse state and local tax revenues. We are asked to condemn the State's judgment in conferring on political subdivisions the power to tax local property to supply revenues for local interests. In so doing, appellees would have the Court intrude in an area in which it has traditionally deferred to state legislatures. This Court has often admonished against such interference with the State's fiscal policies under the Equal Protection Clause. . . .

. . . The very complexity of the problems of financing and managing a statewide public school system suggest that "there will be more than one constitutionally permissible method of solving them," and that, within the limits of rationality, "the legislature's efforts to tackle the problems" should be entitled to respect. . . . On even the most basic questions in this area the scholars and educational experts are divided. Indeed, one of the hottest sources of controversy concerns the extent to which there is a demonstrable correlation between educational expenditures and the quality of education—an assumed correlation underlying virtually every legal conclusion drawn by the District Court in this case. . . .

. . . The Texas plan is not the result of hurried, ill-conceived legislation. It certainly is not the product of purposeful discrimination against any group or class. . . . In its essential characteristics the Texas plan for financing public education reflects what many educators for a half century have thought was an enlightened approach to a problem for which there is no perfect solution. We are unwilling to assume for ourselves a level of wisdom superior to that of legislators, scholars, and educational authorities in 49 States, especially where the alternatives proposed are only recently conceived and nowhere yet tested. The constitutional standard under the Equal Protection Clause is whether the challenged state action rationally furthers a legitimate state purpose or interest. . . . We hold that the Texas plan abundantly satisfies this standard. . . .

Mr. Justice Stewart, concurring. . . .

Mr. Justice Brennan, dissenting.

Although I agree with my Brother White that the Texas statutory scheme is devoid of any rational basis, and for that reason is violative of the Equal Protection Clause, I also record my disagreement with the Court's rather distressing assertion that a right may be deemed "fundamental" for the purposes of equal protection analysis only if it is "explicitly or implicitly guaranteed by the Constitution." . . .

Here, there can be no doubt that education is inextricably linked to the right to participate in the electoral process and to the rights of free speech and association guaranteed by the First Amendment. . . . This being so, any classification affecting education must be subjected to strict judicial scrutiny, and since even the State concedes that the statutory scheme now before us cannot pass constitutional muster under this stricter standard of review, I can only conclude that the Texas school financing scheme is constitutionally invalid.

Mr. Justice White, with whom Mr. Justice Douglas and Mr. Justice Brennan join, dissenting. . . .

Perhaps the majority believes that the major disparity in revenues provided and permitted by the Texas system is inconsequential. I cannot agree, however, that the difference of the magnitude appearing in this case can sensibly be ignored, particularly since the State itself considers it so important to provide opportunities to exceed the minimum state educational expenditures. . . .

. . .[I]n the present case we would blink reality to ignore the fact that school districts, and students in the end, are differentially affected by the Texas school financing scheme with respect to their capability to supplement the Minimum Foundation School Pogram. At the very least, the law discriminates against those children and their parents who live in districts where the per-pupil tax base is sufficiently low to make impossible the provision of comparable school revenues by resort to the real property tax which is the only device the State extends for this purpose.

Mr. Justice Marshall, with whom Mr. Justice Douglas concurs, dissenting.

The Court today decides, in effect, that a State may constitutionally vary the quality of education which it offers its children in accordance with the amount of taxable wealth located in the school districts within which they reside. The majority's decision represents an abrupt departure from the mainstream of recent state and federal court decisions concerning the unconstitutionality of state educational financing schemes dependent upon taxable local wealth. More unfortunately, though, the majority's holding can only be seen as a retreat from our historic commitment to equality of educational opportunity and as unsupportable acquiescence in a system which deprives children in their earliest years of the chance to reach their full potential as citizens. The Court does this despite the absence of any substantial justification for a scheme which arbitrarily channels educational resources in accordance with the fortuity of the amount of taxable wealth within each district.

In my judgment, the right of every American to an equal start in life, so far as the provision of a state service as important as education is concerned, is far too vital to permit state discrimination on grounds as tenuous as those presented by this record. Nor can I accept the notion that it is sufficient to remit these appellees to the vagaries of the political process which, contrary to the majority's suggestion, has proven singularly unsuited to the task of providing a remedy for this discrimination. I, for one, am unsatisfied with the hope of an ultimate "political" solution sometime in the indefinite future while, in the meantime, countless children unjustifiably receive inferior educations that "may affect their hearts and minds in a way unlikely ever to be undone." . . .

The appellants do not deny the disparities in educational funding caused by variations in taxable district property wealth. They do contend, however, that whatever the differences in per pupil spending among Texas districts, there are no discriminatory consequences for the children of the disadvantaged districts. . . .

In my view, though, even an unadorned restatement of this contention is sufficient to reveal its absurdity. Authorities concerned with educational quality no doubt disagree as to the significance of variations in per pupil spending. . . . That a child forced to attend an underfunded school with poorer physical facilities, less experienced teachers, larger classes, and a narrower range of courses than a school with substantially more funds—and thus with greater choice in educational planning—may nevertheless excel is to the credit of the child, not the State. . . .

Even if the Equal Protection Clause encompassed some theory of constitutional adequacy, discrimination in the provision of educational opportunity would certainly seem to be a poor candidate for its application. Neither the majority nor appellants informs us how judicially manageable standards are to be derived for determining how much education is "enough" to excuse constitutional discrimination. . . .

## THE "THREE-TIERED" APPROACH

Dissatisfied with the results in limiting themselves to only two categories in dealing with equal protection issues ("strict scrutiny" and the "compelling state interest" test on the one hand and the "rational basis" test on the other), the Court majority has created a third category—a "middle-tier" of cases which require a search for a "substantial" state interest, although not a "compelling" state interest. (One might also say that such cases demand *some* scrutiny but not *strict* scrutiny.) The lead case on the development is *Craig v. Boren*, decided in 1976.

CRAIG *v.* BOREN
*429 U.S. 190 (1976)*

[Oklahoma law prohibits the sale of 3.2 percent beer to males under twenty-one and to females under eighteen years of age. Craig, a male between the ages of eighteen and twenty-one, brought suit for declaratory and injunctive relief against the governor and other state officials, asserting that the gender-based age classification in the statute violated the Equal Protection Clause. A three-judge federal court denied relief, and the decision was appealed.]

Mr. Justice Brennan delivered the opinion of the Court. . . .

Analysis may appropriately begin with the reminder that *Reed* [v. *Reed*] emphasized that statutory classifications that distinguish between males and females are "subject to scrutiny under the Equal Protection Clause." . . . To withstand constitutional challenge, previous cases establish that classifications by gender must serve important governmental objectives and must be subtantially related to achievement of those objectives. Thus, in *Reed*, the objectives of "reducing the workload on probate courts," . . . and "avoiding intrafamily controversy," . . . were deemed of insufficient importance to sustain use of an overt gender criterion in the appointment of administrators of intestate decedents' estates. Decisions following *Reed* similarly have rejected administrative ease and convenience as sufficiently important objectives to justify gender-based classifications. . . .

. . . We turn then to the question whether, under *Reed*, the difference between males and females with respect to the purchase of 3.2% beer warrants the differential in age drawn by the Oklahoma statute. We conclude that it does not. . . .

The appellees introduced a variety of statistical surveys. First, an analysis of arrest statistics for 1973 demonstrated that 18–20-year-old male arrests for "driving under the influence" and "drunkenness" substantially exceeded female arrests for that same age period. Similarly, youths aged 17–21 were found to be overrepresented among those killed or injured in traffic accidents, with males again numerically exceeding females in this regard. Third, a random roadside survey in Oklahoma City revealed that young males were more inclined to drive and drink beer than were their female counterparts. Fourth, Federal Bureau of Investigation nationwide statistics exhibited a notable increase in arrests for "driving under the influence." Finally, statistical evidence gathered in other jurisdictions . . . was offered to corroborate Oklahoma's experience by indicating the pervasiveness of youthful participation in motor vehicle accidents following the imbibing of alcohol. Conceding that "the case is not free from doubt," . . . the District Court nonetheless concluded that this statistical showing substantiated "a rational basis for the legislative judgment underlying the challenged classification." . . .

. . . Setting aside the obvious methodological problems, the surveys do not adequately justify the salient features of Oklahoma's gender-based traffic-safety law. None purports to measure the use and dangerousness of 3.2% beer as opposed to alcohol generally, a detail that is of particular importance since, in light of its low alcohol level, Oklahoma apparently considers the 3.2% beverage to be "nonintoxicating." . . .

There is no reason to belabor this line of analysis. It is unrealistic to expect either members of the judiciary or state officials to be well versed in the rigors of experimental or statistical technique. But this merely illustrates that proving broad sociological propositions by statistics is a dubious business, and one that inevitably is in tension with the normative philosophy that underlies the Equal Protection Clause. Suffice to say that the showing offered by the appellees does not satisfy us that sex represents a legitimate, accurate proxy for the regulation of drinking and driving. In fact, when it is further recognized that Oklahoma's statute prohibits only the selling of 3.2% beer to young males and not their drinking the beverage once acquired (even after purchase by their 18–20-year-old female companions), the relationship between gender and traffic safety becomes far too tenuous to satisfy *Reed*'s requirement that the gender-based difference be substantially related to achievement of the statutory objective. . . .

We conclude that the gender-based differential contained in [the statute] constitutes a denial of the equal protection of the laws to males aged 18–20 and reverse the judgment of the District Court.

*It is so ordered.*

Mr. Justice Powell, concurring. . . .

With respect to the equal protection standard, I agree that *Reed* v. *Reed* . . . is the most relevant precedent. But I find it unnecessary, in deciding this case, to read that decision as broadly as some of the Court's language may imply. *Reed* and subsequent cases involving gender-based classifications make clear that the Court subjects such classifications to a more critical examination than is normally applied when "fundamental" constitutional rights and "suspect classes" are not present. . . .

. . . [T]his gender-based classification does not bear a fair and substantial relation to the object of the legislation.

As is evident from our opinions, the Court has had difficulty in agreeing upon a standard of equal protection analysis that can be applied consistently to the wide variety of legislative classifications. There are valid reasons for dissatisfaction with the "two-tier" approach that has been prominent in the Court's decisions in the past decade. Although viewed by many as a result-oriented substitute for more critical analysis, that approach—with its narrowly limited "upper-tier"—now has substantial precedential support. As has been true of *Reed* and its progeny, our decision today will be viewed by some as a "middle-tier" approach. While I would not endorse that characterization and would not welcome a further subdividing of equal protection analysis, candor compels the recognition that the relatively deferential "rational basis" standard of review normally applied takes on a sharper focus when we address a gender-based classification. So much is clear from our recent cases. . . .

Mr. Justice Stevens, concurring.

There is only one Equal Protection Clause. It requires every State to govern impartially. It does not direct the courts to apply one standard of review in some cases and a different standard in other cases. Whatever criticism may be leveled at a judicial opinion implying that there are at least three such standards applies with the same force to a double standard. . .

Mr. Justice Blackmun, concurring in part. . . .

Mr. Justice Stewart, concurring in the judgment. . . .

Mr. Chief Justice Burger, dissenting. . . .

Mr. Justice Rehnquist, dissenting. . . .

The Court's conclusion that a law which treats males less favorably than females "must serve important governmental objectives and must be substantially related to achievement of those objectives" apparently comes out of thin air. The Equal Protection Clause contains no such language, and none of our previous cases adopt that standard. I would think we have had enough difficulty with the two standards of review which our cases have recognized—the norm of "rational basis," and the "compelling state interest" required where a "suspect classification" is involved—so as to counsel weightily against the insertion of still another "standard" between those two. How is this Court to divine what objectives are important? How is it to determine whether a particular law is "substantially" related to the achievement of such objective, rather than related in some other way to its achievement? Both of the phrases used are so diaphanous and elastic as to invite subjective judicial preferences or prejudices relating to particular types of legislation, masquerading as judgments whether such legislation is directed at "important" objectives or, whether the relationship to those objectives is "substantial" enough. . . .

It would appear that illegitimacy has arrived at middle-tier status, although an earlier decision in *Labine* v. *Vincent,* 401 U.S. 532 (1971), upholding a Louisiana law providing that illegitimate children could not share equally with legitimate children in the parents' estate, seemingly followed the "rational basis" model. Speaking for a plurality in *Lalli* v. *Lalli,* 439 U.S. 259 (1978), Chief Justice Burger stated: "Although . . . classifications based on illegitimacy are not subject to 'strict scrutiny,' they nevertheless are invalid under the Fourteenth Amendment if they are not substantially related to permissible state interests." And most of the decisions since 1968 have been against statutes discriminating against illegitimate children.

In 1975 the Texas legislature amended its education laws to deny funds to local school districts for the education of illegal alien children. In an equal protection challenge to the law, in *Plyler* v. *Doe,* 457 U.S. 202 (1982), the Court faced the problem of what standard to employ in the case. It had held that alienage was a suspect category, and it had held that education was not a fundamental right. But how should it treat the case of an *illegal* minor alien who was to be denied access to public education altogether? After a lengthy discussion of the peculiar plight of such children and the problem of "promoting the creation and perpetuation of a subclass of illiterates within our boundaries," Justice Brennan, for the majority, adopted the "middle-tier" standard. "If the State is to deny a discrete group of innocent children the free public education that it offers to other children residing within its borders, that denial must be justified by a showing that it furthers some substantial state interest. No such showing was made here." Chief Justice Burger, speaking for the four dissenters, said:

[B]y patching together bits and pieces of what might be termed quasi-suspect-class and quasi-fundamental-rights analysis, the Court spins out a theory custom-tailored to the facts of these cases.

In the end, we are told little more than that the level of scrutiny employed to strike down the Texas law applies only when illegal alien children are deprived of a public education. . . . If ever a court was guilty of an unabashedly result-oriented approach, this case is a prime example.

## RACE DISCRIMINATION

The single most dramatic change in the broad movement toward equal rights since the abolition of slavery has been the reversal in constitutional interpretation which now bars governmental discrimination based on race. For most of the period since 1865 the law looked in two directions with regard to racial discrimination. It was held unconstitutional for the state explicitly to deny to persons because of their race a right enjoyed by members of other races, but, under the decision in *Plessy* v. *Ferguson* in 1896, it was not unconstitutional for the state to dispense governmental benefits and employ its police powers along lines separated on the basis of race. The Louisiana statute upheld in that case required "equal but separate accomodations for the white and colored races" in railway coaches. The phrase has been reversed and since that time has been referred to as the "separate but equal" doctrine. The landmark decision in the area of race discrimination, *Brown* v. *Board of Education of Topeka,* 347 U.S. 483 (1954), although technically confined to education, has been subsequently broadened to a holding that separate facilities are *inherently unequal,* and therefore governmental discrimination on the basis of race cannot meet the test of equal protection of the laws. [The literature on the subject of racial discrimination is enormous, but for an excellent treatment of the development of the law through the *Brown* case, see A. P. Blaustein and C. C. Ferguson, Jr., *Desegregation and the Law* (New Brunswick: Rutgers University Press, 1957). On the *Brown* case itself, see Richard Kluger, *Simple Justice: The History of Brown v. Board of Education and Black America's Struggle for Equality* (New York: Knopf, 1975). An invaluable reference source is the *Race Relations Law Reporter* (Nashville: Vanderbilt University School of Law, published quarterly, 1956–1974).]

The bitterly criticized decision in *Dred Scott* v. *Sandford,* 19 Howard 393 (1857), held that the Constitution did not contemplate acquisition of United States citizenship by Negroes. And after the Civil War the Thirteenth, Fourteenth, and Fifteenth Amendments were adopted. As a package, these amendments were clearly intended to elevate the Negro to at least equal *legal* status with other United States citizens. The extent to which they limit private and quasi-public discrimination based on race is actually still a matter of argument, although the question is largely moot since the adoption of the Civil Rights Act of 1964. The Thirteenth Amendment, of course, does limit private action, but the Fourteenth restricts only "state action." It required nearly a century of litigation to reach a clear holding that all governmental distinctions based on race were unconstitutional. One of the earliest post-Civil War cases on the application of the Fourteenth Amendment to racial discrimination was decided in 1880 and dealt with the constitutionality of a statutory bar to jury service for Negroes. The case was *Strauder* v. *West Virginia* and was decided by a Court whose members had lived through the Civil War and observed the activity of the subsequent Congresses in adopting constitutional amendments and legislation designed to protect the Negro.

### STRAUDER *v.* WEST VIRGINIA
#### *100 U.S. 303 (1880)*

[Strauder, a Negro, was convicted of murder in a West Virginia court by an all-white jury. Under state law only white male citizens were liable for jury service. A petition for removal of the cause to the federal circuit court on the ground of racial discrimination in the selection of jurors was denied, and the trial proceeded in state court. The state supreme court affirmed the conviction and the United States Supreme Court reviewed the conviction on writ of error.]

Mr. Justice Strong delivered the opinion of the Court.

[The Fourteenth Amendment] is one of a series of constitutional provisions having a common purpose; namely, securing to a race recently emancipated, a race that through many generations had been held in slavery, all the civil rights that the superior race enjoy. . . . At the time when they were incorporated into the Constitution, it required little knowledge of human nature to anticipate that those who had long been regarded as an inferior and subject race would, when suddenly raised to the rank of citizenship, be looked upon with jealousy and positive dislike, and that state laws might be enacted or enforced to perpetuate the distinctions that had before existed. Discriminations against them had been habitual. . . . They especially needed protection against unfriendly action in the States where they were resident. It was in view of these considerations the Fourteenth Amendment was framed and adopted.

It was designed to assure to the colored race the enjoyment of all the civil rights that under the law are enjoyed by white persons, and to give to that race the protection of the general government, in that enjoyment, whenever it should be denied by the States. . . .

If this is the spirit and meaning of the amendment, whether it means more or not, it is to be construed liberally, to carry out the purposes of its framers. . . . It ordains that no State shall deprive any person of life, liberty, or property, without due process of law, or deny to any person within its jurisdiction the equal protection of the laws. What is this but declaring that the law in the States shall be the same for the black as for the white; that all persons, whether colored or white, shall stand equal before the laws of the States, and, in regard to the colored race, for whose protection the amendment was primarily designed, that no discrimination shall be made against them by law because of their color? The words of the amendment, it is true, are prohibitory, but they contain a necessary implication of a positive immunity, or right, most valuable to the colored race,—the right to exemption from unfriendly legislation against them distinctively as colored,—exemption from legal discriminations, implying inferiority in civil society, lessening the security of their enjoyment of the rights which others enjoy, and discriminations which are steps towards reducing them to the condition of a subject race. . . .

In view of these considerations, it is hard to see why the statute of West Virginia should not be regarded as discriminating against a colored man when he is put upon trial for an alleged criminal offense against the State. It is not easy to comprehend how it can be said that while every white man is entitled to a trial by a jury selected from persons of his own race or color, or rather, selected without discrimination against his color, and a negro is not, the latter is equally protected by the law with the former. Is not protection of life, and liberty against race or color prejudice a right, a legal right, under the constitutional amendment? And how can it be maintained that compelling a colored man to submit to a trial for his life by a jury drawn from a panel from which the State has expressly excluded every man of his race, because of color alone, however well qualified in other respects, is not a denial to him of equal legal protection? . . .

The Fourteenth Amendment makes no attempt to enumerate the rights it is designed to protect. It speaks in general terms, and those are as comprehensive as possible. Its language is prohibitory; but every prohibition implies the existence of rights and immunities, prominent among which is an immunity from inequality of legal protection, either for life, liberty, or property. Any state action that denies this immunity to a colored man is in conflict with the Constitution. . . .

*Reversed.*

[Justice Field, joined by Justice Clifford, dissented.]

The bar against state discrimination on race in jury service has been applied uniformly by the Court since *Strauder,* although it extends only to a requirement that racial discrimination not be employed in the selection process and does not command that a given racial distribution be found on a particular jury. Thus in *Hernandez* v. *Texas,* 347 U.S. 475 (1954), the Court reversed the conviction of a Mexican-American where the record showed a systematic exclusion of Mexican-Americans from juries. (See the discussion of jury trial in Chapter 3.)

Despite the sweeping statements in Justice Strong's opinion concerning the scope of protection offered by the Fourteenth Amendment against racial discrimination, the Court, less than twenty years later, in 1896, was prepared to uphold, with only one dissent, the power of the state to require racial segregation. The case was *Plessy* v. *Ferguson,* and the dissenter, Justice Harlan, was the only remaining member who had voted with the majority in the *Strauder* case. (Justice Field also remained, but he had dissented in the earlier case.)

PLESSY *v.* FERGUSON
*163 U.S. 537 (1896)*

[A Louisiana statute, passed in 1890, required all railway companies carrying passengers in the state to provide "equal but separate accommodations for the white and colored races," and also that no person should be permitted to occupy seats in coaches other than the ones assigned to his race. Plessy alleged that he was seven-eights Caucasian and one-eighth African blood, that he took a seat in a white coach, and upon his refusal to leave the coach was forcibly ejected, imprisoned, and charged with violation of the act. He petitioned for a writ of prohibition directed against the trial court on the ground that the statute was unconstitutional under the Thirteenth and Fourteenth Amendments. The Louisiana Supreme Court held the statute constitutional and denied the relief sought.]

Mr. Justice Brown . . . delivered the opinion of the court.

That it does not conflict with the Thirteenth Amendment, which abolished slavery and involuntary servitude, . . . is too clear for argument. Slavery implies involuntary servitude,—a state of bondage; the ownership of mankind as a chattel, or, at least, the control of the labor and services of one man for the benefit of another. . . .

By the Fourteenth Amendment . . . the states are forbidden from making or enforcing any law which shall . . . deny to any person within their jurisdiction the equal protection of the laws. . . .

The object of the amendment was undoubtedly to enforce the absolute equality of the two races before the law, but in the nature of things it could not have been intended to abolish distinctions based upon color, or to enforce social, as distinguished from political, equality, or a commingling of the two races upon terms unsatisfactory to either. Laws permitting, and even requiring, their separation in places where they are liable to be brought into contact do not necessarily imply the inferiority of either race to the other, and have been generally, if not universally, recognized as within the competency of the state legislatures in the exercise of their police power. The most common instance of this is connected with the establishment of separate schools for white and colored children, which has been held to be a valid exercise of the legislative power even by courts of states where the political rights of the colored race have been longest and most earnestly enforced.

One of the earliest of these cases is that of *Roberts* v. *City of Boston*, 5 Cush. 198 (1849), in which the Supreme Judicial Court of Massachusetts held that the general school committee of Boston had power to make provision for the instruction of colored children in separate schools established exclusively for them, and to prohibit their attendance upon the other schools. . . . Similar laws have been enacted by Congress under its general power of legislation over the District of Columbia . . . as well as by the legislatures of many of the states, and have been generally, if not uniformly, sustained by the courts. . . .

The distinction between laws interfering with the political equality of the Negro and those requiring the separation of the two races in schools, theatres, and railway carriages has been frequently drawn by this court. . . .

We consider the underlying fallacy of the plaintiff's argument to consist in the assumption that the enforced separation of the two races stamps the colored race with a badge of inferiority. If this be so, it is not by reason of anything found in the act, but solely because the colored race chooses to put that construction upon it. The argument necessarily assumes that if . . . the colored race should become the dominant power in the state legislature, and should enact a law in precisely similar terms, it would thereby relegate the white race to an inferior position. We imagine that the white race, at least, would not acquiesce in this assumption. The argument also assumes that social prejudices may be overcome by legislation and that equal rights cannot be secured to the Negro except by an enforced commingling of the two races. We cannot accept this proposition. If the two races are to meet upon terms of social equality, it must be the result of natural affinities, a mutual appreciation of each other's merits, and a voluntary consent of individuals. . .

Legislation is powerless to eradicate racial instincts or to abolish distinctions based upon physical differences, and the attempt to do so can only result in accentuating the difficulties of the present situation. If the civil and political rights of both races be equal, one cannot be inferior to the other civilly or politically. If one race be inferior to the other socially, the Constitution of the United States cannot put them upon the same plane. . . . .

The judgment of the court below is, therefore,

*Affirmed.*

Mr. Justice Brewer did not hear the argument or participate in the decision of this case.

Mr. Justice Harlan, dissenting: . . .

In respect of civil rights, common to all citizens, the Constitution of the United States does not, I think, permit any public authority to know the race of those entitled to be protected in the enjoyment of such rights. . . .

It was said in argument that the statute of Louisiana does not discriminate against either race but prescribes a rule applicable alike to white and colored citizens. But this argument does not meet the difficulty. Everyone knows that the statute in question had its origin in the purpose, not so much to exclude white persons from railroad cars occupied by blacks, as to exclude colored people from coaches occupied or assigned to white persons. . . . The thing to accomplish was, under the guise of giving equal accommodations for whites and blacks, to compel the latter to keep to themselves while travelling in railroad passenger coaches. No one would be so wanting in candor as to assert the contrary. The fundamental objection, therefore, to the statute is that it interferes with the personal freedom of citizens. . . .

The white race deems itself to be the dominant race in this country. And so it is, in prestige, in achievements, in education, in wealth, and in power. So, I doubt not, it will continue to be for all time, if it remains true to its great heritage and holds fast to the principles of constitutional liberty. But in the views of the Constitution, in the eye of the law, there is in this country no superior, dominant, ruling class of citizens. There is no caste here. Our Constitution is color-blind and neither knows nor tolerates classes among citizens. In respect of civil rights, all citizens are equal before the law. The humblest is the peer of the most powerful. The law regards man as man and takes no account of his surroundings or of his color when his civil rights as guaranteed by the supreme law of the land are involved. . . .

The arbitrary separation of citizens, on the basis of race, while they are on a public highway, is a badge of servitude wholly inconsistent with the civil freedom and the equality before the law established by the Constitution. It cannot be justified upon any legal grounds.

If evils will result from the commingling of the two races upon public highways established for the benefit of all, they be infinitely less than those that will surely come from state legislation regulating the enjoyment of civil rights upon the basis of race. We boast of the freedom enjoyed by our people above all other peoples. But it is difficult to reconcile that boast with a state of the law which, practically, puts the brand of servitude and degradation upon a large class of our fellow citizens, our equals before the law. The thin disguise of "equal" accommodations for passengers in railroad coaches will not mislead anyone, nor atone for the wrong this day done. . . . .

It is difficult to reconcile the holding in *Plessy* with the language of Justice Strong in *Strauder* v. *West Virginia*. As Justice Harlan pointed out in his dissent in *Plessy*, it was clear to everyone that the equal but separate provisions in transportation and other laws were designed to perpetuate a caste system, even though the facilities for the two races might be equal. As a matter of fact, segregated facilities were rarely equal, but it was not until almost fifty years later that the Court came to grips with this issue.

If it was not unconstitutional for the State to segregate by race in transportation, then it was felt that it would be equally permissible to segregate in other areas such as education, parks, and swimming pools. The so-called Jim Crow laws became a pattern in the South and racial segregation in "social" activities was maintained, while under the *Strauder* rule and the Fifteenth Amendment at least most of the "political" arena was presumed to be constitutionally bound to a policy of freedom from racial differentiation. [See C. Vann Woodward, *The Strange Career of Jim Crow*, 3rd ed. (New York: Oxford, 1974).]

Even this kind of rough distinction between "social" and "political" did not always obtain, however, as became evident when the issue of racial zoning in residential property came to the Court in 1917.

## BUCHANAN *v.* WARLEY
### 245 U.S. 60 (1917)

[In 1914 the City of Louisville, Kentucky, in order "to prevent conflict and ill-feeling between the white and colored races in the City of Louisville," enacted an ordinance which prohibited any Negro from moving into and occupying a residence in a block in which more than half the houses were occupied by whites and, conversely, prohibited whites from moving into a block in which the houses were predominantly Negro-occupied. Warley, a Negro, contracted with Buchanan for the purchase of a home in a block largely occupied by white residents. Buchanan then refused to complete the sale on the ground that the ordinance forbade it. Warley brought an action for specific performance on the contention that the ordinance violated the Fourteenth Amendment and thus was no defense to an action for specific performance. The Kentucky courts upheld the ordinance, and the case was carried to the Supreme Court for review on a writ of error.]

Mr. Justice Day delivered the opinion of the Court. . . .

That there exists a serious and difficult problem arising from a feeling of race hostility which the law is powerless to control, and to which it must give a measure of consideration, may be freely admitted. But its solution cannot be promoted by depriving citizens of their constitutional rights and privileges. . . .

The right which the ordinance annulled was the civil rights of a white man to dispose of his property if he saw fit to do so to a person of color and of a colored person to make such disposition to a white person.

It is urged that this proposed segregation will promote the public peace by preventing race conflicts. Desirable as this is, and important as is the preservation of the public peace, this aim cannot be accomplished by laws or ordinances which deny rights created or protected by the federal Constitution.

It is said that such acquisitions by colored persons depreciate property owned in the neighborhood by white persons. But property may be acquired by undesirable white neighbors or put to disagreeable though lawful uses with like results.

We think this attempt to prevent the alienation of the property in question to a person of color was not a legitimate exercise of the police power of the State, and is in direct violation of the fundamental law enacted in the Fourteenth Amendment of the Constitution preventing state interference with property rights except by due process of law. That being the case, the ordinance cannot stand.

It should be noted that the decision came off on the ground that for the State so to restrict the property owner was a deprivation of property without due process of law. Technically, then, the holding did not interfere with the earlier interpretation of the equal protection clause that racial segregation imposed by law in nonpolitical areas was not barred. It did, however, point up the anomaly in such an interpretation, and the Court was sharply criticized for giving greater protection to the property rights of Negroes than to their personal rights. In rebuttal it was contended that the Congress following the Civil War had enacted legislation specifically to protect the right of all citizens "to inherit, purchase, lease, sell, hold, and convey real and personal property" (14 Stat. 27, 1866), while it also established schools for the District of Columbia on a racially segregated basis. Thus it was argued that the Congress intended to protect property rights through the Fourteenth Amendment but did not intend for that Amendment to restrict racial segregation imposed by law. As a consequence of the decision in *Buchanan* v. *Warley,* the practice developed of incorporating racially restrictive covenants in deeds conveying property. (The cases involving the validity of the enforcement of such covenants by the state are taken up below.)

Taking the decisions in *Strauder, Plessy,* and *Buchanan* together, it would appear that by the end of World War I a rough rule had been developed that the State could not make racial distinctions in the area of political or property rights, but racial segregation in "social" areas could be imposed by law on a "separate but equal" basis. Added to this is the holding in the *Civil Rights Cases,* 109 U.S. 3 (1883), that the Fourteenth Amendment barred only *state* action of certain types and not racial barriers set up by *private* action. This decision was double-edged in that it not only limited judicial remedies in actions brought under the Fourteenth Amendment, but it also, and to the same extent, limited the scope of legislation adopted by Congress to enforce the provisions of the Fourteenth Amendment. The rule of *Strauder-Plessy-Buchanan,* and the rule of the *Civil Rights Cases,* however, suggested three broad avenues of attack on racial discrimination. Within the framework of these decisions it was still possible to enter the judicial arena and argue (1) that a given right was political in nature and that the State should be barred from making any kind of racial distinctions in its exercise, or (2) that a given facility, required by state law to be segregated, was operated in such fashion that Negroes were not in fact being treated equally with whites, or (3) that a particular form of racial discrimination, though nominally imposed by private action, was in some manner being furthered by the active assistance or participation of the State in such fashion as to bring the imposition within the category of "state action" prohibited by the Fourteenth or Fifteenth Amendments.

The first approach has been used repeatedly in such areas as racial discrimination in jury selection and in voting rights. Despite the clear holding in *Strauder,* the Court repeatedly found it necessary to review, and reverse, convictions of Negroes where a long-continued pattern of discrimination in the selection of jurors was followed. And in *Pierre* v. *Louisiana,* 306 U.S. 354 (1939), the Court held unanimously that even in the grand jury the Negro defendant was constitutionally entitled to a panel free from selection methods which discriminated against Negroes because of their race. (The discussion of racial discrimination in voting will be reserved for Chapter 7.)

The second approach is the one which was ultimately successful in barring racial segregation in public schools in the landmark case of *Brown* v. *Board of Education* in 1954. It is not suggested that the earlier cases brought on this ground were part of an organized, frontal assault on the whole concept of segregation by race. They were, in fact, sporadic, isolated cases, and not until after the end of World War II was there a conscious strategy employed to press the case for exact equality of facilities to the point that separate facilities were by this very fact unequal.

The earlier cases arguing inequality of facilities were brought in situations where the Negro was offered no facilities whatever in an area where they were available to whites. The Court had little difficulty finding a violation of the Fourteenth Amendment in such instances where there was no pretense of affording separate but equal treatment. In *McCabe v. Atchison, T. & S. F. Ry.*, 235 U.S. 151 (1914), the Court held void a separate coach law of Oklahoma which permitted carriers to provide sleeping and dining cars only for white persons, notwithstanding the state's contention that there was little demand for them by colored persons. Nearly twenty-five years later a similar issue was presented, this time in the field of education, and again the Court held the state provision to be a violation of the equal protection of the laws. The State of Missouri maintained a law school at its university for white students but had none at the state university for Negroes. It provided by statute for the payment of tuition fees for any of its Negro citizens to study law "at the university of any adjacent state," but refused to admit them to the white law school. In *Missouri ex rel. Gaines v. Canada*, 305 U.S. 337 (1938), the Court unanimously held that petitioner had been denied equal protection of the laws. Chief Justice Hughes, speaking for the Court, stated:

The admissibility of laws separating the races in the enjoyment of privileges afforded by the State rests wholly upon the equality of the privileges which the laws give to the separated groups within the State. The question here is not of a duty of the State to supply legal training, or of the quality of the training which it does supply, but of its duty when it provides such training to furnish it to the residents of the State upon the basis of an equality of right. By the operation of the laws of Missouri a privilege has been created for white law students which is denied to negroes by reason of their race. The white resident is afforded legal education within the State; the negro resident having the same qualifications is refused it there and must go outside the State to obtain it. That is a denial of the equality of legal right to the enjoyment of the privilege which the State has set up, and the provision for the payment of tuition fees in another State does not remove the discrimination. . . . That resort may mitigate the inconvenience of the discrimination but cannot serve to validate it.

Nor can we regard the fact that there is but a limited demand in Missouri for the legal education of negroes as excusing the discrimination in favor of whites. We had occasion to consider a cognate question in the case of *McCabe v. Atchison, T. & S. F. Ry. Co*. . . . We found that argument to be without merit. It made, we said, the constitutional right "depend upon the number of persons who may be discriminated against, whereas the essence of the constitutional right is that it is a personal one. Whether or not particular facilities shall be provided may doubtless be conditioned upon there being a reasonable demand therefor; but, if facilities are provided, substantial equality of treatment of persons traveling under like conditions cannot be refused. It is the individual who is entitled to the equal protection of the laws, and if he is denied by a common carrier, acting in the matter under the authority of a state law, a facility or convenience in the course of his journey which, under substantially the same circumstances, is furnished to another traveler, he may properly complain that his constitutional privilege has been invaded." *Id*, 235 U.S. 161, 162. . . .

The *McCabe* and *Gaines* cases can, of course, be confined to the narrow holding that privileges created by law for white persons cannot be denied to Negroes, although they can be constitutionally provided on a segregated basis. There are phrases in the two opinions, however, which suggest that the segregated facilities should in fact be equal. The opinion in *McCabe* states that "substantial equality of treatment . . . cannot be refused." And in *Gaines* the Court refers to "the equality of legal right to the enjoyment of the privilege which the State has set up." Not yet, however, did the Court squarely hold that separate facilities had to be truly equal to meet the requirements of equal protection.

Meanwhile a sort of collateral attack on segregation by race was undertaken in the field of interstate transportation. In *Mitchell* v. *United States,* 313 U.S. 80 (1941), the Court held that for a railroad to deny Pullman car accomodations to a Negro solely because of his race was in violation of the provision of the Interstate Commerce Act forbidding "any undue or unreasonable prejudice or disadvantage in any respect whatsoever." The decision stands with *McCabe* and *Gaines,* however, as a case involving absolute denial of a facility rather than the equality of separately provided facilities. The next approach was to argue that separate facilities required by state law on interstate carriers was an undue burden on interstate commerce. This argument was successful in *Morgan* v. *Virginia,* 328 U.S. 373 (1946), in which the Court held that the mandatory reseating of passengers when a state line was crossed was a burden on interstate commerce not supportable under the police power of the State. In the absence of state laws, however, private regulations of carriers requiring segregation of passengers remained unaffected by this ruling. This gap was closed by the ruling in *Henderson* v. *United States,* 339 U.S. 816 (1950), in which the Court held that the nondiscrimination requirement of the Interstate Commerce Act barred a railroad from enforcing its rule providing for segregated dining facilities on its cars. And *Boynton* v. *Virginia,* 364 U.S. 454 (1960), extended the holding to the terminal and restaurant facilities of interstate bus carriers.

## Discrimination in Public Schools

In the same year that the *Henderson* case was decided, the Court decided two other cases in the field of higher education which squarely opened the way for an attack on segregated facilities on the ground that accommodations for Negroes were not in actuality equal to those for white persons. *McLaurin* v. *Oklahoma State Regents,* 339 U.S. 637 (1950), involved a Negro in the graduate school of the University of Oklahoma. Under the requirements of the *Gaines* holding, the State had provided that qualified Negroes could be admitted to white state schools where the Negro school did not offer the requested course of study. Once McLaurin was admitted, however, rigid segregation practices prevailed within the University. He was assigned a special "colored" seat in each classroom, a special table was provided for him in the library, and he was required to eat in a segregated portion of the cafeteria. The Court declared these conditions unconstitutional on the ground that they would "impair and inhibit his ability to study, to engage in discussions and exchange views with other students."

On the same day as *McLaurin,* the Court rendered its decision in *Sweatt* v. *Painter,* involving the petition of a Negro for admission to the University of Texas Law School.

SWEATT *v.* PAINTER

*339 U.S. 629 (1950)*

[Petitioner applied for admission to the University of Texas Law School, but his application was rejected solely because he was a Negro. He applied for mandamus to compel his admission on the ground that there was no Negro law school in Texas. The court did not issue mandamus, but continued the case for six months to allow the State to supply substantially equal facilities. A Negro law school was opened by the State, and the court denied the writ, but petitioner refused to register in the new school. A new hearing was held on the issue of the equality of the educational facilities at the newly established school as compared with the University of Texas Law School. Finding that the new school offered petitioner "privileges, advantages, and opportunities for the study of law substantially equivalent to those offered by the State to white students at the University of Texas," the trial court denied mandamus, and the Court of Civil Appeals affirmed.]

Mr. Chief Justice Vinson delivered the opinion of the Court. . . .

The University of Texas Law School, from which petitioner was excluded, was staffed by a faculty of sixteen full-time and three part-time professors, some of whom are nationally recognized authorities in their field. Its student body numbered 850. The library contained over 65,000 volumes. Among the other facilities available to the students were a law review, moot court facilities, scholarship funds, and Order of the Coif affiliation. The school's alumni occupy the most distinguished positions in the private practice of the law and in the public life of the State. It may properly be considered one of the nation's ranking law schools.

The law school for Negroes which was to have opened in February, 1947, would have no independent faculty or library. The teaching was to be carried on by four members of the University of Texas Law School faculty, who were to maintain their offices at the University of Texas while teaching at both institutions. Few of the 10,000 volumes ordered for the library had arrived; nor was there any full-time librarian. The school lacked accreditation.

Since the trial of this case, respondents report the opening of a law school at the Texas State University for Negroes. It is apparently on the road to full accreditation. It has a faculty of five full-time professors; a student body of 23; a library of some 16,500 volumes serviced by a full-time staff; a practice court and legal aid association; and one alumnus who has become a member of the Texas Bar.

Whether the University of Texas Law School is compared with the original or the new law school for Negroes, we cannot find substantial equality in the educational opportunities offered white and Negro law students by the State. In terms of number of the faculty, variety of courses and opportunity for specialization, size of the student body, scope of the library, availability of law review and similar activities, the University of Texas Law School is superior. What is more important, the University of Texas Law School possesses to a far greater degree those qualities which are incapable of objective measurement but which make for greatness in a law school. Such qualities, to name but a few, include reputation of the faculty, experience of the administration, position and influence of the alumni, standing in the community, traditions and prestige. It is difficult to believe that one who had a free choice between these law schools would consider the question close.

. . . The law school to which Texas is willing to admit petitioner excludes from its student body members of the racial groups which number 85 percent of the population of the State and include most of the lawyers, witnesses, jurors, judges and other officials with whom petitoner will inevitably be dealing with when he becomes a member of the Texas Bar. With such a substantial and significant segment of society excluded, we cannot conclude that the education offered petitioner is substantially equal to that which he would receive if admitted to the University of Texas Law School. . . .

In holding that the Texas practice violated the equal protection clause, the Court refused, however, to reexamine the separate but equal doctrine. Nonetheless, the decision and the general tenor of the Court's opinion suggested strongly that the time might be ripe for such a reexamination. To make a point of the opportunities of students for "intellectual commingling" in the *McLaurin* case and to examine and recognize "those qualities which are incapable of objective measurement" such as reputation of the faculty, the school's standing in the community, and the "position and influence of the alumni," as the Court did in *Sweatt,* is certainly to give strong intimations that separate facilities in education are inherently unequal and therefore unconstitutional. Actions were brought in several states and in the District of Columbia with the hope that this issue could ultimately be squarely raised in the United States Supreme Court. In December 1952, the Court heard argument in its appellate review of four cases involving segregated school laws in the states of Kansas, Virginia, South Carolina, and Delaware, and one case involving the validity of maintaining segregated public schools in the District of Columbia. In December of the following year, 1953, the cases were reargued on certain questions propounded by the Court. Finally, on May 17, 1954, the Court handed down its momentous decision that govermentally enforced racial segregation in public schools was unconstitutional. The state cases, decided together and reported officially under the name of the Kansas case, *Brown* v. *Board of Education of Topeka, Kansas,* were based on the equal protection clause of the Fourteenth Amendment. The District of Columbia case, *Bolling* v. *Sharpe,* was based on an equal protection requirement as implied in the due process clause of the Fifth Amendment.

### BROWN *v.* BOARD OF EDUCATION OF TOPEKA
### *347 U.S. 483 (1954)*

Mr. Chief Justice Warren delivered the opinion of the Court.

These cases come to us from the States of Kansas, South Carolina, Virginia, and Delaware. They are premised on different facts and different local conditions, but a common legal question justifies their consideration together in this consolidated opinion.

In each of the cases, minors of the Negro race, through their legal representatives, seek the aid of the courts in obtaining admission to the public schools of their community on a nonsegregated basis. In each instance, they had been denied admission to schools attended by white children under laws requiring or permitting segregation according to race. This segregation was alleged to deprive the plantiffs of the equal protection of the laws under the Fourteenth Amendment. In each of the cases other than the Delaware case, a three-judge federal district court denied relief to the plantiffs on the so-called "separate but equal" doctrine announced by this Court in *Plessy* v. *Ferguson*, 163 U.S. 537. Under that doctrine, equality of treatment is accorded when the races are provided substantially equal facilities, even though these facilities be separate. In the Delaware case, the Supreme Court of Delaware adhered to that doctrine, but ordered that the plantiffs be admitted to the white schools because of their superiority to the Negro schools.

The plantiffs contend that segregated public schools are not "equal" and cannot be made "equal," and that hence they are deprived of the equal protection of the laws. Because of the obvious importance of the question presented, the Court took jurisdiction. Argument was heard in the 1952 Term, and reargument was heard this Term on certain questions propounded by the Court.

[The order was issued on June 8, 1953, 345 U.S. 972, and requested counsel "to discuss particularly" five questions. The first three questions are answered in the instant case, but questions 4 and 5 were set out for still further argument in the following Term. The five questions were:

"1. What evidence is there that the Congress which submitted and the State legislatures and conventions which ratified the Fourteenth Amendment contemplated or did not contemplate, understood or did not understand, that it would abolish segregation in public schools?

"2. If neither the Congress in submitting nor the States in ratifying the Fourteenth Amendment understood that compliance with it would require the immediate abolition of segregation in public schools, was it nevertheless the understanding of the framers of the Amendment

(a) that future Congresses might, in the exercise of their power under section 5 of the Amendment, abolish such segregation, or

(b) that it would be within the judicial power, in light of future conditions, to construe the Amendment as abolishing such segregation of its own force?

"3. On the assumption that the answers to questions 2(a) and (b) do not dispose of the issue, is it within the judicial power, in construing the Amendment, to abolish segregation in public schools,

"4. Assuming it is decided that segregation in public schools violated the Fourteenth Amendment

(a) would a decree necessarily follow providing that, within the limits set by normal geographic school districting, Negro children should forthwith be admitted to schools of their choice, or

(b) may this Court, in the exercise of its equity powers, permit an effective gradual adjustment to be brought about from existing segregated systems to a system not based on color distinctions?

"5. On the assumption on which questions 4(a) and (b) are based, and assuming further that this Court will exercise its equity powers to the end described in question 4(b),

(a) should this Court formulate decrees in these cases;

(b) if so, what specific issues should the decrees reach;

(c) should this Court appoint a special master to hear evidence with a view to recommending specific terms for such decrees;

(d) should this Court remand to the courts of first instance with directions to frame decrees in these cases, and if so what general directions should the decrees of this Court include and what procedures should the courts of first instance follow in arriving at the specific terms of more detailed decrees?" 345 U.S. 972.

The Attorney General of the United States participated both Terms as *amicus curiae*.]

Reargument was largely devoted to the circumstances surrounding the adoption of the Fourteenth Amendment in 1868. It covered exhaustively consideration of the Amendment in Congress, ratification by the states, then existing practices in racial segregation, and the views of proponents and opponents of the Amendment. This discussion and our own investigation convince us that, although these sources cast some light, it is not enough to resolve the problem with which we are faced. At best, they are inconclusive. The most avid proponents of the post-War Amendments undoubtedly intended them to remove all legal distinctions among "all persons born or naturalized in the United States." Their opponents, just as certainly, were antagonistic to both the letter and the spirit of the Amendments and wished them to have the most limited effect. What others in Congress and the state legislatures had in mind cannot be determined with any degree of certainty.

An additional reason for the inconclusive nature of the Amendment's history, with respect to segregated schools, is the status of public education at that time. In the South, the movement toward free common schools, supported by general taxation, had not yet taken hold. Education of white children was largely in the hands of private groups. Education of Negroes was almost nonexistent, and practically all of the race were illiterate. In fact, any education of Negroes was forbidden by law in some states. Today, in contrast, many Negroes have achieved outstanding success in the arts and sciences as well as in the business and professional world. It is true that public school education at the time of the Amendment had advanced further in the North, but the effect of the Amendment on Northern States was generally ignored in the congressional debates. Even in the North, the conditions of public education did not approximate those existing today. The curriculum was usually rudimentary; ungraded schools were common in rural areas; the school term was but three months a year in many states; and compulsory school attendance was virtually unknown. As a consequence, it is not surprising that there should be so little in the history of the Fourteenth Amendment relating to its intended effect on public education.

In the first cases in this Court construing the Fourteenth Amendment, decided shortly after its adoption, the Court interpreted it as proscribing all state-imposed discriminations against the Negro race.[*] The doctrine of "separate but equal" did not make its appearance in this Court until 1896 in the case of *Plessy* v. *Ferguson, supra,* involving not education but transportation.[**] American courts have since labored with the doctrine for over half a century. In this Court, there have been six cases involving the "separate but equal" doctrine in the field of public education. In *Cumming* v. *County Board of Education*, 175 U.S. 528, and *Gong Lum* v. *Rice*, 275 U.S. 78, the validity of the doctrine itself was not challenged. In more recent cases, all on the graduate school level, inequality was found in that specific benefits enjoyed by white students were denied to Negro students of the same educational qualifications. *Missouri ex rel. Gaines* v. *Canada, 305 U.S. 337: Sipuel* v. *Oklahoma,* 332 U.S. 631; *Sweatt* v. *Painter,* 339 U.S. 629; *McLaurin* v. *Oklahoma State Regents*, 339 U.S. 637. In none of these cases was it necessary to re-examine the doctrine to grant relief to the Negro plaintiff. And in *Sweatt* v. *Painter, supra,* the Court expressly reserved decison on the question whether *Plessy* v. *Ferguson* should be held inapplicable to public education.

In the instant cases, that question is directly presented. Here, unlike *Sweat* v. *Painter,* there are findings below that the Negro and white schools involved have been equalized, or are being equalized, with respect to buildings, curricula, qualifications and salaries of teachers, and other "tangible" factors. Our decision, therefore, cannot turn on merely a comparison of these tangible factors in the Negro and white schools involved in each of the cases. We must look instead to the effect of segregation itself on public education.

In approaching this problem we cannot turn the clock back to 1868 when the Amendment was adopted, or even to 1896 when *Plessy* v. *Ferguson* was written. We must consider public education in the light of its full development and its present place in American life throughout the Nation. Only in this way can it be determined if segregation in public schools deprives these plaintiffs of the equal protection of the laws.

Today, education is perhaps the most important function of state and local governments. Compulsory school attendance laws and the great expenditures for education both demonstrate our recognition of the importance of education to our

---

[*]*Slaughter-House Cases,* 16 Wall. 36, 67–72 (1873); *Strauder* v. *West Virginia,* 100 U.S. 303, 307–308 (1880). . . . See also *Virginia* v. *Rives*, 100 U.S. 313 (1880); *Ex parte Virginia*, 100 U.S. 339, 344–345 (1880).

[**]The doctrine apparently originated in *Roberts* v. *City of Boston,*59 Mass. 198, 206 (1850), upholding school segregation against attack as being violative of a state constitutional guarantee of equality. . . .

democratic society. It is required in the performance of our most basic public responsibilities, even service in the armed forces. It is the very foundation of good citizenship. Today it is a principal instrument in awakening the child to cultural values, in preparing him for later professional training, and in helping him to adjust normally to his environment. In these days, it is doubtful that any child may reasonably be expected to succeed in life if he is denied the opportunity of an education. Such an opportunity, where the state has undertaken to provide it, is a right which must be made available to all on equal terms.

We come then to the question presented: Does segregation of children in public schools solely on the basis of race, even though the physical facilities and other "tangible" factors may be equal, deprive the children of the minority group of equal education opportunities? We believe that it does.

In *Sweatt* v.*Painter, supra,* in finding that a segregated law school for Negroes could not provide them equal educational opportunities, this Court relied in large part on "those qualities which are incapable of objective measurement but which make for greatness in a law school," In *McLaurin* v. *Oklahoma State Regents, supra,* the Court, in requiring that a Negro admitted to a white graduate school be treated like all other students, again resorted to intangible considerations: ". . . his ability to study, to engage in discussions and exchange views with other students, and, in general, to learn his profession." Such considerations apply with added force to children in grade and high schools. To separate them from others of similar age and qualifications solely because of their race generates a feeling of inferiority as to their status in the community that may affect their hearts and minds in a way unlikely ever to be undone. The effect of this separation on their educational opportunities was well stated by a finding in the Kansas case by a court which nevertheless felt compelled to rule against the Negro plaintiffs:

"Segregation of white and colored children in public schools has a detrimental effect upon the colored children. The impact is greater when it has the sanction of the law; for the policy of separating the races is usually interpreted as denoting the inferiority of the negro group. A sense of inferiority affects the motivation of a child to learn. Segregation with the sanction of law, therefore, has a tendency to [retard] the educational and mental development of negro children and to deprive them of some of the benefits they would receive in a racial[ly] integrated school system."

Whatever may have been the extent of psychological knowledge at the time of *Plessy* v. *Ferguson*, this finding is amply supported by modern authority.*** Any language in *Plessy* v. *Ferguson* contrary to this finding is rejected.

We conclude that in the field of public education the doctrine of "separate but equal" has no place. Separate educational facilities are inherently unequal. Therefore, we hold that the plaintiffs and others similarly situated for whom the actions have been brought are, by reason of the segregation complained of, deprived of the equal protection of the laws guaranteed by the Fourteenth Amendment. This disposition makes unnecessary any discussion whether such segregation also violates the Due Process Clause of the Fourteenth Amendment.

***K. B. Clark, *Effect of Prejudice and Discrimination on Personality Development* (Midcentury White House Conference on Children and Youth, 1950); Witmer and Kotinsky, *Personality in the Making* (1952), c. VI; Deutscher and Chein, "The Psychological Effects of Enforced Segregation: a Survey of Social Science Opinion," 26 J. *Psychol.* 259 (1948); Chein, "What Are the Psychological Effects of Segregation Under Conditions of Equal Facilities?" 3 *Int. J. Opinion and Attitude Res.* 229 (1949); Brameld, *Educational Costs in Discrimination and National Welfare* (MacIver, ed., 1949), 44–48; Frazier, *The Negro in the United States* (1949), 674–681. And see generally Gunnar Myrdal, *An American Dilemma* (1944).

Because these are class actions, because of the wide applicability of this decision, and because of the great variety of local conditions, the formulation of decrees in these cases presents problems of considerable complexity. On reargument, the consideration of appropriate relief was necessarily subordinated to the primary question—the constitutionality of segregation in public education. We have now announced that such segregation is a denial of the equal protection of the laws. In order that we may have the full assistance of the parties in formulating decrees, the cases will be restored to the docket, and the parties are requested to present further argument on Questions 4 and 5 previously propounded by the Court for the reargument this term. . . .

*It is so ordered.*

In *Bolling* v. *Sharpe*, 347 U.S. 497 (1954), decided the same day, the Court held that racial segregation enforced by the federal government in the public schools of the District of Columbia was violative of the Fifth Amendment. The case was treated separately because there is no equal protection clause applicable to the federal government. The Court, however, had no difficulty in reading the requirement into the due process clause of the Fifth Amendment. It was pointed out that classifications may be so arbitrary and unjust as to be violative of due process, and racial discrimination by the federal government fell into this category. Chief Justice Warren, for the Court, stated:

In view of our decision that the Constitution prohibits the states from maintaining racially segregated public schools, it would be unthinkable that the same Constitution would impose a lesser duty on the Federal Government. We hold that racial segregation in the public schools of the District of Columbia is a denial of the due process of law guaranteed by the Fifth Amendment to the Constitution.

In two landmark decisions, then, coming near the end of the term in 1954, the Court held that governmentally enforced racial segregation in the public schools was forbidden by the Constitution. Two points should be noted. First, the Court did not in these decisions state that the Constitution commanded governmental *integration* of the schools. It stated only that the policy of forcible segregation by the governments of the nation was invalid. Second, although *Plessy* v. *Ferguson* was not squarely overruled, and the decisions were technically limited to segregation in public education, the Court did say that any language in *Plessy* "contrary to this finding is rejected," and the clear import of the decision was a renunciation of *Plessy.* The final step in overruling *Plessy* was taken in *Gayle* v. *Browder*, 352 U.S. 903 (1956), which held invalid, under the equal protection clause, a city ordinance requiring segregation on motor buses operated within the city of Montgomery, Alabama.

Having held that racial segregation enforced by government in the public schools was unconstitutional, the Court was then faced with the question of how best to implement the decision. As stated in the *Brown* opinion, the Court decided to hear further argument on this question before issuing any enforcement decree. Argument was heard in April 1955, and the opinion and judgments were announced in May 1955.

## BROWN *v.* BOARD OF EDUCATION OF TOPEKA
### *349 U.S. 294 (1955)*

Mr. Chief Justice Warren delivered the opinion of the Court.

These cases were decided on May 17, 1954. The opinions of that date, declaring the fundamental principle that racial discrimination in public education is unconstitutional, are incorporated herein by reference. All provisions of federal, state, or local law requiring or permitting such discrimination must yield to this principle. There remains for consideration the manner in which relief is to be accorded.

Because these cases arose under different local conditions and their disposition will involve a variety of local problems, we requested further argument on the question of relief. In view of the nationwide importance of the decision, we invited the Attorney General of the United States and the Attorneys General of all states requiring or permitting racial discrimination in public education to present their views on that question. . . .

These presentations were informative and helpful to the Court in its consideration of the complexities arising from the transition to a system of public education freed of racial discrimination. . . .

Full implementation of these constitutional principles may require solution of varied local school problems. School authorities have the primary responsibility for elucidating, assessing, and solving these problems; courts will have to consider whether the action of school authorities constitutes good faith implementation of the governing constitutional principles. Because of their proximity to local conditions and the possible need for further hearings, the courts which originally heard these cases can best perform this judicial appraisal. Accordingly, we believe it appropriate to remand the cases to those courts.

In fashioning and effectuating the decrees, the courts will be guided by equitable principles. Traditionally, equity has been characterized by a practical flexibility in shaping its remedies and by a facility for adjusting and reconciling public and private needs. These cases call for the exercise of these traditional attributes of equity power. At stake is the personal interest of the plaintiffs in admission to public schools as soon as practicable on a nondiscriminatory basis. To effectuate this interest may call for elimination of a variety of obstacles in making the transition to school systems operated in accordance with the constitutional principles set forth in our May 17, 1954, decision. Courts of equity may properly take into account the public interest in the elimination of such obstacles in a systematic and effective manner. But it should go without saying that the vitality of these constitutional principles cannot be allowed to yield simply because of disagreement with them.

While giving weight to these public and private considerations, the courts will require that the defendants make a prompt and reasonable start toward full compliance with our May 17, 1954 ruling. Once such a start has been made, the courts may find that additional time is necessary to carry out the ruling in an effective manner. The burden rests upon the defendants to establish that such time is necessary in the public interest and is consistent with good faith compliance at the earliest practicable date. To that end, the courts may consider problems related to administration, arising from the physical condition of the school plant, the school transportation system, personnel, revision of school districts and attendance areas into compact units to achieve a system of determining admission to the public schools on a nonracial basis, and revision of local laws and regulations which may be necessary in solving the foregoing problems. They will also consider the adequacy of any plans the defendants may propose to meet these problems and to effectuate a transition to a racially nondiscriminatory school system. During this period of transition, the courts will retain jurisdiction of these cases.

The judgments below, except that in the Delaware case, are accordingly reversed and the cases are remanded to the District Courts to take such proceedings and enter such orders and decrees consistent with this opinion as are necessary and proper to admit to public schools on a racially nondiscriminatory basis with all deliberate speed the parties to these cases. . . .

Despite the fact that *Brown* v. *Board of Education* had been decided ten years earlier, little progress toward desegregation in public schools had been made in the deep South by the time of the passage of the Civil Rights Act of 1964. Title IV of the Act provided for various assistance in the preparation and implementation of plans for the desegregation of public schools and, in addition, provided that the Attorney General could initiate suits to obtain relief for persons denied equal protection in the utilization of public schools or colleges. The primary weapon for ending racial segregation in schools and other federally aided state programs, however, was the Title VI provision for cutting off federal funds as penalty for failure to desegregate. The substantive and main procedural provisions are covered in Sections 601 and 602:

Sec. 601. No person in the United States shall, on the ground of race, color, or national origin, be excluded from participation in, be denied the benefits of, or be subjected to discrimination under any program or activity receiving Federal financial assistance.

Sec. 602. Each Federal department and agency which is empowered to extend Federal financial assistance to any program or activity, by way of grant, loan, or contract other than a contract of insurance or guaranty, is authorized and directed to effectuate the provisions of section 601 with respect to such program or activity by issuing rules, regulations, or orders of general applicability which shall be consistent with achievement of the objectives of the statute authorizing the financial assistance in connection with which the action is taken. No such rule, regulation, or order shall become effective unless and until approved by the President. Compliance with any requirement adopted pursuant to this section may be effected (1) by the termination of or refusal to grant or to continue assistance under such program or activity to any recipient as to whom there has been an express finding on the record, after opportunity for hearing, of a failure to comply with such requirement, but such termination or refusal shall be limited to the particular political entity, or part thereof, or other recipient as to whom such a finding has been made and, shall be limited in its effect to the particular program, or part thereof, in which noncompliance has been so found, or (2) by any other means authorized by law: *Provided, however,* That no such action shall be taken until the department or agency concerned has advised the appropriate person or persons of the failure to comply with the requirement and has determined that compliance cannot be secured by voluntary means. In the case of any action terminating, or refusing to grant or continue, assistance because of failure to comply with a requirement imposed pursuant to this section, the head of the Federal department or agency shall file with the committees of the House and Senate having legislative jurisdiction over the program or activity involved a full written report of the circumstances and the grounds for such action. No such action shall become effective until thirty days have elapsed after the filling of such report.

On April 29, 1965, the Office of Education of the Department of Health, Education and Welfare issued a statement of policy for the implementation of the Title VI provisions. A key aspect of the policy statement lies in the fact that instead of approaching the problem with a view of *cutting off* funds during the year for school systems which failed to desegregate, the Office of Education demanded that school systems *prove their eligibility* for the funds by filing appropriate plans or *court orders* for desegregation and assurances of implementation with the Commissioner of Education.

One of the many responses to the *Brown* decisions was the adoption by some states of some form of "freedom of choice" plan, under which parents could formally designate a choice of schools which their children would attend. Since approval or rejection of such choices was presumably based on strictly nonracial factors, it was argued that the plan was not in violation of the *Brown* decisions barring forced segregation. In the case to follow, however, the Court made a major policy shift and held that states with formerly segregated schools would be required by the Constitution to take affirmative steps to *integrate* the public school system rather than merely remaining neutral.

### GREEN *v.* SCHOOL BOARD OF NEW KENT COUNTY
### *391 U.S. 430 (1968)*

Mr. Justice Brennan delivered the opinion of the Court.

The question for decision is whether, under all the circumstances here, respondent School Board's adoption of a "freedom-of-choice" plan which allows a pupil to choose his own public school constitutes adequate compliance with the Board's responsibility "to achieve a system of determining admission to the public schools on a nonracial basis. . ."....

Petitioners brought this action in March, 1965, seeking injunctive relief against respondent's continued maintenance of an alleged racially segregated school system. New Kent County is a rural county in Eastern Virginia. About one-half of its population of some 4,500 are Negroes. There is no residential segregation in the county; persons of both races reside throughout. The school system has only two schools, the New Kent school on the east side of the county and the George W. Watkins school on the west side. . . . The School Board operates one white combined elementary and high school (New Kent), and one Negro combined elementary and high school (George W. Watkins). . . . Each school serves the entire county. . . . Children were each year automatically reassigned to the school previously attended unless upon their application the State Board assigned them to another school. . . . To September, 1964, no Negro pupil had applied for admission to the New Kent school under this statute and no white pupil had applied for admission to the Watkins school. . . .

It was such dual systems that 14 years ago *Brown I* held unconstitutional and a year later *Brown II* held must be abolished; school boards operating such school systems were *required* by *Brown II* "to effectuate a transition to a racially nondiscriminatory school system." . . . It is of course true that for the time immediately after *Brown II* the concern was with making an initial break in a long-estabished pattern of excluding Negro children from schools attended by white children. The principle focus was on obtaining for those Negro children courageous enough to break with tradition a place in the "white" schools. . . . Under *Brown II* that immediate goal was only the first step, however. The transition to a unitary, nonracial system of public education was and is the ultimate end to be brought about; it was because of the "complexities arising from the transition to a system of public education freed of racial discrimination" that we provided for "all deliberate speed" in the implementation of the principles of *Brown I.* . . .

The School Board contends that it has fully discharged its obligation by adopting a plan by which every student, regardless of race, may "freely" choose the school he will attend. The Board attempts to cast the issue in its broadest form by arguing that its "freedom-of-choice" plan may be faulted only by reading the Fourteenth Amendment as universally requiring "compulsory integration," a reading it insists the wording of the Amendment will not support. But that argument ignores the thrust of *Brown II.* . . . *Brown II* was a call for the dismantling of well-entrenched dual systems tempered by an awareness that complex and multifaceted problems would arise which would require time and flexibility for a successful resolution. School boards such as the respondent then operating state-compelled dual systems were nevertheless clearly charged with the affirmative duty to take whatever steps might be necessary to convert to a unitary system in which racial discrimination would be eliminated root and branch. . . . The constitutional rights of Negro school children articulated in *Brown I* permit no less than this; and it was to this end that *Brown II* commanded school boards to bend their efforts. . . . The burden on a school board today is to come forward with a plan that promises realistically to work, and promises realistically to work *now.* . . .

We do not hold that "freedom of choice" can have no place in such a plan. We do not hold that a "freedom-of-choice" plan might of itself be unconstitutional, although that argument has been urged upon us. Rather, all we decide today is that in desegregating a dual system a plan utilizing "freedom of choice" is not an end in itself. . . .

The New Kent School Board's "freedom-of-choice" plan cannot be accepted as a sufficient step to "effectuate a transition" to a unitary system. In three years of operation not a single white child has chosen to attend Watkins school and although 115 Negro children enrolled in New Kent school in 1967 . . . 85% of the Negro children in the system still attend the all-Negro Watkins school. In other words, the school system remains a dual system. Rather than further the dismantling of the dual system, the plan has operated simply to burden children and their parents with a responsibility which *Brown II* placed squarely on the School Board. The Board must be required to formulate a new plan and, in light of other courses which appear open to the Board, such as zoning, fashion steps which promise realistically to convert promptly to a system without a "white" school and a "Negro" school, but just schools. . . . [Reversed and remanded.]

*It is so ordered.*

In response to the *Green* decision, a number of district courts began to include in their desegregation orders a directive that white and black students in different schools be interchanged in order to achieve an integrated, unitary system. The protest over "busing" orders was enormous and led to the examination of that issue in *Swann* in 1971.

### SWANN *v.* CHARLOTTE–MECKLENBURG BOARD OF EDUCATION
### *402 U.S. 1 (1971)*

· [The Charlotte-Mecklenburg school system, which includes the city of Charlotte, North Carolina, had more than 84,000 students in 107 schools in the 1968–1969 school year. Approximately 29 percent of the pupils were Negro, about two-thirds of whom (some 14,000 students) attended 21 schools which were at least 99 percent Negro. This resulted from a desegregation plan approved by the District Court in 1965, at the start of this litigation. In 1968 petitioner Swann moved for further relief based on *Green* v. *School Board of New Kent County.* The District Court ordered the school board in 1969 to provide a plan for faculty and student desegregation. Finding the board's submission unsatisfactory, the Court appointed an expert (Finger) to submit a desegregation plan. The Court in 1970 adopted the board's plan, as modified, for the junior and senior high schools, and the Finger plan for the elementary schools. The latter plan desegregated all the elementary schools by the technique of grouping two or three outlying schools with one black inner city school, by transporting black students from grades one through four to the outlying white schools, and by transporting white students from the fifth and sixth grades from the outlying white schools to the inner city black school. The Court of Appeals affirmed portions of the order but vacated the order respecting elementary schools, fearing that the plan would unreasonably burden the pupils and the Board.]

Mr. Chief Justice Burger delivered the opinion of the Court.

We granted certiorari in this case to review important issues as to the duties of school authorities and the scope of powers of federal courts under this Court's mandates to eliminate racially separate public schools established and maintained by state action. . . .

This case and those argued with it arose in states having a long history of maintaining two sets of schools in a single school system deliberately operated to carry out a governmental policy to separate pupils in schools solely on the basis of race. That was what *Brown* v. *Board of Education* was all about. These cases present us with the problem of defining in more precise terms than heretofore the scope of the duty of school authorities and district courts in implementing *Brown I* and the mandate to eliminate dual systems and establish unitary systems at once. . . .

The problems encountered by the district courts and courts of appeal make plain that we should now try to amplify guidelines, however incomplete and imperfect, for the assistance of school authorities and courts. . . .

If school authorities fail in their affirmative obligations under these holdings, judicial authority may be invoked. Once a right and a violation have been shown, the scope of a district court's equitable powers to remedy past wrongs is broad, for breadth and flexibility are inherent in equitable remedies. . . .

The school authorities argue that the equity powers of federal district courts have been limited by Title IV of the Civil Rights Act of 1964, 42 U.S.C. Sec. 2000c. The language and the history of Title IV shows that it was not enacted to limit but to define the role of the Federal Government in the implementation of the *Brown I* decision. . . . [Section 2000c-6 provides that "nothing herein shall empower any official or court of the United States to issue any order seeking to achieve a racial balance in any school by requiring the transportation of pupils or students from one school to another. . . to achieve such racial balance. . . ."]

The proviso in Sec. 2000c–6 is in terms designed to foreclose any interpretation of the Act as expanding the *existing* powers of federal courts to enforce the Equal Protection Clause. There is no suggestion of an intention to restrict those powers or withdraw from courts their historic equitable remedial powers. The legislative history of Title IV indicates that Congress was concerned that the Act might be read as creating a right of action under the Fourteenth Amendment in the situation of so-called "de facto segregation," where racial imbalance exists in the schools but with no showing that this was brought about by discriminatory action of state authorities. In short, there is nothing in the Act which provides us material assistance in answering the question of remedy for state-imposed segregation in violation of *Brown I.* The basis of our decision must be the prohibition of the Fourteenth Amendment that no State shall "deny to any person within its jurisdiction the equal protection of the laws.". . .

In *Green*, we pointed out that existing policy and practice with regard to faculty, staff, transportation, extra-curricular activities, and facilities were among the most important indicia of a segregated system. . . . Independent of student assignment, where it is possible to identify a "white school" or a "Negro school" simply by reference to the racial composition of teachers and staff, the quality of school buildings and equipment, or the organization of sports activities, a *prima facie* case of violation of substantive constitutional rights under the Equal Protection Clause is shown. . . .

The construction of new schools and the closing of old ones is one of the most important functions of local school authorities and also one of the most complex. . . . The result of this will be a decision which, when combined with one technique or another of student assignment, will determine the racial composition of the student body in each school in the system. Over the long run, the consequences of the choices will be far reaching. People gravitate toward school facilities, just as schools are located in response to the needs of people. . . . It may well promote segregated residential patterns which, when combined with "neighborhood zoning," further lock the school system into the mold of separation of the races. Upon a proper showing a district court may consider this in fashioning a remedy. . . .

(1) *Racial Balances or Racial Quotas.* . . . .

We do not reach in this case the question whether a showing that school segregation is a consequence of other types of state action, without any discriminatory action by the school authorities, is a constitutional violation requiring remedial action by a school desegregation decree. This case does not present that question and we therefore do not decide it. . . .

In this case it is urged that the District Court has imposed a racial balance requirement of 71%–29% on individual schools. The fact that no such objective was actually achieved—and would appear to be impossible—tends to blunt that claim, yet in the opinion and order of the District Court. . . we find that court directing: "that efforts should be made to reach 71–29 ratio in the various schools so that there will be no basis for contending that one school is racially different from the others. . . ."

The District Judge went on to acknowledge that variation "from that norm may be unavoidable." This contains intimations that the "norm" is a fixed mathematical racial balance reflecting the pupil constituency of the system. If we were to read the holding of the District Court to require, as a matter of substantive constitutional right, any particular degree of racial balance or mixing, that approach would be disapproved and we would be obliged to reverse. The constitutional command to desegregate schools does not mean that every school in every community must always reflect the racial composition of the school system as a whole. . . .

Awareness of the racial composition of the whole school system is likely to be a useful starting point in shaping a remedy to correct past constitutional violations. In sum, the very limited use made of mathematical ratios was within the equitable remedial discretion of the District Court.

(2) *One-Race Schools.*

The record in this case reveals that familiar phenomenon that in metropolitan areas minority groups are often found concentrated in one part of the city. . . . Schools all or predominately of one race in a district of mixed population will require close scrutiny to determine that school assignments are not part of state-enforced segregation.

In light of the above, it should be clear that the existence of some small number of one-race, or virtually one-race, schools within a district is not in and of itself the mark of a system which still practices segregation by law. . . .

The court should scrutinize such schools, and the burden upon the school authorities will be to satisfy the court that their racial composition is not the result of present or past discriminatory action on their part. . . .

(3) *Remedial Altering of Attendance Zones.*

The maps submitted in these cases graphically demonstrate that one of the principal tools employed by school planners and by courts to break up the dual school system has been a frank—and sometimes drastic—gerrymandering of school districts and attendance zones. An additional step was pairing, "clustering," or "grouping" of schools with attendance assignments made deliberately to accomplish the transfer of Negro students out of formerly segregated Negro schools and transfer of white students to formerly all-Negro schools. More often than not, these zones are neither compact nor contiguous; indeed they may be on opposite ends of the city. As an interim corrective measure, this cannot be said to be beyond the broad remedial powers of a court.

Absent a constitutional violation there would be no basis for judicially ordering assignment of students on a racial basis. All things being equal, with no history of discrimination, it might well be desirable to assign pupils to schools nearest their homes. But all things are not equal in a system that has been deliberately constructed and maintained to enforce racial segregation. The remedy for such segregation may be administratively awkward, inconvenient, and even bizarre in some situations and may impose burdens on some; but all awkwardness and inconvenience cannot be avoided in the interim period when remedial adjustments are being made to eliminate the dual school systems. . . .

We hold that the pairing and grouping of noncontiguous school zones is a permissible tool and such action is to be considered in light of the objectives sought. . . .

(4) *Transportation of Students.*

The scope of permissible transportation of students as an implement of a remedial decree has never been defined by this Court and by the very nature of the problem it cannot be defined with precision. No rigid guidelines as to student transportation can be given for application to the infinite variety of problems presented in thousands of situations. . . . The District Court's conclusion that assignment of children to the school nearest their home serving their grade would not produce an effective dismantling of the dual system is supported by the record.

Thus the remedial techniques used in the District Court's order were within that court's power to provide equitable relief; implementation of the decree is well within the capacity of the school authority.

The decree provided that the buses used to implement the plan would operate on direct routes. . . . The trips for elementary school pupils average about seven miles and the District Court found that they would take "not over 35 minutes at the most." This system compares favorably with the transportation plan previously operated in Charlotte under which each day 23,600 students on all grade levels were transported an average of 15 miles one way for an average trip requiring over an hour. In these circumstances, we find no basis for holding that the local school authorities may not be required to employ bus transportation as one tool of school desegregation. Desegregation plans cannot be limited to the walk-in school.

An objection to transportation of students may have validity when the time or distance of travel is so great as to risk either the health of the children or significantly impinge on the educational process. District courts must weigh the soundness of any transportation plan in light of what is said in subdivisions (1), (2), and (3) above. . . .

On the facts of this case, we are unable to conclude that the order of the District Court is not reasonable, feasible and workable. . . .

It does not follow that the communities served by such systems will remain demographically stable, for in a growing, mobile society, few will do so. Neither school authorities nor district courts are constitutionally required to make year-by-year adjustments of the racial composition of student bodies once the affirmative duty to desegregate has been accomplished and racial discrimination through official action is eliminated from the system. This does not mean that federal courts are without power to deal with future problems; but in the absence of a showing that either the school authorities or some other agency of the State has deliberately attempted to fix or alter demographic patterns to affect the racial composition of the schools, further intervention by a district court should not be necessary. . . .

The order of the District Court . . . is . . . affirmed.

*It is so ordered.*

In 1976 the Court cited with approval the statement in *Swann* that annual adjustments would not be constitutionally required of school districts in order to maintain a given racial composition. The Pasadena, California, Board of Education was ordered by a federal District Court in 1970 to implement a desegregation plan which would provide that there would be no school "with a majority of any minority students." In 1974 the District Court stated that such requirement was an inflexible one to be applied anew each school year even though changes in the racial mix were occasioned by the operation of normal demographic factors beyond the control of the Board. In *Pasadena City Board of Education* v. *Spanger*, 427 U.S. 424 (1976), the Court reversed, holding that where shifts in the racial composition of schools resulted from changes in the residential patterns of the city and were not attributable to any segregative action on the part of school officials, neither the school officials nor the District Court "were constitutionally required to make year-by-year adjustments of racial composition of student bodies once the affirmative duty to desegregate has been accomplished and racial discrimination through official action is eliminated from the system."

As the Southern public schools began to achieve substantial integration, attention was directed to systems outside the South, many of which, especially in the North, were far more segregated than the reordered systems in the South. *Swann* suggested that where segregation was *de facto* only, as a result of residential housing patterns of one-race neighborhoods rather than as a result of governmental policy, the Court would not necessarily require the "elimination root and branch" of the segregated school system. More and more Negroes, and many Southern whites, began to point out that if segregation was wrong in the public schools, and if a unitary system was in fact required by the Constitution, then the rule should apply throughout the country, irrespective of whether segregation had developed *de jure, de facto,* or in any other manner. In his impassioned statement regarding segregated school systems in *Brown I,* Chief Justice Warren said, "To separate them from others of similar age and qualifications solely because of their race generates a feeling of inferiority as to their status in the community that may affect their hearts and minds in a way unlikely ever to be undone." And if racially segregated neighborhoods lead to racially segregated schools, it was argued, then the same damage is done and it is immaterial whether the result was produced by purposeful governmental policy or not. In fact, evidence began to accumulate that in some areas outside the South governmental units had encouraged the development of segregated schools by such devices as the location of new schools and the drawing of attendance lines. One such case involved Denver, Colorado, and came to the Court as *Keyes* v. *School District No. 1* in 1973.

## KEYES *v.* SCHOOL DISTRICT NO. 1
### *413 U.S. 921 (1973)*

[Petitioners filed suit in District Court for an order directing the desegregation of the schools in the Park Hill area of Denver, Colorado, and also "for the School District as a whole." The court found that for a period of almost a decade, the School Board had engaged in an unconstitutional policy of deliberate racial segregation with respect to the Park Hill schools. The court issued the order to desegregate those schools, but as to the remaining areas, the court fractionated the district and held that petitioners had to make a fresh showing of de jure segregation in each area of the city for which they sought relief. The court found that petitioners did not prove that the Board had followed a like policy with respect to the core city or other areas within the district. Nevertheless, the court went on to hold that the proofs established that the segregated core city schools were educationally inferior to the predominantly white schools in other parts of the district. Therefore, although all-out desegregation would not be decreed, the decree did demand some desegregation and certain educational improvements for those schools. The Court of Appeals affirmed the Park Hill order but reversed the order respecting the core city schools.]

Mr. Justice Brennan delivered the opinion of the Court. . . .

. . . We have never suggested that plaintiffs in school desegregation cases must bear the burden of proving the elements of de jure segregation as to each and every school or each and every student within the school system. Rather, we have held that where plaintiffs prove that a current condition of segregated schooling exists within a school district where a dual system was compelled or authorized by statute at the time of our decision in *Brown* v. *Board of Education*, . . . the State automatically assumes an affirmative duty "to effectuate a transition to a racially nondiscriminatory school system," . . . that is, to eliminate from the public schools within their school system "all vestiges of state-imposed segregation.". . .

This is not a case, however, where a statutory dual system has ever existed. Nevertheless, where plaintiffs prove that the school authorities have carried out a systematic program of segregation affecting a substantial portion of the students, schools, teachers, and facilities within the school system, it is only common sense to conclude that there exists a predicate for a finding of the existence of a dual school system. Several considerations support this conclusion. First, it is obvious that a practice of concentrating Negroes in certain schools by structuring attendance zones or designating "feeder" schools on the basis of race has the reciprocal effect of keeping other nearby schools predominantly white. Similarly, the practice of building a school . . . to a certain size and in a certain location, "with conscious knowledge that it would be a segregated school," . . . has a substantial reciprocal effect on the racial composition of other schools. So also, the use of mobile classrooms, the drafting of student transfer policies, the transportation of students, and the assignment of faculty and staff, on racially identifiable bases, have the clear effect of earmarking schools according to their racial composition, and this, in turn, together with the elements of student assignment and school construction, may have a profound reciprocal effect on the racial composition of residential neighborhoods within a metropolitan area, thereby causing further racial concentration within the schools. . . .

In short, common sense dictates the conclusion that racially inspired school board actions have an impact beyond the particular schools that are the subjects of those actions. . . . [P]roof of state-imposed segregation in a substantial portion of the district will suffice to support a finding by the trial court of the existence of a dual system. Of course, where that finding is made, as in cases involving statutory dual systems, the school authorities have an affirmative duty "to effectuate a transition to a racially nondiscriminatory school system.". . .

On remand, therefore, the District Court should decide in the first instance whether respondent School Board's deliberate racial segregation policy with respect to the Park Hill schools constitutes the entire Denver school system a dual school system. . . . We emphasize that the differentiating factor between de jure segregation and so-called de facto segregation to which we referred in *Swann* is *purpose* or *intent* to segregate. . . .

In discharging that burden, it is not enough, of course, that the school authorities rely upon some allegedly logical, racially neutral explanation for their actions. Their burden is to adduce proof sufficient to support a finding that segregative intent was not among the factors that motivated their actions. The courts below attributed much significance to the fact that many of the Board's actions in the core city area antedated our decision in *Brown.* We reject any suggestion that remoteness in time has any relevance to the issue of intent. If the actions of school authorities were to any degree motivated by segregative intent and the segregation resulting from those actions continues to exist, the fact of remoteness in time certainly does not make those actions any less "intentional.". . .

. . . If the District Court determines that the Denver school system is a dual school system, respondent School Board has the affirmative duty to desegregate the entire system "root and branch." . . . If the court determines, however, that the Denver school system is not a dual school system by reason of the Board's actions in Park Hill, the court . . . will afford respondent School Board the opportunity to rebut petitioners' prima facie case of intentional segregation in the core city schools raised by the finding of intentional segregation in the Park Hill schools. . . . If respondent Board fails to rebut petitioners' prima facie case, the District Court must, as in the case of Park Hill, decree all-out desegregation of the core city schools. . . .

Mr. Chief Justice Burger concurs in the result.

Mr. Justice White took no part in the decision of this case.

Mr. Justice Douglas.

While I join the opinion of the Court, I agree with my Brother Powell that there is, for the purpose of the Equal Protection Clause of the Fourteenth Amendment as applied to the school cases, no difference between de facto and de jure segregation. The school board is a state agency and the lines that it draws, the locations it selects for school sites, the allocation it makes of students, the budgets it prepares are state action for Fourteenth Amendment purposes. . . .

Mr. Justice Powell concurring in part and dissenting in part.

I concur in the remand of this case for further proceedings in the District Court, but on grounds that differ from those relied upon by the Court.

This is the first school desegregation case to reach this Court which involves a major city outside the South. It comes from Denver, Colorado, a city and a State which have not operated public schools under constitutional or statutory provisions which mandated or permitted racial segregation. . . . The Court has inquired only to what extent the Denver public school authorities may have contributed to the school segregation which is acknowledged to exist in Denver. . . .

The situation in Denver is generally comparable to that in other large cities across the country in which there is a substantial minority population and where desegregation has not been ordered by the federal courts. There is segregation in the schools of many of these cities fully as pervasive as that in southern cities prior to the desegregation decrees of the past decade and a half. The focus of the school desegregation problem has now shifted from the South to the country as a whole. Unwilling and footdragging as the process was in most places, substantial progress toward achieving integration has been made in southern States.* No comparable progress has been made in many nonsouthern cities with large minority populations primarily because

---

*According to the 1971 [HEW] estimate, 43.9% of Negro pupils attended majority white schools in the South as opposed to only 27.8% who attended such schools in the North and West. Fifty-seven percent of all Negro pupils in the North and West attend schools with over 80% minority population as opposed to 32.2% who do so in the South. . . .

of the de facto/de jure distinction nurtured by the courts and accepted complacently by many of the same voices which denounced the evils of segregated schools in the South. But if our national concern is for those who attend such schools, rather than for perpetuating a legalism rooted in history rather than present reality, we must recognize that the evil of operating separate schools is no less in Denver than in Atlanta.

In my view we should abandon a distinction which long since has outlived its time, and formulate constitutional principles of national rather than merely regional application. . . . In a series of decisions extending from 1954 to 1971 the concept of state neutrality was transformed into the present constitutional doctrine requiring affirmative state action to desegregate school systems. The keystone case was *Green* v. *County School Board*, . . . where school boards were declared to have "the affirmative duty to take whatever steps might be necessary to convert to a unitary system in which racial discrimination would be eliminated root and branch.". . .

[T]he doubt as to whether the affirmative-duty concept would flower into a new constitutional principle of general application was laid to rest by *Swann* v. *Charlotte-Mecklenburg Board of Education*, . . . in which the duty articulated in *Green* was applied to the urban school system of metropolitan Charlotte, North Carolina. . . .

In *Swann*, the Court further noted it was concerned only with States having "a long history" of officially imposed segregation and the duty of school authorities in those States to implement *Brown I*. . . . In so doing, the Court refrained from even considering whether the evolution of constitutional doctrine from *Brown I* to *Green/Swann* undercut whatever logic once supported the de facto/de jure distinction. In imposing on metropolitan southern school districts an affirmative duty, entailing large-scale transportation of pupils, to eliminate segregation in the schools, the Court required these districts to alleviate conditions which in large part did *not* result from historic, state-imposed de jure segregation. Rather, the familiar root cause of segregated schools in *all* the biracial metropolitan areas of our country is essentially the same: one of segregated residential migratory patterns the impact of which on the racial composition of the schools was often perpetuated and rarely ameliorated by action of public school authorities. This is a national, not a southern, phenomenon. And it is largely unrelated to whether a particular State had or did not have segregative schools laws.

Whereas *Brown I* rightly decreed the elimination of state-imposed segregation in that particular section of the country where it did exist, *Swann* imposed obligations on southern school districts to eliminate conditions which are not regionally unique but are similar both in origin and effect to conditions in the rest of the country. As the remedial obligations of *Swann* extend far beyond the elimination of the outgrowths of the state-imposed segregation outlawed in *Brown,* the rationale of *Swann* points inevitably toward a uniform, constitutional approach to our national problem of school segregation.

The Court's decision today, while adhering to the de jure/de facto distinction, will require the application of the *Green/Swann* doctrine of "affirmative duty" to the Denver School Board despite the absence of any history of state-mandated school segregation. . . . I concur in the Court's position that the public school authorities are the responsible agency of the State, and that if the affirmative-duty doctrine is sound constitutional law for Charlotte, it is equally so for Denver. I would not, however, perpetuate the de jure/de facto distinction nor would I leave to petitioners the initial tortuous effort of identifying "segregative acts" and deducing "segregative intent." I would hold, quite simply, that where segregated public schools exist within a school district to a substantial degree, there is a prima facie case that the duly constituted public authorities . . . are sufficiently responsible to warrant imposing upon them a nationally applicable burden to demonstrate they nevertheless are operating a genuinely integrated school system.

The principal reason for abandonment of the de jure/de facto distinction is that, in view of the evolution of the holding in *Brown I* into the affirmative-duty doctrine, the distinction no longer can be justified on a principled basis. In decreeing remedial requirements for the Charlotte-Mecklenburg school district, *Swann* dealt with a metropolitan, urbanized area in which the basic causes of segregation were generally similar to those in all sections of the country, and also largely irrelevant to the existence of historic, state-imposed segregation at the time of the *Brown* decision. Further, the extension of the affirmative-duty concept to include compulsory student transportation went well beyond the mere remedying of that portion of school segregation for which former state segregation laws were ever responsible. Moreover, as the Court's opinion today abundantly demonstrates, the facts deemed necessary to establish de jure discrimination present problems of subjective intent which the courts cannot fairly resolve. . . .

Public schools are creatures of the State, and whether the segregation is state-created or state-assisted or merely state-perpetuated should be irrelevant to constitutional principle. . . .

It makes little sense to find prima facie violations and the consequent affirmative duty to desegregate solely in those States with state-imposed segregation at the time of the *Brown* decision. The history of state-imposed segregation is more widespread in our country than the de jure/de facto distinction has traditonally cared to recognize. . . .

As the Court's opinion virtually compels the finding on remand that Denver has a "dual school system," that city will then be under an "affirmative duty" to desegregate its entire system "root and branch.". . . Again, the critical question is what ought this constitutional duty to entail. . . .

To the extent that *Swann* may be thought to require large-scale or long-distance transportation of students in our metropolitan school districts, I record my profound misgivings. Nothing in our Constitution commands or encourages any such court-compelled disruption of public education. . . . In the balancing of interests so appropriate to a fair and just equitable decree, transportation orders should be applied with special caution to any proposal as disruptive of family life and interests— and ultimately of education itself—as extensive transportation of elementary-age children solely for desegregation purposes. . . .

The existing state of law has failed to shed light and provide guidance on the two issues addressed in this opinion: (i) whether a constitutional rule of uniform, national application should be adopted with respect to our national problem of school desegregation and (ii), if so, whether the ambiguities of *Swann,* construed to date almost uniformly in favor of extensive transportation, should be redefined to restore a more viable balance among the various interests which are involved. With all deference, it seems to me that the Court today has addressed neither of these issues in a way that will afford adequate guidance to the courts below in this case or lead to a rational, coherent national policy. . . .

Mr. Justice Rehnquist, dissenting. . . .

*Milliken v. Bradley,* 418 U.S. 717 (1974), dealt with an attempt to desegregate the public schools in the city of Detroit. The District Court ultimately concluded that the defendant school system had engaged in unconstitutional activities which had resulted in de jure segregation in the city school district. The court ordered the submission of desegregation plans for the city alone, and also for the three-county metropolitan area, even though the suburban school districts were not parties to the action and there was no claim that they had committed any constitutional violations. The court concluded that to effectively desegregate the Detroit schools it would be necessary to include neighboring districts as well, and ordered the preparation of a plan with a desegregation area including 53 suburban school districts plus Detroit and with the acquisition of a number of school buses to transport students between and among the various districts to achieve integration. The Supreme Court reversed by a five-to-four vote, holding that a federal court could not properly impose a multi-district, areawide remedy to a single district de jure segregation problem unless it was first established that unconstitutional racially discriminatory acts of the other districts had caused inter- district segregation, or that district lines—which could not be considered as mere arbitrary lines drawn for political convenience—had been deliberately drawn on the basis of race. The dissenters pointed out that the majority decision left the District Court with no effective remedy for correcting widespread and pervasive segregation in the metropolitan area, since a remedy limited to the city of Detroit would probably result in the Detroit school system becoming a substantially all-Negro system by increasing flight of whites from the city to the suburbs.

In *Columbus Board of Education* v. *Penick,* 443 U.S. 449 (1979), and *Dayton Board of Education* v. *Brinkman,* 443 U.S. 526 (1979), the Court ordered massive school desegregation in the public schools of Columbus and Dayton, Ohio. The lower courts made findings that children were attending schools that were heavily one-race and that the distribution could only be explained by the adoption of racially discriminatory policies. The majority upheld the desegregation orders in both cases, which included the reassignment of almost half of the 96,000 students in the Columbus system and the busing of some 15,000 students in Dayton. The orders also required reassignments of teachers and other staff personnel, reorganization of grade structures, and the closing of certain schools. Justices Rehnquist and Powell gave separate, vigorous dissents in both cases.

## Affirmative Action

To enforce the antidiscrimination provisions of the Civil Rights Act of 1964, the Department of Labor issued requirements for preferential hiring on the basis of race and sex in the business community. In 1970 the Department of Health, Education, and Welfare issued guidelines to encourage increased employment of women and minorities on the faculty and staff of colleges and universities with the potential sanction of withdrawing federal funds for failure to comply. These "affirmative action" or "reverse discrimination" policies obviously presented equal protection issues. The leading higher education case on the point was *Regents of the University of California* v. *Bakke* (1978).

### REGENTS OF THE UNIVERSITY OF CALIFORNIA *v.* BAKKE
*438 U.S. 265 (1978)*

[The medical school of the University of California at Davis maintained two separate admissions programs. Eighty-four of the 100 class positions were filled through the regular admissions program, but sixteen positions were set aside for "economically and/or educationally disadvantaged" applicants and those members of certain minorities—blacks, Chicanos, Asians, or American Indians. The special admission candidates did not have to meet the regular admission requirements for consideration. Allan Bakke, a white applicant, was rejected although his scores and projected performance were higher than the minimum standard for regular admission and were higher than a number of the minority candidates who were admitted. He sued, alleging denial of admission on grounds of race, and the trial court agreed that there had been a violation of the 1964 Act, the Fourteenth Amendment, and the California Constitution, but refused to order admission since it concluded that even without the minority program he would not have been admitted. The California Supreme Court held on equal protection grounds that the use of race in the admission program could not survive "strict scrutiny" and, further, ordered Bakke's admission to the medical school.]

Mr. Justice Powell announced the judgment of the Court. . . .

For the reasons stated in the following opinion, I believe that so much of the judgment of the California court as holds petitioner's special admissions program unlawful and directs that respondent be admitted to the Medical School must be affirmed. For the reasons expressed in a separate opinion, my Brothers The Chief Justice, Mr. Justice Stewart, Mr. Justice Rehnquist, and Mr. Justice Stevens concur in this judgment.

I also conclude for the reasons stated in the following opinion that the portion of the court's judgment enjoining petitioner from according any consideration to race in its admissions process must be reversed. For reasons expressed in separate opinions, my Brothers Mr. Justice Brennan, Mr. Justice White, Mr. Justice Marshall, and Mr. Justice Blackmun concur in this judgment.

Affirmed in part and reversed in part. . . .

### III

### A

. . . The special admissions program is undeniably a classification based on race and ethnic background. To the extent that there existed a pool of at least minimally qualified minority applicants to fill the 16 special admissions seats, white applicants could compete only for 84 seats in the entering class, rather than the 100 open to minority applicants. Whether this limitation is described as a quota or a goal, it is a line drawn on the basis of race and ethnic status.

The guarantees of the Fourteenth Amendment extend to all persons. Its language is explicit: "No State shall . . . deny to any person within its jurisdiction the equal protection of the laws." It is settled beyond question that the "rights created by the first section of the Fourteenth Amendment are, by its terms, guaranteed to the individual. The rights established are personal rights." . . . The guarantee of equal protection cannot mean one thing when applied to one individual and something else when applied to a person of another color. If both are not accorded the same protection, then it is not equal. . . .

### B

. . .

Petitioner urges us to adopt for the first time a more restrictive view of the Equal Protection Clause and hold that discrimination against members of the white "majority" cannot be suspect if its purpose can be characterized as "benign." The clock of our liberties, however, cannot be turned back to 1868. . . . It is far too late to argue that the guarantee of equal protection to *all* persons permits the recognition of special wards entitled to a degree of protection greater than that accorded others. . . .

Moreover, there are serious problems of justice connected with the idea of preference itself. First, it may not always be clear that a so-called preference is in fact benign. . . . Second, preferential programs may only reinforce common stereotypes holding that certain groups are unable to achieve success without special protection based on a factor having no relationship to individual worth. . . . Third, there is a measure of inequity in forcing innocent persons in respondent's position to bear the burden of redressing grievances not of their making.

### IV

We have held that in "order to justify the use of a suspect classification, a State must show that its purpose or interest is both constitutionally permissible and substantial, and that its use of the classification is 'necessary . . . to the accomplishment' of its purpose or the safeguarding of its interest." . . . The special admissions program purports to serve the purposes of: (i) "reducing the historic deficit of traditionally disfavored minorities in medical schools and in the medical profession," . . . (ii) countering the effects of societal discrimination; (iii) increasing the number of physicians who will practice in communities currently underserved; and (iv) obtaining the educational benefits that flow from an ethnically diverse student body. It is necessary to decide which, if any, of these purposes is substantial enough to support the use of a suspect classification.

[The opinion here concludes that the first purpose is "facially invalid," the second purpose is unjustified, as resulting in harm to innocent persons, and that on the third purpose, "Petitioner simply has not carried its burden of demonstrating that it must prefer members of particular ethnic groups over all other individuals in order to promote better health-care delivery to deprived citizens."]

### D

The fourth goal asserted by petitioner is the attainment of a diverse student body. This clearly is a constitutionally permissible goal for an institution of higher education. Academic freedom, though not a specifically enumerated constitutional right, long has been viewed as a special concern of the First Amendment. The freedom of a university to make its own judgments as to education includes the selection of its student body. . . .

The atmosphere of "speculation, experiment and creation"—so essential to the quality of higher education—is widely believed to be promoted by a diverse student body. . . .

Thus, in arguing that its universities must be accorded the right to select those students who will contribute the most to the "robust exchange of ideas," petitioner invokes a countervailing constitutional interest, that of the First Amendment. In this light, petitioner must be viewed as seeking to achieve a goal that is of paramount importance in the fulfillment of its mission. . . .

### V
### A

. . .

The experience of other university admissions programs, which take race into account in achieving the educational diversity valued by the First Amendment, demonstrates that the assignment of a fixed number of places to a minority group is not a necessary means toward that end. An illuminating example is found in the Harvard College program. . . . [Here the opinion quotes from a brief showing that while the College does not use quotas, in considering applicants who are "admissable," the

Committee on Admissions indicated that "the race of an applicant may tip the balance in his favor just as geographic origin or a life spent on a farm may tip the balance in other candidates' cases."]

In such an admissions program, race or ethnic background may be deemed a "plus" in a particular applicant's file, yet it does not insulate the individual from comparison with all other candidates for the available seats. . . . No facial infirmity exists in an admissions program where race or ethnic background is simply one element—to be weighed fairly against other elements—in the selection process. . . .

Opinion of Mr. Justice Brennan, Mr. Justice White, Mr. Justice Marshall, and Mr. Justice Blackmun, concurring in the judgment in part and dissenting in part. . . .

[Justice Brennan first discusses Title VI of the Civil Rights Act of 1964 and the decisions dealing with it, concluding that "These prior decisions are indicative of the Court's unwillingness to construe remedial statutes designed to eliminate discrimination against racial minorities in a manner which would impede efforts to attain this objective. There is no justification for departing from this course in the case of Title VI and frustrating the clear judgment of Congress that race-conscious remedial action is permissible." He then turns to the Equal Protection Clause for analysis.]

Unquestionably we have held that a government practice or statute which restricts "fundamental rights" or which contains "suspect classifications" is to be subjected to "strict scrutiny" and can be justified only if it furthers a compelling government purpose. . . . But no fundamental right is involved here. . . . Nor do whites as a class have any of the "traditional indicia of suspectness: the class is not saddled with such disabilities, or subjected to such a history of purposeful unequal treatment, or relegated to such a position of political powerlessness as to command extraordinary protection from the majoritarian political process." . . .

On the other hand, the fact that this case does not fit neatly into our prior analytic framework for race cases does not mean that it should be analyzed by applying the very loose rational-basis standard of review that is the very least that is always applied in equal protection cases. . . . Instead, a number of considerations—developed in gender-discrimination cases but which carry even more force when applied to racial classifications—lead us to conclude that racial classifications designed to further remedial purposes " 'must serve important governmental objectives and must be substantially related to achievement of those objectives.' " . . .

In sum, . . . to justify such a classification an important and articulated purpose for its use must be shown. In addition, any statute must be stricken that stigmatizes any group or that singles out those least well represented in the political process to bear the brunt of a benign program. . . .

. . . We . . . conclude that Davis' goal of admitting minority students disadvantaged by the effects of past discrimination is sufficiently important to justify use of race-conscious admissions criteria. . . .

Certainly, on the basis of the undisputed factual submissions before this Court, Davis had a sound basis for believing that the problem of underrepresentation of minorities was substantial and chronic and that the problem was attributable to handicaps imposed on minority applicants by past and present racial discrimination. . . .

The second prong of our test—whether the Davis program stigmatizes any discrete group or individual and whether race is reasonably used in light of the program's objectives—is clearly satisfied by the Davis program.

It is not even claimed that Davis' program in any way operates to stigmatize or single out any discrete and insular, or even any identifiable, nonminority group. Nor will harm comparable to that imposed upon racial minorities by exclusion or separation on grounds of race be the likely result of the program. It does not, for example, establish an exclusive preserve for minority students apart from and exclusive of whites. Rather, its purpose is to overcome the effects of segregation by bringing the races together. True, whites are excluded from participation in the special admissions program, but this fact only operates to reduce the number of whites to be admitted in the regular admissions program in order to permit admission of a reasonable percentage—less than their proportion of the California population—of otherwise underrepresented qualified minority applicants. . . .

Accordingly, we would reverse the judgment of the Supreme Court of California holding the Medical School's special admissions program unconstitutional and directing respondent's admission, as well as that portion of the judgment enjoining the Medical School from according any consideration to race in the admissions process.

Separate opinion of Mr. Justice White. . . .

Mr. Justice Marshall.

I agree with the judgment of the Court only insofar as it permits a university to consider the race of an applicant in making admissions decisions. I do not agree that petitioner's admissions program violates the Constitution. . . .

[Here the opinion traces the history of Negro slavery in America.]

## II

The position of the Negro today in America is the tragic but inevitable consequence of centuries of unequal treatment. Measured by any benchmark of comfort or achievement, meaningful equality remains a distant dream for the Negro. . . .

## III

I do not believe that the Fourteenth Amendment requires us to accept that fate. Neither its history nor our past cases lend any support to the conclusion that a university may not remedy the cumulative effects of society's discrimination by giving consideration to race in an effort to increase the number and percentage of Negro doctors. . . .

## IV

While I applaud the judgment of the Court that a university may consider race in its admissions process, it is more than a little ironic that, after several hundred years of class-based discrimination against Negroes, the Court is unwilling to hold that a class-based remedy for that discrimination is permissible. In declining to so hold, today's judgment ignores the fact that for several hundred years Negroes have been discriminated against, not as individuals, but rather solely because of the color of their skins. It is unnecessary in 20th century America to have individual Negroes demonstrate that they have been victims of racial discrimination; the racism of our society has been so pervasive that none, regardless of wealth or position, has managed to escape its impact. The experience of Negroes in America has been different in kind, not just in degree, from that of other ethnic groups. It is not merely the history of slavery alone but also that a whole people were marked as inferior by the law. And that mark has endured. The dream of America as the great melting pot has not been realized for the Negro; because of his skin color he never even made it into the pot. . . .

I fear that we have come full circle. After the Civil War our Government started several "affirmative action" programs. This Court in the *Civil Rights Cases* and *Plessy* v. *Ferguson* destroyed the movement toward complete equality. For almost a century no action was taken, and this nonaction was with the tacit approval of the courts. Then we had *Brown* v. *Board of Education* and the Civil Rights Acts of Congress, followed by numerous affirmative action programs. *Now,* we have this Court again stepping in, this time to stop affirmative action programs of the type used by the University of California.

Mr. Justice Blackmun. . . .

I am not convinced, as Mr. Justice Powell seems to be, that the difference between the Davis program and the one employed by Harvard is very profound or constitutionally significant. The line between the two is a thin and indistinct one. In each, subjective application is at work. . . .

I suspect that it would be impossible to arrange an affirmative action program in a racially neutral way and have it successful. To ask that this be so is to demand the impossible. In order to get beyond racism, we must first take account of race. There is no other way. And in order to treat some persons equally, we must treat them differently. We cannot—we dare not—let the Equal Protection Clause perpetuate racial supremacy. . . .

Mr. Justice Stevens, with whom The Chief Justice, Mr. Justice Stewart, and Mr. Justice Rehnquist join, concurring in the judgment in part and dissenting in part. . . .

### III

Section 601 of the Civil Rights Act of 1964 . . . provides:

"No person in the United States shall, on the ground of race, color, or national origin, be excluded from participation in, be denied the benefits of, or be subjected to discrimination under any program or activity receiving Federal financial assistance."

The University, through its special admissions policy, excluded Bakke from participation in its program of medical education because of his race. The University also acknowledges that it was, and still is, receiving federal financial assistance. The plain language of the statute therefore requires affirmance of the judgment below. A different result cannot be justified unless that language misstates the actual intent of the Congress that enacted the statute or the statute is not enforceable in a private action. Neither conclusion is warranted. . . .

Petitioner contends, however, that exclusion of applicants on the basis of race does not violate Title VI if the exclusion carries with it no racial stigma. No such qualification or limitation of §601's categorical prohibition of "exclusion" is justified by the statute or its history. . . .

As with other provisions of the Civil Rights Act, Congress' expression of its policy to end racial discrimination may independently proscribe conduct that the Constitution does not. However, we need not decide the congruence—or lack of congruence—of the controlling statute and the Constitution since the meaning of the Title VI ban on exclusion is crystal clear: Race cannot be the basis of excluding anyone from participation in a federally funded program. . . .

Accordingly, I concur in the Court's judgment insofar as it affirms the judgment of the Supreme Court of California. To the extent that it purports to do anything else, I respectfully dissent.

With no majority opinion in the case, one must make a head count to draw conclusions from the voting. Four members of the Court would have held the Davis system valid in its entirety, including the quota feature. Justice Powell concluded only that Davis could *consider* race in its admission policy, and thus we have five members of the Court affirming the use of race as a factor in educational admissions. Four members held that the Davis program was violative of the Civil Rights Act of 1954 in its entirety. Justice Powell held that the quota feature was invalid under the Fourteenth Amendment, and thus (for different reasons) five members of the Court held the establishment of a racial quota to be invalid. The result appears to be that affirmative action programs will be held valid even though race is taken into account if such programs are developed carefully without specific quotas.

A provision of the Public Works Employment Act of 1977 required that 10 percent of the federal funds expended for local public works projects must be used to procure services or supplies from minority-controlled businesses. This provision was challenged as violative of the due process clause of the Fifth Amendment. In *Fullilove* v. *Klutznick,* 448 U.S. 448 (1980), the Court upheld the provision by a vote of six to three, although again there was no majority opinion. Chief Justice Burger, for three members, held that the objective of the law was within the power of Congress under the Commerce Clause and the Fourteenth Amendment, and that nonminority businesses would be subjected to only a light burden, one which was far from an "invidious discrimination." Justice Powell, concurring, argued that the "strict scrutiny" approach was called for, but that the set-aside provision was "justified as a remedy that serves the compelling interest in eradicating the continuing effects of past discrimination identified by Congress." Thus he distinguished the case from *Bakke* on the ground that there was no showing in *Bakke* that Davis had engaged in any racially discriminatory policies prior to their establishment of the quota program.

Although no constitutional issue was presented since the case involved private action, *Kaiser Aluminum & Chemical Co.* v. *Weber,* 443 U.S. 193 (1979), addressed the problem of the application of the Civil Rights Act of 1964 to affirmative action programs in private industry. A collective bargaining agreement was negotiated between the company and a union to redress the problem of a virtual absence of black workers in the skilled craft work force. The program required that at least half of the trainees in an in-plant training program be black, and that the scheme be continued until the proportion of black craft workers in the plant was equal to the proportion of blacks in the local work force. Weber, a white applicant who was denied entry to the training program, although he had more seniority than several blacks who were chosen, challenged the agreement as violative of the Civil Rights Act's nondiscrimination provision. Justice Brennan, for the majority, concluded that despite the wording of the Act, the program was in conformity with the spirit of the law and was legal, and that "Congress chose not to forbid all voluntary race-conscious affirmative action." Justice Rehnquist, joined by Chief Justice Burger in dissent, stated:

[B]y a tour de force reminiscent not of jurists such as Hale, Holmes, and Hughes, but of escape artists such as Houdini, the Court eludes clear statutory language, "uncontradicted" legislative history, and uniform precedent in concluding that employers are, after all, permitted to consider race in making employment decisions. It may be that one or more of the principal sponsors of Title VII would have preferred to see a provision allowing preferential treatment of minorities written into the bill. Such a provision, however, would have to have been expressly or impliedly excepted from Title VII's explicit prohibition on all racial discrimination in employment. There is no such exception in the Act.

The effect of a "last hired, first fired" policy on an affirmative action program required in a consent decree judicially enforced on the City of Memphis was examined in *Firefighters Local Union No. 1784* v. *Stotts,* 467 U.S. 561 (1984). In 1974 a consent decree established a scheme for increasing the number of blacks employed and promoted citywide by the city of Memphis. In 1977 a black firefighter in the city fire department filed a class action charging the city with racial discrimination in its hiring and promotion decisions in violation of the Civil Rights Act of 1964. In due course a consent decree was approved and entered by the District Court in 1980 under which the city agreed to promote certain individuals and to provide backpay for a number of others and, further, to adopt the long-term goal of increasing the proportion of minority representation in each job classification in the Fire Department to approximately the proportion of blacks in the labor force in Shelby County, Tennessee. Neither decree contained provisions for layoffs or reductions in rank, and neither awarded any competitive seniority. In 1981 the city announced that budget deficits required a reduction of personnel throughout the city government. Layoffs were to be based on the "last hired, first fired" rule. If a senior employee's position were eliminated, the employee could "bump down" to a lower ranking position rather than be laid off. The District Court then entered a temporary restraining order forbidding the layoff of any black employee. The Union was permitted to intervene, and at the preliminary injunction hearing it was estimated that forty least-senior employees in the Department would be laid off and that of these, twenty-five were white and fifteen black. The District Court granted an injunction providing for a modified layoff plan aimed at protecting black employees by directing that the city not apply its seniority policy insofar as it would decrease the percentage of black firefighters. In complying with the order the city laid off some nonminority employees with more seniority than minority employees. The decision of the District Court was based on its conclusion that the "last hired, first fired" policy would have a racially discriminatory effect and that the seniority system was not a bona fide one.

The Court of Appeals affirmed, despite its conclusion that the District Court was wrong in holding that the city's seniority system was not bona fide. The city and the Union sought review by certiorari. The Supreme Court reversed, with three members dissenting. Justice White, for the majority, concluded that the District Court exceeded its authority under the consent decree by entering the order calling for the modified layoff plan:

The issue at the heart of this case is whether the District Court exceeded its powers in entering an injunction requiring white employees to be laid off, when the otherwise applicable seniority system would have called for the layoff of black employees with less seniority. We are convinced that the Court of Appeals erred in resolving this issue and in affirming the District Court.

The Court of Appeals first held that the injunction did no more than enforce the terms of the agreed-upon consent decree. This specific-performance approach rests on the notion that because the City was under a general obligation to use its best efforts to increase the proportion of blacks on the force, it breached the decree by attempting to effectuate a layoff policy reducing the percentage of black employees in the Department even though such a policy was mandated by the seniority system adopted by the City and the Union. . . .

The argument that the injunction was proper because it carried out the purposes of the decree is . . . unconvincing. The decree announced that its purpose was "to remedy past hiring and promotion practices" of the Department . . . and to settle the dispute as to the "appropriate and valid procedures for hiring and promotion." . . . The decree went on to provide the agreed- upon remedy, but as we have indicated, that remedy did not include the displacement of white employees with seniority over blacks. Furthermore, it is reasonable to believe that the "remedy," which it was the purpose of the decree to provide, would not exceed the bounds of the remedies that are appropriate under Title VII, at least absent some express provision to that effect. As our cases have made clear, however, . . . Title VII protects bona fide seniority systems, and it is inappropriate to deny an innocent employee the benefits of his seniority in order to provide a remedy in a pattern or practice suit such as this. We thus have no doubt that the City considered its system to be valid and that it had no intention of departing from it when it agreed to the 1980 decree.

Finally, it must be remembered that neither the Union nor the nonminority employees were parties to the suit when the 1980 decree was entered. Hence the entry of that decree cannot be said to indicate any agreement by them to any of its terms. Absent the presence of the Union or the nonminority employees and an opportunity for them to agree or disagree with any provisions of the decree that might encroach on their rights, it seems highly unlikely that the City would purport to bargain away nonminority rights under the then-existing seniority system. We therefore conclude that the injunction does not merely enforce the agreement of the parties as reflected in the consent decree. . . .

The Court of Appeals held that even if the injunction is not viewed as compelling compliance with the terms of the decree, it was still properly entered because the District Court had inherent authority to modify the decree when an economic crisis unexpectedly required layoffs which, if carried out as the City proposed, would undermine the affirmative action outlined in the decree and impose an undue hardship on respondents. This was true, the court held, even though the modification conflicted with a bona fide seniority system adopted by the City. The Court of Appeals erred in reaching this conclusion.

Section 703 (h) of Title VII provides that it is not an unlawful employment practice to apply different standards of compensation, or different terms, conditions, or privileges of employment pursuant to a bona fide seniority system, provided that such differences are not the result of an intention to discriminate because of race. It is clear that the City had a seniority system, that its proposed layoff plan conformed to that system, and that in making the settlement the City had not agreed to award competitive seniority to any minority employee whom the City proposed to lay off. The District Court held that the City could not follow its seniority system in making its proposed layoffs because its proposal was discriminatory in effect and hence not a bona fide plan. Section 703 (h), however, permits the routine application of a seniority system absent proof of an intention to discriminate. . . .

. . . [T]he Court of Appeals was of the view that the District Court ordered no more than that which the City unilaterally could have done by way of adopting an affirmative action program. Whether the City, a public employer, could have taken this course without violating the law is an issue we need not decide. The fact is that in this case the City took no such action and that the modification of the decree was imposed over its objection. . . . Accordingly, the judgment of the Court of Appeals is reversed.

The primary thrust of the dissenting opinion by Justice Blackmun was that the case was moot. All layoffs were terminated, and the city had rehired all workers laid off under the modified plan. Thus the ruling was purely advisory. But on the merits, he would have upheld the Court of Appeals.

A collective-bargaining agreement between the Jackson, Michigan, Board of Education and a teachers' union provided that if it became necessary to lay off teachers, those with the most seniority would be retained, except that at no time would there be a greater percentage of minority personnel laid off than the current percentage of minority personnel employed at the time of the layoff. As a result, during certain school years, nonminority teachers were laid off, while minority teachers with less seniority were retained. Nonminority teachers who were laid off brought suit in a Federal District Court alleging a violation of the Equal Protection Clause. The court upheld the constitutionality of the layoff provision, holding that the racial preferences granted by the Board need not be grounded on a finding of prior discrimination but were permissible under the Equal Protection Clause as an attempt to remedy societal discrimination by providing "role models" for minority schoolchildren. The Court of Appeals affirmed. In *Wygant* v. *Jackson Board of Education*, 476 U.S. 267 (1986), the Supreme Court reversed, holding the provision a violation of the Equal Protection Clause. Justice Powell, for the plurality, stated:

> This Court never has held that societal discrimination alone is sufficient to justify a racial classification. Rather, the Court has insisted upon some showing of prior discrimination by the governmental unit involved before allowing limited use of racial classifications in order to remedy such discrimination. . . .
>
> [T]he role model theory employed by the District Court has no logical stopping point. The role model theory allows the Board to engage in discriminatory hiring and layoff practices long past the point required by any legitimate remedial purpose. . . .
>
> Societal discrimination, without more, is too amorphous a basis for imposing a racially classified remedy. . . . There are numerous explanations for a disparity between the percentage of minority students and the percentage of minority faculty, many of them completely unrelated to discrimination of any kind. . . . No one doubts that there has been serious racial discrimination in this country. But as the basis for imposing discriminatory *legal* remedies that work against innocent people, societal discrimination is insufficient and over expansive. . . .
>
> In cases involving valid *hiring* goals, the burden to be borne by innocent individuals is diffused to a considerable extent among society generally. Though hiring goals may burden some innocent individuals, they simply do not impose the same kind of injury that layoffs impose. Denial of a future employment opportunity is not as intrusive as loss of an existing job.

In *United States* v. *Paradise*, 55 LW 4211 (1987), a court-ordered quota scheme for promotion of blacks in a state highway department was challenged. In 1972 a Federal District Court in Alabama held that the Alabama Department of Public Safety had systematically excluded blacks from employment in violation of the Fourteenth Amendment. Some 11 years later, confronted with the Department's failure to develop promotion procedures that did not have an adverse impact on blacks, the court ordered the promotion of one black trooper for each white trooper elevated in rank, as long as qualified black candidates were available, until the Department implemented an acceptable promotion procedure. The United States maintained that the race-conscious relief ordered in this case violated the Equal Protection Clause of the Fourteenth Amendment. By a 5–4 vote the Court upheld the order. Justice Brennan, for the plurality, said that "although this Court has consistently held that some elevated level of scrutiny is required when a racial or ethnic distinction is made for remedial purposes, it has yet to reach consensus on the appropriate constitutional analysis." He concluded, however, that the relief ordered survived "even strict scrutiny analysis: it is 'narrowly tailored' to serve a 'compelling governmental purpose' "—remedying past and present discrimination by a state actor.

He also stated that the order was flexible in application at all ranks:

> The requirement may be waived if no qualified black candidates are available. The Department has, for example, been permitted to promote only white troopers to the ranks of lieutenant and captain since no black troopers have qualified for those positions. Further, it applies only when the Department needs to make promotions. Thus, if external forces, such as budget cuts, necessitate a promotion freeze, the Department will not be required to make gratuitous promotions to remain in compliance with the court's order.

Justice O'Connor, for three of the dissenters, argued that the one-for-one promotion order was both unsatisfactory and unnecessary as a remedial measure. "The one-for-one promotion quota used in this case far exceeded the percentage of blacks in the trooper force, and there is no evidence in the record that such an extreme quota was necessary to eradicate the effects of the Department's delay." She suggested that the District Court could either have appointed a trustee to supervise or develop promotion procedures for the Department or, alternatively, "the District Court could have found the recalcitrant Department in contempt of court, and imposed stiff fines or other penalties for the contempt."

## Private Discrimination

Hard on the heels of the second *Brown* decision, the Court in 1956, in *Gayle* v. *Browder*, extended the *Brown* rule to the field of transportation, and thus to all areas under governmental regulation. By 1956, then, the Court had officially ruled that any governmentally imposed policy of segregation by race in any area of activity was in violation of the equal protection of the laws. In addition, the transportation cases involving interstate commerce, discussed earlier in this chapter, had laid down a firm rule that racial discrimination in interstate carriers or in restaurant and terminal facilities operated in conjunction with an interstate carrier violated the nondiscrimination clause of the Interstate Commerce Act. Thus the second broad avenue of attack on racial segregation—that separated facilities required by law were not equal—resulted in a firm holding that the separate but equal doctrine was unconstitutional.

Such decisions, however, only affected practices in the public sector or those properly brought by Congress within the application of its commerce power. There still remained an enormous area of private or quasi-public operations in which race discrimination was practiced and which could not readily be fitted into the framework of decisions relating to enforcement of racially discriminatory legislation or governmental regulations. For these areas a third attack was developed in the courts. The basic approach was fairly simple, although the development of the legal doctrines to support it required a great deal of expert legal scholarship and sustained pressure-group strategy of a kind peculiar to the process of "judicial lobbying." [For an account of this aspect of litigation, see Clement Vose, *Caucasians Only: The Supreme Court, the N.A.A.C.P., and the Restrictive Covenant Cases* (Berkeley: University of California Press, 1959).] The approach was simply to bring as much activity as possible within the concept of "state action" rather than private action. The Fourteenth Amendment bars racial discrimination imposed by "state action," so the more agencies and activities which could be classified within that category, the fewer sectors would remain in which discrimination could validly be carried on under the Constitution.

The first area of attack under this approach was racial discrimination in the Democratic primaries in the South, with a long series of cases beginning in the 1920s and culminating in a square holding in 1953 that a Democratic primary was a governmental institution and that no person could be barred from participation because of his race. (The voting cases will be discussed in the following chapter.) Since a political right was involved, and since the Fifteenth Amendment clearly prohibited governmental discrimination based on race in voting, it did not require the abrogation of the "separate but equal" doctrine to support the Negro claimant's argument. Thus in the category of political and property rights the "state action" approach could be, and was, utilized even before the demise of "separate but equal." Once the claimed right was clearly brought into the magic circle of political and property rights, it was then only necessary to make a proper showing that the denial of the right was in some fair manner carried out under the aegis of governmental authority and a decision could be obtained that racially discriminatory enforcement would violate the Fourteenth and Fifteenth Amendments.

It was pointed out earlier that following the decision in *Buchanan* v. *Warley,* holding that racial zoning by ordinance violated the Fourteenth Amendment, the practice developed of incorporating racially restrictive covenants in deeds conveying property. By the terms of the contract, a buyer of such property would agree never to sell the property to persons of African descent, or Oriental descent, or whatever other nationality the covenant excluded. Presumably, if the buyer violated the agreement and attempted to convey the property to a person in the excluded category, the original seller could file an action in a court of equity and have the later conveyance set aside. But this raised an interesting constitutional issue. Does the participation of the State, in a judicial proceeding setting aside a contract as contrary to a racially restrictive covenant, inject sufficient governmental activity into the transaction to bring it within the category of "state action"within the meaning of the Fourteenth Amendment? If so, then the rule of *Buchanan* v. *Warley* should govern and such participation should be unconstitutional. If not, then the Fourteenth Amendment would not apply, and private discrimination is not barred by the Constitution. After a number of abortive attempts to present the issue before the United States Supreme Court, various organizations interested in the problem of discrimination in residential property were successful in bringing two cases to the Court for decision in 1948. The cases were *Shelley* v. *Kraemer* and *McGhee* v. *Sipes*, and they illustrate clearly the attack on discrimination through broadening the scope of coverage of "state action."

## SHELLEY *v.* KRAEMER
### *334 U.S. 1 (1948)*

Mr. Chief Justice Vinson delivered the opinion of the Court.

These cases present for our consideration questions relating to the validity of court enforcement of private agreements, generally described as restrictive covenants, which have as their purpose the exclusion of persons of designated race or color from the ownership or occupancy of real property. Basic constitutional issues of obvious importance have been raised. . . .

### I

Whether the equal protection clause of the Fourteenth Amendment inhibits judicial enforcement by state courts of restrictive covenants based on race or color is a question which this Court has not heretofore been called upon to consider. . . .

It cannot be doubted that among the civil rights intended to be protected from discriminatory state action by the Fourteenth Amendment are the rights to acquire, enjoy, own, and dispose of property. Equality in the enjoyment of property rights was regarded by the framers of that Amendment as an essential pre-condition to the realization of other basic civil rights and liberties which the Amendment was intended to guarantee. . . .

This Court has given specific recognition to the same principle. *Buchanan* v. *Warley,* 245 U.S. 60 (1917).

It is likewise clear that restrictions on the right of occupancy of the sort sought to be created by the private agreements in these cases could not be squared with the requirements of the Fourteenth Amendment if imposed by state statute or local ordinance. . . .

But the present cases, unlike those just discussed, do not involve action by state legislatures or city councils. Here the particular patterns of discrimination and the areas in which the restrictions are to operate, are determined, in the first instance, by the terms of agreements among private individuals. Participation of the State consists in the enforcement of the restrictions so defined. The crucial issue with which we are here confronted is whether this distinction removes these cases from the operation of the prohibitory provisions of the Fourteenth Amendment.

Since the decision of this Court in the *Civil Rights Cases,* 109 U.S. 3 (1883), the principle has become firmly embedded in our constitutional law that the action inhibited by the first section of the Fourteenth Amendment is only such action as may fairly be said to be that of the States. That Amendment erects no shield against merely private conduct, however discriminatory or wrongful. We conclude, therefore, that the restrictive agreements standing alone cannot be regarded as violative of any rights guaranteed to petitioners by the Fourteenth Amendment. So long as the purposes of those agreements are effectuated by voluntary adherence to their terms, it would appear clear that there has been no action by the State and the provisions of the Amendment have not been violated. . . .

But here there was more. These are cases in which the purposes of the agreements were secured only by judicial enforcement by the state courts of the restrictive terms of the agreements. The respondents urge that judicial enforcement of private agreements does not amount to state action; or, in any event, the participation of the State is so attenuated in character as not to amount to state action within the meaning of the Fourteenth Amendment. Finally, it is suggested, even if the States in these cases may be deemed to have acted in the constitutional sense, their action did not deprive petitioners of rights guaranteed by the Fourteenth Amendment. We move to a consideration of these matters.

## II

That the action of state courts and judicial officers in their official capacities is to be regarded as action of the State within the meaning of the Fourteenth Amendment, is a proposition which has long been established by decisions of this Court. That principle was given expression in the earlier cases involving the construction of the terms of the Fourteenth Amendment. . . .

## III

Against this background of judicial construction, extending over a period of some three-quarters of a century, we are called upon to consider whether enforcement by state courts of the restrictive agreements in these cases may be deemed to be the acts of those States; and if so, whether that action has denied these petitioners the equal protection of the laws which the Amendment was intended to secure.

We have no doubt that there has been state action in these cases in the full and complete sense of the phrase. The undisputed facts disclose that petitioners were willing purchasers of properties upon which they desired to establish homes. The owners of the properties were willing sellers; and contracts of sale were accordingly consummated. It is clear that but for the active intervention of the state courts, supported by the full panoply of state power, petitioners would have been free to occupy the properties in question without restraint.

These are not cases, as has been suggested, in which the States have merely abstained from action, leaving private individuals free to impose such discriminations as they see fit. Rather, these are cases in which the States have made available to such individuals the full coercive power of government to deny to petitioners, on the grounds of race or color, the enjoyment of property rights in premises which petitioners are willing and financially able to acquire and which the grantors are willing to sell. . . .

The enforcement of the restrictive agreements by the state courts in these cases was directed pursuant to the common-law policy of the States as formulated by those courts in earlier decisions. . . . We have noted that previous decisions of this Court have established the proposition that judicial action is not immunized from the operation of the Fourteenth Amendment simply because it is taken pursuant to the state's common-law policy. Nor is the Amendment ineffective simply because the particular pattern of discrimination, which the State has enforced, was defined initially by the terms of a private agreement. State action, as that phrase is understood for the purposes of the Fourteenth Amendment, refers to exertions of state power in all forms. And when the effect of that action is to deny rights subject to the protection of the Fourteenth Amendment, it is the obligation of this Court to enforce the constitutional commands.

We hold that in granting judicial enforcement of the restrictive agreements in these cases, the States have denied petitioners the equal protection of the laws and that, therefore, the action of the state courts cannot stand. . . .

*Reversed.*

Mr. Justice Reed, Mr. Justice Jackson, and Mr. Justice Rutledge took no part in the consideration or decision of these cases.

Since the Court stated that the covenants were not violative of the Constitution but that state enforcement of such clauses was, the *Shelley* decision resulted in a revised method of attempting to maintain racially restrictive covenants. *Barrows* v. *Jackson,* 346 U.S. 249 (1953), raised the question of whether the state violated the Fourteenth Amendment by permitting an action for damages for breach of contract to be maintained in its courts against a property owner who conveyed the property in violation of a racial covenant. A California property owner sold a home to a Negro, contrary to the deed restrictions. She was sued by three neighbors on the ground that the value of their property had dropped sharply since Negroes moved in. The Court held that since California could not incorporate in a statute or enforce in equity such discriminatory policies, it could not furnish its coercive power to force payment of damages and thereby accomplish the same result.

The *Shelley* decision also had its impact on federal policies which affected housing. The national government has provided both for supervision of mortgage lenders and for assistance in financing homes. The Fourteenth Amendment does not reach private discrimination, but national power to support and regulate lending practices extends to the individual pieces of property covered by such loans or financial support. A year and a half after *Shelley*, the FHA ruled that it would not provide mortgage insurance for property on which racially restrictive covenants were recorded after February 15, 1950 [FHA *Underwriting Manual,* sec. 303 (December 1949).] This represented a substantial change in policy, since the earlier *Manual* even contained a model restrictive covenant. The VA has followed similar policies designed to promote open occupancy without respect to race. These kinds of pressures are relatively slight to date, but they illustrate the fact that the executive branch can pick up where the courts leave off and can employ additional tools to further a policy of equal opportunity irrespective of race. [For additional material on government and housing, see the 1961 United States Commission on Civil Rights Report No. 4, *Housing* (Washington: United States Government Printing Office, 1961).]

The decisions in *Shelley* and *Barrows* stimulated further litigation in the program to attack racial discrimination via the "state action" route. *Burton* v. *Wilmington Park Authority,* 365 U.S. 715 (1961), raised the question of whether the policy of racial discrimination followed by a private leaseholder of state property in operating a restaurant was "state action" barred by the Fourteenth Amendment. Eagle Coffee Shoppe, Inc., was a restaurant located in a state-owned automobile parking building in Wilmington, Delaware. The Wilmington Parking Authority, a state agency, leased a portion of the building to Eagle for twenty years, renewable for another ten. The lease contained no requirement that the restaurant services be made available to the general public on a nondiscriminatory basis, and Eagle refused to serve Negroes. In an action for injunctive relief, petitioner claimed that in the circumstances of the lease of state property to serve the public, the action of Eagle was state action violative of the equal protection clause of the Fourteenth Amendment. The Delaware Supreme Court held that Eagle was acting in "a purely private capacity" under its lease, that its action was not that of the Authority, and therefore the discriminatory policies were not furthered by state action within the contemplation of the Fourteenth Amendment. The United States Supreme Court reversed. Pointing out some of the interrelationships between the Parking Authority and Eagle, Justice Clark, speaking for the majority, stated, "The State has so far insinuated itself into a position of interdependence with Eagle that it must be recognized as a joint participant in the challenged activity, which, on that account, cannot be considered to have been so 'purely private' as to fall without the scope of the Fourteenth Amendment."

The California experience with the controversial area of open-housing policy presented a novel aspect of the combination of state action and private discrimination. The problem came to the Court in *Reitman* v. *Mulkey*, 387 U.S. 369 (1967). In 1963 the California legislature adopted the Rumford Fair Housing Act, which prohibited racial discrimination in the sale or rental of any private dwelling containing more than four units. In 1964, however, by initiative, the voters of California adopted a constitutional amendment guaranteeing property owners the right to decline to sell or lease such property "to such person or persons as he, in his absolute discretion, chooses." The California Supreme Court held the amendment unconstitutional under the Fourteenth Amendment's equal protection clause, and by a five to four vote the United States Supreme Court affirmed. Justice White, for the majority, stated that the provision "was intended to authorize, and does authorize, racial discrimination in the housing market. The right to discriminate is now one of the basic policies of the State." He agreed with the California court that the section "will significantly encourage and involve the State in private discriminations."

More recently, in *Jones* v. *Alfred Mayer Co.*, 392 U.S. 409 (1968), the Court upheld the validity of an 1866 Act of Congress (now 42 U.S.C. §1982) which guaranteed to all citizens the same right enjoyed by white citizens to inherit, purchase, lease, sell, hold, and convey real and personal property.

Another portion of the Civil Rights Act of 1866 (now Title 42 U.S.C. Section 1981) provides in pertinent part that all persons within the jurisdiction of the United States "shall have the same right in every State and Territory to make and enforce contracts . . . as is enjoyed by white citizens." In *Runyon* v. *McCrary*, 427 U.S. 160 (1976), the Court held that Section 1981 prohibits private, commercially operated, nonsectarian schools from denying admission to black applicants solely on the basis of race. And in *McDonald* v. *Santa Fe Trail Company*, 427 U.S. 173 (1976), it was held that whites as well as nonwhites could maintain an action to challenge racial discrimination in private employment under Section 1981.

The language of both sections of the 1866 Act makes it clear that they were designed to protect against certain aspects of racial discrimination. Two cases decided in 1987 dealt with the issue of defining "race" for purposes of applying the two sections. In *Saint Francis College* v. *Al-Khazraji*, 55 LW 4626 (1987), a former associate professor in the

College, a United States citizen born in Iraq, sued the College and its tenure committee alleging that by denying him tenure they had discriminated against him on the basis of his Arabian race in violation of § 1981. The District Court ruled that the section did not reach claims of discrimination based on Arabian ancestry. The Court of Appeals reversed, holding that the legislative history of the section indicated that Congress intended to forbid "at the least, membership in a group that is ethnically and physiognomically distinctive." Justice White delivered the opinion for a unanimous Court affirming. He examined a number of 19th century dictionaries and encyclopedias that defined race in terms of ethnic groups. "These dictionary and encyclopedic sources are somewhat diverse, but it is clear that they do not support the claim that for the purposes of § 1981, Arabs, Englishmen, Germans and certain other ethnic groups are to be considered a single race." The case was remanded, however, for a determination of whether the respondent was subjected to intentional discrimination based on the fact that he was born an Arab, rather than "solely on the place or nation of his origin, or his religion."

The second case was *Shaare Tefila Congregation* v. *Cobb*, 55 LW 4629 (1987), decided on the same day. After their synagogue was painted with anti-Semitic slogans, phrases, and symbols, the Congregation brought suit in Federal District Court, alleging that the desecration violated § 1982. The District Court dismissed, and the Court of Appeals affirmed, holding that discrimination against Jews is not racial discrimination under § 1982. The Supreme Court reversed, citing *Saint Francis College* on the issue of racial discrimination. "It is evident from the legislative history of the section reviewed in *Saint Francis College* . . . that Jews and Arabs were among the peoples then considered to be distinct races and hence within the protection of the statute." Further, the section "forbids both official and private racially discriminatory interference with property rights, *Jones* v. *Alfred H. Mayer Co.*"

On April 11, 1968, Congress adopted the Civil Rights Act of 1968, 82 Stat. 73, Title VIII of which is a "Fair Housing" provision. Section 804 is the substantive section of the Title, and it makes unlawful: (a) the refusal to sell or rent a dwelling to any person because of race, color, religion, or national origin; (b) discrimination in terms, conditions, or privileges of sale or rental of a dwelling because of race, color, religion, or national origin; (c) printing or publishing of any notice or advertisement with respect to the sale or rental of a dwelling that indicates any preference or limitation based on race, color, religion, or national origin; (d) representation to any person because of race, color, religion, or national origin that any dwelling is not available for inspection, sale, or rental when such dwelling is in fact so available; and (e) the inducement, for profit, of any person to sell or rent by representation regarding the entry into the neighborhood of a person of a particular race, color, religion, or national origin.

In general, enforcement of Title VIII is by negotiation or, if necessary, by civil suit filed by the Secretary of Housing and Urban Development in a United States District Court. Where a pattern or practice of resistance to the provisions of Title VIII appears, the Attorney General may bring a civil action.

Since 1960 several cases growing out of convictions for restaurant "sit-in" demonstrations have been carried to the United States Supreme Court. Various arguments were presented by the Negro appellants in these cases, including (1) that the restaurants had, by virtue of state licensing and special state regulation, become state instrumentalities, (2) that for the state police and courts to enforce trespass laws in support of restaurant-keepers' racially discriminatory policies was to inject unconstitutional state action under the *Shelley* rule, and (3) where segregated facilities exist in response to general and widespread community custom, state enforcement of such rules is tantamount to state legislation adopting the rule as law and thus violates the Fourteenth Amendment to the same extent as the segregation ordinance did in *Gayle* v. *Browder*. One such case was

*Lombard* v. *Louisiana*, 373 U.S. 267 (1963). In *Peterson* v. *Greenville*, 373 U.S. 244 (1963), decided the same day, the Court reversed trespass convictions in a municipal court, following lunch counter "sit-ins," on the ground that a city ordinance required segregated eating facilities, and the convictions had the effect of enforcing the ordinance in violation of the Fourteenth Amendment. In *Lombard,* however, no such ordinance was involved. After having been refused service at the refreshment counter of a Five-and-Ten-Cent store in New Orleans, three Negroes and one white person refused to leave when requested to do so by the restaurant manager. They were convicted in a Louisiana state court of criminal mischief under a statute including within that designation the taking of temporary possession of, or the remaining in, a place of business after being ordered to leave by the person in charge of such business. On appeal the Supreme Court of Louisiana affirmed. On certiorari, the Supreme Court of the United States reversed. In an opinion by Chief Justice Warren, for eight members of the Court, it was held that despite the absence of an ordinance requiring segregation of restaurant facilities, "we conclude that this case is governed by the principles announced in *Peterson* v. *Greenville.*" This conclusion was reached on the ground that public statements of various city officials in effect reached the level of an official command that segregation be continued and such command "has at least as much coercive effect as an ordinance."

The issue of the validity of state enforcement of trespass laws in support of a restaurant owner's policy of racial discrimination has largely become moot as a consequence of the enactment of the Civil Rights Act of 1964 (78 Stat. 241). [For an account of the legislative history of the Act, see Congressional Quarterly Service, *Revolution in Civil Rights* (Washington, D.C.: Congressional Quarterly, Inc., 1965), pp. 41-70.] The Act reaches discrimination in places of public accommodation if the operations affect interstate commerce or if supported by state action. The issue of what constitutes state action is still viable, however, in areas not covered by the definition of "public accommodations" in the Act, such as barber shops or local dance halls or private clubs. [See Richard A. Lang, Jr., "State Action Under the Equal Protection Clause and the Remaining Scope of Private Choice," 50 *Cornell L.Q.* 473-505 (1965).]

The public accommodations title of the Civil Rights Act of 1964 is similar in coverage to the first two sections of the old Civil Rights Act of 1875 which were held unconstitutional in the *Civil Rights Cases* in 1883. The former is primarily grounded in Congress' power to regulate commerce, however, while the latter was largely based on the Civil War Amendments. The relevant provisions of the new Act are found in Title II.

### Title II—Injunctive Relief Against Discrimination in Places of Public Accommodation

Sec. 201. (a) All persons shall be entitled to the full and equal enjoyment of the goods, services, facilities, privileges, advantages, and accommodations of any place of public accommodation, as defined in this section, without discrimination or segregation on the ground of race, color, religion, or national origin.

(b) Each of the following establishments which serves the public is a place of public accommodation within the meaning of this title if its operations affect commerce, or if discrimination or segregation by it is supported by State action:

(1) any inn, hotel, motel, or other establishment which provides lodging to transient guests, other than an establishment located within a building which contains not more than five rooms for rent or hire and which is actually occupied by the proprietor of such establishment as his residence;

(2) any restaurant, cafeteria, lunchroom, lunch counter, soda fountain, or other facility principally engaged in selling food for consumption on the premises including, but not limited to, any such facility located on the premises of any retail establishment; or any gasoline station;

(3) any motion picture house, theater, concert hall, sports arena, stadium or other place of exhibition or entertainment; and

(4) any establishment (A)(i) which is physically located within the premises of any establishment otherwise covered by this subsection, or (ii) within the premises of which is physically located any such covered establishment, and (B) which holds itself out as serving patrons of such covered establishment.

(c) The operations of an establishment affect commerce within the meaning of this title if (1) it is one of the establishments described in paragraph (1) of subsection (b); (2) in the case of an establishment described in paragraph (2) of subsection (b), it serves or offers to serve interstate travelers or a substantial portion of the food which it serves, or gasoline or other products which it sells, has moved in commerce; (3) in the case of an establishment described in paragraph (3) of subsection (b), it customarily presents films, performances, athletic teams, exhibitions, or other sources of entertainment which move in commerce; and (4) in the case of an establishment described in paragraph (4) of subsection (b), it is physically located within the premises of, or there is physically located within its premises, an establishment the operations of which affect commerce within the meaning of this subsection. For purposes of this section, "commerce" means travel, trade, traffic, commerce, transportation, or communication among the several States or between the District of Columbia and any State, or between any foreign country or any territory or possession and any State or the District of Columbia, or between points in the same State but through any other State or the District of Columbia or a foreign country.

(d) Discrimination or segregation by an establishment is supported by State action within the meaning of this title if such discrimination or segregation (1) is carried on under color of any law, statute, ordinance, or regulation; or (2) is carried on under color of any custom or usage required or enforced by officials of the State or political subdivision thereof; or (3) is required by action of the State or political subdivisions thereof.

(e) The provisions of this title shall not apply to a private club or other establishment not in fact open to the public, except to the extent that the facilities of such establishment are made available to the customers or patrons of an establishment within the scope of subsection (b).

Sec. 202 All persons shall be entitled to be free, at any establishment or place, from discrimination or segregation of any kind on the ground of race, color, religion, or national origin, if such discrimination or segregation is or purports to be required by any law, statute, ordinance, regulation, rule, or order of a State or any agency or political subdivision thereof.

[Sec. 203 prohibits the intimidation or coercion of any person with the purpose of interfering with any right or privilege secured by Sections 201 and 202. Sec. 204 provides for the issuance of restraining orders in the event of such attempted intimidation or coercion, upon application of the aggrieved person, and permits the Attorney General to intervene if he certifies that the case is of general public importance. The court is also permitted, in justifiable cases, to appoint an attorney for the complainant and to authorize the commencement of the civil action without the payment of fees, costs, or security. The court may also allow the prevailing party a reasonable attorney's fee as part of the costs.]

Sec. 206 (a) Whenever the Attorney General has reasonable cause to believe that any person or group of persons is engaged in a pattern or practice of resistance to the full enjoyment of any of the rights secured by this title, and that the pattern or practice is of such a nature and is intended to deny the full exercise of the rights herein described, the Attorney General may bring a civil action in the appropriate district court of the United States by filing with it a complaint . . . requesting such preventive relief . . . as he deems necessary to insure the full enjoyment of the rights herein described. . . .

Sec. 207. (a) The district courts of the United States shall have jurisdiction of proceedings instituted pursuant to this title and shall exercise the same without regard to whether the aggrieved party shall have exhausted any administrative or other remedies that may be provided by law.

(b) The remedies provided in this title shall be the exclusive means of enforcing the rights based on this title, but nothing in this title shall preclude any individual or any State or local agency from asserting any right based on any other Federal or State law not inconsistent with this title, including any statute or ordinance requiring nondiscrimination in public establishments or accommodations, or from pursuing any remedy, civil or criminal, which may be available for the vindication or enforcement of such right.

As expected, cases were initiated very quickly questioning the constitutionality of Title II of the Civil Rights Act of 1964. Two such cases were argued on the opening day of the 1964 Term of the Court, only three months after the passage of the Act. *Heart of Atlanta Motel* v. *United States,* 379 U.S. 241 (1964), came on direct appeal from a three-judge district court in Georgia which had sustained the constitutionality of the Title II provisions and had enjoined the motel owner-operator from discriminating against Negroes on account of race or color. *Katzenbach* v. *McClung,* 379 U.S. 294 (1964), came on direct appeal from a three-judge district court in Alabama which had held the Act unconstitutional as applied to "Ollie's Barbecue" in Birmingham and enjoined enforcement against the restaurant. Decisions were handed down in these two companion cases in December 1964, only two months after argument and five months after enactment of the law.

### HEART OF ATLANTA MOTEL *v.* UNITED STATES
*379 U.S. 241 (1964)*

[The owner of a motel which solicited and received patronage from interstate travelers brought suit in a District Court for declaratory and injunctive relief against the enforcement of the public accommodations sections of the Civil Rights Act of 1964, contending that the sections exceeded the commerce power of Congress, deprived him of liberty and property without due process of law, took his property without just compensation, and subjected him to involuntary servitude. The three-judge court held the provisions constitutional and enjoined the owner from discriminating against Negroes on account of race or color. The Court reviewed the decision on direct appeal.]

Mr. Justice Clark delivered the opinion of the Court. . . .

[The opinion takes up the Civil Rights Act of 1875, with somewhat similar language to that in the 1964 Act, and the decision in the *Civil Rights Cases* holding the earlier act unconstitutional.]

We think that decision inapposite, and without precedential value in determining the constitutionality of the present Act. Unlike Title II of the present legislation, the 1875 Act broadly proscribed discrimination in "inns, public conveyances on land or water, theaters, and other public places of amusement," without limiting the categories of affected businesses to those impinging upon interstate commerce. In contrast, the applicability of Title II is carefully limited to enterprises having a direct and substantial relation to the interstate flow of goods and people, except where state action is involved. Further, the fact that certain kinds of businesses may not in 1875 have been sufficiently involved in interstate commerce to warrant bringing them within the ambit of the commerce power is not necessarily dispositive of the same question today. . . . The sheer increase in volume of interstate traffic alone would give discriminatory practices which inhibit travel a far larger impact upon the nation's commerce than such practices had in the economy of another day. Finally, there is language in the *Civil Rights Cases* which indicates that the Court did not fully consider whether the 1875 Act could be sustained as an exercise of the commerce power. . . .

[The opinion then takes up the evidence and testimony reported in various congressional committee hearings to the effect that racial discrimination had "a qualitative as well as quantitative effect on interstate travel by Negroes." The evidence indicated that the uncertainty of finding facilities for food and lodging, stemming from racial discrimination, "had the effect of discouraging travel on the part of a substantial portion of the Negro community."]

The power of Congress to deal with these obstructions depends on the meaning of the Commerce Clause. Its meaning was first enunciated 140 years ago by the great Chief Justice John Marshall in *Gibbons* v. *Ogden,* 9 Wheat. 1 (1824). . . .

In short, the determinative test of the exercise of power by the Congress under the Commerce Clause is simply whether the activity sought to be regulated is "commerce which concerns more than one state" and has a real and substantial relation to the national interest. . . .

It is said that the operation of the motel here is of a purely local character. But, assuming this to be true, "if it is interstate commerce that feels the pinch, it does not matter how local the operation that applies the squeeze." *United States* v. *Women's Sportswear Mfrs. Ass'n.,* 336 U.S. 460, 464 (1949). . . . As Chief Justice Stone put it in *United States* v. *Darby, supra:*

"The power of Congress over interstate commerce is not confined to the regulation of commerce among the states. It extends to those activities intrastate which so affect interstate commerce or the exercise of the power of Congress over it as to make regulation of them appropriate means to the attainment of a legitimate end, the exercise of the granted power of Congress to regulate interstate commerce. . . ."

Thus the power of Congress to promote interstate commerce also includes the power to regulate the local incidents thereof, including local activities in both the States of origin and destination, which might have a substantial and harmful effect upon that commerce. One need only examine the evidence which we have discussed above to see that Congress may—as it has—prohibit racial discrimination by motels serving travelers, however "local" their operations may appear.

Nor does the Act deprive appellant of liberty or property under the Fifth Amendment. The commerce power invoked here by the Congress is a specific and plenary one authorized by the Constitution itself. The only questions are: (1) whether Congress had a rational basis for finding that racial discrimination by motels affected commerce, and (2) if it had such a basis, whether the means it selected to eliminate that evil are reasonable and appropriate. If they are, appellant has no "right" to select its guests as it sees fit free from governmental regulation.

There is nothing novel about such legislation. Thirty-two States now have it on their books either by statute or executive order and many cities provide such regulations. Some of these Acts go back fourscore years. It has been repeatedly held by this Court that such laws do not violate the Due Process Clause of the Fourteenth Amendment. . . .

. . . As a result the constitutionality of such state statutes stands unquestioned. "The authority of the Federal Government over interstate commerce does not differ," it was held in *United States* v. *Rock Royal Co-op, Inc.*, 307 U.S. 533 (1939), "in extent or character from that retained by the states over intrastate commerce." . . .

. . . Neither do we find any merit in the claim that the Act is a taking of property without just compensation. The cases are to the contrary. . . .

We find no merit in the remainder of appellant's contentions, including that of "involuntary servitude." . . . We could not say that the requirements of the Act in this regard are in any way "akin to African slavery." *Butler* v. *Perry,* 240 U.S. 328, 332 (1916).

*Katzenbach* v. *McClung*, 379 U.S. 294 (1964), raised many of the same questions which were disposed of in the companion motel case. The appellees did raise on additional issue, however, which the Court took care of separately. The restaurant was located some distance from interstate highways and railroad and bus stations, and it catered to local family and white-collar trade. In the preceding year the restaurant had purchased locally approximately $150,000 worth of food, of which about $70,000 was for meat that it bought from a local supplier who had procured it from outside the state. In his opinion for the Court upholding the application of the Act to Ollie's Barbecue, Justice Clark stated the question and gave the response:

. . . There is no claim that interstate travelers frequented the restaurant. The sole question, therefore, narrows down to whether Title II, as applied to a restaurant receiving about $70,000 worth of food which has moved in commerce, is a valid exercise of the power of Congress. The Government has contended that Congress had ample basis upon which to find that racial discrimination at restaurants which receive from out of state a substantial portion of the food served does, in fact, impose commercial burdens of national magnitude upon interstate commerce. The appellees' major argument is directed to this premise. They urge that no such basis existed. It is to that question that we now turn. . . .

[The opinion then refers to testimony at hearings before the Senate Committee on Commerce, including testimony that in areas where discrimination is widely practiced there was less spending per capita by Negroes, after discounting income differences, in restaurants and like establishments. "The diminutive spending springing from a refusal to serve Negroes and their total loss as customers, has, regardless of the absence of direct evidence, a close connection to interstate commerce. The fewer customers a restaurant enjoys the less food it sells and consequently the less it buys."]

We believe that this testimony afforded ample basis for the conclusion that established restaurants in such areas sold less interstate goods because of the discrimination, that interstate travel was obstructed directly by it, that business in general suffered and that many new businesses refrained from establishing there as a result of it. . . .

It goes without saying that, viewed in isolation, the volume of food purchased by Ollie's Barbecue from sources supplied from out of state was insignificant when compared with the total foodstuffs moving in commerce. But, as our late Brother Jackson said for the Court in *Wickard* v. *Filburn,* 317 U.S. 111, 127-128 (1942):

"That appellee's own contribution to the demand for wheat may be trivial by itself is not enough to remove him from the scope of federal regulation where, as here, his contribution, taken together with that of many others similarly situated, is far from trivial." . . .

. . . The activities that are beyond the reach of Congress are "those which are completely within a particular State, which do not affect other States, and with which it is not necessary to interfere, for the purpose of executing some of the general powers of the government." *Gibbons* v. *Ogden*, 9 Wheat 1, 195 (1824). This rule is as good today as it was when Chief Justice Marshall laid it down almost a century and a half ago.

Bona fide private clubs are not within the coverage of the Act and thus are not barred from discriminating racially. But in *Moose Lodge No. 107* v. *Irvis*, 407 U.S. 163 (1972), it was argued that by granting the club a liquor license the State had become an "active participant" in the policy and the Fourteenth Amendment applied. The majority refused to hold that such licensure converted the club to a state agency, although three members dissented.

A number of States and local governments, however, have adopted laws and ordinances prohibiting discrimination in private clubs. New York City's Human Rights Law prohibited discrimination based on race, creed, sex, and other grounds by any place of public accommodation, but specifically exempted any institution or club "which is in its nature distinctly private." A 1984 amendment, however, provided that any institution, club or place of accommodation, other than a benevolent order or a religious corporation, "shall not be considered in its nature distinctly private" if it "has more than four hundred members, provides regular meal service and regularly receives payment . . . directly or indirectly from or on behalf of nonmembers for the furtherance of trade or business." In *New York State Club Association, Inc.* v. *City of New York*, 56 LW 4653 (1988), the Association filed suit on behalf of its member clubs challenging the law on First and Fourteenth Amendment grounds, arguing that the law abridged the members' right of association and the exemption for benevolent or religious orders violated the Equal Protection Clause. The New York Courts upheld the law, and the Supreme Court unanimously affirmed. In his opinion for the Court, Justice White emphasized the application of the law to large-sized clubs that provide "regular meal service" and receive regular payments "directly or indirectly from or on behalf of nonmembers for the furtherance of trade or business." He stated that "These characteristics are at least as significant in defining the nonprivate nature of these associations, because of the kind of role that strangers play in their ordinary existence, as is the regular participation of strangers at meetings." Further, the equal protection challenge must fail unless the city could not reasonably believe that the exempted organizations are different in relevant respects from the Association's members. And the Court held that the Association had not carried the burden of showing that the exempted organizations were identical in critical respects to the covered private clubs.

A third important provision of the Civil Rights Act of 1964 is the Title VII provision setting up a right of equal employment opportunity irrespective of race, color, religion, sex, or national origin. Though the impact of this Title has not been so immediate or dramatic as that of the equal accommodations sections, the long-term effect of this provision, if implemented, will probably be of more importance in assuring real equality of opportunity for all persons than any of the other provisions of the Act. Equal educational opportunity alone does not instill motivation to learn or to remain in school through advanced grades. And equal access to public accommodations is no great personal triumph for the man whose menial occupation does not pay enough to permit him to stay in motels or eat in restaurants. Assurance of equal chances to compete and to advance in the economic arena, however, at least offers the potential for encouraging the fuller utilization of educational opportunities and the realization of some of the benefits of the equal accommodations provisions.

The first section of Title VII defines the persons and organizations to which the terms of the Title extend. It covers labor unions, employers engaged in an industry affecting commerce, employment agencies, and others. In general the provisions apply to employers and labor unions with twenty-five or more employees or members, but operating on a sliding scale with exemption the first year for those with less than one hundred, the second year for those with less than seventy-five, the third year for those with less than fifty, and those with less than twenty-five thereafter. (Amended in 1972 to reach employers of fifteen or more persons.) Section 701 (b) further states that the term "employer" does not include:

(1) the United States, a corporation wholly owned by the Government of the United States, an Indian tribe, or a State or political subdivision thereof, (2) a bona fide private membership club (other than a labor organization) which is exempt from taxation under section 501 (c) of the Internal Revenue Code of 1954: . . . *Provided further,* That it shall be the policy of the United States to insure equal employment opportunities for Federal employees without discrimination because of race, color, religion, sex or national origin and the President shall utilize his existing authority to effectuate this policy. (The 1972 amendments extended the coverage of the Act to States and their political subdivisions.)

The substantive provisions of the Title are found in the following section:

Sec. 703. (a) It shall be an unlawful employment practice for an employer—
(1) to fail or refuse to hire or to discharge any individuals, or otherwise to discriminate against any individual with respect to his compensation, terms, conditions, or privileges of employment, because of such individual's race, color, religion, sex, or national origin; or
(2) to limit, segregate, or classify his employees in any way which would deprive or tend to deprive any individual of employment opportunities or otherwise adversely affect his status as an employee, because of such individual's race, color, religion, sex, or national origin. . . .

Subsections (b), (c), and (d) impose similar limitations on the referral policies of employment agencies, membership policies of labor unions, and training program policies of either employers or labor organizations.

There are two primary exceptions to the nondiscrimination provisions. First, classification on the basis of religion, sex, or national origin may be made if such classification is "a bona fide occupational qualification reasonably necessary to the normal operation of that particular business or enterprise." (Note that the provision does not permit an exception based on race.) Second, schools may hire employees of a particular religion if they are "in whole or in substantial part, owned, supported, controlled, or managed by a particular religion," or if the curriculum of any such school "is directed toward the propagation of a particular religion."

The final subsection, (j), states that nothing in the title shall be interpreted to require *preferential* treatment based on race, religion, sex, or national origin "on account of an imbalance which may exist" in the number of persons in any category employed by any employer (or admitted to membership in any labor union, etc.) in comparison with the total number of persons in such category in the community. Thus a "quota" system of hiring is not demanded by the title.

Section 705 of Title VII provides for the creation of a five-member Equal Employment Opportunity Commission. It is given the power to furnish various kinds of technical assistance to further compliance with the title, to make such technical studies "as are appropriate to effectuate the purposes and policies of this title," and to perform other advising and consulting functions. It is charged with reporting annually to the Congress and to the President concerning the action it has taken, "and shall make such further reports on the cause of and means of eliminating discrimination and such recommendations for further legislation as may appear desirable." The Commission also has authority to examine witnesses under oath and to require the production of documentary evidence relevant or material to the investigation. The Commission has further authority to issue suitable procedural regulations to carry out the provisions of Title VII.

## GRIGGS v. DUKE POWER CO.
### 401 U.S. 424 (1971)

Mr. Chief Justice Burger delivered the opinion of the Court.

We granted the writ in this case to resolve the question whether an employer is prohibited by the Civil Rights Act of 1964, Title VII, from requiring a high school education or passing of a standardized general intelligence test as a condition of employment in or transfer to jobs when (a) neither standard is shown to be significantly related to successful job performance, (b) both requirements operate to disqualify Negroes at a substantially higher rate than white applicants, and (c) the jobs in question formerly had been filled only by white employees as part of a long-standing practice of giving preference to whites. . . .

The District Court found that prior to . . . the effective date of the Civil Rights Act of 1964, the Company openly discriminated on the basis of race in the hiring and assigning of employees at its Dan River plant. . . .

The objective of Congress in the enactment of Title VII is plain from the language of the statute. It was to achieve equality of employment opportunities and remove barriers that have operated in the past to favor an identifiable group of white employees over other employees. Under the Act, practices, procedures, or tests neutral on their face, and even neutral of intent, cannot be maintained if they operate to "freeze" the status quo of prior discriminatory employment practices. . . .

. . . Congress did not intend by Title VII, however, to guarantee a job to every person regardless of qualifications. In short, the Act does not command that any person be hired simply because he was formerly the subject of discrimination, or because he is a member of a minority group. Discriminatory preference for any group, minority or majority, is precisely and only what Congress has proscribed. What is required by Congress is the removal of artificial, arbitrary, and unnecessary barriers to employment when the barriers operate invidiously to discriminate on the basis of racial or other impermissible classification. . . . The touchstone is business necessity. If an employment practice which operates to exclude Negroes cannot be shown to be related to job performance, the practice is prohibited.

On the record before us, neither the high school completion requirement nor the general intelligence test is shown to bear a demonstrable relationship to successful performance of the jobs for which it was used. Both were adopted, as the Court of Appeals noted, without meaningful study of their relationship to job-performance ability. Rather, a vice president of the Company testified, the requirements were instituted on the Company's judgment that they generally would improve the overall quality of the work force.

The evidence, however, shows that employees who have not completed high school or taken the tests have continued to perform satisfactorily and make progress in departments for which the high school and test criteria are now used. . . .

The facts of this case demonstrate the inadequacy of broad and general testing devices as well as the infirmity of using diplomas or degrees as fixed measures of capability. History is filled with examples of men and women who rendered highly effective performance without the conventional badges of accomplishment in terms of certificates, diplomas, or degrees. Diplomas and tests are useful servants, but Congress has mandated the common-sense proposition that they are not to become masters of reality.

The company contends that its general intelligence tests are specifically permitted by §703(h) of the Act. That section authorizes the use of "any professionally developed ability test" that is not "designed, intended *or used* to discriminate because of race. . . ." (Emphasis added.) . . .

Nothing in the Act precludes the use of testing or measuring procedures; obviously they are useful. What Congress has forbidden is giving these devices and mechanisms controlling force unless they are demonstrably a reasonable measure of job performance. Congress has not commanded that the less qualified be preferred over the better qualified simply because of minority origins. Far from disparaging job qualifications as such, Congress has made such qualifications the controlling factor, so that race, religion, nationality, and sex become irrelevant. What Congress has commanded is that any tests used must measure the person for the job and not the person in the abstract. . . .

Mr. Justice Brennan took no part in the consideration or decision of this case.

In *Washington v. Davis,* 426 U.S. 229 (1976), various unsuccessful black candidates for positions as police officers in the District of Columbia challenged the constitutionality of certain of the written tests, claiming discriminatory racial impact. It should be noted that while there was considerable discussion of Title VII standards in the opinion of the Court, the case was brought on due process grounds rather than under Title VII because, at the time the action was brought, Title VII did not apply to governmental units. (Amendments to the Act in 1972 did extend the provisions to such units.) The Court held that the mere fact that a governmental test had a racially disproportionate impact (four times as many blacks as whites failed the test) was insufficient, standing alone, to require a decision that the test violated the Fifth Amendment's prohibition against invidious discrimination. The claimants were required to make a further showing that the test was adopted with a racially discriminatory purpose. Justice White, for the majority, indicated that Title VII imposed a more rigorous standard than did the Fifth and Fourteenth Amendments. He stated:

Under Title VII, Congress provided that when hiring and promotion practices disqualifying substantially disproportionate numbers of blacks are challenged, discriminatory purpose need not be proved, and that it is an insufficient response to demonstrate some rational basis for the challenged practices. It is necessary, in addition, that they be "validated" in terms of job performance in any one of several ways, perhaps by ascertaining the minimum skill, ability or potential necessary for the position at issue and determining whether the qualifying tests are appropriate for the selection of qualified applicants for the job in question. However this process proceeds, it involves a more probing judicial review of, and less deference to, the seemingly reasonable acts of administrators and executives than is appropriate under the Constitution where special racial impact, without discriminatory purpose, is claimed. We are not disposed to adopt this more rigorous standard for the purposes of applying the Fifth and the Fourteenth Amendments in cases such as this.

The Court accepted the District Court's finding that the challenged test, measuring verbal skills, was directly related to the requirements of the police training program and that a positive relationship between the test and that program was sufficient to validate the test.

It has already been noted in the Memphis *Firefighters* case that the Act of 1964 provides special protection to bona fide seniority systems. And in *American Tobacco Company* v. *Patterson,* 456 U.S. 63 (1982), the Court held that in dealing with minority challenges to seniority systems, the test is not whether the system has a discriminatory impact, but whether the system was adopted with a discriminatory purpose.

In *Watson* v. *Fort Worth Bank and Trust,* 56 LW 4922 (1988), the Court extended the *Griggs* holding to cover *subjective* employment criteria as well as standardized or written aptitude tests. Clara Watson, a black employee of the bank, was rejected in favor of white applicants for four promotions to different supervisory positions in the bank. The bank had not developed precise and formal criteria for evaluating candidates for the positions for which Watson unsuccessfully applied. It relied instead on the subjective judgment of supervisors who were acquainted with the candidates and with the nature of the jobs to be filled. All the supervisors involved in denying Watson the four promotions at issue were white. After exhausting her administrative remedies, she filed suit in Federal District Court alleging that the bank's promotion policies had unlawfully discriminated against blacks generally and her, personally, in violation of Title VII of the 1964 Act. The court held that she had not met her burden of proof under the discriminatory *treatment* evidentiary standard and dismissed the action. The Court of Appeals affirmed, rejecting Watson's contention that the trial court erred in failing to apply disparate *impact* analysis to her claims. The court held that under its precedent, a Title VII challenge to a discretionary or subjective promotion system can only be analyzed under the disparate *treatment* model. The Supreme Court vacated the judgment and remanded the case. Justice O'Connor's opinion for the plurality stated:

> In *Griggs* v. *Duke Power Co* . . . this Court held that a plaintiff need not necessarily prove intentional discrimination in order to establish that an employer has violated §703. In certain cases, facially neutral employment practices that have significant adverse effects on protected *groups* have been held to violate the Act without proof that the employer adopted those practices with a discriminatory intent. The factual issues and the character of the evidence are inevitably somewhat different when the plaintiff is exempted from the need to prove intentional discrimination . . . The evidence in these "disparate impact" cases usually focuses on statistical disparities, rather than specific incidents, and on competing explanations for those disparities. . . .

> We are persuaded that our decisions in *Griggs* and succeeding cases could largely be nullified if disparate impact analysis were applied only to standardized selection practices. However one might distinguish "subjective" from "objective" criteria, it is apparent that selection systems that combine both types would generally have to be considered subjective in nature. Thus, for example, if the employer in *Griggs* had consistently preferred applicants who had a high school diploma and who passed the company's general aptitude test, its system could nonetheless have been considered "subjective" if it also included brief interviews with the candidates. So long as an employer refrained from making standardized criteria absolutely determinative, it would remain free to give such tests almost as much weight as it chose without risking a disparate impact challenge. If we announced a rule that allowed employers so easily to insulate themselves from liability under *Griggs,* disparate impact analysis might effectively be abolished. . . .

> We conclude, accordingly, that subjective or discretionary employment practices may be analyzed under the disparate impact approach in appropriate cases.

Having decided that disparate impact analysis may in principle be applied to subjective as well as to objective practices, we turn to the evidentiary standards that should apply in such cases. . . . Standardized tests and criteria . . . can often be justified through formal "validation studies," which seek to determine whether discrete selection criteria predict actual on-the-job performance. . . . Respondent warns, however, that "validating" subjective selection criteria in this way is impracticable. Some qualities—for example, common sense, good judgment, originality, ambition, loyalty, and tact—cannot be measured accurately through standardized testing techniques. . . . Because of these difficulties, we are told, employers will find it impossible to eliminate subjective selection criteria and impossibly expensive to defend such practices in litigation. Respondent insists, and the United States agrees, that employers' only alternative will be to adopt surreptitious quota systems in order to ensure that no plaintiff can establish a statistical prima facie case.

We agree that the inevitable focus on statistics in disparate impact cases could put undue pressure on employers to adopt inappropriate prophylactic measures. . . .

We do not believe that disparate impact theory need have any chilling effect on legitimate business practices. . . .

First, we note that the plaintiff's burden in establishing a prima facie case goes beyond the need to show that there are statistical disparities in the employer's work force. The plaintiff must begin by identifying the specific employment practice that is challenged. . . .

Once the employment practice at issue has been identified, causation must be proved; that is, the plaintiff must offer statistical evidence of a kind and degree sufficient to show that the practice in question has caused the exclusion of applicants for jobs or promotions because of their membership in a protected group. Our formulations, which have never been framed in terms of any rigid mathematical formula, have consistently stressed that statistical disparities must be sufficiently substantial that they raise such an inference of causation. . . .

In the context of subjective or discretionary employment decisions, the employer will often find it easier than in the case of standardized tests to produce evidence of a "manifest relationship to the employment in question." It is self-evident that many jobs, for example those involving managerial responsibilities, require personal qualities that have never been considered amenable to standardized testing. . . . In sum, the high standards of proof in disparate impact cases are sufficient in our view to avoid giving employers incentives to modify any normal and legitimate practices by introducing quotas or preferential treatment.

The case was remanded to permit the lower courts to determine whether Watson made out a prima facie case of discriminatory promotion practices under disparate impact theory.


## Other Aspects of Race Discrimination

There is one area of state legislation classifying by race into which the Court did not venture until 1967. This is the statutory bar to marriages between whites and nonwhites, commonly known as antimiscegenation laws. Since miscegenous marriages represent one of the great fears of those who support race discriminations, it is understandable that neither the Court nor the nonwhite racial pressure groups were anxious to press the issue of the validity of such laws, at least until nondiscrimination in the more important areas of social and economic activity had been achieved. The line of decisions respecting classification by race in regulatory legislation, however, clearly presaged a holding that the miscegenation laws were unconstitutional.

At one period in the nineteenth century some thirty-eight states had statutes barring whites from marrying members of defined categories of nonwhites. During the Civil War period nine states repealed such statutes, and as of 1951 twenty-nine states retained them. [See Harvey H. Applebaum, "Miscegenation Statutes: A Constitutional and Social Problem," 53 Geo. L. J. 49 (1946).] Since that time a number of those states had repealed their statutes, and as of 1967 sixteen states remained with statutes outlawing interracial marriage. The statutes differed widely, both in the persons to whom they applied and in the definitions of categories. In general they prohibited whites from marrying nonwhites but did not bar intermarriage among the nonwhite categories, as, for example, between Indians and Negroes. The definition of Negro (or Indian or Oriental) varied, however, and a person of mixed white and Negro ancestry could be a white under the law of one state and a Negro under the law of another.

Shortly after the end of World War II, the California Supreme Court held the California antimiscegenation law unconstitutional, as a denial of equal protection of the law, in Perez v. Lippold [Sharp], 32 Cal. 2d 711, 198 P.2d 17 (1948). The United States Supreme Court had an opportunity to rule on the question in a case involving the Virginia law as applied to an attempted marriage between a white and an Oriental, but avoided a decision on the merits. The case was first remanded to the Virginia court on the ground of deficiencies in the record, and an appeal from the later decision was dismissed. [Naim v. Naim, 350 U.S. 985 (1956).]

More recently the Court took an appeal and rendered a decision in a case which bore closely on the miscegenation question. Defendants were convicted in a Florida state court of having violated a statute which made it a criminal offense for a white person and a Negro of opposite sexes, not married to each other, to habitually live in and occupy in the nighttime the same room. The Florida Supreme Court sustained the statute against a claim of denial of equal protection under the Fourteenth Amendment. On appeal the Court unanimously reversed in McLaughlin v. Florida, 379 U.S. 184 (1964). In his opinion for the Court, Justice White discussed the legislative power to classify and then stated: "Our inquiry, therefore, is whether there clearly appears in the relevant materials some overriding statutory purpose requiring the proscription of the specified conduct when engaged in by the white person and a Negro, but not otherwise. Without such justification the racial classification . . . is reduced to an invidious discrimination forbidden by the Equal Protection Clause." He concluded that promiscuity by the interracial couple presented no particular problems which required separate or different treatment. Florida argued, however, that the interracial cohabitation law was valid because it was ancillary to and served the same purpose as the miscegenation law itself. Justice White responded, "We reject this argument without reaching the question of the validity of the State's prohibition against interracial marriage. . . ."

The Court did reach the question in 1967, however, in an appeal involving the antimiscegenation policy of the state of Virginia. The case testing Virginia's statutes began, ironically, as Virginia v. Loving, a criminal prosecution for violation of the state's ban on interracial marriages. In Loving v. Virginia, 388 U.S. 1 (1967), the Court held the prohibition unconstitutional.

Despite the long list of cases denying governments the power to classify by race in regulatory legislation, it should not be assumed that they are barred from taking any cognizance whatever of race or color. There are valid uses for such notations, and as long as data concerning race or color are maintained for legitimate statistical or other valid public purposes, such record-keeping does not violate the constitution. Drivers' licenses presumably may properly require an entry showing race or color as an aid to identification, and certainly birth records and census reports would seem justifiably to contain the same information. In *Tancil* v. *Woolls*, 379 U.S. 19 (1964), the Court, in a Per Curiam opinion, affirmed a three-judge district court's judgment [230 F.Supp. 156 (E.D. Va., 1964)] upholding a Virginia statute which required that the race of the parties be identified in divorce decrees. It is clear, however, that record-keeping by race which may be maintained must not in any way suggest differential treatment, such as occurred in the jury selection cases, for example, or the procedure will not pass muster under the equal protection clause.

In 1971 the Court examined the question of whether a city's closing of a public swimming pool, following a court order to integrate the facility, was a violation of the equal protection clause. There was disagreement among the justices as to whether the primary motivation behind the decision to close the pool was to avoid financial loss or to evade the integration order, but the majority held that the action was not unconstitutional.

## PALMER *v.* THOMPSON
### 403 U.S. 217 (1971)

[After federal litigation had resulted in a judgment declaring unconstitutional a Mississippi city's operation of public swimming pools on a racially segregated basis—four for whites only and one for Negroes only—the city council decided not to operate public swimming pools at all, and the pools were closed. Some Negro residents brought suit in federal court seeking to require the city to reopen the pools and to operate them on a desegregated basis. The District Court declined to issue an injunction, and the Court of Appeals affirmed.]

Mr. Justice Black delivered the opinion of the Court.

Petitioners rely chiefly on the first section of the Fourteenth Amendment which forbids any State to "deny to any person within its jurisdiction the equal protection of the laws." There can be no doubt that a major purpose of this Amendment was to safeguard Negroes against discriminatory state laws—state laws that fail to give Negroes protection equal to that afforded white people. . . . Here there has unquestionably been "state action" because the official local government legislature, the city council, has closed the public swimming pools of Jackson. The question, however, is whether this closing of the pools is state action that denies "the equal protection of the laws" to Negroes. It should be noted first that neither the Fourteenth Amendment nor any act of Congress purports to impose an affirmative duty on a State to begin to operate or to continue to operate swimming pools. Furthermore, this is not a case where whites are permitted to use public facilities while blacks are denied access. It is not a case where a city is maintaining different sets of facilities for blacks and whites and forcing the races to remain separate in recreational or educational activities. . . .

Unless, therefore, as petitioners urge, certain past cases require us to hold that closing the pools to all denied equal protection to Negroes, we must agree with the courts below and affirm.

Although petitioners cite a number of our previous cases, the only two which even plausibly support their argument are *Griffin* v. *County School Board of Prince Edward County*, 377 U.S. 218 (1964), and *Reitman* v. *Mulkey*, 387 U.S. 369 (1967). For the reasons that follow, however, neither case leads to reverse the judgment here.

A. In *Griffin* the public schools of Prince Edward County, Virginia, were closed under authority of state and county law, and so-called "private schools" were set up in their place to avoid a court desegregation order. . . . In Prince Edward County the "private schools" were open to whites only and these schools were in fact run by a practical partnership between state and county, designed to preserve segregated education. We pointed out in *Griffin* the many facets of state involvement in the running of the "private schools." . . . That case can give no comfort to petitioners here. This record supports no intimation that Jackson has not completely and finally ceased running swimming pools for all time. . . .

B. Petitioners also claim that Jackson's closing of the public pools authorizes or encourages private pool owners to discriminate on account of race and that such "encouragement" is prohibited by *Reitman* v. *Mulkey, supra.*

In *Reitman,* California had repealed two laws relating to racial discrimination in the sale of housing by passing a constitutional amendment establishing the right of private persons to discriminate on racial grounds in real estate transactions. This Court [held] that the constitutional amendment was an official authorization of racial discrimination which significantly involved the State in the discriminatory acts of private parties. . . . *Reitman* v. *Mulkey* was based on a theory that the evidence was sufficient to show the State was abetting a refusal to rent an apartment on racial grounds. On this record, *Reitman* offers no more support to petitioners than does *Griffin.*

Petitioners have also argued that respondents' action violates the Equal Protection Clause because the decision to close the pools was motivated by a desire to avoid integration of the races. But no case in this Court has held that a legislative act may violate equal protection solely because of the motivations of the men who voted for it. . . .

It is true there is language in some of our cases interpreting the Fourteenth and Fifteenth Amendments which may suggest that the motive or purpose behind a law is relevant to its constitutionality. *Griffin* v. *Prince Edward County, supra; Gomillion* v. *Lightfoot,* 364 U.S. 339 (1960). But the focus in those cases was on the actual effect of the enactments, not upon the motivation which led the States to behave as they did. . . . Here the record indicates only that Jackson once ran segregated public swimming pools and that no public pools are now maintained by the city. . . . It shows no state action affecting blacks differently from whites. . . . The judgment is

*Affirmed.*

Mr. Chief Justice Burger, concurring. . . .

Mr. Justice Blackmun, concurring. . . .

Mr. Justice Douglas, dissenting. . . .

I conclude that though a State may discontinue any of its municipal services—such as schools, parks, pools, athletic fields, and the like—it may not do so for the purpose of perpetuating or installing apartheid or because it finds life in a multiracial community difficult or unpleasant. If that is its reason, then abolition of a designated public service becomes a device for perpetuating a segregated way of life. That a State may not do. . . .

Mr. Justice White, with whom Mr. Justice Brennan and Mr. Justice Marshall join, dissenting. . . .

Let us assume a city has been maintaining segregated swimming pools and is ordered to desegregate them. Its express response is an official resolution declaring desegregation to be contrary to the city's policy and ordering the facilities closed rather than continued in service on a desegregated basis. To me it is beyond cavil that on such facts the city is adhering to an unconstitutional policy and is implementing it by abandoning the facilities. It will not do in such circumstances to say that whites and Negroes are being treated alike because both are denied use of public services. The fact is that closing the pools is an expression of official policy that Negroes are unfit to associate with whites. . . . The Equal Protection Clause is a hollow promise if it does not forbid such official denigrations of the race the Fourteenth Amendment was designed to protect. . . .

Mr. Justice Marshall, with whom Mr. Justice Brennan and Mr. Justice White join, dissenting. . . .

. . . [W]hen the officials of Jackson, Mississippi, in the circumstances of this case, detailed by Mr. Justice White, denied a single Negro child the opportunity to go swimming simply because he is a Negro, rights guaranteed to that child by the Fourteenth Amendment were lost. The fact that the color of his skin is used to prevent others from swimming in public pools is irrelevant. . . .

## SEX DISCRIMINATION

A variety of earlier cases held that the State does not violate the equal protection clause by singling out women for special treatment in the exercise of the state's protective power. Classification has been upheld based on differences either in their physical characteristics or in the social conditions surrounding their employment. One of the earliest pieces of social legislation to be held valid by the Court was a law limiting hours of work for women in laundries to a ten-hour workday. [*Muller* v. *Oregon*, 208 U.S. 412 (1908).] In *Radice* v. *New York*, 264 U.S. 292 (1924), a law prohibiting women from working in restaurants at night was upheld. More recently, in *Goesaert* v. *Cleary*, 335 U.S. 464 (1948), the Court sustained a state statute forbidding women to act as bartenders, but making an exception in favor of wives and daughters of the male owners of liquor establishments, although three justices dissented. Justice Frankfurter, for the majority, stated:

We are, to be sure, dealing with a historic calling. We meet the alewife, sprightly and ribald, in Shakespeare, but centuries before him she played a role in the social life of England. . . . The Fourteenth Amendment did not tear history up by the roots, and the regulation of the liquor traffic is one of the oldest and most untrammeled of legislative powers. Michigan could, beyond question, forbid all women from working behind a bar. This is so despite the vast changes in the social and legal position of women. The fact that women may now have achieved the virtues that men have long claimed as their prerogatives and now indulge in vices that men have long practiced, does not preclude the States from drawing a sharp line between the sexes, certainly in such matters as the regulation of the liquor traffic. . . . The Constitution does not require legislatures to reflect sociological insight, or shifting social standards, any more than it requires them to keep abreast of the latest scientific standards.

The experiences of World War II, however, had shown to many people clear proof that women could perform just as competently and safeguard their morals at least as well as men in occupations which formerly had been denied them. Women drove taxis, welded, riveted, flew airplanes, and even did heavy construction work. And they did these jobs at all hours of the day and night. Understandably, many such women chafed under the resumption after the war of the so-called "protective" laws limiting the types of employment for women or the hours in which they could work. Their criticisms began to reach legislative bodies and political party platform committees, and they charged that the only thing "protective" about such restrictions was the protection of men from female competition for their jobs. The dissenting opinion of Justice Rutledge, joined by Justices Douglas and Murphy, in the *Goesaert* case indicated a willingness to look more closely into the reasonableness of classifications based on sex. He stated, in part:

The statute arbitrarily discriminates between male and female owners of liquor establishments. A male owner, although he himself is always absent from his bar, may employ his wife and daughter as barmaids. A female owner may neither work as a barmaid herself nor employ her daughter in that position, even if a man is always present in the establishment to keep order. The inevitable result of the classification belies the assumption that the statute was motivated by a legislative solicitude for the moral and physical well-being of women who, but for the law, would be employed as barmaids. Since there could be no other conceivable justification for such discrimination against women owners of liquor establishments, the statute should be held invalid as a denial of equal protection.

In 1967 the United States Supreme Court denied a petition for certiorari to review a Tennessee rule of tort liability involving an unusual aspect of discrimination on the basis os sex. The case was *Krohn* v. *Richardson-Merrell, Inc.,* 406 S.W.2d 166 (Tennessee, 1966), a tort action against a drug company following the rendering of a man impotent as a consequence of using the company's drug. As one assignment of injury, the wife claimed damages for loss of consortium. Following the common-law rule, the Tennessee Supreme Court held that the wife could not maintain such an action and rejected her contention that permitting a husband but not a wife to recover for loss of consortium is an impermissible discrimination under the equal protection clause.

## The Constitutional Development

In 1971 the Supreme Court for the first time in history held a law unconstitutional on the ground that it discriminated against women in violation of the equal protection clause. The case grew out of the appointment of an administrator for the estate of a minor child under a construction of the relevant Idaho law which accorded preference for the appointment of the father rather than the mother to such positions.

### REED *v.* REED
#### *404 U.S. 71 (1971)*

[After the death of an adopted, minor son, the mother, who had separated from the father, filed a petition in the Probate Court of Ada County, Idaho, seeking appointment as administratrix of her son's estate. Prior to a hearing on the mother's petition, the father filed a competing petition seeking to have himself appointed administrator. Under the Idaho Probate Code, the parents of a decedent are in the same entitlement class for appointment as administrator. The Probate Court, apparently without attempting to determine the relative capability of the competing applicants, ordered that letters of administration be issued to the father, on the basis of a provision of the Probate Code that males must be preferred to females where persons of equal entitlement seek to administer an estate. On appeal by the mother, the District Court of Idaho reversed, holding that the statute violated the Fourteenth Amendment equal protection clause. The Supreme Court of Idaho reversed.]

Mr. Chief Justice Burger delivered the opinion of the Court. . . .

. . . The court treated . . . the Idaho Code as the controlling statutes and read those sections as compelling a preference for Cecil Reed because he was a male. . . .

. . . Having examined the record and considered the briefs and oral arguments of the parties, we have concluded that the arbitrary preference established in favor of males by . . . the Idaho Code cannot stand in the face of the Fourteenth Amendment's command that no State deny the equal protection of the laws to any person within its jurisdiction.

Idaho does not, of course, deny letters of administration to women altogether. Indeed, under §15-312, a woman whose spouse dies intestate has a preference over a son, father, brother, or any other male relative of the decedent. Moreover, we can judicially notice that in this country, presumably due to the greater longevity of women, a large proportion of estates, both intestate and under wills of decedents, are administered by surviving widows.

Section 15-314 is restricted in its operation to those situations where competing applications for letters of administration have been filed by both male and female members of the same entitlement class. . . . In such situations, §15-314 provides that different treatment may be accorded to the applicants on the basis of their sex; it thus establishes a classification subject to scrutiny under the Equal Protection Clause.

In applying that clause, this Court has consistently recognized that the Fourteenth Amendment does not deny to States the power to treat different classes of persons in different ways. . . . The Equal Protection Clause of that Amendment does, however, deny to States the power to legislate that different treatment be accorded to persons placed by a statute into different classes on the basis of criteria wholly unrelated to the objective of that statute. . . . The question presented by this case, then, is whether a difference in the sex of competing applicants for letters of administration bears a rational relationship to a state objective that is sought to be advanced by the operation of [the statutes].

In upholding the latter section, the Idaho Supreme Court concluded that its objective was to eliminate one area of controversy when two or more persons, equally entitled, . . . seek letters of administration and thereby present the probate court "with the issue of which one should be named." The court also concluded that where such persons are not of the same sex, the elimination of females from consideration "is neither an illogical nor arbitrary method devised by the legislature to resolve an issue that would otherwise require a hearing as to the relative merits . . . of the two or more petitioning relatives. . . ." . . .

Clearly the objective of reducing the workload on probate courts by eliminating one class of contests is not without some legitimacy. The crucial question, however, is whether §15-314 advances that objective in a manner consistent with the command of the Equal Protection Clause. We hold that it does not. To give a mandatory preference to members of either sex over members of the other, merely to accomplish the elimination of hearings on the merits, is to make the very kind of arbitrary legislative choice forbidden by the Equal Protection Clause of the Fourteenth Amendment; and whatever may be said as to the positive values of avoiding intrafamily controversy, the choice in this context may not lawfully be mandated solely on the basis of sex. . . .

The judgment of the Idaho Supreme Court is reversed and the case remanded for further proceedings not inconsistent with this opinion.

*Reversed and remanded.*

In *Stanley* v. *Illinois*, 405 U.S. 645 (1972), Illinois statutes were challenged which permitted custody of illegitimate children by the unwed mother but did not even allow the unwed father a hearing to determine fitness for custody, presuming him to be unfit. A majority of the Court held that such discrimination violated the equal protection clause, and that both the father and the mother should be accorded equal rights to hearing on the issue of fitness before removing children from custody.

In 1972 opponents of sex discrimination finally achieved a victory in the Congress by the proposal of the Equal Rights Amendment. Section 1 of the proposed Amendment, the substantive section, stated: "Equality of rights under the law shall not be denied or abridged by the United States or by any State on account of sex."

The second section would have given Congress the power to pass appropriate legislation to enforce the first section. The amendment was proposed on March 22, 1972, and by December 1, twenty-two States had ratified. The process slowed considerably, however, and by the end of 1977 thirty-five States had ratified, and three States had passed resolutions rescinding earlier ratification. The proposal contained a seven-year deadline, and as that date came closer, pro-ERA forces successfully campaigned for a three-year extension by the Congress (to June 30, 1982). Even so, the required three-fourths vote of the States was not obtained, and the ERA failed of ratification.

## FRONTIERO v. RICHARDSON
### 411 U.S. 677 (1973)

[A servicewoman's application for increased quarters allowances and medical and dental benefits for her husband as a dependent was denied because she failed to demonstrate that her husband was dependent on her for more than one-half of his support, as required by various sections of the United States Code. Thereupon the servicewoman sued in the United States District Court in Alabama, contending that the statutes—which allow a serviceman to claim his wife as a dependent for such benefits without regard to whether she is in fact dependent upon him for any part of her support—unreasonably discriminated on the basis of sex in violation of the due process clause of the Fifth Amendment. The three-judge District Court upheld the constitutionality of the statutes.]

Mr. Justice Brennan announced the judgment of the Court and an opinion in which Mr. Justice Douglas, Mr. Justice White, and Mr. Justice Marshall join.

The question before us concerns the right of a female member of the uniformed services to claim her spouse as a "dependent" for the purposes of obtaining increased quarters allowances and medical and dental benefits . . . on an equal footing with male members. Under these statutes, a serviceman may claim his wife as a "dependent" without regard to whether she is in fact dependent upon him for any part of her support. . . . A servicewoman, on the other hand, may not claim her husband as a "dependent" under these programs unless he is in fact dependent upon her for over one-half of his support. . . . Thus, the question for decision is whether this difference in treatment constitutes an unconstitutional discrimination against servicewomen in violation of the Due Process Clause of the Fifth Amendment. . . .

At the outset, appellants contend that classifications based upon sex, like classifications based upon race, alienage, and national origin, are inherently suspect and must therefore be subjected to close judicial scrutiny. We agree and, indeed, find at least implicit support for such an approach in our unanimous decision only last Term in Reed v. Reed . . . (1971). . . .

There can be no doubt that our Nation has had a long and unfortunate history of sex discrimination. Traditionally, such discrimination was rationalized by an attitude of "romantic paternalism" which, in practical effect, put women, not on a pedestal, but in a cage. Indeed, this paternalistic attitude became so firmly rooted in our national consciousness that, 100 years ago, a distinguished Member of this Court was able to proclaim:

"Man is, or should be, woman's protector and defender. The natural and proper timidity and delicacy which belongs to the female sex evidently unfits it for many of the occupations of civil life. The constitution of the family organization, which is founded in the divine ordinance, as well as in the nature of things, indicates the domestic sphere as that which properly belongs to the domain and functions of womanhood. The harmony, not to say identity, of interests and views which belong, or should belong, to the family institution is repugnant to the idea of a woman adopting a distinct and independent career from that of her husband. . . .

". . . The paramount destiny and mission of woman are to fulfill the noble and benign offices of wife and mother. This is the law of the Creator." *Bradwell* v. *Illinois*, 16 Wall. 141 (1873) (Bradley, J., concurring).

As a result of notions such as these, our statute books gradually became laden with gross, stereotyped distinctions between the sexes and, indeed, throughout much of the 19th century the position of women in our society was, in many respects, comparable to that of blacks under the pre-Civil War slave codes. Neither slaves nor women could hold office, serve on juries, or bring suit in their own names, and married women traditionally were denied the legal capacity to hold or convey property or to serve as legal guardians of their own children. . . . And although blacks were guaranteed the right to vote in 1870, women were denied even that right—which is itself "preservative of other basic civil and political rights" until adoption of the Nineteenth Amendment half a century later.

It is true, of course, that the position of women in America has improved markedly in recent decades. Nevertheless, it can hardly be doubted that, in part because of the high visibility of the sex characteristic, women still face pervasive, although at times more subtle, discrimination in our educational institutions, in the job market and, perhaps most conspicuously, in the political arena. . . .

. . . [W]hat differentiates sex from such nonsuspect statutes as intelligence or physical disability, and aligns it with the recognized suspect criteria, is that the sex characteristic frequently bears no relation to ability to perform or contribute to society. As a result, statutory distinctions between the sexes often have the effect of invidiously relegating the entire class of females to inferior legal status without regard to the actual capabilities of its individual members.

We might also note that, over the past decade, Congress has itself manifested an increasing sensitivity to sex-based classifications. [The opinion here cites Title VII of the Civil Rights Act of 1964, the Equal Pay Act of 1963, and the Equal Rights Amendment, passed by Congress in 1972 and submitted to the States for ratification.] Thus, Congress itself has concluded that classifications based upon sex are inherently invidious, and this conclusion of a coequal branch of Government is not without significance to the question presently under consideration. . . .

With these considerations in mind, we can only conclude that classifications based upon sex, like classifications based upon race, alienage, or national origin, are inherently suspect, and must therefore be subjected to strict judicial scrutiny. Applying the analysis mandated by that stricter standard of review, it is clear that the statutory scheme now before us is constitutionally invalid. . . .

. . . [T]he Government concedes that the differential treatment accorded men and women under these statutes serves no purpose other than mere "administrative convenience." In essence, the Government maintains that, as an empirical matter, wives in our society frequently are dependent upon their husbands, while husbands rarely are dependent upon their wives. Thus, the Government argues that Congress might reasonably have concluded that it would be both cheaper and easier simply conclusively to presume that wives of male members are financially dependent upon their husbands, while burdening female members with the task of establishing dependency in fact. . . .

. . . [O]ur prior decisions make clear that, although efficacious administration of governmental programs is not without some importance, "the Constitution recognizes higher values than speed and efficiency." *Stanley* v. *Illinois*, . . . (1972). And when we enter the realm of "strict judicial scrutiny," there can be no doubt that "administrative convenience" is not a shibboleth, the mere recitation of which dictates constitutionality. . . . On the contrary, any statutory scheme which draws a sharp line between the sexes, *solely* for the purpose of achieving administrative convenience, necessarily commands "dissimilar treatment for men and women who are . . . similarly situated," and therefore involves the "very kind of arbitrary legislative choice forbidden by the [Constitution]. . . ." *Reed* v. *Reed*. . . . We therefore conclude that, by according differential treatment to male and female members of the uniformed services for the sole purpose of achieving administrative convenience, the challenged statutes violate the Due Process Clause of the Fifth Amendment insofar as they require a female member to prove the dependency of her husband.

*Reversed.*

Mr. Justice Stewart concurs in the judgment, agreeing that the statutes before us work an invidious discrimination in violation of the Constitution. *Reed* v. *Reed*.

Mr. Justice Rehnquist dissents. . . .

Mr. Justice Powell, with whom The Chief Justice and Mr. Justice Blackmun join, concurring in the judgment.

I agree that the challenged statutes constitute an unconstitutional discrimination against servicewomen in violation of the Due Process Clause of the Fifth Amendment, but I cannot join the opinion of Mr. Justice Brennan, which would hold that all classifications based upon sex, "like classifications based upon race, alienage, and national origin," are "inherently suspect and must therefore be subjected to close judicial scrutiny." . . . It is unnecessary for the Court in this case to characterize sex as a suspect classification, with all of the far-reaching implications of such a holding. *Reed* v. *Reed* . . . , which abundantly supports our decision today, did not add sex to the narrowly limited group of classifications which are inherently suspect. In my view, we can and should decide this case on the authority of *Reed* and reserve for the future any expansion of its rationale.

There is another, and I find compelling, reason for deferring a general categorizing of sex classifications as invoking the strictest test of judicial scrutiny. The Equal Rights Amendment, which if adopted will resolve the substance of this precise question, has been approved by the Congress and submitted for ratification by the States. If this Amendment is duly adopted, it will represent the will of the people accomplished in the manner prescribed by the Constitution. By acting prematurely and unnecessarily, as I view it, the Court has assumed a decisional responsibility at the very time when state legislatures, functioning within the traditional democratic process, are debating the proposed Amendment. It seems to me that this reaching out to preempt by judicial action a major political decision which is currently in process of resolution does not reflect appropriate respect for duly prescribed legislative processes. . . .

In *Cleveland Board of Education* v. *La Fleur*, 414 U.S. 632 (1974), certain pregnant teachers had challenged the constitutionality of the Board's maternity leave policy which provided that a pregnant teacher must take maternity leave beginning five months before the expected birth of the child, that the teacher give notice of her pregnancy at least two weeks prior to the time when she must begin her maternity leave, and that she could become eligible for reemployment no sooner than the beginning of the next school semester after her child was three months old, provided that a doctor issued a certificate attesting to the teacher's health. The Court held the policy unconstitutional, but the decision came on due process grounds rather than equal protection. The majority found the notice provision reasonable, but held the mandatory employment termination provisions and the waiting period rule violative of the due process clause as not being necessary for continuity of instruction or for keeping physically unfit teachers out of the classroom since they established a conclusive presumption of the physical incapacity of the teacher during these periods and such presumptions were neither necessarily nor universally true. Justice Stewart, for the majority, stated, "While the medical experts in these cases differed on many points, they unanimously agreed on one—the ability of any particular pregnant woman to continue at work past any fixed time in her pregnancy is very much an individual matter." As to the three-months-of-age provision for eligibility to return, the opinion stated, "To the extent that the three-month provision reflects the school board's thinking that no mother is fit to return until that point in time, it suffers from the same constitutional deficiencies that plague the irrebuttable presumption in the termination rules." It was also considered unnecessary, since the requirement of a physician's certificate fully protected the school's interest in this regard.

In the following year in *Turner* v. *Department of Employment Security*, 423 U.S. 44 (1975), the Court held invalid a Utah law that automatically denied unemployment compensation to pregnant women for twelve weeks before childbirth and for six weeks afterward.

In *Stanton* v. *Stanton*, 421 U.S. 7 (1975), Utah statutes were challenged which provided that males attained majority at age twenty-one and females at age eighteen, and thus a father's responsibility for child support payments following a divorce decree ceased at age eighteen for females but continued to age twenty-one for males. The Court held that *Reed* v. *Reed* was controlling, and that "in the context of child support the classification effectuated . . . denies the equal protection of the laws, as guaranteed by the Fourteenth Amendment." The Court was unimpressed with the Utah court's "old notions" that females tend to marry earlier than males, and that since it is the man's primary responsibility to provide a home, it is salutary for him to have education and training before he assumes that responsibility. Justice Blackmun, for the Court, stated, "To distinguish between the two on educational grounds is to be self-serving: if the female is not to be supported so long as the male, she hardly can be expected to attend school as long as he does, and bringing her education to an end earlier coincides with the role-typing society has long imposed."

It should not be assumed that only women were adversely affected by gender-based legislation. Males were occasionally the disadvantaged group, and they also began to ride the wave of equal rights litigation—winning some and losing some. In *Kahn* v. *Shevin*, 416 U.S. 351 (1974), a Florida law was challenged that gave to widows, but not to widowers, a $500 property tax exemption. The Court upheld the classification as rational on the ground that women have suffered greater financial disabilities than men, and older women, particularly, have a more difficult time getting jobs. Further, the States have large leeway in making classifications with respect to taxation.

In *Schlesinger* v. *Ballard*, 419 U.S. 498 (1975), the Court upheld federal statutes providing for mandatory discharge of male Naval officers who were passed over twice for promotion, although women officers were guaranteed thirteen years of service. The differentiation was considered to be rational in view of the fact that women have less chance for sea duty and combat service, and therefore their opportunities for promotion are more limited.

The Social Security Act contains a number of provisions with gender-based classifications and several cases have arisen challenging these provisions. The first decision to grant males equal rights with women involved one section of the Act. It grants survivors benefits to widows and minor children where the working husband dies, but provides benefits only to the minor children in the event the husband survives his working wife. In *Weinberger* v. *Wiesenfeld*, 420 U.S. 636 (1975), the Court unanimously held the provision invalid. The majority opinion found a violation of the equal protection secured by the Fifth Amendment, since the distinction results in the efforts of women workers, required to pay social security taxes, producing less protection for their families than is produced by the efforts of men. Thus the decision was still slanted toward protecting the rights of women, although males were to be the direct beneficiary.

*Craig* v. *Boren* (1976) was discussed earlier and came off squarely as a decision giving males equal status with women in exercising their right to purchase 3.2% beer in the State of Oklahoma. Another provision of the Social Security Act was attacked in *Califano* v. *Goldfarb*, 430 U.S. 199 (1977). The Act provides that survivors' benefits are payable to the widow of a husband covered under the Act regardless of the degree of her dependency upon the deceased husband, but such benefits are payable to the widower of a wife covered by the Act only if the widower was receiving at least one-half of his support from the deceased wife. Although there was no majority opinion, five members of the Court agreed that the sex-based distinction violated the Fifth Amendment. The plurality opinion relied heavily on *Weinberger*, suggesting that the distinction was supported by no more substantial justification than archaic and overbroad generalizations or old notions, "that are more consistent with 'the role-typing society has long imposed.'"

In *Califano* v. *Webster*, 430 U.S. 313 (1977), however, the Court upheld a distinction in the Act favoring women. The formula for computing old-age benefits under the Act permits women workers to exclude from the "average monthly wage" three more low-earning years than the male worker is allowed. The Court unanimously upheld the differentiation. The per curiam opinion quoted *Goldfarb* in stating that the more favorable treatment was the permissible one "of redressing our society's longstanding disparate treatment of women," and operated directly to compensate women for past economic discrimination.

In *Orr* v. *Orr* (1979), a decision considered by many to be a major victory for males in the equal protection area, the Court held unconstitutional a state law providing that husbands, but not wives, may be required to pay alimony upon the granting of a divorce.

## ORR *v.* ORR
### 440 U.S. 268 (1979)

[The portions of the Court's opinion dealing with "case or controversy" issues are omitted from the cutting.]

Mr. Justice Brennan delivered the opinion of the Court. . . .

In authorizing the imposition of alimony obligations on husbands, but not on wives, the Alabama statutory scheme "provides that different treatment be accorded . . . on the basis of . . . sex; it thus establishes a classification subject to scrutiny under the Equal Protection Clause," *Reed* v. *Reed*. . . . The fact that the classification expressly discriminates against men rather than women does not protect it from scrutiny. *Craig* v. *Boren*. . . . "To withstand scrutiny" under the Equal Protection Clause, "classifications by gender must serve important governmental objectives and must be substantially related to achievement of those objectives.' " . . . We shall, therefore, examine the three governmental objectives that might arguably be served by Alabama's statutory scheme.

Appellant views the Alabama alimony statutes as effectively announcing the State's preference for an allocation of family responsibilities under which the wife plays a dependent role, and as seeking for their objective the reinforcement of that model among the State's citizens. . . . We agree, as he urges, that prior cases settle that this purpose cannot sustain the statutes. *Stanton* v. *Stanton* . . . held that the "old notion" that "generally it is the man's primary responsibility to provide a home and its essentials," can no longer justify a statute that discriminates on the basis of gender. . . .

The opinion of the Alabama Court of Civil Appeals . . . states that the Alabama statutes were "designed" for "the wife of a broken marriage who needs financial assistance. . . ." We concede, of course, that assisting needy spouses is a legitimate and important governmental objective. . . .

But in this case, even if sex were a reliable proxy for need, and even if the institution of marriage did discriminate against women, these factors still would "not adequately justify the salient features of" Alabama's statutory scheme, *Craig* v. *Boren*. . . . Under the statute, individualized hearings at which the parties' relative financial circumstances are considered *already* occur. . . . There is no reason, therefore, to use sex as a proxy for need. Needy males could be helped along with needy females with little if any additional burden on the State. In such circumstances, not even an administrative-convenience rationale exists to justify operating by generalization or proxy. Similarly, since individualized hearings can determine which women were in fact discriminated against vis-à-vis their husbands, as well as which family units defied the stereotype and left the husband dependent on the wife, Alabama's alleged compensatory purpose may be effectuated without placing burdens solely on husbands. Progress toward fulfilling such a purpose would not be hampered, and it would cost the State nothing more, if it were to treat men and women equally by making alimony burdens independent of sex. "Thus, the gender-based distinction is gratuitous; without it, the statutory scheme would only provide benefits to those men who are in fact similarly situated to the women the statute aids," *Weinberger* v. *Wiesenfeld* . . . , and the effort to help those women would not in any way be compromised.

Moreover, use of a gender classification actually produces perverse results in this case. As compared to a gender-neutral law placing alimony obligations on the spouse able to pay, the present Alabama statutes give an advantage only to the financially secure wife whose husband is in need. Although such a wife might have to pay alimony under a gender-neutral statute, the present statutes exempt her from that obligation. Thus, "[t]he [wives] who benefit from the disparate treatment are those who were . . . nondependent on their husbands," *Califano* v. *Goldfarb* . . . They are precisely those who are not "needy spouses" and who are "least likely to have been victims of . . . discrimination," by the institution of marriage. A gender-based classification which, as compared to a gender-neutral one, generates additional benefits only for those it has no reason to prefer cannot survive equal-protection scrutiny. . . .

Mr. Justice Blackmun, concurring. . . .

Mr. Justice Stevens, concurring. . . .

Mr. Justice Powell, dissenting. [Justice Powell would remand the case for the disposition of "unsettled questions of state law" before reaching the constitutional issues.]

Mr. Justice Rehnquist, with whom the Chief Justice joins, dissenting. ["I think the Court's eagerness to invalidate Alabama's statutes has led it to deal too casually with the "case and controversy" requirement of Art. III of the Constitution."]

In *Kirchberg* v. *Feenstra*, 450 U.S. 455 (1981), the Court unanimously held unconstitutional a Louisiana law that gave a husband, as "head and master" of property jointly owned with his wife, the unilateral right to dispose of such property without his spouse's consent. In *Michael M.* v. *Superior Court*, 450 U.S. 464 (1981), by the narrow margin of five to four the Court sustained a California statutory rape law that makes it criminal for a male to have sexual relations with a female not his wife, where the female is under the age of eighteen, while the female involved is not liable criminally. Nor would a female be liable if she were over eighteen and the male was under eighteen. Justice Rehnquist, for the plurality of four members, stated:

> The question . . . boils down to whether a State may attack the problem of sexual intercourse and teenage pregnancy directly by prohibiting a male from having sexual intercourse with a minor female. We hold that such a statute is sufficiently related to the State's objectives to pass constitutional muster.
>
> Because virtually all of the significant harmful and inescapably identifiable consequences of teenage pregnancy fall on the young female, a legislature acts well within its authority when it elects to punish only the participant who, by nature, suffers few of the consequences of his conduct. It is hardly unreasonable for a legislature acting to protect minor females to exclude them from punishment. Moreover, the risk of pregnancy itself constitutes a substantial deterrence to young females. No similar natural sanctions deter males. A criminal sanction imposed solely on males thus serves to roughly "equalize" the deterrents on the sexes.

The dissenters argued that the State had not met its burden of proving that a gender-neutral statute would be less effective in achieving its goals.

The Military Selective Service Act authorizes the President to require the registration of males, but not females, for possible military service. Registration for the draft was discontinued by Presidential Proclamation in 1975, but in 1980 President Carter decided to reactivate the registration requirement and requested Congress to provide funding. He also recommended that Congress amend the Act to permit registration of both men and women, but Congress refused the amendment. Thereafter men in designated age groups were ordered to register. In a suit challenging the constitutionality of the Act brought by several men, a three-judge District Court held that the gender-based discrimination violated the Fifth Amendment and enjoined registration under the Act. In *Rostker* v. *Goldberg*, 453 U.S. 57 (1981), the Supreme Court, with three dissenting votes, upheld the constitutionality of the Act. Justice Rehnquist, for the majority, agreed that Congress was not "free to disregard the Constitution when it acts in the area of military affairs, . . . but the tests and limitations to be applied may differ because of the military context." He concluded that *Schlesinger* v. *Ballard* was the appropriate precedent in this instance. He stated:

> Congress determined that any future draft, which would be facilitated by the registration scheme, would be characterized by a need for combat troops. . . . Congress' determination that the need would be for combat troops if a draft took place was sufficiently supported by testimony adduced at the hearings so that the courts are not free to make their own judgment on the question. . . .
>
> Women as a group, however, unlike men as a group, are not eligible for combat. The restrictions on the participation of women in combat in the Navy and Air Force are statutory. . . . The Army and Marine Corps preclude the use of women in combat as a matter of established policy. . . . Congress specifically recognized and endorsed the exclusion of women from combat in exempting women from registration. . . . The reason women are exempt from registration is not because military needs can be met by drafting men. This is not a case of Congress arbitrarily choosing to burden one of two similarly situated groups, such as would be the case with an all-black or

all-white, or an all-Catholic or all-Lutheran, or an all-Republican or all-Democratic registration. Men and women, because of the combat restrictions on women, are simply not similarly situated for purposes of a draft or registration for a draft.

Congress' decision to authorize the registration of only men, therefore, does not violate the Due Process Clause.

The Court also upheld the State of Massachusetts' policy of according "veterans preference" in making state civil service appointments. The contention was that since some 57% of the appointees were male and only 2% were female veterans, the policy was discriminatory against women. In *Personnel Administrator of Massachusetts* v. *Feeney*, 442 U.S. 256 (1979), the Court held that the classification was gender-neutral in view of the fact that women veterans, as well as male veterans, would benefit from the preference.

Veteran status is not uniquely male. Although few women benefit from the preference, the nonveteran class is not substantially all-female. To the contrary, significant numbers of nonveterans are men, and all nonveterans—male as well as female—are placed at a disadvantage. Too many men are affected . . . to permit the inference that the statute is but a pretext for preferring men over women.

In *Mississippi University for Women* v. *Hogan*, 458 U.S. 718 (1982), the Court ordered the admission of a male to the School of Nursing that had from its inception limited its enrollment to women. Although the male applicant could have enrolled in other state-supported schools of nursing at Jackson or Hattiesburg, he chose to apply at MUW. By a five to four vote the Court held that state-financed MUW was guilty of unconstitutional sex discrimination. Justice O'Connor, for the majority, was not impressed with the contention that the policy compensates for discrimination against women and, therefore, constitutes educational affirmative action.

Rather than compensate for discriminatory barriers faced by women, MUW's policy of excluding males from admission to the School of Nursing tends to perpetuate the stereotyped view of nursing as an exclusively woman's job. By assuring that Mississippi allots more openings in its state-supported nursing schools to women than it does to men, MUW's admissions policy lends credibility to the old view that women, not men, should become nurses, and makes the assumption that nursing is a field for women a self-fulfilling prophecy. . . .

The policy is invalid also because it fails the second part of the equal protection test, for the State has made no showing that the gender-based classification is substantially and directly related to its proposed compensatory objective. To the contrary, MUW's policy of permitting men to attend classes as auditors fatally undermines its claim that women, at least those in the School of Nursing, are adversely affected by the presence of men.

In the strongest of the dissenting opinions, Justice Powell stated:

The Court's opinion bows deeply to conformity. Left without honor—indeed, held unconstitutional—is an element of diversity that has characterized much of American education and enriched much of American life. The Court in effect holds today that no State now may provide even a single institution of higher learning open only to women students. . . .

Coeducation, historically, is a novel educational theory. From grade school through high school, college, and graduate and professional training, much of the Nation's population during much of our history has been educated in sexually segregated classrooms. At the college level, for instance, until recently some of the most prestigious colleges and universities—including most of the Ivy League—had long histories of single-sex education. . . .

The arguable benefits of single-sex colleges also continue to be recognized by students of higher education. The Carnegie Commission on Higher Education has reported that it "favor[s] the continuation of colleges for women. They provide an element of diversity . . . and [an environment in which women] generally . . . speak up more in their classes, . . . hold more positions of leadership on campus, . . . and . . . have more role models and mentors among women teachers and administrators." . . .

By applying heightened equal protection analysis to this case, the Court frustrates the liberating spirit of the Equal Protection Clause. It prohibits the States from providing women with an opportunity to choose the type of university they prefer. And yet it is these women whom the Court regards as the *victims* of an illegal, stereotyped perception of the role of women in our society. The Court reasons this way in a case in which no woman has complained, and the only complainant is a man who advances no claims on behalf of anyone else. His claim, it should be recalled, is not that he is being denied a substantive educational opportunity, or even the right to attend an all-male or a coeducational college. . . . It is *only* that the colleges open to him are located at inconvenient distances.

### The Civil Rights Act of 1964 and Sex Discrimination

The Civil Rights Act of 1964, while primarily designed to prevent racial discrimination, includes in the Title VII provisions on Equal Employment Opportunity a provision that it shall be an unlawful employment practice for an employer, as defined by the Act, "to fail or refuse to hire or to discharge any individual, or otherwise to discriminate against any individual with respect to his compensation, terms, conditions, or privileges of employment, because of such individual's . . . sex. . . ." Employment agencies and labor unions are also barred from making classifications or otherwise discriminating on the basis of sex. The Title permits an exception, however, "in those certain instances where . . . sex . . . is a bona fide occupational qualification reasonably necessary to the normal operation of that particular business or enterprise." In order to implement these and other provisions of Title VII, the Equal Opportunity Commission is created by the Act and is given authority to "issue, amend, or rescind suitable procedural regulations to carry out the provisions of this title."

On November 22, 1965, Franklin D. Roosevelt, Jr., Chairman of the Commission, published the first guidelines (30 Federal Register 14926) on how the Commission construed its statutory duties under the provisions barring discrimination based on sex. The statement is made that "The commission does not believe that Congress intended to disturb such laws and regulations which are intended to, and have the effect of, protecting women against exploitation and hazard." It goes on to point out, however, that many laws originally enacted to protect women have ceased to be relevant to the nation's technology or to the expanding role of the woman worker in the economy. And in cases where the clear effect of a law in current circumstances is not to protect women but to subject them to discrimination, the law will not be considered a justification for discrimination. As an example, the Commission said it would honor state restrictions on lifting weights except where the limit is set at an unreasonably low level that could not endanger women.

In *Dothard* v. *Rawlinson,* 433 U.S. 321 (1977), the Court held invalid under Title VII an Alabama statute specifying minimum height and weight requirements of five feet, two inches, and 120 pounds for employment as a state prison guard. The majority concluded that the plaintiff had established a prima facie case of unlawful sex discrimination upon showing that the statutory requirements would exclude over forty-one percent of the nation's female population while excluding less than one percent of the male population. No evidence had been presented by the State to correlate the statutory requirements with the amount of strength thought to be essential to the position. A regulation prohibiting the hiring of women as prison guards at the State's maximum security male penitentiaries in "contact positions" which require continual close physical proximity to inmates, however, was upheld. The majority felt that placing women in such positions would pose a substantial security problem, both to the women and to the basic control of the prison.

In *Phillips* v. *Marietta Corp.*, 400 U.S. 542 (1971), the Court held that §703 (a) of the Civil Rights Act of 1964, which prohibits discriminatory hiring practices because of sex, was violated by an employer who refused to accept applications from women with preschool-age children, although it did employ men with preschool-age children. In the per curiam opinion, however, the case was remanded with the suggestion that the existence of such conflicting family obligations, "if demonstrably more relevant to job performance for a woman than for a man, could arguably be a basis for distinction under §703 (e) of the Act."

In *Geduldig* v. *Aiello*, 417 U.S. 484 (1974), the Court held that a California law establishing a disability program was not sex discrimination violative of the Equal Protection Clause even though the plan excluded pregnancy disabilities. In *General Electric Co.* v. *Gilbert*, 429 U.S. 125 (1976), however, it was argued that a similar exclusion in a private company's disability plan violated the prohibition against sex discrimination in the Civil Rights Act of 1964. The Court rejected the claim, holding that the exclusion did not constitute sex discrimination. "There is no more showing in this case than there was in *Geduldig* that the exclusion of pregnancy benefits is a mere '[pretext] designed to effect an invidious discrimination against the members of one sex or the other.' " The conclusion was that the plan was "nothing more than an insurance package, which covers some risks, but excludes others."

In response to the *Gilbert* decision, Congress passed the Pregnancy Discrimination Act of 1978 [42 USC §2000e(k)] which specifies that sex discrimination includes discrimination on the basis of pregnancy. Thus the Congress approved the views of the dissenters in *Gilbert* who contended that the disability plan discriminated on the basis of sex by giving men protection for all categories of risk but giving women only partial protection.

As a result of Nashville Gas Company's sick pay and seniority policies, a female employee who had been required to take a formal leave of absence during her pregnancy did not receive sick pay while on leave and also lost all accumulated job seniority. She brought an action in a federal District Court alleging that both of the Company's policies violated Title VII of the Civil Rights Act. The District Court so held, and the Court of Appeals affirmed. On certiorari, the United States Supreme Court affirmed with respect to the seniority policy but reversed with respect to the issue of sick pay. It held that the seniority policy adversely affected the status of employees because of their sex, and since in the absence of any proof of business necessity for the policy, it could be assumed that there was no justification to support it. *Nashville Gas Company* v. *Satty*, 434 U.S. 136 (1977).

Illustrative of another area of private discrimination, although not an issue under the Civil Rights Act, was the right of the United States Jaycees to exclude women in the face of a state law prohibiting the denial of full and equal enjoyment of the facilities and privileges of "places of public accommodation" because of sex. Minnesota had passed such a law and it was construed by the state supreme court to apply to the Jaycees' organization. In *Roberts* v. *United States Jaycees,* 468 U.S. 609 (1984) the Court rejected a claim that the law violated the members' freedom of association. Further, it held that Minnesota's compelling interest in eradicating discrimination against women justified the impact that the statute might have on the male members' associational freedoms.

Similarly, in *Board of Directors of Rotary International* v. *Rotary Club of Duarte,* 55 LW 4606 (1987), the Court upheld a California statute that was construed to require California Rotary Clubs to admit women against a claim that the statute violated the First Amendment's guarantee of associational rights. The Unruh Act entitled all persons, regardless of sex, to "full and equal accommodations, advantages, facilities, privileges, or services in all business establishments." The California Court of Appeal stated that testimony "leaves no doubt that business concerns are a motivating factor in joining local clubs," and that "business benefits [are] enjoyed and capitalized upon by Rotarians and their businesses or employers." The Supreme Court accepted this application of the statute and held "Even if the Unruh Act does work some slight infringement on Rotary members' right of expressive association, that infringement is justified because it serves the State's compelling interest in eliminating discrimination against women."

In *Los Angeles Department of Water & Power* v. *Manhart,* 435 U.S. 702 (1978), the Court held that Title VII of the Civil Rights Act prohibits an employer from requiring women to make larger contributions in order to obtain the same monthly pension benefits as men, although women as a class live longer than men and would draw greater total benefits as a result. In *Arizona Governing Committee* v. *Norris,* 463 U.S. 1073 (1983), the question presented was whether Title VII also prohibits an employer from offering various deferred compensation plans for retirement benefits, all of which paid a woman lower monthly benefits than a man who had made the same contributions. All of the companies selected by the State to participate in the plan used sex-based mortality tables to calculate monthly retirement benefits; the tables did not incorporate other factors correlating with longevity such as smoking habits, alcohol consumption, weight, medical history, or family history. The Court held that this practice constituted discrimination on the basis of sex in violation of Title VII, but it held further that a requirement of gender-neutral retirement plans should operate prospectively only, and that benefits derived from contributions made prior to this decision could be calculated as provided by the existing terms of the Arizona plan.

In 1978 an affirmative-action plan for hiring and promoting minorities and women was voluntarily adopted by the Santa Clara County Transportation Agency. The plan provided that in making promotions to positions within a traditionally segregated job classification in which women had been significantly underrepresented, the Agency was authorized to consider as one factor the sex of a qualified applicant. No quotas were set, but the goal was to increase the number of women and minorities in such job classifications. When a vacancy in the position of road dispatcher opened up, Diane Joyce applied. At the time, the Agency employed no women in any of the 238 Skilled Craft positions, and had never employed a woman as a road dispatcher. After interviews by a two-person board, seven applicants were certified as eligible, including Joyce and one Paul Johnson. Johnson ranked second with a score of 75, and Joyce ranked third with a score of 73 on the interview. Joyce was appointed, and Johnson filed suit in Federal District Court alleging sex discrimination in violation of Title VII. The court held the plan invalid on the ground that it was not a temporary remedy for sexual imbalance. The Court of Appeals reversed, and the Supreme Court in *Johnson* v. *Transportation Agency, Santa Clara County,* 55 LW 4379 (1987), upheld the plan. The majority held that the Agency appropriately took into account Joyce's sex as one factor in determining that she should be promoted. The Agency's affirmative-action plan "represents a moderate, flexible, case-by-case approach to effecting a gradual improvement in the representation of minorities and women in the Agency's work force," and "[s]uch a plan is fully consistent with Title VII."

A number of complaints have been filed with the EEOC alleging "sexual harassment" in the workplace as a form of sex discrimination prohibited by Title VII. In 1986 the Court had occasion to define the application of the Act to such conduct.

MERITOR SAVINGS BANK v. VINSON

477 U.S. 57 (1986)

[Vinson, a former employee of the Bank, brought an action against the Bank and her supervisor claiming that during her employment at the Bank she had been subjected to sexual harassment by the supervisor in violation of Title VII and seeking injunctive relief and damages. At trial, the parties presented conflicting testimony about the supervisor's (Taylor) behavior during Vinson's employment. She testified that during her probationary period as a teller-trainee, Taylor treated her in a fatherly way and made no sexual advances. Shortly thereafter, however, he invited her out to dinner and, during the course of the meal, suggested that they go to a motel to have sexual relations. At first she refused, but out of what she described as fear of losing her job, she eventually agreed. She said that Taylor thereafter made repeated demands upon her for sexual favors, usually at the branch, both during and after business hours; she estimated that over the next several years she had intercourse with him some 40 or 50 times. In addition, she testified that Taylor touched and fondled other women employees of the Bank. Taylor denied that he had had sexual intercourse with her or asked her to do so.

The Federal District Court denied relief, finding that if Taylor did engage in intimate relations with her, that relationship was a voluntary one having nothing to do with her continued employment or her advancement or promotions. Evidence showed that Vinson was employed in 1974. With Taylor as her supervisor, she started as a teller-trainee, and thereafter was promoted to teller, head teller, and assistant branch manager before her discharge in 1978.

The Court of Appeals reversed, and the Supreme Court granted certiorari.]

Justice Rehnquist delivered the opinion of the Court.

This case presents important questions concerning claims of workplace "sexual harassment" brought under Title VII of the Civil Rights Act of 1964. . . .

[I]n 1980 the EEOC issued guidelines specifying that "sexual harassment," as there defined, is a form of sex discrimination prohibited by Title VII. . . .

In defining "sexual harassment," the guidelines first describe the kinds of workplace conduct that may be actionable under Title VII. These include "[u]nwelcome sexual advances, requests for sexual favors, and other verbal or physical conduct of a sexual nature." . . . Relevant to the charges at issue in this case, the guidelines provide that such sexual misconduct constitutes prohibited "sexual harassment," whether or not it is directly linked to the grant or denial of an economic *quid pro quo*, where "such conduct has the purpose or effect of unreasonably interfering with an individual's work performance or creating an intimidating, hostile, or offensive working environment." . . .

Since the guidelines were issued, courts have uniformly held, and we agree, that a plaintiff may establish a violation of Title VII by proving that discrimination based on sex has created a hostile or abusive work environment. . . .

The question remains, however, whether the District Court's ultimate finding that respondent "was not the victim of sexual harassment," . . . effectively disposed of respondent's claim. The Court of Appeals recognized, we think correctly, that this ultimate finding was likely based on one or both of two erroneous views of the law. First, the District Court apparently believed that a claim for sexual harassment will not lie absent an *economic* effect on the complainant's employment. . . . Since it appears that the District Court made its findings without ever considering the "hostile environment" theory of sexual harassment, the Court of Appeal's decision to remand was correct.

Second, the District Court's conclusion that no actionable harassment occurred might have rested on its earlier "finding" that "[i]f [respondent] and Taylor did engage in an intimate or sexual relationship. . . . that relationship was a voluntary one." . . . But the fact that sex-related conduct was "voluntary," in the sense that the complainant was not forced to participate against her will, is not a defense to a sexual harassment suit brought under Title VII. The gravamen of any sexual harassment claim is that the alleged sexual advances were "unwelcome." . . . While the question whether particular conduct was indeed unwelcome presents difficult problems of proof and turns largely on credibility determinations committed to the trier of fact, the District Court in this case erroneously focused on the "voluntariness" of respondent's participation in the claimed sexual episodes. The correct inquiry is whether respondent by her conduct indicated that the alleged sexual advances were unwelcome, not whether her actual participation in sexual intercourse was voluntary. . . .

Accordingly, the judgment of the Court of Appeals reversing the judgment of the District Court is affirmed, and the case is remanded for further proceedings consistent with this opinion.

*It is so ordered.*

Justice Stevens, concurring. . . .

Justice Marshall, with whom Justice Brennan, Justice Blackmun, and Justice Stevens join, concurring in the judgment. . . .

## Sex Discrimination in Education Programs

One of the most controversial developments in the movement toward abolition of sex discrimination has been the establishment of new guidelines by HEW for "Nondiscrimination on the Basis of Sex in Education Programs and Activities Receiving or Benefitting from Federal Financial Assistance." The regulations were issued to effectuate Title IX of the Education Amendments of 1972 and became operative as of July 21, 1975 (40 *Federal Register* 24128, 1975). While a variety of topics are covered, the application of the regulations to the athletic programs of colleges and universities seemed to stir the greatest opposition. Equal athletic opportunities must be provided for members of both sexes, including provision of equipment and supplies, travel and per diem allowance, provision of housing and dining facilities and services, and others. And if the school awards athletic scholarships or grants-in-aid, §86.37 requires that "it must provide reasonable opportunities for such awards for members of each sex in proportion to the number of students of each participating in interscholastic or intercollegiate athletics." In other areas, neither students nor employees may be discriminated against on the basis of pregnancy, and the schools are directed to treat pregnancy under the same policies as any other temporary disability. Admission and hiring policies must be absolutely nondiscriminatory, except to the extent that "sex is a bonafide occupational qualification." Schools may provide separate housing facilities by sex, but such facilities must be comparable in quality and cost to the student and must be proportionate in quantity to the number of students of each sex applying for housing. In general, the guidelines represent a full-scale effort to accomplish the purposes of Title IX, which provides that "No person in the United States shall on the basis of sex, be excluded from participation in, be denied the benefits of, or be subjected to discrimination under any education program or activity receiving Federal financial assistance." The only exceptions are for certain religious institutions, military and merchant marine educational institutions, and certain voluntary organizations such as social fraternities and sororities, the YMCA, the YWCA, and the Boy Scouts and Girl Scouts.

GROVE CITY COLLEGE *v.* BELL

*465 U.S. 555 (1984)*

[The Title IX provision requires that schools receiving federal financial assistance file an Assurance of Compliance with the nondiscrimination provisions with the Department of Education. Grove City College is a private, coeducational, liberal arts college that accepts no direct federal assistance. However, the college enrolls students who receive Basic Educational Opportunity Grants (BEOG) paid directly to the students. The Department concluded that the College was nonetheless under the requirements of Title IX and initiated administrative proceedings that resulted in an order terminating assistance until the College execu.ted an Assurance of Compliance and satisfied the Department that it was in compliance with the regulations.]

Justice White delivered the opinion of the Court. . . .

II

In defending its refusal to execute the Assurance of Compliance required by the Department's regulations, Grove City first contends that neither it nor any "education program or activity" of the College receives any federal financial assistance within the meaning of Title IX by virtue of the fact that some of its students receive BEOGs and use them to pay for their education. We disagree.

Grove City provides a well-rounded liberal arts education and a variety of educational programs and student services. The question is whether any of those programs or activities "receiv[es] Federal financial assistance" within the meaning of Title IX when students finance their education with BEOGs. The structure of the Education Amendments of 1972, in which Congress both created the BEOG program and imposed Title IX's nondiscrimination requirement, strongly suggests an affirmative conclusion. BEOGs were aptly characterized as a "centerpiece of the bill," . . . and Title IX "relate[d] directly to [its] central purpose." . . . In view of this connection and Congress' express recognition of discrimination in the administration of student financial aid programs, it would indeed be anomalous to discover that one of the primary components of Congress' comprehensive "package of federal aid" . . . was not intended to trigger coverage under Title IX. . . .

With the benefit of clear statutory language, powerful evidence of Congress' intent, and a longstanding and coherent administrative construction of the phrase "receiving Federal financial assistance," we have little trouble concluding that Title IX coverage is not foreclosed because federal funds are granted to Grove City's students rather than directly to one of the College's educational programs. There remains the question, however, of identifying the "education program or activity" of the College that can properly be characterized as "receiving" federal assistance through grants to some of the students attending the college.

III

An analysis of Title IX's language and legislative history led us to conclude in *North Haven Board of Education* v. *Bell* . . . that "an agency's authority under Title IX both to promulgate regulations and to terminate funds is subject to the program-specific limitations of §§901 and 902." Although the legislative history contains isolated suggestions that entire institutions are subject to the nondiscrimination provision whenever one of their programs receives federal assistance, . . . we cannot accept the Court of Appeals' conclusion that in the circumstances present here Grove City itself is a "program or activity" that may be regulated in its entirety. . . .

. . . Only by ignoring Title IX's program-specific language could we conclude that funds received under the [Regular Disbursement System], awarded to eligible students, and paid back to the school when tuition comes due represent federal aid to the entire institution. . . .

. . . Student financial aid programs, we believe, are *sui generis*. In neither purpose nor effect can BEOGs be fairly characterized as unrestricted grants that institutions may use for whatever purpose they desire. The BEOG program was designed, not merely to increase the total resources available to educational institutions, but to enable them to offer their services to students who had previously been unable to afford higher education. It is true, of course, that substantial portions of the BEOGs received by Grove City's students ultimately find their way into the College's general operating budget and are used to provide a variety of services to the students through whom the funds pass. However, we have found no persuasive evidence suggesting that Congress intended that the Department's regulatory authority follow federally aided students from classroom to classroom, building to building, or activity to activity. . . .

We conclude that the receipt of BEOGs by some of Grove City's students does not trigger institution-wide coverage under Title IX. In purpose and effect, BEOGs represent federal financial assistance to the College's own financial aid program, and it is that program that may properly be regulated under Title IX. . . .

Justice Powell, with whom Chief Justice Burger and Justice O'Connor join, concurring. . . .

The sole purpose of the statute is to make unlawful "discrimination" by recipients of federal financial assistance on the "basis of sex." The undisputed fact is that Grove City does not discriminate—and so far as the record in this case shows—never has discriminated against anyone on account of sex, race, or national origin. This case has nothing whatever to do with discrimination past or present. The College therefore has complied to the letter with the sole purpose of §901(a). . . .

. . . At the outset of this litigation, the Department insisted that by accepting students who received BEOG awards, Grove City's entire institution was subject to regulation under Title IX. The College, in view of its policies and principles of independence and its record of nondiscrimination, objected to executing this Assurance. One would have thought that the Department, confronted as it is with cases of national importance that involve actual discrimination, would have respected the independence and admirable record of this college. But common sense and good judgment failed to prevail. . . .

The effect of the Department's termination of the student grants and loans would not have been limited to the College itself. Indeed, the most direct effect would have been upon the students themselves. Absent the availability of other scholarship funds, many of them would have had to abandon their college education or choose another school. It was to avoid these serious consequences, that this suit was instituted. The College prevailed in the District Court but lost in the Court of Appeals. Only after Grove City had brought its case before this Court, did the Department retreat to its present position that Title IX applies only to Grove City's financial aid office. On this narrow theory, the Department has prevailed, having taken this small independent college, which it acknowledges has engaged in no discrimination whatever, through six years of litigation with the full weight of the federal government opposing it. I cannot believe that the Department will rejoice in its "victory."

Justice Stevens, concurring in part and concurring in the result. . . .

Justice Brennan, with whom Justice Marshall joins, concurring in part and dissenting in part. . . .

## II

A proper application of Title IX to the circumstances of this case demonstrates beyond peradventure that the Court has unjustifiably limited the statute's reach. . . . Although the grant monies are paid directly to the students, the Court properly concludes that the use of these federal monies at the College means that the College "receives Federal financial assistance" within the meaning of Title IX. The Court also correctly notes that a principal purpose underlying congressional enactment of the BEOG program is to provide funds that will benefit colleges and universities as a whole. It necessarily follows, in my view, that the entire undergraduate institution operated by Grove City College is subject to the antidiscrimination provisions included in Title IX. . . .

The Congress effectively overruled the *Grove City College* decision by passing the Civil Rights Restoration Act of 1987 in which Title IX was amended to provide: "For the purposes of this title, the term 'program or activity' and 'program' mean all of the operations of . . . a college, university, or other postsecondary institution, or a public system of higher education."

[The literature on sex discrimination and women's rights is now voluminous. A few useful items are: J. D. Johnston, Jr., "Sex Discrimination and the Supreme Court— 1971–1974," 49 *N. Y. U. L. Rev.* 617 (1974); Panel, "Men, Women, and the Constitution: the Equal Rights Amendment," 10 *Colum. J. L. & Soc. Prob.* 77 (1973); Karen De-Crow, *Sexist Justice* (New York: Random House, 1974); Barbara S. Deckard, *The Women's Movement,* 3rd ed. (New York: Harper & Row, 1983); Joyce Gelb and Marian L. Palley, *Women and Public Policies* (Princeton: Princeton Univ. Press, 1982); Ellen Boneparth, ed., *Women, Power and Policy* (New York: Pergamon, 1982); Irene Diamond, ed., *Families, Politics, and Public Policy* (New York Longman, 1983); Janet K. Boles, *The Politics of the Equal Rights Amendment* (New York: Longman, 1979).]

## APPORTIONMENT OF LEGISLATIVE SEATS AND THE EQUAL PROTECTION CLAUSE

Prior to 1962, attacks on patterns of apportioning seats for legislative bodies based on the claim that such patterns violated the Article IV guarantee of "a republican form of government" or that population inequalities between districts had the effect of producing inequalities in the effective voting power of persons residing in different districts were unsuccessful in the federal courts. *Colegrove* v. *Green*, 328 U.S. 549 (1946), presented a challenge to the arrangement of Illinois' congressional districts, essentially unchanged since 1901. Petitioners asked that the Court restrain the state from holding a general election on the ground that the districts lacked compactness of territory and approximate equality of population, and that the inequality of voting power resulting was in violation of the Fourteenth Amendment and the provisions of Article I respecting the election of members of the House of Representatives. Three justices held that the matter was nonjusticiable. Justice Frankfurter, speaking for these, stated:

We are of opinion that the petitioners ask of this Court what is beyond its competence to grant. This is one of those demands on judicial power which cannot be met by verbal fencing about "jurisdiction." It must be resolved by considerations on the basis of which this Court, from time to time, has refused to intervene in controversies. It has refused to do so because due regard for the effective working of our Government revealed this issue to be of a peculiarly political nature and therefore not meet for judicial determination. . . .

. . . Nothing is clearer than that this controversy concerns matters that bring courts into immediate and active relations with party contests. From the determination of such issues this Court has traditionally held aloof. It is hostile to a democratic system to involve the judiciary in the politics of the people. And it is not less pernicious if such judicial intervention in an essentially political contest be dressed up in the abstract phrases of the law. . . .

The one stark fact that emerges from a study of the history of Congressional apportionment is its embroilment in politics, in the sense of party contests and party interests. . . .

Justice Rutledge concurred in the result, holding that the question *was* justiciable but that the bill should be dismissed because the Court could not provide a proper equitable remedy for the problem.

Justices Black, Douglas, and Murphy dissented, asserting that the question was justiciable, that appellants had made out a case for their allegations of injury, and that they were entitled to equitable relief. Justice Black suggested that if the state did not properly redistrict, the courts could order elections at large for members of the House, thereby equalizing voting power within the state.

Only seven members of the Court participated in the *Colegrove* decision. On the question of the Court's power to offer assistance in such a case the vote was four-to-three in the negative. With Justice Rutledge's split vote, however, the Court was divided four-to-three in *favor* of holding that the question presented a justiciable controversy. Thus the bill was dismissed, but the case was hardly a conclusive disposition of the whole question of judicial remedies for malapportionment.

In *South* v. *Peters*, 339 U.S. 276 (1950), an injunction was sought in a federal court to restrain the enforcement of the Georgia county-unit statute. The county-unit system provided that in primary elections the candidate receiving the largest vote in a county received its entire "electoral vote," which ranged from two for the small county to six for the most populous county. The complaint charged that gross inequality of voting power resulted from the system. The Court, citing *Colegrove* v. *Green*, affirmed a dismissal of the petition, with Justices Black and Douglas dissenting.

In *Baker* v. *Carr*, 369 U.S. 186 (1962), the Court for the first time held that allegations that malapportionment of legislative seats denied equal protection presented a justiciable cause of action and one for which the federal courts could fashion appropriate equitable relief upon finding that such apportionment was a denial of equal protection under the Fourteenth Amendment. The case presented a challenge to the apportionment of seats in the Tennessee House of Representatives. It was alleged that Tennessee continued to allocate representation on the basis of a 1901 statute and that subsequent population changes without reapportionment resulted in a denial to the plaintiffs of the equal protection of the laws by virtue of "the debasement of their votes." The trial court had dismissed the petition on grounds of nonjusticiability. By a six-to-two vote the Court reversed and remanded.

BAKER *v.* CARR

*369 U.S. 186 (1962)*

Mr. Justice Brennan delivered the opinion of the Court. . . .

. . . [Petitioners] seek a declaration that the 1901 statute is unconstitutional and an injunction restraining the appellees from acting to conduct any further elections under it. They also pray that unless and until the General Assembly enacts a valid reapportionment, the District Court should either decree a reapportionment by mathematical application of the Tennessee constitutional formulae to the most recent Federal Census figures, or direct the appellees to conduct legislative elections, primary and general, at large. . . .

I

. . . In light of the District Court's treatment of the case, we hold today only (a) that the court possessed jurisdiction of the subject matter; (b) that a justiciable cause of action is stated upon which appellants would be entitled to appropriate relief; and (c) because appellees raise the issue before this Court, that the appellants have standing to challenge the Tennessee apportionment statutes. Beyond noting that we have no cause at this stage to doubt the District Court will be able to fashion relief if violations of constitutional rights are found, it is improper now to consider what remedy would be most appropriate if appellants prevail at the trial.

II

Jurisdiction of the Subject Matter

The District Court was uncertain whether our cases withholding federal judicial relief rested upon a lack of federal jurisdiction or upon the inappropriateness of the subject matter for judicial consideration—what we have designated "nonjusticiability." The distinction between the two grounds is significant. In the instance of nonjusticiability, consideration of the cause is not wholly and immediately foreclosed; rather, the Court's inquiry necessarily proceeds to the point of deciding whether the duty asserted can be judicially identified and its breach judicially determined, and whether protection for the right asserted can be judicially molded. In the instance of lack of jurisdiction the cause either does not "arise under" the Federal Constitution, law or treaties (or fall within one of the other enumerated categories or Art. III, Section 2), or is not a "case or controversy" within the meaning of that section; or the cause is not one described by any jurisdictional statute. . . .

An unbroken line of our precedents sustains the federal courts' jurisdiction of the subject matter of federal constitutional claims of this nature. The first case involved the redistricting of States for the purpose of electing Representatives to the Federal Congress. . . . When the Minnesota Supreme Court affirmed the dismissal of a suit to enjoin the Secretary of State of Minnesota from acting under Minnesota redistricting legislation, we reviewed the constitutional merits of the legislation and reversed the State Supreme Court. *Smiley* v. *Holm*, 285 U.S. 355. . . . When a three-judge District Court . . . permanently enjoined officers of the State of Mississippi from conducting an election of Representatives under a Mississippi redistricting act, we reviewed the federal questions on the merits and reversed the District Court. *Wood* v. *Broom*, 287 U.S. 1. . . .

The appellees refer to *Colegrove* v. *Green*, 328 U.S. 549, as authority that the District Court lacked jurisdiction of the subject matter. Appellees misconceive the holding of that case. The holding was precisely contrary to their reading of it. Seven members of the Court participated in the decision. Unlike many other cases in this field which have assumed without discussion that there was jurisdiction, all three opinions filed in *Colegrove* discussed the question. Two of the opinions expressing the views of four of the Justices, a majority, flatly held that there was jurisdiction of the subject matter. . . .

Several subsequent cases similar to *Colegrove* have been decided by the Court in summary *per curiam* statements. None was dismissed for want of jurisdiction of the subject matter. . . .

. . . In *South* v. *Peters*, 339 U.S. 276, we affirmed the dismissal of an attack on the Georgia "county unit" system but founded our action on a ground that plainly would not have been reached if the lower court lacked jurisdiction of the subject matter. . . .

We hold that the District Court has jurisdiction of the subject matter of the federal constitutional claim asserted in the complaint. . . .

## IV
## Justiciability

. . . We understand the District Court to have read the cited cases as compelling the conclusion that since the appellants sought to have a legislative apportionment held unconstitutional, their suit presented a "political question" and was therefore nonjusticiable. We hold that this challenge to an apportionment presents no nonjusticiable "political question." The cited cases do not hold the contrary.

Of course the mere fact that the suit seeks protection of a political right does not mean it presents a political question. Such an objection "is little more than a play upon words." . . . Rather, it is argued that apportionment cases, whatever the actual wording of the complaint, can involve no federal constitutional right except one resting on the guaranty of a republican form of government, and that complaints based on that clause have been held to present political questions which are nonjusticiable.

We hold that the claim pleaded here neither rests upon nor implicates the Guaranty Clause and that its justiciability is therefore not foreclosed by our decisions of cases involving that clause. . . .

Our discussion . . . requires review of a number of political question cases, in order to expose the attributes of the doctrine. . . . That review reveals that in the Guaranty Clause cases and in the other "political question" cases, it is the relationship between the judiciary and the coordinate branches of the Federal Government, and not the federal judiciary's relationship to the States, which gives rise to the "political question." . . .

. . . The nonjusticiability of a political question is primarily a function of the separation of powers. . . .

. . . Prominent on the surface of any case held to involve a political question is found a textually demonstrable constitutional commitment of the issue to a coordinate political department; or a lack of judicially discoverable and manageable standards for resolving it; or the impossibility of deciding without an initial policy determination of a kind clearly for nonjudicial discretion; or the impossibility of a court's undertaking independent resolution without expressing lack of the respect due coordinate branches of government; or an unusual need for unquestioning adherence to a political decision already made; or the potentiality of embarrassment from multifarious pronouncements by various departments on one question. . . .

We conclude that the nonjusticiability of claims resting on the Guaranty Clause which arises from their embodiment of questions that were thought "political," can have no bearing upon the justiciability of the equal protection claim presented in this case. . . . Only last Term, in *Gomillion* v. *Lightfoot*, 364 U.S. 339 (1960), we applied the Fifteenth Amendment to strike down a redrafting of municipal boundaries which effected a discriminatory impairment of voting rights, in the face of what a majority of the Court of Appeals thought to be a sweeping commitment to state legislatures of the power to draw and redraw such boundaries. . . .

. . . We conclude that the complaint's allegations of a denial of equal protection present a justiciable constitutional cause of action upon which appellants are entitled to a trial and a decision. The right asserted is within the reach of judicial protection under the Fourteenth Amendment.

The judgment of the District Court is reversed and the cause is remanded for further proceedings consistent with this opinion.

*Reversed and remanded.*

Mr. Justice Whittaker did not participate in the decision of this case.

Mr. Justice Douglas, concurring. . . .

The traditional test under the Equal Protection Clause has been whether a State has made "an invidious discrimination," as it does when it selects "a particular race or nationality for oppressive treatment." . . .

I agree with my Brother Clark that if the allegations in the complaint can be sustained a case for relief is established. We are told that a single vote in Moore County, Tennessee, is worth 19 votes in Hamilton County, that one vote in Stewart or in Chester County is worth nearly eight times a single vote in Shelby or Knox County. The opportunity to prove that an "invidious discrimination" exists should therefore be given the appellants. . . .

Mr. Justice Clark, concurring. . . .

The controlling facts cannot be disputed. It appears from the record that 37 per cent of the voters of Tennessee elect 20 of the 33 Senators while 40 per cent of the voters elect 63 of the 99 members of the House. But this might not on its face be "invidious discrimination," . . . for a "statutory discrimination will not be set aside if any state of facts reasonably may be conceived to justify it." *McGowan* v. *Maryland*, 366 U.S. 420, 426 (1961).

It is true that the apportionment policy incorporated in Tennessee's Constitution, *i.e.*, state-wide numerical equality of representation with certain minor qualifications, is a rational one. . . . Try as one may, Tennessee's apportionment just cannot be made to fit the pattern cut by its Constitution. . . . We must examine what the Assembly has done. The frequency and magnitude of the inequalities in the present districting admit of no policy whatever. . . . [T]he apportionment picture in Tennessee is a topsy-turvical of gigantic proportions. This is not to say that some of the disparity cannot be explained, but when the entire Table is examined . . . it leaves but one conclusion, namely that Tennessee's apportionment is a crazy quilt without rational basis. . . .

Although I find the Tennessee apportionment statute offends the Equal Protection Clause, I would not consider intervention by this Court into so delicate a field if there were any other relief available to the people of Tennessee. But the majority of the people of Tennessee have no "practical opportunities for exerting their political weight at the polls" to correct the existing "invidious discrimination." Tennessee has no initiative and referendum. I have searched diligently for other "practical opportunities" present under the law. I find none other than through the federal courts. The majority of the voters have been caught up in a legislative strait jacket. Tennessee has an "informed, civically militant electorate" and "an aroused popular conscience," but it does not sear "the conscience of the people's representatives." This is because the legislative policy has riveted the present seats in the Assembly to their respective constituencies, and by the votes of their incumbents a reapportionment of any kind is prevented. The people have been rebuffed at the hands of the Assembly; they have tried the constitutional convention route, but since the call must originate in the Assembly it, too, has been fruitless. They have tried Tennessee courts with the same result, and Governors have fought the tide only to flounder. It is said that there is recourse in Congress and perhaps that may be, but from a practical standpoint this is without substance. To date Congress has never undertaken such a task in any State. We therefore must conclude that the people of Tennessee are stymied and without judicial intervention will be saddled with the present discrimination in the affairs of their state government. . . .

. . . If judicial competence were lacking to fashion an effective decree, I would dismiss this appeal. However . . . I see no such difficulty in the position of this case. One plan might be to start with the existing assembly districts, consolidate some of them, and award the seats thus released to those counties suffering the most egregious discrimination. Other possibilities are present and might be more effective. But the plan here suggested would at least release the strangle hold now on the Assembly and permit it to redistrict itself. . . .

Mr. Justice Stewart, concurring. . . .

The complaint in this case asserts that Tennessee's system of apportionment is utterly arbitrary—without any possible justification in rationality. The District Court did not reach the merits of that claim, and this Court quite properly expresses no view on the subject. Contrary to the suggestion of my Brother Harlan, the Court does not say or imply that "state legislatures must be so structured as to reflect with approximate equality of the voice of every voter." . . . The Court does not say or imply that there is anything in the Federal Constitution "to prevent a State, acting not irrationally, from choosing any electoral legislative structure it thinks best suited to the interests, temper, and customs of its people." . . .

Mr. Justice Frankfurter, whom Mr. Justice Harlan joins, dissenting.

The Court today reverses a uniform course of decision established by a dozen cases, including one by which the very claim now sustained was unanimously rejected only five years ago. The impressive body of rulings thus cast aside reflected the equally uniform course of our political history regarding the relationship between population and legislative representation—a wholly different matter from denial of the franchise to individuals because of race, color, religion or sex. Such a massive repudiation of the experience of our whole past in asserting destructively novel judicial power demands a detailed analysis of the role of this Court in our constitutional scheme. Disregard of inherent limits in the effective exercise of the Court's "judicial

Power" not only presages the futility of judicial intervention in the essentially political conflict of forces by which the relation between population and representation
has time out of mind been and now is determined. It may well impair the Court's position as the ultimate organ of "the supreme Law of the Land" in that vast range of legal problems, often strongly entangled in popular feeling, on which this Court must
pronounce. The Court's authority—possessed neither of the purse nor the sword—
ultimately rests on sustained public confidence in its moral sanction. Such feeling
must be nourished by the Court's complete detachment, in fact and in appearance,
from political entanglements and by abstention from injecting itself into the clash of
political forces in political settlements. . . .

Manifestly, the Equal Protection Clause supplies no clearer guide for judicial examination of apportionment methods than would the Guarantee Clause itself. Apportionment, by its character, is a subject of extraordinary complexity, involving—
even after the fundamental theoretical issues concerning what is to be represented
in a representative legislature have been fought out or compromised—considerations of geography, demography, electoral convenience, economic and social cohe-
sions or divergencies among particular local groups, communications, the practical
effects of political institutions like the lobby and the city machine, ancient traditions
and ties of settled usage, respect for proven incumbents of long experience and senior status, mathematical mechanics, censuses compiling relevant data, and a host of
others. Legislative responses throughout the country to the reapportionment demands of the 1960 Census have glaringly confirmed that these are not factors that
lend themselves to evaluations of a nature that are the staple of judicial determinations or for which judges are equipped to adjudicate by legal training or experience
or native wit. And this is the more so true because in every strand of this complicated, intricate web of values meet the contending forces of partisan politics. The practical significance of apportionment is that the next election results may differ
because of it. Apportionment battles are overwhelmingly party or intra-party contests. It will add a virulent source of friction and tension in federal-state relations to
embroil the federal judiciary in them. . . .

Dissenting opinion of Mr. Justice Harlan, whom Mr. Justice Frankfurter joins. . . .

In the last analysis, what lies at the core of this controversy is a difference of opinion as to the function of representative government. It is surely beyond argument
that those who have the responsibility for devising a system of representation may
permissibly consider that factors other than bare numbers should be taken into account. . . .

In short, there is nothing in the Federal Constitution to prevent a State, acting not
irrationally, from choosing any electoral legislative structure it thinks best suited to the
interests, temper, and customs of its people. I would have thought this proposition
settled by *MacDougall* v. *Green*, . . . in which the Court observed that to "assume
that political power is a function exclusively of numbers is to disregard the practica-
lities of government." . . .

Indeed, I would hardly think it unconstitutional if a state legislature's expressed
reason for establishing or maintaining an electoral imbalance between its rural and
urban population were to protect the State's agricultural interests from the sheer
weight of numbers of those residing in the cities. . . .

In conclusion, it is appropriate to say that one need not agree, as a citizen, with
what Tennessee has done or failed to do, in order to deprecate, as a judge, what the
majority is doing today. Those observers of the Court who see it primarily as the last
refuge for the correction of all inequality or injustice, no matter what its nature or
source, will no doubt applaud this decision and its break with the past. Those who

consider that continuing national respect for the Court's authority depends in large measure upon its wise exercise of self-restraint and discipline in constitutional adjudication, will view the decision with deep concern. . . .

[Mr. Justice Harlan attached an Appendix entitled "The Inadequacy of Arithmetical Formulas as Measures of the Rationality of Tennessee's Apportionment."]

The potential impact of *Baker* v. *Carr* on state and local government and politics was readily apparent. The decision was rendered on March 26, 1962, and a spate of articles, editorials, studies, and speeches in legislative bodies soon followed. Reaction ranged from anger or dismay at the Court's entry into the "political thicket" to warm expressions of enthusiasm for the cutting of the Gordian knot of malapportionment. Many observers, however, raised questions about the application of the *Baker* decision to such problems as the county unit system of Georgia, malapportionment of congressional districts, and the "little federal system" of according equal representation by counties in one house of the state legislature. Answers to these questions were not long in coming. In *Gray* v. *Sanders*, 372 U.S. 368 (1963), the Court held invalid the Georgia county unit system of weighting smaller county votes disproportionately in the Democratic primary where United States Senators and statewide officers were nominated. And while some of the opinions in *Baker* indicated that factors other than population might be relevant in setting up electoral districts, the majority in *Gray* v. *Sanders* held that the only acceptable test in statewide elections was equality of population. Justice Douglas, speaking for eight members of the Court, stated:

. . . If a State in a statewide election weighted the male vote more heavily than the female vote or the white vote more heavily than the Negro vote, none could successfully contend that that discrimination was allowable. . . . How then can one person be given twice or 10 times the voting power of another person in a statewide election merely because he lives in a rural area or because he lives in the smallest rural county? Once the geographical unit for which a representative is to be chosen is designated, all who participate in the election are to have an equal vote—whatever their race, whatever their sex, whatever their occupation, whatever their income, and wherever their home may be in that geographical unit. This is required by the Equal Protection Clause of the Fourteenth Amendment. The concept of "we the people" under the Constitution visualizes no preferred class of voters but equality among those who meet the basic qualifications. The idea that every voter is equal to every other voter in his State, when he casts his ballot in favor of one of several competing candidates, underlies many of our decisions. . . .

The conception of political equality from the Declaration of Independence, to Lincoln's Gettysburg Address, to the Fifteenth, Seventeenth, and Nineteenth Amendments can mean only one thing—one person, one vote. . . .

[Justice Harlan was the only dissenter in the case. In an "I-told-you-so" opinion he pointed to the rash of litigation spawned by the *Baker* decision:]

When *Baker* v. *Carr* . . . was argued at the last Term we were assured that if this Court would only remove the roadblocks of *Colegrove* v. *Green* . . . and its predecessors to judicial review in "electoral" cases, this Court in all likelihood would never have to get deeper into such matters. State legislatures, it was predicted, would be prodded into taking satisfactory action by the mere prospect of legal proceedings.

These predictions have not proved true. As of November 1, 1962, [only eight months after *Baker*] the apportionment of seats in at least 30 state legislatures had been challenged in state and federal courts, and, besides this one, 10 electoral cases of one kind or another are already on this Court's docket. The present case is the first of these to reach plenary consideration. . . .

In the following year, in another Georgia case, *Wesberry v. Sanders*, 376 U.S. 1 (1964), the Court applied the "one man, one vote" rule to the matter of equalizing of population among congressional districts within a state. Petitioners lived in Georgia's Fifth Congressional District, in which Atlanta is located, which had a population of 823,680—as contrasted with a population of 394,312 for the average Georgia congressional district. They brought suit in a federal district court to enjoin defendants from conducting an election under the existing congressional districting statute on the ground that it was violative of the Constitution. The district court dismissed for nonjusticiability and want of equity, and on appeal the Supreme Court reversed. In an opinion by Justice Black, for six members of the Court, it was held that the statute was invalid as abridging the requirement of Article 1, Section 2, that congressmen be chosen "by the People of the several States." In construing this section, Justice Black stated:

We hold that, construed in its historical context, the command of Art. I, Section 2, that Representatives be chosen "by the People of the several States" means that as nearly as is practicable one man's vote in a congressional election is to be worth as much as another's. This rule is followed automatically, of course, when Representatives are chosen as a group on a statewide basis, as was a widespread practice in the first 50 years of our Nation's history. . . . We do not believe that the Framers of the Constitution intended to permit . . . vote-diluting discrimination to be accomplished through the device of districts containing widely varied numbers of inhabitants. To say that a vote is worth more in one district than in another would not only run counter to our fundamental ideas of democratic government, it would cast aside the principle of a House of Representatives elected "by the People," a principle tenaciously fought for and established at the Constitutional Convention. The history of the Constitution, particularly that part of it relating to the adoption of Art. I, Section 2, reveals that those who framed the Constitution meant that, no matter what the mechanics of an election, whether statewide or by districts, it was population which was to be the basis of the House of Representatives.

[The opinion then treats the debates in the Philadelphia Convention on the structure of the Congress and gives some contemporaneous construction of the sections dealing with the House of Representatives indicating that equality of voting power was intended.]

While it may not be possible to draw congressional districts with mathematical precision, that is no excuse for ignoring our Constitution's plain objective of making equal representation for equal numbers of people the fundamental goal for the House of Representatives. That is the high standard of justice and common sense which the Founders set for us.

Apparently there was fairly general acceptance of the idea that fairness demanded that one house of the legislature and congressional districts be apportioned on the "one man, one vote" formula. But criticism erupted when in June 1964, in a group of Alabama cases cited as *Reynolds* v. *Sims*, the Court held that both houses of a bicameral state legislature were required by the equal protection clause to be apportioned strictly on the basis of population.

### REYNOLDS *v.* SIMS
### *377 U.S. 533 (1964)*

[Taxpayers and registered voters of two urban Alabama counties brought suit in the United States District Court challenging the validity of (1) the existing apportionment provisions for the Alabama legislature, which created a 35-member state senate elected from 35 districts varying in population from 15,417 to 634,864, and a 106-member state house of representatives with population-per-representative variances from 6,731 to 104,767; (2) a proposed state constitutional amendment creating a 67-member state senate with one senator per county, the counties varying in population from 10,726 to 634,864, and a 106-member state house of representatives with population-per-representative variances from 10,726 to 42,303; and (3) a "standby" statutory measure creating a 35-member state senate elected from 35 districts varying in population from 31,175 to 634,864, and a 106-member house of representatives with population-per-representative variances from under 20,000 to over 52,000. The three-judge court held that all three schemes were unconstitutional, but in order to "break the strangle hold" of the rural counties on the legislature so that it could reapportion itself, the court ordered a temporary reapportionment following the proposed amendment's provisions with respect to the house of representatives and the "standby" statute's provisions with respect to the state senate. Direct appeal to the Supreme Court.]

Mr. Chief Justice Warren delivered the opinion of the Court. . . .

*Gray* and *Wesberry* are of course not dispositive of or directly controlling on our decision in these cases involving state legislative apportionment controversies. Admittedly, those decisions, in which we held that, in statewide and in congressional elections, one person's vote must be counted equally with those of all other voters in a State, were based on different constitutional considerations and were addressed to rather distinct problems. But neither are they wholly inapposite. . . . *Wesberry* clearly established that the fundamental principle of representative government in this country is one of equal representation for equal numbers of people, without regard to race, sex, economic status, or place of residence within a State. Our problem, then, is to ascertain, in the instant cases, whether there are any constitutionally cognizable principles which would justify departures from the basic standard of equality among voters in the apportionment of seats in state legislatures. . . .

Legislators represent people, not trees or acres. Legislators are elected by voters, not farms or cities or economic interests. As long as ours is a representative form of government, and our legislatures are those instruments of government elected directly by and directly representative of the people, the right to elect legislators in a free and unimpaired fashion is a bedrock of our political system. . . . [I]f a State should provide that the votes of citizens in one part of the State should be given two times, or five times, or 10 times the weight of votes of citizens in another part of the State, it could hardly be contended that the right to vote of those residing in the disfavored areas had not been effectively diluted.

[In response to the claim that a state senate based on one member per county was reasonable because analogous to the Federal Senate, Chief Justice Warren stated:]

Much has been written since our decision in *Baker* v. *Carr* about the applicability of the so-called federal analogy to state legislative apportionment arrangements.[*] After considering the matter, the court below concluded that no conceivable analogy could be drawn between the federal scheme and the apportionment of seats in the Alabama Legislature under the proposed constitutional amendment. We agree with the District Court, and find the federal analogy inapposite and irrelevant to

---

[*] For a thorough statement of the arguments against holding the so-called federal analogy applicable to state legislative apportionment matters, see, e.g., McKay, Reapportionment and the Federal Analogy (National Municipal League pamphlet 1962); McKay, The Federal Analogy and State Apportionment standards, 38 Notre Dame Law. 487 (1963). See also Merrill, Blazes for a Trail through the Thicket of Reapportionment, 16 Okla. L. Rev. 59, 67–70 (1963).

state legislative districting schemes. Attempted reliance on the federal analogy appears often to be little more than an after-the-fact rationalization offered in defense of maladjusted state apportionment arrangements. The original constitutions of 36 of our States provided that representation in both houses of the state legislatures would be based completely, or predominantly, on population. And the Founding Fathers clearly had no intention of establishing a pattern or model for the apportionment of seats in state legislatures when the system of representation in the Federal Congress was adopted. Demonstrative of this is the fact that the Northwest Ordinance, adopted in the same year, 1787, as the Federal Constitution, provided for the apportionment of seats in territorial legislatures solely on the basis of population.

The system of representation in the two Houses of the Federal Congress is one ingrained in our Constitution, as part of the law of the land. It is one conceived out of compromise and concession indispensable to the establishment of our federal republic. Arising from unique historical circumstances, it is based on the consideration that in establishing our type of federalism a group of formerly independent States bound themselves together under one national government. . . .

Political subdivisions of States—counties, cities, or whatever—never were and never have been considered as sovereign entities. Rather, they have been traditionally regarded as subordinate governmental instrumentalities created by the State to assist in the carrying out of state governmental functions. . . . The relationship of the States to the Federal Government could hardly be less analogous. . . .

Since we find the so-called federal analogy inapposite to a consideration of the constitutional validity of state legislative apportionment schemes, we necessarily hold that the Equal Protection Clause requires both houses of a state legislature to be apportioned on a population basis. The right of a citizen to equal representation and to have his vote weighted equally with those of all other citizens in the election of members of one house of a bicameral state legislature would amount to little if States could effectively submerge the equal-population principle in the apportionment of seats in the other house. If such a scheme were permissible, an individual citizen's ability to exercise an effective voice in the only instrument of state government directly representative of the people might be almost as effectively thwarted as if neither house were apportioned on a population basis. Deadlock between the two bodies might result in compromise and concession on some issues. But in all too many cases the more probable result would be frustration of the majority will through minority veto in the house not apportioned on a population basis. . . .

We do not believe that the concept of bicameralism is rendered anachronistic and meaningless when the predominant basis of representation in the two state legislative bodies is required to be the same—population. A prime reason for bicameralism, modernly considered, is to insure mature and deliberate consideration of, and to prevent precipitate action on, proposed legislative measures. Simply because the controlling criterion for apportioning representation is required to be the same in both houses does not mean that there will be no differences in the composition and complexion of the two bodies. Different constituencies can be represented in the two houses. One body could be composed of single-member districts while the other could have at least some multimember districts. The length of terms of the legislators in the separate bodies could differ. The numerical size of the two bodies could be made to differ, even significantly, and the geographical size of districts from which legislators are elected could also be made to differ. And apportionment in one house could be arranged so as to balance off minor inequities in the representation of certain areas in the other house. In summary, these and other factors could be, and are presently in many States, utilized to engender differing complexions and collective attitudes in the two bodies of a state legislature, although both are apportioned substantially on a population basis.

By holding that as a federal constitutional requisite both houses of a state legislature must be apportioned on a population basis, we mean that the Equal Protection Clause requires that a State make an honest and good faith effort to construct districts, in both houses of its legislature, as nearly of equal population as is practicable. We realize that it is a practical impossibility to arrange legislative districts so that each one has an identical number of residents, or citizens, or voters. Mathematical exactness or precision is hardly a workable constitutional requirement. . . .

[Justices Clark and Stewart concurred in the result, but on the ground that the Alabama legislature as constituted and the proposals for reapportionment offered by the state were not rationally based. Justice Clark stated, in part:]

It seems to me that all the Court need say in this case is that each plan considered by the trial court is "a crazy quilt," clearly revealing invidious discrimination in each house of the Legislature and therefore violative of the Equal Protection Clause. . . .

I, therefore, do not reach the question of the so-called "federal analogy." But in my view, if one house of the State Legislature meets the population standard, representation in the other house might include some departure from it so as to take into account, on a rational basis, other factors in order to afford some representation to the various elements of the State. . . .

Mr. Justice Harlan, dissenting. . . .

Had the Court paused to probe more deeply into the matter, it would have found that the Equal Protection Clause was never intended to inhibit the States in choosing any democratic method they pleased for the apportionment of their legislatures. This is shown by the language of the Fourteenth Amendment taken as a whole, by the understanding of those who proposed and ratified it, and by the political practices of the States at the time the Amendment was adopted. It is confirmed by numerous state and congressional actions since the adoption of the Fourteenth Amendment, and by the common understanding of the Amendment as evidenced by subsequent constitutional amendments and decisions of this Court before *Baker* v. *Carr* made an abrupt break with the past in 1962. . . .

The Court's elaboration of its new "constitutional" doctrine indicates how far— and how unwisely—it has strayed from the appropriate bounds of its authority. The consequence of today's decision is that in all but the handful of States which may already satisfy the new requirements the local District Court or, it may be, the state courts, are given blanket authority and the constitutional duty to supervise apportionment of the State Legislatures. It is difficult to imagine a more intolerable and inappropriate interference by the judiciary with the independent legislatures of the States. . . .

Finally, these decisions give support to a current mistaken view of the Constitution and the constitutional function of this Court. This view, in a nutshell, is that every major social ill in this country can find its cure in some constitutional "principle," and that this Court should "take the lead" in promoting reform when other branches of government fail to act. The Constitution is not a panacea for every blot upon the public welfare, nor should this Court, ordained as a judicial body, be thought of as a general haven for reform movements. . . . This Court . . . does not serve its high purpose when it exceeds its authority, even to satisfy justified impatience with the slow workings of the political process. For when, in the name of constitutional interpretation, the Court *adds* something to the Constitution that was deliberately excluded from it, the Court in reality substitutes its view of what should be so for the amending process. . . .

The apportionment decisions are, by any test, landmark cases in the history of the Court's work. And they will inevitably have enormous impact on the organization, structure, and operation of state and local government in the United States. The Court has been both praised for its statesmanlike courage and condemned for its heavy-handed entry into matters deemed within the sole prerogative of the states. Illustrative of the former position, Dean Robert B. McKay, in the summary of his book *Reapportionment: The Law and Politics of Equal Representation* (New York: Twentieth Century Fund, 1965), stated: "It has been the theme of this volume that the *Reapportionment Cases* have opened the way for revitalization of representative democracy in the United States at the national, state, and even local levels." Other writers, while accepting the general line of the apportionment decisions, expressed doubt whether the Court had given adequate thought to some of the ramifications of its statements. In a thoughtful article by Professor Robert G. Dixon, Jr. ["Reapportionment Perspectives: What is Fair Representation?" 51 *A. B. A. J.* 319 (1965)] for example, the point was made that the Court was actually dealing with representation, not voting, and thus was involved in "the most interesting, the most complex, the most baffling aspect of any democratic political system."

[For an exceptionally careful and thorough analysis of the cases and the views of the critics, through the *Reynolds* decision, see Carl Auerbach, "The Reapportionment Cases: One Person, One Vote—One Vote, One Value," 1964 *Supreme Court Review* 1 (Chicago: University of Chicago Press, 1964.)]

The "one man, one vote" rule of the Court in the apportionment cases raised the obvious question of just what degree of mathematical precision would be demanded to satisfy the constitutional test of equality. If, for example, only a one- or two-percent population deviation among districts was allowable, then it might be impossible to construct a valid system without splitting political subdivision lines. And once this approach is required, or even permitted, the potential for gerrymandered districts increases enormously.

In decisions subsequent to *Reynolds* the Court has adopted two different standards of permissible variance. In cases involving state or local legislative districts, substantial population variances have been upheld. But in the drawing of congressional district lines a much more restrictive rule of equality has been imposed. Those cases, however, reach more deeply into the matter of organization and structure of government, and the purpose of this section is to demonstrate the principle that the equal protection clause applies to the apportionment issue.

# CHAPTER 7

# *The Right to Vote*

The framers of the United States Constitution clearly contemplated that the basic power to regulate elections and fix voter qualifications would rest with the states. Except for the "dead letter" provisions of Section 2 of the Fourteenth Amendment, the only affirmative statements of qualifications of voters are found in Article I, Section 2, and the Seventeenth Amendment, and these provisions only go so far as to require that persons voting for members of the Congress "shall have the Qualifications requisite for Electors of the most numerous Branch of the State Legislature." Thus the states were left with broad leeway in determining the manner in which elections would be conducted and the persons who could participate in them. From 1964 to the present a number of changes have occurred, brought about by constitutional amendments, enactments by Congress, and judicial revision of some of the older provisions of the Constitution, which have resulted in greater uniformity in voter requirements. Before that time, while the general outlines were similar, there was considerable variation in the requirements for voting and candidacy and in the situations which would disqualify persons from continuing to exercise the franchise. For example, the age requirement was usually twenty-one years, but Georgia and Kentucky set the voting age at eighteen, Alaska at nineteen, and Hawaii at twenty. And while the usual residence requirement was one year, some states required only six months and others two years. Approximately one-third of the states employed literacy tests of one kind or another, and eleven southern states made prior payment of a poll tax a condition of voting. Although all states now require citizenship, there have been some twenty states which at one time or other have allowed aliens to vote before their naturalization was complete. [See Constance E. Smith, *Voting* and *Election Laws* (New York: Oceana Publications, 1960).]

If this were the whole of the picture of regulations concerning voting and elections, then any problems would be resolved simply by reference to the respective state laws. Complications are introduced, however, by the fact that the Constitution both gives to Congress certain powers to regulate elections and sets certain limits on the states in the exercise of their regulatory powers over certain voting and elections. It is in the treatment accorded these two areas by the Congress and the courts in the past hundred years, rather than in positive state laws, that the major developments have occurred in safeguarding and expanding the basic right to vote.

## CONSTITUTIONAL LIMITATIONS ON STATE VOTING REGULATIONS

The provisions of the United States Constitution which serve to limit the states in the area of voting and elections are the Fourteenth Amendment's equal protection clause, the Fifteenth Amendment, the Nineteenth Amendment, the Twenty-fourth Amendment, and the Twenty-sixth Amendment. In brief, the equal protection clause denies the state the power to make unreasonable classifications in the matter of voting, the Fifteenth Amendment prohibits both the states and the United States from abridging the right to vote because of race or color, and the Nineteenth Amendment prohibits both the states and the United States from abridging the right to vote because of sex. The Twenty-fourth Amendment bars the states and the United States from requiring the payment of a poll tax as a condition of voting for federal officials, and the Twenty-sixth Amendment forbids the states and the United States from denying persons eighteen years of age or older the right to vote because of age. It should be noted that in each of the Amendments the prohibitions lie against action carried through by *governments,* and none of the restrictions runs against purely *private* action to interfere with voting. In a case alleging a violation of the equal protection clause, the court must make affirmative findings in response to two questions before it can offer a remedy: (1) Was the alleged interference accomplished by means of state action? and (2) Was the interference a result of improper classification either in a statute or in its administration? In a case alleging a violation of the other Amendments, the court must also make affirmative findings in response to certain questions, but they are slightly different from those which would be raised in an equal protection claim. In a Fifteenth Amendment case, for example, the issues would be: (1) Was the alleged interference accomplished by means of either state or federal action? (2) Was the attempted electoral participation of the kind guaranteed in the phrase "right to vote"? and (3) Was the alleged denial of electoral participation based on race or color? Only if the answer to all three questions is in the affirmative can the court offer a remedy.

### Race Discrimination: The White Primary Cases

In the latter part of the nineteenth century the southern states adopted a variety of provisions directed largely toward disfranchisement of the Negro. These included such voter requirements as long residence, payment of a poll tax, literacy tests (often discriminatorily administered), and the production of a receipt proving payment of the previous year's taxes. But as the selection of candidates by primary elections instead of party conventions become general, the main thrust of the southern effort was directed toward preventing the Negro from participating in the Democratic primaries. In the "solid South" until fairly recently, winning the Democratic primary was tantamount to election, and thus, even if participation in the general elections was permitted, it was largely futile. The first of the white primary cases to reach the Court was *Nixon* v. *Herndon,* 273 U.S. 536 (1927). The Texas election law of 1923 provided that "in no event shall a negro be eligible to participate in a Democratic Party primary election held in the State of Texas." This provision might appear at first glance to have been a clear-cut violation of the Fifteenth Amendment. But until 1941 the Court did not take a clear stand that the Fifteenth Amendment "right to vote" included the right to vote in a primary. With this uncertainty the Court in *Nixon* v. *Herndon* chose the safer course of ruling the provision unconstitutional as a denial of equal protection of the laws under the Fourteenth Amendment. A substitute statute was then passed authorizing the state executive committee of every political party to fix qualifications for participating in their respective primaries. The state executive committee of the Democratic Party then adopted a rule barring Negroes from participation in its primaries. In *Nixon* v. *Condon,* 286 U.S. 73 (1932), the Court held that this was a delegation of state power to the state executive committee and made its determination conclusive irrespective of any expression of the party's will by its convention, and therefore the committee's action barring Negroes from the party primaries was "state action" prohibited by the Fourteenth Amendment. Undaunted, the Texas legislature then repealed its statutes regarding party membership and left the matter solely to the parties. In 1932 the state Democratic convention of Texas adopted a resolution limiting membership in the Democratic Party, and thereby participation in the primaries, to white persons. When this resolution as well was challenged, in *Grovey* v. *Townsend*, 294 U.S. 699 (1935), the Court's uncertainties regarding the right to participate in a primary election as well as the status of a state party convention's determinations under the "state action" definition combined to produce a decision that the petitioner was not denied "any right guaranteed by the Fourteenth and Fifteenth Amendments." The Court held that arguments directed toward the right to membership in a party and participation in its primaries were confused with the right to vote for one who is to hold a public office. "With the former the state need have no concern, with the latter it is bound to concern itself. . . ." With regard to the status of the Democratic convention, the opinion stated, "We are not prepared to hold that in Texas the state convention of a party has become a mere instrumentality or agency for expressing the voice or will of the state."

In 1941, however, the Court held in *United States* v. *Classic* that a citizen's right to vote in a congressional primary and to have his vote properly counted is a federal right protected by the Constitution.

## UNITED STATES *v.* CLASSIC
### *313 U.S. 299 (1941)*

[Classic and others, election commissioners, were charged with willfully altering and falsely counting and certifying the ballots in a Democratic primary in Louisiana at which a candidate for representative in Congress was being nominated. The indictment was brought in a federal district court under Sections 19 and 20 of the United States Criminal Code. Section 19 makes criminal any conspiracy to injure a citizen in the exercise "of any right or privilege secured to him by the Constitution or laws of the United States." Section 20 makes it a crime for anyone "acting under color of any law" willfully to subject any person to the deprivation of any rights protected by the Constitution and laws of the United States. The constitutional question turned on the issue of whether Congress' power to regulate "elections" for Senators and Representatives under Article I, Section 4, extended to the regulation of primaries in which candidates for such positions were nominated. Convictions were obtained in the trial court, but the Court of Appeals reversed.]

Mr. Justice Stone delivered the opinion of the Court. . . .

. . . [T]he practical operation of the primary in Louisiana, is and has been since the primary election was established in 1900 to secure the election of the Democratic primary nominee for the Second Congressional District of Louisiana.

Interference with the right to vote in the congressional primary in the Second Congressional District for the choice of Democratic candidate for Congress is thus as a matter of law and in fact an interference with the effective choice of the voters at the only stage of the election procedure when their choice is of significance, since it is at the only stage when such interference could have any practical effect on the ultimate result, the choice of the Congressman to represent the district. The primary in Louisiana is an integral part of the procedure for the popular choice of Congressman. The right of qualified voters to vote at the congressional primary in Louisiana and to have their ballots counted is thus the right to participate in that choice.

We come then to the question whether that right is one secured by the Constitution. Section 2 of Article I commands that Congressmen shall be chosen by the people of the several states by electors, the qualifications of which it prescribes. The right of the people to choose, whatever its appropriate constitutional limitations, where in other respects it is defined, and the mode of its exercise is prescribed by state action in conformity to the Constitution, is a right established and guaranteed by the Constitution and hence is one secured by it to those citizens and inhabitants of the state entitled to exercise the right. *Ex parte Yarbrough*, 110 U.S. 651. . . .

While, in a loose sense, the right to vote for representatives in Congress is some-times spoken of as a right derived from the states, see *Minor v. Happersett,* 21 Wall, 162, . . . this statement is true only in the sense that the states are authorized by the Constitution, to legislate on the subject as provided by Section 2 of Article I, to the extent that Congress has not restricted state action by the exercise of its powers to regulate elections under Section 4 and its more general power under Article I, Sec-tion 8, clause 18 of the Constitution "to make all laws which shall be necessary and proper for carrying into execution the foregoing powers." . . .

Obviously included within the right to choose, secured by the Constitution, is the right of qualified voters within a state to cast their ballots and have them counted at congressional elections. This Court has consistently held that this is a right secured by the Constitution. . . . And since the constitutional command is without restric-tion or limitation, the right, unlike those guaranteed by the Fourteenth and Fifteenth Amendments, is secured against the action of individuals as well as of states. *Ex parte Yarbrough.* . . .

. . . The right to participate in the choice of representatives for Congress includes, as we have said, the right to cast a ballot and to have it counted at the general elec-tion whether for the successful candidate or not. Where the state law has made the primary an integral part of the procedure of choice, or where in fact the primary ef-fectively controls the choice, the right of the elector to have his ballot counted at the primary, is likewise included in the right protected by Article I, Section 2. And this right of participation is protected just as is the right to vote at the election, where the primary is by law made an integral part of the election machinery, whether the voter exercises his right in a party primary which invariably, sometimes or never deter-mines the ultimate choice of the representatives. . . .

. . . The words of Sections 2 and 4 of Article I, read in the sense which is plainly permissible and in the light of the constitutional purpose, requires us to hold that a primary election which involves a necessary step in the choice of candidates for election as representatives in Congress, and which in the circumstances of this case controls that choice, is an election within the meaning of the constitutional provi-sion and is subject to congressional regulation as to the manner of holding it. . . .

*Reversed.*

[Mr. Justice Douglas wrote a dissenting opinion in which Justices Black and Mur-phy joined, arguing that as a matter of statutory construction, Congress did not in-tend to reach congressional primaries when it enacted the sections applied in this case.]

While the *Classic* case did not deal directly with the question of the validity of white primaries, the relevance of the decision to the problem in *Grovey* v. *Townsend* was ob-vious. If "elections" in Article I, Section 4, included primaries, then the "right to vote" protected by the Fifteenth Amendment should also extend to the right to participate in primaries. In short order, another case was brought up from Texas for a reexamination of the *Grovey* rule, and in *Smith* v. *Allwright* in 1944 *Grovey* was overruled.

### SMITH *v.* ALLWRIGHT
### *321 U.S. 649 (1944)*

Mr. Justice Reed delivered the opinion of the Court. . . .

. . . When *Grovey* v. *Townsend* was written, the Court looked upon the denial of a vote in a primary as a mere refusal by a party of party membership. As the Louisiana statutes for holding primaries are similar to those of Texas, our ruling in *Classic* as to the unitary character of the electoral process calls for a reexamination as to whether or not the exclusion of Negroes from a Texas party primary was state action. . . .

It may now be taken as a postulate that the right to vote in such a primary for the nomination of candidates without discrimination by the State, like the right to vote in a general election, is a right secured by the Constitution. . . .

Primary elections are conducted by the party under state statutory authority. The county executive committee selects precinct election officials and the county, district or state executive committees, respectively, canvass the returns. These party committees or the state convention certify the party's candidates to the appropriate officers for inclusion on the official ballot for the general election. No name which has not been so certified may appear upon the ballot for the general election as a candidate of a political party. No other name may be printed on the ballot which has not been placed in nomination by qualified voters who must take oath that they did not participate in a primary for the selection of a candidate for the office for which the nomination is made.

The state courts are given exclusive original jurisdiction of contested elections and of mandamus proceedings to compel party officers to perform their statutory duties.

We think that this statutory system for the selection of party nominees for inclusion on the general election ballot makes the party which is required to follow these legislative directions an agency for the state in so far as it determines the participants in a primary election. . . . If the state requires a certain electoral procedure, prescribes a general election ballot made up of party nominees so chosen and limits the choice of the electorate in general elections for state offices, practically speaking, to those whose names appear on such a ballot, it endorses, adopts and enforces the discrimination against Negroes, practiced by a party entrusted by Texas law with the determination of the qualifications of participants in the primary. This is state action within the meaning of the Fifteenth Amendment. . . .

The privilege of membership in a party may be, as this Court said in *Grovery* v. *Townsend,* no concern of a state. But when, as here, that privilege is also the essential qualification for voting in a primary to select nominees for a general election, the state makes the action of the party the action of the state. . . . *Grovey* v. *Townsend is overruled.*

*Judgment reversed.*

Mr. Justice Frankfurter concurs in the result.

Mr. Justice Roberts, dissenting. . . .

The reason for my concern is that the instant decision, overruling that announced about nine years ago, tends to bring adjudications of this tribunal into the same class as a restricted railroad ticket, good for this day and train only. I have no assurance, in view of current decisions, that the opinion announced today may not shortly be repudiated and overruled by justices who deem they have new light on the subject. In the present Term the Court has overruled three cases. . . .

*Smith* v. *Allwright* would seem to have settled the matter of the white primary once and for all, but this was not the case. The South Carolina legislature was called into special session and, taking its cue from the way Justice Reed found "state action" in the Texas case, repealed all statutes (nearly 150 in all) relating in any way to primaries and proposed amendments to the state constitution to remove any similar provisions in the constitution. The theory was that such action would leave the political party in the same position as any other private club, and its acts would in no way be construed as state action. This done, a Democratic state convention adopted a rule barring Negroes from membership in the Democratic Club and, therefore, from participation in its primaries.

A federal district court issued an injunction against an official of the Democratic Party to prevent his denying Negroes the right to vote in the primaries. [*Elmore* v. *Rice,* 72 F. Supp. 516 (E.D.S.C., 1947).] In *Rice* v. *Elmore,* 165 F.2d 387 (4th Cir., 1947), this ruling was affirmed by the Court of Appeals. [*Cert. denied,* 333 U.S. 875 (1948).] Judge Parker, speaking for the Court of Appeals, stated:

The fundamental error in defendant's position consists in the premise that a po-litical party is a mere private aggregation of individuals, like a country club, and that the primary is a mere piece of party machinery. . . . [W]ith the passage of the years, political parties have become in effect state institutions, governmental agencies through which sovereign power is exercised by the people. . . .

The closing chapter in the white primary story saw a return to Texas and a challenge to the racially exclusionary practices of the Jaybird Democratic Association of Fort Bend County, Texas. The Jaybird Association was organized in 1889 and limited its member-ship to white registered voters. Candidates for county offices submitted their names to the Jaybird Committee and ran in a primary held by the Association prior to the regular Democratic primary. The winners normally ran subsequently in the regular Democratic primary without opposition and won both that and the general election following. In *Terry* v. *Adams,* 345 U.S. 461 (1953), the Court held such a procedure violative of the Fif-teenth Amendment. Justice Black, for three of the majority, stated:

For a state to permit such a duplication of its election processes is to permit a fla-grant abuse of those processes to defeat the purposes of the Fifteenth Amendment. The use of the county-operated primary to ratify the results of the prohibited elec-tion merely compounds the offense. It violates the Fifteenth Amendment for a state, by such circumvention, to permit within its borders the use of any device that pro-duces an equivalent of the prohibited election. . . .
. . . It is immaterial that the state does not control that part of this elective process which it leaves for the Jaybirds to manage. The Jaybird primary has become an inte-gral, indeed the only effective part, of the elective process that determines who shall rule and govern in the county. The effect of the whole procedure, Jaybird primary plus Democratic primary plus general election, is to do precisely that which the Fif-teenth Amendment forbids—strip Negroes of every vestige of influence in selecting the officials who control the local county matters that intimately touch the daily lives of citizens. . . .

Five other members of the Court concurred in the result, but for slightly different rea-sons. Justice Minton was the lone dissenter, arguing that the actions of the Jaybird Asso-ciation could not properly be held to be state action. [On the white primary, see Douglas Weeks, "The White Primary: 1944–1948," 42 *Am. Pol. Sci. Rev.* 500 (1948); V. O. Key, *Southern Politics* (New York: Knopf, 1949), pp. 625–643; and Thurgood Mar-shall, "The Rise and Collapse of the 'White Primary,' " 26 *J. of Negro Ed.* 249 (1957).]

### The Grandfather Clauses

Among other devices employed to impede voting by Negroes was the "grandfather clause," used by several States beginning in 1895. Without expressly disfranchising the Negro, it facilitated the permanent placement of white residents on the lists of regis-tered voters while continuing to impose serious obstacles upon Negro registration. The typical provision required all prospective electors to be able to read and write any sec-tion of the state constitution, but no person who voted prior to January 1, 1866, or who was a lineal descendant of such person, could be denied the right to register and vote because of his inability to meet this literacy requirement. The clause did not, therefore, bar Negroes from being registered, but because of the operative date, all Negroes had to pass the literacy test while most white persons were exempt. In *Guinn* v *United*

*States,* 238 U.S. 347 (1915), the Court held that the employment by the state of Oklahoma of a standard based purely upon a period of time before the enactment of the Fifteenth Amendment and which so clearly set up a classification following racial lines was
in violation of the protection accorded by that Amendment. Oklahoma promptly
adopted a new statute in 1916 which provided that all persons, except those who voted
in 1914, who were qualified to vote in 1916 but who failed to register between April 30
and May 11, 1916 (a twelve-day registration period) should be perpetually disfran-
chised. The Court was not impressed with this obvious subterfuge, and in *Lane* v. *Wilson,* 307 U.S. 268 (1939), held this statute also violative of the Fifteenth Amendment. In
a sharply worded opinion, Justice Frankfurter stated that that Amendment "nullifies sophisticated as well as simple-minded modes of discrimination. It hits onerous procedural requirements which effectively handicap exercise of the franchise by the colored
race although the abstract right to vote may remain unrestricted as to race."

## Poll Taxes

There were at one time in the period following Reconstruction some eleven southern
states which imposed a poll tax as a prerequisite to voting. The amount of the tax ranged
from one to two dollars, and some statutes exempted women and older persons.
Whether the tax had greater impact on Negroes than on white persons has been a matter of some dispute. Certainly in the manner of administration, and in the fact that it was
cumulative in some states, it was a factor in discouraging voter registration whether
there was special racial impact or not. Payment was normally voluntary and, since tax
bills were not usually sent out, the voter had to keep track of annual deadlines and take
the initiative in seeking out the proper officials to whom the poll tax was to be paid. Until a 1953 amendment was adopted, the Alabama tax was cumulative starting with age
twenty-one and going through age forty-five. After 1953 the cumulative period was reduced to two years. V. O. Key, in his book *Southern Politics* (New York: Knopf, 1949),
pp. 617–618, concluded that the poll tax had little or no bearing on the paucity of Negro
voters because of the much greater effect of other methods of disfranchisement. He did
feel, however, that removal of the poll tax would increase voting in most southern states
by five to ten percent of the potential number of white voters.

The Court in *Breedlove* v. *Suttles,* 302 U.S. 277 (1937), upheld the Georgia poll tax
law against the claims of a white male citizen that the law violated the equal protection
clause, that it abridged the privileges and immunities of United States citizens, and that
it violated the Nineteenth Amendment. The law exempted blind persons and women
who did not register for voting.

Proposals in Congress for abolishing the poll tax as a prerequisite to voting were advanced for many years, beginning in 1939, but many members expressed reservations
concerning the constitutionality of the proposals. Finally, in 1962, a constitutional
amendment passed the Congress prohibiting the exacting of any tax as a requirement
for voting in federal elections. It was ratified in 1964 as the Twenty-fourth Amendment.
At the time, five states still required payment of the poll tax [Alabama, Arkansas, Mississippi, Texas, and Virginia), and they indicated plans to continue the requirement with
respect to voting in state and local elections.

In 1963, in anticipation of the promulgation of the Twenty-fourth Amendment, a special session of the Virginia General Assembly was convened. it adopted a requirement
that in order to qualify to vote in federal elections one must either pay a poll tax or file a
witnessed or notarized certificate of residence. In *Harman* v. *Forssenius,* 380 U.S. 528
(1965), the Court unanimously held the requirement repugnant to the Twenty-fourth
Amendment. Chief Justice Warren, for the Court, stated that the requirement of a poll

tax clearly violated that Amendment, and "no equivalent or milder substitute may be imposed." He said further, "Any material requirement imposed upon the federal voter solely because of his refusal to waive the constitutional immunity subverts the effectiveness of the Twenty-fourth Amendment and must fall under its ban."

The closing chapter in the long history of the poll tax as a prerequisite to voting was presumably written in 1966. In *Harper* v. *Virginia State Bd. of Elections*, 383 U.S. 663 (1966), the Court by a six-to-three vote held the requirement of payment of a poll tax as a prerequisite to participation in state elections unconstitutional under the equal protection clause of the Fourteenth Amendment. Justice Douglas, for the majority, stated:

We conclude that a State violates the Equal Protection Clause of the Fourteenth Amendment whenever it makes the affluence of the voter or payment of any fee an electoral standard. Voter qualifications have no relation to wealth nor to paying or not paying this or any other tax. . . . The principle that denies the State the right to dilute a citizen's vote on account of his economic status or other such factors by analogy bars a system which excludes those unable to pay a fee to vote or who fail to pay. . . . To introduce wealth or payment of a fee as a measure of a voter's qualifications is to introduce a capricious or irrelevant factor. The degree of the discrimination is irrelevant. In this context—that is, as a condition of obtaining a ballot—the requirement of fee paying causes an "invidious" discrimination (*Skinner* v. *Oklahoma* . . .) that runs afoul of the Equal Protection Clause. Levy "by the poll," as stated in *Breedlove* v. *Suttles*, . . . is an old familiar form of taxation; and we say nothing to impair its validity so long as it is not made a condition to the exercise of the franchise. *Breedlove* v. *Suttles* sanctioned its uses as "a prerequisite of voting." . . . To that extent the *Breedlove* case is overruled.

## Literacy Tests

Literacy tests for voting have been used by a number of states for many years. While there is a fairly obvious relationship between literacy and voting (although even here the case may be overstated), the literacy test at the same time lends itself more readily than most other requirements to discriminatory administration. The constitutionality of a Mississippi literacy requirement was attacked in *Williams* v. *Mississippi*, 170 U.S. 213 (1898) on the ground that unfettered discretion was vested in the registrars and that the provisions were administered in a racially discriminatory manner. The Court found the claim of discriminatory administration inadequately pleaded and held that literacy tests which are drafted so as to apply alike to all applicants for the voting franchise would be deemed to be fair on their face, and in the absence of proof of discriminatory enforcement could not be viewed as denying the equal protection of the laws guaranteed by the Fourteenth Amendment.

As recently as 1959, in *Lassiter* v. *Northampton Election Board*, 360 U.S. 45, the Court refused to hold invalid on its face a North Carolina requirement that all voters be able "to read and write any section of the Constitution of North Carolina in the English language." Justice Douglas, speaking for a unanimous Court, stated:

The states have long been held to have broad powers to determine the conditions under which the right of suffrage may be exercised. . . .

We do not suggest that any standards which a State desires to adopt may be required of voters. But there is wide scope for exercise of its jurisdiction. Residence requirements, age, previous criminal record . . . are obvious examples indicating factors which a State may take into consideration in determining the qualifications of voters. The ability to read and write likewise has some relation to standards designed to promote intelligent use of the ballot. Literacy and illiteracy are neutral on race, creed, color, and sex, as reports around the world show. Literacy and intelligence are obviously not synonymous. Illiterate people may be intelligent voters. Yet in our society where newspapers, periodicals, books, and other printed matter canvass and debate campaign issues, a State might conclude that only those who are literate should exercise the franchise. . . . It was said last century in Massachusetts that a literacy test was designed to insure an "independent and intelligent" exercise of the right of suffrage. . . . North Carolina agrees. We do not sit in judgment on the wisdom of that policy. We cannot say, however, that it is not an allowable one measured by constitutional standards. . . .

In *Louisiana* v. *United States*, 380 U.S. 145 (1965), the Court held invalid a Louisiana requirement that applicants for registration be able to give a "reasonable interpretation" of any section of the Louisiana Constitution or the United States Constitution when read to them by the registrar. In his opinion for the Court, Justice Black stated:

. . . The applicant facing a registrar in Louisiana thus has been compelled to leave his voting fate to that official's uncontrolled power to determine whether the applicant's understanding of the Federal or State Constitution is satisfactory. As the evidence showed, colored people, even some with the most advanced education and scholarship, were declared by voting registrars with less education to have an unsatisfactory understanding of the constitution of Louisiana or of the United States. This is not a test but a trap, sufficient to stop even the most brilliant man on his way to the voting booth. The cherished right of people in a country like ours to vote cannot be obliterated by the use of laws like this, which leave the voting fate of a citizen to the passing whim or impulse of an individual registrar. . . .

Other practices designed to hinder Negro registration in Louisiana are described in the chapter "The Louisiana Story" in the 1961 United States Commission on Civil Rights Report, *Voting* (Washington, D.C.: U.S. Government Printing Office, 1961). One feature of the registration requirements which appears to be unique is the requirement that the applicant state his exact age in years, months, and days. The report states that a registrar of voters of Plaquemines Parish, who was called on to give a step-by-step demonstration of the proper way to complete the application form, erred in her age computation by almost a month. And there appeared to be some confusion as to whether to include or exclude the day on which the application was filed. Nor was there agreement on whether an error of one day would be fatal to registration.

A group of provisions added to the Mississippi Constitution in 1954 and 1960 resulted in requirements that applicants for registration had to: (1) be able to read and copy in writing any section of the Mississippi Constitution, and (2) give a reasonable interpretation of that section to the county registrar, and (3) demonstrate to the registrar "a reasonable understanding of the duties and obligations of citizenship under a constitutional form of government," and (4) be "of good moral character."

The repeated use of literacy tests in a racially discriminatory manner led to the adoption of, first, the Voting Rights Act of 1965, which prohibited the use of any "test or device" for voter qualification in defined areas (predominantly the South), and, second, the 1970 Voting Rights Amendments, which operated nationwide to bar the use of literacy tests in all elections, state and national.

### Residence Requirements

All states have established durational residence requirements as a condition of registering to vote. These have customarily included a period of residence in the state (from six months to two years), a period of residence in the county, and frequently a period of residence in the precinct. In earlier cases, the Court had indicated that such requirements did not violate the Constitution. [See *Pope* v. *Williams,* 193 U.S. 621 (1904), for example.] But in the 1970 Federal Voting Rights Act, Congress outlawed state durational residence requirements for presidential and vice-presidential elections and prohibited the States from closing registration more than thirty days before such elections. This provision was upheld in *Oregon* v. *Mitchell,* 400 U.S. 112 (1970). This still left the states free to impose such requirements for persons wishing to vote in state and congressional elections, however. In *Dunn* v. *Blumstein* these provisions were challenged as violative of the equal protection clause.

## DUNN *v.* BLUMSTEIN
### *405 U.S. 330 (1972)*

Mr. Justice Marshall delivered the opinion of the Court.

Various Tennessee public officials . . . appeal from a decision by a three-judge federal court holding that Tennessee's durational residence requirements for voting violate the Equal Protection Clause of the United States Constitution. The issue arises in a class action for declaratory and injunctive relief brought by appellee James Blumstein. Blumstein moved to Tennessee on June 12, 1970, to begin employment as an assistant professor of law at Vanderbilt University in Nashville. With an eye toward voting in the upcoming elections, he attempted to register to vote on July 1, 1970. The county registrar refused to register him, on the ground that Tennessee law authorizes the registration of only those persons who, at the time of the next election, will have been residents of the State for a year and residents of the county for three months. . . .

Durational residence laws penalize those persons who have traveled from one place to another to establish a new residence during the qualifying period. Such laws divide residents into two classes, old residents and new residents, and discriminate against the latter to the extent of totally denying them the opportunity to vote. The constitutional question presented is whether the Equal Protection Clause of the Fourteenth Amendment permits a State to discriminate in this way among its citizens.

To decide whether a law violates the Equal Protection Clause, we look, in essence, to three things: the character of the classification in question; the individual interests affected by the classification; and the governmental interests asserted in support of the classification. . . . First, then, we must determine what standard of review is appropriate. In the present case, whether we look to the benefit withheld by the classification (the opportunity to vote) or the basis for the classification (recent interstate travel) we conclude that the State must show a substantial and compelling reason for imposing durational residence requirements. . . .

We turn, then, to the question of whether the State has shown that durational residence requirements are needed to further a sufficiently substantial state interest. We emphasize again the difference between bona fide residence requirements and durational residence requirements. We have in the past noted approvingly that the States have the power to require that voters be bona fide residents of the relevant political subdivision. . . . But *durational* residence requirements, representing a separate voting qualification imposed on bona fide residents, must be separately tested by the stringent standard. . . .

It is worth noting at the outset that Congress has, in a somewhat different context, addressed the question whether durational residence laws further compelling state interests. In §202 of the Voting Rights Act of 1965, added by the Voting Rights Act amendments of 1970, Congress outlawed state durational residence requirements for presidential and vice-presidential elections, and prohibited the State from closing registration more than 30 days before such elections. . . . In our present case, of course, we deal with congressional, state, and local elections, in which the State's interests are arguably somewhat different; and, in addition, our function is not merely to determine whether there was a reasonable basis for Congress' findings. However, the congressional finding which forms the basis for the Federal Act is a useful background for the discussion that follows.

Tennessee tenders "two basic purposes" served by its durational residence requirements:

"(1) INSURE PURITY OF BALLOT BOX—Protection against fraud through colonization and inability to identify persons offered to vote, and

"(2) KNOWLEDGEABLE VOTER—Afford some surety that the voter has, in fact, become a member of the community and that as such, he has a common interest in all matters pertaining to its government and is, therefore, more likely to exercise his right more intelligently." Brief for Appellants. . . .

We consider each in turn.

A

Preservation of the "purity of the ballot box" is a formidable-sounding state interest. The impurities feared, variously called "dual voting" and "colonization," all involve voting by nonresidents, either singly or in groups. The main concern is that nonresidents will temporarily invade the State or county, falsely swear that they are residents to become eligible to vote, and, by voting, allow a candidate to win by fraud. Surely the prevention of such fraud is a legitimate and compelling government goal. But it is impossible to view durational residence requirements as necessary to achieve that state interest. . . . This contention is particularly unconvincing in light of Tennessee's total statutory scheme for regulating the franchise.

Durational residence laws may once have been necessary to prevent a fraudulent evasion of state voter standards, but today in Tennessee, as in most other States, this purpose is served by a system of voter registration. . . . There is no indication in the record that Tennessee routinely goes behind the would-be voter's oath to determine his qualifications. Since false swearing is no obstacle to one intent on fraud, the existence of burdensome voting qualifications like durational residence requirements cannot prevent corrupt nonresidents from fraudulently registering and voting. . . . Indeed, the durational residence requirement becomes an effective voting obstacle only to residents who tell the truth and have no fraudulent purposes. . . .

. . . If the State itself has determined that a three-month period is enough time in which to confirm bona fide residence in the State and county, obviously a one-year period cannot also be justified as "necessary" to achieve the same purpose. Beyond that, the job of detecting nonresidents from among persons who have registered is a relatively simple one. It hardly justifies prohibiting all new-comers from voting for even three months. . . . Objective information tendered as relevant to the question of bona fide residence under Tennessee law—places of dwelling, occupation, car registration, driver's license, property owned, etc.—is easy to double-check, especially in light of modern communications. . . . It is sufficient to note here that 30 days appears to be an ample period of time for the State to complete whatever tasks are necessary to prevent fraud—and a year, or three months, too much. . . .

Our conclusion that the waiting period is not the least restrictive means necessary for preventing fraud is bolstered by the recognition that Tennessee has at its disposal a variety of criminal laws that are more than adequate to detect and deter whatever fraud may be feared. . . .

## B

The argument that durational residence requirements further the goal of having "knowledgeable voters" appears to involve three separate claims. . . .

Finally, the State urges that a longtime resident is "more likely to exercise his right [to vote] more intelligently." To the extent that this is different from the previous argument, the State is apparently asserting an interest in limiting the franchise to voters who are knowledgeable about the issues. . . .

. . . [T]he durational residence requirements in this case founder because of their crudeness as a device for achieving the articulated state goal of assuring the knowledgeable exercise of the franchise. The classifications created by durational residence requirements obviously permit any longtime resident to vote regardless of his knowledge of the issues—and obviously many longtime residents do not have any. On the other hand, the classifications bar from the franchise many other, admittedly new, residents who have become at least minimally, and often fully, informed about the issues. Indeed, recent migrants who take the time to register and vote shortly after moving are likely to be those citizens, such as appellee, who make it a point to be informed and knowledgeable about the issues. Given modern communications, and given the clear indication that campaign spending and voter education occur largely during the month before an election, the State cannot seriously maintain that it is "necessary" to reside for a year in the State and three months in the county in order to be knowledgeable about congressional, state, or even purely local elections. There is simply nothing in the record to support the conclusive presumption that residents who have lived in the State for less than a year and their county for less than three months are uninformed about elections. . . .

It is pertinent to note that Tennessee has never made an attempt to further its alleged interest in an informed electorate in a universally applicable way. Knowledge or competence has never been a criterion for participation in Tennessee's electoral process for longtime residents. . . . If the State seeks to assure intelligent use of the ballot, it may not try to serve this interest only with respect to new arrivals. . . .

*Affirmed.*

Mr. Justice Powell and Mr. Justice Rehnquist took no part in the consideration or decision of this case.

Mr. Justice Blackmun, concurring in the result. . . .

Mr. Chief Justice Burger, dissenting. . . .

Although *Dunn* held that a state could not constitutionally impose a one-year residence requirement for voting, in *Kanapaux v. Ellisor,* 419 U.S. 891 (1974), the Court in a summary action, without opinion, affirmed the judgment of a three-judge court which held that South Carolina's five-year durational residence requirement for candidates for Governor was not violative of the Fourteenth Amendment equal protection clause.

### Closed Primaries

In *Rosario v. Rockefeller,* 410 U.S. 752 (1973), the Court in a five-to-four decision upheld provisions of the New York election laws which required a person wishing to vote in a party primary to register his party affiliation eight months before a presidential primary and eleven months before primaries for other offices. The majority held that the requirement was not so severe as to constitute "a constitutionally onerous burden on petitioners' exercise of the franchise." It concluded that the goal of preventing "raiding" by members of the opposition party was a legitimate purpose and was neither invidious nor arbitrary.

An Illinois statute, as construed by the state supreme court, prohibited a person from voting in the primary election of a political party if he had voted in the primary of any other party within the preceding twenty-three months, an exception being made if the primary was held within a city only by a purely local political party. In *Kusper* v. *Pontikes*, 414 U.S. 51 (1973), the Court held that the statute unconstitutionally abridged the right of free political association. Justice Stewart, for the majority, stated:

> There can no longer be any doubt that freedom to associate with others for the common advancement of political beliefs and ideas is a form of "orderly group activity" protected by the First and Fourteenth Amendments. . . . The right to associate with the political party of one's choice is an integral part of this basic constitutional freedom. . . .
>
> There can be little doubt that [the statute] substantially restricts an Illinois voter's freedom to change his political party affiliation. One who wishes to change his party registration must wait almost two years before his choice will be given effect. Moreover, he is forced to forego participation in any primary elections occurring within the statutory 23-month hiatus. The effect of the Illinois statute is thus to "lock" the voter into his pre-existing party affiliation for a substantial period of time following participation in any primary election, and each succeeding primary vote extends this period of confinement.

The Court distinguished the case from *Rosario*, holding that the New York rule did not prevent voters from exercising their constitutional freedom to associate with the party of their choice, while the Illinois law did. It further held that while prevention of "raiding" was a legitimate state interest, Illinois would have to attain the objective by "less drastic means."

A Connecticut statute required voters in any political party primary to be registered members of that party. The Republican Party of Connecticut adopted a Party rule that permits independent voters to vote in Republican primaries for federal and statewide offices. (Thus the rule did not apply to voting in primaries for nominations to the state legislature.) The Party sued in Federal District Court alleging that the statute violated the Party's associational rights under the First and Fourteenth Amendments. In *Tashjian* v. *Republican Party of Connecticut*, 55 LW 4057 (1986), the Court held 5–4 that the statute was unconstitutional. The State argued that the law ensures the administrability of the primary, prevents voter raiding, avoids voter confusion, and protects the integrity of the two-party system and the responsibility of party government. The majority found these interests "insubstantial." A further argument presented was that the rule violated the Qualifications Clause of the Constitution, Article I, Section 2, providing that the qualifications for voting in congressional elections were those in effect for "electors of the most numerous branch of the State Legislature," and under the rule the qualifications would be different. The majority concluded that the purpose of the Qualifications Clause was "to prevent the mischief which would arise if state voters found themselves disqualified from participation in federal elections." The Clause does not require a "perfect symmetry of voter qualifications in state and federal legislative elections." Two of the dissenters thought the rule clearly violated the Qualifications Clause by permitting persons to vote for members of Congress who were not persons eligible to vote for candidates to most numerous branch of the state legislature. Others argued that no associational interest of the Party was violated, since the voters involved were not members of the Party but independents.

### Filing Fees for Candidates

It has long been the practice for political parties to charge filing fees for persons who wished to enter party primaries as candidates for public office. While in some states these fees were fairly nominal, there were other states in which the filing fees amounted to very substantial sums of money. In support of such charges it was argued that since the parties usually had to bear the expenses for administering the primaries, such levies against the candidates were a reasonable method of financing the elections. In *Bullock v. Carter*, in 1972, the Court addressed the question of whether such fees, which had the effect of denying the poor entry into political contests, were violative of the equal protection clause.

BULLOCK *v.* CARTER

*405 U.S. 134 (1972)*

Mr. Chief Justice Burger delivered the opinion of the Court.

Under Texas law, a candidate must pay a filing fee as a condition to having his name placed on the ballot in a primary election. The constitutionality of the Texas filing-fee-system is the subject of this appeal from the judgment of a three-judge District Court.

Appellee Pate met all qualifications to be a candidate in the . . . Democratic primary for the office of County Commissioner . . . except that he was unable to pay the $1,424.60 assessment required of candidates in that primary. Appellee Wischkaemper sought to be placed on the Democratic primary ballot as a candidate for County Judge . . . but he was unable to pay the $6,300 assessment for candidacy for that office. Appellee Carter wished to be a Democratic candidate for Commissioner of the General Land Office; his application was not accompanied by the required $1,000 filing fee.

After being denied places on the Democratic primary ballots in their respective counties, these appellees instituted . . . actions in the District Court challenging the validity of the Texas filing-fee system. . . . Following a hearing on the merits, the three-judge court declared the Texas filing-fee scheme unconstitutional and enjoined its enforcement. . . .

Under the Texas statute, payment of the filing fee is an absolute prerequisite to a candidate's participation in a primary election. There is no alternative procedure by which a potential candidate who is unable to pay the fee can get on the primary ballot by way of petitioning voters, and write-in votes are not permitted in primary elections for public office. . . .

Unlike a filing-fee requirement that most candidates could be expected to fulfill from their own resources or at least through modest contributions, the very size of the fees imposed under the Texas system gives it a patently exclusionary character. . . . To the extent that the system requires candidates to rely on contributions from voters in order to pay the assessments, a phenomenon that can hardly be rare in light of the size of the fees, it tends to deny some voters the opportunity to vote for a candidate of their choosing; at the same time it gives the affluent the power to place on the ballot their own names or the names of persons they favor. . . .

Because the Texas filing-fee scheme has a real and appreciable impact on the exercise of the franchise, and because this impact is related to the resources of the voters supporting a particular candidate, we conclude . . . that the laws must be "closely scrutinized" and found reasonably necessary to the accomplishment of legitimate state objectives in order to pass constitutional muster.

Appellants contend that the filing fees required by the challenged statutes are necessary both to regulate the ballot in primary elections and to provide a means for financing such elections. . . .

. . . There may well be some rational relationship between a candidate's willingness to pay a filing fee and the seriousness with which he takes his candidacy. But the candidates in this case affirmatively alleged that they were *unable,* not simply *unwilling,* to pay the assessed fees, and there was no contrary evidence. It is uncontested that the filing fees exclude legitimate as well as frivolous candidates. And even assuming that every person paying the large fees required by Texas law takes his own candidacy seriously, that does not make him a "serious candidate" in the popular sense. If the Texas fee requirement is intended to regulate the ballot by weeding out spurious candidates, it is extraordinarily ill-fitted to that goal; other means to protect those valid interests are available. . . .

. . . Appellants strenuously urge that apportioning the cost among the candidates is the only feasible means for financing the primaries. They argue that if the State must finance the primaries, it will have to determine which political bodies are "parties" so as to be entitled to state sponsorship for their nominating process, and that this will result in new claims of discrimination. . . . [T]he Court has recently upheld the validity of a state law distinguishing between political parties on the basis of success in prior elections. *Jenness* v. *Fortson* [1971]. We are not persuaded that Texas would be faced with an impossible task in distinguishing between political parties for the purpose of financing primaries.

We also reject the theory that since the candidates are availing themselves of the primary machine, it is appropriate that they pay that share of the cost that they have occasioned. . . .

Appellants seem to place reliance on the self-evident fact that if the State must assume the cost, the voters, as taxpayers, will ultimately be burdened with the expense of the primaries. But it is far too late to make out a case that the party primary is such a lesser part of the democratic process that its cost must be shifted away from the taxpayers generally. . . . Viewing the myriad governmental functions supported from general revenues, it is difficult to single out any of a higher order than the conduct of elections at all levels to bring forth those persons desired by their fellow citizens to govern. Without making light of the State's interest in husbanding its revenues, we fail to see such an element of necessity in the State's present means of financing primaries as to justify the resulting incursion on the prerogatives of voters.

Since the State has failed to establish the requisite justification for this filing-fee system, we hold that it results in a denial of equal protection of the laws. It must be emphasized that nothing herein is intended to cast doubt on the validity of reasonable candidate filing fees or licensing fees in other contexts. By requiring candidates to shoulder the costs of conducting primary elections through filing fees and by providing no reasonable alternative means of access to the ballot, the State of Texas has erected a system that utilizes the criterion of ability to pay as a condition to being on the ballot, thus excluding some candidates otherwise qualified and denying an undetermined number of voters the opportunity to vote for candidates of their choice. These salient features of the Texas system are critical to our determination of constitutional invalidity.

*Affirmed.*

Mr. Justice Powell and Mr. Justice Rehnquist took no part in the consideration or decision of this case.

In *Lubin* v. *Panish,* 415 U.S. 709 (1974), the Court followed the *Bullock* rule in holding invalid the California filing-fee requirement which, like that of Texas, provided no alternative access to the ballot. The State argued that the requirement was a useful device for minimizing the possibility of lengthy "laundry list" ballots cluttered with frivolous or otherwise nonserious candidates. The Court, as in *Bullock,* held that the State would have to use devices to accomplish this purpose other than mere distinctions based on wealth.

## Property Requirements for Voting

While the States no longer make ownership of property a condition for eligibility for general voter participation, it has not been uncommon for them to require some specified ownership of taxable property as a prerequisite to voting in elections on the issuance of governmental bonds or other special categories of elections. In *Kramer* v. *Union Free School District*, 393 U.S. 818 (1969), discussed earlier, the Court held invalid New York statutes limiting the electorate for choosing school board members to qualified voters who, in addition, either owned or leased taxable real property within the school district or who were parents of children enrolled in the local public schools.

*Hill* v. *Stone*, 421 U.S. 289 (1975), involved a challenge by residents of Fort Worth, Texas, to a "dual box election procedure" required by law to be used in all the State's local bond elections. Under this procedure, all persons owning taxable property, and so "rendered," voted in one box, and all other registered voters cast their ballots in a separate box. The results in both boxes were tabulated, and the bond issue would be deemed to have passed only if it was approved by a majority vote both in the "renderers' box" and in the aggregate of both boxes. On authority of *Kramer* and others, the Court held the procedure invalid. The bond issue was for the purpose of building a library, and although a general obligation issue, it was to have been paid for entirely out of property taxes. Appellant claimed that in view of this fact, the election was one of special interest and thus outside the rule of *Kramer*. The majority opinion cited *City of Phoenix* v. *Kolodziejski*, 339 U.S. 204 (1970), which had also held invalid a statute restricting the franchise in a general obligation bond election to real property owners, in which it was stated:

**Property taxes may be paid initially by property owners, but a significant part of the ultimate burden of each year's tax on rental property will very likely be borne by the tenant rather than the landlord since . . . the landlord will treat the property tax as a business expense and normally will be able to pass all or a large part of this cost on to the tenants in the form of higher rent.**

In addition, it was noted that property taxes on commercial property would normally be treated as a cost of doing business and would "be reflected in the prices of goods and services purchased by nonproperty owners and property owners alike." Appellant argued further that any resident could become eligible merely by listing personal property of even negligible value, and therefore it could not be considered a serious impediment to participation. The Court's answer was that if this were true, the requirement "can hardly be said to select voters according to the magnitude of their prospective liability for the city's indebtedness."

However, in *Salyer Land Co.* v. *Tulare Water District*, 410 U.S. 719 (1973), the Court upheld a scheme for electing the Board of Directors of the Water District in which the franchise was limited to landholders and their votes were weighted according to the assessed valuations of their property. The District was established for the purpose of acquiring, storing and distributing water for farming in the Tulare Lake Basin. It was empowered to fix tolls and charges for the use of water and to collect them from all persons receiving the benefit of the water. The costs of the various projects were assessed against district land in accordance with the benefits accruing to each tract held in separate ownership. And land not benefited could be withdrawn from the district on petition. The Court distinguished *Kramer*, holding that the activities of the District fell so disproportionately on landowners as a group that it was not unreasonable to focus on the land benefited rather than on people as such. Further, weighting the vote according to assessed valuation of the land did not violate the principle that wealth has no relation to voter qualifications where, as here, the expense as well as the benefit is proportional to the land's assessed value.

## FEDERAL LEGISLATION TO PROTECT VOTING RIGHTS

Shortly after the Fifteenth Amendment was ratified in 1870, Congress passed a law to enforce its provisions [Act of May 31, 1870, 42 U.S.C. 1971(a)(1958)]. The relevant section provided:

All citizens of the United States who are otherwise qualified by law to vote at any election by the people in any State, Territory, district, county, city, parish, township, school district, municipality, or other territorial subdivision, shall be entitled and allowed to vote at all such elections, without distinction of race, color, or previous condition of servitude; any constitution, law, custom, usage, or regulation of any State or Territory, or by or under its authority, to the contrary notwithstanding.

[The discussion of this section and other legislation through the Civil Rights Act of 1960 is largely in the words of the 1961 Civil Rights Commission Report, *Voting*, pp. 73–78. See also, Note, "Voting Rights," 3 *Race Rel. L. Rep.* 371 (1958).]

While the Supreme Court has long since struck down much Reconstruction legislation as unconstitutional, this provision, Section 1971(a) of Title 42, survives as a cornerstone of Federal legislation to protect the right to vote.

But this section merely declared a right; it provided no legal remedy. And other relevant Reconstruction legislation has proved difficult to apply or depends on private initiative. Until the passage of the Civil Rights Act of 1957, therefore, the federal government could do little to combat discriminatory denials of the right to vote. The 1957 Act, and its successor Act in 1960, opened the way to more direct and effective federal action to protect the fundamental right of electoral participation.

For seventy years the federal government relied almost solely on two sections of the Criminal Code to prevent discrimination in voting. Both were Reconstruction measures, now Sections 241 and 242 of Title 18 of the United States Code. Section 241 penalizes *conspiracies* of two or more persons to "injure, oppress, threaten, or intimidate any citizen in the free exercise or enjoyment of any right . . . secured . . . by the Constitution or laws of the United States. . . ." This provision applies to actions by either state officials or private persons that interfere with voting in federal elections, and also to state officials in state and local elections. The other criminal provision, now Section 242, prohibits action "under color of law" which interferes with "rights . . . secured or protected by the Constitution or laws of the United States," including the right not to be discriminated against on grounds of race or color.

Section 241 was involved in the case of *Ex parte Yarbrough*, 110 U.S. 651 (1884), where the Court declared that the right to vote in federal elections arose from the federal Constitution and was, therefore, subject to protection by federal legislation. This was true, said the Court, despite the fact that state laws prescribe the qualifications of electors. Both sections were involved in *United States* v. *Classic*, 313 U.S. 299 (1941), where the Court held for the first time that the guarantees of the Constitution cover primary as well as general elections.

In 1939 Congress enacted, as part of the Hatch Act, another criminal provision to protect the right to vote. It is Section 594 of Title 18 of the Code and assesses criminal penalties as a misdemeanor for persons who intimidate, threaten, or coerce any other person for the purpose of interfering with his right to vote in federal elections. It does not appear to have been used to date.

Before 1957, in addition to these criminal remedies, three other provisions of the Code laid a basis for *civil* remedies for improper denials of the right to vote. Section 1971(a), quoted above, while it did not provide for specific remedies, did set up the federal right to vote without distinctions as to race or color. And two other sections set up the civil remedies. Section 1983 (the civil counterpart of Section 242) of Title 42 of the Code permits suits to be brought against persons acting "under color of any statute, or-dinance, regulation, custom or usage" to deprive citizens of rights secured by the Con-stitution and laws of the United States. The injured party may bring "an action at law, suit in equity, or other proper proceeding for redress." The suit for injunctive relief or for damages is the usual type of action under this section. It was the basis for action, along with Section 1971(a), in a number of landmark cases, including *Nixon* v. *Herndon, Smith* v. *Allwright,* and *Rice* v. *Elmore.* The other section, Section 1985 (3) of Title 42, provides for a suit for damages (but not equitable action) in the case of a conspiracy to deprive persons of the equal protection of the laws or to prevent by force, intimidation, or threat, any qualified voter from voting as he chooses in a federal election. This sec-tion has been little used.

In summing up the effect of these provisions, the 1961 Civil Rights Commission *Voting* Report states (p. 75):

These provisions set the framework for a series of important cases expanding and defining the Federal right to vote—but they were weak. Most of these cases were civil, not criminal. The Federal Government was empowered only to bring criminal cases, and the criminal statutes were unwieldly and difficult to apply. Civil cases, with their flexible remedies and relative ease of proof, could be brought only by pri-vate persons, who are not always able to bear the expense and difficulty involved in long and complicated litigation.

Congress made a substantial change in adopting the Civil Rights Act of 1957 (71 Stat. 635). Basically, the Act is an amendment to the old Section 1971. It retains that section as subsection (a) and adds several other subsections. Subsection (b) is also a declaration of rights, adopting substantially the same language as 18 U.S.C. Section 594, the Hatch Act provision to punish for intimidation of voters in federal elections, except that it ex-plicitly mentions primaries as well as general elections and provides for civil suits to be brought by either private parties or the Attorney General. Other provisions of the Act give the federal district courts jurisdiction of such civil proceedings without a require-ment that state administrative or other remedies first be exhausted; provide for con-tempt proceedings in the event of disobedience of court orders under the section; and, by authorizing the appointment of an additional Assistant Attorney General, led to rais-ing the Department of Justice's Civil Rights Section to the status of a full division. The Act also created the Civil Rights Commission.

Experience under the 1957 Act indicated that it was still insufficient to stop discrimi-natory denials of the right to vote. When the Commission issued its first report late in 1959, the Civil Rights Division had instituted only three actions under the section per-mitting the Attorney General to institute suits, and none had been successful. In one case, because the registrars against whom the suit was brought had previously resigned from office, a federal district court had held that there was no one the federal govern-ment could sue. [*United States* v. *Alabama,* 171 F. Supp. 720 (M.D. Ala., 1959), *aff'd,* 267 F.2d 808 (5th Cir., 1960), *vacated,* 362 U.S. 602 (1960).]

As a result of the experience under the 1957 Act, the Commission strongly urged the passage of another act to close up several loopholes. The Civil Rights Act of 1960 (74 Stat. 86) reflected the Commission's recommendations. It took care of the problem of resigning registrars by amending the 1957 law to provide that in actions brought under Section 1971(a) and (c), "the act or practice shall also be deemed that of the State and the State may be joined as a party defendant and if, prior to the institution of such pro-ceeding, such official has resigned or has been relieved of his office and no successor as-sumed such office, the proceeding may be instituted against the State."

Another provision of the 1960 Act—Title III—declared voting records public and required their preservation for a period of twenty-two months following any general or special election. The provision opened the way for inspection and copying by the Attorney General both to help him to decide which cases might warrant prosecution and also to help him in gathering evidence for suits ultimately filed.

Title VI of the 1960 Act made provision for the substitution of federal voting referees for local registration officials when various judicial findings of discriminatory practices were made. The procedural requirements which had to be met preparatory to an actual registration order were quite formidable, however. First, the government had to file suit under Section 1971(a) and (c) and obtain a court finding that "a person has been deprived on account of race or color" of the right to vote. Second, the court was required to find that "such deprivation was or is pursuant to a pattern or practice." Third, any person found to be discriminated against because of race could apply for an order declaring him qualified to vote. To get such an order he had to prove: "(1) he is qualified under State law to vote, and (2) he has since such finding by the court been (a) deprived of or denied under color of law the opportunity to register to vote or otherwise to qualify to vote, or (b) found not qualified to vote by any person acting under color of law." Finally, the court (or an appointed referee) had to hold a hearing on the application and permit the state to appear to challenge the applicant's qualifications. Only then could a specific person be ordered to be registered and allowed to vote. Thus the machinery was provided to combat discrimination against voters, but it was cumbersome machinery indeed.

In the 1963 Report of the United States Commission on Civil Rights this statement is made (p. 27):

Abridgment of the right to vote on the grounds of race persists in the United States in direct violation of the Constitution. In fulfillment of its statutory obligation, the Commission has previously recommended to the President and the Congress a variety of corrective measures. In 1963 the continuing discriminatory denial of the right to vote has led this Commission to reexamine and reconsider each of its prior voting recommendations. The Commission now believes that the only effective method of guaranteeing the vote for all Americans is the enactment by Congress of some form of uniform voter qualification standards. The Commission further believes that the right to vote must, in many instances, be safeguarded and assured by the Federal Government. Adequate legislation must include both standards and implementation. . . .

In partial response to this and other recommendations, Title I of the Civil Rights Act of 1964 (78 Stat. 241) adds further amendments to Section 1971 of Title 42. It prohibits the employment of differential standards of qualification for applicants for registration, prohibits denial of right to vote in federal elections because of trivial errors or omissions on the part of applicants which are not material to the determination of qualification, and requires that literacy tests be administered wholly in writing and, further, that a certified copy of the tests and his answers be furnished to the applicant upon his request. In addition, the provision set up a rebuttable presumption that completion of the sixth grade in school is sufficient to meet the requirement of literacy which any state might impose.

Political pressures mounted, however, for even stronger federal legislation guaranteeing the right to vote. The answer came with the signing into law of the Voting Rights Act of 1965 (79 Stat. 437) on August 6 of that year. The Act was clearly aimed at the South, where most of the racially discriminatory denials of the franchise occurred, and was designed to sweep away all procedures which in the past had been used to deny the right to vote on racial grounds, whatever rational justification might be presented for the procedures. The key provision of the Act, in this respect, is Section 4, which prohibits the use of "any test or device" in certain defined states or political subdivisions thereof. The section states, in part:

Sec. 4. (a) To assure that the right of citizens of the United States to vote is not denied or abridged on account of race or color, no citizen shall be denied the right to vote in any Federal, State, or local election because of his failure to comply with any test or device in any State with respect to which the determinations have been made under subsection (b) or in any political subdivision with respect to which such determinations have been made as a separate unit, unless the United States District Court for the District of Columbia in an action for a declaratory judgment brought by such State or subdivision against the United States has determined that no such test or device has been used during the five years preceding the filing of the action for the purpose or with the effect of denying or abridging the right to vote on account of race or color. . . .

(b) The provisions of subsection (a) shall apply in any State or in any political subdivision of a state which (1) the Attorney General determines maintained on November 1, 1964, any test or device, and with respect to which (2) the Director of the Census determines that less than 50 per centum of the persons of voting age residing therein were registered on November 1, 1964, or that less than 50 per centum of such persons voted in the presidential election of November 1964. . . .

(c) The phrase "test or device" shall mean any requirement that a person as a prerequisite for voting or registration for voting (1) demonstrate the ability to read, write, understand, or interpret any matter, (2) demonstrate any educational achievement or his knowledge of any particular subject, (3) possess good moral character, or (4) prove his qualifications by the voucher of registered voters or members of any other class.

The Act authorizes the appointment of examiners with authority to examine the qualifications of applicants for registration and, if they are found qualified under state laws not in conflict with the Constitution or federal laws, to place their names on a list of eligible voters. The appointment of such examiners may be authorized by a federal court in appropriate proceedings begun by the Attorney General under Section 3 of the Act, or the Civil Service Commission will appoint such examiners if the Attorney General certifies that in specified areas as defined by Section 4(b) residents are being denied registration on account of race or color and that the appointment of examiners is necessary to enforce the guarantees of the Fifteenth Amendment.

Section 5 of the Act demands that, if states or political subdivisions falling within the category defined by Section 4 "enact or seek to administer any voting qualification or prerequisite to voting, or standard, practice, or procedure with respect to voting different from that in force or effect on November 1, 1964," they must either seek a declaratory judgment from the United States District Court for the District of Columbia that such provision will not abridge the right to vote on account of race or color, or submit such provision to the Attorney General, in which case if he does not interpose an objection within sixty days thereafter, the provision may be put into operation. In the latter case, however, the Attorney General's failure to object does not act as a bar to subsequent action to enjoin the enforcement of the new provision.

The Attorney General moved swiftly after the adoption of the Act, and several southern states were brought within the prohibitions of the Act in the late summer of 1965. South Carolina brought an action in the original jurisdiction of the United States Supreme Court challenging the constitutionality of the "triggering" provision, Section 4(b) of the Act (the characterization was by counsel for South Carolina, and referred to the coverage formula and the provisions for findings by the Attorney General and the Director of the Census which would "trigger" application of the coverage formula), as well as the Section 5 provision "freezing" the election procedures as they were on November 1, 1964, and the Section 6 provisions for registration by federal examiners. Five other southern states were permitted to file supporting briefs and participate in oral argument in the case—Alabama, Georgia, Louisiana, Mississippi, and Virginia. Twenty northern and western states filed briefs in support of the government's position that the Act was constitutional, and argument was heard beginning on January 17, 1966.

In less than two months, an exceptionally rapid disposition of the case, the Court handed down its decision upholding the constitutionality of the Act in *South Carolina* v. *Katzenbach*.

## SOUTH CAROLINA *v* KATZENBACH
### *383 U.S. 301 (1966)*

[By leave of the Court, South Carolina filed on original bill a bill of complaint seeking a declaration that the Voting Rights Act of 1965 was unconstitutional and asking for an injunction against enforcement of its provisions. The attack centered on the provisions for suspension of literacy and other voting tests in the applicable geographic areas, the provisions suspending all new voting regulations in such areas pending review by federal authorities, the provisions for assignment of federal examiners to list qualified applicants for voting, and the designation of the United States District Court for the District of Columbia over litigation as to termination of the statutory coverage. It was contended that the coverage formula violated the principle of the equality of states, denied due process by employing an invalid presumption, constituted a forbidden bill of attainder, and impaired the separation of powers by adjudicating guilt through legislative action rather than through the courts.]

Mr. Chief Justice Warren delivered the opinion of the Court. . . .

Two points emerge vividly from the voluminous legislative history of the Act contained in the committee hearings and floor debates. First: Congress felt itself confronted by an insidious and pervasive evil which had been perpetuated in certain parts of our country through unremitting and ingenious defiance of the Constitution. Second: Congress concluded that the unsuccessful remedies which it had prescribed in the past would have to be replaced by sterner and more elaborate measures in order to satisfy the clear commands of the Fifteenth Amendment. . . .

In recent years, Congress has repeatedly tried to cope with the problem by facilitating case-by-case litigation against voting discrimination. . . .

Despite the earnest efforts of the Justice Department and of many federal judges, these new laws have done little to cure the problem of voting discrimination. . . .

. . . [T]he basic question presented by the case [is]: Has Congress exercised its powers under the Fifteenth Amendment in an appropriate manner with relation to the States?

The ground rules for resolving this question are clear. The language and purpose of the Fifteenth Amendment, the prior decisions construing its several provisions, and the general doctrines of constitutional interpretation, all point to one fundamental principle. As against the reserved powers of the States, Congress may use any rational means to effectuate the constitutional prohibition of racial discrimination in voting. . . .

Congress exercised its authority under the Fifteenth Amendment in an inventive manner when it enacted the Voting Rights Act of 1965. First: The measure prescribes remedies for voting discrimination which go into effect without any need for prior adjudication. This was clearly a legitimate response to the problem, for which there is ample precedent under other constitutional provisions. . . . After enduring nearly a century of systematic resistance to the Fifteenth Amendment, Congress might well decide to shift the advantage of time and inertia from the perpetrators of the evil to its victims. . . .

Second: The Act intentionally confines these remedies to a small number of States and political subdivisions which in most instances were familiar to Congress by name. This, too, was a permissible method of dealing with the problem. Congress has learned that substantial voting discrimination presently occurs in certain sections of the country, and it knew no way of accurately forcasting whether the evil might spread elsewhere in the future. In acceptable legislative fashion, Congress chose to limit its attention to the geographic areas where immediate action seemed necessary. . . . The doctrine of the equality of States, invoked by South Carolina, does not bar this approach, for that doctrine applies only to the terms upon which States are admitted to the Union, and not to the remedies for local evils which have subsequently appeared. . . .

Mr. Justice Black, concurring and dissenting.

I agree with substantially all of the Court's opinion sustaining the power of Congress . . . to suspend state literacy tests and similar voting qualifications and to authorize the Attorney General to secure the appointment of federal examiners to register qualified voters in various sections of the country. . . . I dissent from its holding that every part of §5 of the Act is constitutional. Section 4(a), to which §5 is linked, suspends for five years all literacy tests and similar devices in those States coming within the formula of §4(b). Section 5 goes on to provide that a State covered by §4(b) can in no way amend its constitution or laws relating to voting without first trying to persuade the Attorney General of the United States or the Federal District Court for the District of Columbia that the new proposed laws do not have the purpose and will not have the effect of denying the right to vote to citizens on account of their race or color. I think this section is unconstitutional on at least two grounds.

(a) The Constitution gives federal courts jurisdiction over cases and controversies only. . . . [I]t is hard for me to believe that a justiciable controversy can arise in the constitutional sense from a desire by the United States Government or some of its officials to determine in advance what legislative provisions a State may enact or what consitutional amendments it may adopt. . . .

(b) My second and more basic objection to §5 is that Congress has here exercised its power under §2 of the Fifteenth Amendment through the adoption of means that conflict with the most basic principles of the Constitution. . . . Section 5, by providing that some of the States cannot pass state laws or adopt state constitutional amendments without first being compelled to beg federal authorities to approve their policies, so distorts our constitutional structure of government as to render any distinction drawn in the Constitution between state and federal power almost meaningless. . . .

In the Voting Rights Act Amendments of 1970 Congress adopted a law of national application to (1) lower the voting age to 18 in both state and federal elections, (2) bar the use of literacy tests in all elections, state and national, and (3) abolish residency requirements for voters in elections for presidential electors. In *Oregon v. Mitchell*, 400 U.S. 112 (1970), a badly split Court held the 18-year-old vote provisions constitutional as applied to federal elections but unconstitutional as applied to state elections. It upheld the provisions barring literacy tests and also the residency prohibition for voters in presidential elections. The decision on voter age qualification was remedied by the adoption of the Twenty-sixty Amendment. It was ratified on June 10, 1971, in the record time of three months, seven days, and reinstates the 18-year-old vote provision held unconstitutional in *Oregon* v. *Mitchell.*

One of the more troublesome aspects of procedure under the Voter Rights Act of 1965 has been the requirement of "preclearance" before any changes in the law affecting voting or elections can be effectuated by governmental units covered by the Act. In 1971 the Court decided *Perkins* v. *Matthews,* which illustrates the application of the Act to the decision of a Mississippi city to change the location of some of its polling places.

## PERKINS *v.* MATTHEWS
### *400 U.S. 379 (1971)*

[Section 5 of the Voting Rights Act of 1965 requires that changes in voting standards or procedures in those States covered by the Act receive prior approval from the District Court for the District of Columbia or be submitted to the Attorney General and receive no objection from him before becoming operative. The city of Canton, Mississippi, (1) changed the locations of certain polling places, (2) annexed adjacent areas, thereby enlarging the number of eligible voters, and (3) changed from ward to at-large election of aldermen, all without following the prior submission procedures outlined in the Voting Rights Act. Certain voters and candidates for election to city offices filed an action in federal court to enjoin the city elections, on the ground that the Act had been violated by instituting the electoral changes without a judgment that such changes did not have a discriminatory purpose or effect. Pending the convening of a three-judge court, a single judge issued a temporary restraining order. The three-judge court, after hearing, dissolved the injunction and dismissed the complaint. The elections were then held in October, 1969, with the challenged changes in effect. The case was heard on direct appeal by the Supreme Court.]

Mr. Justice Brennan delivered the opinion of the Court. . . .

The three-judge court misconceived the permissible scope of its inquiry into appellant's allegations. . . . The inquiry should have been limited to the determination whether "a state requirement is covered by Sec. 5, but has not been subjected to the required federal scrutiny." . . . What is foreclosed to such district court is what Congress expressly reserved for consideration by the District Court of the District of Columbia or the Attorney General—the determination whether a covered change does or does not have the purpose or effect "of denying or abridging the right to vote on account of race or color." . . .

[The opinion then gives an examination of each of the three changes in electoral procedure and concludes that since there is a potential for racial discrimination in the purpose or effect of each change, they should have followed the approval procedures outlined in Section 5 of the Voting Rights Act.]

The appellants have urged that, in addition to reversing the District Court judgment, the Court should set aside the elections held in October, 1969, and order new elections held forthwith in which the changes challenged in this case may not be enforced. . . . Since the District Court is more familiar with the nuances of the local situation than are we, and has heard the evidence in this case, we think the question of the appropriate remedy is for that court to determine, in the first instance, after hearing the views of both parties.

The judgment of the District Court is reversed, and the case is remanded to that court with instructions to issue injunctions restraining the further enforcement of the changes until such time as the appellees adequately demonstrate compliance with Sec. 5, and for further proceedings consistent with this opinion.

*It is so ordered.*

Mr. Justice Blackmun with whom the Chief Justice joins, concurring. . . .

Mr. Justice Harlan, concurring in part and dissenting in part.

Our role in this case, as the Court correctly recognizes, is limited to determination whether Sec. 5 of the Voting Rights Act of 1965 . . . required the city of Canton to obtain federal approval of the way it proposed to run its 1969 elections. For this reason, I am unable to join the dissenting opinion of Mr. Justice Black, . . . although like him I see little likelihood that the changes here involved had a discriminatory purpose or effect.

I agree with the Court, and for substantially the reasons it gives, that the city should have submitted the relocation of polling places for federal approval. But I cannot agree that it was obliged to follow that course with respect to the other two matters here at issue.

. . . Section 5 requires submission of changes "with respect to voting" only.

The Court seems to interpret this restriction as including any change in state law which has an effect on voting, if changes of that type have "a potential for racial discrimination in voting." . . . At least in the absence of a contrary administrative interpretation, I would not go beyond *Allen* [v. *State Board of Elections*] to hold that annexations are within the scope of Sec. 5. The Court's assertion that the Attorney General does in fact interpret the Act differently seems to me to give too much weight to the passing remark of an Assistant Attorney General. [The opinion here points out that there were over forty municipal annexations in South Carolina in 1967–1968 and over one hundred boundary changes in Georgia cities in 1965–1969, only one of which was submitted to the Attorney General.]

I must confess that I am somewhat mystified by the Court's discussion of the appropriate remedy in this case. . . . I would direct the holding of new elections if and only if the city fails to obtain approval from the appropriate federal officials within a reasonable time. . . . In any event, the District Court is entitled to more guidance on this score than the Court provides.

Mr. Justice Black dissenting.

In *South Carolina* v. *Katzenbach* . . . I dissented vigorously from the majority's conclusion that every part of Sec. 5 of the Voting Rights Act was constitutional. The fears which precipitated my dissent in *Katzenbach* have been fully realized in this case. The majority, relying on *Katzenbach,* now actually holds that the City of Canton, Mississippi, a little town of 10,000 persons, cannot change four polling places for its election of aldermen without obtaining federal approval. . . .

The city altered four of the local polling places. Two were moved because the old polling places had been located on private property and the owners would no longer consent to the use of their property for voting. I find it incredible to believe that Congress intended that the people of Canton would have to travel to Washington to get the Attorney General's consent to rent new polling places. Another polling place was moved because the old one did not have sufficient space to accommodate voting machines. Finally, the fourth place was moved from a courthouse to a public school to eliminate interference with courtroom proceedings. It is difficult for me to imagine a matter more peculiarly and exclusively fit for local determination than the location of polling places for the election of town aldermen. Nor is there the slightest indication that any of these changes were motivated by or resulted in racial discrimination. . . . Presumably, the majority is ready to hold, if necessary, that the City of Canton could not change from ballots to voting machines without obtaining similar federal approval. I dissent from any such utter degradation of the power of the States to govern their own affairs. . . .

. . . It is beyond my comprehension how the change from wards to an at-large election can discriminate against Negroes on account of their race in a city that has an absolute majority of Negro voters. . . .

This Act attempts to reverse the proper order of things. Now the Congress presumes—a presumption which the Court upholds—that statutes regulating voting are discriminatory and enjoins their enforcement until the State can convince distant federal judges or politically appointed officials that the statute is not discriminatory. This permits the Federal Government to suspend the effectiveness or enforcement of a state act *before* discrimination is proved. But I think the Federal Government is without power to suspend a state statute before discrimination is proved. The inevitable effect of such a reversal of roles is what has happened in this case—a nondiscriminatory state practice or statute is voided wholly without constitutional authority.

Except as applied to a few southern States in a renewed spirit of Reconstruction, the people of this country would never stand for such a perversion of the separation of authority between state and federal governments. Never would New York or California be required to come begging to the City of Washington before they could enforce the valid enactments of their own legislatures. Never would this law have emerged from congressional committees had it applied to the entire United States. Our people are more jealous of their own local governments than to permit such a bold seizure of their authority.

Finally, I dissent from the remedy adopted by the Court. . . . I am convinced that if the majority were to confront the issue of an appropriate remedy now, the Court would not void the election or compel the city to hold a new election. To the contrary, the 1969 election would be upheld because the alleged violations of the Act are so very minor and so clearly technical. We should not forget that while it is easy for judges to order new elections, it will be neither easy nor inexpensive for the little city of Canton to comply with such an order. . . .

Even before the passage of the Voting Rights of 1965, the Court had invalidated an Alabama law redrawing a city's boundaries on the ground that the law had a racially discriminatory effect in violation of the Fifteenth Amendment. The statute had reduced the corporate limits of the City of Tuskegee, which had formerly been predominantly black, to exclude virtually all blacks without removing a single white resident. The Court unanimously found that the law clearly was designed to accomplish the unconstitutional purpose of disfranchising black voters. *Gomillion* v. *Lightfoot,* 364 U.S. 339 (1960).

In *Perkins* v. *Matthews* the Court held that annexation of additional territory was subject to the requirements of §5 of the Voting Rights Act. In a rather complicated fact situation involving annexation by the city of Richmond, Virginia, *City of Richmond* v. *United States,* 422 U.S. 358 (1975), the Court addressed the problem of whether adverse racial impact of annexation constituted per se a violation of the Act. In 1969 a Virginia court approved Richmond's annexation of an adjacent area in Chesterfield County, which reduced the proportion of Negroes in Richmond from 52% to 42%. Before and immediately after annexation, the city had a nine-man council, which was elected at large. In 1968, three candidates endorsed by a black civic organization, were elected to the council. In the post-annexation, at-large election in 1970, three of the nine members elected had also received the endorsement of the organization. Following the decision in *Perkins* that §5 of the Act applied to annexations, the city sought the approval of the Attorney General for the annexation, but he declined on the ground that black voting had been diluted. Meanwhile, Holt, a black resident, sued in a federal district court in Virginia alleging that the annexation was unconstitutional. The District Court so ruled and ordered a new election for the city council, seven councilmen to be elected at large from the old city and two primarily from the annexed area. A Court of Appeals reversed, finding no violation of the Fifteenth Amendment. Holt then filed another suit, this time seeking to have the annexation declared invalid under §5 for failure to have secured approval of either the Attorney General or the District Court for the District of Columbia. Based on the Court of Appeals decision in Holt I, the city again asked the Attorney General for approval. Receiving no response from the Attorney General, the city filed suit in the District Court for the District of Columbia seeking approval of the annexation and relying on the Fourth Circuit's decision in Holt I. Shortly after the suit was filed, however, that court held invalid another annexation in Virginia where council elections were held at large but indicated approval if the city modified its elections by the adoption of a ward system to reduce the adverse racial impact that at-large elections would have on blacks. The Supreme Court affirmed in *City of Petersburg v. United States,* 410 U.S. 962 (1973). After the *Petersburg* decision, Richmond and the Attorney General agreed to an amendment of the city's electoral scheme that would partition the city into nine wards, four with substantial black majorities, four with substantial white majorities, and one ward with a 59% white, 41% black division. The District Court held, nonetheless, that the annexation diluted the voting power of blacks but left the matter of fashioning a remedy to await an appeal to the Supreme Court. The City of Richmond appealed. The Court held that an annexation reducing the relative political strength of the minority race in the enlarged city as compared with their pre-annexation status does not violate §5 of the Act so long as Negroes are not underrepresented in the new council. Justice White, for the majority, stated:

As long as this is true, we cannot hold that the effect of the annexation is to deny or abridge the right to vote. To hold otherwise would be either to forbid all such annexations or to require, as the price for approval of the annexation, that the black community be assigned the same proportion of council seats as before, hence perhaps permanently overrepresenting them and underrepresenting other elements in the community, including the nonblack citizens in the annexed area. We are unwilling to hold that Congress intended either consequence in enacting §5.

The majority remanded the case, however, concluding that it was not clear from the findings of the Special Master and the District Court whether the decision to annex was based on "objectively verifiable, legitimate reasons for the annexation" or whether it was primarily dictated for the purpose of discriminating against Negroes on account of their race.

In 1975 Congress extended the Voting Rights Act for an additional seven years and made the ban on literacy tests permanent. It also extended the coverage to include areas in twenty-four states where foreign languages were spoken by large numbers of voters. The Act required bilingual voting information and also federal enforcement personnel in some areas.

*City of Mobile v. Bolden,* 446 U.S. 55 (1980), involved an attack on the city's electoral scheme under which a three-member city commission was elected at large. Although the population of the city was 40% black, no black had ever been elected to the commission. A District Court held the system to be racially discriminatory and ordered the city to change to a mayor-council form of government. The Supreme Court reversed and remanded, although there was no majority opinion. A four-justice plurality held that the "ultimate question" was whether a discriminatory purpose or intent had been proved, and that the mere existence of at-large elections was insufficient to establish that proof. Further, "the Equal Protection Clause of the Fourteenth Amendment does not require proportional representation as an imperative of political organization." The case was remanded, however, for a determination of whether in fact there was purposeful discrimination in the operation of the electoral system.

In *Rogers* v. *Lodge*, 458 U.S. 613 (1982), however, the Court upheld a District Court finding that the at-large election scheme for choosing members of a county's Board of Commissioners was maintained for invidious racial purposes, despite the fact that blacks constituted a majority in the county. While blacks made up a substantial majority of the population, they were a minority of the registered voters. The District Court found that past discrimination had restricted their opportunity to participate effectively in the political process, and although the state policy behind the at-large electoral system was "neutral in origin," the policy was being maintained for invidious purposes in violation of the Constitution. The Supreme Court reiterated its *Bolden* position that at-large elections were not per se unconstitutional and that discriminatory intent had to be proved, but affirmed the finding of the lower courts on the ground that they did not appear to be clearly erroneous. It also affirmed the relief ordered—that the county be divided into five single-member districts for the purpose of electing county commissioners. Three justices dissented on the ground that the subjective evidence used by the District Court was not a valid criterion for constitutional adjudication.

In 1982 the Voting Rights Act was extended again, this time for twenty-five years. It also contained two important amendments. First, it added a new "bail out" provision to allow not only States but also "any political subdivision of such State" (covered by the Act) to free itself from the preclearance requirements if it could demonstrate to a three-judge panel in the District Court of the District of Columbia that it had maintained a clean record on voting rights for ten years. The Act sets out the type of proof required: no objections by the Attorney General to any submission, elimination of all voting procedures inhibiting or diluting equal access to the political process, constructive efforts to bring minorities into the political process, and no federal examiners assigned to the governmental unit. This provision resulted from objections to the decision in *City of Rome* v. *United States*, 446 U.S. 156 (1980), holding that the preclearance provisions still applied to a city that had been free of any signs of voting discrimination for at least seventeen years, since only States, and not political subdivisions, could utilize the "bail out" provisions of the earlier act.

A second amendment made it clear that §5 of the Act applied to any voting standard or practice or procedure that *results* in a denial or abridgment of the right of any citizen to vote on account of race or color. And a violation of that section is established if it is shown that the political processes leading to nomination or election are not equally open to participation by members of the class of citizens protected by the Act. This section did, however, add the proviso that "nothing in this section establishes a right to have members of a protected class elected in numbers equal to their proportion in the population."

Actually, the 1965 Act itself provided that the Attorney General could preclear a voting practice only if it "does not have the purpose and will not have the effect of denying or abridging the right to vote on account of race or color." Thus a voting practice could not be precleared unless both discriminatory purpose and effect were absent. This was clearly stated by the majority in the *Rome* case in discussing the City's application for preclearance of several annexation proposals. *Mobile* v. *Bolden* was decided on the same day and the plurality stressed the necessity of proving discriminatory purpose only. But that case was brought under the Fifteenth Amendment rather than the 1965 Act, and some members differentiated between the coverage of the two.

In *City of Pleasant Grove* v. *United States,* 55 LW 4133 (1987), the Court denied relief to the City which had unsuccessfully sought preclearance from the Attorney General for the annexation of two parcels of land, one vacant and the other inhabited by a few whites. According to the District Court, the City had "a long history of racial discrimination." Out of a population of some 7,000 there were only thirty-two black inhabitants, all of them residents of a nursing home. One area to be annexed was a 40-acre parcel containing one white family. The other was an uninhabited 45-acre parcel. The City had refused to annex a third area that contained black residents. The City argued that the annexations would have no effect on black voting in the city, since there were no black citizens registered to vote, either in the city or in the proposed areas for annexation. The District Court found that the refusal to annex the third area was racially motivated, and the City's plans for the uninhabited area, for relatively expensive housing, "indicate that it is likely to be developed for use by white persons only." It concluded that the City had failed to carry the burden of proving that the two annexations at issue did not have the purpose of denying the right to vote on account of race. In a 6–3 vote, the Court affirmed, holding that in light of the record, the District Court's findings were not clearly erroneous.

Justice Powell, joined by the Chief Justice and Justice O'Connor, dissented. He stated that the Court affirms the decision of the District Court that a city can act with a purpose to deny or abridge black voting rights "even when the city's actions can have no present effect on the voting rights of any black individual and any future effect on black voting rights is purely speculative. Because the Court's finding of a violation of the Voting Rights Act is inconsistent with the language and purpose of the Act, I dissent."

[On the application of the 1965 Act prior to the 1982 amendments, see Gayle Binion, "The Implementation of Section 5 of the 1965 Voting Rights Act," 32 *Western Political Quarterly* 154 (1979) and Howard Ball, Dale Krane, and Thomas P. Lauth, *Compromised Compliance: Implementation of the 1965 Voting Rights Act* (Westport, Conn.: Greenwood Press, 1982).]

# CHAPTER 8

# *The Right of Privacy*

When the Constitution and the Bill of Rights were ratified, neither statutes nor common-law rules established a right of privacy as such. And certainly there was no constitutional provision which clearly provided a vehicle for its inclusion. The common law with regard to trespass, assault, slander and libel, and even nuisance (as applied to offensive noises and odors, for example) could be said to have tangential reference to privacy, but this would offer a piecemeal approach rather than an argument based on a full-fledged right of privacy.

The development of the law of privacy can be said to have originated with a law review article by Samuel D. Warren and Louis D. Brandeis, "The Right of Privacy," published in 1890 in the *Harvard Law Review* (4 *Harv. L. Rev.* 193). Out of a few fragments of the common law, the authors invented a brand new tort, the invasion of privacy. Dean Roscoe Pound reportedly said that the article did nothing less than add a chapter to the law. In the years following the publication of the article, a law of privacy gradually developed by statute and by common-law decisions in state courts. [For an excellent history of these developments, see Morris L. Ernst and Alan U. Schwartz, *Privacy: The Right to Be Let Alone* (New York: Macmillan, 1962).] But it was not until 1965 that the Supreme Court squarely held that the Constitution contained at least a limited right to privacy.

### GRISWOLD *v.* CONNECTICUT
### *381 U.S. 479 (1965)*

[Connecticut statutes prohibited the use of contraceptive devices and also provided punishment for anyone giving information or instruction on the use of such devices. Appellant Griswold was Executive Director of the Planned Parenthood League of Connecticut. Appellant Buxton was a licensed physician and a professor at the Yale Medical School and served as Medical Director for the League at its Center in New Haven. They gave instruction and medical advice to married persons as to the means of preventing conception and were convicted of violation of the law and fined $100.]

Mr. Justice Douglas delivered the opinion of the Court. . . .

. . . We do not sit as a super-legislature to determine the wisdom, need, and propriety of laws that touch economic problems, business affairs, or social conditions. This law, however, operates directly on an intimate relation of husband and wife and their physician's role in one aspect of that relation.

The association of people is not mentioned in the Constitution nor in the Bill of Rights. The right to educate a child in a school of the parents' choice—whether public or private or parochial—is also not mentioned. Nor is the right to study any particular subject or any foreign language. Yet the First Amendment has been construed to include certain of those rights.

[Here the opinion cites a number of cases expanding the application of the First Amendment.]

The foregoing cases suggest that specific guarantees in the Bill of Rights have penumbras, formed by emanations from those guarantees that help give them life and substance. . . . Various guarantees create zones of privacy. The right of association contained in the penumbra of the First Amendment is one, as we have seen. The Third Amendment in its prohibition against the quartering of soldiers "in any house" in time of peace without the consent of the owner is another facet of that privacy. The Fourth Amendment explicitly affirms the "right of the people to be secure in their persons, houses, papers, and effects, against unreasonable searches and seizures." The Fifth Amendment in its Self-Incrimination Clause enables the citizen to create a zone of privacy which government may not force him to surrender to his detriment. The Ninth Amendment provides: "The enumeration in the Constitution, of certain rights, shall not be construed to deny or disparage others retained by the people."

The Fourth and Fifth Amendments were described in *Boyd* v. *United States* . . . as protection against all governmental invasions "of the sanctity of a man's home and the privacies of life." We recently referred in *Mapp* v. *Ohio* . . . to the Fourth Amendment as creating a "right to privacy, no less important than any other right carefully and particularly reserved to the people." See Beaney, The Constitutional Right to Privacy, 1962 Sup. Ct. Rev. 212; Griswold, The Right to Be Let Alone, 55 Nw U.L. Rev. 216 (1960). . . .

The present case, then, concerns a relationship lying within the zone of privacy created by several fundamental constitutional guarantees. And it concerns a law which, in forbidding the *use* of contraceptives rather than regulating their manufacture or sale, seeks to achieve its goals by means having a maximum destructive impact upon that relationship. Such a law cannot stand in light of the familiar principle, so often applied by this Court, that a "governmental purpose to control or prevent activities constitutionally subject to state regulation may not be achieved by means which sweep unnecessarily broadly and thereby invade the area of protected freedoms." *NAACP* v. *Alabama*. . . . Would we allow the police to search the sacred precincts of marital bedrooms for telltale signs of the use of contraceptives? The very idea is repulsive to the notions of privacy surrounding the marriage relationship.

We deal with a right of privacy older than the Bill of Rights—older than our political parties, older than our school system. Marriage is a coming together for better or for worse, hopefully enduring, and intimate to the degree of being sacred. It is an association that promotes a way of life, not causes; a harmony in living, not political faiths; a bilateral loyalty, not commercial or social projects. Yet it is an association for as noble a purpose as any involved in our prior decisions.

*Reversed.*

Mr. Justice Goldberg, whom the Chief Justice and Mr. Justice Brennan join, concurring. . . .

This Court, in a series of decisions, has held that the Fourteenth Amendment absorbs and applies to the States those specifics of the first eight amendments which express fundamental personal rights. The language and history of the Ninth Amendment reveal that the Framers of the Constitution believed that there are additional fundamental rights, protected from governmental infringement, which exist alongside those fundamental rights specifically mentioned in the first eight constitutional amendments.

The Ninth Amendment reads, "The enumeration in the Constitution, of certain rights, shall not be construed to deny or disparage others retained by the people." . . . It was proffered to quiet expressed fears that a bill of specifically enumerated rights could not be sufficiently broad to cover all essential rights and that the specific mention of certain rights would be interpreted as a denial that others were protected. . . .

. . . The Ninth Amendment to the Constitution may be regarded by some as a recent discovery but since 1791 it has been a basic part of the Constitution which we are sworn to uphold. To hold that a right so basic and fundamental and so deep-rooted in our society as the right of privacy in marriage may be infringed because that right is not guaranteed in so many words by the first eight amendments to the Constitution is to ignore the Ninth Amendment and to give it no effect whatsoever. Moreover, a judicial construction that this fundamental right is not protected by the Constitution because it is not mentioned in explicit terms by one of the first eight amendments or elsewhere in the Constitution would violate the Ninth Amendment, which specifically states that "[t]he enumeration in the Constitution, of certain rights shall not be *construed* to deny or disparage others retained by the people." (Emphasis added.) . . .

. . . The State, at most, argues that there is some rational relation between this statute and what is admittedly a legitimate subject of state concern—the discouraging of extra-marital relations. It says that preventing the use of birth-control devices by married persons helps prevent the indulgence by some in such extra-marital relations. The rationality of this justification is dubious, particularly in light of the admitted widespread availability to all persons in the State of Connecticut, unmarried as well as married, of birth-control devices for the prevention of disease, as distinguished from the prevention of conception. . . . But, in any event, it is clear that the state interest in safeguarding marital fidelity can be served by a more discriminately tailored statute, which does not, like the present one, sweep unnecessarily broadly, reaching far beyond the evil sought to be dealt with and intruding upon the privacy of all married couples. . . .

In sum, I believe that the right of privacy in the marital relation is fundamental and basic—a personal right "retained by the people" within the meaning of the Ninth Amendment. Connecticut cannot constitutionally abridge this fundamental right, which is protected by the Fourteenth Amendment from infringement by the States. I agree with the Court that petitioners' convictions must therefore be reversed.

Mr. Justice Harlan, concurring in the judgment. . . .

Mr. Justice White, concurring in the judgment. . . .

Mr. Justice Black, with whom Mr. Justice Stewart joins, dissenting.

I agree with my Brother Stewart's dissenting opinion. And like him I do not to any extent whatever base my view that this Connecticut law is constitutional on a belief that the law is wise or that its policy is a good one. In order that there may be no room at all to doubt why I vote as I do, I feel constrained to add that the law is every bit as offensive to me as it is to my Brethren of the majority and my Brothers Harlan, White and Goldberg who, reciting reasons why it is offensive to them, hold it unconstitutional. . . .

. . . I get nowhere in this case by talk about a constitutional "right of privacy" as an emanation from one or more constitutional provisions. I like my privacy as well as the next one, but I am nevertheless compelled to admit that government has a right to invade it unless prohibited by some specific constitutional provision. For these reasons I cannot agree with the Court's judgment and the reasons it gives for holding this Connecticut law unconstitutional. . . .

My Brother Goldberg has adopted the recent discovery that the Ninth Amendment as well as the Due Process Clause can be used by this Court as authority to strike down all state legislation which this Court thinks violates "fundamental principles of liberty and justice," or is contrary to the "traditions and [collective] con-science of our people." He also states, without proof satisfactory to me, that in making decisions on this basis judges will not consider "their personal and private notions." One may ask how they can avoid considering them. Our Court certainly has no machinery with which to take a Gallup Poll. And the scientific miracles of this age have not yet produced a gadget which the Court can use to determine what tradi-tions are rooted in the "[collective] conscience of our people." . . .

I realize that many good and able men have eloquently spoken and written, some-times in rhapsodical strains, about the duty of this Court to keep the Constitution in tune with the times. The idea is that the Constitution must be changed from time to time and that this Court is charged with a duty to make those changes. For myself, I must with all deference reject that philosophy. The Constitution makers knew the need for change and provided for it. Amendments suggested by the people's elected representatives can be submitted to the people or their selected agents for ratifica-tion. That method of change was good for our Fathers, and being somewhat old-fashioned I must add it is good enough for me. And so, I cannot rely on the Due Process Clause or the Ninth Amendment or any mysterious and uncertain natural law concept as a reason for striking down this state law. . . .

Mr. Justice Stewart, whom Mr. Justice Black joins, dissenting. . . .

In *Eisenstadt* v. *Baird,* 405 U.S. 438 (1972), the Court held unconstitutional a Massa-chusetts law that made it a felony to provide anyone other than a married person con-traceptive devices, and even then such distribution was to be made only through a registered pharmacist or by a licensed physician. The decision came off as a violation of the Equal Protection Clause, but *Griswold* and privacy interests were also cited. "If the right of privacy means anything, it is the right of the *individual,* married or single, to be free from unwarranted governmental intrusion into matters so fundamentally affecting a person as the decision whether to bear or beget a child."

An extension of the "right to privacy" argument was successfully employed in the controversial abortion cases in 1973, in which the Court held unconstitutional the Texas and Georgia statutes which severely restricted the right of pregnant women to have le-gal abortions. The Texas case was *Roe* v. *Wade* and is illustrative of the reasoning in both cases.

ROE *v.* WADE
*410 U.S. 113 (1973)*

[A pregnant single woman (Roe) brought a class action challenging the constitu-tionality of the Texas criminal abortion laws, which prohibit procuring or attempt-ing an abortion except on medical advice for the purpose of saving the mother's life. A licensed physician (Hallford), who had two state abortion prosecutions pending against him, was permitted to intervene in the class action. A separate action was filed by a married, childless couple, who alleged that if the wife became pregnant at some future date, they would wish to have an abortion. A three-judge District Court held that Roe and Hallford had standing to sue, but that the married, childless couple did not. As to the statutes, the court held them unconstitutionally vague and over-broad and issued a declaratory judgment so holding. In the Supreme Court the ma-jority agreed that Roe had standing to sue. It was contended that Roe's claim was moot because her pregnancy had been terminated. The majority opinion stated: "If that termination makes a case moot, pregnancy litigation seldom will survive much beyond the trial stage, and appellate review will be effectively denied. . . . Preg-nancy provides a classic justification for a conclusion of nonmootness."]

Mr. Justice Blackmun delivered the opinion of the Court. . . .

The principal thrust of appellant's attack on the Texas statutes is that they improperly invade a right, said to be possessed by the pregnant woman, to choose to terminate her pregnancy. Appellant would discover this right in the concept of personal "liberty" embodied in the Fourteenth Amendment's Due Process Clause; or in personal, marital, familial, and sexual privacy said to be protected by the Bill of Rights or its penumbras, see *Griswold* v. *Connecticut*, . . . ; or among those rights reserved to the people by the Ninth Amendment. . . .

It is perhaps not generally appreciated that the restrictive criminal abortion laws in effect in a majority of States today are of relatively recent vintage. Those laws, generally proscribing abortion or its attempt at any time during pregnancy except when necessary to preseve the pregnant woman's life, are not of ancient or even of common law origin. Instead, they derive from statutory changes effected, for the most part, in the latter half of the 19th century. . . .

It is undisputed that at the common law, abortion performed *before* "quickening"—the first recognizable movement of the fetus in utero, appearing usually from the 16th to the 18th week of pregnancy—was not an indictable offense. . . .

Whether abortion of a *quick* fetus was a felony at common law, or even a lesser crime, is still disputed. Bracton, writing early in the 13th century, thought it homicide. But the later and predominant view, following the great common law scholars, has been that it was at most a lesser offense. . . .

England's first criminal abortion statute . . . came in 1803. It made abortion of a quick fetus, §1, a capital crime, but in §2 it provided lesser penalties for the felony of abortion before quickening, and thus preserved the quickening distinction. . . .

Three reasons have been advanced to explain historically the enactment of criminal abortion laws in the 19th century and to justify their continued existence.

It has been argued occasionally that these laws were the product of a Victorian social concern to discourage illict sexual conduct. . . . The appellants and amici contend . . . that this is not a proper state purpose at all and suggest that, if it were, the Texas statutes are overbroad in protecting it since the law fails to distinguish between married and unwed mothers.

A second reason is concerned with abortion as a medical procedure. When most criminal abortion laws were first enacted, the procedure was a hazardous one for the woman. This was particulary true prior to the development of antisepsis. . . . Thus it has been argued that a State's real concern in enacting a criminal abortion law was to protect the pregnant woman, that is, to restrain her from submitting to a procedure that placed her life in serious jeopardy.

Modern medical techniques have altered this situation. Appellants and various amici refer to medical data indicating that abortion in early pregnancy, that is, prior to the end of first trimester, although not without its risk, is now relatively safe. . . .

The third reason is the State's interest—some phrase it in terms of duty—in protecting prenatal life. Some of the argument for this justification rests on the theory that a new human life is present from the moment of conception. The State's interest and general obligation to protect life then extends, it is argued, to prenatal life. Only when the life of the pregnant mother herself is at stake, balanced against the life she carries within her, should the interest of the embryo or fetus not prevail. . . .

Parties challenging state abortion laws have sharply disputed in some courts the contention that a purpose of these laws, when enacted, was to protect prenatal life. Pointing to the absence of legislative history to support the contention, they claim that most state laws were designed solely to protect the woman. . . . They claim that adoption of the "quickening" distinction through received common law and state statutes tacitly recognizes the greater health hazards inherent in late abortion and impliedly repudiates the theory that life begins at conception.

It is with these interests, and the weight to be attached to them, that this case is concerned.

The Constitution does not explicitly mention any right of privacy. In a line of decisions, however, going back perhaps as far as . . . [1891], the Court has recognized that a right of personal privacy, or a guarantee of certain areas or zones of privacy, does exist under the Constitution. In varying contexts the Court or individual Justices have indeed found at least the roots of that right in the First Amendment . . . ; in the Fourth and Fifth Amendments . . . ; in the penumbras of the Bill of Rights . . . ; in the Ninth Amendment . . . ; or in the concept of liberty guaranteed by the first section of the Fourteenth Amendment. . . . These decisions make it clear that only personal rights that can be deemed "fundamental" or "implicit in the concept of ordered liberty" . . . are included in this guarantee of personal privacy. They also make it clear that the right has some extension to activities relating to marriage . . . , procreation, . . . family relationships . . . , and child rearing and education. . . .

This right of privacy, whether it be founded in the Fourteenth Amendment's concept of personal liberty and restrictions upon state action, as we feel it is, or as the District Court determined, in the Ninth Amendment's reservation of rights to the people, is broad enough to encompass a woman's decision whether or not to terminate her pregnancy. The detriment that the State would impose upon the pregnant woman by denying this choice is apparent. Specific and direct harm medically diagnosable even in early pregnancy may be involved. Maternity, or additional offspring, may force upon the woman a distressful life and future. Psychological harm may be imminent. Mental and physical health may be taxed by child care. There is also the distress, for all concerned, associated with the unwanted child, and there is the problem of bringing a child into a family already unable, psychologically and otherwise, to care for it. In other cases, as in this one, the additional difficulties and continuing stigma of unwed motherhood may be involved. All these are factors the woman and her responsible physician necessarily will consider in consultation.

On the basis of elements such as these, appellants and some amici argue that the woman's right is absolute and that she is entitled to terminate her pregnancy at whatever time, in whatever way, and for whatever reason she alone chooses. With this we do not agree. . . . The Court's decisions recognizing a right of privacy also acknowledge that some state regulation in areas protected by that right is appropriate. As noted above, a state may properly assert important interests in safeguarding health, in maintaining medical standards, and in protecting potential life. . . . The privacy right involved, therefore, cannot be said to be absolute. . . .

We therefore conclude that the right of personal privacy includes the abortion decision, but that this right is not unqualified and must be considered against important state interests in regulation. . . .

The appellee and certain *amici* argue that the fetus is a "person" within the language and meaning of the Fourteenth Amendment. In support of this they outline at length and in detail the well-known facts of fetal development. If this suggestion of personhood is established, the appellant's case, of course, collapses, for the fetus' right to life is then guaranteed specifically by the Amendment. The appellant conceded as much on reargument. On the other hand, the appellee conceded on reargument that no case could be cited that holds that a fetus is a person within the meaning of the Fourteenth Amendment.

The Constitution does not define "person" in so many words. . . . None [of the references to "person" in the various clauses] indicates, with any assurance, that it has any possible prenatal application.

All this, together with our observation, supra, that throughout the major portion of the 19th century prevailing legal abortion practices were far freer than they are today, persuades us that the word "person" as used in the Fourteenth Amendment, does not include the unborn. . . .

This conclusion, however, does not of itself fully answer the contentions raised by Texas, and we pass on to other considerations. . . .

With respect to the State's important and legitimate interest in the health of the mother, the "compelling" point, in the light of present medical knowledge, is at approximately the end of the first trimester. This is so because of the now established medical fact . . . that until the end of the first trimester mortality in abortion is less than mortality in normal childbirth. It follows that, from and after this point, a State may regulate the abortion procedure to the extent that the regulation reasonably relates to the preservation and protection of maternal health. Examples of permissible state regulation in this area are requirements as to the qualifications of the person who is to perform the abortion; as to the licensure of that person; as to the facility in which the procedure is to be performed, that is, whether it must be a hospital or may be a clinic or some other place of less-than-hospital status; as to the licensing of the facility; and the like. . . .

With respect to the State's important and legitimate interest in potential life, the "compelling" point is at viability. This is so because the fetus then presumably has the capability of meaningful life outside the mother's womb. State regulation protective of fetal life after viability thus has both logical and biological justifications. If the State is interested in protecting fetal life after viability, it may go so far as to proscribe abortion during that period except when it is necessary to preserve the life or health of the mother. . . .

To summarize and to repeat:

1. A state criminal abortion statute of the current Texas type, that excepts from criminality only a *life saving* procedure on behalf of the mother, without regard to pregnancy stage and without recognition of the other interests involved, is violative of the Due Process Clause of the Fourteenth Amendment.

(a) For the stage prior to approximately the end of the first trimester, the abortion decision and its effectuation must be left to the medical judgment of the pregnant woman's attending physician.

(b) For the stage subsequent to approximately the end of the first trimester, the State, in promoting its interest in the health of the mother, may, if it chooses, regulate the abortion procedure in ways that are reasonably related to maternal health.

(c) For the stage subsequent to viability the State, in promoting its interest in the potentiality of human life, may, if it chooses, regulate, and even proscribe, abortion except where it is necessary, in appropriate medical judgment, for the preservation of the life or health of the mother.

2. The State may define the term "physician," as it has been employed in . . . this opinion, to mean only a physician currently licensed by the State, and may proscribe any abortion by a person who is not a physician as so defined. . . .

Mr. Chief Justice Burger, concurring. . . .

Mr. Justice Douglas, concurring. . . .

Mr. Justice Stewart, concurring. . . .

Mr. Justice White, with whom Mr. Justice Rehnquist joins, dissenting. . . .

With all due respect, I dissent. I find nothing in the language or history of the Constitution to support the Court's judgment. The Court simply fashions and announces a new constitutional right for pregnant mothers and, with scarcely any reason or authority for its action, invests that right with sufficient substance to override most existing state abortion statutes. The upshot is that the people and the legislatures of the 50 States are constitutionally disentitled to weigh the relative importance of the continued existence and development of the fetus on the one hand against a spectrum of possible impacts on the mother on the other hand. As an exercise of raw judicial power, the Court perhaps has authority to do what it does today; but in my view its judgment is an improvident and extravagant exercise of the power of judicial review which the Constitution extends to this Court.

The Court apparently values the convenience of the pregnant mother more than the continued existence and development of the life or potential life which she carries. Whether or not I might agree with that marshalling of values, I can in no event join the Court's judgment because I find no constitutional warrant for imposing such an order of priorities on the people and legislatures of the States. . . .

Mr. Justice Rehnquist, dissenting. . . .

In *Planned Parenthood of Central Missouri* v. *Danforth*, 428 U.S. 52 (1976), the Court held unconstitutional a section of Missouri's abortion law which required the husband's consent before permitting abortion and a section which required one parent's consent as a condition for an unmarried minor's abortion. As to the spouse's consent, the opinion stated that the requirement did not comport with the standards enunciated in *Roe* v. *Wade*, since the State cannot "delegate to a spouse a veto power which the state itself is absolutely and totally prohibited from exercising during the first trimester of pregnancy." On the requirement of parental consent, the opinion stated, "Just as with the requirement of consent from the spouse, so here, the State does not have the constitutional authority to give a third party an absolute, and possibly arbitrary, veto over the decision of the physician and his patient to terminate the patient's pregnancy, regardless of the reason for withholding the consent." The opinion stated further that any independent interest the parent may have in the termination of the minor daughter's pregnancy "is no more weighty than the right of privacy of the competent minor mature enough to have become pregnant."

The Court did uphold, however, the provision of the Missouri law which required that the woman submitting to abortion must consent in writing to the procedure and certify that "her consent is informed and freely given and is not the result of coercion."

*Carey* v. *Population Services International*, 431 U.S. 678 (1977) held unconstitutional a New York statute which made it a crime (1) to sell or distribute any contraceptive to a minor under the age of 16 years, (2) for anyone other than a licensed pharmacist to distribute contraceptives to persons over 16, and (3) to advertise or display contraceptives. As to the section on sale to minors, Justice Brennan, for the plurality, stated:

Since the State may not impose a blanket prohibition, or even a blanket requirement of parental consent, on the choice of a minor to terminate her pregnancy, the constitutionality of a blanket prohibition of the distribution of contraceptives to minors is *a fortiori* foreclosed. The State's interest in protection of the mental and physical health of the pregnant minor, and in protection of potential life are clearly more implicated by the abortion decision than by the decision to use a nonhazardous contraceptive.

In *Bellotti* v. *Baird*, 443 U.S. 622 (1979), the Court held unconstitutional a Massachusetts law that required unmarried female minors who wished to get an abortion to obtain the consent of parents or guardians or, if they refused, an order from a superior court judge which could be obtained if good cause were shown. But in *H. L. v. Matheson*, 450 U.S. 398 (1981), a Utah statute that required a physician to notify the parents or guardian of a minor before performing an abortion was held constitutional. The Court held that the statute did not give parents a veto power over the minor's abortion decision. Further, as applied to immature and dependent minors, the statute served important considerations of family integrity and protecting adolescents, as well as providing an opportunity for parents to supply essential medical and other information to the physician.

In 1982 the Pennsylvania Abortion Control Act was passed as an effort to limit abortions. This omnibus statute contained numerous procedural requirements to be met before abortions could be performed: (1) the woman had to give her "informed consent," which required that she be given the name of the doctor, the "particular medical risks" of the abortion, the facts that there might be "detrimental physical and psychological effects," information on the availability of prenatal and postnatal care for the child, and printed material describing the fetus; (2) the printed materials to be available should include a description of the characteristics of an unborn child at "two-week gestational increments;" (3) the physician should report the identification of the performing and referring physicians, information as to the woman's residence, age, race, marital status, and number of prior pregnancies and the method of payment for the abortion, and these records would be available for public inspection without disclosure of the person filing the report; (4) a physician performing a post viability abortion would be required to attempt to preserve the life and health of any unborn child intended to be born unless it would endanger the pregnant woman's life or health; and (5) required that a second physician be present during an abortion performed when viability was possible, this physician to take all reasonable steps to preserve the child's life and health. In *Thornburgh v. American College of Obstetricians and Gynecologists*, 476 U.S. 747 (1986), the Court held the law unconstitutional. "The States are not free, under the guise of protecting maternal health or potential life, to intimidate women into continuing pregnancies. Appellants claim that the statutory provisions before us today further legitimate compelling interests of the Commonwealth. Close analysis of those provisions, however, shows that they wholly subordinate constitutional privacy interests and concerns with maternal health in an effort to deter a woman from making a decision that, with her physician, is hers to make."

In *Hartigan v. Zbaraz*, 56 LW 4053 (1987), the judgment of the Court of Appeals for the Seventh Circuit declaring unconstitutional an Illinois abortion statute that required unemancipated pregnant minors to wait 24 hours after notifying both parents of her decision to obtain an abortion was affirmed by an equally divided Court.

The argument has repeatedly been made that the constitutional right to privacy extends to all private sexual activity between consenting adults. Thus far the United States Supreme Court has refused to accept this extension. In *Doe v. Commonwealth's Attorney*, 425 U.S. 901 (1976), the Court affirmed a lower court decision upholding Virginia's law prohibiting consensual sodomy. The New York Court of Appeals, however, in *People v. Onofre*, 51 N.Y.2d 476, 415 N.E.2d 936 (1980), held unconstitutional a statute that makes consensual sodomy a crime. The majority opinion stated:

Personal feelings of distaste for the conduct sought to be proscribed . . . and even disapproval by a majority of the populace, if that disapproval were to be assumed, may not substitute for the required demonstration of a valid basis for intrusion by the State in an area of important personal decision protected under the right of privacy drawn from the United States Constitution. . . .

The majority found no threat, either to participants or the public in general, in consequence of the voluntary engagement by adults in "private, discreet, sodomous conduct."

In *Bowers* v. *Hardwick,* 478 U.S. 186 (1986), the Court by a 5–4 vote upheld a Georgia statute that made sodomy even between consenting persons a criminal offense. Justices Blackmun, Brennan, Marshall and Stevens dissented. Justice White, for the majority, stated:

> [R]espondent would have us announce, as the Court of Appeals did, a fundamental right to engage in homosexual sodomy. This we are quite unwilling to do. . . . [U]ntil 1961, all 50 States outlawed sodomy, and today, 24 States and the District of Columbia continue to provide criminal penalties for sodomy performed in private and between consenting adults. . . . Against this background, to claim that a right to engage in such conduct is "deeply rooted in this Nation's history and tradition" or "implicit in the concept of ordered liberty" is, at best, facetious.

Justice Blackmun, for the dissenters, stated that the majority's stress on homosexual conduct was misplaced, since the statute applied to heterosexual conduct as well. Further, he said:

> In a variety of circumstances we have recognized that a necessary corollary of giving individuals freedom to choose how to conduct their lives is acceptance of the fact that different individuals will make different choices. . . . The Court claims that its decision today merely refuses to recognize a fundamental right to engage in homosexual sodomy; what the Court really has refused to recognize is the fundamental interest all individuals have in controlling the nature of their intimate associations with others.
>
> The behavior for which Hardwick faces prosecution occurred in his own home, a place to which the Fourth Amendment attaches special significance. The Court's treatment of this aspect of the case is symptomatic of its overall refusal to consider the broad principles that have informed our treatment of privacy in specific cases.

Many States have had statutes prohibiting the publication of the names of victims of rape in order to protect such victims or their families from further humiliation and anguish. A Georgia law that made it a misdemeanor to publish or broadcast the identity of a rape victim was held unconstitutional in *Cox Broadcasting Corporation* v. *Cohn,* 420 U.S. 469 (1975), discussed earlier. The majority opinion stated that the "States may not impose sanctions for the publication of truthful information contained in official court records open to public inspection."

Similar statutes have been enacted prohibiting the publication of the names of juvenile offenders. In *Smith* v. *Daily Mail Publishing Co.,* 443 U.S. 97 (1979), the Court held such a statute unconstitutional, at least where, as here, there was no issue of unlawful press access to confidential judicial proceedings. Justice Rehnquist concurred in the judgment, but only because the West Virginia law involved in the case prohibited only newspapers from publishing juvenile offenders' names and did not bar broadcasting of the names by the electronic media.

*Cantrell* v. *Forest City Publishing Co.,* 419 U.S. 245 (1974), involved a suit for invasion of privacy, although in this case the suit was grounded on a claim of damages for false reporting. The *Cleveland Plain Dealer* published a news story concerning the collapse of a bridge across the Ohio River in which forty-three persons were killed, including the plaintiff's husband. Some months later, a reporter and photographer were sent to the Cantrell home to do a follow-up story. They talked with the Cantrell children while Mrs. Cantrell was away. The story contained several misstatements of fact, particularly regarding nonexistent conversations with Mrs. Cantrell concerning the family's poverty.

She sued, alleging mental distress and humiliation by the false statements in the article, which had made them objects of pity and ridicule. The jury awarded compensation based on a "false light" theory of invasion of privacy, finding that the story had been published while known to be false. The Sixth Circuit reversed, but the Supreme Court reversed that holding, stating that a publisher is vicariously liable for damages caused by its reporters' knowing falsehoods. The Court cited with approval the trial judge's charge to the jury, to the effect that liability could be imposed only if the jury concluded that the false statements in the article had been made with knowledge of their falsity or in reckless disregard of the truth, although it did not rule on whether a State might constitutionally apply a more relaxed standard of liability for a publisher of false statements injurious to a private individual under a false-light theory of invasion of privacy.

Several federal statutes have been passed to offer some degree of privacy for records maintained on individuals by private and governmental entities. Some of these go in two directions: first, by guaranteeing access to records in order to assure their accuracy and providing means for correcting errors, and second, by limiting disclosure without the individual's consent. The Privacy Act of 1974 was designed to cover records maintained by federal agencies and to permit the individual access to his records and to restrict disclosure to other persons except for specified exemptions. The Right to Financial Privacy Act of 1978 was designed to protect the confidentiality of customer records held by financial institutions. But the records may be released in response to administrative subpoenas, search warrants, judicial subpoenas, or formal written request from a government authority if "the request is authorized by regulations promulgated by the head of the agency or department," or if "there is reason to believe that the records sought are relevant to a legitimate law enforcement inquiry." This would seem to offer little more protection than did the Bank Secrecy Act of 1970 which actually required disclosure of bank records to the government rather than protecting their secrecy. It required banks to microfilm checks and to report currency transactions over $5,000 coming in or going out of the country. The implementing regulations required domestic financial institutions, with certain exemptions, to report each deposit, withdrawal, exchange of currency, or other payment or transfer "which involves a transaction in currency of more than $10,000." The Act was upheld in *California Bankers Assn.* v. *Shultz,* 416 U.S. 21 (1974).

Quite clearly a major aspect of the problems of privacy is that of searches conducted by public authority, and the validity of such searches under the Fourth Amendment has been treated in some detail in a previous chapter. Additional situations, however, may be noted here. The Privacy Protection Act of 1980 was designed to limit governmental search and seizure of documentary materials possessed by persons involved in the dissemination of communications to the public—employees of newspapers, publishers or broadcasters. The Act was a response to the decision by the Supreme Court in *Zurcher* v. *Stanford Daily,* 436 U.S. 537 (1978), in which the Court upheld a search by police, under a general warrant, of the files and desks of a student newspaper for photographs that might assist in the identification of participants in a campus riot. The Court refused to accept the argument that such a warrant was improper in the case of third parties who were not themselves suspected of criminal activity. The Act of 1980 prohibited a search for or seizure of "work product," and for other documents the Act required that the police first obtain a subpoena rather than a search warrant. This would insure that police would not rummage through the files of people preparing materials for publication, and those subject to the subpoena would have the opportunity to contest the government's need for the information. The exceptions to the prohibitions were (1) when authorities wanted a hostage note or other material whose seizure might prevent harm to a person, (2) when the journalist or writer was suspected of a crime, and (3) if there was reason to believe that the notice requirement of a subpoena would result in the destruction or concealment of the materials.

In a number of state court decisions and lower federal court cases the issue of the extent to which public school authorities may constitutionally search students, their lockers and their automobiles has been litigated. A case finally reached the United States Supreme Court for decision in 1985, although the holding in the case was fairly narrow, and further decisions will be necessary to fill out the matter of the Fourth Amendment's application to such students.

NEW JERSEY *v.* T. L. O.
*469 U.S. 325 (1985)*

[A teacher at a New Jersey high school, upon discovering T. L. O., then a 14-year-old freshman, and her companion smoking cigarettes in a school lavatory in violation of a school rule, took them to the Principal's office, where they met with Mr. Choplick, the Assistant Vice Principal. When T. L. O., in response to questioning, denied that she had been smoking and claimed that she did not smoke at all, Choplick demanded to see her purse. Upon opening the purse, he found a pack of cigarettes and also noticed a package of cigarette rolling papers that are commonly associated with the use of marihuana. He then proceeded to search the purse thoroughly and found some marihuana, a pipe, plastic bags, a fairly substantial amount of money, an index card containing a list of students who owed her money, and two letters that implicated her in marihuana dealing. Thereafter, the State brought delinquency charges against her in the Juvenile Court, which, after denying a motion to suppress the evidence found in the purse, held that the Fourth Amendment applied to searches by school officials but that the search in question was a reasonable one, and adjudged T. L. O. to be a delinquent. The New Jersey Supreme Court reversed, holding that the search violated the Fourth Amendment.]

Justice White delivered the opinion of the Court.

We granted certiorari in this case to examine the appropriateness of the exclusionary rule as a remedy for searches carried out in violation of the Fourth Amendment by public school authorities. Our consideration of the proper application of the Fourth Amendment to the public schools, however, has led us to conclude that the search that gave rise to the case now before us did not violate the Fourth Amendment. Accordingly, we here address only the questions of the proper standard for assessing the legality of searches conducted by public school officials and the application of that standard to the facts of this case. . . .

In determining whether the search at issue in this case violated the Fourth Amendment, we are faced initially with the question whether that Amendment's prohibition on unreasonable searches and seizures applies to searches conducted by public school officials. We hold that it does. . . .

To hold that the Fourth Amendment applies to searches conducted by school authorities is only to begin the inquiry into the standards governing such searches. Although the underlying command of the Fourth Amendment is always that searches and seizures be reasonable, what is reasonable depends on the context within which a search takes place. The determination of the standard of reasonableness governing any specific class of searches requires "balancing the need to search against the invasion which the search entails." *Camara* v. *Municipal Court* . . . On one side of the balance are arrayed the individual's legitimate expectations of privacy and personal security; on the other, the government's need for effective methods to deal with breaches of public order.

We have recognized that even a limited search of the person is a substantial invasion of privacy. . . . A search of a child's person or of a closed purse or other bag carried on her person,* no less than a similar search carried out on an adult, is undoubtedly a severe violation of subjective expectations of privacy. . . .

. . . [S]choolchildren may find it necessary to carry with them a variety of legitimate, noncontraband items, and there is no reason to conclude that they have necessarily waived all rights to privacy in such items merely by bringing them onto school grounds.

Against the child's interest in privacy must be set the substantial interest of teachers and administrators in maintaining discipline in the classroom and on schoolgrounds. Maintaining order in the classroom has never been easy, but in recent years, school disorder has often taken particularly ugly forms: drug use and violent crime in the schools have become major social problems. . . . Even in schools that have been spared the most severe disciplinary problems, the preservation of order and a proper educational environment requires close supervision of schoolchildren, as well as the enforcement of rules against conduct that would be perfectly permissible if undertaken by an adult. . . .

How, then, should we strike the balance between the schoolchild's legitimate expectations of privacy and the school's equally legitimate need to maintain an environment in which learning can take place? It is evident that the school setting requires some easing of the restrictions to which searches by public authorities are ordinarily subject. The warrant requirement, in particular, is unsuited to the school environment: requiring a teacher to obtain a warrant before searching a child suspected of an infraction of school rules (or of the criminal law) would unduly interfere with the maintenance of the swift and informal disciplinary procedures needed in the schools. Just as we have in other cases dispensed with the warrant requirement when "the burden of obtaining a warrant is likely to frustrate the governmental purpose behind the search," . . . we hold today that school officials need not obtain a warrant before searching a student who is under their authority.

The school setting also requires some modification of the level of suspicion of illicit activity needed to justify a search. Ordinarily, a search—even one that may permissibly be carried out without a warrant—must be based upon "probable cause" to believe that a violation of the law has occurred. . . . However, "probable cause" is not an irreducible requirement of a valid search. The fundamental command of the Fourth Amendment is that searches and seizures be reasonable. . . . Thus, we have in a number of cases recognized the legality of searches and seizures based on suspicions that, although "reasonable," do not rise to the level of probable cause. . . . Where a careful balancing of governmental and private interests suggests that the public interest is best served by a Fourth Amendment standard of reason-

---

*We do not address the question, not presented by this case, whether a schoolchild has a legitimate expectation of privacy in lockers, desks, or other school property provided for the school property provided for the storage of school supplies. . . . Compare *Zamora* v. *Pomeroy*, 639 F.2d 662, 670 (CA10 1981) ("Inasmuch as the school had assumed joint control of the locker it cannot be successfully maintained that the school did not have a right to inspect it."), and *People* v. *Overton*, 24 N.Y.2d 522, 249 N.E.2d 366 (1969) (school administrators have power to consent to search of a student's locker), with *State* v. *Engerud*, 94 N.J. 331, 348, 463 A.2d 934, 943 (1983) ("We are satisifed that in the context of this case the student had an expectation of privacy in the contents of his locker. . . . For the four years of high school, the school locker is a home away from home. In it the student stores the kind of personal 'effects' protected by the Fourth Amendment.").

ableness that stops short of probable cause, we have not hesitated to adopt such a standard.

We join the majority of courts that have examined this issue in concluding that the accommodation of the privacy interests of schoolchildren with the substantial need of teachers and administrators for freedom to maintain order in the schools does not require strict adherence to the requirement that searches be based on probable cause to believe that the subject of the search has violated or is violating the law. Rather, the legality of a search of a student should depend simply on the reasonableness, under all the circumstances, of the search. Determining the reasonableness of any search involves a twofold inquiry: first, one must consider "whether the . . . action was justified at its inception," . . . ; second, one must determine whether the search as actually conducted "was reasonably related in scope to the circumstances which justified the interference in the first place." . . . Under ordinary circumstances, a search of a student by a teacher or other school official will be "justified at its inception" when there are reasonable grounds for suspecting that the search will turn up evidence that the student has violated or is violating either the law or the rules of the school. Such a search will be permissible in its scope when the measures adopted are reasonably related to the objectives of the search and not excessively intrusive in light of the age and sex of the student and the nature of the infraction. . . .

[Here the opinion examines the facts of the case to determine whether the search and seizure met the "reasonable grounds" standard. The conclusion was that the report of T. L. O.'s smoking in the lavatory gave Mr. Choplick reason to suspect that she was carrying cigarettes with her, and if she did so, her purse was the obvious place in which to find them. Further, the discovery of the cigarette papers gave rise to a reasonable suspicion that she was carrying marihuana as well as cigarettes in her purse and justified further exploration of the purse. "In short, we cannot conclude that the search for marihuana was unreasonable in any respect."]

Because the search resulting in the discovery of the evidence of marihuana dealing by T. L. O. was reasonable, the New Jersey Supreme Court's decision to exclude that evidence from T. L. O.'s juvenile delinquency proceedings on Fourth Amendment grounds was erroneous. Accordingly, the judgment of the Supreme Court of New Jersey is

*Reversed.*

Justice Powell, with whom Justice O'Connor joins, concurring. . . .

Justice Blackmun, concurring in the judgment. . . .

Justice Brennan, with whom Justice Marshall joins, concurring in part and dissenting in part. . . .

I agree that schoolteachers or principals, when not acting as agents of law enforcement authorities, generally may conduct a search of their students' belongings without first obtaining a warrant. To agree with the Court on this point is to say that school searches may justifiably be held to that extent to constitute an exception to the Fourth Amendment's warrant requirement. . . .

I emphatically disagree with the Court's decision to cast aside the constitutional probable-cause standard when assessing the constitutional validity of a schoolhouse search. The Court's decision jettisons the probable-cause standard—the only standard that finds support in the text of the Fourth Amendment—on the basis of its Rohrschach-like "balancing test." Use of such a "balancing test" to determine the standard for evaluating the validity of a full-scale search represents a sizable innovation in Fourth Amendment analysis. This innovation finds support neither in precedent nor policy and portends a dangerous weakening of the purpose of the Fourth Amendment to protect the privacy and security of our citizens. Moreover, even if this Court's historic understanding of the Fourth Amendment were mistaken and a balancing test of some kind were appropriate, any such test that gave adequate weight to the privacy and security interests protected by the Fourth Amendment would not reach the preordained result the Court's conclusory analysis reaches today. Therefore, because I believe that the balancing test used by the Court today is flawed both in its inception and its execution, I respectively dissent. . . .

On my view of the case, we need not decide whether the initial search conducted by Mr. Choplick—the search for evidence of the smoking violation that was completed when Mr. Choplick found the pack of cigarettes—was valid. For Mr. Choplick at that point did not have probable cause to continue to rummage through T. L. O.'s purse. Mr. Choplick's suspicion of marihuana possession at this time was based *solely* on the presence of the package of cigarette papers. The mere presence without more of such a staple item of commerce is insufficient to warrant a person of reasonable caution in inferring both that T. L. O. had violated the law by possessing marihuana and that evidence of that violation would be found in her purse. Just as a police officer could not obtain a warrant to search a home based solely on his claim that he had seen a package of cigarette papers in that home, Mr. Choplick was not entitled to search possibly the most private possessions of T. L. O. based on the mere presence of a package of cigarette papers. Therefore, the fruits of this illegal search must be excluded and the judgment of the New Jersey Supreme Court affirmed. . . .

Justice Stevens, with whom Justice Marshall joins, and with whom Justice Brennan joins as to Part I, concurring in part and dissenting in part. . . .

Of importance to students was the adoption of the Family Educational Rights Act of 1974 which limits the record-keeping and record-disclosing activities of schools and universities that receive federal funds. It requires educational institutions to allow parents or students, if over eighteen, to see their files, and the student's consent must be obtained prior to giving information on the files to third parties.

## O'CONNOR *v.* ORTEGA
### 55 LW 4405 (1987)

Justice O'Connor announced the judgment of the Court and delivered an opinion in which the Chief Justice, Justice White, and Justice Powell join.

This suit . . . presents two issues concerning the Fourth Amendment rights of public employees. First, we must determine whether the respondent, a public employee, had a reasonable expectation of privacy in his office, desk, and file cabinets at his place of work. Second, we must address the appropriate Fourth Amendment standard for a search conducted by a public employer in areas in which a public employee is found to have a reasonable expectation of privacy.

[Dr. Magno Ortega, a physician and psychiatrist, was an employee of a state hospital and had primary responsibility for training physicians in the psychiatric residency program. Hospital officials became concerned about possible improprieties in his management of the program, particularly with respect to his acquisition of a computer, charges against him concerning sexual harassment of female hospital employees and inappropriate disciplinary action against a resident. While he was on administrative leave pending investigation of the charges, hospital officials, allegedly in order to inventory and secure state property (including the computer, that Ortega reportedly had taken to his home), searched his office and seized personal items from his desk and file cabinets that were used in administrative proceedings resulting in his discharge. Ortega filed an action against the hospital officials in Federal

District Court under 42 USC §1982, alleging that the search of his office violated the Fourth Amendment. On cross-motions for summary judgment, the court granted judgment for the officials, concluding that the search was proper because there was a need to secure state property in the office, although no formal inventory of the property in the office was ever made. The Court of Appeals concluded that Ortega had a reasonable expectation of privacy in his office and the search violated his Fourth Amendment rights.]

Within the workplace context, this Court has recognized that employees may have a reasonable expectation of privacy against intrusions by police. . . . As with the expectation of privacy in one's home, such as expectation in one's place of work is "based upon societal expectations that have deep roots in the history of the Amendment." . . .

Given the societal expectations of privacy in one's place of work . . . we reject the contention made by the Solicitor general and petitioners that public employees can never have a reasonable expectation of privacy in their place of work. Individuals do not lose Fourth Amendment rights merely because they work for the government instead of a private employer. The operational realities of the workplace, however, may make *some* employees' expectations of privacy unreasonable when an intrusion is by a supervisor rather than a law enforcement official. Public employees' expectations of privacy in their offices, desks, and file cabinets, like similar expectations of employees in the private sector, may be reduced by virtue of actual office practices and procedures, or by legitimate regulation. . . . The employee's expectation of privacy must be assessed in the context of the employment relation. An office is seldom a private enclave free from entry by supervisors, other employees and business and personal invitees. Instead, in many cases offices are continually entered by fellow employees and other visitors during the workday for conferences, consultations, and other work-related visits. Simply put, it is the nature of government offices that others—such as fellow employees, supervisors, consensual visitors, and the general public—may have frequent access to an individual's office. . . .

But regardless of any legitimate right of access the Hospital staff may have had to the office as such, we recognize that the undisputed evidence suggests that Dr. Ortega had a reasonable expectation of privacy in his desk and file cabinets. The undisputed evidence discloses that Dr. Ortega did not share his desk or file cabinets with any other employees. Dr. Ortega had occupied the office for 17 years and he kept materials in his office, which included personal correspondence, medical files, and correspondence from private patients unconnected to the Hospital, personal financial records, teaching aids and notes, and personal gifts and mementos. . . .

On the basis of this undisputed evidence, we accept the conclusion of the Court of Appeals that Dr. Ortega had a reasonable expectation of privacy at least in his desk and file cabinets. . . .

But as we have stated in *T.L.O.,* "[t]o hold that the Fourth Amendment applies to searches conducted by [public employers] is only to begin the inquiry into the standards governing such searches. . . . [W]hat is reasonable depends on the context within which a search takes place." *New Jersey* v. *T.L.O.* . . . . Thus, we must determine the appropriate standard of reasonableness applicable to the search. . . . In the case of searches conducted by a public employer, we must balance the invasion of the employees' legitimate expectations of privacy against the government's need for supervision, control and the efficient operation of the workplace. . . .

There is surprisingly little case law on the appropriate Fourth Amendment standard of reasonableness for a public employer's work-related search of its employee's offices, desks, or file cabinets. Generally, however, the lower courts have held that any "work-related" search by an employer satisfies the Fourth Amendment reasonableness requirement. . . .

In our view, requiring an employer to obtain a warrant whenever the employer wished to enter an employee's office, desk, or file cabinets for a work-related purpose would seriously disrupt the routine conduct of business and would be unduly burdensome. Imposing unwieldy warrant procedures in such cases upon supervisors, who would otherwise have no reason to be familiar with such procedures, is simply unreasonable. . . .

Whether probable cause is an inappropriate standard for public employer searches of their employees' offices presents a more difficult issue. For the most part, we have required that a search be based upon probable cause, but as we noted in *New Jersey* v. *T.L.O.,* "[t]he fundamental command of the Fourth Amendment is that searches and seizures be reasonable, and although 'both the concept of probable cause and the requirement of a warrant bear on the reasonableness of a search, . . . in certain limited circumstances neither is required.' " . . . Thus, "[w]here a careful balancing of governmental and private interests suggests that the public interest is best served by a Fourth Amendment standard of reasonableness that stops short of probable cause, we have not hesitated to adopt such a standard." . . .

The governmental interest justifying work-related intrusions by public employers is the efficient and proper operation of the workplace. . . . To ensure the efficient and proper operation of the agency, therefore, public employers must be given wide latitude to enter employee offices for work-related, noninvestigatory reasons.

We come to a similar conclusion for searches conducted pursuant to an investigation of work-related employee misconduct. Even when employers conduct an investigation, they have an interest substantially different from "the normal need for law enforcement,". . . . Public employers have an interest in ensuring that their agencies operate in an effective and efficient manner, and the work of these agencies inevitably suffers from the inefficiency, incompetence, mismanagement or other work-related misfeasance of its employees. . . . In our view, therefore, a probable cause requirement for searches of the type at issue here would impose intolerable burdens on public employers. The delay in correcting the employee misconduct caused by the need for probable cause rather than reasonable suspicion will be translated into tangible and often irreparable damage to the agency's work, and ultimately to the public interest. . . .

A standard of reasonableness will neither unduly burden the efforts of government employers to ensure the efficient and proper operation of the workplace, nor authorize arbitrary intrusions upon the privacy of public employees. We hold, therefore, that public employer intrusions on the constitutionally protected privacy interests of government employees for noninvestigatory, work-related purposes, as well as for investigations of work-related misconduct, should be judged by the standard of reasonableness under all the circumstances. . . .

In the procedural posture of this case, we do not attempt to determine whether the search of Dr. Ortega's office, and the seizure of his personal belongings, satisfy the standard of reasonableness we have articulated in this case. No evidentiary hearing was held in this case because the District Court acted on cross-motions for summary judgment, and granted petitioner summary judgment. . . .

Accordingly, the judgment of the Court of Appeals is reversed, and the case is remanded to that court for further proceedings consistent with this opinion.

*It is so ordered.*

Justice Scalia, concurring in the judgment. . . .

The government, like any other employer, needs frequent and convenient access to its desks, offices, and file cabinets for work-related purposes. I would hold that government searches to retrieve work-related materials or to investigate violations of workplace rules—searches of the sort that are regarded as reasonable and normal in the private-employer context—do not violate the Fourth Amendment. Because the conflicting and incomplete evidence in the present case could not conceivably support summary judgment that the search did not have such a validating purpose, I agree with the plurality that the decision must be reversed and remanded.

Justice Blackmun, with whom Justice Brennan, Justice Marshall, and Justice Stevens join, dissenting. . . .

A careful balancing with respect to the warrant requirement is absent from the plurality's opinion, an absence that is inevitable in light of the gulf between the plurality's analysis and any concrete factual setting. It is certainly correct that a public employer cannot be expected to obtain a warrant for every routine entry into an employee's workplace. This situation, however, should not justify dispensing with a warrant in *all* searches by the employer. The warrant requirement is perfectly suited for many work-related searches, including the instant one. Moreover, although the plurality abandons the warrant requirement, it does not explain what it will substitute or how the standard it adopts retains anything of the normal "neutral scrutiny of the judge." In sum, the plurality's general result is preordained because, cut off from a particular factual setting, it cannot make the necessary distinctions among types of searches, or formulate an alternative to the warrant requirement that derives from a precise weighing of competing interests.

In *Griffin* v. *Wisconsin*, 55 LW 5156 (1987), the Court upheld a warrantless search of a probationer's home by a probation officer, holding that it was "reasonable" within the meaning of the Fourth Amendment because it was conducted pursuant to a regulation that was itself a reasonable response to the "special needs" of a probation system. Wisconsin puts probationers in the legal custody of the State Department of Health and Social Services and renders them subject to conditions set by the court and rules and regulations set by the Department. One of the Department's regulations permits any probation officer to search a probationer's home without a warrant as long as his supervisor approves and as long as there are "reasonable grounds" to believe the presence of contraband—including any item that the probationer cannot possess under the probation conditions. Further, a regulation makes it a violation of the terms of probation to refuse to consent to a home search. After receiving an unauthenticated tip that Griffin might have a gun in his home, a probation officer conducted a warrantless search of the home and found a handgun. Griffin was charged with possession of a firearm by a convicted felon, his motion to suppress the evidence was denied, and he was convicted. The Court held that "the probation regime would be unduly disrupted by a requirement of probable cause," and "it is both unrealistic and destructive of the whole object of the continuing probation relationship to insist upon the same degree of demonstrable reliability of particular items of supporting data, and upon the same degree of certainty of violation, as is required in other contexts."

In *California* v. *Greenwood*, 56 LW 4409 (1988), the Court addressed the issue of whether the Fourth Amendment prohibits the warrantless search and seizure of garbage left for collection outside the curtilage of a home. Justice White, for the majority, concluded "in accordance with the vast majority of lower courts that have addressed the issue that it does not." Acting on information that Greenwood might be engaged in narcotics trafficking, police twice obtained from his regular trash collector garbage bags left on the curb in front of his house. On the basis of items in the bags which were indicative of narcotics use, the police obtained warrants to search the house. They discovered controlled substances and arrested the occupants. Greenwood argued that he had an expectation of privacy with respect to the trash since it was contained in opaque plastic bags, which the collector was expected to pick up, mingle with the trash of others, and deposit at the garbage dump. Justice White stated: "An expectation of privacy does not give rise to Fourth Amendment protection, however, unless society is prepared to accept that expectation as objectively reasonable." Further, he said:

Here, we conclude that respondents exposed their garbage to the public sufficiently to defeat their claim to Fourth Amendment protection. It is common knowledge that plastic garbage bags left on or at the side of a public street are readily accessible to animals, children, scavengers, snoops, and other members of the public.

He also noted that even the refuse of prominent Americans has not been invulnerable, citing a reporter's seizure of five bags of garbage from the sidewalk outside the home of Secretary of State Henry Kissinger. In dissent, Justice Brennan stated:

Scrutiny of another's trash is contrary to commonly accepted notions of civilized behavior. I suspect, therefore, that members of our society will be shocked to learn that the Court, the ultimate guarantor of liberty, deems unreasonable our expectation that the aspects of our private lives that are concealed safely in a trash bag will not become public.

More and more frequently in recent years there has been pressure for mandatory testing of various employees, athletes, airline pilots, jockeys and others for a variety of purposes. In some cases the effort is to identify drug users by giving blood and urine tests. In others polygraph tests are employed to discourage theft or the revealing of industrial or security and defense secrets. A different demand for testing stems from the fear of the further spread of AIDS—Acquired Immunodeficiency Syndrome. Whatever the focus, when mandatory testing is imposed by governmental authorities, there are clearly constitutional implications for the right of privacy. As of this writing, the Supreme Court has heard argument, but not yet decided, two cases involving drug testing programs. *Burnley* v. *Railway Labor Executives' Association,* _____ U.S. _____ (1989), dealt with a Fourth Amendment challenge to Federal Railroad Administration regulations requiring railroads to give drug and alcohol tests to all "covered employees" involved in major accidents, impact accidents, and accidents that resulted in the death of a railroad employee. All members of the train crew are to be tested following an accident. The second case, *National Treasury Employees Union* v. *Von Raab.* _____ U.S. _____ (1989). was a challenge to the Customs Service policy that requires employees who seek transfer to "sensitive" jobs to submit to urine sampling. The Ninth Circuit held the railroad regulations violative of the Fourth Amendment in the absence of particularized suspicion. But the Fifth Circuit upheld the Customs Service policy. [See Miller, "Mandatory Urinalysis Testing and the Privacy Rights of Subject Employees: Toward a General Rule of Legality Under the Fourth Amendment," 48 *U. Pitt. L. Rev.* 201 (1986) and Susan J. Levy, "The Constitutional Implications of Mandatory Testing for Acquired Immunodeficiency Syndrome — AIDS," 37 *Emory L. J.* 217 (1988).]

# Constitution of the United States

WE THE PEOPLE of the United States, in order to form a more perfect union, establish justice, insure domestic tranquility, provide for the common defense, promote the general welfare, and secure the blessings of liberty to ourselves and our posterity, do ordain and establish this Constitution for the United States of America.

## ARTICLE I

SECTION 1. All legislative powers herein granted shall be vested in a Congress of the United States, which shall consist of a Senate and House of Representatives.

SECTION 2. (1) The House of Representatives shall be composed of members chosen every second year by the people of the several States, and the electors in each State shall have the qualifications requisite for electors of the most numerous branch of the State legislature.

(2) No person shall be a Representative who shall not have attained to the age of twenty-five years, and been seven years a citizen of the United States, and who shall not, when elected, be an inhabitant of that State in which he shall be chosen.

(3) Representatives and direct taxes[1] shall be apportioned among the several States which may be included within this Union, according to their respective numbers, which shall be determined by adding to the whole number of free persons, including those bound to service for a term of years, and excluding Indians not taxed, three fifths of all other persons.[2] The actual enumeration shall be made within three years after the first meeting of the Congress of the United States, and within every subsequent term of ten years, in such manner as they shall by law direct. The number of Representatives shall not exceed one for every thirty thousand, but each State shall have at least one Representative; and until such enumeration shall be made, the State of New Hampshire shall be entitled to choose three, Massachusetts eight, Rhode Island and Providence Plantations one, Connecticut five, New York, six, New Jersey four, Pennsylvania eight, Delaware one, Maryland six, Virginia ten, North Carolina five, South Carolina five, and Georgia three.

(4) When vacancies happen in the representation from any State, the executive authority thereof shall issue writs of election to fill such vacancies.

(5) The House of Representatives shall choose their Speaker and other officers; and shall have the sole power of impeachment.

SECTION 3. (1) The Senate of the United States shall be composed of two Senators from each State, chosen by the Legislature thereof,[3] for six years; and each Senator shall have one vote.

(2) Immediately after they shall be assembled in consequence of the first election, they shall be divided as equally as may be into three classes. The seats of the Senators of the first class

---

[1]Modified as to income taxes by the 16th Amendment.
[2]Replaced by the 14th Amendment.
[3]Modified by the 17th Amendment.

shall be vacated at the expiration of the second year, of the second class at the expiration of the fourth year, and of the third class at the sixth year, so that one third may be chosen every second year; and if vacancies happen by resignation, or otherwise, during the recess of the legislature of any State, the executive thereof may make temporary appointments until the next meeting of the legislature, which shall then fill such vacancies.

(3) No person shall be a Senator who shall not have attained to the age of thirty years, and been nine years a citizen of the United States, and who shall not, when elected, be an inhabitant of that State for which he shall be chosen.

(4) The Vice President of the United States shall be president of the Senate, but shall have no vote, unless they be equally divided.

(5) The Senate shall choose their other officers, and also a president pro tempore, in the absence of the Vice President, or when he shall exercise the office of President of the United States.

(6) The Senate shall have the sole power to try all impeachments. When sitting for that purpose, they shall be on oath or affirmation. When the President of the United States is tried, the Chief Justice shall preside: and no person shall be convicted without the concurrence of two thirds of the members present.

(7) Judgment in cases of impeachment shall not extend further than to removal from office, and disqualification to hold and enjoy any office of honor, trust or profit under the United States: but the party convicted shall nevertheless be liable and subject to indictment, trial, judgment and punishment, according to law.

SECTION 4. (1) The times, places and manner of holding elections for Senators and Representatives, shall be prescribed in each State by the legislature thereof; but the Congress may at any time by law make or alter such regulations, except as to the places of choosing Senators.

(2) The Congress shall assemble at least once in every year, and such meeting shall be on the first Monday in December, unless they shall by law appoint a different day.

SECTION 5. (1) Each House shall be the judge of the elections, returns and qualifications of its own members, and a majority of each shall constitute a quorum to do business; but a smaller number may adjourn from day to day, and may be authorized to compel the attendance of absent members, in such manner, and under such penalties as each House may provide.

(2) Each House may determine the rules of its proceedings, punish its members for disorderly behavior, and, with the concurrence of two thirds, expel a member.

(3) Each House shall keep a journal of its proceedings, and from time to time publish the same, excepting such parts as may in their judgment require secrecy; and the yeas and nays of the members of either House on any question shall, at the desire of one fifth of those present, be entered on the journal.

(4) Neither House, during the session of Congress, shall, without the consent of the other, adjourn for more than three days, nor to any other place than that in which the two Houses shall be sitting.

SECTION 6. (1) The Senators and Representatives shall receive a compensation for their services, to be ascertained by law, and paid out of the Treasury of the United States. They shall in all cases, except treason, felony and breach of the peace, be privileged from arrest during their attendance at the session of their respective Houses, and in going to and returning from the same; and for any speech or debate in either House, they shall not be questioned in any other place.

(2) No Senator or Representative shall, during the time for which he was elected, be appointed to any civil office under the authority of the United States, which shall have been created, or the emoluments whereof shall have been increased during such time; and no person holding any office under the United States, shall be a member of either House during his continuance in office.

SECTION 7. (1) All bills for raising revenue shall originate in the House of Representatives; but the Senate may propose or concur with amendments as on other bills.

(2) Every bill which shall have passed the House of Representatives and the Senate, shall, before it become a law, be presented to the President of the United States; if he approves he

shall sign it, but if not he shall return it, with his objections to that House in which it shall have originated, who shall enter the objections at large on their journal, and proceed to reconsider it. If after such reconsideration two thirds of that House shall agree to pass the bill, it shall be sent, together with the objections, to the other House, by which it shall likewise be reconsidered, and if approved by two thirds of that House, it shall become a law. But in all such cases the votes of both Houses shall be determined by yeas and nays, and the names of the persons voting for and against the bill shall be entered on the journal of each House respectively. If any bill shall not be returned by the President within ten days (Sundays excepted) after it shall have been presented to him, the same shall be a law, in like manner as if he had signed it, unless the Congress by their adjournment prevent its return, in which case it shall not be a law.

(3) Every order, resolution, or vote to which the concurrence of the Senate and House of Representatives may be necessary (except on a question of adjournment) shall be presented to the President of the United States; and before the same shall take effect, shall be approved by him, or being disapproved by him, shall be repassed by two thirds of the Senate and House of Representatives, according to the rules and limitations prescribed in the case of a bill.

SECTION 8. (1) The Congress shall have power to lay and collect taxes, duties, imposts and excises, to pay the debts and provide for the common defense and general welfare of the United States; but all duties, imposts and excises shall be uniform throughout the United States;

(2) To borrow money on the credit of the United States;

(3) To regulate commerce with foreign nations, and among the several States, and with the Indian tribes;

(4) To establish an uniform rule of naturalization, and uniform laws on the subject of bankruptcies throughout the United States;

(5) To coin money, regulate the value thereof, and of foreign coin, and fix the standard of weights and measures;

(6) To provide for the punishment of counterfeiting the securities and current coin of the United States;

(7) To establish post offices and post roads;

(8) To promote the progress of science and useful arts, by securing for limited times to authors and inventors the exclusive right to their respective writings and discoveries;

(9) To constitute tribunals inferior to the Supreme Court;

(10) To define and punish piracies and felonies committed on the high seas, and offenses against the law of nations;

(11) To declare war, grant letters of marque and reprisal, and make rules concerning captures on land and water;

(12) To raise and support armies, but no appropriation of money to that use shall be for a longer term than two years;

(13) To provide and maintain a navy;

(14) To make rules for the government and regulation of the land and naval forces;

(15) To provide for calling forth the militia to execute the laws of the Union, suppress insurrections and repel invasions;

(16) To provide for organizing, arming, and disciplining the militia, and for governing such part of them as may be employed in the service of the United States, reserving to the States respectively, the appointment of the officers, and the authority of training the militia according to the discipline prescribed by Congress;

(17) To exercise exclusive legislation in all cases whatsoever, over such district (not exceeding ten miles square) as may, by cession of particular States, and the acceptance of Congress, become the seat of the government of the United States,[4] and to exercise like authority over all places purchased by the consent of the legislature of the State in which the same shall be, for the erection of forts, magazines, arsenals, dockyards, and other needful buildings; and

[4] Modified by the 23rd Amendment.

(18) To make all laws which shall be necessary and proper for carrying into execution the foregoing powers, and all other powers vested by this Constitution in the government of the United States, or in any department or officer thereof.

SECTION 9. (1) The migration or importation of such persons as any of the States now existing shall think proper to admit, shall not be prohibited by the Congress prior to the year one thousand eight hundred and eight, but a tax or duty may be imposed on such importation, not exceeding ten dollars for each person.

(2) The privilege of the writ of habeas corpus shall not be suspended, unless when in cases of rebellion or invasion the public safety may require it.

(3) No bill of attainder or ex post facto law shall be passed.

(4) No capitation, or other direct, tax shall be laid, unless in proportion to the census or enumeration herein before directed to be taken.[5]

(5) No tax or duty shall be laid on articles exported from any State.

(6) No preference shall be given by any regulation of commerce or revenue to the ports of one State over those of another: nor shall vessels bound to, or from, one State, be obliged to enter, clear, or pay duties in another.

(7) No money shall be drawn from the Treasury, but in consequence of appropriations made by law; and a regular statement and account of the receipts and expenditures of all public money shall be published from time to time.

(8) No title of nobility shall be granted by the United States: and no person holding any office of profit or trust under them, shall, without the consent of the Congress, accept of any present, emolument, office, or title, of any kind whatever, from any king, prince, or foreign State.

SECTION 10. (1) No State shall enter into any treaty, alliance, or confederation; grant letters of marque and reprisal; coin money; emit bills of credit; make anything but gold and silver coin a tender in payment of debts; pass any bill of attainder, ex post facto law, or law impairing the obligation of contracts, or grant any title of nobility.

(2) No State shall, without the consent of the Congress, lay any imposts or duties on imports or exports, except what may be absolutely necessary for executing its inspection laws; and the net produce of all duties and imposts, laid by any State on imports or exports, shall be for the use of the Treasury of the United States; and all such laws shall be subject to the revision and control of the Congress.

(3) No State shall, without the consent of Congress, lay any duty of tonnage, keep troops, or ships of war in time of peace, enter into any agreement or compact with another State, or with a foreign power, or engage in war, unless actually invaded, or in such imminent danger as will not admit of delay.


## ARTICLE II

SECTION 1. (1) The executive power shall be vested in a President of the United States of America. He shall hold his office during the term of four years,[6] and, together with the Vice President, chosen for the same term, be elected, as follows:

(2) Each State shall appoint, in such manner as the legislature thereof may direct, a number of electors, equal to the whole number of Senators and Representatives to which the State may be entitled in the Congress: but no Senator or Representative, or person holding an office of trust or profit under the United States, shall be appointed an elector.

The electors[7] shall meet in their respective States, and vote by ballot for two persons, of whom one at least shall not be an inhabitant of the same State with themselves. And they shall make a list of all the persons voted for, and of the number of votes for each; which list they shall sign and certify, and transmit sealed to the seat of the government of the United States, directed to the president of the Senate. The president of the Senate shall, in the pres-

---

[5] Modified by the 16th Amendment.
[6] Modified by the 22nd Amendment.
[7] This paragraph was replaced in 1804 by the 12th Amendment.

ence of Senate and House of Representatives, open all the certificates, and the votes shall then be counted. The person having the greatest number of votes shall be the President, if such number be a majority of the whole number of electors appointed; and if there be more than one who have such majority, and have an equal number of votes, then the House of Representatives shall immediately choose by ballot one of them for President; and if no person have a majority, then from the five highest on the list the said House shall in like manner choose the President. But in choosing the President, the votes shall be taken by States, the representation from each State having one vote; a quorum for this purpose shall consist of a member or members from two thirds of the States, and a majority of all the States shall be necessary to a choice. In every case, after the choice of the President, the person having the greatest number of votes of the electors shall be the Vice President. But if there should remain two or more who have equal votes, the Senate shall choose from them by ballot the Vice President.

(3) The Congress may determine the time of choosing the electors, and the day on which they shall give their votes; which day shall be the same throughout the United States.

(4) No person except a natural born citizen, or a citizen of the United States, at the time of the adoption of this Constitution, shall be eligible to the office of President; neither shall any person be eligible to that office who shall not have attained to the age of thirty five years, and been fourteen years a resident within the United States.

(5) In the case of the removal of the President from office, or of his death, resignation, or inability to discharge the powers and duties of the said office, the same shall devolve on the Vice President, and the Congress may by law provide for the case of removal, death, resignation, or inability, both of the President and Vice President, declaring what officer shall then act as President, and such officer shall act accordingly, until the disability be removed, or a President shall be elected.[8]

(6) The President shall, at stated times, receive for his services, a compensation, which shall neither be increased nor diminished during the period for which he shall have been elected, and he shall not receive within that period any other emolument from the United States, or any of them.

(7) Before he enter on the execution of his office, he shall take the following oath or affirmation:—"I do solemnly swear (or affirm) that I will faithfully execute the office of President of the United States, and will to the best of my ability, preserve, protect and defend the Constitution of the United States."

SECTION 2. (1) The President shall be commander in chief of the army and navy of the United States, and of the militia of the several States, when called into the actual service of the United States; he may require the opinion, in writing, of the principal officer in each of the executive departments, upon any subject relating to the duties of their respective offices, and he shall have power to grant reprieves and pardons for offenses against the United States, except in cases of impeachment.

(2) He shall have power, by and with the advice and consent of the Senate, to make treaties, provided two thirds of the Senators present concur; and he shall nominate, and by and with the advice and consent of the Senate, shall appoint ambassadors, other public ministers and consuls, judges of the Supreme Court, and all other officers of the United States, whose appointments are not herein otherwise provided for, and which shall be established by law: but the Congress may by law vest the appointment of such inferior officers, as they think proper, in the President alone, in the courts of law, or in the heads of departments.

(3) The President shall have the power to fill up all vacancies that may happen during the recess of the Senate, by granting commissions which shall expire at the end of their next session.

SECTION 3. He shall from time to time give to the Congress information of the state of the Union, and recommend to their consideration such measures as he shall judge necessary and expedient; he may, on extraordinary occasions, convene both Houses, or either of them, and in case of disagreement between them, with respect to the time of adjournment, he may adjourn them to such time as he shall think proper; he shall receive ambassadors

---

[8] Replaced by the 25th Amendment.

and other public ministers; he shall take care that the laws be faithfully executed, and shall commission all the officers of the United States.

SECTION 4. The President, Vice President and all civil officers of the United States, shall be removed from office on impeachment for, and conviction of, treason, bribery, or other high crimes and misdemeanors.

## ARTICLE III

SECTION 1. The judicial power of the United States, shall be vested in one Supreme Court, and in such inferior courts as the Congress may from time to time ordain and establish. The judges, both of the Supreme and inferior courts, shall hold their offices during good behavior, and shall, at stated times, receive for their services, a compensation, which shall not be diminished during their continuance in office.

SECTION 2. (1) The judicial power shall extend to all cases, in law and equity, arising under this Constitution, the laws of the United States, and treaties made, or which shall be made, under their authority;—to all cases affecting ambassadors, other public ministers and consuls;—to all cases of admiralty and maritime jurisdiction;—to controversies to which the United States shall be a party;—to controversies between two or more States;—between a State and citizens of another State;[9]—between citizens of different States;—between citizens of the same State claiming lands under grants of different States, and between a State, or the citizens thereof, and foreign States, citizens or subjects.

(2) In all cases affecting ambassadors, other public ministers and consuls, and those in which a State shall be party, the Supreme Court shall have original jurisdiction. In all the other cases before mentioned, the Supreme Court shall have appellate jurisdiction, both as to law and fact, with such exceptions, and under such regulations as Congress shall make.

(3) The trial of all crimes, except in cases of impeachment, shall be by jury; and such trial shall be held in the State where the said crimes shall have been committed; but when not committed within any State, the trial shall be at such place or places as the Congress may by law have directed.

SECTION 3. (1) Treason against the United States, shall consist only in levying war against them, or in adhering to their enemies, giving them aid and comfort. No person shall be convicted of treason unless on the testimony of two witnesses to the same overt act, or on confession in open court.

(2) The Congress shall have power to declare the punishment of treason, but no attainder of treason shall work corruption of blood, or forfeiture except during the life of the person attained.

## ARTICLE IV

SECTION 1. Full faith and credit shall be given in each State to the public acts, records, and judicial proceedings of every other State. And the Congress may by general laws prescribe the manner in which such acts, records and proceedings shall be proved, and the effect thereof.

SECTION 2. (1) The citizens of each State shall be entitled to all privileges and immunities of citizens in the several States.

(2) A person charged in any State with treason, felony, or other crime, who shall flee from justice, and be found in another State, shall on demand of the executive authority of the State from which he fled, be delivered up, to be removed to the State having jurisdiction of the crime.

(3) No person held to service or labor in one State, under the laws thereof, escaping into another, shall, in consequence of any law or regulation therein, be discharged from such service or labor, but shall be delivered up on claim of the party to whom such service or labor may be due.

[9] Restricted by the 11th Amendment.

SECTION 3. (1) New States may be admitted by the Congress into this Union; but no new State shall be formed or erected within the jurisdiction of any other State; nor any State be formed by the junction of two or more States, or parts of States, without the consent of the legislatures of the States concerned as well as of the Congress.

(2) The Congress shall have power to dispose of and make all needful rules and regulations respecting the territory or other property belonging to the United States; and nothing in this Constitution shall be so construed as to prejudice any claims of the United States, or of any particular State.

SECTION 4. The United States shall guarantee to every State in this Union a republican form of government, and shall protect each of them against invasion; and on application of the legislature, or of the executive (when the legislature cannot be convened) against domestic violence.

## ARTICLE V

The Congress, whenever two thirds of both Houses shall deem it necessary, shall propose amendments to this Constitution, or, on the application of the legislatures of two thirds of the several States, shall call a convention for proposing amendments, which, in either case, shall be valid to all intents and purposes, as part of this Constitution, when ratified by the legislatures of three fourths of the several States, or by conventions in three fourths thereof, as the one or the other mode of ratification may be proposed by the Congress; Provided that no amendment which may be made prior to the year one thousand eight hundred and eight shall in any manner affect the first and fourth clauses in the ninth section of the first article; and that no State, without its consent, shall be deprived of its equal suffrage in the Senate.

## ARTICLE VI

SECTION 1. All debts contracted and engagements entered into, before the adoption of this Constitution, shall be as valid against the United States under this Constitution, as under the Confederation.

SECTION 2. This Constitution, and the laws of the United States which shall be made in pursuance thereof; and all treaties made, or which shall be made, under the authority of the United States, shall be the supreme law of the land; and the judges in every State shall be bound thereby, anything in the constitution or laws of any State to the contrary notwithstanding.

SECTION 3. The Senators and Representatives before mentioned, and the members of the several State legislatures, and all executive and judicial officers, both of the United States and of the several States, shall be bound by oath or affirmation to support this Constitution; but no religious test shall ever be required as a qualification to any office or public trust under the United States.

## ARTICLE VII

The ratification of the conventions of nine States, shall be sufficient for the establishment of this Constitution between the States so ratifying the same.

done in Convention by the unanimous consent of the States present the seventeenth day of September in the year of our Lord one thousand seven hundred and eighty-seven, and of the independence of the United States of America the twelfth. In witness whereof we have hereunto subscribed our names.

Go Washington—
Presidt. and Deputy from Virginia

## AMENDMENTS

### ARTICLE I[10]

Congress shall make no law respecting an establishment of religion, or prohibiting the free exercise thereof; or abridging the freedom of speech, or of the press; or the right of the people peaceably to assemble, and to petition the government for a redress of grievances.

### ARTICLE II

A well regulated militia, being necessary to the security of a free State, the right of the people to keep and bear arms, shall not be infringed.

### ARTICLE III

No soldier shall, in time of peace be quartered in any house, without the consent of the owner, nor in time of war, but in a manner to be prescribed by law.

### ARTICLE IV

The right of the people to be secure in their persons, houses, papers, and effects, against unreasonable searches and seizures, shall not be violated, and no warrants shall issue, but upon probable cause, supported by oath or affirmation, and particularly describing the place to be searched, and the persons or things to be seized.

### ARTICLE V

No person shall be held to answer for a capital, or otherwise infamous crime, unless on a presentment or indictment of a grand jury, except in cases arising in the land or naval forces, or in the militia, when in actual service in time of war or public danger; nor shall any person be subject for the same offense to be twice put in jeopardy of life or limb; nor shall be compelled in any criminal case to be a witness against himself, nor be deprived of life, liberty, or property, without due process of law; nor shall private property be taken for public use, without just compensation.

### ARTICLE VI

In all criminal prosecutions the accused shall enjoy the right to a speedy and public trial, by an impartial jury of the State and district wherein the crime shall have been committed, which district shall have been previously ascertained by law, and to be informed of the nature and cause of the accusation; to be confronted with the witnesses against him; to have compulsory process for obtaining witnesses in his favor, and to have the assistance of counsel for his defense.

### ARTICLE VII

In suits at common law, where the value in controversy shall exceed twenty dollars, the right of trial by jury shall be preserved, and no fact tried by a jury shall be otherwise reexamined in any court of the United States, than according to the rules of the common law.

[10]The first ten Amendments were adopted in 1791.

## ARTICLE VIII

Excessive bail shall not be required, nor excessive fines imposed, nor cruel and unusual punishments inflicted.

## ARTICLE IX

The enumeration in the Constitution, of certain rights, shall not be construed to deny or disparage others retained by the people.

## ARTICLE X

The powers not delegated to the United States by the Constitution, nor prohibited by it to the States, are reserved to the States respectively, or to the people.

## ARTICLE XI[11]

The judicial power of the United States shall not be construed to extend to any suit in law or equity, commenced or prosecuted against one of the United States by citizens of another State, or by citizens or subjects of any foreign State.

## ARTICLE XII[12]

The electors shall meet in their respective States and vote by ballot for President and Vice-President, one of whom, at least, shall not be an inhabitant of the same State with themselves; they shall name in their ballots the person voted for as President, and in distinct ballots the person voted for as Vice-President, and they shall make distinct lists of all persons voted for as President, and of all persons voted for as Vice-President, and of the number of votes for each, which lists they shall sign and certify, and transmit sealed to the seat of the government of the United States, directed to the president of the Senate;—The president of the Senate shall, in the presence of the Senate and House of Representatives, open all the certificates and the votes shall then be counted;—The person having the greatest number of votes for President, shall be the President, if such number be a majority of the whole number of electors appointed; and if no person have such majority, then from the persons having the highest numbers not exceeding three on the list of those voted for as President, the House of Representatives shall choose immediately, by ballot, the President. But in choosing the President, the votes shall be taken by States, the representation from each State having one vote; a quorum for this purpose shall consist of a member or members from two thirds of the States, and a majority of all the States shall be necessary to a choice. And if the House of Representatives shall not choose a President whenever the right of choice shall devolve upon them, before the fourth day of March next following, then the Vice-President shall act as President, as in the case of the death or other constitutional disability of the President.—The person having the greatest number of votes as Vice-President, shall be the Vice-President, if such number be a majority of the whole number of electors appointed, and if no person have a majority, then from the two highest numbers on the list, the Senate shall choose the Vice-President; a quorum for the purpose shall consist of two thirds of the whole number of Senators, and a majority of the whole number shall be necessary to a choice. But no person constitutionally ineligible to the office of President shall be eligible to that of Vice-President of the United States.

[11]Ratified in 1795; proclaimed in 1798.
[12]Adopted in 1804.

## ARTICLE XIII[13]

SECTION 1. Neither slavery nor involuntary servitude, except as a punishment for crime whereof the party shall have been duly convicted, shall exist within the United States, or any place subject to their jurisdiction.

SECTION 2. Congress shall have power to enforce this article by appropriate legislation.

## ARTICLE XIV[14]

SECTION 1. All persons born or naturalized in the United States, and subject to the jurisdiction thereof, are citizens of the United States and of the State wherein they reside. No State shall make or enforce any law which shall abridge the privileges or immunities of citizens of the United States; nor shall any State deprive any person of life, liberty, or property, without due process of law; nor deny to any person within its jurisdiction the equal protection of the laws.

SECTION 2. Representatives shall be apportioned among the several States according to their respective numbers, counting the whole number of persons in each State, excluding Indians not taxed. But when the right to vote at any election for the choice of electors for President and Vice President of the United States, Representatives in Congress, the executive and judicial officers of a State, or the members of the legislature thereof, is denied to any of the male inhabitants of such State, being twenty-one years of age, and citizens of the United States, or in any way abridged, except for participation in rebellion, or other crime, the basis of representation therein shall be reduced in the proportion which the number of such male citizens shall bear to the whole number of male citizens twenty-one years of age in such State.

SECTION 3. No person shall be a Senator or Representative in Congress, or elector of President and Vice President, or hold any office, civil or military, under the United States, or under any State, who, having previously taken an oath, as a member of Congress, or as an officer of the United States, or as a member of any State legislature, or as an executive or judicial officer of any State, to support the Constitution of the United States, shall have engaged in insurrection or rebellion against the same, or given aid or comfort to the enemies thereof. But Congress may by a vote of two thirds of each House, remove such disability.

SECTION 4. The validity of the public debt of the United States, authorized by law, including debts incurred for payment of pensions and bounties for services in suppressing insurrection or rebellion, shall not be questioned. But neither the United States nor any State shall assume or pay any debt or obligation incurred in aid of insurrection or rebellion against the United States, or any claim for the loss or emancipation of any slave; but all such debts, obligations and claims shall be held illegal and void.

SECTION 5. The Congress shall have power to enforce, by appropriate legislation, the provisions of this article.

## ARTICLE XV[15]

SECTION 1. The right of citizens of the United States to vote shall not be denied or abridged by the United States or by any State on account of race, color, or previous condition of servitude.

SECTION 2. The Congress shall have power to enforce this article by appropriate legislation.

[13]Adopted in 1865.
[14]Adopted in 1868.
[15]Adopted in 1870.

## ARTICLE XVI[16]

The Congress shall have power to lay and collect taxes on incomes, from whatever source derived, without apportionment among the several States, and without regard to any census or enumeration.

## ARTICLE XVII[16]

The Senate of the United States shall be composed of two Senators from each State, elected by the people thereof, for six years; and each Senator shall have one vote. The electors in each State shall have the qualifications requisite for electors of the most numerous branch of the State legislatures.

When vacancies happen in the representation of any State in the Senate, the executive authority of such State shall issue writs of election to fill such vacancies: *Provided,* That the legislature of any State may empower the executive thereof to make temporary appointments until the people fill the vacancies by election as the legislature may direct.

This amendment shall not be so construed as to affect the election or term of any Senator chosen before it becomes valid as part of the Constitution.

## ARTICLE XVIII[17]

SECTION 1. After one year from the ratification of this article the manufacture, sale, or transportation of intoxicating liquors within, the importation thereof into, or the exportation thereof from the United States and all territory subject to the jurisdiction thereof for beverage purposes is hereby prohibited.

SECTION 2. The Congress and the several States shall have concurrent power to enforce this article by appropriate legislation.

SECTION 3. This article shall be inoperative unless it shall have been ratified as an amendment to the Constitution by the legislatures of the several States, as provided in the Constitution, within seven years from the date of the submission hereof to the States by the Congress.

## ARTICLE XIX[18]

The right of citizens of the United States to vote shall not be denied or abridged by the United States or by any State on account of sex.

The Congress shall have power to enforce this article by appropriate legislation.

## ARTICLE XX[19]

SECTION 1. The terms of the President and Vice President shall end at noon on the 20th day of January, and the terms of Senators and Representatives at noon on the 3rd day of January, of the years in which such terms would have ended if this article had not been ratified; and the terms of their successors shall then begin.

SECTION 2. The Congress shall assemble at least once in every year, and such meeting shall begin at noon on the 3rd day of January, unless they shall by law appoint a different day.

SECTION 3. If, at the time fixed for the beginning of the term of the President, the President elect shall have died, the Vice President elect shall become President. If a President shall not have been chosen before the time fixed for the beginning of his term, or if the

[16]Adopted in 1913.
[17]Adopted in 1919. Repealed by Article XXI.
[18]Adopted in 1920.
[19]Adopted in 1933.

President elect shall have failed to qualify, then the Vice President elect shall act as President until a President shall have qualified; and the Congress may by law provide for the case wherein neither a President elect nor a Vice President elect shall have qualified, declaring who shall then act as President, or the manner in which one who is to act shall be selected, and such person shall act accordingly until a President or Vice President shall have qualified.

SECTION 4. The Congress may by law provide for the case of the death of any of the persons from whom the House of Representatives may choose a President whenever the right of choice shall have developed upon them, and for the case of the death of any of the persons from whom the Senate may choose a Vice President whenever the right of choice shall have devolved upon them.

SECTION 5. Sections 1 and 2 shall take effect on the 15th day of October following the ratification of this article.

SECTION 6. This article shall be inoperative unless it shall have been ratified as an amendment to the Constitution by the legislatures of three-fourths of the several States within seven years from the date of its submission.

## ARTICLE XXI[20]

SECTION 1. The eighteenth article of amendment to the Constitution of the United States is hereby repealed.

SECTION 2. The transportation or importation into any State, Territory or Possession of the United States for delivery or use therein of intoxicating liquors in violation of the laws thereof is hereby prohibited.

SECTION 3. This article shall be inoperative unless it shall have been ratified as an amendment to the Constitution by conventions in the several States, as provided in the Constitution, within seven years from the date of submission hereof to the States by the Congress.

## ARTICLE XXII[21]

SECTION 1. No person shall be elected to the office of the President more than twice, and no person who has held the office of President, or acted as President for more than two years of a term to which some other person was elected President shall be elected to the office of the President more than once. But this Article shall not apply to any person holding the office of President when this Article was proposed by the Congress, and shall not prevent any person who may be holding the office of President, or acting as President, during the term within which this Article becomes operative from holding the office of President or acting as President during the remainder of such term.

SECTION 2. This Article shall be inoperative unless it shall have been ratified as an amendment to the Constitution by the legislatures of three-fourths of the several States within seven years from the date of its submission to the States by the Congress.

## ARTICLE XXIII[22]

SECTION 1. The District constituting the seat of Government of the United States shall appoint in such manner as the Congress may direct:

A number of electors of President and Vice-President equal to the whole number of Senators and Representatives in Congress to which the District would be entitled if it were a State, but in no event more than the least populous state; they shall be in addition to those appointed by the states, but they shall be considered, for the purposes of the election of

[20]Adopted in 1933.
[21]Adopted in 1951.
[22]Adopted in 1961.

President and Vice-President, to be electors appointed by a state; and they shall meet in the District and perform such duties as provided by the twelfth article of amendment.

SECTION 2. The Congress shall have the power to enforce this article by appropriate legislation.

## ARTICLE XXIV[23]

SECTION 1. The right of citizens of the United States to vote in any primary or other election for President or Vice-President, for electors for President or Vice-President, or for Senator or Representative in Congress, shall not be denied or abridged by the United States or any state by reason of failure to pay any poll tax or other tax.

SECTION 2. The Congress shall have power to enforce this article by appropriate legislation.

## ARTICLE XXV[24]

SECTION 1. In case of the removal of the President from office or his death or resignation, the Vice President shall become President.

SECTION 2. Whenever there is a vacancy in the office of the Vice President, the President shall nominate a Vice President who shall take the office upon confirmation by a majority vote of both houses of Congress.

SECTION 3. Whenever the President transmits to the President pro tempore of the Senate and the Speaker of the House of Representatives his written declaration that he is unable to discharge the powers and duties of his office, and until he transmits to them a written declaration to the contrary, such powers and duties shall be discharged by the Vice President as Acting President.

SECTION 4. Whenever the Vice President and a majority of either the principal officers of the executive departments, or of such other body as Congress may by law provide, transmit to the President pro tempore of the Senate and the Speaker of the House of Representatives their written declaration that the President is unable to discharge the powers and duties of his office, the Vice President shall immediately assume the powers and duties of the office as Acting President.

Thereafter, when the President transmits to the President pro tempore of the Senate and the Speaker of the House of Representatives his written declaration that no inability exists, he shall resume the powers and duties of his office unless the Vice President and a majority of either the principal officers of the executive department, or of such other body as Congress may by law provide, transmit within four days to the President pro tempore of the Senate and the Speaker of the House of Representatives their written declaration that the President is unable to discharge the powers and duties of his office. Thereupon Congress shall decide the issue, assembling within 48 hours for that purpose if not in session. If the Congress, within 21 days after receipt of the latter written declaration, or, if Congress is not in session, within 21 days after Congress is required to assemble, determines by two-thirds vote of both houses that the President is unable to discharge the powers and duties of his office, the Vice President shall continue to discharge the same as Acting President; otherwise, the President shall resume the powers and duties of his office.

## ARTICLE XXVI[25]

SECTION 1. The right of citizens of the United States, who are eighteen years of age, or older, to vote shall not be denied or abridged by the United States or by any state on account of age.

SECTION 2. The Congress shall have the power to enforce this article by appropriate legislation.

[23]Adopted in 1964.
[24]Adopted in 1967.
[25]Adopted in 1971.

# Selected References

CHAPTER 1

*General*

Henry J. Abraham, *The Judicial Process*, 4th ed. (New York: Oxford University Press, 1980).

Lawrence Baum, *The Supreme Court*, 2d ed. (Washington, D.C.: Congressional Quarterly, 1984).

Alexander M. Bickel, *The Least Dangerous Branch* (Indianapolis: Bobbs-Merrill, 1963).

John Brigham, *Civil Liberties and American Democracy* (Washington, D.C.: Congressional Quarterly, 1984).

Charles S. Bullock III and Charles M. Lamb, *Implementation of Civil Rights Policy* (Monterey: Brooks/Cole, 1984).

Edmond Cahn, *Can the Supreme Court Defend Civil Liberties?* (New York: Sidney Hiloman Foundation, 1956).

Jerome Frank, *Courts on Trial: Myth and Reality in American Justice* (Princeton: Princeton University Press, 1959).

Sheldon Goldman and Thomas P. Jahnige, *The Federal Courts as a Political System*, 2d ed. (New York: Harper & Row, 1976).

Harold J. Grilliot, *Introduction to Law and the Legal System*, 3rd ed. (Boston: Houghton Mifflin, 1983).

Robert H. Jackson, *The Supreme Court in the American System of Government* (Cambridge: Harvard University Press, 1955).

Herbert Jacob, *Justice in America: Courts, Lawyers, and the Judicial Process*, 3rd ed. (Boston: Little, Brown, 1978).

Charles A. Johnson and Bradley C. Canon, *Judicial Policies: Implementation and Impact* (Washington, D.C.: Congressional Quarterly, 1984).

Herbert McClosky and Alida Brill, *Dimensions of Tolerance: What Americans Believe about Civil Liberties* (New York: Russell Sage, 1983).

C. Herman Pritchett, *Constitutional Law of the Federal System* (Englewood Cliffs: Prentice-Hall, 1984), Chaps. 6–8.

Richard J. Richardson and Kenneth N. Vines, *The Politics of Federal Courts* (Boston: Little, Brown, 1970).

Ellis Sandoz, *Conceived in Liberty: American Individual Rights Today* (North Scituate, Mass.: Duxbury, 1978).

Stephen L. Wasby, *The Impact of the United States Supreme Court: Some Perspectives* (Homewood: Dorsey, 1970).

*Activism and Self-Restraint*

Charles L. Black, Jr., *The People and the Court: Judicial Review in a Democracy* (New York: Macmillan, 1960).

Howard Dean, *Judicial Review and Democracy* (New York: Random House, 1966).

John Hart Ely, *Democracy and Distrust: A Theory of Judicial Review* (Cambridge: Harvard University Press, 1980).

D. F. Forte, ed., *The Supreme Court in American Politics: Judicial Activism* v. *Judicial Restraint* (Lexington, Mass.: Heath, 1972).

Stephen C. Halpern and Charles M. Lamb, *Supreme Court Activism and Restraint* (Lexington, Mass.: Heath, 1982).

Wallace Mendelson, "The Politics of Judicial Activism," 24 *Emory L. J.* 43 (1975).

Richard Neely, *How Courts Govern America* (New Haven: Yale University Press, 1981).

Michael J. Perry, *The Constitution, the Courts, and Human Rights* (New Haven: Yale University Press, 1982).

Robert J. Steamer, *The Supreme Court: Constitutional Revision and the New "Strict Constructionism"* (Minneapolis: Burgess, 1973).

Herbert Wechsler, "Toward Neutral Principles of Constitutional Law," 73 *Harv. L. Rev.* 1 (1959).

### Standing and Justiciability

Raoul Berger, "Standing to Sue in Public Actions: Is It a Constitutional Requirement?" 78 *Yale L. J.* 816 (1969).

Louis L. Jaffee, "The Citizen as Litigant in Public Actions: The Non-Hohfeldian or Ideological Plaintiff," 16 *U. Pa. L. Rev.* 1033 (1968).

T. P. Lewis, "Constitutional Rights and the Misuse of 'Standing'," 14 *Stan. L. Rev.* 433 (1962).

Note, "Advisory Opinions on the Constitutionality of Statutes," 69 *Harv. L. Rev.* 1302 (1956).

C. G. Post, Jr. *The Supreme Court and Political Questions* (New York: Da Capo, 1969).

Gregory J. Rathjen and Harold J. Spaeth, "Access to the Federal Courts: An Analysis of Burger Court Policy Making," 23 *Amer. J. Pol. Sci.* 360 (1979).

Victor G. Rosenblum, "Justiciability and Justice: Elements of Restraint and Indifference," 15 *Catholic U. L. Rev.* 141 (1966).

Fritz Scharpf, "Judicial Review and the Political Question: A Functional Analysis," 75 *Yale L. J.* 517 (1966).

Philippa Strum, *The Supreme Court and "Political Questions:" A Study in Judicial Evasion* (Tuscaloosa: University of Alabama Press, 1974).

Christopher L. Stone, "Should Trees Have Standing?—Toward Legal Rights for Natural Objects," 45 *So. Cal. L. Rev.* 450 (1972).

### Delay

Hans Zeisel, Harry Kalven, Jr., and Bernard Buchholz, *Delay in the Court* (Boston: Little, Brown, 1959).

### Appeals

William J. Brennan, "The National Court of Appeals: Another Dissent," 40 *Univ. of Chi. L. Rev.* 473 (1973).

Paul Freund, "Why We Need the National Court of Appeals," 59 *Am. Bar Assn. J.* 247 (1973).

J. Woodford Howard, Jr., *Courts of Appeals in the Federal Judicial System* (Princeton: Princeton University Press, 1981).

Samuel Krislov, "The Amicus Curiae Brief: From Friendship to Advocacy," 72 *Yale L. J.* 694 (1963).

Karl Llewellyn, *The Common Law Tradition: Deciding Appeals* (Boston: Little, Brown, 1960).

S. Sydney Ulmer, William Hintze, and Louise Kirklosky, "The Decision to Grant or Deny Certiorari: Further Consideration of Cue Theory," 6 *Law and Society Rev.* 640 (1972).

*Poverty and Justice*

Norman Dorsen, ed., "Poverty, Civil Liberties, and Civil Rights: A Symposium," 41 *N.Y.U. L. Rev.* 328 (1966).

Leonard Downie, Jr., *Justice Denied: The Case for Reform of the Courts* (New York: Praeger, 1971), Chap. 4.

Robert Lefcourt, ed., *Law Against the People* (New York: Random House, 1971).

Report of the Attorney General's Committee on Poverty and the Administration of Criminal Justice, *Poverty and the Administration of Federal Criminal Justice* (Submitted to U.S. Attorney General, February 25, 1963).

Patricia Wald, *Law and Poverty: 1965* (Report to the National Conference on Law and Poverty, Washington, D.C., June, 1965).

*Judicial Review of Administrative Action*

Raoul Berger, "Administrative Arbitrariness and Judicial Review," 65 *Colum. L. Rev.* 55 (1965).

Walter Gellhorn, Clark Byse, and Peter L. Strauss, *Administrative Law: Cases and Comments*, 7th ed. (Mineola, N.Y.: Foundation Press, 1979), Chap. 9.

Louis L. Jaffee, *Judicial Control of Administrative Action* (Boston: Little, Brown, 1965).

CHAPTER 2

Henry J. Abraham, *Freedom and the Court*, 4th ed. (New York: Oxford University Press, 1982).

William J. Brennan, Jr., *The Bill of Rights and the States* (Santa Barbara: Center for Study of Democratic Institutions, 1961).

Richard C. Cortner, *The Supreme Court and the Second Bill of Rights: The 14th Amendment and the Nationalization of Civil Liberties* (Madison: University of Wisconsin Press, 1981).

Charles Fairman, "Does the Fourteenth Amendment Incorporate the Bill of Rights? The Original Understanding," 2 *Stan. L. Rev.* 5 (1949).

Horace Flack, *The Adoption of the Fourteenth Amendment* (Baltimore: Johns Hopkins Press, 1908).

Felix Frankfurter, "Memorandum on 'Incorporation' of the Bill of Rights into the Due Process Clause of the Fourteenth Amendment," 78 *Harv. L. Rev.* 746 (1965).

Roger Howell, "The Privileges and Immunities of State Citizenship," *The John Hopkins University Studies in History and Political Science*, Vol. 36, No. 3 (Baltimore: Johns Hopkins Press, 1918).

Alex B. Lacy, Jr., "The Bill of Rights and the Fourteenth Amendment: The Evolution of the Absorption Doctrine," 23 *Wash. and Lee L. Rev.* 37 (1966).

CHAPTER 3

*General*

George F. Cole, ed., *Criminal Justice: Law and Politics*, 2d ed. (North Scituate, Mass.: Duxbury, 1976).

David Fellman, *The Defendant's Rights Today* (Madison: University of Wisconsin Press, 1976).

David Fellman, *The Defendant's Rights Under English Law* (Madison: University of Wisconsin Press, 1966).

J. A. C. Grant, *Our Common Law Constitution* (Boston: Boston University Press, 1956).

Stuart Nagel, Erika Fairchild, and Anthony Champagne, eds., *The Political Science of Criminal Justice* (Springfield, Ill.: Charles Thomas, 1983).

C. Herman Pritchett, *Constitutional Civil Liberties* (Englewood Cliffs: Prentice-Hall, 1984), Chap. 9.

Leon Radzinowicz and Marven E. Wolfgang, eds., *Crime and Justice*, 3 vols. (New York: Basic Books, 1971).

John Robertson, ed., *Rough Justice: Perspectives on Lower Criminal Courts* (Boston: Little, Brown, 1974).

Jerome H. Skolnick, *Justice Without Trial* (New York: Wiley, 1966).

H. Frank Way, *Criminal Justice and the American Constitution* (North Scituate, Mass.: Duxbury, 1980).

Lloyd L. Weinreb, *Denial of Justice: Criminal Process in the United States* (New York: Free Press, 1977).

## Notice

Oliver P. Field, "Ex Post Facto in the Constitution," 20 *Mich L. Rev.* 315 (1922).

Note, "The Void-for-Vagueness Doctrine in the Supreme Court," 109 *U. Pa. L. Rev.* 67 (1960).

## Searches and Seizures

William G. Buss, "The Fourth Amendment and Searches of Students in Schools," 59 *Iowa L. Rev.* 739 (1974).

Erwin N. Griswold, *Search and Seizure: A Dilemma of the Supreme Court* (Lincoln: University of Nebraska Press, 1975).

Michele G. Herman, *Search and Seizure Checklist*, 3rd ed. (New York: Boardman, 1983).

Jerold H. Israel, "Legislative Regulation of Searches and Seizures: The Michigan Proposals," 73 *Mich. L. Rev.* 222 (1974).

Yale Kamisar, "A Defense of the Exclusionary Rule," 15 *Crim. L. Bull.* 5 (1979).

John Kaplan, "The Limits of the Exclusionary Rule," 26 *Stan. L. Rev.* 1027 (1974).

Wayne R. LaFave, *Search and Seizure: a Treatise on the Fourth Amendment*, 2d ed., 4 vols. (St. Paul: West Publishing Co., 1987).

Jacob W. Landynski, *Search and Seizure and the Supreme Court* (Baltimore: Johns Hopkins Press, 1966).

Nelson B. Lasson, *The History and Development of the Fourth Amendment to the United States Constitution* (Baltimore: Johns Hopkins Press, 1937).

Note, "Border Searches Revisited: The Constitutional Propriety of Fixed and Temporary Checkpoint Searches," 2 *Hastings Con. L. Q.* 251 (1975).

Note, "Protecting Privacy Under the Fourth Amendment," *91 Yale L. J.* 313 (1981).

Note, "Warrantless Searches and Seizures of Automobiles," 87 *Harv. L. Rev.* 835 (1974).

Symposium, "Fourth Amendment Reform," 17 *U. Mich. J. of Law Reform* 409–625 (1984).

John B. Wefing, "Consent Searches and the Fourth Amendment: Voluntariness and Third Party Problems," 5 *Seton Hall L. Rev.* 211 (1974).

Welsh S. White, "Effective Consent to Search and Seizure," 113 *U. Pa. L. Rev.* 260 (1964).

*Self-Incrimination and Confessions*

Erwin N. Griswold, *The Fifth Amendment Today* (Cambridge: Harvard University Press, 1955).

Yale Kamisar, *Police Interrogation and Confessions* (Ann Arbor: University of Michigan Press, 1980).

Leonard W. Levy, *Origins of the Fifth Amendment* (New York: Oxford University Press, 1968).a

R. C. Pittman, "The Colonial and Constitutional History of the Privilege Against Self-Incrimination in America," 21 *Va. L. Rev.* 763 (1935).

Otis H. Stephens, Jr., *The Supreme Court and Confessions of Guilt* (Knoxville: University of Tennessee Press, 1973).

Lawrence Taylor, *Witness Immunity* (Springfield, Ill.: Charles Thomas, 1983).

*Right to Counsel*

Fred P. Graham, *The Self-Inflicted Wound* (New York: Macmillan, 1970).

Robert Hermann, Eric Single and John Boston, *Counsel for the Poor* (Lexington, Mass.: Lexington Books, 1977).

Anthony Lewis, *Gideon's Trumpet* (New York: Random House, 1964).

S. Sidney Ulmer, *Military Justice and the Right to Counsel* (Lexington: University of Kentucky Press, 1970).

*Double Jeopardy*

Walter T. Fisher, "Double Jeopardy, Two Sovereignties and the Intruding Constitution," 28 *U. Chi. L. Rev.* 591 (1961).

M. L. Friedland, *Double Jeopardy* (New York: Oxford University Press, 1969).

J. A. C. Grant, "Successive Prosecutions by State and Nation," 4 *U.C.L.A. L. Rev.* 377 (1966).

Jay A. Sigler, *Double Jeopardy: The Development of a Legal and Social Policy* (Ithaca: Cornell University Press, 1969).

L. G. Miller, *Double Jeopardy and the Federal System* (Chicago: University of Chicago Press, 1968).

Peter Westen and Richard Drubel, "Toward a General Theory of Double Jeopardy," 1978 *Sup. Ct. Rev.* 81 (1979).

*Trial by Jury*

Sir Patrick Devlin, *Trial by Jury* (London: Stevens, 1956).

Harry Kalven, Jr., and Hans Zeisel, *The American Jury* (Boston: Little, Brown, 1966).

Rita J. Simon, *The Jury: Its Role in American Society* (Lexington, Mass.: Lexington Books, 1980).

James Bradley Thayer, *A Preliminary Treatise on Evidence at the Common Law* (Cambridge: Harvard University Press, 1898), Chap. 1.

*Sentencing and Plea Bargaining*

Robert O. Dawson, *Sentencing* (Boston: Little, Brown, 1969).

Alfred Blumstein, Jacqueline Cohen, Susan E. Martin, and Michael H. Tonry, eds., *Research on Sentencing*, 2 vols. (Washington, D.C.: National Academy Press, 1983).

Steven J. Schulhofer, "Is Plea Bargaining Inevitable?," 97 *Harv. L. Rev.* 1037 (1984).

*Cruel and Unusual Punishment*

Larry C. Berkson, *The Concept of Cruel and Unusual Punishment* (Lexington, Mass.: Heath, 1975).

Michael Meltsner, *Cruel and Unusual: The Supreme Court and Capital Punishment* (New York: Morrow, 1974).

Charles L. Black, Jr., *Capital Punishment: The Inevitability of Caprice and Mistake* (New York: Norton & Co., 1974).

*Habeas Corpus*

Paul M. Bator, "Finality in Criminal Law and Federal Habeas Corpus for State Prisoners," 76 *Harv. L. Rev.* 441 (1963).

Zechariah Chafee, Jr., "The Most Important Human Right in the Constitution," 32 *B. U. L. Rev.* 144 (1952).

H. J. Friendly, "Is Innocence Irrelevant? Collateral Attack on Criminal Judgments," 38 *U. of Chi. L. Rev.* 142 (1970).

Daniel J. Meador, *Habeas Corpus and Magna Carta* (Charlottesville: University Press of Virginia, 1966).

Note, "Habeas Corpus and the Military: The Crippled Attack on Courts Martial," 61 *Ky. L. J.* 333 (1972–73).

James Turner, "Habeas Corpus after *Stone* v. *Powell*: The 'Opportunity for Full and Fair Litigation' Standard," 13 *Harv. Civil Rights–Civil Liberties Rev.* 521 (1978).

*Rights of Prisoners*

Burton N. Atkins and Emily Wilson Boyle, "Prisoners' Perceptions of their Constitutional Rights: A Client's View of the World of Criminal Justice," 24 *Emory L. Rev.* 67 (1975).

Susan N. Herman, "The New Liberty: The Procedural Due Process Rights of Prisoners and Others Under the Burger Court," 59 *N.Y.U. L. Rev.* 482 (1984).

David Rudovsky, *The Rights of Prisoners,* 4th ed. (Carbondale: Southern Illinois University Press, 1988).


CHAPTER 4

Jesse H. Choper, "Defining 'Religion' in the First Amendment," 1982 *U. Ill. L. Rev.* 579 (1982).

"Developments in the Law—Religion and the State," 100 *Harv. L. Rev.* 1606–1781 (1987).

Kenneth M. Dolbeare and P. E. Hammond, *The School Prayer Decisions: From Court Policy to Local Practice* (Chicago: University of Chicago Press, 1971).

David Fellman, *Religion in American Public Law* (Boston: Boston University Press, 1965).

Sidney Hook, *Religion in a Free Society* (Lincoln: University of Nebraska Press, 1967).

Mark DeWolfe Howe, *The Garden and the Wilderness* (Chicago: University of Chicago Press, 1964).

Paul G. Kauper, "The Supreme Court and the Establishment Clause: Back to Everson?" 25 *Case West. Reserve L. Rev.* 107 (1974).

David R. Manwaring, *Render unto Caesar: The Flag Salute Controversy* (Chicago: University of Chicago Press, 1962).

Richard E. Morgan, *The Supreme Court and Religion* (New York: Free Press, 1972).

Note, "The Establishment Clause: Analysis of Legislative and Administrative Aid to Religion," 74 *Colum. L. Rev.* 1175 (1974).

Note, "Government Neutrality and Separation of Church and State: Tuition Tax Credits," 92 *Harv. L. Rev.* 696 (1979).

Note, "Released Time Cases Revisited: A Study of Group Decisionmaking by the Supreme Court," 83 *Yale L. J.* 1202 (1974).

Note, "Private Colleges, State Aid, and the Establishment Clause," 1975 *Duke L. J.* 976 (1975).

Leo Pfeffer, "Freedom and/or Separation: The Constitutional Dilemma of the First Amendment," 64 *Minn. L. Rev.* 561 (1980).

Frank J. Sorauf, *The Constitutional Politics of Church and State* (Princeton: Princeton University Press, 1976).

Anson P. Stokes, *Church and State in the United States*, 3 vols. (New York: Harper & Row, 1950). See also the one-volume condensation by Leo Pfeffer, *Church and State in the United States* (New York: Harper & Row, 1964).

Hearings before the Subcommittee on Constitutional Amendments of the Committee on the Judiciary, United States Senate, 89th Congress, 2d Session, August, 1966, on Senate Joint Resolution 148 relating to Prayers in Public Schools.

Symposium, "The Religion Clauses," 72 *Cal. L. Rev.* 753 (1984).

Symposium, "Religion and the State," 27 special issue, *Wm. & Mary L. Rev.* 833 (1985–86).

CHAPTER 5

*General*

Henry J. Abraham, *Freedom and the Court,* 4th ed. (New York: Oxford University Press, 1982), Chap. 5.

Edmond Cahn, ed., *The Great Rights* (New York: Macmillan, 1963).

J. Denvir, "Justice Brennan, Justice Rehnquist and Free Speech," 80 *Nw. U. L. Rev.* 285 (1985).

David Fellman, *The Limits of Freedom* (New Brunswick: Rutgers University Press, 1959).

Leonard W. Levy, *Freedom of Speech and Press in Early American History: Legacy of Suppression* (New York: Harper & Row, 1963).

Paul L. Murphy, *The Meaning of Freedom of Speech: First Amendment Freedoms from Wilson to FDR* (Westport, Conn.: Greenwood, 1972).

*Doctrines of Interpretation*

Thomas I. Emerson, *Toward a General Theory of the First Amendment* (New York: Random House, 1967).

Laurent B. Frantz, "The First Amendment in the Balance," 71 *Yale L. J.* 1424 (1962).

Alexander Meiklejohn, *Free Speech and Its Relation to Self-Government* (New York: Harper & Row, 1948).

Wallace Mendelson, "On the Meaning of the First Amendment: Absolutes in the Balance," 50 *Cal. L. Rev.* 821 (1962).

Henry P. Monaghan, "Overbreadth," 1981 *Sup. Ct. Rev.* 1 (1981).

Martin Shapiro, *Freedom of Speech: The Supreme Court and Judicial Review* (Englewood Cliffs: Prentice-Hall, 1966).

*Internal Security*

Association of the Bar of the City of New York, Report of the Special Committee on *The Federal Loyalty-Security Program* (New York: Dodd, Mead, 1956).

Ralph S. Brown, Jr., *Loyalty and Security* (New Haven: Yale University Press, 1958).

*Digest of the Public Record of Communism in the United States* (New York: Fund for the Republic, 1955).

Sidney Hook, *Political Power and Personal Freedom: Critical Studies in Democracy, Communism, and Civil Rights* (New York: Criterion, 1959).

Harold D. Laswell, *National Security and Individual Freedom* (New York: McGraw-Hill, 1950).

Note, "The National Security Interest and Civil Liberties," 85 *Harv. L. Rev.* 1130 (1972).

Telford Taylor, *Grand Inquest* (New York: Simon & Schuster, 1955).

*Press*

Jerome Barron, *Freedom of the Press for Whom: The Right of Access to Mass Media* (Bloomington: Indiana University Press, 1973).

Francis X. Beytagh, "Privacy and a Free Press: A Contemporary Conflict in Values," 20 *N.Y. L. Forum* 453 (1975).

Zechariah Chafee, Jr., *Government and Mass Communication* (Chicago: University of Chicago Press, 1947).

Council of State Governments, *Shield Laws* (Lexington, Ky.: Council of State Governments, 1973).

Robert G. Dixon, "The Constitution Is Shield Enough for Newsmen," 60 *Amer. Bar Assn. J.* 707 (1974).

Sam J. Ervin, Jr., "In Pursuit of a Press Privilege," 11 *Harv. J. on Leg.* 278 (1974).

Hearings on Freedom of the Press before the Subcommittee on Constitutional Rights, Senate Committee on the Judiciary, 92d Congress, 1st and 2d Sessions (1972).

Leonard W. Levy, ed., *Freedom of the Press from Zenger to Jefferson* (New York: Bobbs-Merrill, 1966).

Note, "Privacy and the Freedom of Information Act," 27 *Admin. L. Rev.* 275 (1975).

Glenn Robinson, "The FCC and the First Amendment: Observations on 40 Years of Radio and Television Regulation," 52 *Minn. L. Rev.* 67 (1967).

*Free Press and Fair Trial*

American Bar Association Committee on Fair Trial and Free Press, *Standards Relating to Fair Trial and Free Press, Tentative Draft* (New York: Institute of Judicial Administration, 1966).

Association of the Bar of the City of New York, Special Committee on Radio, Television, and the Administration of Justice, *Freedom of the Press and Fair Trial: Final Report with Recommendations* (New York: Columbia University Press, 1967).

C. R. Bush, ed., *Free Press and Fair Trial* (Athens: University of Georgia Press, 1970).

Hearings on S. 290 before the Subcommittee on Constitutional Rights and the Subcommittee on Improvements in Judicial Machinery, United States Senate Committee on the Judiciary, 89th Congress, 1st Session (1965), *Free Press and Fair Trial*.

Robert T. Roper, "The Gag Order: Asphyxiating the First Amendment," 34 *West. Pol. Q.* 372 (1981).

*Assembly and Association*

Glenn Abernathy, *The Right of Assembly and Association*, rev. ed. (Columbia: University of South Carolina Press, 1981).

Zechariah Chafee, Jr., "The Internal Affairs of Associations Not for Profit," 43 *Harv. L. Rev.* 993 (1930).

Zechariah Chafee, Jr., "The Problem of the Hostile Audience," 49 *Colum. L. Rev.* 1118 (1949).

David Fellman, *The Constitutional Right of Association* (Chicago: University of Chicago Press, 1963).

Robert A. Horn, *Groups and the Constitution* (Stanford University Press, 1956).

Note, "The Future of Prisoners' Unions," 13 *Harv. Civil Rights L. Rev.* 799 (1978).

Note, "Heckling: A Protected Right or Disorderly Conduct?" 60 *S. Cal. L. Rev.* 215 (1986).

Note, "Regulation of White House Demonstrations," 119 *U. Pa. L. Rev.* 668 (1971).

Note, "Hostile Audience Confrontations: Police Conduct and First Amendment Rights," 75 *Michigan L. Rev.* 180 (1976).

Charles E. Rice, *Freedom of Association* (New York: New York University Press, 1962).

*Censorship of Books: Obscenity*

John Chandos, ed., *To Deprave and Corrupt* (New York: Association Press, 1962).

Harry M. Clor, ed., *Censorship and Freedom of Expression* (Chicago: Rand McNally, 1971).

David Copp and Susan Wendell, eds., *Pornography and Censorship* (Buffalo: Prometheus Books, 1984).

Morris L. Ernst and Alan U. Schwartz, *Censorship: The Search for the Obscene* (New York: Macmillan, 1964).

Walter Gellhorn, *Individual Freedom and Governmental Restraints* (Baton Rouge: Louisiana State University Press, 1958), Chap. 2.

Robert W. Haney, *Comstockery in America* (Boston: Beacon Press, 1960).

The Report of the Commission on Obscenity and Pornography (Washington, D.C.: U.S. Government Printing Office, 1970).

Norman St. John-Stevas, *Obscenity and the Law* (London: Secker & Warburg, 1956).

Jay A. Sigler, "Freedom of the Mails: A Developing Right," 54 *Georgetown L. J.* 30 (1965).

C. R. Sunstein, "Pornography and the First Amendment," 1986 *Duke L. J.* 589

## CHAPTER 6

*General*

John Frank and Robert F. Munro, "The Original Understanding of 'Equal Protection of the Laws'." 50 *Colum. L. Rev.* 131 (1950).

Joseph Tussman and Jacobs ten Broek, "The Equal Protection of the Laws," 37 *Cal. L. Rev.* 341 (1949).

*Race Discrimination*

William Van Alstyne, "Rites of Passage: Race, the Supreme Court and the Constitution," 46 *U. of Chi. L. Rev.* 775 (1979).

Morris Berger, *Equality by Statute: The Revolution in Civil Rights*, rev. ed. (Garden City: Doubleday, 1967).

Jack A. Greenberg, ed., "Blacks and the Law," *The Annals*, Vol. 407 (May 1973).

John C. Livingston, *Fair Game? Inequality and Affirmative Action* (San Francisco: W. H. Freeman, 1979).

Note, "Is the U.S. Committed to Fair Housing? Enforcement of the Fair Housing Act Remains a Crucial Problem," 29 *Cath. U. L. Rev.* 641 (1980).

Gary Orfield, *Must We Bus? Segregated Schools and National Policy* (Washington, D.C.: Brookings Institution, 1978).

Clement E. Vose, *Caucasians Only: The Supreme Court, the NAACP, and the Restrictive Covenant Cases* (Berkeley: University of California Press, 1959).

J. Harvie Wilkinson III, *From Brown to Bakke: The Supreme Court and School Integration, 1954–1978* (New York: Oxford University Press, 1979).

C. Vann Woodward, *The Strange Career of Jim Crow*, 3rd rev. ed. (New York: Oxford University Press, 1974).

*Sex Discrimination*

Janet K. Boles, *The Politics of the Equal Rights Amendment* (New York: Longman, 1979).

Roxanne B. Conlin, "Equal Protection Versus Equal Rights Amendment—Where Are We Now?" 24 *Drake L. Rev.* 259 (1975).

Kenneth Davidson, Ruth Ginsburg, and Herma Kay, *Sex-Based Discrimination* (St. Paul: West Publishing Co., 1974).

Karen DeCrow, *Sexist Justice* (New York: Random House, 1974).

Sylvia A. Law, "Rethinking Sex and the Constitution," 132 *U. Pa. L. Rev.* 955 (1984).

Panel, "Men, Women, and the Constitution: The Equal Rights Amendment," 10 *Colum. J. L. & Soc. Prob.* 77 (1973).

## CHAPTER 7

Howard Ball, Dale Krane, and Thomas P. Lauth, *Compromised Compliance: Implementation of the 1965 Voting Rights Act* (Westport, Conn.: Greenwood, 1982).,

Paul. W. Bonapfel, "Minority Challenges to At-Large Elections—The Dilution Problem," 10 *Ga. L. Rev.* 353 (1976).

William Gillette, *The Right to Vote: Politics and the Passage of the Fifteenth Amendment* (Baltimore: Johns Hopkins Press, 1965).

Alan P. Grimes, *The Puritan Ethic and Woman Suffrage* (New York: Oxford University Press, 1967).

Charles V. Hamilton, *The Bench and the Ballot: Southern Federal Judges and Black Voters* (New York: Oxford University Press, 1973).

V. O. Key, Jr., *Southern Politics in State and Nation* (New York: Knopf, 1949).

Thurgood Marshall, "The Rise and Collapse of the 'White Primary'," 26 *J. of Negro Ed.* 249 (1957).

1961 U.S. Commission on Civil Rights Report No. 1, *Voting* (Washington, D.C.: U.S. Government Printing Office, 1961).

Hearings before the United States Commission on Civil Rights, held in 1965 in Jackson, Mississippi, Vol. 1, *Voting* (Washington, D.C.: U.S. Government Printing Office, 1965).

## CHAPTER 8

P. Allan Dionisopoulos and Craig Ducat, *The Right to Privacy: Essays and Cases* (St. Paul: West Publishing Co., 1976).

Thomas I. Emerson, "Right of Privacy and Freedom of the Press," 14 *Harv. Civil Rights–Civil Liberties L. Rev.* 329 (1979).

David W. O'Brien, *Privacy, Law and Public Policy* (New York: Praeger, 1979).

R. A. Posner, "Uncertain Protection of Privacy by the Supreme Court," 1978 *Sup. Ct. Rev.* 173 (1979).

Symposium, "The Right to Privacy," 15 *U. Tol. L. Rev.* 437–915 (1984).

Alan F. Westin, *Privacy and Freedom* (New York: Atheneum, 1967).

Hearings before the Subcommittee on Administrative Practice and Procedure of the Senate Judiciary Committee, "Invasions of Privacy," 6 parts, 89th Cong., 1st and 2nd Sessions, 1965–1966.

Hearings before a Subcommittee of the Committee on Government Operations, House of Representatives, "Special Inquiry on Invasion of Privacy," 89th Congress, 1st and 2nd Sessions, 1965–1966.

# INDEX

123569